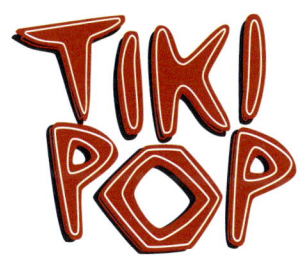

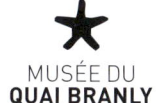

MUSÉE DU
QUAI BRANLY

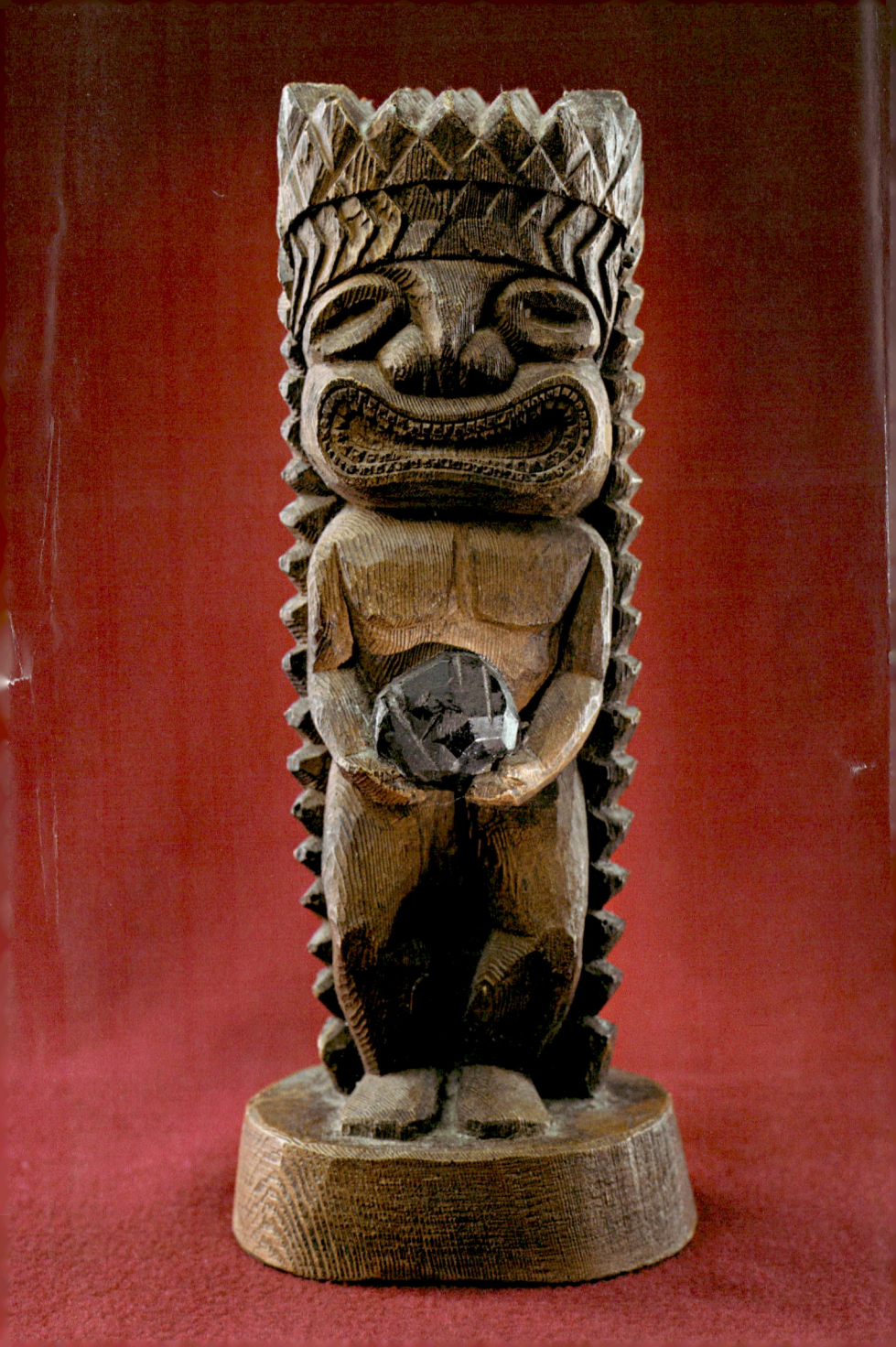

SVEN A. KIRSTEN

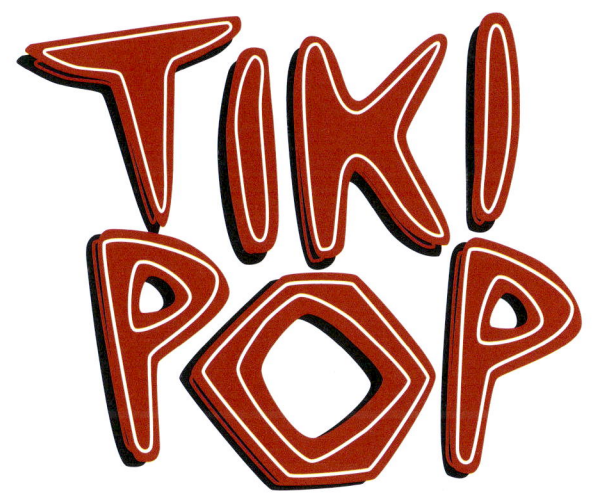

AMERICA IMAGINES ITS OWN POLYNESIAN PARADISE

AMERIKA ERSCHAFFT SICH SEIN EIGENES
POLYNESISCHES PARADIES

L'AMÉRIQUE RÊVE SON PARADIS POLYNÉSIEN

TASCHEN
Bibliotheca Universalis

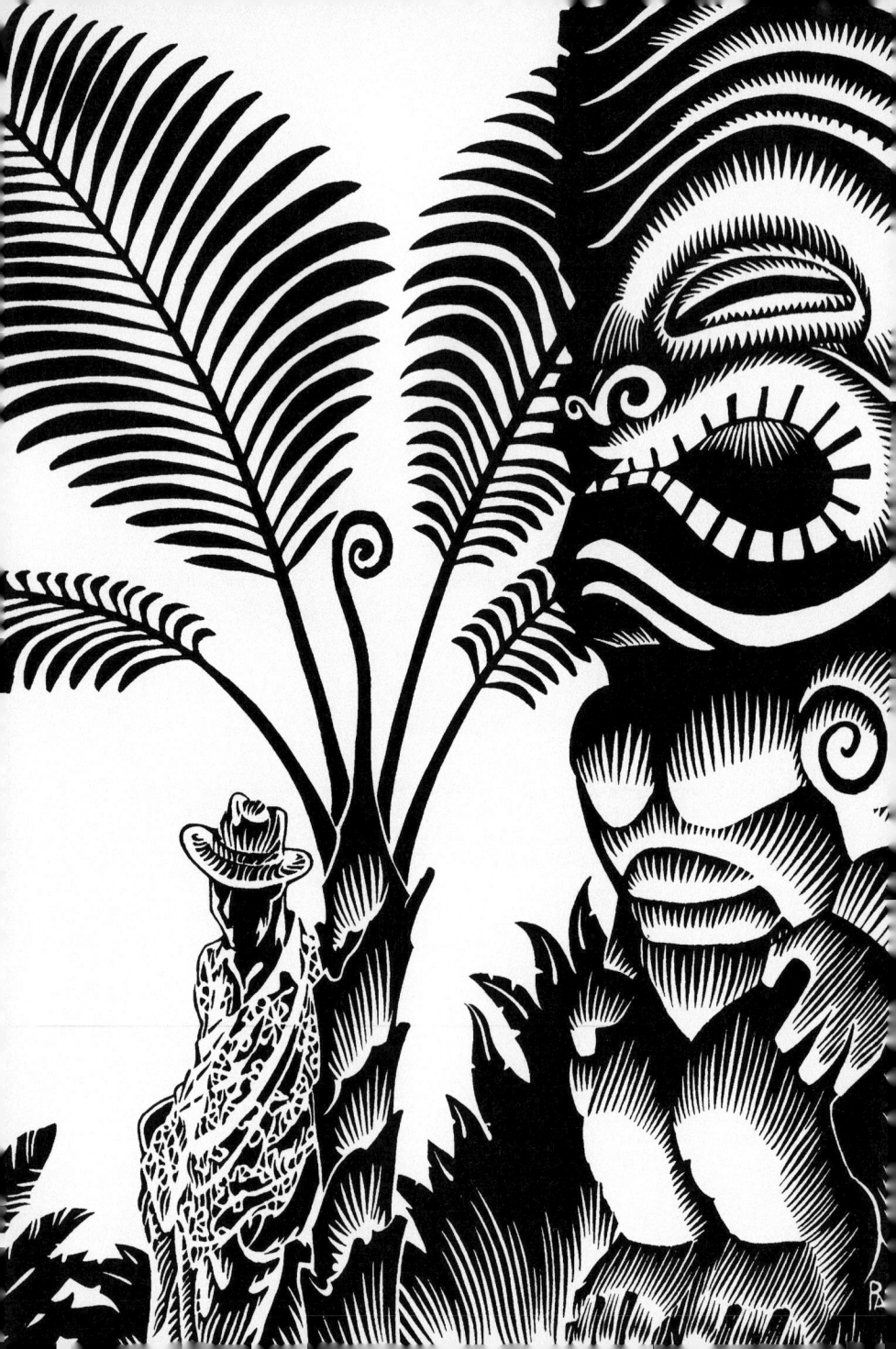

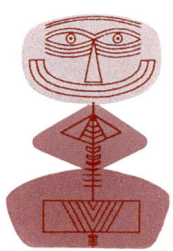

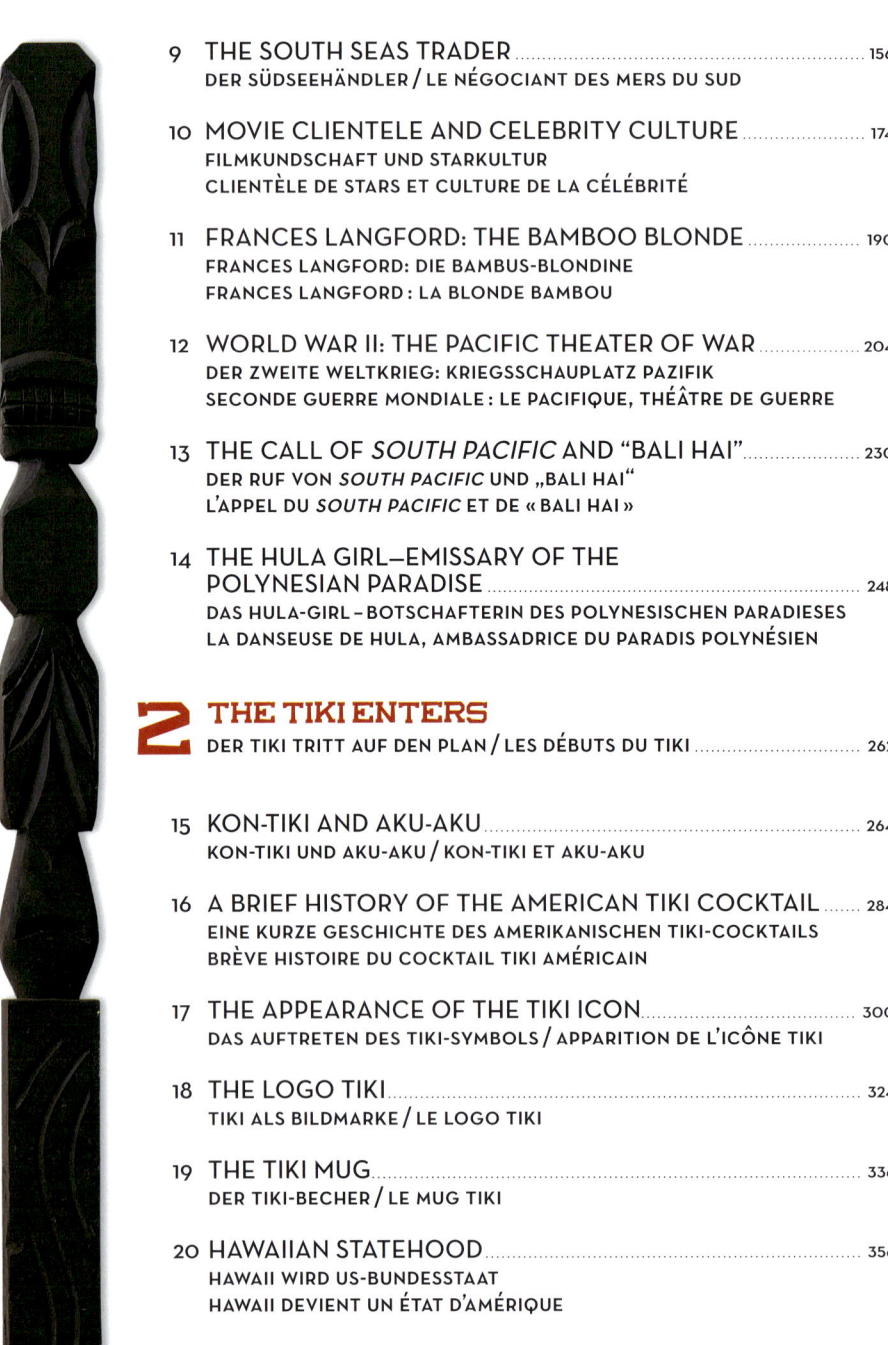

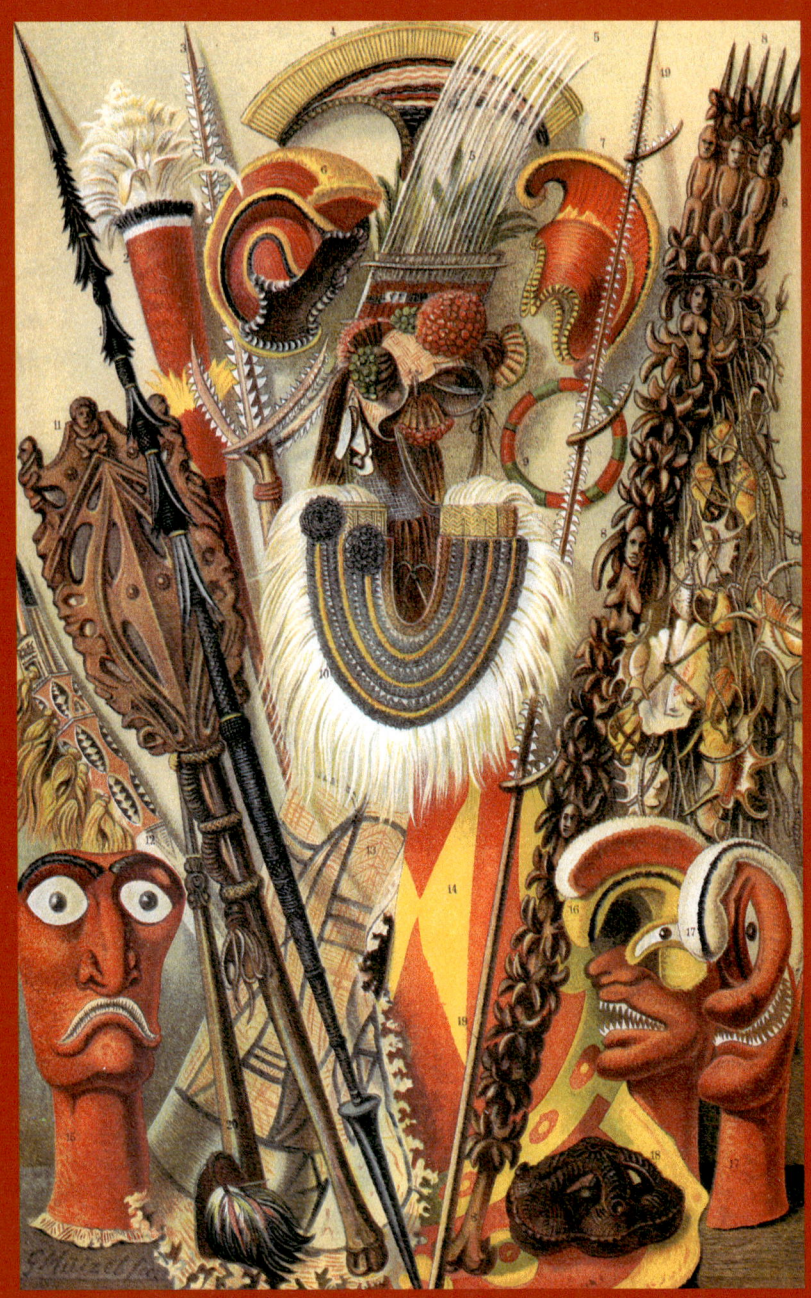

FOREWORD

In America in the 1950s, a "synthetic exoticism" took shape that mirrored the humor and optimism of the time. Riding the economic expansion of the era, Hawaii's accession to American statehood, combined with Hollywood South Seas concepts and a modern vogue for the "primitive arts," produced a new symbol for a less constrained way of life: the American Tiki!

The Old World's intoxication with Polynesia reaches back into the 19th century and before, when explorers' experiences were utilized for one of the rare forms of eroticism accepted by bourgeois society. The New World's 20th-century Tiki craze brought this fantasy to surprising heights in popular arts and architecture.

After its sudden collapse in the midst of the anti-Vietnam War movement and the much more radical eroticization of the 1960s generation, the public quickly disinherited Tiki style as politically incorrect and in bad taste.

This book will allow the reader to discover a large part of this once-forgotten facet of American pop culture through numerous documents, objects, and images. Its first publication coincides with the launch of the first full-scale exhibition on Tiki Pop at the Musée du Quai Branly in Paris, curated by Sven Kirsten, an "urban archaeologist" and expert on Tiki style, and author of this, his third book on the subject. The mass of material collected in this and his previous works bears unwavering witness to the verve and charm of a style that has recently been undergoing a spectacular renaissance. Long live the Tiki!

Stéphane Martin
President, Musée du Quai Branly

Vintage illustration of Polynesian weapons, personal adornments and cult objects. *Meyers Konversations-Lexikon,* 1896

VORWORT

In den 1950er-Jahren entstand in Amerika eine „künstliche Exotik-Welle", die den Humor und Optimismus jener Zeit widerspiegelte. Die Wirtschaft war auf dem aufsteigenden Ast, und so brachte Hawaiis Beitritt zu den USA, kombiniert mit den Südseefantasien Hollywoods und der damaligen Vorliebe für Primitive Kunst, ein neues Symbol für ein sorgenfreies Leben hervor: die amerikanische Tiki-Kultur.

Die Besessenheit der Alten Welt von Polynesien reicht ins 19. Jahrhundert und weiter zurück. Die Erfahrungsberichte der Entdecker boten damals eine der wenigen Erotikformen, die von der bürgerlichen Gesellschaft akzeptiert wurde. Der Tiki-Fimmel der Neuen Welt verhalf diesen Fantasien im 20. Jahrhundert zu ungeahnter Beliebtheit in Populärkunst und Architektur. Im Zuge der Anti-Kriegsbewegung des Vietnamkriegs und der radikalen Sexualisierung der Generation der 1960er-Jahre brach die Tiki-Kultur jedoch plötzlich wieder zusammen und wurde von der Öffentlichkeit als politisch inkorrekt und geschmacklos deklariert.

In diesem Buch kann der Leser einen großen Teil dieser in Vergessenheit geratenen Facette amerikanischer Popkultur anhand zahlreicher Dokumente, Objekte und Bilder entdecken. Die Erstveröffentlichung des Buchs ging mit dem Start der ersten Tiki-Pop-Großausstellung im Musée du Quai Branly in Paris einher, die von Sven Kirsten kuratiert wurde. Kirsten ist Stadtarchäologe, Tiki-Style-Experte und Autor seines dritten Buchs zum Thema. Die Fülle an gesammeltem Material in diesem und früheren Werken bringt die Leichtigkeit und den Charme eines Stils zum Ausdruck, der seit Kurzem eine spektakuläre Renaissance erlebt. Lang lebe Tiki!

Stéphane Martin
Direktor des Musée du Quai Branly

PAGE 2: Coal mine Tiki by MAPCO Inc., Tulsa, Oklahoma, which incorporated the word "-tiki" into the name of all of its coal mines in order to secure good luck.

AVANT-PROPOS

En Amérique, dans les années 1950, est apparu un « exotisme synthétique » qui reflétait l'humour et l'optimisme de l'époque. Surfant sur la croissance économique de ces années, l'accession d'Hawaii au statut d'État américain combinée aux concepts hollywoodiens des mers du Sud et à une vogue moderne des « arts primitifs », a produit le nouveau symbole d'un mode de vie moins contraignant : le tiki américain !

L'engouement de l'Ancien Monde pour la Polynésie remonte au XIXᵉ siècle, si ce n'est plus tôt encore, lorsque les expériences des explorateurs servirent à exprimer l'une des rares formes d'érotisme acceptée par la société bourgeoise. La folie du Nouveau Monde et du XXᵉ siècle pour le tiki ont hissé ce fantasme à des sommets étonnants dans l'art populaire et l'architecture. Après son effondrement soudain au milieu du mouvement contre la guerre du Vietnam et l'érotisation radicale de la génération des années 1960, le public a rapidement discrédité le style tiki, désormais jugé politiquement incorrect et de mauvais goût.

Ce livre permettra au lecteur de découvrir diverses facettes de ce versant oublié de la culture pop américaine à travers un large éventail de documents, d'objets et d'images. Sa première publication coïncide avec la première exposition de grande envergure sur le tiki pop au musée du quai Branly, organisée par Sven Kirsten, « archéologue urbain » expert du style tiki et auteur de cet ouvrage – son troisième sur le sujet. L'ensemble des documents recueillis dans cet ouvrage, ajouté à ses précédents, constitue un témoignage sans faille sur la verve et le charme d'un style qui a récemment connu une renaissance spectaculaire. Longue vie au tiki !

Stéphane Martin
Président du musée du quai Branly

PAGE 4: *Fern Twilight* by Brad Parker

PAGE 12: Ballyhoo Cover

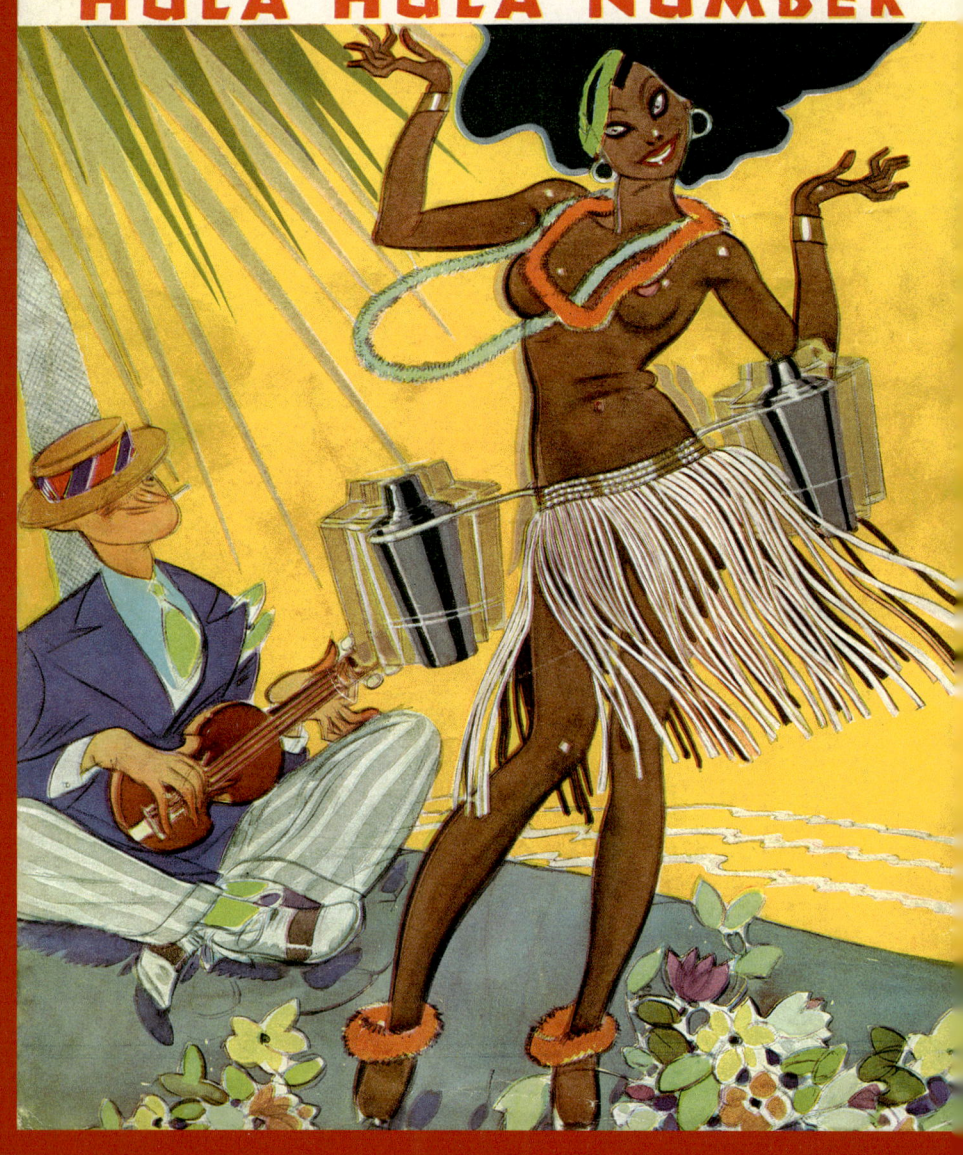

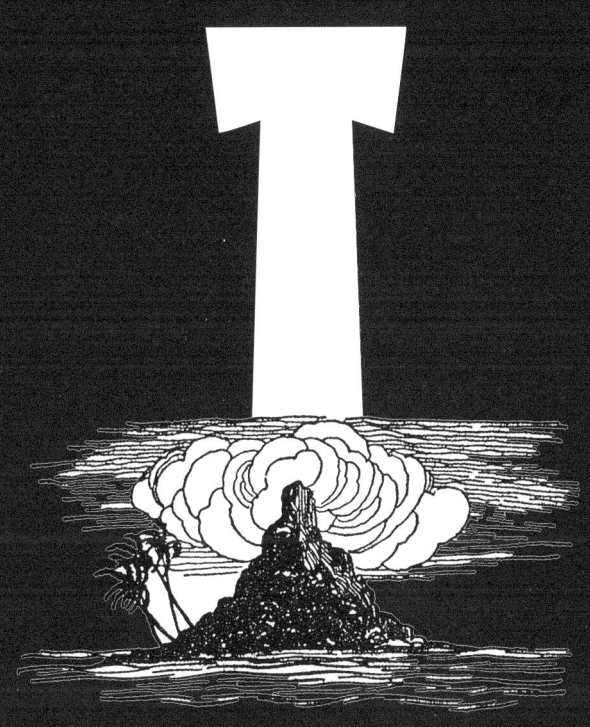

PRE-TIKI:
SETTING THE STAGE

PRÄ-TIKI: DIE WEGBEREITER
LE PRÉTIKI : ÉTAT DES LIEUX

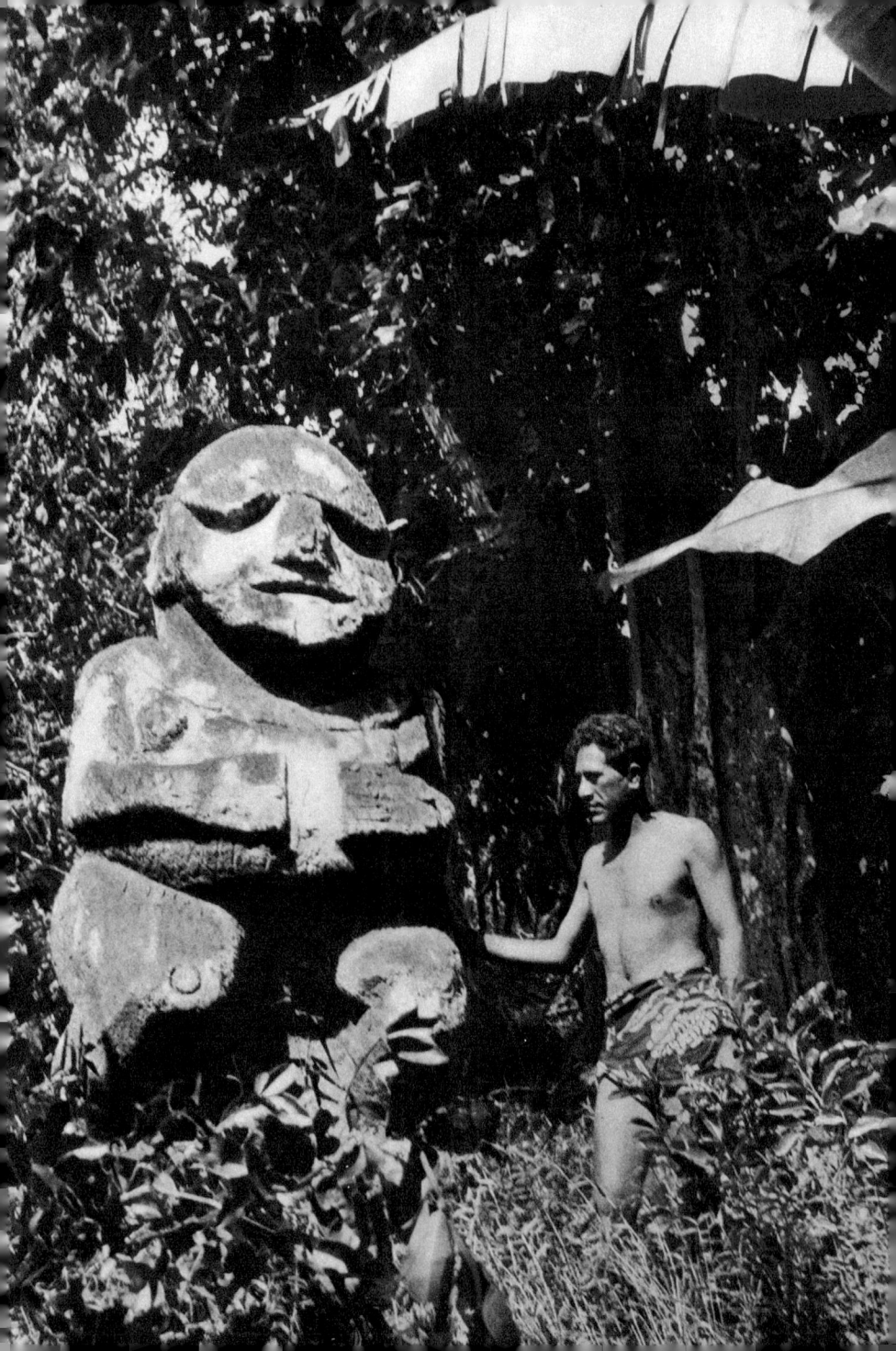

I

TIKI-MAN, MYTH, MERRYMAKER

TIKI-MENSCH, MYTHOS, MUSE
TIKI, L'HOMME, LE MYTHE, LE FÊTARD

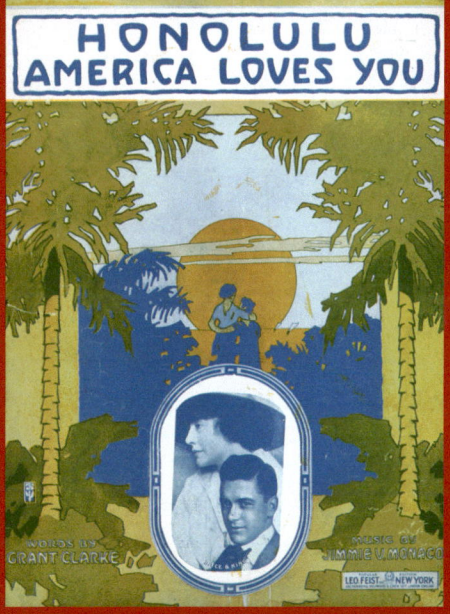

ABOVE: American sheet music cover, 1920s

OPPOSITE: Ancient Tahitian ancestor statue

I

TIKI—THE ANCESTOR OF MANKIND

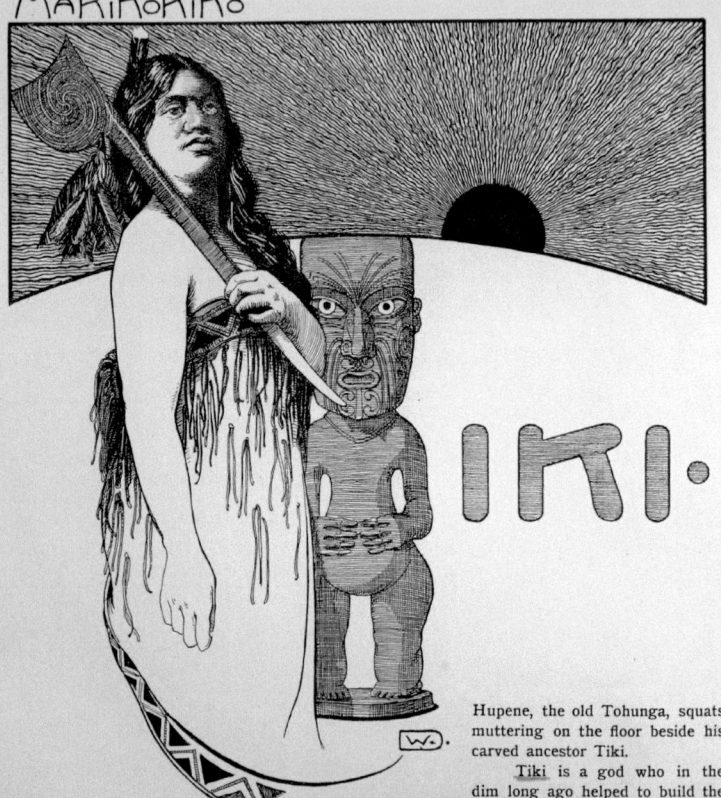

Marikoriko, the first woman, and Tiki, her Creator.

Hupene, the old Tohunga, squats muttering on the floor beside his carved ancestor Tiki.

Tiki is a god who in the dim long ago helped to build the world, and whose carved image is now supporting the middle pillar of the house. His eyes of pawa-shell, which once commanded in the ten Heavens and were full of fire and wisdom, glisten out of the silent twilight; they stare far, far into the darkness, which Hine-nui-te-po is slowly spreading over the world, Hine-nui-te-po, the Great Mother of Night, who at one time was young and beautiful, and gave life to Nature.

5

From *Te Tohunga: The Ancient Legends and Traditions of the Maoris* by W. Dittmer, 1907

POLYNESIANS WORSHIPPED

their ancestors as gods, sculpting them into idols of wood and stone. In some of their myths, a demigod named Tiki appeared comparable to the Bible's Adam, this half mortal / half deity was said to be the first man, and possessed human faults and a sense of humor. This eventually inspired the islanders—namely those in the Marquesas and New Zealand—to call all carvings depicting the human form *Tikis*.

In the 20th century, Americans developed a strong affection for the Hawaiian islands. Fueled by popular literature, music, and Hollywood movies, the people of mainland U.S.A. fabricated a romantic vision of Polynesia that ignored complex realities of native culture in favor of an idealized island fantasy.

By the mid-1950s, the Tiki figure became the pop-culture icon of this American yearning for an earthly paradise. This book explores the genesis, evolution, and eventual devolution of this unique transcultural phenomenon.

Tales told by tribal elders recounting their history and ancestors were part of Polynesian culture. Repeated through the generations, the tales eventually deified their ancient heroes, and Tiki, the first man, became a god. According to tribal lore, he created the first woman and then proceeded to make children with her. Henceforth, the Tiki figure was imbued with procreative and phallic powers. But still he possessed the humanlike traits of being a prankster and trickster. Thus, all manlike images became identified with him. In American pop culture, Tiki's meaning was somewhat simplified. American Tiki restaurants preached Tiki's powers in a more Bacchus-like fashion, associating him with good

food and good luck—which conveniently paralleled the services they provided to the American public. Customers saw the Tiki as a symbol of the pagan pleasures disapproved of by postwar America: here, dining among idols, they indulged in potent potions and finger food, forgetting their work world outside.

Possessing creative powers, Tiki was revered as god of the artists by some Polynesians. The carving of ancestor images was a sacred activity performed only by the best native artisans, who created imposing works of art meant to instill respect and awe for the ancestors and their powerful *mana*.

Accurately portraying these statues posed a challenge to Western artists who accompanied the early European expeditions to the Pacific because they were trained as realists and not accustomed to such stylized depictions of the human form. Louis Choris's renderings of Hawaiian gods are among the most faithful of their time. They skillfully reproduced the idols' exaggerated facial features that more than a century later inspired European—and eventually American—artists.

By the early 1960s, Americans were consumed with Tiki. Their love affair with Hawaii and Polynesia had unknowingly converted them into committing a unique form of idolatry. Tikis not only adorned bars and restaurants, but also decorated apartment buildings and motels, and appeared in all sorts of advertising. Importers of exotic handicrafts could not keep up with the increased demand for carved Polynesian godheads, and so with typical American ingenuity, they picked up pen and chisel and fabricated island idols based on native art examples in Oceanic art books—and their own imaginations.

Countless artists added a flair of modernism and a touch of cartoonish whimsy to the savage countenance of the Tiki figure.

In the architecture of Oceanic cultures, ancestor images were carved on support posts, wall panels, and roof gables to protect the structures and those who dwelled within them. The Maori were particularly skillful wood-carvers; their meeting houses were storytelling tools of tribal history.

Larger statues were erected on temple platforms, where they served to invoke the spirits of the various gods of the Polynesian pantheon. Intended less as personifications of the deities, these figures functioned primarily as empty vessels to be temporarily inhabited by the native divinities.

When Hawaii became an American state in 1959, real-estate developers banked on the public equating Polynesian style with a new quality of living. What had proven successful for restaurants was effective for apartments and motels too. Tiki statues were installed as poster boys of the Hawaiian lifestyle, and the name Tiki was invoked to represent an environment of fun and leisure to wannabe islanders stuck in urban centers.

American Tiki architecture utilized the Tiki as support posts—just like their Polynesian predecessors—as well as free-standing sentinels in tropical landscaping, and on signage advertising these various establishments, which all promised a Polynesian paradise on the mainland. A new, modern-primitive style of design had come into being.

In the Polynesian islands, the use of the Tiki image was not limited to just statuary, but also included necklaces and utensils, such as tool handles and poi pounders. Maori *Hei-Tiki* pendants were made from

green jade and followed a specific design. They were treated as special heirlooms, handed down from generation to generation, and as such they were carriers of powerful ancestor *mana*. In American Tiki pop culture, the use of the Tiki in daily life went far beyond that of its Polynesian predecessors. From Tiki mugs to Tiki lamps to Tiki soap, the idol was molded into every possible shape. At that period in time, any

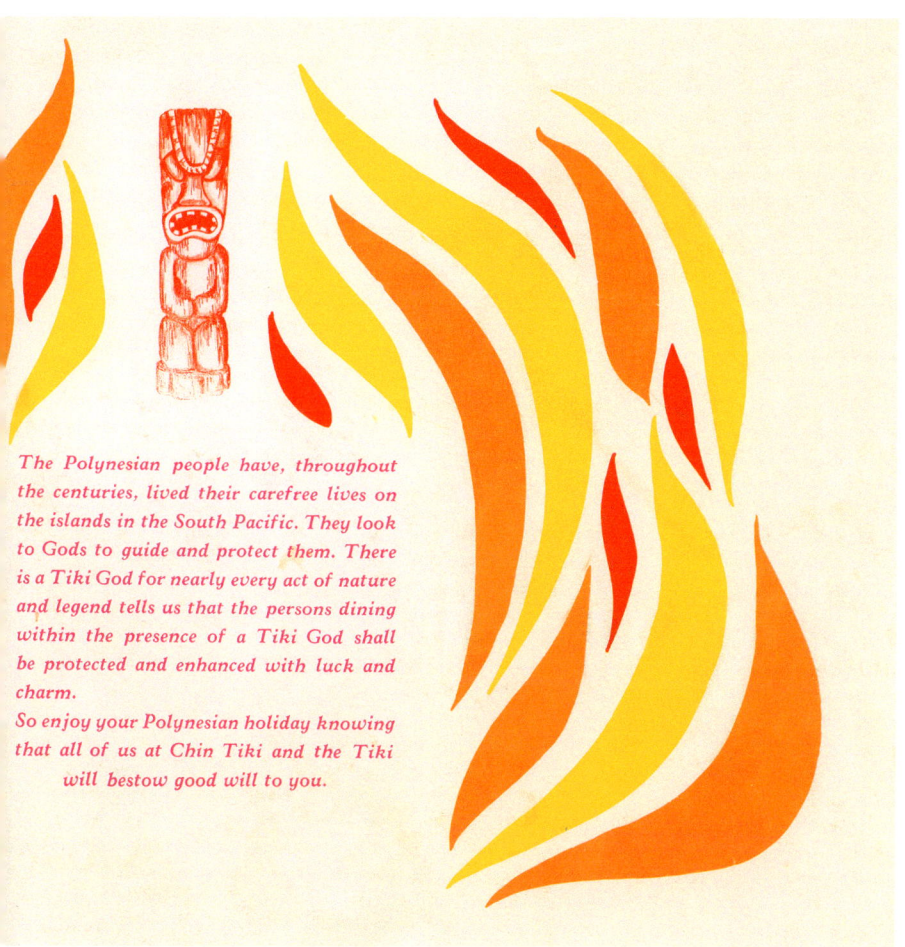

The Polynesian people have, throughout the centuries, lived their carefree lives on the islands in the South Pacific. They look to Gods to guide and protect them. There is a Tiki God for nearly every act of nature and legend tells us that the persons dining within the presence of a Tiki God shall be protected and enhanced with luck and charm.

So enjoy your Polynesian holiday knowing that all of us at Chin Tiki and the Tiki will bestow good will to you.

deeper interest in other cultures' religious beliefs was uncommon. If any spiritual attributes were attached to these items, it was that of "good luck" charms, imbued with a sense of the superstitious.

Although the original Tikis were denounced as pagan idols by the early missionaries and destroyed by priests and natives alike during the islands' conversion to Christianity, some were collected as

Chin Tiki menu, Detroit, 1967
(Frank Brajevic Collection)

curios and brought back to Europe, where they were displayed in museums and galleries. The expressive power that the native artists had conveyed in these works inspired continuous fascination in the public, not least among early-20th-century modern artists, who drew great inspiration from what they saw. To some, these figures functioned as reminders of an archaic, simpler way of life, offering a temporary return to a purer, original existence unfettered by the ills of civilization.

So what was American Tiki Pop? An example of the cultural naïveté of Western culture? Or did this curious outgrowth of popular taste represent a universal impulse of mankind: the search for the betterment of oneself, and the hope that beyond the ills of modern society created by man's shortcomings, there are still people and places pure and innocent? Could Tiki Pop, then, be the desire to attain that state—through whatever silly voodoo was available at the time?

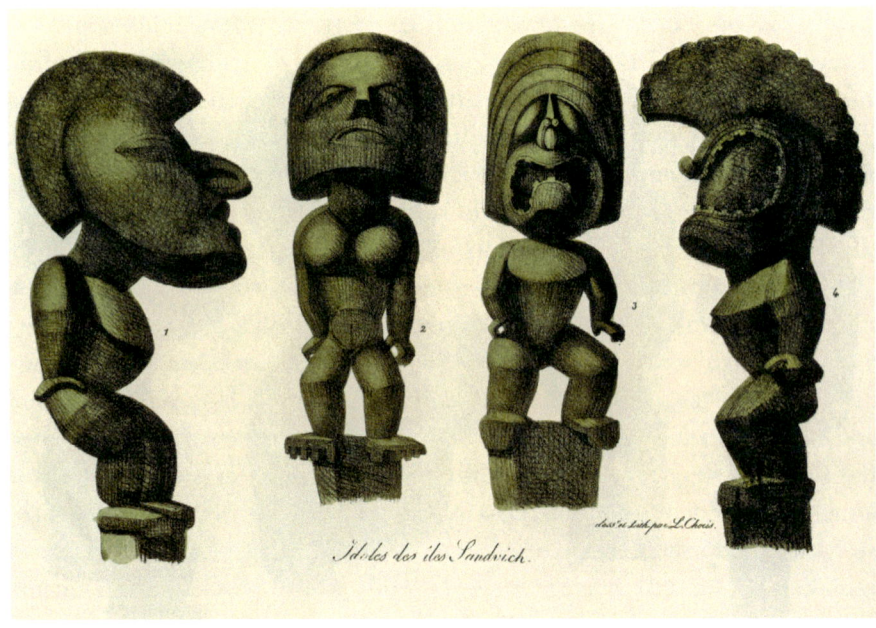

Idoles des îles Sandvich.

ABOVE: Rendering of Hawaiian temple carvings by Louis Choris, ca. 1816

OPPOSITE: Famous gateway at Pukeroa village depicting Tutanekai; Lake Rotorua, New Zealand

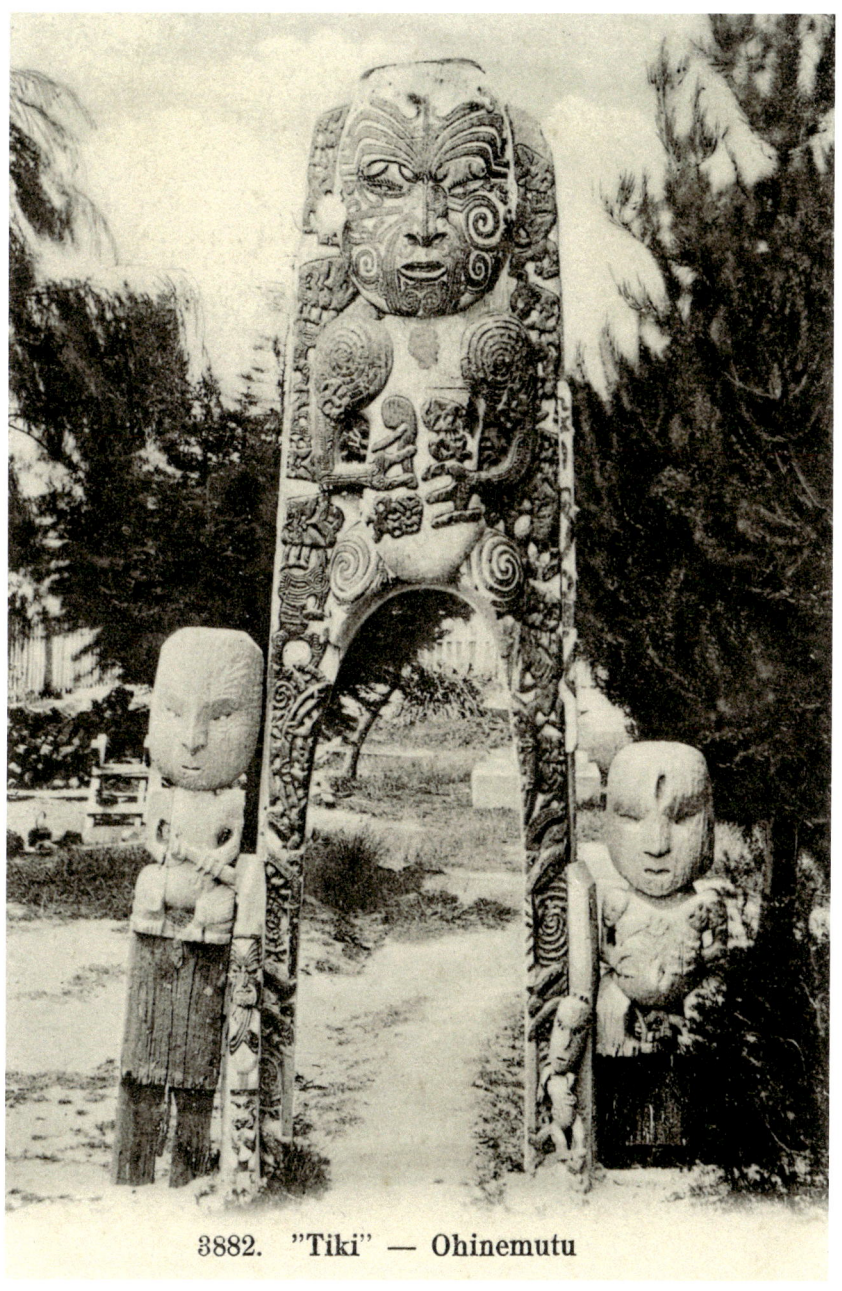

3882. "Tiki" — Ohinemutu

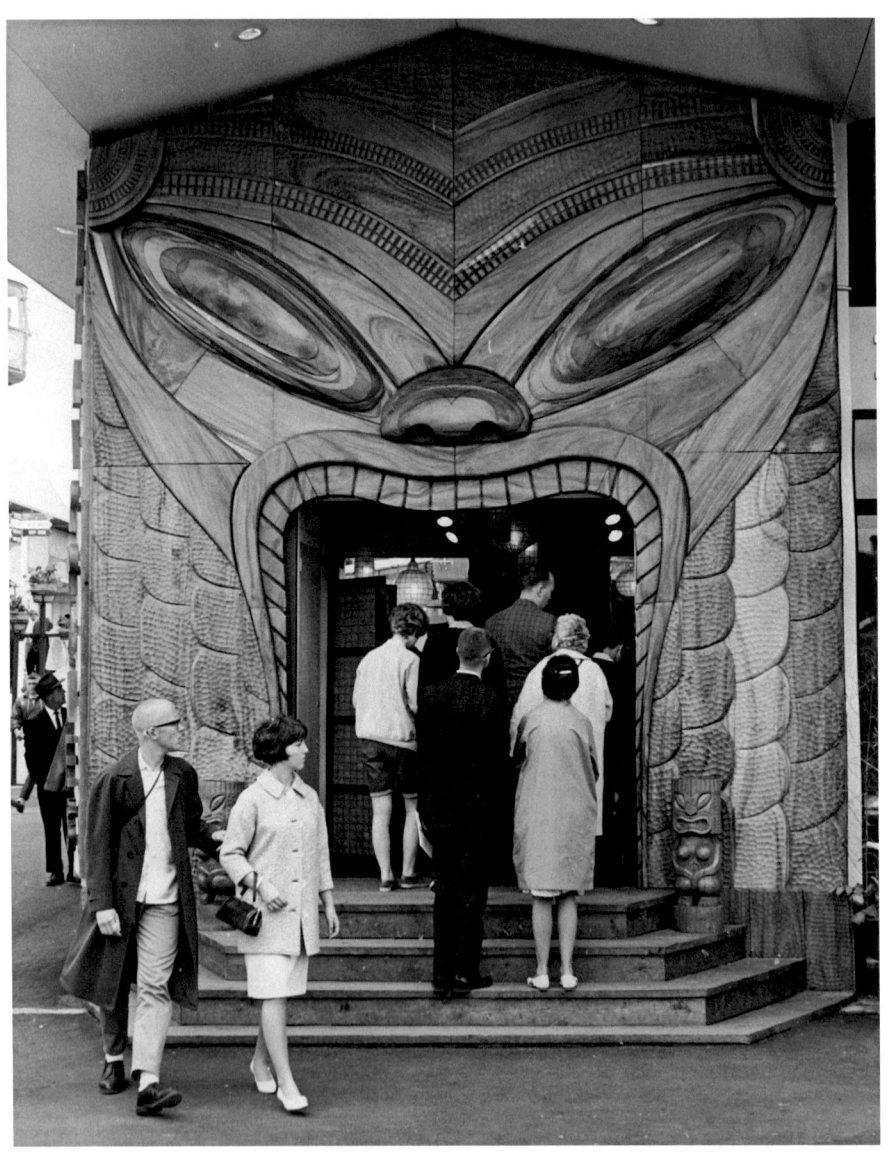

Giant Tiki mouth at the 1962
Seattle World's Fair

DIE POLYNESIER VEREHRTEN

ihre Vorfahren wie Götter und verewigten sie in Götterfiguren aus Holz und Stein. In manchen ihrer Mythen taucht ein Halbgott namens Tiki auf, der dem biblischen Adam gleichkommt. Halb Mann, halb Gott soll er der erste Mensch auf Erden gewesen sein. Er war fehlerbehaftet und hatte Sinn für Humor. Dies führte dazu, dass die Insulaner – genauer gesagt, die Bewohner der Marquesas-Inseln und Neuseelands – fortan alle geschnitzten Darstellungen der menschlichen Figur „Tiki" nannten. Im 20. Jahrhundert entwickelten die Amerikaner eine Vorliebe für die hawaiischen Inseln. Befeuert durch Populärliteratur, Musik und Hollywood-Filme entstand im Kopf der Bewohner des US-amerikanischen Festlands eine romantische Vorstellung von Polynesien – der perfekten Inselidylle –, die die komplexen Realitäten polynesischer Kulturen ignorierte.

Mitte der 1950er-Jahre war die Tiki-Figur bereits zur Popkultur-Ikone der amerikanischen Sehnsucht nach einem Paradies auf Erden geworden. Dieses Buch erforscht die Entstehung, Entwicklung und letztlich den Niedergang dieses einzigartigen transkulturellen Phänomens.

In der polynesischen Kultur war es üblich, dass die Stammesältesten von der Geschichte und den Vorfahren ihres Volkes erzählten. Über die Generationen hinweg wurden die antiken Helden schließlich zu Göttern erhoben und Tiki, der erste Mann, zum Gott. Überlieferungen zufolge erschuf er die erste Frau und pflanzte sich mit ihr fort. Die Tiki-Figur wurde fortan zum Symbol für Fruchtbarkeit und Manneskraft. Die menschlichen Züge blieben jedoch erhalten und Tiki galt weiterhin als Schelm und Gauner,

mit dem alle Abbildungen der menschlichen Gestalt identifiziert wurden.

In der amerikanischen Popkultur wurde Tikis Bedeutung etwas abgewandelt. Tiki-Restaurants bewarben seine Kräfte eher in Bacchus-ähnlicher Weise und verbanden ihn mit gutem Essen und viel Glück, was praktischerweise eine Repräsentation ihrer eigenen Dienstleistungen war. Für die Kunden wurde Tiki zum Symbol heidnischer Vergnügungen, die von der Nachkriegsgesellschaft missbilligt wurden. Man aß Fingerfood zwischen Götterfiguren, trank starke Cocktails und kehrte der Arbeitswelt für einen Moment den Rücken.

Wegen der ihm zugeschriebenen schöpferischen Kraft wurde Tiki von manchen Polynesiern als Gott der Künstler verehrt. Das Schnitzen von Götterfiguren galt als heiliger Akt. Nur die besten einheimischen Kunsthandwerker führten diese Arbeit aus und erschufen eindrucksvolle Werke, die den Menschen Ehrfurcht und Bewunderung für ihre Vorfahren und deren mächtiges Mana einflößen sollten.

Die akkurate Darstellung dieser Statuen stellte die westlichen Künstler, die frühe europäische Pazifikexpeditionen begleiteten, vor eine Herausforderung. Sie waren ausgewiesene Realisten und taten sich mit den stilisierten Darstellungen der menschlichen Form schwer. Ludwig Choris' Darstellungen hawaiischer Götter gehören zu den originalgetreuesten ihrer Zeit. Geschickt brachte er ihre markanten Gesichtszüge zu Papier; mehr als ein Jahrhundert später sollten sie europäische und schließlich auch amerikanische Künstler inspirieren.

Anfang der 1960er-Jahre waren die US-Amerikaner von Tiki nahezu besessen. Ihre Liebe zu Hawaii und Polynesien hatte sie unbewusst zu einer einzigartigen Form des

Götzendienstes verführt. Tikis dekorierten nicht nur Bars und Restaurants, sondern auch Wohngebäude und Motels und tauchten auf allen möglichen Werbeträgern auf.

Die Importeure für exotisches Kunsthandwerk konnten die gesteigerte Nachfrage nach geschnitzten polynesischen Götterfiguren kaum bedienen. So griffen sie schließlich – typisch amerikanisch – selbst zu Stift und Meißel und erschufen ihre eigenen Insel-Ikonen, wobei sie sich von ihrer Vorstellungskraft ebenso leiten ließen wie von Abbildungen in Kunstbüchern. Unzählige Künstler verliehen Tikis primitiver Miene ein modernes Flair und eine karikaturartige Verspieltheit.

Die ozeanischen Kulturen schnitzten ihre Götterfiguren in Stützpfosten, Wandplatten und Dachgiebel zum Schutz von Häusern und Bewohnern. Die Maori waren besonders talentierte Holzschnitzer und verzierten ihre Begegnungsstätten mit Darstellungen der Geschichte ihres Stammes.

Für ihre Tempel errichteten sie größere Statuen, um die Geister diverser Götter des polynesischen Pantheons zu beschwören. Die Figuren waren keine Personifizierungen eines bestimmten Gottes; vielmehr wurden sie als leere Gefäße betrachtet, die von den einheimischen Gottheiten vorübergehend bewohnt werden konnten.

Als Hawaii 1959 amerikanischer Bundesstaat wurde, rechneten Immobilienentwickler damit, dass die Bevölkerung den polynesischen Gebäudestil mit neuer Lebensqualität gleichsetzen würde. Was für Restaurants funktionierte, sollte auch für Wohnungen und Motels funktionieren. Tiki-Statuen wurden zur Titelfigur des hawaiischen Lebensstils der Möchtegern-Insulaner ernannt, der Name Tiki stand für Leichtigkeit und Vergnügen.

Die amerikanische Tiki-Architektur setzte die Götterfiguren – wie auch ihre polynesischen Vorgänger – sowohl als Stützpfeiler als auch als freistehende Wächter in tropisch gestalteten Gärten ein. Tiki verzierte auch die Schilder, die diese Immobilien bewarben und ein polynesisches Paradies auf dem Festland versprachen. Ein neues, primitivmodernes Design war geboren.

Auf den polynesischen Inseln beschränkte sich die Verwendung von Tikis Abbild nicht nur auf Statuen, sondern umfasste auch Halsketten und andere Gebrauchsgegenstände wie Werkzeuggriffe und Stößel. Die Maori fertigten ihre Hei-Tiki-Anhänger aus grüner Jade nach einem speziellen Design. Als wertvolle Erbstücke reichten sie diese von Generation zu Generation weiter. So wurden sie zu Trägern des mächtigen Mana ihrer Vorfahren.

Die Amerikaner schöpften die Tiki-Motive um Einiges weiter aus als ihre polynesischen Vorgänger. Von Tiki-Bechern über Tiki-Lampen bis hin zu Tiki-Seife – die Götterfigur wurde in jede nur mögliche Form gebracht. Zur damaligen Zeit war ein tiefgründiges Interesse an religiösen Glaubenssätzen anderer Kulturen eher ungewöhnlich. Falls die Tiki-Produkte einen spirituellen Charakter hatten, dann höchstens in der Funktion als Talisman.

Die ursprünglichen Tikis wurden von den frühen Missionaren als Götzenbilder gebrandmarkt und während der Christianisierung der Inseln von Priestern wie auch von Einheimischen zerstört. Zahlreiche Skulpturen wurden jedoch von neugierigen Entdeckern mit nach Europa genommen, wo Museen und Galerien sie ausstellten. Die ausdrucksstarken Werke der Ureinwohner faszinierten die Bevölkerung und nicht zuletzt die modernen Künstler des

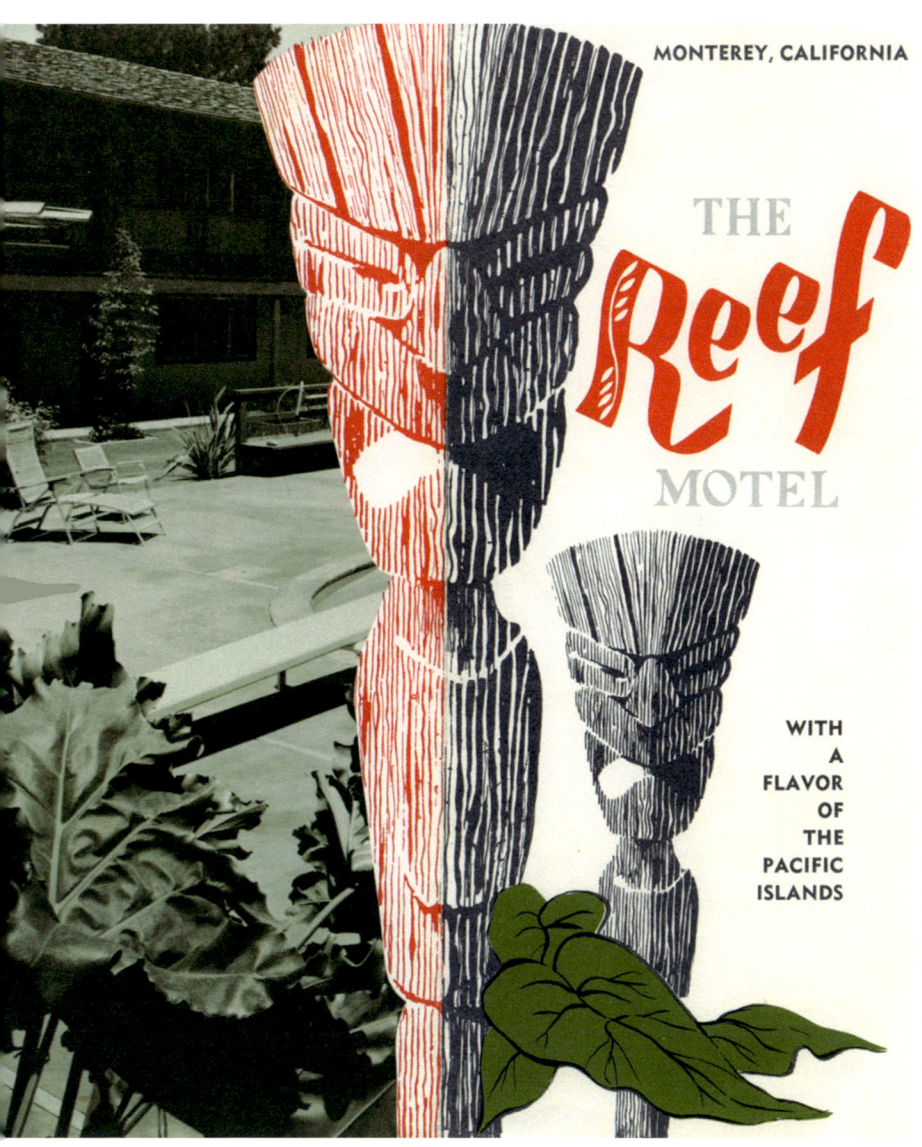

THE Reef MOTEL

WITH
A
FLAVOR
OF
THE
PACIFIC
ISLANDS

Brochure for the Reef Motel, 1960s
(Jackie Zumwalt Collection)

frühen 20. Jahrhunderts, die sich von ihnen inspirieren ließen. Etliche sahen sich durch diese Figuren an einen archaischen, schlichten Lebensstil erinnert. Es war eine vorübergehende Rückkehr zu einer vermeintlich reinen, ursprünglichen Existenz, frei von den Missständen der westlichen Zivilisation.

Was war nun der amerikanische Tiki-Pop? Ein Beispiel für die kulturelle Naivität des Westens? Oder repräsentierte diese kuriose Mode einen universellen Antrieb der Menschheit: den Wunsch, ein besserer Mensch zu werden, und die Hoffnung, dass es abseits aller Missstände der modernen Gesellschaft noch reine und unschuldige Völker und Orte gibt? Könnte Tiki-Pop dann der Versuch gewesen sein, diesen Zustand zu erreichen, so bizarr die Mittel auch scheinen mögen?

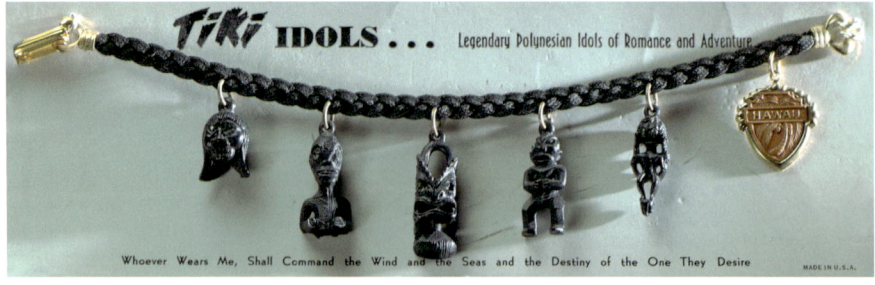

ABOVE: Hawaiian souvenir bracelet, 1960s

OPPOSITE: Maori meeting house *Rauru*, with native guide

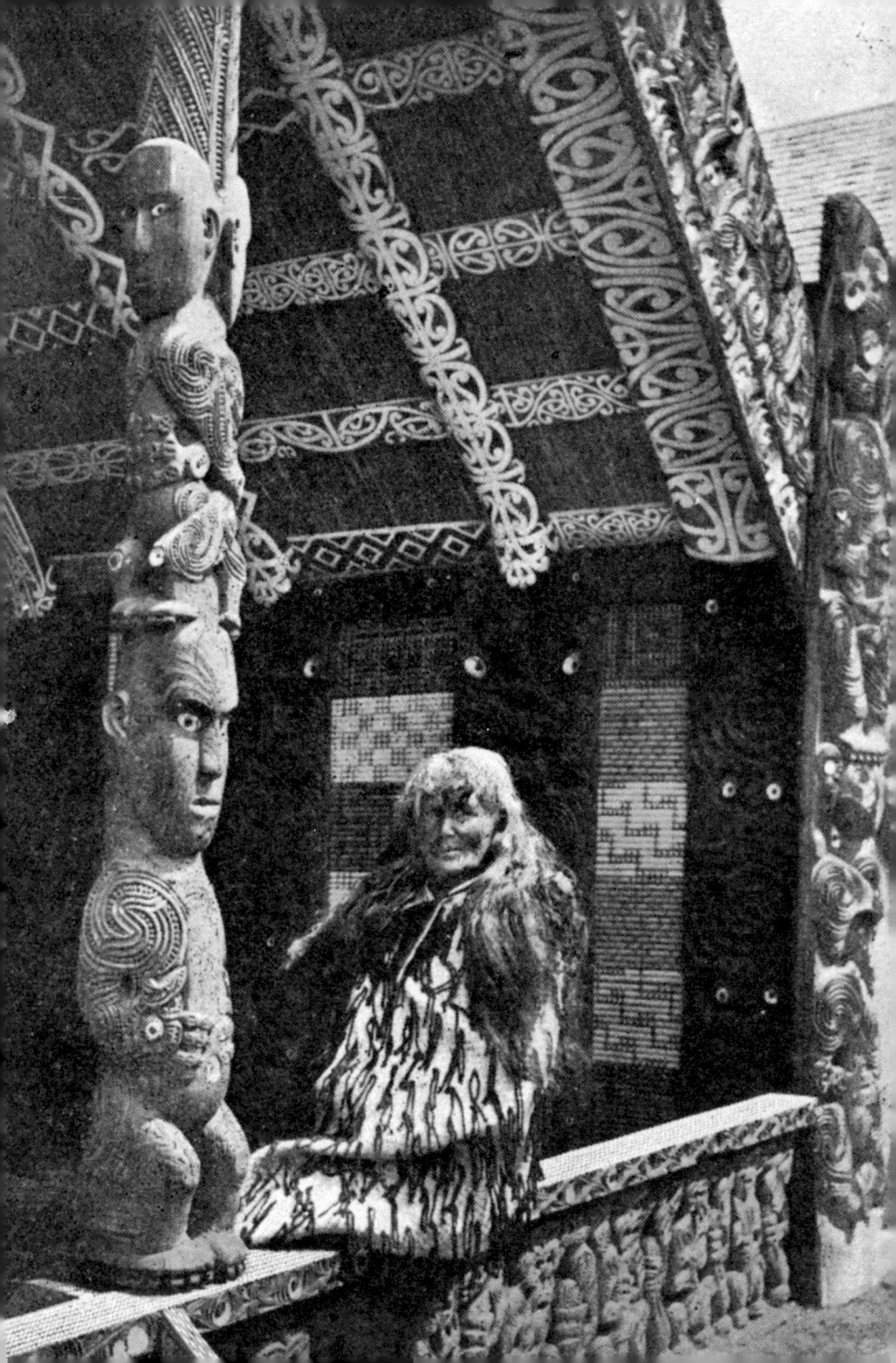

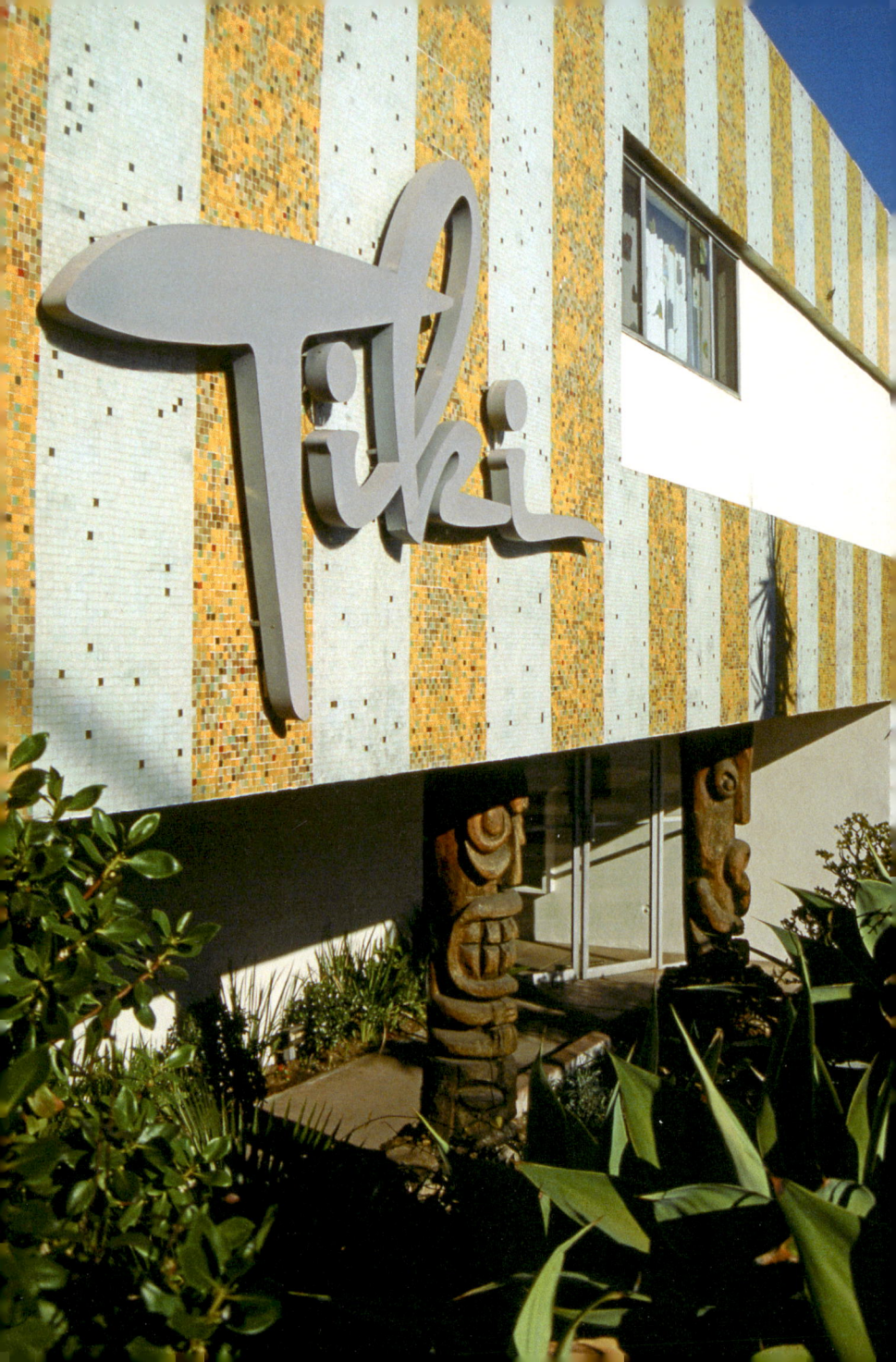

LES POLYNÉSIENS QUI VÉNÉRAIENT leurs ancêtres à l'égal de dieux les ont représentés dans leurs idoles de bois ou de pierre. Dans certains de leurs mythes apparaît un demi-dieu nommé « Tiki ». Comparable à l'Adam de la Bible, cette créature semi-mortelle et semi-divine, réputée être le premier homme, possédait des défauts humains et le sens de l'humour. Ce qui a finalement incité les insulaires, précisément ceux originaires des Marquises et de Nouvelle-Zélande, à baptiser « tikis » ces sculptures à figure humaine.

Au XXᵉ siècle, les Américains se sont pris d'une profonde affection pour les îles hawaiiennes. Pétris de littérature populaire, de musique et de cinéma hollywoodien, les continentaux ont élaboré une vision romancée de la Polynésie qui délaissait les réalités complexes de la culture autochtone au profit d'une île de fantaisie largement idéalisée.

Vers le milieu des années 1950, la figure de Tiki est devenue une icône de la culture pop, incarnant cette nostalgie américaine d'un paradis terrestre. Ce livre relate la genèse, l'évolution et le déclin de ce phénomène transculturel unique.

Les récits des anciens relatant l'histoire et dépeignant les ancêtres de la tribu faisaient partie de la culture polynésienne. Leur transmission sur des générations a fini par déifier les héros anciens, à commencer par Tiki, le premier homme, élevé au rang de dieu. Selon la légende tribale, il a créé la première femme avec laquelle il a ensuite entrepris de faire des enfants. Dès lors, la figure de Tiki se chargeait d'une puissance phallique et procréatrice. Il possédait néanmoins des attributs humains puisqu'il est représenté sous les traits d'un farceur et d'un filou. C'est ainsi que toutes les figures humaines ont fini par s'identifier à lui.

Dans la culture pop américaine, Tiki a été quelque peu simplifié. Les restaurants tiki vantaient la puissance d'un personnage plutôt bachique, associé à la bonne chère et à la chance, une image en parfaite adéquation avec ce qu'ils offraient au public américain. Les clients voyaient donc en Tiki le symbole des plaisirs païens que réprouvait l'Amérique au lendemain de la Seconde Guerre mondiale : entourés de divinités, ils étaient autorisés à faire bombance et à manger avec les doigts, oubliant le temps d'un repas leur quotidien professionnel.

Du fait de sa puissance créatrice, Tiki est vénéré à l'égal d'un dieu des artistes par certaines peuplades polynésiennes. Sculpter les figures d'ancêtres était une activité sacrée exclusivement réservée aux meilleurs artisans autochtones, lesquels créaient d'imposantes œuvres d'art destinées à inspirer le respect et la crainte envers les ancêtres et leur puissant *mana*.

La reproduction fidèle de ces statues a posé un problème aux artistes occidentaux attachés aux premières expéditions européennes dans le Pacifique parce qu'ils étaient formés à l'esthétique réaliste et n'étaient pas habitués à ces représentations stylisées de la figure humaine. Les représentations des dieux hawaiiens par Louis Choris comptent parmi les plus fidèles de leur époque. Elles reproduisent avec brio les visages aux expressions outrées

Tiki apartments,
Redondo Beach, 1963

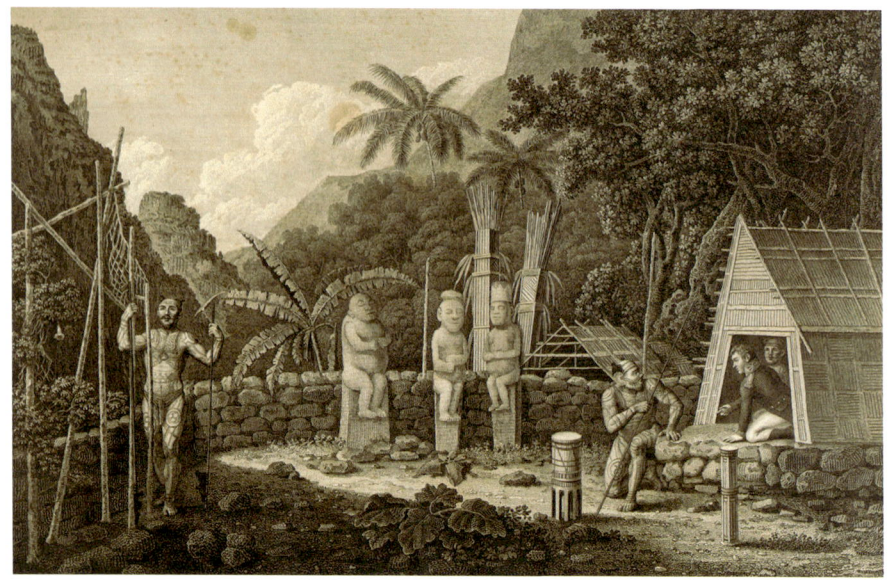

des idoles qui devaient inspirer, plus d'un siècle après, les artistes européens puis américains.

Au début des années 1960, les Américains étaient dévorés par la passion tiki. Leur histoire d'amour avec Hawaii et la Polynésie les avait inconsciemment poussés à développer une forme unique d'idolâtrie. Les tikis ornaient les bars et restaurants, les résidences et les motels… et s'incrustaient dans pléthore de publicités. Les importateurs d'objets d'artisanat, qui ne pouvaient satisfaire la demande croissante en têtes d'idoles polynésiennes sculptées,

se résolurent, avec une ingénuité américaine typique, à faire usage du crayon et du ciseau de sculpteur pour réaliser des idoles insulaires inspirées d'exemples d'art autochtone océanien – ainsi que de leur propre imagination. D'innombrables artistes ajoutèrent ainsi une touche de modernisme et de fantaisie « BD » à l'apparence sauvage des figures de Tiki.

Dans l'architecture vernaculaire océanique, les images d'ancêtres étaient sculptées sur les piliers, les panneaux muraux et les auvents dans le but de protéger les constructions et ceux qui y vivaient. Les

ABOVE: Marquesan temple from Krusenstern's voyage around the world, 1803–1806

OPPOSITE: View-Master 3-D slide set for Tiki Gardens amusement park, Florida, mid-1960s

Maoris étaient des sculpteurs particulièrement habiles. Leurs maisons de réunion
faisaient fonction de supports narratifs de
l'histoire tribale.

Les statues les plus imposantes étaient
érigées sur les estrades des temples où elles
servaient à invoquer les esprits des divers
dieux du panthéon polynésien. Ces figures
étaient conçues comme des réceptacles
vides destinés à offrir un refuge temporaire

aux divinités autochtones, et non pas
comme des personnifications de déités.

Quand Hawaii est devenu, en 1959, un
État américain, des promoteurs immobiliers
ont parié que le public assimilerait le style
polynésien à une nouvelle qualité de vie.
Ce qui s'était avéré si fructueux pour l'aménagement de restaurants réussit tout aussi
bien en matière de décoration d'appartements
et de motels. Les statues de Tiki servaient

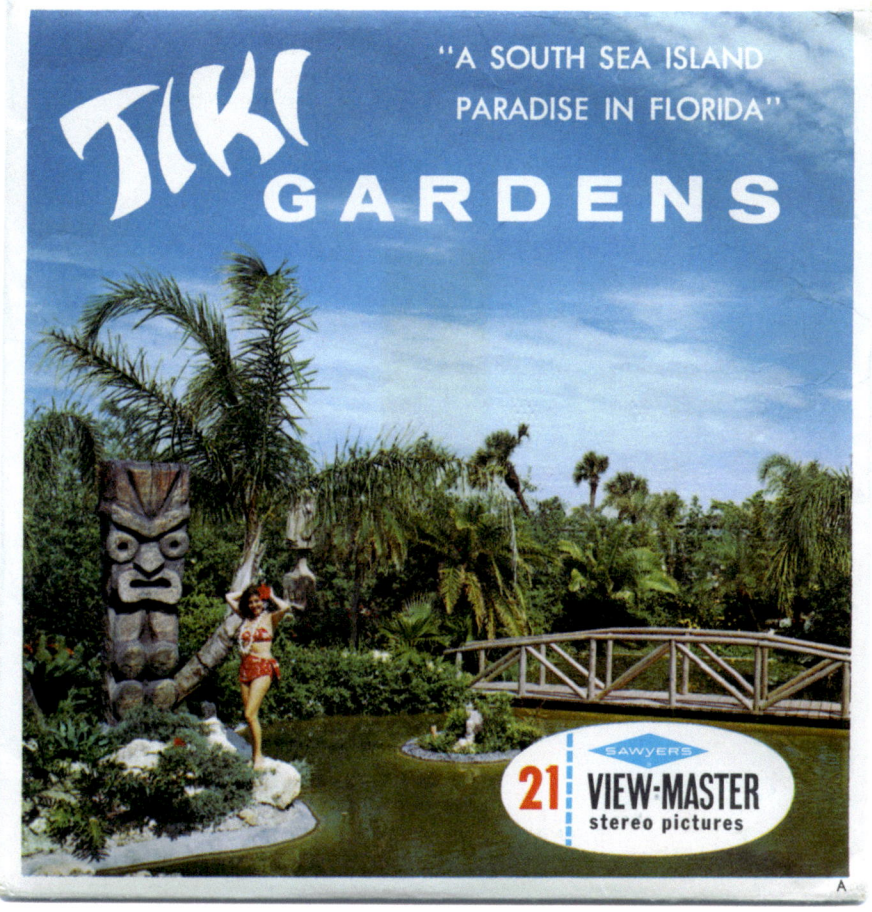

de panneaux publicitaires glorifiant le style de vie hawaiien, et l'appellation tiki était invoquée pour représenter tout cadre plaisant et relaxant destiné aux aspirants à la vie insulaire coincés dans des agglomérations urbaines. L'architecture américaine tiki déclinait l'idole sous forme de piliers sculptés – exactement comme en Polynésie –, de sentinelles dressées ici ou là dans un paysage tropical, ainsi que sur les panonceaux publicitaires des divers établissements qui louaient à l'unisson le paradis polynésien aux continentaux. Un style de design nouveau, à la fois moderne et primitif, venait de naître.

Sur les îles polynésiennes, la figure du Tiki n'était pas réservée à la seule statuaire, elle décorait aussi pendentifs et ustensiles divers, manches d'outils ou pilons à *poi*. Les pendentifs maoris *hei tiki* en jade vert gravé obéissaient à une conception spécifique. Ces objets de famille, transmis de génération en génération, étaient particulièrement vénérés et à ce titre chargés du puissant *mana* des ancêtres.

Dans la culture américaine tiki pop, l'usage du Tiki dans la vie quotidienne allait bien au-delà de celui qu'en faisaient ses prédécesseurs polynésiens. Des mugs aux lampes ou aux savons tiki, l'idole était moulée dans toutes les formes imaginables. À cette époque, un intérêt aussi profond pour les croyances religieuses d'autres cultures était inhabituel. Si un attribut spirituel quelconque était attaché à ce type d'objets, avec une connotation superstitieuse, c'était celui de « porte-bonheur ».

Bien que les tikis originels aient été condamnés comme idoles païennes par les premiers missionnaires et détruits par les prêtres aussi bien que par les autochtones au moment de leur conversion au christianisme, certains d'entre eux ont été collectés à titre de *curios* et rapportés en Europe où ils furent exposés dans les musées et les galeries. La puissance expressive que les artistes du Pacifique avaient su leur conférer a exercé une fascination constante sur le public, et tout autant sur

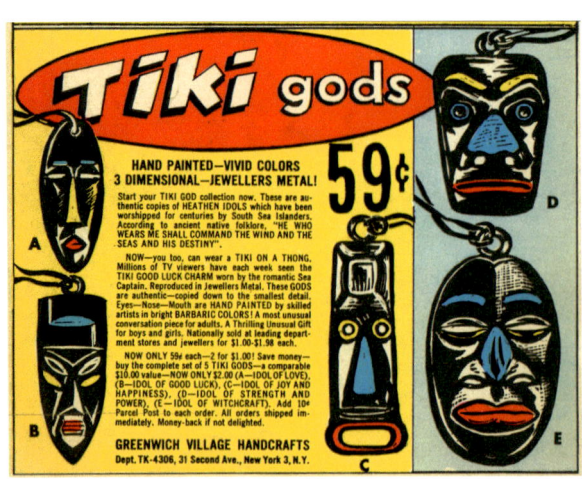

LEFT: Ad for Tiki pendants, referencing Gardner McKay in the TV series *Adventures in Paradise*

OPPOSITE: Maori maiden wearing typical *Hei-Tiki* pendant

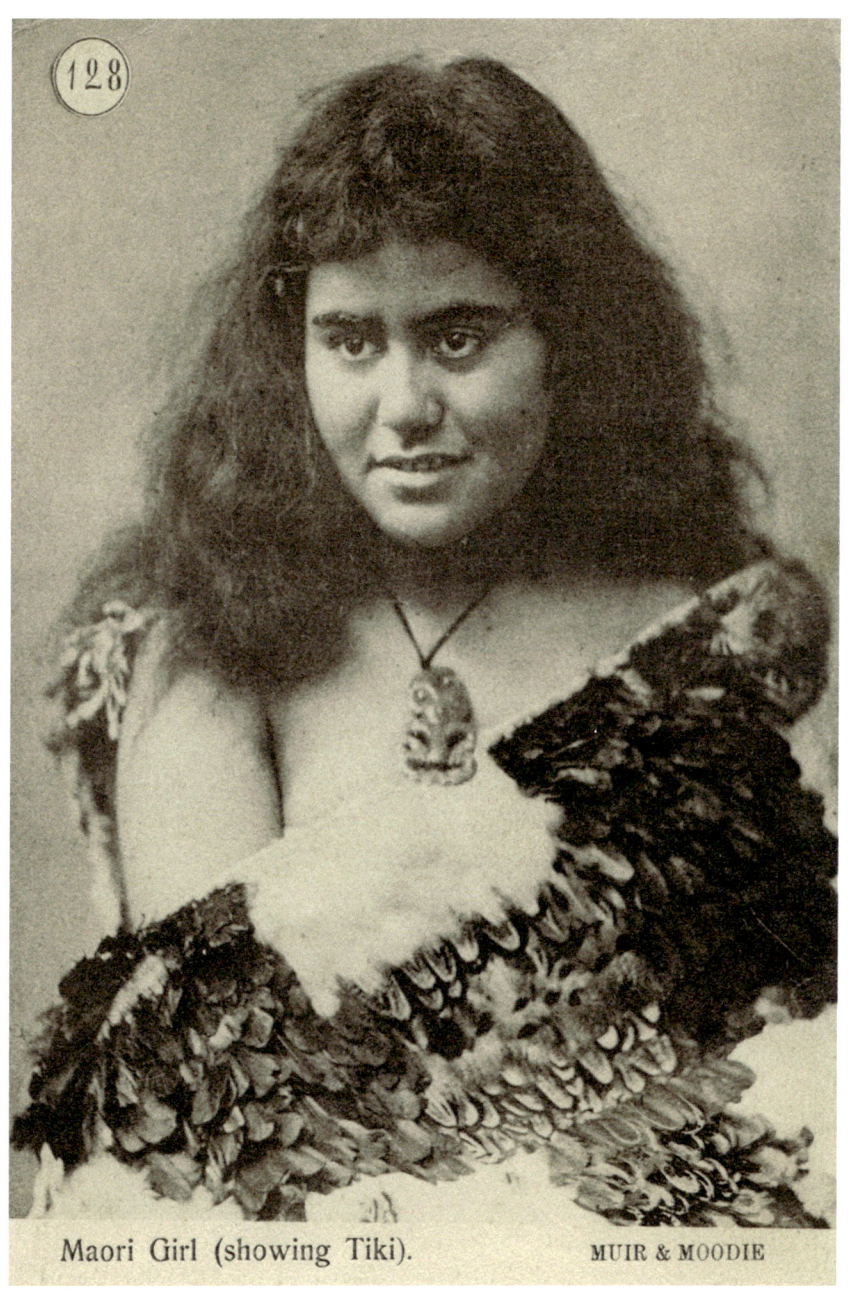

Maori Girl (showing Tiki).   MUIR & MOODIE

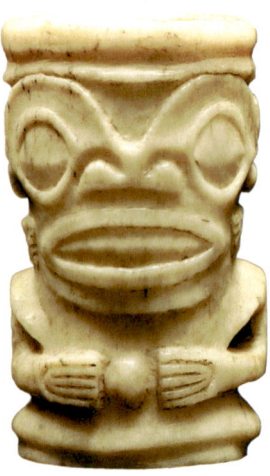

LEFT: Marquesan Tiki toggle, sometimes carved from human bone (*Musée du Quai Branly Collection*)

BELOW: Ceramic condiment dish set, late 1960s

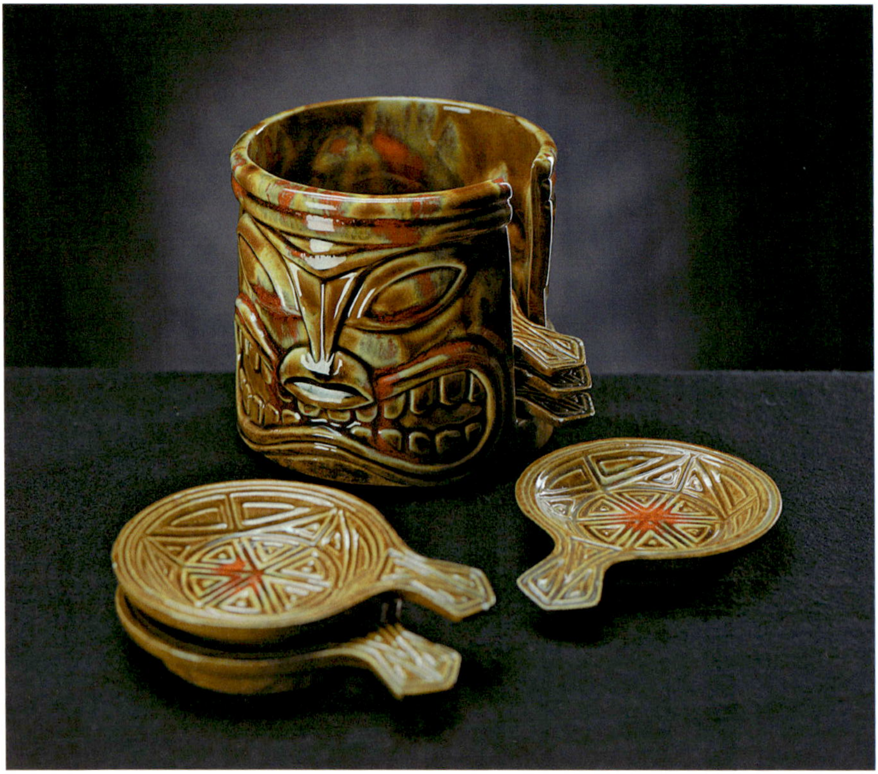

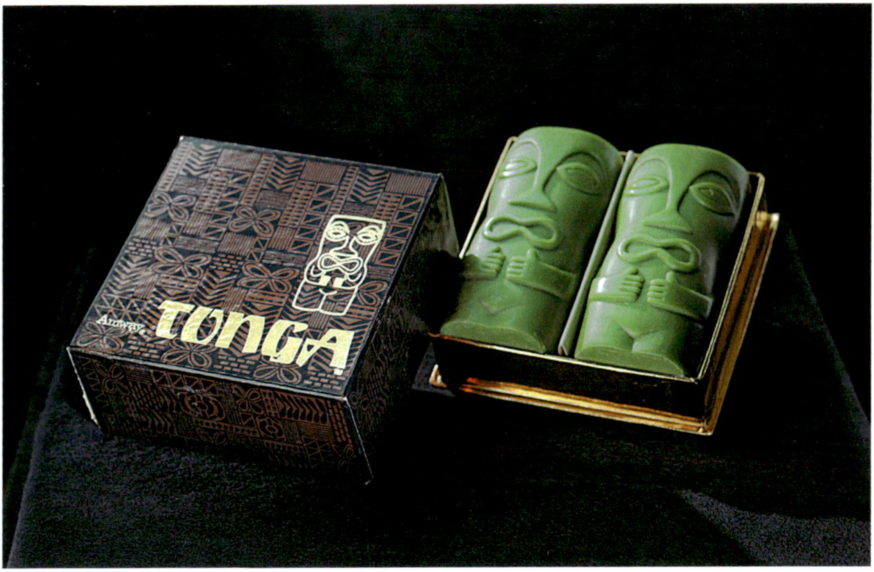

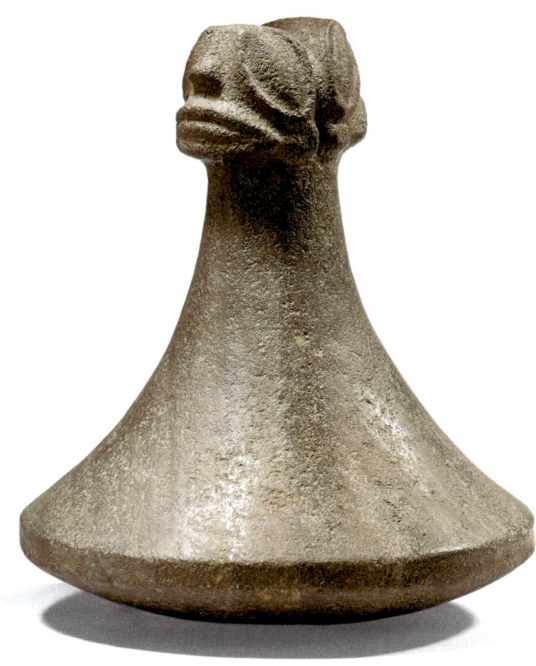

ABOVE: Tiki soap set by Amway, mid-1960s *(Kate Simmons Collection)*

LEFT: Stone pounder used to make poi paste, Marquesas Islands *(Musée du Quai Branly Collection)*

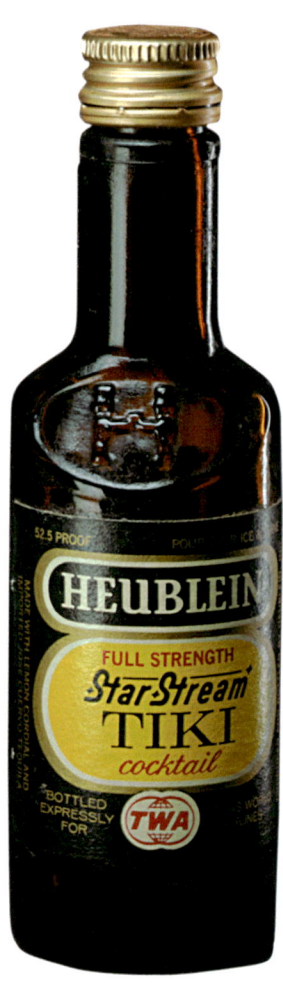

les artistes modernes du début du XXᵉ siècle qui ont été profondément inspirés par cette découverte. Pour certains d'entre eux, ces figures fonctionnaient comme des rappels d'un mode de vie archaïque, plus simple, offrant un retour temporaire à une existence plus pure, originale, encore indemne des maux de la civilisation.

Comment définir exactement le tiki pop américain ? Une expression de la naïveté culturelle de la culture occidentale ? Ou bien cette étrange excroissance du goût populaire représente-t-elle ce à quoi l'humanité aspire de façon universelle : la quête d'une amélioration du moi et l'espoir qu'au-delà des maux de la société moderne dus aux imperfections humaines, il subsiste encore des êtres et des lieux purs et innocents ? Le tiki pop représenterait-il alors le désir d'atteindre cet état par le truchement d'une quelconque imagerie vaudou plus ou moins niaise disponible à l'époque ?

ABOVE: Inflight cocktail for the jet-setter

RIGHT: Tiki lighter and ad from Hawaii Kai Restaurant, New York, 1960s

OPPOSITE: 1967 booklet containing copies of the American Declaration of Independence, the Constitution, and other historic documents

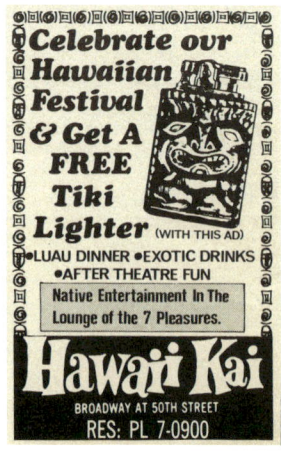

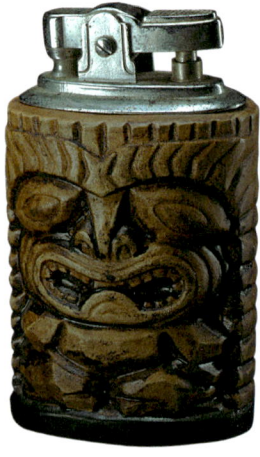

THE FREEDOM COLLECTION

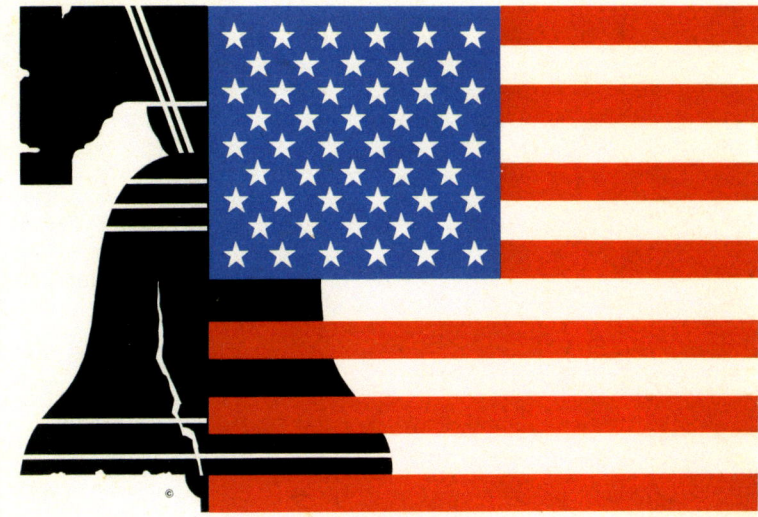

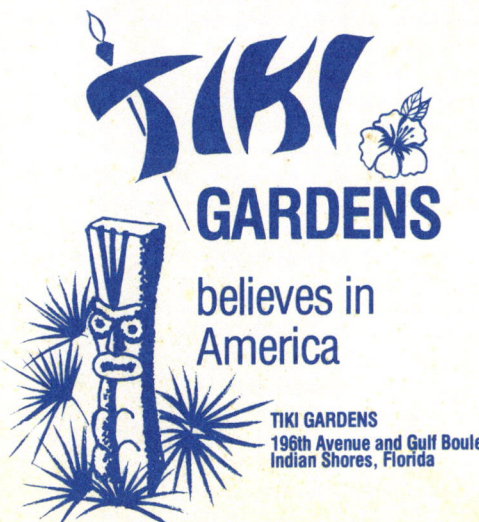

TIKI GARDENS
believes in
America

TIKI GARDENS
196th Avenue and Gulf Boulevard
Indian Shores, Florida

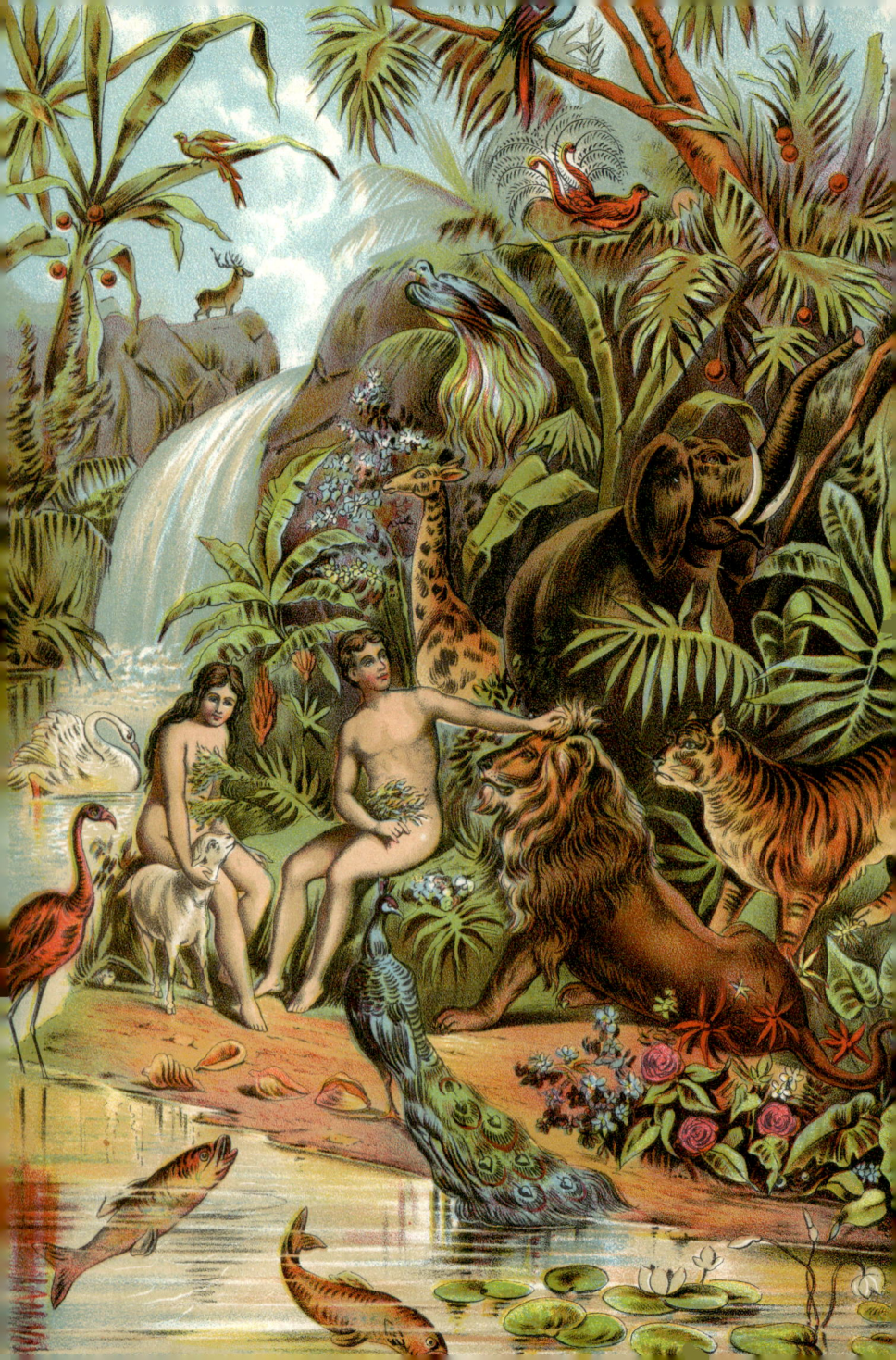

COOK, BOUGAINVILLE, AND THE EARLY EXPLORERS

COOK, BOUGAINVILLE UND DIE FRÜHEN ENTDECKER
COOK, BOUGAINVILLE ET LES PREMIERS EXPLORATEURS

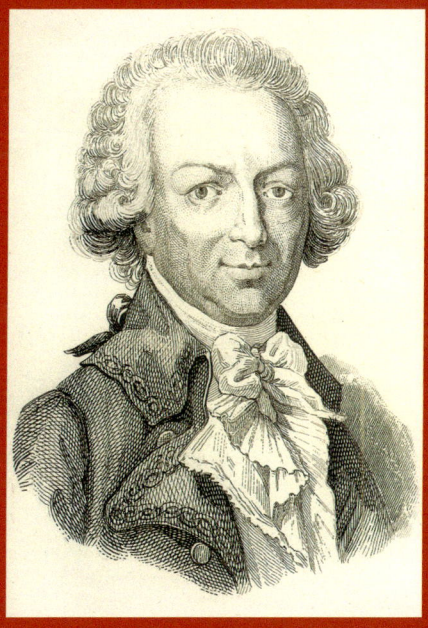

OPPOSITE: Book illustration of the biblical concept of Paradise, 1871

ABOVE: Portrait of Louis Antoine de Bougainville

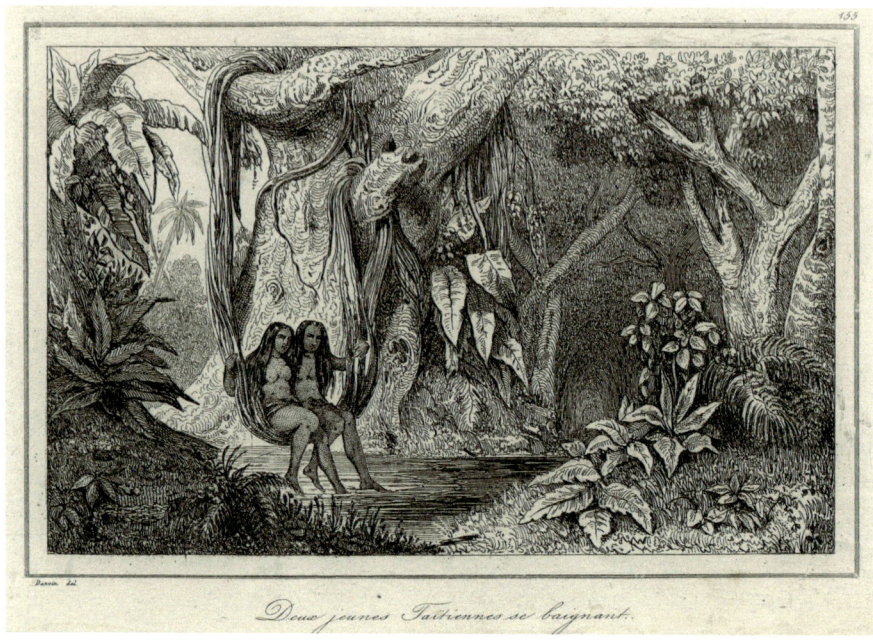

Deux jeunes Taïtiennes se baignant.

CHRISTIANITY'S DOCTRINE OF

man's expulsion from Paradise had ingrained in Western Europe a sense of civilization's loss and separation from its own true condition. When the first European explorers encountered the Pacific Islanders living in harmony with nature, unencumbered by heavy clothes due to the mild climate, they were led to believe that the "original state" was not lost after all. Here were a people that could live off nature's bounty without much effort: happy, healthy, and beautiful.

In the 18th century, the Pacific Ocean and its islands were still uncharted territory. The first navigators came upon the Polynesian islands by chance and thought them to be the unknown coast of a continent. It was a welcome mistake, nevertheless: after months at sea, the sight of lush, tropical

landscapes—and bare-breasted native women soon thereafter—did indeed seem like paradise on earth to the exhausted sailors. It took the experience and leadership of such men as Captain James Cook to keep the crew at bay.

To the Tahitians, sexuality was something to be enjoyed freely and openly, and gladly shared with their guests. Captivated by this carefree behavior, French navigator Louis Antoine de Bougainville named the island New Cythera, after the birthplace of Aphrodite, the Greek goddess of love. However, recent theory suggests that the natives' offering of their women was a tactical maneuver, developed after having lost several of their men a year before to the superior firepower of the British, when they attacked the ship of Captain Samuel Wallis. Having seen that there were no women onboard the ship, the islanders deduced that the seafarers had come in search of what they were lacking. It was easy to curry the interlopers' favor by sharing what they had an abundance of and did not attach special value to.

One circumstance that worked in the explorers' favor was that native priests had foretold of the arrival of certain divinities by sea. Thus, the strangers were greeted as gods, equal to or greater than the local rulers. The superior technology of their ships and weapons did not suggest otherwise to the Polynesians, and the "white gods" did nothing to dispel their beliefs.

The ship navigators' mission was finding new trade routes, but as educated men of culture, they took interest in the tropical environments and foreign customs that they encountered and recorded them in their logs. These expeditions also counted among their crew natural scientists, who were trained in documenting exotic people, places, and implements as faithfully as possible. Their renderings visually complemented the travelogues of the seafarers when they were published on the mainland. Although the explorers' intent was largely scientific, they did not refrain from adding their own personal observations and opinions about island life. Their writings were received with interest by the educated classes in Europe, with special attention being paid to the liberal sexual mores found in Polynesian society.

At this time, French philosopher Jean-Jacques Rousseau was advocating the idea of the "noble savage" living in a state of nature, "unencumbered by civilization and divine revelation." The glowing reports in which Bougainville and his botanist, Philibert Commerson, described South Seas island life gave further credence to the vision of a utopian return to nature, and liberal thinkers employed the material as critique of the ills of civilized society. The literary salons of Europe were abuzz with discussions about Polynesia.

The mainland's reception and interpretation of the early explorers' travelogues was the first step toward changing the perception of the Pacific Islands from fact to fiction. Henceforth, inhabitants of the Western Hemisphere dreamed of tropical island beaches as romantic getaways and as an escape from old traditions that were holding them back and had lost their luster. This, then, was the beginning of the projection of Polynesian Pop, which laid the groundwork for the appearance of Tiki Pop.

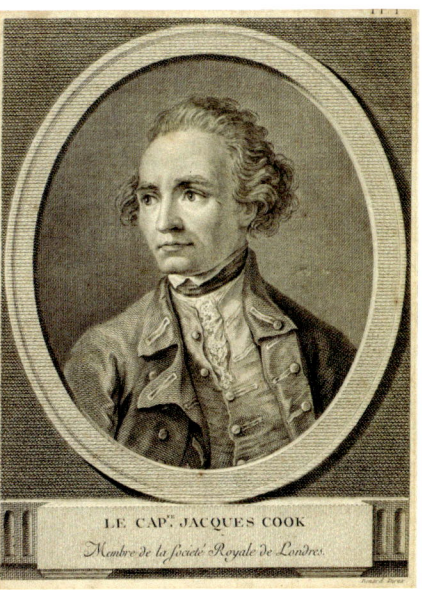

LE CAP.ᵗ JACQUES COOK
Membre de la société Royale de Londres.

OPPOSITE: Two young Tahitians bathing, engraving, ca. 1850

RIGHT: Portrait of James Cook

LAUT CHRISTLICHER LEHRE WURDE der Mensch aus dem Paradies verbannt. Die Westeuropäer wuchsen demzufolge in dem Glauben auf, dass sie nicht so lebten, wie es ihnen ursprünglich bestimmt war. Als die ersten europäischen Entdecker den Inselbewohnern des Pazifiks begegneten, die im Einklang mit der Natur lebten und sich angesichts des milden Klimas nur leicht bekleideten, glaubten die Entdecker, dass der Ursprungszustand des Menschen doch nicht ganz verloren gegangen war. Hier gab es ein Volk, das ohne Anstrengung von der Natur leben konnte. Die Menschen waren glücklich, gesund und schön. Im 18. Jahrhundert war der Pazifische Ozean

mit seinen Inseln noch unbekanntes Terrain. Die ersten Seefahrer stießen durch Zufall auf die polynesischen Inseln und hielten sie für die unbekannte Küste eines Kontinents. Es war ein willkommener Irrglaube. Nach Monaten auf See schien der Anblick üppiger tropischer Landschaften – und kurz darauf barbusiger Frauen – den erschöpften Seemännern das Paradies auf Erden zu verkünden. Es bedurfte der Führung erfahrener Männer wie Kapitän James Cook, um die Crew in Schach zu halten.

Die Tahitianer lebten ihre Sexualität offen und frei aus und teilten sie auch gern mit ihren Gästen. Angezogen von diesem sorglosen Verhalten, nannte der

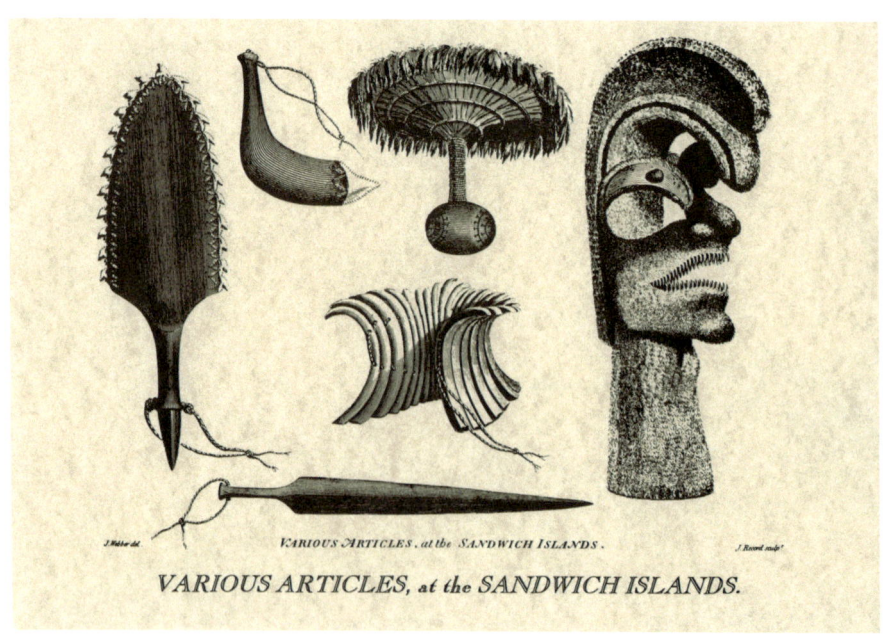

VARIOUS ARTICLES, at the SANDWICH ISLANDS.

ABOVE: Various implements from the Hawaiian Islands, rendered by John Webber, 1780

OPPOSITE: Johann Forster and his son Georg, naturalists on Cook's second voyage

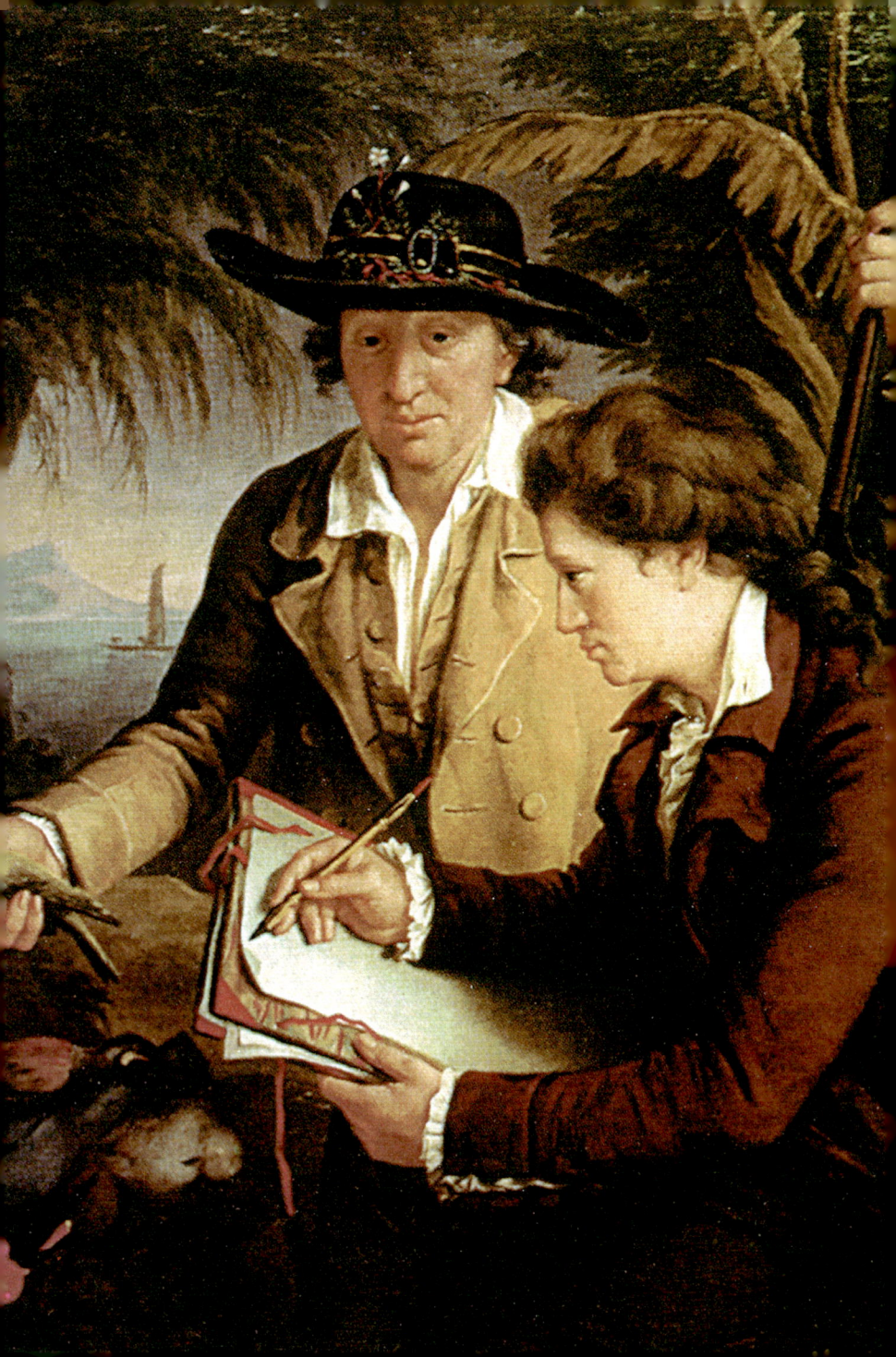

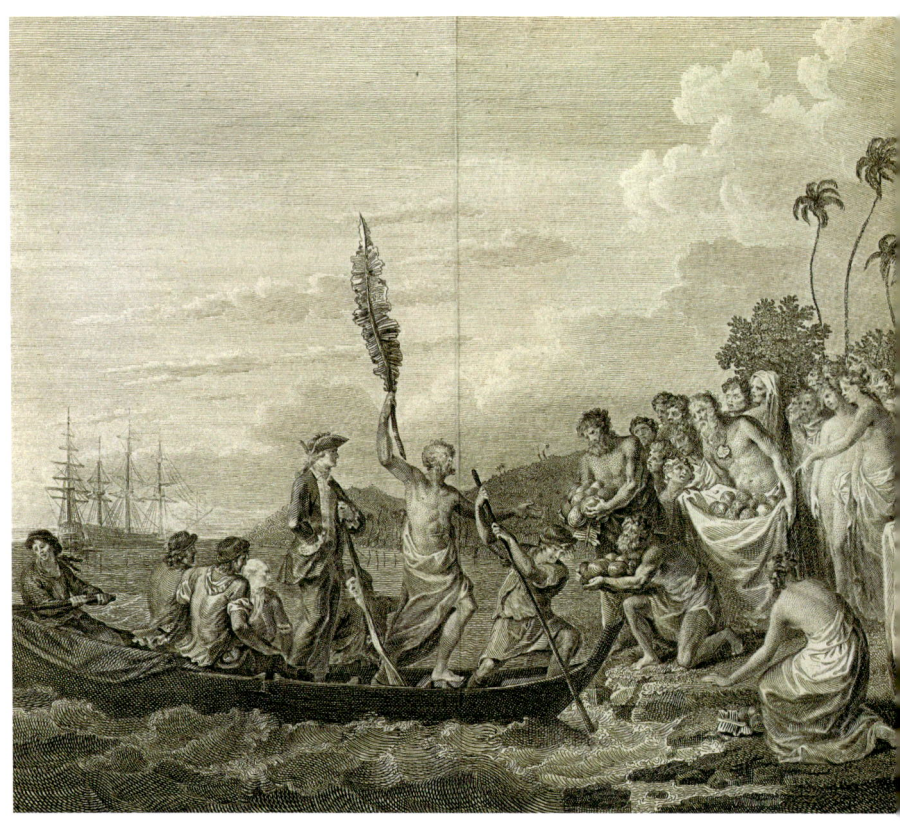

französische Seefahrer Louis Antoine de Bougainville die Insel Neu-Kythira, nach dem Geburtsort von Aphrodite, der griechischen Liebesgöttin. Moderne Theorien vermuten jedoch, dass die Avancen der einheimischen Frauen ein taktisches Manöver waren, nachdem die Einwohner ein Jahr zuvor eine Reihe ihrer Männer an die Feuerkraft der Briten verloren hatten. Die Tahitianer hatten damals das Schiff von Kapitän Samuel Wallis angegriffen, wobei sie feststellten, dass sich an Bord keine Frauen befanden. Sie schlossen daraus, dass die Seefahrer gekommen waren, um dieses Defizit auszugleichen. Indem die Insulaner also anboten, wovon sie selbst genug hatten und womit sie freigiebig umgingen, war es ihnen ein Leichtes, sich bei den Eindringlingen einzuschmeicheln.

Den Entdeckern kam zugute, dass polynesische Priester die Ankunft seefahrender Gottheiten vorhergesagt hatten. Die Fremden wurden wie Götter begrüßt. Ihr Ansehen kam dem der Stammesführer gleich oder übertraf es. Die fortschrittliche Bauart der Schiffe und Waffen bestätigte dies und die „weißen Götter" unternahmen nichts, um diesen Glauben zu zerstreuen.

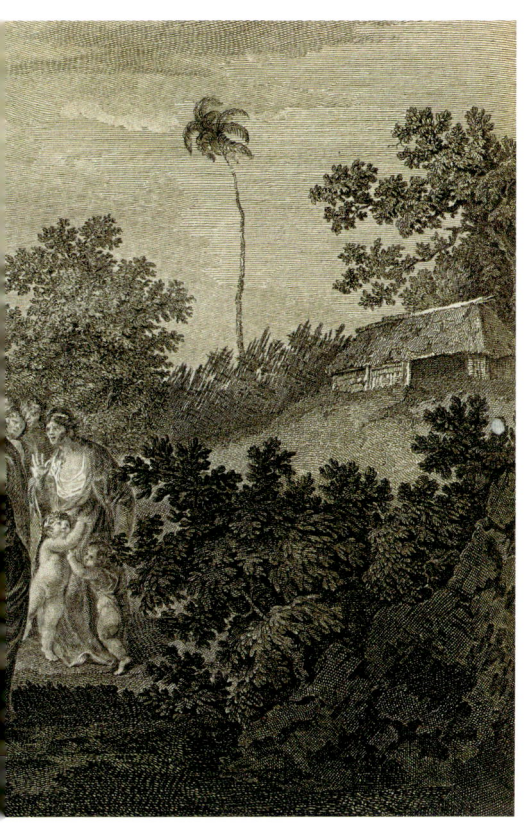

LEFT: European explorers being welcomed by Polynesian natives, rendered in the classical Greek style of the time

BELOW: A modern vision of what the explorers saw

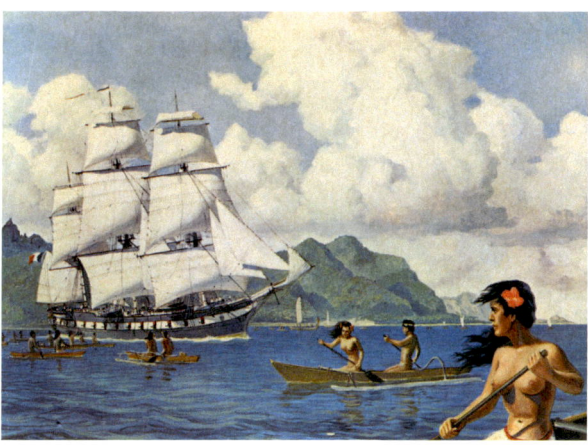

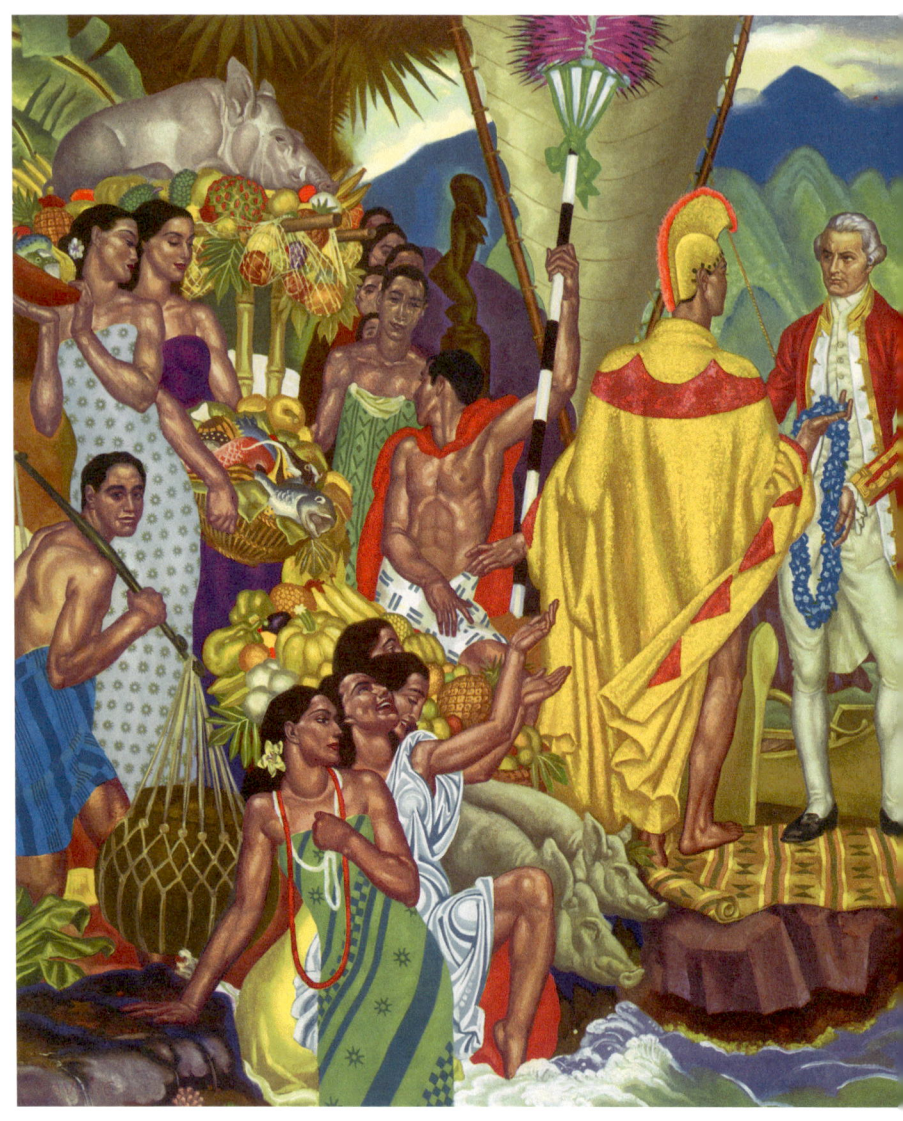

Captain Cook being greeted as a god
upon his landing in Kealakekua Bay,
Hawaii, 1778 (Matson Line menu
illustration by Eugene Savage, 1940s)

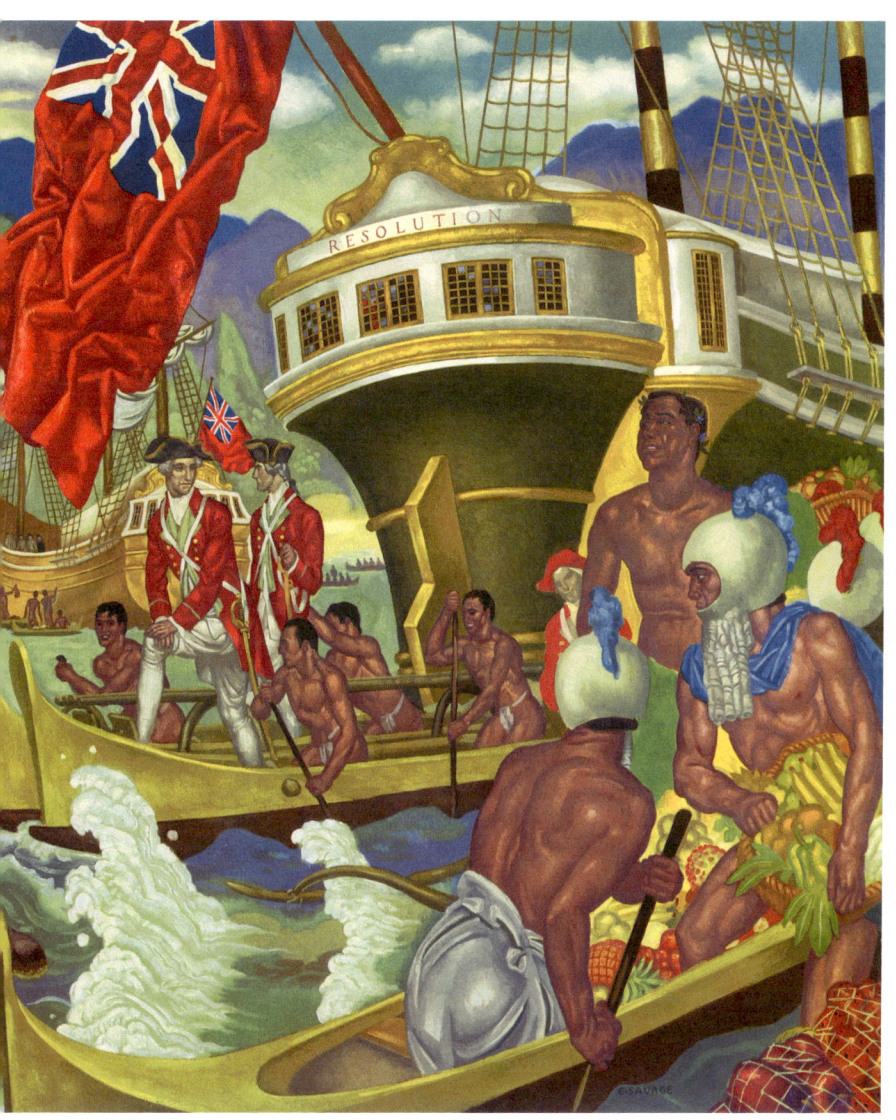

Die Seefahrer hatten die Aufgabe, neue Handelsrouten auszukundschaften. Und als gebildete, kultivierte Männer interessierten sie sich auch für die tropische Natur und die Bräuche der Einheimischen – all das hielten sie in ihren Tagebüchern fest. Unter den Crewmitgliedern waren auch Naturwissenschaftler, die ihre Beobachtungen so getreu wie möglich dokumentierten. Ihre Zeichnungen ergänzten die Reisetagebücher der Seefahrer, die – zurück auf dem Festland – veröffentlicht wurden. Ihren wissenschaftlichen Beobachtungen fügten die Entdecker persönliche Betrachtungen und Ansichten über das Inselleben bei. Das Bildungsbürgertum Europas nahm die Berichte mit Interesse auf, wobei den liberalen sexuellen Sitten der polynesischen Gesellschaft besondere Aufmerksamkeit geschenkt wurde.

Zu dieser Zeit stellte der französische Philosoph Jean-Jacques Rousseau seine Idee des „edlen Wilden" vor, der sich durch seine naturnahe Lebensweise

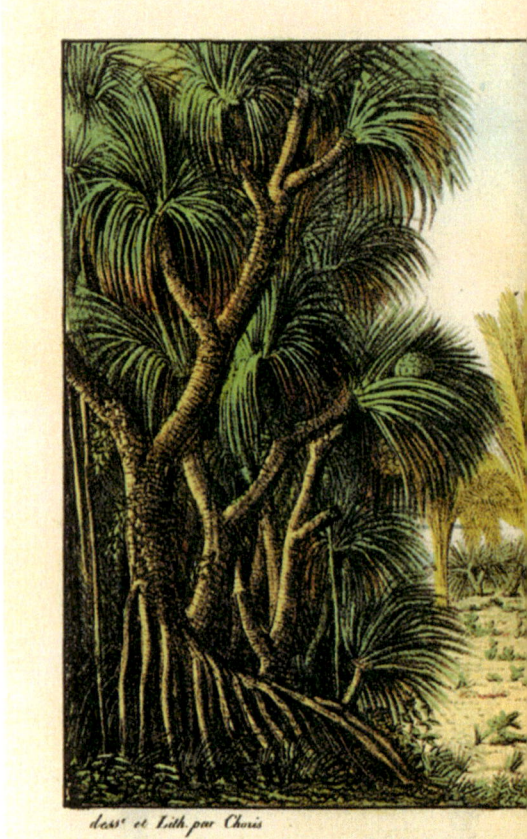

Pacific Islanders leading a seemingly better life

auszeichnet, „unbelastet von der Zivilisation und der göttlichen Offenbarung". Die begeisterten Berichte von Bougainville und seinem Botaniker Philibert Commerson über die Südseeinseln verliehen der utopischen Vision einer Rückkehr zur Natur weitere Glaubwürdigkeit. Liberale Denker bedienten sich der Beschreibungen, um die Missstände in der zivilisierten Gesellschaft aufzudecken. In den literarischen Salons Europas diskutierte man mit Begeisterung über Polynesien.

Die Reiseberichte der frühen Forscher sorgten dafür, dass die Inseln des Pazifiks in Europa eine veränderte Wahrnehmung erfuhren und zu einem Traumbild wurden. Fortan sehnten sich die Bewohner der westlichen Hemisphäre nach Urlauben an romantischen, tropischen Stränden, an denen sie alten, beengenden Traditionen entfliehen konnten, die ihren Glanz bereits verloren hatten. Dies war der Grundstein für die Entstehung des „Polynesian Pop", aus dem später der Tiki-Pop hervorging.

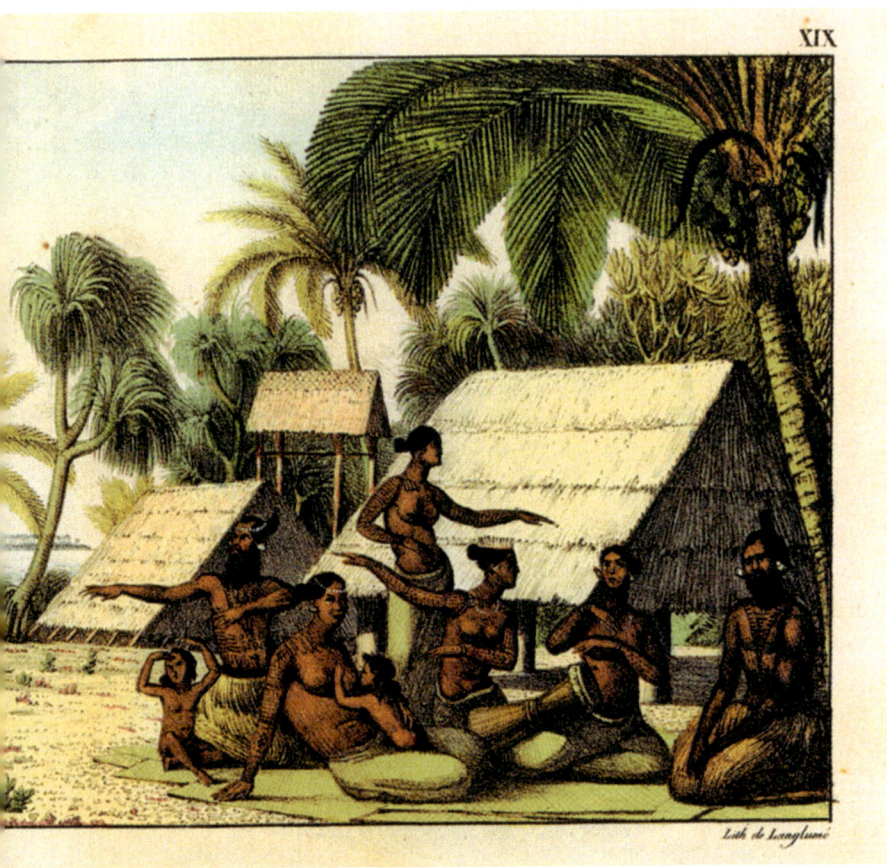

XIX

Lith de Langlumé

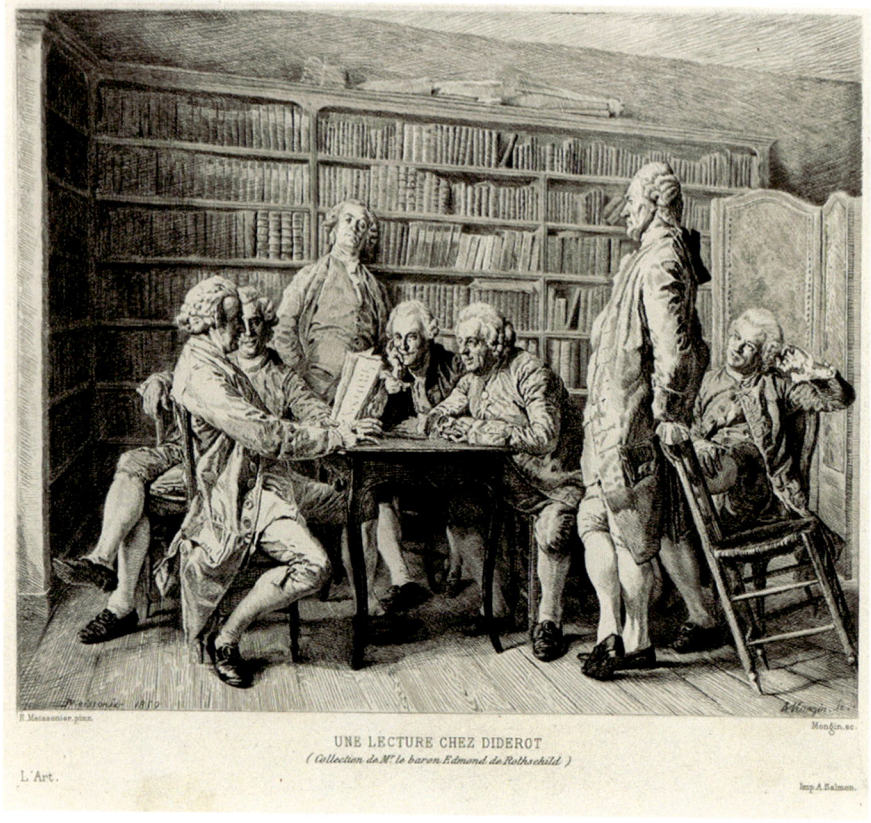

UNE LECTURE CHEZ DIDEROT
(Collection de M. le baron Edmond de Rothschild)

L'Art.

LA DOCTRINE CHRÉTIENNE

sur l'expulsion de l'Homme du paradis
avait enraciné en Europe occidentale la
notion d'une perte liée à la civilisation
et d'une séparation de l'Homme de sa
véritable condition. Lorsque les premiers
explorateurs européens ont découvert
les Océaniens vivant en harmonie avec la
nature, libérés des lourds vêtements grâce
à la douceur du climat, ils en ont conclu
que l'« état originel » n'avait somme toute
pas été perdu. Voilà un peuple qui pouvait
profiter des bienfaits de la nature sans
trop d'effort : il était heureux, sain et beau.

Au XVIIIᵉ siècle, l'océan Pacifique et
ses îles étaient une région du monde
encore inexplorée. Les premiers navigateurs arrivés sur les îles polynésiennes par
hasard croyaient accoster sur un continent inconnu. Ce fut une heureuse erreur,
cependant : après des mois de navigation,
la vision de luxuriants paysages tropicaux –
et peu après de ces femmes autochtones
aux seins nus – fit en effet aux marins épui-
sés l'effet d'un paradis terrestre. Il fallut
l'expérience et l'autorité de chefs comme le
capitaine James Cook pour tenir les équi-
pages à distance.

Les Tahitiens qui avaient un rapport libre et dénué de honte à leur sexualité étaient heureux de la partager avec leurs hôtes. Séduit par ce comportement insouciant, le navigateur français Louis Antoine de Bougainville baptisa l'île « la Nouvelle Cythère », d'après le lieu de naissance d'Aphrodite, la déesse grecque de l'amour. Cependant, des recherches récentes laissent supposer qu'en proposant leurs femmes à leurs hôtes, les indigènes se livraient à une manœuvre tactique, consécutive aux pertes humaines essuyées un an plus tôt lors de l'assaut du navire du capitaine Samuel Wallis. Les insulaires avaient dû battre en retraite devant des Britanniques à la puissance de feu supérieure. Ayant constaté qu'il n'y avait pas de femmes à bord du navire, ils en avaient déduit que les marins étaient venus s'emparer de ce qui leur faisait défaut. D'où l'idée de s'attirer facilement les faveurs des intrus en partageant ce qu'ils possédaient en abondance et à quoi ils n'attachaient pas d'importance particulière.

Une circonstance joua en faveur des explorateurs : les prêtres indigènes avaient prédit l'arrivée de certaines divinités par la mer. Les étrangers furent donc accueillis comme des dieux, égaux voire supérieurs aux chefs locaux. La technologie supérieure de leurs navires et de leurs armes confirma

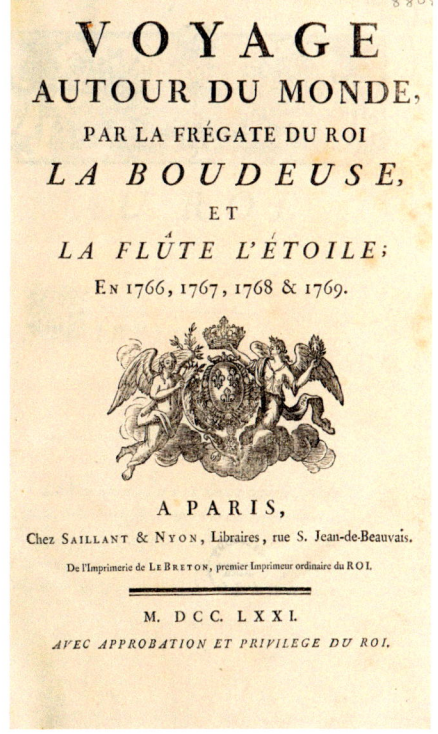

OPPOSITE: Denis Diderot, here in his literary circle, wrote a philosophical commentary on Bougainville's book

RIGHT: Bougainville's *Voyage around the World*, title page, 1771

les légendes polynésiennes, et les fameux « dieux blancs » se gardèrent bien de dissiper leurs croyances.

La mission des marins de cette époque était de découvrir de nouvelles routes commerciales, mais en hommes de culture éduqués, nos explorateurs se prirent d'intérêt pour les sites tropicaux et les coutumes étrangères qu'ils décrivirent dans leurs journaux. Ces expéditions comptaient aussi des chercheurs en sciences naturelles qui avaient été formés à recueillir des informations sur les peuplades et les contrées exotiques, et à les restituer le plus fidèlement possible dans leurs carnets de croquis. Leurs interprétations complétaient visuellement les récits de voyage des marins qui furent publiés sur le continent. Bien que les intentions des explorateurs fussent pour une large part scientifiques, ils ne se privèrent pas d'y ajouter leurs propres observations et leurs opinions sur la vie insulaire. Leurs écrits furent accueillis avec intérêt par les classes éduquées d'Europe qui accordèrent une attention particulière aux mœurs sexuelles libérales découvertes dans la société polynésienne.

À cette époque, le philosophe français Jean-Jacques Rousseau prônait l'idée du « bon sauvage », vivant dans un état de nature, et non encore dépravé par la civilisation et par la révélation divine. Les rapports élogieux de Bougainville et de son botaniste Philibert Commerson, dans leurs descriptions de la vie des insulaires des mers du Sud, ajoutaient de la crédibilité à la vision d'un retour utopique à la nature, et les penseurs progressistes s'appuyèrent sur ces découvertes pour étayer leur critique des maux de la société civilisée. Les discussions sur la Polynésie alimentaient les discussions des salons littéraires de l'Europe entière.

La réception et l'interprétation des récits des premiers explorateurs sur le continent furent la première étape vers une transformation de la perception des îles du Pacifique qui bascula de la réalité dans la fiction. Désormais, les habitants du continent américain rêvaient d'insouciance, des plages des îles tropicales, destinations rêvées pour des escapades romantiques ou simplement pour fuir les traditions séculaires qui les retenaient prisonniers et avaient perdu leur lustre. Ce fut donc le début de la projection du pop polynésien, qui prépara l'éclosion du phénomène tiki pop.

American sheet music cover, 1936

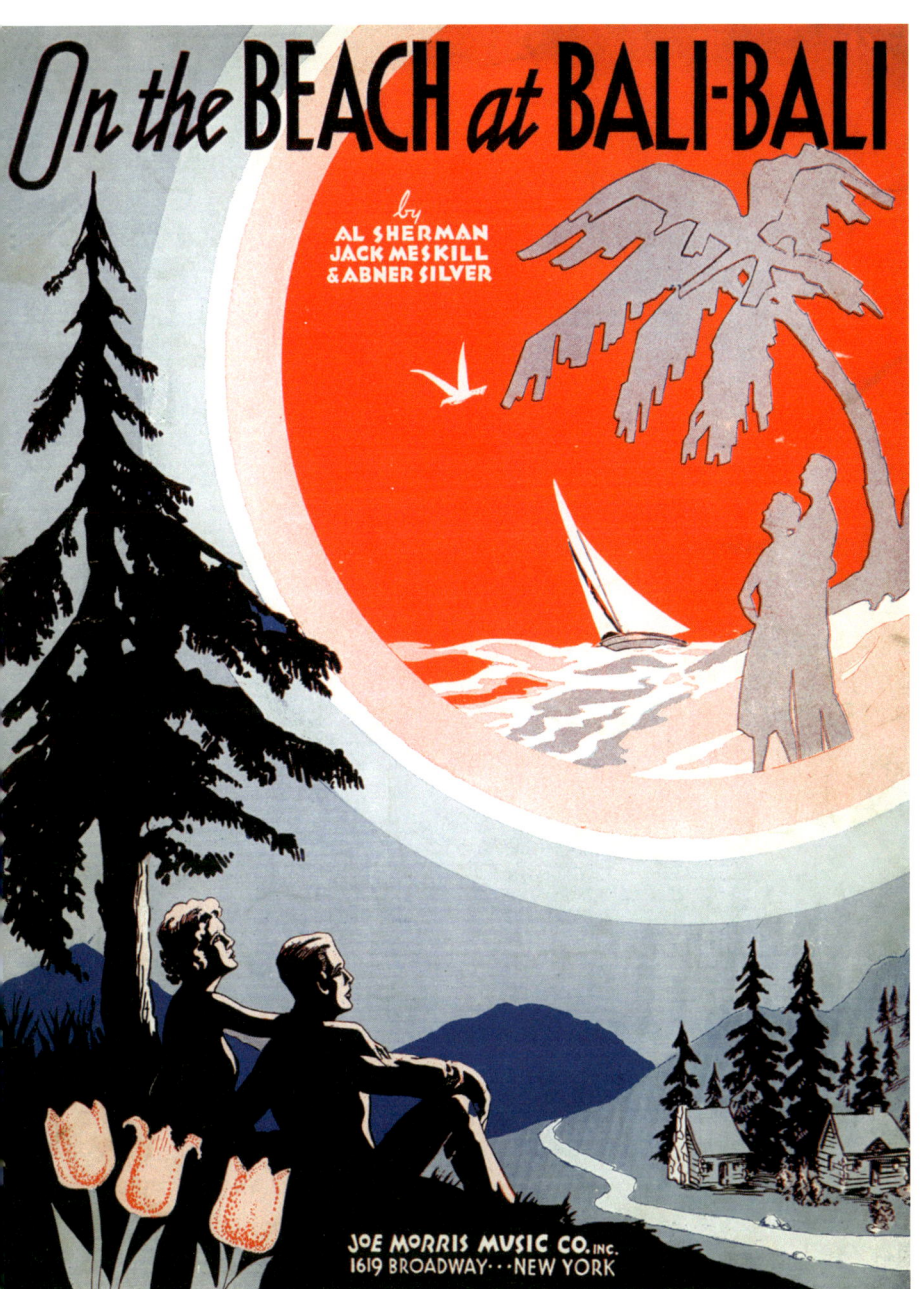

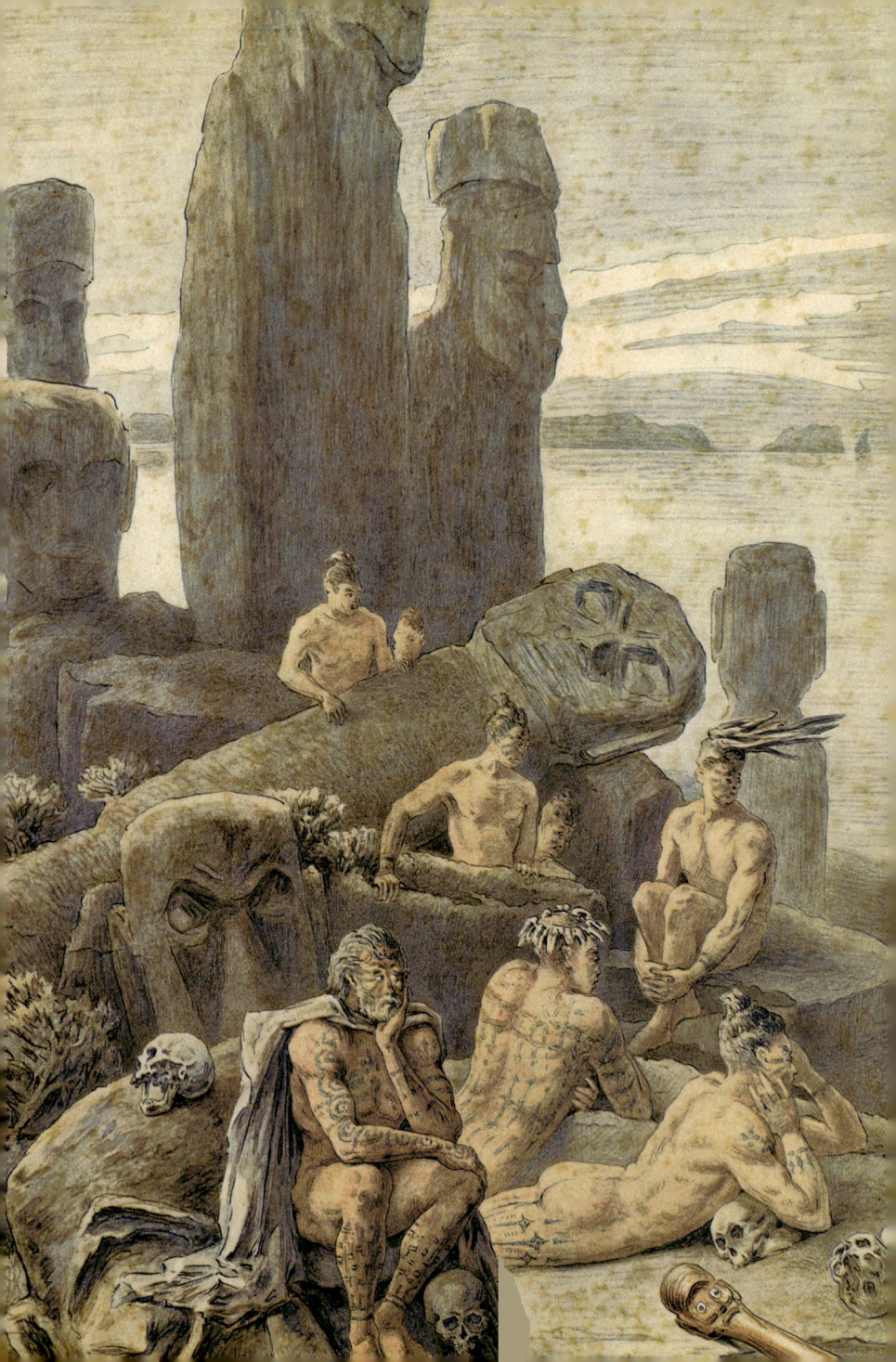

ARTISTS
AND AUTHORS

KÜNSTLER UND SCHRIFTSTELLER
ARTISTES ET AUTEURS

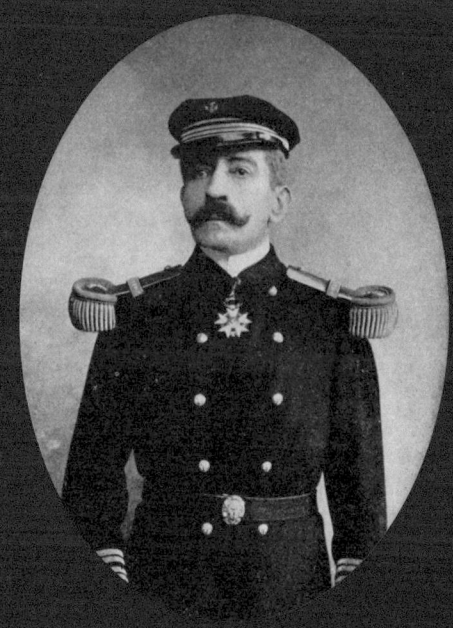

OPPOSITE: Illustration depicting natives on Easter Island
by Pierre Loti, dedicated to actress Sarah Bernhardt

ABOVE: Loti came to Tahiti as an officer in the French navy

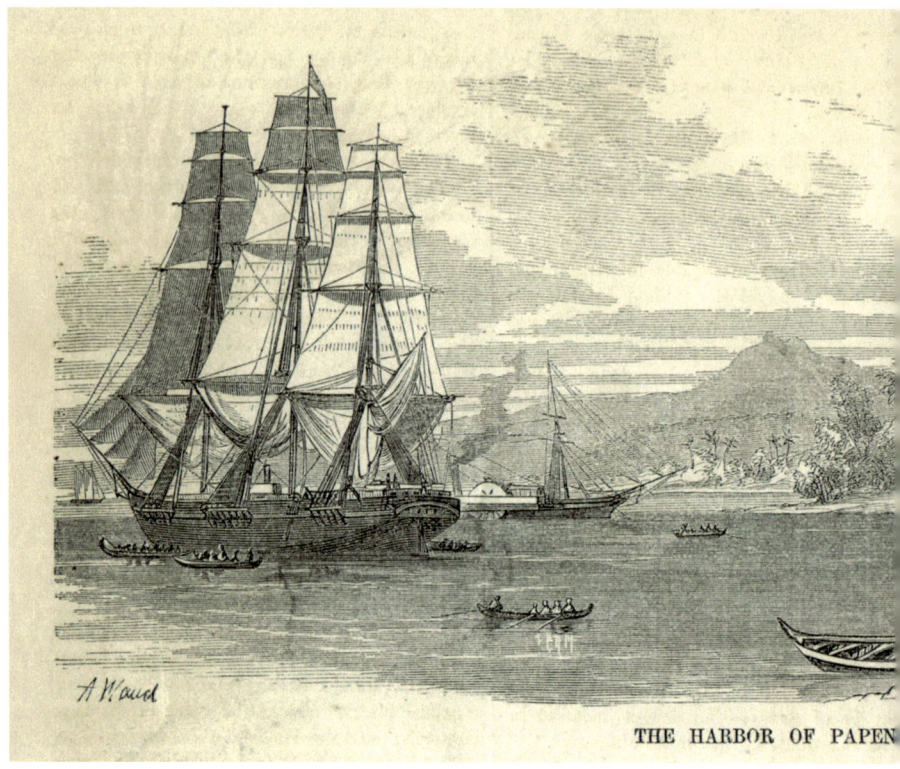

THE HARBOR OF PAPEN

THE NEXT GENERATION OF

myth-makers to perpetuate the South Seas fantasy abandoned any pretense of scientific exploration or accuracy. Their mission was to chase the dream, to experience the tales of adventure and free love they had heard in Europe. They were artists and writers, finding their muse in the islands. Their creations would influence generations of South Seas dreamers, and encouraged some of them to follow in their footsteps. One of these creative minds was Pierre Loti.

Loti was a flamboyant lover of foreign cultures—so much so that he liked to dress in exotic costumes and decorate his home in a non-Western style. He was much read

and appreciated in France in his day, and his novel about his romantic adventures in Tahiti, *The Marriage of Loti,* was influential to many.

One of the Frenchmen inspired by Loti's book was painter Paul Gauguin. Weary of modern civilization, he quit his job as a stockbroker in Paris, said farewell to his wife and children, and settled in Tahiti. Gauguin's aim was to return to the origin of creation, the childhood of mankind, to create truth in his art. He pursued this goal mostly on canvas, but also carved his vision of natural life into wood.

Gauguin's story became the quintessential example of an artist's struggle and

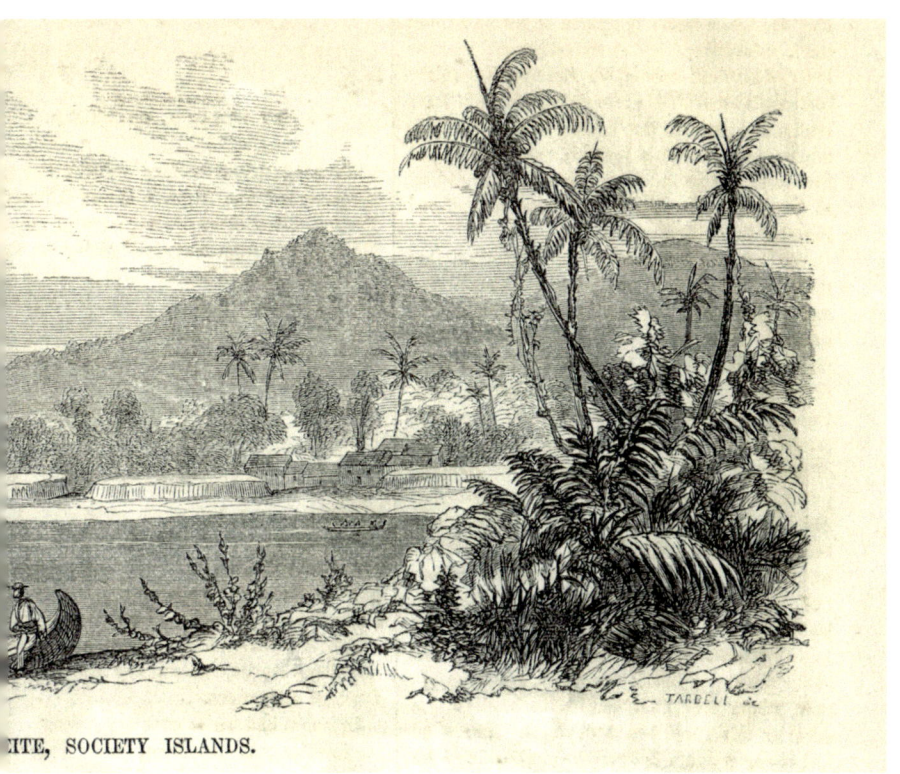

ITE, SOCIETY ISLANDS.

bohemian existence in the tropics: shunning
conventional modes of living, sharing his
bed with his nude models, the true South
Seas painter was uncompromising in his art
and life. His genius was only recognized
after his death.

Gauguin's ascension to pop-culture hero
happened in the same fashion as for other
characters in the Polynesian melodrama: his
biography progressed from book form into
a movie, and the cliché of a freer life in the
islands was burned into the minds of those
craving refuge from civilization.

An American contemporary of Loti
and Gauguin, Herman Melville was also
a refugee. He had experienced his father's

Tahiti in Loti's day

PIERRE LOTI

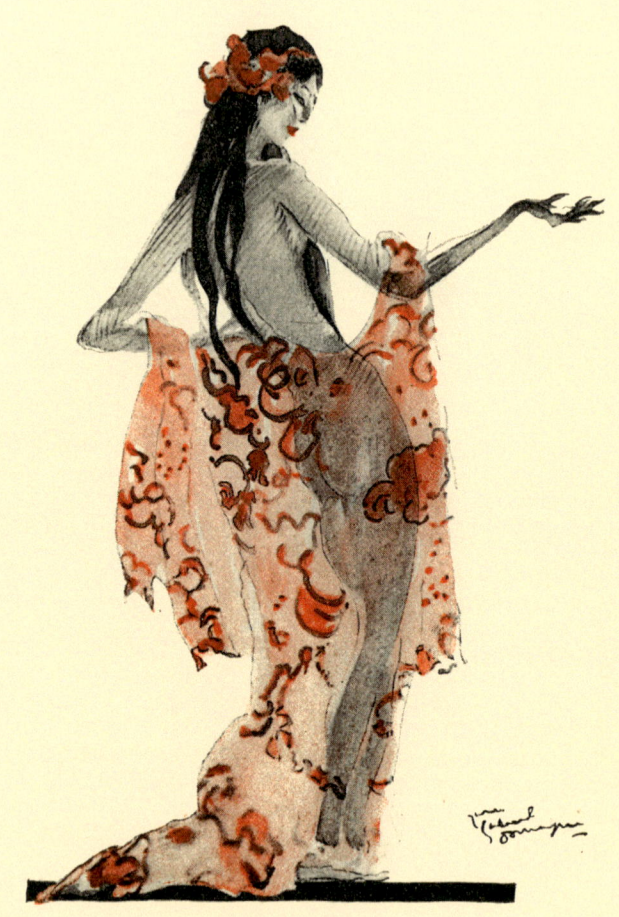

LE MARIAGE
DE LOTI

ILLUSTRATIONS DE J.-G. DOMERGUE

descent from successful businessman into ruined lunatic on his deathbed. Young Herman became a seaman on a whaler to the South Seas and jumped ship in the Marquesas, north of Tahiti. His account of his stay among the natives, *Typee* (1846), included these observations:

> *There were none of those thousand irritations that the ingenuity of civilized man has created to mar his own felicity. There were no foreclosures of mortgages, no bills payable, no debts of honor in Typee. . .*

The public devoured Melville's *Peep at Polynesian Life* (the subtitle of *Typee*), and he embarked on expanding his South Seas stories into a trilogy, with *Omoo* (1847) and *Mardi* (1849).

In his works, Melville echoed the same adoration for the Polynesians as was expressed by the first explorers, like Commerson, Bougainville's botanist:

> *. . . they recognize no other god but love. Every day is consecrated to him, the entire island is his temple, every woman his altar, and every man his celebrant. And women of what kind I hear you ask? The rivals of the Georgians in beauty. . . there neither shame nor modesty exercise their tyranny at all. . .*

Ironically, *Moby Dick*, the book Melville is best known for and which is considered a classic, was not recognized in his own time, and Melville died in poverty and obscurity. Mostly taking place on the open sea, the story provides hope for reconciliation of the white man with the "noble savage" in the person of Queequeg, the Polynesian prince.

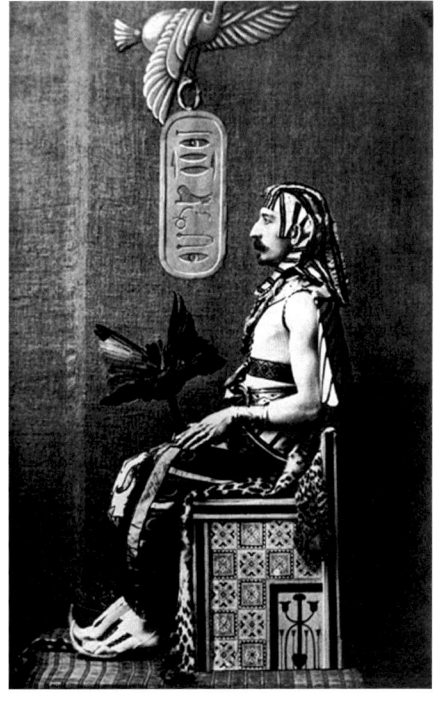

DIE NÄCHSTE GENERATION VON

Mythenschöpfern für Südseefantasien verzichtete auf den Vorwand wissenschaftlichen Entdeckergeistes. Ihre Mission war es, dem Traumbild hinterherzujagen. Sie hatten in Europa von Abenteuern und freier Liebe gehört – das wollten sie auch erleben. Es waren Künstler und Schriftsteller, die auf den Inseln ihre Muse fanden. Ihre Werke sollten Generationen von Südseeträumern beeinflussen und manche von ihnen dazu ermutigen, es ihnen gleichzutun. Einer dieser kreativen Köpfe war Pierre Loti.

Loti war ein extravaganter Liebhaber fremder Kulturen, der sich exotisch kleidete und sein Zuhause entsprechend dekorierte. In Frankreich wurde er zu seiner Zeit viel gelesen und geschätzt. Sein Roman über seine romantischen Abenteuer in Tahiti, *Le Mariage de Loti*, hatte großen kulturgeschichtlichen Einfluss.

Ein Franzose, der sich von Lotis Buch inspirieren ließ, war der Paul Gauguin. Der modernen Zivilisation überdrüssig, kündigte er seinen Job als Börsenmakler in Paris, sagte Frau und Kindern Lebewohl und zog nach Tahiti. Gauguin wollte zum Ursprung der Schöpfung zurückkehren, in die Kinderstube der Menschheit, um seiner Kunst Wahrhaftigkeit zu verleihen. Diesem Ziel versuchte er sich hauptsächlich auf der Leinwand zu nähern, schnitzte seine Visionen eines naturnahen Lebens jedoch auch in Holz.

Gauguins Geschichte wurde zum Paradebeispiel für Leben und Kampf eines Künstlers in den Tropen: Er scheute konventionelle Lebensformen, teilte das Bett mit seinen Aktmodellen und war weder in seiner Arbeit noch im Alltag zu Kompromissen bereit. Seine Genialität wurde erst nach seinem Tod erkannt.

Gauguins Aufstieg zum Helden der Popkultur glich dem anderer Charaktere des polynesischen Melodramas. Seine Biografie wurde zum Stoff zahlreicher Romane und Filme. Das Klischee eines freieren Lebens auf den Inseln brannte sich in die Köpfe jener, die der Zivilisation entfliehen wollten.

Ein amerikanischer Zeitgenosse Lotis und Gauguins, Herman Melville, war ebenfalls ein Suchender. Er hatte mit ansehen müssen, wie sein Vater, ein erfolgreicher Geschäftsmann, am Ende seines Lebens dem Wahnsinn verfiel. Der junge Herman fuhr auf einem Walfangschiff als Seemann in die Südsee und ging auf den Marquesas-Inseln, nördlich von Tahiti, von Bord. In seinem Bericht über seinen Aufenthalt unter den Einheimischen, *Taipi* (1846), schreibt er:

> *„All die tausend Quellen der Verärgerung, die der zivilisierte Mensch sich ausgedacht hat, um sein eigenes Glück zu zerstören, gab es hier nicht. Keine Hypotheken, die fällig wurden, keine Wechsel zum Protestieren, keine Rechnungen, keine Ehrenschulden…“*

Die Öffentlichkeit verschlang Melvilles *Abenteuer in der Südsee* (so der Untertitel von *Taipi*), was ihn dazu veranlasste, sie mit *Omoo* (1847) und *Mardi* (1849) zu einer Trilogie auszubauen.

In seinen Büchern brachte Melville dieselbe Verehrung für die Polynesier zum

Paul Gauguin, *Mata Mua (In Olden Times)*, 1892

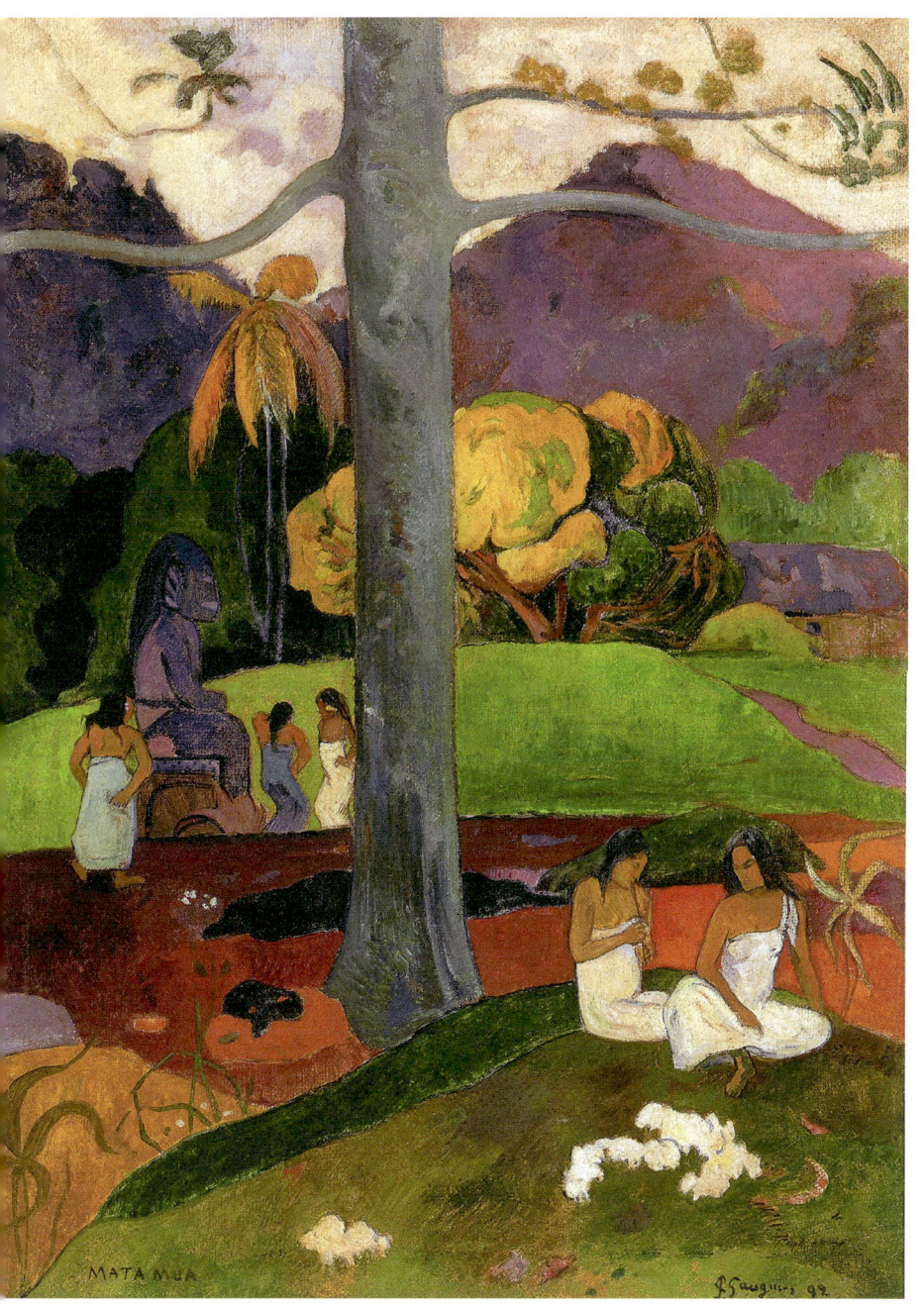

MATA MUA

P Gauguin 92

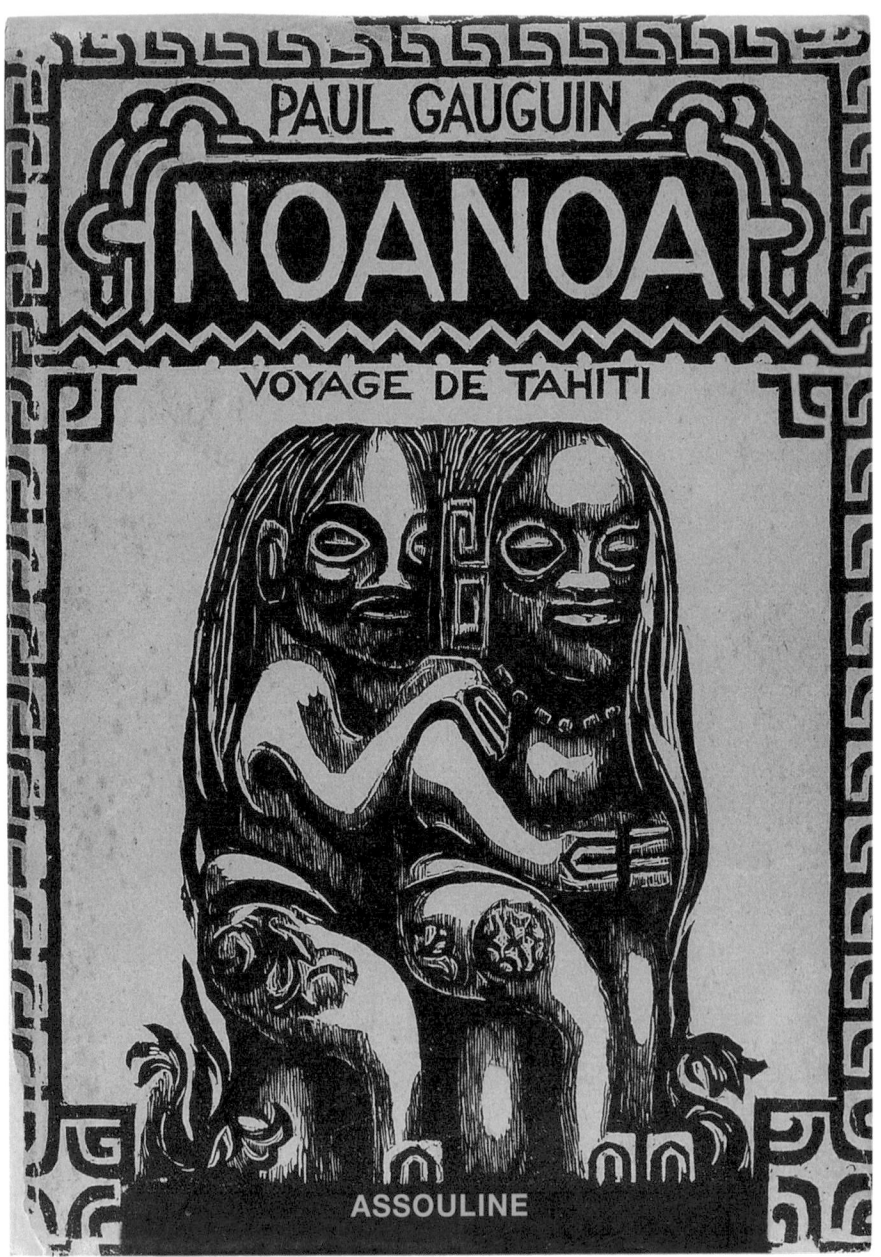

Ausdruck, wie auch schon der frühe Entdecker Commerson, Bougainvilles Botaniker:

> *„Sie erkennen keinen anderen Gott an als die Liebe. Jeder Tag wird ihm geweiht, die ganze Insel ist sein Tempel, jede Frau sein Altar und jeder Mann sein Zelebrant. Frauen welcher Art, fragen Sie? An Schönheit wetteifern sie mit den Georgianerinnen… Weder Scham noch Bescheidenheit herrschen an diesem Ort".*

Ironischerweise fand *Moby Dick*, Melvilles bekanntestes Buch und heute ein Klassiker der Weltliteratur, zu seiner Zeit keine Anerkennung – Melville starb arm und vergessen. Die Geschichte spielt vorwiegend auf offener See und bietet mit der Figur des Queequeg, einem polynesischen Prinzen, Hoffnung auf eine Versöhnung des weißen Mannes mit dem „edlen Wilden".

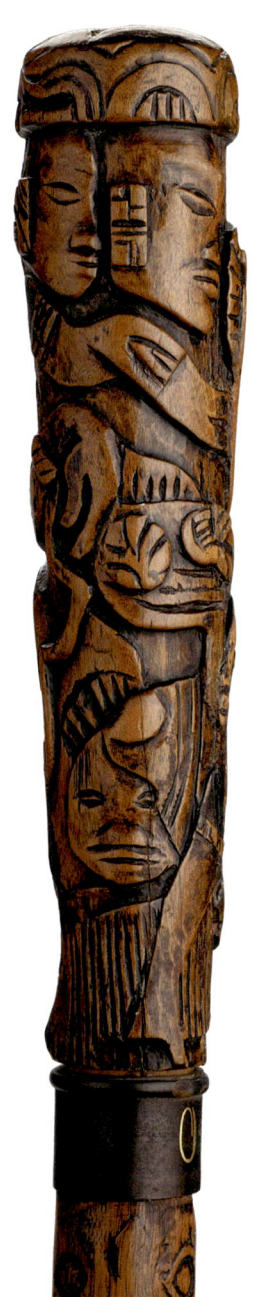

OPPOSITE : *Noa Noa*, Gauguin's Tahitian journal

RIGHT: Walking stick carved by Gauguin. His carvings represent the first examples of Polynesian art interpreted by a Western artist (*Musée d'Orsay Collection*)

PAGES 64–65: Illustration of Gauguin in a 1960s men's magazine

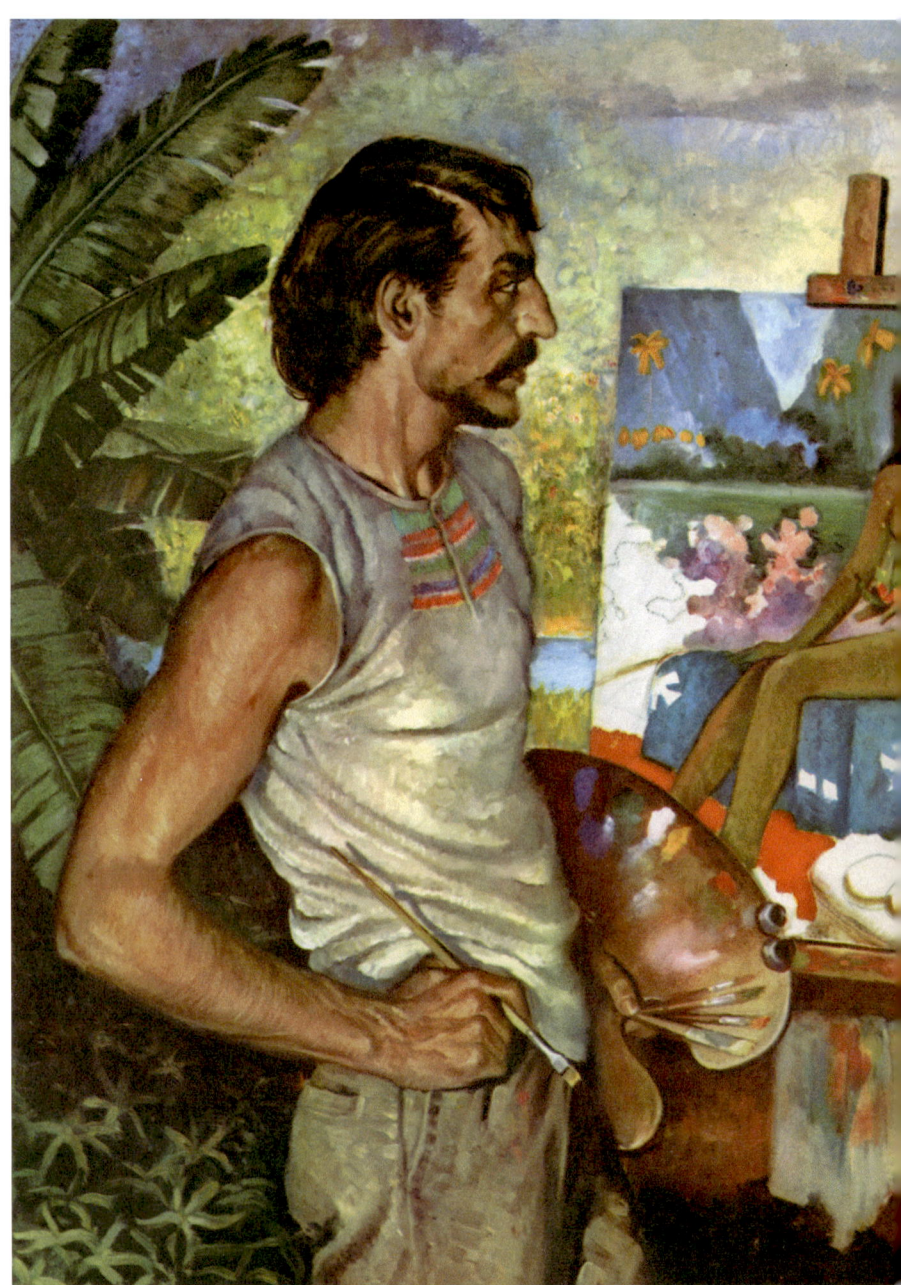

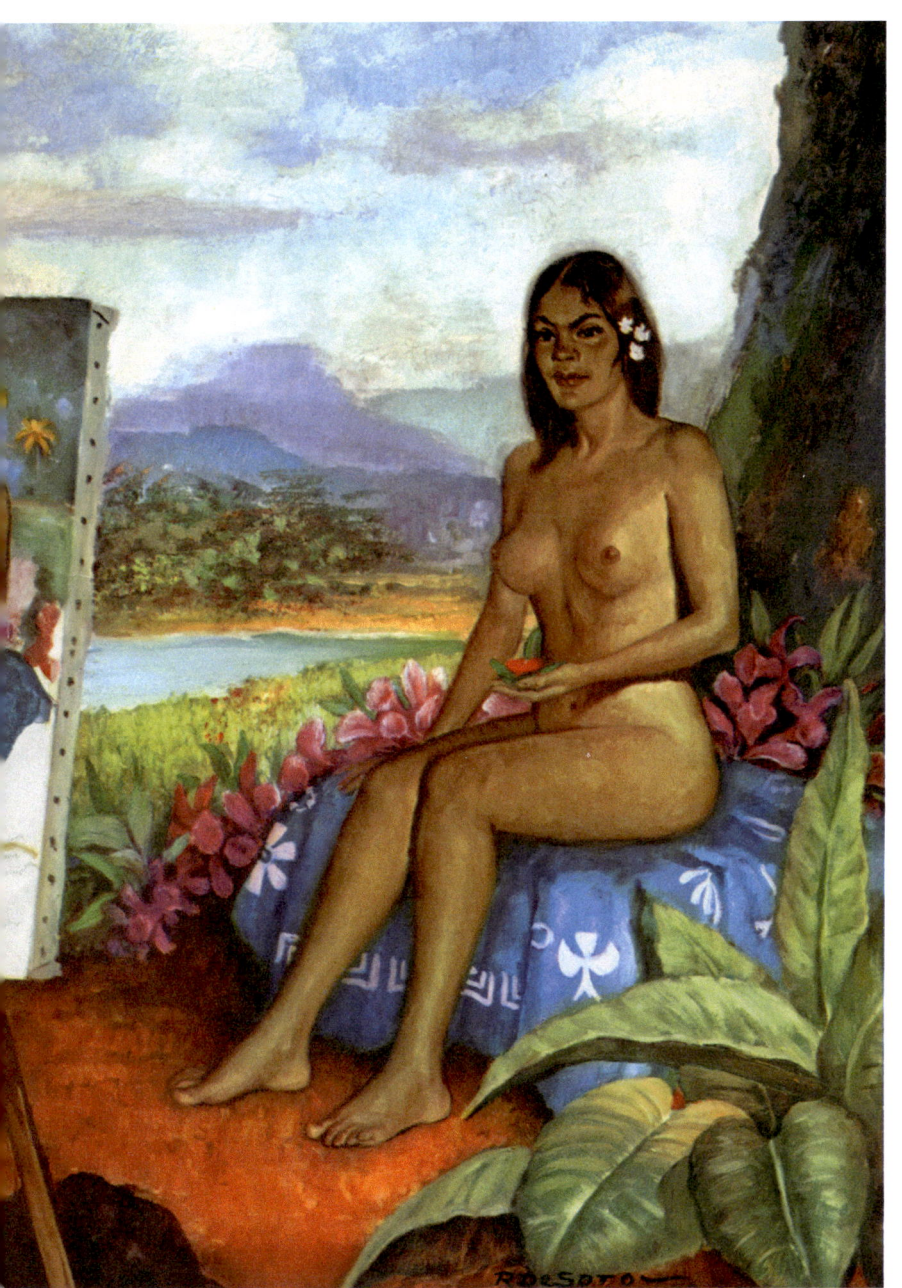

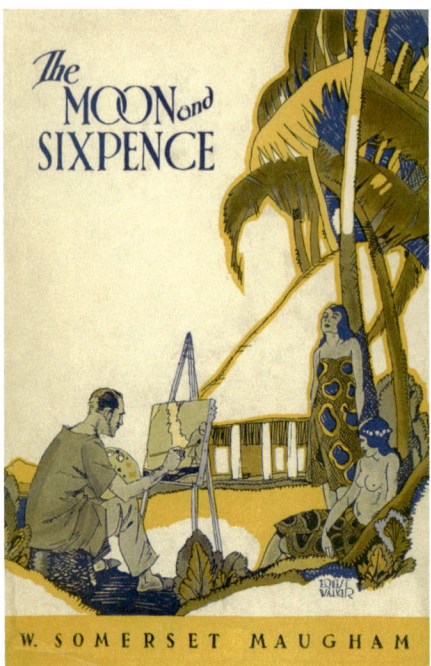

LA GÉNÉRATION SUIVANTE DES

fabricants de mythes occupés à perpétuer le fantasme des mers du Sud abandonna toute prétention à l'exploration comme à l'exactitude scientifique. Leur mission était de traquer le rêve, de faire l'expérience concrète des récits d'aventure et d'amour libre qu'ils avaient entendus en Europe. Ces artistes et ces écrivains trouvèrent leur muse dans les îles. Leurs créations devaient influencer des générations de « rêveurs » des mers du Sud, et encourager certains d'entre eux à suivre leurs traces.

L'un de ces esprits créatifs fut Pierre Loti. Loti était un amoureux transi des cultures étrangères – à tel point qu'il affectionnait les tenues exotiques et qu'il avait décoré sa maison dans un style non occidental. Il était

très lu et apprécié en France à son époque, et son roman relatant ses aventures sentimentales à Tahiti, *Le Mariage de Loti,* rencontra la faveur d'un large public.

L'un des Français qu'inspira l'ouvrage de Loti fut le peintre Paul Gauguin. Lassé de la civilisation moderne, celui-ci quitta son emploi d'agent de change à Paris, fit ses adieux à sa femme et à son enfant, et partit s'installer à Tahiti. Gauguin entendait revenir aux origines de la création, à l'enfance de l'humanité, pour créer un art authentique. Il poursuivit cet objectif essentiellement dans sa peinture, mais traduisit aussi sa vision de la vie naturelle dans ses sculptures sur bois.

L'histoire de Gauguin est devenue l'exemple même de la lutte pour la survie

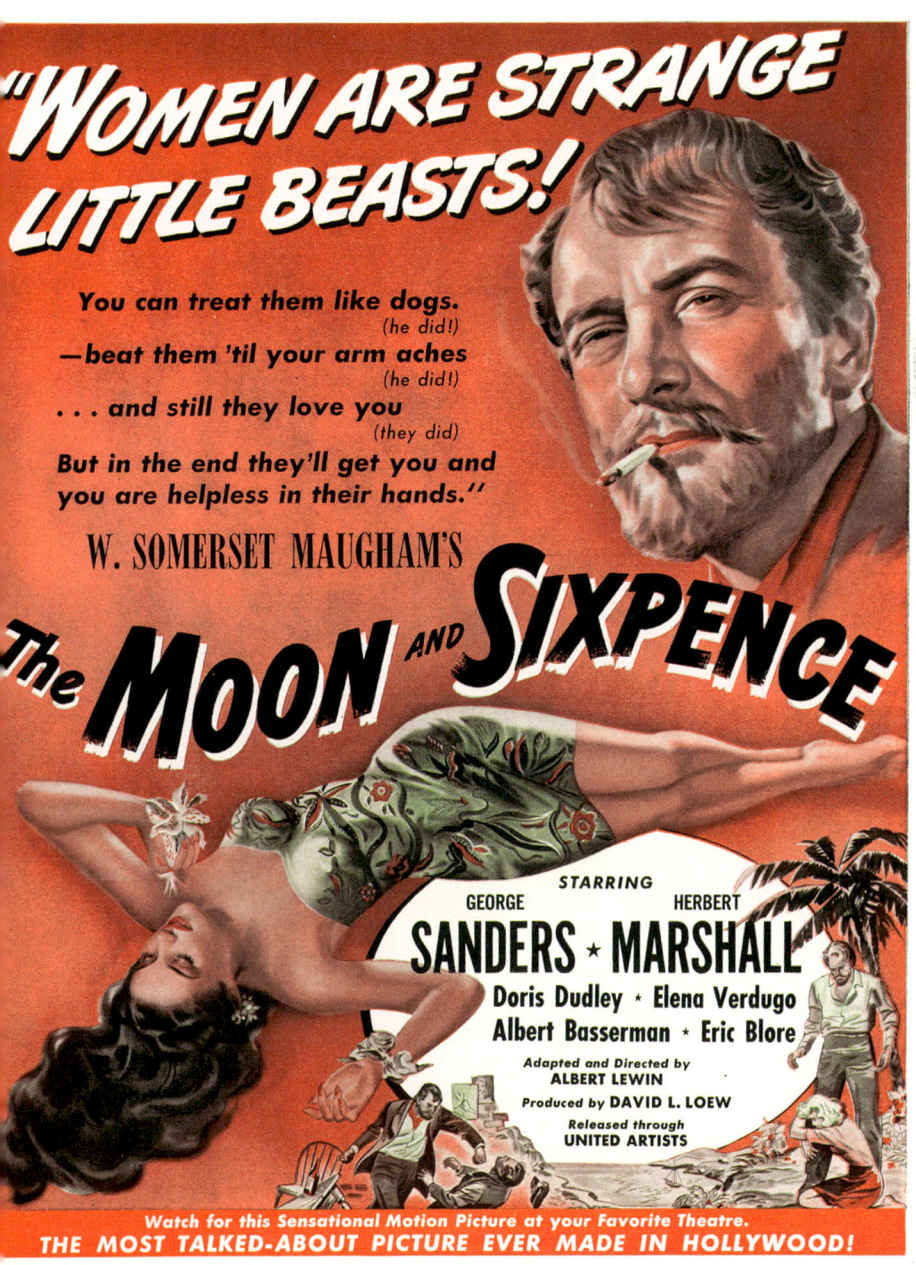

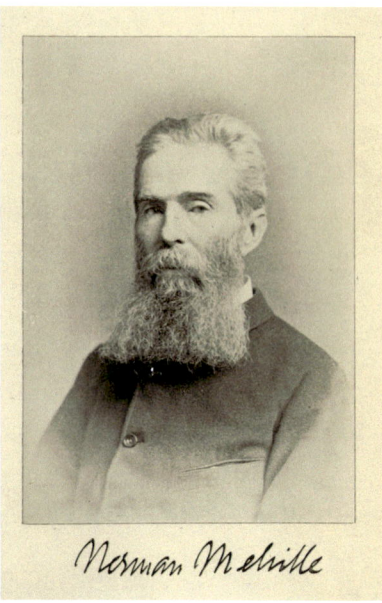

Norman Melville

de l'artiste sous les tropiques. De la vie de bohème aussi : refusant le style de vie bourgeois, partageant sa couche avec ses modèles nus, ce véritable peintre des mers du Sud fut aussi intransigeant dans son art que dans la vie. Son génie n'a été reconnu qu'après sa mort.

L'apothéose de Gauguin en héros de la culture pop connut les mêmes avatars que les autres personnages du mélodrame polynésien : sa biographie fut d'abord un livre avant d'être portée à l'écran et de devenir par la suite le cliché d'une existence insulaire sans contraintes, image qui se grava profondément dans l'esprit de ceux qui cherchaient un refuge aux antipodes de la civilisation.

Contemporain américain de Loti et Gauguin, Herman Melville était lui aussi un réfugié. Il avait été le témoin de la déchéance de son père, ex-homme d'affaires

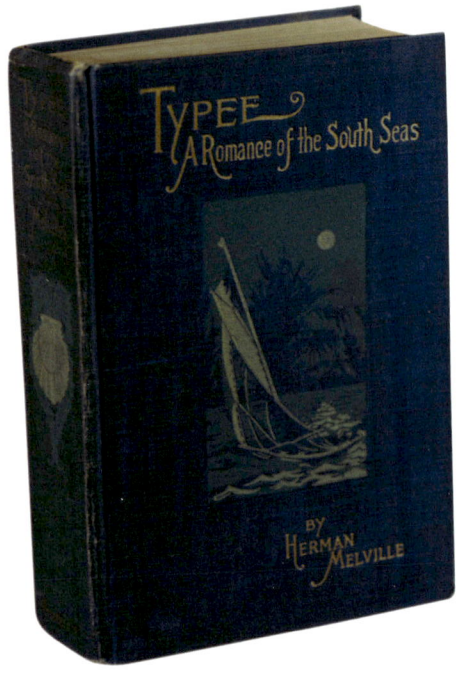

ABOVE: Portrait of the author

RIGHT: *Typee*, Melville's first novel, became a best seller

OPPOSITE: Melville extolled the beauty of the Polynesian women, here illustrated by Miguel Covarrubias in the 1935 edition

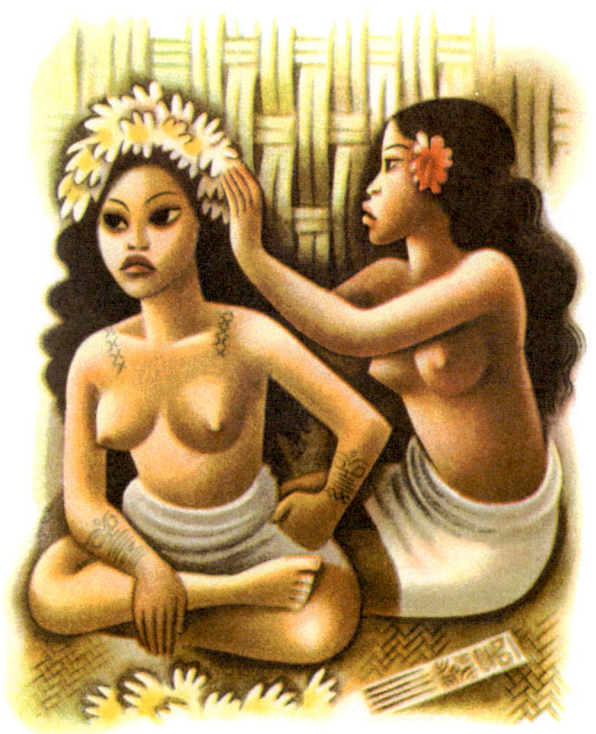

jadis prospère mort ruiné dans un asile d'aliénés. Le jeune Herman embarqua comme marin sur une baleinière en partance pour les mers du Sud, qu'il quitta une fois parvenu aux Marquises, au nord de Tahiti. Dans *Taïpi* (1846), le récit de son séjour chez les indigènes, on peut lire ceci :

« *On n'éprouvait aucune de ces mille irritations que l'ingéniosité de l'homme civilisé a créées pour ternir sa propre félicité. Il n'y avait pas de saisies d'hypothèques, pas de factures à payer, pas de dettes d'honneur à Taïpi...* »

Le public a dévoré cet *Aperçu de la vie polynésienne* (sous-titre de *Taïpi*), et Melville s'est alors lancé dans la suite de son récit sur les mers du Sud qui devint finalement une trilogie, avec *Omoo* (1847) puis *Mardi* (1849).

L'adoration pour les Polynésiens que Melville exprime dans son œuvre fait écho à celle que montraient les premiers explorateurs, comme Commerson, le botaniste de Bougainville :

« *Ils ne reconnaissent pas d'autre dieu que l'amour. Chaque jour lui est consacré, l'île entière est son temple, chaque femme son*

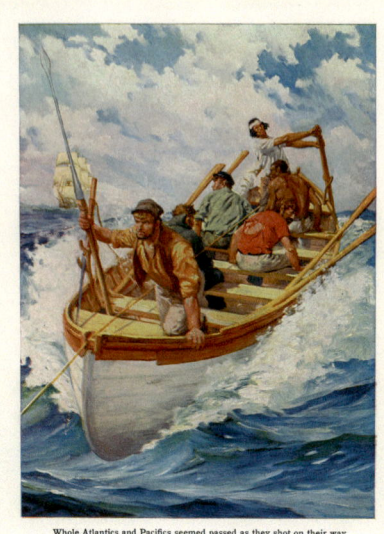

Whole Atlantics and Pacifics seemed passed as they shot on their way

MOBY DICK
~ OR ~
THE WHITE WHALE

BY
HERMAN MELVILLE

WITH AN INTRODUCTION BY
WILLIAM McFEE
AND NOTES BY
M. DODGE HOLMES, Ph.D.
AUTHOR OF JOAN OF ARC, ETC.

ILLUSTRATIONS BY
ANTON OTTO FISCHER

THE JOHN C. WINSTON COMPANY
CHICAGO   PHILADELPHIA   TORONTO

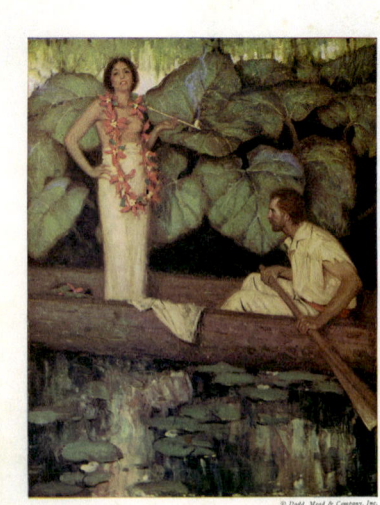

FAYAWAY AND I HAD A DELIGHTFUL LITTLE PARTY ON THE LAKE
Page 142

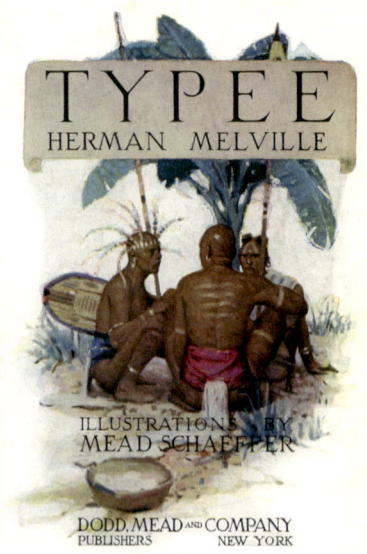

TYPEE
HERMAN MELVILLE

ILLUSTRATIONS BY
MEAD SCHAEFFER

DODD, MEAD AND COMPANY
PUBLISHERS   NEW YORK

*autel, et chaque homme son célébrant.
Mais quel genre de femmes, vous
entends-je demander ? Rivales des
Géorgiennes en beauté… ici ni honte ni
pudeur n'exercent nulle tyrannie… »*

Ironiquement, *Moby Dick,* le plus
célèbre livre de Melville, considéré comme
un classique, n'a pas été reconnu en son
temps, et son auteur est mort pauvre et
anonyme. L'histoire qui se déroule pour
l'essentiel sur la mer laisse espérer une
réconciliation de l'homme blanc avec le
« bon sauvage » représenté par Queequeg,
le prince polynésien.

OPPOSITE ABOVE: The master work
that made Melville famous, *Moby
Dick,* first published in 1851 as
The Whale

OPPOSITE BELOW: *Typee,* Melville's
first novel

BELOW "Noble savage" Queequeg in
John Huston's film version of *Moby
Dick* (1956)

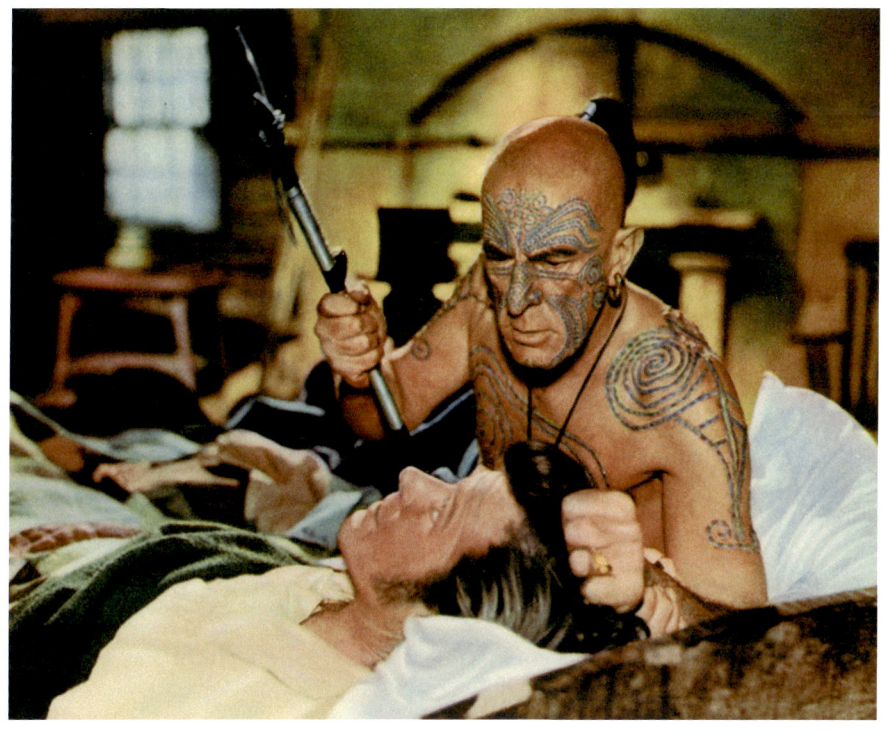

SOUTH SEA TALES

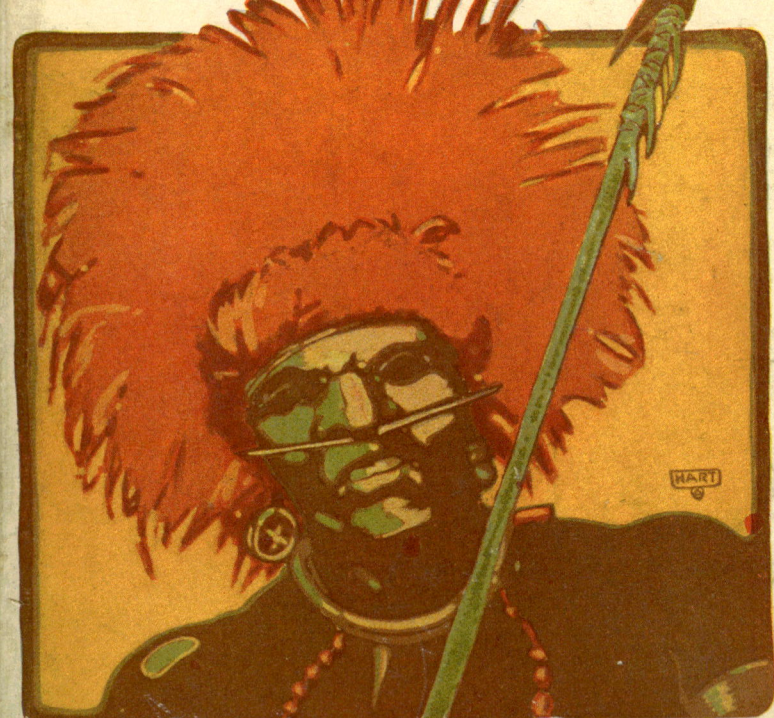

JACK LONDON

4

STORYTELLERS IN THE SOUTH SEAS

GESCHICHTENERZÄHLER IN DER SÜDSEE
CONTEURS DES MERS DU SUD

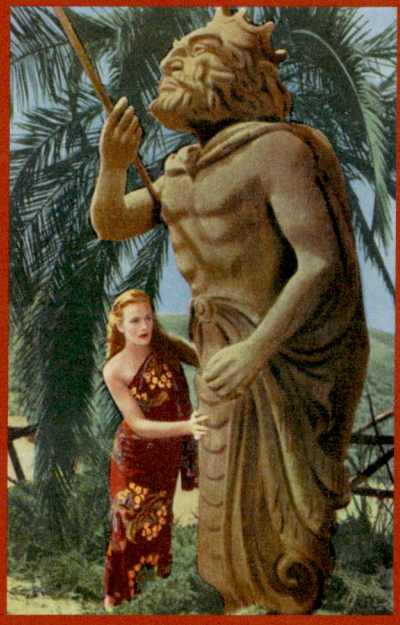

OPPOSITE: 1920s edition of Jack London's *South Sea Tales*

ABOVE: Frances Farmer in the film version of Stevenson's *Ebb Tide* (1937)

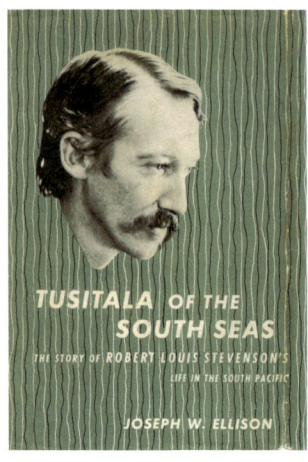

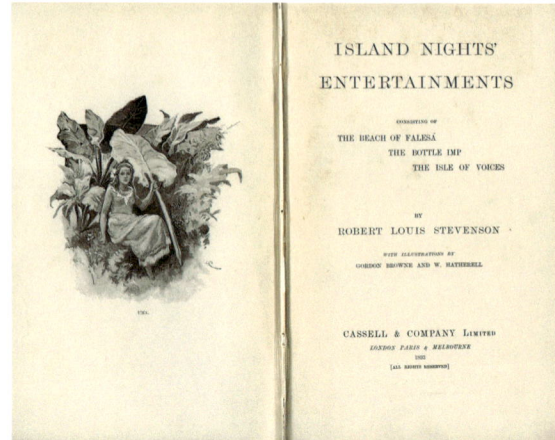

BY THE BEGINNING OF THE 20TH

century, South Seas tales had become their
own literary genre. The popularity of books
in this vein was such that by 1931, one had
to promise to describe the "real" South Seas
in their pages.

This fad was due in part to two famous
authors whose stories of adventure and
exploration captured the imagination of the
American public: Robert Louis Stevenson
and Jack London spearheaded the "call
of the wild" and penned tales about their
journeys among the enchanted atolls
of the Pacific.

Although Robert Louis Stevenson's first
popular success, *Treasure Island* (1883), is a
classic of the pirate genre, Stevenson was
a Polynesiac at heart. Embracing the easy-
going lifestyle of the islands, he is noted
to have said: "It is perhaps a more fortunate
destiny to have a taste for collecting shells
than to be born a millionaire." Stevenson
traveled to Hawaii, where he became
friends with the islands' last monarch, King
Kalakaua. He spent time in the Marquesas

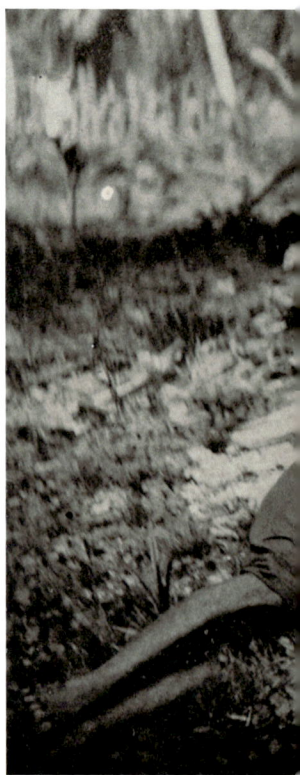

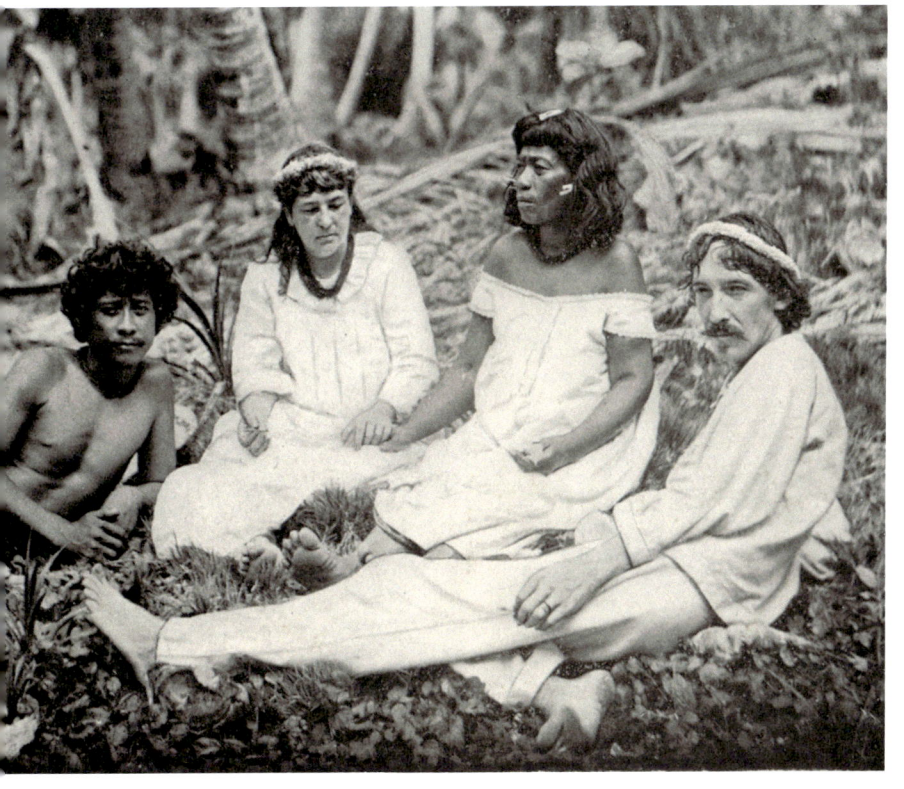

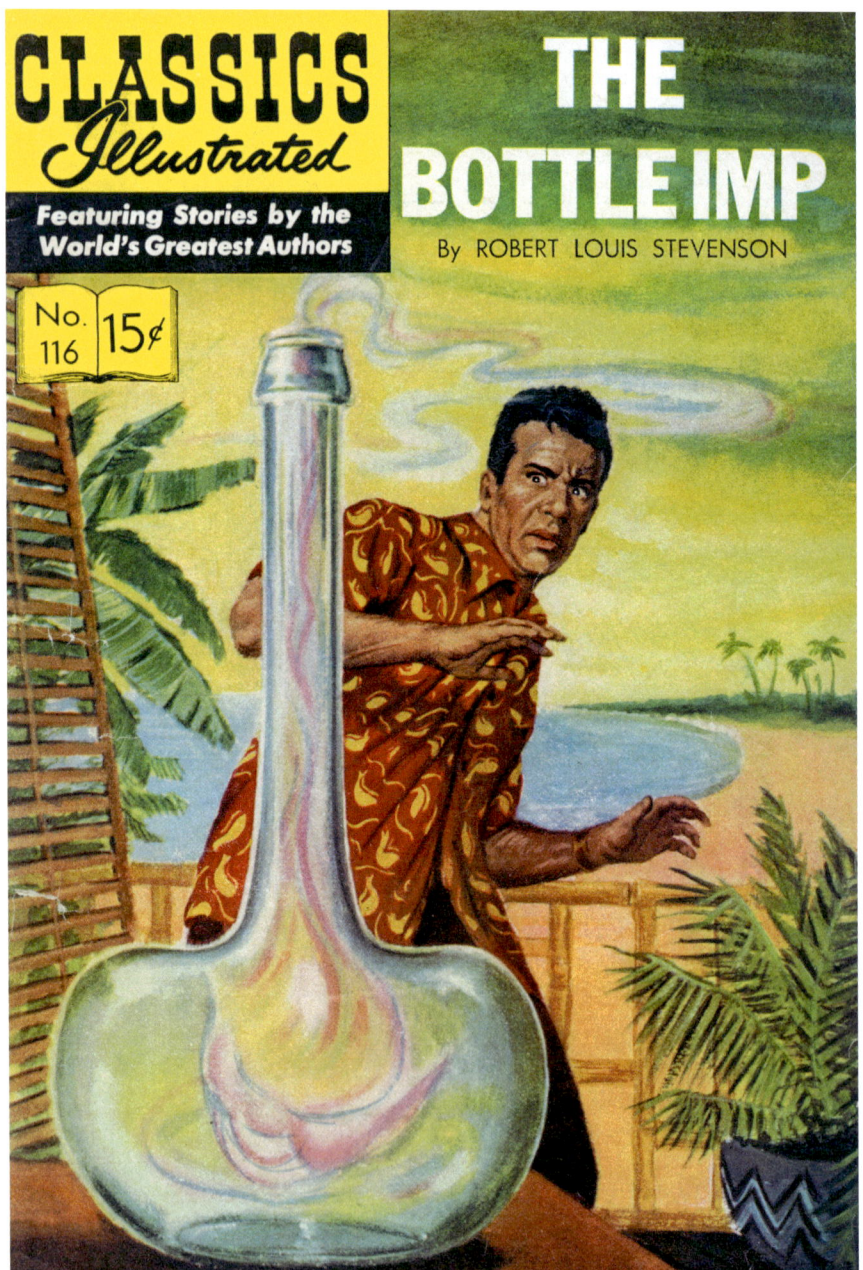

and Kiribati, and finally settled in Samoa, where he was held in high regard by the native population to his last days.

As a young lad, Jack London frequented John Heinold's First and Last Chance Saloon at the port of Oakland, California. Here he listened to sailors from all over the Pacific weave tall tales about their adventures in distant ports of call. Eventually he used some of these old mariners as characters in his books. In time, London made the decision to become a seafaring man himself. From the same pier from which Robert Louis Stevenson had set sail to the Pacific aboard the *Casco* 20 years before, Jack London set out on his South Seas cruise with his sloop, the *Snark*.

We don't know how many actual South Seas "cruises" were inspired by the works of Stevenson and London, but one book clearly references them: the 1921 send-up of the genre, *The Cruise of the Kawa* In the guise of a serious travelogue, this spoof parodies the romanticism of South Seas writers like Arnold Safroni-Middleton, whose flowery prose reiterates the Polynesian paradise theme in his 1920 book, *South Sea Foam*:

> *Here at least I shall find rest from the hot-footed turbulency of civilized humanity; here I can dwell beneath the Eden-like shades of feathery palms, and listen to the wind-blown melodies as they come in from the sea ... I felt that I had come across a pagan world where no more should I hear servile mumblings of a conventional people.*

Another contributor to the slew of South Seas writings was Frederick O'Brien. Having lived in Samoa and the Marquesas, O'Brien saw himself as walking in the footsteps of Melville, Gauguin, and Stevenson. With the success of his book *White Shadows in the South Seas*, he became the American South Seas sage of the 1920s, publishing two more volumes about the Polynesian Islands. In a cartoon by decorated naval officer and author Admiral Gene Markey, O'Brien was caricatured as Captain Traprock, fictional writer of *The Cruise of the Kawa*. O'Brien's *Shadows* was the first of many South Seas best sellers to make the transition from book to movie screen in 1929.

Stevenson's stories remained popular into the mid-20th century

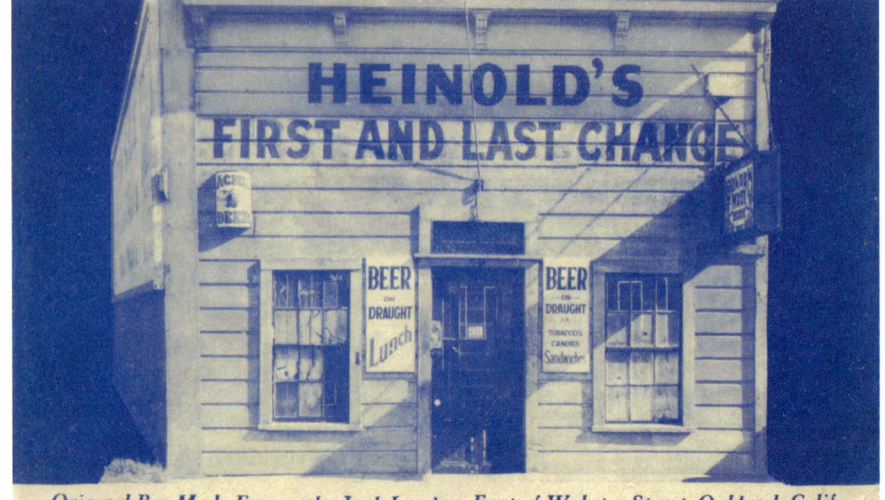

Original Bar Made Famous by Jack London, Foot of Webster Street, Oakland, Calif.

ANFANG DES 20. JAHRHUNDERTS
waren die Südseegeschichten zu einem
eigenen Genre der Literatur geworden. Auf
dem Buchmarkt fanden sich so viele Titel,
dass Verlage bereits 1931 damit warben,
in ihren Büchern werde die „echte" Südsee beschrieben.

Dieser Trend ist zum Teil zwei berühmten Autoren zu verdanken, deren Abenteu-
ergeschichten die amerikanische Bevölkerung in ihren Bann zogen: Jack London und
Robert Louis Stevenson waren die Ersten,
die diesem „Ruf der Wildnis" folgten und
Erzählungen über ihre Reisen durch die
bezaubernden Atolle des Pazifiks schrieben.

Obwohl Robert Louis Stevensons erster
Erfolg, *Die Schatzinsel* (1883), ein klassischer
Piratenroman ist, war Stevenson im Herzen
Polynesier. Den unbeschwerten Lebensstil
der Inseln annehmend, soll er einst gesagt
haben: „Es ereilt einen vermutlich ein glück-
licheres Schicksal, wenn man eine Vorliebe
für das Sammeln von Muscheln hat, als

wenn man als Millionär geboren wurde."
Auf Hawaii freundete Stevenson sich mit
dem letzten Monarchen der Insel, König
Kalākaua, an; einige Zeit verbrachte er auf
den Marquesas-Inseln und auf Abemama
(Gilbertinseln), bis er sich schließlich auf
Samoa niederließ. Dort genoss er bis zu
seinem Tod 1894 hohes Ansehen.

Als junger Mann besuchte Jack London
häufig John Heinolds Kneipe Heinold's
First and Last Chance Saloon im Hafen
von Oakland, Kalifornien. Hier hörte er
Seemannsgeschichten aus allen Ecken des
Pazifiks über vermeintlich unglaubliche
Abenteuer in fernen Häfen. Manche der
alten Seebären sollten später als Charak-
tere in seinen Büchern auftauchen. Mit der
Zeit fasste London den Entschluss, selbst
Seefahrer zu werden. Vom selben Kai
aus, von dem 20 Jahre zuvor schon Robert
Louis Stevenson an Bord der *Casco* in Rich-
tung Pazifik gesegelt war, stach auch Jack
London in See. Die Schaluppe, mit der er

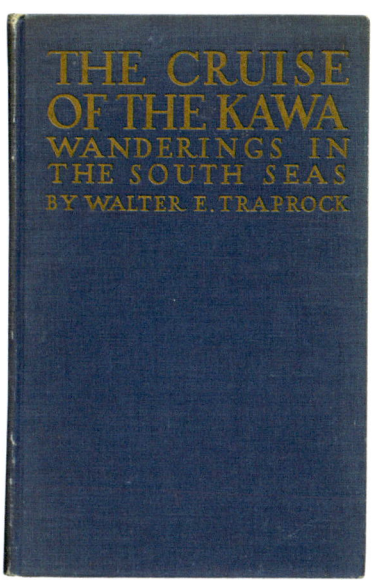

THE CRUISE
OF THE KAWA
WANDERINGS IN
THE SOUTH SEAS
BY WALTER E. TRAPROCK

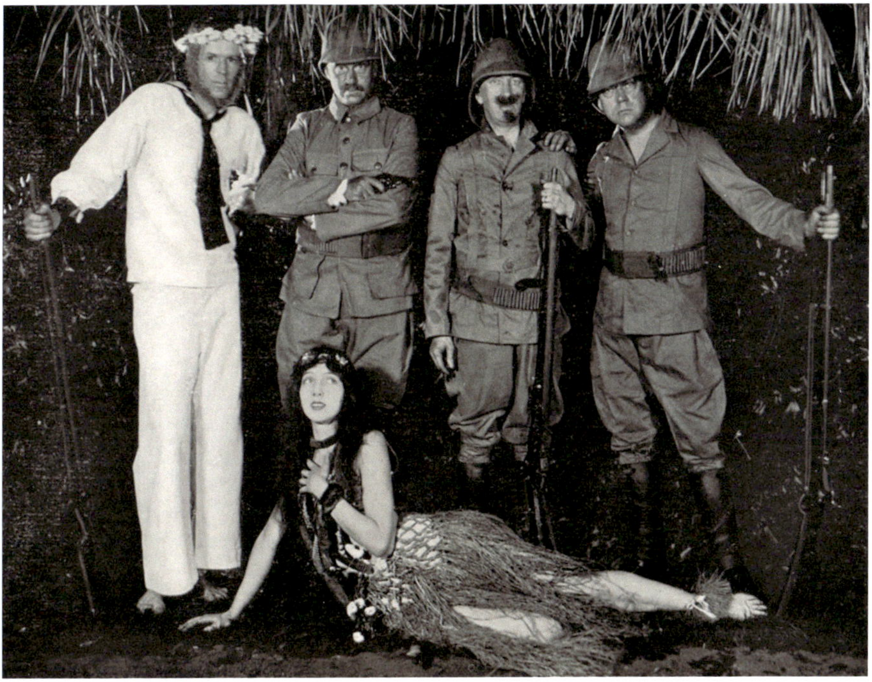

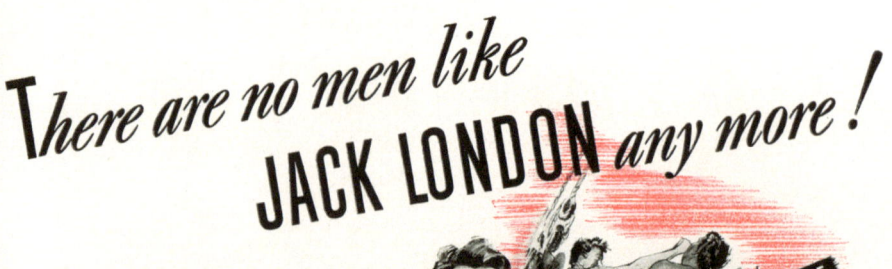
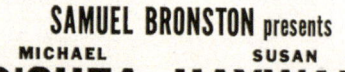

seine Südseereise antrat, hieß *Snark*. Wie viele Südseefahrten von Stevensons und Londons Werken tatsächlich beeinflusst wurden, ist nicht bekannt. Allerdings gibt es ein Buch, in dem beide direkt erwähnt werden: in der Genreparodie *The Cruise of the Kawa* von 1921. Als realistisches Reisetagebuch getarnt, parodiert dieses Werk die Romantik von Südseeautoren wie Arnold Safroni-Middleton. In seinem 1920 erschienenen Buch *South Sea Foam* bekräftigte Safroni-Middleton mit blumiger Prosa die Idee des polynesischen Paradieses:

> *„Hier zumindest kann ich Ruhe abseits der schnelllebigen Turbulenzen menschlicher Zivilisation finden; hier kann ich wie im Garten Eden unter den federleichten Palmwedeln weilen und den Melodien des Windes lauschen, der über die See weht… Ich stieß auf eine heidnische Welt, in der mir das kriecherische Gemurmel der gewöhnlichen Leute nie mehr zu Ohren kommen soll."*

Ein weiterer Autor, der seinen Teil zu den Südseegeschichten beitrug, war Frederick O'Brien. O'Brien hatte auf Samoa und den Marquesas-Inseln gelebt und verstand sich als Nachfolger von Melville, Gauguin und Stevenson. Mit seinem Buch *White Shadows in the South Seas* wurde er Amerikas Südseeguru der 1920er-Jahre, später veröffentlichte er noch zwei weitere Bücher über die polynesischen Inseln. In einer Karikatur des hochdekorierten Marineoffiziers Admiral Gene Markey stellte ihn dieser als Captain Traprock dar, den fiktiven Autor von *The Cruise of the Kawa*. O'Brien's *Shadows* war der erste von vielen Südseebestsellern, der es 1929 auf die Kinoleinwand schaffte.

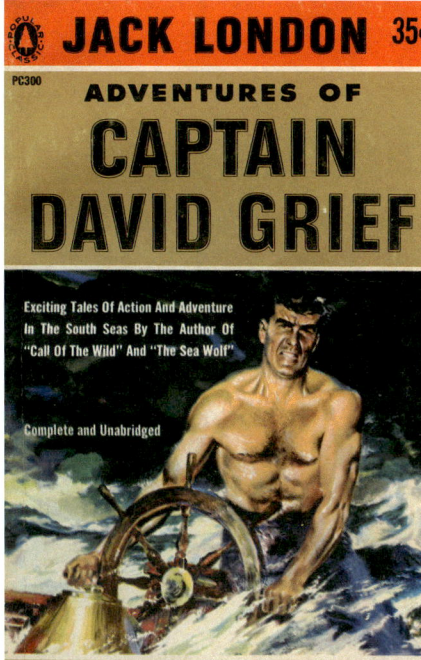

AU DÉBUT DU XXᵉ SIÈCLE, LES
récits se jouant dans les mers du Sud sont
devenus un genre littéraire à part entière.
Le succès populaire des livres composés
dans cette veine est tel qu'en 1931, un
auteur se devait de décrire dans ses histoires les « véritables » mers du Sud.

Cet engouement est en grande partie
imputable à deux écrivains célèbres dont
les récits d'aventure et d'exploration fasci-
nèrent le public américain : Robert Louis
Stevenson et Jack London firent résonner
les premiers cet « appel de la nature » en
racontant, notamment, leurs voyages dans
les atolls enchantés du Pacifique.

Bien que le premier succès populaire de
Robert Louis Stevenson, *L'Île au trésor,* soit
un classique de l'histoire de pirates, l'auteur
avait l'âme polynésienne. Il appréciait
pleinement la douceur de vivre insulaire

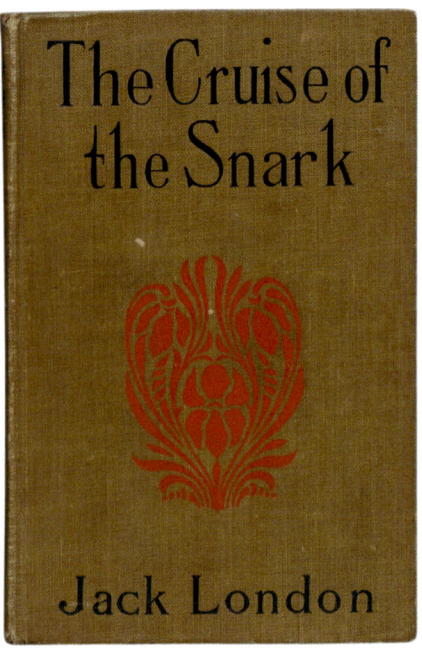

et aurait déclaré : « C'est peut-être une destinée plus heureuse d'aimer collectionner
les coquillages que de naître millionnaire. »
Stevenson se rendit à Hawaii, où il se lia
d'amitié avec le dernier monarque de l'archipel, le roi Kalakaua. Il séjourna aussi aux
Marquises et dans les Kiribati, avant de
s'installer à Samoa, dont la population lui
témoigna admiration et affection aux dernières heures de sa vie.

Jeune homme, Jack London fréquentait
le First & Last Chance Saloon de John Heinold dans le port d'Oakland, en Californie.
Il y écoutait les vieux loups de mer raconter
le Pacifique qu'ils avaient écumé au gré de
leurs missions, et s'inspira d'eux plus tard
pour ses personnages de marins. London
finit par décider de prendre la mer lui
aussi. Depuis le même quai où Robert Louis
Stevenson avait embarqué sur le *Casco* à
destination du Pacifique vingt ans plus tôt,
Jack London mit les voiles pour sa propre
aventure dans les mers du Sud à bord de
son sloop, le *Snark*.

Impossible de dire combien d'escapades
dans les mers du Sud ont été inspirées par
les œuvres de Stevenson et London, mais il
est un livre qui témoigne de l'ampleur du
phénomène : le roman parodique *The Cruise
of the Kawa,* paru en 1921. Sous couvert d'un
récit de voyage tout à fait sérieux, cette
satire se joue du romantisme échevelé d'auteurs comme Arnold Safroni-Middleton,
qui relança le thème du paradis polynésien
avec sa prose fleurie dans son roman de
1920, *South Sea Foam :*

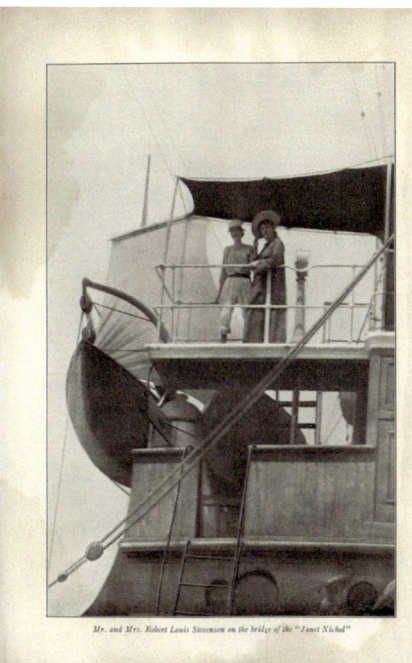

Mr. and Mrs. Robert Louis Stevenson on the bridge of the "Janet Nichol"

The Cruise of the "Janet Nichol" Among the South Sea Islands

A Diary by
Mrs. Robert Louis Stevenson

New York
Charles Scribner's Sons
1914

« Ici, las, je saurai me reposer des turbulences trépidantes de l'humanité civilisée ; ici, je peux demeurer à l'ombre idyllique de palmiers gracieux, et écouter les mélodies que chante le vent lorsqu'il vient de la mer… J'eus la sensation d'avoir atteint un monde païen où me seraient enfin épargnés les marmonnements serviles des gens conventionnels. »

Parmi les autres auteurs ayant contribué à ce raz-de-marée exotique figure Frederick O'Brien. Après avoir vécu aux Marquises et Samoa, O'Brien se jugea digne de marcher dans les pas de Melville, Gauguin et Stevenson. Grâce au succès de son roman *Ombres blanches*, il devint l'expert ès mers du Sud américain des années 1920, et publia deux livres supplémentaires sur ce sujet si porteur. L'amiral Gene Markey, officier de marine décoré et dessinateur humoristique, caricatura d'ailleurs O'Brien en Capitaine Traprock, le narrateur de *The Cruise of the Kawa*. Les *Ombres blanches* de O'Brien fut le premier d'une longue série de bestsellers « pacifiques » à passer du papier au grand écran, en 1929.

OPPOSITE AND ABOVE: Travelogues of London and Stevenson

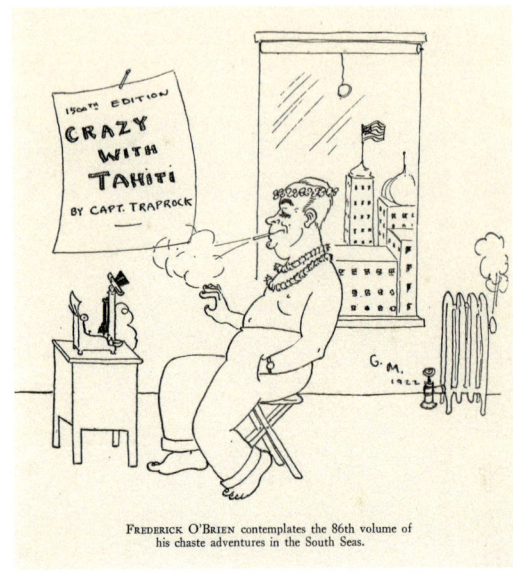

FREDERICK O'BRIEN contemplates the 86th volume of
his chaste adventures in the South Seas.

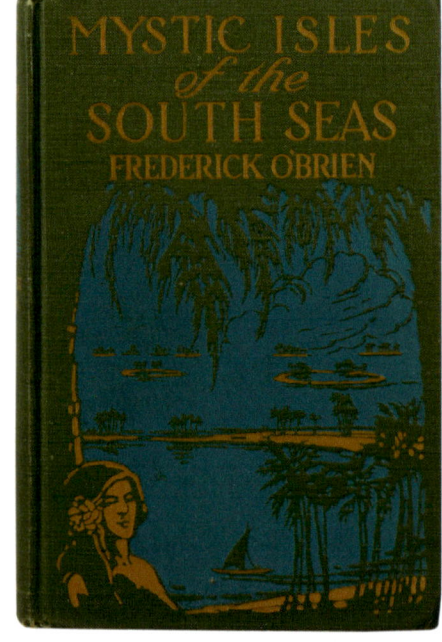

ABOVE: Caricature of O'Brien
as Captain Traprock

RIGHT: *Mystic Isles of the South
Seas* (1921) was the second novel
in O'Brien's island trilogy

OPPOSITE: Frederick O'Brien
advocated the South Seas dream
in periodicals

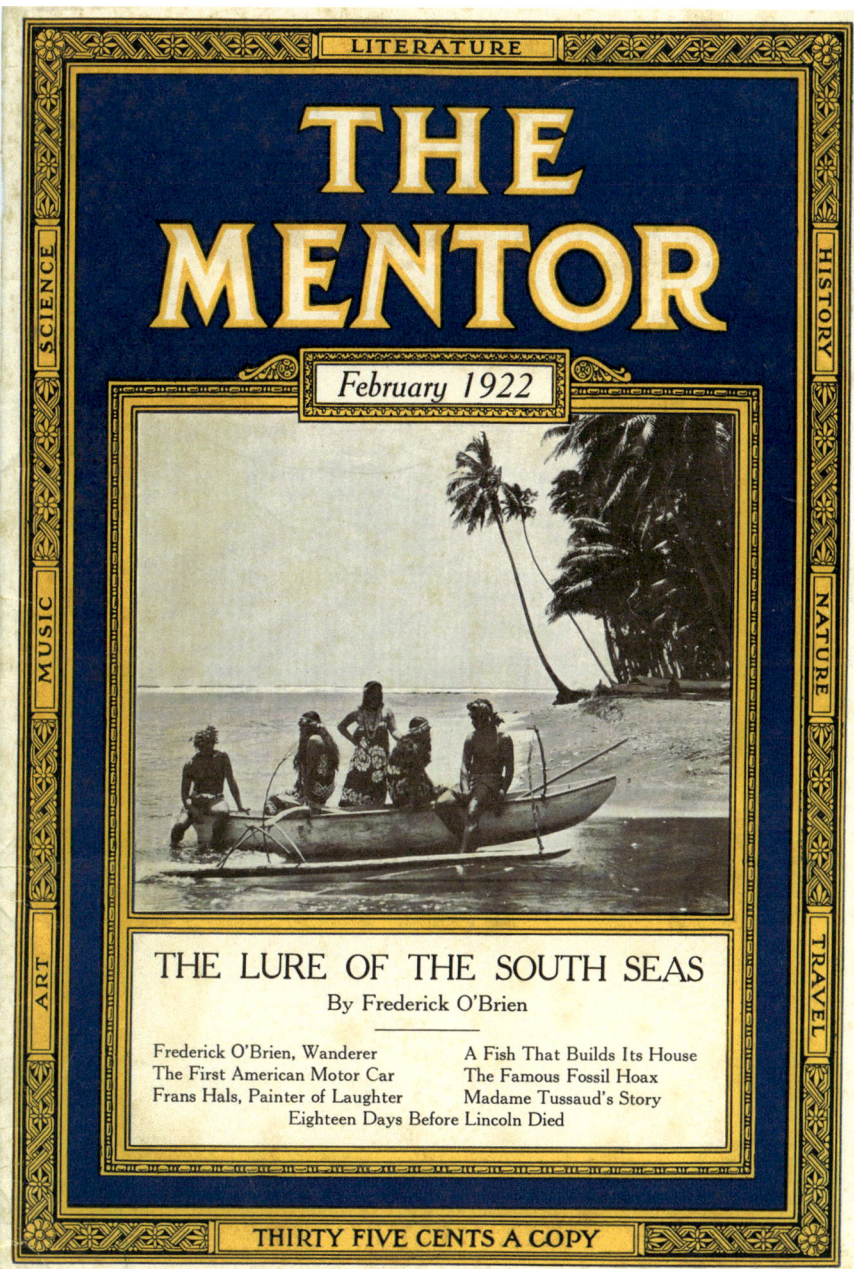

LITERATURE

THE MENTOR

February 1922

SCIENCE

MUSIC

ART

HISTORY

NATURE

TRAVEL

THE LURE OF THE SOUTH SEAS
By Frederick O'Brien

Frederick O'Brien, Wanderer   A Fish That Builds Its House
The First American Motor Car   The Famous Fossil Hoax
Frans Hals, Painter of Laughter   Madame Tussaud's Story
Eighteen Days Before Lincoln Died

THIRTY FIVE CENTS A COPY

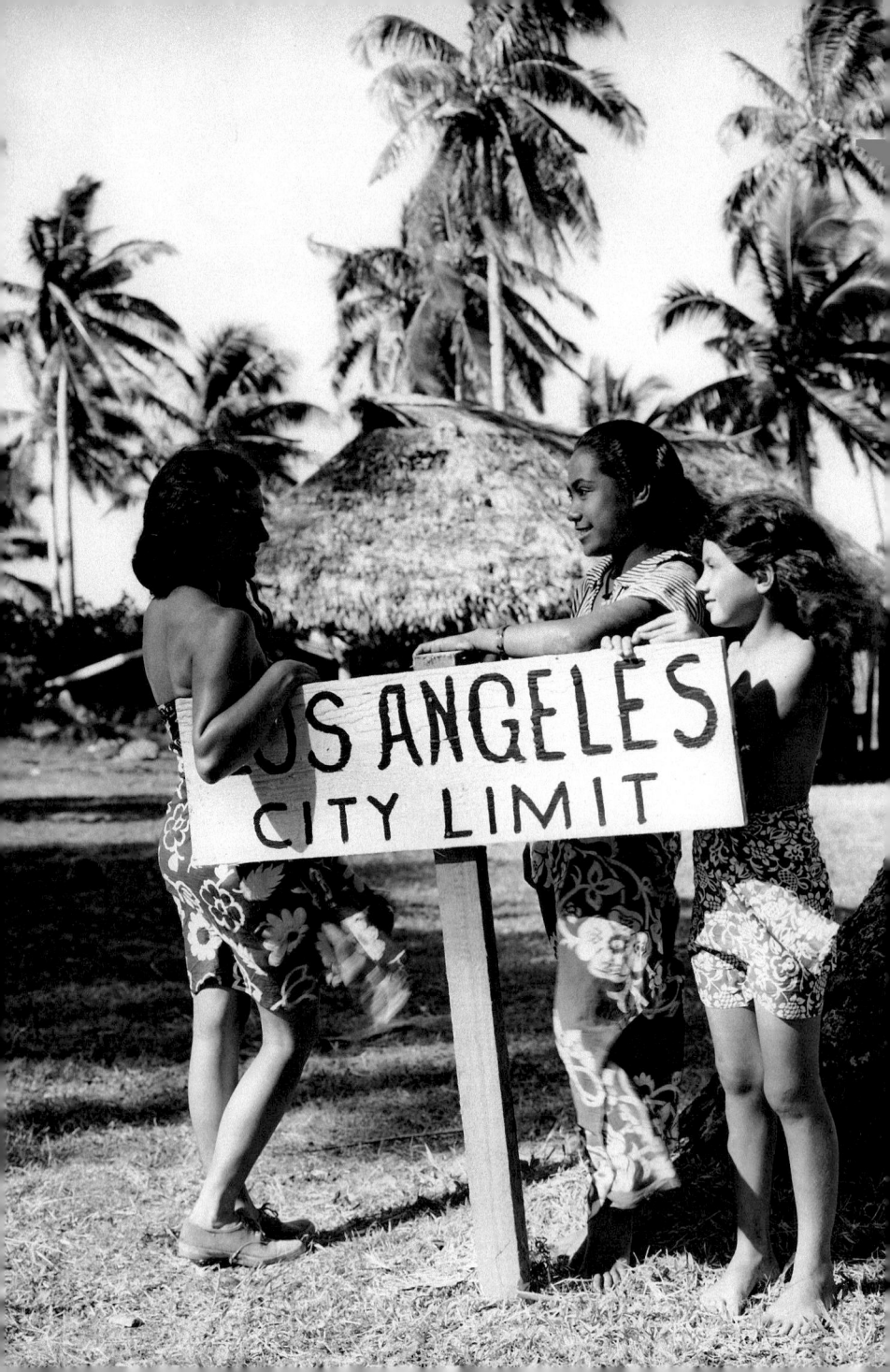

5

SOUTH SEAS MADE IN HOLLYWOOD: FROM BOOK TO FILM TO BAR

SÜDSEE „MADE IN HOLLYWOOD" - VOM BUCH ZUM FILM ZUR BAR
LES MERS DU SUD VUES PAR HOLLYWOOD: DU LIVRE AU FILM, PUIS AU BAR

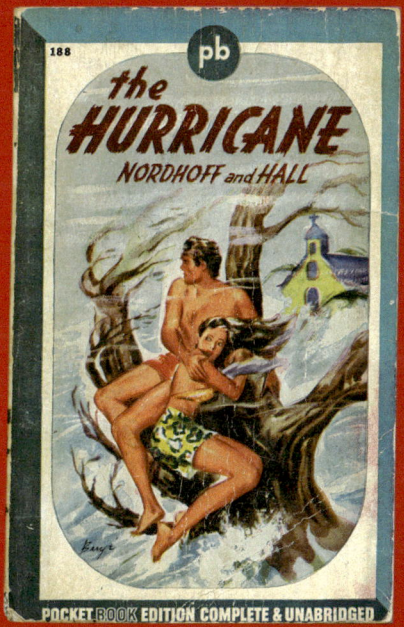

OPPOSITE: A mock boundary sign pretends that Los Angeles bordered
directly on Polynesia, on the set of *The Hurricane* (1937)

ABOVE: Paperback cover of the novel, perpetuating the visual theme

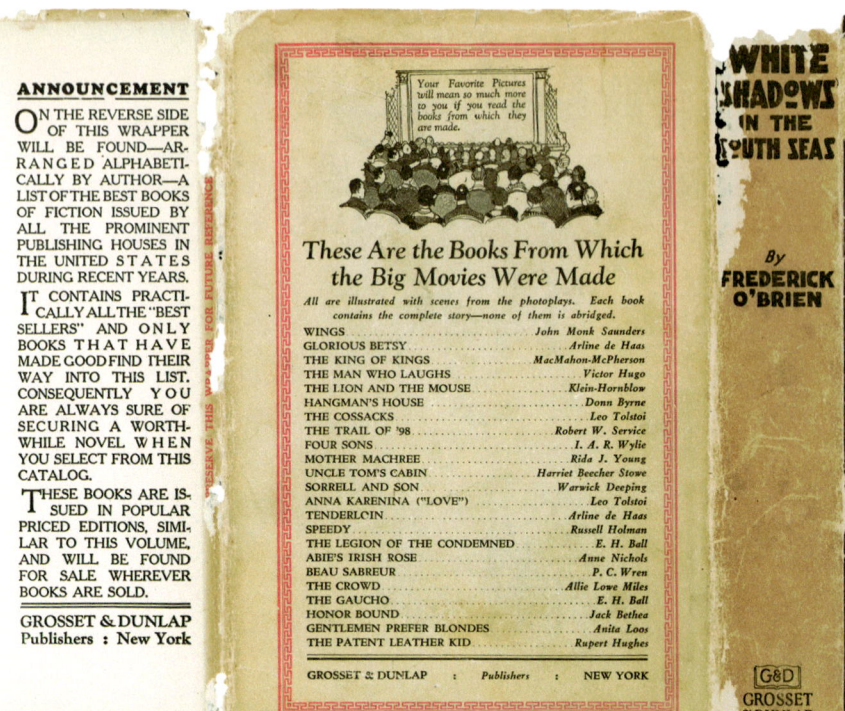

These Are the Books From Which the Big Movies Were Made

WHITE SHADOWS IN THE SOUTH SEAS

By FREDERICK O'BRIEN

GROSSET & DUNLAP

IN THE EARLY 20TH CENTURY A

completely new form of entertainment arrived that was soon to surpass all others in popularity: the motion picture, or "movie" for short. Moviemakers chose Hollywood, a suburb of Los Angeles, California, as their preferred filming location. Here, the sunny climate and diversity of the surrounding landscape offered plenty of backgrounds for their stories: from green valleys to snowy mountains, rocky canyons to sandy deserts, Southern California had it all. It also provided its own "South Seas" island: Catalina, just 22 miles off the Los Angeles coast.

The 1920s were the dawn of Hollywood's Golden Age. Movie producers searched for gripping stories that would appeal to the public; best-selling books were the logical choice. *White Shadows in the South Seas* had enjoyed great success, so it was chosen to make the transition from book to film.

Leading the next generation of South Seas novelists was the author team Charles Nordhoff and James Norman Hall. *The Mutiny on the Bounty*, their true-life parable about a man's rebellion against government and subsequent escape to an island paradise, was realized as an elaborate Hollywood spectacle for the big screen. The isthmus of Catalina Island served as the location for the H.M.S. *Bounty's* landing on the island of Tahiti. Art LaShelle, an

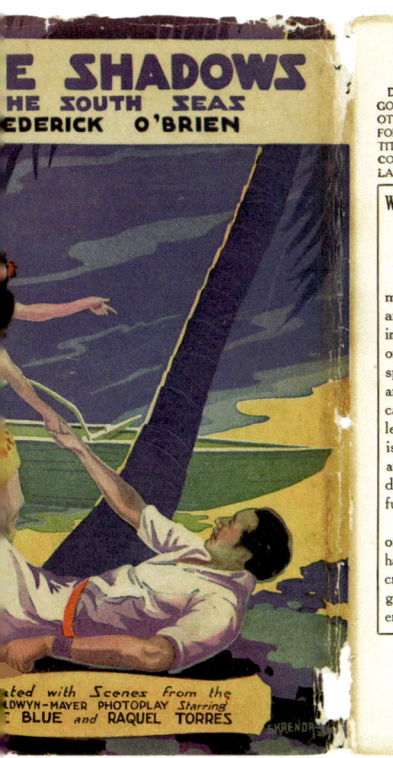

E SHADOWS
HE SOUTH SEAS
EDERICK O'BRIEN

ted with Scenes from the
DWYN-MAYER PHOTOPLAY Starring
BLUE and RAQUEL TORRES

DO YOU WANT ANOTHER
GOOD STORY? LOOK ON THE
OTHER SIDE OF THIS WRAPPER
FOR A LIST OF MORE THAN 500
TITLES OF THE BEST RECENT
COPYRIGHT FICTION IN POPU-
LAR PRICED EDITIONS.

**WHITE SHADOWS IN THE
SOUTH SEAS**

By FREDERICK O'BRIEN

A travel classic which
made its author famous
and which set a fashion
in literature. , It is a record of one happy year
spent by the author
among the simple friendly
cannibals of Atuona val-
ley, in those marvelous
islands, the Marquesas,
among the fascinating
descendants of a beauti-
ful, artistic, noble race.

No other travel book
of the past twenty years
has been received by the
critical press and the
general public with such
enthusiastic delight.

LOOK ON THE REVERSE SIDE OF THIS JACKET

The republished movie edition
of the book, listing many other
book-to-film projects

early Catalina resident, befriended Clark
Gable during the shooting of *Bounty* and
became his double in the movie. It was
his and Gable's idea to turn the film set
into a Polynesian bar named after Gable's
movie character. This was such a success
that LaShelle opened a second Christian's
Hut in the Los Angeles beach community
of Balboa. The establishment attracted
celeb-rities like John Wayne, Errol Flynn,
and Humphrey Bogart, and franchises
opened in Laguna Beach, Corona del Mar,
and even Hawaii.

Authors Nordhoff and Hall quickly
followed the success of *Bounty* with another
South Seas drama, *The Hurricane*, which was
just as swiftly adapted for the screen. The
story of a tragic native love affair turned
Dorothy Lamour and Jon Hall into South
Seas stars and gave Lamour her signature
hit song, "Moon of Manakoora." A native
village built for the film occupied two and
a half acres of the United Artists Studios
backlot. The movie's storm and tidal wave
special effects were the most spectacular of
their time.

Banking on the enormous popular success of *The Hurricane*, a number of tropical
nightclub owners opened "Hurricane" bars
in New York, Boston, San Francisco, and
Los Angeles. The film's dramatic theme
was carried so far that many establishments

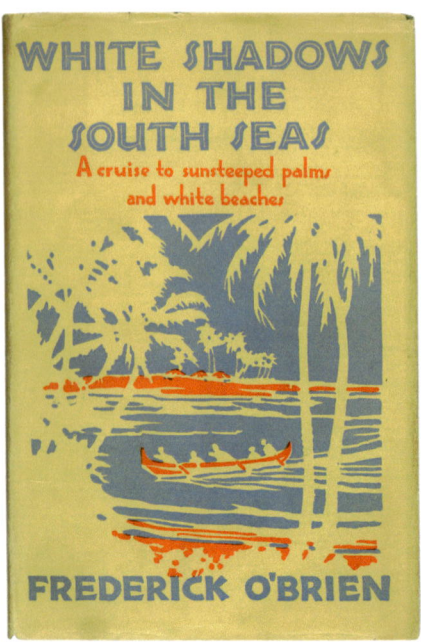

LEFT: The first edition of *White Shadows in the South Seas* (1919)

BELOW: The *White Shadows in the South Seas* movie program (1928)

OPPOSITE: Sheet music cover for the *White Shadows in the South Seas* theme song

installed simulated storm effects, from thunder sounds to strobe "lightning" and "rain" dripping down eaves and windowpanes from sprinklers overhead. The South Seas story was being retold in 3-D Sensurround, and the rum cocktail-soaked customers were willing believers.

The visual iconography of the various "Hurricane" establishments was obviously inspired by the memorable storm sequences of the Hollywood film. Suddenly, nude native maidens in distress, wearing their hair and grass skirts horizontally, were portrayed on matchbooks, menus, and cocktail mugs.

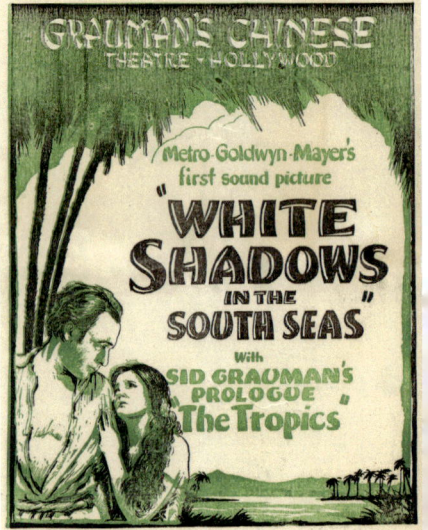

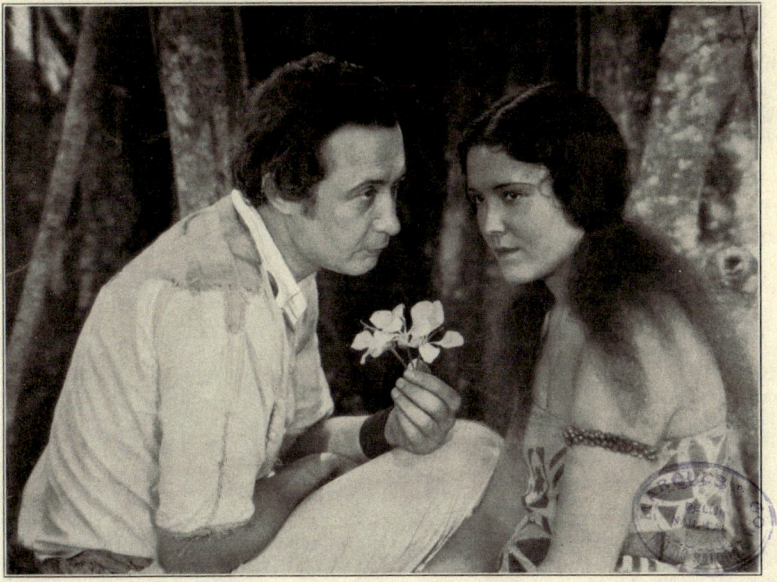

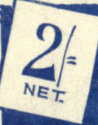

THE ISTHMUS—FOR SOUTH SEAS GLAMOUR

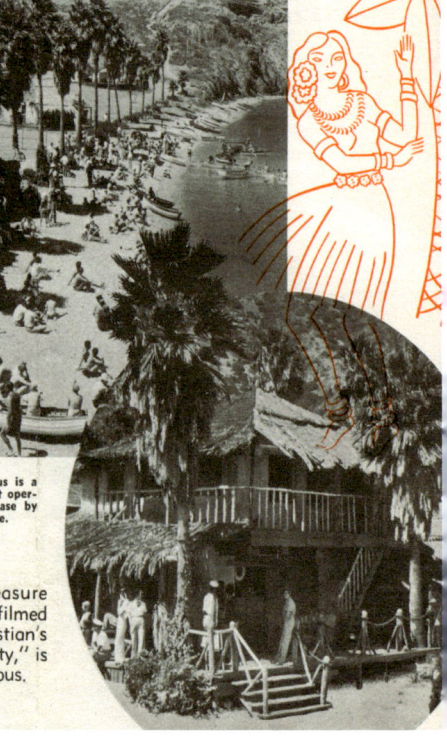

ISTHMUS PORT

Twenty-five miles by motor from Avalon, at the Island's "other end," lies the Isthmus, where but half a mile of land divides the shores. Because of its startling scenic beauty, it has become Hollywood's chosen "location" for South Sea films, a favored anchorage for countless yachts, and the perfect spot for vacationists who want to "go native" in comfort.

PAPEETE BEACH

Lined with palms and thatched huts, broad, sandy Papeete Beach reflects the exotic glamour of languorous tropical isles — inviting you to happy hours under the lazy sun, caressed by cooling, carefree breezes. The Isthmus offers the ideal place for healthful relaxation — with plenty of diversions.

LIVING CONVENIENCES

Comfortable cabins, a dining room, and telephone service to Avalon and mainland make Isthmus living complete. Boat and auto rates to Isthmus —inside back cover; steamer schedule on facing page.

	Per Day: Single	Double
Bungalettes without lavatory and toilet	$2.50	$3.50
Deluxe bungalettes with lavatory and toilet	4.00 up	4.50 up
Sadie Thompson Cottage ..	4.50	5.50

Cot charge, $1.00 for third person in room.

Duplex bungalette	$ 7.00 (1 to 4 persons)
Round House	10.00 (1 to 5 persons)
Brown Jug Cottage	10.00 (1 to 6 persons)

Other cottages $10.00 and up.
A la Carte and Table d'Hote Service for Meals

● The Isthmus is a separate resort operated under lease by ABSCO Service.

CHRISTIAN'S HUT

"Ten Commandments," "Treasure Island" and other movies were filmed here and many sets remain. Christian's Hut, from "Mutiny on the Bounty," is now an unique cocktail rendezvous.

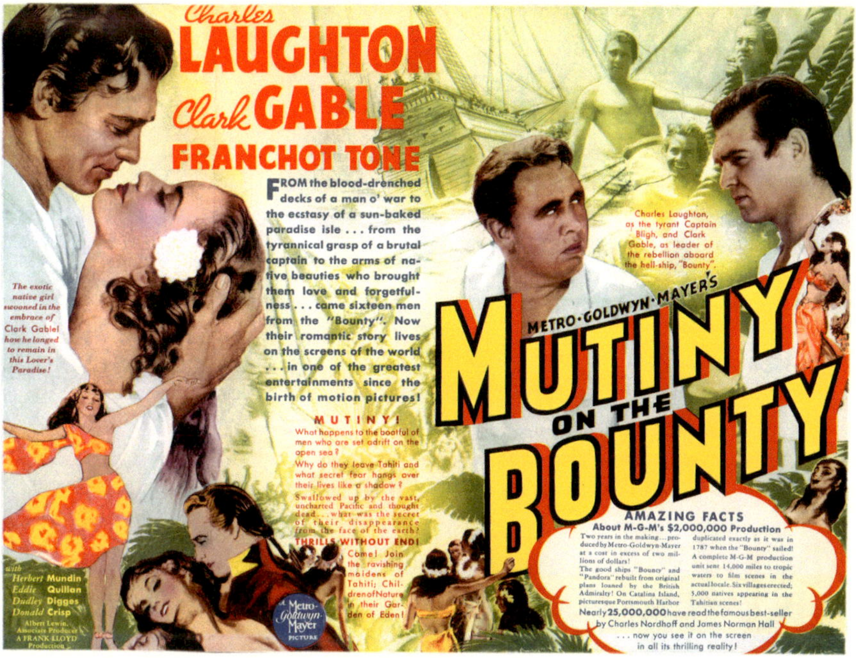

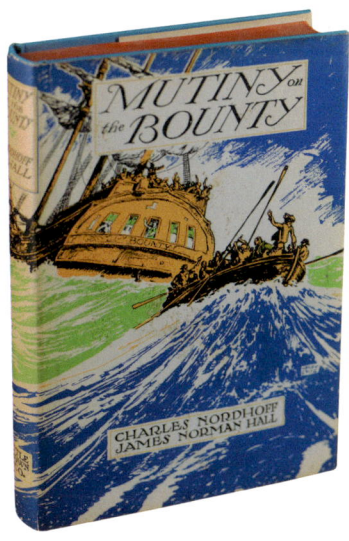

OPPOSITE: The palm trees and thatched-hut sets erected by movie-makers led to the Catalina Isthmus being nicknamed "Papeete Beach"

ABOVE: *Mutiny* lobby card with lurid copy, 1935

LEFT: The next big South Seas book-to-film hit

ANFANG DES 20. JAHRHUNDERTS
kam eine neue, beliebte Unterhaltungsform
auf, die schon bald alle anderen übertreffen sollte: der Film. Hollywood, ein Vorort
von Los Angeles, wurde bald zum bevorzugten Drehort der Filmemacher. Das son-
nige Klima und die die Stadt umgebende
abwechslungsreiche Landschaft boten pas-
sende Hintergründe für ihre Geschichten.
Von grünen Tälern bis zu schneebedeckten
Bergen, von felsigen Canyons bis zu Sand-
wüsten – Südkalifornien hatte alles. Selbst
eine „Südseeinsel" gab es hier: Catalina
liegt nur 35 Kilometer vor der Küste von
Los Angeles.

Die 1920er-Jahre waren der Beginn von
Hollywoods goldenem Zeitalter. Filmpro-

duzenten waren auf der Suche nach fesseln-
den Geschichten – und Literaturbestseller
waren die logische Wahl. Der erfolgreiche
Roman *White Shadows in the South Seas*
wurde 1928 verfilmt.

Die nächste Generation von Südsee-
Autoren wurde von dem Schriftsteller-Duo
Charles Nordhoff und James Norman Hall
angeführt. Die *Meuterei auf der Bounty,* eine
Parabel über das Aufbegehren des Men-
schen gegen die Regierung und seine Flucht
in ein Inselparadies, wurde ein aufwendiges
Hollywood-Spektakel für die Kinoleinwand.
Die Landenge von Catalina Island diente als
Anlegestelle der *HMS Bounty* auf Tahiti.

Art LaShelle, ein alteingesessener Bewohner Catalinas, freundete sich während

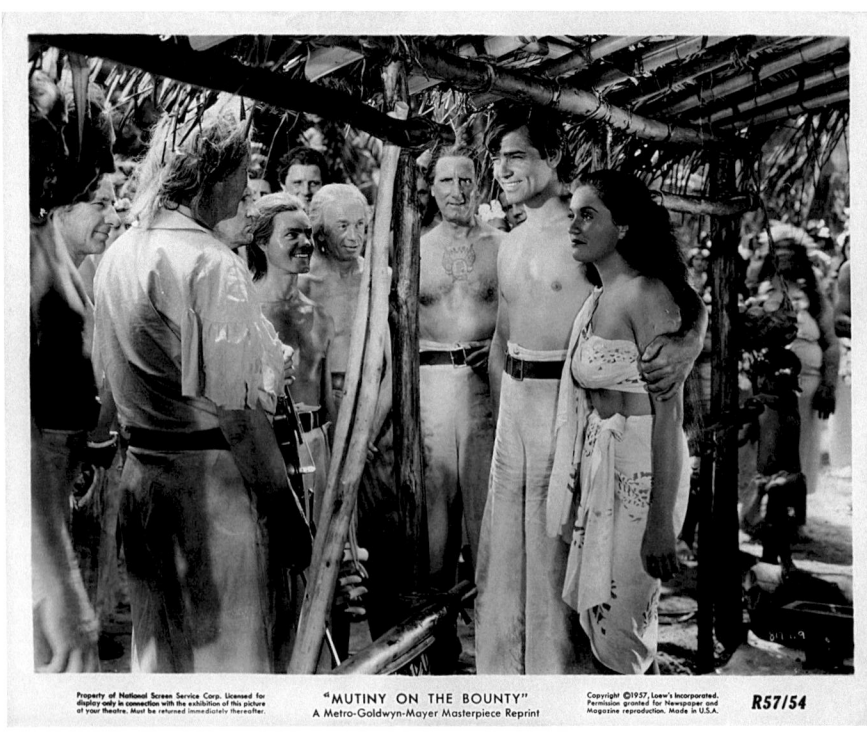

Property of National Screen Service Corp. Licensed for display only in connection with the exhibition of this picture of your theatre. Must be returned immediately thereafter. **"MUTINY ON THE BOUNTY"** A Metro-Goldwyn-Mayer Masterpiece Reprint Copyright ©1957, Loew's Incorporated. Permission granted for Newspaper and Magazine reproduction. Made in U.S.A. **R57/54**

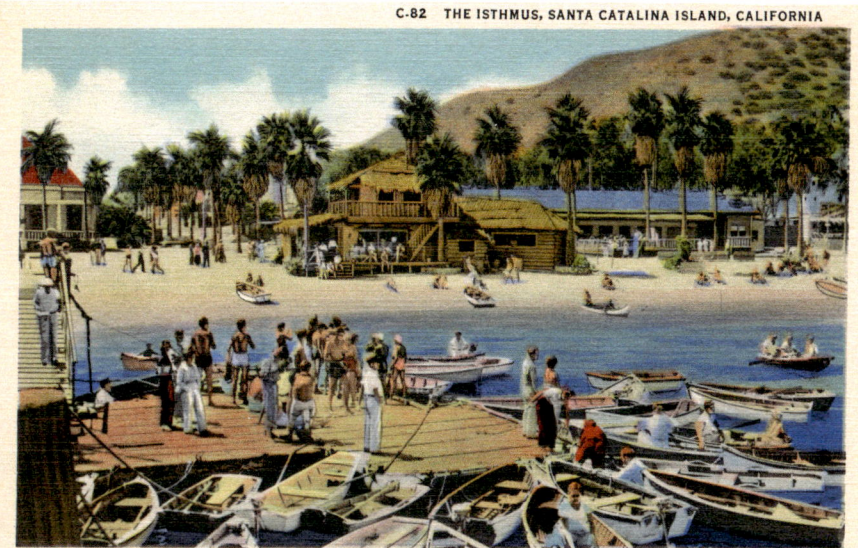

7A-H1687

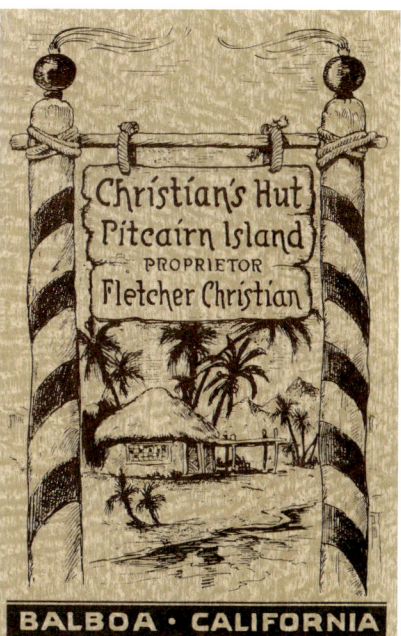

Christian's Hut
Pitcairn Island
PROPRIETOR
Fletcher Christian

BALBOA · CALIFORNIA

OPPOSITE: Heartthrob Clark Gable played mutiny leader Fletcher Christian

ABOVE: Fletcher Christian slept here: This building was a movie set built for the filming of *Mutiny on the Bounty* (1935) *(JonPaul Balak Collection)*

LEFT: Menu cover from Christian's Hut in Balboa *(Duane Orzol Collection)*

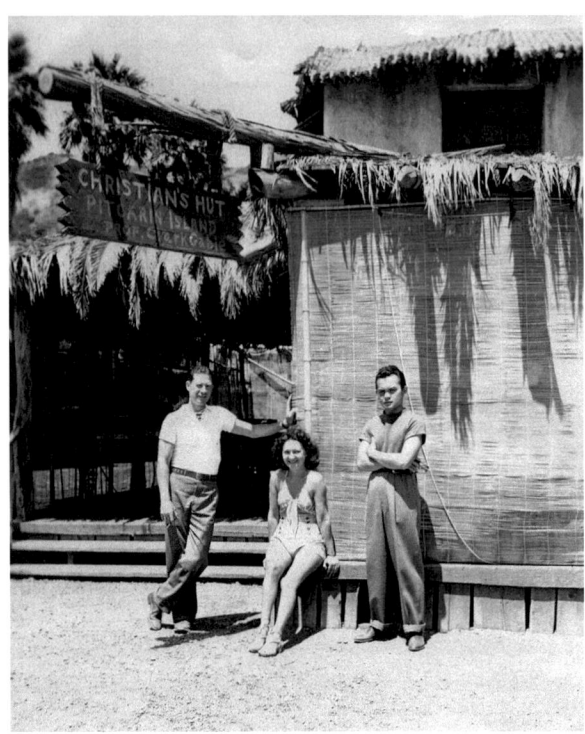

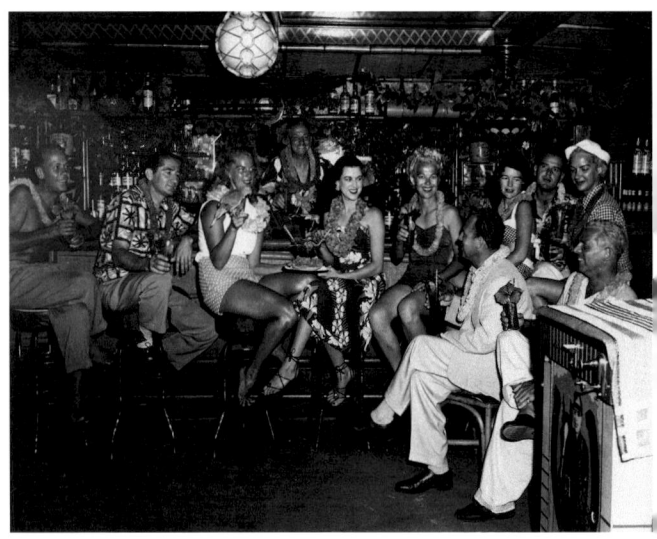

LEFT: The original Christian's Hut on Catalina Island. Barkeep Ray Buhen (far right) eventually opened the Tiki Ti, still in business today

BELOW: Happy customers at Christian's Hut, Balboa *(Frank Brajevic Collection)*

OPPOSITE: Comical character "The Goof" was the Hut's pre-Tiki logo figure *(Scott Schell Collection)*

der Dreharbeiten mit Clark Gable an und wurde dessen Filmdouble. Gemeinsam kamen sie auf die Idee, die Filmkulisse in eine polynesische Bar mit dem Namen von Gables Filmcharakter umzuwandeln. Das Unterfangen war ein solcher Erfolg, dass LaShelle eine zweite Christian's Hut in Los Angeles' Strandgemeinde Balboa eröffnete. Die Bar zog Stars wie John Wayne, Errol Flynn und Humphrey Bogart an und bald eröffneten weitere Franchise-Kneipen in Laguna Beach, Corona del Mar und sogar auf Hawaii.

Die Autoren Nordhoff und Hall lieferten nach dem Erfolg der *Bounty* schnell ein weiteres Südseedrama nach. *The Hurricane* (deutscher Filmtitel *… dann kam der Orkan*) wurde ebenso schnell für die Leinwand adaptiert wie sein Vorgänger. Die tragische Liebesgeschichte im Südpazifik machte Dorothy Lamour und Jon Hall zu Südseestars und verhalf Lamour zu ihrem größten Musikerfolg, „The Moon of Manakoora". Das für den Film gebaute Einheimischendorf nahm einen knappen Hektar des Studiogeländes von United Artists in Anspruch. Die Spezialeffekte für Sturm und Wellen waren die spektakulärsten ihrer Zeit.

Eine Reihe von Besitzern tropischer Nachtclubs machte sich den enormen Erfolg von *… dann kam der Orkan* zunutze und eröffnete „Hurricane"-Bars in

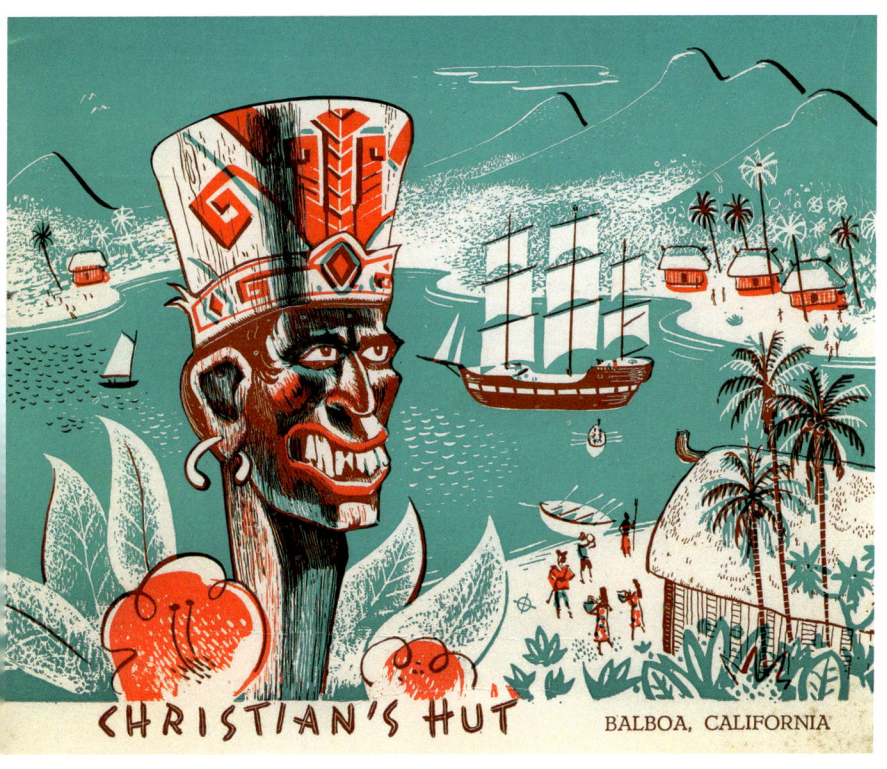

CHRISTIAN'S HUT · BALBOA, CALIFORNIA

New York, Boston, San Francisco und Los Angeles. Es ging sogar so weit, dass viele dieser Bars Sturmsimulationen installierten. Es gab Donnergrollen, Stroboskop-Blitze und Regentropfen aus Sprinklern an Dach und Fenstern. Die Südseegeschichte wurde gleichsam zum Anfassen nacherzählt und die von Rum-Cocktails beschwipsten Gäste waren begeistert.

Die Dekoration der Hurricane-Bars war von den denkwürdigen Sturmszenen der Hollywood-Filme inspiriert. Und plötzlich tauchten auch nackte polynesische Frauen – Haar und Bambusrock vom Wind in die Höhe geblasen – auf Streichholzbriefchen, Getränkekarten und Cocktailbechern auf.

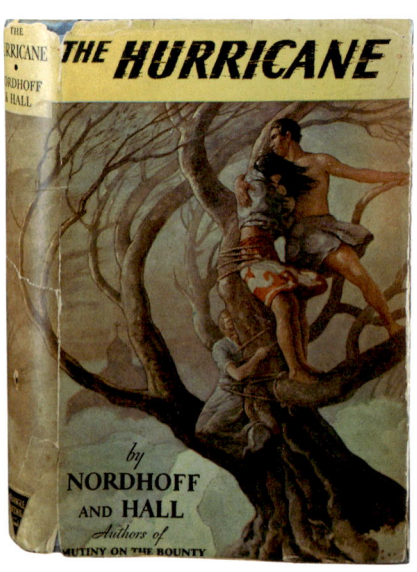

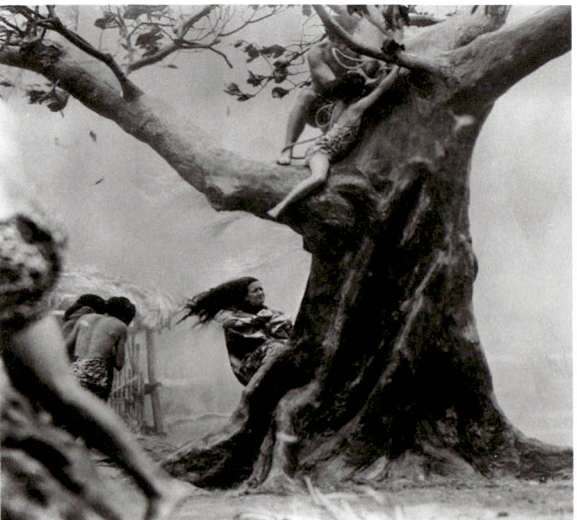

ABOVE: Book by Charles Nordhoff and James Norman Hall titled *The Hurricane*

LEFT: *The Hurricane* special effects impressed audiences and established a recurring theme

OPPOSITE: *The Hurricane* lifted Jon Hall (nephew of author James Norman Hall) and Dorothy Lamour to stardom. Numerous South Seas movie roles followed in its wake

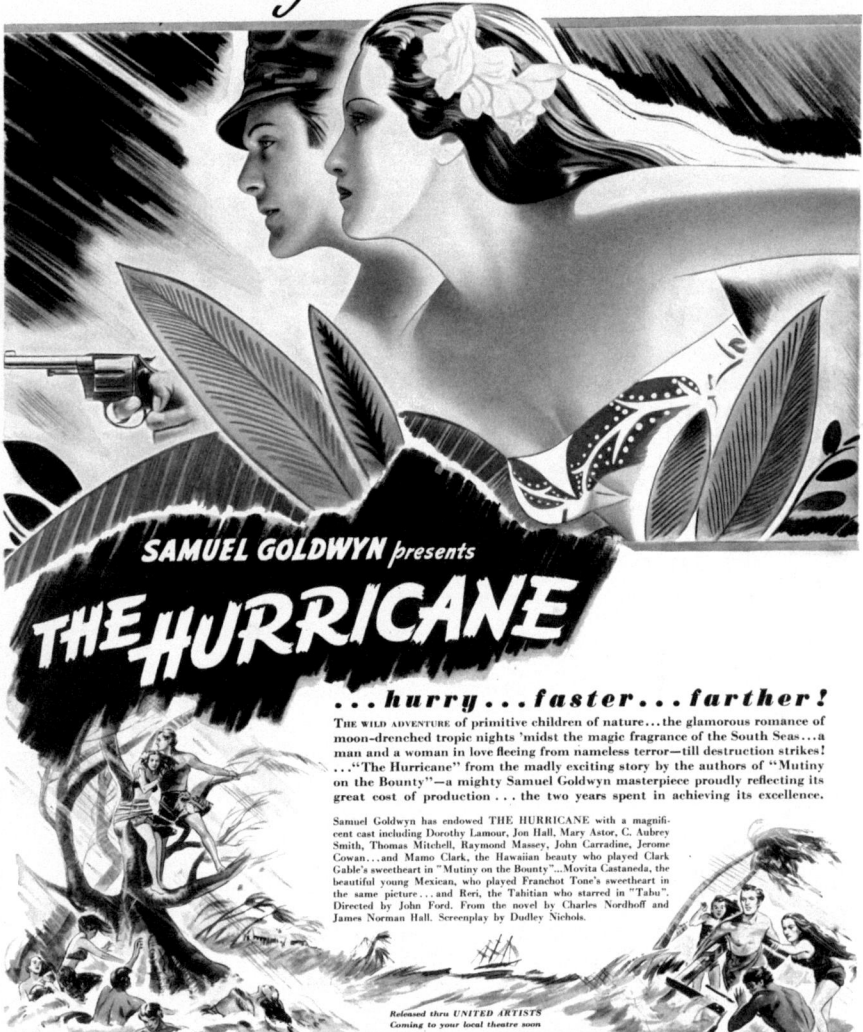

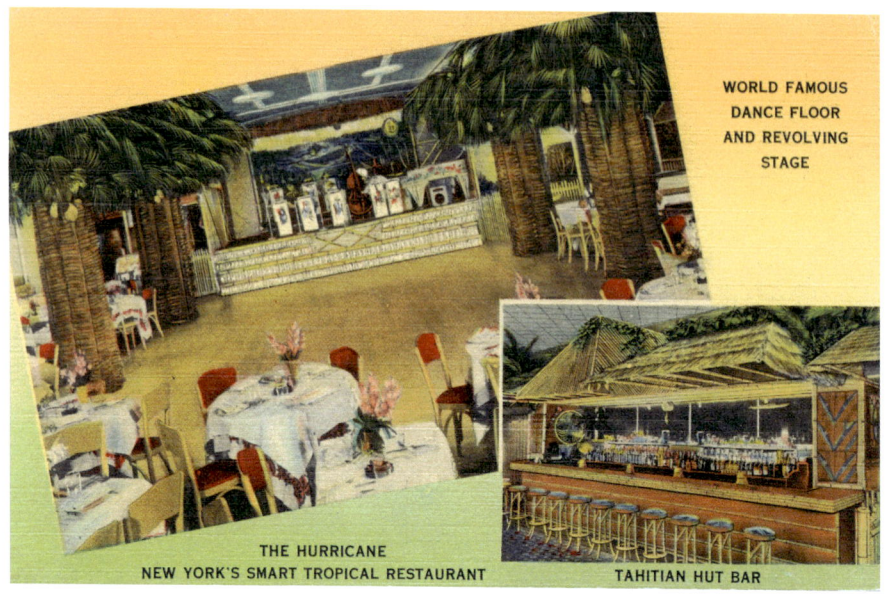

World Famous Dance Floor and Revolving Stage

THE HURRICANE
NEW YORK'S SMART TROPICAL RESTAURANT

TAHITIAN HUT BAR

AU DÉBUT DU XXe SIÈCLE, UNE

forme de divertissement totalement nouvelle apparaît, qui surpasse bientôt toutes les autres en popularité : le cinématographe, « cinéma » pour les intimes. L'industrie choisit d'installer ses studios à Hollywood, en banlieue de Los Angeles, en Californie, qui, outre son climat ensoleillé, a l'avantage de regorger de décors naturels variés où mettre en scène ses histoires : vallées verdoyantes, monts enneigés, canyons escarpés, déserts de sable ou forêts millénaires, on trouve de tout en Californie du Sud. La Californie possède aussi sa propre île aux allures de paradis primitif : Catalina, à quelque 20 milles nautiques au large de Los Angeles.

À Hollywood, les années 1920 marquent l'aube de l'âge d'or. Les producteurs, en quête d'intrigues captivantes qui sauront attirer massivement le public, se tournent

très logiquement vers les romans à succès. C'est ainsi qu'un de ces best-sellers, *White Shadows in the South Seas,* est adapté pour le grand écran (diffusé en France sous le titre *Ombres blanches*).

À la tête de la nouvelle génération de romanciers férus d'exotisme figure le duo formé par Charles Nordhoff et James Norman Hall. *Les Révoltés du Bounty,* leur parabole biographique narrant la rébellion d'un homme contre son gouvernement, puis son exil volontaire dans une île paradisiaque, devient ainsi un spectacle foisonnant sous les auspices de Hollywood, et l'accostage sur l'île de Tahiti du *Bounty,* navire de Sa Majesté, est tourné dans l'isthme de l'île de Catalina.

Art LaShelle, qui vit à Catalina depuis des années, sert de doublure à Clark Gable sur le tournage du *Bounty* et les deux hommes se lient d'amitié. Ensemble, ils

OPPOSITE: Interior of the Hurricane Restaurant in New York

RIGHT: Matchbook cover promising ample amounts of tropical atmosphere *(Scott Schell Collection)*

BELOW: Rain and rum helped the customer get into the "tropical hideaway" mood *(Frank Brajevic Collection)*

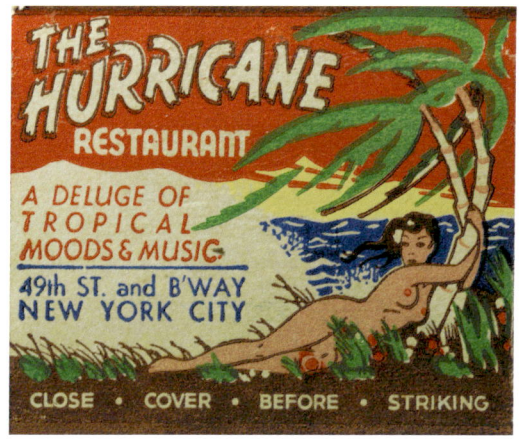

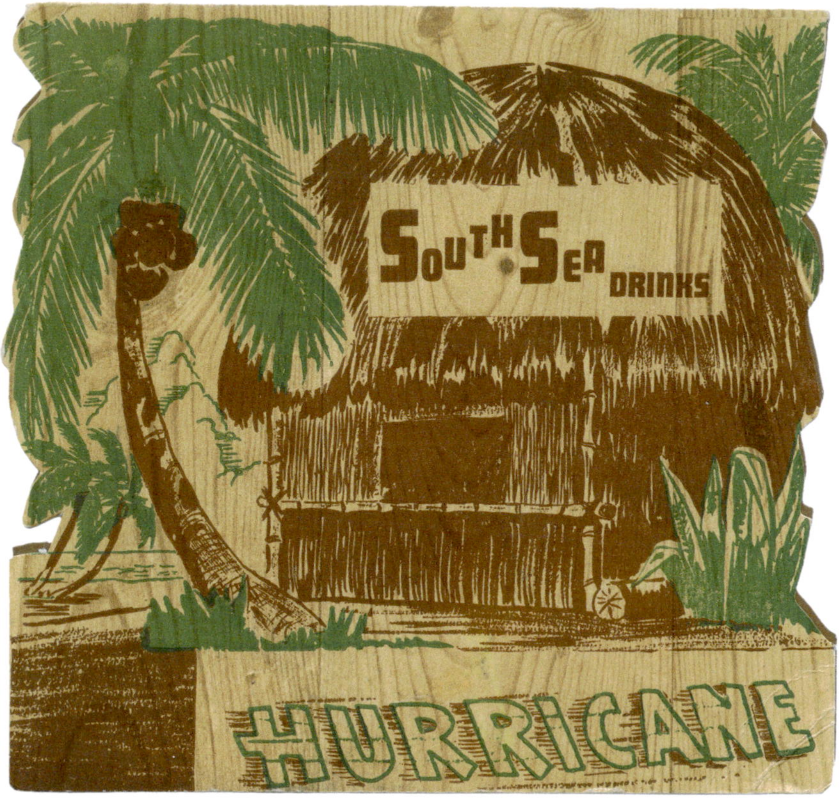

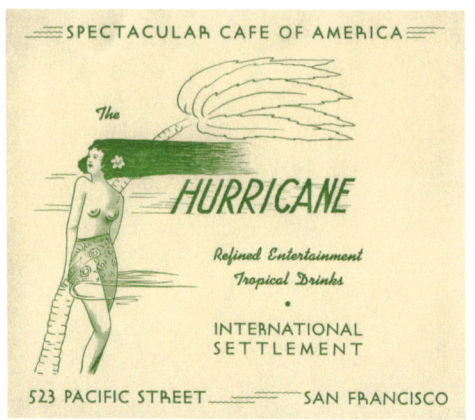

décident de transformer les décors du film en bar à thème portant le nom du personnage principal du film, campé par Gable. Le lieu remporte un succès tel que LaShelle ouvre un second Christian's Hut sur la plage de Balboa, toujours dans le comté de Los Angeles. L'établissement est fréquenté par des célébrités comme John Wayne, Errol Flynn ou Humphrey Bogart, et des franchises ouvrent à Laguna Beach, Corona del Mar, et même Hawaii.

Nordhoff et Hall n'en restent pas à leur premier succès, et le *Bounty* est rapidement suivi d'un deuxième drame sis dans les mers du Sud : *The Hurricane*, qui est tout aussi vite projeté sur grand écran. Il s'agit cette fois de la tragique histoire d'amour entre deux « indigènes » incarnés par Dorothy Lamour et Jon Hall, qui deviennent ainsi des vedettes du genre. Dorothy Lamour y interprète la célèbre chanson « Moon of Manakoora ». Le village construit pour le tournage occupe un terrain de plus d'un hectare appartenant aux studios des Artistes associés. Les effets spéciaux employés pour recréer la tempête et le raz-de-marée sont très spectaculaires pour l'époque.

Nombreux sont les propriétaires de boîtes de nuit qui, misant sur l'énorme succès populaire de *The Hurricane*, ouvrent des bars « Hurricane », à New York, Boston, San Francisco ou Los Angeles. Certains poussent la thématique si loin qu'ils installent des simulateurs d'orage, à grand renfort de grondements de tonnerre (préenregistrés), d'éclairs (stroboscopiques) et d'averses (en réalité des arroseurs automatiques) martelant l'avant-toit et dégoulinant sur les fenêtres, afin que leurs clients revivent en Sensurround 3D le déchaînement des éléments qui les a captivés au cinéma. Après quelques cocktails maison à base de rhum, la plupart n'y voyaient que du feu.

L'iconographie qui fait la marque des divers établissements baptisés « Hurricane » s'inspire à l'évidence des mémorables scènes de tempête du film hollywoodien. Soudain, de jeunes vierges en détresse, créatures à demi nues, chevelure et pagne au vent, apparaissent sur les boîtes d'allumettes, les cartes, et les mugs à cocktail.

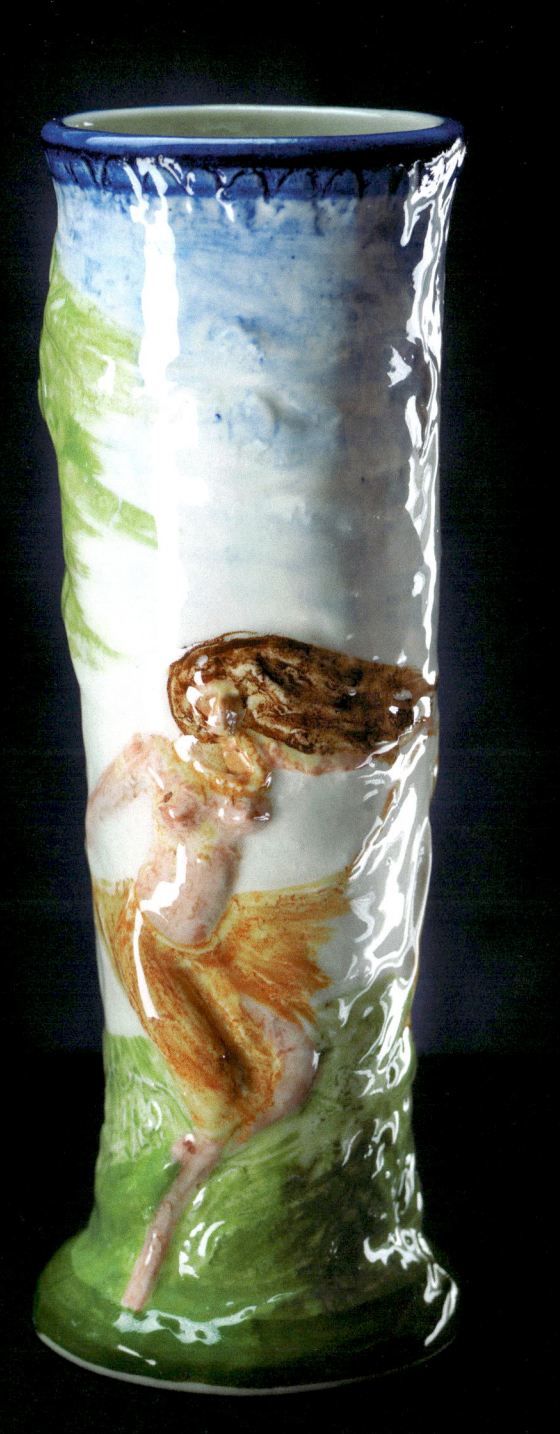

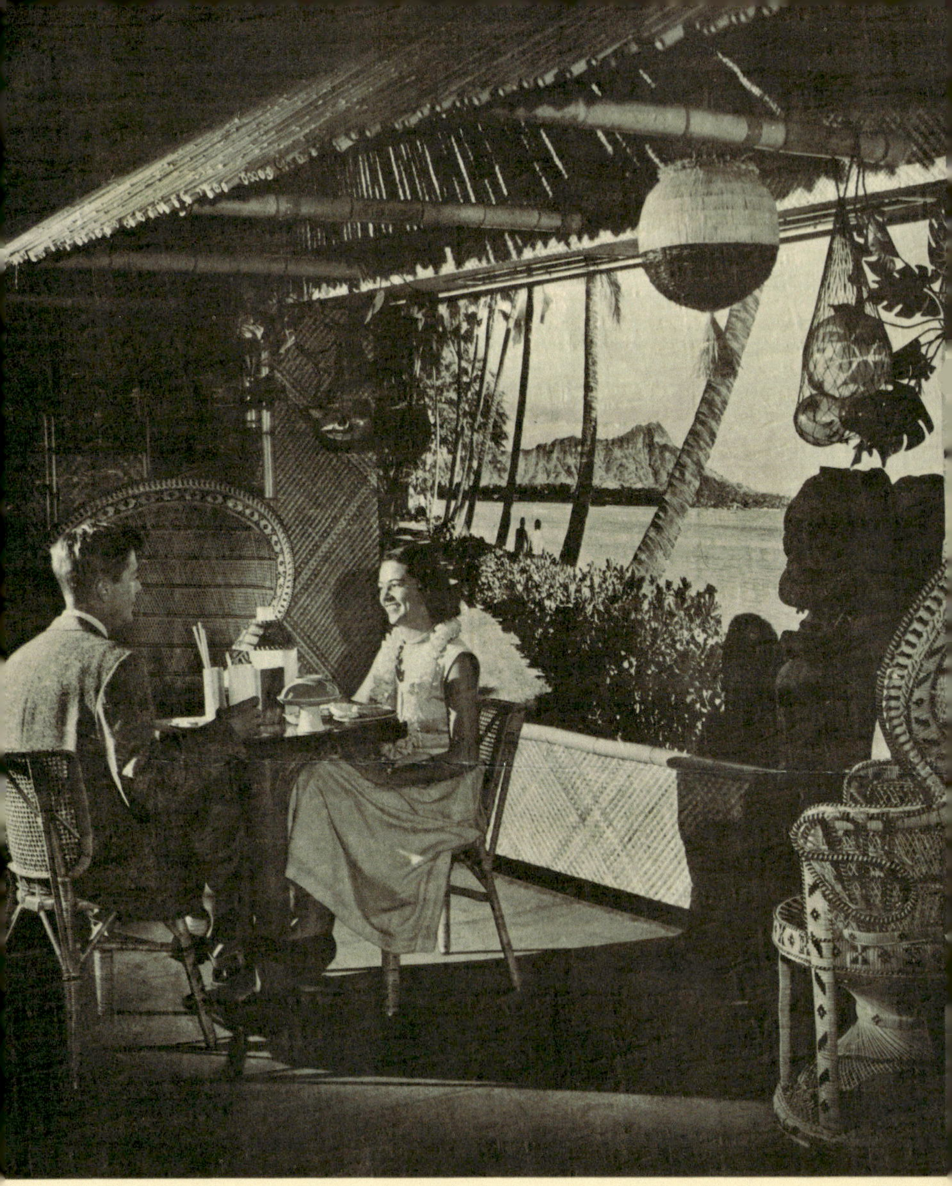

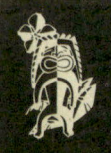

Waikiki Room

Hotel NICOLLET

TRICKS OF THE FILM TRADE: SET DESIGN AND SPECIAL EFFECTS

TRICKS DES FILMGESCHÄFTS: BÜHNENBILD UND SPECIAL EFFECTS
LES TRUCS DES MARCHANDS DE RÊVE : DÉCORS ET EFFETS SPÉCIAUX

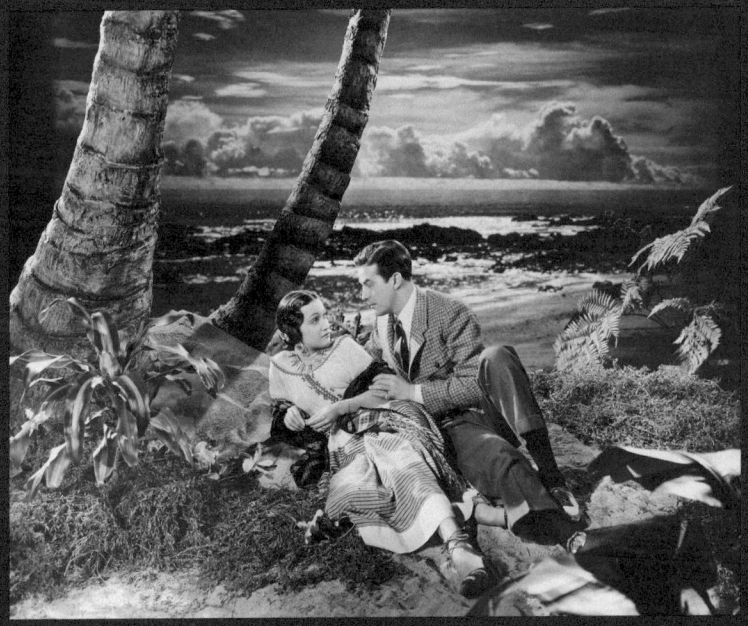

OPPOSITE: A South Seas diorama providing the illusion of a tropical-beach setting at the Waikiki Room, Minneapolis, Minnesota *(Mimi Payne Collection)*

ABOVE: Rear projection scenery was an accepted way to bring the tropics onto a soundstage and into a movie scene

TO CREATE THE ULTIMATE ESCAPIST
experience for their customers, proprietors
of tropical restaurants used theatrical effects
not unlike those being employed on movie
sets. In Los Angeles in particular, where
Polynesian supper clubs flourished, close
proximity to the film industry and its artisans was a crucial influence. Set designers,
builders, and special-effects artists gladly
freelanced their talents to the Polynesian-
restaurant industry.

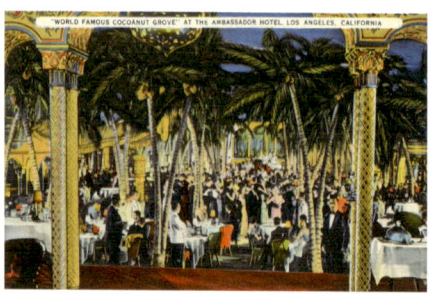

The earliest and simplest icon of the
tropical-island fantasy, the palm tree, was
not native to Los Angeles. They were
imported from Mexico in the late 1800s to
beautify streets and became synonymous
with the area thanks to tourism ads and
motion pictures. Of course, movies used
the palm as an exotic prop for all kinds
of locales. Restaurants also favored them
for their exotic effect. The famous Cocoanut Grove nightclub was supposedly
decorated with faux palm trees from the
set of Rudolph Valentino's *The Sheik*.

Another film trick used in Polynesian
restaurants was the backdrop: Murals
depicting island scenery gave the customers
the impression of beholding beautiful

ABOVE: The Cocoanut Grove, the
nightspot of the '20s, used film props
as tropical décor

BELOW: Faux palms became standard
décor for South Seas cocktail lounges
(*Scott Schell Collection*)

OPPOSITE: The earliest specimen of
a palm tree in L.A.

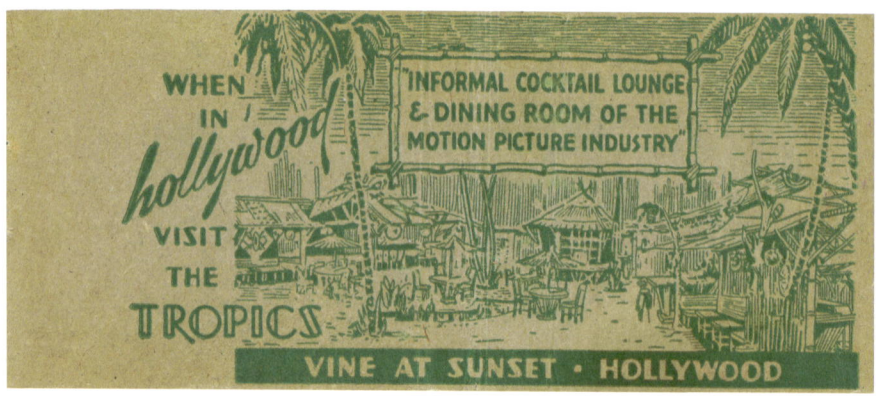

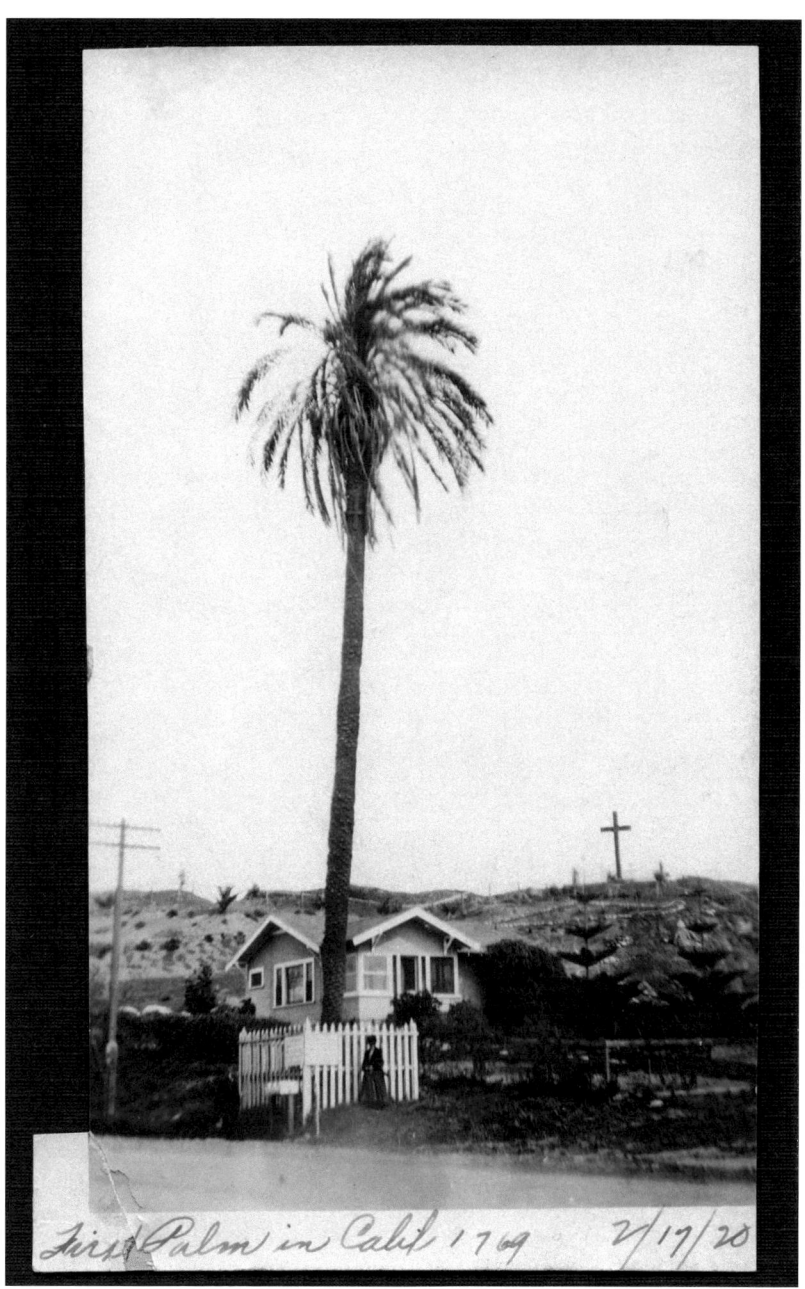

First Palm in Calif 1769   2/17/20

tropical views while actually sitting in urban dining rooms. Sometimes these vistas were equipped with day-to-night special effects with stars sparkling where sunrays had beamed just a few minutes before.

Before the many Hurricane nightclubs unleashed their storms onto customers, it was rainy season in tropical-club land. W. Somerset Maugham's novel *Rain* was filmed twice: in 1928 and again in 1932. Its locale, the port of Pago Pago in Samoa, lent its name to numerous Polynesian bars that offered the patter of "rain on the roof" for tropical atmosphere.

Along with rain effects and artificial diorama windows, some establishments featured whole jungle environments that included live tropical plantings dowsed by showers at regular intervals. In the more elaborate Tiki temples, like the Kahiki in Columbus, Ohio, exotic birds like parakeets

flittered from branch to branch. This type of make-believe island flora and fauna was especially effective in the long winter months of the Midwestern and Eastern United States.

Clifford E. Clinton's Pacific Seas Cafeteria (aka Clifton's Cafeteria) in downtown Los Angeles was the city's most elaborate urban island of the 1930s and '40s. Built like a movie set inside and out, it featured multiple floors of tropical fakery, with interior palms, bamboo huts, waterfalls, and neon flowers throughout. Esther Baldwin York rhymed: *"Step from the street with its dust and cries / Into an island paradise / Amid these tropic trees and flowers / Find rest and peace and happy hours / From here you'll seek the streets again / Refreshed to meet your fellow men..."* According to urban myth, Walt Disney took some of his inspiration for Disneyland from Clifton's.

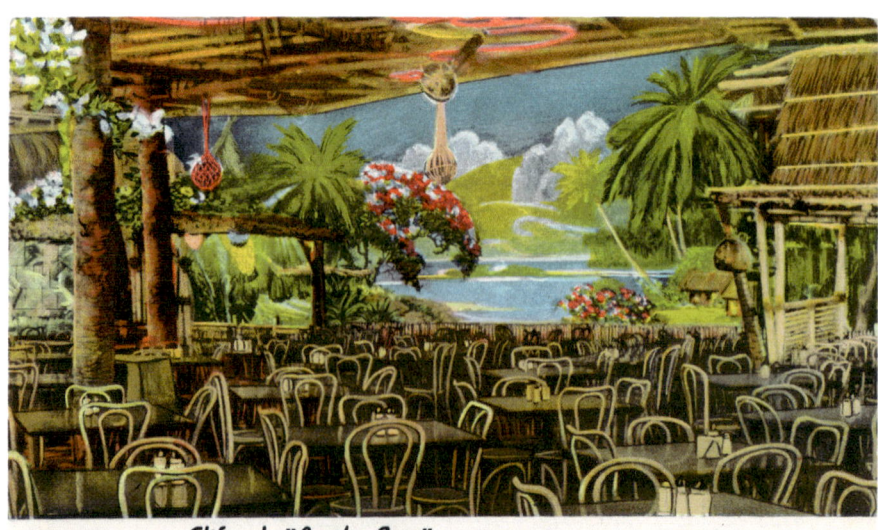

Lagoon — Clifton's *"Pacific Seas"*
618 So. Olive St., Los Angeles

8B393-N

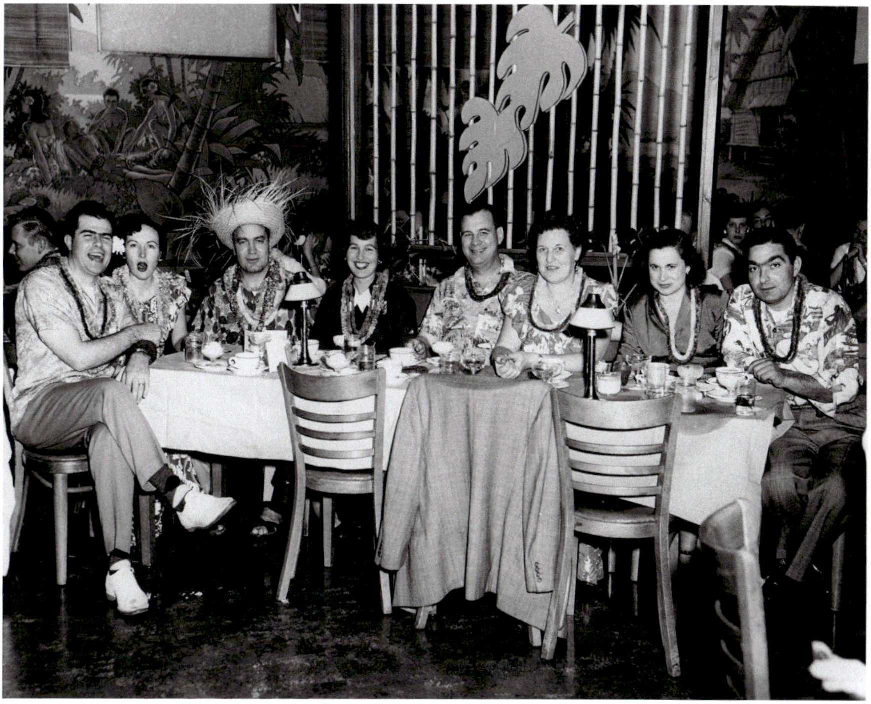

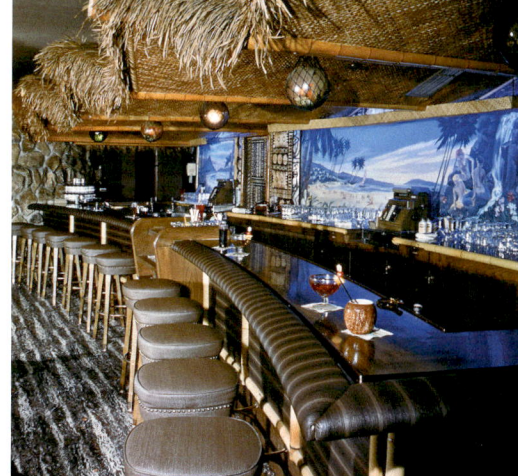

OPPOSITE: One of many tropical murals at Clifton's Cafeteria, L.A. *(Scott Schell Collection)*

ABOVE: Native Californians mingling with painted island natives

RIGHT: Sitting at this bar, one could gaze at waterfalls and sandy beaches

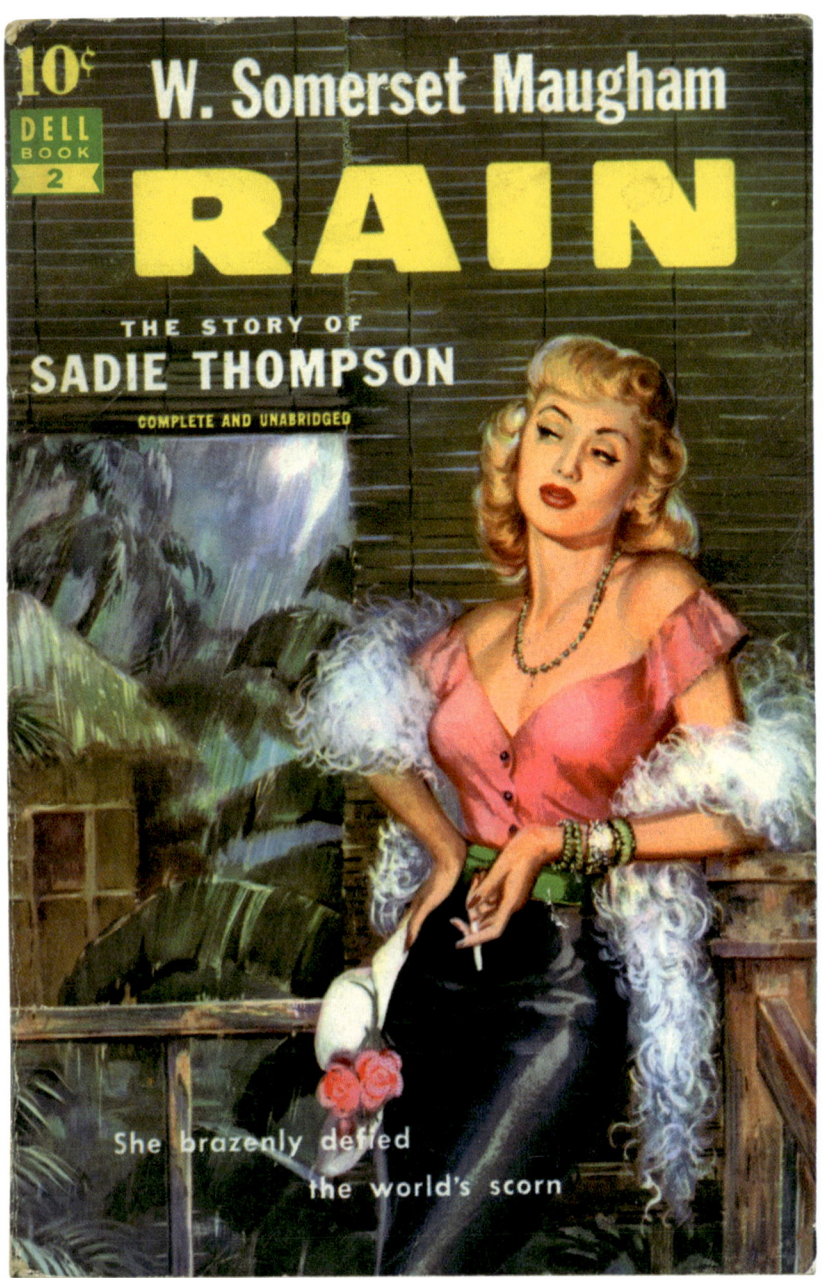

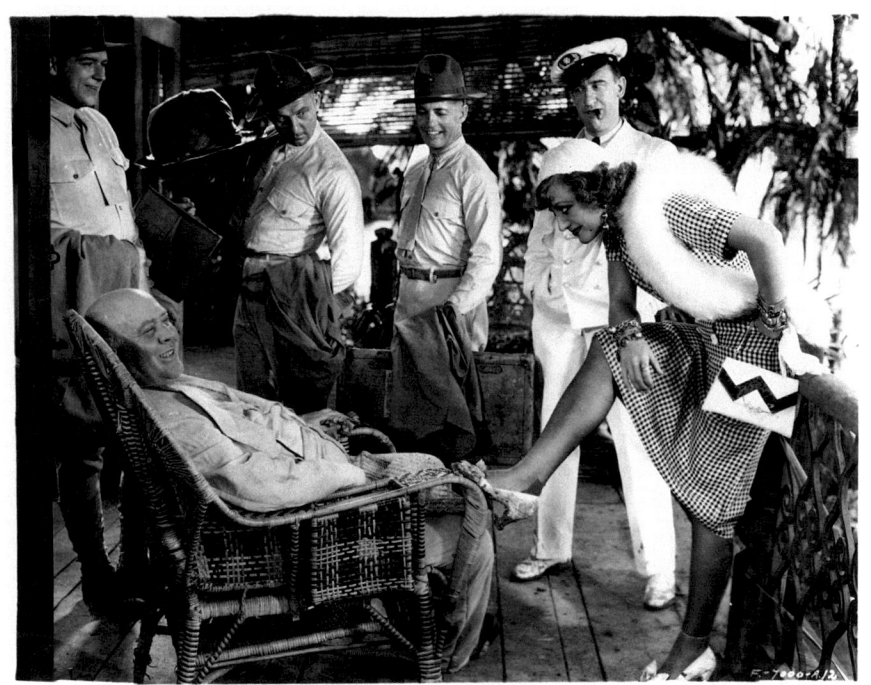

Joseph M. Schenck presents JOAN CRAWFORD (by courtesy Metro-Goldwyn-Mayer Corp.) in "RAIN"
UNITED ARTISTS PICTURE
Made in U. S. A.

OPPOSITE: Paperback cover for the
South Seas classic

ABOVE: Joan Crawford as prostitute
Sadie Thompson, 1932

UM DEN GÄSTEN DIE ULTIMATIVE
Aussteigererfahrung bieten zu können, griffen die Besitzer tropischer Restaurants zu ähnlichen Effekten wie beim Film. Insbesondere in Los Angeles, wo polynesische Supper Clubs florierten, hatte die Nähe zur Filmindustrie und ihren Künstlern großen Einfluss. Szenenbildner, Baumeister und Special-Effect-Künstler boten der Gastronomie gern ihre Dienste an.

Das älteste und schlichteste Symbol der Inselfantasien, die Palme, war ursprünglich nicht in Los Angeles heimisch. Sie wurde im 19. Jahrhundert aus Mexiko importiert, um die Straßen zu verschönern. Später sorgten Reiseprospekte und Filmindustrie dafür, dass man die Region mit diesen Bäumen assoziierte. In Filmen wurden Palmen in exotischen Kulissen für viele verschiedene Schauplätze eingesetzt. Auch in Restaurants waren sie wegen ihrer Exotik beliebt. Der berühmte Nachtclub Cocoanut Grove soll angeblich mit künstlichen Palmen vom Filmset von Rudolph Valentinos *Der Scheich* ausgestattet gewesen sein.

Ein weiteres aus dem Film übernommenes Gestaltungselement in polynesischen Restaurants waren Hintergründe: Wandbilder mit Insel-Impressionen gaukelten den Gästen tropische Aussichten vor. Manche waren sogar mit Tag-Nacht-Effekten ausgestattet, sodass plötzlich Sterne funkelten, wo noch wenige Minuten zuvor die Sonne geschienen hatte.

Vor dem Aufkommen der vielen „Hurricane"-Nachtclubs herrschte Regenzeit in den Bars. W. Somerset Maughams Roman *Regen* wurde zweimal verfilmt: 1928 und noch einmal 1932. Der Drehort, der Hafen von Pago Pago auf Samoa, war Namensgeber zahlreicher polynesischer Bars, in denen die Gäste – der tropischen Atmosphäre wegen – den Regen aufs Dach prasseln hörten.

Neben Regeneffekten und künstlichen Panoramen fanden sich in manchen Lokalen ganze Dschungellandschaften mit tropischen Pflanzen, über die sich in regelmäßigen Abständen ein künstlicher Regen ergoss. In aufwendigen Tiki-Tempeln wie dem Kahiki in Columbus, Ohio, flatterten exotische Vögel zwischen den Ästen umher. Die importierte Inselflora und -fauna erwies sich besonders in den langen Wintermonaten des Mittleren Westens und Ostens der USA als umsatzsteigernd.

Clifford E. Clintons Pacific Seas Cafeteria (alias Clifton's Cafeteria) in Downtown Los Angeles war in den 1930er- und 1940er-Jahren die ausgefeilteste Insellandschaft der Stadt. Von außen und innen wie ein Filmset gebaut, erstreckte sich die tropische Illusion über mehrere Stockwerke. Es gab Palmen, Bambushütten, Wasserfälle und bunt leuchtende Blumen, wohin man sah.

Esther Baldwin York dichtete einst: *„Von Straßen voll Staub und lautem Geschrei / Tritt in ein Inselparadies hinein / Zwischen tropischen Blumen und Bäumen / Lässt sich von Ruhe und Frieden träumen / Dann kannst du wieder nach draußen treten / Erfrischt dich unter die Leute begeben …"* Angeblich hat sich sogar Walt Disney einige seiner Ideen für Disneyland bei Clifton's geholt.

The motto of many urban Pago Pago islands
(Mimi Payne Collection)

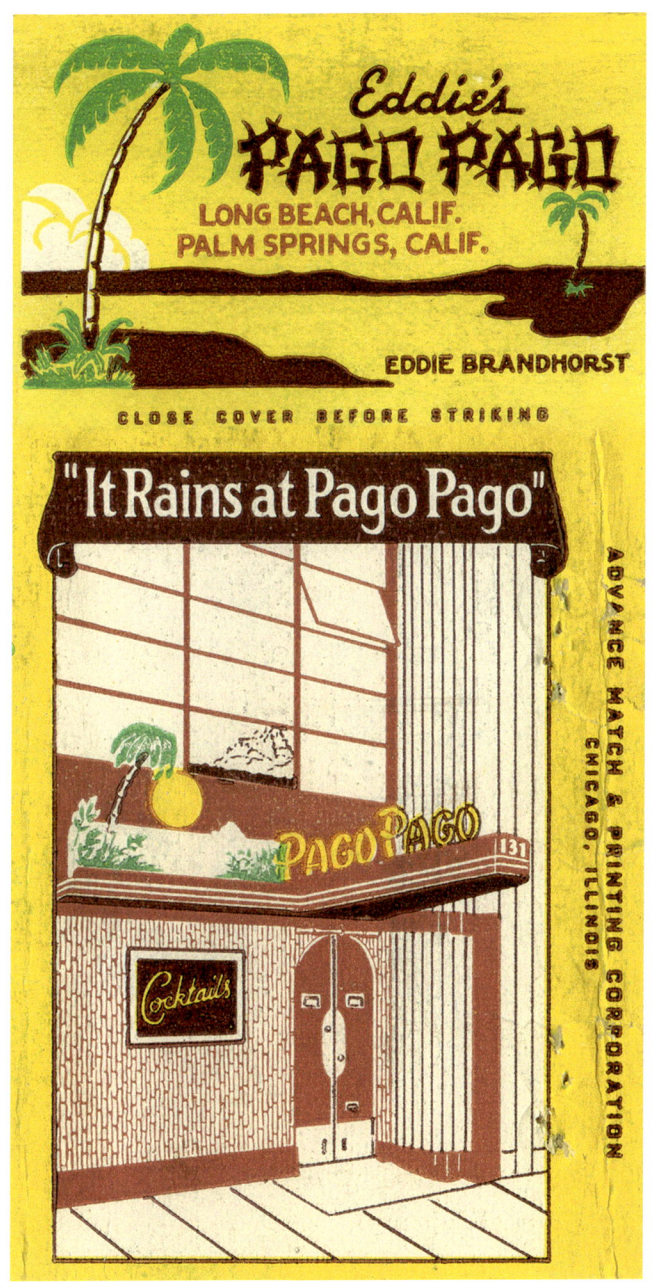

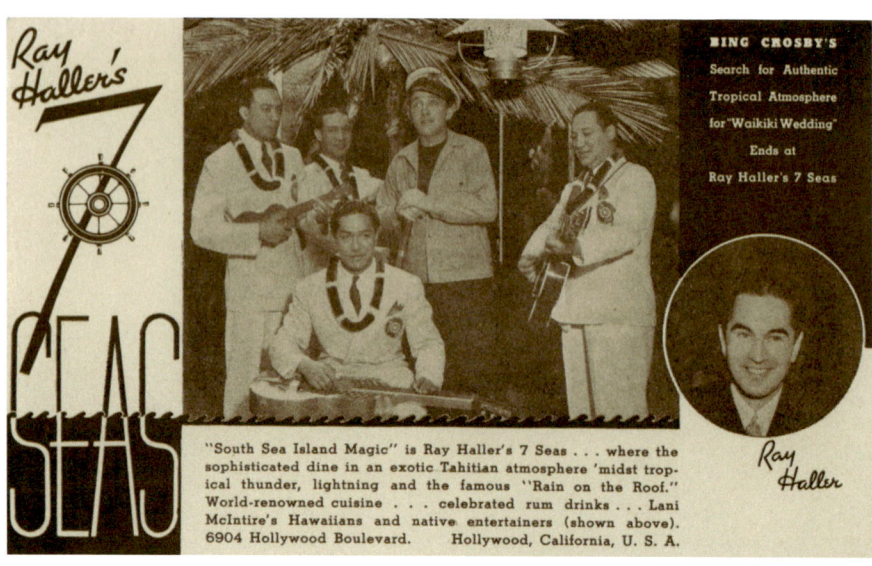

Ray Haller's 7 Seas

BING CROSBY'S Search for Authentic Tropical Atmosphere for "Waikiki Wedding" Ends at **Ray Haller's 7 Seas**

"South Sea Island Magic" is Ray Haller's 7 Seas . . . where the sophisticated dine in an exotic Tahitian atmosphere 'midst tropical thunder, lightning and the famous "Rain on the Roof." World-renowned cuisine . . . celebrated rum drinks . . . Lani McIntire's Hawaiians and native entertainers (shown above). 6904 Hollywood Boulevard. Hollywood, California, U. S. A.

Ray Haller

7 Seas RAIN ON THE ROOF SAN FRANCISCO

ABOVE AND RIGHT: South Seas nightclubs in San Francisco and Los Angeles advertised their atmospheric special effects together with their island music acts (*Martijn Veltman Collection*)

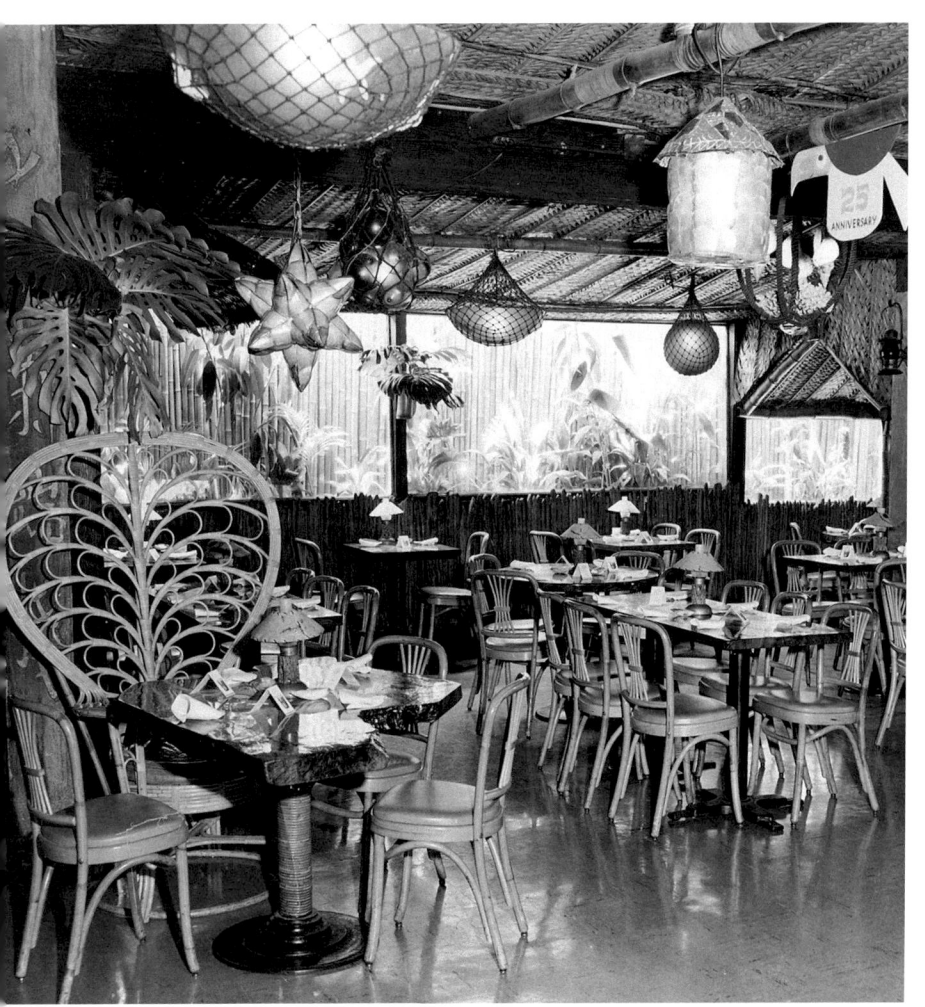

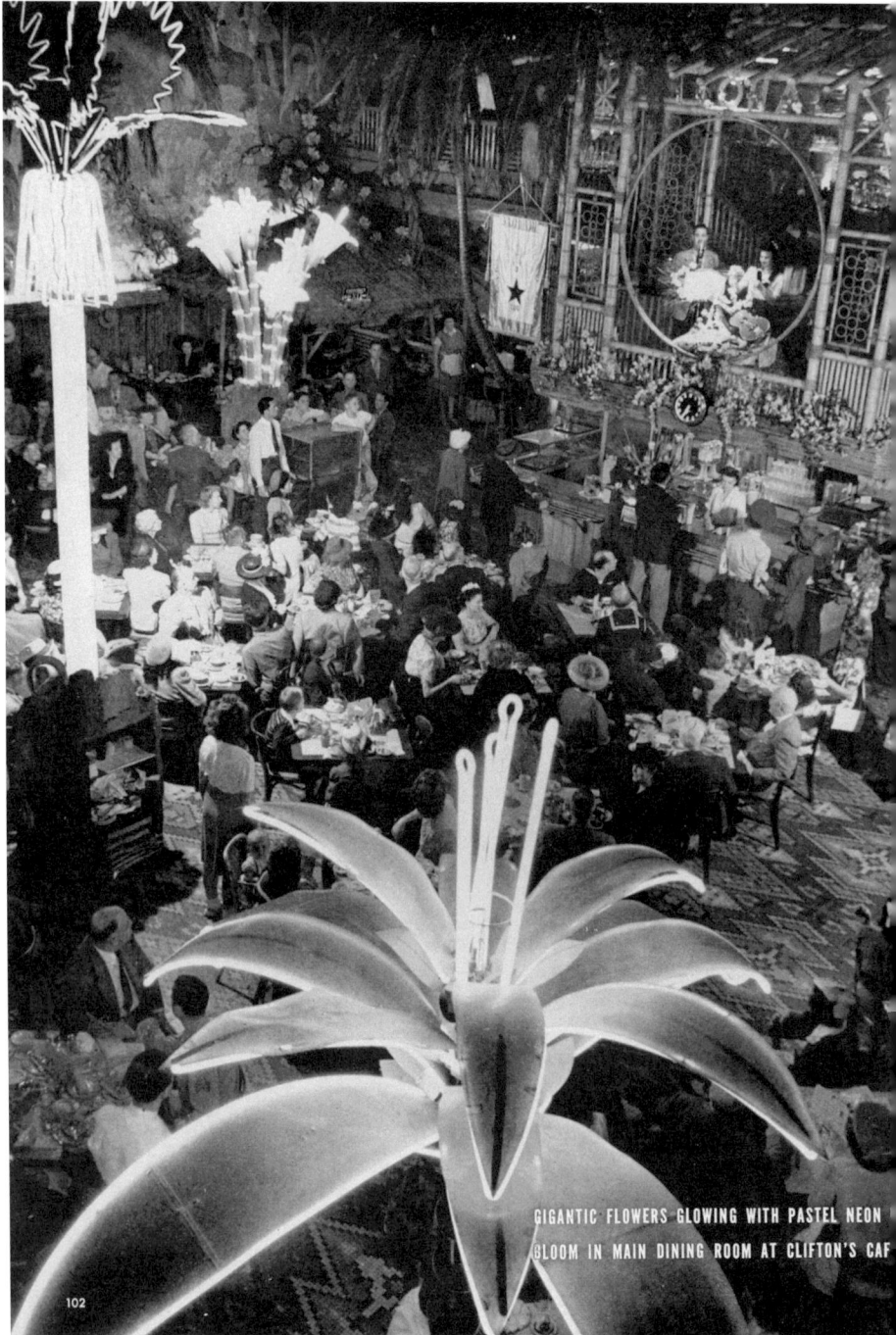

GIGANTIC FLOWERS GLOWING WITH PASTEL NEON
GLOOM IN MAIN DINING ROOM AT CLIFTON'S CAF

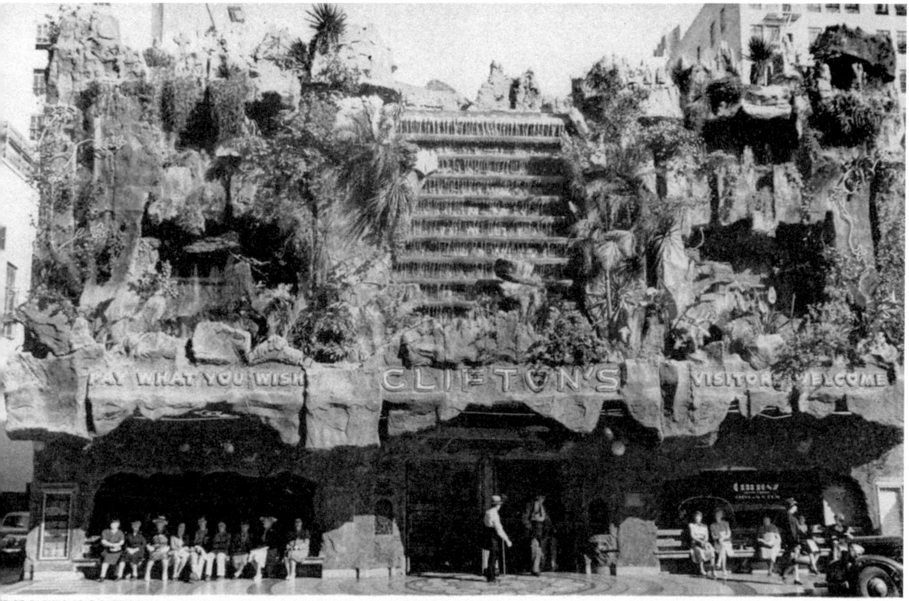

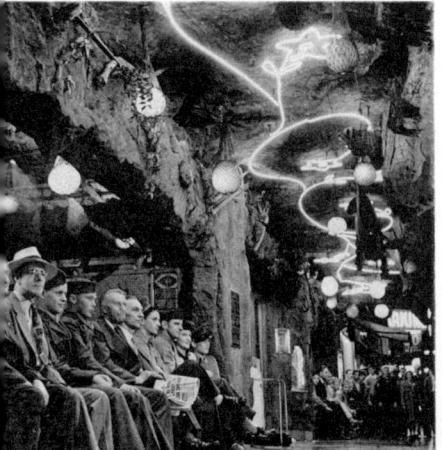

Life Visits Clifton's Cafeteria

omers at the Pacific Seas in Los Angeles get tropical surroundings and music with low-cost meals

, and even less, a customer at Clifton's Pacific restaurant in Los Angeles can sit in a dining urnished with man-made waterfalls and rain-aviaries and aquariums, thatched huts and on-lighted flowers. He can hear an organ play-birds singing. He can also get a pretty sub-meal of meat, vegetables, dessert and bever-thinks he is being overcharged for a com-n of low-priced food and extravagant night-

club surroundings, he can pay only what he thinks the meal was worth, or he can pay nothing.

Only about 7 of the 8,000 daily customers at Clifton's Pacific Seas take advantage of the privilege of writing their own checks. But a great many take advantage of other Clifton services which include free birthday cakes on customers' birthdays, free advice on diets and nutrition problems, free directories of jobs and apartments. Every night (as in ceremony

being enacted on the opposite page) four lucky dinner customers are awarded free leis of gardenias by a master of ceremonies at microphone over counter.

The man who gives all of these things away and makes a big profit besides is Clifford E. Clinton, from whose two names "Clifton" is derived. Restaurateur Clinton conducts his cafeteria business with a sincere respect for the principles of the golden rule and a shrewd respect for the principles of good business.

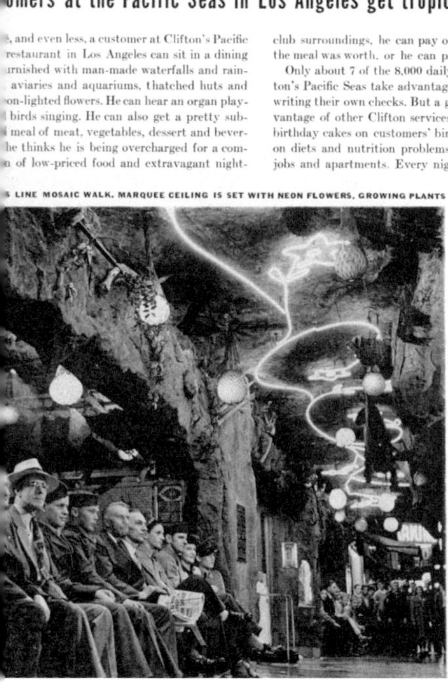

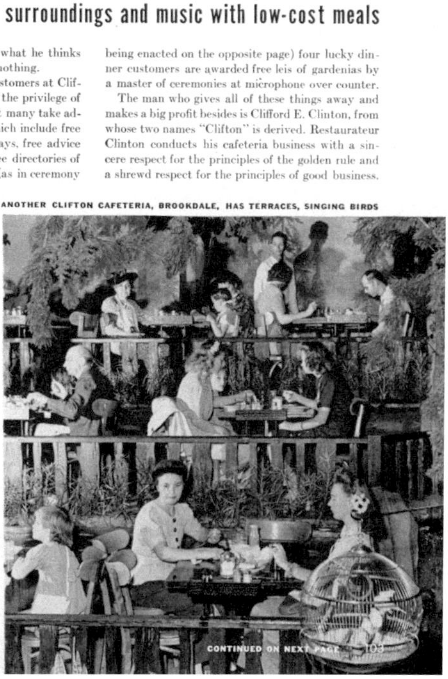

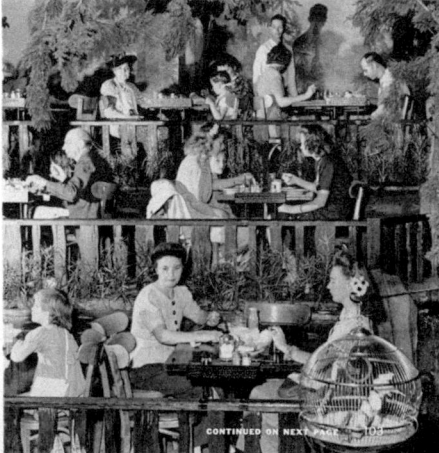

CONTINUED ON NEXT PAGE

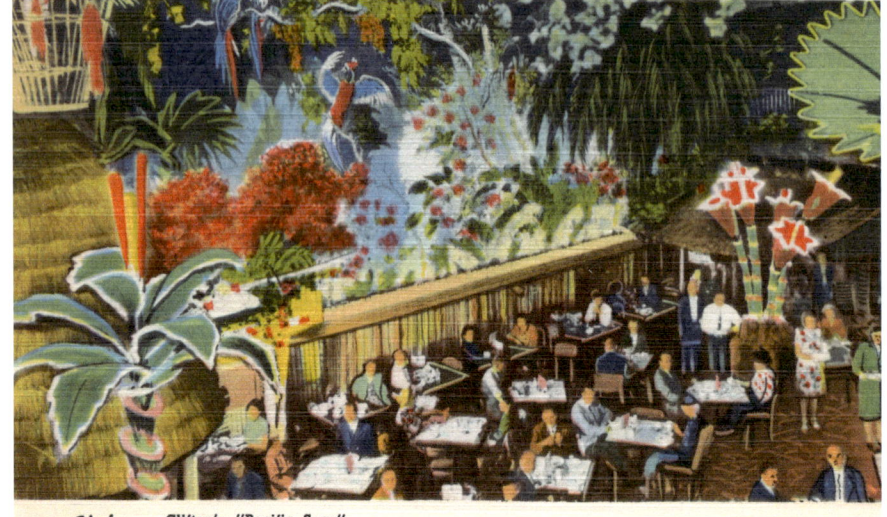

Aloha- Clifton's "Pacific Seas"
618 So. Olive St., Los Angeles

DÉSIREUX DE CRÉER LA MEILLEURE expérience dépaysante qui soit pour leur clientèle, les propriétaires d'établissements dits tropicaux recourent à des effets scéniques assez semblables à ceux utilisés sur les plateaux de cinéma. À Los Angeles, surtout, où les clubs à thème polynésiens prolifèrent, la proximité géographique avec l'industrie du film exerce sur eux une influence cruciale. Décorateurs, artisans et spécialistes en effets spéciaux sous-traitent d'ailleurs avec plaisir leurs talents aux restaurateurs surfant sur la vague polynésienne.

Le symbole le plus précoce et le plus simple du fantasme tropical, le palmier, n'est pas endémique à Los Angeles. Il a été importé du Mexique au tout début du XIXe siècle pour embellir les nouvelles artères de la ville, avant de devenir une des icônes de la région, grâce aux agences de voyage et au cinéma. Les décorateurs hollywoodiens n'hésitaient pas – bien sûr – à mettre le palmier à toutes les sauces. Ils étaient aussi du plus bel effet dans tout établissement « exotique ». Ainsi, le Cocoanut Grove, célèbre boîte de nuit, aurait récupéré ses palmiers factices sur le plateau du *Cheik*, avec Rudolph Valentino.

L'autre élément que les restaurateurs empruntent alors fréquemment au 7e art, ce sont les fonds en trompe-l'œil : une fresque représentant un paysage tropical donnait aux clients l'illusion de passer un moment enchanteur dans un paysage idyllique alors qu'ils se trouvaient dans une banale salle de restaurant citadine. Ces toiles de fond étaient parfois enrichies d'effets spéciaux simulant le crépuscule et l'apparition d'étoiles scintillantes là où le soleil dardait ses rayons quelques minutes plus tôt.

Avant que la marée de clubs Hurricane ne déferle sur le grand public, le monde du club tropical a traversé une longue saison des pluies. La nouvelle de W. Somerset Maugham *Miss Thomson* (ou *Pluie,* titre original : *Rain*) est adaptée deux fois au cinéma, en 1928, puis en 1932. L'intrigue se déroule dans le port de Pago Pago, aux Samoa, qui donna ensuite son nom à des dizaines de bars polynésiens dont l'attraction phare était le crépitement d'une « pluie tropicale » sur le toit.

Outre la pluie sur commande et les toiles de fond en diorama, certains établissements recréent de véritables jungles d'intérieur, où de luxuriantes plantes tropicales sont rafraîchies par des averses (douches) régulières. Dans les plus élaborés des temples dédiés à Tiki, comme le Kahiki de Columbus (Ohio), des oiseaux exotiques, notamment des perroquets, voletaient de branche en branche. Ainsi agencés, paysage, faune et flore exotiques étaient particulièrement

prisés du public dans le Centre et l'Est des États-Unis pendant les longs mois d'hiver.

La Pacific Seas Cafeteria de Clifford E. Clinton (alias « Clifton's Cafeteria »), dans le centre de Los Angeles, est, dans les années 1930 et 1940, l'île reconstituée la plus élaborée de la ville. Bâtie comme un décor de cinéma, elle dispose de plusieurs étages dédiés au kitch tropical, avec palmiers, huttes de bambou, chutes d'eau et cascades de fleurs fluorescentes. Sur ce sujet, les vers d'Esther Baldwin York sont éloquents : « Quittez la rue, sa poussière et ses cris / Pour pénétrer dans une île paradis / Venez parmi de tropicales fleurs / Trouver repos, paix et bonheur / De là heureux vous reviendrez / Rencontrer votre prochain sur le pavé… » D'après la légende, Walt Disney se serait inspiré de la cafétéria de Clifton pour Disneyland.

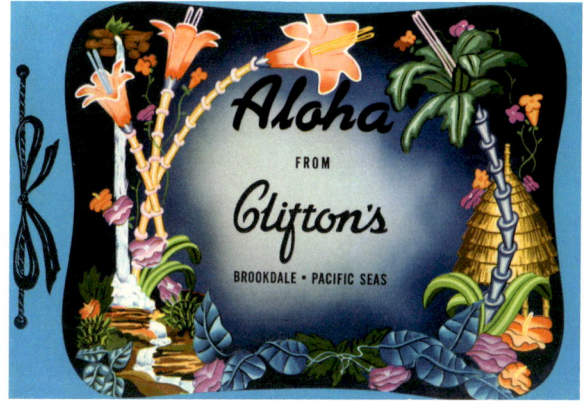

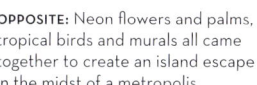

OPPOSITE: Neon flowers and palms, tropical birds and murals all came together to create an island escape in the midst of a metropolis

RIGHT: Tourist booklet for Clifton's Cafeteria in Los Angeles *(Frank Brajevic Collection)*

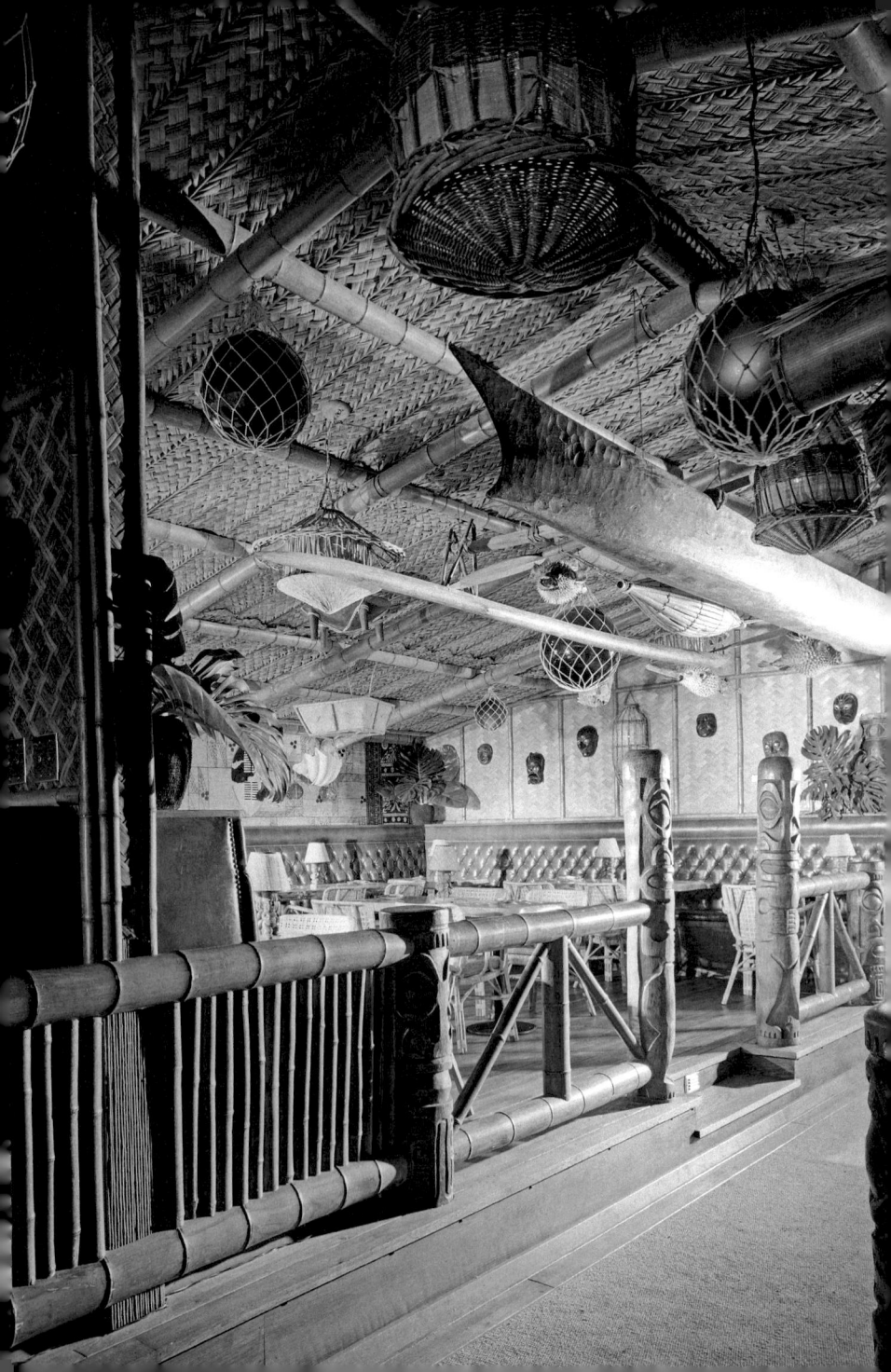

7

NATURAL MATERIALS OF THE TROPICAL BAR

NATURMATERIALIEN FÜR DIE TROPENBAR
LES MATÉRIAUX NATURELS DU BAR TROPICAL

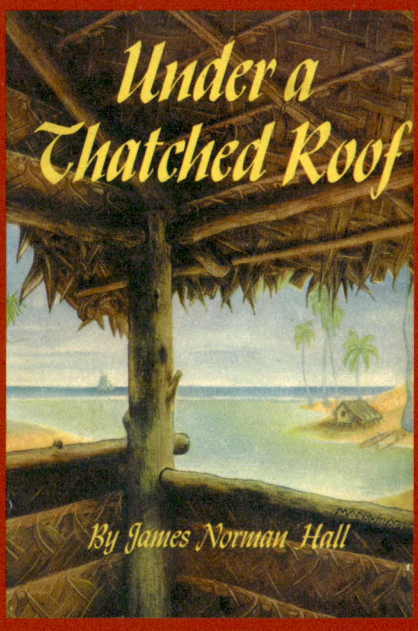

OPPOSITE: Dine inside a tropical hut at Trader Vic's, Beverly Hills, 1955

ABOVE: South Seas literature espousing the theme

MUCH OF EARLY TROPICAL SUPPER
clubs' appeal lay in their interior décor:
a natural environment that offered an
alternative to the big city's industrial
steel-and-concrete habitat. The idea was to
make visitors feel as if they had stepped
into a native hut by surrounding them with
all-natural textures from floor to ceiling.
Framed by bamboo poles, the walls were
clad with *lahaula* and other woven plant
fabrics. Palm-frond canopies sheltered seat-
ing areas, and carved shields and hanging
basket lamps formed an overlapping layer.

Because nesting in your own little grass
shack was part of the South Seas fantasy,
the need for tropical building materials
gave birth to suppliers and importers of
such exotic fare. In Southern California,
these importers' customer base was not
just the restaurant industry, but also the
movie studios, who trimmed boatloads of
bamboo into native-hut sets for their South
Seas movies. The craftsmen who worked
in this medium were equally employed by
Hollywood art directors and Polynesian
drinking establishments.

In addition to restaurants and cocktail
lounges, homeowners refashioned their
basements and backyards in the tropical
theme; by the early 1960s, a wave of
Polynesian-style apartment buildings
added to the demand for tropical materials.
By then, a multitude of goods were offered
to construct one's own island hideaway,
including Polynesian *tapa* cloth, a natural
fabric made from pounded tree bark and
decorated with abstract patterns unique to
every island group. *Tapa's* handmade block-
print aesthetic was chosen as the ideal
wallpaper for many urban-hut interiors.

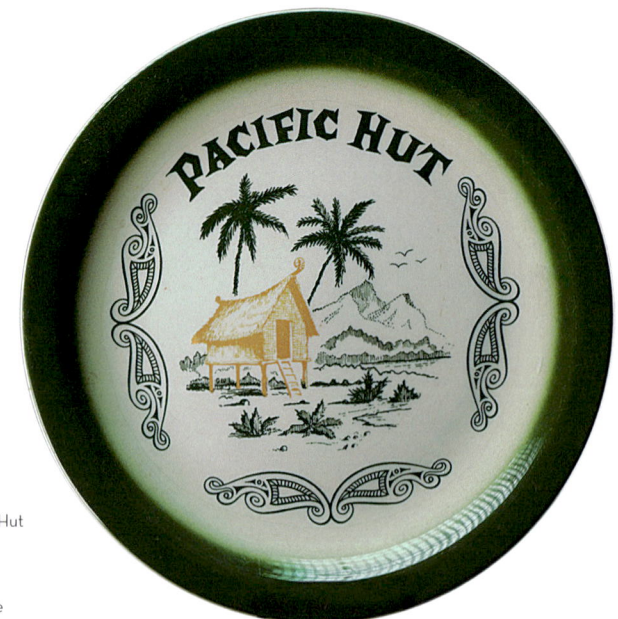

RIGHT: Dinner plate from Pacific Hut
restaurant near Boston
(Rick Hamilton Collection)

OPPOSITE: This 1933 song became
a *hapa haole* classic

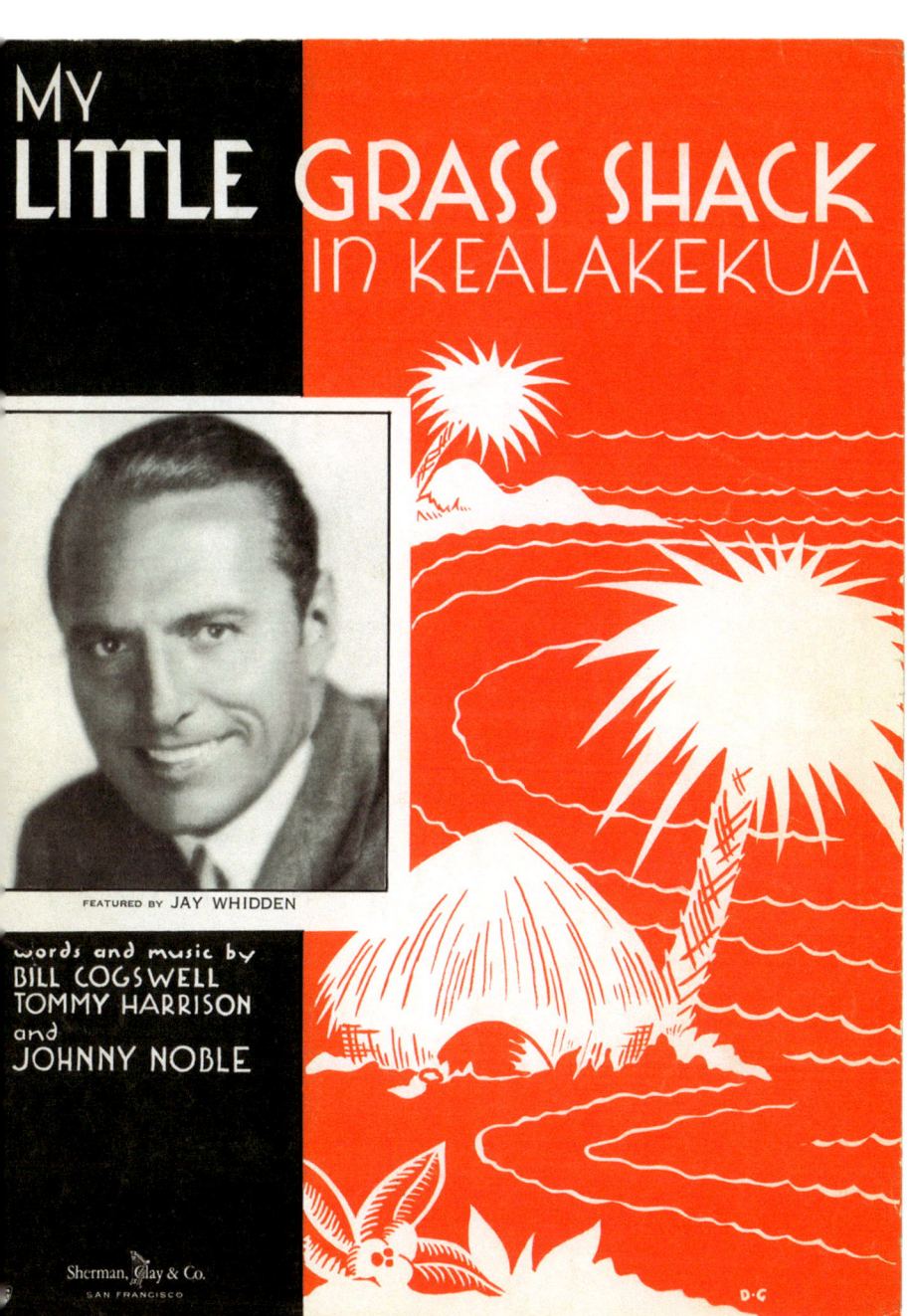

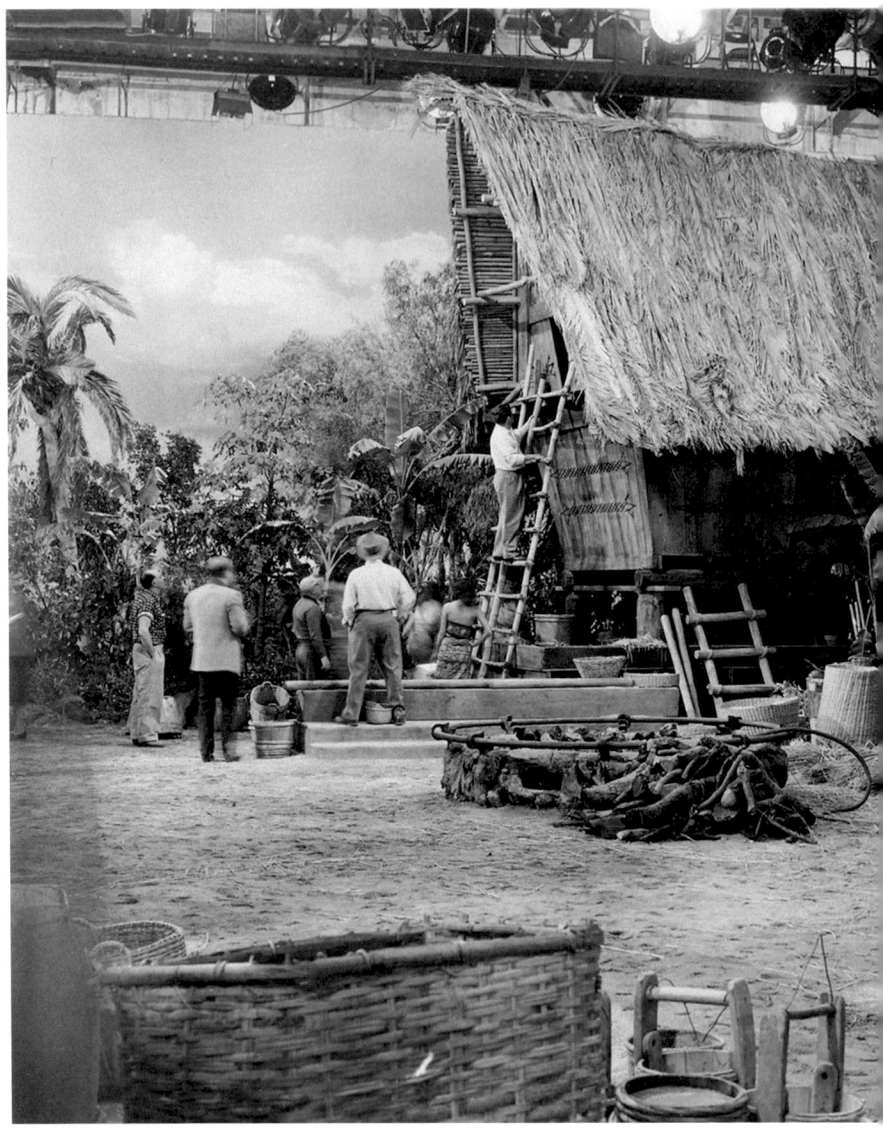

ABOVE: Movie set for *East of Sumatra* (1953)

OPPOSITE: A bamboo menu for a Hollywood Hut
(Martijn Veltman Collection)

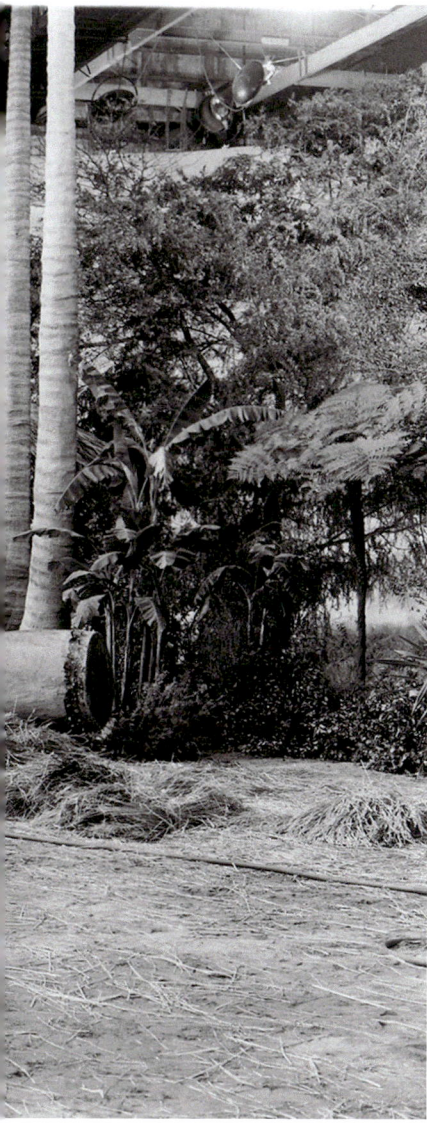

Polynesian palaces advertised the exotic origin of their décor in their menus and other promotional materials. The Vagabond's House in Los Angeles wrote (not necessarily factually): "*Tapa* from the Pelopenesus [sic], Bamboo from the Jungles of Luzon, Rattan from the Isle of Jolo, a Turtle from Galapagos & War Shields from Fiji." An environment composed of foreign wares helped urbanites leave their known world behind for an evening and go on an imaginary vacation without ever leaving home.

The draw of the Polynesian paradise in the 20th century seems to have been motivated by the same "turning away from civilization" mentality that was prevalent in previous centuries. The organic materials of the early tropical bars offered a sensuous experience that was missing from the ambitious world of modern America. The chance to drop it all and relax in a natural setting seemed like a desirable alternative to the hard-working middle-class life.

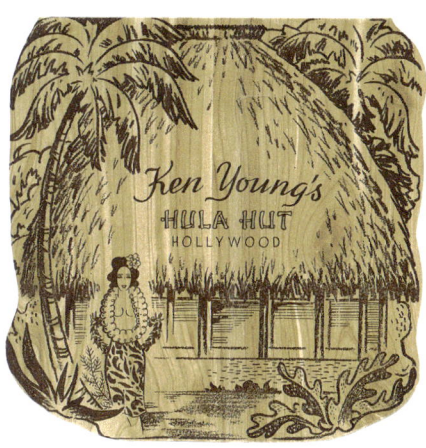

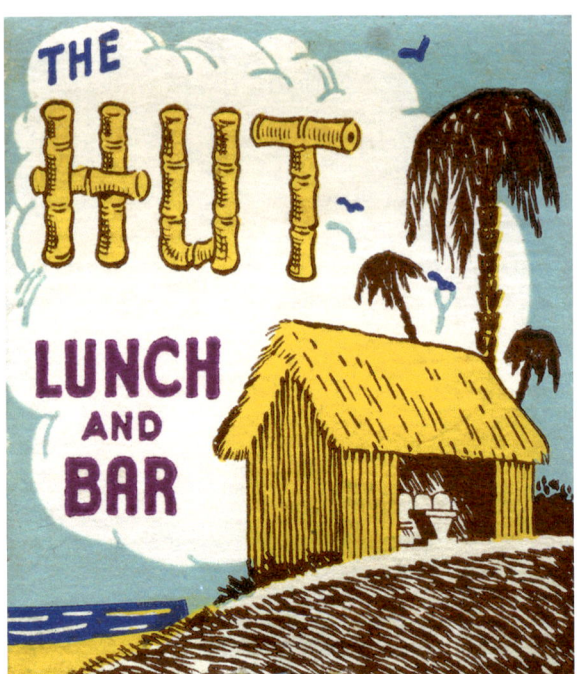

LEFT: The name was the concept *(Scott Schell Collection)*

BELOW: The real thing: a Polynesian chieftain's abode

OPPOSITE: Bob Carter was one of the earliest purveyors of tropical wares *(Frank Brajevic Collection)*

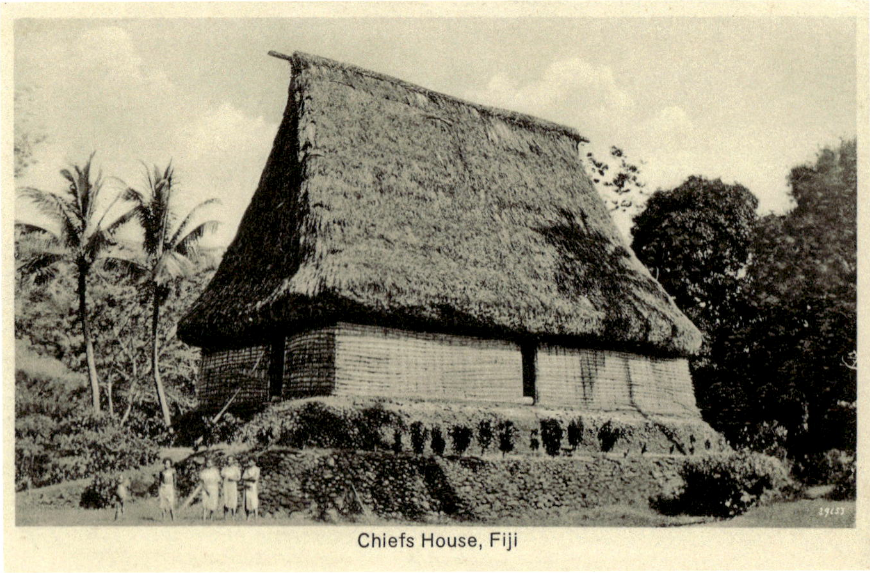

Chiefs House, Fiji

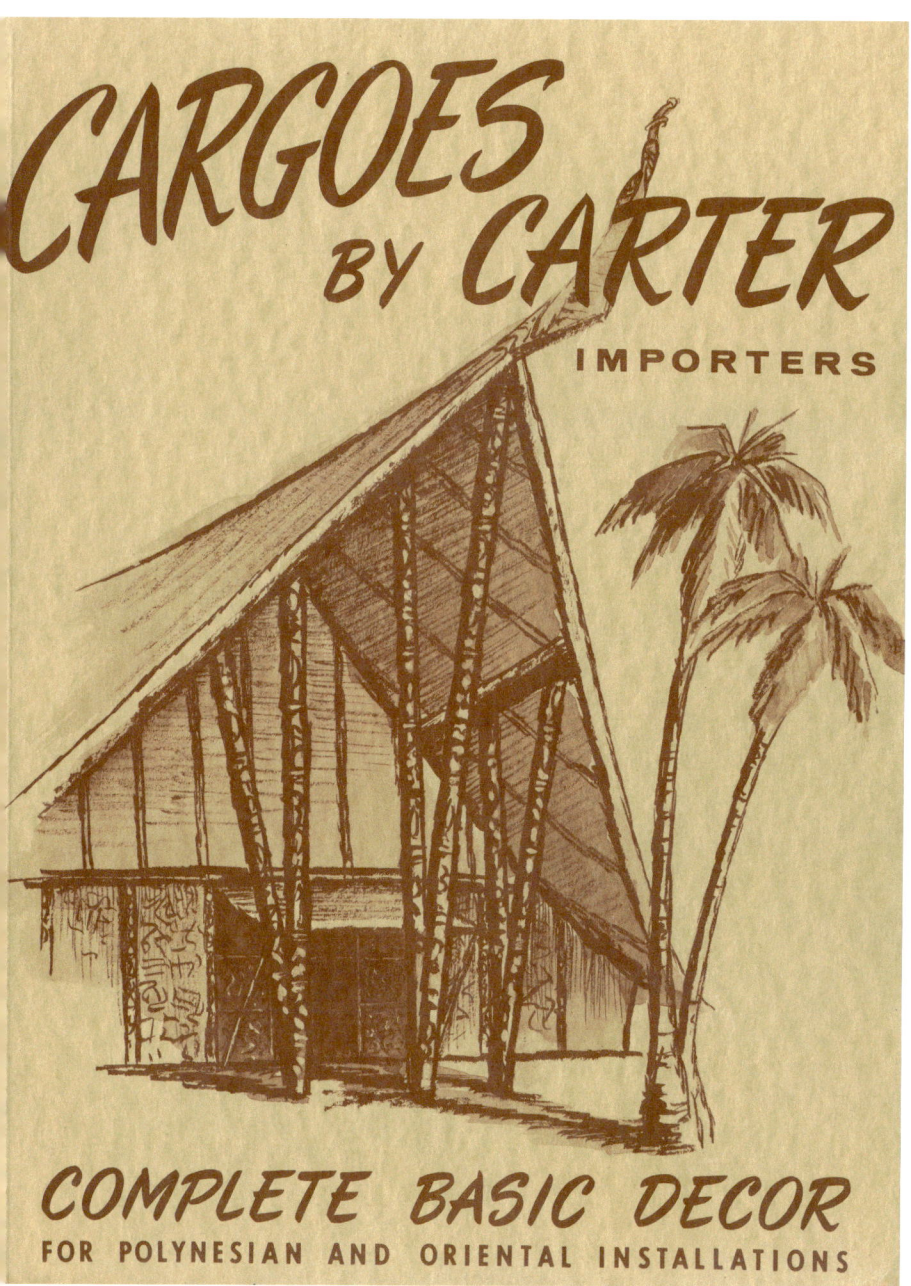

CARGOES BY CARTER

IMPORTERS

COMPLETE BASIC DECOR
FOR POLYNESIAN AND ORIENTAL INSTALLATIONS

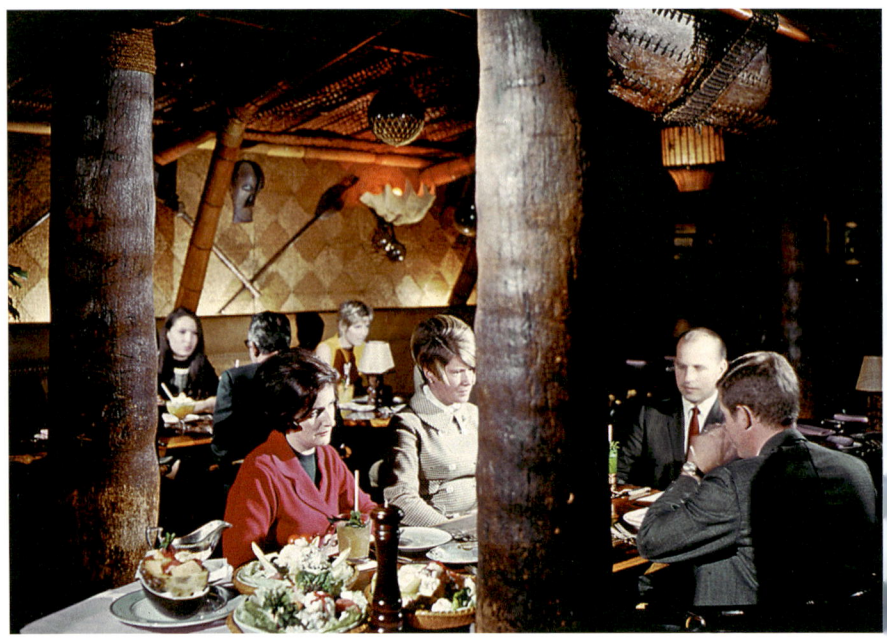

DIE DAMALIGEN TROPISCHEN

Supper Clubs waren in erster Linie wegen ihrer Inneneinrichtung beliebt: eine natürliche Umgebung statt Stahl und Beton der Großstadt. Besucher sollten sich wie in der Hütte eines Südseeinsulaners fühlen und fanden sich deshalb inmitten eines Raums wieder, der vom Boden bis zur Decke mit natürlichen Materialien ausgestattet war. Von Bambuspfeilern eingerahmt, waren die Wände mit *Lahaula*-Matten verkleidet. Baldachine aus Palmwedeln schufen Privatsphäre zwischen den einzelnen Sitzbereichen und mit Schnitzereien verzierte Holzschilde und Hängelampen aus Korbgeflecht rundeten das Bild ab.

Wichtiger Bestandteil der Südseefantasie war eine gemütliche kleine Bambushütte, sodass die Nachfrage nach tropischen Baumaterialien stieg, was den Lieferanten und Importeuren dieser exotischen Waren einen neuen Markt eröffnete. In Südkalifornien belieferten sie nicht nur die Gastronomie, sondern auch die Filmstudios, die ganze Wagenladungen Bambus in Hütten für ihre Südseefilme verwandelten. Die Handwerker, die auf dem Gebiet arbeiteten, wurden sowohl von Hollywood als auch von polynesischen Themenlokalen eingestellt.

Doch auch Hausbesitzer gestalteten ihre Keller und Gärten nach tropischen Vorbildern um. In den frühen 1960er-Jahren gab

ABOVE AND OPPOSITE: Americans dining in a hut setting

es einen regelrechten Trend im polynesisch inspirierten Wohnungsbau. Für die Gestaltung des eigenen Inselparadieses gab es zu dieser Zeit bereits ein großes Warenangebot, zu dem auch polynesische Tapa-Stoffe gehörten, Baststoffe aus zerstoßener Baumrinde. Sie waren mit abstrakten Mustern verziert, die einzelne Inselgruppen repräsentierten. Der handgemachte Blockdruck-Look der Tapa wurde von vielen Besitzern der städtischen Inselhütten als die perfekte Wandbekleidung angesehen.

Die polynesischen Paläste warben mit der exotischen Herkunft ihrer Innenausstattung. Das Vagabond's House in Los Angeles schrieb (nicht unbedingt wahrheitsgetreu): „Tapa von der Peloponnes [sic], Bambus aus den Dschungeln Luzons, Rattan von der Insel Jolo, eine Schildkröte von den Galapagos & Kriegsschilde aus Fidschi." In einer exotischen Umgebung fiel es den Städtern leichter, ihre bekannte Welt für einen Abend hinter sich zu lassen und sich auf eine Reise zu begeben, ohne ihr Zuhause verlassen zu müssen.

Die Anziehungskraft des polynesischen Paradieses im 20. Jahrhundert schien wie in den vorangegangenen Jahrhunderten aus dem Wunsch zu resultieren, der Zivilisation den Rücken zu kehren. Die in den frühen Tropenbars verwendeten Naturmaterialien boten eine sinnliche Erfahrung, die der vom beruflichen Ehrgeiz geprägten Welt des modernen Amerika fehlte. Die Aussicht auf Entspannung in einer natürlichen Umgebung schien eine erstrebenswerte Alternative zum arbeitsamen Leben des Mittelstands.

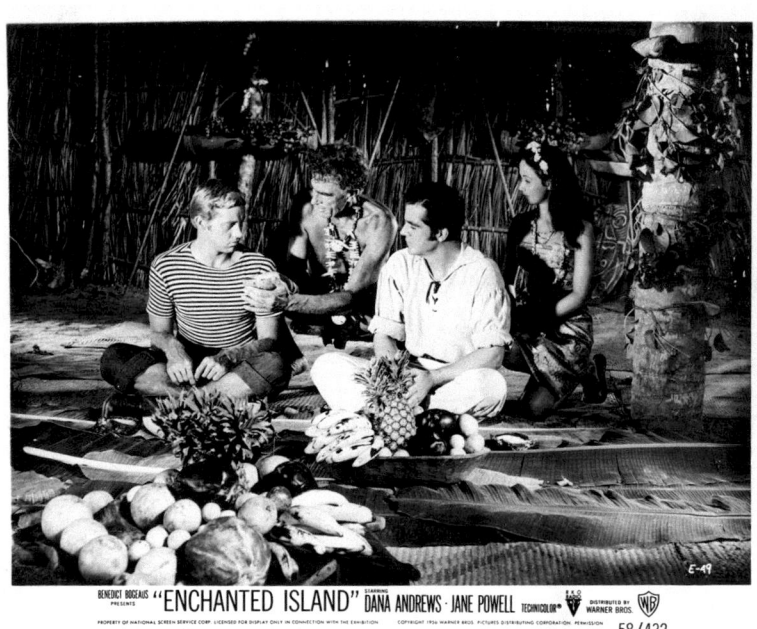

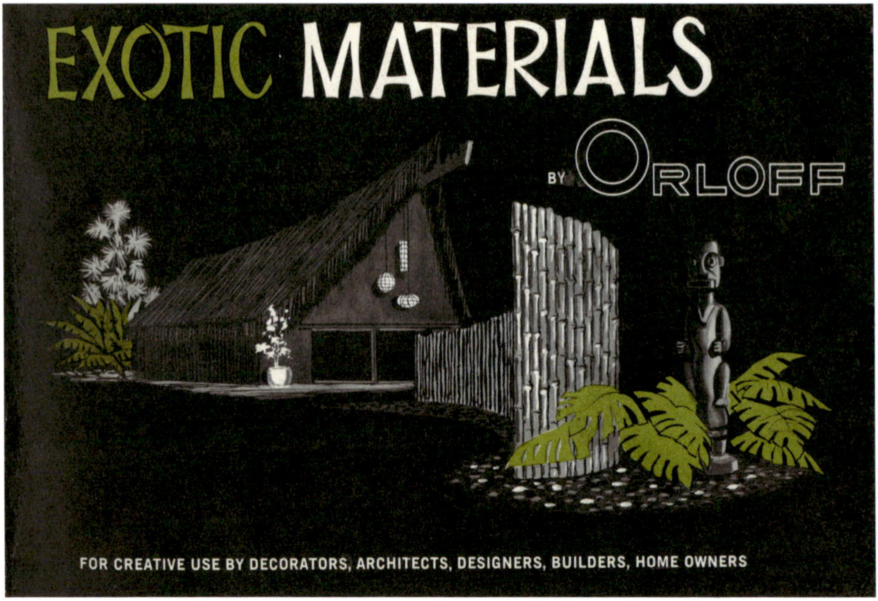

EXOTIC MATERIALS BY ORLOFF

FOR CREATIVE USE BY DECORATORS, ARCHITECTS, DESIGNERS, BUILDERS, HOME OWNERS

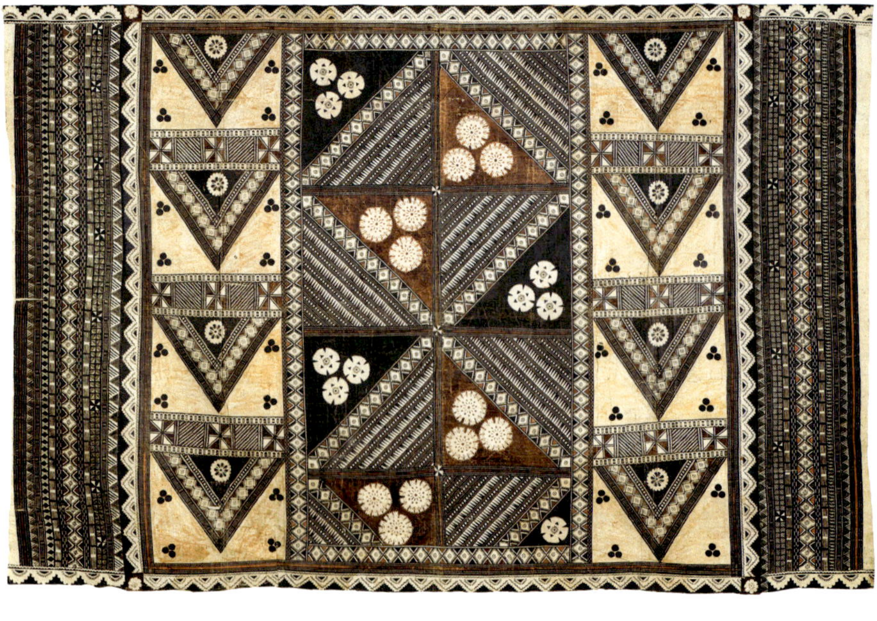

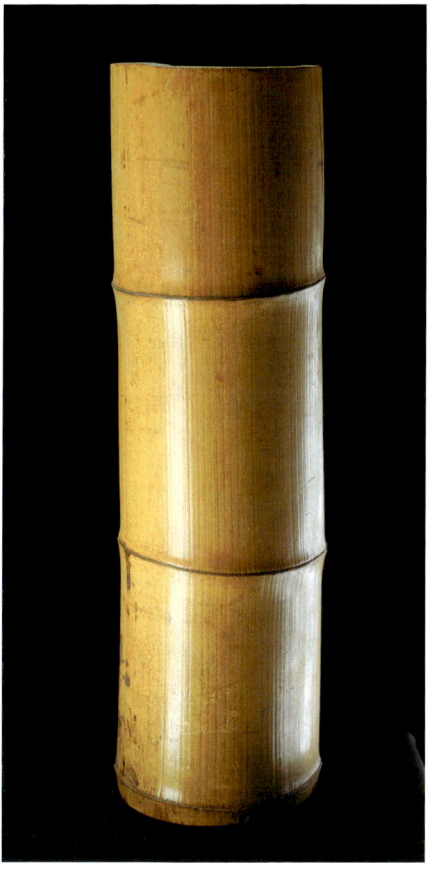

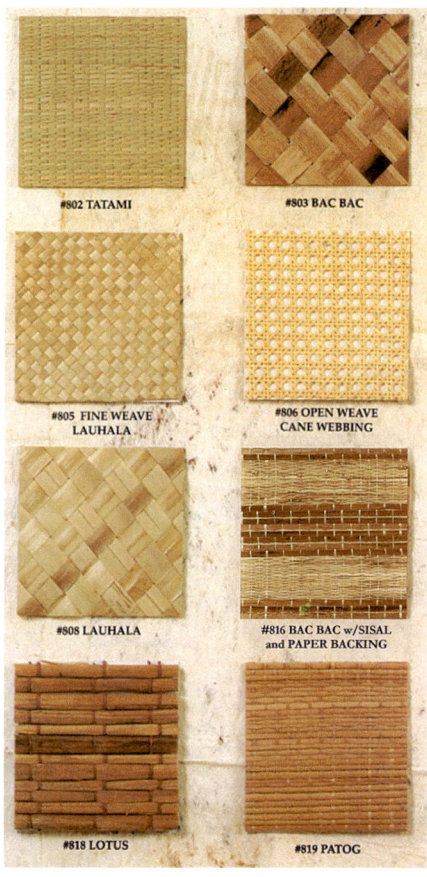

#802 TATAMI

#803 BAC BAC

#805 FINE WEAVE LAUHALA

#806 OPEN WEAVE CANE WEBBING

#808 LAUHALA

#816 BAC BAC w/SISAL and PAPER BACKING

#818 LOTUS

#819 PATOG

LES BARS RESTAURANTS TROPICAUX DE la première heure séduisent principalement par leur décoration intérieure : un environnement « naturel » qui offre une alternative fort appréciée à l'habitat industriel en béton et acier typique des mégapoles américaines. L'idée est de donner aux clients l'impression d'entrer dans une hutte indigène en les entourant de matériaux naturels du sol au plafond. Encadrées par des poteaux de bambou, les cloisons sont bardées de *lahaula* et d'autres fibres végétales tissées. Une canopée luxuriante porte son ombre sur les tables, et l'ensemble est encore accessoirisé de boucliers sculptés et de lampes paniers accrochés çà et là.

Se lover dans une alcôve de verdure fait partie du fantasme polynésien, et avec la demande en matériaux de construction tropicaux, les entreprises important et fournissant de tels équipements exotiques fleurissent. Dans le sud de la Californie, leur clientèle ne se limite pas au secteur de la restauration, mais s'étend aussi aux studios de cinéma, qui débitent des bateaux entiers de bambou en villages de huttes pour leurs productions estampillées « Mers du Sud ». De la même manière, les artisans œuvrant dans cette spécialité sont autant employés par les directeurs artistiques de Hollywood que par les tenanciers d'établissements tiki.

À la suite des restaurants et des bars à cocktails, les particuliers redécorent leurs sous-sols et leurs arrière-cours dans le thème tropical ; au début des années 1960, la tendance polynésienne prend d'assaut les intérieurs américains et gonfle encore la demande en matériaux tropicaux. Chacun dispose alors d'une très vaste gamme de produits pour se construire son propre paradis insulaire, notamment la toile polynésienne *tapa*, une étoffe naturelle fabriquée à partir d'écorce écrasée et décorée de motifs abstraits spécifiques à chaque tribu. L'aspect artisanal et unique de l'impression du *tapa* au moyen de blocs de bois a rapidement la faveur des ménages pour tapisser les cloisons de leur hutte maison.

Les palais polynésiens mettaient en avant l'origine exotique de leur décor sur leurs menus et leurs brochures, voire le reste de leur documentation commerciale. Ainsi, le Vagabond's House de Los Angeles (oubliant sans doute son orthographe par trop-plein d'enthousiasme) : « *Tapa* du Pélopénèse [sic], bambou des jungles de Luzon, rotin de l'île de Jolo, une tortue des Galapagos & des boucliers de guerre des Fidji. » Un environnement émaillé d'éléments venus de loin aide les citadins à abandonner le monde qu'ils connaissent le temps d'une soirée, pour s'offrir des vacances imaginaires sans passeport ni décalage horaire.

Cette passion soudaine (et relativement durable) pour le paradis polynésien au XXᵉ siècle semble avoir été motivée par le désir de tourner le dos à la civilisation, celui-là même qui a prévalu par flambées au cours des siècles précédents. Les matériaux organiques des premiers bars tropicaux offrent au public une expérience sensuelle et sensorielle absente d'une Amérique moderne farouchement ambitieuse. Les classes moyennes laborieuses s'octroient avec un grand plaisir ces occasions de relâcher la pression et de se détendre dans une ambiance apaisante et naturelle.

An interior bamboo village in Chicago
(Scott Schell Collection)

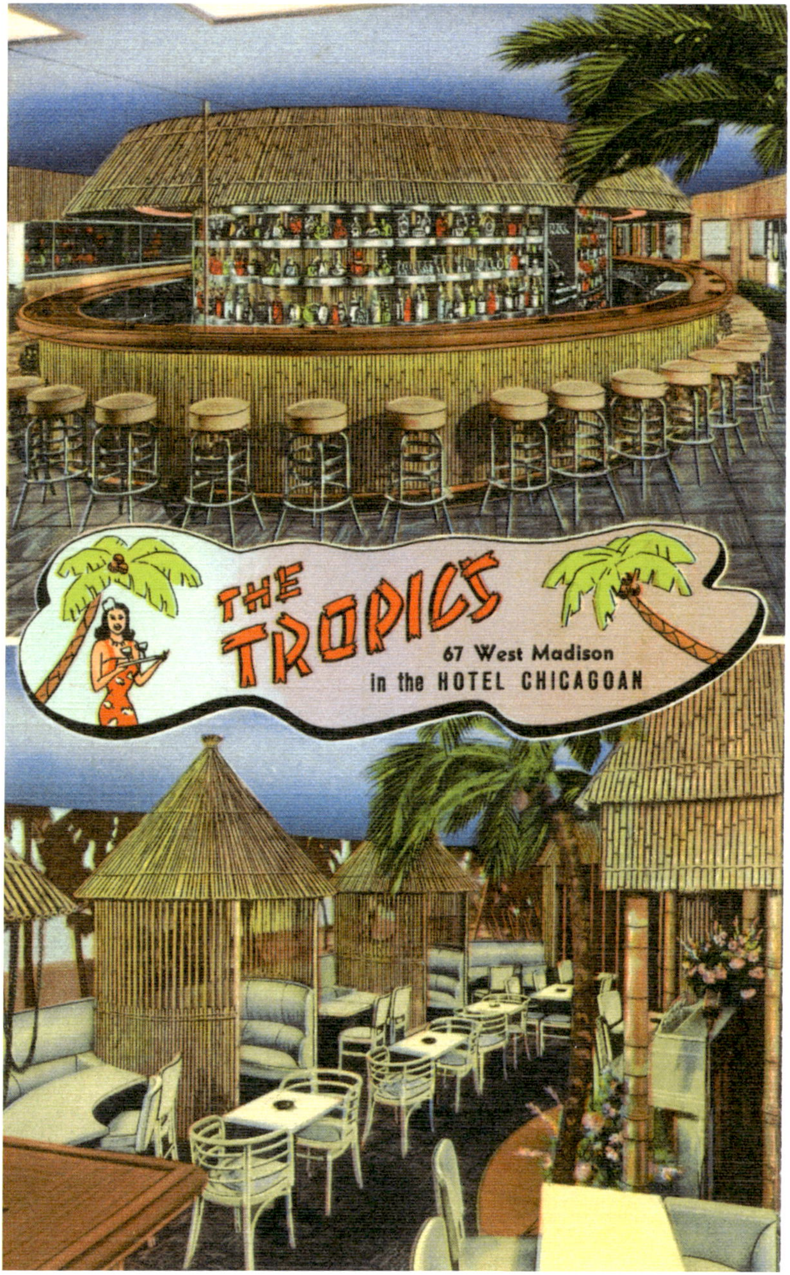
THE TROPICS
67 West Madison
in the HOTEL CHICAGOAN

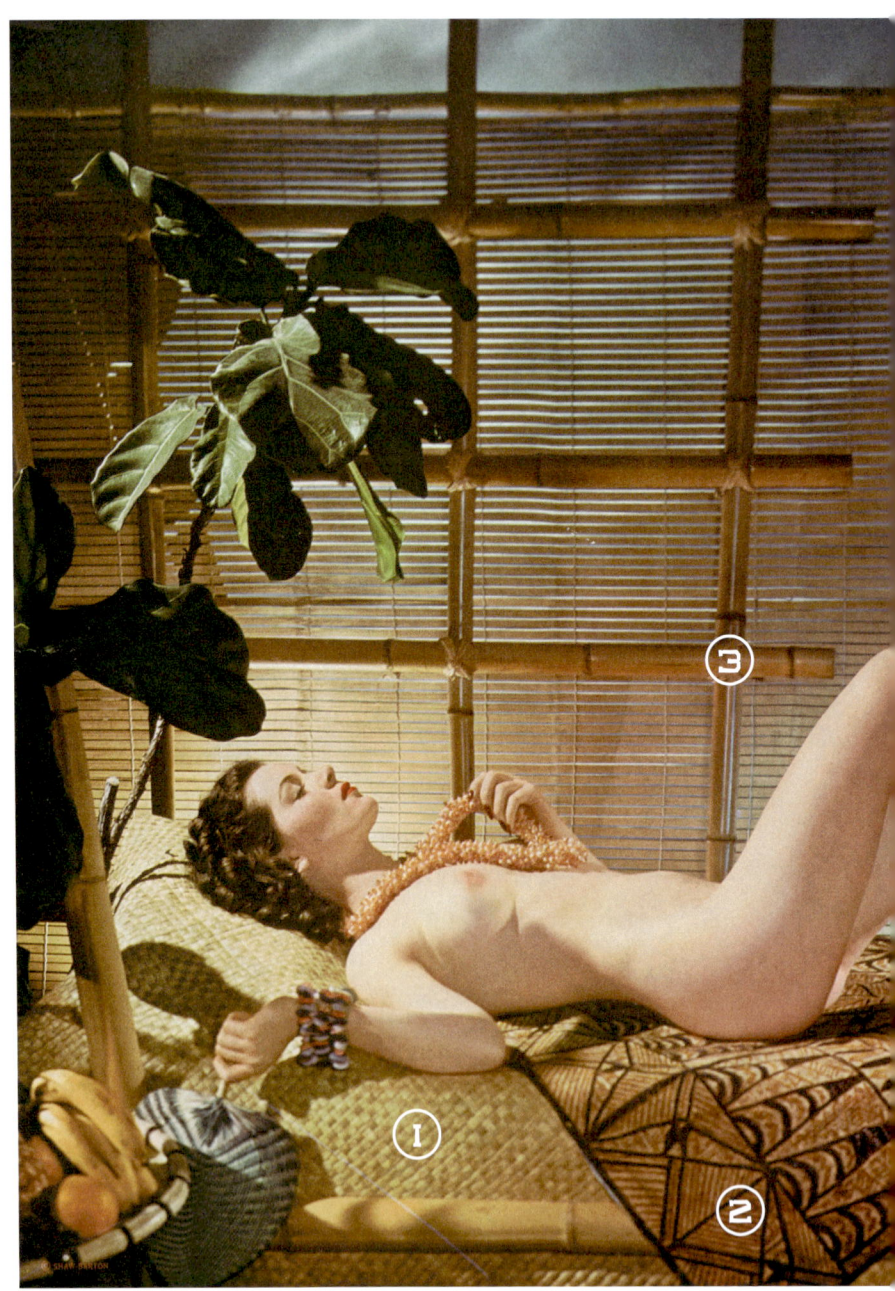

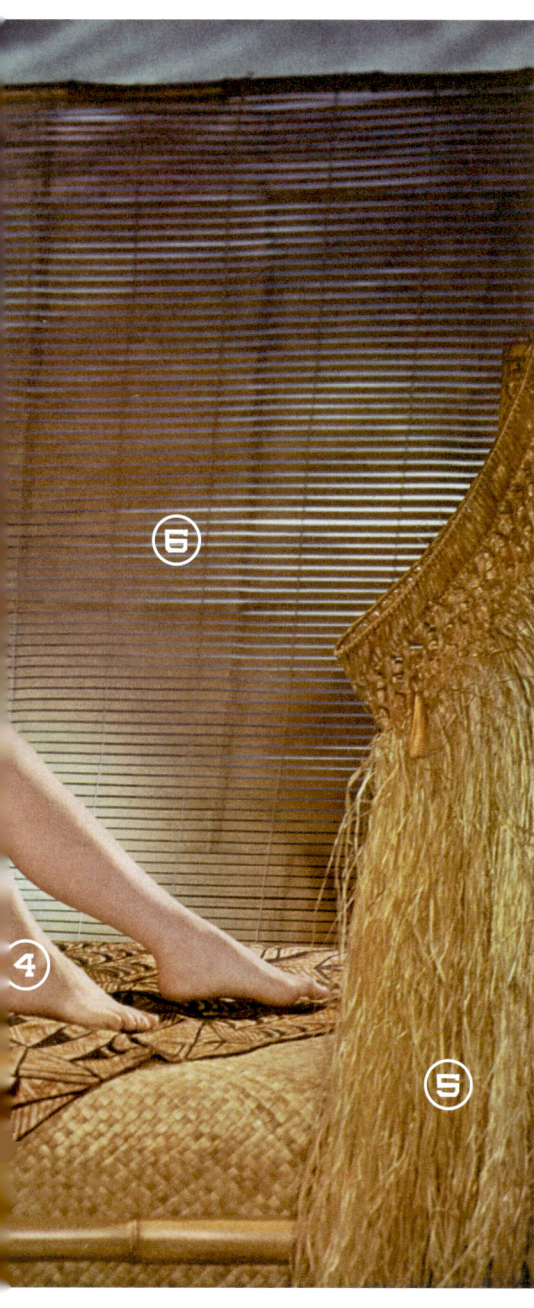

A slice of paradise

TROPICAL TEXTURES OF
THE PRE-TIKI LOUNGE
① *Lauhala* matting
② *Tapa* Cloth
③ Bamboo
④ Human skin
⑤ Raffia
⑥ Split bamboo shade

HEILMAN'S
Beachcomber

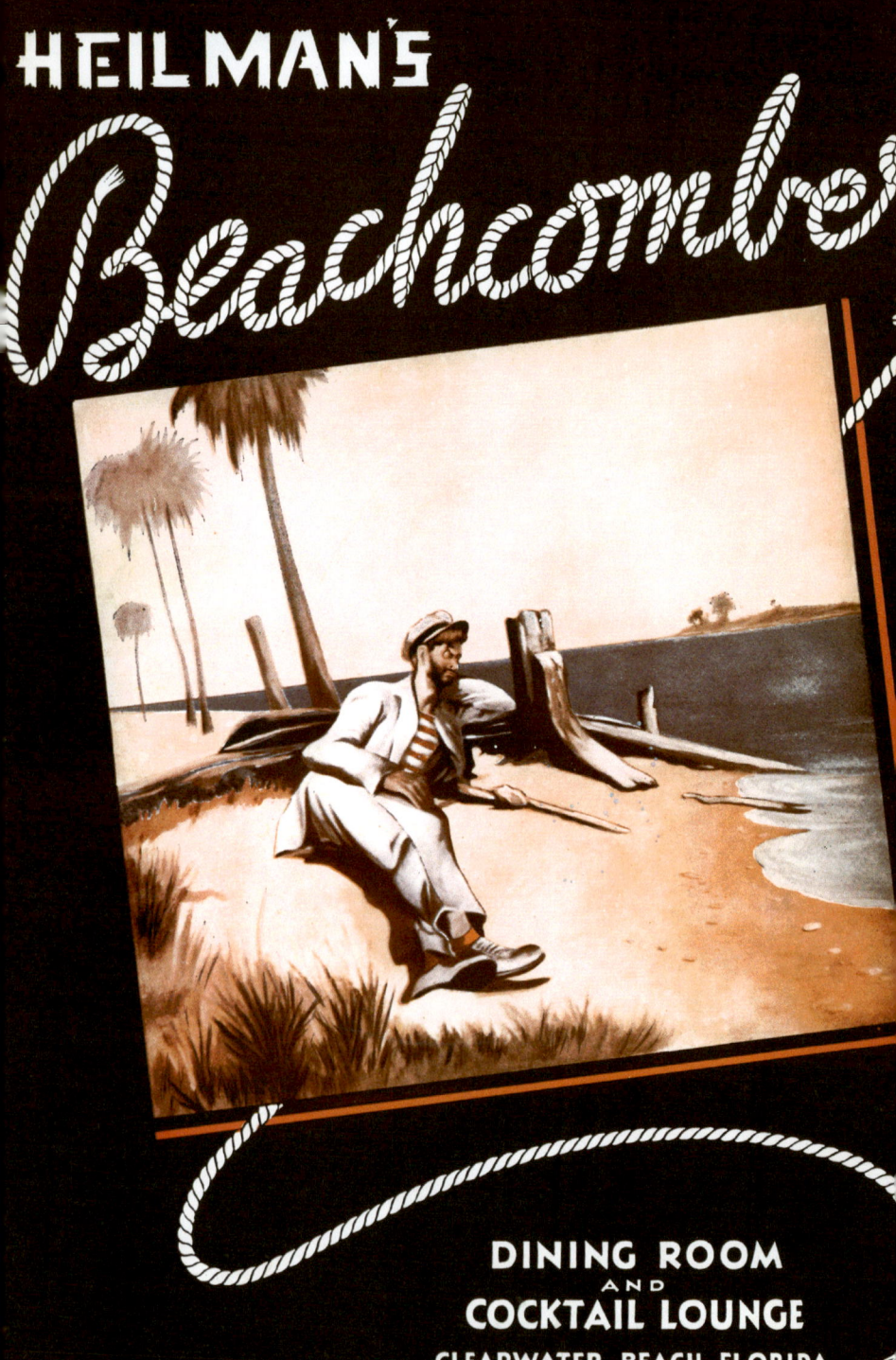

DINING ROOM
AND
COCKTAIL LOUNGE
CLEARWATER BEACH, FLORIDA

BEACHCOMBER BOHEMIA

BEACHCOMBER-BOHÈME
LA BOHÈME DU BATTEUR DE GRÈVE

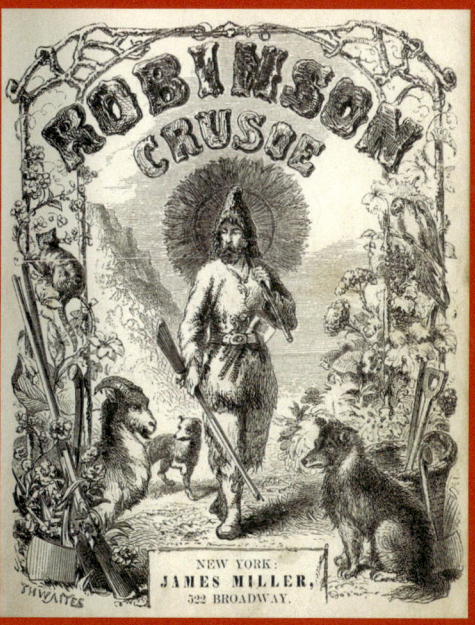

OPPOSITE: One of the fictional depictions of the beachcomber character, on the menu of the Heilman's Beach-comber restaurant in Clearwater Beach, Florida *(Mimi Payne Collection)*

ABOVE: The first famous work of beachcomber fiction, *Robinson Crusoe*

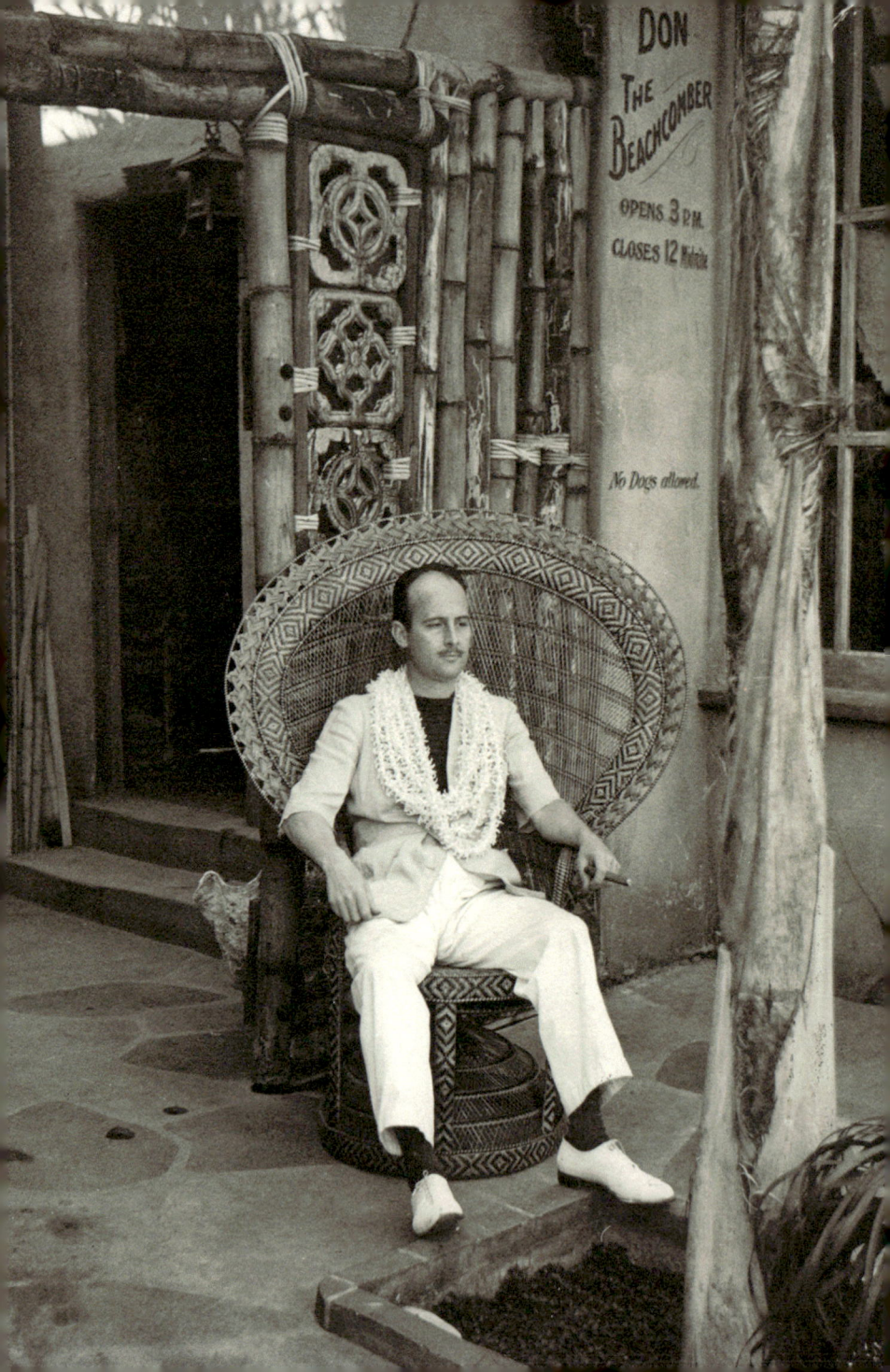

NOW THAT THE STAGE WAS

appropriately set, the South Seas story needed a hero. Taken from real-life accounts of ship-jumpers and castaways in the Pacific, the figure of the beachcomber was the perfect hybrid bridging the gap between white man and island native. He was the quintessential dropout from civilization, who chose a life of leisure and idleness on a palm-lined beach over societal conventions—an ideal host for an urban island escape, indeed.

A beachcomber could be the king of his little island paradise—and this is what Ernest Beaumont Gantt turned himself into when he created his first bamboo hideaway in Hollywood, which in turn became the blueprint for all future Polynesian bars. He landed in Tinseltown after traveling the South Seas, first renting the artifacts he had collected on his trips to the movie studios, then working as an advisor on South Seas films. When Prohibition ended, he opened his Beachcomber Café in 1934 and cast himself as Don the Beachcomber.

Another unique individual who helped popularize the "Beachcomber Moderne" style was Eli Hedley, also known as "The Real Beachcomber." Having built a home at Paradise Cove in San Pedro, California, entirely from driftwood and other "gifts from the sea," he then proceeded to turn his talent into a profitable business by selling hand-assembled beach décor to Disneyland and department stores through his Tradewinds Trading Company.

Beachcomber style combined the art genres of *art trouvé* ("found art") with assemblage (mixed-media sculpture). Seashore finds like shells and cork floats were combined into utilitarian and decorative objects that conveyed a bohemian,

OPPOSITE AND BELOW: Don the Beachcomber at the entrance to his bar *(Frank Brajevic Collection)*, and his literary precedent

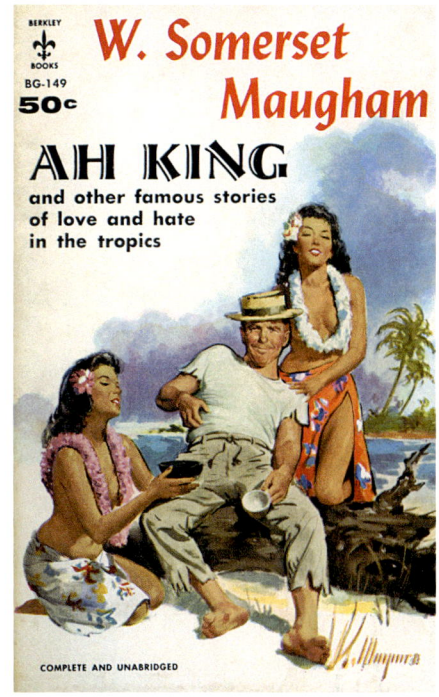

BERKLEY BOOKS
BG-149
50c

W. Somerset Maugham

AH KING

and other famous stories of love and hate in the tropics

COMPLETE AND UNABRIDGED

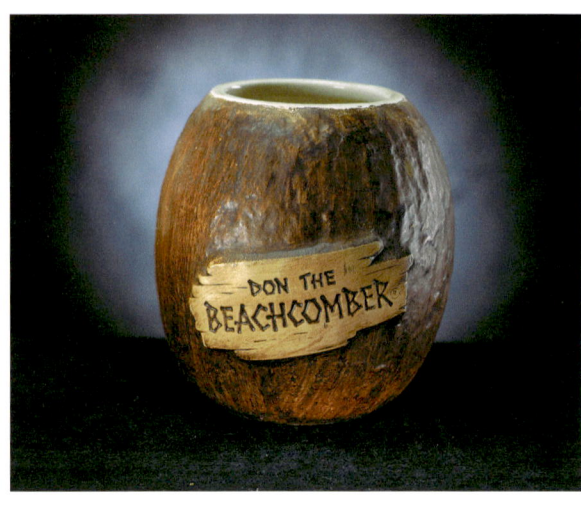

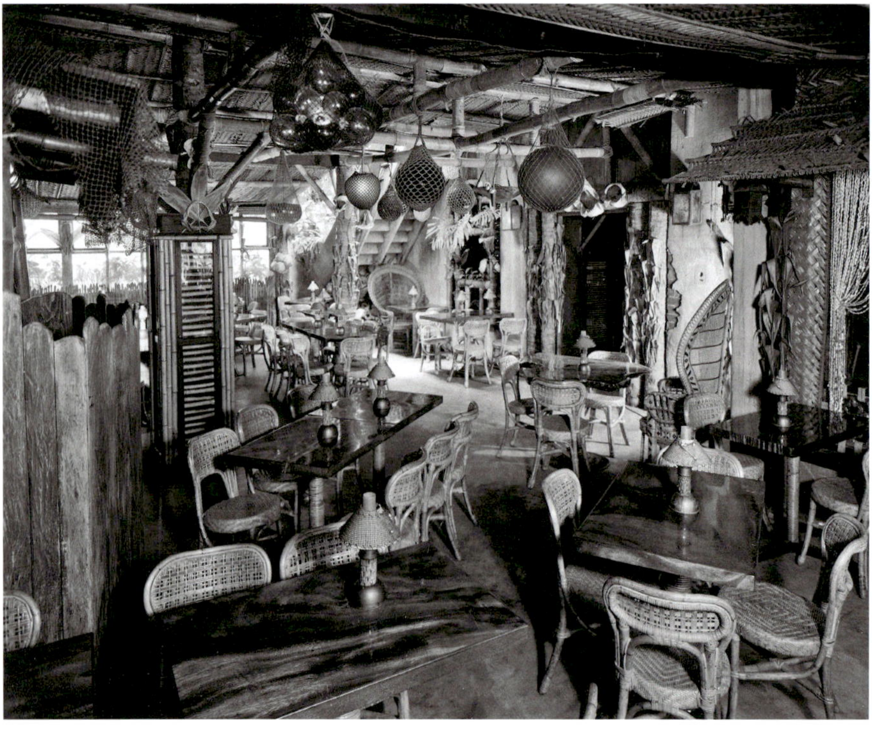

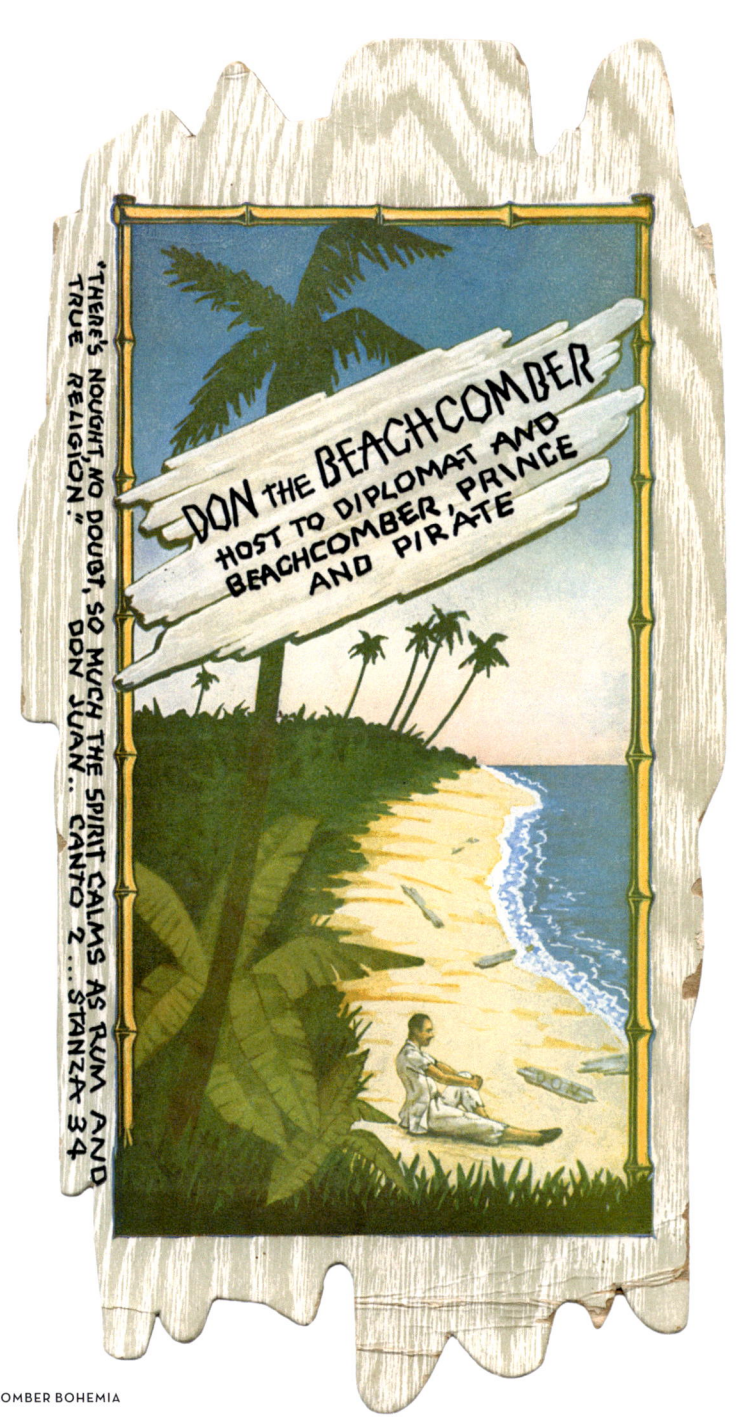

DON THE BEACHCOMBER

HOST TO DIPLOMAT AND
BEACHCOMBER, PRINCE
AND PIRATE

"THERE'S NOUGHT NO DOUBT, SO MUCH THE SPIRIT CALMS AS RUM AND TRUE RELIGION." DON JUAN...CANTO 2...STANZA 34 world-traveled atmosphere of faraway harbor hangouts. One could imagine exotic adventures and the smell of sea air in his own landlocked home or neighborhood bar.

Japanese glass floats that had been torn of their nets by storms drifted to the Hawaiian coast, where they were collected by locals. First used for home décor, they later were turned into lamps for bars. Soon, a whole galaxy of beachcomber lanterns was created from bamboo fish traps, dried puffer fish, and exotic basketry. As floats became standard décor items for every good Tiki bar, they began to be made from colorful plastic resins, giving off a dim, romantic light to maintain the mood.

While the success of the original Don the Beachcomber led to the opening of DTB franchises in numerous American cities, the concept inspired other driftwood lounges to use the castaway theme. It was a form of pre-hippie *boheme* that the middle class

could playfully partake in without really compromising career and family goals or responsibilities. The fruits of the postwar economic boom were fresh and yet to be enjoyed by the hardworking Americans of the 1940s and '50s.

Don the Beachcomber himself might have drawn his inspiration from the writings of a poet: espousing the Hawaiian way of life, Don Blanding's poetry collection *Vagabond's House* was first published in 1928, and within four years went into its 12th printing to satisfy his growing fan base. Blanding's poem of the same name conjures up a home full of mementos from travels to exotic places: "When I have a house. . . I'll fill it with things that have caught my eye / in drifting from Iceland to Molokai. . . " Two years later, Ernest Beaumont Gantt did just that at his Beachcomber Café, and chose the name of "Don" for himself.

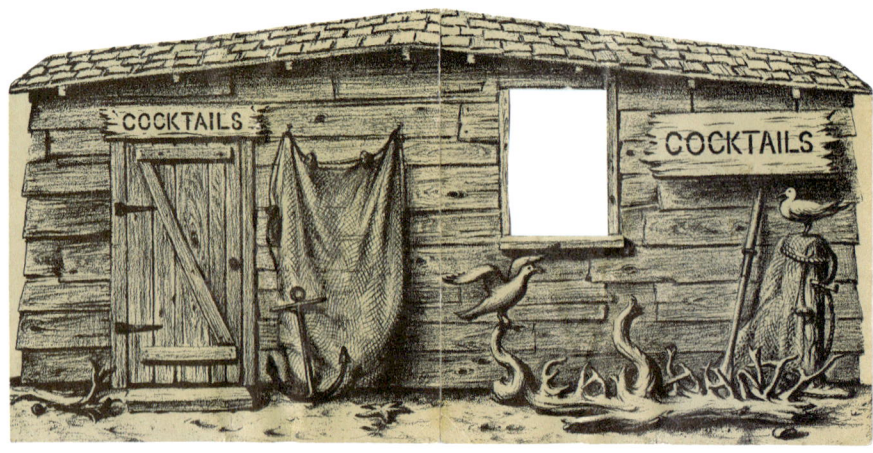

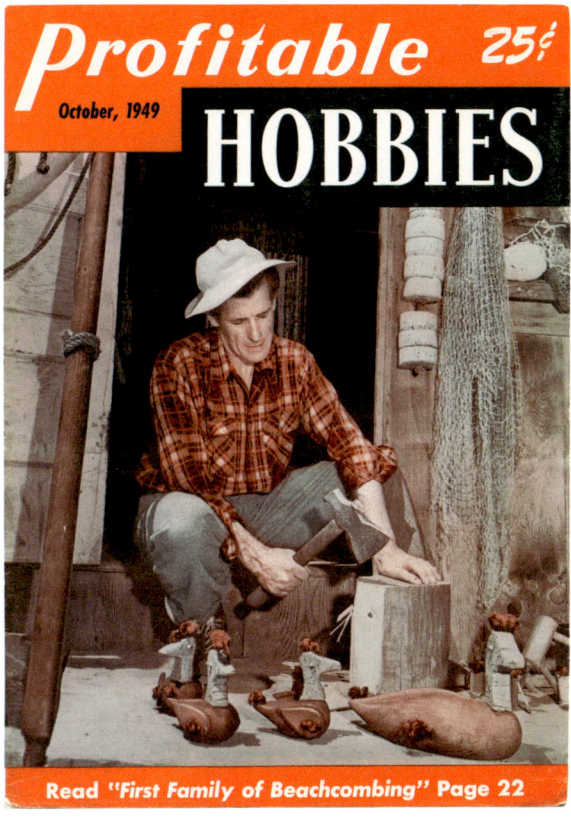

OPPOSITE: Cocktail menu for the Sea Shanty, a bar in the beachcomber-shack style
(both Frank Brajevic Collection)

LEFT: Self-made beachcomber/business owner Eli Hedley, posing in the doorway of his hand-built beach home

BELOW: Various beachcomber lamps made with hurricane-glass shades, cork, and sea shells

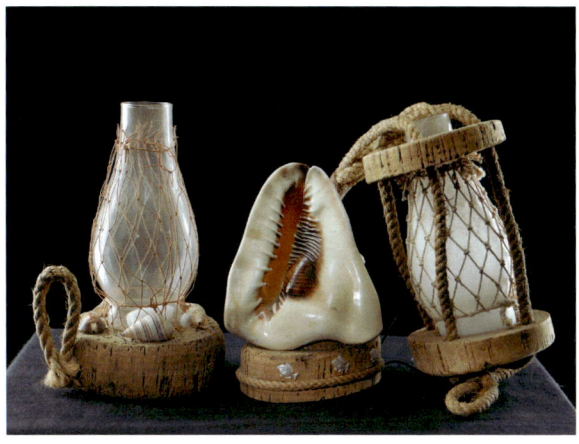

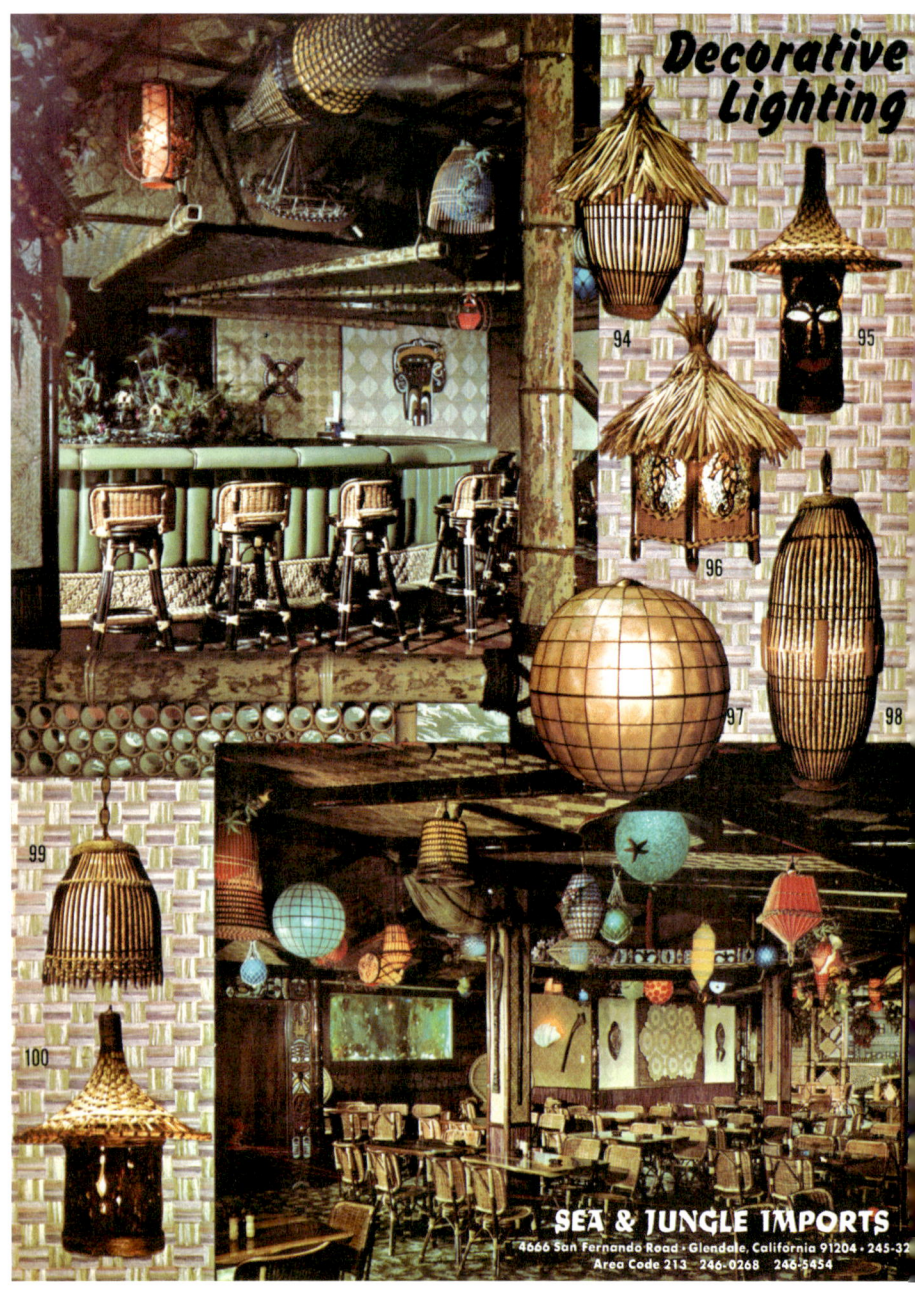

Decorative Lighting

SEA & JUNGLE IMPORTS
4666 San Fernando Road · Glendale, California 91204 · 245-32
Area Code 213   246-0268   246-5454

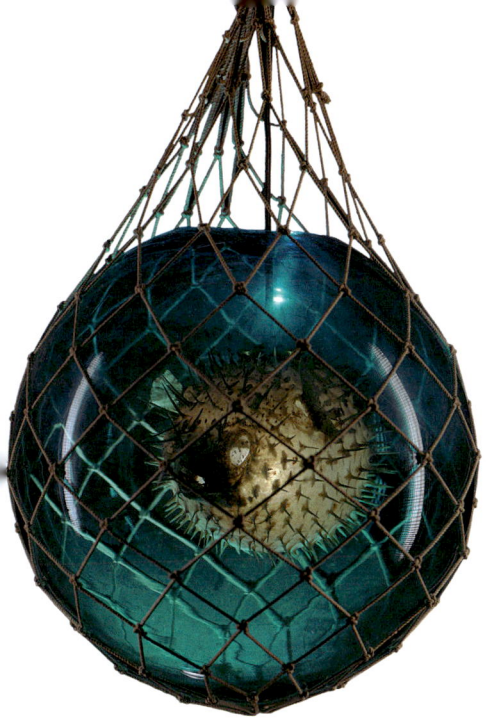

DA DER BODEN JETZT BEREITET

war, brauchte die Südseegeschichte einen Helden. Berichte von Schiffbrüchigen und Aussteigern im Pazifik lieferten die Figur des Beachcomber („Strandbummler") – das perfekte Bindeglied zwischen weißem Mann und Inselbewohner. Er war ein Aussteiger, der die Zivilisation hinter sich ließ und ein Leben des Müßiggangs und Nichtstuns an einem von Palmen gesäumten Strand gesellschaftlichen Konventionen vorzog – der ideale Gastgeber für die Südseeinsel in der Stadt.

Ein Beachcomber konnte der König seines kleinen Inselparadieses sein – und zu einem solchen machte sich Ernest Beaumont Gantt mit seinem ersten Bambusrefugium in Hollywood. Dieses wurde zum Vorbild für alle zukünftigen polynesischen Bars. Gantt landete nach einer Südseereise

in der Traumfabrik. Die Artefakte, die er auf seinem Trip gesammelt hatte, verlieh er zunächst an Filmstudios. Später arbeitete er als Berater für Südseefilme. Als die Prohibition aufgehoben wurde, eröffnete er 1934 sein Beachcomber-Café und gab sich selbst die Rolle des Don the Beachcomber.

Eine weitere Koryphäe, die die Beachcomber populär machten, war Eli Hedley, auch „The Real Beachcomber" genannt. Nachdem er sich in Paradise Cove im kalifornischen San Pedro ein Haus komplett aus Treibholz und anderen „Geschenken des Meeres" gebaut hatte, investierte er sein Talent in ein profitables Unternehmen. Seine Tradewinds Trading Company verkaufte handgemachtes Stranddekor an Disneyland und Kaufhäuser.

Der Beachcomber-Stil ist eine Kombination aus Objet trouvé und Assemblage.

Strandgut wie Muscheln und Schwimmer von Fischernetzen wurden zu zweckmäßigen und dekorativen Objekten zusammengefügt. Sie waren unkonventionell und sahen aus, als kämen sie von weit her. Im eigenen Festlandheim oder in der Eckkneipe verkörperten sie exotische Abenteuer. Man konnte das Meer fast riechen.

Japanische Glasschwimmkörper, die aus ihren Netzen gerissen wurden, trieben an die hawaiische Küste, wo Einheimische sie aufsammelten. Sie ließen sich leicht zu Lampen für Bars umarbeiten. Bald gab es ein ganzes Universum an Beachcomber-Lichtern aus Bambusfischreusen, getrocknetem Kugelfisch und exotischen Körben. Als die Glasschwimmer in keiner anständigen Tiki-Bar mehr fehlen durften, wurden sie aus buntem Plastikharz gegossen. Ihr gedämpftes, romantisches Licht sorgte für die richtige Stimmung.

Don the Beachcomber war so erfolgreich, dass aus seinem Café ein Franchise-Unternehmen mit Standorten in zahlreichen amerikanischen Städten wurde. Das Motiv des Schiffbrüchigen tauchte in vielerlei Variationen in den Bars auf. Der Mittelstand konnte sich dieser Form der Prä-Hippie-Bohème ausgelassen hingeben, ohne die Karriere, die Familie oder die gesellschaftliche Verantwortung hinter sich lassen zu müssen. Die Früchte des Wirtschaftsbooms nach dem Zweiten Weltkrieg schmeckten süß und wollten von den arbeitsamen Amerikanern der 1940er- und 1950er-Jahre in vollen Zügen genossen werden.

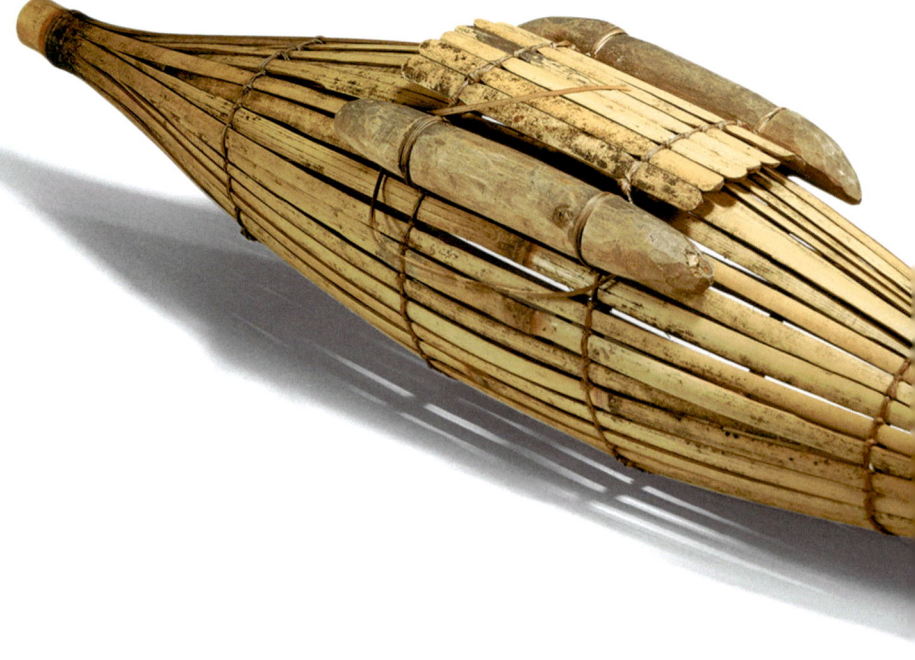

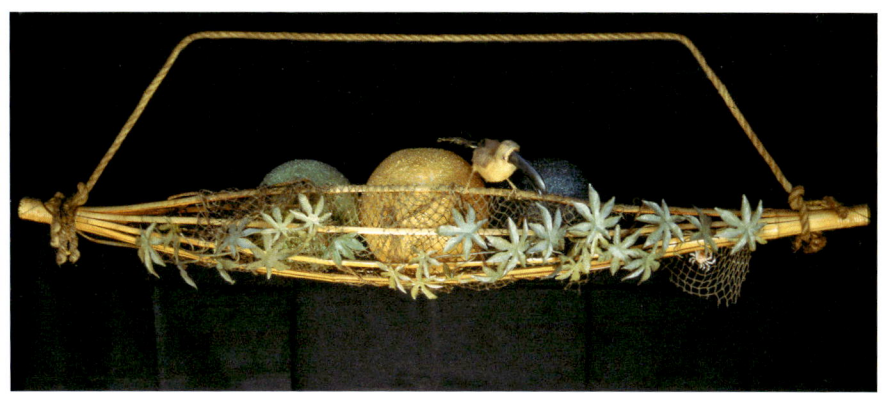

ABOVE: A beachcomber bamboo-fish trap lamp with resin floats

BELOW: Authentic Tahitian fish trap (*Musée du Quai Branly Collection*)

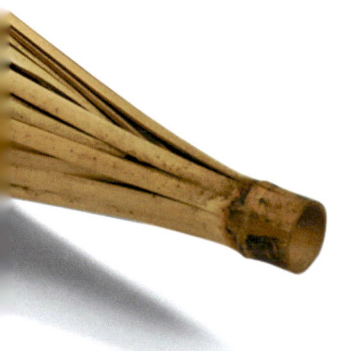

Don the Beachcomber selbst könnte seine Inspiration aus den Werken eines Dichters gezogen haben. Don Blandings Gedichtsammlung *Vagabond's House* pries den hawaiischen Lebensstil. Sie wurde erstmals 1928 veröffentlicht und ging innerhalb von vier Jahren in ihre 12. Auflage. Das titelgebende Gedicht beschwört ein Haus voller exotischer Reisesouvenirs herauf: „Wenn ich einmal ein Haus habe… Dann fülle ich es mit Dingen, die mir ins Auge stachen / auf dem Weg von Island nach Moloka'i". Zwei Jahre später hat Ernest B. Gantt genau das mit seinem Beachcomber-Café getan und sich selbst den Namen „Don" verliehen.

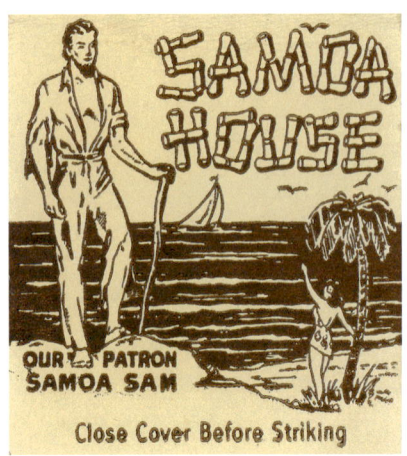

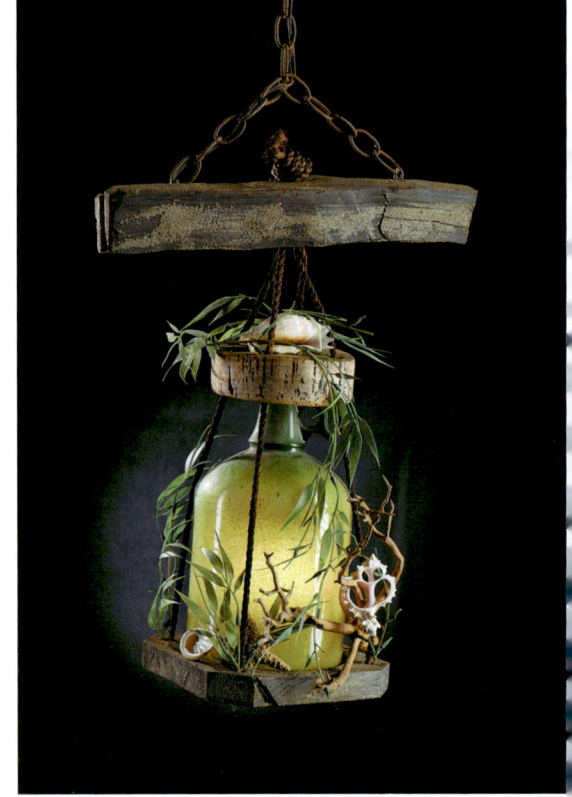

ABOVE: A fine figure of a beachcomber, Samoa Sam did not become as famous as Don or Vic

RIGHT: A beachcomber jug lamp

OPPOSITE: Glass fishnet floats set the mood in this advertising photo

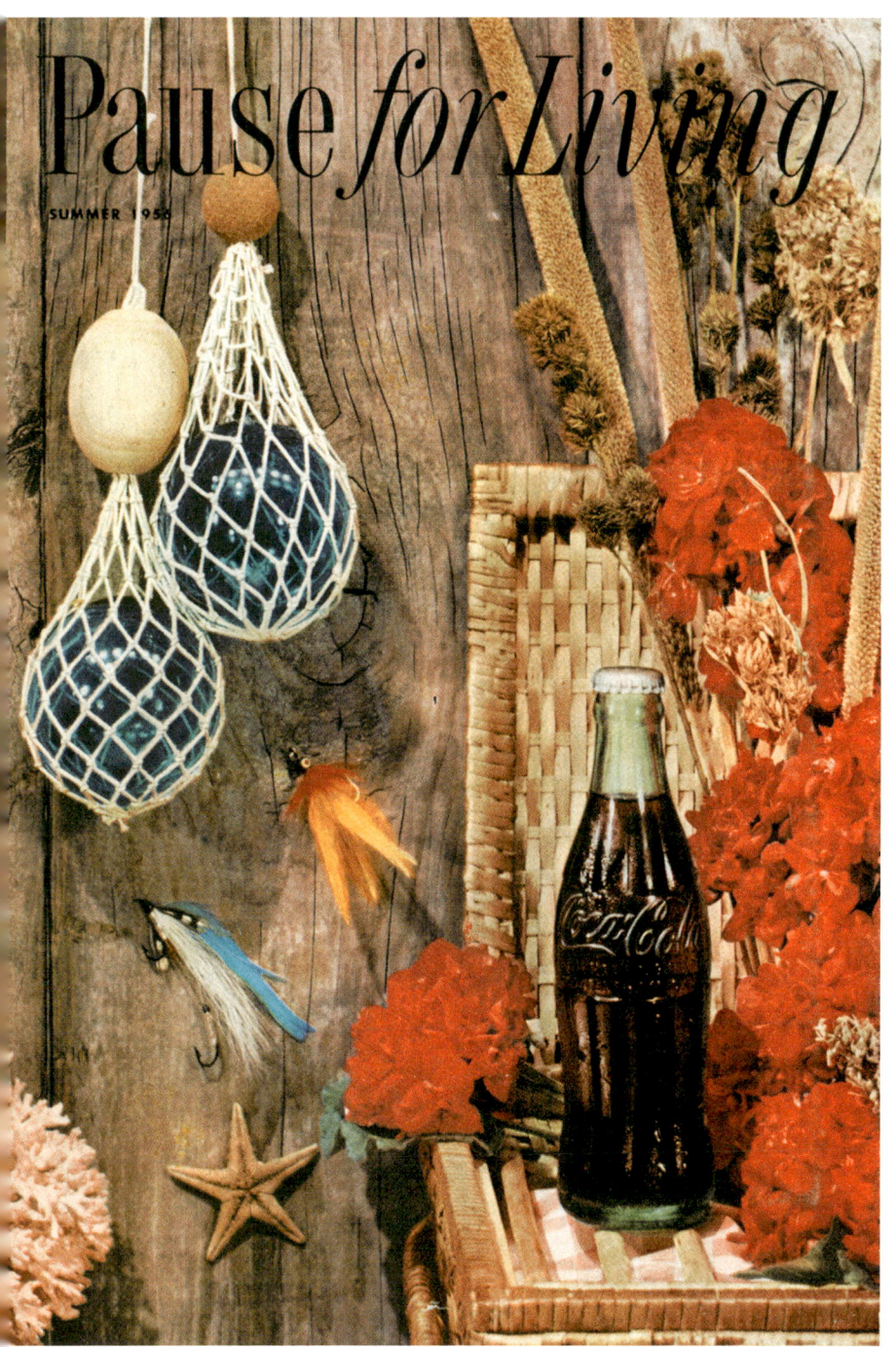

Pause *for Living*

SUMMER 1956

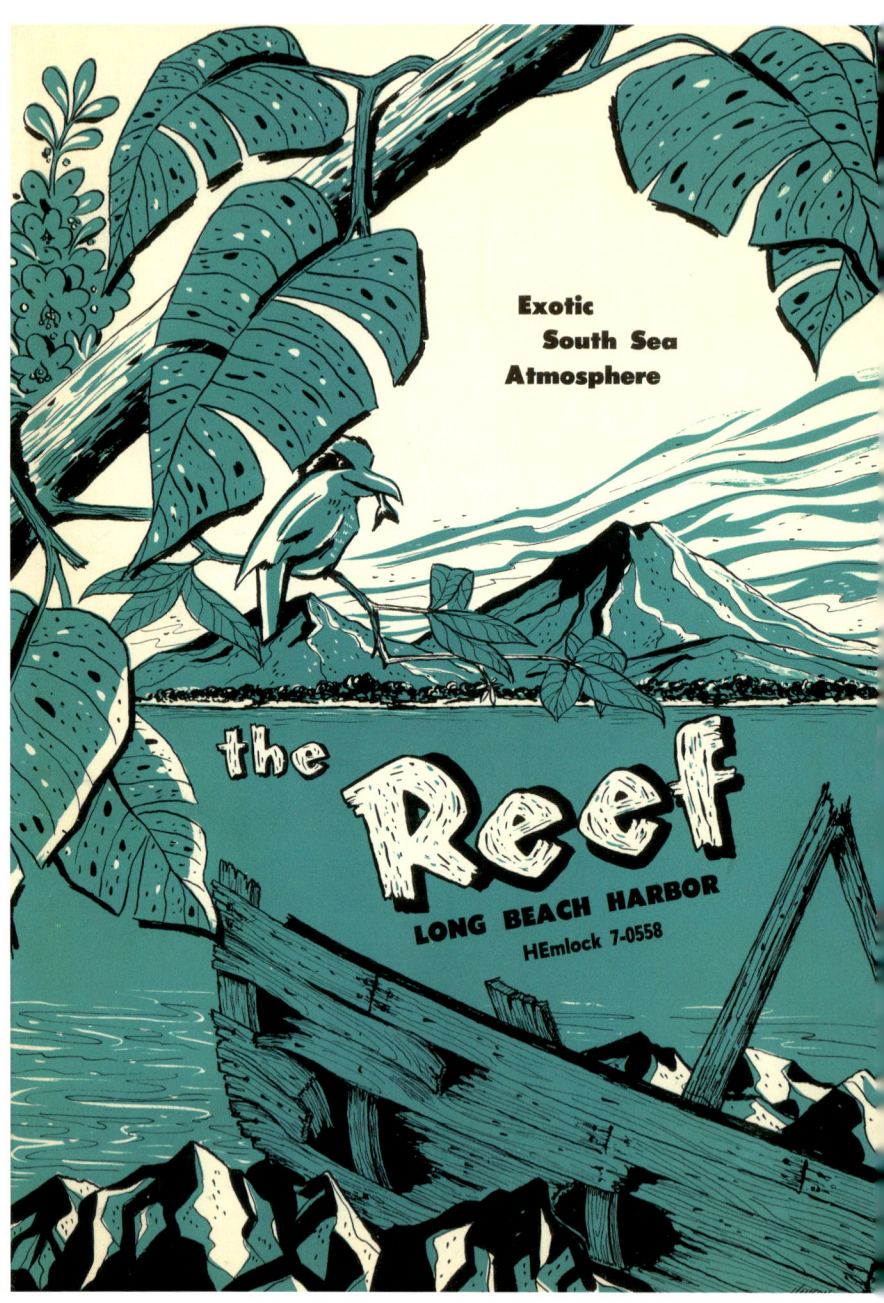

Exotic
South Sea
Atmosphere

the **Reef**
LONG BEACH HARBOR
HEmlock 7-0558

MAINTENANT QUE LE DÉCOR

idoine était en place, ne manquait plus aux mers du Sud que leur héros. Empruntée aux histoires vécues des naufragés et autres passagers clandestins du Pacifique, la figure du *beachcomber*, ou batteur de grève, était le trait d'union idéal apte à combler le fossé entre l'homme blanc et l'indigène des îles. Il incarnait l'archétype de l'individu qui tourne le dos à la civilisation et fait le choix d'une existence de loisir et de paresse sur une plage bordée de palmiers, à rebours des conventions sociales – l'hôte rêvé d'un refuge exotique en milieu urbain.

Le batteur de grève pouvait s'introniser roi de son petit paradis insulaire, ce que fit Ernest Beaumont Gantt en créant à Hollywood son premier refuge en bambou, lequel allait devenir le prototype de tous les futurs bars polynésiens. Il s'installa dans la capitale du cinéma après avoir parcouru les mers du Sud et commença par louer les objets rapportés de ses voyages aux studios de cinéma, avant de travailler comme conseiller sur les films « Mers du Sud ». Dès la fin de la prohibition, en 1934, il ouvrit son Beachcomber Café et s'attribua le rôle de « Don the Beachcomber » (Don le batteur de grève).

Autre personnage unique ayant contribué à populariser le style « Beachcomber Moderne », Eli Hedley fut également connu sous la dénomination « The Real Beachcomber ». Après avoir bâti une maison à Paradise Cove, à San Pedro (Californie), entièrement faite de bois flotté et autres « présents de la mer », il sut ensuite mettre à profit ses talents en vendant à Disneyland et aux grands magasins des décors de plage assemblés à la main, par le truchement de sa société Tradewinds Trading Company.

Le style Beachcomber mêlait les genres artistiques du « ready-made » ou « art trouvé » et de l'assemblage – la sculpture combinant divers matériaux. Les trouvailles rejetées par la mer, tels les coquillages et flotteurs de liège, étaient assemblées et converties en objets décoratifs exprimant l'atmosphère bohème et cosmopolite de ports du bout du monde. Ils permettaient d'imaginer des aventures exotiques et de humer la brise marine chez soi ou dans un bar fort peu maritime.

Les flotteurs de verre japonais, arrachés de leurs filets par la tempête, dérivaient souvent vers les côtes hawaiiennes, où ils étaient recueillis par les habitants. D'abord utilisés pour la décoration de la maison, ils furent par la suite transformés en lampes pour les bars. Bientôt, c'est toute une galaxie de lanternes Beachcomber qui fut créée à partir de pièges à poissons en bambou, de poissons-globes séchés, ou de vanneries exotiques. Les flotteurs étant devenus des articles de décoration standard pour chaque vrai bar tiki, l'industrie se mit à fabriquer des globes en résine plastique colorée qui émettaient la lumière tamisée indispensable à l'ambiance romantique recherchée.

Le succès de Don the Beachcomber a conduit à l'ouverture de franchises DTB dans diverses villes américaines, ce concept ayant poussé d'autres bars d'ambiance « bois flotté » à utiliser le thème du naufragé. La classe moyenne y goûtait alors au charme d'une bohème préhippie, sans

The Reef, Long Beach harbor menu

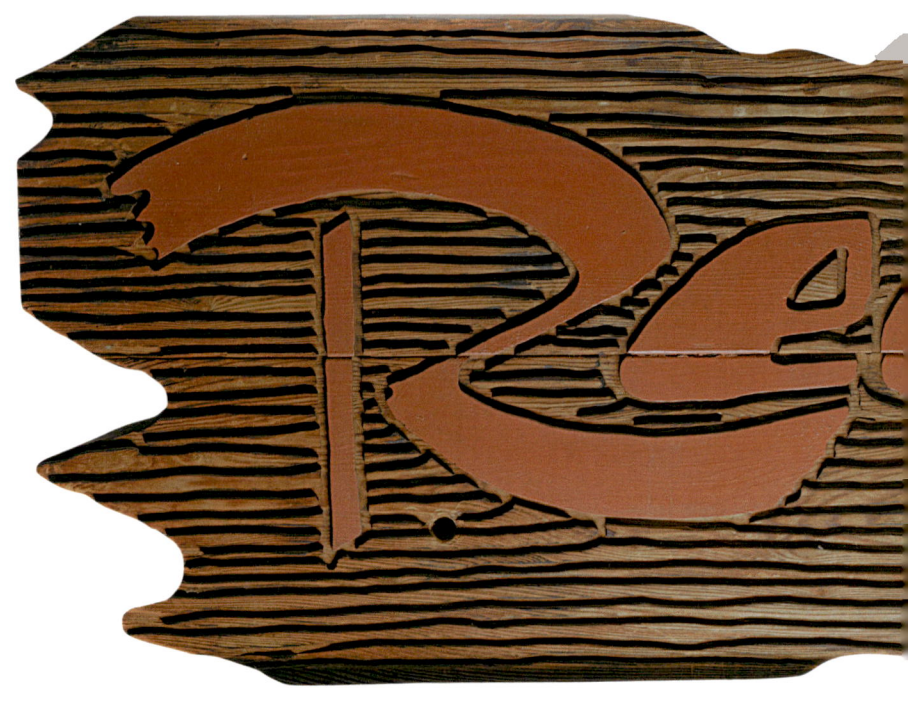

compromettre sa carrière ni ses responsabilités ou ses objectifs familiaux. Les bienfaits du boom économique de l'après-guerre étaient encore trop récents pour que les Américains des années 1940 et 1950 qui travaillaient dur aient encore pu vraiment en profiter.

Don the Beachcomber lui-même a peut-être tiré son inspiration des écrits d'un poète : vibrant éloge du mode de vie hawaiien, le recueil de poésies de Don Blanding *Vagabond's House,* paru en 1928,

a été réimprimé ensuite douze fois en quatre ans à la demande d'un public de fans qui ne cessait de croître. Le poème éponyme de Blanding évoque une maison remplie de souvenirs de voyages dans des lieux exotiques :

« Quand j'aurai une maison… je la remplirai d'objets qui m'ont séduit dans mes dérives de l'Islande à Molokai… » C'est exactement ce que fit deux ans plus tard Ernest B. Gantt dans son Beachcomber Café, non sans se rebaptiser « Don » au passage.

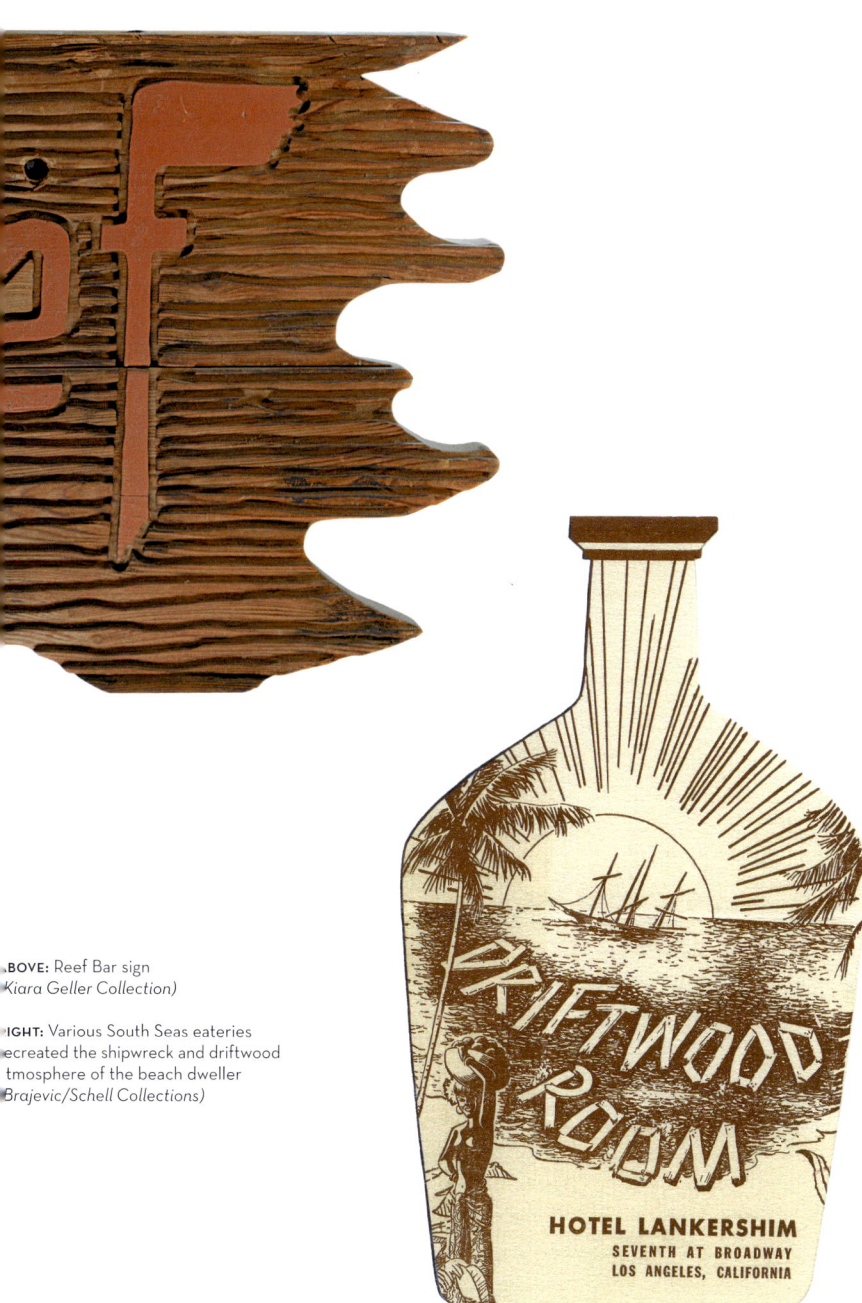

ABOVE: Reef Bar sign
(*Kiara Geller Collection*)

RIGHT: Various South Seas eateries
recreated the shipwreck and driftwood
atmosphere of the beach dweller
(*Brajevic/Schell Collections*)

DRIFTWOOD ROOM

HOTEL LANKERSHIM
SEVENTH AT BROADWAY
LOS ANGELES, CALIFORNIA

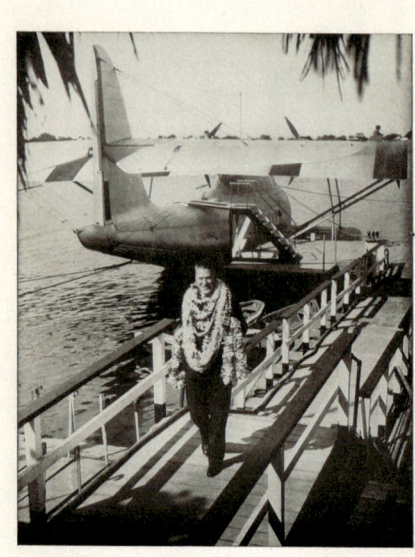

Winged Return to Paradise. The author arriving in Hawaii by Clipper from California.

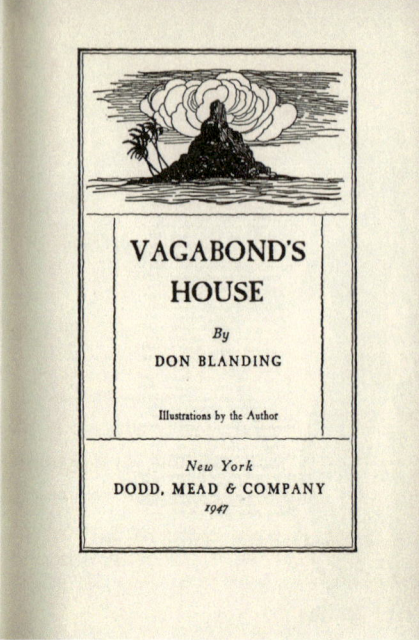

VAGABOND'S HOUSE

By

DON BLANDING

Illustrations by the Author

New York
DODD, MEAD & COMPANY
1947

ABOVE: Don Blanding, the Hawaiian poet laureate. *Vagabond's House* was popular into the '50s, but its romantic word-weaving appeared dated by the time Tiki rolled around

RIGHT AND OPPOSITE: Testament to its popularity, a restaurant and a record carried the book's name

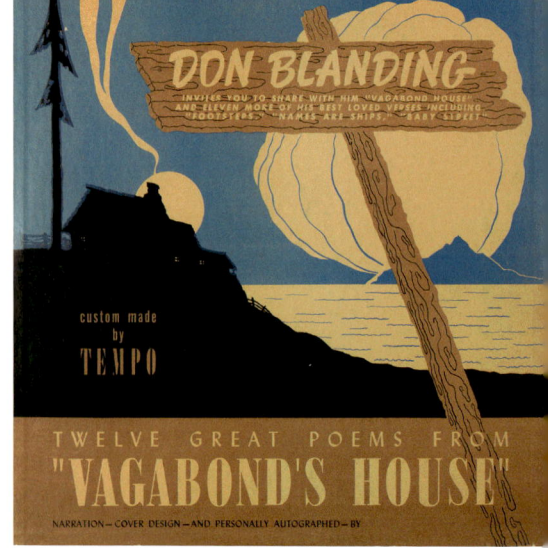

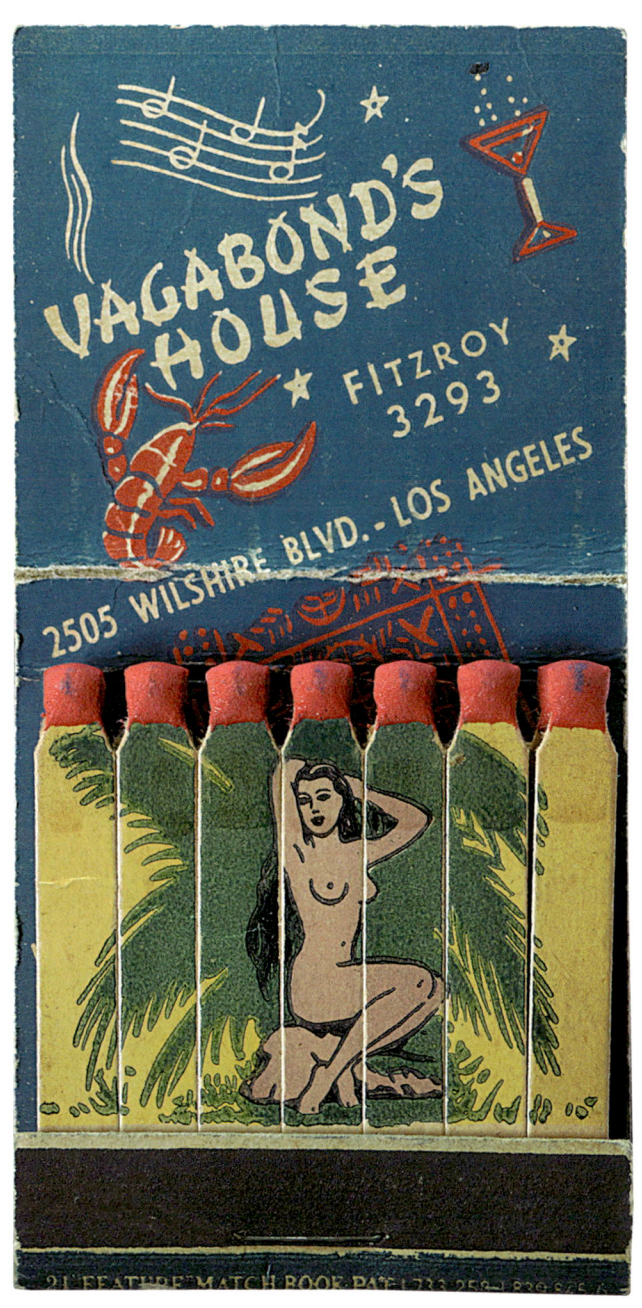

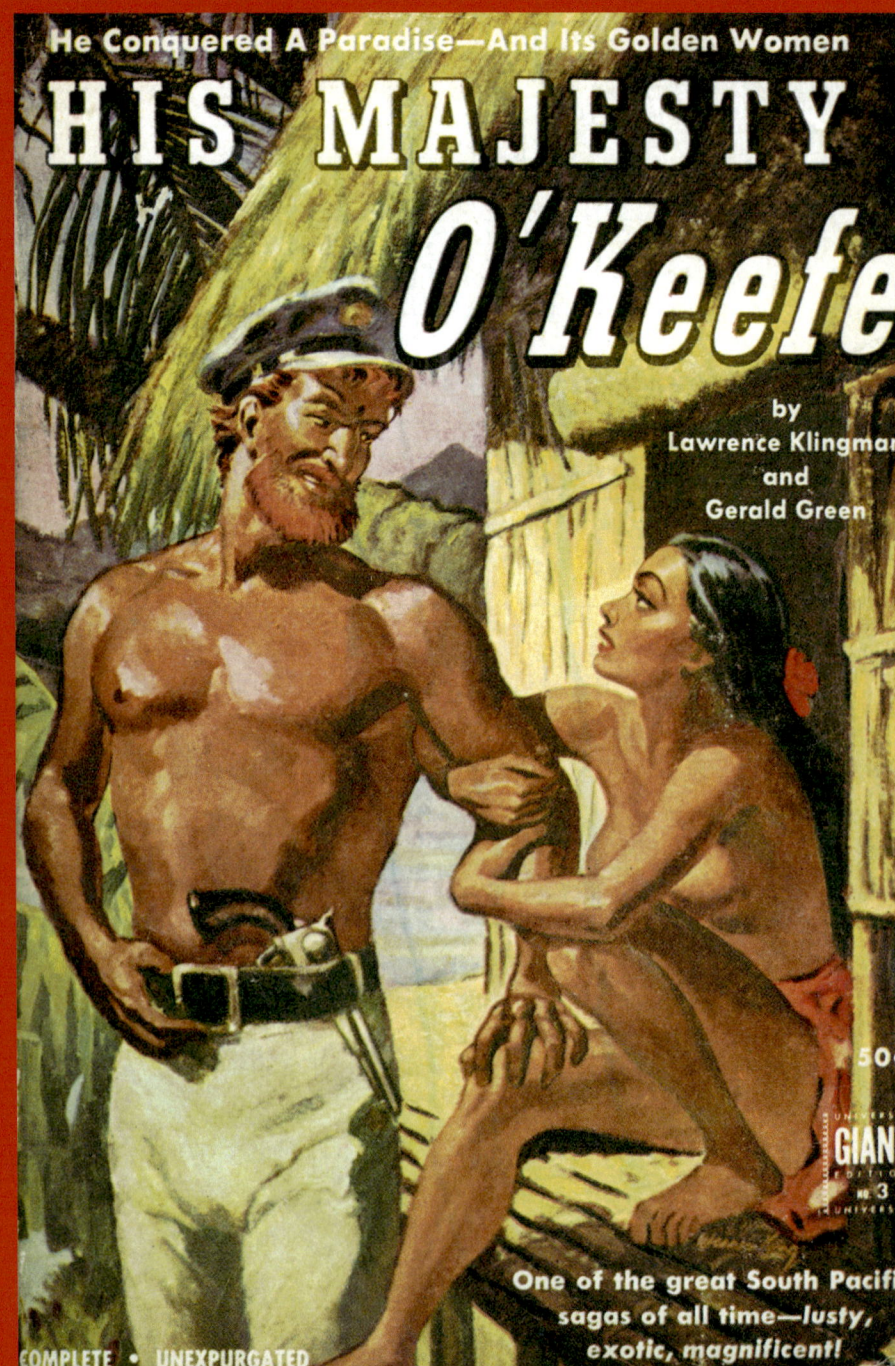

He Conquered A Paradise—And Its Golden Women

HIS MAJESTY
O'Keefe

by
Lawrence Klingman
and
Gerald Green

50¢

GIANT
№ 3

One of the great South Pacific
sagas of all time—*lusty,
exotic, magnificent!*

COMPLETE • UNEXPURGATED

9

THE SOUTH SEAS TRADER

DER SÜDSEEHÄNDLER
LE NÉGOCIANT DES MERS DU SUD

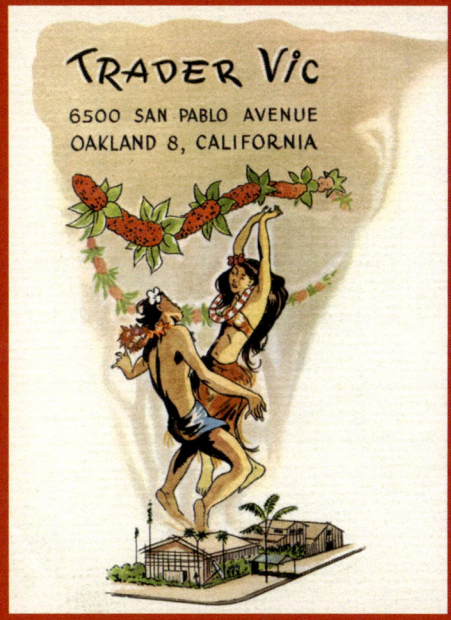

OPPOSITE: The paperback cover of the O'Keefe story
exploits the fact that he had several native wives

ABOVE: Trader Vic's humble beginnings

ANOTHER CHARACTER FROM THE pages of post-contact Pacific island history was the trader. Like the beachcomber, he had "gone native" and chosen to leave modern society behind for an island existence. Less a self-reliant loner and leisure lover, the trader was the industrious intermediary between the Western seafarers and the native island population. In Polynesian Pop, he was portrayed as firmly in control of his little chiefdom, wise to the ways of the islanders and weary of the white men whose world he had forsaken.

Many of the South Seas trader's popular attributes were based on the figure of David Dean O'Keefe, an Irish immigrant to America who had settled on the island of Yap in 1873 and turned it into a center of the copra trade. The book written in 1952 about his adventurous life opens with this statement by retired Royal Navy Admiral Cyprian A. B. Bridge: "Those who believe

that the beachcomber or the copra trader of the South Seas is necessarily a scoundrel, err grievously."

Although the 1954 movie version of the book was partly shot in the Fijian Islands, it is a classic Hollywood production, fulfilling all the expectations the mid-century public could have had about a South Seas adventure film. However, no cocktail lounges were opened in the name of this film. The Polynesian-restaurant industry was coming into its own, developing its own form of authenticity, which often used the South Seas clichés in a more tongue-in-cheek way.

Trader restaurant décor built and expanded on the beachcomber look with a heavily nautical bend. As traders like O'Keefe shipped their wares on their own schooners, anything that came from an old sailing vessel was used to create that "from the Seven Seas" ambience: anchors, signal lamps, wooden ship's wheels,

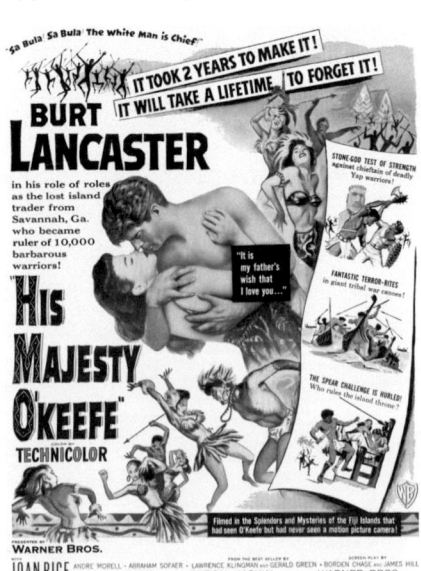

LEFT: The press book for *His Majesty O'Keefe*, with typical South Seas exploitation movie copy and graphic

OPPOSITE: The first movie trader, Trader Horn, plied his wares in Africa

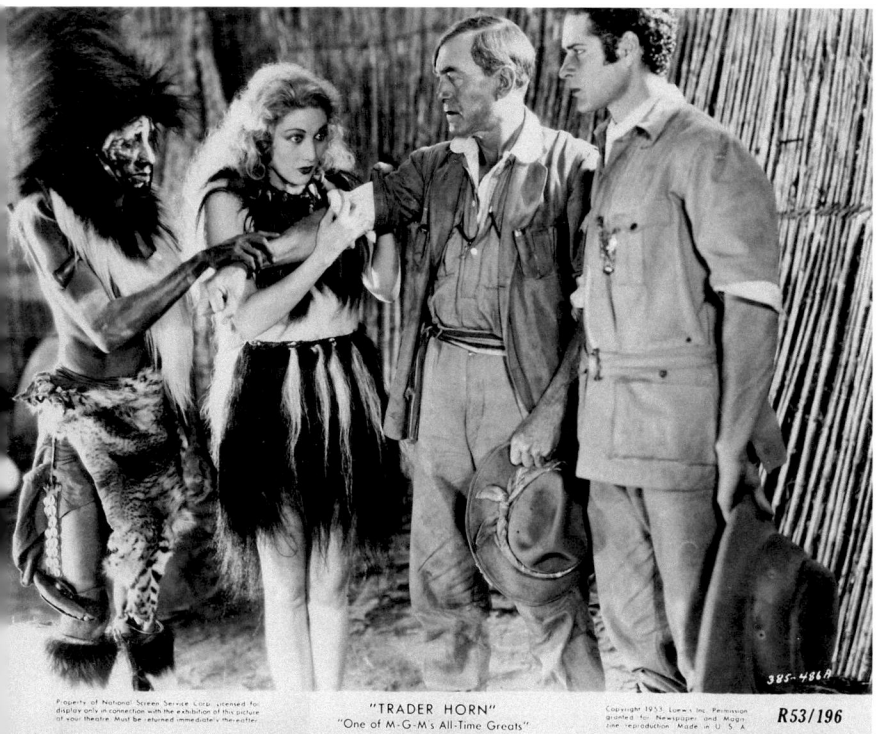

"TRADER HORN"
"One of M-G-M's All-Time Greats"

R53/196

pulleys, and rope fenders were just some of the props used for trader-style interiors. These items formed yet another story layer to the driftwood and tropical textures of the Tiki lounge.

Another important Trader prop was the rum barrel — rum being the lifeblood of sailors as well as Polynesian bars. Every tropical restaurant worth its salt had to have its own signature barrel mug, usually used for the "Rum Barrel" cocktail. Wooden barrels were also used as tables or hung from the ceiling in fishnets. Care was taken to not let the décor drift into the "pirate" genre, an entirely different theme belonging to the Caribbean.

All of this exotic merchandise scattered about the place gave the restaurant an aura of unconventionality and informality, and inspired conversation. To make good on the name, Trader Vic's and other South Seas posts installed gift shops in their restaurants. In his "Zombie Village," Skipper Kent offered, "Tapa cloth. . . shell beads, leis, bamboo, Hawaiian blouses, spices, ship's curios, etc. for sale or trade." But the main items for sale were the comestibles.

Entering a warehouse filled with overseas goods, the customer was looking forward to the experience of intriguing tastes of foreign food and drink.

Trader Vic's remained the most successful of the trader outposts in America, opening franchises in many U.S. cities and expanding to foreign shores in Europe and Asia. It is the only Polynesian-restaurant chain that survived the abolishment of Tiki in the 1980s and '90s. Vic's classic urban islands in Atlanta, London, and Munich still maintain the original atmosphere of romance and adventure in the South Seas, serving Vic's time-tested cocktails and food. New openings, like the one in Portland, Oregon, prove that the concept can be carried into the 21st century with style and class.

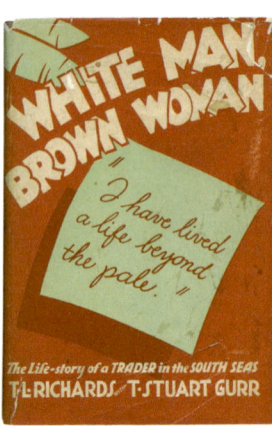

ABOVE: Another book title preying on the public's fascination with interracial relationships

LEFT: A real trader and his real native wife

OPPOSITE: 1949 menu cover for Trader Vic's restaurant in Oakland, California. Proprietor Victor Bergero. became "Trader Vic" after visiting Don the Beachcomber in Hollywood

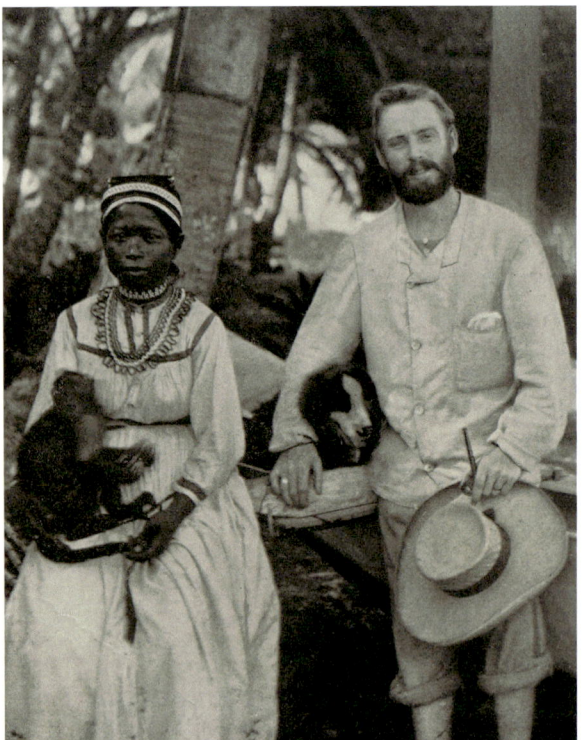

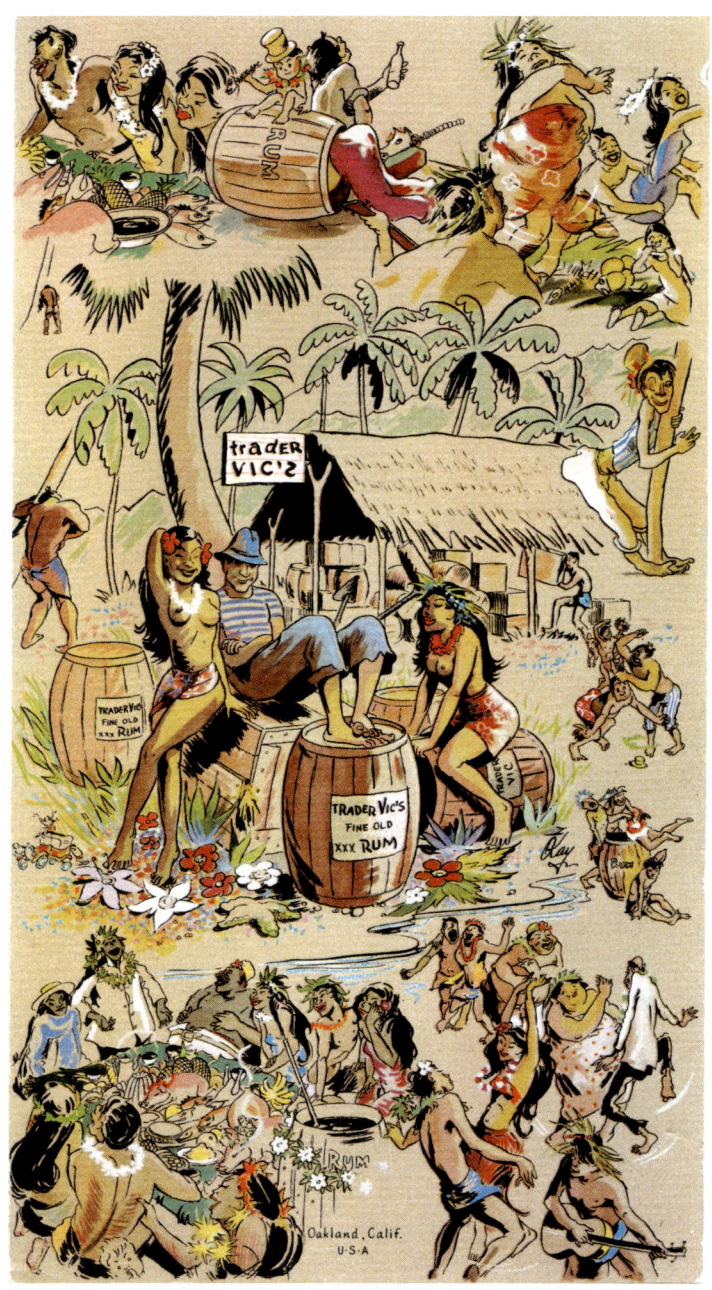

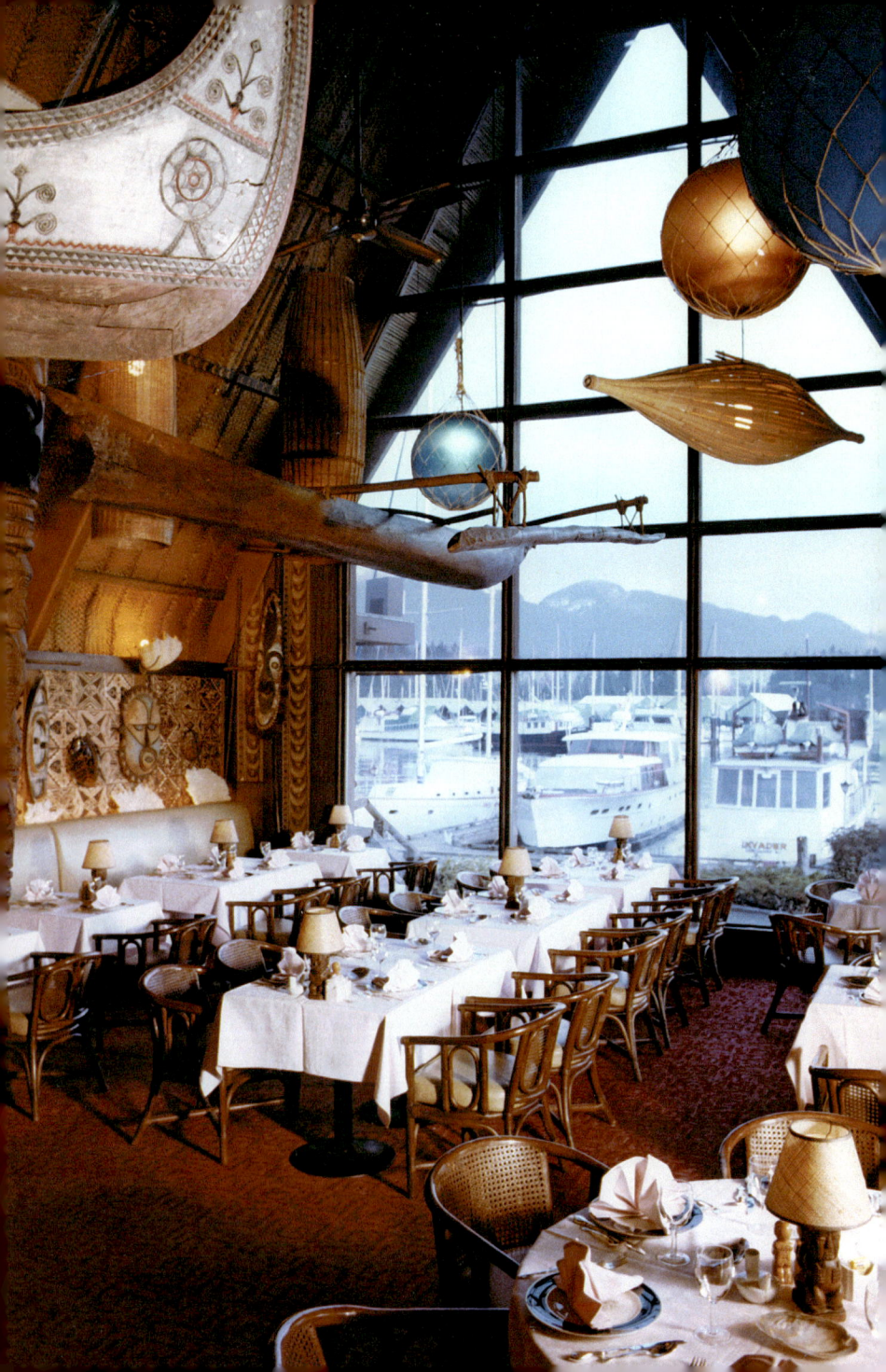

EINE WEITERE FIGUR, DIE NACH

der Entdeckung der pazifischen Inseln auf-
tauchte, war der Trader, also ein Händler.
Wie auch der Beachcomber ist er ein
Aussteiger, der die moderne Gesellschaft
zugunsten des Insellebens hinter sich
gelassen hat. Weniger ein Einzelgänger und
Faulenzer ist der Trader ein arbeitsamer
Mittelsmann zwischen den westlichen
Seefahrern und der einheimischen Insel-
bevölkerung. Der „Polynesian Pop" definierte ihn als einen Mann, der sein kleines
Reich fest im Griff hatte, die Einwohner
kannte und der Welt des weißen Mannes
überdrüssig geworden war.

Viele Eigenschaften des Südseehändlers
basierten auf der Person des David Dean
O'Keefe, einem Immigranten aus Irland,
der 1848 in die USA gekommen war und
sich 1873 auf der mikronesischen Insel Yap
niedergelassen hatte, die er in ein Zentrum
des Handels mit Kopra verwandelt hatte.
Ein 1952 erschienenes Buch über sein beweg-
tes Leben beginnt mit einer Stellungnahme
eines pensionierten Admirals der Royal
Navy, Cyprian A. B. Bridge: „Wer glaubt,
dass der Strandbummler oder Koprahänd-
ler der Südsee zwangsläufig ein Halunke
sein muss, irrt gewaltig."

Auch wenn die Verfilmung des Buchs
von 1954 zum Teil auf den Fidschi-Inseln
gedreht wurde, ist sie eine klassische
Hollywood-Produktion. Sie erfüllte alle
Erwartungen, die an einen Südsee-Aben-
teuerfilm gestellt wurden. Und doch wurden keine Cocktailbars nach ihr benannt.
Die Industrie für polynesische Restaurants
entwickelte ihre eigene Form der Authentizität, die sich der Südseeklischees oft mit
einem Augenzwinkern bediente.

Aufbauend auf dem Beachcomber-Look
nahmen die Trader-Interieurs vermehrt

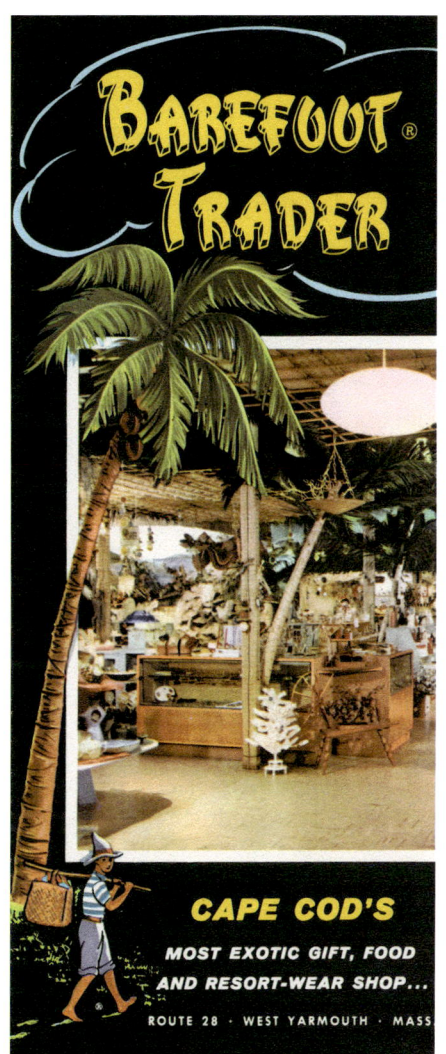

OPPOSITE: The view at Trader Vic's,
Vancouver

ABOVE: Barefoot Trader stores
supplied discerning 20th-century
beachcombers with home décor

nautische Gestaltungselemente in sich auf. Männer wie O'Keefe transportierten ihre Waren auf ihren eigenen Schonern. Also wurde alles, was zu einem alten Segelschiff gehören konnte, eingesetzt, um die sieben Weltmeere in die Zivilisation zu holen; Anker, Signallampen, hölzerne Steuerräder, Taljen, Fender etc. verliehen den Tiki-Bars aus Treibholz und tropischen Materialien eine neue Dimension.

Ein weiteres wichtiges Requisit war das Rumfass. Rum war das Lebenselixier der Seefahrer – und der polynesischen Bars. Jedes Tropen-Restaurant, das etwas auf sich hielt, musste seine eigenen, unverwechselbaren Trinkbecher haben, die an Rumfässer erinnerten und in denen der Rum-Barrel-Cocktail serviert wurde. Holzfässer wurden als Tische genutzt oder hingen in Fischernetzen von der Decke. Dabei wurde penibel darauf geachtet, die Inneneinrichtung nicht ins Piratengenre abrutschen zu lassen – ein ganz anderes karibisches Motiv.

Die exotische Ausstattung des Restaurants strahlte eine zwanglose Atmosphäre aus, die zu Gesprächen anregte. Um dem Motto gerecht zu werden, waren Trader Vic's und anderen Südseelokalen Souvenirläden angeschlossen. In seinem „Zombie Village" bot Skipper Kent „Tapa-Rindenbaststoff … Muschelperlen, Blumenketten, Bambus, Hawaiihemden, Gewürze, nautische Kuriositäten usw. zum Verkauf oder Tausch" an. Die Hauptprodukte waren jedoch die Esswaren.

Angesichts der Fülle von Artikeln aus Übersee freuten sich die Gäste, in diesen Läden neue exotische Gerichte und Getränke entdecken zu können.

Trader Vic's war eines der erfolgreichsten Händlerrestaurants in den USA. Es eröffnete Franchise-Lokale in vielen amerikanischen Städten und expandierte auch nach Europa und Asien. Es ist die einzige polynesische Restaurantkette, die den Untergang der Tiki-Kultur in den 1980er- und 1990er-Jahren überlebte. Vics urbane Inseln in Atlanta, London und München halten die ursprüngliche Atmosphäre romantischer Südseeabenteuer nach wie vor am Leben und servieren die bewährten Cocktails und Gerichte. Neueröffnungen wie zum Beispiel die in Portland, Oregon, beweisen, dass das Konzept mit Stil und Klasse auch ins 21. Jahrhundert übertragen werden kann.

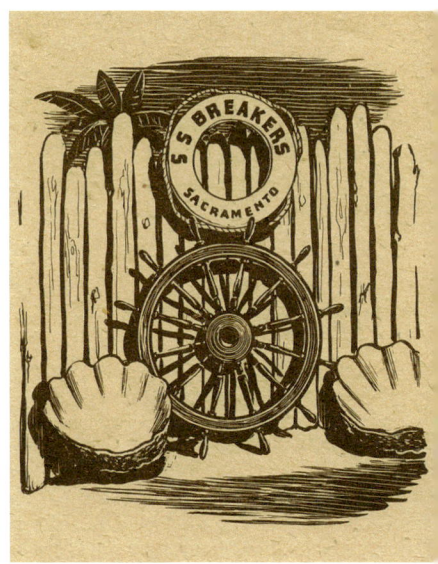

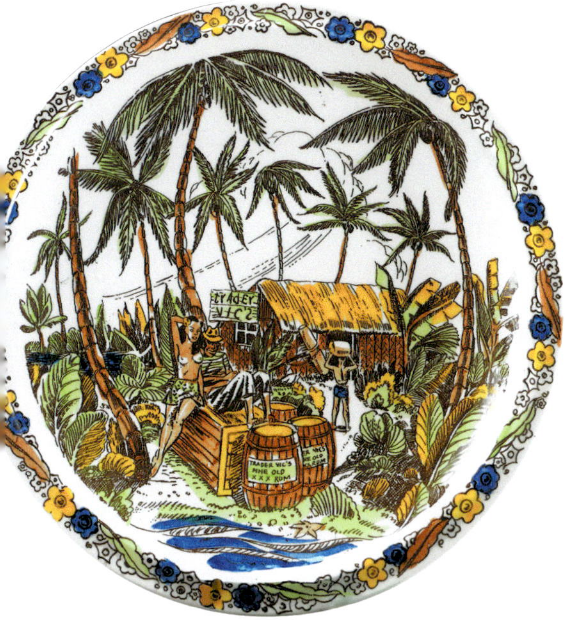

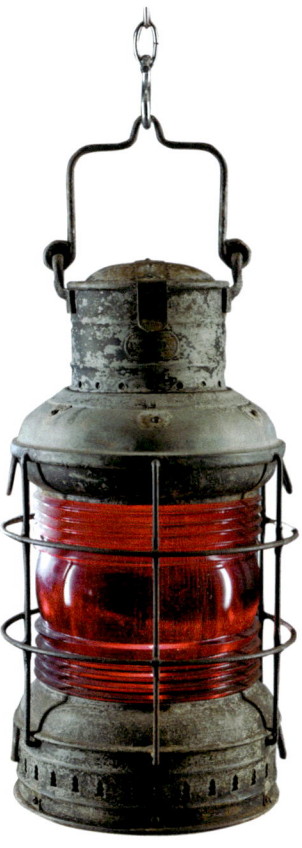

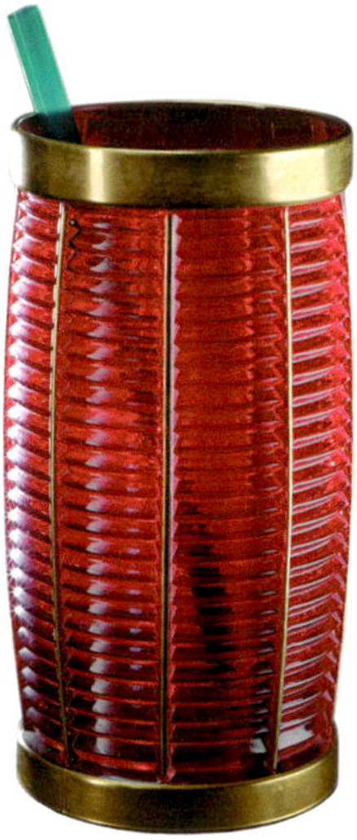

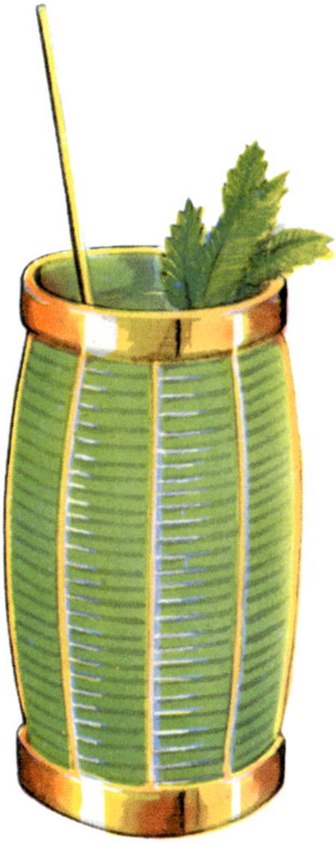

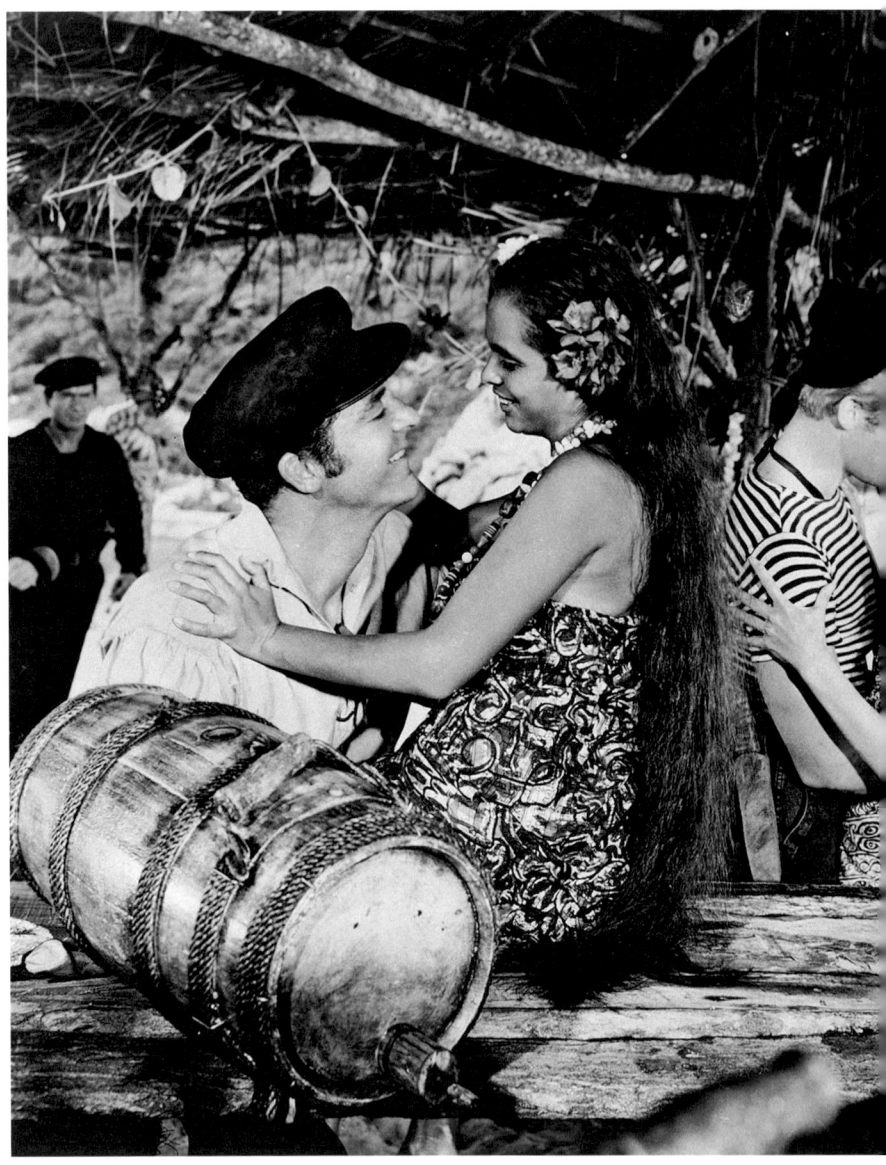

ABOVE: A scene from *Enchanted Island*, the 1958 film version of Herman Melville's *Typee*

OPPOSITE: Rum barrel mugs

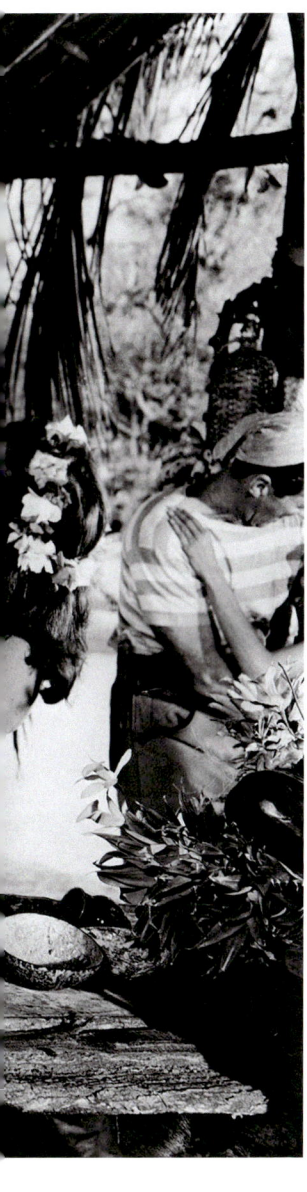

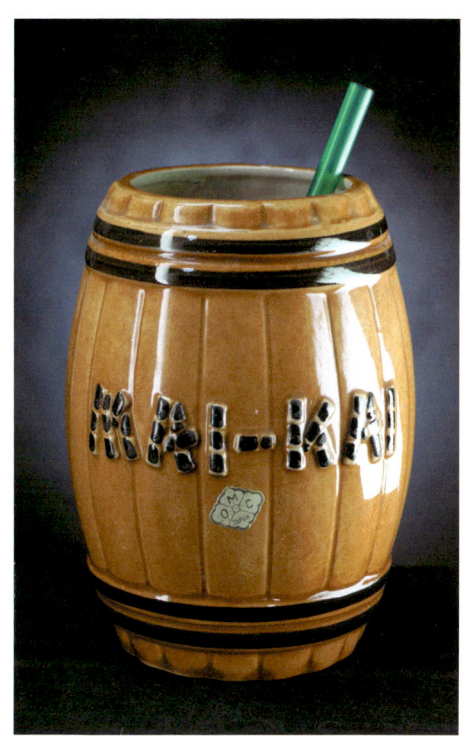

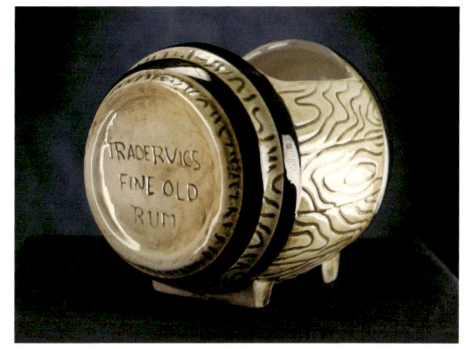

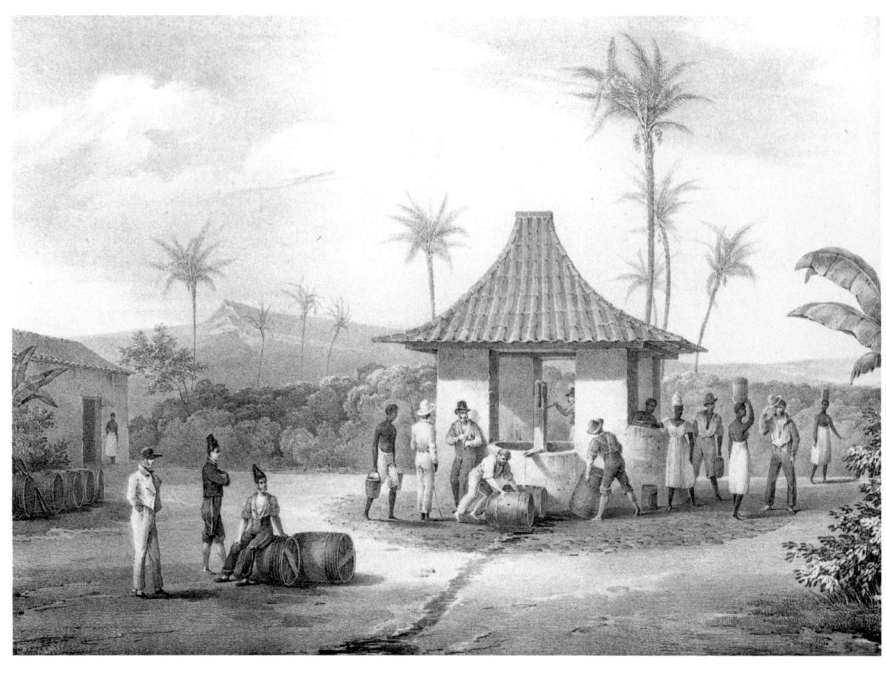

UN AUTRE PERSONNAGE MARQUANT de l'histoire avec les îles du Pacifique fut le négociant. À l'instar du batteur de grève, il s'était « converti en indigène », choisissant de laisser derrière lui la société moderne pour mener une existence insulaire. Contrairement à ce dernier, pourtant, le négociant n'est pas un amoureux du farniente vivant en autarcie, mais un intermédiaire industrieux entre les marins occidentaux et les populations autochtones des îles. Dans la culture populaire polynésienne il est représenté comme fin connaisseur des coutumes locales, gouvernant d'une main ferme son petit fief et faisant preuve de méfiance envers les Blancs dont il a quitté le monde. Nombre des caractéristiques qui ont popularisé la figure du négociant s'inspiraient de

la figure de David Dean O'Keefe, un immigrant irlandais en Amérique installé en 1873 sur l'île de Yap dont il fit une plaque tournante du commerce du coprah. *His Majesty O'Keefe*, l'ouvrage paru en 1952 qui relate sa vie aventureuse, débute par ce jugement de Cyprian A. B. Bridge, amiral en retraite de la Royal Navy : « Ceux qui croient que le batteur de grève ou le négociant de coprah des mers du Sud est nécessairement un gredin se trompent lourdement. »

Bien que le film de 1954 tiré du livre (film diffusé en France sous le titre *Le Roi des îles*) ait été partiellement tourné aux îles Fidji, il est l'exemple même d'une production hollywoodienne répondant aux attentes du public du milieu du siècle envers un film d'aventures dans les mers

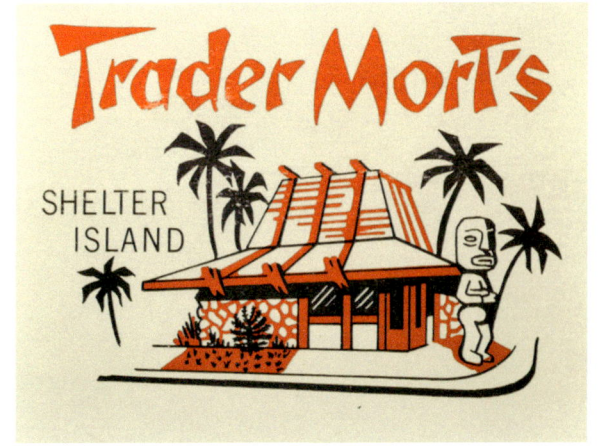

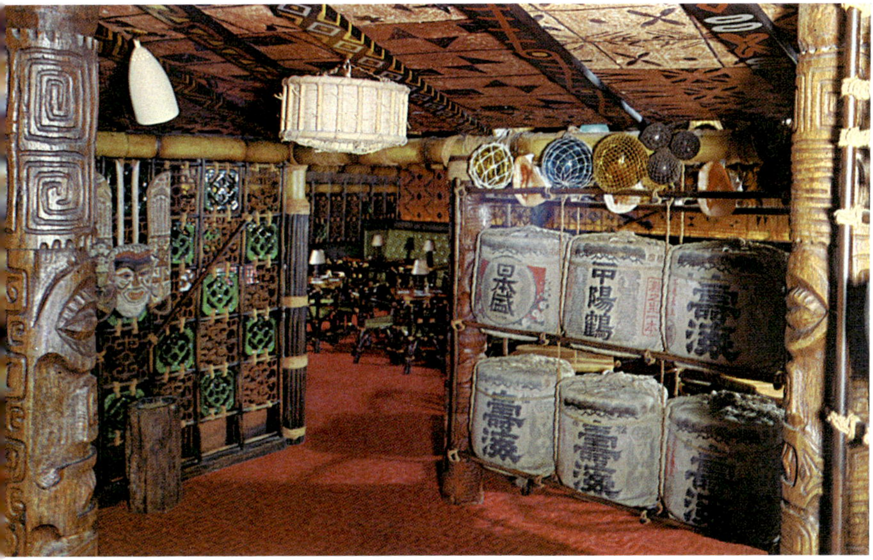

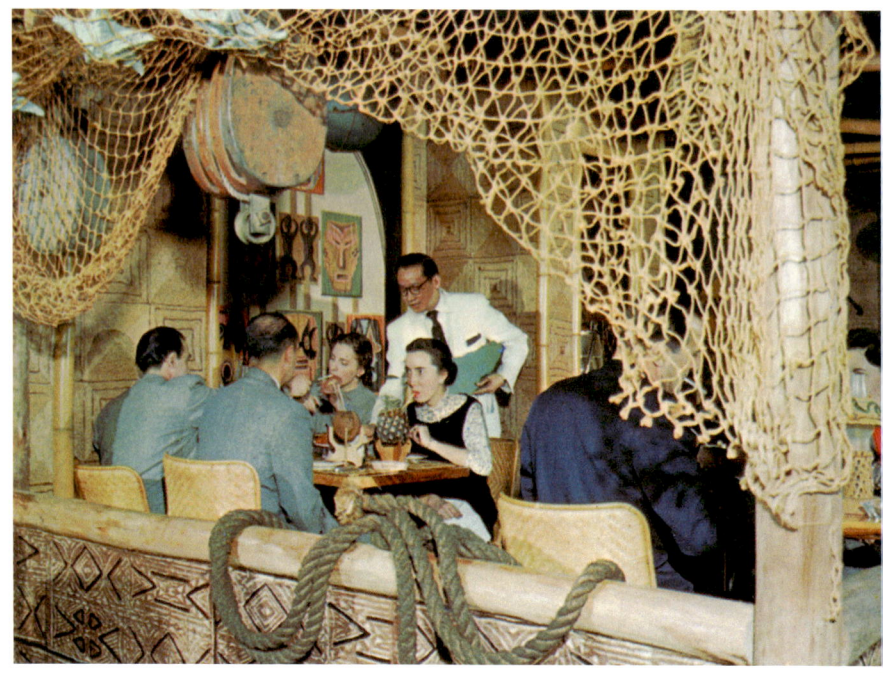

du Sud. Aucune enseigne de bar à cocktails n'a pourtant jamais repris son titre. L'industrie de la restauration polynésienne était en passe de trouver son authenticité propre avec une utilisation plus ironique des clichés des mers du Sud.

Le décor du restaurant Trader s'inspire du look Beachcomber en y mêlant une forte influence nautique. Les négociants comme O'Keefe expédiant leurs marchandises par bateau, tous les objets récupérés sur un vieux voilier se prêtaient idéalement à recréer l'atmosphère « sept mers » : ancres, fanaux, gouvernails en bois, poulies et cordages tressés étaient quelques-uns des accessoires utilisés pour la décoration intérieure de style Trader. Ces objets ont contribué à l'apparition d'une nouvelle variante du décor en bois flotté et textures tropicales qu'on retrouvera dans les bars tiki.

Autre accessoire important du bar Trader, le baril de rhum, le rhum étant le remontant de prédilection des marins comme des bars polynésiens. Tous les restaurants tropicaux dignes de ce nom se devaient de proposer leur mug maison en forme de tonneau, en général dévolu au cocktail « baril de rhum ». Les tonnelets de bois faisaient aussi office de tables ou pouvaient être suspendus dans des filets de pêche accrochés au

ABOVE: Ship's pulleys and other nautical décor at the Polynesian Village, Boston

OPPOSITE: The gift shop at the Beverly Hills Trader Vic's, 1955

plafond. On prenait soin de ne pas laisser ce décor dériver vers le genre « pirate », un thème entièrement différent appartenant aux Caraïbes.

L'accumulation de ces marchandises exotiques dans le restaurant créait une ambiance originale, informelle et alimentait les conversations. Pour tirer profit de leur image, Trader Vic's et d'autres lieux « Mers du Sud » installèrent d'ailleurs des boutiques de cadeaux dans leurs restaurants. Dans son Village Zombie, Skipper Kent proposait « toile *tapa*… perles en coquillages, colliers de fleurs hawaiiens, chemises hawaiiennes, épices, curiosités de marine à troquer ou à vendre ». Mais les principales marchandises à vendre restaient les comestibles.

En pénétrant dans la salle-entrepôt débordant de marchandises exotiques, le client savourait d'avance le dépaysement et les arômes surprenants des aliments et breuvages exotiques.

Trader Vic's est resté le plus populaire des restaurants Trader fondés aux États-Unis, multipliant les franchises dans de nombreuses villes américaines avec quelques incursions sur les rivages lointains d'Europe et d'Asie. C'est la seule chaîne de restaurants polynésiens qui a survécu à la disparition du style tiki dans les années 1980 et 1990. Les îlots urbains de Vic's à Atlanta, Londres et Munich ont su préserver l'atmosphère originale combinant amours et aventures dans les mers du Sud et servent toujours les cocktails et les plats de Vic qui ont fait leurs preuves. De nouvelles ouvertures récentes comme celle d'un restaurant à Portland (Oregon) prouvent que ce concept peut affronter les défis du XXIe siècle avec style et classe.

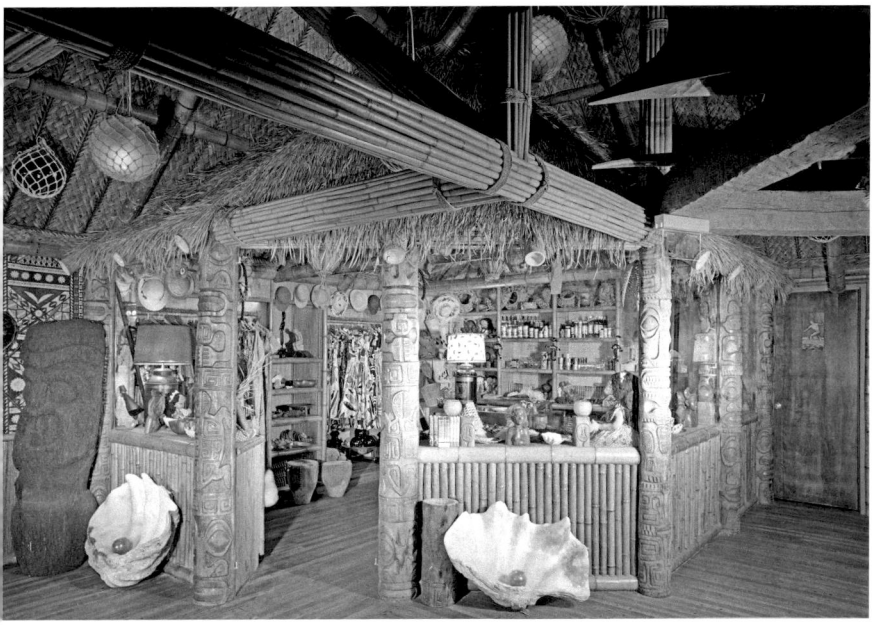

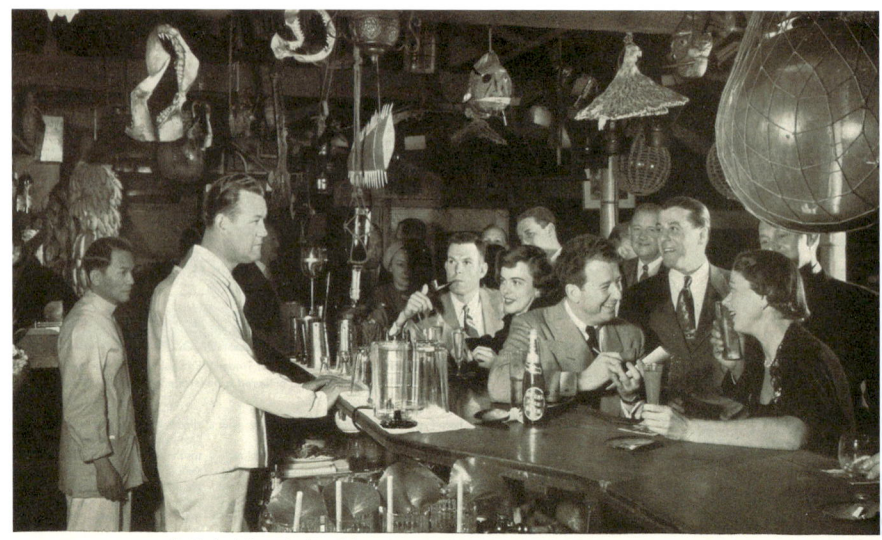

The Trader believes that lots of decoration causes lots of talk, and that lots of talk sells lots of drinks.

TRADER VIC'S

By Lucius Beebe { **A restaurant which offers hilarity, exotic food and drink blended with a remarkable atmosphere of adventure**

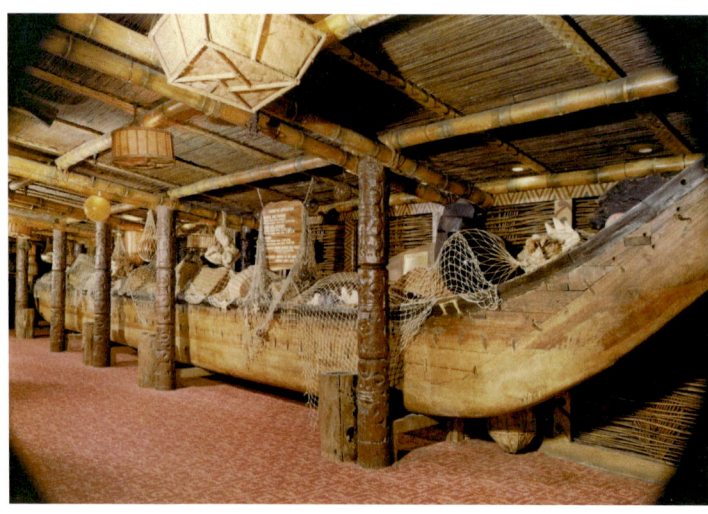

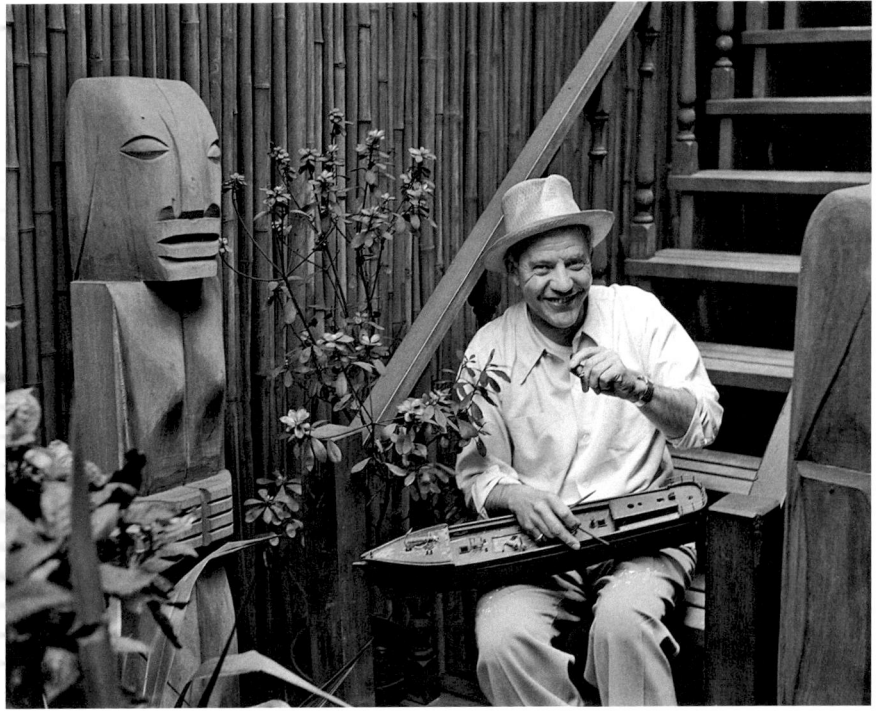

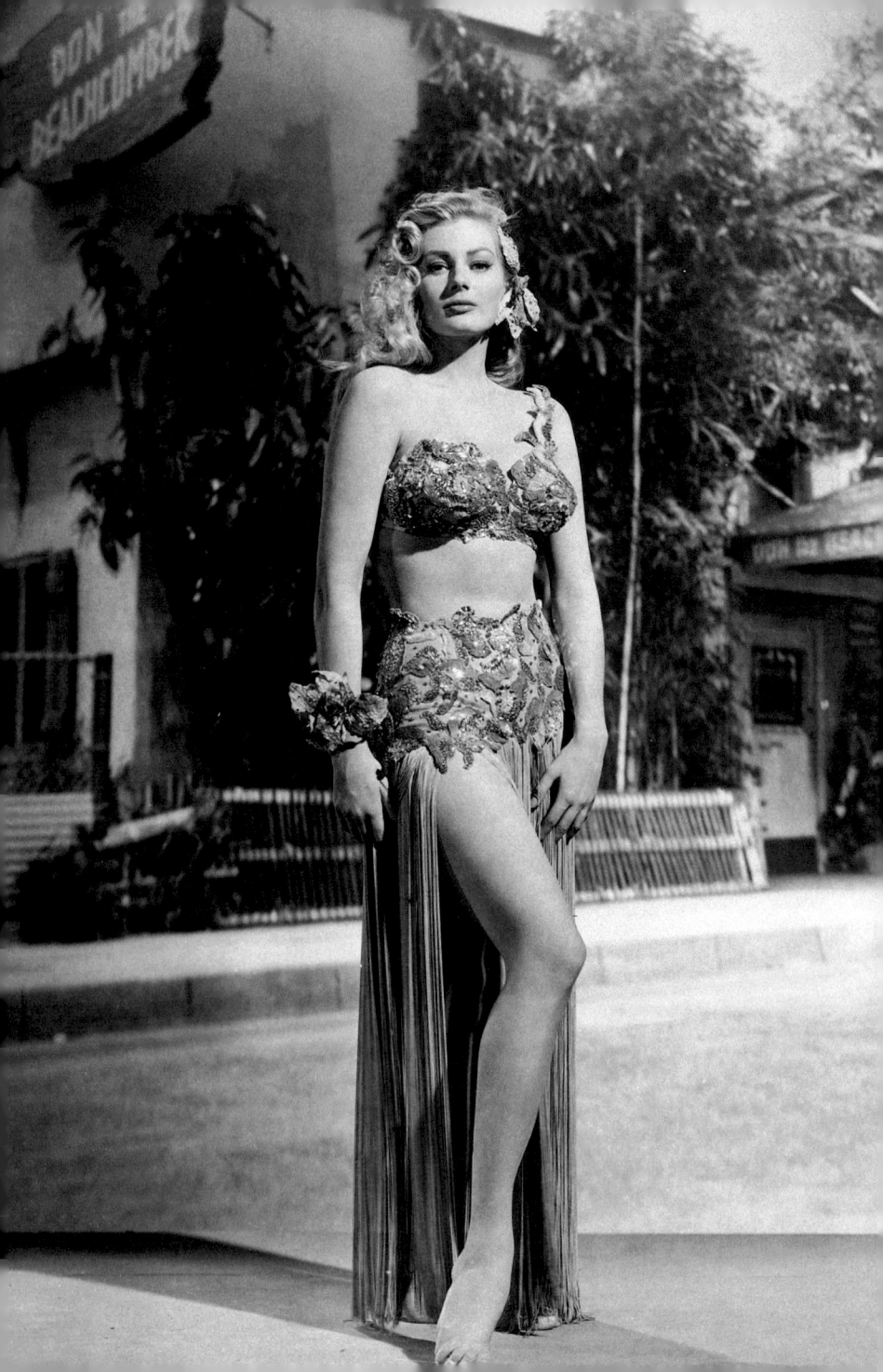

IO

MOVIE CLIENTELE
AND CELEBRITY CULTURE

FILMKUNDSCHAFT UND STARKULTUR
CLIENTÈLE DE STARS ET CULTURE DE LA CÉLÉBRITÉ

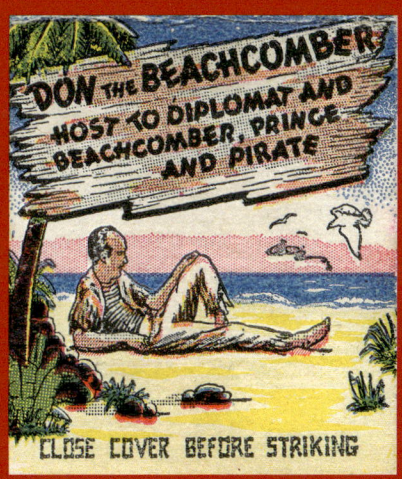

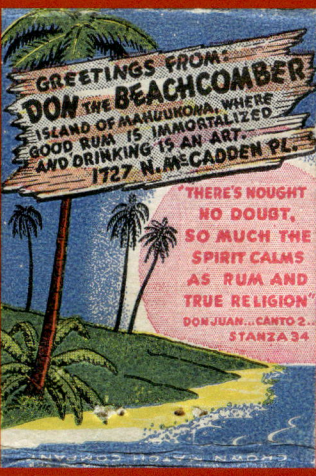

OPPOSITE: Anita Ekberg, the "bust" in *Hollywood or Bust*, 1956, posing in island attire in front of a Don the Beachcomber's backdrop, from the title sequence in the film *(Frank Brajevic Collection)*

ABOVE: An original matchbook touting Don's mottos

THE PRACTICE OF GETTING ONE'S

business endorsed by celebrity customers was not unheard of when Don the Beachcomber opened his Hollywood hideaway; but he elevated it to a new level. Don had become friendly with many members of the film community while working for the studios, and his little bar soon became the favorite nightspot for movie stars to go hang out. By the 1950s, it was so synonymous with "Hollywood," it was used in the title sequence of the Jerry Lewis / Dean Martin comedy *Hollywood or Bust*—on equal standing with such Hollywood icons as Grauman's Chinese Theater, the Beverly Hills Hotel, and the Brown Derby.

In time, Don bought himself a property next to Clark Gable's ranch in Encino, California. In his sizable tropical backyard he held lavish *luau* parties for his Hollywood friends. The media was always invited as an eager collaborator of the celebrity cult, and *Life* and *Look* magazines covered the affairs in double-page spreads. At that time, these glossy, oversized magazines reached every American household, exerting a formative influence on popular taste.

One of the famous gimmicks of the Hollywood Beachcomber was the installation of the "personal chopsticks" cabinet, where celebrities like Ava Gardner and Fred Astaire would keep their eating utensils in bamboo tubes marked with their names.

When Don returned from service in World War II, he found that his partner and ex-wife Sunny Sund had taken over the reins of the business. Never much of a stationary man, he decided to open a new Beachcomber in Hawaii, where he proceeded to innovate the hospitality business.

If anybody could measure up to Don in marketing Hollywood celebrity clientele, it was Harry "Sugie" Sugarman, proprietor of the Tropics nightclub in Beverly Hills. As the manager of Grauman's Chinese Theater, he had maintained the famous "Footprints of the Stars" in the theater's courtyard; and now he utilized the star power for his bar menu: Hollywood actors, framed in stars, were assigned to their favorite cocktails, which sported humorous names and descriptions.

In the early 1950s, Sugie became involved with the Hollywood Chamber of Commerce. While heading the Hollywood Improvement Association, he proposed the "Hollywood Walk of Fame": Based on his menu concept, actors' names were immortalized in star-shaped frames in the pavement of Hollywood Boulevard, giving tourists the experience of having arrived in Tinseltown.

Sugie opened a second Tropics in Hollywood proper, which also could boast an impressive roster of celebs among its regulars. Its interior of bamboo huts and faux palm trees conveyed the impression

Life article describing Don's "South Seas party." Note Stephen Crane, future owner of the Luau, and scandal starlet Lila Leeds as guests.

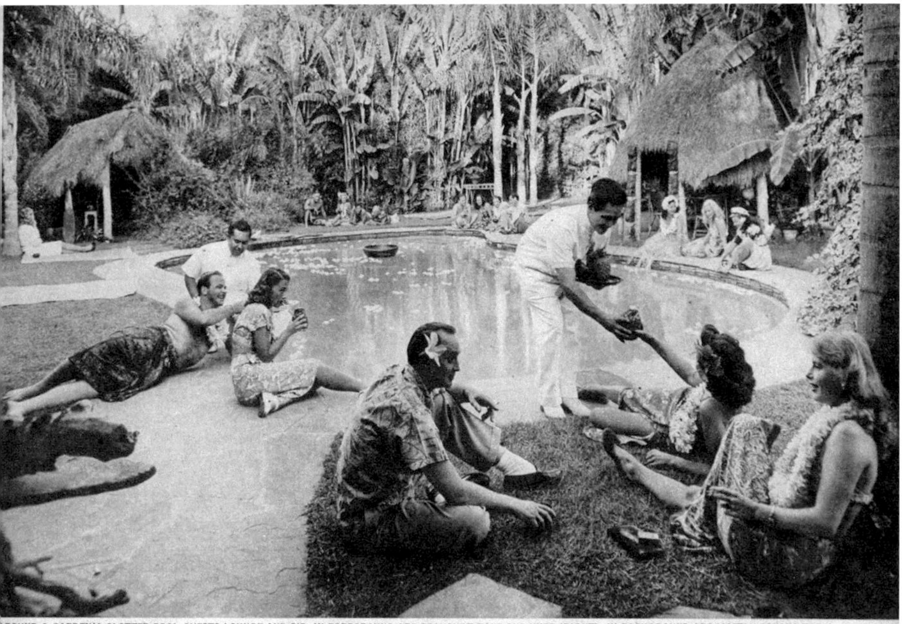

AROUND A GARDENIA-CLOTTED POOL GUESTS LOUNGE AND SIP. IN FOREGROUND ARE FRANCHOT TONE AND WIFE (RIGHT). IN BACKGROUND ARE MOSTLY BANANA TREES

Life Goes to a Hollywood South Seas Party

Movie stars enjoy a tropical dreamworld as they help a beautiful film executive celebrate her birthday

When guests arrived for Anita Colby's 32nd birthday party they walked into the favorite dreamworld of most civilized citizens, the South Seas. The party was given by a Hollywood character who calls himself Don Beach-Comber, at his one-acre plantation at Encino, near Hollywood. The guests lolled in sarongs and *pareus* (*above*) around a pool bordered by banana trees, palm trees, hibiscus and night-blooming jasmine. They sat cross-legged on the ground (*opposite page*) to eat suckling pig, salmon stuffed with coconut, baked bananas, papaya. They ate with their hands, drank out of hollowed pineapples and, to show their

pleasure with the food, they kissed the ear of a pig, as polite Samoans always do.

The host, whose real name is Don Richard Beaumont-Gantt, runs a Hollywood restaurant called The Beachcomber. On his single acre he has jammed as much South Seas scenery as he possibly could, enthusiastically mixing in a good deal of atmosphere from other parts of the Pacific. His party for Anita Colby, the former model who is now one of the movie industry's youngest, ablest and best-looking executives, was given two weeks after her birthday, but in the languorous South Seas atmosphere of the party this seemed time enough.

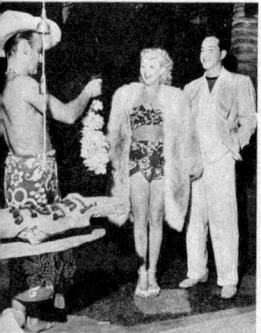

THE HOST (*left*) gives *leis* to guests. Lila Leeds came in native clothing and fur jacket, escorted by Stephen Crane.

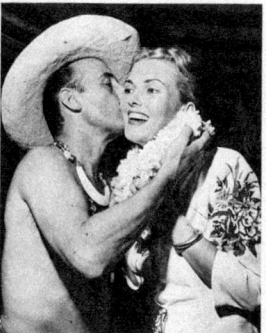

GUEST OF HONOR, Anita Colby, is given a welcoming buss by the host as he places a *lei* around her neck.

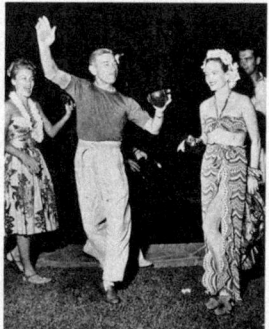

ENTERTAINERS are guests. Mike Romanoff does impromptu hula. Watching (*right*) is Mrs. Reginald Gardiner.

CONTINUED ON NEXT PAGE 135

MOVIE CLIENTELE AND CELEBRITY CULTURE

177

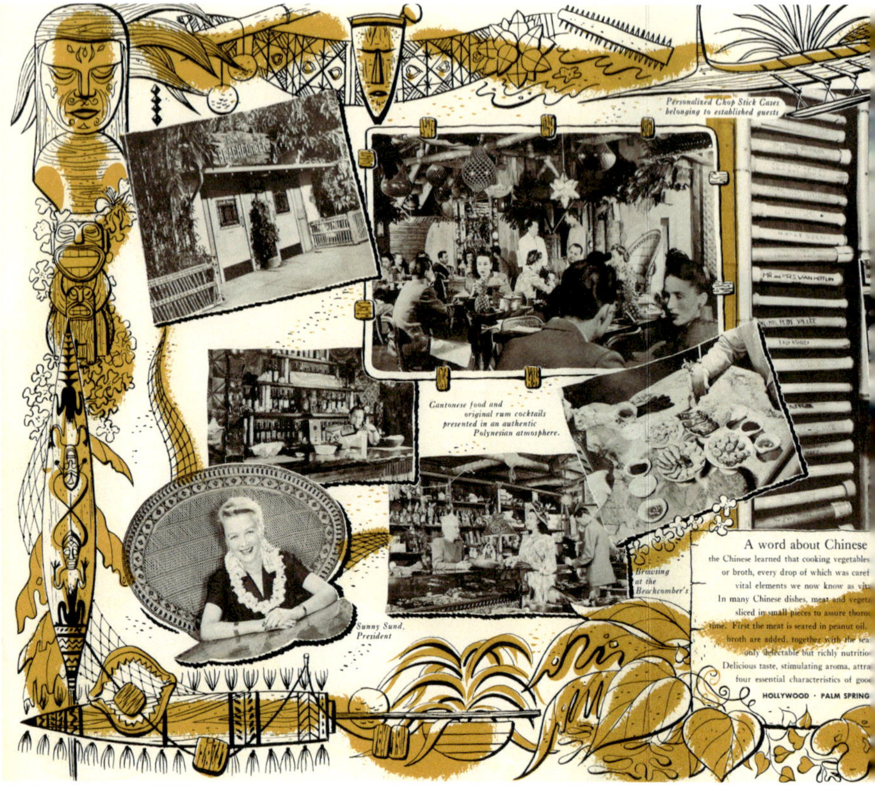

DON THE BEACHCOMBER
Personalized Chop Stick Cases belonging to established guests
MR and MRS VAN HEFLIN
Cantonese food and original rum cocktails presented in an authentic Polynesian atmosphere.
Sunny Sund, President
Browsing at the Beachcomber's
A word about Chinese
the Chinese learned that cooking vegetables
or broth, every drop of which was caref
vital elements we now know as
In many Chinese dishes, meat and
sliced in small pieces to assure
time. First the meat is seared in peanut oil.
broth are added, together with the
only delectable but richly
Delicious taste, stimulating aroma,
four essential characteristics of
HOLLYWOOD · PALM SPRING

ABOVE: Part of the Don the Beachcomber menu, showing the famous chopstick case
(Frank Brajevic Collection)

OPPOSITE: Leading man Gary Cooper (on right) with friends at Don's
(Vincent Jefferds Collection)

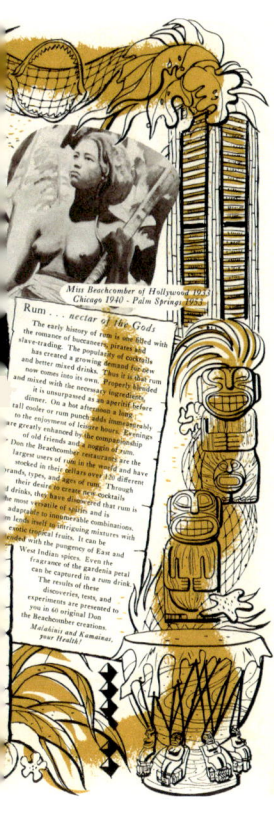

Miss Beachcomber of Hollywood 1939
Chicago 1940 - Palm Springs 1938

Rum . . . *nectar of the Gods*

The early history of rum is one filled with the romance of buccaneering, pirates and slave-trading. The popularity of cocktails has created a growing demand for new and better mixed drinks. Thus it is that rum now comes into its own. Properly blended and mixed with the necessary ingredients it is unsurpassed as an aperitif before dinner. On a hot afternoon immeasurably to the enjoyment of leisure hours. Evenings are greatly enhanced by the companionship of old friends and a noggin of rum.

Don the Beachcomber restaurants are the largest users of rum in the world and have stocked in their cellars over 150 different brands, types, and ages of rum. Through their desire to create new cocktails and drinks, they have discovered that rum is the most versatile of spirits and is adaptable to innumerable combinations. It lends itself so intriguing mixtures with exotic tropical fruits. It can be blended with the pungency of East and West Indian spices. Even the fragrance of the gardenia petal can be captured in a rum drink.

The results of these discoveries, tests, and experiments are presented to you in 60 original Don the Beachcomber creations.

Malakinis and Kamaina,
your Health!

of dining in a native village. Hollywood and Hawaii became so intertwined that the popular *Donna Parker* book series for girls illustrated a Hollywood-themed story with a poolside *luau*.

The "Home of the Stars" tradition of the Beverly Hills Tropics continued when actor Stephen Crane took over the business in the mid-1950s and renamed it the Luau. Known in town as a ladies' man, Crane took his commitment to the concept one step further and married Lana Turner, then at the height of her film career.

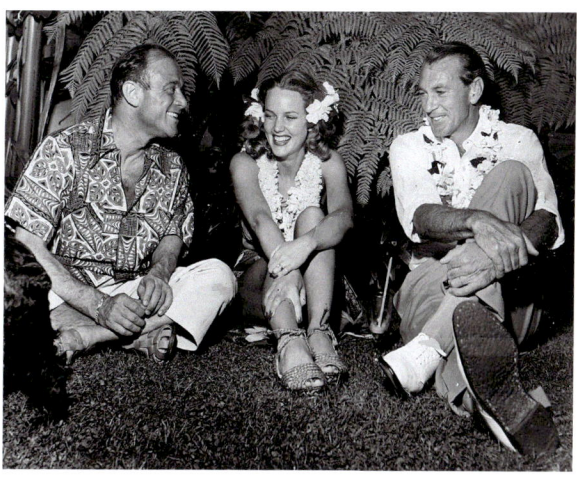

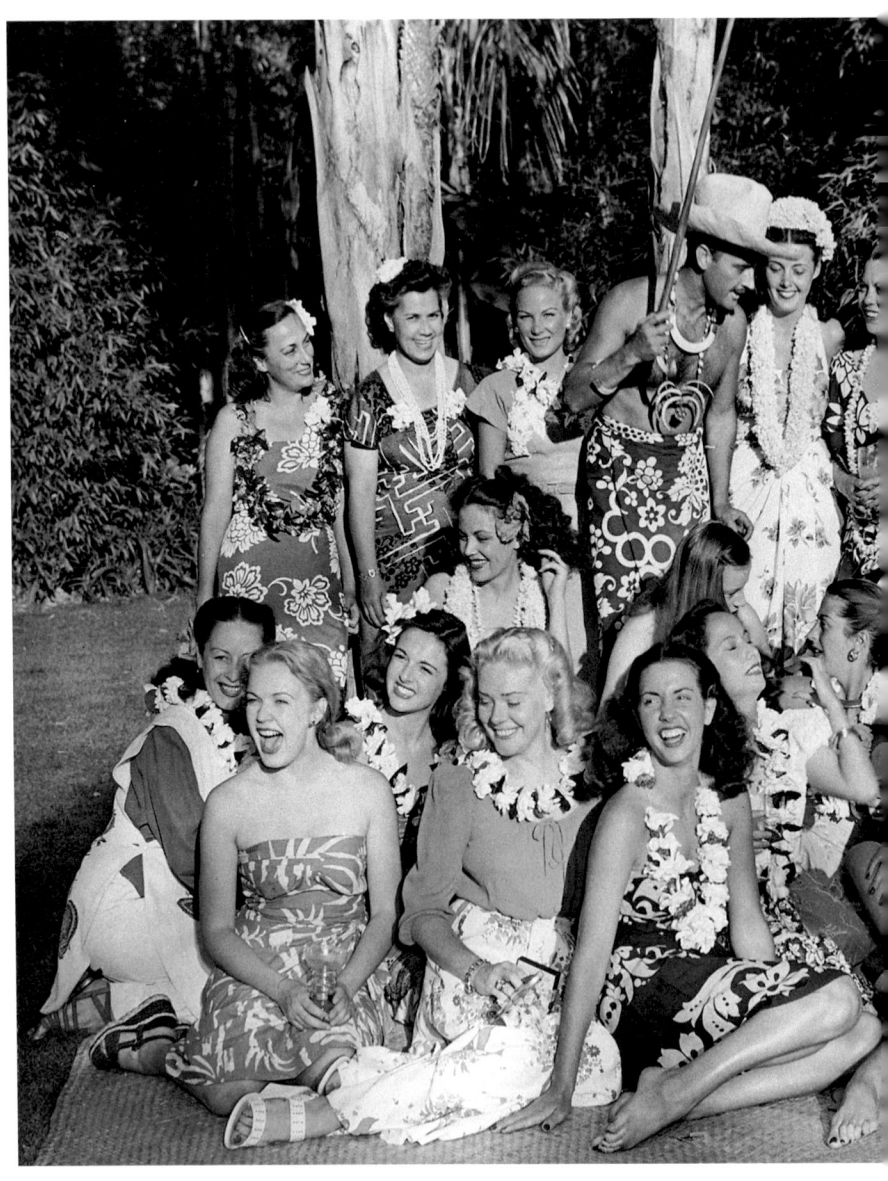

Don amid a flock of Hollywood
starlets at one of his backyard *luaus*
(Vincent Jefferds Collection)

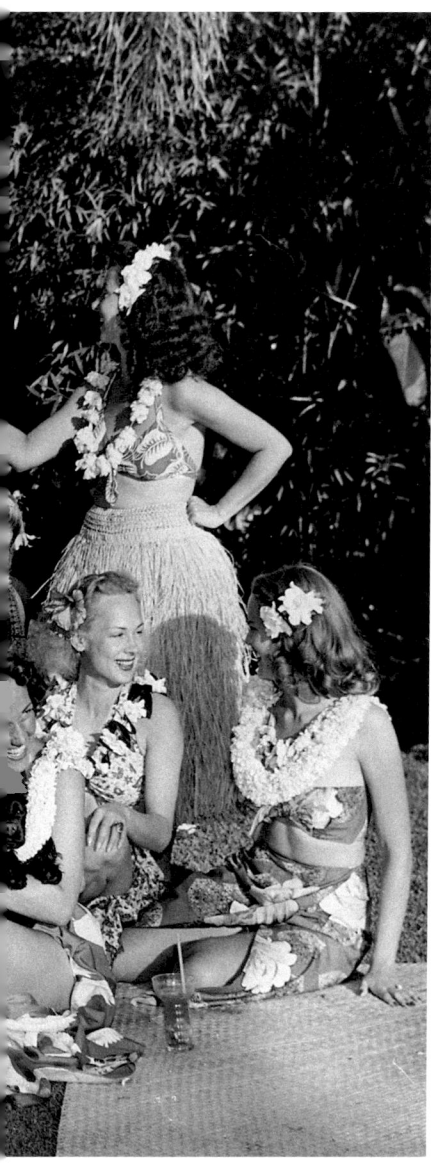

DASS LOKALBESITZER IHRE
Einrichtungen durch prominente Gäste
aufwerten ließen, war nichts Neues. Doch
als Don the Beachcomber seine Hollywood-
Insel eröffnete, hob er diese Praxis auf ein
neues Level. Don hatte sich während seiner
Zusammenarbeit mit den Studios mit vielen
Mitgliedern der Filmszene angefreundet.
Seine kleine Bar wurde bald zur Lieblings-
kneipe vieler Filmstars und in den 1950er-
Jahren war sie gleichsam ein Synonym für
Hollywood selbst. Sie war im Vorspann von
Jerry Lewis' und Dean Martins Komödie
Hollywood or Bust (dt. Titel: *Alles um Anita*)
zu sehen und rangierte gleichauf mit be-
rühmten Hollywood-Etablissements wie
Grauman's Chinese Theater, dem Beverly
Hills Hotel und dem Brown Derby.

Irgendwann kaufte sich Don ein Grundstück neben Clark Gables Ranch im kalifornischen Encino. In seinem großzügigen
Garten veranstaltete er üppige Luau-Partys
für seine Hollywood-Freunde. Die Medien
waren stets eingeladen, um den Promikult
weiter zu befeuern. Die Magazine *Life* und
Look berichteten regelmäßig darüber. Zu
dieser Zeit erreichten diese Hochglanzma-
gazine nahezu jeden Haushalt in den USA
und trugen so maßgeblich zur Definition
des „guten Geschmacks" bei.

Ein berühmtes Kuriosum des Hollywood-
Beachcomber war ein Schrank für „persönliche Essstäbchen", in dem Stars wie Ava
Gardner und Fred Astaire ihre Essutensilien
in Bambusröhrchen verwahrten.

Als Don von seinem Einsatz im Zweiten
Weltkrieg zurückkehrte, stellte er fest, dass
seine Partnerin und Ex-Frau Sunny Sund
die Zügel in die Hand genommen hatte.
Don war nie ein sonderlich sesshafter Typ
gewesen und so beschloss er, eine neue
Beachcomber-Bar auf Hawaii zu eröffnen.

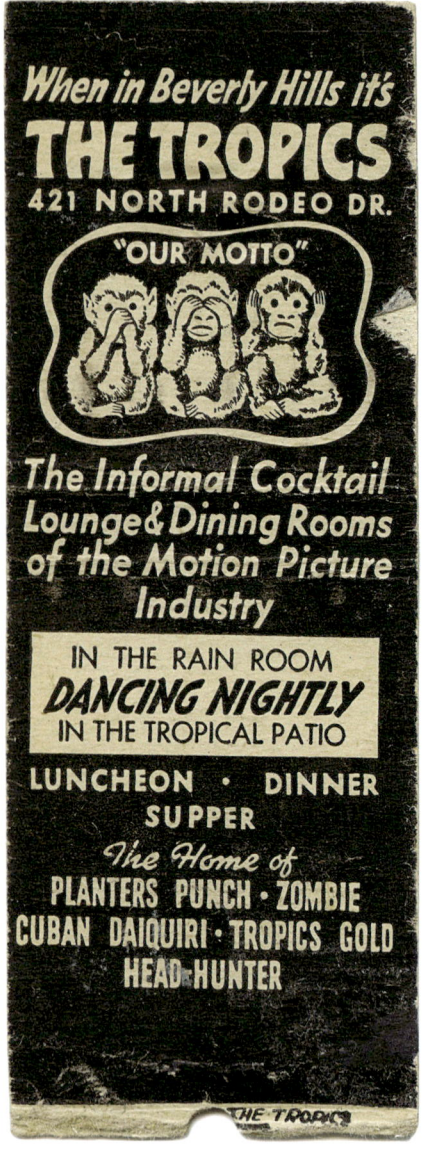

Von hier aus sollte er das Gastgewerbe weiter revolutionieren.

Falls es jemanden gab, der Don in der Vermarktung prominenter Hollywood-Gäste übertreffen konnte, dann war es Harry „Sugie" Sugarman, Besitzer des Nachtclubs The Tropics in Beverly Hills. Als Manager des Grauman's Chinese Theater hatte er die berühmten Fußabdrücke der Stars im Innenhof des Kinos instand gehalten. Jetzt machte er sich den Einfluss der Prominenz auf der Cocktailkarte seiner Bar zunutze. In Sternform wiedergegebene Porträts von Hollywood-Schauspielern waren hier neben ihrem Lieblingsgetränk mit humorvollem Namen und lustiger Beschreibung abgebildet.

In den frühen 1950er-Jahren begann Sugie, sich in Hollywoods Handelskammer zu engagieren. Als Leiter der Hollywood Improvement Association schlug er den „Walk of Fame" vor: Basierend auf dem Konzept seiner Getränkekarte werden die Namen der Schauspieler in sternförmigen Rahmen im Bürgersteig des Hollywood Boulevard verewigt und zeigen den Touristen so überdeutlich, dass sie in der Traumfabrik angekommen sind.

Sugie eröffnete ein zweites Tropics in Hollywood, das ebenfalls mit beeinruckend vielen Stars unter seinen Stammgästen aufwarten konnte. Die Bambushütten und falschen Palmen im Innern ließen die Gäste glauben, in einem polynesichen Dorf zu speisen. Hollywood und Hawaii waren so eng aneinander gekoppelt, dass in der berühmten Mädchenbuchreihe *Donna Parker* in einer Geschichte zum Thema

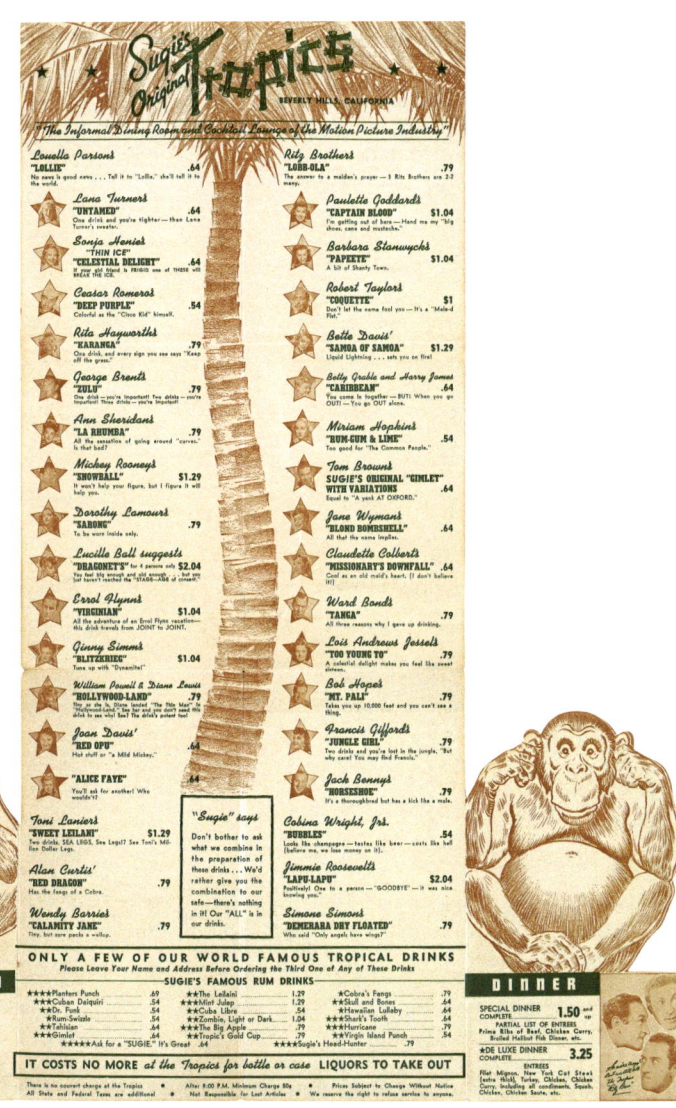

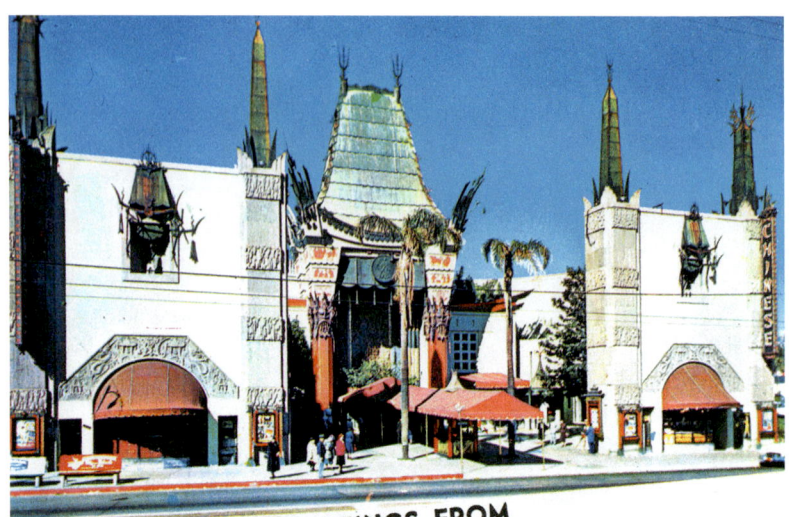

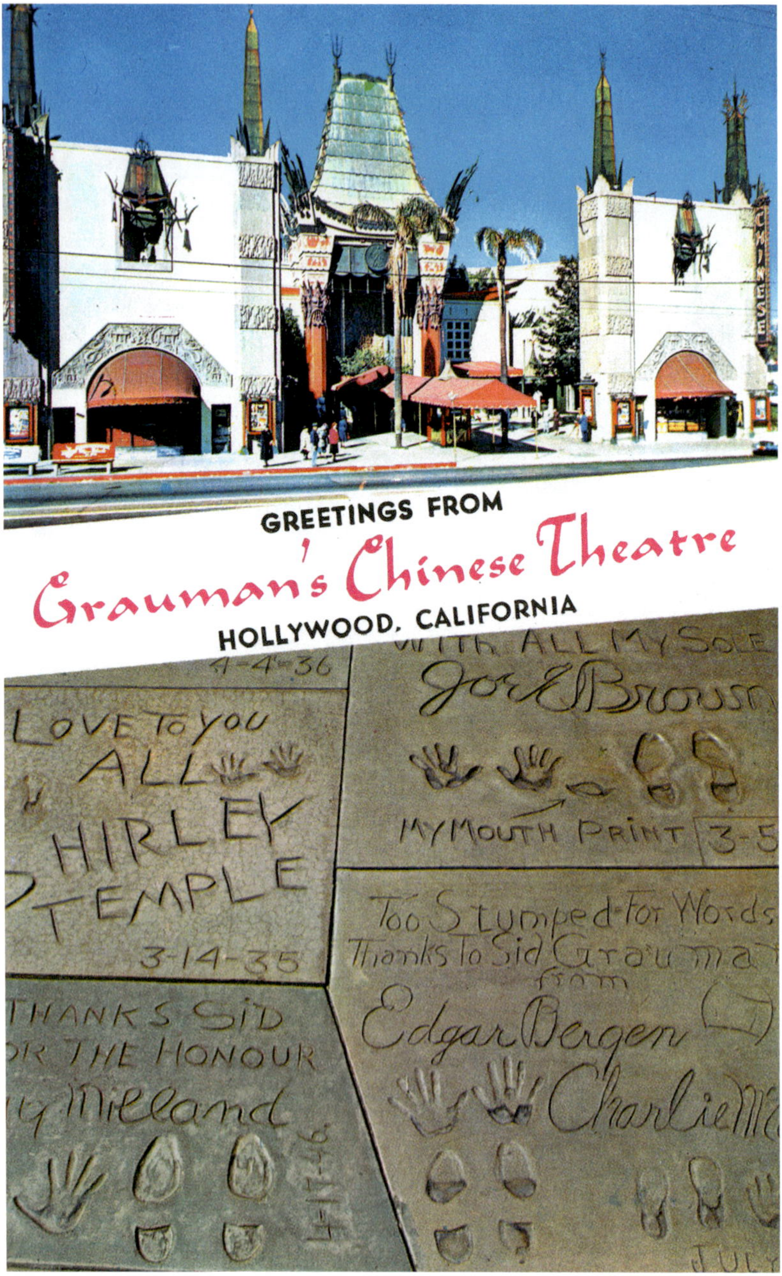

GREETINGS FROM

Grauman's Chinese Theatre

HOLLYWOOD, CALIFORNIA

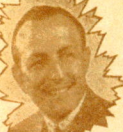
Hollywood auf dem Umschlag auch eine Luau am Pool dargestellt wurde.

Das Tropics blieb auch dann noch das „Zuhause der Stars", als Stephen Crane das Geschäft Mitte der 1950er-Jahre übernahm und das Lokal in The Luau umbenannte. Als stadtbekannter Frauenheld war Crane dem Konzept sogar so weit verpflichtet, dass er Lana Turner, damals auf dem Höhepunkt ihrer Filmkarriere, geheiratet hatte.

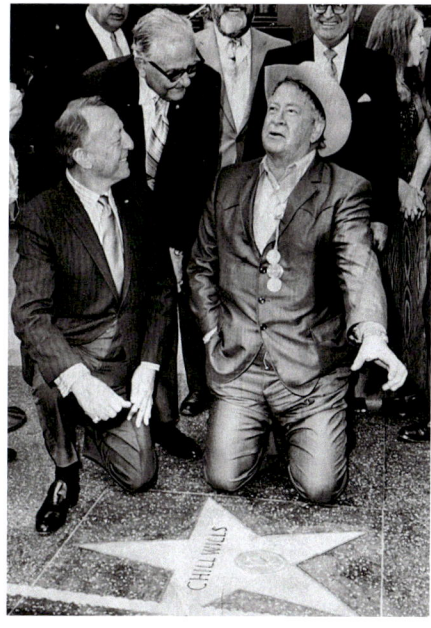

OPPOSITE: Movie theaters were among the earliest users of exotic architecture

ABOVE: Sugie was a showman with flourish

RIGHT: Sugie (at left) at the star-unveiling ceremony of actor Chill Wills

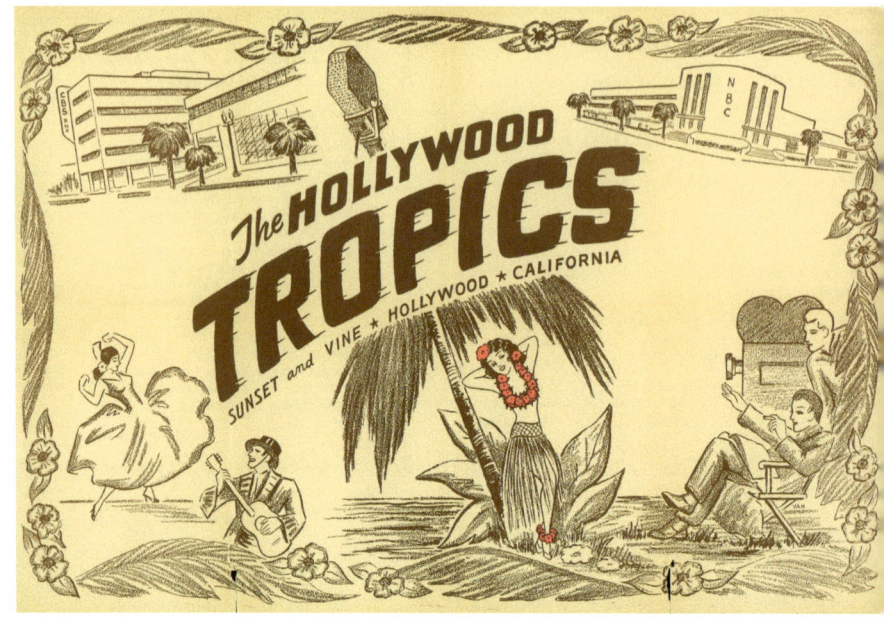

L'HABITUDE CONSISTANT À
valoriser son affaire en obtenant la bénédic-
tion de clients célèbres n'était pas inédite
quand Don the Beachcomber ouvrit son
refuge hollywoodien. Mais il sut lui donner
une nouvelle dimension. Don avait sym-
pathisé avec de nombreux professionnels
du cinéma lorsqu'il travaillait pour les
studios, et son petit bar devint bientôt le
QG des stars en mal de sorties nocturnes.
Dans les années 1950, son lieu était si
associé à « Hollywood » qu'il apparaît
dans la bande-annonce de la comédie
Un vrai cinglé de cinéma avec Jerry Lewis
et Dean Martin, sur un pied d'égalité avec
des icônes de Hollywood, tels le Théâtre
chinois de Grauman, le Beverly Hills Hotel
ou le Brown Derby.

Don fit bientôt l'acquisition d'une propriété jouxtant le ranch de Clark Gable à
Encino (Californie). Dans son imposant
jardin tropical, il donnait des fêtes somp-
tueuses pour ses amis de Hollywood. Il ne
manquait jamais d'inviter aussi les médias,
fervents adeptes du culte de la célébrité.
Les magazines *Life* et *Look* rendaient compte
de ces fêtes sur de spectaculaires doubles
pages. À l'époque, on trouvait ces magazines grand format sur papier glacé dans
tous les foyers américains et ils exerçaient
une grande influence sur le goût du public.

L'une des trouvailles célèbres du
Hollywood Beachcomber consista dans
l'installation d'un « casier à baguettes
personnelles » où des vedettes comme
Ava Gardner et Fred Astaire rangeaient
leurs couverts dans des tubes de bambou
marqués à leur nom. Quand Don revint
de la Seconde Guerre mondiale où il avait
servi comme soldat, il découvrit que son

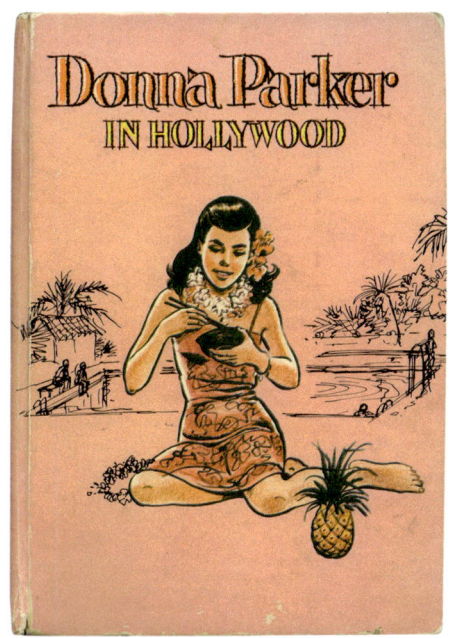

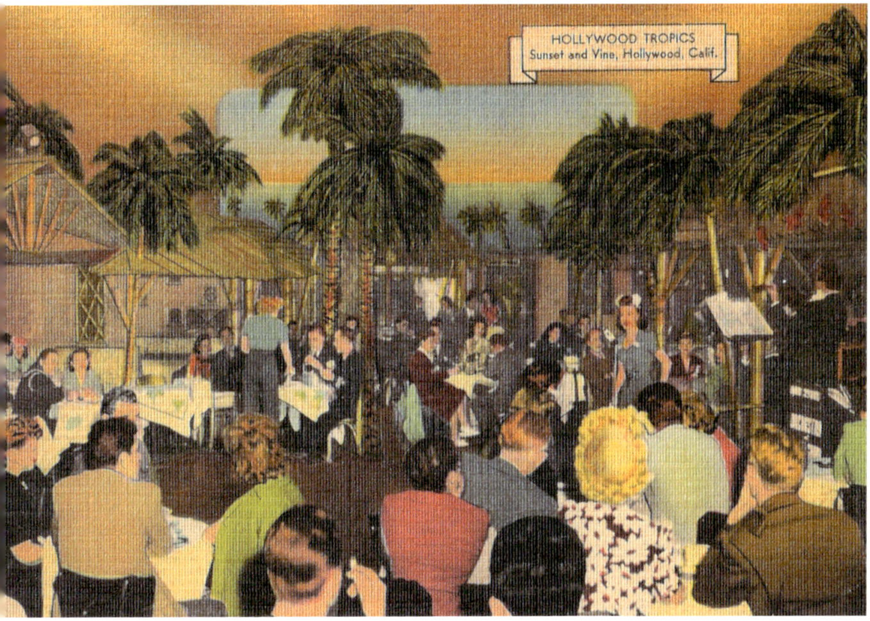

ex-femme et associée Sunny Sund avait repris les rênes de l'affaire. Peu enclin à végéter, il décida alors d'ouvrir un nouveau Beachcomber à Hawaii où il lança de nouveaux concepts d'hôtels.

Si un personnage rivalisa avec Don dans la gestion marketing de sa clientèle célèbre, ce fut sans aucun doute Harry « Sugie » Sugarman, propriétaire du night-club The Tropics à Beverly Hills. Ex-directeur du Théâtre chinois de Grauman, c'est lui qui avait pris l'initiative d'immortaliser les empreintes de pieds des stars dans la cour du théâtre. Désormais c'est pour orner sa carte qu'il utilise leur prestige : les acteurs hollywoodiens y apparaissent dans des étoiles accolées à leurs cocktails préférés, aux noms et aux descriptions humoristiques.

Au début des années 1950, Sugie s'associe avec la Chambre de commerce de Hollywood. À la tête de la Hollywood Improvement Association, il invente le « Hollywood Walk of Fame » qui s'inspire du concept de sa carte : les noms des acteurs sont désormais gravés dans les étoiles qui parsèment le trottoir du Hollywood Boulevard, signalant aux touristes qu'ils sont bien arrivés à « Tinseltown ».

Sugie ouvre à Hollywood même un deuxième Tropics qui peut lui aussi arborer fièrement une liste de clients réguliers célèbres. Son décor de huttes en bambou et de faux palmiers donne au client l'impression de dîner dans un village indigène. Hollywood et Hawaii se confondent désormais si étroitement que *Donna Parker*, la série populaire de livres pour adolescentes, illustrera l'une de ses histoires sur Hollywood avec un *luau* (fête hawaiienne) donné au bord d'une piscine.

La tradition qui a fait du Tropics de Beverly Hills le « QG des stars » se perpétue au milieu des années 1950 avec la reprise par l'acteur Stephen Crane du bar qu'il rebaptise The Luau. Connu comme séducteur impénitent, Crane rehaussera d'un cran son idolâtrie en épousant la belle Lana Turner, alors à l'apogée de sa carrière d'actrice.

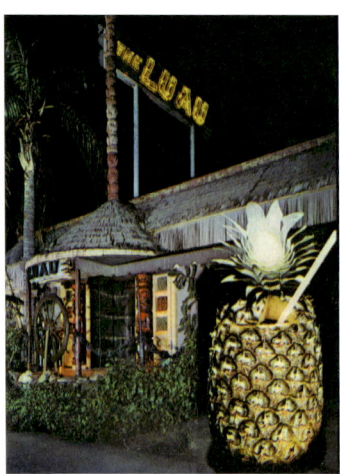
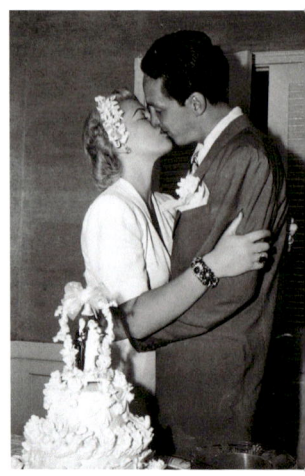

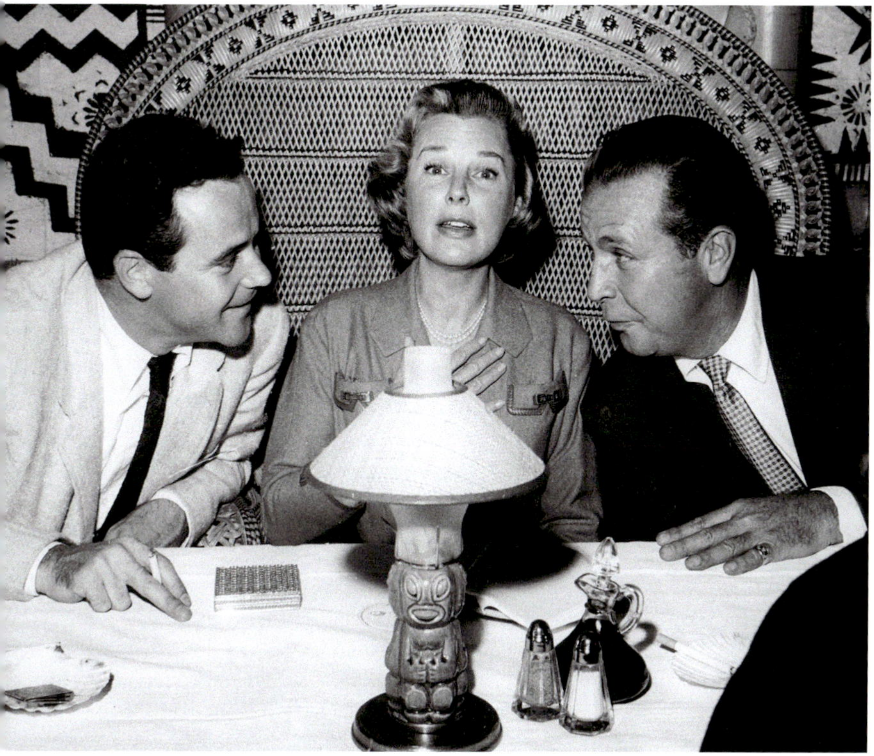

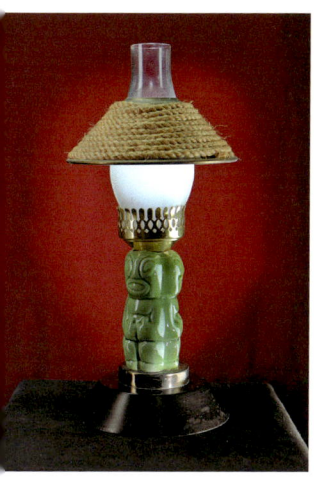

OPPOSITE LEFT: The Luau, formerly the Tropics

OPPOSITE RIGHT: Stephen Crane and Lana Turner exchange their wedding kiss

ABOVE: Actor Jack Lemmon with June Allyson and Dick Powell at the Luau

LEFT: Tiki table lamp from the Luau *(Frank Brajevic Collection)*. The changeover from "Tropics" to "Luau" marked the appearance of Tiki style

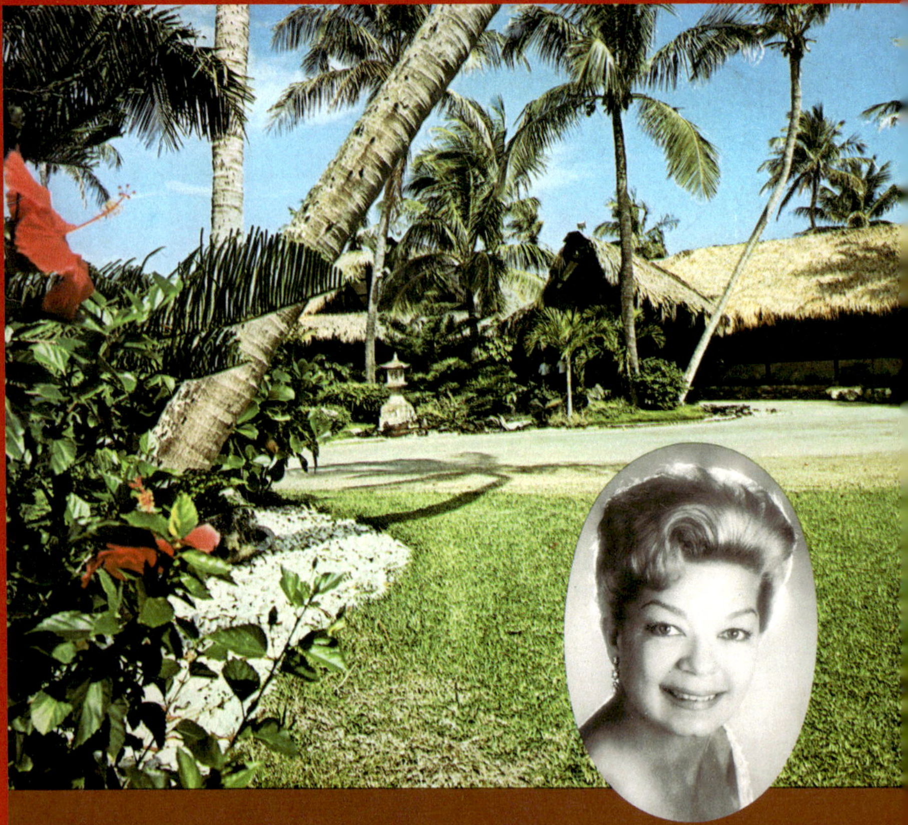

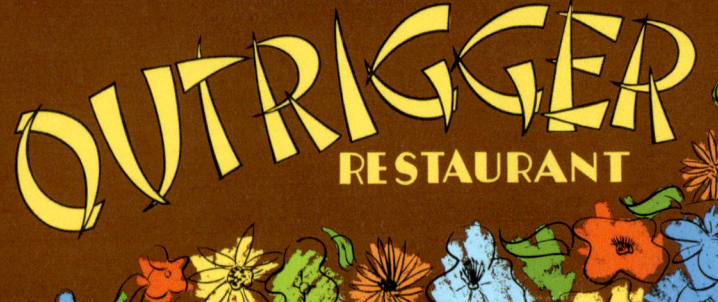

FRANCES LANGFORD'S

OUTRIGGER
RESTAURANT

JENSEN BEACH, FLORIDA

II

FRANCES LANGFORD: THE BAMBOO BLONDE

FRANCES LANGFORD: DIE BAMBUS-BLONDINE
FRANCES LANGFORD : LA BLONDE BAMBOU

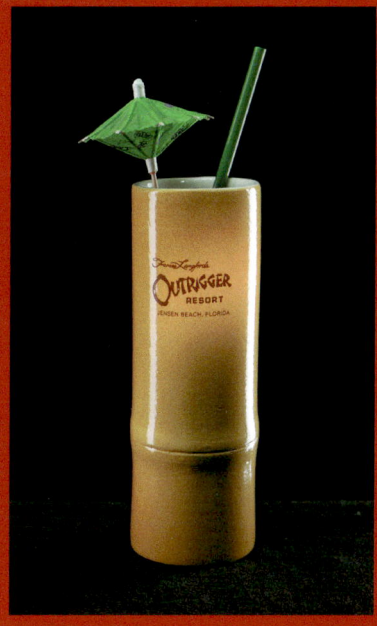

OPPOSITE: Frances on the menu cover of her restaurant
(Geoff Sundstrom Collection)

ABOVE: Ceramic bamboo mug from the Outrigger

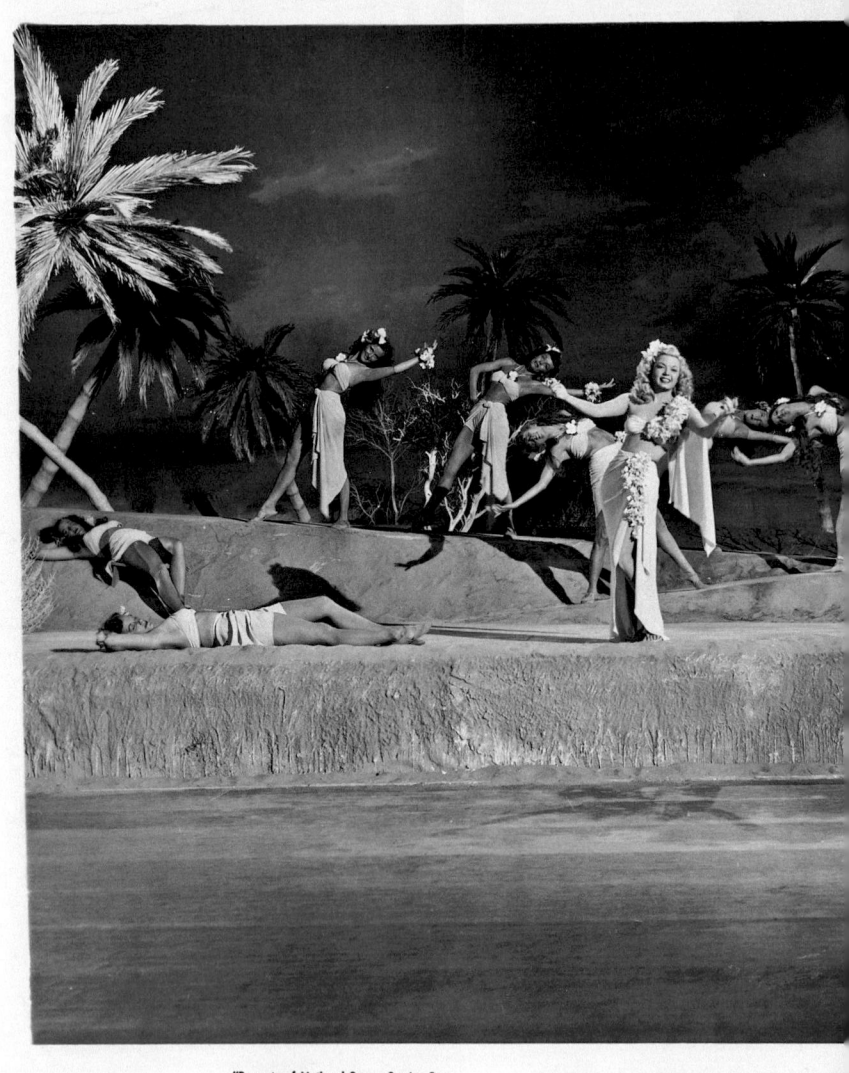

"Property of National Screen Service Corp. Licensed for display only in connection with the exhibition of this picture at your theatre. Must be returned immediately thereafter."

"THE BAMBOO BLOND
An RKO Radio Picture

ABOVE: The South Seas, classic Hollywood style. "The Bamboo Blonde" became Langford's popular handle

OPPOSITE: In 1946, Langford played a nightclub singer whose portrait becomes a pin-up on a bomber plane

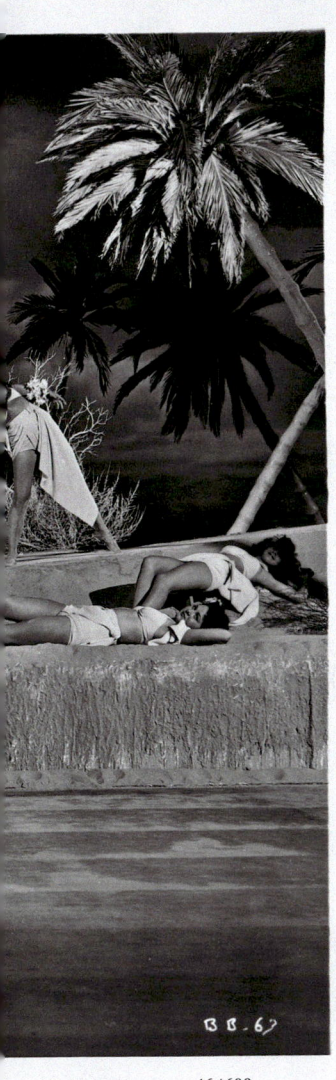

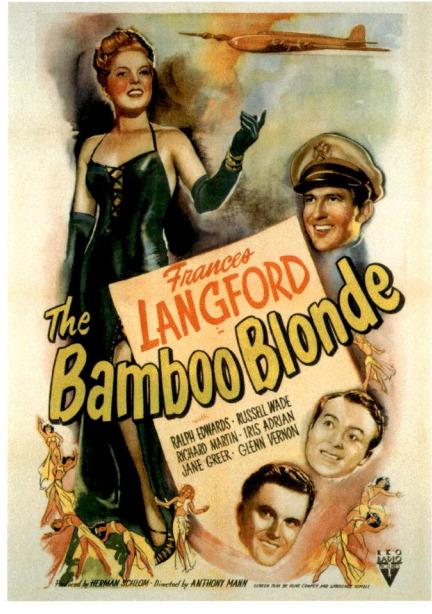

IT IS HARD TO IMAGINE ANY ONE

personality whose life and career reflected America's 20th-century romance with Polynesia and Hollywood better than singer and actress Frances Langford. She recorded Hawaiian songs with Dick McIntire in the 1930s. She was married to South Seas movie star Jon Hall. She entertained the U.S. troops in the Pacific in the 1940s and eventually opened her own Polynesian restaurant in Florida in the early 1960s.

Before television became the center of home entertainment, there was the radio. Trained as an opera singer, the talented Frances Langford was discovered by singing superstar Rudy Vallee in the early 1930s, and she became a radio performer. She moved to California, where she appeared on Louella Parsons's radio show *Hollywood Hotel* before making her first film, *The Subway Symphony* (1932).

Some 30 movies followed, in most of which she sang, often appearing as herself. In 1938, she married Jon Hall, who became the quintessential South Seas movie hunk with his success in John Ford's *The Hurricane* (1937). Hall was the offspring of a Swiss actor and a Tahitian royal, and the nephew of South Seas author James Norman Hall. Having been raised in Tahiti, Hall liked tropical environs, and the couple bought property in Jensen Beach, Florida.

In the early '40s, Frances Langford worked on Bob Hope's radio show, and in 1943 she joined his troupe to tour Army bases in Europe and the Pacific. The appreciation she received from the homesick,

women-less G.I. audiences led her to continue to work for the USO for the rest of her life, which earned her the moniker "Darling of the Fighting Fronts." After the war she wrote a newspaper column called "Purple Heart Diary," helping the cause of World War II veterans. She reenacted her wartime experiences in the 1951 film of the same name.

After her long Hollywood career faded, Langford remarried a wealthy businessman and opened a Polynesian resort on her Florida property. Across from where her husband's yacht, the *Chanticleer*, was docked, Don the Beachcomber restaurant designer Ed Lawrence built her the

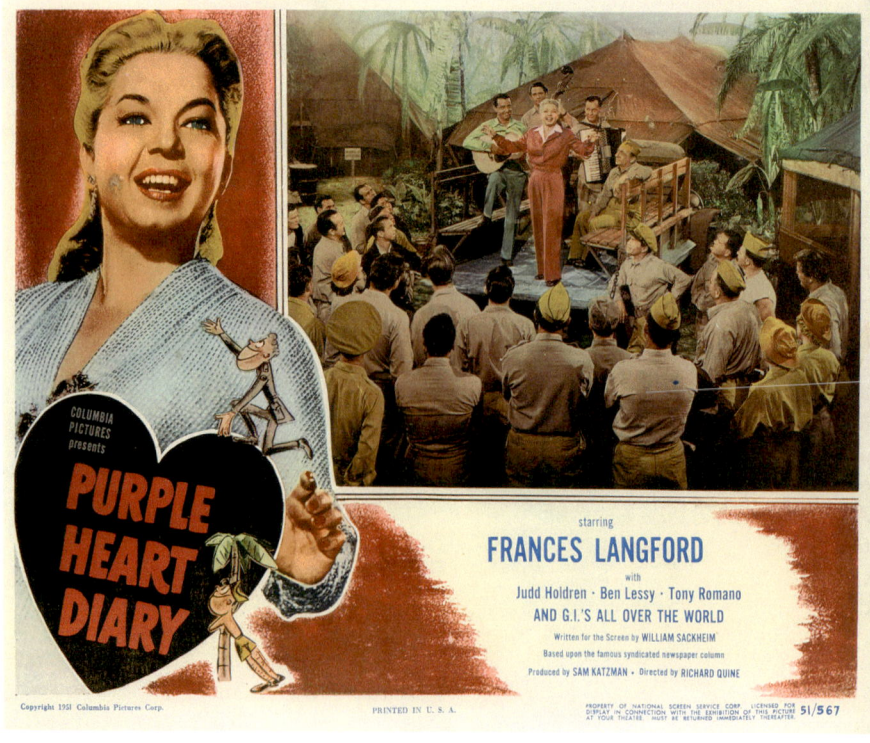

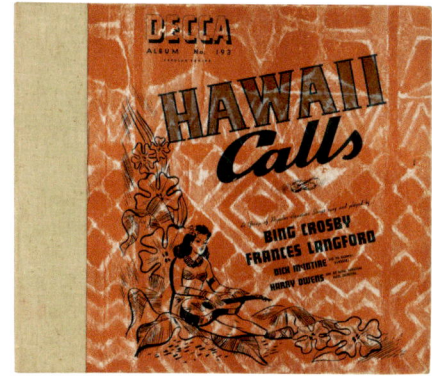

romantic Outrigger Restaurant and rental cottages, which opened in 1961. Here Frances performed well into the 1980s. After she passed away at age 92, the restaurant lost its Polynesian look and name.

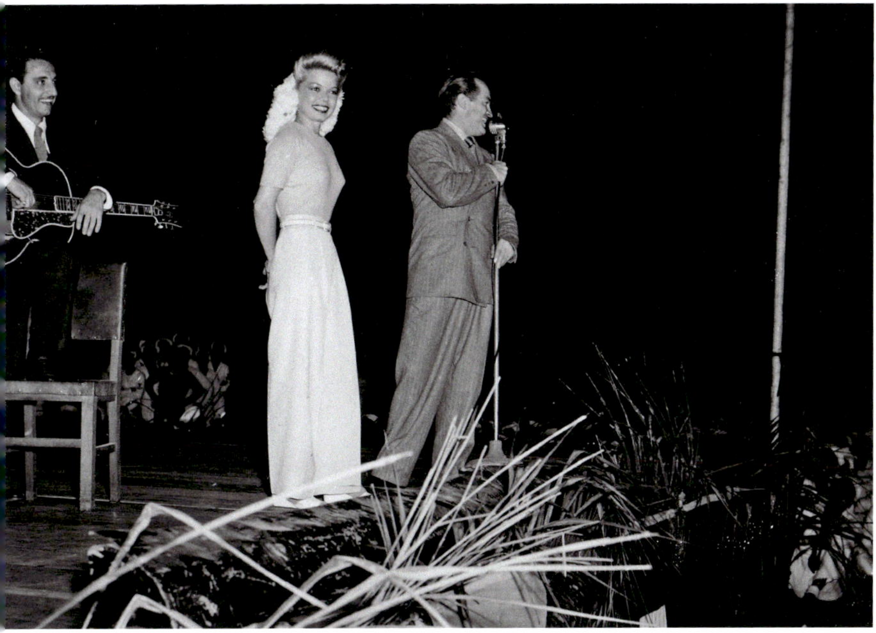

As Frances Langford's presence in the public eye waned, so did her generation's politics and lifestyle. She gave benevolently to her Florida community, and accompanied Bob Hope on his USO performances as late as 1989, continuing her life-long support of the troops. She had experienced the American Army as heroes, saving the world from the scourge of World War II, and could not imagine the American president doing anything wrong.

OPPOSITE: This 1951 movie dramatized Langford's USO tours

ABOVE: Langford on stage with Bob Hope on a Pacific island base in 1943

BELOW: Frances doing hapa haole with "Der Bingle," Bing Crosby (*Geoff Sundstrom Collection*)

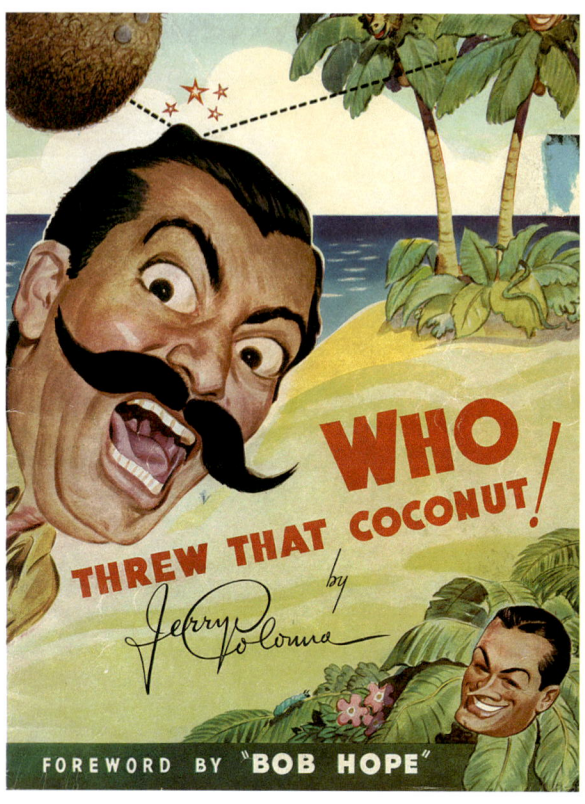

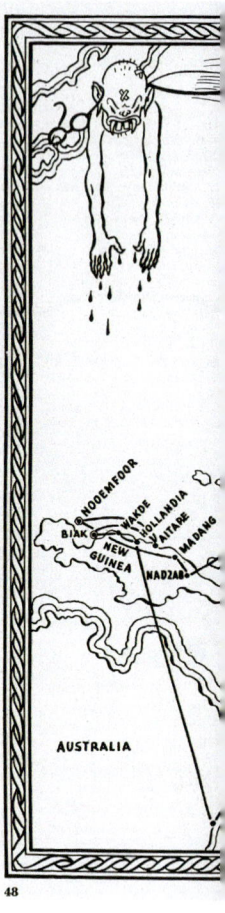

48

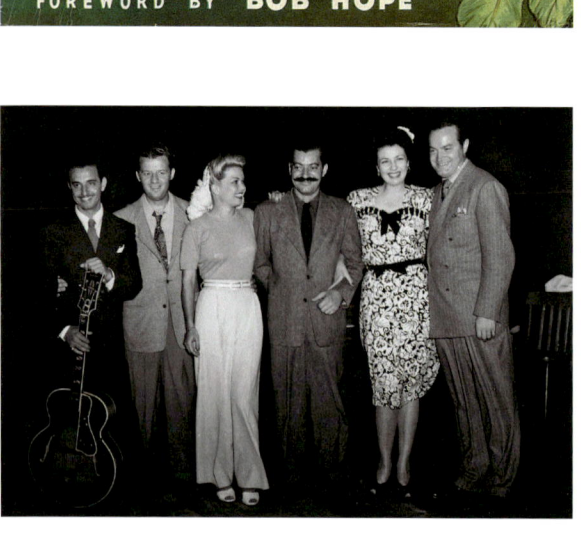

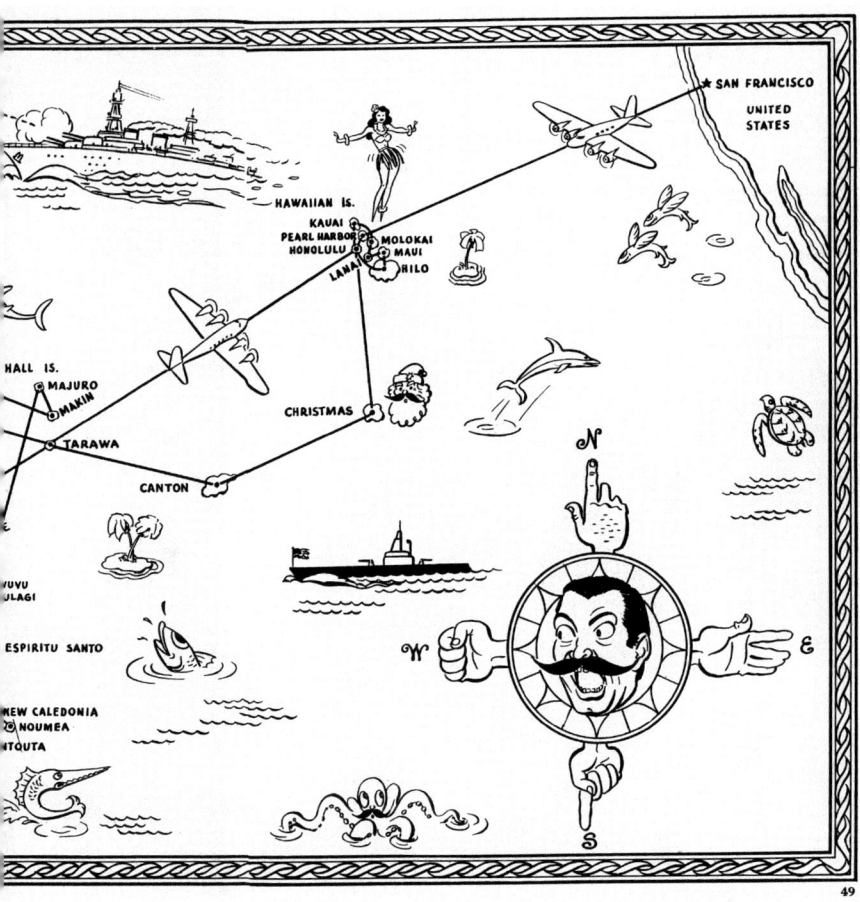

49

ABOVE: This map from comedian Jerry Colonna's 1945 book about the Bob Hope tour (opposite above) well illustrates the many U.S. Army and Navy bases in the Pacific

OPPOSITE BELOW: USO tour members, left to right: guitarist Tony Romero, unknown male, Frances Langford, Jerry Colonna, unknown female, Bob Hope

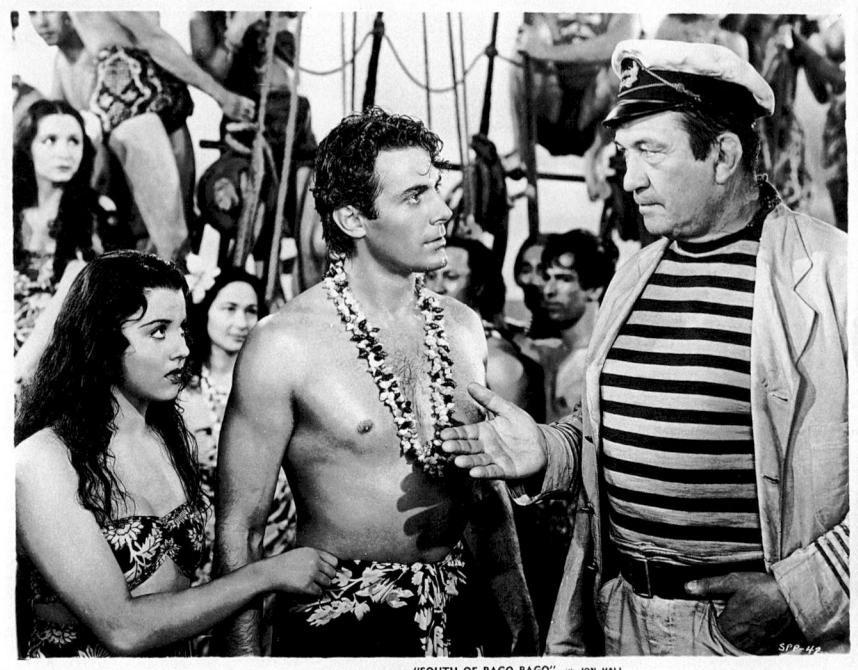

EDWARD SMALL presents "SOUTH OF PAGO PAGO" with JON HALL
FRANCES FARMER — VICTOR McLAGLEN — Olympe Bradna — Gene Lockhart
Released thru United Artists

ES GIBT KEINE PERSON, DEREN

Leben und Karriere Amerikas moderne Romanze mit Polynesien und Hollywood besser widerspiegelt als die der Sängerin und Schauspielerin Frances Langford. In den 1930er-Jahren hat sie mit Dick McIntire Hawaiilieder aufgenommen, zudem war sie mit dem Südseestar Jon Hall verheiratet. In den 1940er-Jahren unterhielt sie die US-Truppen im Pazifik und schließlich eröffnete sie in den frühen 1960ern ihr eigenes polynesisches Restaurant in Florida.

Vor dem Fernsehen diente das Radio der heimischen Unterhaltung. Die ausgebildete Opernsängerin Frances Langford wurde vom berühmten Sänger Rudy Vallée Anfang der 1930er-Jahre entdeckt,

ABOVE: Beauty, beau, and bad guy: Hall in his element in the 1940 film *South of Pago Pago*, shot mostly in Long Beach, near Los Angeles

OPPOSITE: Record marketing Jon Hall's Polynesian cachet

woraufhin sie ihre Karriere beim Radio begann. Sie zog nach Kalifornien und trat dort in Louella Parsons Radioshow *Hollywood Hotel* auf, bevor sie ihren ersten Film, *The Subway Symphony* (1932), drehte.

Es folgten etwa 30 weitere Filme. In den meisten spielte sie sich selbst und sang. 1938 heiratete sie Jon Hall, der nach seinem Erfolg in John Fords … *dann kam der Orkan* (1937) als der Südseestar schlechthin galt. Hall war der Sohn eines Schweizer Schauspielers und einer tahitischen Prinzessin und außerdem der Neffe des Südseeautors James Norman Hall. Da er in Tahiti aufgewachsen war, fühlte er sich in tropischen Umgebungen wohl und das Paar kaufte ein Grundstück in Jensen Beach, Florida.

In den frühen 1940er-Jahren arbeitete Frances Langford für Bob Hopes Radioshow und 1943 schloss sie sich seiner Truppe für eine Tour zu den Militärbasen der US Army in Europa und im Pazifik an. Durch die Dankbarkeit, die ihr die heimwehkranken, frauenlosen Soldaten entgegenbrachten, fühlte sie sich in ihrer Arbeit so sehr bestätigt, dass sie sich bis an ihr Lebensende für die USO (Unterhaltungsabteilung des US-Militärs) engagierte. Dies verschaffte ihr den Spitznamen „Darling of the Fighting Fronts". Nach dem Zweiten Weltkrieg schrieb sie eine wöchentliche Zeitungskolumne unter dem Titel „Purple Heart Diary", in der sie sich für die Belange der Veteranen einsetzte. Ihre Kriegserfahrungen verarbeitete sie 1951 in dem gleichnamigen Film.

Als sich ihre lange Hollywood-Karriere dem Ende näherte, heiratete Langford in zweiter Ehe einen wohlhabenden Geschäftsmann und eröffnete ein polynesisches Resort auf ihrem Grundstück in Florida, The Frances Langford Outrigger Resort.

Gegenüber vom Anlegeplatz der Jacht ihres Mannes (die *Chanticleer*), baute ihr Ed Lawrence, der Restaurantdesigner von Don the Beachcomber, das romantische Outrigger Restaurant und die dazugehörigen Miethütten. Die Eröffnung der Anlage war im Jahr 1961. Frances trat hier noch bis weit in die 1980er-Jahre auf. Als sie im Alter von 92 Jahren starb, verlor das Restaurant mit ihrem Namen auch seinen polynesischen Look.

Zeitgleich mit dem Verblassen von Langfords Namen in der Öffentlichkeit veränderten sich auch Politik und Lifestyle ihrer Generation. Langford spendete für ihre Gemeinde in Florida und begleitete Bob Hope noch bis 1989 auf seinen USO-Auftritten. Für sie waren die US-Soldaten Helden, die die Welt von der Geißel des Krieges befreit hatten. Dass ein amerikanischer Präsident Fehler machen konnte, war für sie unvorstellbar.

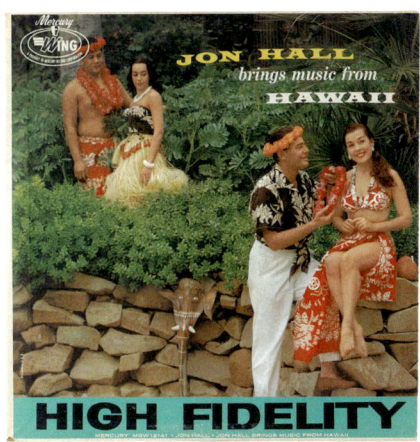

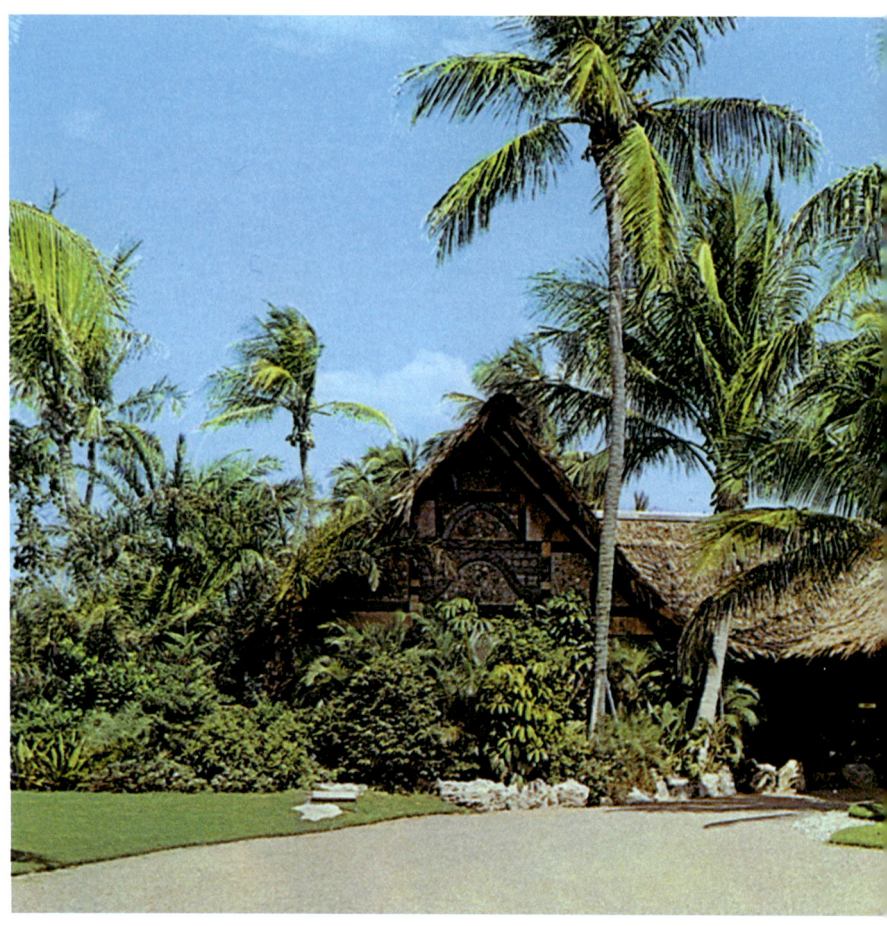

DIFFICILE D'IMAGINER UNE

personnalité dont la vie et la carrière reflètent mieux la passion de l'Amérique du XXe siècle pour la Polynésie et Hollywood que la chanteuse et actrice Frances Langford. Après avoir enregistré des chansons hawaiiennes dans les années 1930, elle épousa la vedette du cinéma exotique Jon Hall, alla divertir les troupes américaines cantonnées dans le Pacifique dans les années 1940, et finit par ouvrir son

propre restaurant polynésien en Floride, au début des années 1960.

Avant que la télévision devienne le cœur du divertissement domestique, il y avait la radio. Formée au chant lyrique, la talentueuse Frances Langford est découverte par Rudy Vallee, célébrissime chanteuse du début des années 1930, et commence à se produire à la radio. Elle s'installe en Californie, où elle participe à l'émission *Hollywood Hotel* présentée

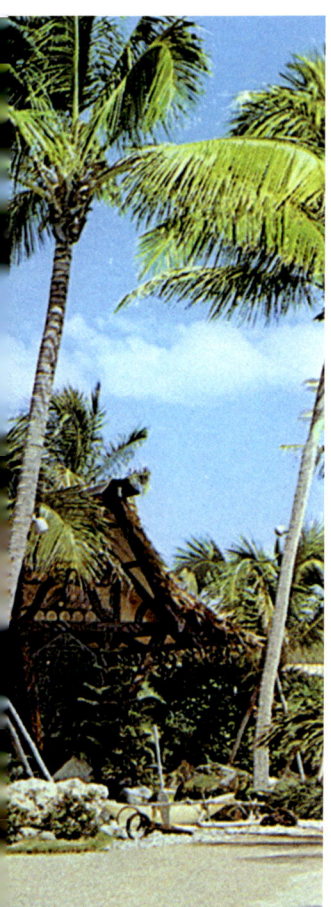

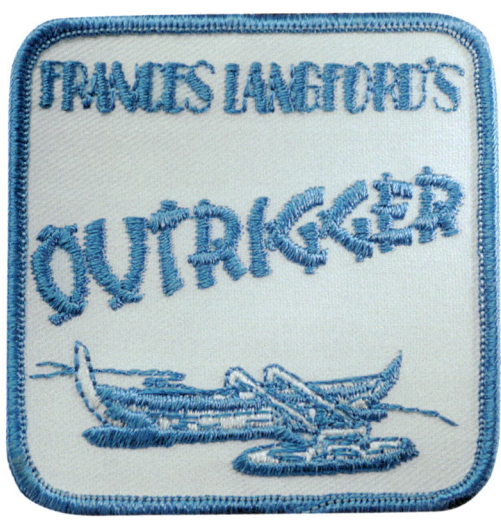

par Louella Parsons, et fait rapidement ses débuts au cinéma dans *The Subway Symphony* (1932).

Suit une trentaine de films, dans la plupart desquels elle chante et joue le plus souvent son propre rôle. En 1938, elle épouse Jon Hall, devenu lui aussi la quintessence du beau gosse des mers du Sud avec le succès de *The Hurricane* de John Ford (1937). Hall était le fils d'un acteur suisse et d'une princesse tahitienne, et le

neveu de l'auteur spécialiste du genre, James Norman Hall. Élevé à Tahiti, Hall aime les environnements tropicaux et le couple s'installe à Jensen Beach, en Floride.

Au début des années 1940, Frances Langford travaille sur l'émission de radio de Bob Hope, et en 1943 se joint à sa troupe pour une tournée des bases militaires américaines en Europe et dans le Pacifique. L'affection et la reconnaissance que lui témoignent ces soldats nostalgiques de

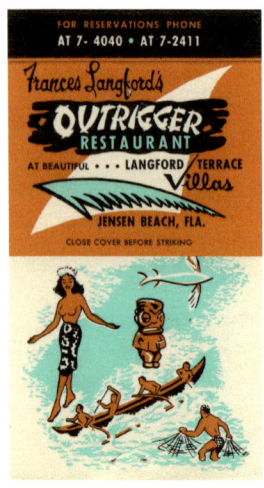

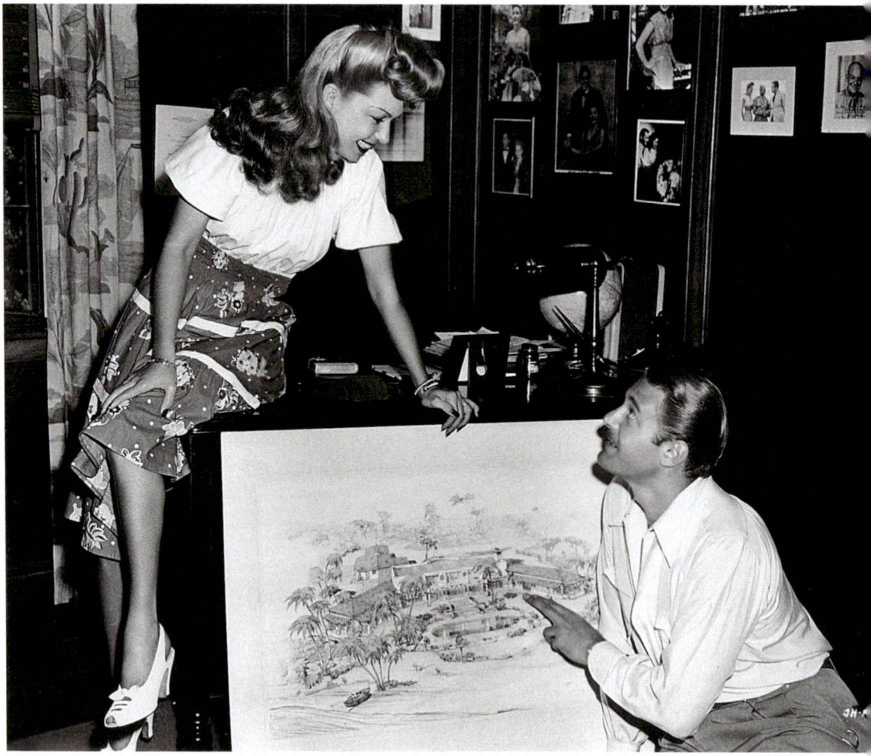

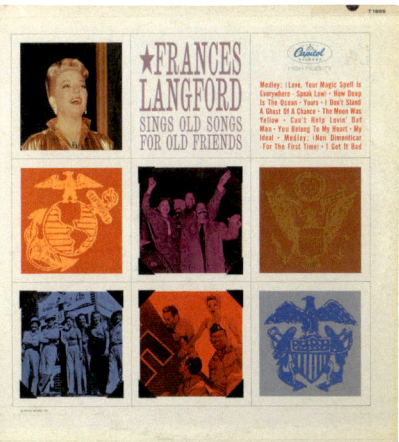

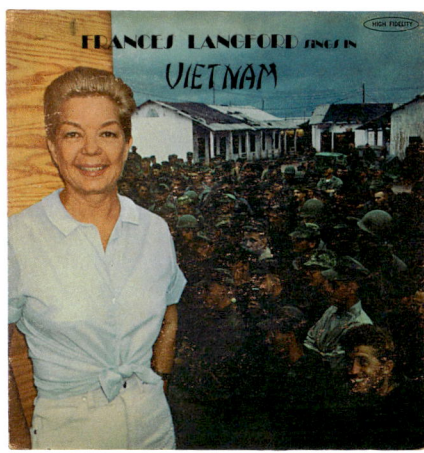

leur pays et privés de femmes la touchent tant qu'elle continuera à collaborer avec l'USO toute sa vie, ce qui lui valut le surnom de « Chérie des lignes de front ». Après la guerre, elle rédige une chronique intitulée « Purple Heart Diary », qui soutient la cause des vétérans de la Seconde Guerre mondiale. Elle rejouera ses expériences en temps de guerre pour le film éponyme, sorti en 1951.

Lorsque sa carrière hollywoodienne finit par s'essouffler, Langford se remarie avec un riche homme d'affaires et ouvre un hôtel sur le thème polynésien dans sa propriété de Floride. Face au ponton auquel est amarré le yacht de son mari, le *Chanticleer*, le décorateur de l'illustre restaurant Don the Beachcomber, Ed Lawrence, lui construit le romantique Outrigger Restaurant et une série de petits cottages en loca-

tion, qui ouvrent en 1961. Frances y chante jusque dans les années 1980. À son décès, à l'âge de 92 ans, le restaurant perdit son style et son nom polynésiens.

Lorsque l'intérêt du public pour Frances s'estompe, c'est aussi le style de vie et la façon dont sa génération concevait le monde qui disparaissent peu à peu. Généreuse bénévole auprès de ses voisins de Floride, elle continuera à accompagner Bob Hope dans ses tournées avec l'USO jusqu'en 1989, fidèle à son engagement au côté des troupes américaines déployées dans le monde. Pour elle, ces soldats étaient des héros, ceux qui avaient sauvé le monde du désastre pendant la Seconde Guerre mondiale, et il était pour elle inimaginable qu'un président américain prenne jamais la moindre mauvaise décision.

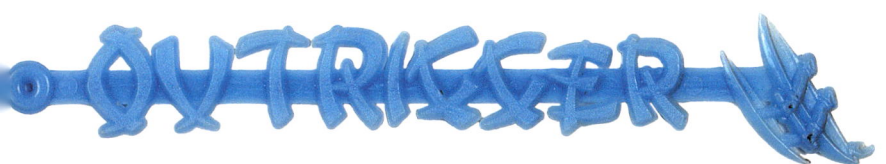

The October

Leatherneck

MAGAZINE OF THE MARINES

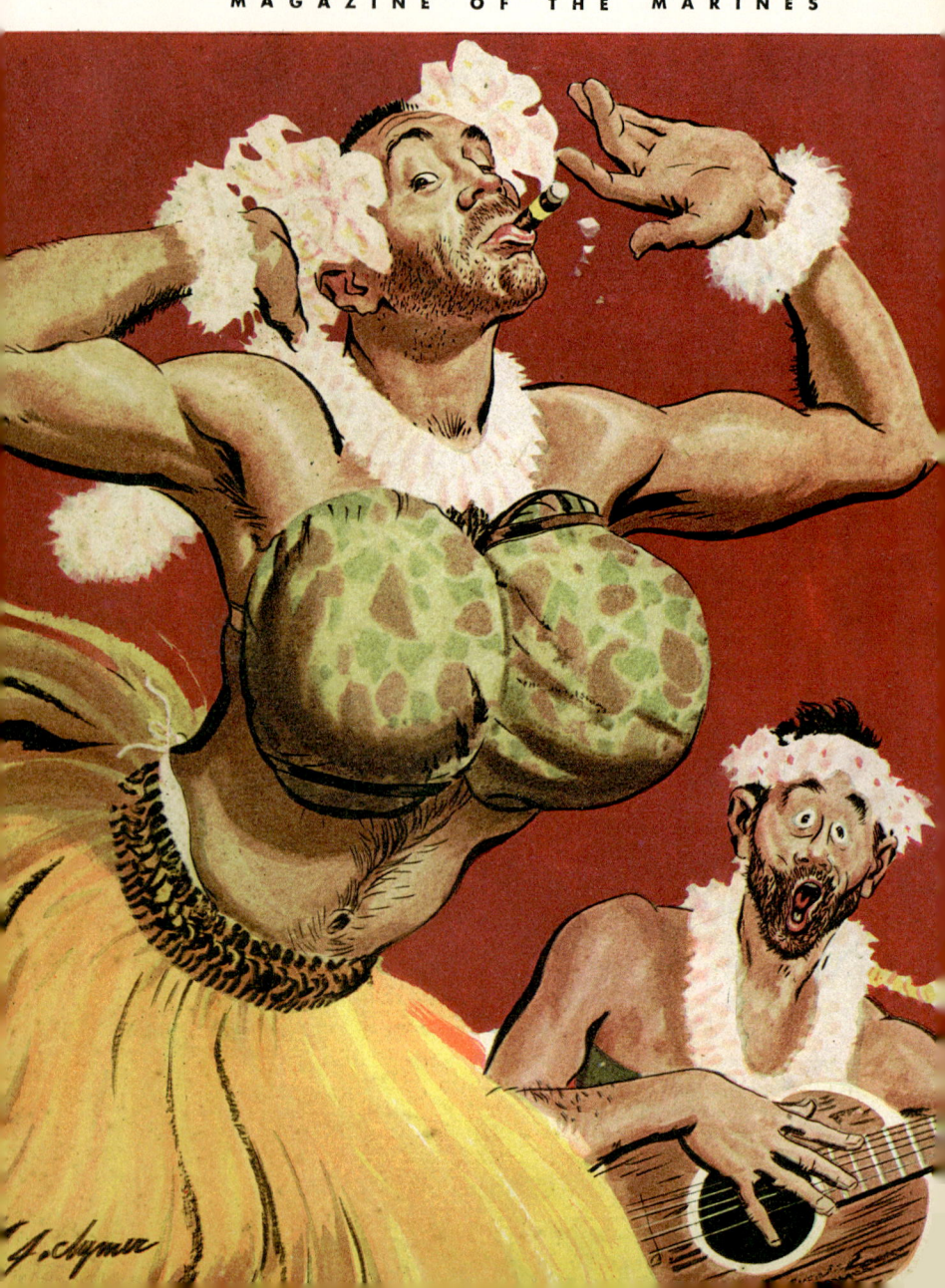

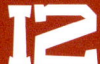

12

WORLD WAR II:
THE PACIFIC THEATER OF WAR

DER ZWEITE WELTKRIEG: KRIEGSSCHAUPLATZ PAZIFIK
SECONDE GUERRE MONDIALE :
LE PACIFIQUE, THÉÂTRE DE GUERRE

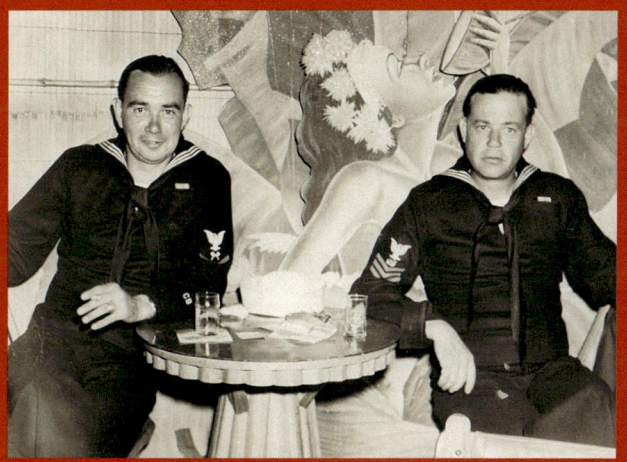

OPPOSITE: When native hula girls did not materialize, soldiers
created their own island entertainment. *Leatherneck:
Magazine of the Marines*, October 1945

ABOVE: Two American sailors at the Jade Hula Shack in
Oakland, California, 1944 *(Mimi Payne Collection)*

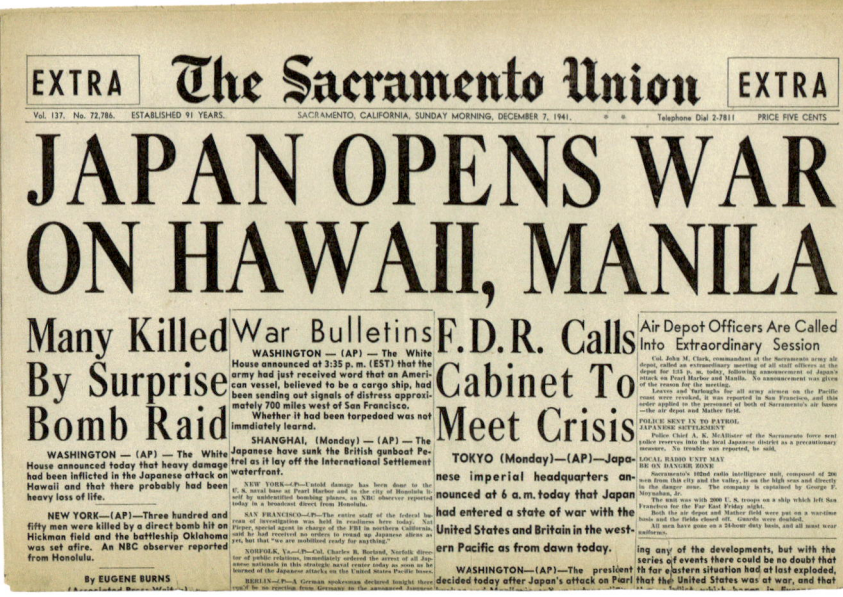

EVER SINCE THE FIRST TALL SHIPS landed on Polynesian shores, the romantic relations between sailors and native maidens were the stuff of popular lore. The reports of early navigators describing the open reception of the seafarers by scantily clad island females had been perpetuated into the 20th century, and American bamboo bars used the motif to attract the boys in blue as their drinking customers.

So when the U.S. Navy's favorite Polynesian port of call, the Pearl Harbor naval base in the Hawaiian Islands, was attacked without warning by the Japanese on December 7, 1941, Americans were seriously taken aback. The Murphy Sisters crooned in their swing tune: "You're a sap, Mister Jap / You make a Yankee cranky / You're a sap, Mister Jap / Uncle Sam is gonna spanky / Oh what a load to carry /

Don't you know, don't you know, you're committing Hari-Kari?"

Japanese admiral Yamamoto Isoroku did not share the sense of victory that the other military leaders at the Imperial General Headquarters expressed after the destruction of Pearl Harbor.

His sentiments are found in this quote accredited to him: "I am afraid we have awakened a sleeping giant, and filled him with terrible resolve!"

And indeed, America entered World War II with all its energy and resources, and soon a generation of young enlisted men who only knew exotic places like Zamboanga as tropical nightclubs was shipping out to the actual locale.

Suddenly these men, many of whom had never left their rural homes in middle America before, found themselves on thin

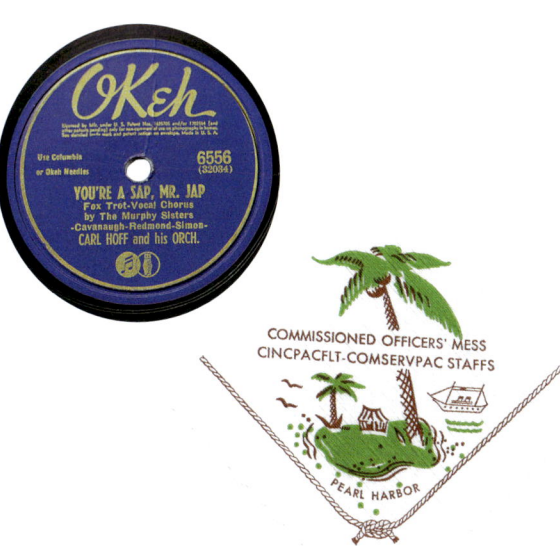

OKeh

Licensed for Mfr. under U. S. Patent Nos. 1,695,795 and/or 1,703,934 [and other patents pending] only for non-commercial of use on phonographs in homes. Use of this device shown in this record [and patent notice on envelope. Made in U.S.A.]

Use Columbia
or Okeh Needles

6556
(32034)

YOU'RE A SAP, MR. JAP
Fox Trot-Vocal Chorus
by The Murphy Sisters
-Cavanaugh-Redmond-Simon-
CARL HOFF and his ORCH.

COMMISSIONED OFFICERS' MESS
CINCPACFLT·COMSERVPAC STAFFS

PEARL HARBOR

OPPOSITE: California newspaper headline, December 7, 1941

LEFT: Swing song recorded December 23, 1941 and Cocktail napkin from Officers' Mess, Pearl Harbor, Hawaii

BELOW: Explosion of *U.S.S. Shaw* during Pearl Harbor attack

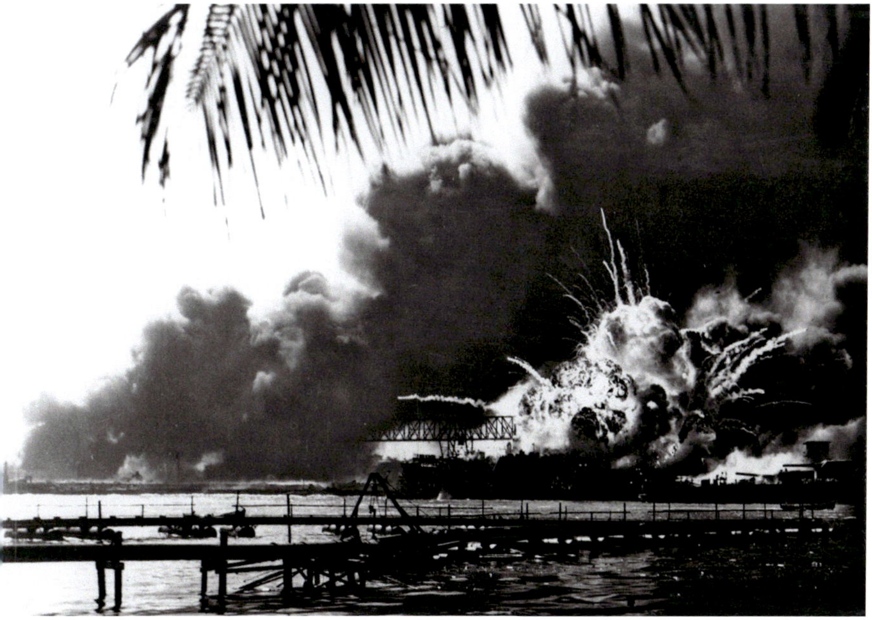

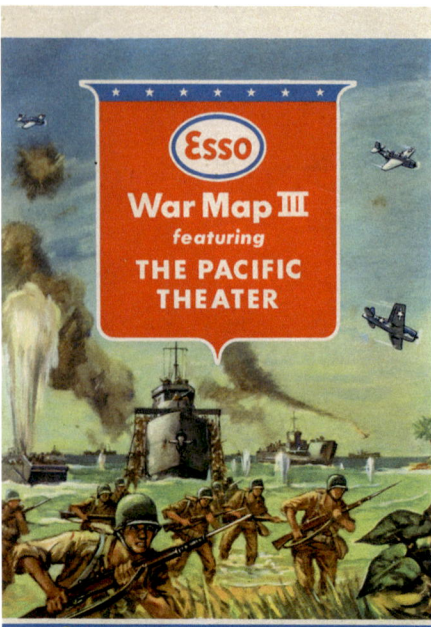

ABOVE: Pacific Ocean map by Esso Oil

OPPOSITE ABOVE: U.S. Navy troops heading for the real Zamboanga, Philippines

OPPOSITE BELOW: Postcard for Zamboanga nightclub, Los Angeles *(Scott Schell Collection)*

coral atolls like Enewetok in Micronesia, or in the dense, steaming jungles and malaria-breeding swamps of Bougainville Island in the Solomons. These places were not necessarily tropical paradises, but the South Seas myth accompanied the soldiers wherever they went, thanks to the popular entertainment provided by the USO and Special Services Division.

Unfortunately, for many G.I.s, their first contact with a Pacific island was not balmy breezes wafting from a palm studded beach, but machine gun bullets raking them from Japanese fox holes. Many died after their first few steps on the hot sand. Within hours, tropical beaches had been turned into deforested moonscapes littered with the dead and wounded. The surviving soldiers dug in for days on what one of them called the "Sunuvabeach." They fought beyond exhaustion, to the point where they could not be distinguished from the dead. At the end of the Pacific war campaign, close to a 100,000 men did not return alive to their homeland from the "South Seas paradise." Many of those who did never wanted to talk about what they had experienced.

Hardy farm boys and studied city men alike dealt with the hardships of war the American way, lightening their load with humor and imagination. If there were no dusky maidens waiting for them, one could still dream about them. There were also a lucky few that remained on posts behind the lines, never seeing action. Stationed on remote islets, their contact with the Pacific island world was a peaceful and educational one. One of these fortunate few was James Michener, who wrote the quintessential Pacific War best seller that was used to revitalize the South Seas myth for decades to come.

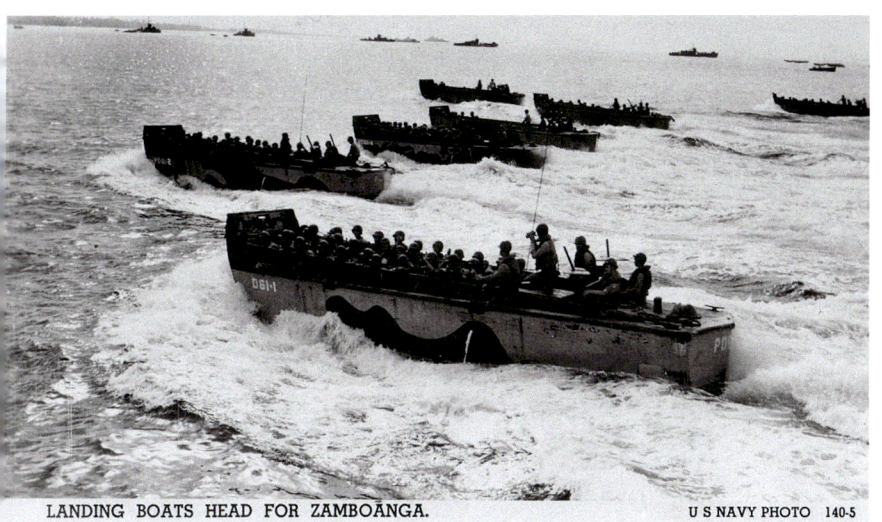

LANDING BOATS HEAD FOR ZAMBOÄNGA.

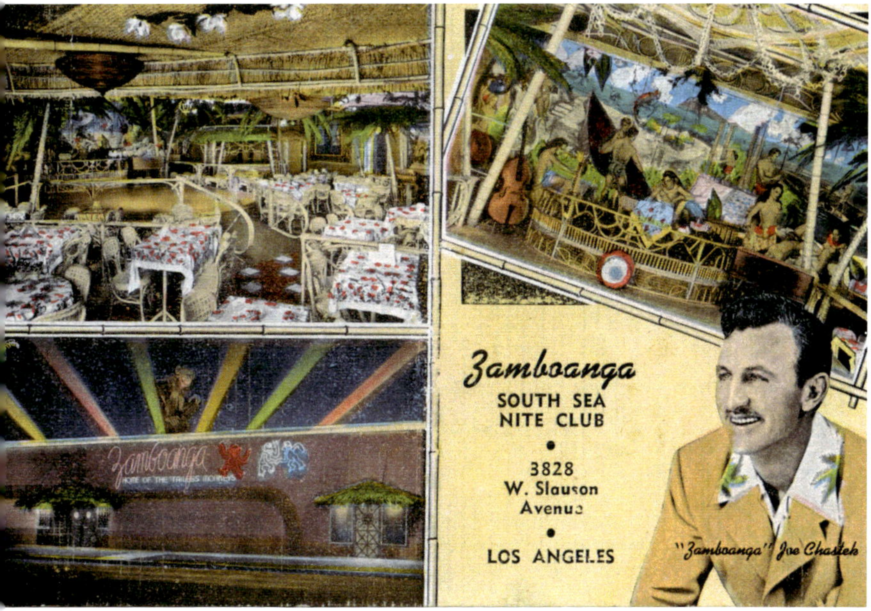

Zamboanga
SOUTH SEA
NITE CLUB
•
3828
W. Slauson
Avenue
•
LOS ANGELES

"Zamboanga" Joe Chastek

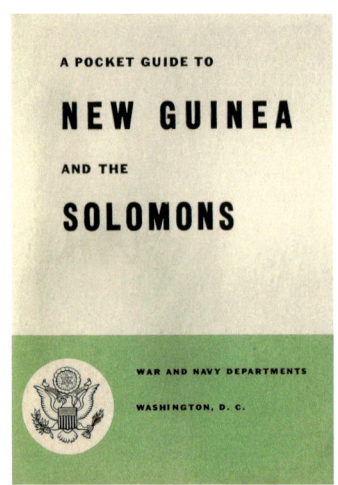

A POCKET GUIDE TO

NEW GUINEA

AND THE

SOLOMONS

WAR AND NAVY DEPARTMENTS

WASHINGTON, D. C.

LEFT: Guide for the inexperienced tropical traveler *(Timothy Haack Collection)*

BELOW: G.I.s schlepping heavy equipment in the jungle heat

OPPOSITE: Classic South Seas fiction for the foot soldier

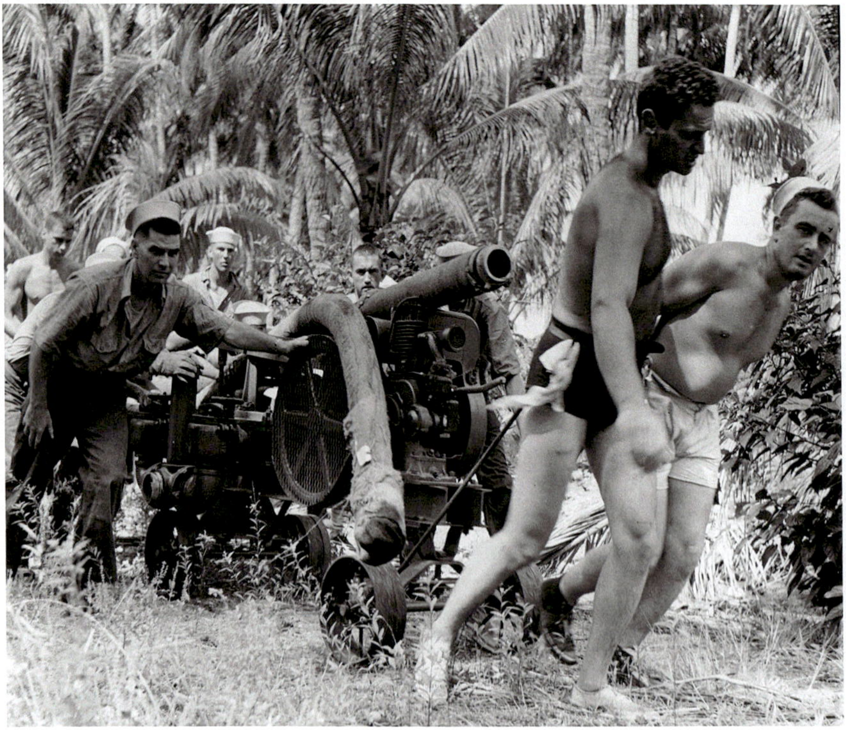

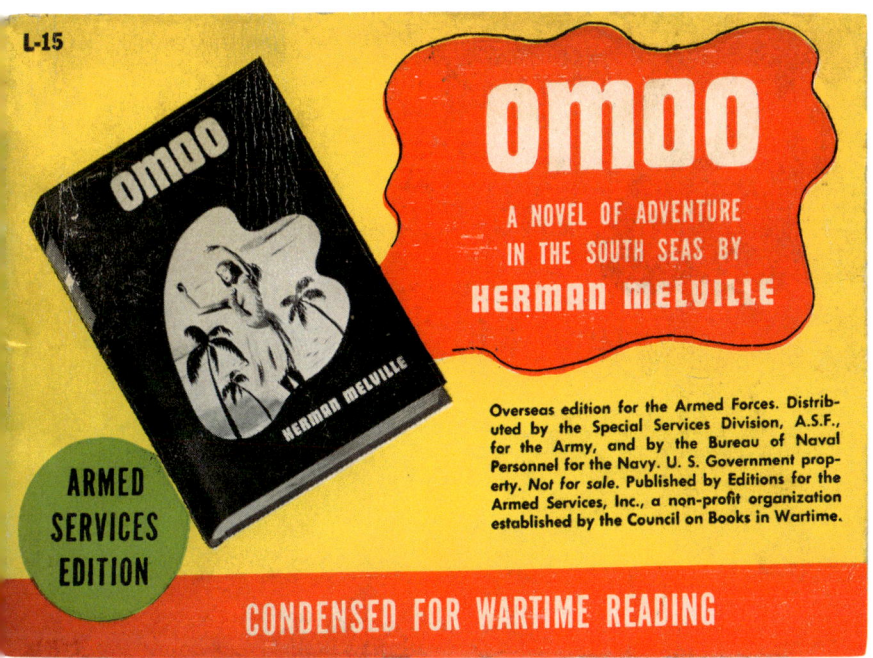

L-15

OMOO

A NOVEL OF ADVENTURE
IN THE SOUTH SEAS BY
HERMAN MELVILLE

Overseas edition for the Armed Forces. Distrib-
uted by the Special Services Division, A.S.F.,
for the Army, and by the Bureau of Naval
Personnel for the Navy. U. S. Government property. *Not for sale.* Published by Editions for the
Armed Services, Inc., a non-profit organization
established by the Council on Books in Wartime.

ARMED
SERVICES
EDITION

CONDENSED FOR WARTIME READING

Meanwhile on the mainland, the media perpetuated the South Seas clichés the same way it had always done: where friendly islanders and beautiful wahines frolicked, life was a beach and fun could be had. When the shell-shocked war veterans returned home, no one really wanted to hear stories of bloodied corpses and blown-off limbs.

Eager to re-enter normal life, the G.I.s themselves willingly forgot about the horrors of battle. By selectively embellishing the humorous aspects of their "exotic adventure," the soldiers' experiences were swiftly woven into the mainland's pop culture mythology. Wartime souvenirs were used to illustrate heroic lore and ribald jokes told in suburban rumpus rooms and Polynesian bars. For many veterans their war experiences represented the most intense period of their lives. They had "been there," and felt that now they deserved to rest on their palm-frond laurels.

The South Seas fantasy, having existed long before the war, proved to be stronger than any grim memories, and mid-century Americans, happy to perpetuate it, chimed along to the melodies of "*South Pacific,*" the musical and the movie.

By the 1960s, the wacky shenanigans of *McHale's Navy*, shored up in a Hollywood lagoon and stationed in bamboo huts at the Universal studio lot, successfully represented the lighter side of the Pacific War theater.

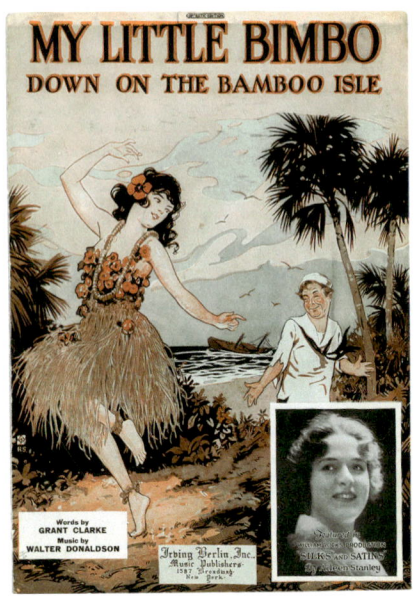

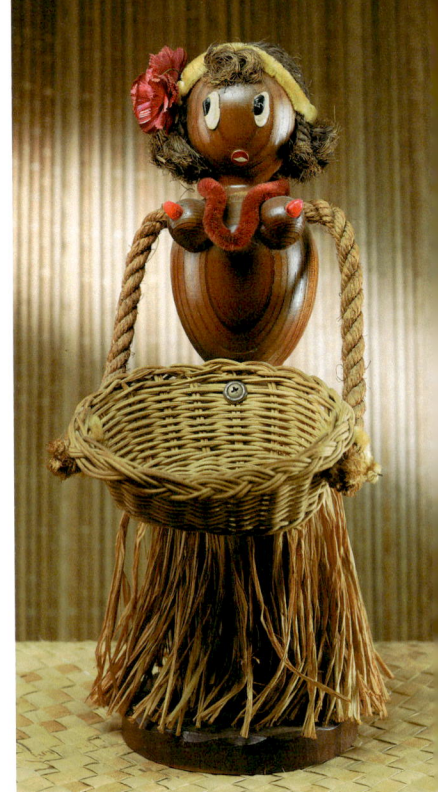

ABOVE: Sheet music cover, 1920

RIGHT: Whimsical island-souvenir bar figurine

OPPOSITE: South Seas movie screening for the troops… and some real natives

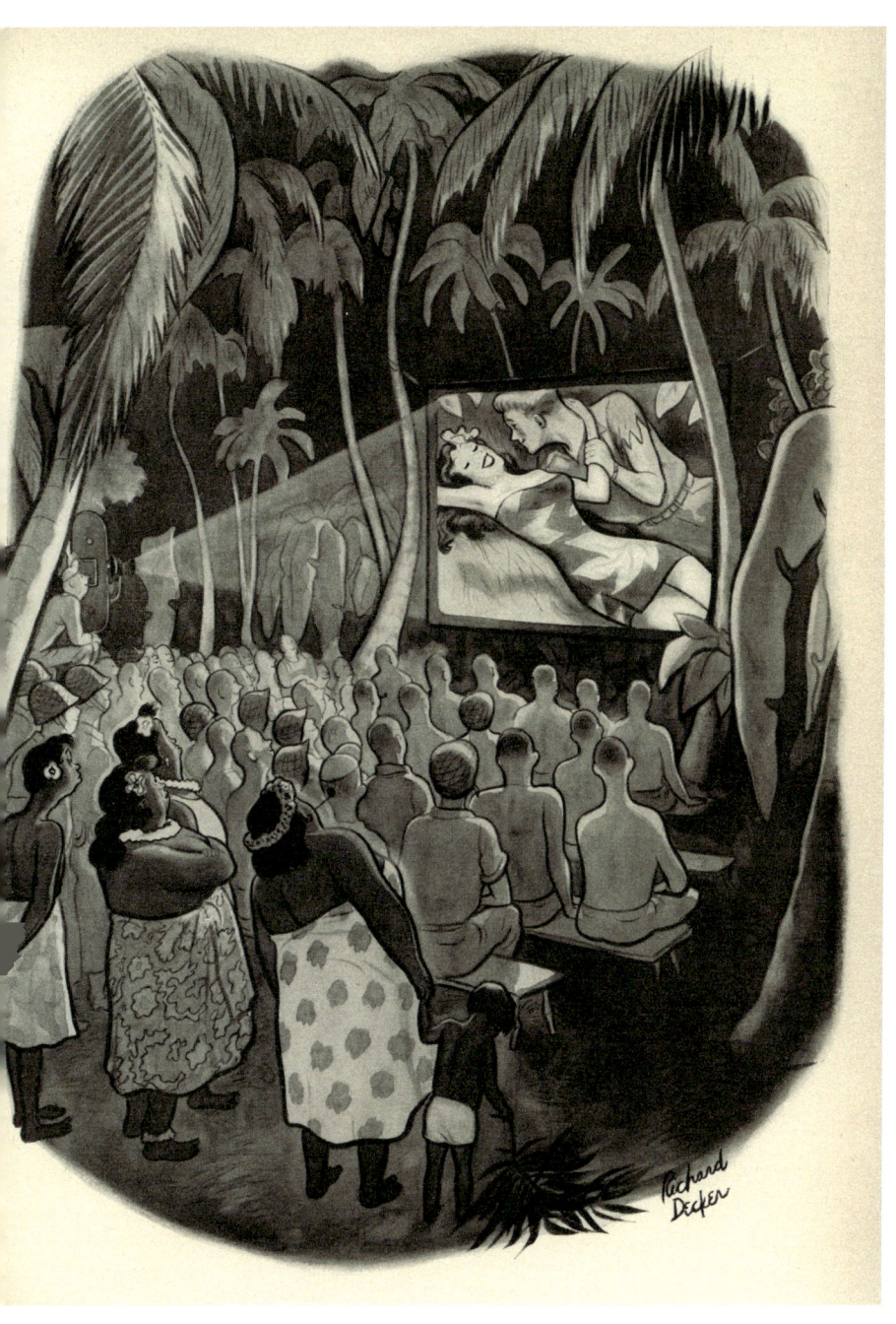

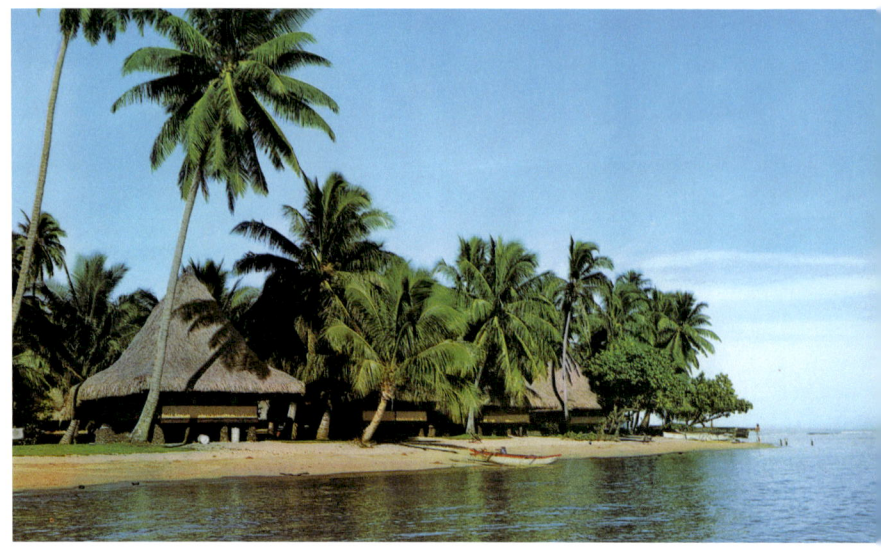

ABOVE: A cliché image of a beautiful South Seas beach, Tahiti

SEIT DIE ERSTEN GROSSSEGLER

an den polynesischen Küsten an Land gingen, gibt es Geschichten über Liebesaffären zwischen Seemännern und einheimischen Frauen. Die Berichte der frühen Seefahrer vom offenherzigen Empfang der leicht bekleideten Inselschönheiten überdauerten bis ins 20. Jahrhundert. Amerikanische Bambus-Bars machten sich das Motiv zunutze, um die Jungs in Blau als Gäste zu gewinnen.

Als der beliebteste Anlaufhafen der US Navy, der Marinestützpunkt Pearl Harbor auf Hawaii, am 7. Dezember 1941 ohne Vorwarnung von den Japanern angegriffen wurde, waren die Amerikaner ernsthaft bestürzt. Die Murphy Sisters sangen in ihrem *You're A Sap, Mr. Jap*: „Du bist ein Trottel, Mister Jap / Du machst einen Yankee wütend / Du bist ein Trottel, Mister Jap / Uncle Sam wird dich verhauen / Oh, welch Last zu tragen / Weißt du nicht, weißt du nicht, du begehst Harakiri?"

OPPOSITE ABOVE AND BELOW: The reality of how many G.I.s experienced Pacific island beaches looked different. It was a common enough sight to be used for an army cartoon

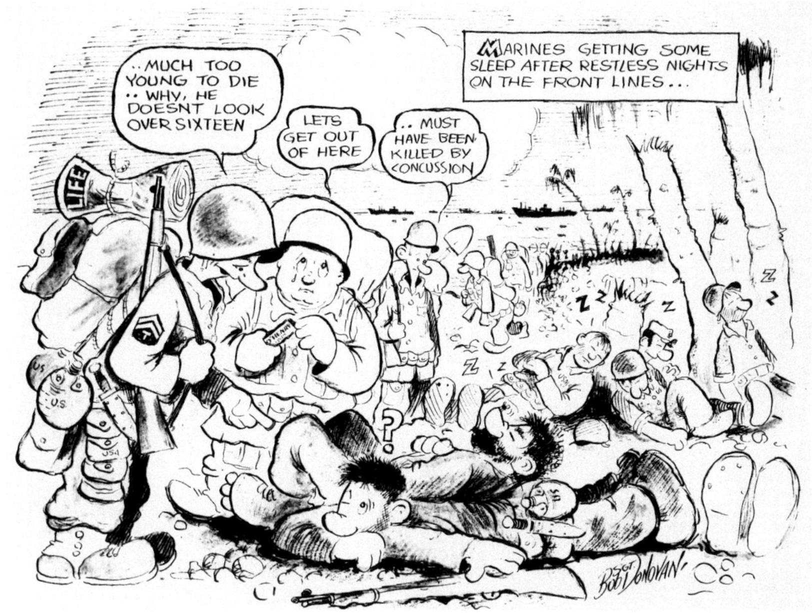
MARINES GETTING SOME SLEEP AFTER RESTLESS NIGHTS ON THE FRONT LINES...
..MUCH TOO YOUNG TO DIE .. WHY, HE DOESNT LOOK OVER SIXTEEN
LETS GET OUT OF HERE
.. MUST HAVE BEEN KILLED BY CONCUSSION
LIFE
SGT. BOB DONOVAN

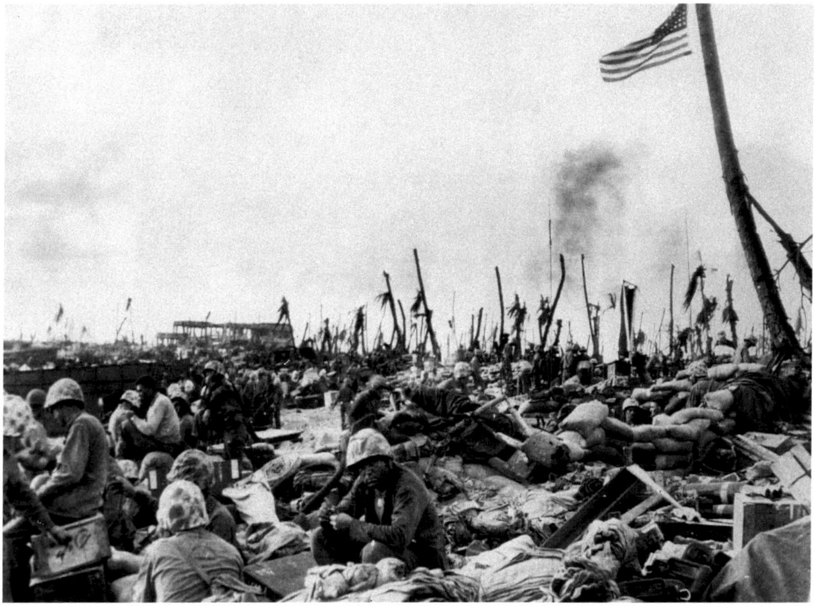

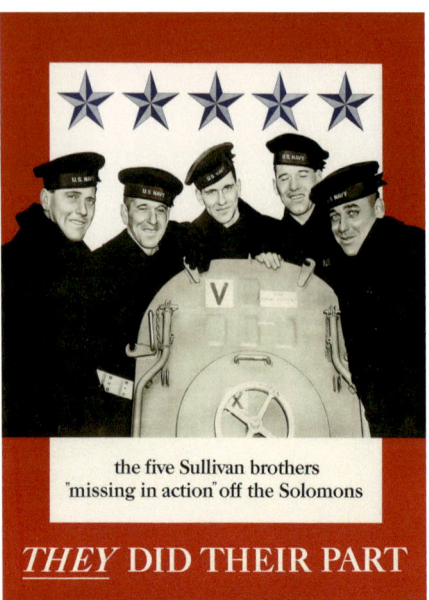

the five Sullivan brothers
'missing in action' off the Solomons

THEY DID THEIR PART

Der japanische Admiral Yamamoto Isoroku konnte in das Siegesgeschrei der anderen Militärs, die Pearl Harbors Zerstörung im Oberkommando des Kaiserreichs feierten, nicht einstimmen. Das folgende Zitat wird ihm zugeschrieben: „Ich fürchte, wir haben einen schlafenden Riesen geweckt und ihn zu schrecklicher Entschlossenheit getrieben!"

Und tatsächlich traten die USA mit all ihrer militärischen Stärke in den Zweiten Weltkrieg ein. Schon bald wurde eine Generation junger Soldaten, die exotische Plätze wie Zamboanga nur als tropische Nachtclubs kannten, an die echten Schauplätze verschifft. Plötzlich fanden sich diese Männer, von denen viele ihr Zuhause im Mittleren Westen nie verlassen hatten, auf kleinen Korallenatollen wieder, wie Eniwetok in Mikronesien, oder in den Dschungeln und malariaverseuchten Sümpfen von Bougainville auf den Salomonen. Diese Orte waren nicht gerade ein Paradies, doch der Südseemythos reiste mit den Soldaten, wohin sie auch gingen – in Form des beliebten Unterhaltungsprogramms der USO und der Special Services Division.

ABOVE: The five Sullivan brothers were killed in action in the Pacific when their ship was hit by a Japanese torpedo

RIGHT: Dead Japanese soldiers on a Pacific beach

OPPOSITE: Cannon Towel advertisement, 1944

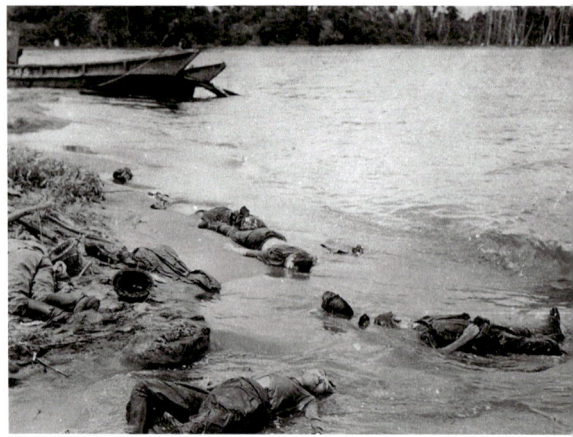

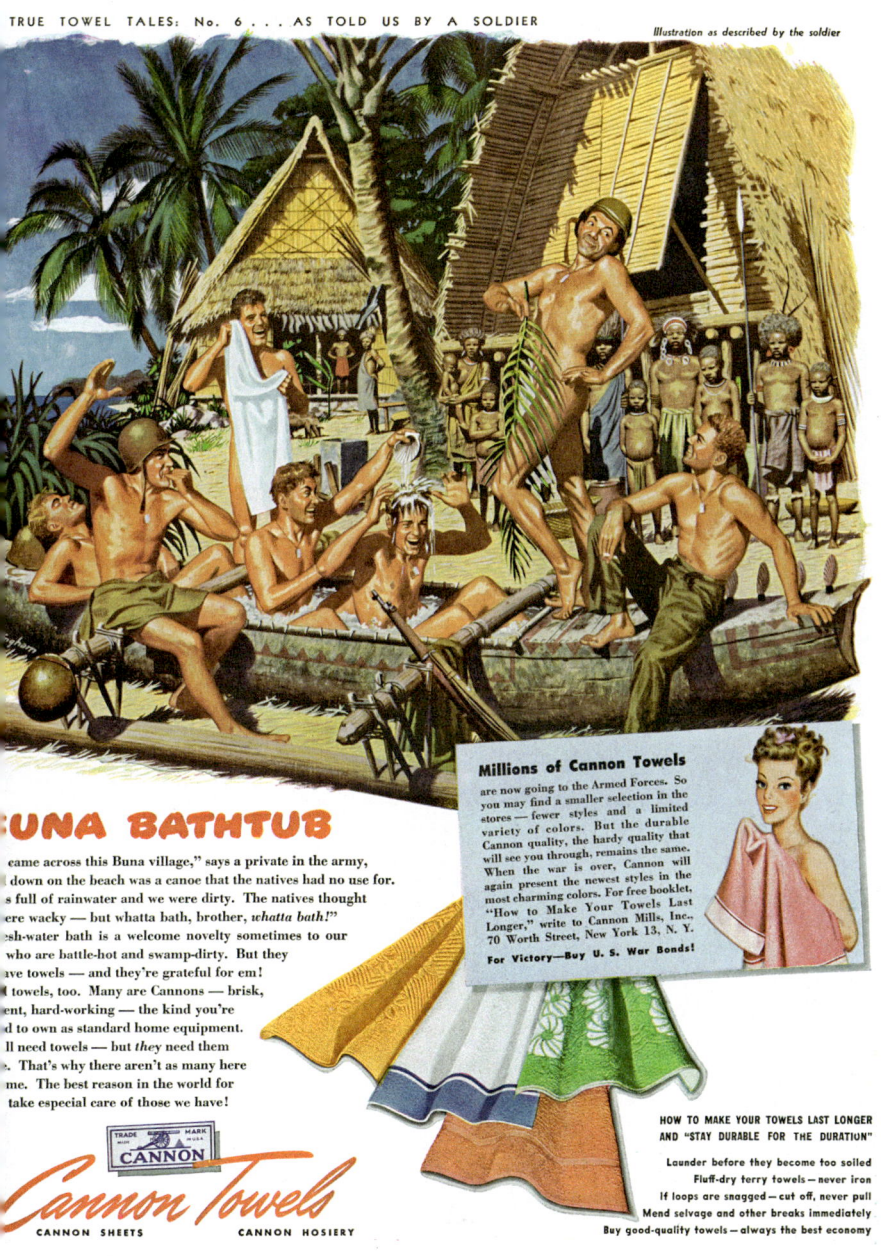

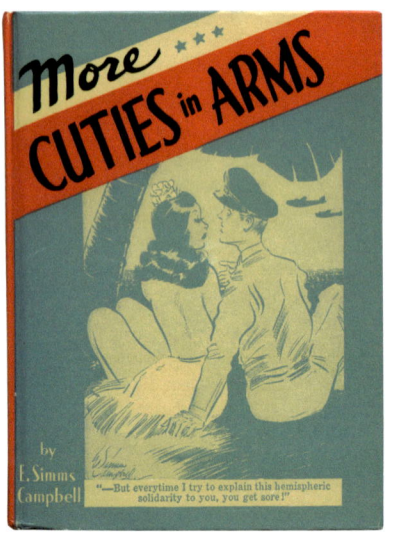

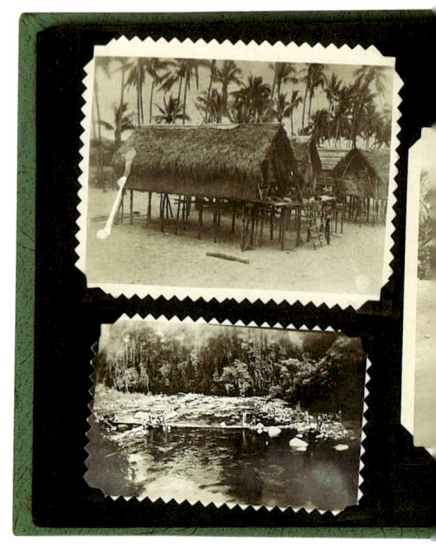

Leider war der erste Kontakt mit den pazifischen Inseln für viele Soldaten nicht die sanfte Brise an einem von Palmen gesäumten Strand, sondern das Maschinengewehrfeuer aus den japanischen Schützengräben. Viele starben nach nur wenigen Schritten auf dem heißen Sand. Innerhalb von Stunden verwandelten sich tropische Strände in Mondlandschaften, die von Toten und Verwundeten übersät waren. Die Überlebenden verschanzten sich tagelang am „Sunuvabeach", wie ein Soldat ihn nannte. Sie kämpften bis zur Erschöpfung; am Ende des Pazifikkriegs waren es fast 100 000 Männer, die aus dem „Südseeparadies" nicht mehr lebend heimkehrten. Viele Überlebende wollten nie über ihre Erlebnisse sprechen.

Zähe Bauernjungs und gebildete Stadtmänner gingen mit dem Kriegselend auf sehr amerikanische Weise um – sie setzten ihren Humor und ihre Vorstellungskraft

dagegen. Wenn keine dunkelhäutigen Jung frauen auf sie warteten, konnten sie immer noch von ihnen träumen. Es gab aber auch ein paar Glückliche, deren Posten sich hinter der Frontlinie befand und die nie kämpfen mussten. Auf den kleinen Inseln war ihr Südseeaufenthalt friedlich und lehrreich. Einer dieser wenigen Glücklicher war James Michener, Autor jenes Bestsellers über den Pazifikkrieg, der den Südseemythos für die folgenden Jahrzehnte wiederbeleben sollte.

Auf dem Festland wurde die Pazifikregion weiterhin mit denselben Klischees wie immer gepriesen: als Ort, an dem freundliche Insulaner und wunderschöne Wahine umhertollten und das Leben aus Spaß am Strand bestand. Als die verstörten Kriegsveteranen heimkehrten, wollte keiner so recht ihre grausamen Geschichten hören.

Begierig darauf, in ihr normales Leben zurückzukehren, vergaßen auch die Soldaten

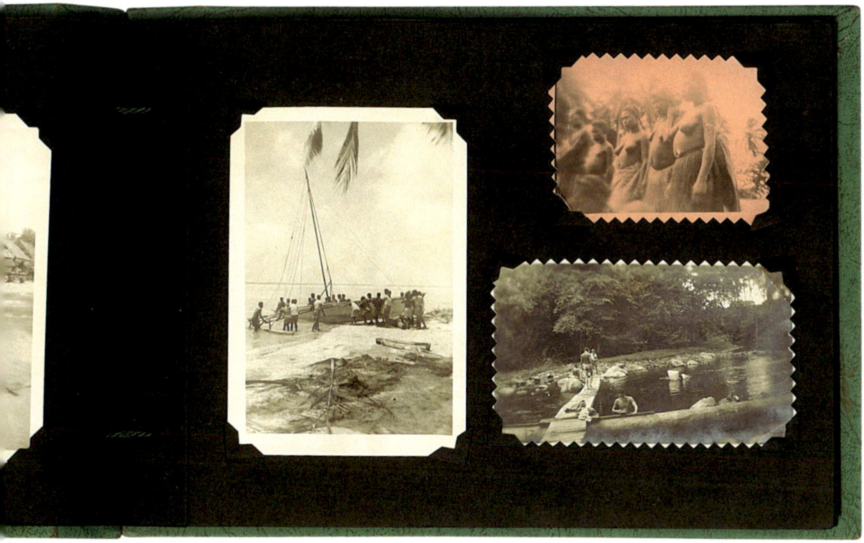

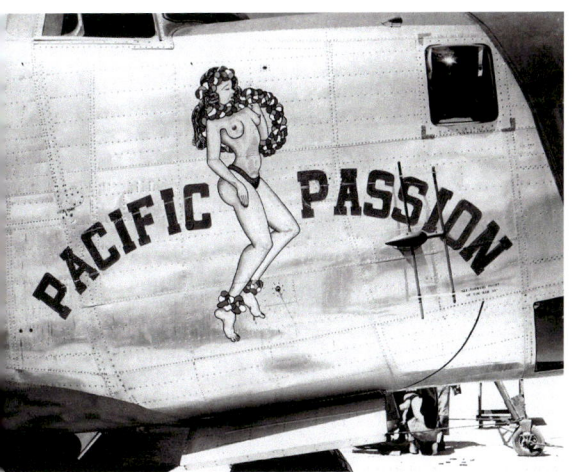

OPPOSITE ABOVE: A book of armed forces cartoons, 1943

ABOVE: G.I. souvenir photo album from unknown Pacific island (*Rick Hamilton Collection*)

LEFT: Nose art depicting a dream wahine, on a B-24 Liberator Bomber, Mariana Islands, 1945 nur zu gern die Schrecken der Schlacht. Da sie die heiteren Momente ihres „exotischen Abenteuers" gezielt ausschmückten, wurden die Erfahrungen der Veteranen ein integraler Teil der Popkultur-Mythologie. Mitbringsel aus dem Krieg dienten der Untermalung heldenhafter Taten und obszöner Witze, die in vorstädtischen Partyräumen und in polynesischen Bars zum Besten gegeben wurden. Für viele Veteranen war die Zeit im Krieg die intensivste Phase ihres Lebens. Sie waren „vor Ort" gewesen und hatten nun das Gefühl, sich auf ihren Palmwedel-Lorbeeren ausruhen zu dürfen.

Die Südseefantasie, die es schon lange vor dem Krieg gab, war robuster als jede dunkle Erinnerung. Und die Menschen dieser Zeit, gewillt das Traumbild aufrechtzuerhalten, sangen die Lieder von *South Pacific* mit – dem Musical und dem Film.

In den 1960er-Jahren lagen die ulkigen Faxentreiber der Fernsehserie *McHale's Navy* in einer Hollywood-Lagune auf dem Studiogelände von Universal vor Anker. In Bambushütten wohnend, repräsentierten sie erfolgreich die heitere Seite des Pazifikkriegs.

BELOW: Army comic book cover caricature of souvenir-hunting soldiers

OPPOSITE: Army weekly magazine cover showing American soldier as collector of native carvings

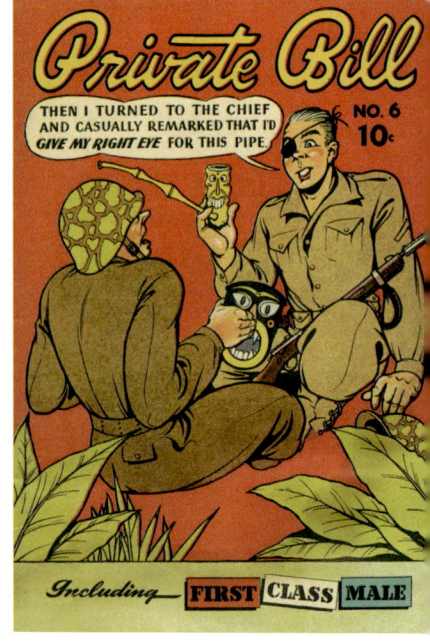

BRITISH EDITION

YANK

THE ARMY WEEKLY

3d AUG. 29 **1943**
VOL. 2, NO. 11

By the men .. for the
men in the service

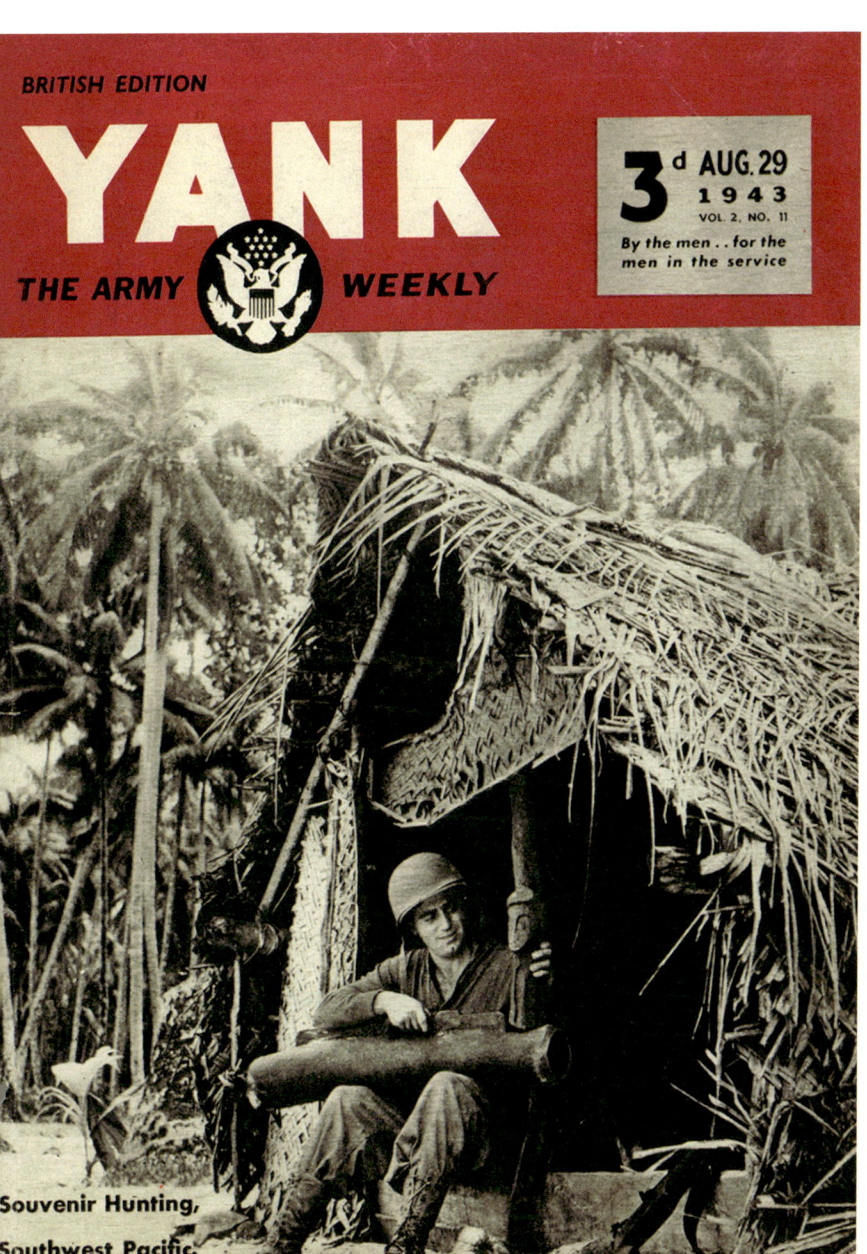

Souvenir Hunting,
Southwest Pacific.

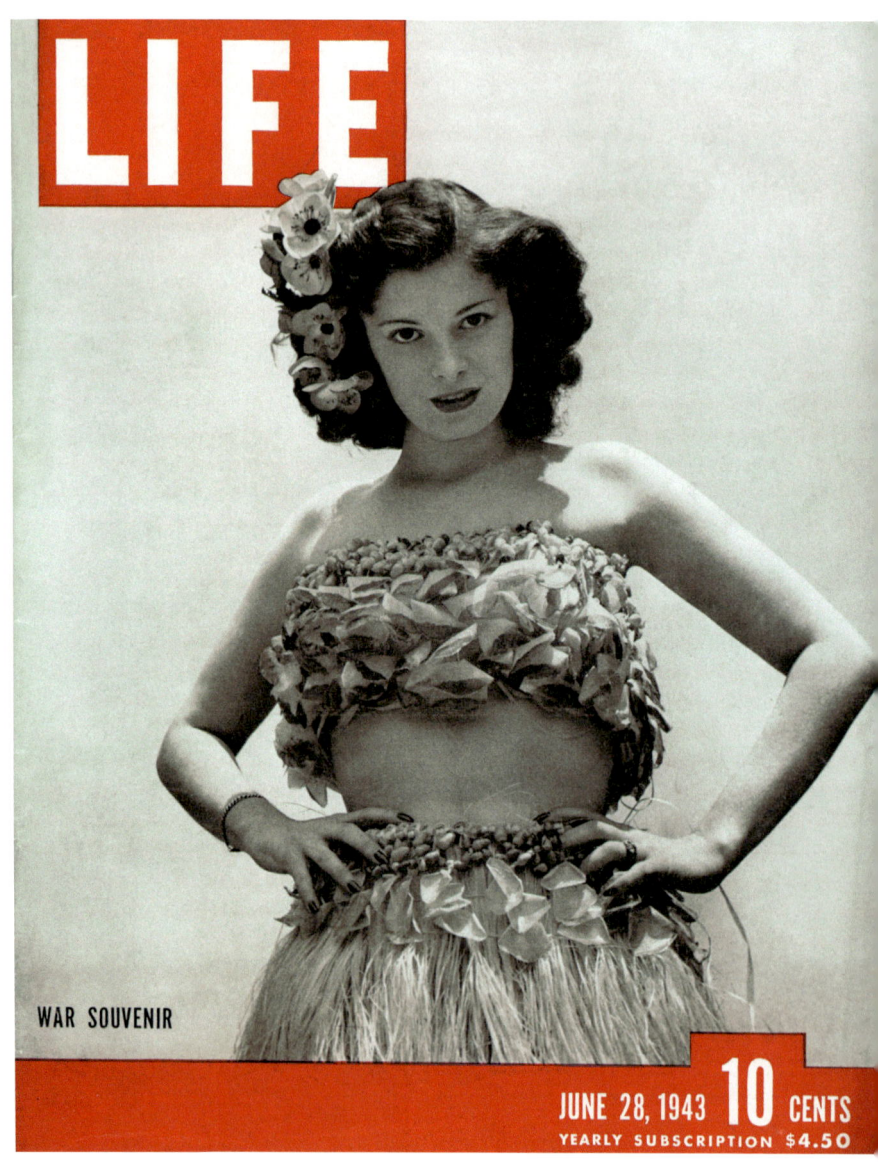

LIFE

WAR SOUVENIR

JUNE 28, 1943 **10** CENTS

YEARLY SUBSCRIPTION $4.50

À PARTIR DU MOMENT OÙ LES

premiers gros navires accostent sur les rivages polynésiens, les relations romantiques entre marins et jeunes autochtones font la joie du public. Les récits d'explorateurs décrivant l'accueil chaleureux que réservent des insulaires à moitié nues aux voyageurs des mers ont fait leur chemin jusqu'au XXᵉ siècle, et les bars en bambou américains utilisent ce fantasme entré dans l'imaginaire collectif pour attirer les gars de la marine.

Ainsi, lorsque le port d'attache polynésien préféré de la marine américaine, la base navale de Pearl Harbor, dans l'archipel hawaiien, est attaquée sans avertissement par les Japonais le 7 décembre 1941, les Américains sont abasourdis. Les Murphy Sisters chanteront sur un air de swing : « Tu nous sapes le moral, Monsieur le Jap / À cause de toi, les Yankees sont fâchés / Tu nous sapes le moral, Monsieur le Jap / Oncle Sam, c'est sûr, va te fesser / Oh quel risque tu as pris / Tu ne sais donc pas, tu ne sais pas, que tu t'es fait Hara-kiri ».

L'amiral japonais Yamamoto Isoroku ne partage d'ailleurs pas le sentiment de victoire qu'expriment les autres officiers réunis au quartier général impérial après l'attaque sur Pearl Harbor.

Une réticence qui apparaît dans cette citation que l'histoire lui attribue : « Je crains que nous ayons réveillé un géant en sommeil, et que nous l'ayons empli d'une détermination féroce ! »

De fait, les États-Unis se lancent dans la Seconde Guerre mondiale avec toute leur énergie et leurs ressources et, bientôt, une génération entière de jeunes enrôlés, qui ne connaissaient du Pacifique que les décors factices des boîtes de nuit, embarque

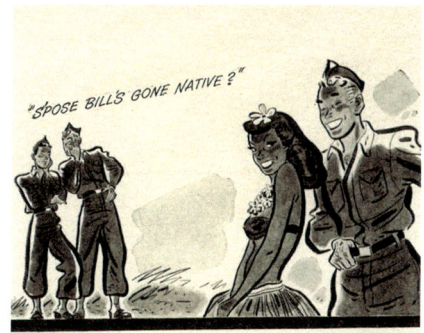

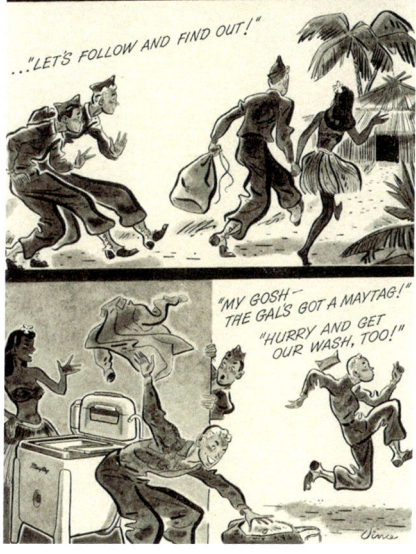

OPPOSITE: *Life* magazine cover with a suggestive title

ABOVE: Maytag washing machine advertisement

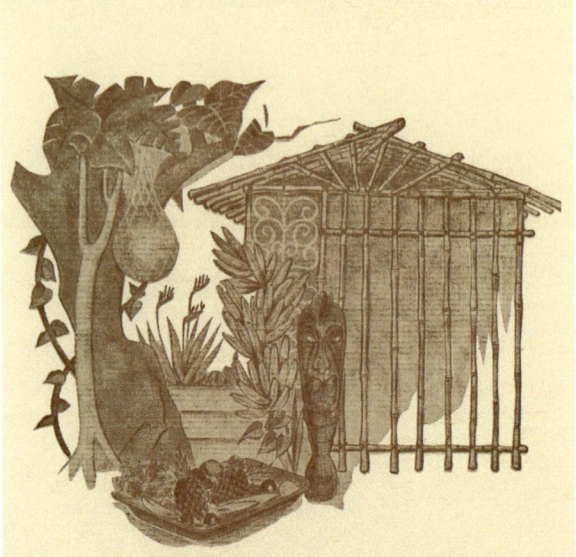

ALOHA *Ka Hale o ke Kia'aina*

LUAU

Welcome to the Governor's Mansion
FEAST

The restaurant — Ka Hale o ke Kia'aina — derives its name from an experience of one of the Luau's owners — Ben Holmes. When Holmes was with the United States Navy Seebees, his unit landed at Talegi, the capital of the Solomon Islands. Holmes and his companions were told that this was to be their home for awhile and they were to find a place to live. And so they did (after diligent searching); but the hut which Holmes and his six friends built turned out to be the finest on the island.

So, the simple home became known as the governor's mansion . . . and Holmes became known then — as now — as the "governor". ALOHA Ka o ke Kia'aina. Welcome to the governor's mansion.

The Governor
BEN A. HOLMES

LEFT: Menu introduction by Pacific War veteran, from the Luau Lounge at the Hawaii Kai Motel on Myrtle Beach, Florida *(Scott Schell Collection)*

OPPOSITE ABOVE: Bobby Hammack Jazz LP of South Pacific, the musica

OPPOSITE BELOW: Postwar rumpus-room fun *(Scott Schell Collection)*

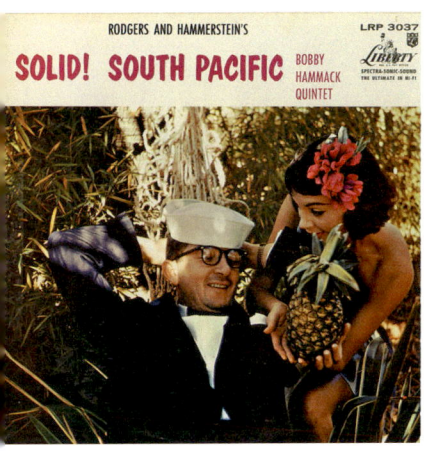

RODGERS AND HAMMERSTEIN'S
SOLID! SOUTH PACIFIC BOBBY HAMMACK QUINTET
LRP 3037

à destination des contrées lointaines qui les ont inspirés.

Soudain, ces hommes dont beaucoup n'avaient jamais quitté leur cambrousse américaine auparavant, se retrouvèrent sur de filiformes atolls coralliens comme Enewetak, en Micronésie, dans la jungle dense et étouffante ou les marais infestés par la malaria de Bougainville, dans les îles Salomon. Il ne s'agit pas toujours de paradis tropicaux, mais le mythe des mers du Sud accompagne les soldats partout, grâce aux divertissements que leur fournissent régulièrement l'USO et la division des services spéciaux de l'armée.

Pour bien des jeunes soldats américains, le premier contact avec une île du Pacifique n'est malheureusement pas le souffle parfumé de la brise sur une plage émaillée de palmiers, mais des rafales de balles tirées depuis les tranchées japonaises. Beaucoup sont abattus après seulement deux ou trois pas sur le sable chaud. En quelques heures, les plages de sable blanc sont changées en paysages désolés jonchés de cadavres et de blessés. Les survivants s'enterrent pendant des journées entières dans ce qu'ils

appellent la « Sunuvabeach ». Ils s'épuisent au combat, dépassent leurs limites, jusqu'à ce qu'on ne distingue plus les morts des vivants. Lorsque la guerre du Pacifique prend fin, près de 100 000 hommes ont péri dans les « paradis des mers du Sud ». La plupart de ceux qui en reviennent refuseront de raconter ce qu'ils ont vécu.

Robustes garçons de ferme et citadins éduqués affrontent les horreurs de la guerre à l'américaine, en allégeant leur fardeau par l'humour et l'imagination. Si les beautés basanées ne sont pas là pour les accueillir, rien n'empêche ces garçons de rêver d'elles. Certains ont aussi la chance de rester en arrière, bien loin du front et de toute action. Stationnés dans des îlets isolés, ils ont la possibilité d'établir avec ces lieux et leurs habitants une relation pacifique, et formatrice. Parmi eux se trouve James Michener, l'auteur du grand best-seller sur la guerre du Pacifique qui revitalisa le mythe des mers du Sud pour les décennies à venir.

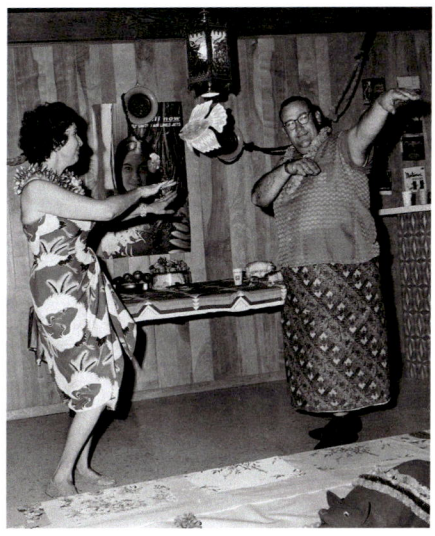

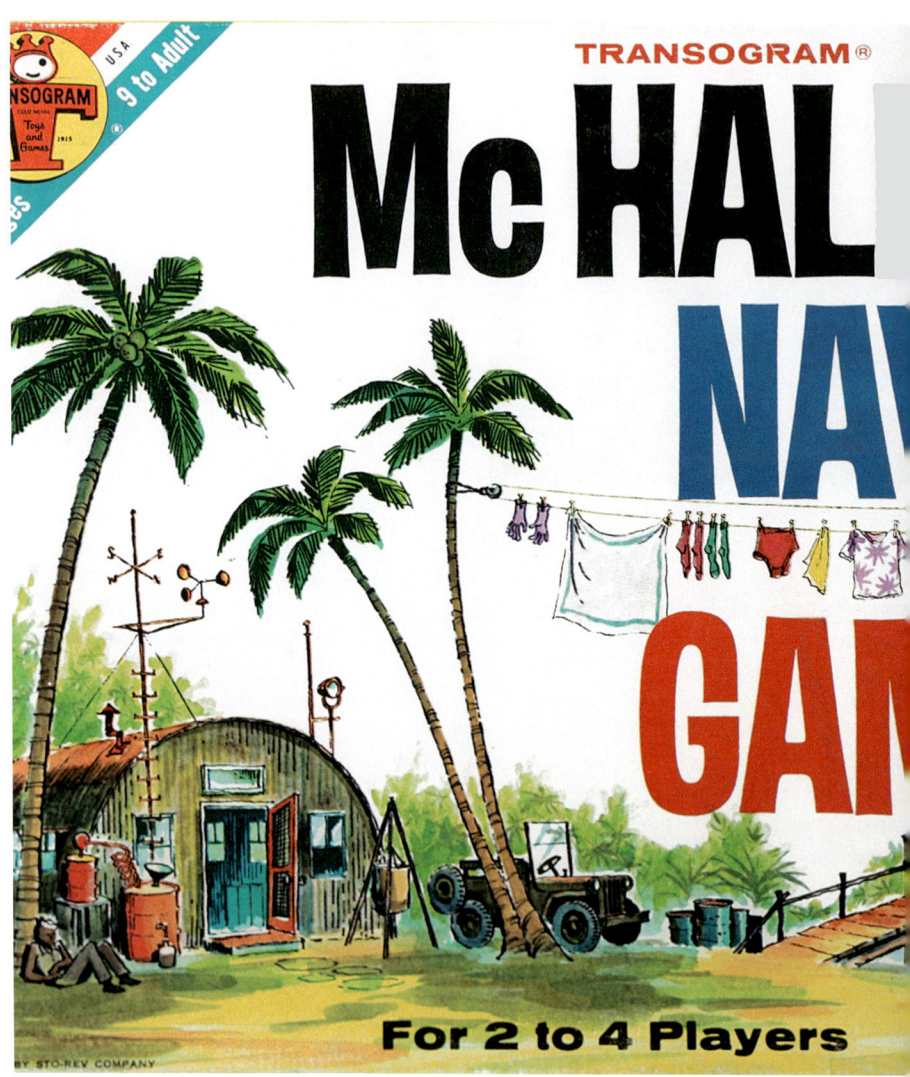

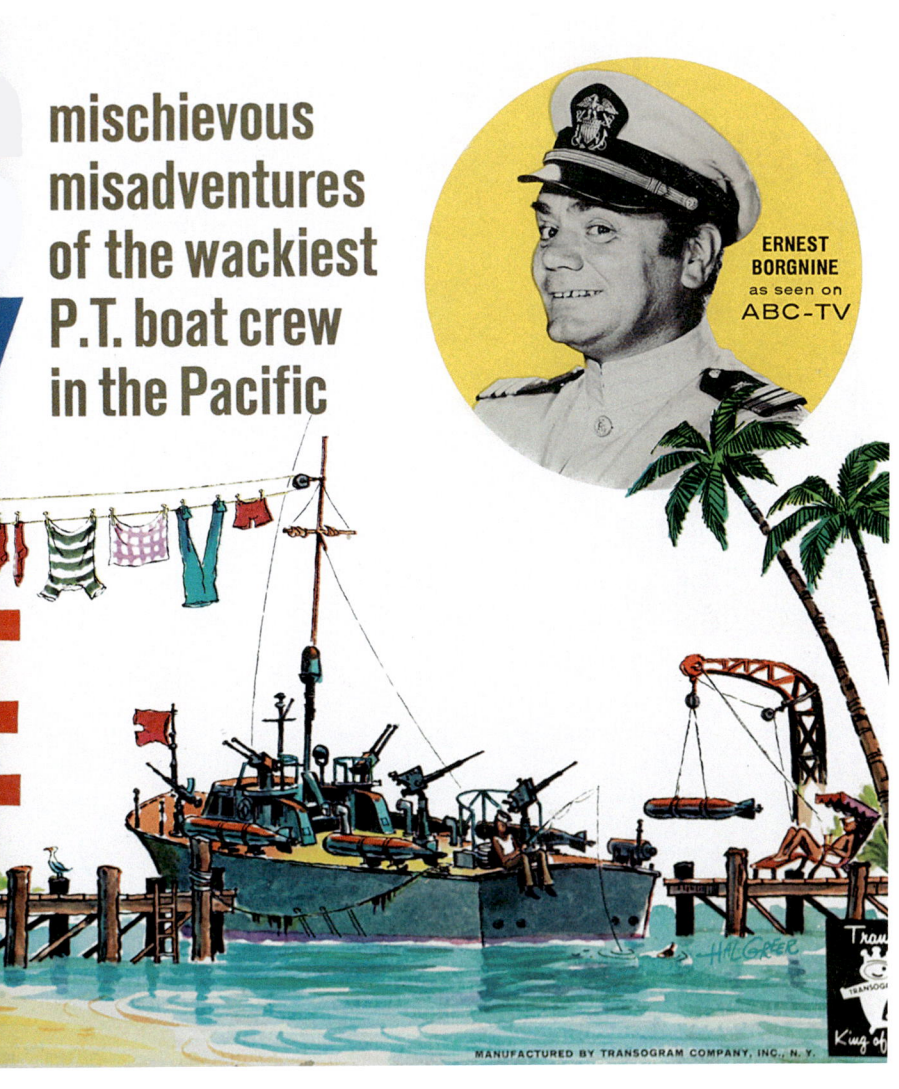

mischievous misadventures of the wackiest P.T. boat crew in the Pacific

ERNEST BORGNINE
as seen on ABC-TV

MANUFACTURED BY TRANSOGRAM COMPANY, INC., N. Y.

McHale's Navy board game, based on the TV series

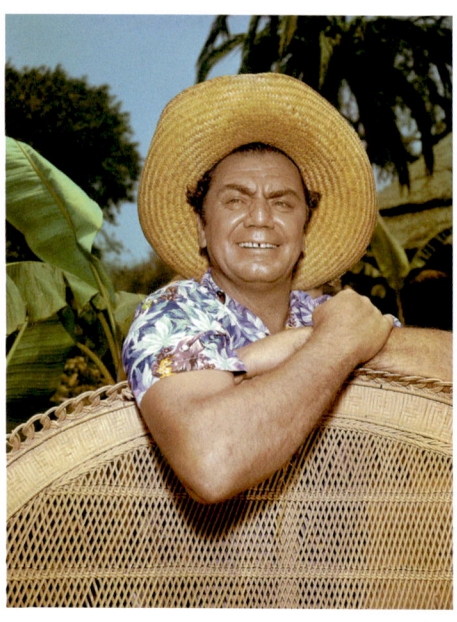

LEFT: Ernest Borgnine as Lt. Quinton McHale, sporting his best beach-comber gear

BELOW: *McHale's Navy* set on the Universal Studios back lot

OPPOSITE: Ernest Borgnine lines up a bevy of hula maidens for a scene from *McHale's Navy*—the Movie, 1964

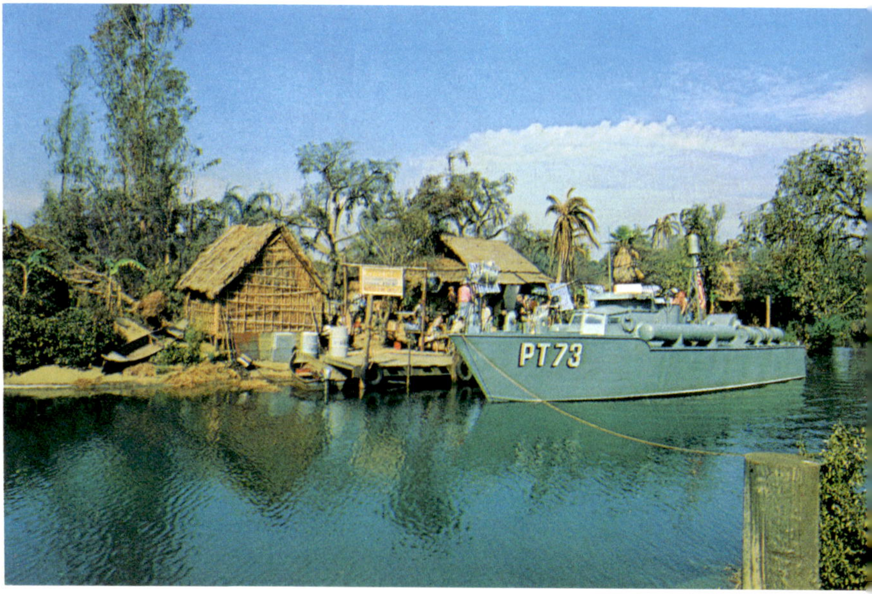

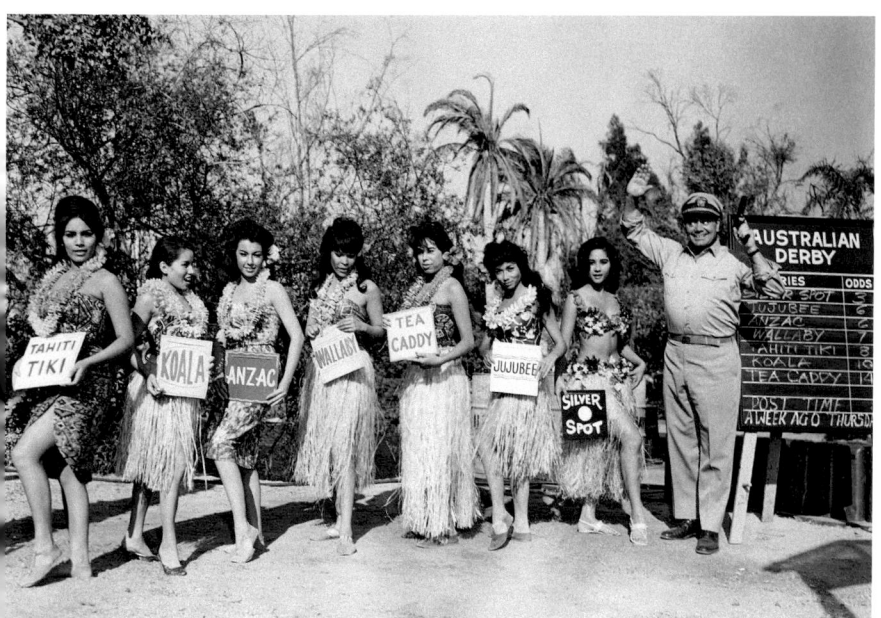

Pendant ce temps, aux États-Unis, la presse continue à véhiculer les clichés des mers du Sud comme si rien n'avait changé : des insulaires sympathiques et des vahinés magnifiques à foison, la vie était une plage, le bonheur possible. Lorsque les vétérans secoués par les affres du combat rentrent au pays, personne n'a envie d'entendre leurs histoires de corps sanguinolents et de membres arrachés.

Impatients de revenir à une vie normale, les soldats eux-mêmes font tout pour oublier les horreurs qu'ils ont vécues. Avec une mémoire volontairement sélective, ils embellissent leur « aventure exotique », en narrent les aspects humoristiques, et participent ainsi à cette mythologie assimilée par la culture populaire. Les souvenirs de guerre viennent illustrer l'héroïsme des anciens combattants, dont les blagues salaces se racontent dans les bars polynésiens et les

salles de jeu de banlieue. Pour bien des vétérans, cette expérience représente la période la plus intense de leur vie. Ils « y étaient », et ils estiment qu'ils ont mérité de se reposer sur leurs lauriers.

Le fantasme des mers du Sud, qui était né bien avant la guerre, se révèle plus fort que les mauvais souvenirs et les Américains de la moitié du siècle, heureux de l'entretenir, entonnent les mélodies de *South Pacific,* la comédie musicale et le film.

Dans les années 1960, les magouilles farfelues qui constituent la trame de la série américaine *Sur le pont, la marine !,* tournée dans un lagon hollywoodien et dans les huttes en bambou des studios Universal, parviennent à illustrer un aspect plus léger de la guerre.

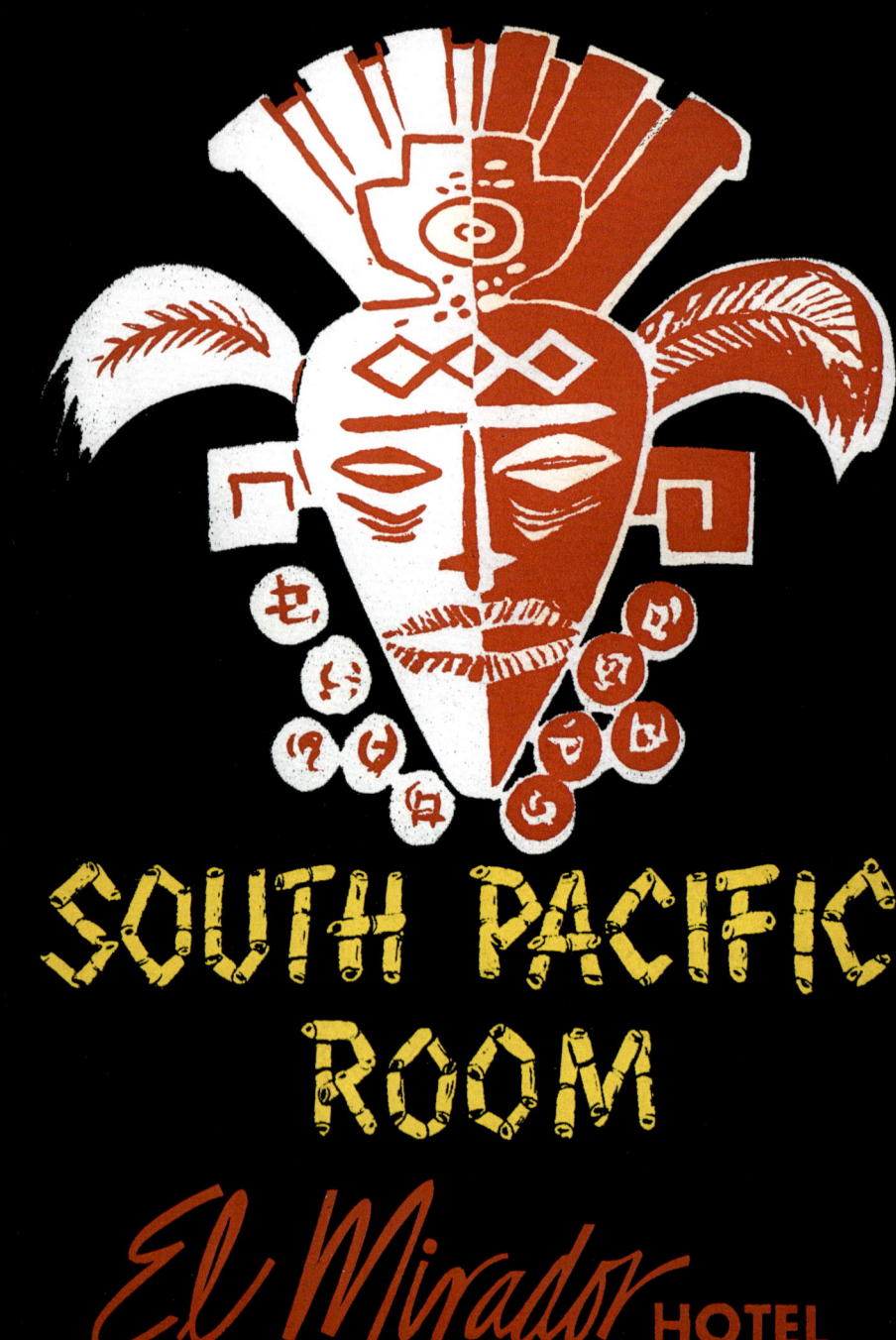

SOUTH PACIFIC
ROOM
El Mirador HOTEL

THE CALL OF *SOUTH PACIFIC* AND "BALI HAI"

DER RUF VON *SOUTH PACIFIC* UND „BALI HAI"
L'APPEL DU *SOUTH PACIFIC* ET DE « BALI HAI »

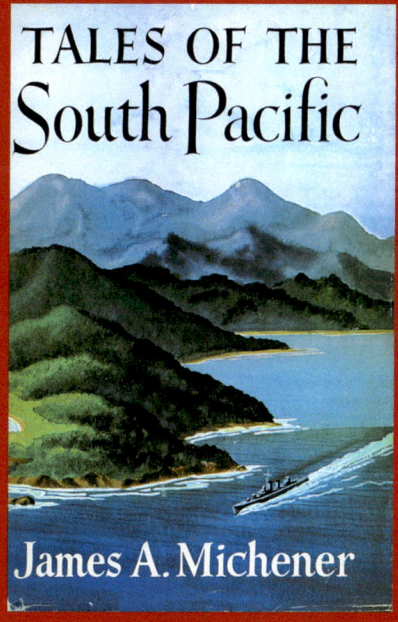

OPPOSITE: South Pacific Room menu, El Mirador Hotel, Palm Springs, California, 1950s *(Mimi Payne Collection)*

ABOVE: The book that brought the Pacific Theater home to America

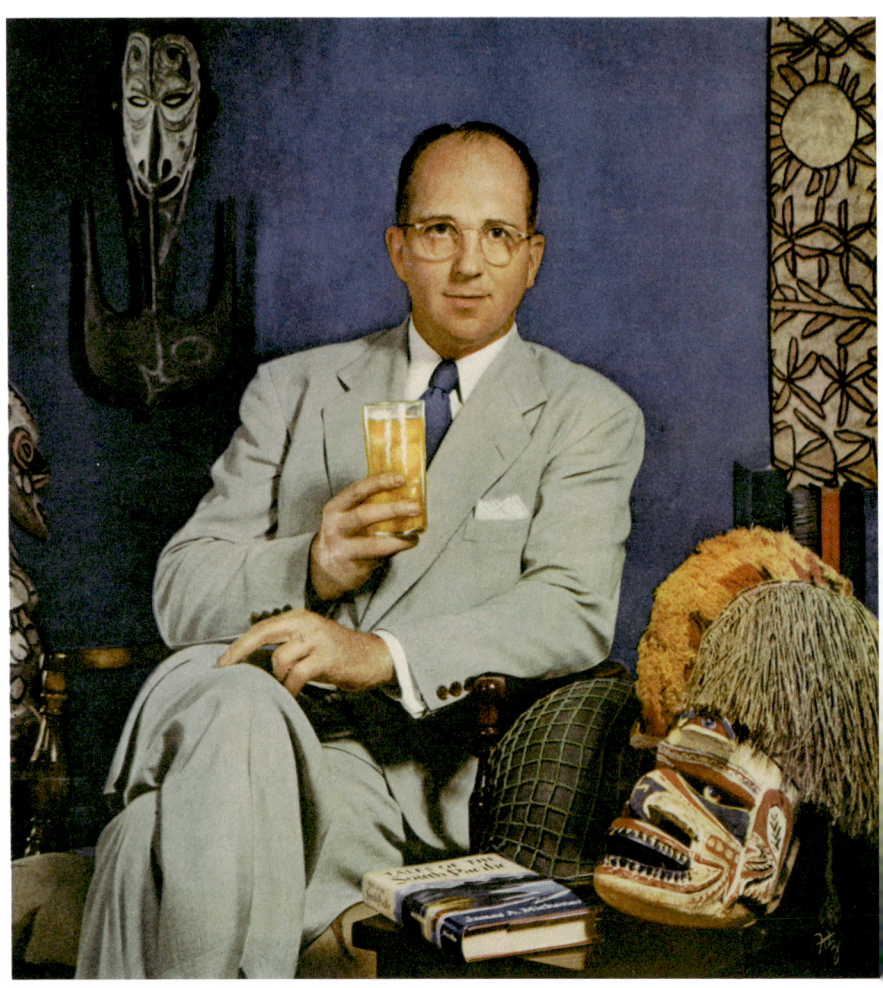

ABOVE: Author James Michener portrayed as Oceanic art connoisseur

OPPOSITE ABOVE: *South Pacific* goes Broadway

OPPOSITE BELOW: The play became a standard of the musical stage

AS FAR AS WARTIME NAVAL TOURS

of duty go, James Michener was lucky: his superiors judged him to be an intellectual, and he was assigned to write the history of the navy in the Pacific as an observer from behind the front lines. The characters and stories he encountered inspired Michener to spin off his own novel from the material. The resulting story collection, *Tales of the South Pacific,* was published in 1947 and earned Michener the Pulitzer Prize for fiction.

The book hit a nerve in postwar America and became a best seller. As such, it sparked the immediate interest of producers of other popular media. Its first adaptation was to the stage, in the unlikely form of a Broadway musical. The play's songbook proved to be infectious, turning the cast album into a hit record. Music critic Donal Henahan wrote: "Few inhabitants of America in 1949 could have failed to know every dramatic nuance and singable note of *South Pacific*... the Rodgers score penetrated every layer of American culture... for years, no American ear could escape... The songs oozed out of every radio and television set, assailed one in elevators, restaurants, and washrooms." Selections from the score were covered by every well-known singer and musician in the country. In 1951, composer Leonard Bernstein gave his social-criticism opera the title *Trouble in Tahiti,* referring to trouble in the typical, seemingly wholesome suburban family.

It was the musical, not the book, that was adapted to the big screen in 1958, marking a slight detour from the book-to-film-to-bar tradition. The result was a grand Hollywood spectacular in Cinemascope, projecting the war-torn Pacific through rose-colored glasses—literally.

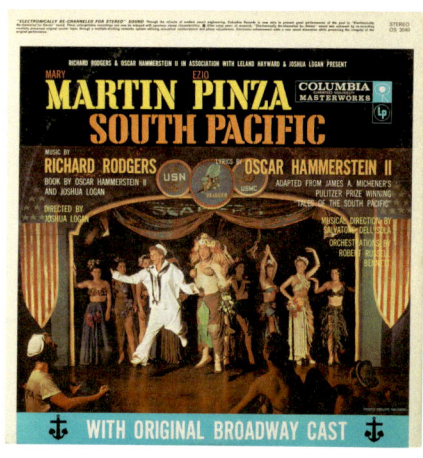

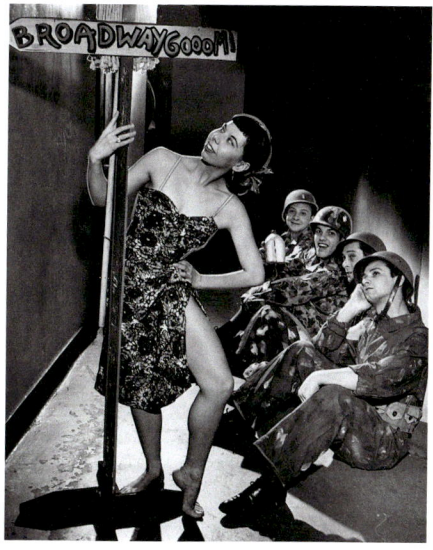

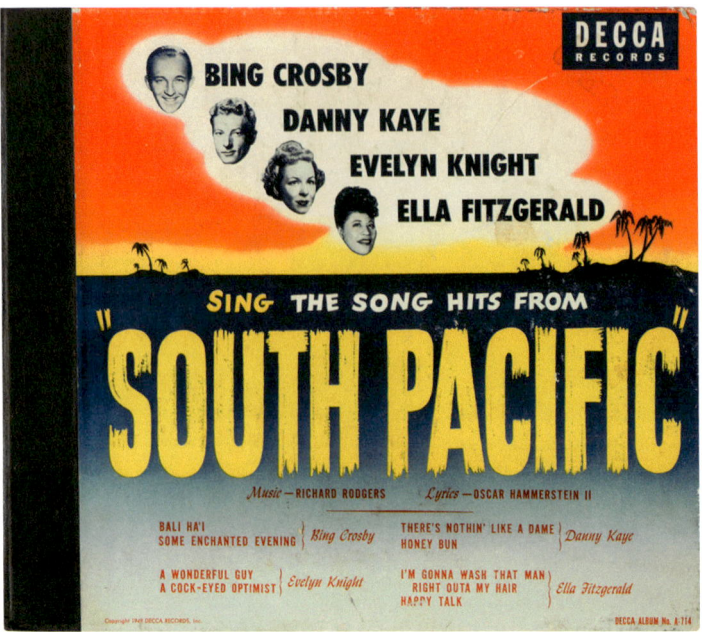

The time of the Tiki was just dawning in America. The postwar *South Pacific* fever inspired even more Polynesian supper clubs to pop up in America. The *South Pacific* restaurant in Hallandale, Florida, declared: "The *South Pacific* is a complete replica of a South Sea Island village. The native huts, the lyrical rock gardens and the lush tropical setting all speak the glamour of the Islands."

Another pop-culture idiom that sprang out of the *South Pacific* opus was that of the dream isle of Bali Hai. The hit song by that name had a hypnotic effect on the American psyche, suggestively conveying the promise that everyone could find their own special island where one would realize one's "own special hopes, own special dreams / Where the sky meets the sea / Come to me, Come to me..."

And so the people came, escaping to the many urban Bali Hais that popped up throughout America, to catch a moment on that magic isle if just for an evening. With the siren song of Bali Ha'i echoing in their ears, they imbibed potent potions with names like Boar's Tooth, Headhunter, and Bali Hai Swizzle, seeking "ecstatic fulfillment of the hungers of body and soul."

The introduction of the new Polynesian pop paradigm of Bali Hai was perhaps best signified by the fact that the Bali Hai in San Diego took over the location of a Christian's Hut franchise, a prewar concept of Polynesian pop. The Bali Hai continued to use the logo of the native chief called "The Goof" from its predecessor, but also added its own cartoony mascot, "Mr. Bali Hai." One film-inspired destination had taken over another, carrying on the tradition of Polynesia Americana.

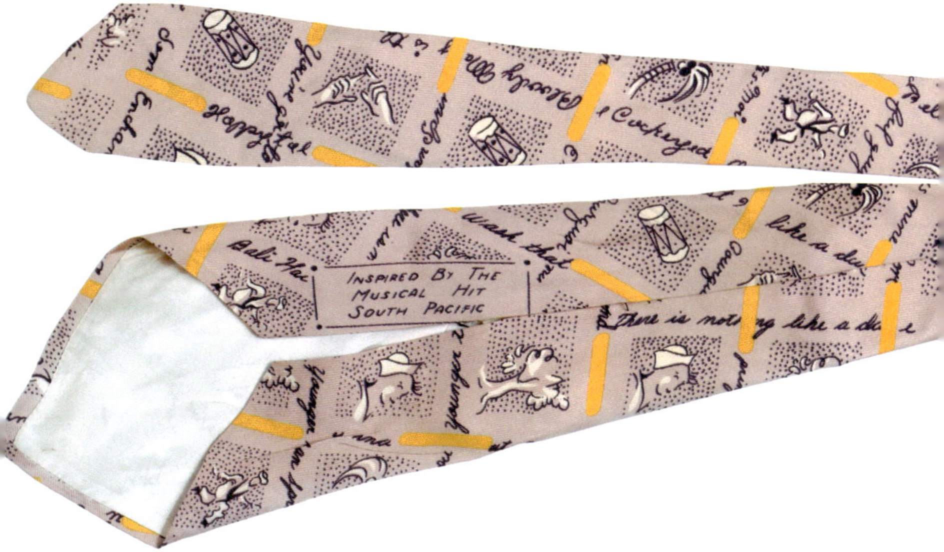

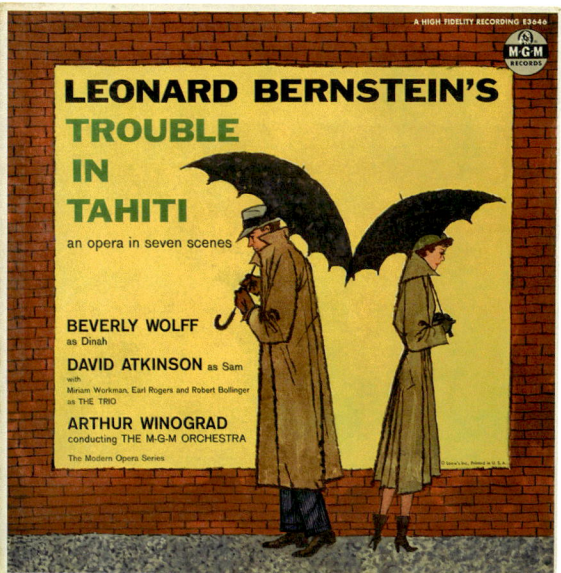

OPPOSITE: Singing stars big and small interpreted its songs

ABOVE: It was such a pop-culture phenomenon, branded merchandise followed

LEFT: Tahiti as the metaphor for the nuclear family?

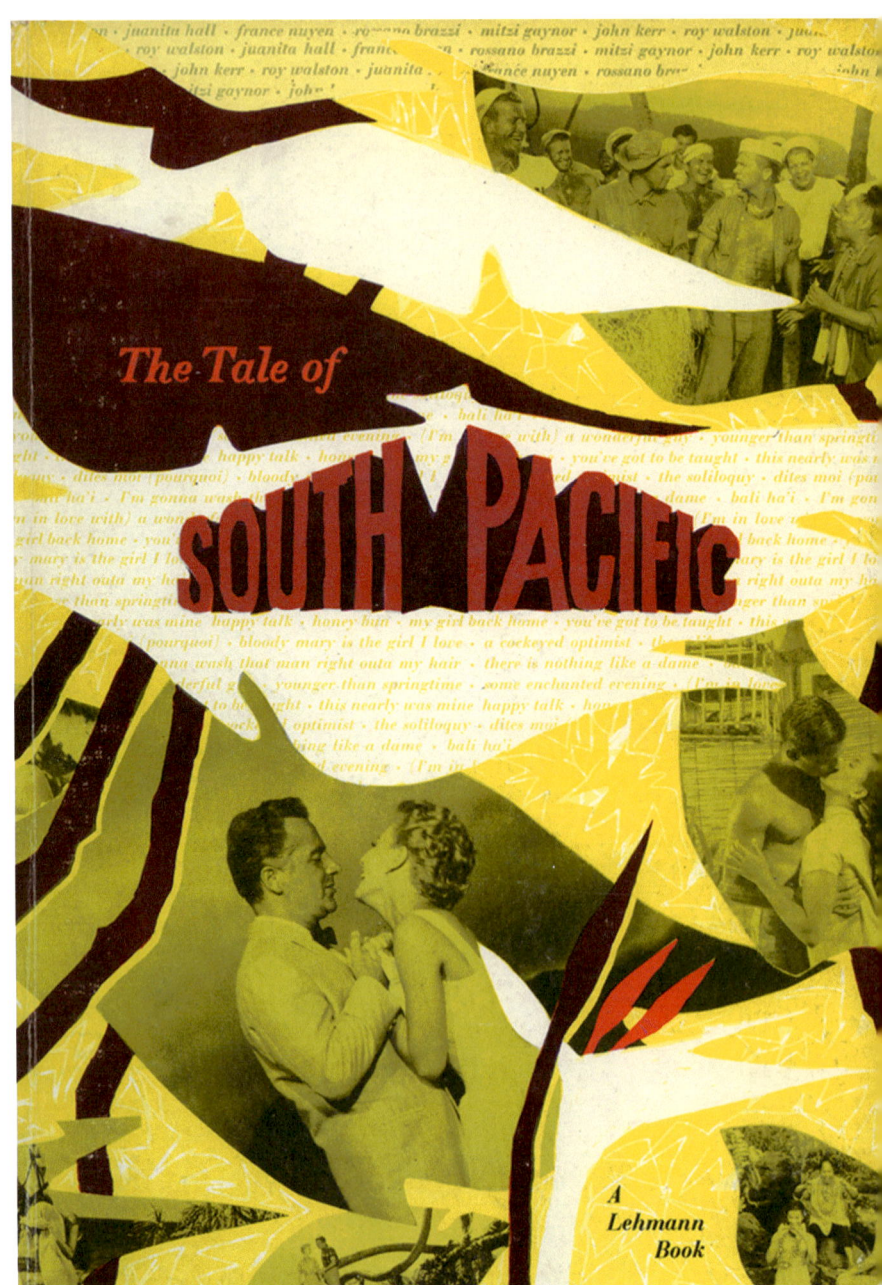

JAMES MICHENER HATTE BEI SEINEN Marineeinsätzen Glück: Seine Vorgesetzten sahen in ihm einen Intellektuellen und übertrugen ihm die Aufgabe, die Geschehnisse im Pazifik als Beobachter hinter der Front festzuhalten. Die Menschen, denen er begegnete und die Geschichten, die er erlebte, inspirierten ihn zu den Kurzgeschichten, die als sein erstes Buch unter dem Titel *Tales of the South Pacific* (dt. *Die Südsee*) 1947 veröffentlicht wurden und ihm den Pulitzer-Preis für Belletristik einbrachten.

Das Buch traf im Nachkriegsamerika einen empfindlichen Nerv und wurde ein Bestseller. Als solcher erregte es sofort das Interesse von Filmproduzenten und anderen Medienschaffenden. Es wurde zuerst für die Bühne adaptiert und – unpassenderweise – zu einem Broadway-Musical gemacht. Die Lieder des Stücks erwiesen sich als so mitreißend, dass aus dem Soundtrack ein Spitzenreiter in den Charts wurde. Der Musikkritiker Donal Henahan schrieb: „Es gab 1949 nur wenige Einwohner in den USA, die nicht jede dramatische Nuance und sangbare Note von *South Pacific* mittönen konnten… Rodgers Musik durchzog jede Schicht der amerikanischen Kultur…

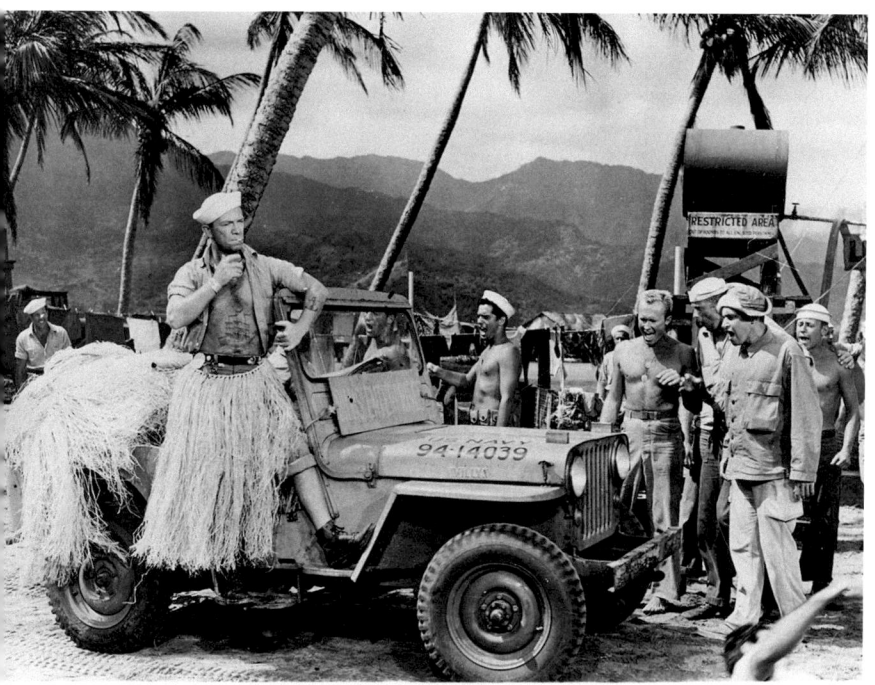

A Scene from Rodgers and Hammerstein's **"SOUTH PACIFIC"**, filmed in TODD-AO
a MAGNA Release
Directed by Joshua Logan   Color by Technicolor   Produced at Twentieth Century-Fox

OPPOSITE: Promotional picture book for *South Pacific*

ABOVE: The rest of the G.I.s were not so lucky

The male
South Seas dream comes true:
Lt. Cable is sent on a mission to
the "Isle of the women," Bali Hai.
Here Cable gets to meet the lovely
and exotic Liat

jahrelang konnte ihr kein Amerikaner ent-
kommen… Die Lieder tönten aus jedem
Radio und Fernseher, überfielen einen in
Fahrstühlen, Restaurants und in öffent-
lichen Toiletten." Unzählige Musiker cover-
ten sie; 1951 gab der Komponist Leonard
Bernstein seiner sozialkritischen Oper den
Titel *Trouble in Tahiti*, eine Anspielung auf
die Probleme einer scheinbar perfekten vorstädtischen Familie.

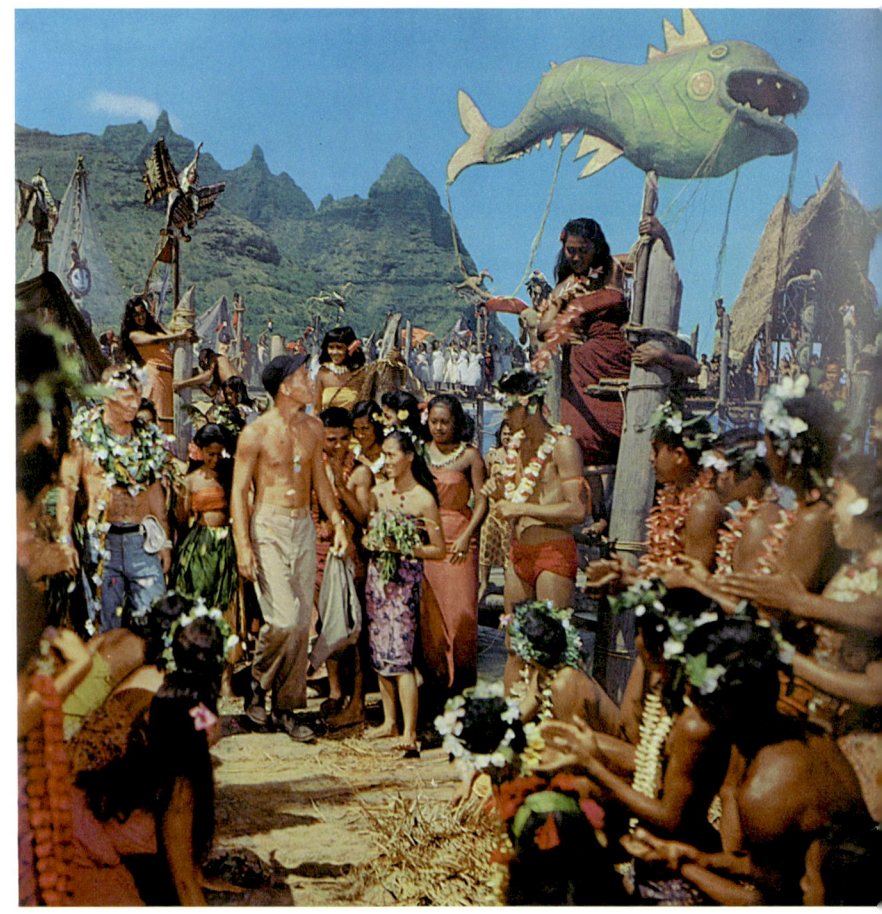

Es war das Musical, nicht das Buch, das schließlich im Jahr 1958 für die Kinoleinwand adaptiert wurde – eine leichte Abweichung der „Buch-zum-Film-zur-Bar-Tradition". Das Ergebnis war ein Hollywood-Spektakel in CinemaScope, in dem der kriegsgebeutelte Pazifik wortwörtlich durch die rosarote Brille gezeigt wurde.

Das Tiki-Zeitalter hatte in Amerika gerade erst begonnen. Der Rummel um *South Pacific* resultierte in der Eröffnung von noch mehr polynesischen Supper Clubs. Ein gleichnamiges Restaurant in Hallandale, Florida, deklarierte: „Das *South Pacific* ist eine vollständige Replik eines Inseldorfes in der Südsee. Die authentischen Hütten, die malerischen Steingärten und das üppige tropische Dekor erwecken den Zauber dieser Inseln zum Leben."

Ein weiterer Popkulturbegriff, den wir *South Pacific* zu verdanken haben, ist die Trauminsel Bali Hai. Peggy Lees gleichnamiger Hit hatte einen hypnotischen Effekt auf die amerikanische Psyche. Seine Zeilen suggerierten, dass jeder seine eigene Trauminsel finden konnte, um „seine Hoffnungen, seine Träume zu realisieren / Wo Himmel und Meer sich treffen / Komm zu mir, komm zu mir".

Und so kamen die Menschen und flüchteten sich in die vielen Bali Hais, die nun überall in den USA eröffneten, um nur einen Moment, nur einen Abend, auf dieser magischen Insel zu verbringen. Mit Sirenengesängen à la Bali Hai in den Ohren kippten sie mächtige Cocktails mit Namen wie Boar's Tooth, Headhunter und Bali Hai Swizzle, immer auf der Suche nach Wegen, „den Hunger von Körper und Geist zu stillen".

Die Bedeutung von Bali Hai als einem neuen Musterbeispiel für den „Polynesian Pop" wird vermutlich am treffendsten durch die Tatsache unterstrichen, dass die Filiale in San Diego in den Räumlichkeiten des dortigen Christian's Hut eingerichtet wurde – *dem* Sinnbild der Bewegung vor dem Krieg. Das Bali Hai übernahm das Logo des The Goof genannten Eingeborenenhäuptlings von seinem Vorgänger, entwickelte jedoch auch ein eigenes Maskottchen, „Mr. Bali Hai". Sowohl Christian's Hut als auch Bali Hai waren von einem Film inspiriert worden. Das eine hatte das andere ersetzt und die Tradition des Polynesia Americana fortgeführt.

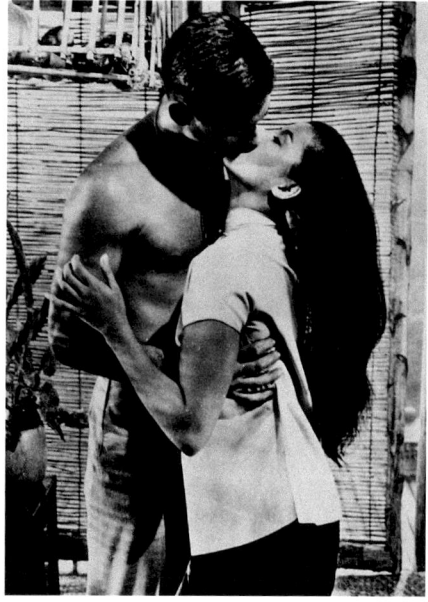

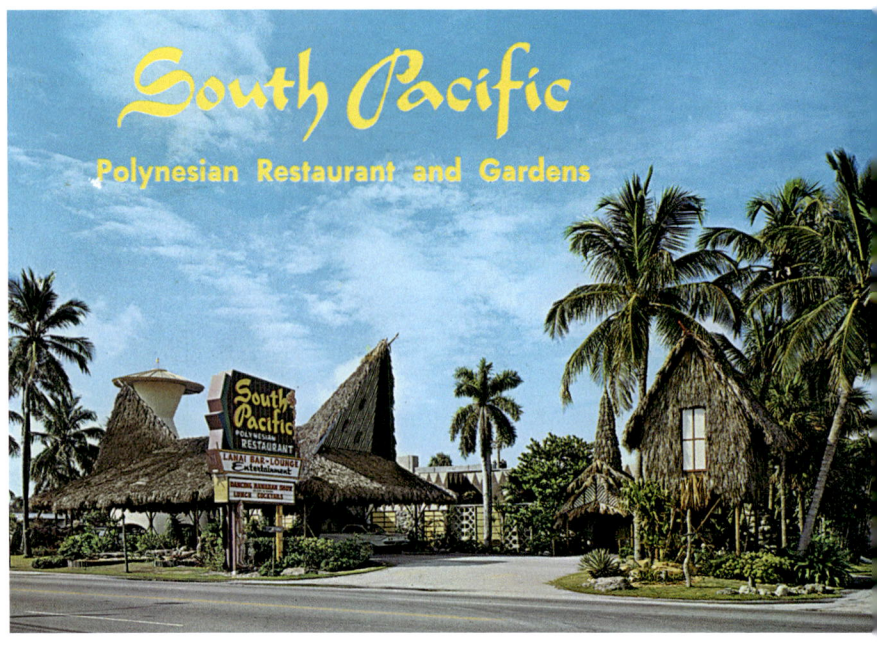

POUR CE QUI EST DES ORDRES DE
mission pendant son temps de service,
James Michener a eu de la chance, puisque
ses supérieurs ont jugé qu'il était un pur
intellectuel et lui ont assigné le devoir
d'écrire une histoire de la marine dans le
Pacifique en tant qu'observateur, loin derrière les lignes de combat. Les personnages
et les intrigues qu'il découvre alors lui
inspirent aussi un roman plus personnel.
Le recueil de nouvelles Pacifique Sud est publié
en 1947 et vaut à Michener le Prix Pulitzer
dans la catégorie fiction.

Dans l'Amérique d'après-guerre, le
livre touche une corde sensible et devient
un best-seller. Son succès en librairie attire
immédiatement l'attention des producteurs de cinéma et des autres médias de
masse. Le roman est d'abord adapté sur
les planches, sous la forme improbable

d'une comédie musicale de Broadway.
La musique qui accompagne l'intrigue
se révèle d'une séduction contagieuse
et bientôt le disque bat lui aussi tous les
records de vente. Le critique musical Donal
Henahan écrit : « Rares sont les citoyens
d'Amérique qui, en 1949, ne connaissaient
pas par cœur la moindre nuance drama-
tique et chaque note de *South Pacific*… La
partition composée par Rodgers s'insinua
dans toutes les couches de la culture américaine… pendant des années, aucune oreille
ne put y échapper… Les chansons suin-
taient de tous les postes de radio et de télévision, vous prenaient en embuscade dans
les ascenseurs, les restaurants, et même
les toilettes. »

Pas un chanteur ou musicien célèbre qui
n'ait repris un titre ou un autre la pièce.
En 1951, le compositeur Leonard Bernstein

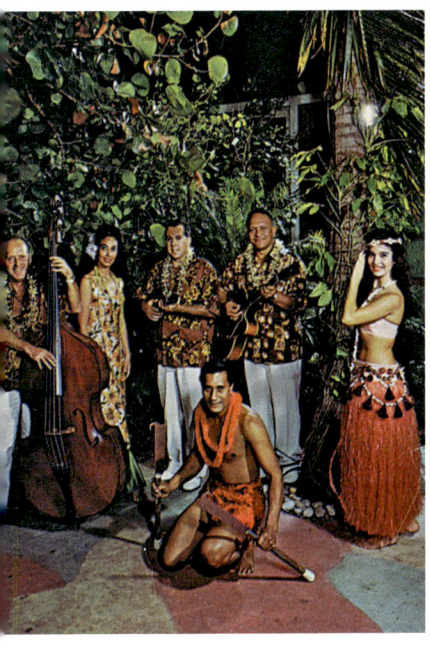

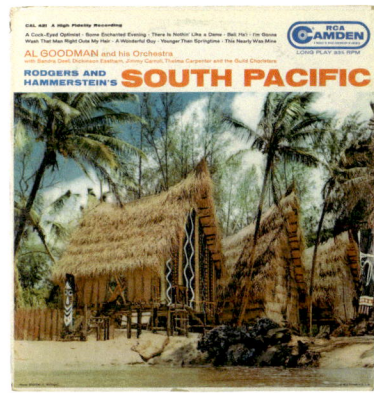

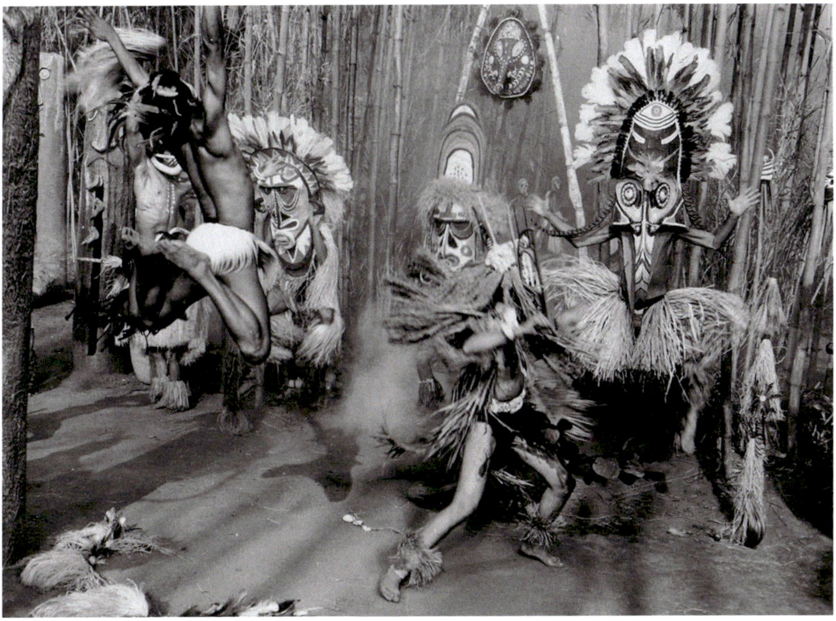

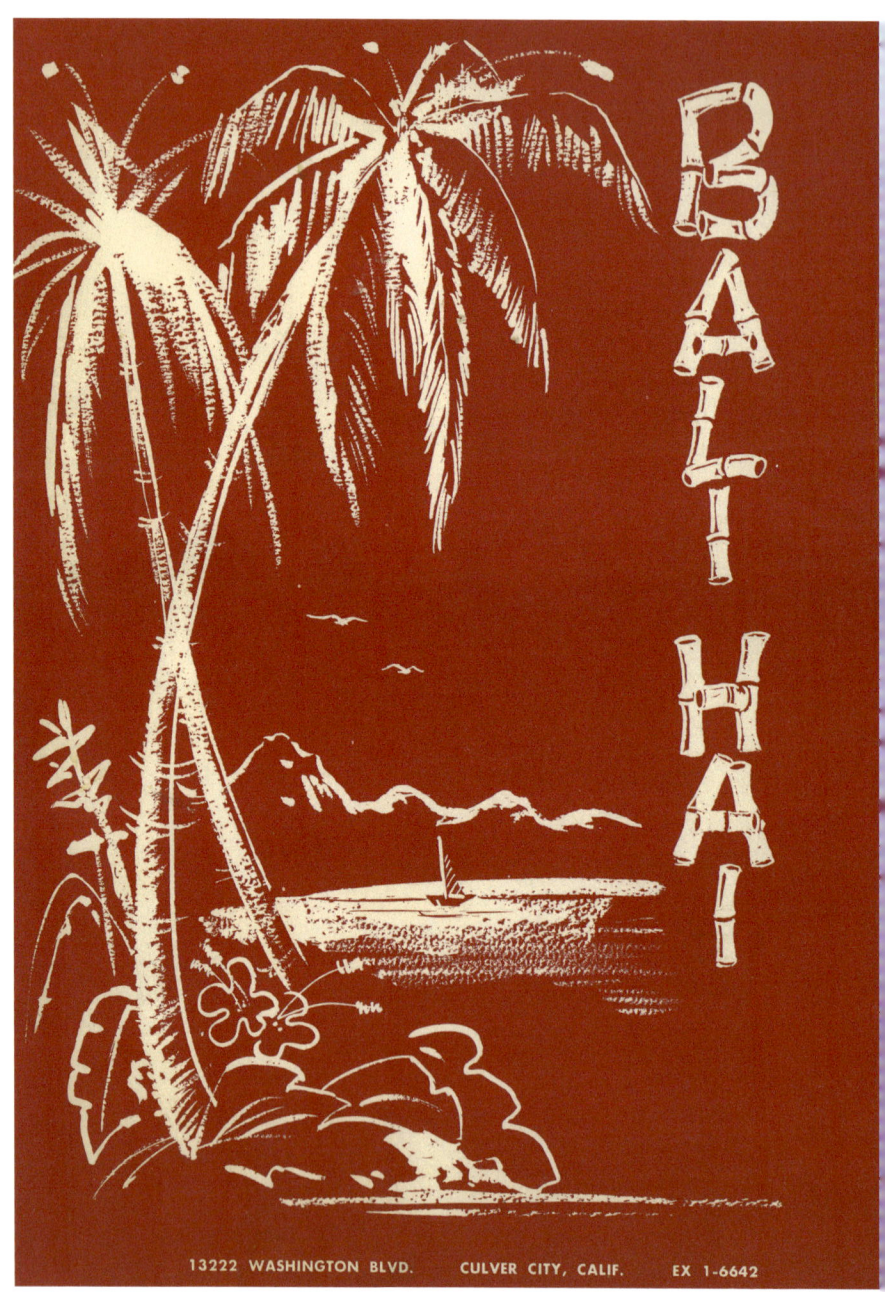

BALI HAI

13222 WASHINGTON BLVD.   CULVER CITY, CALIF.   EX 1-6642

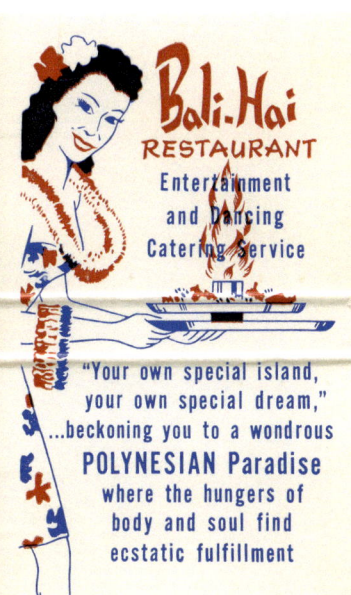

OPPOSITE: Menu for the Bali Hai in Culver City, Los Angeles (Frank Brajevic Collection)

LEFT: Matchbook quoting the song

BELOW: Cocktail mug from the Bali Hai in Lynnfield, Massachusetts (Frank Brajevic Collection)

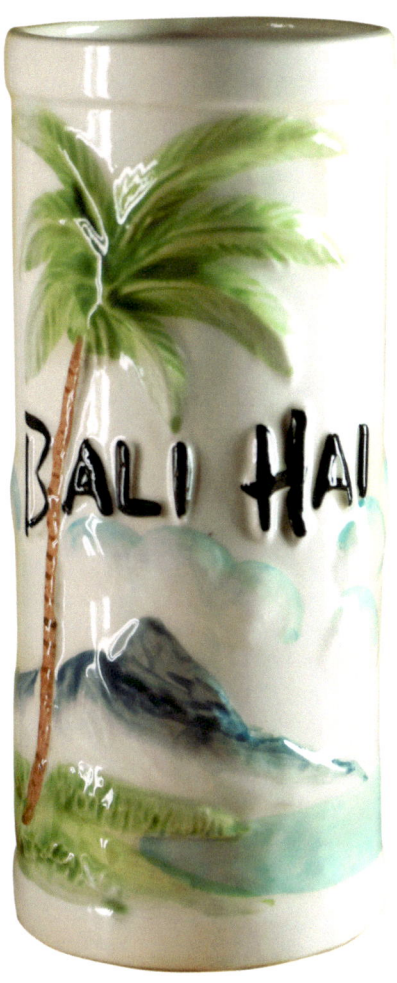

intitule son opéra empreint de critique sociale *Trouble in Tahiti*, en référence aux problèmes qui secouent une typique famille de banlieue, en apparence unie et heureuse.

C'est la comédie musicale, et non le roman, qui est adaptée sur grand écran en 1958, divergeant ainsi de l'habituel enchaînement livre/film/bar. Le résultat est un film à grand spectacle en cinémascope, dans la plus pure tradition hollywoodienne, qui présente le Pacifique ravagé par la guerre à travers des lunettes aux verres teintés de rose…

L'ère du tiki ne fait que commencer en Amérique. La fièvre tropicale d'après-guerre provoque une nouvelle poussée de dîners dansants et autres clubs polynésiens dans tout le pays. Le restaurant South Pacific d'Hallandale, en Floride, annonce : « Le South Pacific est la réplique complète d'un village d'une île des mers du Sud. Les huttes en feuillage, les lyriques jardins de rocaille et les paysages tropicaux luxuriants expriment tout le charme supposé des îles lointaines. »

Parmi les idiomes que *South Pacific* intègre à la culture populaire figure l'île rêvée de Bali Hai. La chanson ainsi intitulée a un effet hypnotique sur la psyché américaine, et suggère l'idée, promet même, que toute personne peut trouver son île, où elle verra se réaliser « ses propres espoirs, ses propres rêves / Là où le ciel rencontre la mer / Viens à moi, Viens à moi… ».

Et les gens affluent, s'évadent dans les nombreuses Bali Hai urbaines qui pullulent aux quatre coins du pays, pour vivre la magie, ne serait-ce que le temps d'une soirée. Avec dans les oreilles les accords familiers et envoûtants de la chanson « Bali Ha'i », ils ingurgitent de puissantes potions baptisées « Dent de Sanglier », « Chasseur de tête » ou « Cocktail de Bali Hai », en quête d'un « épanouissement extatique des appétits du corps et de l'esprit ».

Détail révélateur de l'importance de ce nouveau paradigme polynésien pop, le Bali Hai de San Diego s'installe en lieu et place d'un Christian's Hut, célèbre franchise d'avant-guerre. L'établissement conserve le personnage du chef coutumier simplet baptisé « The Goof », mais lui adjoint sa propre mascotte dessinée, M. Bali Hai. Une destination inspirée du cinéma en remplace une autre, entretenant la factice culture américano-polynésienne.

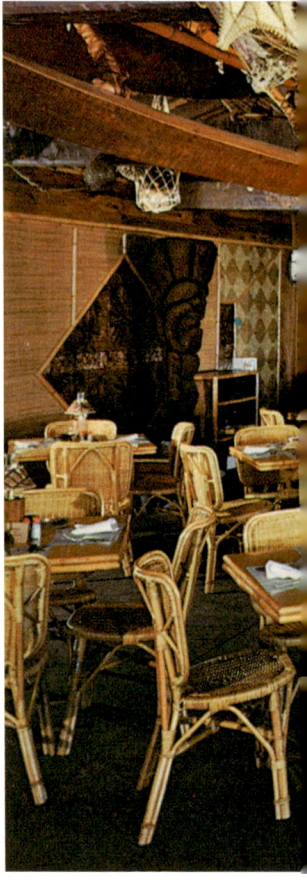

ABOVE: Interior of the Bali Hai at Lake Pontchartrain, New Orleans *(Scott Schell Collection)*

RIGHT: Exterior of the Bali Hai at Lake Pontchartrain, New Orleans *(Jody Daly Collection)*

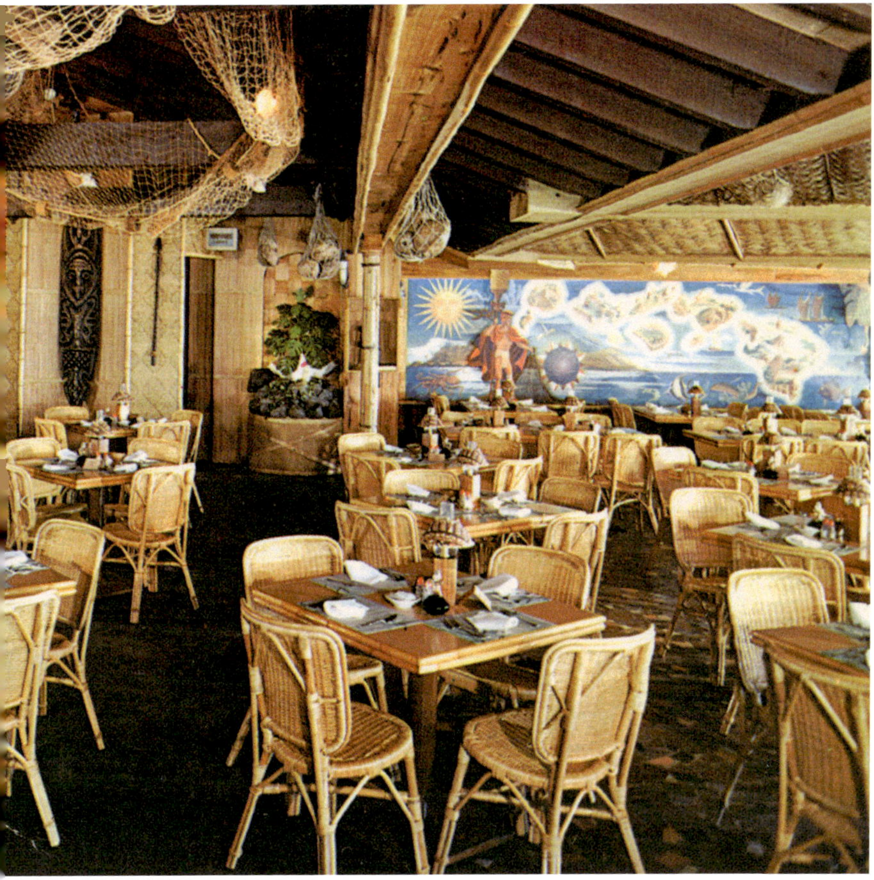

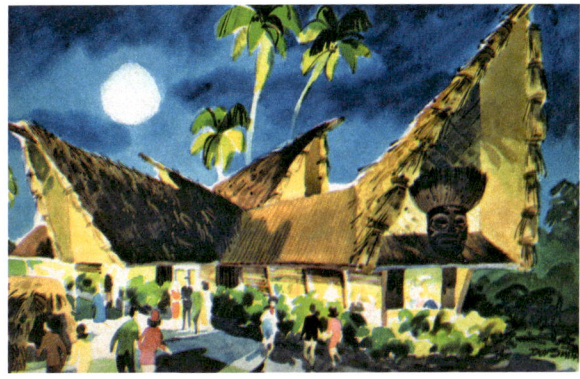

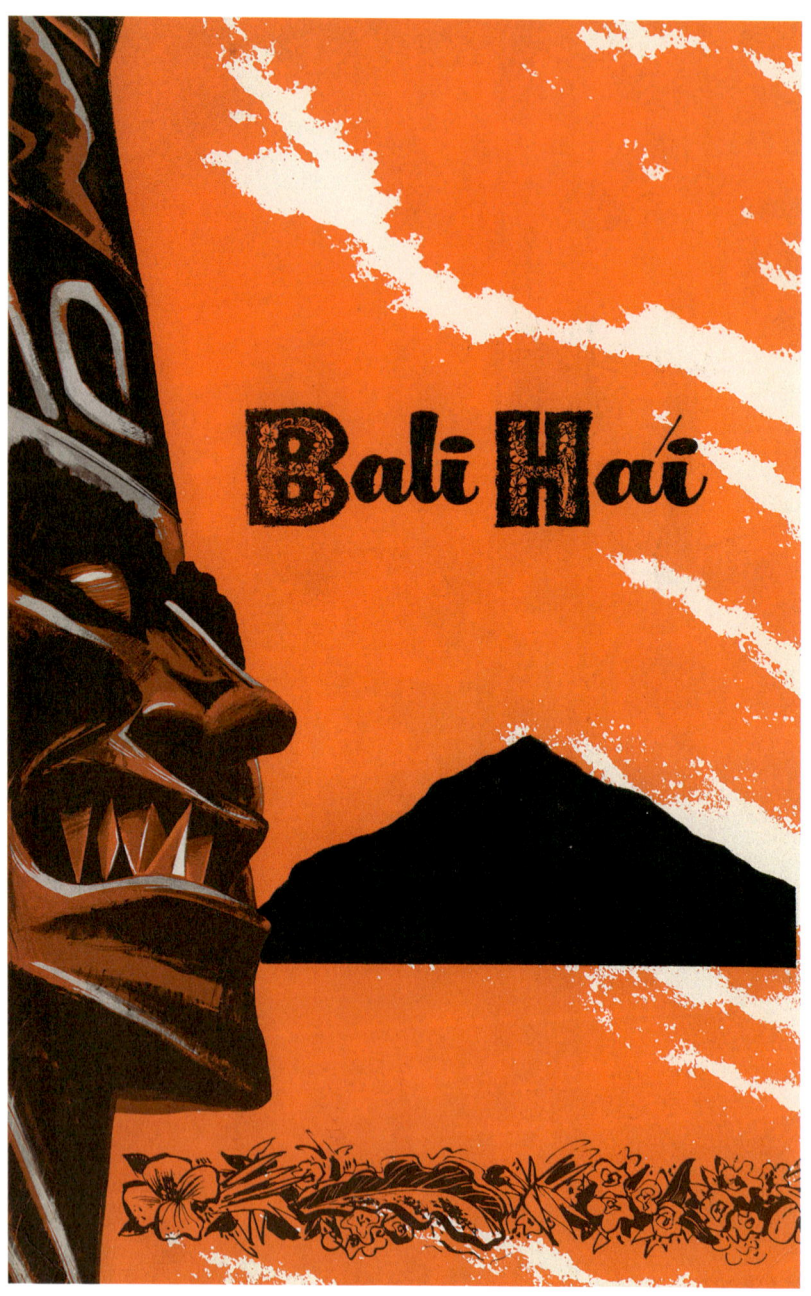

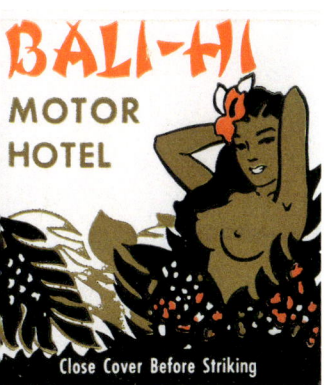

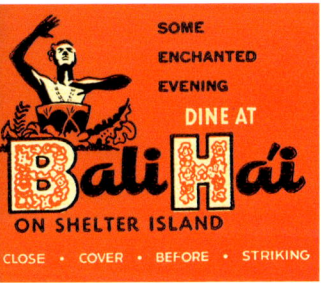

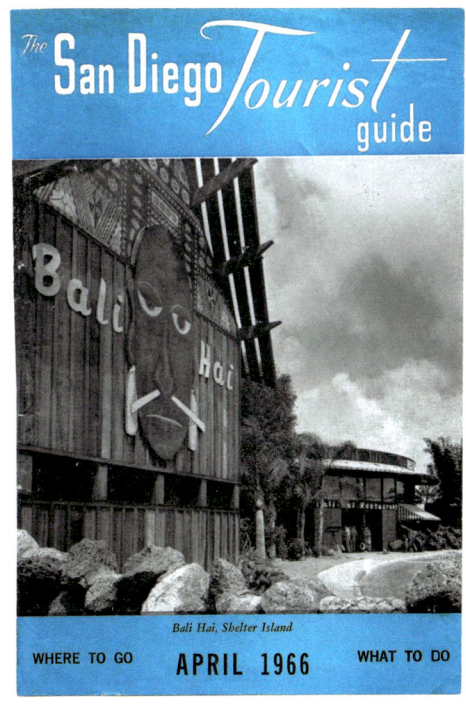

Bali Hai, Shelter Island

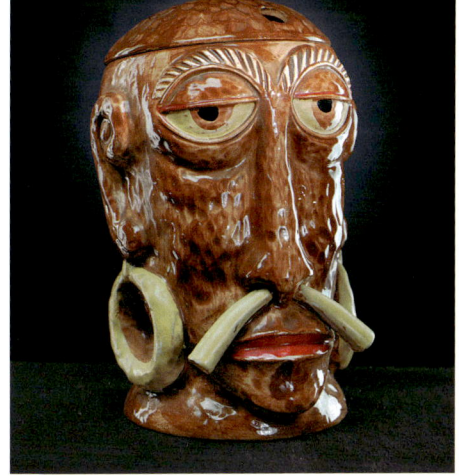

OPPOSITE AND RIGHT: Both Christian's Hut's "The Goof" and the Bali Hai's "Mr. Bali Hai" were classic pre-Tiki cartoon characters

ABOVE: The name Bali Hai became another South Seas fantasy label

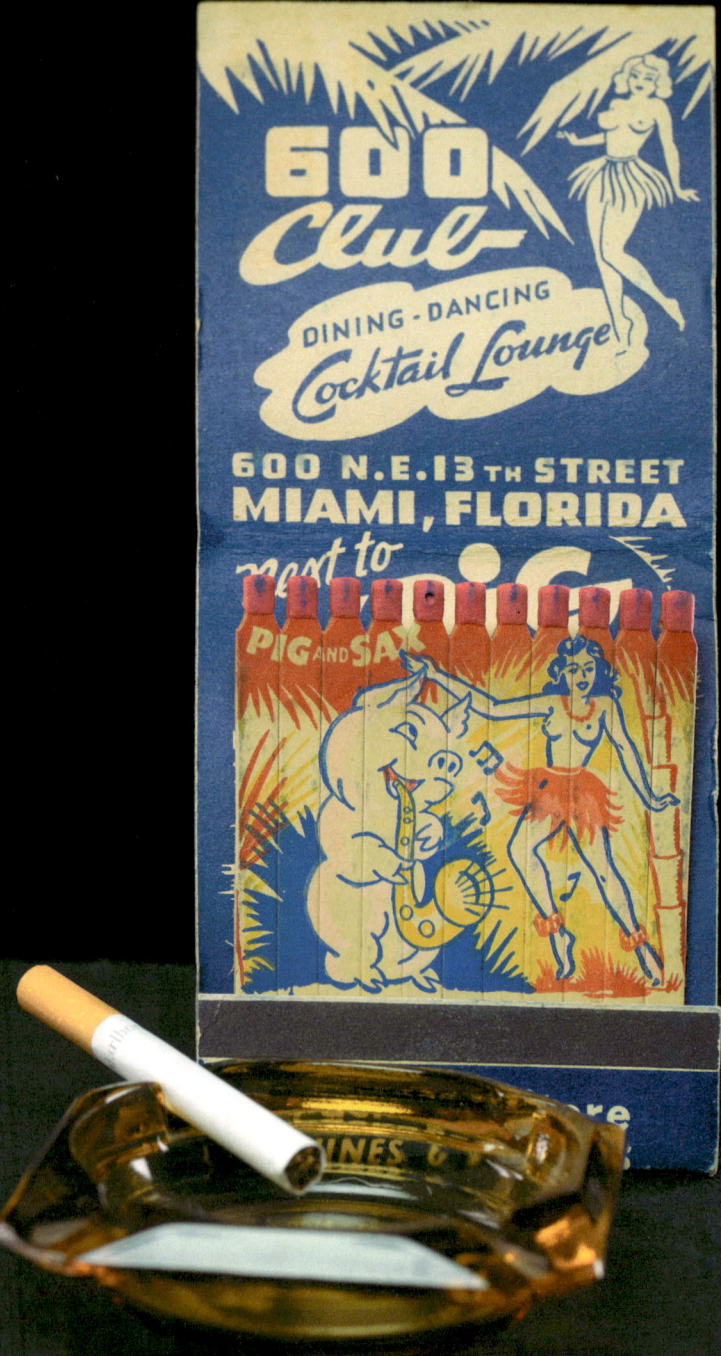

14

THE HULA GIRL—EMISSARY OF THE POLYNESIAN PARADISE

DAS HULA-GIRL – BOTSCHAFTERIN DES POLYNESISCHEN PARADIESES

LA DANSEUSE DE HULA, AMBASSADRICE DU PARADIS POLYNÉSIEN

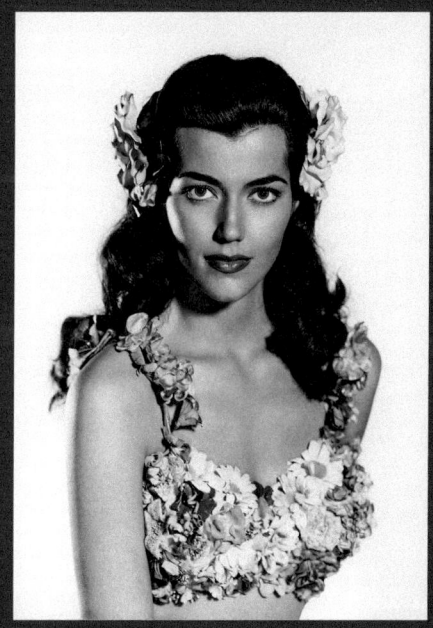

OPPOSITE: Whimsical giant feature matchbook (3.5 x 8 inches)

ABOVE: A stunning modern hula girl, Hollywood-glamour style.
Sandra Edwards in *Up Periscope*, 1959

THE BALMY CLIMATE AND BLUE

waters... the gently swaying palm trees on the sandy beach... the tropical fruits and flowers... While all of this would have made a passable Polynesian paradise, without its Eve, the earthly Eden would have been incomplete. She was the personification of female beauty, the promise of unconditional love so yearned for by man since the Fall from Grace.

Around the mid-20th century, the full-frontal nudity of the native island girl made her a welcome sex symbol in the entertainment industry. If clothed, there still was enough exposed skin and leg to hypnotize the average male gawker. The image of the free-loving Polynesian temptress had been ingrained in men's minds for generations, and the media did nothing to dissuade its tractable customers.

Edgar Leeteg, the "American Gauguin," became the court painter of the Polynesian-restaurant scene. During the American Depression of the 1930s he had escaped to Tahiti, where he paid his bar bills with nude portraits of local beauties painted on black velvet. These voluptuous island madonnas enhanced the bohemian character of the bamboo hideaways they graced.

South Seas restaurants utilized the motif of the Polynesian wahine in many different ways. Her likeness graced menu covers, communal drinking bowls, and cocktail mugs. She was the symbol for having entered a world apart from the bustle outside, an exotic, erotic retreat that indulged one's senses.

RIGHT: Swizzle stick from the Pago Pago bar (*Frank Brajevic Collection*)

OPPOSITE: She is calling... Sheet music cover, 1920

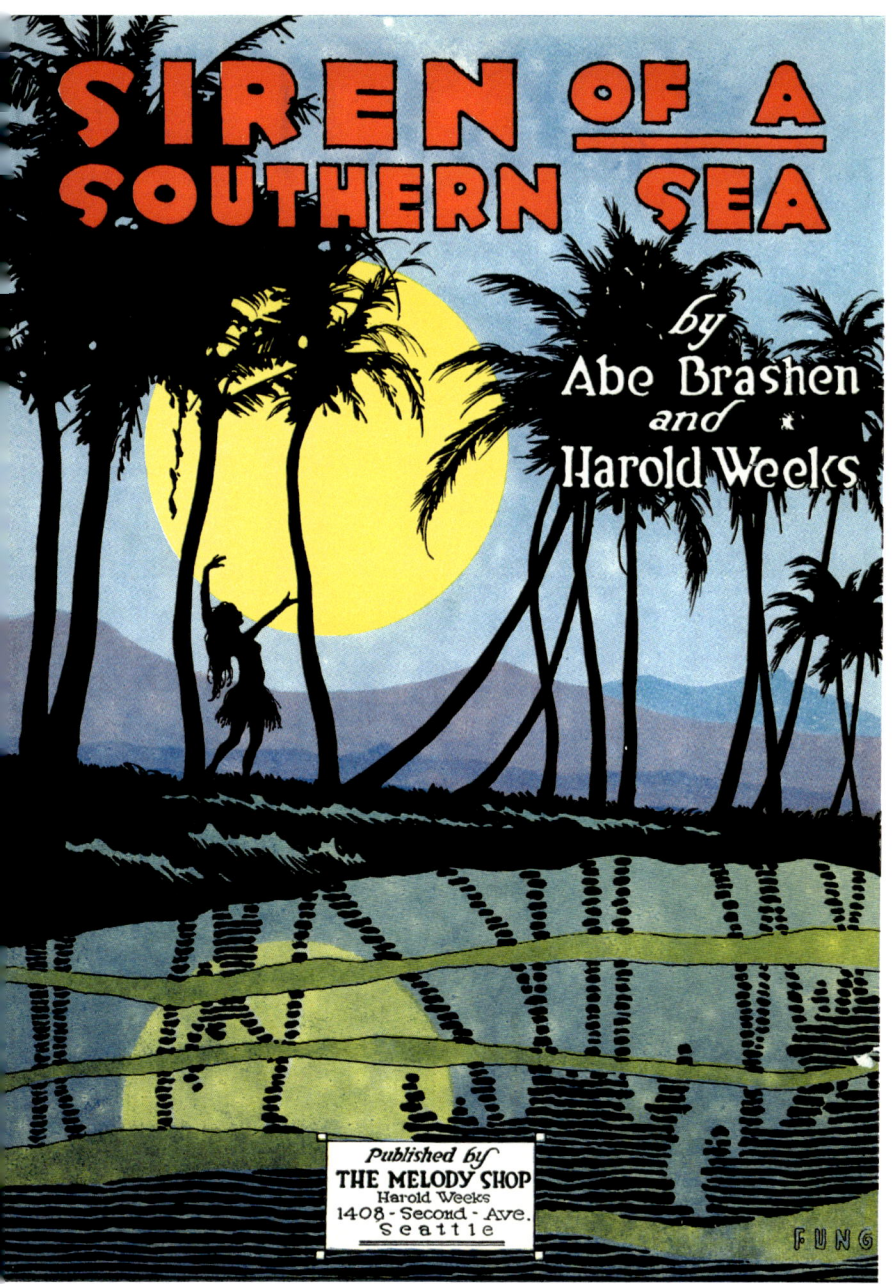

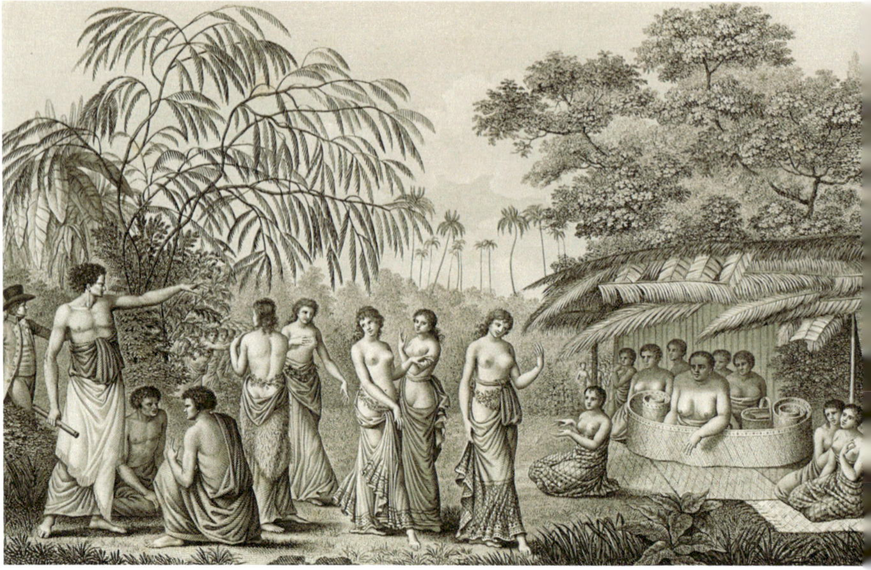

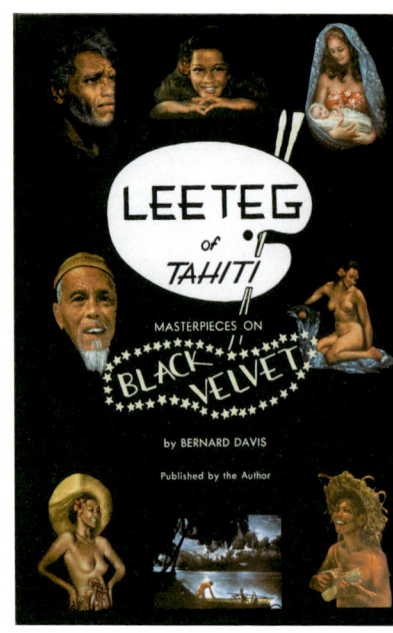

Well-sculpted drink stirrers, provocative cocktail napkins, and whimsical giant "feature" matchbooks all added to the gallery of native nudes found in Polynesian bars throughout the States. Perhaps the most unique artifacts remaining of America's hula-girl fetish are the "embossed breasts" matchbooks, which provided a tactile experience of the model's assets. Lulled in an alcoholic daze and smoky haze, one could dream the South Seas dream.

OPPOSITE ABOVE: Reception of early explorers, La Perouse, 18th century *(Musée du Quai Branly Collection)*

OPPOSITE BELOW: Leeteg's biography

BELOW: Average Americans trying to loosen up among Leetegs at the Seven Seas nightclub, Hollywood *(Schell Collection)*

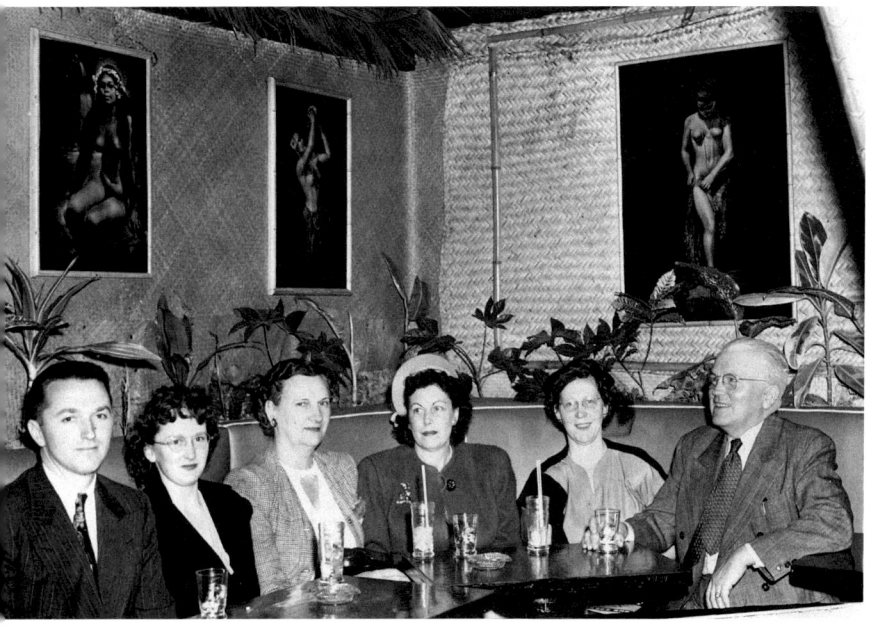

DAS MILDE KLIMA, DAS BLAUE

Wasser… Palmen in der leichten Brise am Strand… exotische Früchte und Blumen – all das hätte ein passables polynesisches Paradies abgegeben. Doch ohne seine Eva wäre das irdische Eden einfach nicht dasselbe. Sie ist die Personifizierung weiblicher Schönheit, das Versprechen bedingungsloser Liebe, nach dem sich der Mensch seit dem Sündenfall sehnt.

Mitte des 20. Jahrhunderts machte die Nacktheit der polynesischen Frauen sie zu einem willkommenen Sexsymbol. Selbst bekleidet gab es noch genug nackte Haut und Beine, um den durchschnittlichen männlichen Gaffer zu hypnotisieren. Das Bild der freigiebigen polynesischen Verführerin brannte sich für Generationen in die Köpfe der Männer – und die Medien taten nichts, um es ihren gefügigen Kunden auszureden

Edgar Leeteg, der „amerikanische Gauguin", wurde zum Hofmaler polynesischer Restaurants. Während der Weltwirtschaftskrise in den 1930er-Jahren war er nach Tahiti geflohen, wo er seine Zeche mit Nacktporträts einheimischer Schönheiten auf schwarzem Samt beglich. Die sinnlichen Insel-Madonnen verstärkten den unkonventionellen Charakter der Bambus-Refugien, die sie schmückten.

Südseerestaurants nutzten das Motiv der polynesischen Wahine auf vielerlei Art

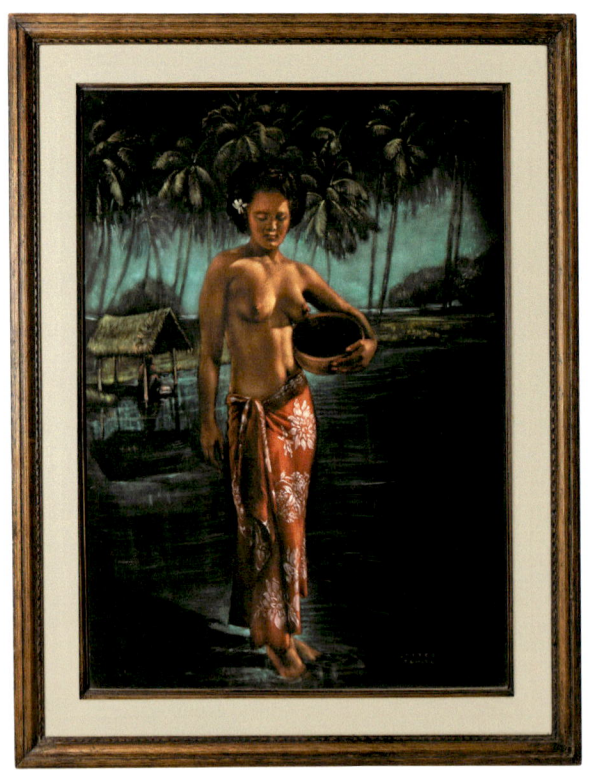

LEFT: *Tahitia*, a classic Leeteg painting (*Velveteria Collection*)

OPPOSITE ABOVE: South Seas movies were made from a man's perspective

OPPOSITE BELOW: Beachcomber Revue flyer, 1946 (*Frank Brajevic Collection*)

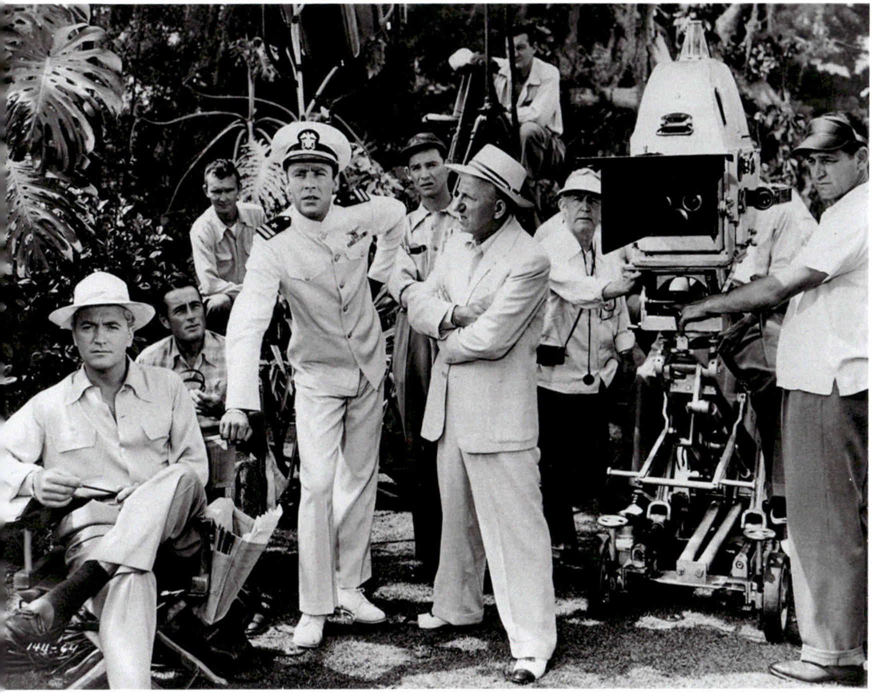

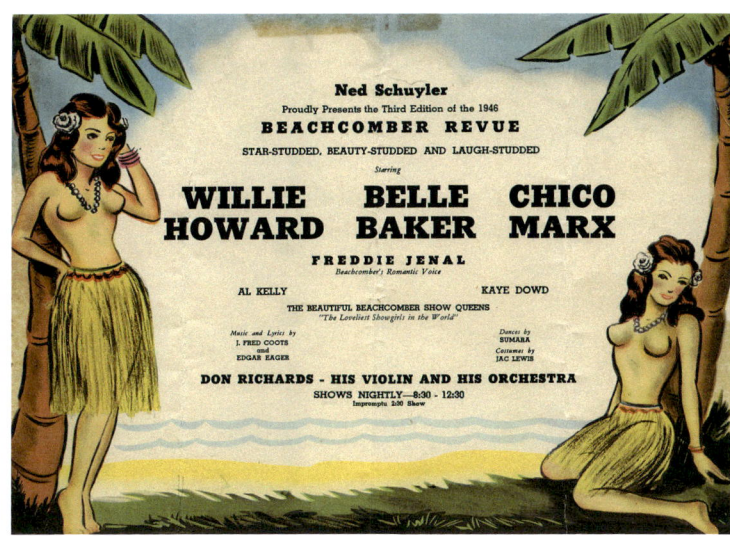

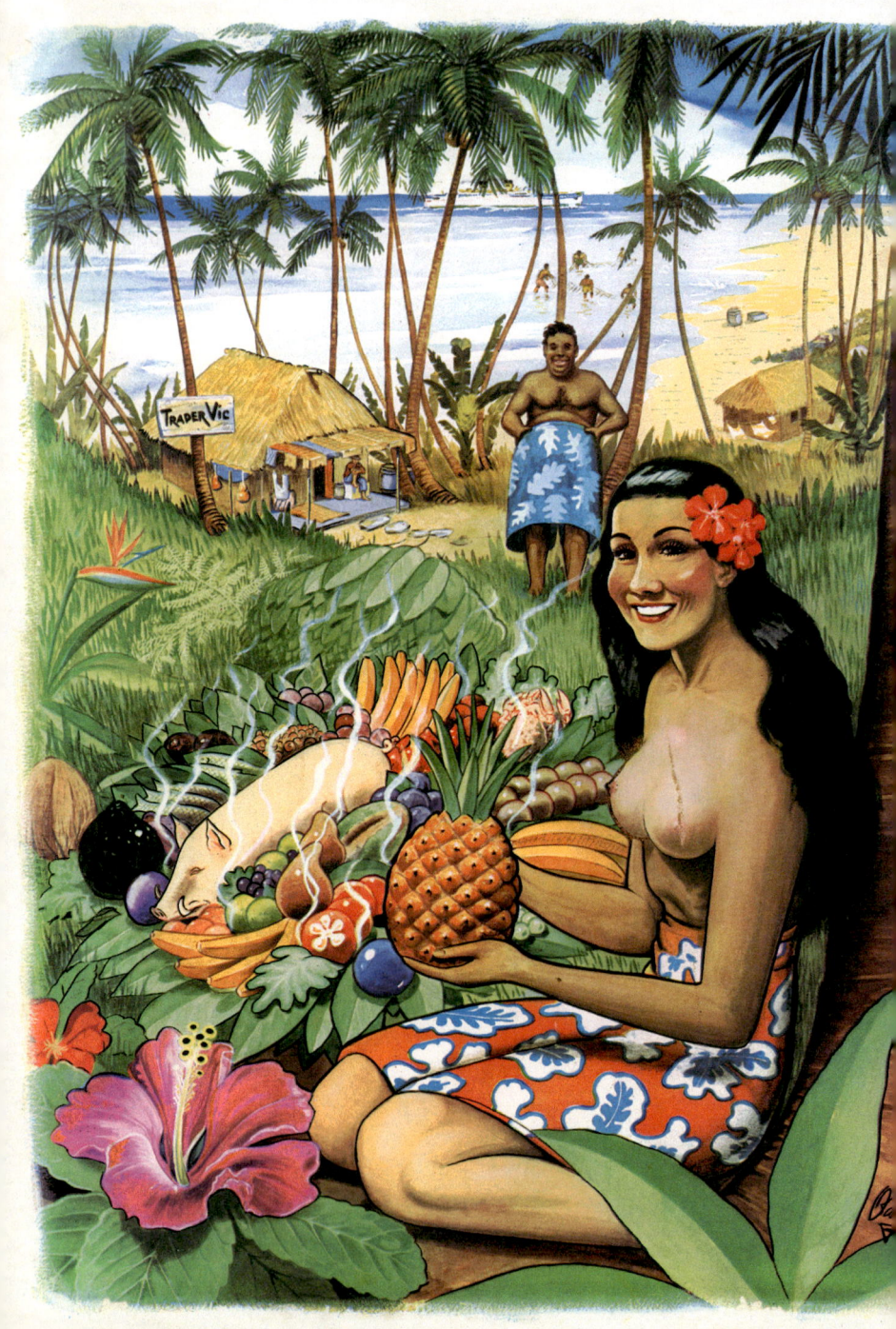

und Weise. Ihr Abbild zierte Speisekarten, Trinkschalen und Cocktailbecher. Sie war das Symbol einer Welt jenseits des schnöden Alltags – eines exotischen, erotischen Kurzurlaubs für die Sinne.

Wohlgeformte Cocktailstäbchen, provokative Servietten und exzentrische Streichholzbriefchen ergänzten die Riege nackter Einheimischer, die in den polynesischen Bars der USA ausgestellt wurden. Vermutlich eines der einzigartigsten Artefakte aus dem Bereich des amerikanischen Hula-Fetischs sind Streichholzbriefchen mit aufgeprägten Brüsten, die die Vorzüge des Modells haptisch erfahrbar machten. Von Alkohol und Nikotin benebelt, schien der Südseetraum hier zum Greifen nah.

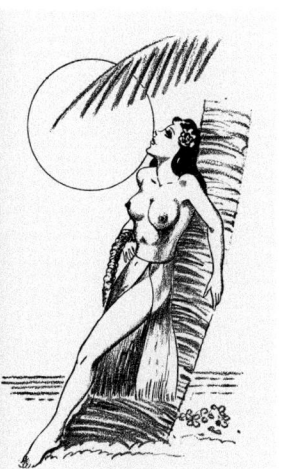
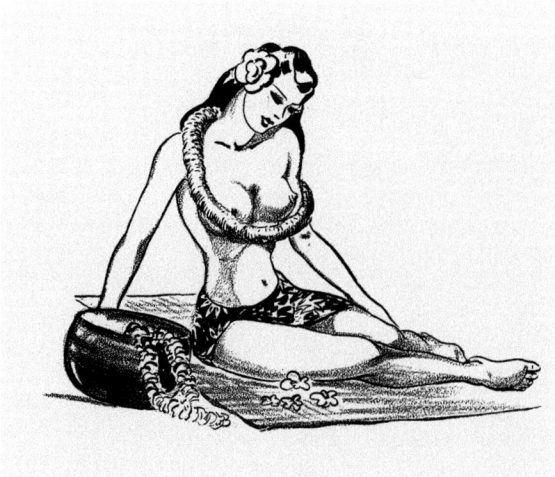

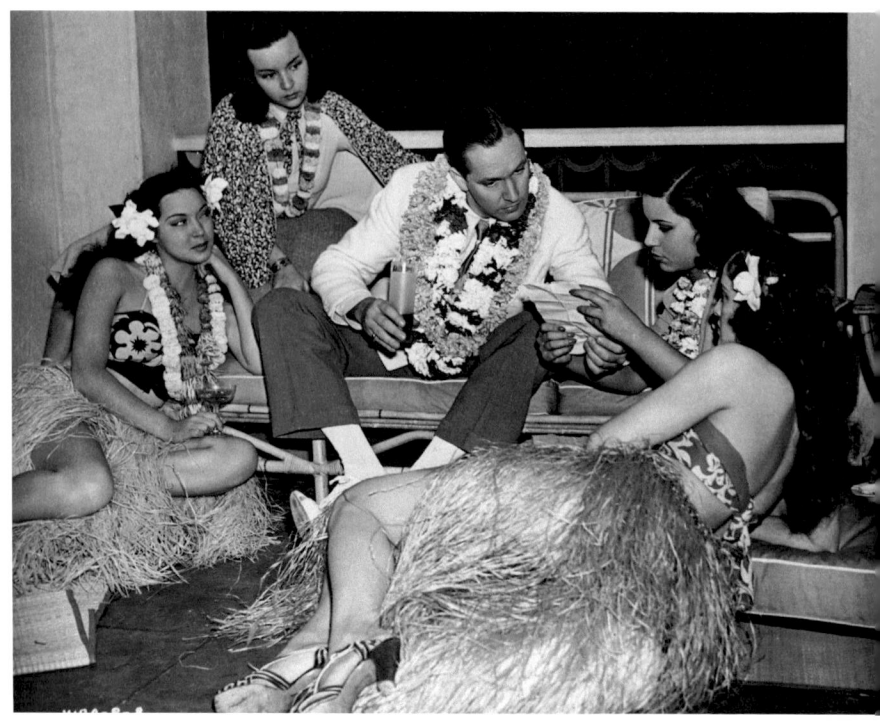

UN CLIMAT DOUX, UNE EAU

bleue… de gracieux palmiers jetant leur
ombre ondoyante sur le sable fin… des
fleurs et des fruits tropicaux… Tout cela
aurait pu évidemment suffire à composer
un paradis polynésien acceptable, mais
sans une Ève, cet éden terrestre aurait été
incomplet. Incarnation de la beauté fémi-
nine, elle promet cet amour inconditionnel
que tout homme recherche si désespéré-
ment depuis sa chute.

Au milieu du XXᵉ siècle, la nudité arbo-
rée sans complexe par la femme des îles
fait d'elle un sex-symbol bienvenu dans
l'industrie du divertissement. Même habil-
lée, elle révélait toujours assez de peau et
de cuisse pour hypnotiser le mâle de base.

Le cliché de la tentatrice polynésienne aux
amours libres s'est insinué dans l'esprit
des hommes depuis des générations, et les
médias ne font rien pour les détromper.
Edgar Leeteg, le « Gauguin américain »,
devient le peintre attitré des restaurants
polynésiens. Pendant la Grande Dépression
des années 1930, il s'est exilé à Tahiti, où il
payait ses consommations dans les bars en
réalisant des portraits de beautés locales
dénudées sur du velours noir. Ces volup-
tueuses madones tropicales venaient apporter un caractère bohème aux établissements
qu'elles gratifiaient de leur présence.

Les restaurants sur le thème des mers
du Sud recourent au motif de la vahiné
de bien des façons. Elle apparaît sur les

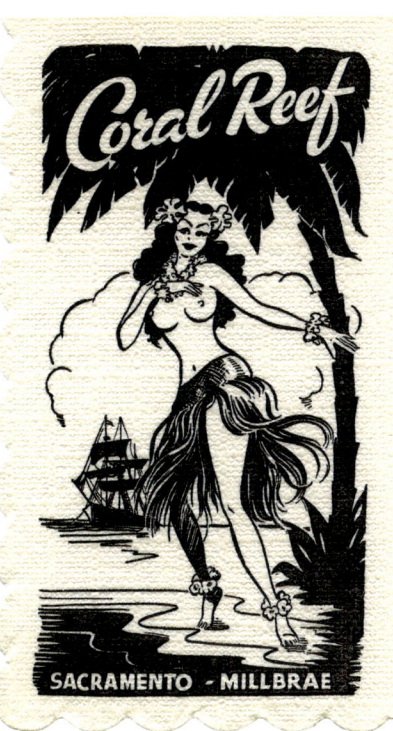

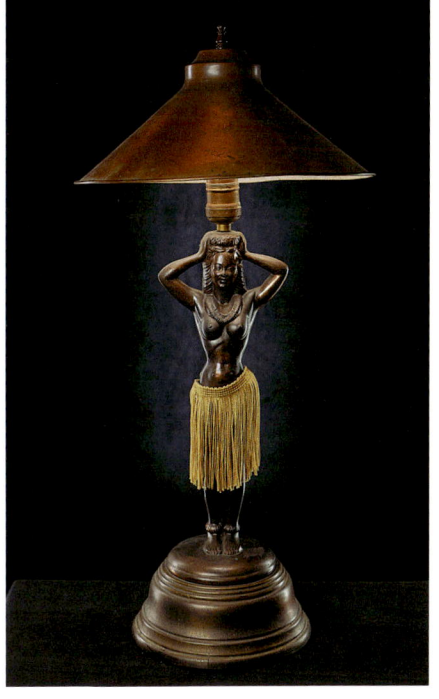

ouvertures des menus, les bols et les mugs à cocktails. Elle symbolise l'entrée dans un monde détaché du tohu-bohu moderne, un refuge exotique et érotique où les sens exultent.

Mélangeurs finement sculptés, serviettes de tables évocatrices et pochettes d'allu-nettes géantes arborent aussi les formes pulpeuses de ces dames dans la plupart des bars et clubs hula-olé d'Amérique. Le spécimen le plus étonnant de ce fétichisme américain reste sans doute la pochette d'allumettes avec seins en relief, qui ajoute au plaisir des yeux l'expérience tactile des modèles et de leurs atouts. Étourdis par l'alcool, hébétés et embrumés, les clients pouvaient enfin vivre leur rêve tropical.

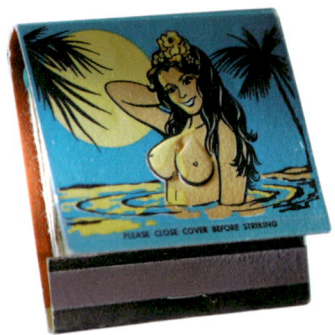

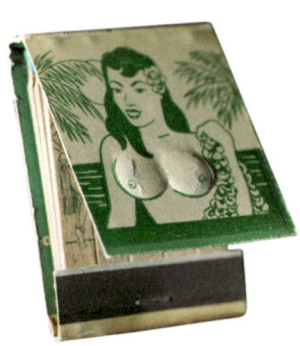

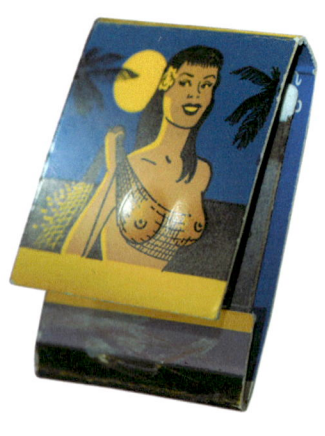

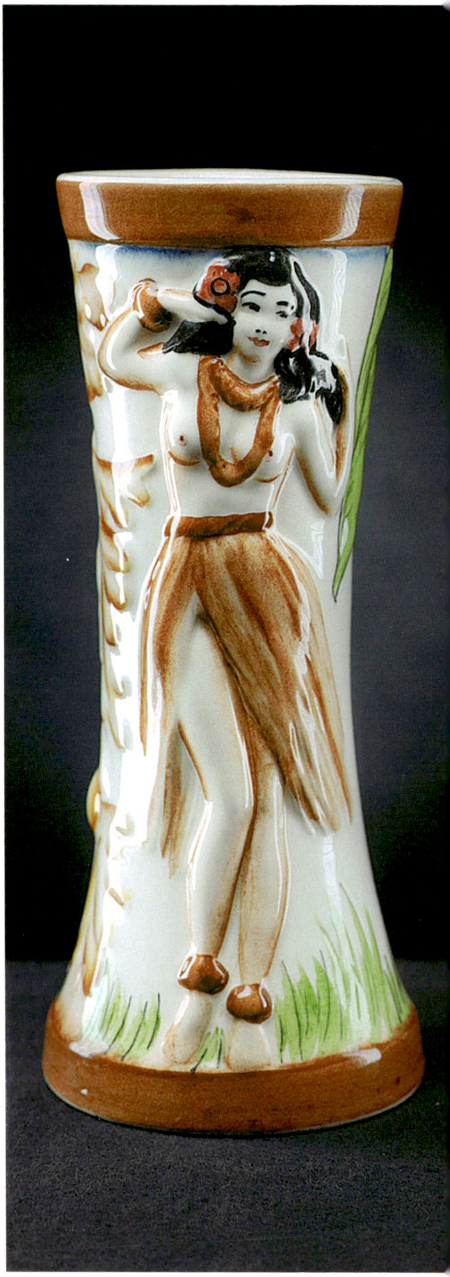

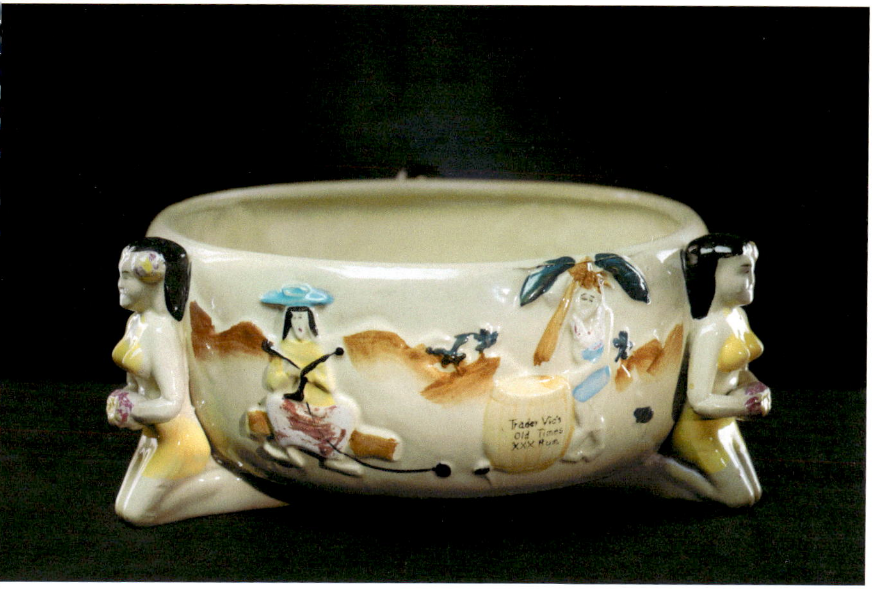

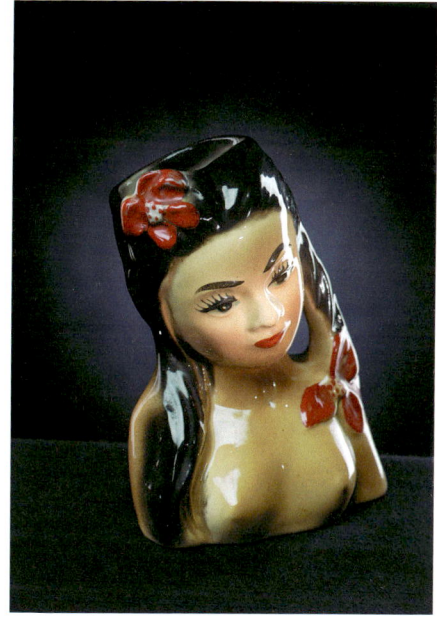

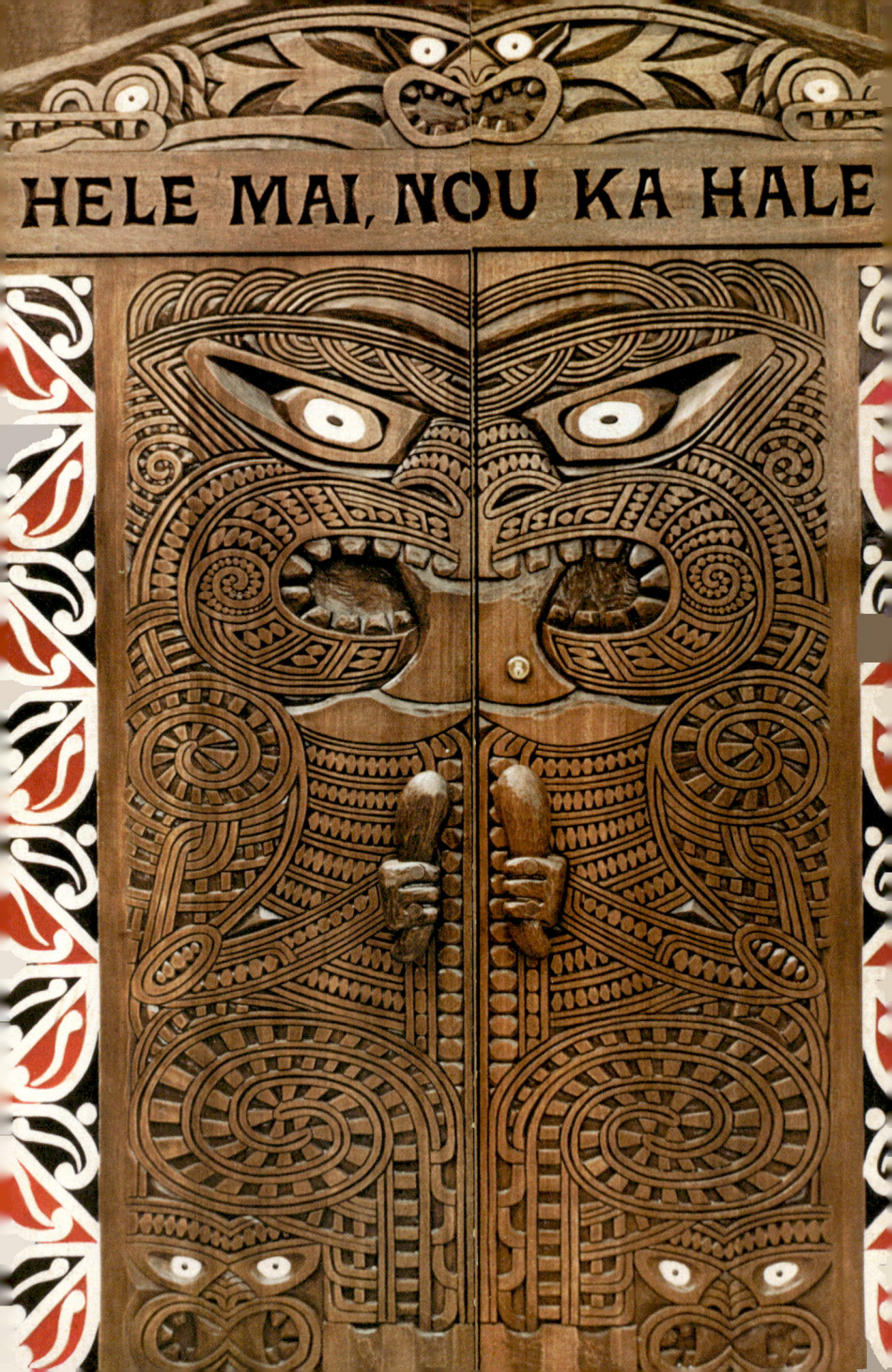

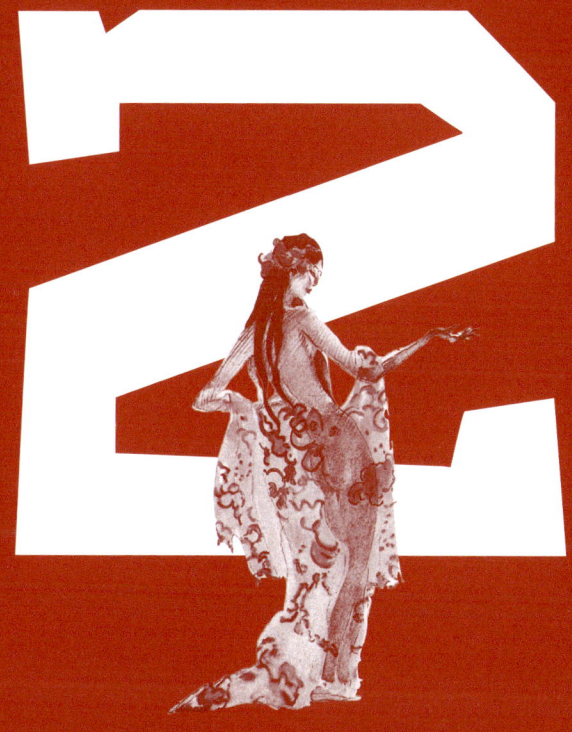

THE
TIKI ENTERS

DER TIKI TRITT AUF DEN PLAN
LES DÉBUTS DU TIKI

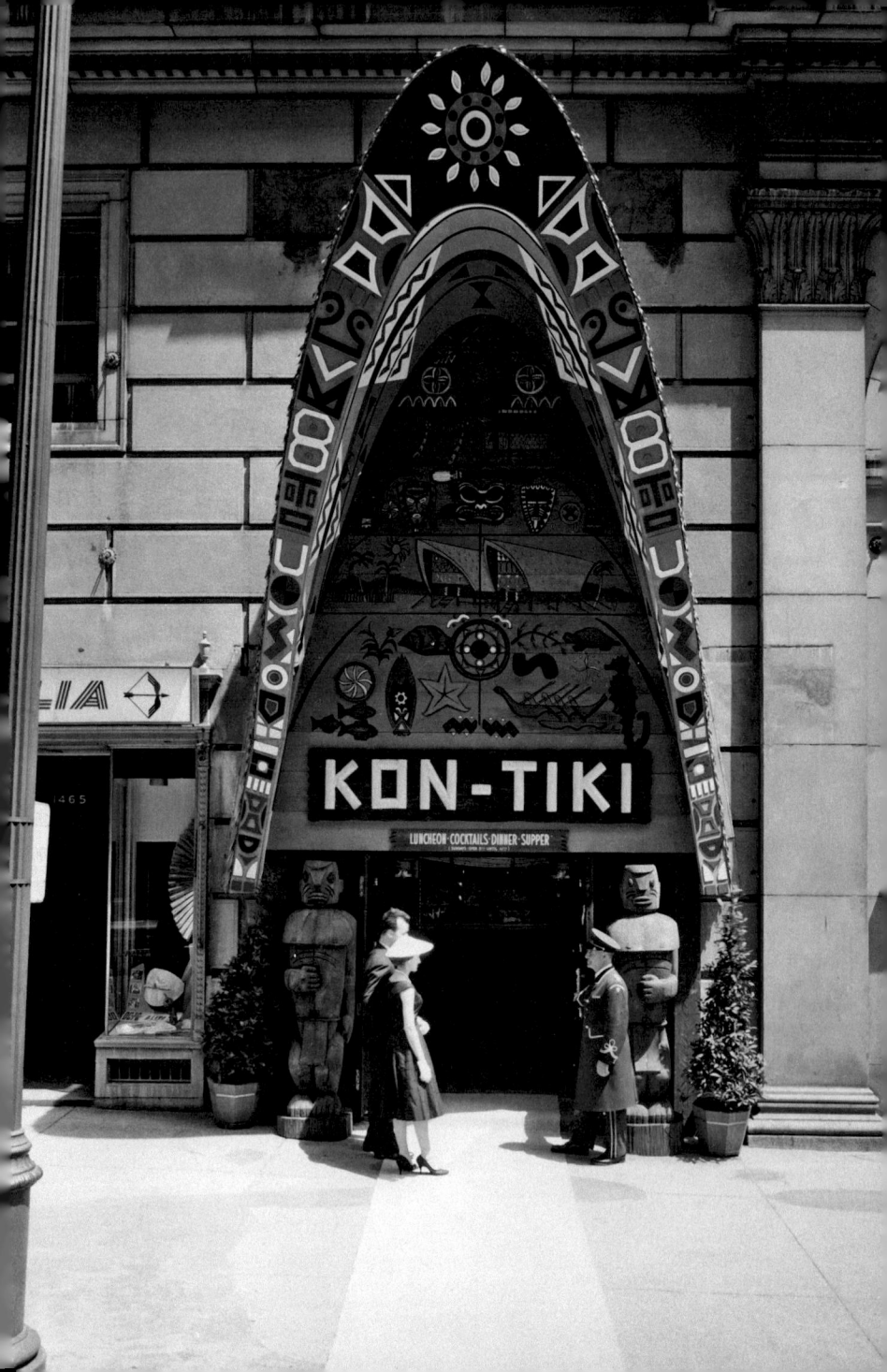

KON-TIKI AND AKU-AKU

KON-TIKI UND AKU-AKU
KON-TIKI ET AKU-AKU

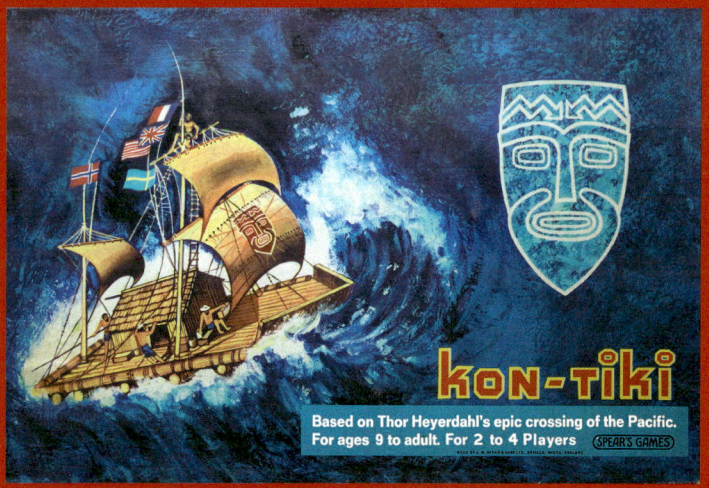

OPPOSITE: A gate to another world: Kon-Tiki Polynesian restaurant,
Montreal, 1958 *(JP Balak Collection)*

ABOVE: Dramatic rendering of the Kon-Tiki raft
and mask on a board game, 1967

IN 1947, THE WORLD WAS STILL
recovering from the trauma of World War II.
In that year, a young Norwegian anthropologist named Thor Heyerdahl captured
international attention by embarking on
a daring scientific adventure: to prove
his theory that Polynesians could have
migrated from South America, he built a
raft entirely from indigenous materials.
He christened the raft Kon-Tiki, after the
Incan sun god, and sailed it from Peru to
Tahiti, relying on only the sea currents.

According to Heyerdahl's research, Kon-
Tiki the sun god arrived in Polynesia with
the ancient mariners and became the Tiki of
Polynesian mythology. The book recounting
the journey became a worldwide best seller,
printed in more countries than the Bible.
The documentary shot by the crew during
the voyage earned an Academy Award.

Here was an adventure that was non-
violent but dramatic, something that every
boy and man would want to take part in.
The idea was so compelling, in fact, that
several imitators tried to raft across the
Pacific, notwithstanding the fact that their
deeds somewhat lacked in originality.

The name Kon-Tiki made "Tiki" a
household word in America. In Polynesia,
Heyerdahl had lived in a primitive hut;
now his concept was used for the most
modern of lodgings. The raft's moniker
was applied to Polynesian-style restaurants,
motels, and apartments. Shirt designers,
watchmakers, and boat builders also used
it as a brand name, denoting adventure.

The electric guitar hymn "Kon-Tiki"
became a number-one hit for the British
band The Shadows, and it inspired countless cover versions. The logo mask of the
sun god that had emblazoned the raft's sail
decorated Polynesian lounges and eateries.

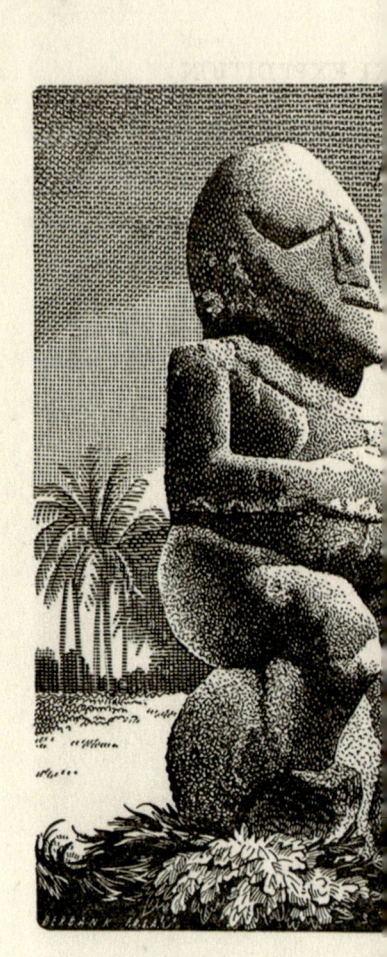

TIKI WAS THE NAME OF THE FIRST GREAT
BY THE INHABITANTS AS THEIR DIVINE AND
AMERICAN TYPE WERE ERECTED IN HIS

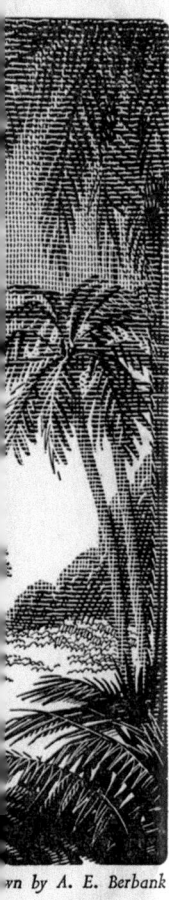

THE
KON-TIKI
EXPEDITION

BY RAFT ACROSS THE SOUTH SEAS

THOR HEYERDAHL
TRANSLATED BY F. H. LYON

THE REPRINT SOCIETY LONDON

The book and its protagonist

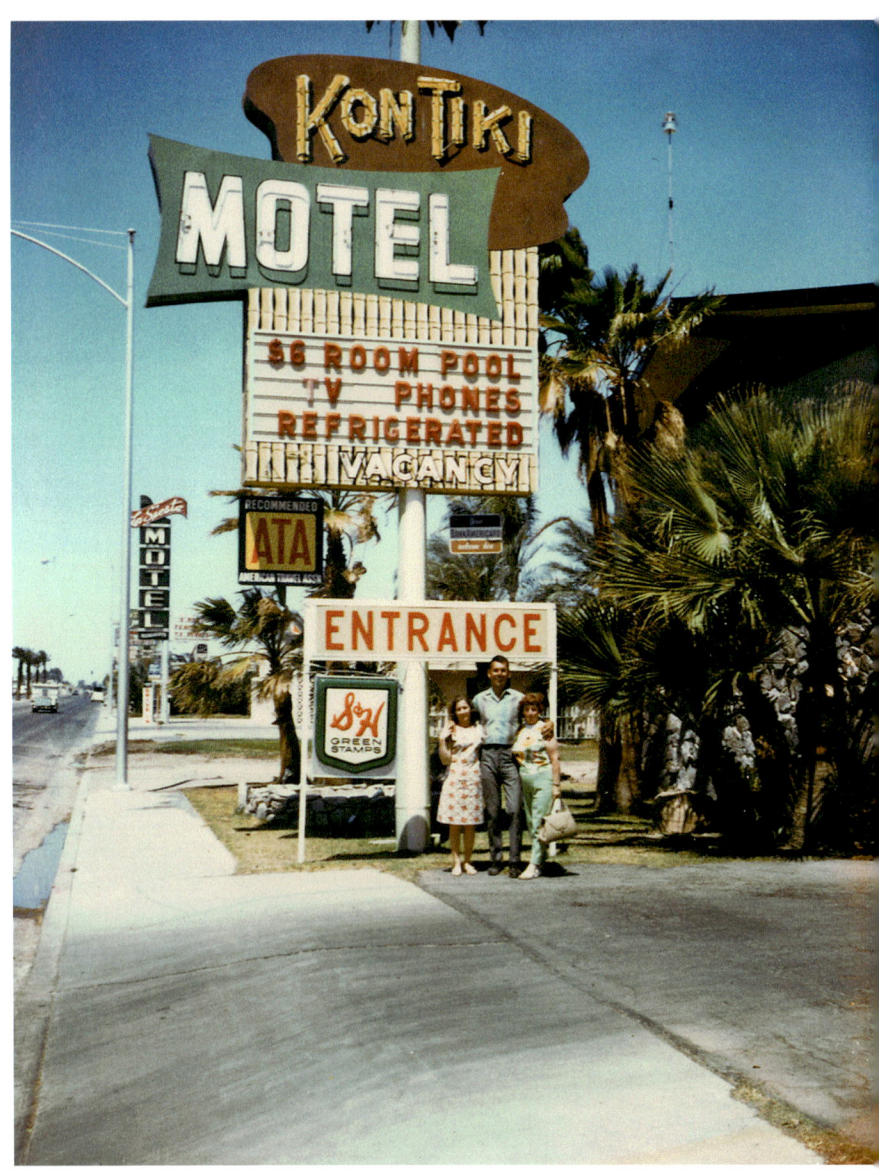

ABOVE: Modern Kon-Tiki dwellers, El Centro, California, 1960s

OPPOSITE: The crew and a model of their vessel

In some cases, the popularization of the name went a little too far.

Heyerdahl continued his Polynesian research on Easter Island, and published it in his 1958 book, *Aku-Aku*. It was another best seller, and the iconic cover art by mid-century graphic designer Charley Harper was quickly appropriated into the Tiki Pop culture. Heyerdahl's research inspired a form of edutainment, where elemental knowledge about Polynesian culture was considered *de rigueur*.

The Aku Aku restaurant at the Stardust Casino in Las Vegas was a typical example of this facet of Tiki Pop. With Don the Beachcomber as advisor, Eli Hedley ("The Original Beachcomber") sculpted the giant Moai for the entrance, and Hawaiian artist Edward Brownlee worked on the modernist interior. Moai Tiki mugs and drinking bowls completed the theme.

The fact that Easter Island heads were correctly called "Moai" did not keep restaurateurs from integrating them into the Tiki Pop family as Tikis, or "Aku-Tikis," as restaurant relics from Nebraska to Florida demonstrate.

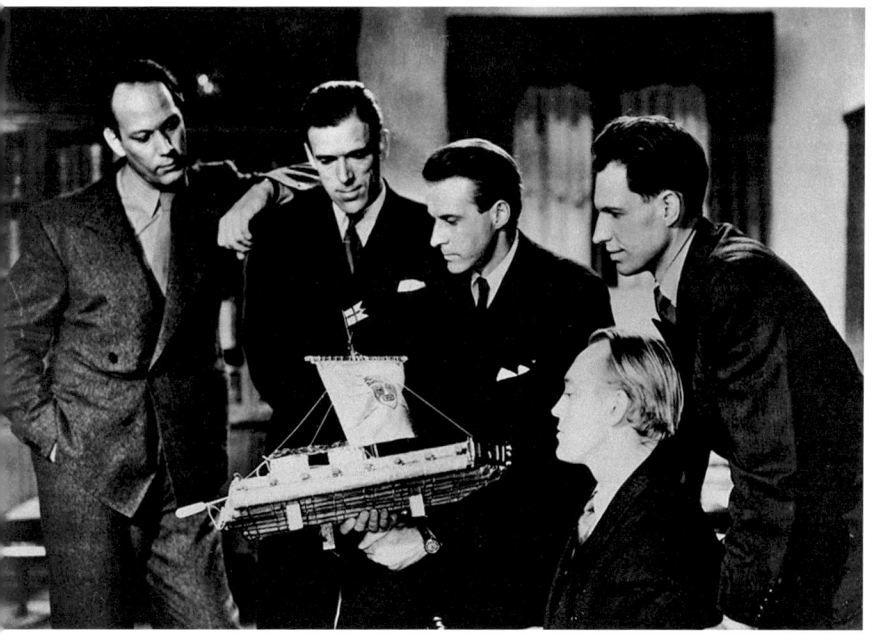

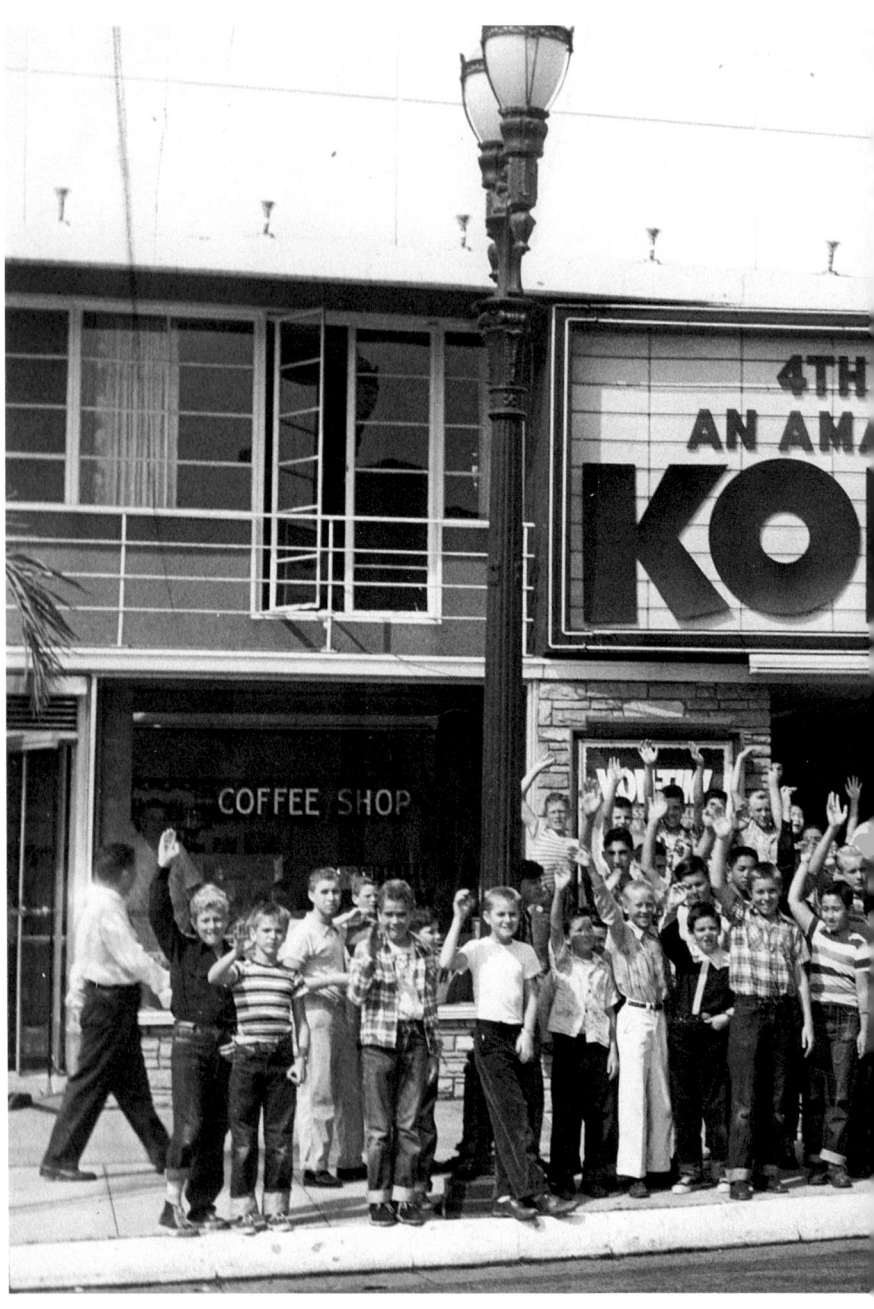

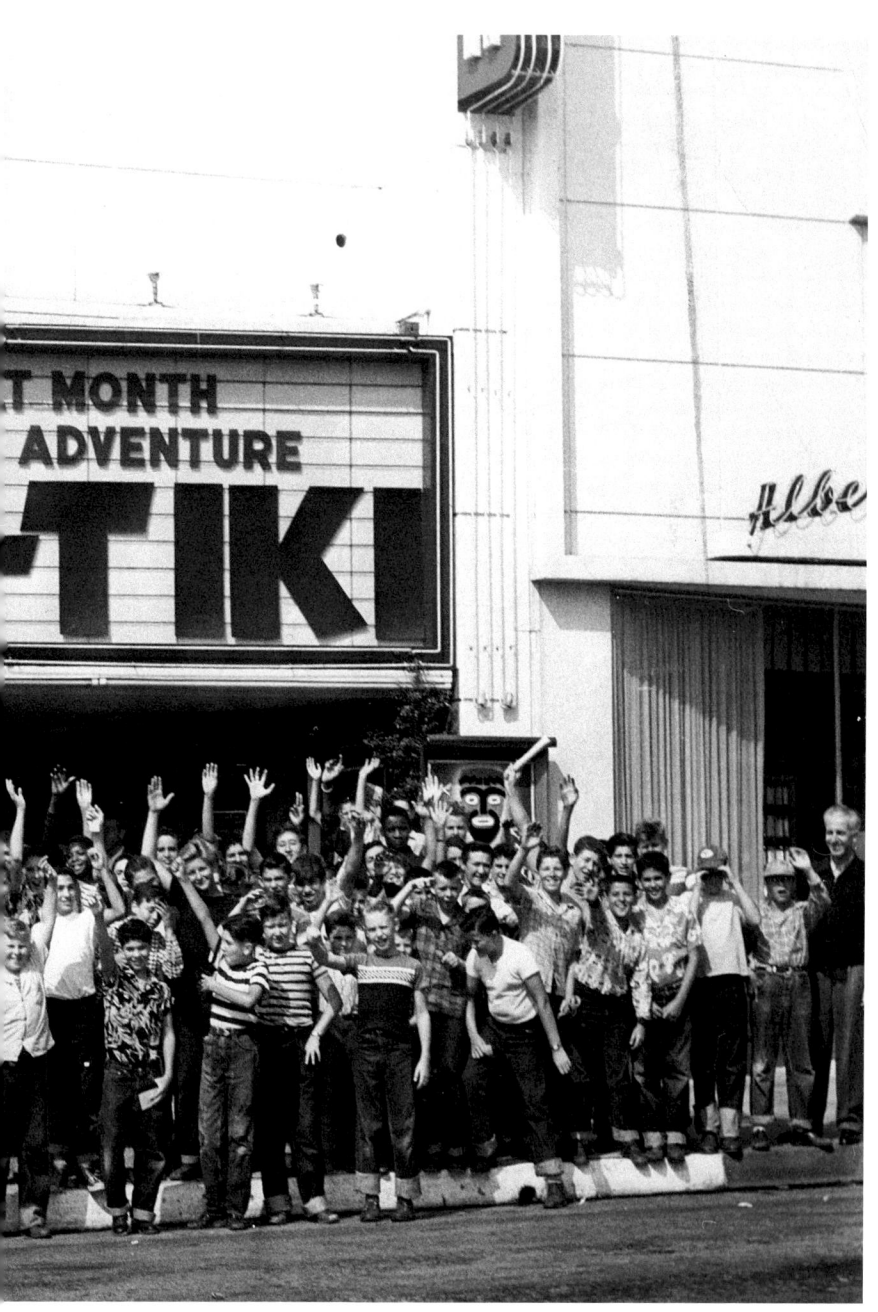

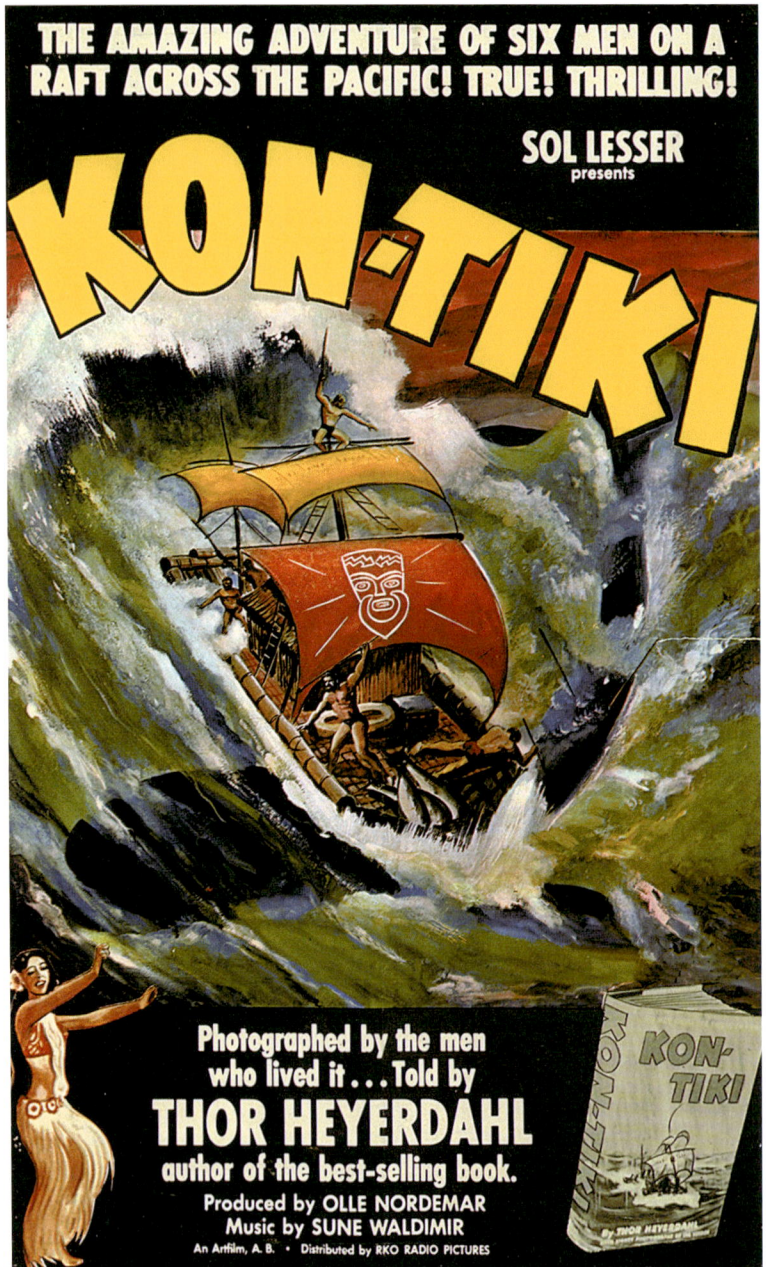

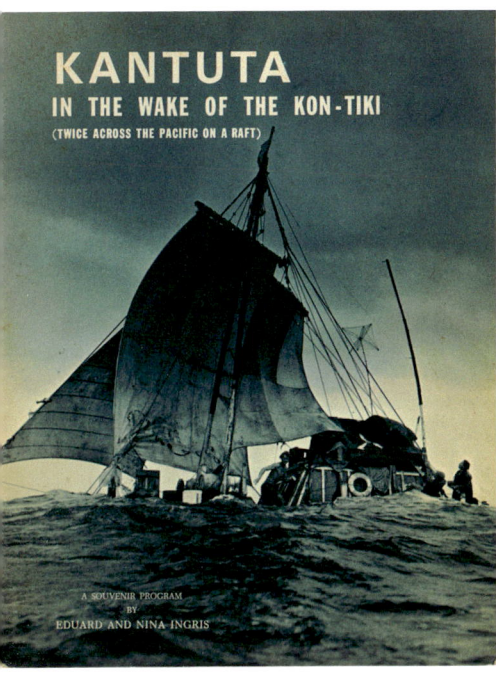

KANTUTA

IN THE WAKE OF THE KON-TIKI

(TWICE ACROSS THE PACIFIC ON A RAFT)

A SOUVENIR PROGRAM
BY
EDUARD AND NINA INGRIS

PAGES 270–271: Young Kon-Tiki fans at a Los Angeles movie theater, 1958

OPPOSITE: The movie about the voyage

LEFT AND BELOW: Way beyond fandom: the active imitators

ALS SICH IM JAHR 1947 DIE WELT NOCH vom Trauma des Zweiten Weltkriegs erholte, erregte ein junger norwegischer Anthropologe namens Thor Heyerdahl internationale Aufmerksamkeit, indem er sich auf ein gewagtes wissenschaftliches Abenteuer begab: Um die Theorie zu belegen, dass die Vorfahren der Polynesier einst aus Südamerika eingewandert waren, baute er sich ein Floß ausschließlich aus den Materialien, die den Menschen in präkolumbischer Zeit zur Verfügung gestanden hatten. Er taufte sein Gefährt „Kon-Tiki", nach dem Sonnengott der Inka, und segelte damit, sich allein auf die Meeresströmungen verlassend, von Peru nach Tahiti.

Heyerdahls Nachforschungen zufolge landete der Sonnengott Kon-Tiki zusammen

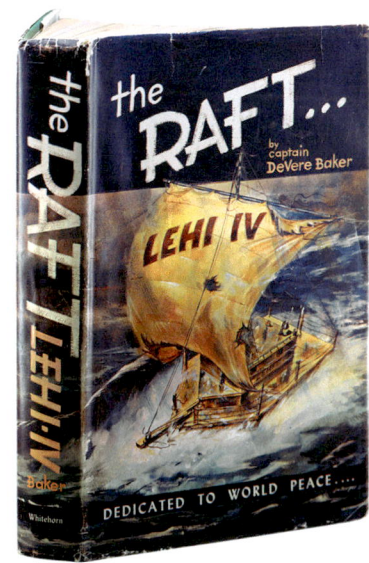

the RAFT...

by captain DeVere Baker

LEHI IV

DEDICATED TO WORLD PEACE....

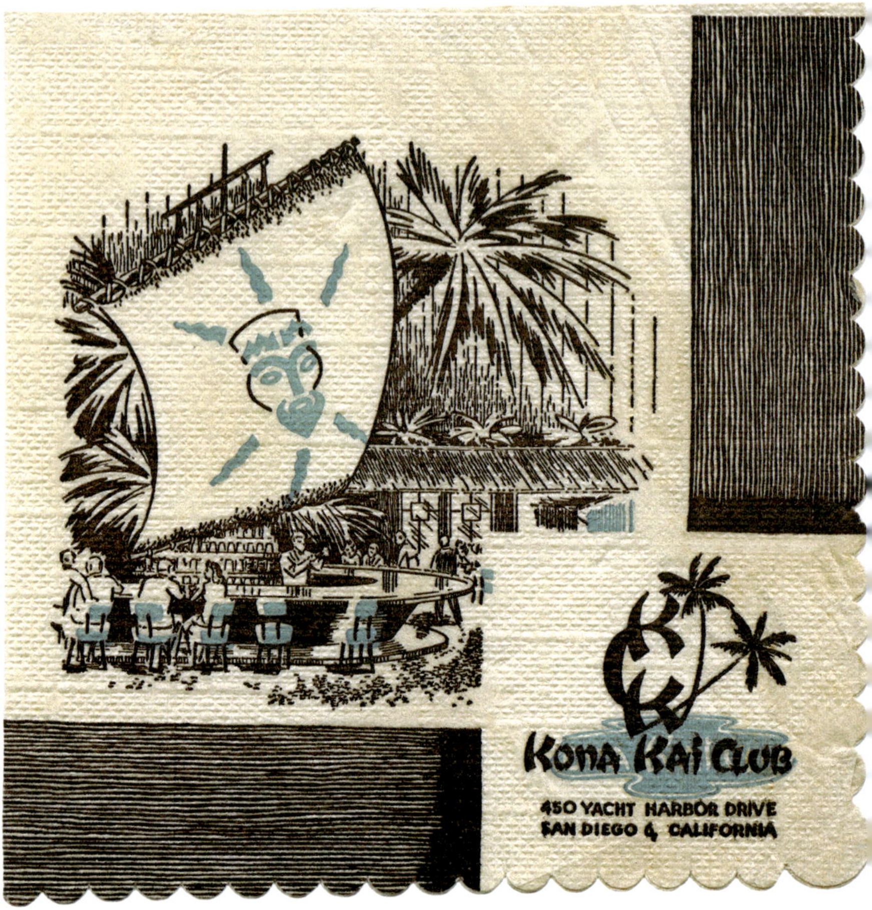

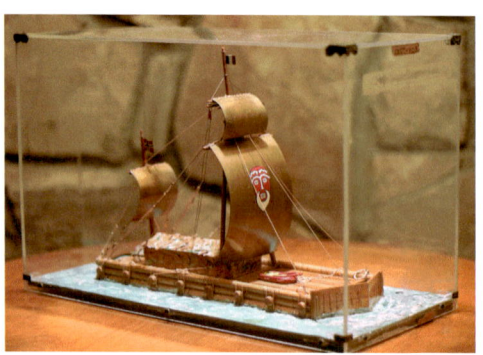

ABOVE: The bar at the Kona Kai club in San Diego flew a Kon-Tiki sail

LEFT: Kon-Tiki model
(Mark Noland collection)

OPPOSITE: Cover of "Kon Tiki" by Seattle band The Exotics mit den Seeleuten in Polynesien und wurde zum „Tiki" der polynesischen Mythologie. Das Buch, in dem Heyerdahl seine Reise beschreibt, wurde ein weltweiter Bestseller und in mehr Ländern verlegt als die Bibel. Die Dokumentation, die von der Crew während der Reise gedreht wurde, gewann einen Oscar.

Es war ein spannendes Abenteuer – wie jeder Junge und jeder Mann es gern erleben würde. Die Idee klang so verlockend, dass mehrere Nachahmer nun ebenfalls versuchten, auf dem Pazifik mit einem Floß zu segeln, auch wenn das nicht besonders originell war. Der Name „Kon-Tiki" machte „Tiki" zu einem geläufigen Ausdruck in den USA. In Polynesien lebte Heyerdahl in einer einfachen Hütte – nun wurde sein Konzept für die modernsten Unterkünfte genutzt. Der Name des Floßes war Namensgeber für polynesische Restaurants, Motels und Wohnanlagen. Shirt-Designer, Uhrenmacher und Bootsbauer nutzten ihn als einen Markennamen, der Sinn für Abenteuer versprühte.

Die britische Band The Shadows veröffentlichte 1961 einen Song mit dem Titel „Kon Tiki"; das Instrumentalstück wurde zum Nummer-eins-Hit und unzählige Male gecovert. Die Maske des Sonnengottes, die auf das Segel des Floßes gezeichnet war, dekorierte polynesische Bars und Restaurants. In manchen Fällen trieb man es mit der Popularisierung des Namens etwas zu weit.

Heyerdahl setzte seine polynesischen Forschungsarbeiten auf den Osterinseln fort und veröffentlichte 1958 sein Buch *Aku-Aku* – ein weiterer Bestseller. Der von dem Grafikdesigner Charley Harper gestaltete Einband wurde schnell der Tiki-Popkultur zugerechnet. Heyerdahls Forschung inspirierte eine Form des Edutainment, die ein grundlegendes Wissen über die polynesische Kultur als absolutes Muss ansah.

Das Aku-Aku-Restaurant im Stardust Casino von Las Vegas war ein typisches Beispiel für diese Facette des Tiki-Pop. Mit Don the Beachcomber als Berater an seiner Seite, meißelte Eli Hedley („The Original Beachcomber") den riesigen Moai für den Eingang. Der hawaiische Künstler Edward Brownlee zeichnete für das moderne Interieur verantwortlich. Moai-Tiki-Becher und -Trinkschalen rundeten den Look ab.

Die Tatsache, dass die Kopfskulpturen der Osterinseln eigentlich Moai hießen, hielt die Gastronomen nicht davon ab, sie in die Tiki-Pop-Familie als Tikis oder Aku-Tikis aufzunehmen. Das zeigen Relikte aus Restaurants von Nebraska bis Florida.

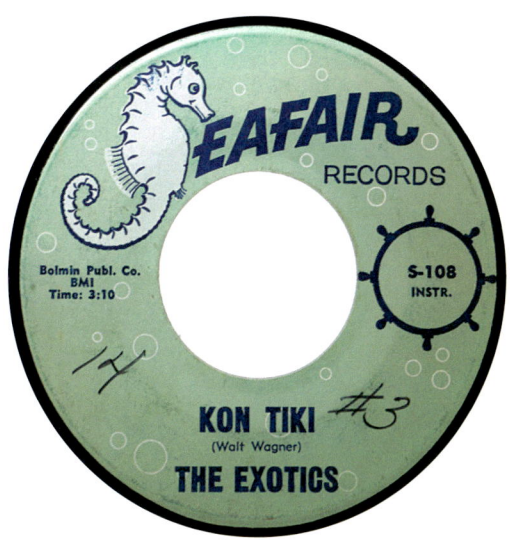

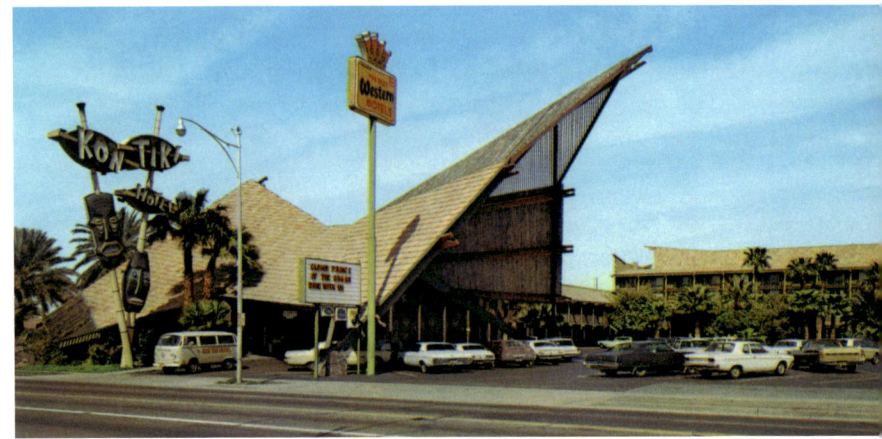

ABOVE: Kon Tiki Hotel, Phoenix, Arizona, 1961 *(Scott Schell Collection)*

BELOW: "The south sea islanders never had it so good" as at the Kon Titi Motel, Florida *(Scott Schell Collection)*

OPPOSITE: Aku-Tiki ashtray

KON TITI MOTEL & APTS.

A bit of Polynesia on Florida famous east coast-ocean. Bathing on our own private beach or in our beautiful heated pool. The south sea islanders never had it so good. But you will at the KON TITI apts. efficiencies-one and two bedroom apts. all with heat and air conditioning-all electric kitchens-tubs and showers. Cable color TV and guest dial phones. Accommodations to fit every need, you will hate to leave us.....
Convenient to all recreational facilities -restaurants-shopping and churches-boating-fishing-races-etc.

Come enjoy a polynesian holiday with your hosts Dale and Beth McMullen. Open year round for your convenience-COME ON LETS GO NATIVE...................

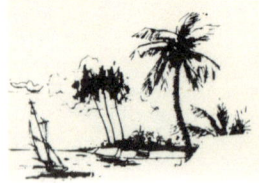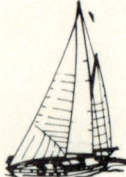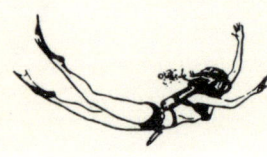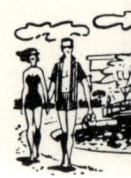

EN 1947, LE MONDE SE REMET ENCORE
du traumatisme de la Seconde Guerre
mondiale. Cette année-là, un jeune anthro-
pologue norvégien, Thor Heyerdahl, attire
l'attention internationale en s'embarquant
pour une audacieuse aventure scientifique :
afin de vérifier sa théorie, selon laquelle les
Polynésiens ont pu migrer d'Amérique du
Sud, il construit un radeau en n'utilisant que
des matériaux locaux naturels. Il baptise son
embarcation *Kon-Tiki,* d'après le dieu inca du
Soleil, et vogue à son bord du Pérou à Tahiti,
ne s'en remettant qu'aux courants marins.

D'après les recherches menées par
Heyerdahl, les navigateurs des temps
anciens auraient apporté avec eux le dieu
solaire Kon-Tiki, qui serait devenu le Tiki
de la mythologie polynésienne. Le livre
qui relate sa traversée téméraire devient
un best-seller dans le monde entier, publié
dans davantage de pays que la Bible, et le
documentaire tourné par l'équipage pendant le voyage remporte un oscar.

Il s'agit là d'une épopée – pacifique –
spectaculaire, l'aventure à laquelle tous les
mâles, enfants et adultes, rêvent de participer. L'idée est même si irrésistible que plusieurs enthousiastes, certes peu imaginatifs,
tentent à leur tour la traversée du Pacifique
sur des embarcations de fortune.

Avec la popularité du *Kon-Tiki,* le mot
« tiki » devient courant en Amérique. En
Polynésie, Heyerdahl a vécu dans une
hutte primitive, et ce modèle de construction minimaliste est utilisé pour concevoir
les logements les plus modernes. Le radeau
donne bientôt son nom à des restaurants,
à des hôtels et à des immeubles d'appartements d'inspiration polynésienne. Les fabricants de chemises, de montres et de bateaux
l'utilisent aussi pour conférer à leur marque
une touche aventureuse.

L'hymne rock'n'roll au *Kon-Tiki,* avec
son entêtante ligne mélodique à la guitare
électrique, vaut au groupe britannique
The Shadows de se placer en tête des ventes

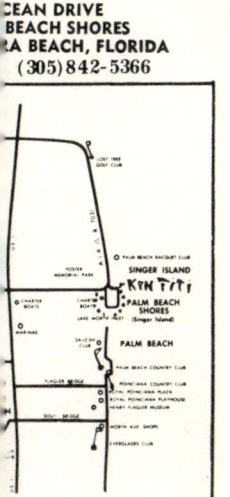

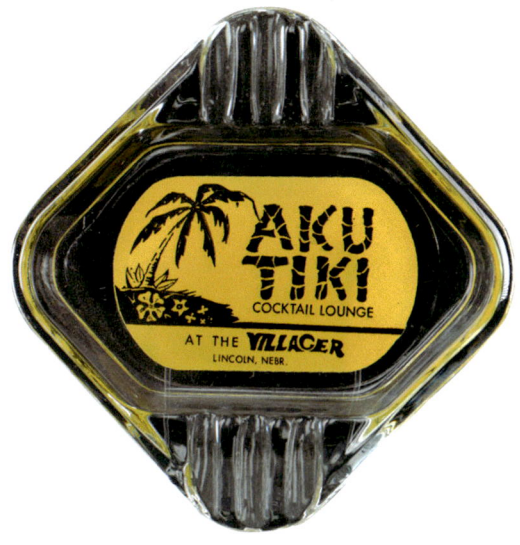

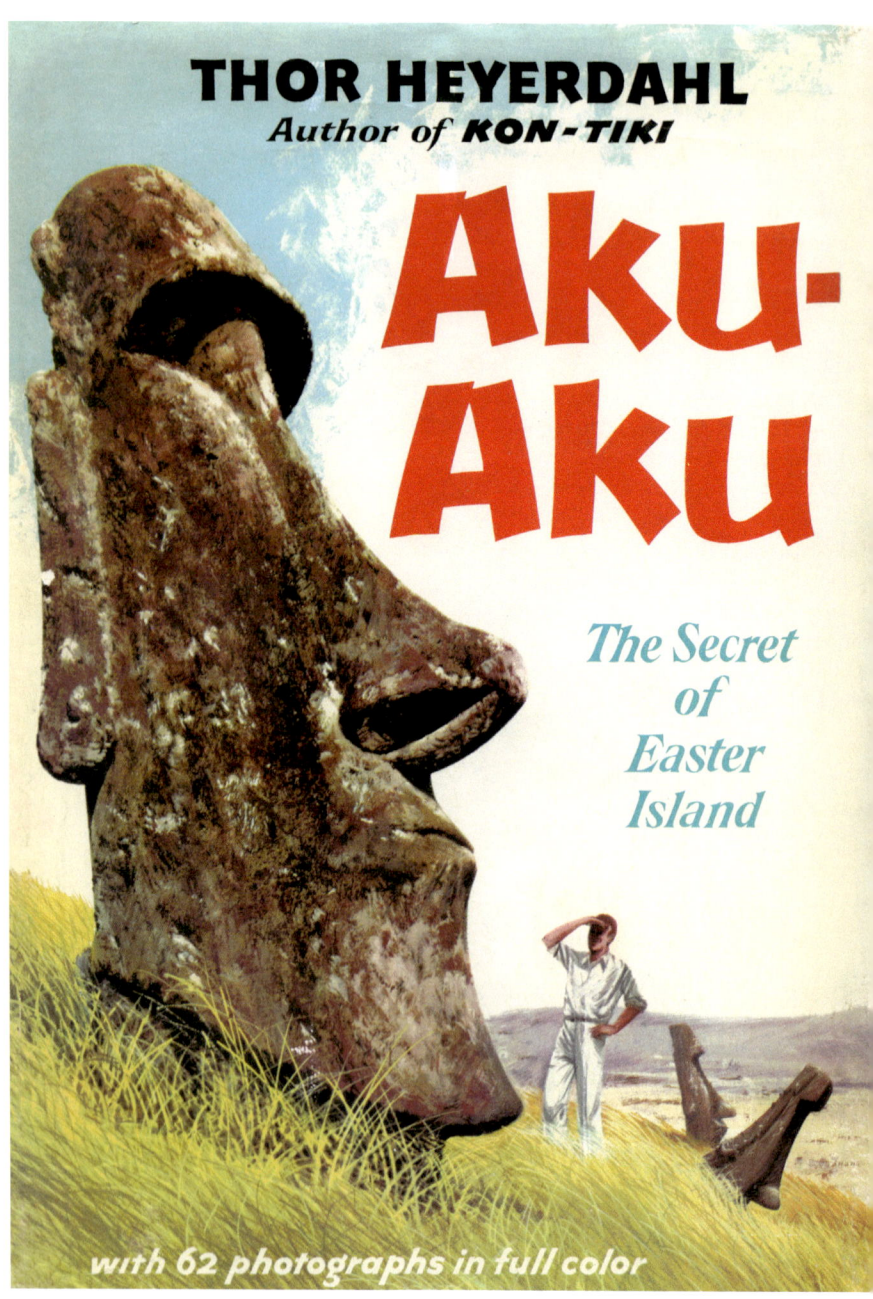

THOR HEYERDAHL
Author of **KON-TIKI**

Aku-Aku

The Secret of Easter Island

with 62 photographs in full color

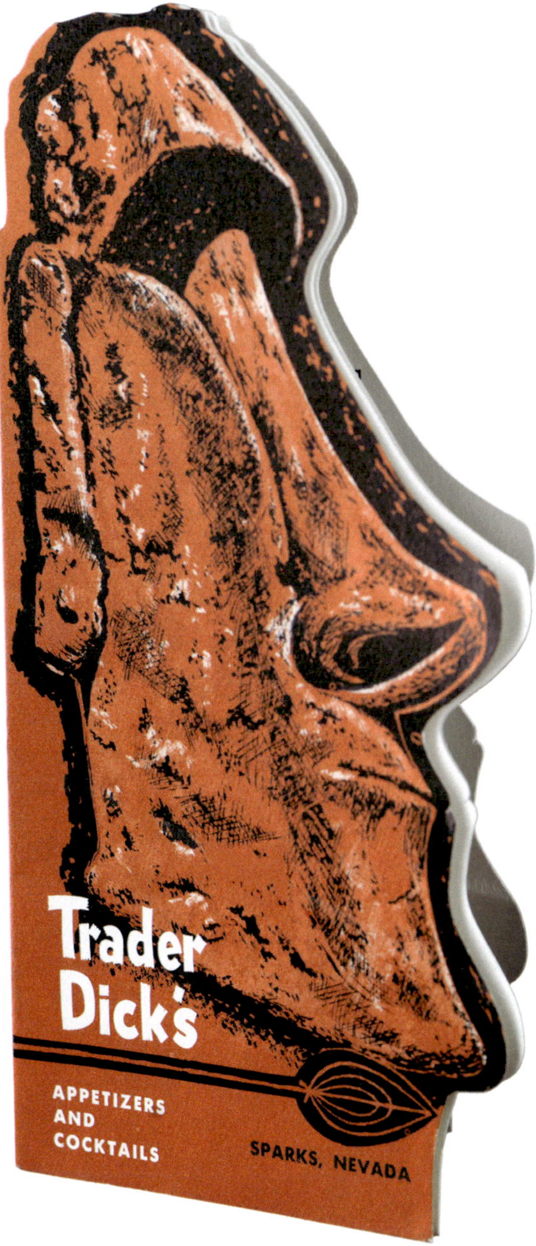

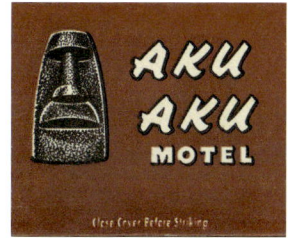

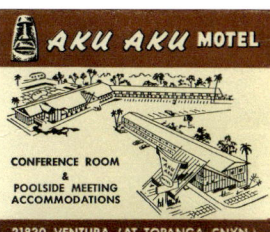

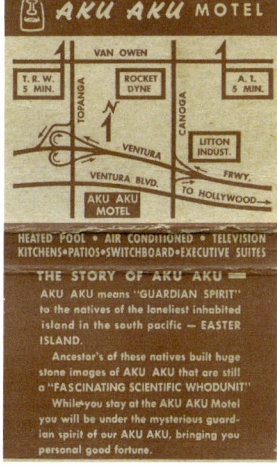

OPPOSITE: *Aku-Aku* book cover by Charley Harper

LEFT: Trader Dick's menu, Reno, Nevada

ABOVE: Aku Aku Motel matchbook, Woodland Hills, California

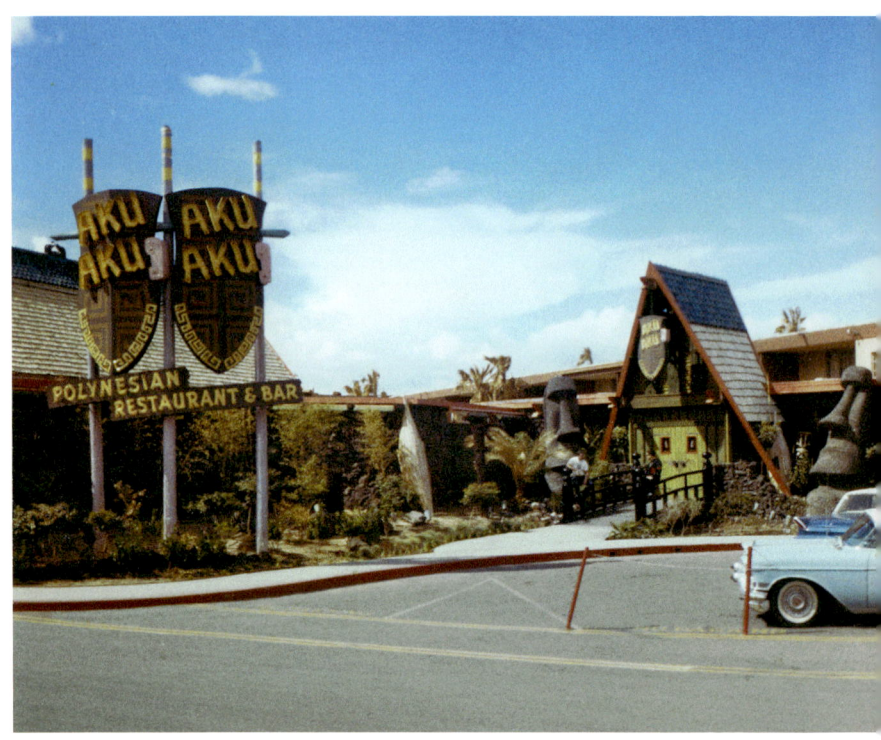

et inspirera d'innombrables reprises. Le masque du dieu solaire qui figurait sur la voile du radeau devient un motif récurrent dans les salons et les restaurants. L'enthousiasme est tel que le réemploi du nom Kon-Tiki va parfois un peu trop loin.

Heyerdahl poursuit ses recherches sur l'île de Pâques, et en publie les résultats dans son livre de 1958, *Aku-Aku*. C'est à nouveau un best-seller, et la couverture signée par Charley Harper, graphiste majeur de l'époque, s'intègre vite à la culture tiki pop. Les travaux de Heyerdahl inspirent une sorte de divertissement éducatif, et il devient bientôt normal, sinon indispensable, de connaître les rudiments de la culture polynésienne.

Le restaurant Aku Aku à l'intérieur du Stardust Casino de Las Vegas illustrent parfaitement cette facette du tiki à la sauce pop. Sur les conseils de Don the Beachcomber, Eli Hedley (« The Original Beachcomber ») sculpte deux moai géant pour l'entrée, et l'artiste hawaiien Edward Brownlee conçoit l'intérieur moderniste. Les fameux mugs et bols à cocktail moai et tiki viennent parachever l'ensemble.

Les restaurateurs ne se gênent pas pour intégrer les têtes typiques des statues de l'île de Pâques (les moai) à la famille pop des tikis, et ils les qualifient même parfois de « aku-tikis », comme le montrent certaines reliques de restaurants ouverts du Nebraska à la Floride.

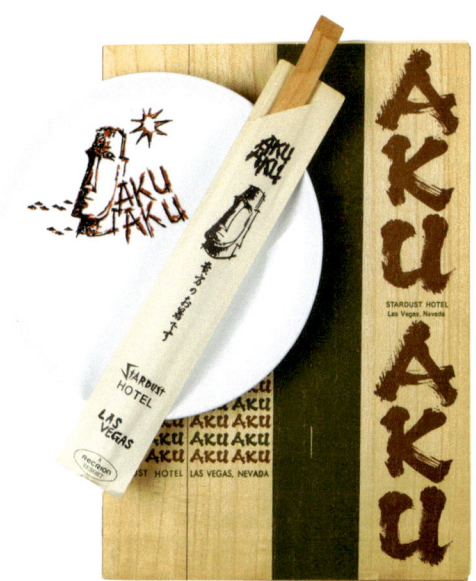

PU-PU'S

POLYNESIAN BAR
and RESTAURANT
LAS VEGAS, NEVADA

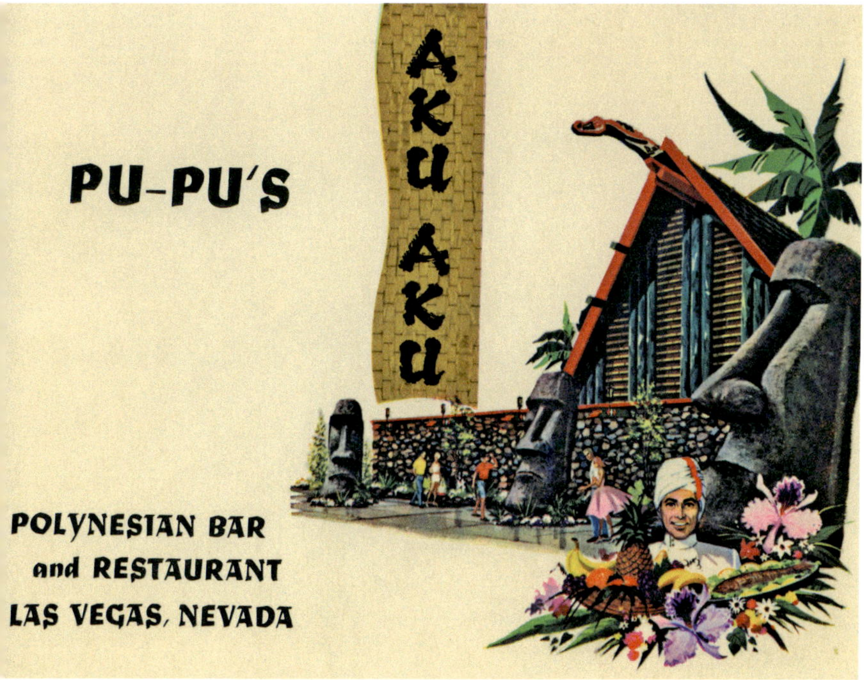

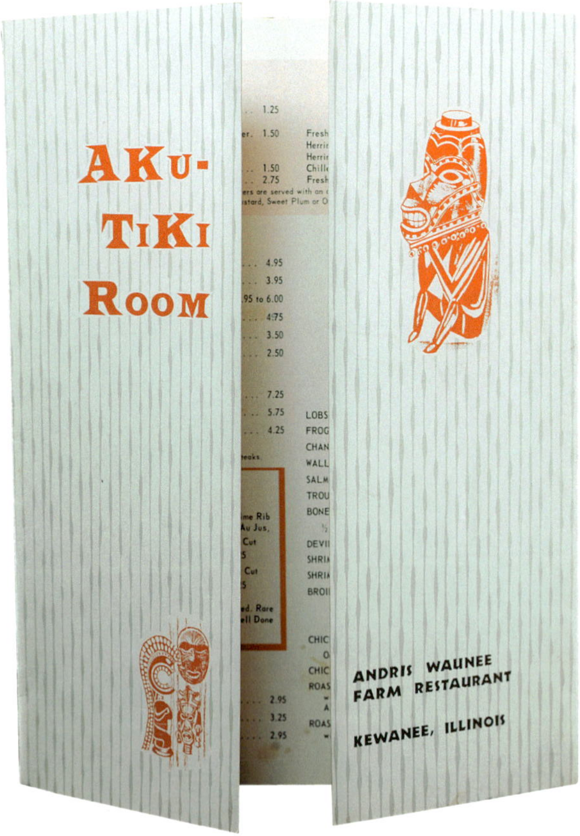

AKU-
TiKi
Room

Fresh
1.25
... 1.50   Herring
... 1.50   Herring
... 2.75   Chilled
            Fresh
           ers are served with on
           stard, Sweet Plum or O

... 4.95
... 3.95
95 to 6.00
... 4.75
... 3.50
... 2.50

... 7.25
... 5.75   LOBS
... 4.25   FROG
            CHAN
reaks.   WALL
            SALM
            TROU
ime Rib   BONE
Au Jus,   ½
Cut   DEVII
S   SHRIA
Cut   SHRIA
S   BROII

d. Rare
ll Done

            CHIC
              O
            CHIC
            ROAS
... 2.95   A
... 3.25   ROAS
... 2.95

**ANDRIS WAUNEE
FARM RESTAURANT**

KEWANEE, ILLINOIS

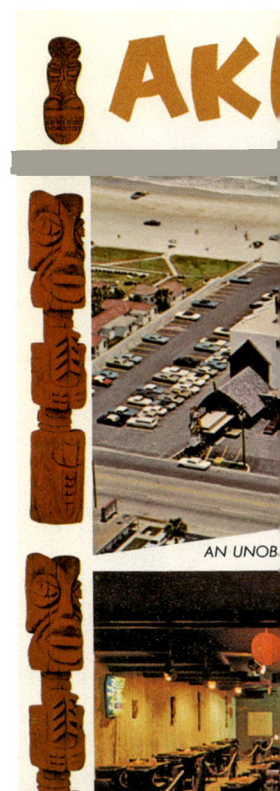

AN UNOB

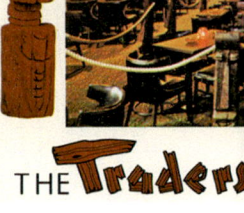

THE Traders

ΙΚΙ INN

The new Aku Tiki Inn offers an enchanted Island atmosphere on the world's most famous beach. Five hundred feet of soft, white sand at your doorstep, generous playground, game room, a sparkling all tile olympic - size pool, 3 meter or 1 meter diving boards. Free sun lounges and umbrellas around our pool deck assure you of outdoor fun in the sun all year round. Our large informal lobby is a gathering place for friendly guests. A large TV and stereo music offer relaxation for those who may have worshipped the sun too long.

Enter the Tiki restaurant from the lobby, pass over the moon bridge at the waterfall and here breakfast, lunch or dinner is served in an atmosphere of Polynesia. You may dine overlooking the ocean, pool and beautifully landscaped garden. Exotic fruit trees bloom in season with a perfume known only to the tropics. Everything can be found here to make a perfect vacation.

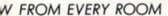

W FROM EVERY ROOM

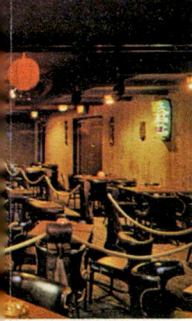

h night 'till 2:00 A.M., featuring r favorite spirits.

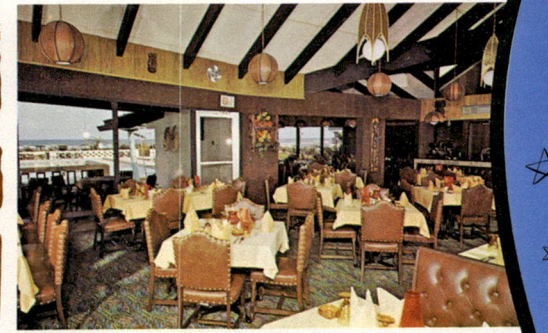

Traders **RESTAURANT** *Overlooking The Ocean*
Open 7 A.M. To 11 P.M.

OPPOSITE: Aku-Tiki establishments existed in remote places in America

ABOVE: The Aku Tiki Inn still stands today, beckoning Daytona visitors with its giant Moai sign

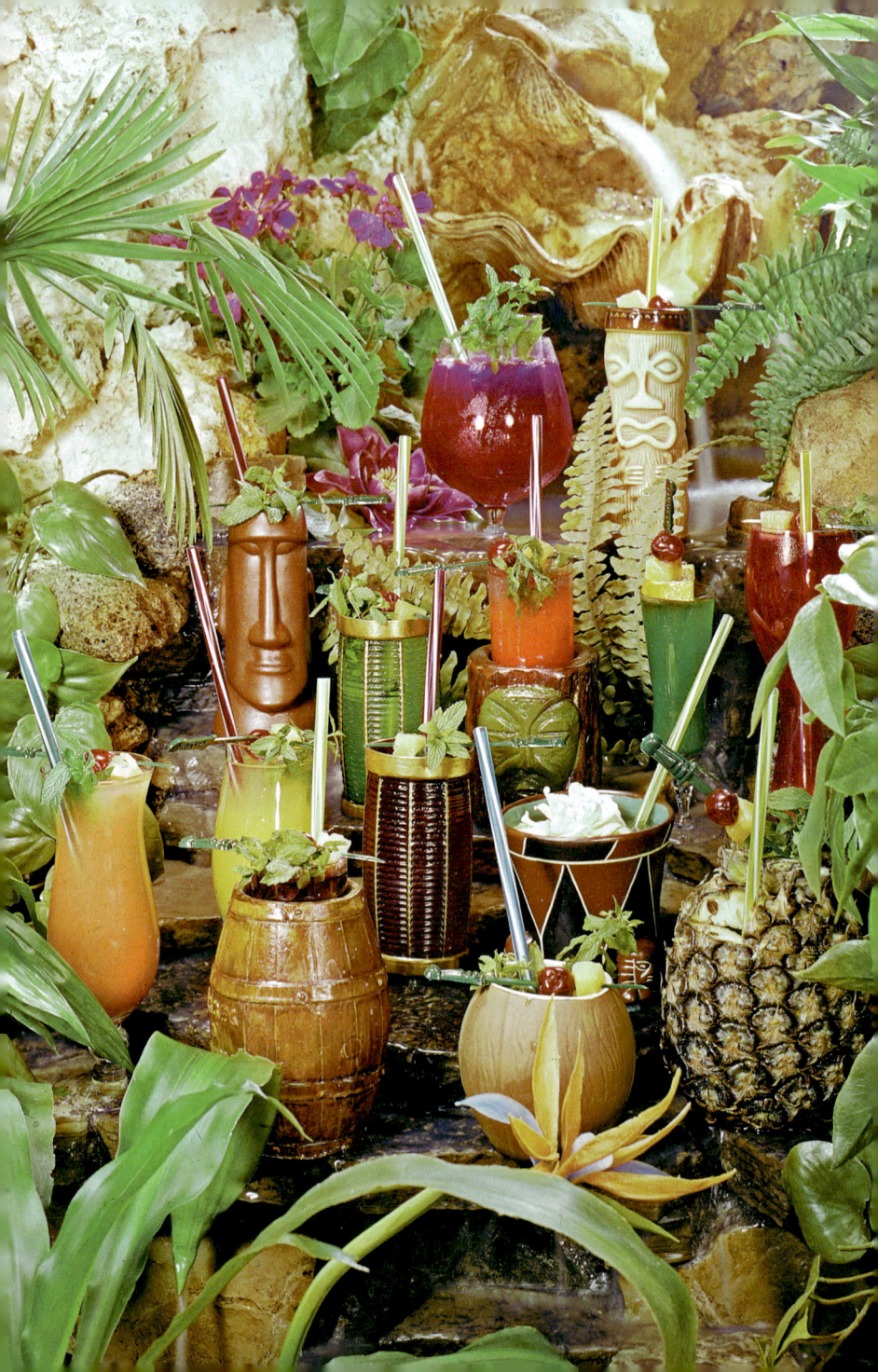

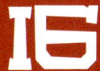

16

A BRIEF HISTORY OF THE AMERICAN TIKI COCKTAIL

EINE KURZE GESCHICHTE DES AMERIKANISCHEN TIKI-COCKTAILS
BRÈVE HISTOIRE DU COCKTAIL TIKI AMÉRICAIN

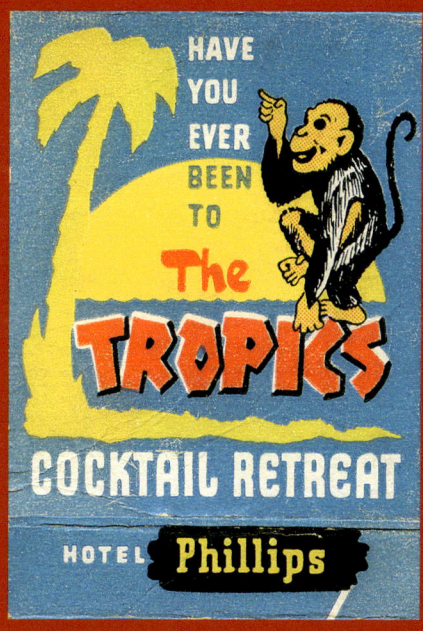

OPPOSITE: Welcome to the rum jungle!

ABOVE: Matchbook from a cocktail retreat

THE TROPICAL COCKTAIL WAS,

without doubt, the sustaining substance of the Tiki lounge. With its tempting profit margin, ever more elaborate Tiki temples arose out of the American asphalt jungles. Its potent alcohol content, masked behind complex flavors, and its seductive visual presentation made it an addictive stimulant for business and pleasure. Only a few of the classic concoctions from the pages of Tiki history can be mentioned here, along with a brief description of the antecedent of what was the Golden Age of rum mixology.

The years between 1920 and 1933 marked the Dark Ages of alcohol prohibition in the United States. Not without reason: Americans had been drinking too much and needed to sober up. Liquor became an illegal drug. Upon Prohibition's repeal, alcohol

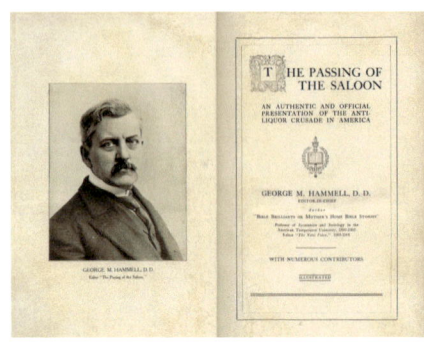

appreciation went into overdrive. Ever fancier and more potent combinations of spirits were tested on the eagerly imbibing public. The time of the cocktail had arrived.

Being able to mix good drinks for your guests became a sign of sophistication. By mid-century, a cocktail culture had evolved:

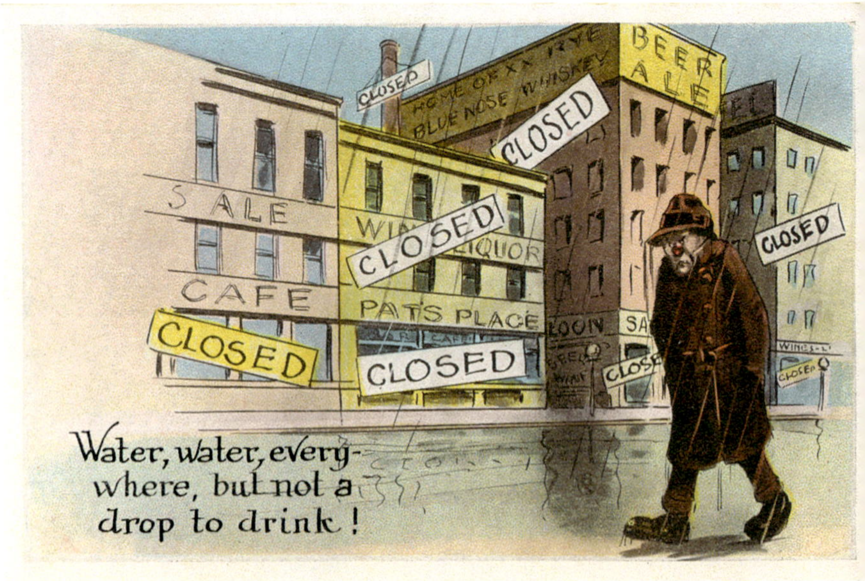

Water, water, every-where, but not a drop to drink!

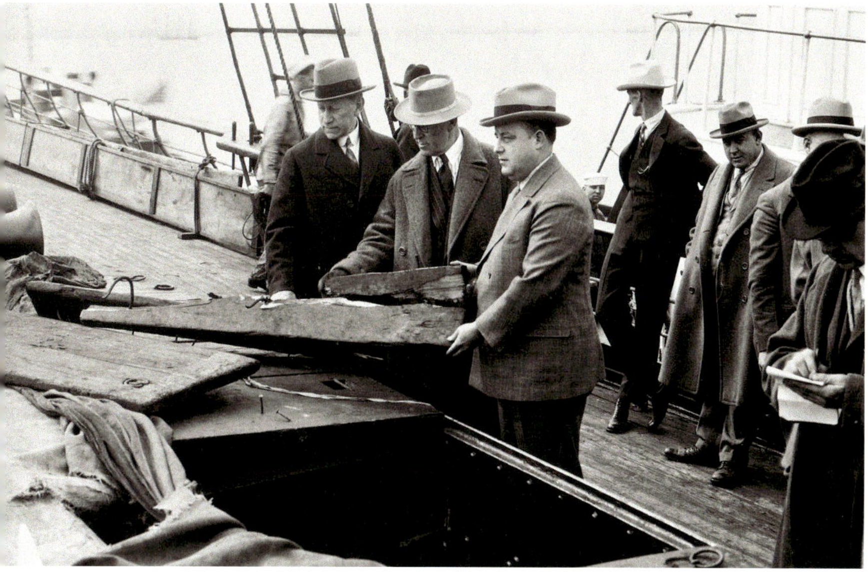

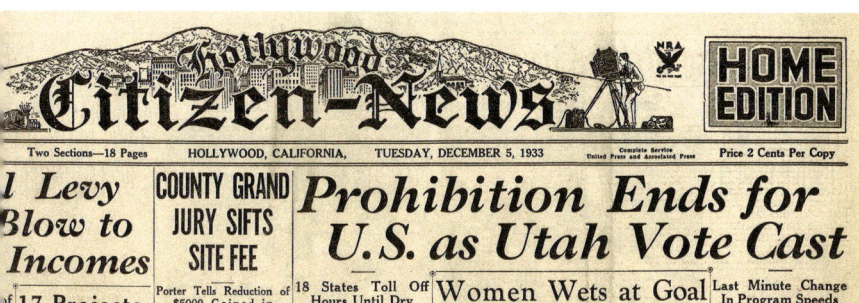

OPPOSITE ABOVE: A chronicle of the crusade that led to Prohibition, 1908

OPPOSITE BELOW: Postcard from the Prohibition period

ABOVE: Federal agents busting a "rum runner" smuggling ship, 1927

BELOW: Newspaper announcing the repeal of Prohibition, 1933

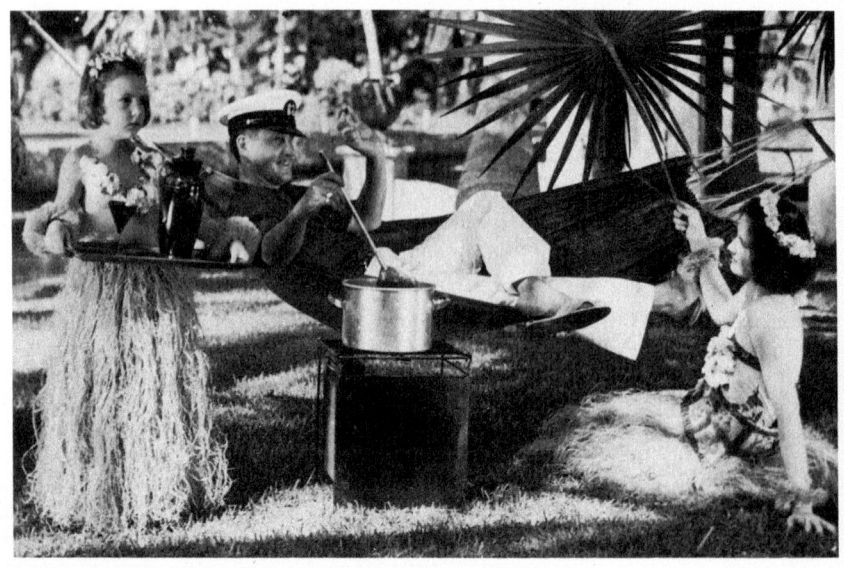

At "cocktail parties," women wore "cocktail dresses" and one listened to "cocktail music." As the liner notes on one such record extol: "The cocktail hour is the vine-clad bridge in the day of the active modern... It is a time of discovery of new moods, of desires..."

From his youth in Jamaica, Don the Beachcomber was familiar with rum. He created a lethal libation by blending several different kinds of the golden cane distillate with fruit juices. He called it "the Zombie." Having worked for the studios, Don might have gotten his idea from the 1932 film *White Zombie*. The next classic movie of this genre, *I Walked with a Zombie* (1943), already made mention of the cocktail in its dialogue—a sure sign of its popularity.

Imitation being the sincerest form of flattery, Don the Beachcomber should have been thrilled that so many tropical bars claimed the Zombie as their own. None

of them really knew Don's secret formula, but that didn't deter them from selling their attempts. New York impresario Mont Proser trumped them all by calling his nightclub "The Beachcomber" and boldly advertising it to be "The Home of the Zombie." The case was settled out of court

Perhaps the only Tiki cocktail created in Polynesia is the "Dr. Funk." Its many variations are based on a mixture of rum, absinthe, and lime juice, originally concocte by Dr. Bernard Funk, a German physician to Robert Louis Stevenson in Samoa. He shared the recipe with a friend in Papeete, Tahiti; from there, it spread throughout the South Seas.

The Mai Tai was the cocktail of the Tiki generation. Its origin was hotly contested until its creator, Trader Vic, had an affidavi signed by his friend Carrie Wright, who witnessed its creation in 1944 and exclaime

pon drinking it: "Mai Tai roa ae!", —Tahit-
an for "Out of this world!" The Mai Tai was
oon the most requested drink—not just in
American Tiki bars, but on the Hawaiian
slands as well.

Of the many poetic descriptions bestowed
n Polynesian cocktails in restaurant menus,
he one for the "Tiki Lo-lo" perhaps says
t most succinctly: "Tikis are Hawaiian
Gods—If you can't be one, drink up and
eel like one!"

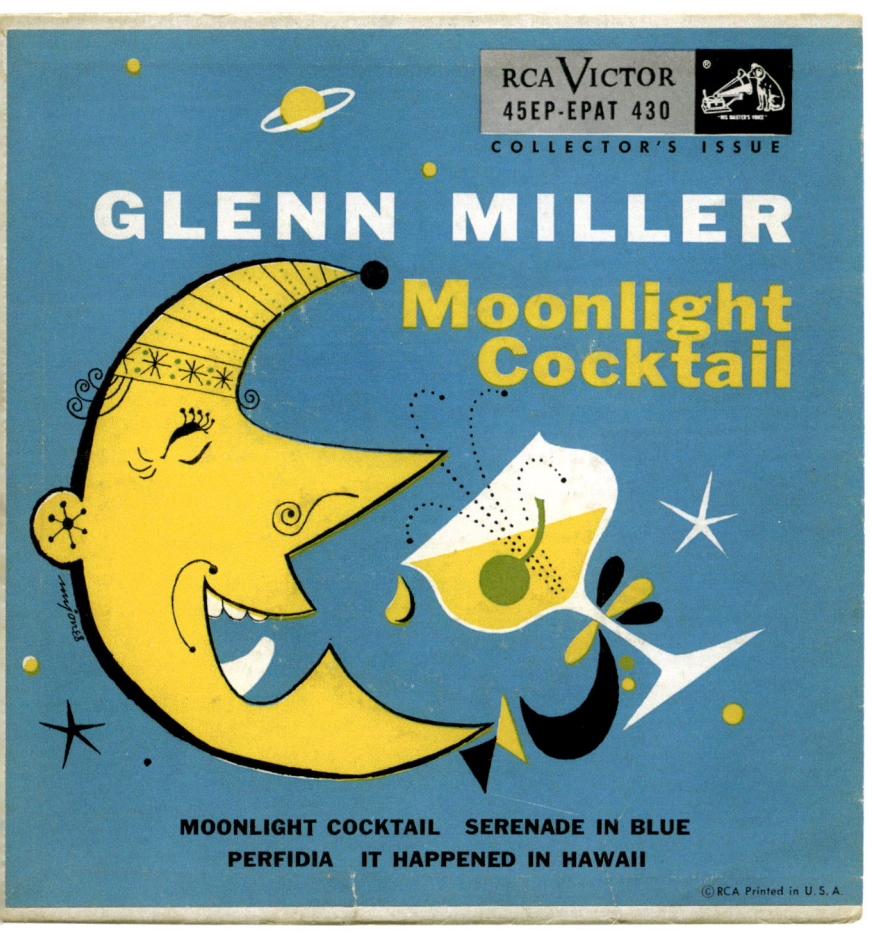

DER TROPISCHE COCKTAIL WAR OHNE
Zweifel *die* Stütze der Tiki-Lounges. Aufgrund der verlockenden Gewinnspanne
schossen immer aufwendigere Tiki-Tempel
aus dem amerikanischen Asphaltdschungel.
Der hohe Alkoholgehalt, der sich hinter
den komplexen Geschmackskombinationen
verbarg, und die verführerische Optik ließen den Cocktail zu einem Stimulans für
Geschäft und Freizeit werden. Dieses Buch
bietet lediglich Platz für einige wenige Ge-
tränke-Klassiker der Tiki-Geschichte sowie
eine kurze Beschreibung ihrer Vorläufer
aus den goldenen Zeiten der Rum-Drinks.

In den Jahren zwischen 1920 und 1933
herrschte in den USA das dunkle Zeitalter der Alkoholprohibition. Nicht ohne
Grund: Die Amerikaner tranken zu viel
und hatten den Entzug bitter nötig. Alkohol
wurde zur illegalen Droge deklariert. Mit

der Aufhebung der Prohibition schoss der
Alkoholgenuss rasant in die Höhe. Immer
ausgefallenere und stärkere Kombinationen
wurden an der gierig schlürfenden Öffentlichkeit getestet. Die große Zeit des Cocktails war gekommen.

Als kultiviert galt fortan, wer seinen
Gästen gute Drinks mixen konnte. Bis
zur Jahrhundertmitte hatte sich eine ganze
Cocktailkultur herausgebildet: Auf „Cocktailpartys" trugen die Damen „Cocktailklei-
der" und die Gäste hörten „Cocktailmusik".
Auf der Hülle einer solchen Schallplatte
findet sich folgende Beschreibung: „Die
Cocktailstunde ist die weinumrankte Brücke in Zeiten der aktiven Moderne… Es ist
eine Zeit für die Entdeckung neuer Stim-
mungen, Sehnsüchte…"

Don the Beachcomber kannte Rum aus
seiner Jugend auf Jamaika. Indem er verschiedene Arten des Zuckerrohrdestillats
mit Fruchtsäften mixte, kreierte er einen
Trunk, den er „Zombie" nannte. Die Idee
für den Namen könnte er durch seine
Zusammenarbeit mit den Filmstudios für
The White Zombie (1932) gehabt haben. Der
nächste Klassiker dieses Genres *Ich folgte
einem Zombie* (1943) erwähnte den Cocktail
bereits in einem Dialog – ein sicheres Zeichen für seine Popularität.

Nachahmung ist bekanntermaßen die
schönste Form der Anerkennung und Don
the Beachcomber hätte sich geehrt fühlen
sollen, dass so viele Tropenbars den
„Zombie" als ihre Eigenkreation ausgaben.
Keine von ihnen kannte Dons Geheimre-
zept, aber das hielt sie nicht davon ab, ihre

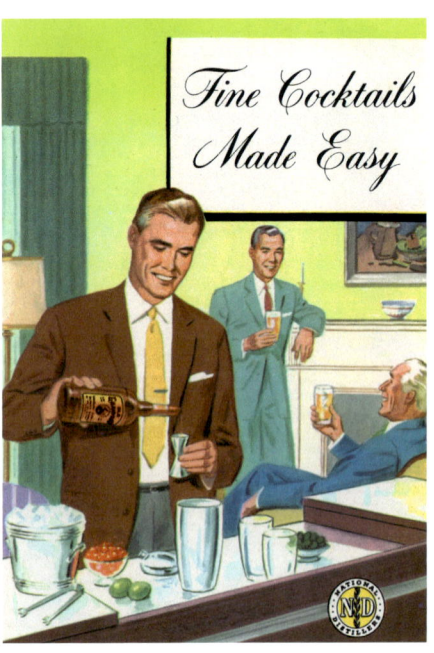

Fine Cocktails Made Easy

1950s recipe booklet

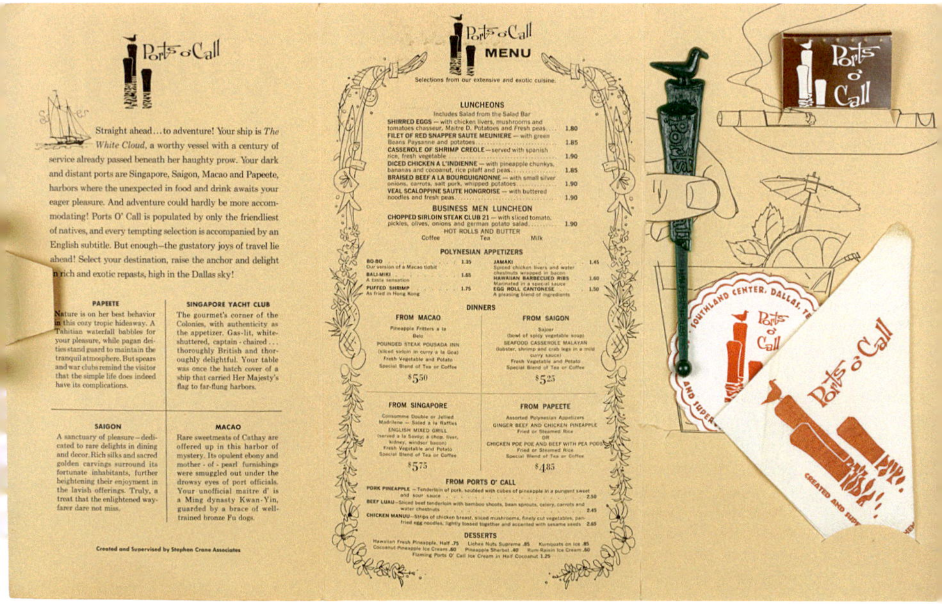

Mixturen als „Zombies" zu verkaufen. Der New Yorker Impresario Monte Proser überrumpfte sie alle und nannte seinen Nachtclub „The Beachcomber", den er wagemutig als „The Home of the Zombie" anpries. Der Fall wurde außergerichtlich gelöst.

Der wahrscheinlich einzige Tiki-Cocktail aus Polynesien ist „Dr. Funk". Seine vielen Variationen basieren alle auf einer Mischung aus Rum, Absinth und Limettensaft. Der Erfinder war Bernhard Funk, der deutsche Arzt von Robert Louis Stevenson, der wie ein Patient auf Samoa lebte. Er teilte sein Rezept mit einem Freund in Papeete, Tahiti.

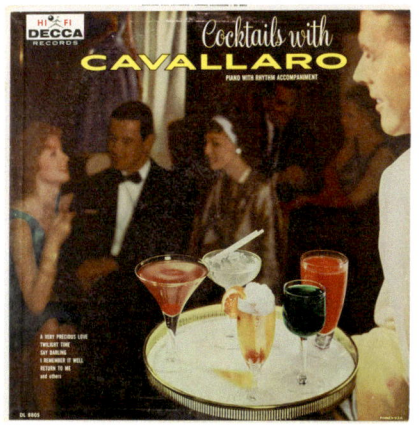

TOP: Souvenir menu providing the accouterments of cocktail culture (*Timothy Haack Collection*)

ABOVE: Cocktail music album

ZOMBIE

Of the 56 world-famous rum creations concocted by Don the Beachcomber, the most famous of all is the Zombie. It came into being one festive night in 1934 at Don's Hollywood restaurant-bar and since then imitations of the heady mixture of rums, juices, absinthe, grenadine, etc., have been blended in bars the world over. Still, there is no beating the original, and Don the Beachcomber has consented to Cabaret's request for the true recipe. Here, for the first time in print, is the secret to the real Zombie.

CABARET

MIXES THE ORIGINAL AND ONLY ZOMBIE

¾ ounce fresh lime juice; ½ ounce fresh grapefruit juice; 1½ ounces fresh pineapple juice; ¼ ounce Falernum; 1¼ ounces Puerto Rican dark rum; 1 ounce Jamaica Planter's Punch rum; 1 ounce Demarrara 151-proof rum; 2 dashes Angostura bitters; 1 dash absinthe (Pernod); 3 dashes grenadine; ¾ ounce maraschino.

Pour above ingredients into shaker or cup of an electric blender. Add handful of small cracked ice. Shake, using medium speed on blender. Pour into 14-ounce glass, with three or four cubes of ice. Decorate with spear of fresh pineapple, orange and cherry, and sprig of mint. Serve with straw. Sip with eyes half-closed. Repeat process until desired effects have been attained.

The 14-ounce glass which is used throughout the country for the Zombie was also designed by Don the Beachcomber in 1934.

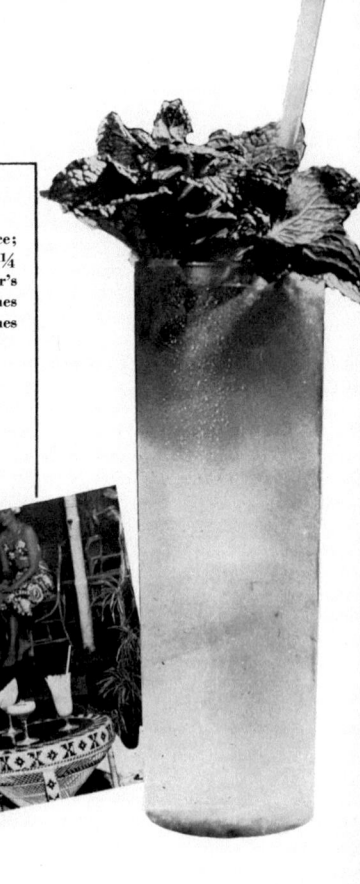

Von dort verbreitete es sich im gesamten Südseeraum.

„Mai Tai" war der Cocktail der Tiki-Generation. Seine Herkunft war heftig umstritten, bis sein Erfinder, Trader Vic, seine Freundin Carrie Wright eine eidesstattliche Erklärung abgeben ließ. Sie war 1944 Zeugin der Entstehung des Cocktails. Nachdem sie ihn probiert hatte, soll sie ausgerufen haben: „Mai Tai roa ae!" – Tahitisch für: „Nicht von dieser Welt!" Der „Mai Tai" war schon bald der beliebteste Drink – nicht nur in amerikanischen Tiki-Bars, sondern auch auf den hawaiischen Inseln.

Von all den poetischen Beschreibungen der polynesischen Cocktails auf den Getränkekarten, war die des „Tiki Lo-lo" vermutlich am prägnantesten: „Tikis sind hawaiische Götter – wenn du selbst keiner sein kannst, trink aus und fühl dich wie einer!"

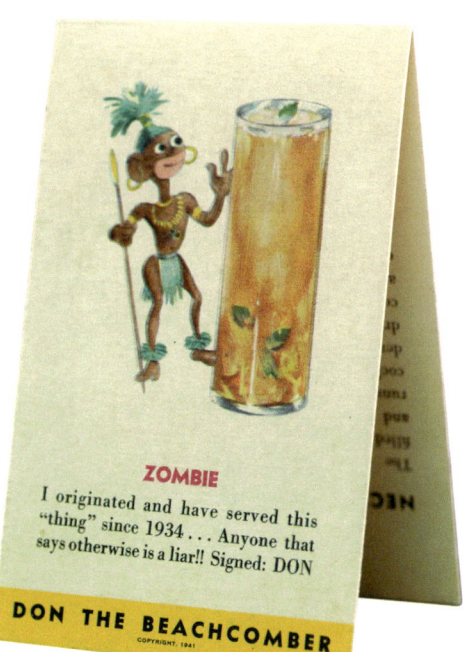

ZOMBIE

I originated and have served this "thing" since 1934 . . . Anyone that says otherwise is a liar!! Signed: DON

DON THE BEACHCOMBER
COPYRIGHT, 1941

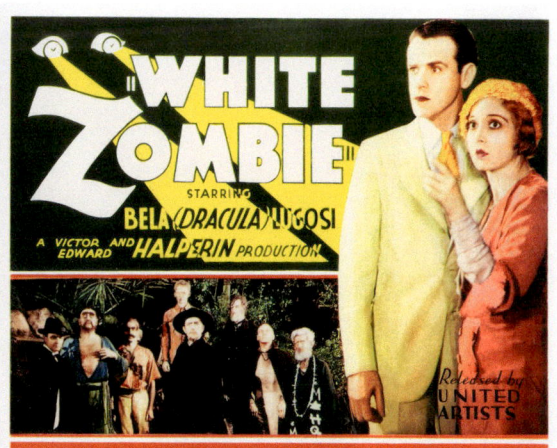

OPPOSITE: First publication of the Zombie recipe, *Cabaret* magazine, 1956

ABOVE: Zombie table card *(Frank Brajevic Collection)*

LEFT: "White Zombie" lobby card, 1932

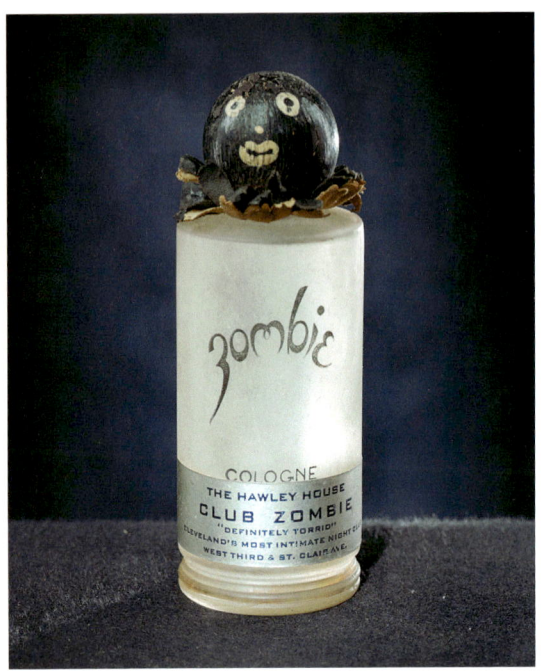

LEFT: Zombie Cologne bottle, Hawley House, Cleveland

BELOW: Photo folder from Monte Proser's Beachcomber, New York (*Frank Brajevic Collection*)

OPPOSITE: Zombie Club menu (*Scott Schell Collection*)

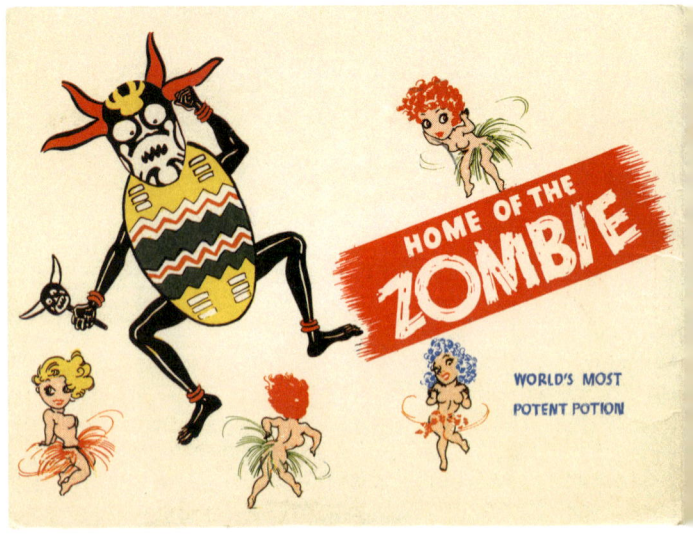

HOME OF THE ZOMBIE

WORLD'S MOST POTENT POTION

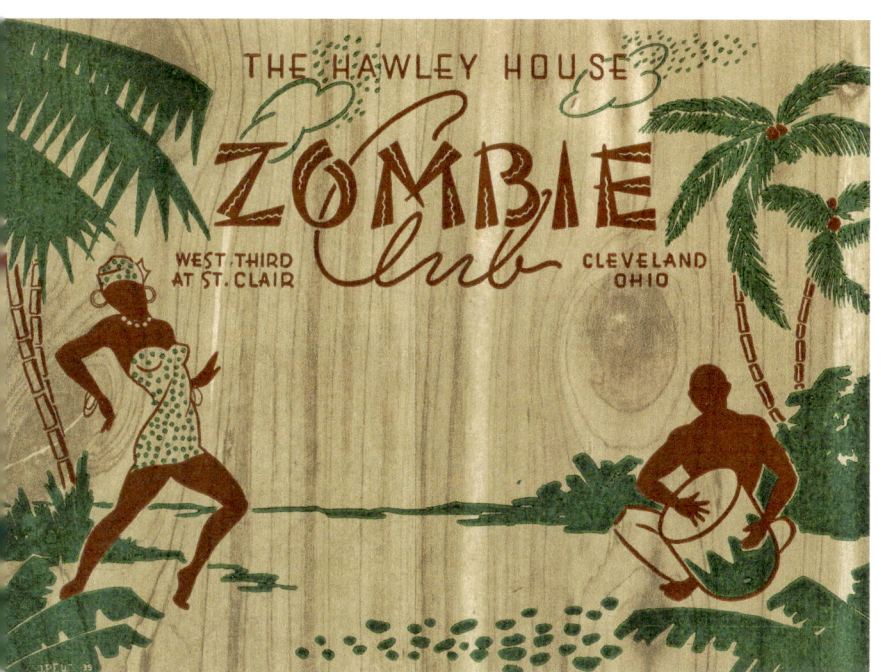

LE COCKTAIL TROPICAL ÉTAIT, SANS

l'ombre d'un doute, le carburant des salons et autres bars tiki. La confortable marge de profit qu'il autorise voit fleurir des temples tiki de plus en plus élaborés dans les jungles d'asphalte américaines. Sa forte teneur en alcool, masquée par un ensemble de saveurs subtiles, et sa présentation visuellement attrayante en font un stimulant addictif dans les affaires comme dans les loisirs. Nous ne pouvons mentionner ici qu'une infime proportion des décoctions qui ont épicé l'histoire américaine du tiki, avec une brève description des pionniers de ce qui fut l'âge d'or de la mixologie à base de rhum.

Les États-Unis vivent de 1920 à 1933 la sombre époque de la prohibition. Il y a une raison à cela : les Américains ont abusé de l'alcool et ont grand besoin de se dégriser. L'alcool devient alors une drogue illégale. Lorsque la prohibition est levée, le goût du public pour les breuvages alcoolisés atteint des sommets inégalés. Les combinaisons de boissons, toujours plus jolies à regarder et brûlantes à avaler sont testées sur des clients avides. L'heure de gloire du cocktail est venue.

Savoir confectionner de bons « drinks » pour ses clients ou ses invités devient un signe de sophistication. Au milieu du siècle, une véritable culture du cocktail s'est développée, au point qu'on organise des soirées apéritives éponymes, les « cocktail parties », pour lesquelles les femmes portent des « robes cocktail » et où l'on écoute de la « cocktail music ». Comme le chante un titre alors très en vogue : « L'heure du cocktail

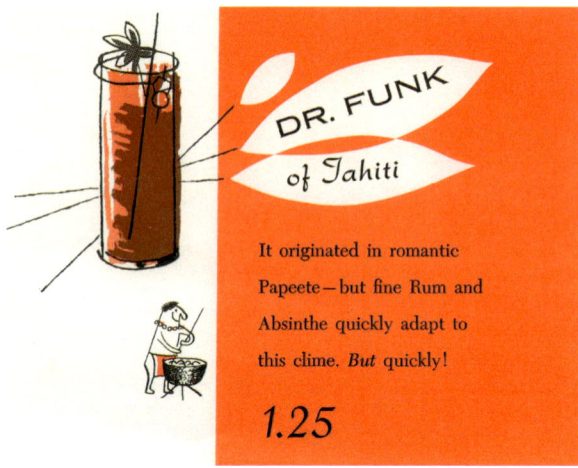

It originated in romantic Papeete—but fine Rum and Absinthe quickly adapt to this clime. *But* quickly!

1.25

est un pont paré de vigne dans la journée active de l'homme moderne… Une heure vouée à la découverte de nouvelles modes, de nouveaux désirs… »

De sa jeunesse en Jamaïque, Don the Beachcomber avait gardé une bonne connaissance du rhum. Il mélangea plusieurs sortes de sucre de canne avec différents jus de fruit et créa une boisson fatale qu'il baptisa le « Zombie ». Don avait travaillé pour les studios et s'est sans doute inspiré du film de 1932, *Les Morts-Vivants*. Dans la catégorie des films d'épouvante, le prochain classique du genre sera *Vaudou* (1943), lequel mentionne ce cocktail dans ses dialogues – un indice imparable de popularité.

L'imitation étant la forme la plus sincère de la flatterie, Don the Beachcomber aurait pu se réjouir que tant de bars tropicaux s'emparent de sa recette phare et en réclament même la paternité. Aucun d'entre eux ne connaissait réellement sa formule secrète, mais cela ne les empêchait pas de vendre le fruit de leurs tentatives. L'impresario new-yorkais Monte Proser les surpassa tous en

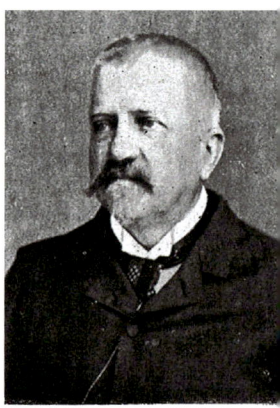

DR. B. FUNK, M.D.

ABOVE LEFT: 1950s table card

ABOVE RIGHT: The good Dr. Funk

OPPOSITE: Recipe for a variation, by Trader Vic, 1940s

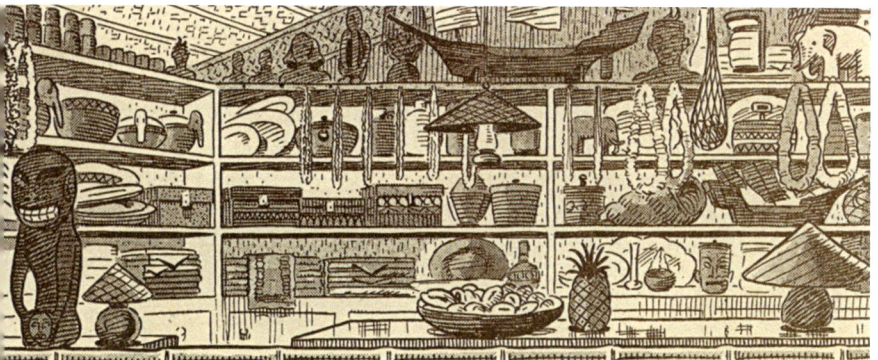

THE STORE

Bora Bora Cooler
(DR. FUNK)

Dr. Funk of Tahiti made a drink like this, only he used some absinthe.
I don't like the darn stuff, so I think this is better.

2½ oz. Gold Rum (use Ron Merito)   ½ oz. Curacoa
Juice of one orange   Small spoon of sugar
Juice of one lemon   2 Dashes of Grenadine

Mix first in a mixing glass with ice then pour into a 14-oz. glass full of ice.

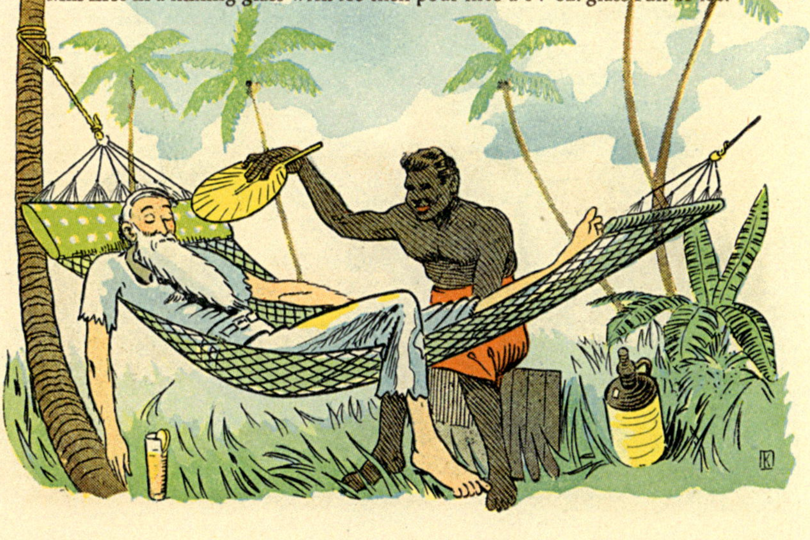

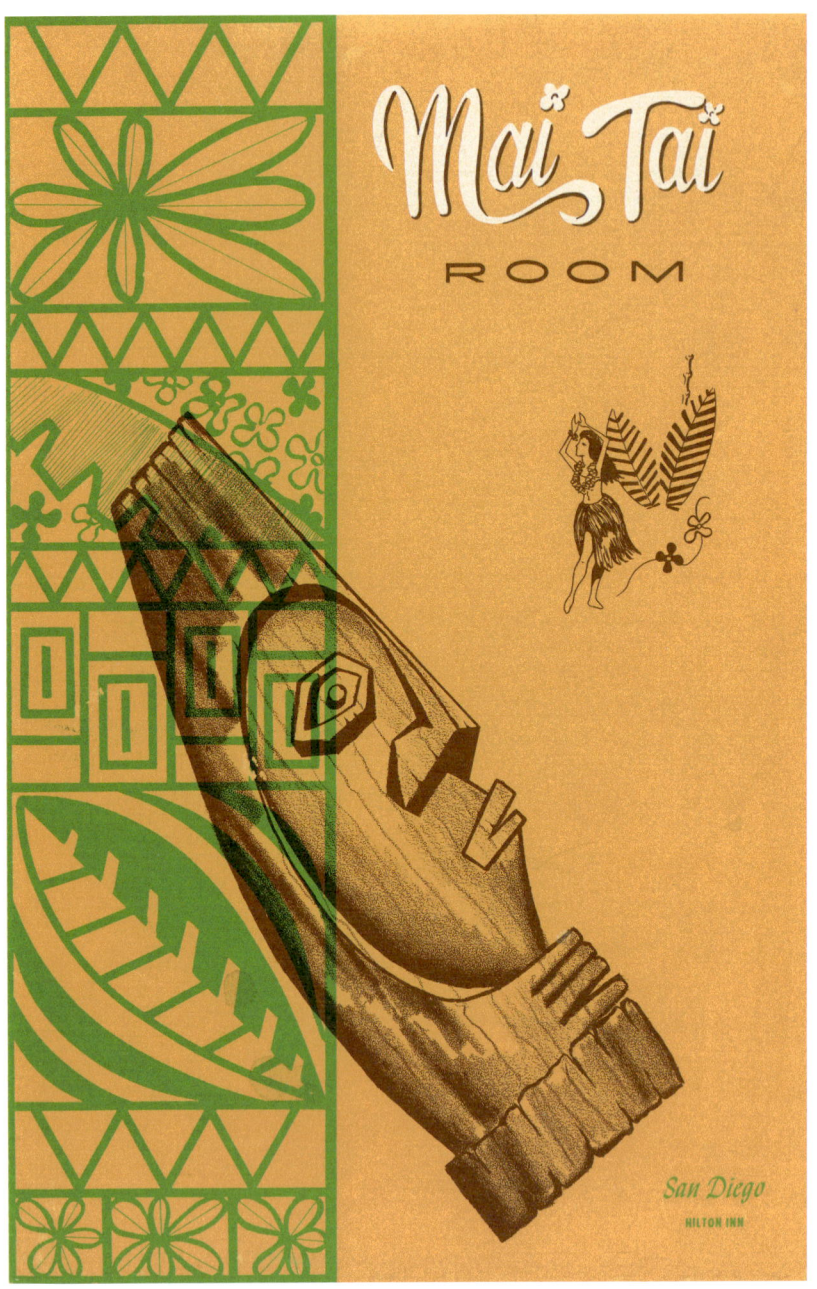

Maĭ Taĭ
ROOM

San Diego
HILTON INN

appelant sa boîte de nuit « The Beachcomber » et en fondant sa campagne publicitaire sur le slogan « La patrie du Zombie ». L'affaire se régla devant un juge.

Le « Dr Funk » est peut-être le seul cocktail réellement venu de Polynésie. Il a connu bien des variantes mais la recette originelle, qui consiste à mélanger rhum, absinthe et jus de citron vert, a été imaginée par le Dr Bernard Funk, un médecin allemand qui soigna Robert Louis Stevenson aux Samoa. Il partagea la recette de cette décoction avec son ami à Papeete, et de Tahiti elle se répandit sur toutes les côtes des mers du Sud.

Pourtant, *le* cocktail de la génération tiki reste le Mai Tai. Ses origines ont longtemps été sujettes à controverse, jusqu'à ce que son créateur, Trader Vic, fît signer un affidavit à son amie Carrie Wright, qui y témoignait avoir assisté à la création de ce cocktail en 1944 et s'être exclamée, après l'avoir goûté, « Mai Tai roa ae ! » – ce qui signifie en tahitien « C'est extraordinaire ! ». Le Mai Tai devient vite la boisson la plus demandée dans les bars tiki américains, mais aussi dans l'archipel hawaiien.

Parmi les nombreuses descriptions lyriques de cocktails polynésiens inscrites sur les menus des restaurants de cette catégorie, celle du « Tiki Lo-lo » est sans doute la plus directe : « Les Tikis sont des dieux hawaiiens – à défaut de pouvoir en être un, buvez et vous aurez la sensation d'en devenir un ! »

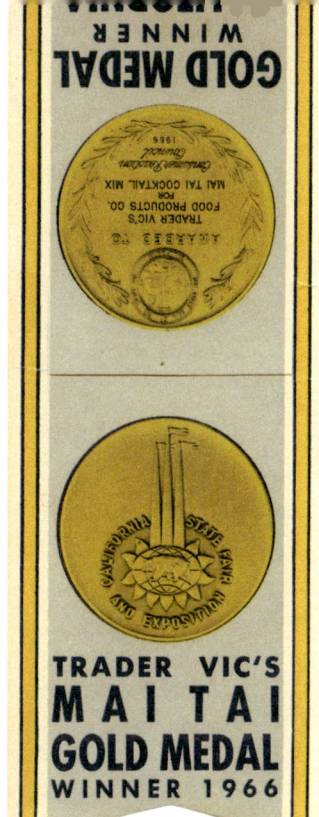

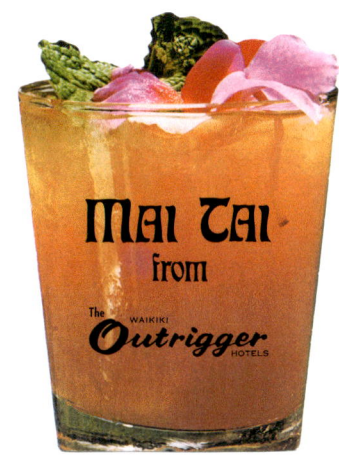

OPPOSITE: Mai Tai Room menu cover (Frank Brajevic Collection)

ABOVE: State fair award for the Mai Tai, 1966

RIGHT: A Mai Tai of Hawaii

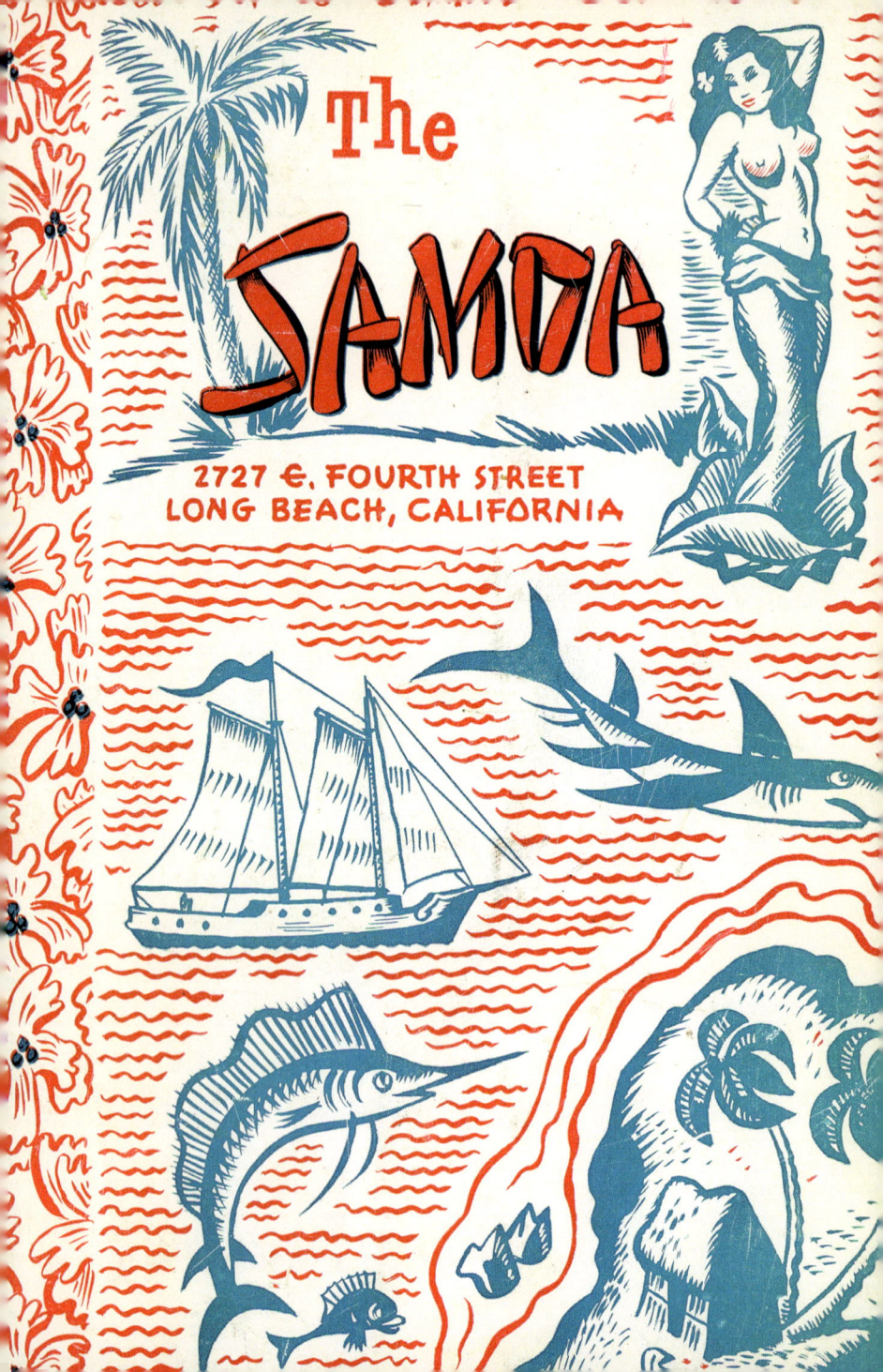

The
SAMOA

2727 E. FOURTH STREET
LONG BEACH, CALIFORNIA

17

THE APPEARANCE OF THE TIKI ICON

DAS AUFTRETEN DES TIKI-SYMBOLS
APPARITION DE L'ICÔNE TIKI

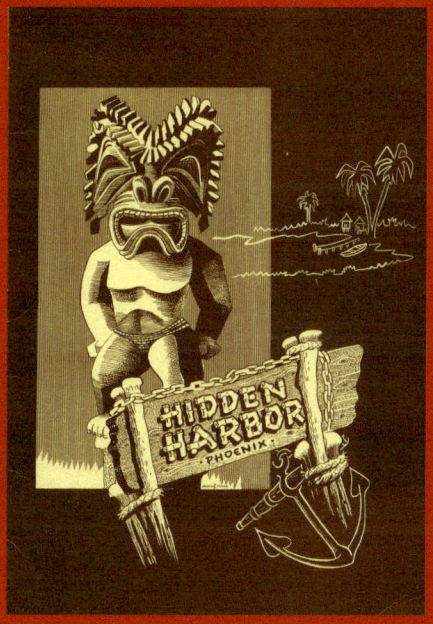

OPPOSITE: Menu cover sporting some of the icons of pre-Tiki Polynesian pop *(Mimi Payne Collection)*

ABOVE: A Tiki looms over other island symbols, menu cover, Phoenix, Arizona *(Frank Brajevic Collection)*

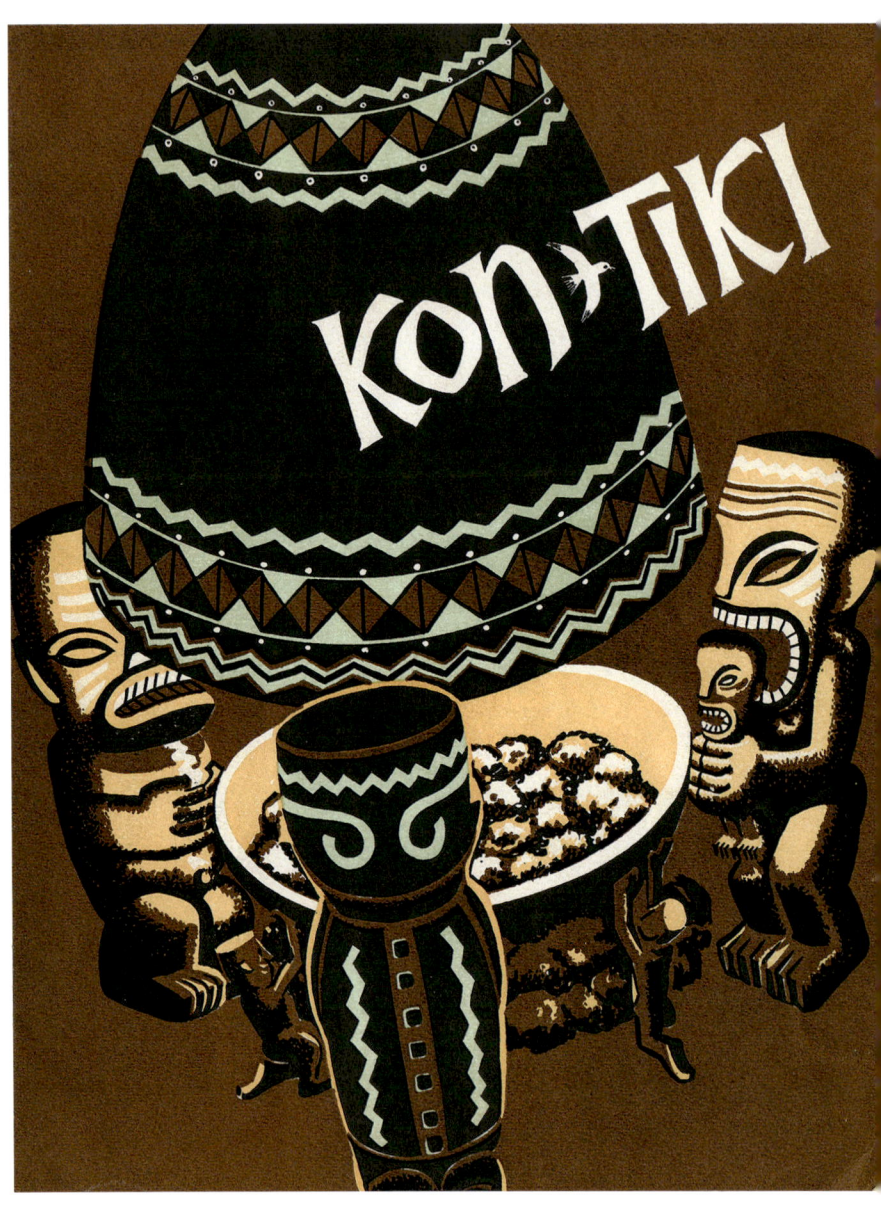

ABOVE: Tahitian cannibal Tikis menu cover, Kon-Tiki restaurant, Montreal

OPPOSITE ABOVE: Bali Hai menu cover *(Kiara Geller Collection)*

OPPOSITE BELOW: "Beachcomber" yearbook, Coronado High School, San Diego, California, 1962

IN THE MID-1950s, A NEW, IMPOSING protagonist appeared on the abundantly decorated stage of Polynesia Americana: the Tiki. Joining the wahine, the beachcomber, and the trader in the story of Polynesian pop, the figure of the primitive idol became the new star of the show.

Nobody specifically sanctioned a changing of the guard, and it is impossible to pinpoint a single cause that induced Tiki's coming. It seems that he emerged from the common subconscious, aided by a variety of compelling conditions.

At the time of Tiki's arrival, a number of archetypes of South Seas escapism had been successfully established in the Western world's mind. With the hula girl as its main icon, various other symbols represented "island paradise": the palm tree; the native hut; the outrigger; the ukelele; the pineapple... These images evoked an exotic pleasure world where one was far removed from any societal obligations.

Suddenly, new editions of South Seas classics featured primitive sculptures on their covers—and so did restaurant menus. Fixtures of Polynesian pop, from beachcomber to Bali Hai, now used the Tiki as their symbol. Where once bamboo huts and hula girls reigned, Tiki carvings now stood guard. Stylistically, godheads from all of the various cultures in the Polynesian triangle were appropriated by American graphic artists and designers, who also added their own dose of whimsy. Far removed from the source of inspiration, the islands, their creativity was free to develop. A new pop art form was taking shape.

A new generation of restaurateurs was adding a plethora of Oceanic artifacts to the layers of tropical textures already covering the walls. From carved Tiki statues and

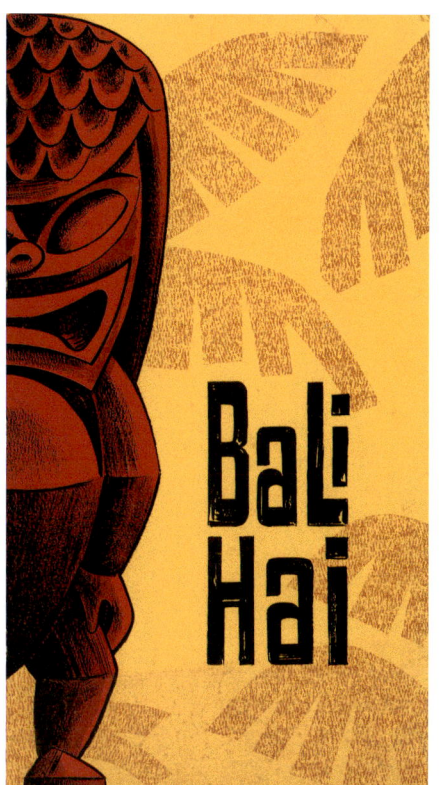

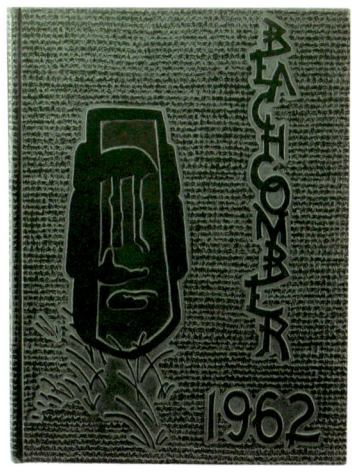

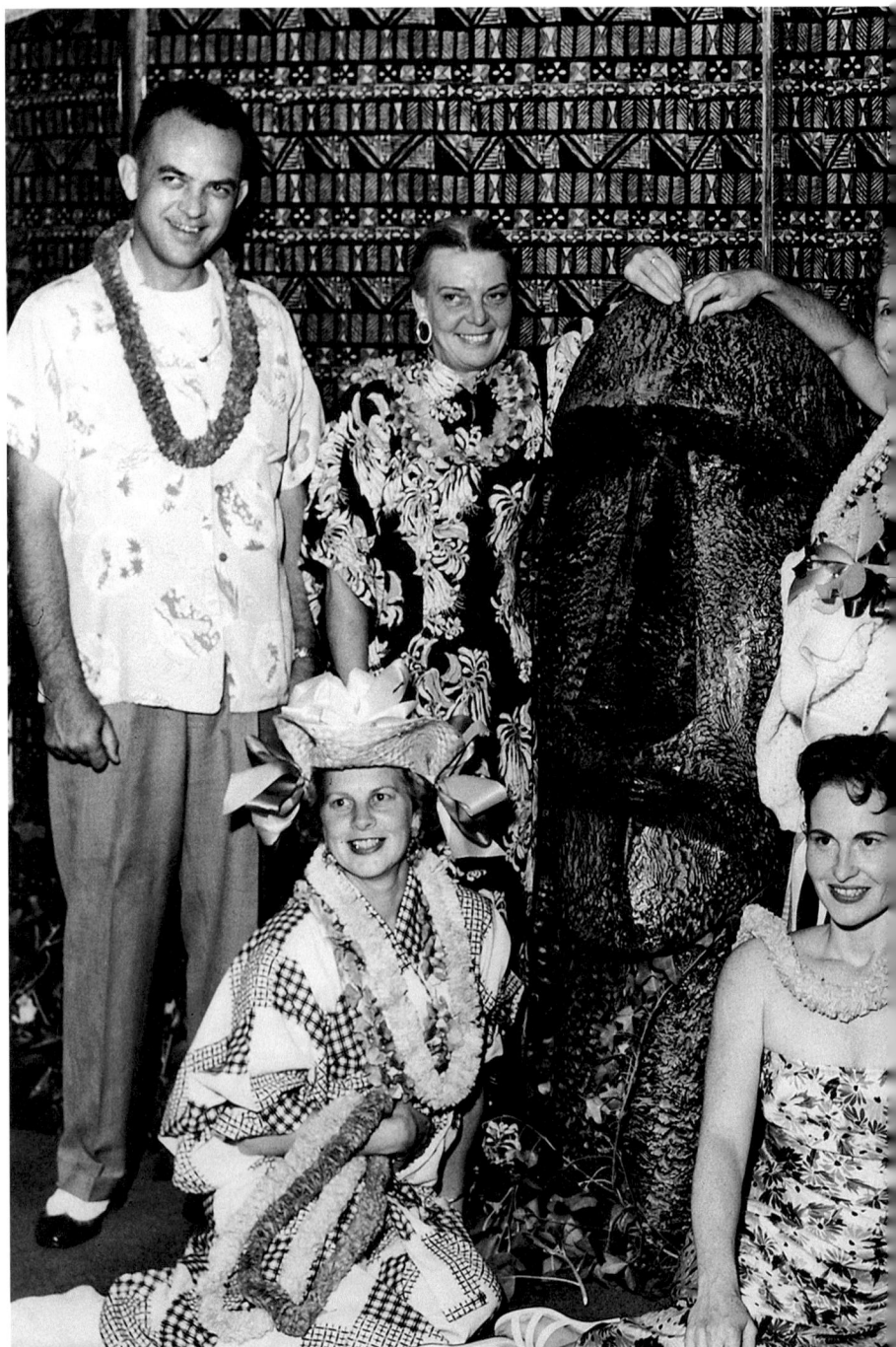

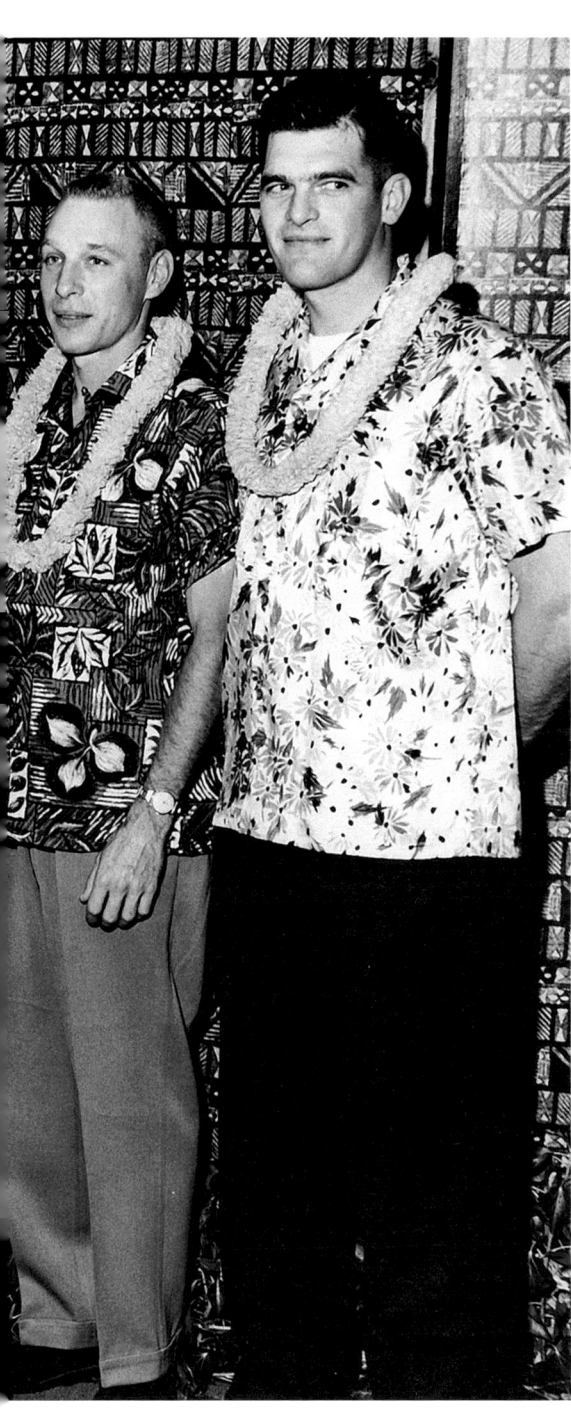

By the late 1950s, Americans
embraced the Tiki

posts to smaller details like Tiki-shaped ceramic salt-and-pepper shakers and Tiki door handles, the image of the Polynesian demigod was perpetuated everywhere.

On the outside of modern island eateries, larger Tiki statues functioned as beacons to the refuge-seeking urbanites. The majority of these idols were sculpted by American artists who were happy to supply the sudden demand for pagan gods. Meanwhile, the unsuspecting drinking public accepted them as "authentic."

Young sculptors fresh from art school felt free to realize their individual interpretations of "primitive art." The results, a mixture of modernism and cartoon style created for commercial purposes, were either ignored or described with mixed feelings by cultural critics, who did not share the general public's enthusiasm. Tiki Pop came and went virtually ignored by the art world.

The Tiki image was applied to an incredible array of not only restaurant items, but also articles for daily use. Tiki was known as the god of the artists in some Polynesian societies; and now he was clearly an inspiration to American designers, who enthusiastically rendered and sculpted his likeness for the pleasure of the recreation industry. While precise, slick mid-century modern style was the mode of the period, a few artists tried their hand at the other end of the spectrum, going back to the rough, naïve beginnings of art.

As the Tiki figure proliferated, so did the Tiki name: first, Polynesian watering holes applied it to their monikers, like Tiki Bob's in San Francisco. Polynesian motels and apartment buildings soon followed. Considering that "tik" is thought by some to be one of the archetypal words of the human language, it is no surprise that "Tiki" became a buzzword, spreading across America during the 1960s.

Eventually, the label "Tiki" was exploited as a brand for businesses with little or no relation to the Polynesian islands: proof of its ubiquity in the period, and a source of amusement for the urban archaeologist in search of remnants of Tiki culture.

Whether in painted or in sculpted form, the Tiki became an undeniable presence in the world of Polynesian pop. He completed the character of the wahine, each balancing and nourishing the other, forming the yin and yang of Tiki Pop. The fact that in Polynesia, Tiki also functioned as a phallic symbol—and, on some islands, was also the name for the male member—certainly might have had something to do with this effect.

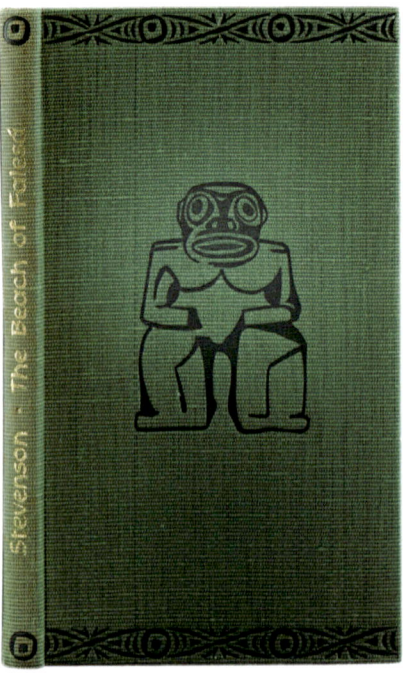

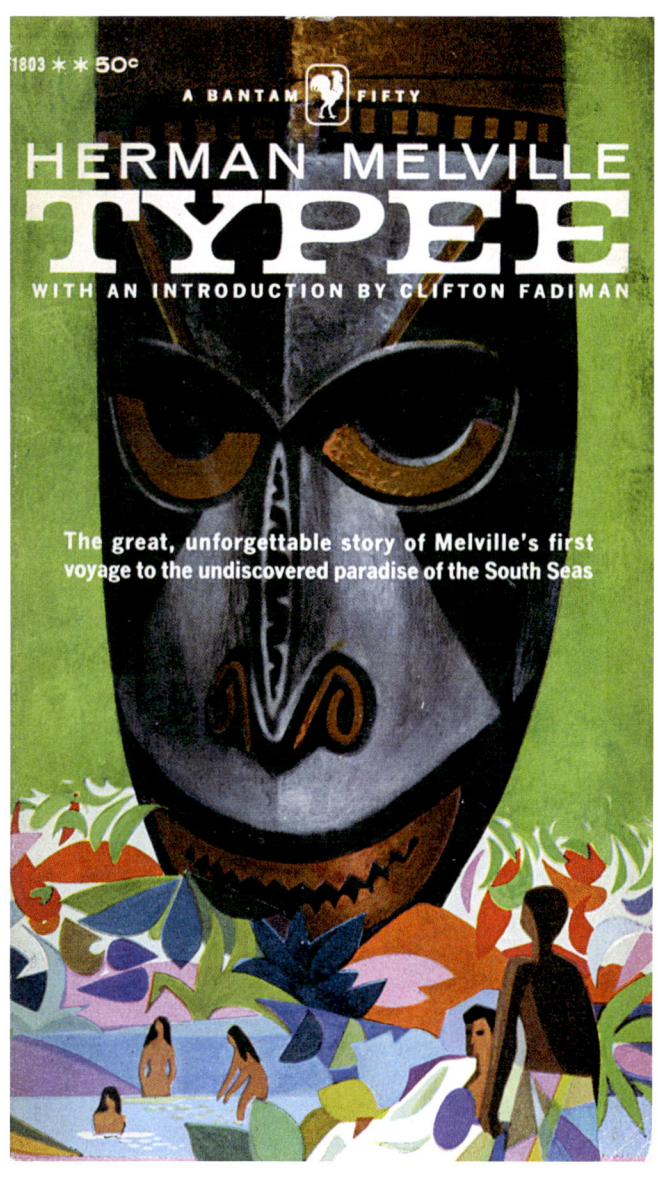

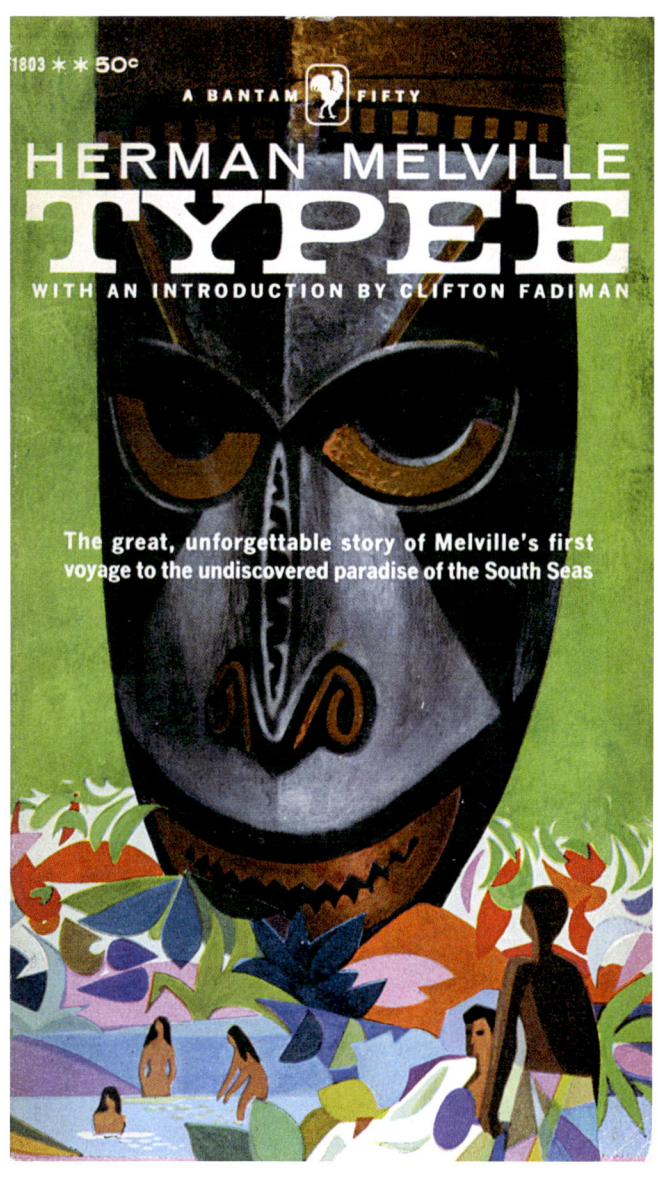1803 ✱✱ 50¢

A BANTAM FIFTY

HERMAN MELVILLE
TYPEE

WITH AN INTRODUCTION BY CLIFTON FADIMAN

The great, unforgettable story of Melville's first voyage to the undiscovered paradise of the South Seas

OPPOSITE: South Seas novel, 1959 edition

ABOVE: Classic South Seas literature with a Tiki cover, 1958

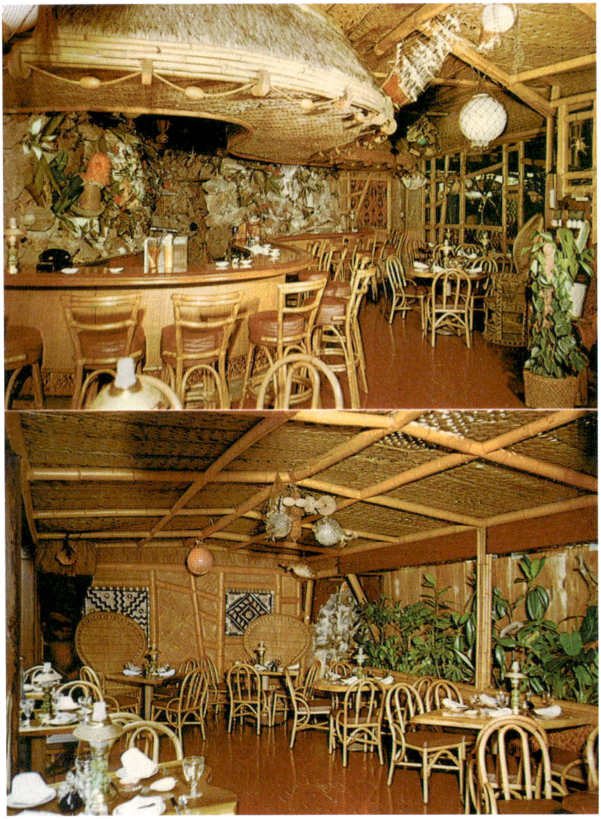

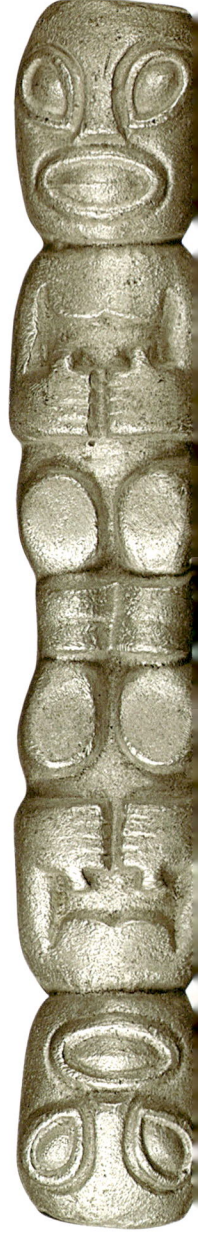

A good example: the Luau, Beverly
Hills, before Tiki moved in (above);
and after (opposite) along with some
of the Luau's Tiki details
(JP Balak Collection)

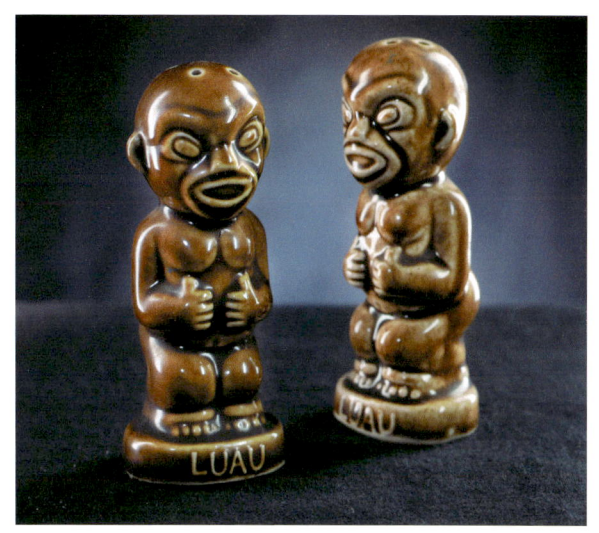

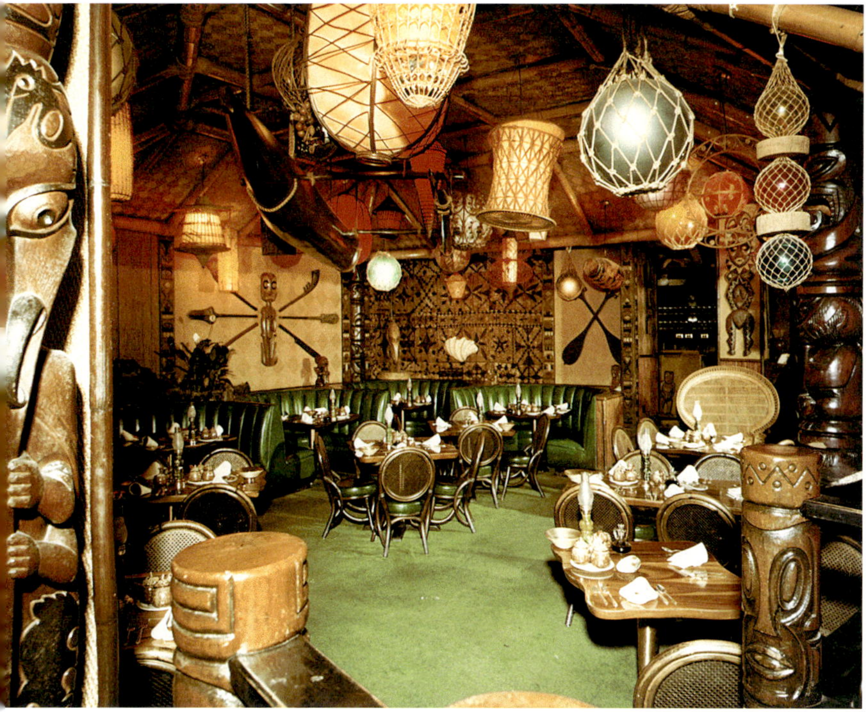

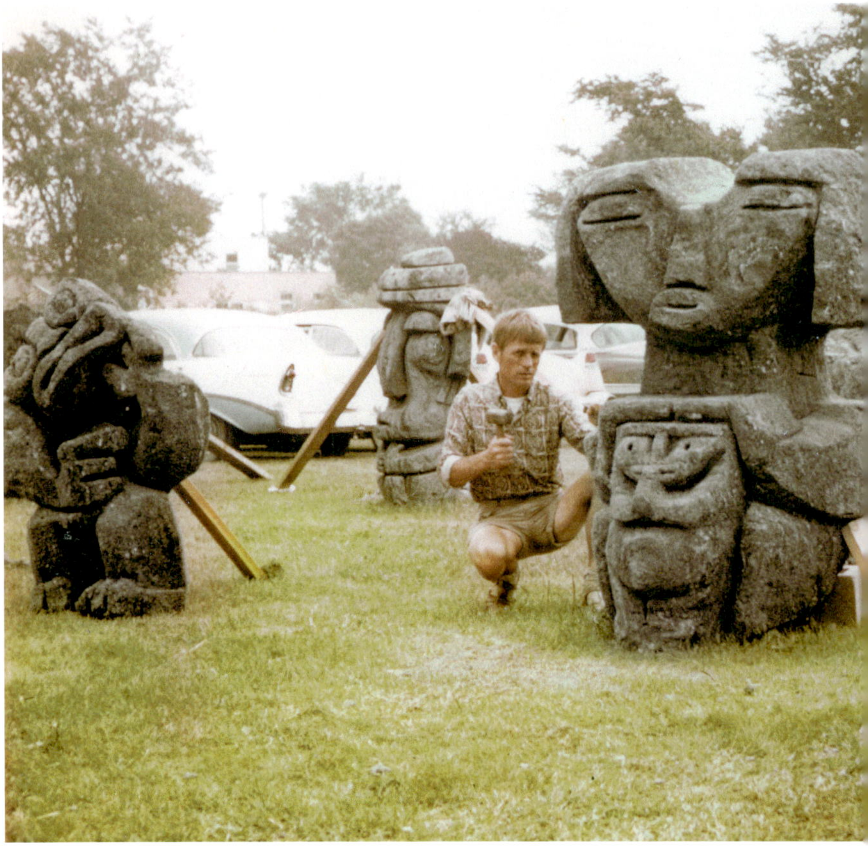

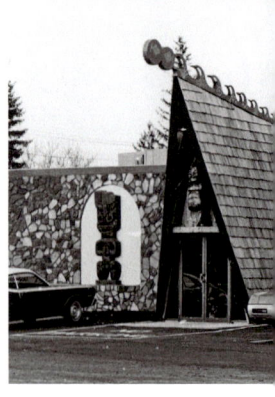

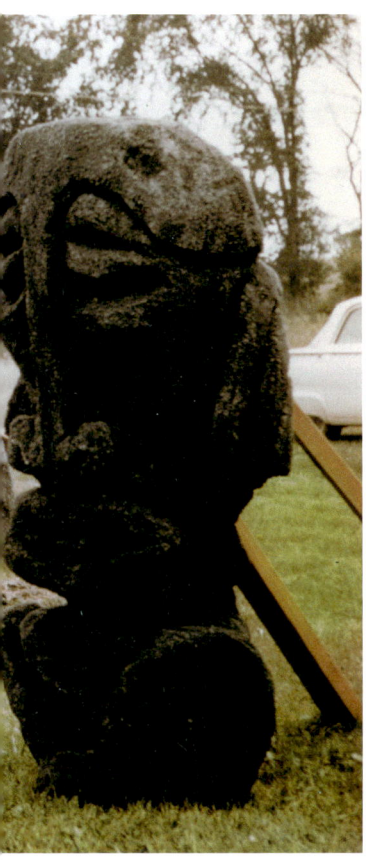

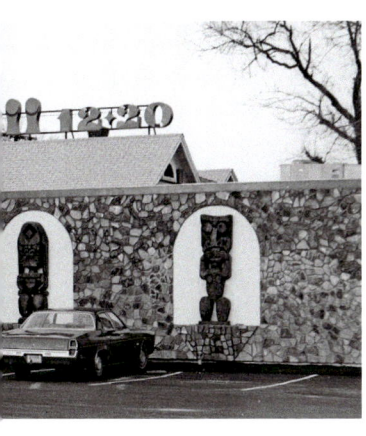

MITTE DER 1950ER-JAHRE TAUCHTE

ein weiterer imposanter Protagonist auf der reich dekorierten Bühne von Polynesia Americana auf: der Tiki. Sich in die Riege aus Wahine, Beachcomber und Trader einreihend, wurde die Figur des Halbgotts zum neuen Star in der Geschichte des „Polynesian Pop".

Es ist unmöglich, für Tikis Aufstieg eine einzige Ursache auszumachen. Es scheint, als sei er eines Tages aus dem kollektiven Unterbewusstsein der USA hervorgegangen, unterstützt durch eine Vielzahl günstiger Bedingungen.

Als Tiki auftrat, hatte sich bereits eine Reihe von typischen Vertretern des Südsee-Eskapismus erfolgreich im Geist der westlichen Welt verankert. Mit dem Hula-Girl als Hauptfigur repräsentierten weitere Symbole das Inselparadies: die Palme, die Bambushütte, das Auslegerkanu, die Ukulele, die Ananas... Symbole, die mit einer Welt exotischer Freuden konnotiert waren, weit weg von gesellschaftlichen Verpflichtungen.

Plötzlich trugen Neuauflagen von Südseeklassikern primitive Skulpturen auf dem Umschlag – genauso wie die Karten der Restaurants. Feste Institutionen des Polynesian Pop – vom Beachcomber bis zum Bali Hai – nutzten Tiki nun als Symbol. Wo einst Bambushütten und Hula-Girls regierten, hielten jetzt geschnitzte Tikis Wache. Gottheiten aus allen Kulturen des polynesischen Dreiecks wurden von amerikanischen Designern mit jeweils eigener Note versehen. Weit entfernt von der eigentlichen Inspirationsquelle, den Inseln, konnten sie ihrer Kreativität freien Lauf lassen. Eine neue Pop-Art-Richtung nahm langsam Gestalt an.

Die nachrückende Generation von Gastronomen fügte den tropischen Materialien an den Wänden eine Fülle von ozeanischen Artefakten hinzu, von geschnitzten Tiki-Statuen und -pfählen bis zu kleineren Objekten wie Salz- und Pfefferstreuern in Tiki-Form oder Tiki-Türgriffen – das Abbild des polynesischen Halbgottes war überall zu finden.

Vor modernen Insellokalen dienten größere Tiki-Statuen als Leuchtfeuer für die Zuflucht suchenden Stadtbewohner. Die Mehrheit dieser Figuren wurde von amerikanischen Künstlern gefertigt, die die plötzliche Nachfrage nach heidnischen Gottheiten gern bedienten. Die trinkende Bevölkerung akzeptierte sie als „authentisch".

Junge Bildhauer, frisch von der Kunstschule gekommen, fühlten sich beflügelt, ihre eigenen individuellen Interpretationen der Primitiven Kunst frei auszuleben. Die Ergebnisse waren eine Mischung aus

Modernismus und Karikatur und dienten kommerziellen Zwecken. Sie wurden entweder von den Medien ignoriert oder von Kulturkritikern, die den Enthusiasmus der Öffentlichkeit nicht teilten, mit gemischten Gefühlen beschrieben. Der Tiki-Pop kam und ging, ohne in der Kunstwelt nennenswerte Beachtung zu finden.

Das Tiki-Motiv fand sich nicht nur in unglaublich vielen Varianten in Restaurants, sondern auch in Form von Alltagsgegenständen wieder. Tiki war in manchen polynesischen Gesellschaften als Gott der Künste bekannt. Nun inspirierte er amerikanische Designer, die sein Bildnis für die Freizeitindustrie begeistert adaptierten. In dieser Zeit war der präzise, glatte Mid-century-modern-Stil in Mode. Aber einige Künstler versuchten sich auch am anderen Ende des

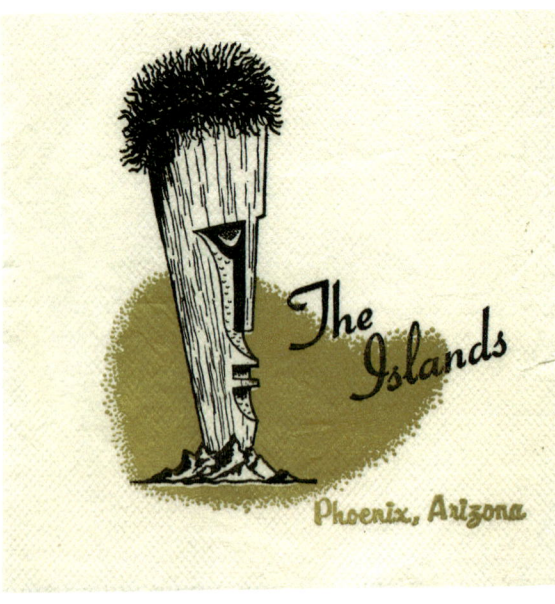

Ugly Statues Are in Vogue

EL PORTO, Calif. (AP)—From this little beach community — known primarily for its bongo drum night life — has come a bow to another exotic culture.

It's the Polynesian tiki, a grotesque statue carved from palm logs, and it's making a comfortable living for bearded young sculptor Mike Gildea.

Landscapers and interior decorators from near-by Los Angeles snap up the bulgy-eyed figures he hacks out with axes, chisels, saws, rasp files and mallets. Prices range from $10 to $15 a foot, and some of the statues are 20 feet tall.

They represent heroes and gods popular in the South Sea islands.

The 22-year-old Gildea claims his work beats imports:

"Native craftsmen are just like others in the world. They have gone commercial. The result is loss of primitive character in their work."

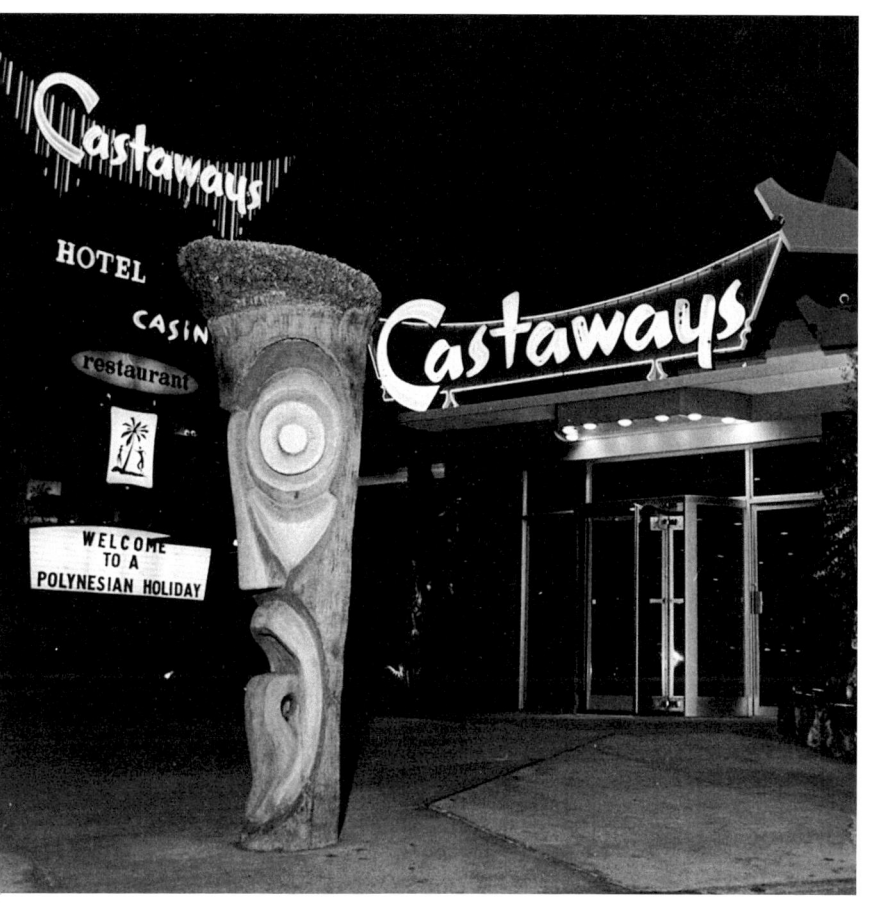

Spektrums und wandten sich wieder den rauen, naiven Anfängen der Kunst zu.

Mit der Ausbreitung der Tiki-Figuren wurde auch ihr Name populärer. Die polynesischen Kneipen waren die ersten, die ihn für sich entdeckten, beispielsweise das Tiki Bob's in San Francisco. Polynesische Motels und Wohnanlagen sollten es ihnen bald gleichtun. Bedenkt man, dass manche Forscher „tik" als archetypisches Wort der menschlichen Sprache betrachten, ist es kaum verwunderlich, dass „Tiki" zu einem Modewort wurde, das sich in den 1960er-Jahren in allen US-Bundesstaaten verbreitete.

Schließlich wurde die Bezeichnung „Tiki" selbst von Unternehmen genutzt, die nur wenig oder gar keinen Bezug zu den polynesischen Inseln hatten. Dies beweist die Allgegenwart des Wortes in jenem Jahrzehnt und amüsiert die Stadtarchäologen, die nach Überbleibseln der Tiki-Kultur forschen.

Ob in gemalter, geschnitzter oder gehauener Form – Tiki wurde ein unbestreitbarer Bestandteil des Polynesian Pop. Er und die Figur der Wahine ergänzten einander; sie waren das Yin und Yang des Tiki-Pop. Die Tatsache, dass Tiki in Polynesien auch als Phallussymbol fungierte – und auf manchen Inseln sogar als Name für das männliche Geschlechtsteil diente – mag sicher etwas damit zu tun gehabt haben.

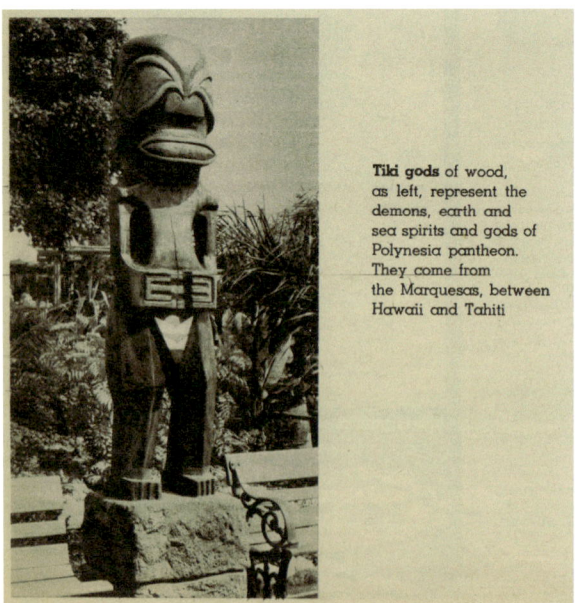

Tiki gods of wood, as left, represent the demons, earth and sea spirits and gods of Polynesia pantheon. They come from the Marquesas, between Hawaii and Tahiti

LEFT: A Tiki God in Disneyland

OPPOSITE ABOVE, LEFT: Ashtray for Islander restaurant, Los Angeles

OPPOSITE ABOVE, RIGHT: Cigarette pouch called "Tiki Tote," 1963

OPPOSITE BELOW, LEFT: Table lamp for unknown restaurant (both Frank Brajevic Collection)

OPPOSITE BELOW, RIGHT: Tiki pendant and lipstick holder in one

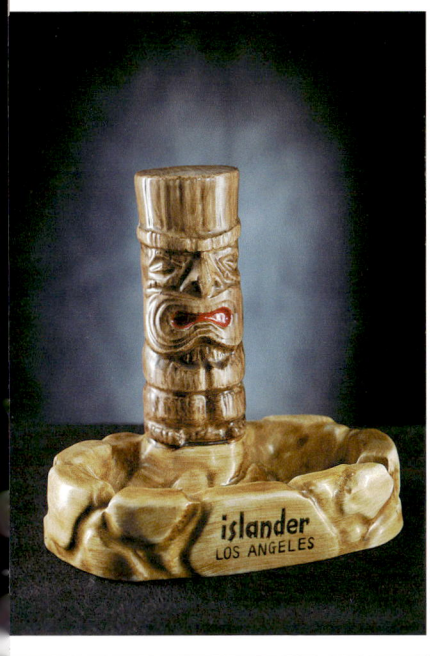

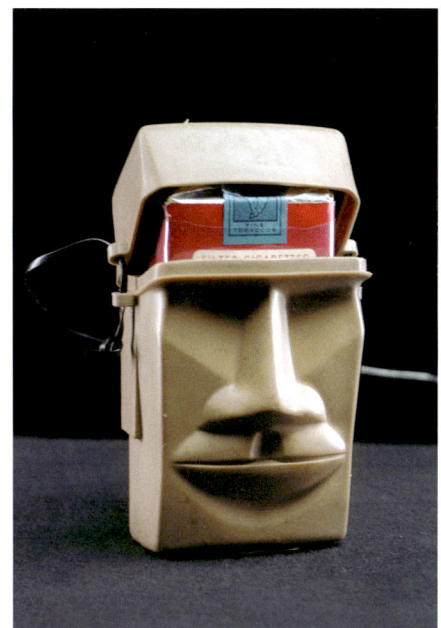

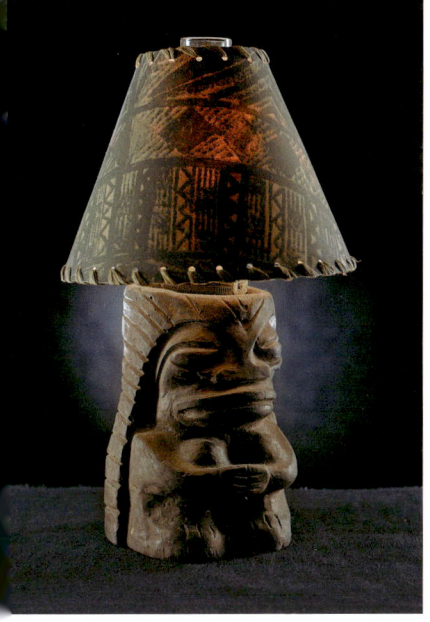

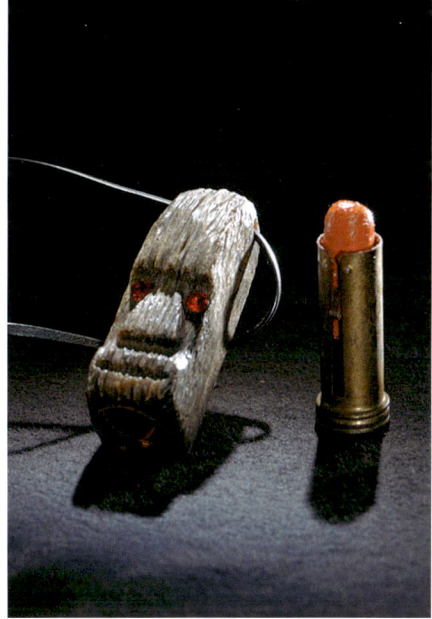

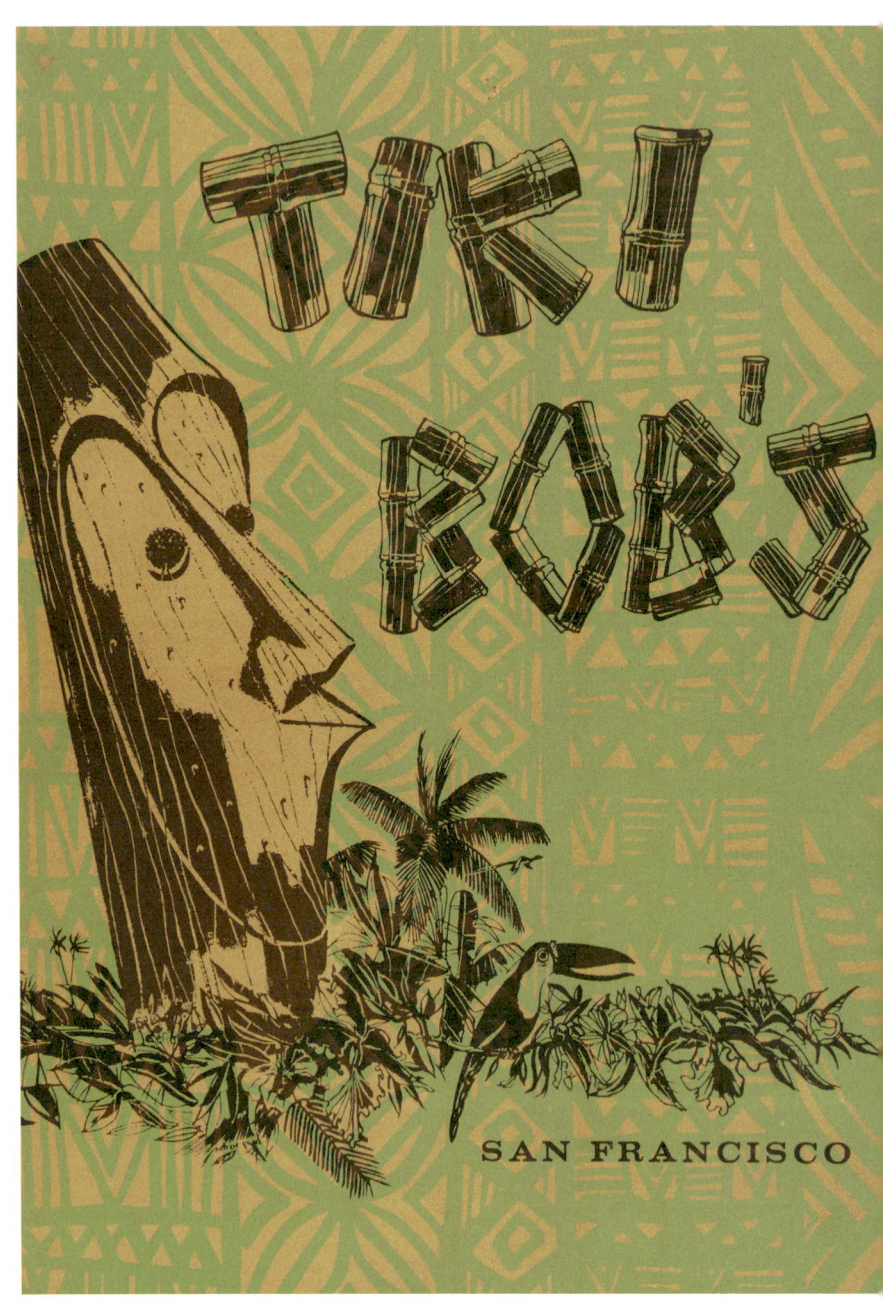

SAN FRANCISCO

AU MILIEU DES ANNÉES 1950, UN nouveau protagoniste, de taille, apparaît sur la scène déjà foisonnante de la culture américano-polynésienne : le tiki. Cette figure primitive élevée au rang d'idole, qui rejoint la vahiné, le batteur de grève et le négociant, devient la vedette de la troupe.

Personne ne note officiellement ce changement de hiérarchie dans une culture de bric et de broc, et il est impossible de pointer une cause unique qui aurait permis l'avènement du tiki. Il semble avoir émergé du subconscient collectif, grâce à la conjonction de conditions nécessaires favorables.

Lorsque surgit le tiki, nombre d'archétypes de l'exotisme pacifique sont déjà ancrés dans le paysage culturel occidental. Si la danseuse de hula est alors la grande prêtresse de cet aréopage, d'autres symboles viennent meubler le « paradis des îles » formé dans l'esprit des Américains : le palmier, la hutte de bambou, la pirogue, l'ukulélé, l'ananas… Ces images évoquent un monde de plaisirs exotiques où s'échapper des contraintes de la vie en société.

Soudain, les rééditions de romans exotiques exhibent en couverture des sculptures primitives… et les menus des restaurants suivent au pas de course. Tous les établissements polynésiens à la sauce pop, du Beachcomber au Bali Hai, prennent le tiki pour symbole. Là où régnaient peu auparavant les huttes de bambou et les vahinés se dressèrent bientôt de massifs

tikis, gardiens d'un monde enchanteur ; mystérieux, et vaguement dangereux. Les artistes et graphistes locaux s'inspirent sans vergogne de toutes les cultures du triangle polynésien pour façonner leurs typos et leurs totems, et n'hésitent pas à convoquer aussi leur fantaisie personnelle. Bien loin de leur source originelle, les îles, ils donnèrent librement cours et corps à un nouvel art populaire.

Chaque nouvelle génération de restaurateurs ajoute son lot d'objets et de matériaux exotiques aux couches successives de rêve tropical qui tapissent déjà les murs de ces établissements. Statues, poteaux et totems, le tiki se retrouve jusque dans les détails décoratifs tels les salières et poivrières en céramique ou les poignées de porte.

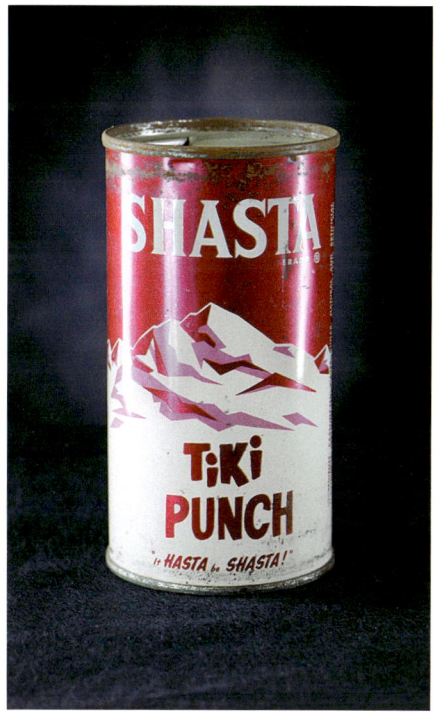

OPPOSITE: Tiki Bob's menu cover, San Francisco (*Frank Brajevic Collection*)

RIGHT: Punch can bearing the tiki name

Aux portes des établissements exotiques modernes trônent des tikis monumentaux, comme des balises dans le paysage urbain. La majorité de ces idoles sont sculptées par des artistes américains qui sont ravis d'alimenter la demande en dieux païens. De son côté, le public de ces refuges de pacotille, où il vient principalement boire et oublier, veut bien les croire « authentiques ».

Les jeunes sculpteurs frais émoulus des écoles se sentent libres de réaliser leurs interprétations personnelles de cet « art primitif ». Les résultats – un mélange de modernisme et de créature de dessin animé créé dans un objectif commercial – sont ignorés ou, au mieux, décrits avec des sentiments mitigés par la critique culturelle, qui partage peu l'engouement du grand public. De la même manière, la tendance pop tiki vient et passe sans que le monde de l'art s'en soucie.

Le style et l'image tiki sont appliqués à un éventail invraisemblable d'objets, hors des restaurants et bars « spécialisés ». Certaines sociétés polynésiennes considèrent Tiki comme la divinité des artistes, et voilà qu'il attise l'imagination des créateurs américains de diverses disciplines, qui ne se font pas prier pour façonner des imitations du demi-dieu à l'usage de l'industrie du divertissement, au sens large. Alors que la mode contemporaine est aux silhouettes précises et lisses, quelques artistes s'essaient, à l'autre bout du spectre stylistique, à un retour aux sources de l'art, brutes et naïves.

Si l'image de Tiki fleurit partout, il en va de même pour le mot « tiki » : les abreuvoirs polynésiens qui jalonnent le territoire américain le collent sur leurs enseignes, comme le Tiki Bob's de San Francisco. Les motels et résidences polynésiennes

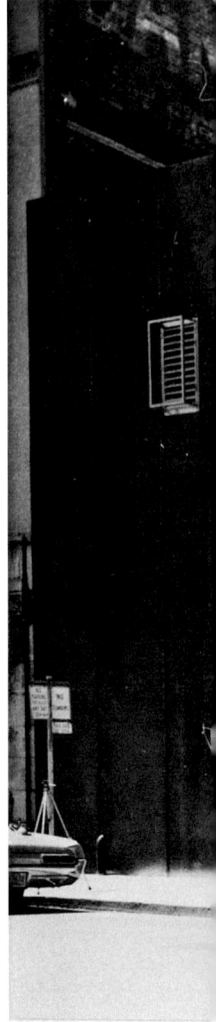

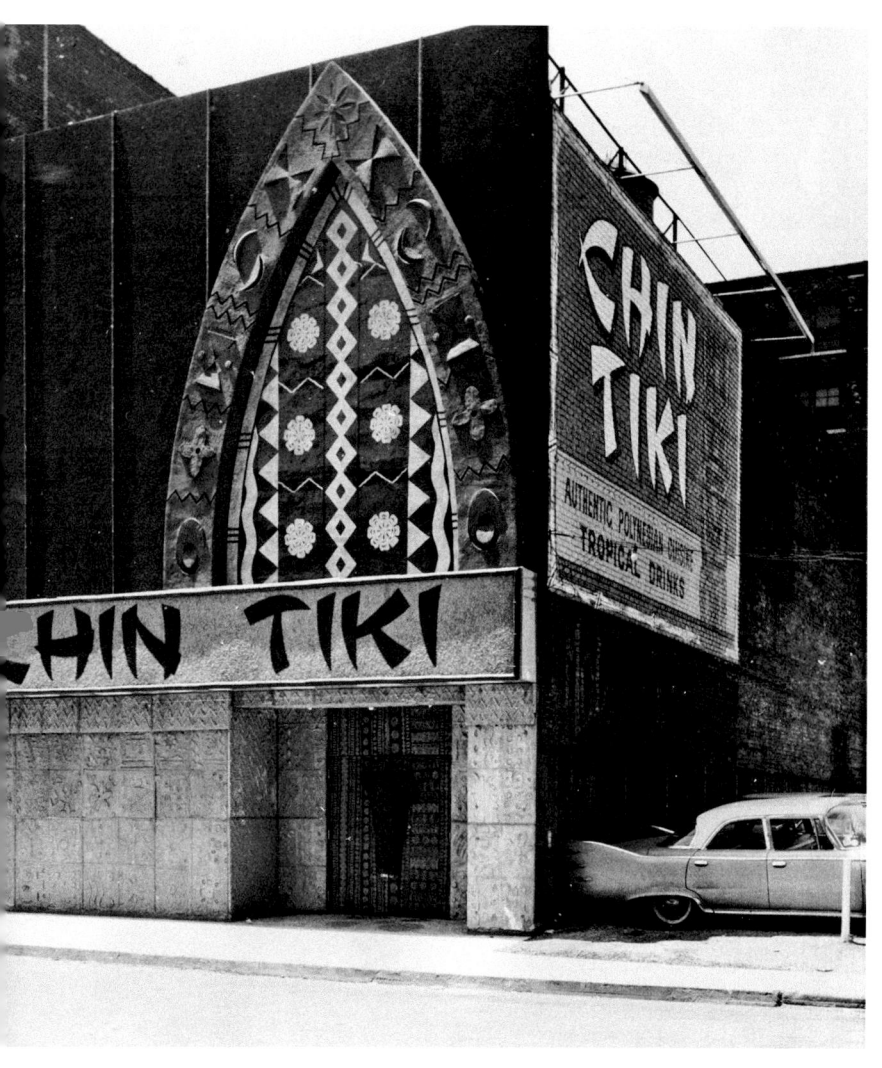

Chin Tiki restaurant, Detroit, 1967

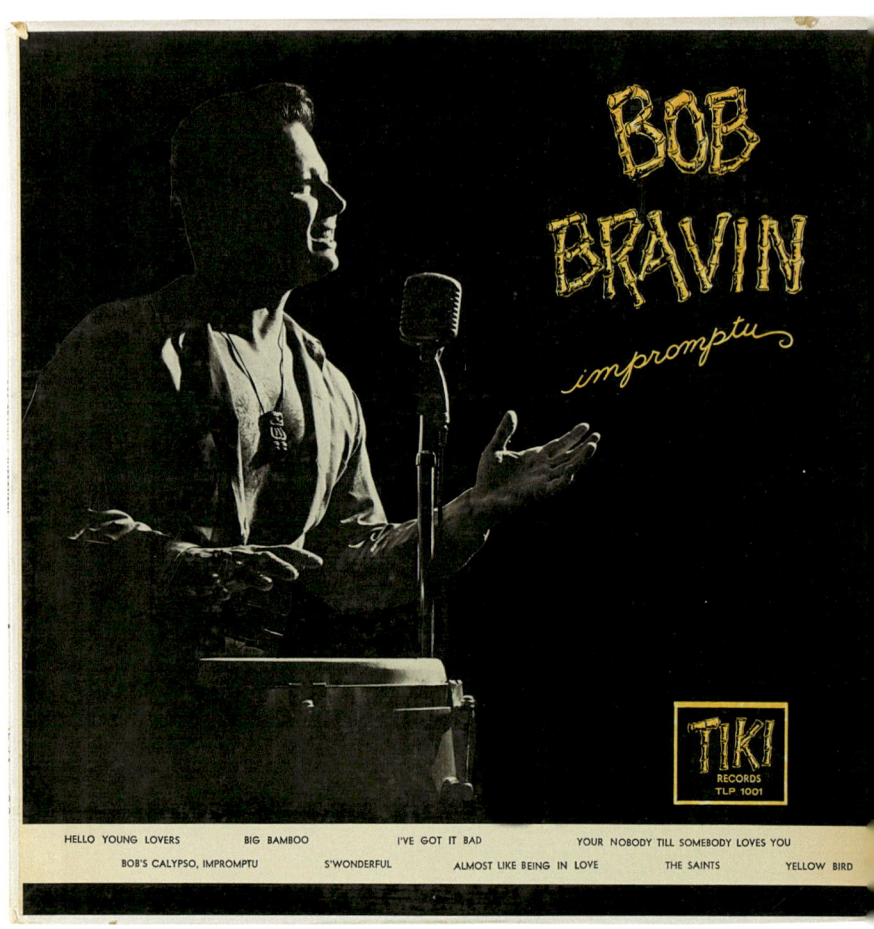

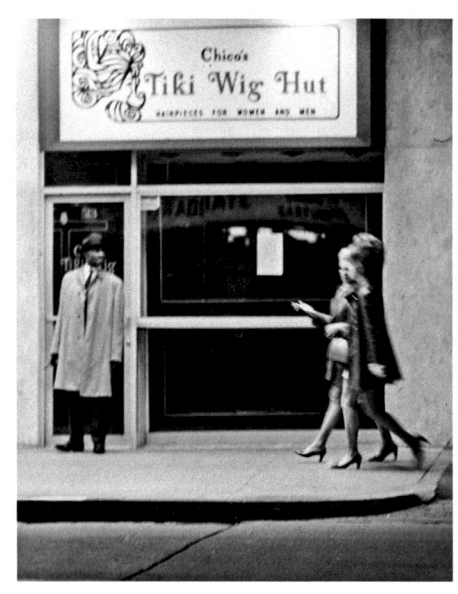

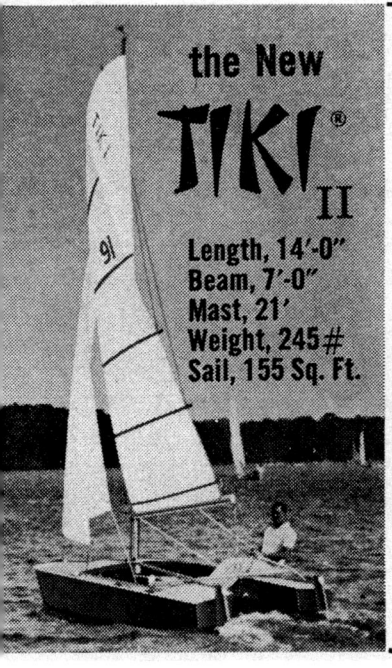

the New

TIKI® II

Length, 14'-0"
Beam, 7'-0"
Mast, 21'
Weight, 245#
Sail, 155 Sq. Ft.

THIS CAT HAS EVERYTHING!

PERFORMANCE: Nimble—Fast—Sea-
worthy

SAFETY: Stable—Self-bailing—Foam
Flotation

VERSATILITY: Waterskiing—Fishing
—Swimming

QUALITY: Only the finest

Write for complete description and
brochure now!

DEALERS: Exclusive Territories Now
Available

CATAMARAN CORPORATION
OF AMERICA
2324 Summit Street,
Kansas City, Missouri

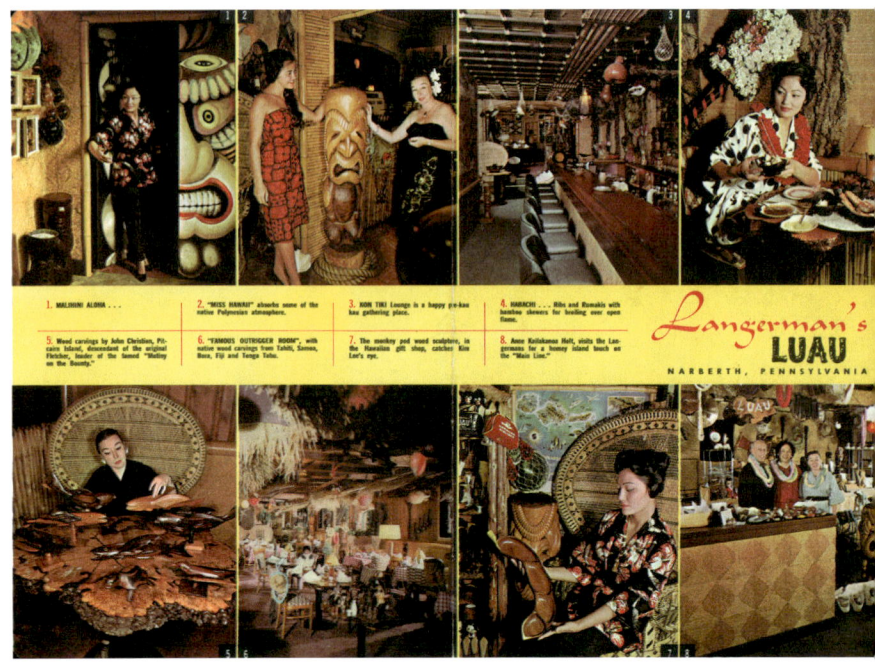

1. MALIHINI ALOHA . . .

2. "MISS HAWAII" absorbs some of the native Polynesian atmosphere.

3. KON TIKI Lounge is a happy pu-kao kau gathering place.

4. HABACHU . . . Ribs and Rumakis with bamboo skewers for basking over open flame.

5. Wood carvings by John Christian, Pitcairn Island, descendant of the original Fletcher, leader of the famed "Mutiny on the Bounty."

6. "FAMOUS OUTRIGGER ROOM", with native wood carvings from Tahiti, Samoa, Java, Fiji and Tonga Tabu.

7. The monkey pod wood sculpture, in the Hawaiian gift shop, catches Kim Lee's eye.

8. Anne Keilakamea Halt, visits the Longoroans for a homey island touch on the "Main Line."

Langerman's
LUAU
NARBERTH, PENNSYLVANIA

suivent. Lorsqu'on sait que le mot « tik » est considéré par certains chercheurs comme un des phonèmes archétypaux du langage humain, il n'est pas étonnant que « tiki » ait été si vite sur toutes les lèvres dans les années 1960.

Le label « tiki » ne tarda pas, bien entendu, à être exploité par des branches commerciales n'ayant que peu ou pas de rapport avec de quelconques îles : une preuve de son ubiquité à cette période qui est aussi une source d'amusement pour l'archéologue urbain en quête de reliques de la culture tiki pop.

Qu'il soit peint ou sculpté, le tiki devient une présence incontournable dans le monde pop polynésien. Avec la vahiné, il forme un couple équilibré, complémentaire, une sorte de yin et yang tiki pop. Le fait qu'en Polynésie le tiki soit aussi considéré comme un symbole phallique et que ce mot désigne sur certaines îles le sexe masculin n'est sans doute pas pour rien dans cette interprétation.

ABOVE: Placemat from Langerman's Luau, Narberth, Pennsylvania

OPPOSITE: Young American wahine posing with a Tiki carved by Barney West at the Barefoot Trader store, Cape Cod

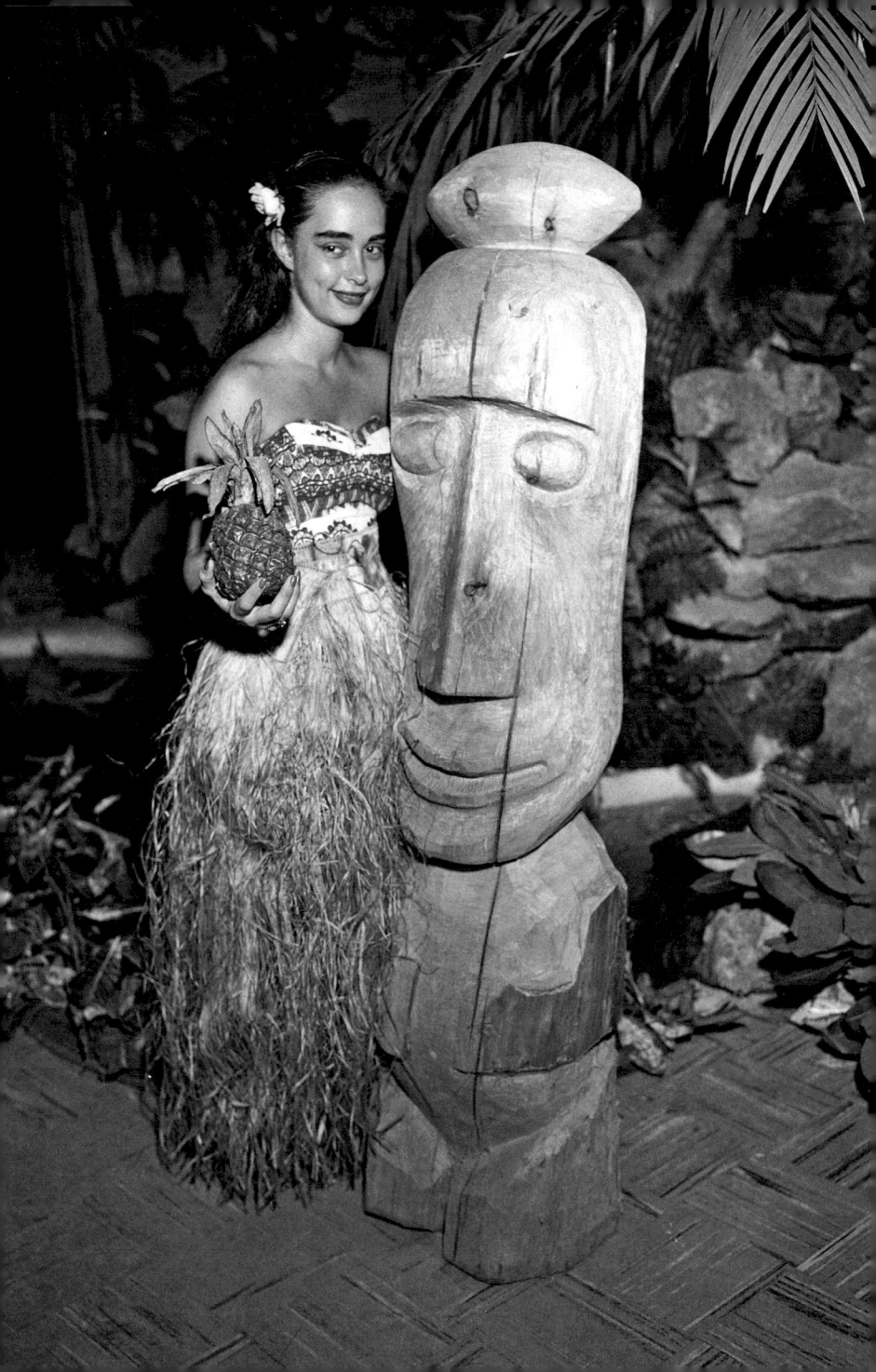

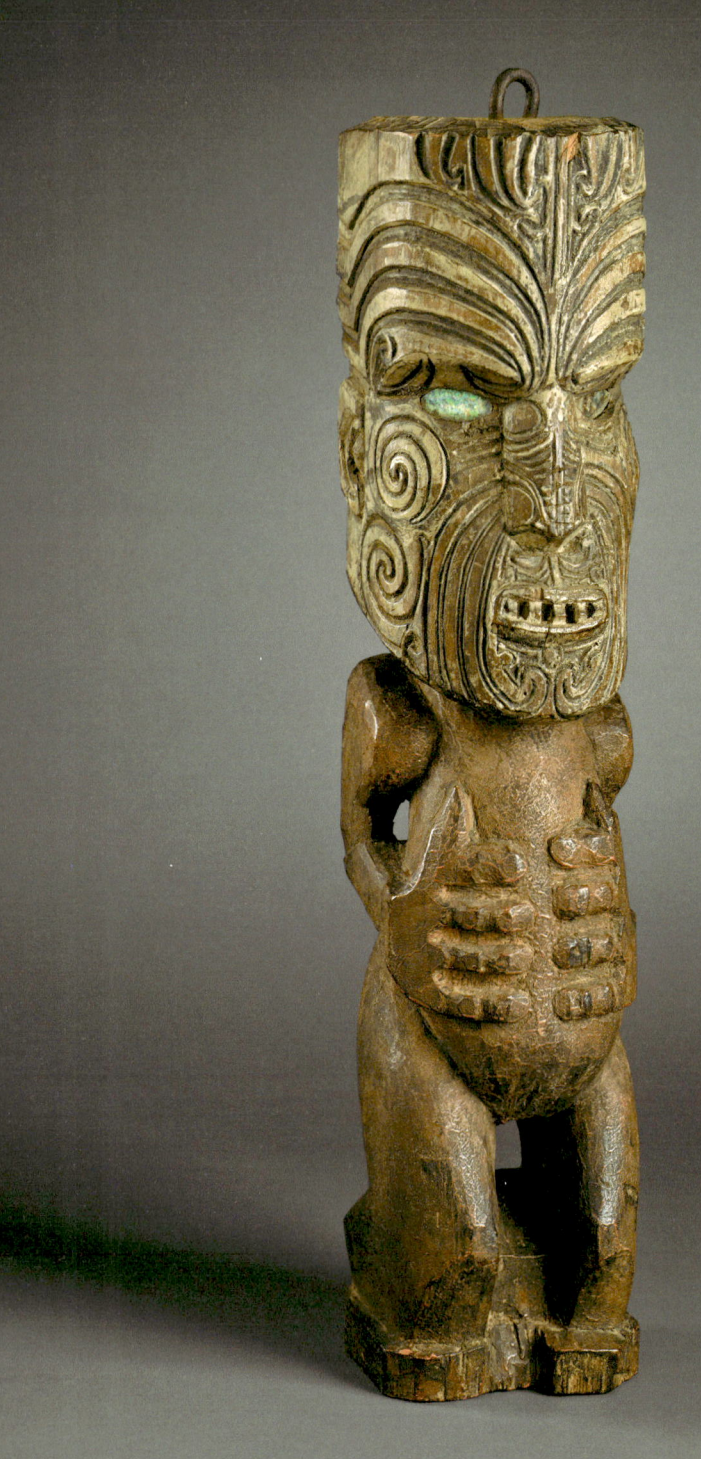

THE LOGO TIKI

TIKI ALS BILDMARKE
LE LOGO TIKI

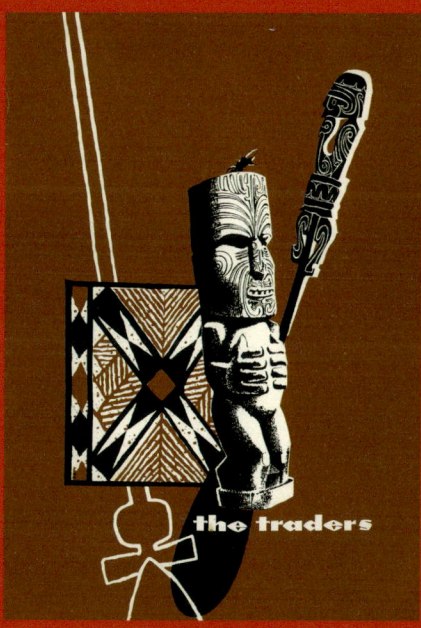

OPPOSITE: Tekoteko, or Maori meeting house gable figure. California
Midwinter International Exposition, 1894 *(de Young Museum Collection)*

ABOVE: Trader Vic's menu cover making use of the image opposite

IN 1955, THE BEVERLY HILLS TRADER

Vic's, located at the Beverly Hilton, was among the first to use a Tiki image on their menu. It was based on a Tekoteko gable figure that had arrived in San Francisco as part of the Maori culture presentation for the California Midwinter International Exposition in 1894. Remaining on display at the de Young Museum from then on, it inspired a plethora of Tiki Pop products.

As the Tiki became the prominent figurehead of Polynesian pop, a statue would be used repeatedly by restaurants, making it their brand logo. The Maori Tekoteko design was applied to many of Trader Vic's paper items, such as menus and cocktail napkins, but its use found its culmination in the Tiki stem glass: the perfect marriage between mid-century cocktail culture and Tiki Pop.

The Trader Vic's Maori Tiki was slightly altered in shape when it was used for cigarette lighters and cuff links, but its origin was still traceable. Its presence was part of the promise the trader had made: to bring his customers "all the atmosphere, the foods and the splendor of the South Sea Islands." Examples of "primitive art" like the Maori Tiki lent an air of authenticity to the restaurant's faux-exotic-island surroundings.

With the success of the Trader Vic's chain, other restaurateurs sought to emulate the trader. They swiped Vic's logo Tiki for their menus and other promotional items, perhaps hoping that some of its mana would rub off on them. The concept of plagiarizing competitors was somewhat integral to Tiki Pop. It must be viewed as a form of creative cross-pollination, aiding the expansion of the Tiki phenomenon.

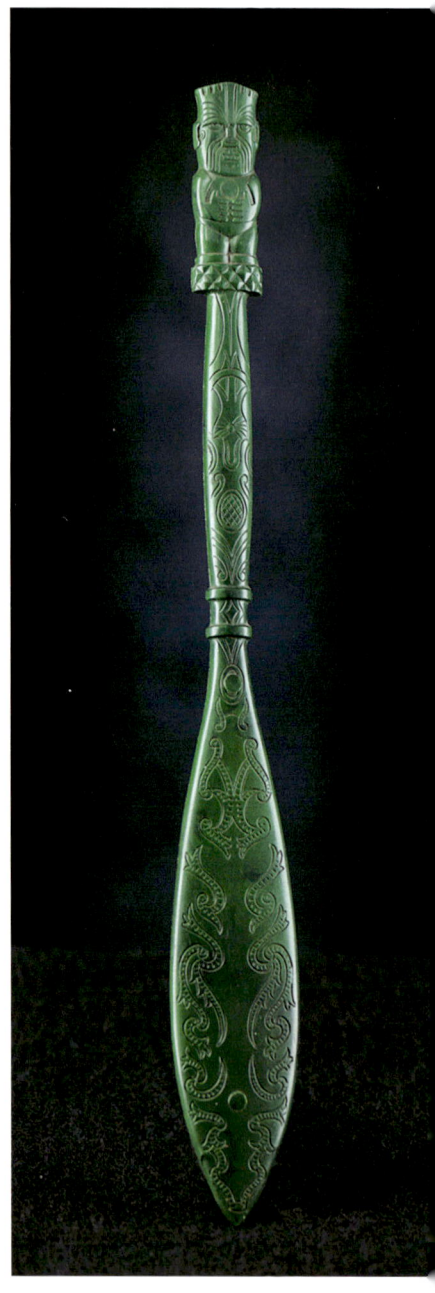

TRADER VIC'S • TRADER VIC'S • TRADER VIC'S •
TRADER VIC'S • TRADER VIC'S • TRADER VIC'S

PALMER HOUSE • CHICAGO
A HILTON HOTEL

trader vic's outrigger

Luncheon

HOTEL BENJAMIN FRANKLIN, SEATTLE

OPPOSITE: Trader Vic's swizzle stick with a Tiki inspired by the statue

ABOVE: Cocktail napkin, Trader Vic's, Chicago

RIGHT: Another menu design with the logo Tiki *(Mimi Payne Collection)*

When the Marriott hotel chain decided that it too deserved a share of the Polynesian-restaurant market, it looked no further than Trader Vic for inspiration. His company had held its own against the competing Don the Beachcomber and Stephen Crane chains and was continually expanding its reach.

The Kona Kai's logo Tiki differed just enough from the original Tekoteko to not be an outright copy, but its big hands and cheek tattoos clearly indicate its origin. The concept of the logo Tiki was fully realized when the Kona Kai used theirs not only on menus and matchbooks, but also in three-dimensional ceramics: a cocktail mug, salt and pepper shakers, and even an ashtray.

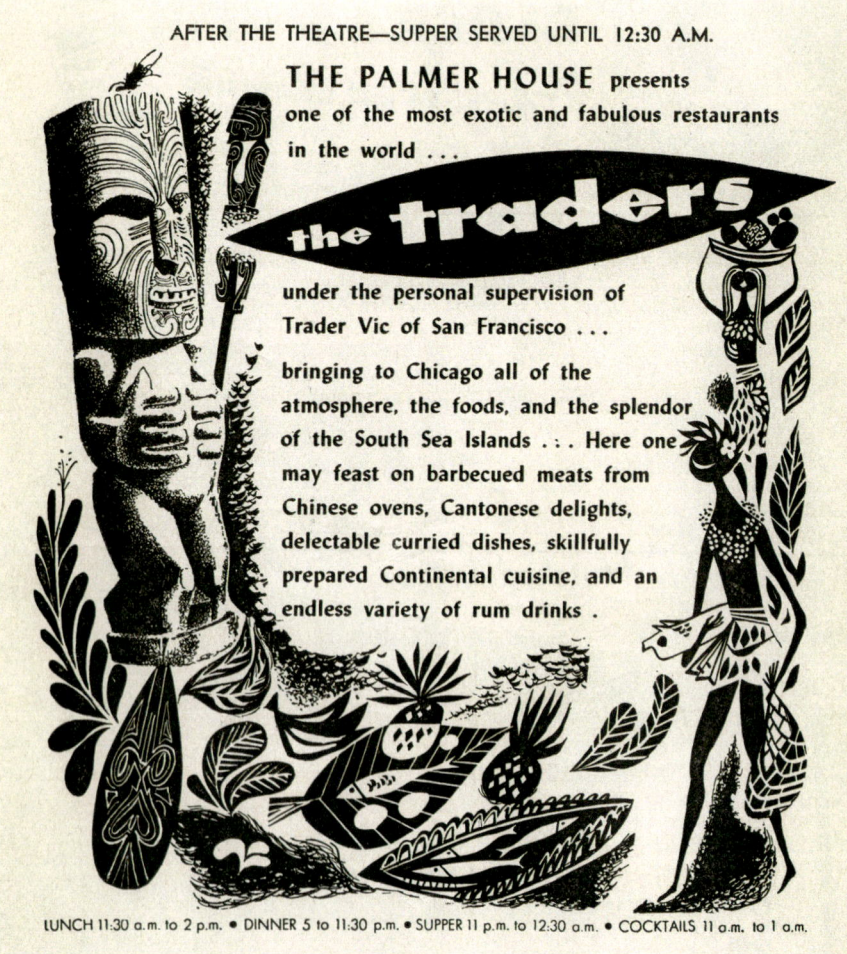

AFTER THE THEATRE—SUPPER SERVED UNTIL 12:30 A.M.

THE PALMER HOUSE presents

one of the most exotic and fabulous restaurants in the world . . .

the traders

under the personal supervision of Trader Vic of San Francisco . . .

bringing to Chicago all of the atmosphere, the foods, and the splendor of the South Sea Islands . : . Here one may feast on barbecued meats from Chinese ovens, Cantonese delights, delectable curried dishes, skillfully prepared Continental cuisine, and an endless variety of rum drinks .

LUNCH 11:30 a.m. to 2 p.m. • DINNER 5 to 11:30 p.m. • SUPPER 11 p.m. to 12:30 a.m. • COCKTAILS 11 a.m. to 1 a.m.

United States Patent Office

Des. 187,481
Patented Mar. 22, 1960

187,481

COCKTAIL GLASS OR SIMILAR ARTICLE

Victor J. Bergeron, Orinda, Calif.

Application July 9, 1958, Serial No. 51,712

Term of patent 14 years

(Cl. D36—8)

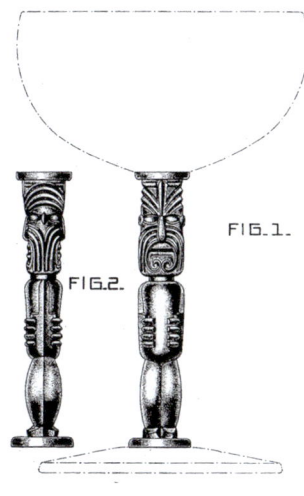

FIG_1_

FIG_2_

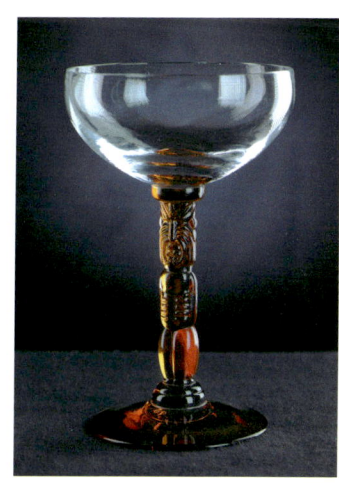

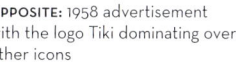

OPPOSITE: 1958 advertisement
with the logo Tiki dominating over
other icons

ABOVE AND RIGHT: The 1960 Trader
Vic's Tiki stem cocktail glass and
its patent

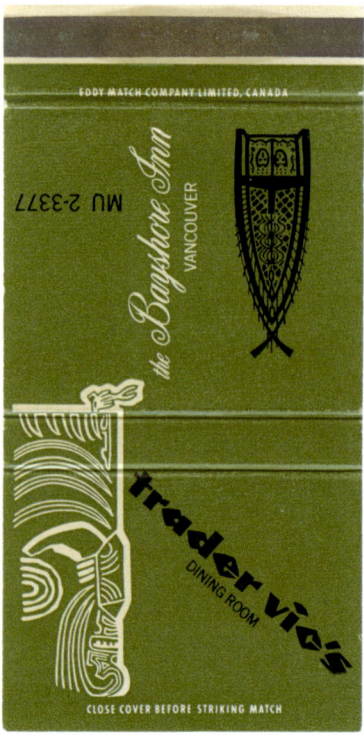

ABOVE: The Tekoteko's head used in profile on a matchbook for Trader Vic's, Vancouver

BELOW: Trader Vic's cuff links (*Jeff Berry Collection*)

OPPOSITE: Trader Vic's cigarette lighter (*Frank Brajevic Collection*)

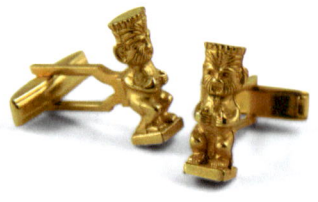

DAS TRADER VIC'S IM BEVERLY HILTON

im Jahr 1955 war eines der ersten Restaurants, das ein Tiki-Symbol auf der Karte verwendete. Es basierte auf der Tekoteko-Giebelfigur, die in San Francisco als Teil der Maori-Kultur-Präsentation für die California Midwinter International Exposition 1894 eingetroffen war. Die Skulptur war anschließend im M. H. de Young Museum in San Francisco ausgestellt und inspirierte unzählige Tiki-Pop-Produkte.

Als Tiki zum Aushängeschild des „Polynesian Pop" wurde, verwendeten viele Restaurants eine Statue als Markenzeichen. Das Tekoteko-Design der Maori fand sich auf vielen Papierwaren von Trader Vic's wieder, etwa auf Speisekarten und Cocktailservietten; seine vollendete Adaption erreichte er jedoch als Stiel eines Tiki-Glases – die perfekte Kombination aus Mid-century-Cocktailkultur und Tiki-Pop.

Für Zigarettenanzünder und Manschettenknöpfe wurde Trader Vic's maorischer Tiki leicht abgewandelt, aber seine Herkunft war noch immer erkennbar. Damit versprach Trader seinen Gästen, „die Atmosphäre, das Essen und die Pracht der Südseeinseln" zu ihnen zu holen. Werke Primitiver Kunst wie der maorische Tiki verliehen dem Restaurant einen Hauch Authentizität inmitten der falschen exotischen Insellandschaft.

Trader Vic's Erfolg verführte andere Gastronomen zur Nachahmung. Sie klauten Vic's Logo und druckten es auf ihre Karten und andere Werbemittel – vielleicht in der Hoffnung, dass etwas von seinem Mana auf sie abfärben werde. Plagiate waren ein integraler Bestandteil des Tiki-Pop. Es war eine Art kreative Fremdbestäubung, welche die Verbreitung des Tiki-Phänomens förderte.

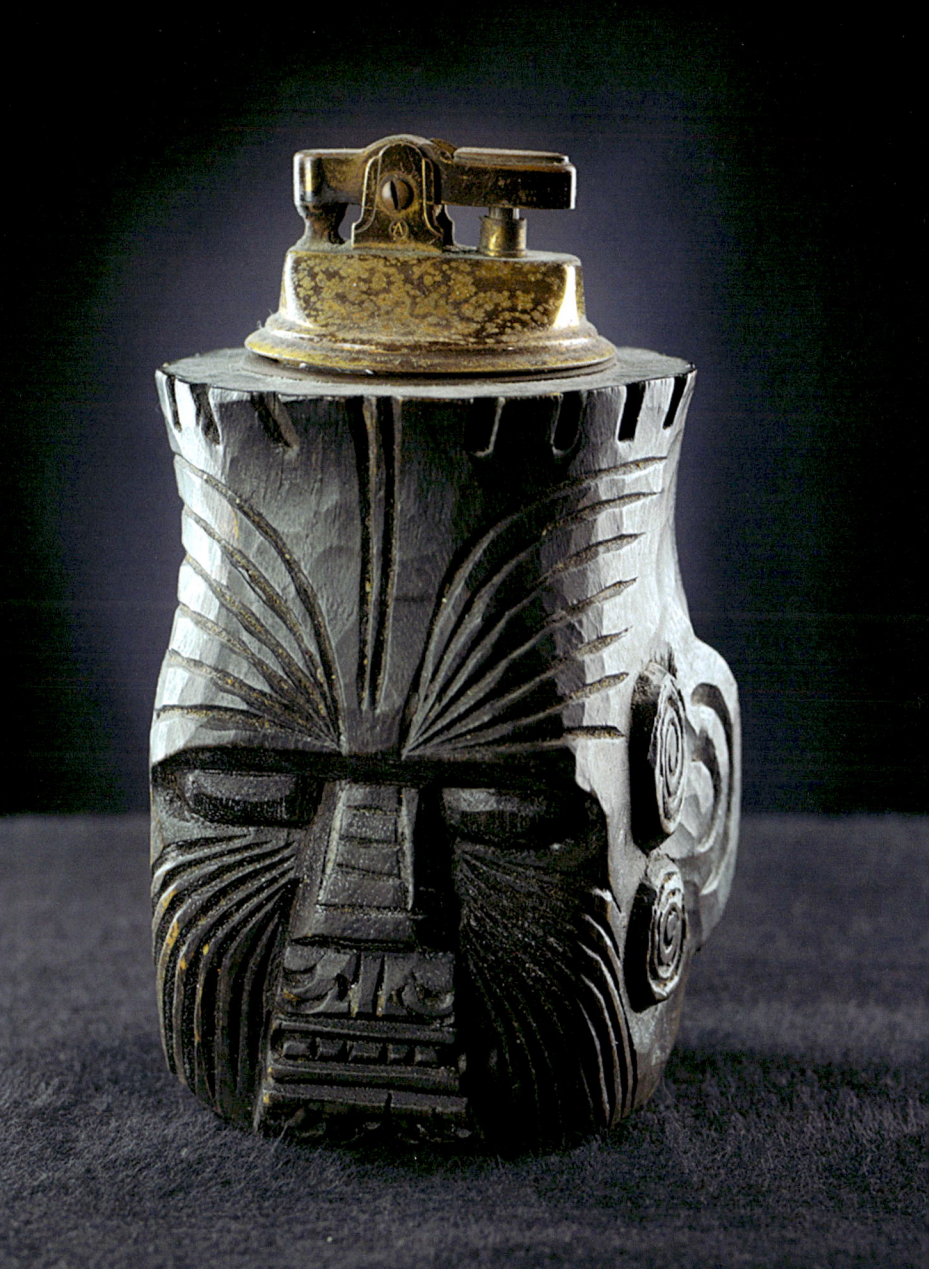

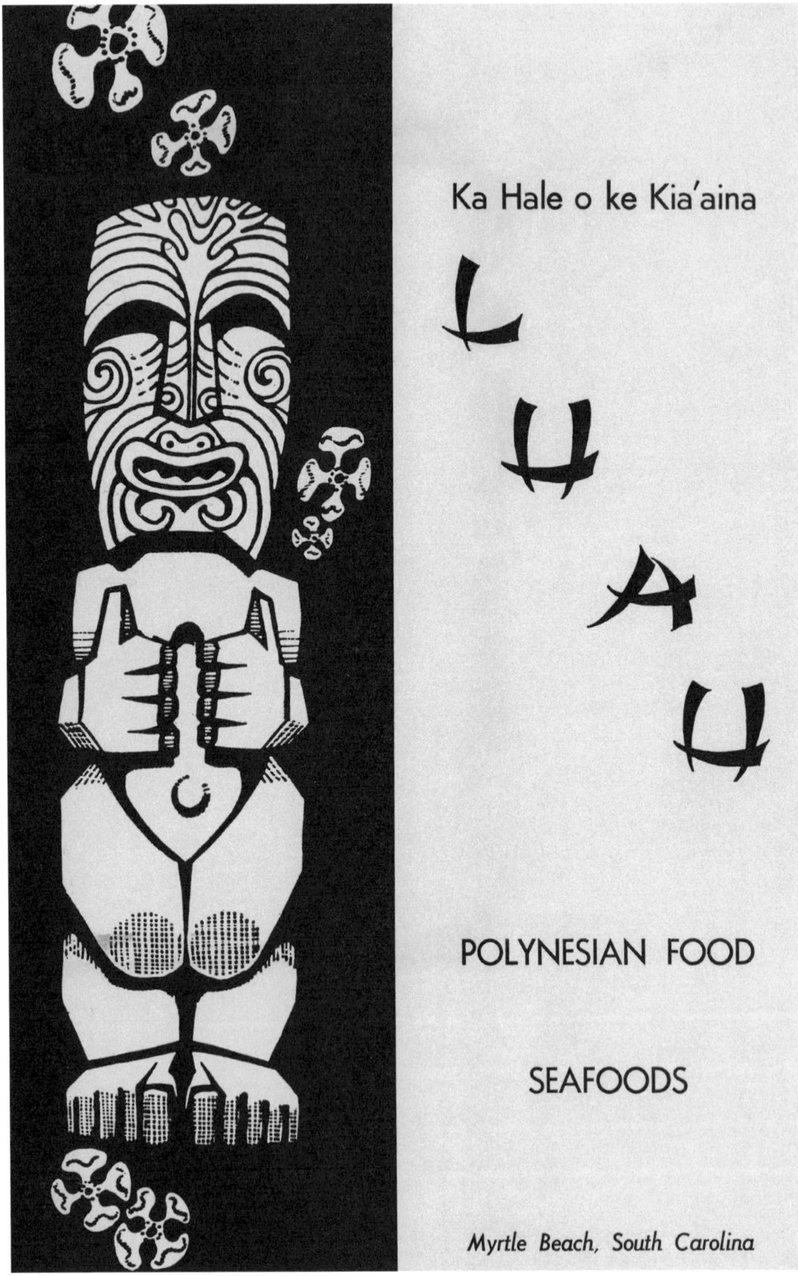

Ka Hale o ke Kia'aina

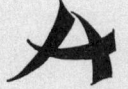
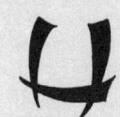

LUAU

POLYNESIAN FOOD

SEAFOODS

Myrtle Beach, South Carolina

Als die Hotelkette Marriott beschloss, dass auch sie am Markt für polynesische Restaurants teilhaben sollte, suchte sie ebenfalls bei Trader Vic nach Inspiration. Das Unternehmen hielt Don the Beachcomber und den Ketten von Stephen Crane wacker stand und baute seine Reichweite kontinuierlich aus.

Das Tiki-Logo des Kona Kai unterschied sich gerade genug vom ursprünglichen Tekoteko, als dass es keine vollständige Kopie war. Aber die großen Hände und Wangentattoos gaben seine Herkunft eindeutig preis. Das Konzept des Tiki als Bildmarke hatte sich vollständig etabliert, als das Kona Kai die Figur nicht nur für Speisekarten und Streichholzbriefchen einsetzte, sondern auch für Keramiken: als Cocktailbecher, Salz- und Pfefferstreuer und sogar als Aschenbecher.

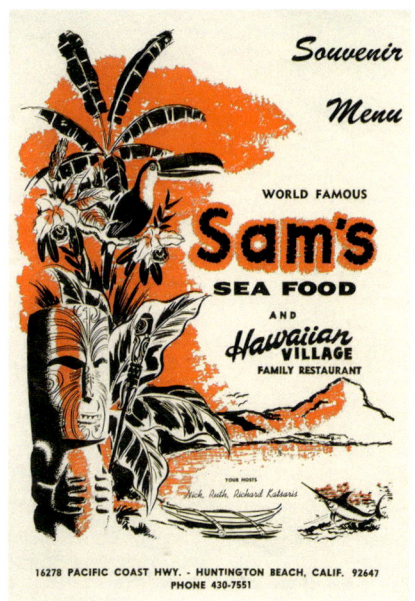

OPPOSITE AND ABOVE: Other restaurants on both American coasts employed the Maori carving for their menu covers *(Frank Brajevic and Scott Schell Collections)*

RIGHT: Kona Kai logo Tiki salt and pepper shakers *(Mimi Payne Collection)*

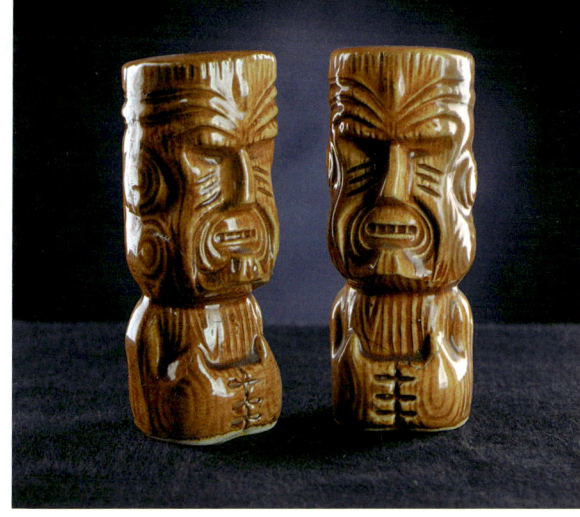

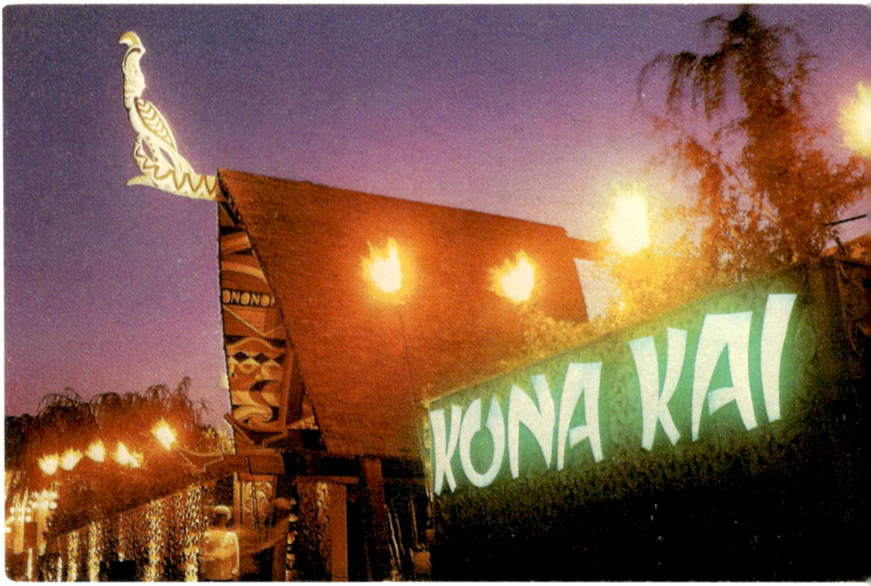

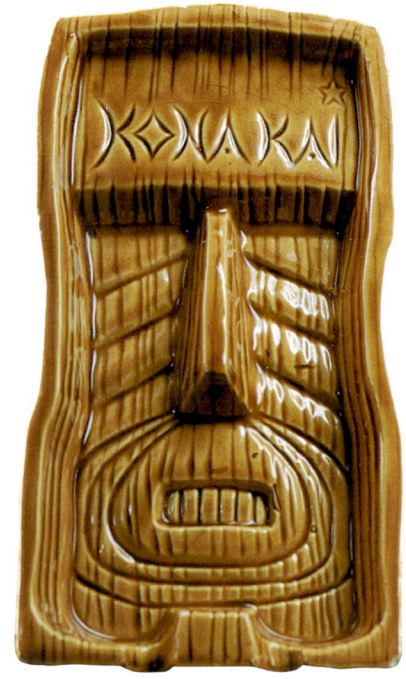

EN 1955, LE TRADER VIC'S, RESTAURANT
et bar de l'hôtel Beverly Hilton de Beverly
Hills, est un des premiers à placer un tiki
sur son menu. Il s'inspire d'un Tekoteko,
une figure de pignon arrivée à San Francisco
dans le cadre d'une présentation de la
culture maorie pour l'exposition internationale de Californie, au milieu de l'hiver
1894. Exposé depuis sa fermeture au musée
De Young de San Francisco, il a inspiré
pléthore de produits tiki pop.

Alors que le tiki devient une figure de
proue de la culture populaire polynésienne,
une figure en particulier est utilisée de façon
récurrente par les restaurants, qui en font
souvent leur insigne. Il s'agit de la statue
maorie Tekoteko, qui apparaît bientôt sur
les documents imprimés du Trader Vic's,
comme les menus et les serviettes à cocktail,
mais son exploitation atteint des sommets
avec le verre à pied tiki : le mariage parfait
entre culture cocktail et culture tiki pop.

Le tiki maori du Trader Vic's change légèrement de forme selon qu'il doit servir à allumer des cigarettes ou à boutonner des manchettes, mais son origine reste très identifiable. Son omniprésence fait partie de la promesse faite par le « Trader » : fournir à ses clients « toute l'atmosphère, les mets et la splendeur des îles des mers du Sud ». Les spécimens d'art « primitif » comme les tikis maoris donnaient un semblant d'authenticité au décor factice ou fantaisiste du restaurant.

Face au succès de la chaîne Trader Vic's, plusieurs restaurants vont s'en inspirer. Ils illustrent leurs menus et d'autres articles promotionnels de clones de l'insigne tiki du Vic's, espérant sans doute que la manne déteindra sur eux. Cette façon de plagier la concurrence fait partie intégrante de la culture tiki pop. Elle doit être vue comme une sorte de pollinisation croisée, qui a participé à l'expansion du phénomène tiki.

Lorsque la chaîne hôtelière Marriott décide qu'elle a droit à sa part du gâteau polynésien, elle se tourne tout naturellement vers Trader Vic's, qui a écrasé la concurrence – dont Don the Beachcomber et Stephen Crane – et ne cesse d'étendre son empire.

Le motif tiki du Kona Kai diffère suffisamment du Tekoteko original pour ne pas être considéré comme du plagiat pur et simple, mais ses grandes mains et ses joues tatouées trahissent clairement sa source. Le concept du « logo tiki » atteint son plein accomplissement quand le Kona Kai l'utilise non seulement sur ses menus et sur ses pochettes d'allumettes, mais aussi sous forme de poteries : mugs à cocktail, salières et poivrières, cendriers…

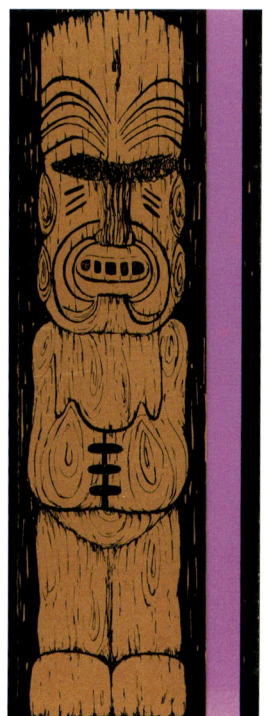

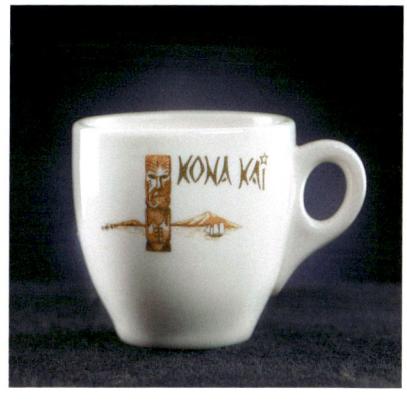

Cannibal Room Cocktail Lounge

These famous Polynesian drinks may be served ONLY if you have your own Rum or Beverage Locker.

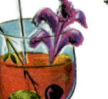

BLACK WOMAN
A dusky belle from deep in the jungle. Sweeter than most, gets along with anything, but favors Vodka.
$1.25

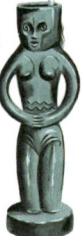

MAI TAI
This means the "best" in Tahitian . . . and you'll agree it is. A real blues chaser. One of the most popular drinks, anywhere!
$1.50

SKULLDUGGERY
Your taste buds will make no bones about this one. Favors Rum.
$1.15

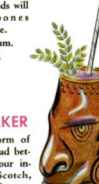

WIDOWMAKER
Not actually a form of suicide, but you had better check with your insurance man — Scotch, Bourbon or Brandy.
$1.00

ALLIGATOR'S TAIL
Normally timid — when provoked, the alligator lashes out with a mighty swipe of his tail. Charged with Rum.
.90

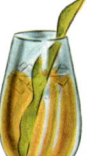

VIRGIN'S LAMENT
You'll never resist one if sufficiently softened by enough of your favorite additive.
.75

PLANTER'S PUNCH
Yo ho ho and a bottle of Rum!
$1.25

CANNIBAL BOWL
For four or more hearty souls — should use Rum on this one but Scotch or Bourbon brings the same effect.
$5.00

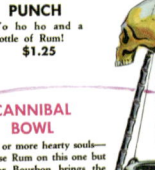

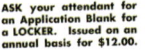

ASK your attendant for an Application Blank for a LOCKER. Issued on an annual basis for $12.00.

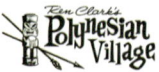

Ren Clark's Polynesian Village

WESTERN HILLS HOTEL FORT WORTH

All drinks shown here are Polynesian Village specialties, but should you wish another type, we will be happy to prepare the drink of your choice.

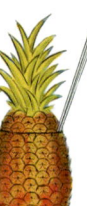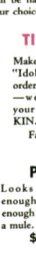

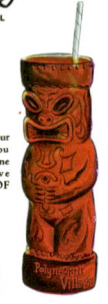

TIKI REN
Make this one your "Idol." When you order the third one — we must have your "NEXT OF KIN." Favors Rum.
$1.25

PI-YI
Looks innocent enough but packs enough Rum to floor a mule.
$1.50

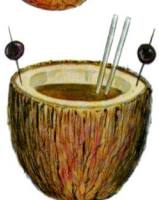

Ko-Ko-No-Ko KOOLER
A cool refreshing long one to dispel the heat of the day — mixes with Gin or Vodka.
$1.30

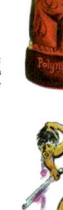

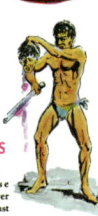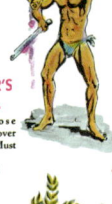

HEAD HUNTER'S SPECIAL
You'll lose your head over this one. Must be Rum.
$1.50

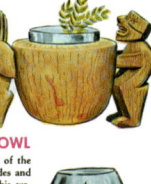

TIKI BOWL
The battle of the sexes recedes and man and his woman work together — mixes with most anything.
$1.15

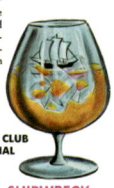

A KEY CLUB SPECIAL

SHIPWRECK
Appropriately named — suitable for hopeless castaways with no interest in further living — mixes with anything but turpentine.
$1.10

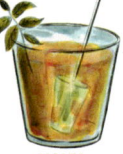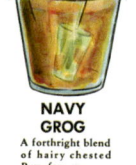

NAVY GROG
A forthright blend of hairy chested Rum for men over 21.
$1.50

MAUNA LOA
The famous mountain of flowers blows its top every time it is provided with Rum.
$1.25

FOR THE YOUNG ONES:
Pieces of Eight
A Pirate's Treasure, Non-Alcoholic but not spiritless.
.50

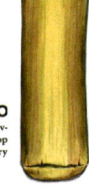

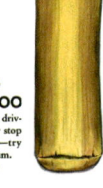

BIG BAMBOO
If you're driving, better stop on three — try it with Rum.
.90

THE TIKI MUG

DER TIKI-BECHER
LE MUG TIKI

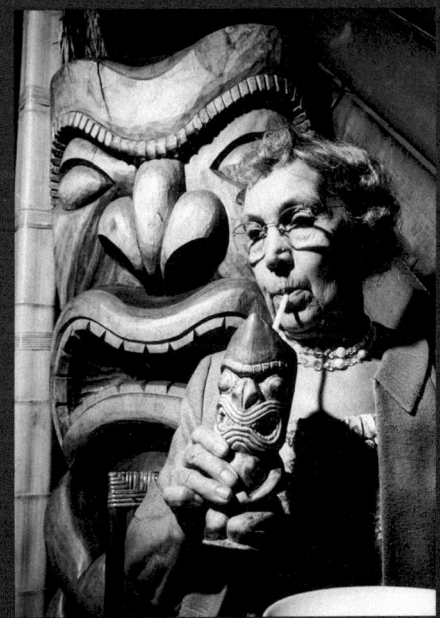

OPPOSITE: A rich compendium of rare Tiki pottery: the cocktail menu for Ren Clark's Polynesian Village in Fort Worth, Texas

ABOVE: A content customer at the Islander

THE TIKI MUG PLAYS AN IMPORTANT
role in the archaeological record of Tiki
culture. The Tiki researcher seeks out such
pottery as important evidence of long-
vanished Tiki temples. These discarded Tiki
vessels were the first remains of such places
discovered by urban archaeologists in secondhand stores and flea markets before the
advent of eBay. The infinite variety of Tiki
mug designs points to the dynamic creativity inherent in Tiki Pop.

Trader Vic can be seen as the pioneer of
the South Seas-themed cocktail container,
as a 1944 *Life* article (see opposite) aptly
illustrates. Although more than a decade
lies between these designs and the first Tiki
mug, the skull mug that Vic introduced
does have certain ritualistic connotations:
it is in keeping with the headhunting tradition of the Maori and Melanesians, who
valued the human head as the seat of mana.

The next step toward the development
of the Tiki mug was inspired by original
Polynesian bowls and containers. In the
18th and 19th centuries, Maori carvers
excelled in ornamental bowls and boxes
decorated with figures, and Hawaiian chiefs
used wooden bowls supported by effigies
for ceremonial food and kava. Only a
handful of these sacred objects survived the
abolition of Hawaiian religion to be housed
in collections and museums in Europe. The
Marquesan Islanders were also skilled in
adapting the Tiki image into all kinds of
utensils. These Oceanic artifacts prompted
Trader Vic in the early 1950s to commission
California artist Dickman Walker to create a
Tiki bowl for his bar menu. This became the
first Tiki cocktail container, and was reproduced in several different versions.

The origin of the first cocktail mug
actually shaped like a Tiki is lost in history.

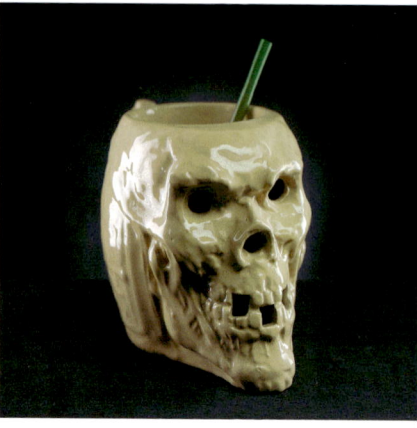

ABOVE: Trader Vic's skull mug

BELOW: Literature for the
armchair explorer, 1942

OPPOSITE: The early pre-Tiki
generation of Polynesian-themed
cocktail mugs by Trader Vic, 1944

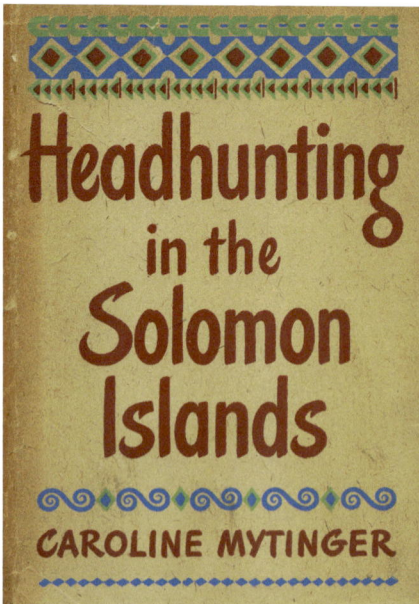

Headhunting
in the
Solomon
Islands

CAROLINE MYTINGER

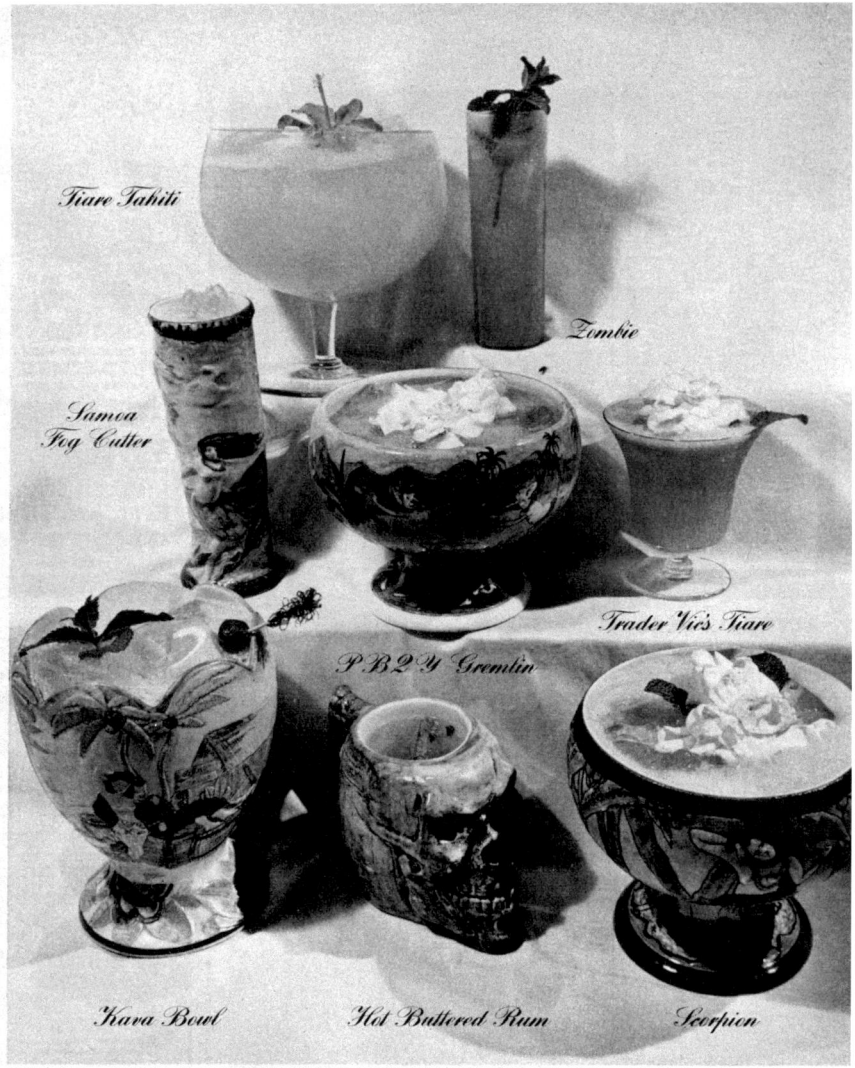

Tiare Tahiti

Zombie

Samoa
Fog Cutter

Trader Vic's Tiare

P.B.2.Y Gremlin

Kava Bowl

Hot Buttered Rum

Scorpion

THESE ARE SOME OF TRADER VIC'S RUM DRINKS. MANY HAVE GARDENIAS FLOATING ON TOP. HOT BUTTERED RUM IN SKULL MUG IS OFTEN LIGHTED TO GIVE EERIE EFFECT

TRADER VIC'S

California restaurant's fancy rum drinks are famous in South Seas

Trader Vic's is a restaurant in Oakland, Calif. which owes its reputation to its proprietor's resourcefulness with rum. Here, in surroundings simulating a South Seas trading post, patrons drink such formidable-looking potions as the ones shown above. Many of these are served in two-quart bowls from which four people sip through straws. Trader Vic, a burly San Franciscan whose name is Victor Bergeron, wisely limits each foursome to three bowls of the more potent drinks. As morale builder, he sends packages

of the ingredients for his drinks to U. S. fliers in the South Pacific. In the densest jungles appreciative airmen have set up Trader Vic outposts where they make up and drink his concoctions.

When Trader Vic's customers decide that it might be a good idea to get some food into them, they have a selection of exotic Hawaiian dishes. In restaurant's outdoor kitchen, where macaws fan the pungent air, Chinese chefs barbecue and roast steaks, squab, ham, spareribs and even whole suckling pigs or wild boars.

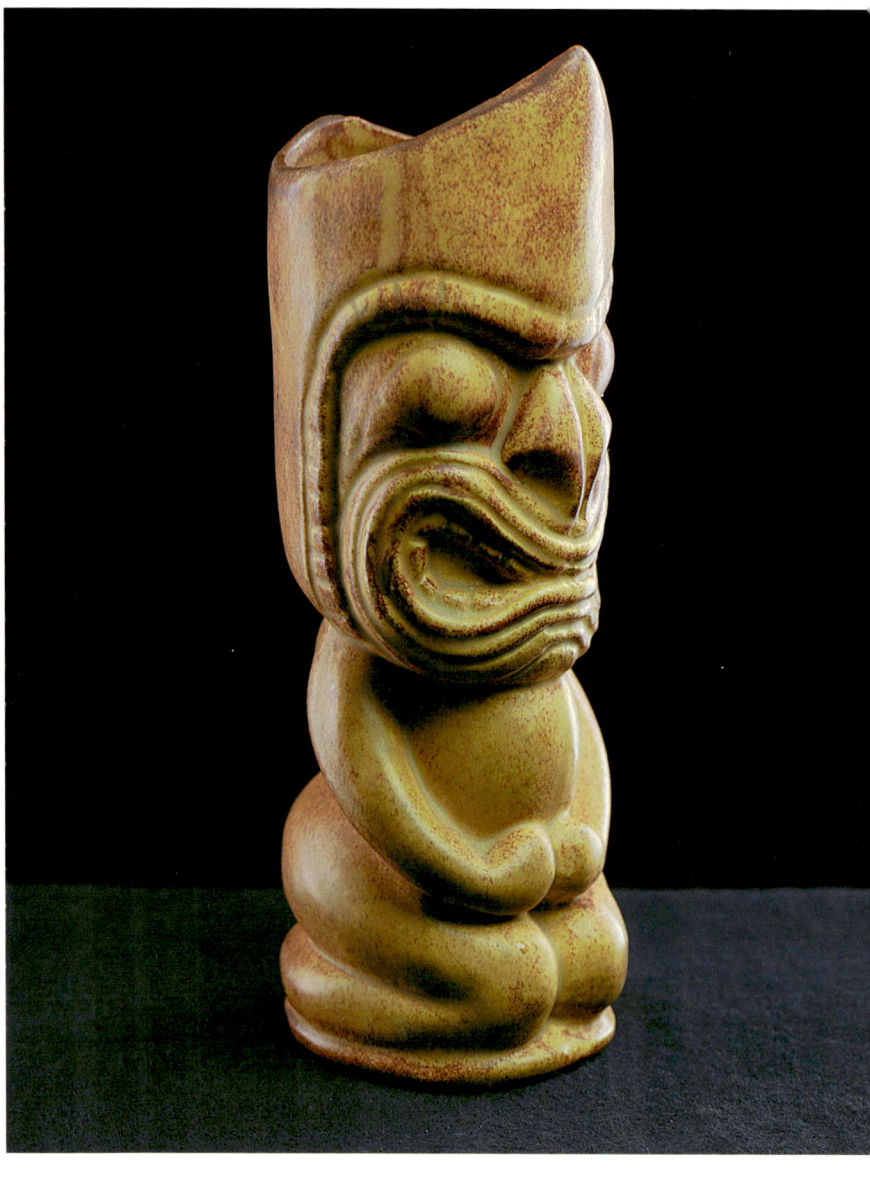

ABOVE: One of the earliest mugs in Tiki form, from the Islander restaurant, Los Angeles, 1960 *(Martijn Veltman Collection)*

OPPOSITE: Cocktail magic

PAGES 342–343: Cocktail menu from the Outrigger bar, New Orleans, showing a later version of the Tiki bow *(Scott Schell Collection)*

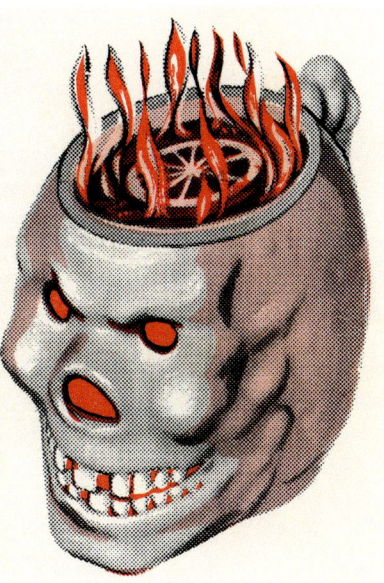

Try Our Mystery Drink

GODDESS OF LOVE

From the secret ingredients of the
PASSION TREE

$3²⁵

No more than TWO drinks per person

If you are over 52 forget it!

The glass belongs to you — take it home

Hawaii Kai

World's Greatest Polynesian Restaurant

Is it the Tiki Bob mug from San Francisco? Or the Islander mug designed by Stella Bodie in Los Angeles? Neither Don's nor Vic's menu featured actual Tiki mugs, but many other new Polynesian places spruced up their already colorful cocktail offerings with ceramic godheads. Tikis now scowled between hollowed-out pineapples and coconuts festooned with gardenias and paper umbrellas.

The custom of elaborately decorating drinks was introduced by Don the Beachcomber. One time, celebrity customer Groucho Marx invited his friend Salvador Dalí to dine at Don's. When the liberally garnished cocktail arrived, Dalí was convinced that it had been especially enhanced just for him, the master Surrealist. Theme cocktails also amused the ladies, and, coupled with their potent content, were a preferred date-night device to coax the object of affection to relax her defenses.

Tiki mugs were intended to carry the "unique and strangely haunting beverages of the huge, island-dotted territory of Polynesia," in the words of the Islander menu. After imbibing, the customer could take his mug home as a souvenir of his sojourn at whichever urban island he had visited. To promote themselves, restaurants imprinted their names and locations on the mugs—which proved to be immensely valuable to Tiki archaeologists decades later. Because such items needed to be affordable, most mugs were manufactured in postwar Japan by restaurant suppliers like Otagiri Mercantile. Some restaurants, like the Kahiki, manufactured their drinkware themselves. A rich legacy of Tiki Pop was the result.

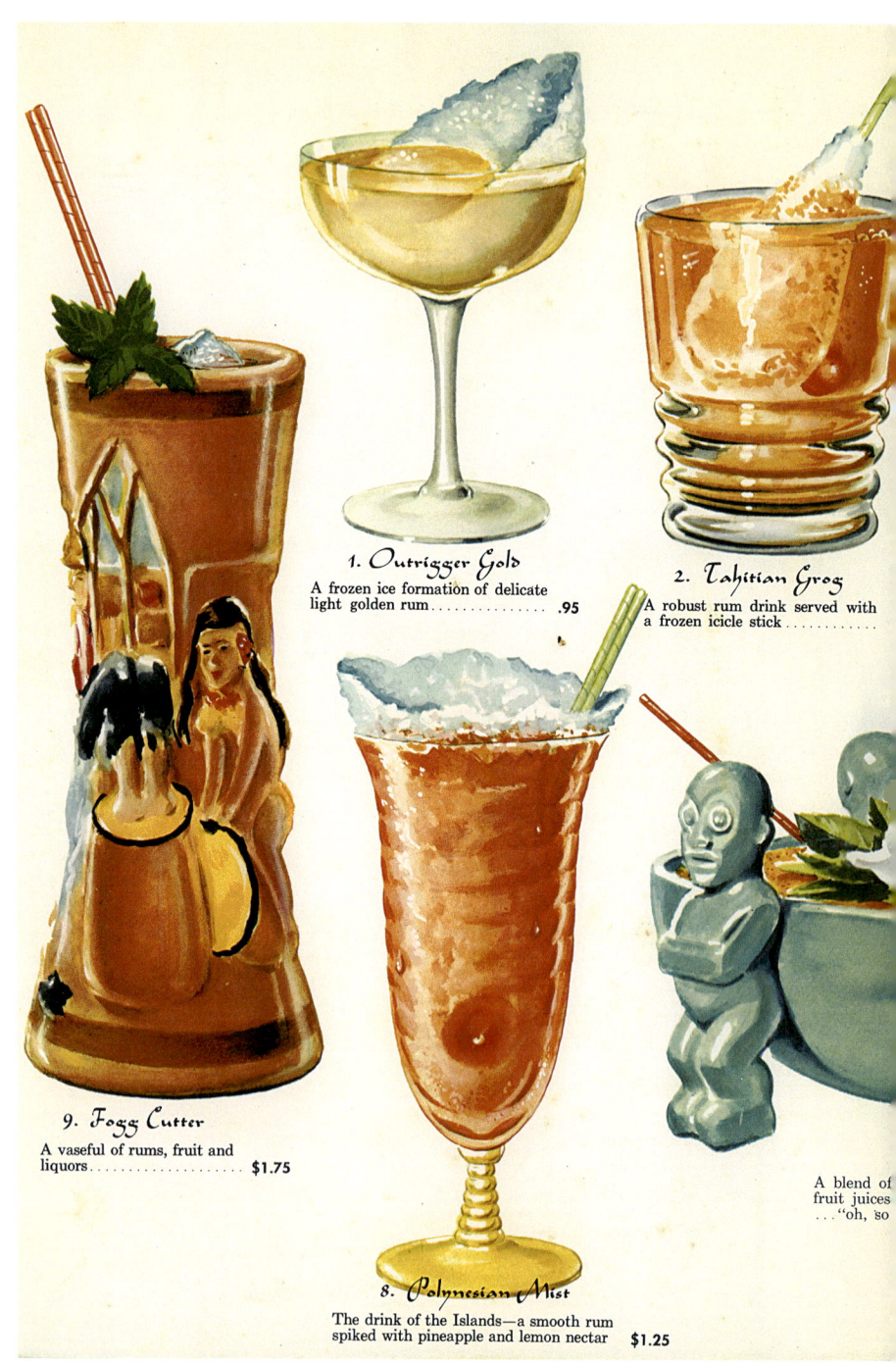

1. Outrigger Gold

A frozen ice formation of delicate
light golden rum . . . . **.95**

2. Tahitian Grog

A robust rum drink served with
a frozen icicle stick . . . .

9. Fogg Cutter

A vaseful of rums, fruit and
liquors **$1.75**

8. Polynesian Mist

The drink of the Islands—a smooth rum
spiked with pineapple and lemon nectar   **$1.25**

A blend of
fruit juices
. . . "oh, so

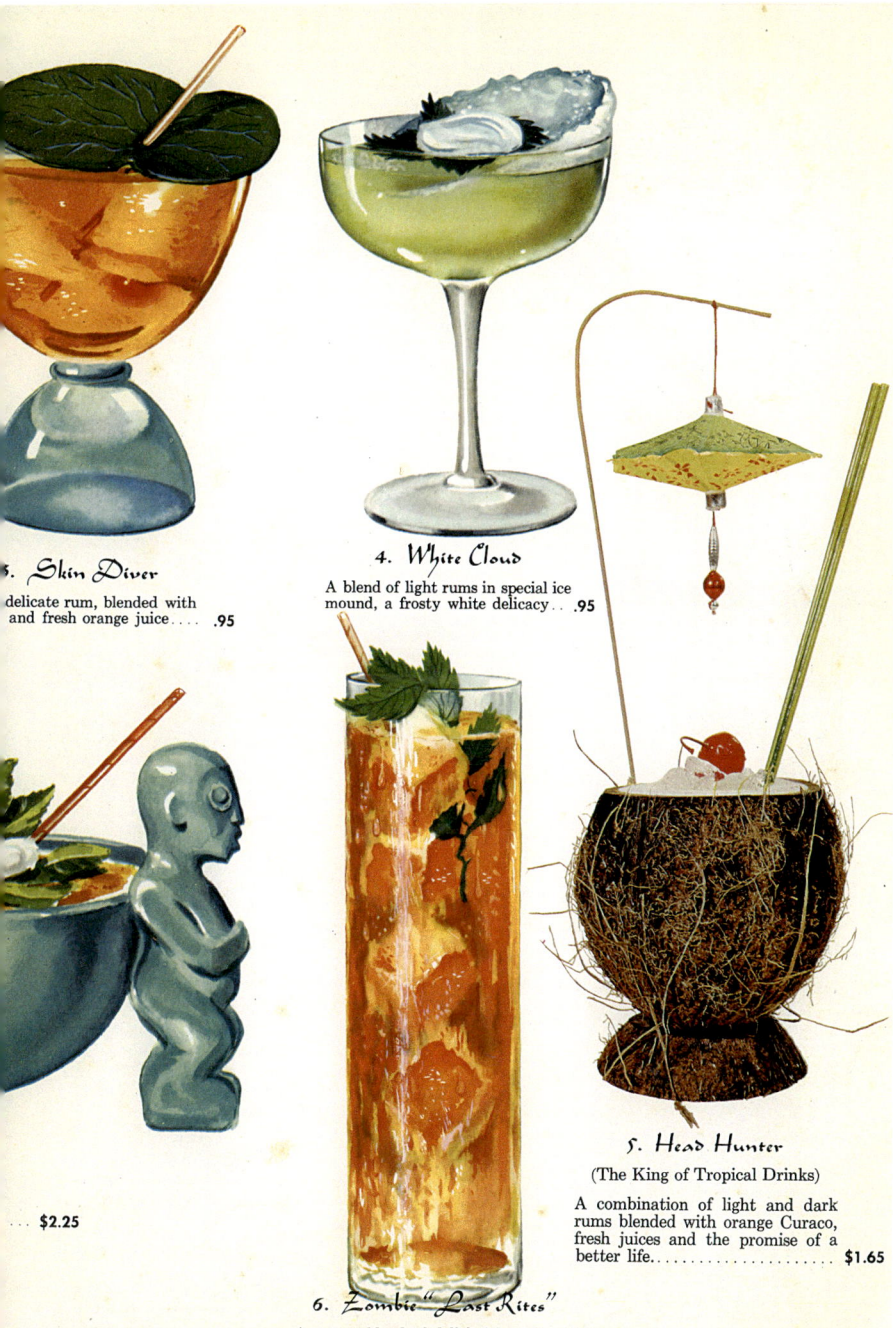

3. Skin Diver

delicate rum, blended with
and fresh orange juice.... **.95**

4. White Cloud

A blend of light rums in special ice
mound, a frosty white delicacy.. **.95**

... **$2.25**

5. Head Hunter

(The King of Tropical Drinks)

A combination of light and dark
rums blended with orange Curaco,
fresh juices and the promise of a
better life..................... **$1.65**

6. Zombie "Last Rites"

A potent blend of delightful rums **$1.25**

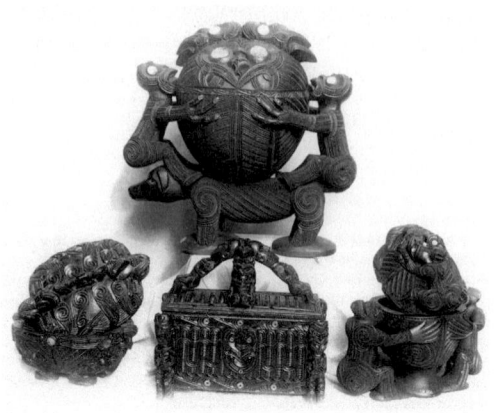

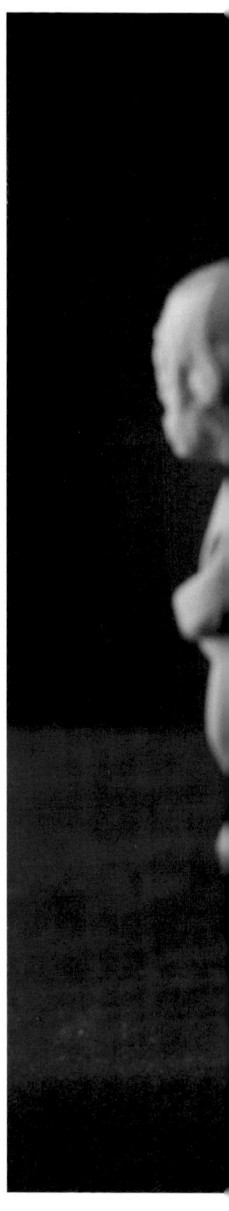

DER TIKI-BECHER SPIELT EINE WICHTIGE
Rolle in den archäologischen Aufzeichnungen der Tiki-Kultur. Für Tiki-Forscher liefern diese Keramiken wichtige Hinweise auf seit Langem verschwundenen Tiki-Tempel. Die ausrangierten Gefäße waren die ersten Überbleibsel, die Stadtarchäologen zu Zeiten, als es noch kein E-Bay gab, in Secondhandläden und auf Flohmärkten ausgegraben haben. Die unendliche Vielfalt der Designs bezeugt die Kreativität des Tiki-Pop.

Trader Vic gilt als Pionier der tropisch gestalteten Cocktailgefäße, die das *Life*-Magazin in einem Artikel von 1944 anschaulich darstellte. Obwohl mehr als ein Jahrzehnt zwischen diesen Modellen und dem Aufkommen der ersten richtigen Tiki-Becher lag, schwingt bei Vics Totenkopf-Gefäß eine gewisse rituelle Konnotation mit: Er passt zur Kopfjagd der Maori und Melanesier, für die das menschliche Haupt der Sitz des Mana war.

Der nächste Schritt in der Entwicklung des Tiki-Bechers wurde von polynesischen Schalen und Gefäßen inspiriert. Im 18. und

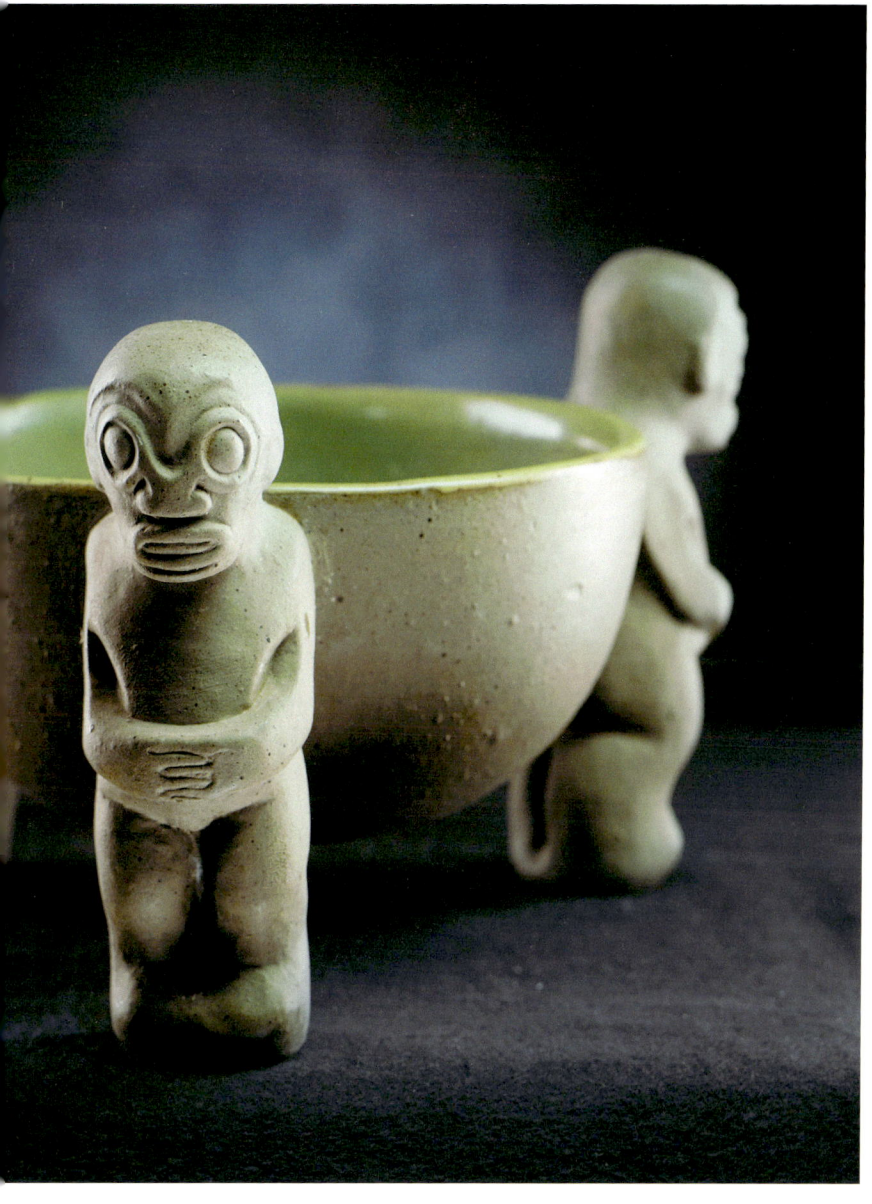

LEFT: Various Maori masterpieces

ABOVE: Original Trader Vic Tiki bowl, signed "Dickman Walker"
(Martijn Veltman Collection)

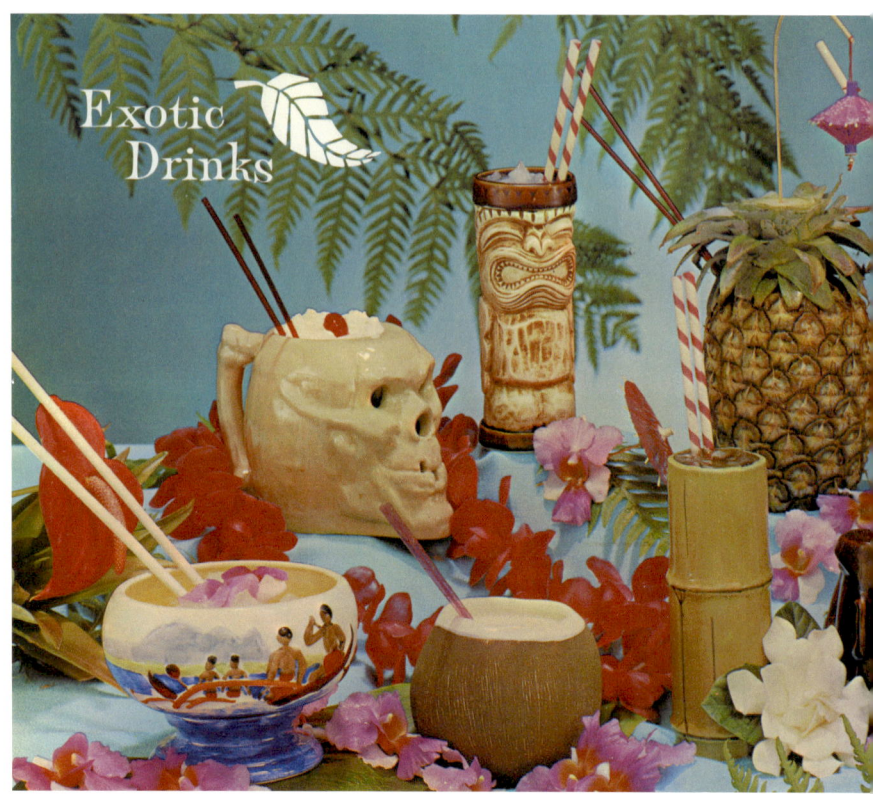

19. Jahrhundert fertigten maorische Künstler wunderschöne dekorative Schüsseln und Kisten an, die mit Figuren verziert waren. Hawaiische Häuptlinge reichten zeremonielle Speisen und Kava in Holzschüsseln, die von kleinen Figuren gestützt wurden. Nur wenige dieser heiligen Objekte haben den Niedergang der hawaiischen Religion überlebt und sind in europäischen Museen ausgestellt.

Die Bewohner der Marquesas-Inseln waren ebenfalls versiert darin, Tikis Abbild in Utensilien zu integrieren. Ozeanische Artefakte wie diese veranlassten Trader Vic in den frühen 1950er-Jahren dazu, den

kalifornischen Künstler Dickman Walker mit dem Entwurf einer Tiki-Schale für die Bar zu beauftragen. Sie gilt als das erste Tiki-Cocktailgefäß und wurde in verschiedenen Versionen reproduziert.

Wer den ersten Cocktailbecher in Form eines Tiki fertigen ließ, ist unbekannt. War es Tiki Bob in San Francisco? Oder der Islander aus Los Angeles, dessen Becher Stella Bodie entworfen hatte? Weder auf Dons noch auf Vics Karte war Tikis Gestalt zu finden. Viele andere polynesische Lokale jedoch polierten ihr bereits sehr farbenfrohes Cocktailangebot mit Gottheiten aus Keramik auf. Zwischen ausgehöhlten

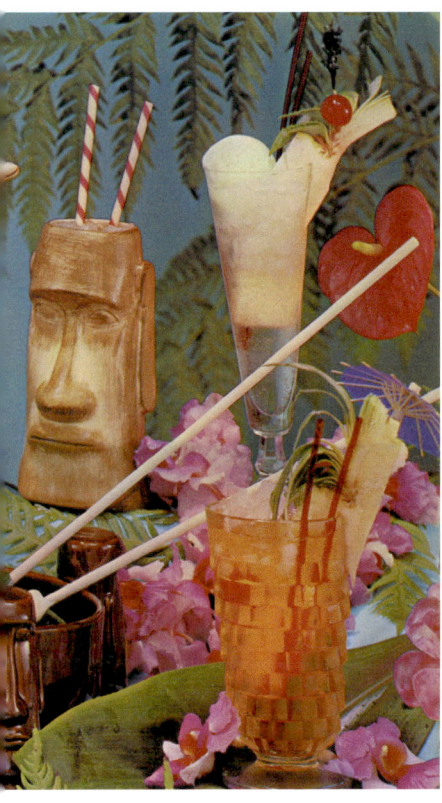

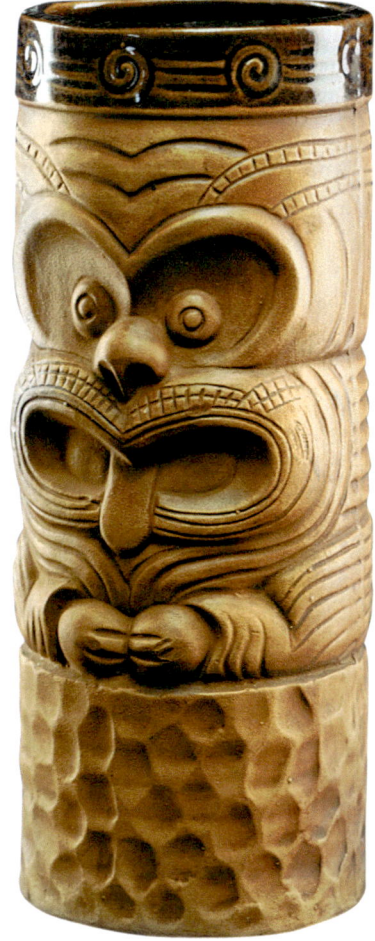

ABOVE: Around the early 1960s, tiki mugs joined the picturesque presentation of Polynesian cocktails

RIGHT: Maori-style mug design used at the Mauna Loa in Detroit

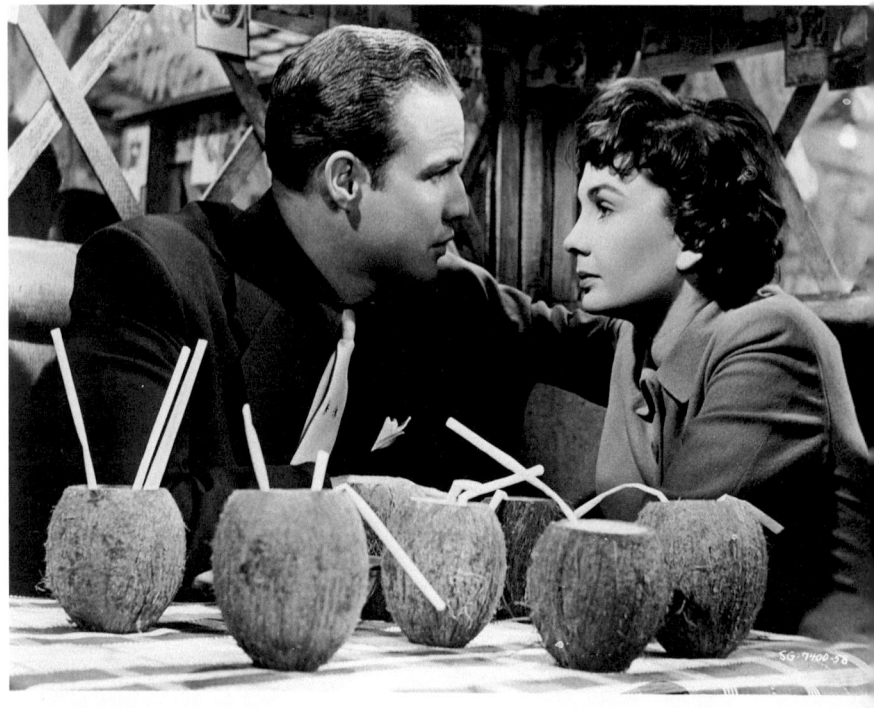

"GUYS AND DOLLS"

55/381

ABOVE: Girls like sweet drinks, and guys like girls

OPPOSITE LEFT: Hawaiian "Ku"-style mug from the Aloha Hut
(*Martijn Veltman Collection*)

OPPOSITE RIGHT: Stylized modern moai mug

Ananas und mit Gardenien und Papier-
chirmchen geschmückten Kokosnüssen
og Tiki nun finster die Stirn in Falten.

Don the Beachcomber war es, der das
ufwendige Dekorieren von Drinks in
Mode brachte. Eines Tages lud der Schau-
pieler Groucho Marx seinen Freund
alvador Dalí zum Abendessen bei Don
in. Als der großzügig verzierte Cocktail
erviert wurde, war Dalí überzeugt, dass
nan ihn einzig für ihn, den großen Surrea-
sten, aufgehübscht hatte. Die thematisch
ekorierten Cocktails amüsierten auch
ie Damenwelt. Aufgrund ihres hohen
Alkoholgehalts wurden sie bei Rendez-
ous gerne bestellt, um die Stimmung
twas aufzulockern.

Tiki-Becher waren für die „einzigartigen
und unvergesslichen Getränke der riesigen
polynesischen Inselwelt" gedacht – so stand
es auf der Karte des Islander. Der Gast
konnte seinen Becher als Erinnerung an
seinen Ausflug auf diese oder jene urbane
Insel mit nach Hause nehmen. Aus Werbe-
zwecken druckten Restaurants ihren Namen und Standort auf die Becher – was
für Tiki-Archäologen Jahrzehnte später
von unschätzbarem Wert sein sollte. Da die
Becher bezahlbar sein mussten, wurden
die meisten im Nachkriegsjapan von Res-
taurantzulieferern wie Otagiri Mercantile
hergestellt. Manche Restaurants wie das
Kahiki produzierten ihre Becher selbst. Das
Resultat: ein reiches Erbe für den Tiki-Pop.

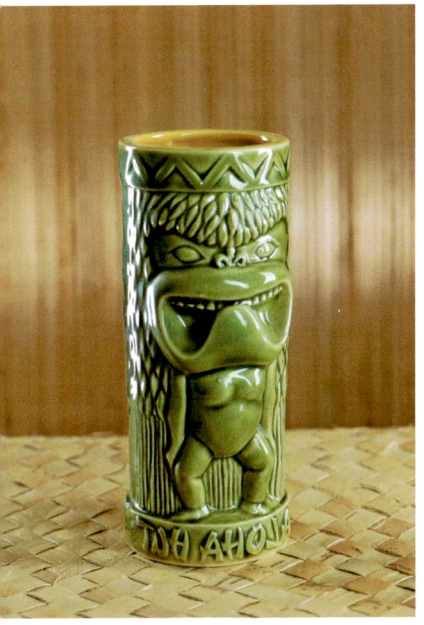
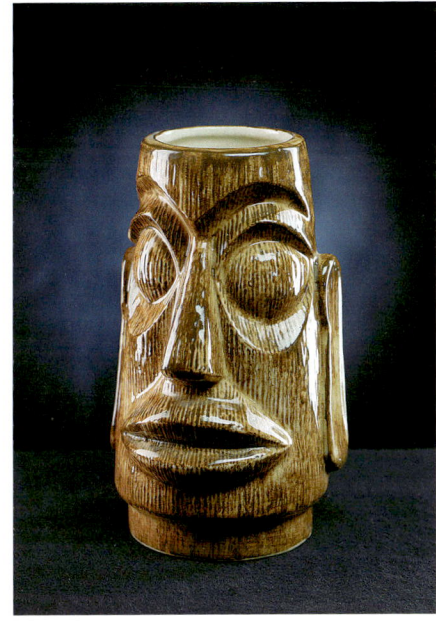

LE MUG TIKI JOUE UN RÔLE IMPORTANT dans l'archéologie et l'archivage de la culture tiki pop. Les spécialistes du domaine considèrent ces céramiques comme les vestiges cruciaux de temples de Tiki depuis longtemps disparus. Ces poteries dépareillées ont été les premiers éléments redécouverts par les fouilleurs de vide-greniers et brocanteurs avant la création d'eBay. La variété infinie de tasses à cocktail de cette veine témoigne aussi de la dynamique créative inhérente à cette sous-culture.

Trader Vic's est justement considéré comme le pionnier du verre à cocktail « Mers du Sud », comme l'atteste cet article publié en 1944 dans *Life*. Plus d'une décennie sépare le premier mug tiki des objets présentés ici, et le nouveau « mug Crâne » du Vic's assume déjà des connotations rituelles : il s'agit de s'accrocher à tous les aspects de la culture maorie et mélanésienne, en l'occurrence la tradition des chasseurs de tête, qui considéraient le crâne comme le siège du mana.

Le pas suivant dans l'évolution du mug tiki est inspiré par les bols et contenants utilisés traditionnellement en Polynésie. Au cours des XVIIIe et XIXe siècles, les sculpteurs maoris excellent dans l'art de façonner des bols et des boîtes ornementales décorées de figures et de formes géométriques complexes, et les chefs hawaiiens utilisaient des bols en bois soutenus par des effigies pour les repas de cérémonie et le kava. Seule une poignée de ces objets sacrés a survécu à la colonisation d'Hawaii et à l'abolition de la religion locale ; ils sont aujourd'hui conservés dans des collections privées et des musées européens. Les habitants des Marquises étaient aussi réputés pour leur reprise de l'image tiki sur toutes sortes d'ustensiles. Ces objets courants en Océanie donnèrent l'idée à Vic le négociant de commander à l'artiste californien Dickman Walker un bol tiki pour ses bars au début des années 1950. Cet objet devint le premier contenant tiki destiné aux cocktails, et a connu plusieurs variantes.

L'origine du premier mug à cocktail tiki est tombée dans les oubliettes de l'histoire. Faut-il la chercher à San Francisco, chez Tiki Bob ? Ou à Los Angeles avec le mug dessiné par Stella Bodie pour l'Islander ? Les menus du Don's et du Vic's ne montrent pas de mug tiki à proprement parler, mais plusieurs nouveaux lieux de la culture tiki pop enrichissent leur carte déjà abondante et haute en couleur de divinités en céramique. Les tikis se retrouvent entre ananas et noix de coco, enguirlandés de gardénias et piqués d'ombrelles en papier.

L'habitude de soigner à outrance la présentation des boissons a été inaugurée par Don the Beachcomber. Un jour, son célèbre client Groucho Marx invita son ami Salvador Dalí à dîner chez Don. Lorsque le cocktail exubérant arriva, Dalí crut qu'il avait été ainsi présenté spécialement pour lui, le maître du surréalisme. Et puis les cocktails à thème amusaient ces dames et leur forte teneur en alcool en faisait un accessoire de choix pour les sorties en amoureux.

Les mugs tiki servent à « contenir des breuvages uniques et étrangement entêtants créés dans les immensités sauvages du territoire polynésien », pour reprendre

Ku mug from the Hawaii Kai, New Yo*
(Frank Brajevic Collection)

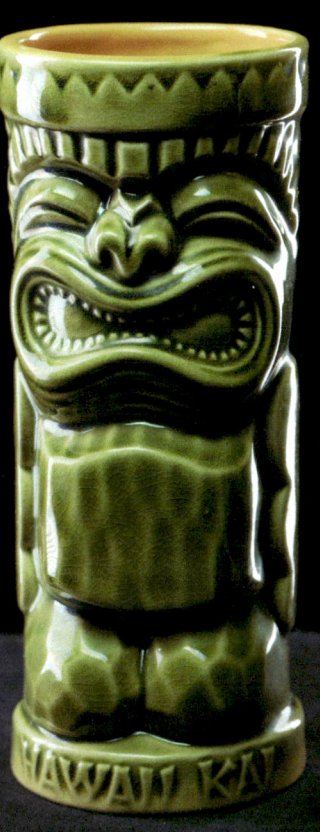

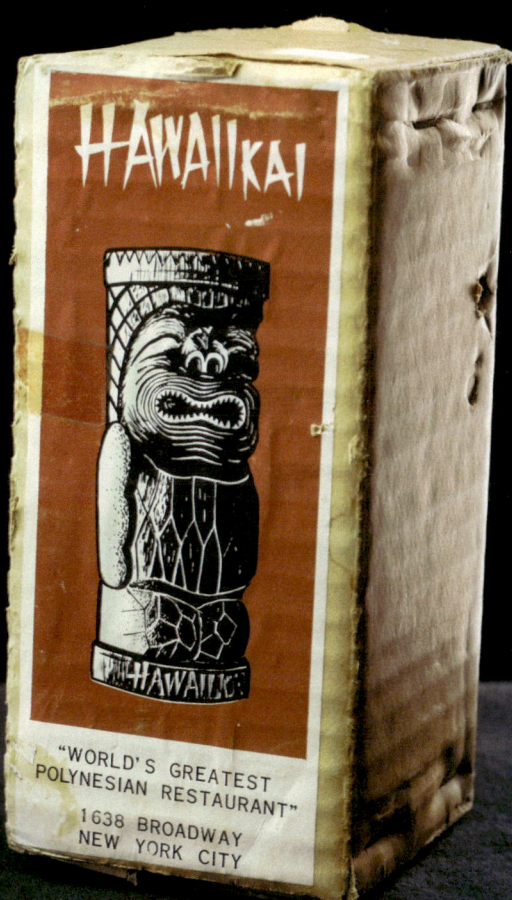

HAWAII KAI

"WORLD'S GREATEST
POLYNESIAN RESTAURANT"

1638 BROADWAY
NEW YORK CITY

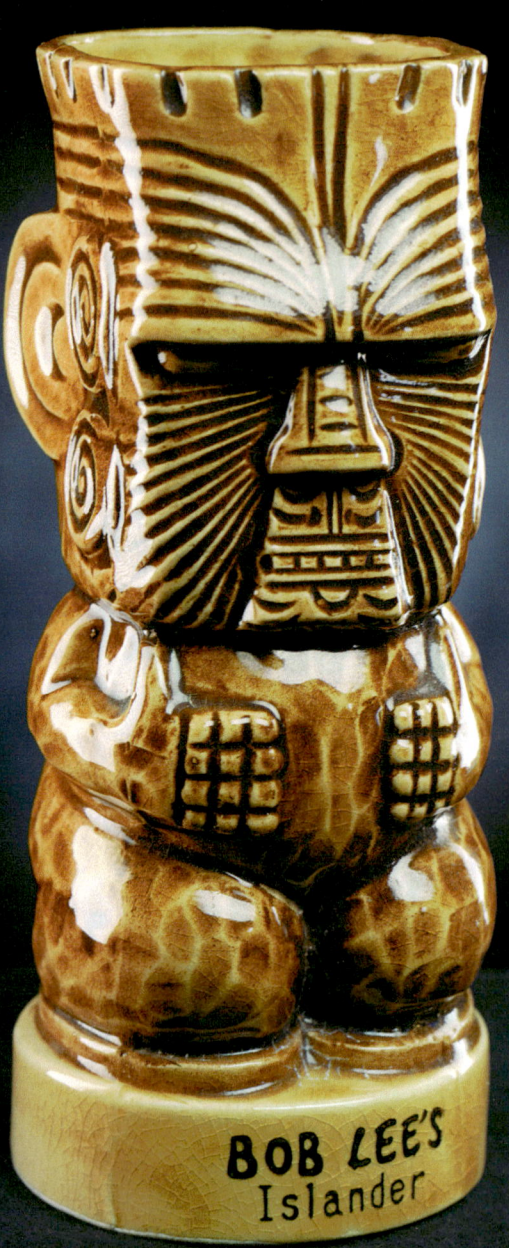

BOB LEE'S
Islander

l'argumentaire inscrit sur le menu de l'Islander. Une fois bien imbibés, les clients pouvaient rapporter leur mug à la maison en souvenir d'un séjour enchanteur dans une autre dimension. Pour se faire connaître, les restaurants faisaient imprimer leurs nom et adresse sur les mugs, ce qui s'avéra immensément précieux pour les collectionneurs des décennies suivantes. Parce qu'il était important que ces objets soient proposés à un prix abordable, la plupart de ces mugs étaient fabriqués dans les usines du Japon d'après-guerre par des fournisseurs de restaurants comme Otagiri Mercantile. Certaines enseignes, comme le Kahiki, fabriquaient elles-mêmes leur vaisselle et leur verrerie. La variété des objets retrouvés résulte de ce double héritage.

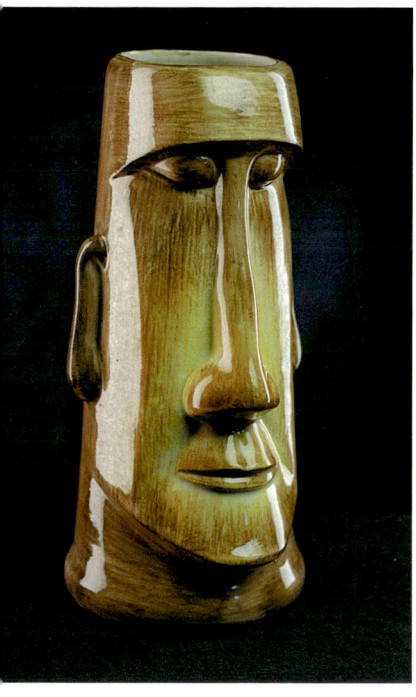

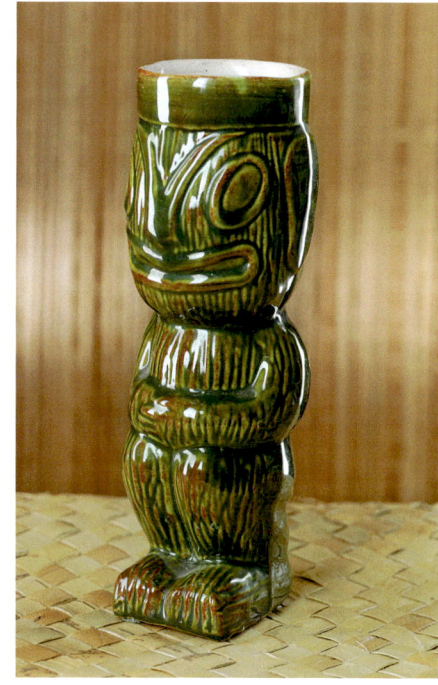

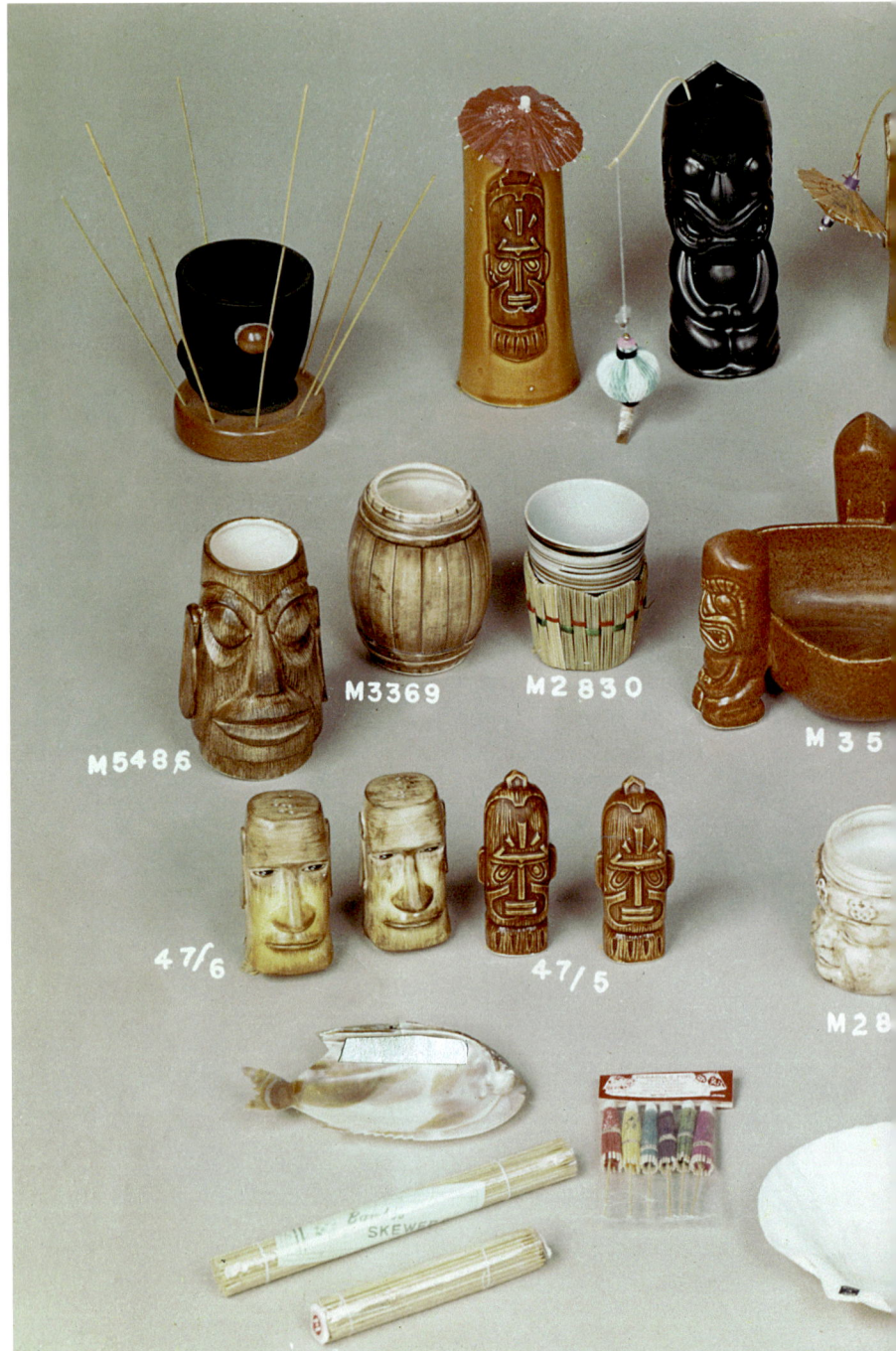

M3369

M2830

M35

M548ß

M35

47/6

47/5

M28

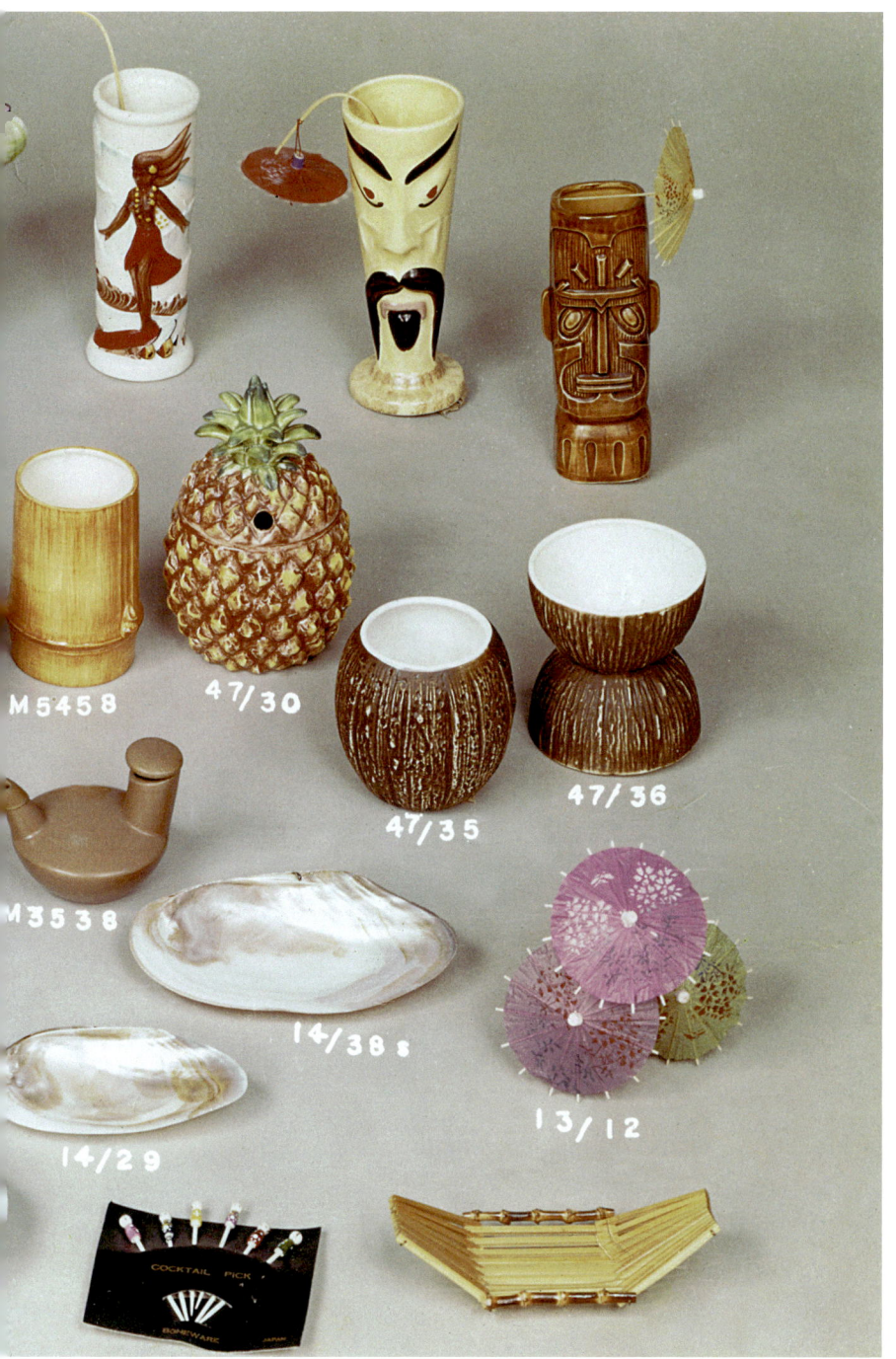

M5458 47/30

47/35 47/36

M3538

14/38s

13/12

14/29

COCKTAIL PICK

BONEWARE   JAPAN

march 1959 . . . 50 c

paradise

... of the pacific

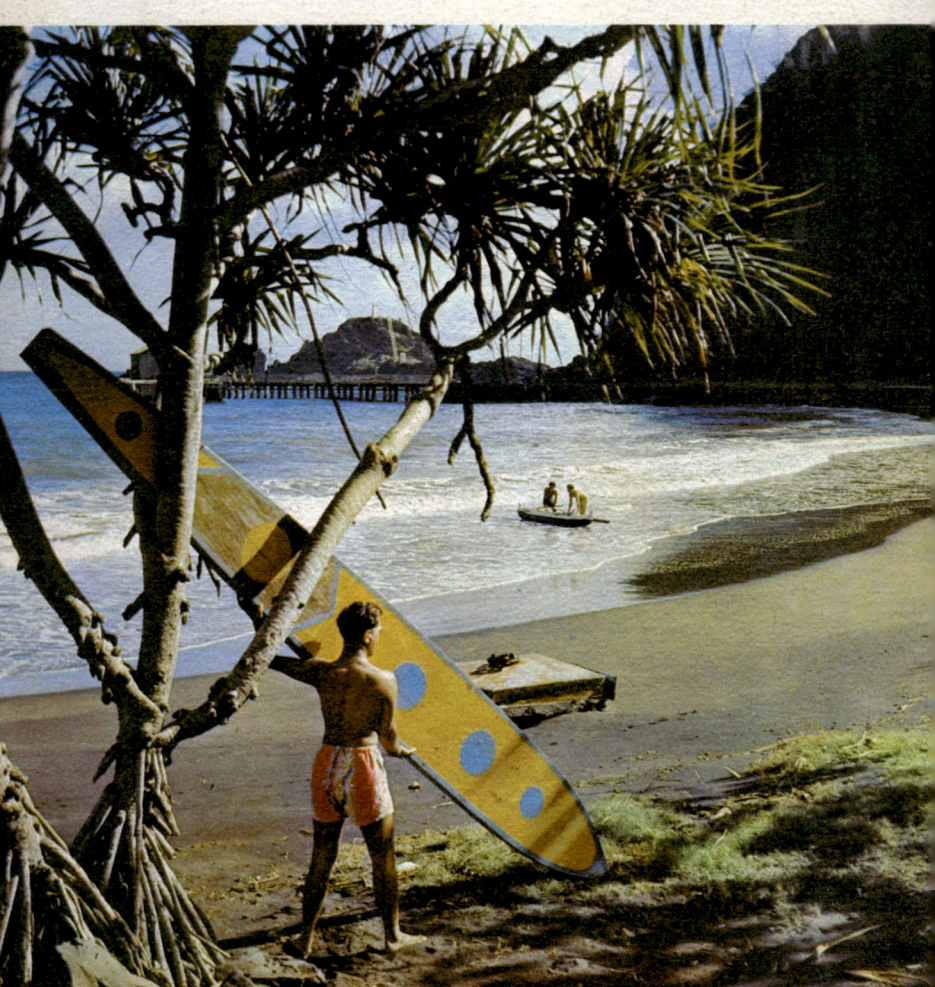

special issue:
HAWAII AND STATEHOOD

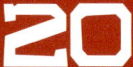

HAWAIIAN STATEHOOD

HAWAII WIRD US-BUNDESSTAAT
HAWAII DEVIENT UN ÉTAT D'AMÉRIQUE

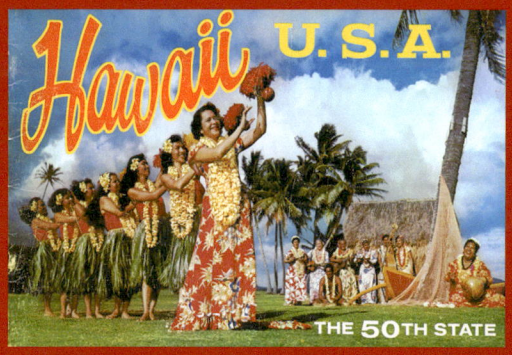

OPPOSITE: Special issue of a local Hawaiian magazine

ABOVE: The 50th State postcard

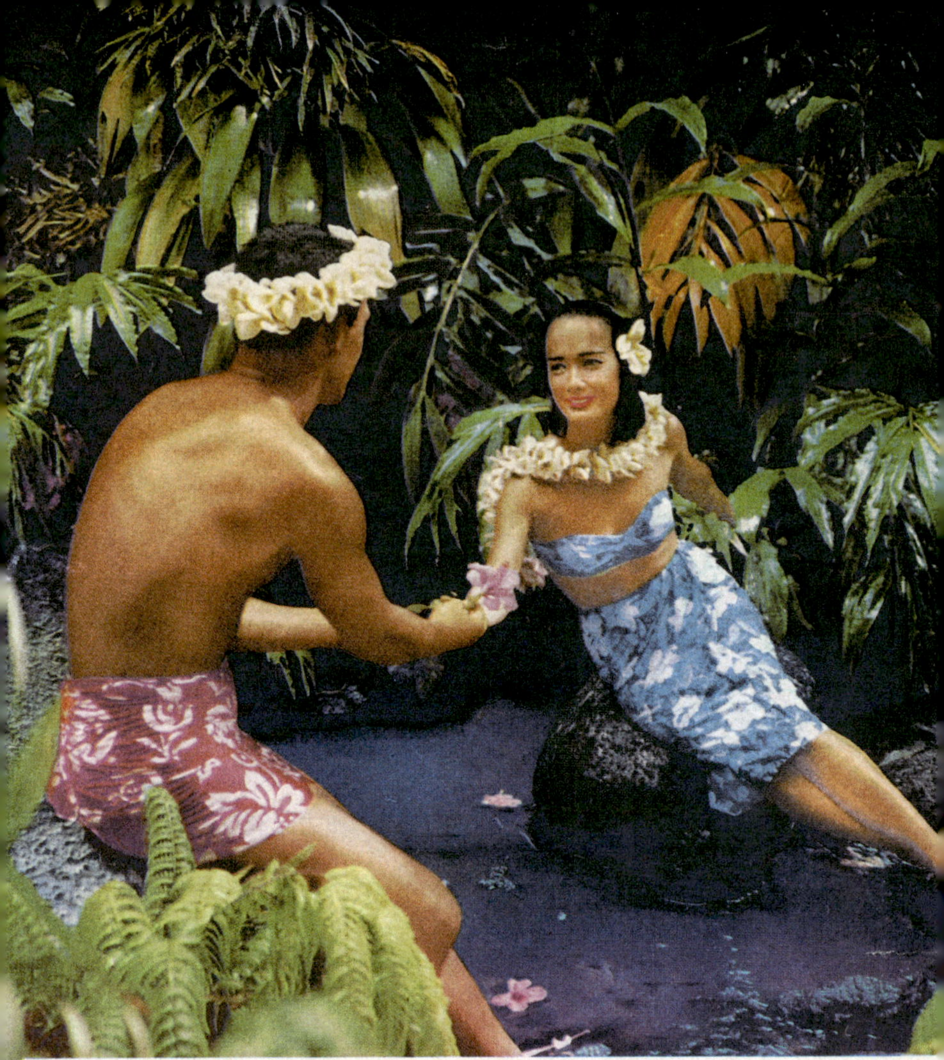

Make **Your Lifetime Dream** come true

Hawaii is your dream come true...peaceful, friendly, excitingly beautiful, enticingly close. Only 8 air-hours from the Pacific Coast or 4½ days by ship, it's a travel adventure beyond compare, yet costs far less than American resorts of comparable class. Why postpone the pleasure? Fulfill your heart's desire...come enjoy all of Hawaii's Islands, Kauai, Oahu, Maui and Hawaii this fall or winter. It's always like summer.

Aloha Week — Polynesian Pageant — October 19-26

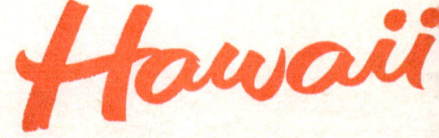

Round trip from Pacific Coast and 10 hotel days (European Plan) can cost as little as $325

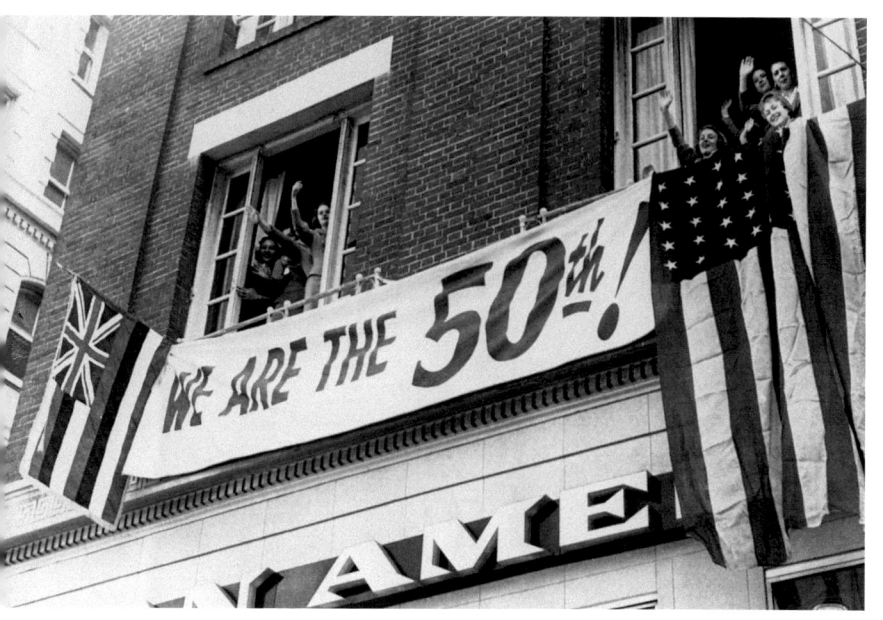

AMERICA HAD FOSTERED A FASCINATION with Hawaii for quite some time, which culminated in Hawaii's being admitted into the Union in 1959. The psychological boon of an American paradise translated into an economic one: Hawaiians were Americans; therefore, all of America was now Hawaiian. Entrepreneurs and developers on the mainland invested their money in helping island-happy Americans make their homeland more Hawaiian.

The Hawaiian Islands had been a dream vacation destination for Americans since the beginning of the 20th century. In the 1920s and '30s, passage on the luxurious Matson Line cruise ships was affordable only for the well-off. With the advent of commercial air service, more and more lucky paradise-seekers could make the trip; and when jetliners took off in the late 1950s, Hawaiian tourism doubled. The West Coast hubs of

·PPOSITE: The dream finally in reach

·BOVE: Pan American Airways ·mployees in a San Francisco office ·elebrate Hawaiian statehood

Los Angeles, San Francisco, and Seattle were easy jumping-off points, and Hawaii practically became these cities' backyard. In this context, Hawaii's statehood consummated and perpetuated America's love for the islands. U.S. citizens who could not make it to Hawaii wanted to; and so they created their own Hawaii on the mainland. Those who had been to the real Hawaii joined them to revel in vacation memories.

Elvis Presley sang "Hawaii, U.S.A.!" and the flower lei, the symbol of the Polynesian welcome, was wrapped around America. "Hawaii" epitomized fun in the sun, and leisure and lounging on the beach. The Hawaiian mind-set was that of a perpetual vacation, in a place one did not want to leave—and didn't have to: every American city could have its own islands; every backyard could be a little Polynesia.

Just like during the Hawaiian-music boom of the '20s, Hawaiian names and phrases were once again selected for use at restaurants and backyard luaus. "Drinks of the Islands" were eagerly consumed by the Hawaiian-shirt-wearing public listening to hapa haole tunes. When Alaska became the 49th state in 1959, it received nowhere near as much attention. But how did the focus on the Hawaiian Islands broaden to include all of Polynesia?

The devastation of World War II and the sudden possibility of a nuclear extinction of the species was so traumatic to mankind that it vowed to prevent such slaughter once and for all. The United Nations was created in a spirit of idealism that such a war would not be repeated, trusting that the world wanted to live in peace for perpetuity. In 1955, Edward Steichen curated the exhibition "The Family of Man" for The Museum of Modern Art in New York. With 503 photos from 68

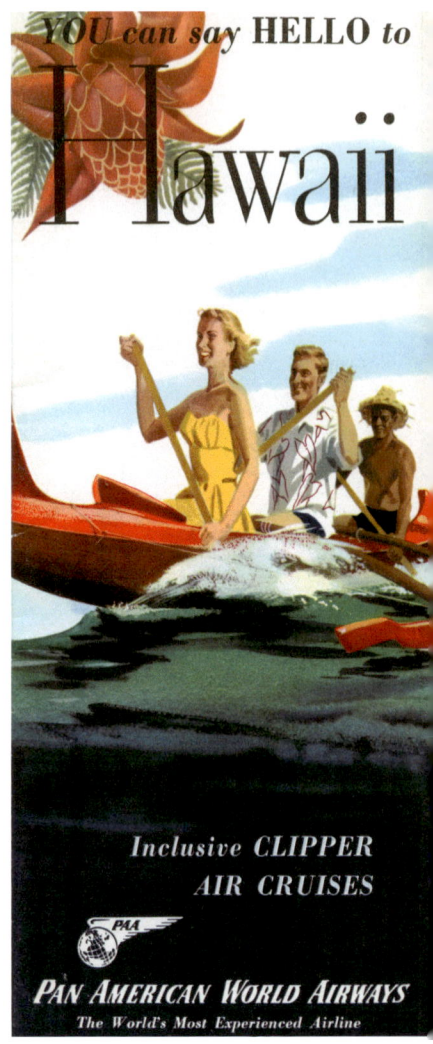

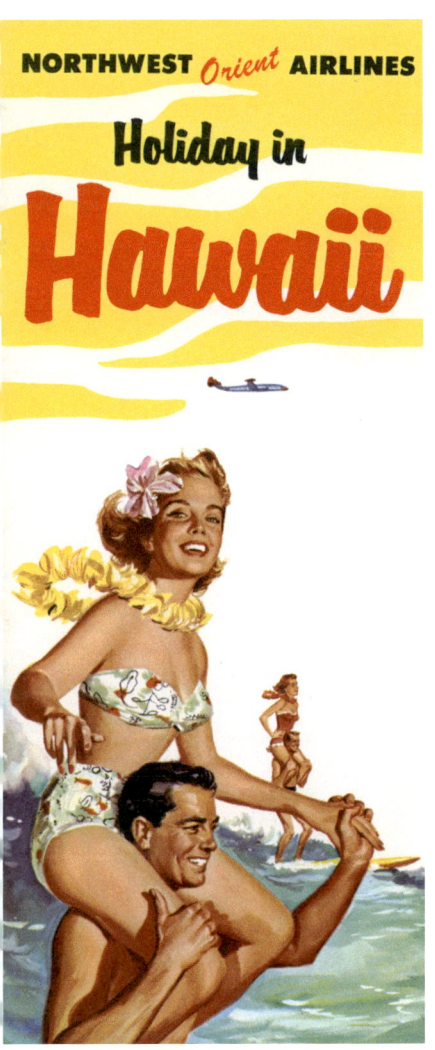

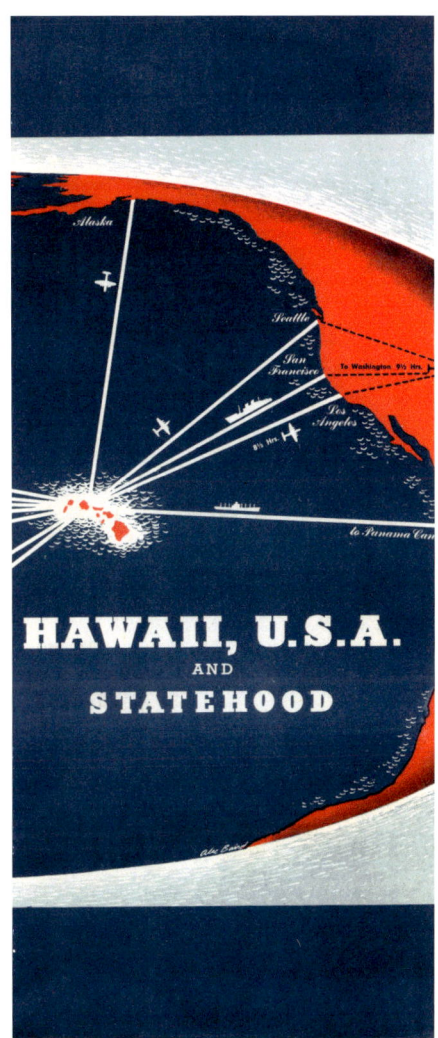

Hawaii meant happiness, and the rush was on

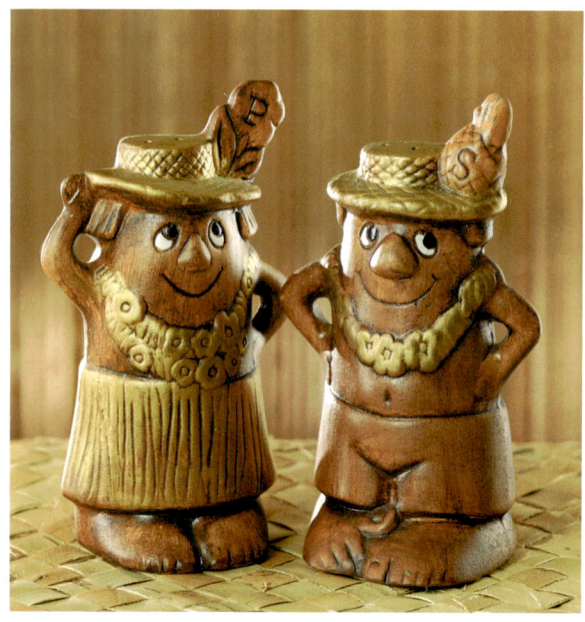

LEFT: Mr. and Mrs. Tourist salt and pepper shakers

BELOW: Life's a beach in Hawaii

OPPOSITE ABOVE: Hawaii extending a lei welcome

OPPOSITE BELOW: Miss Hawaii and Miss Alaska say "Hello" to statehood

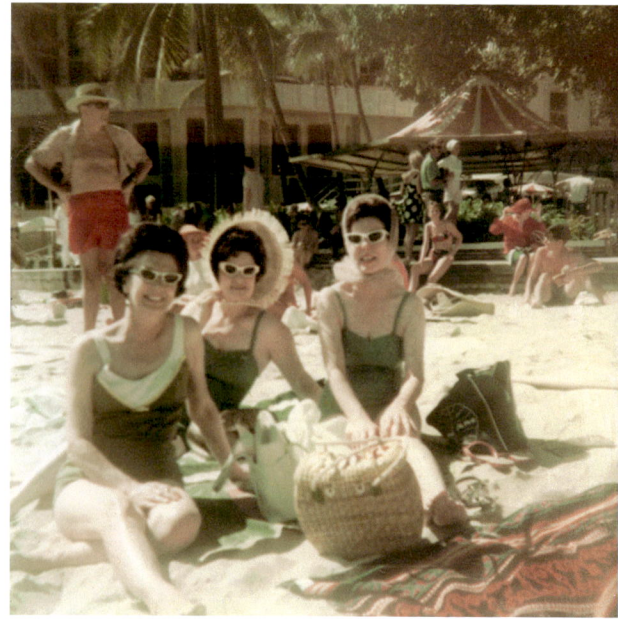

countries, the exhibit's theme was the universality of the human experience.

Hawaii was a peaceful melting pot of several races, and, as such, was held up as an example of the "Family of Man" concept. In 1959, James Michener published his novel *Hawaii*, about the settling of the islands. He developed the theory of "The Golden People": "A group of sociologists in Hawaii were perfecting a concept... a new type of man was being developed..." Hawaii itself instated "Brotherhood Week," celebrating its racial diversity.

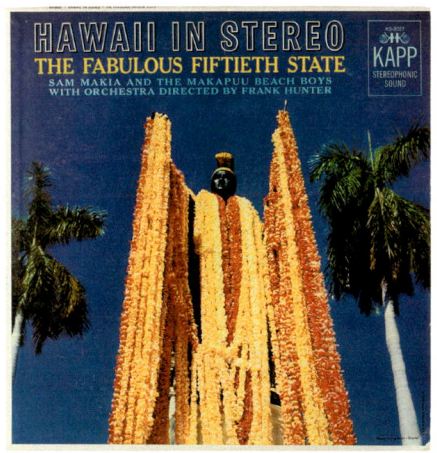

The different migrations of native societies that led to the varied island cultures of Tahiti, Fiji, Tonga, Samoa, Hawaii, and the Marquesas had long fascinated anthropologists. Some idealized Polynesia as a microcosmic version of the "Family of Man." In 1963, the Mormon Church built the Polynesian Cultural Center on Hawaii, a theme park based on that concept. Its various "villages" represented different island cultures and their people, architecture, and handicrafts. All of Polynesia could be visited in a day.

On the U.S. mainland, Tiki establishments utilized the Western enthusiasm for the concept of a multicultural Polynesia as edutainment for their customers: their menus depicted the intermingling of artifacts and cuisine from the Pacific islands, served in dining rooms named after and decorated with objects from the various locales. Tiki artists carved idols in the many different island styles, from Hawaiian "Ku" figures to the Cook Islands' fishermen gods. It was the United Nations of Polynesia!

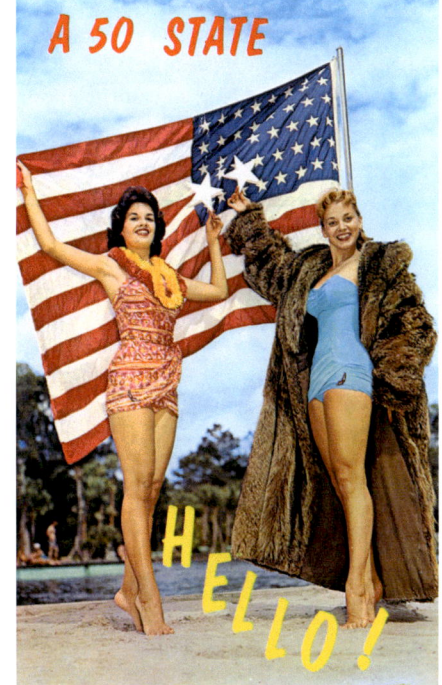

DIE HAWAIISCHEN INSELN WURDEN

1959 zu einem Bundesstaat der USA und der psychologische Segen eines amerikanischen Paradieses wurde zu einem wirtschaftlichen: Hawaiianer waren Amerikaner und somit war nun ganz Amerika Hawaii. Unternehmer und Entwickler auf dem Festland investierten ihr Geld in Projekte, die den Amerikanern helfen sollten, ihre Heimat hawaiischer zu gestalten.

Hawaii war seit Anfang des 20. Jahrhunderts ein Traumreiseziel der Amerikaner. In den 1920er- und 1930er-Jahren konnten sich nur Wohlhabende eine Überfahrt auf den luxuriösen Kreuzfahrtschiffen der Matson Line leisten. Mit dem Aufkommen des kommerziellen Luftverkehrs wurde der Trip für mehr und mehr Paradieshungrige realisierbar. Als Ende der 1950er-Jahre Passagierflugzeuge mit Düsenantrieb auf die Startbahn rollten, verdoppelte sich Hawaiis Touristenaufkommen. Die Metropolen der Westküste, Los Angeles, San Francisco und

Seattle, waren geeignete Ausgangspunkte und Hawaii wurde gleichsam zum Hinterhof dieser Städte. Somit vollendete Hawaiis Aufnahme in das Staatensystem die Liebe der Amerikaner für die Inseln und hielt sie lebendig. Alle wollten nach Hawaii. Wem das nicht möglich war, der schuf sich seine eigene Version auf dem Festland. Jene, die auf den echten Inseln gewesen waren, gesellten sich dazu, um in Urlaubserinnerungen zu schwelgen.

Elvis Presley sang „Hawaii, USA!" und die Blumenkette, der polynesische Willkommensgruß, legte sich um Amerika. Hawaii war ein Sinnbild für Spaß in der Sonne, Freizeit und Faulenzen am Strand. Die hawaiische Denkart kam einem Urlaub an einem Ort gleich, den keiner verlassen wollte. So bekam jede amerikanische Stadt ihre eigene Insel, jeder Garten konnte zu einem kleinen Polynesien werden. Genau wie zur Hochphase der Hawaiimusik in den 1920er-Jahren bedienten sich Restaurants

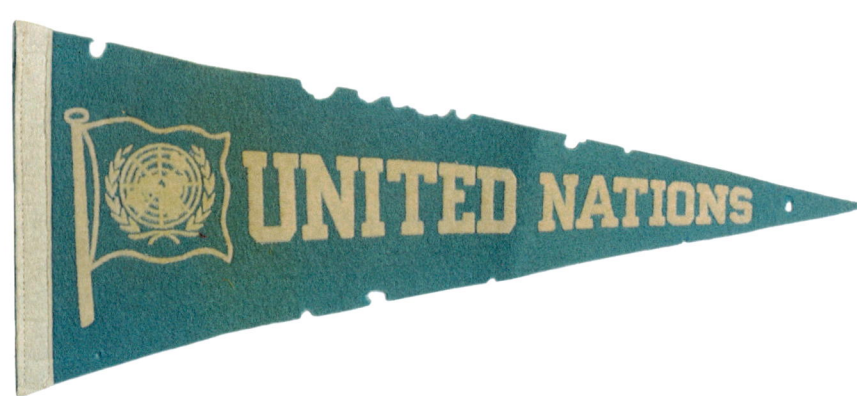

ABOVE: Moth-eaten United Nations pennant

OPPOSITE: Brotherhood Week comic strip (Ben Dickow Collection)

ALOHA... Hawaii!

(IN CELEBRATION OF BROTHERHOOD WEEK, FEB. 21-28)

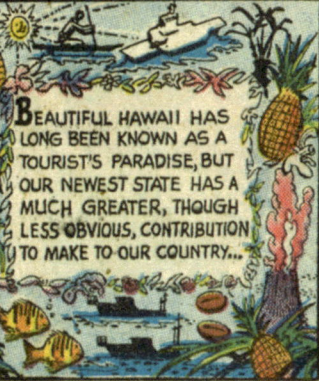

BEAUTIFUL HAWAII HAS LONG BEEN KNOWN AS A TOURIST'S PARADISE, BUT OUR NEWEST STATE HAS A MUCH GREATER, THOUGH LESS OBVIOUS, CONTRIBUTION TO MAKE TO OUR COUNTRY...

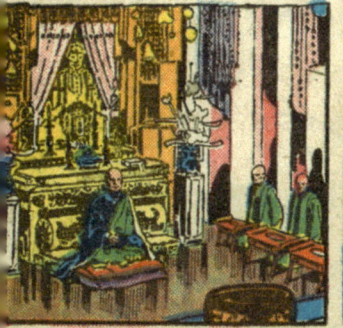

...G THE HAWAIIAN PEOPLE, THERE ARE MANY ...RENT RELIGIONS, ABOUT A TENTH OF THE ...ATION BELONGING TO THE BUDDHIST FAITH...

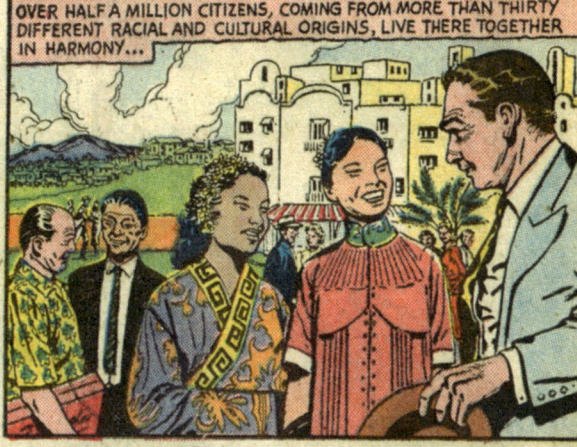

OVER HALF A MILLION CITIZENS, COMING FROM MORE THAN THIRTY DIFFERENT RACIAL AND CULTURAL ORIGINS, LIVE THERE TOGETHER IN HARMONY...

IN ITS FIRST ELECTION AFTER BECOMING A STATE, HAWAII CHOSE ONE SENATOR OF CHINESE PARENTAGE, ANOTHER, A CAUCASIAN, AND A REPRESENTATIVE WHOSE PARENTS WERE JAPANESE...

SENATOR HIRAM L. FONG

SENATOR OREN E. LONG.

REP. DANIEL K. INOUYE

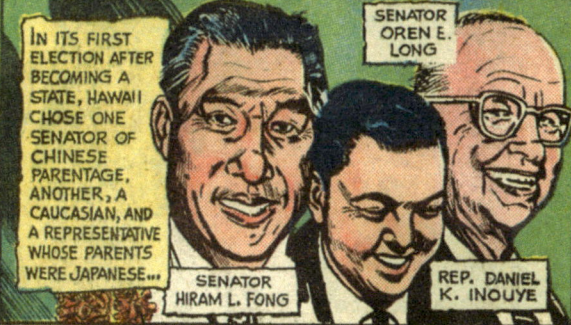

...OUR 50TH ...TE IS AN ...AMPLE OF ...THERHOOD ...RMONY OF ...CH OUR ...NTRY MAY ...L BE PROUD!

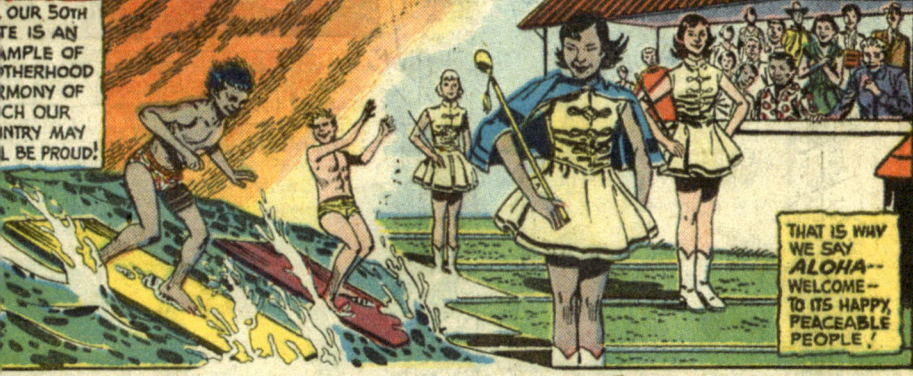

THAT IS WHY WE SAY *ALOHA*-- WELCOME-- TO ITS HAPPY, PEACEABLE PEOPLE!

...ISHED AS A PUBLIC SERVICE IN COOPERATION WITH THE NATIONAL SOCIAL WELFARE ASSEMBLY, ...RDINATING ORGANIZATION FOR NATIONAL HEALTH, WELFARE AND RECREATION AGENCIES OF THE U.S.

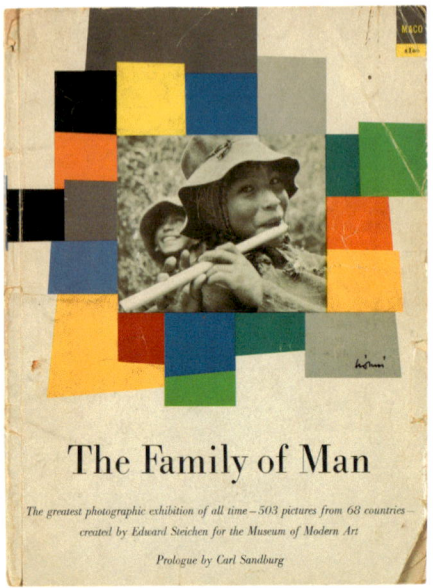

The Family of Man

The greatest photographic exhibition of all time – 503 pictures from 68 countries – created by Edward Steichen for the Museum of Modern Art

Prologue by Carl Sandburg

LEFT: "The Family of Man" exhibition book, which sold over 4 million copies

BELOW: The founding of the United Nations, 1945

OPPOSITE: End pages from James Michener's novel *Hawaii*, 1959

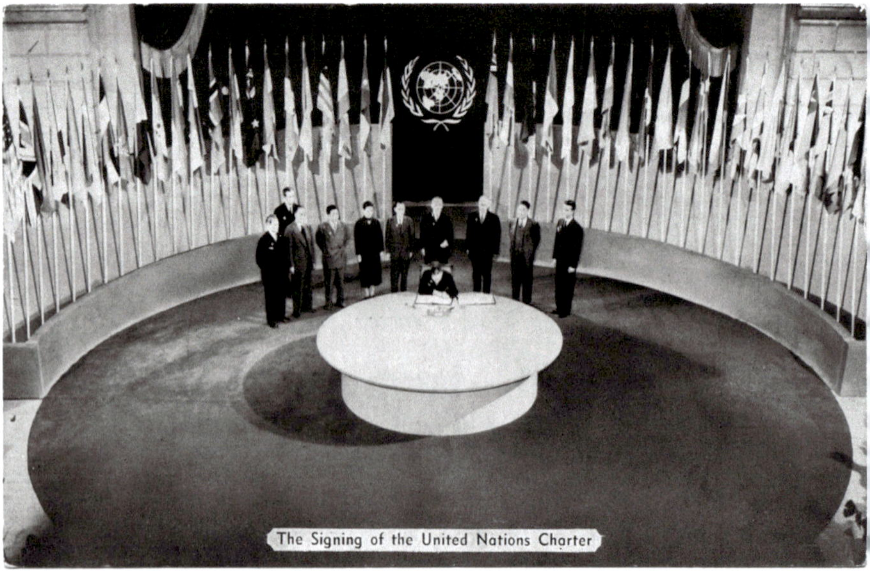

The Signing of the United Nations Charter

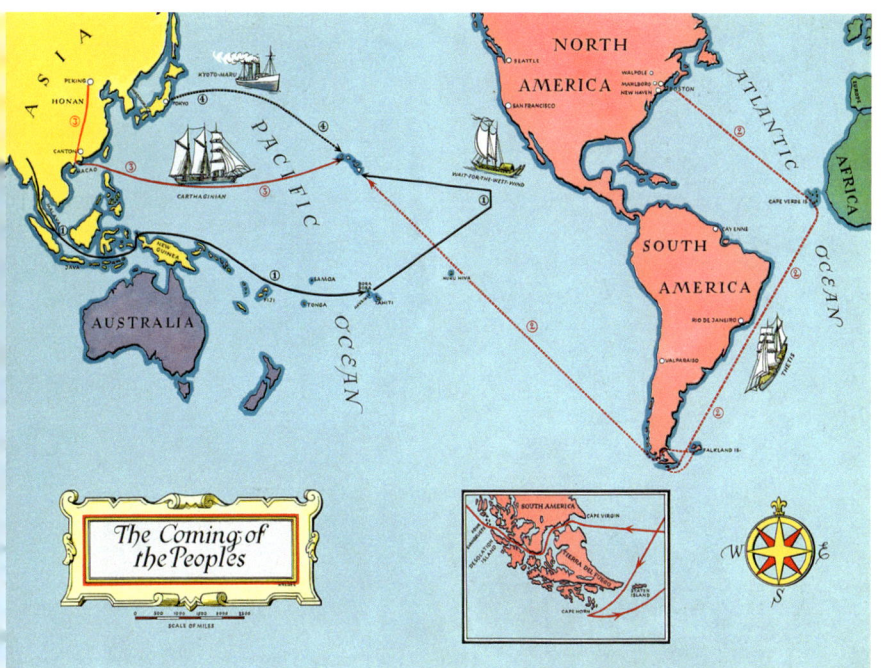

The Coming of the Peoples

SCALE OF MILES

und Garten-Luaus erneut hawaiischer Namen und Ausdrücke. Die „Drinks der Inseln" wurden von den Hawaiihemdträgern, die sich im Rhythmus der Hapa-Haole-Lieder wiegten, mit Begeisterung getrunken. Als Alaska im Januar zuvor zum 49. Bundesstaat wurde, erregte das bei weitem nicht so viel Aufmerksamkeit. Doch wie hat sich das Faible der Amerikaner für die hawaiischen Inseln auf ganz Polynesien ausgeweitet?

Die Verwüstungen des Zweiten Weltkriegs und die plötzliche Bedrohung der menschlichen Spezies durch die Atombombe waren so traumatisch, dass sich die Menschheit schwor, ein solches Gemetzel nie wieder zuzulassen. Die Vereinten Nationen wurden gegründet, damit sich solch ein Krieg nicht mehr wiederholen würde.

Man vertraute darauf, dass die Welt nun in alle Ewigkeit in Frieden leben wollte. Im Jahr 1955 kuratierte Edward Steichen die Ausstellung „The Family of Man" für das Museum of Modern Art in New York. Mit 503 Fotos aus 68 Ländern war das Thema der Ausstellung die Universalität menschlicher Erfahrungen.

Hawaii war ein Schmelztiegel der Kulturen und somit ein gutes Beispiel für das Konzept der friedlichen „Family of Man". 1959 schrieb James Michener in seinem Roman *Hawaii* über die Besiedlung der Inseln. Er entwickelte die Theorie der „Goldenen Menschen": „Eine Gruppe Soziologen in Hawaii perfektionierte ein Konzept… eine neue Form Mensch entwickelte sich…" Hawaii selbst rief die „Brotherhood Week" ins Leben, um seine kulturelle Vielfalt zu feiern.

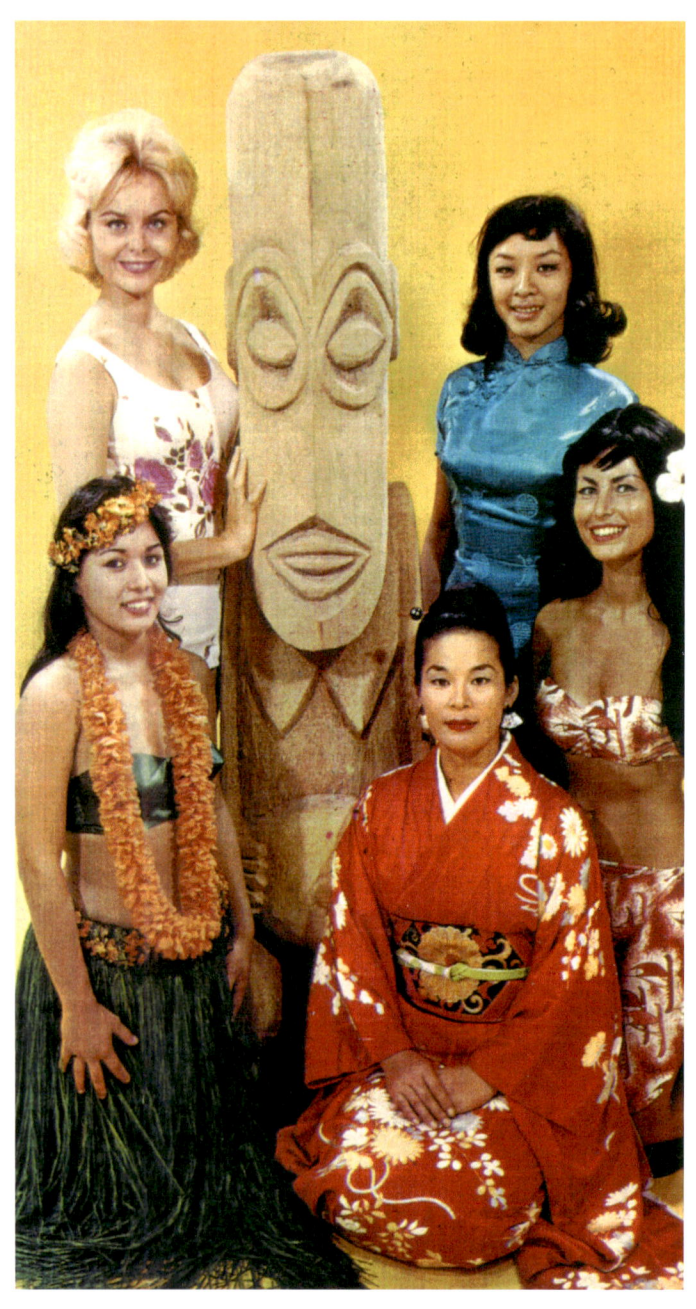

Die Migration unterschiedlicher Gruppen, auf die die Bevölkerungen von Tahiti, Fidschi, Tonga, Samoa, Hawaii und der Marquesas-Inseln zurückgehen, faszinierte Anthropologen seit Langem. Manche idealisierten Polynesien als eine mikrokosmische Version der „Family of Man". 1963 baute die Kirche Jesu Christi der Heiligen der Letzten Tage das Polynesian Cultural Center auf Hawaii – ein Themenpark, der auf diesem Konzept basierte. In verschiedenen „Dörfern" wurden Artefakte und die Architektur unterschiedlicher Inselkulturen präsentiert. Innerhalb eines Tages konnte man ganz Polynesien bereisen.

Auf dem amerikanischen Festland nutzten Tiki-Lokale den westlichen Enthusiasmus für die polynesische Multikulturalität als Edutainment für ihre Gäste. Speisekarten vermischten Artefakte und Gerichte der pazifischen Inseln miteinander. Die Speiseräume waren nach einzelnen Regionen benannt und entsprechend dekoriert. Tiki-Künstler schnitzten Figuren in diversen Stilen, von hawaiischen Ku-Figuren bis zu den Fischergöttern der Cookinseln. Man wähnte sich in den Vereinten Nationen Polynesiens!

OPPOSITE: A sampling of Hawaii's different cultures
(Dug Miller Collection)

RIGHT: Polynesian Cultural Center record album booklet

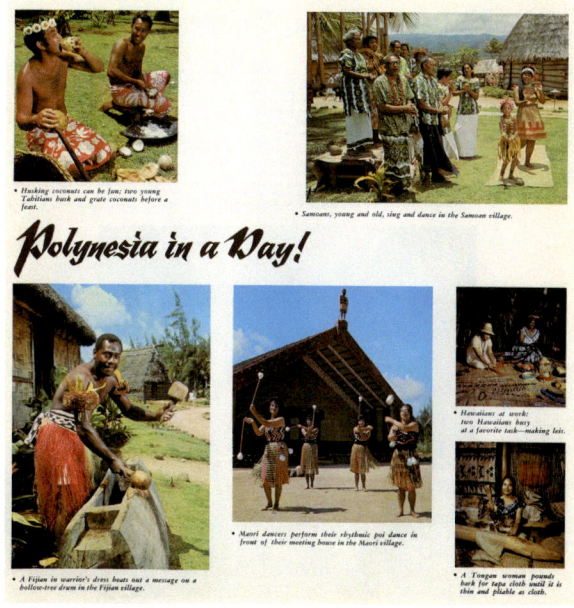

• Husking coconuts can be fun; two young Tahitians husk and grate coconuts before a feast.

• Samoans, young and old, sing and dance in the Samoan village.

Polynesia in a Day!

• A Fijian in warrior's dress beats out a message on a hollow-tree drum in the Fijian village.

• Maori dancers perform their rhythmic poi dance in front of their meeting house in the Maori village.

• Hawaiians at work: two Hawaiians busy at a favorite task—making leis.

• A Tongan woman pounds bark for tapa cloth until it is thin and pliable as cloth.

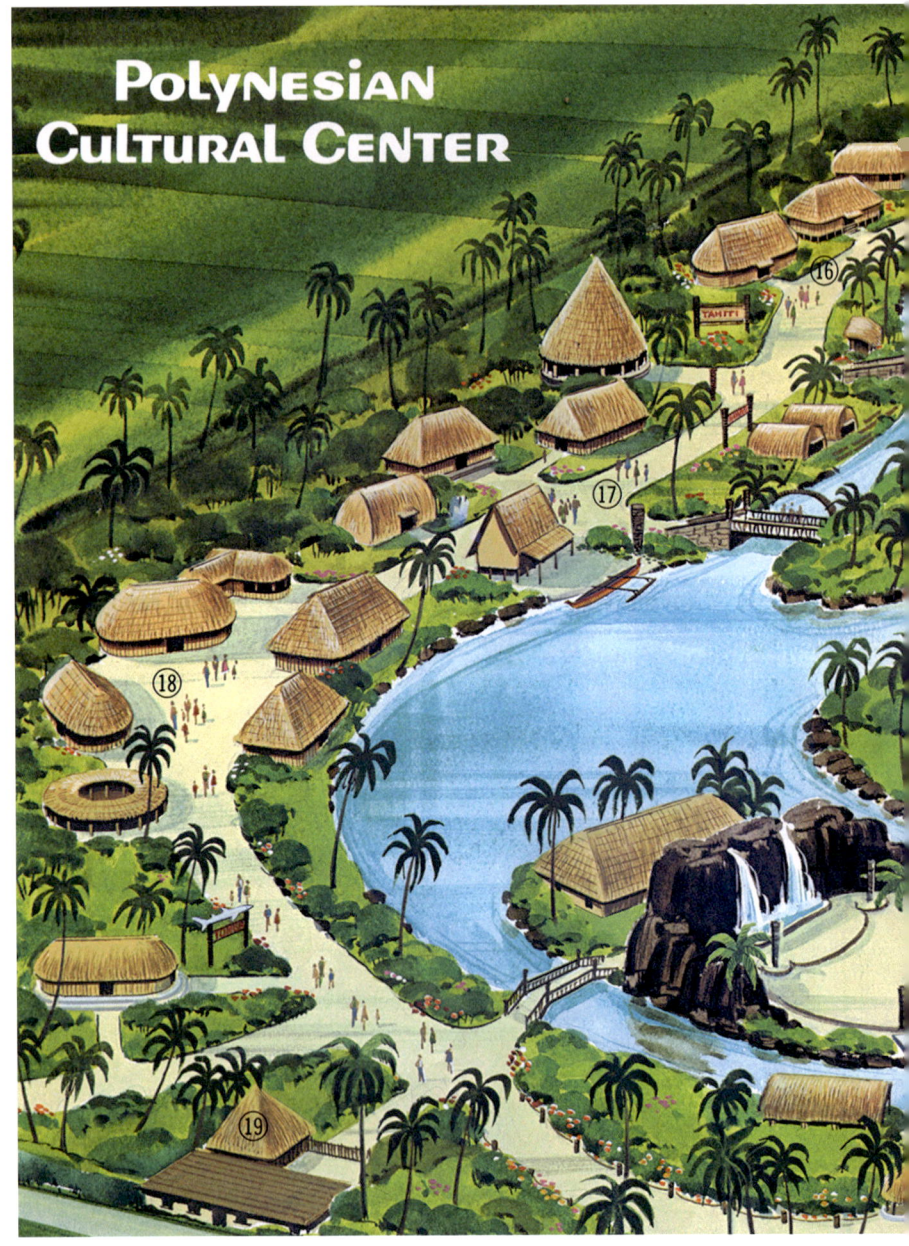

PoLyNesiaN CuLTuRaL CenTer

A pictorial map of the Polynesian
Cultural Center

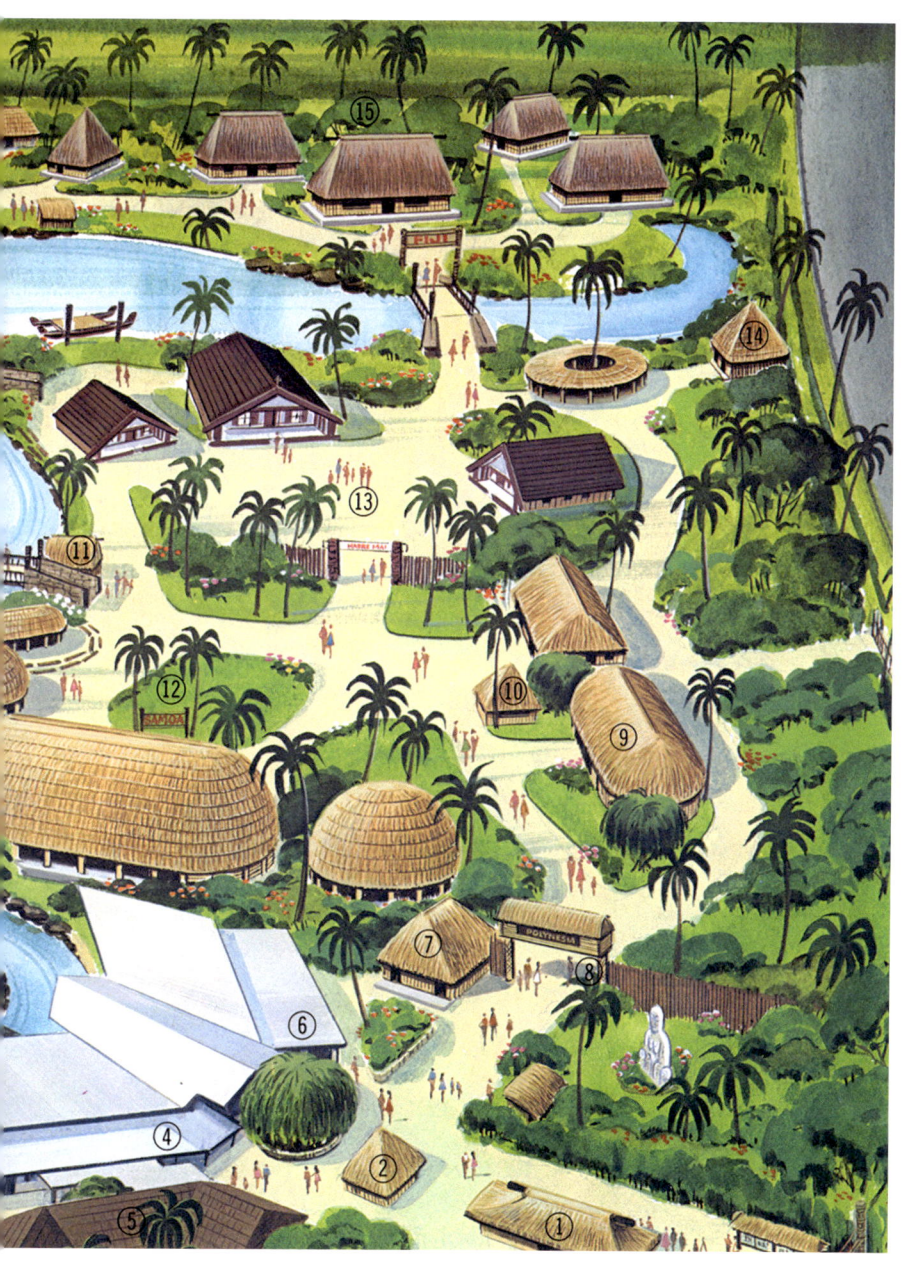

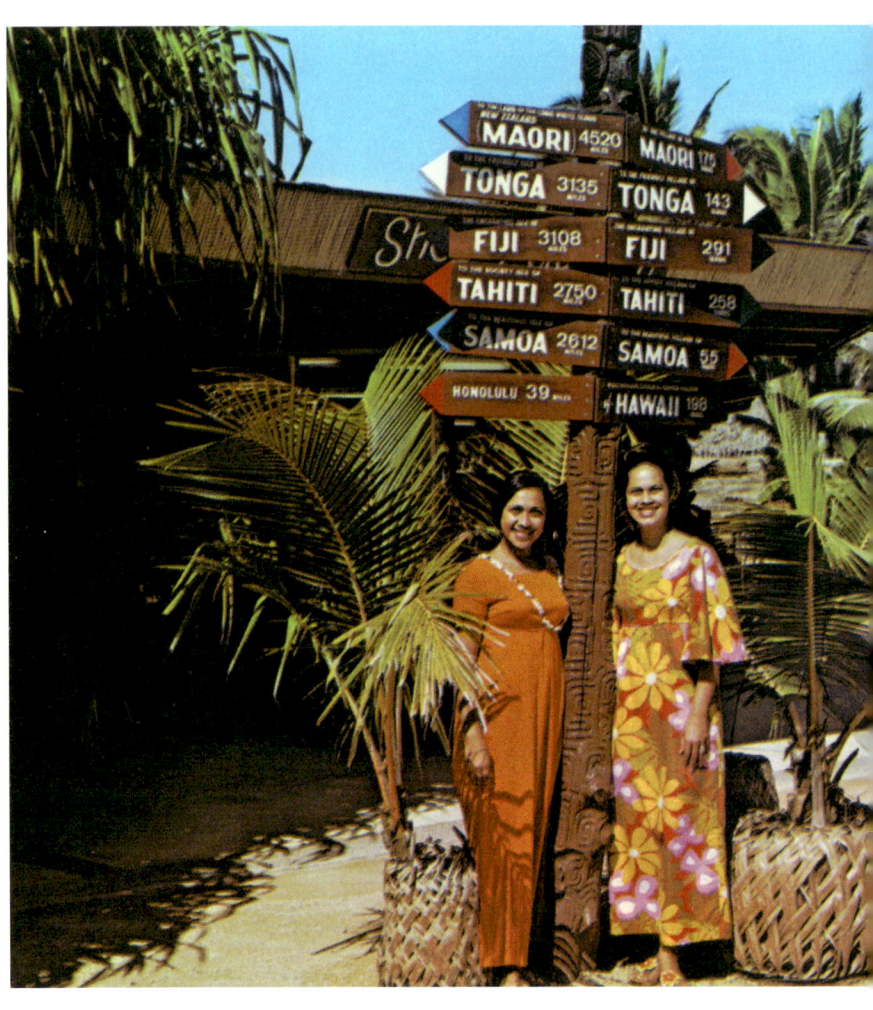

Signpost at the Polynesian
Cultural Center

LA FASCINATION DE L'AMÉRIQUE POUR
Hawaii, déjà ancienne, atteint son apogée
en 1959 quand l'archipel est admis au sein
de l'Union. L'aubaine psychologique que
représente ce nouveau paradis américain se
traduit aussi par une manne économique :
puisque les Hawaiiens *sont* américains,
l'Amérique entière devient hawaiienne.
Entrepreneurs et promoteurs du continent

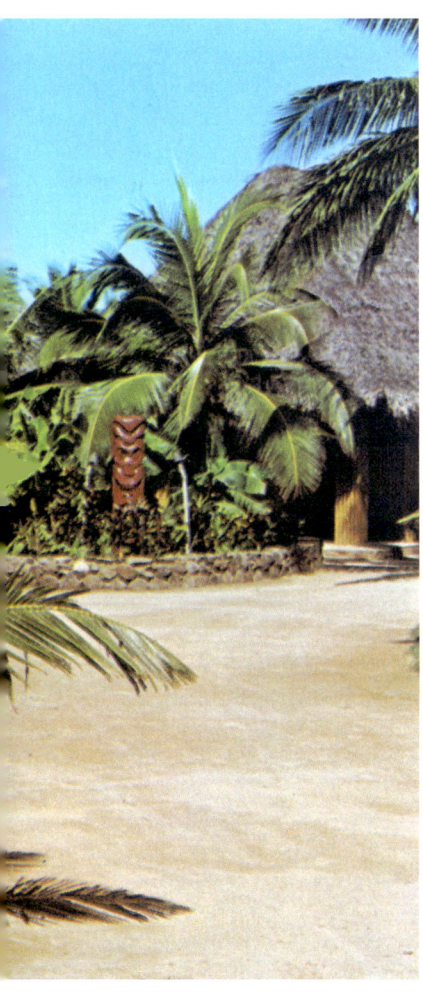

l'arrivée des vols commerciaux, de plus en plus d'heureux amateurs d'exotisme peuvent se permettre le voyage et lorsque l'industrie décolle, à la fin des années 1950, le tourisme à destination d'Hawaii double. Les pôles urbains de la côte Ouest – Los Angeles, San Francisco et Seattle – sont des escales naturelles et faciles, si bien que Hawaii devient pratiquement leur arrière-cour, leur jardin enchanteur. Dans ce contexte, l'entrée d'Hawaii dans l'Union des États d'Amérique ne fait que perpétuer, et attiser, la passion du pays pour l'archipel. Les citoyens américains qui ne pouvaient s'offrir de vraies vacances sur une de ses îles ne comptaient pas se priver de leur atmosphère pour autant. C'est ainsi qu'ils se créèrent des Hawaii domestiques et locaux, où ceux qui avaient fait le voyage prenaient plaisir à revivre et partager leurs souvenirs.

Elvis Presley chante « Hawaii, USA! » et le collier de fleurs (le *lei*), symbole de l'hospitalité polynésienne, s'enroule autour de l'Amérique tout entière. Le mot Hawaii évoque le soleil, la détente, les siestes sur la plage. L'état d'esprit hawaiien est celui de vacances sans fin, dans un endroit que personne ne voudrait quitter ; et d'ailleurs, personne n'y était obligé, puisque chaque jardin pouvait se transformer en Polynésie miniature.

Tout comme au moment de l'explosion de la musique hawaiienne dans les années 1920, les mots et les expressions hawaiiennes sont à nouveau choisis par les restaurants et les *luau* d'arrière-cour. Des clients en chemise hawaiienne sirotaient avec délice des « boissons des îles » sur fond de musique *hapa haole*. L'Alaska n'a pas reçu les mêmes attentions lorsqu'il est devenu le 49e État d'Amérique, en 1959,

nvestissent pour permettre aux Américains ous des îles de rendre leur ville et leur ntérieur aussi hawaiiens que possible.

Les îles hawaiiennes sont une destina-ion de rêve pour les Américains depuis e début du XXe siècle. Dans les années 920 et 1930, les places à bord des luxueux ateaux de croisière de la Matson Line taient réservées aux plus aisés. Avec loin de là. Pourtant, la passion pour l'archipel hawaiien ne tarde pas à s'étendre à toute la Polynésie.

Le cataclysme de la Seconde Guerre mondiale et la possibilité soudaine d'un anéantissement nucléaire de toutes les espèces terrestres sont si traumatisants que l'humanité fait le vœu de ne plus jamais vivre de telles horreurs et crée les Nations unies dans cet esprit idéaliste, par des pays qui jurent que le monde ne connaîtra plus que la paix, éternellement. En 1955, Edward Steichen est le curateur d'une exposition intitulée « La Famille de l'homme » pour le musée d'Art moderne de New York. Les 503 photos prises dans 68 pays ont été choisies pour illustrer l'universalité de l'expérience humaine.

Hawaii est un creuset pacifique où se mêlent plusieurs ethnies, ce qui le rend très représentatif de cette « famille de l'homme ». En 1959, James Michener publie son roman *Hawaii,* qui relate la colonisation de l'archipel. Il y développe la théorie du « Peuple d'or » : « Un groupe de sociologues d'Hawaii a élaboré un concept… un nouvel humain est en train de voir le jour… » Le nouvel État d'Hawaii instaure même une « Semaine de la fraternité » pour célébrer sa diversité.

Les vagues migratoires successives qui ont peuplé et façonné les cultures riches et variées de Tahiti, des Fidji, des Tonga, des Samoa, d'Hawaii et des Marquises fascinent depuis longtemps les anthropologues. Certains ont développé une vision idéalisée de la Polynésie comme microcosme de la famille humaine. En 1963, l'église mormone établit un Centre culturel polynésien à Hawaii, une sorte de parc d'attraction thématique composé de « villages » représentant la culture, le peuple, l'architecture et l'artisanat des différents archipels. Le tour de la Polynésie en un seul jour.

Sur le continent, les établissements tiki profitent de l'enthousiasme occidental pour l'universalisme et le multiculturalisme pour ajouter l'instruction au divertissement de ses clients : leurs menus sont illustrés d'un mélange d'objets et d'aliments venus du Pacifique, les repas sont pris dans des pièce portant le nom de destinations exotiques lointaines. Les artistes qui se sont spécialisé dans le tiki façonnent des idoles dans toutes sortes de styles, du « Ku » hawaiien aux dieux pêcheurs des îles Cook : les Nations unies de Polynésie !

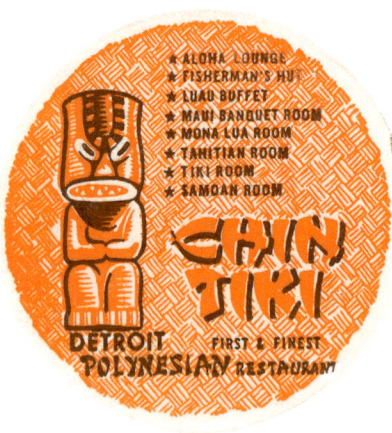

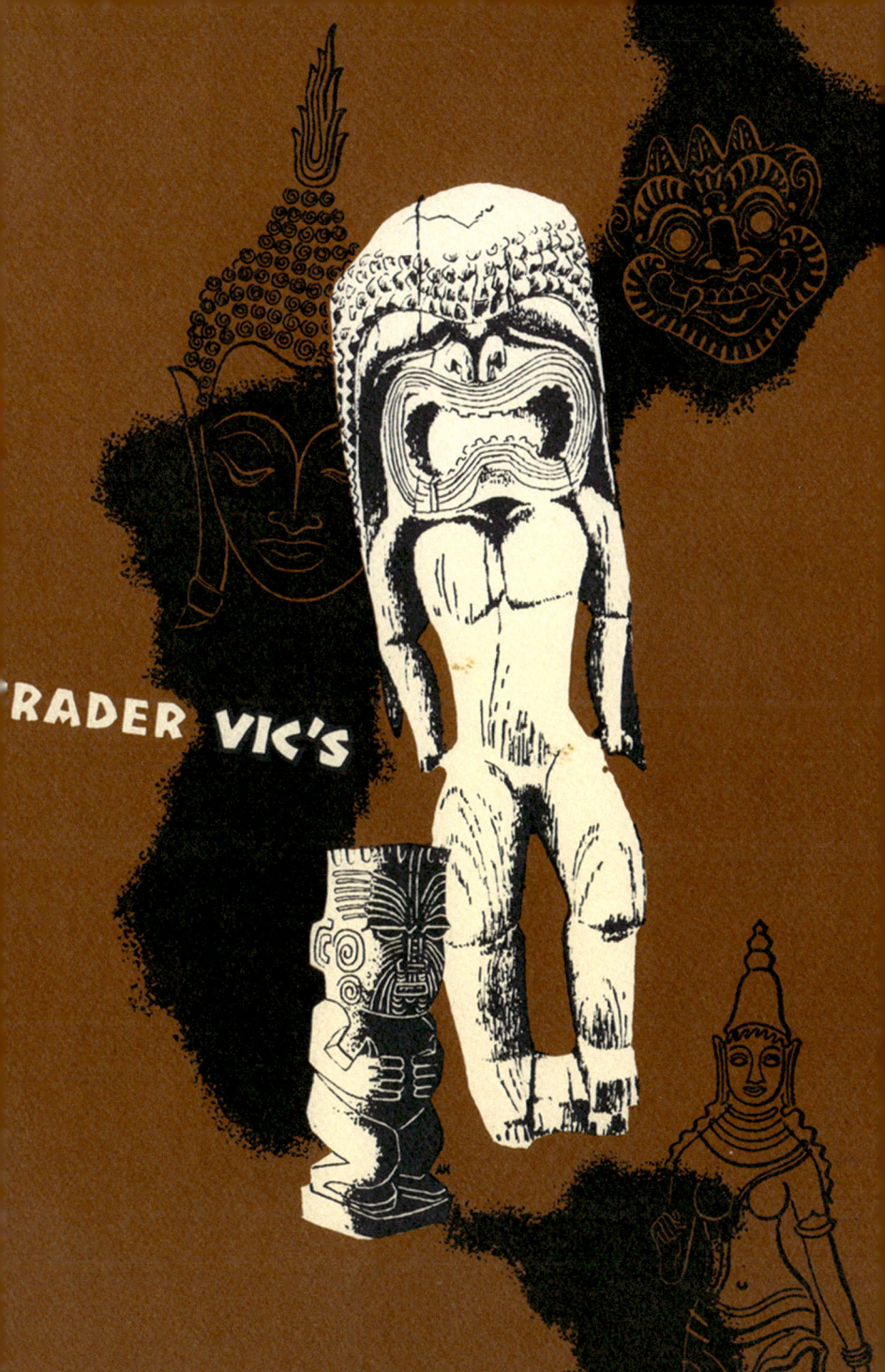

TRADER VIC'S

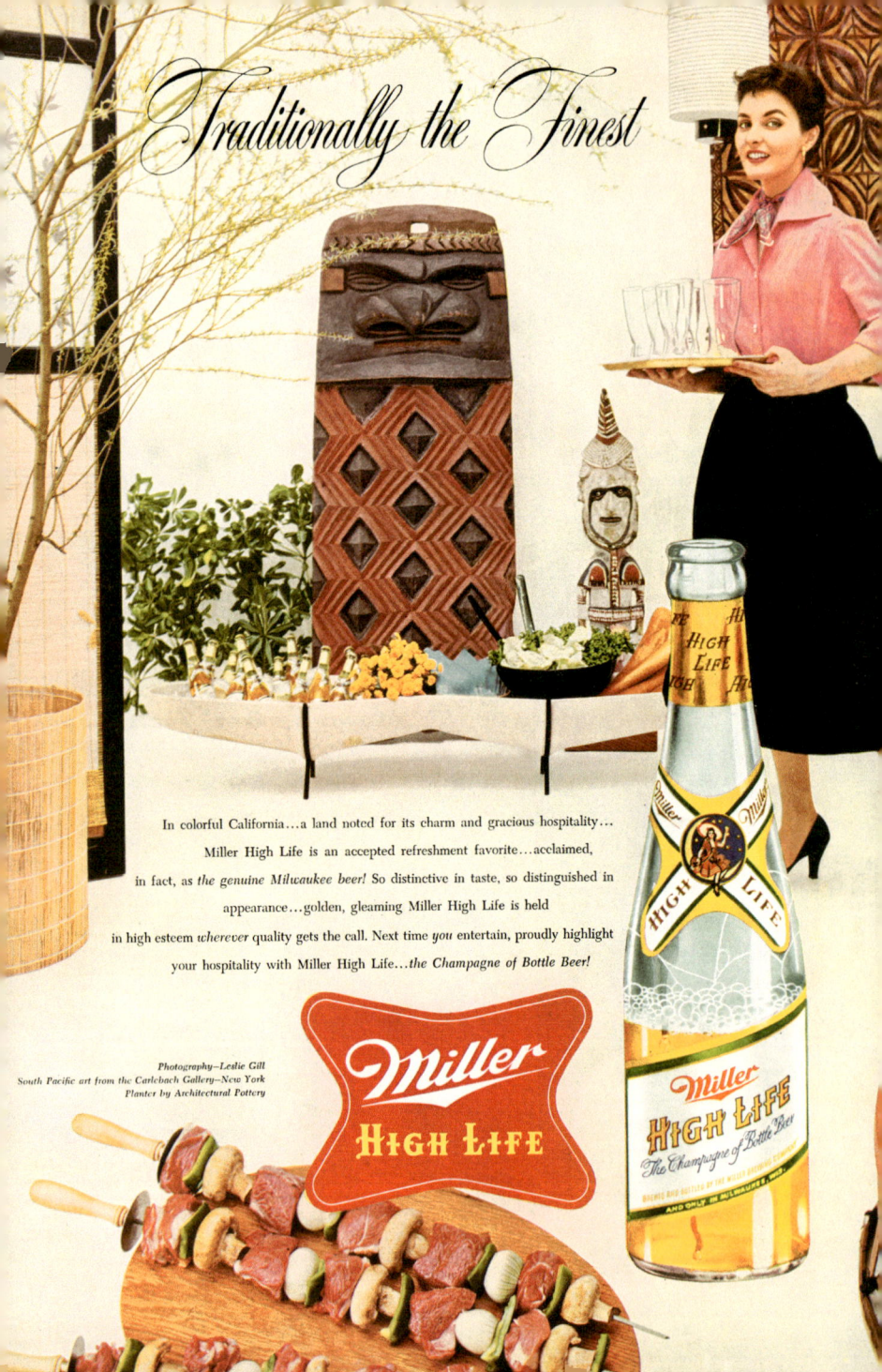

Traditionally the Finest

In colorful California...a land noted for its charm and gracious hospitality...
Miller High Life is an accepted refreshment favorite...acclaimed,
in fact, as *the genuine Milwaukee beer!* So distinctive in taste, so distinguished in
appearance...golden, gleaming Miller High Life is held
in high esteem *wherever* quality gets the call. Next time *you* entertain, proudly highlight
your hospitality with Miller High Life...*the Champagne of Bottle Beer!*

Photography—Leslie Gill
South Pacific art from the Carlebach Gallery—New York
Planter by Architectural Pottery

Miller
HIGH LIFE

Miller
HIGH LIFE
The Champagne of Bottle Beer

21

THE MODERN
AND THE PRIMITIVE

DAS MODERNE UND DAS PRIMITIVE
LE MODERNE ET LE PRIMITIF

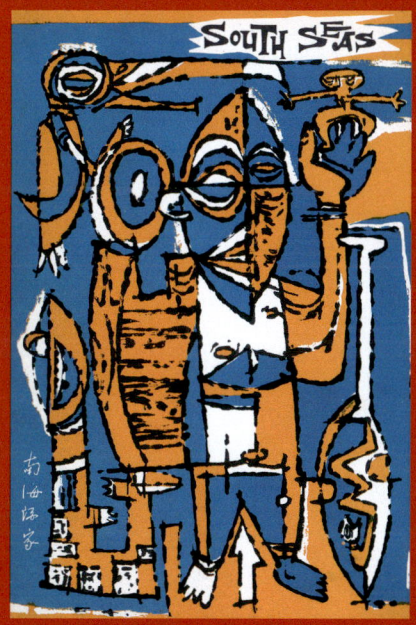

OPPOSITE: Miller beer ad showing Oceanic art
and *tapa* cloth in a modern setting, 1954

ABOVE: Menu cover for South Seas restaurant, Boston, 1969

WHILE THE STATEHOOD OF HAWAII
provided the social and economic push
that lifted America's fondness for Polynesia
to a new level, what led to the Tiki taking
over the reins from the hula girl as its icon
beginning in the mid-'50s? One factor was
that there seems to have been a gradual
opening of American taste toward what
was then called "primitive art." The middle
class discovered that indigenous sculpture
complemented modern home décor.

This evolution in taste was initiated
earlier in the 20th century by the first generation of modern artists in Europe. Pablo
Picasso and his contemporaries in Paris
were inspired by African and Oceanic tribal
sculpture and saw it as proof that there was
more to artistic expression than naturalism
and true-to-nature portraiture. The leader of
the Surrealists, André Breton, wrote a poem
entitled "Tiki." Artist groups like Die Brücke
in Berlin proclaimed their right and duty
to apply the subjective and spiritual forms

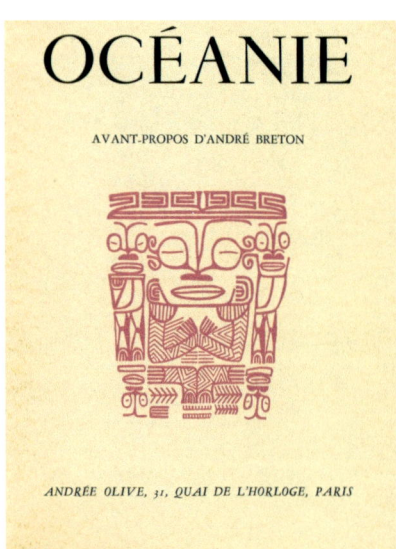

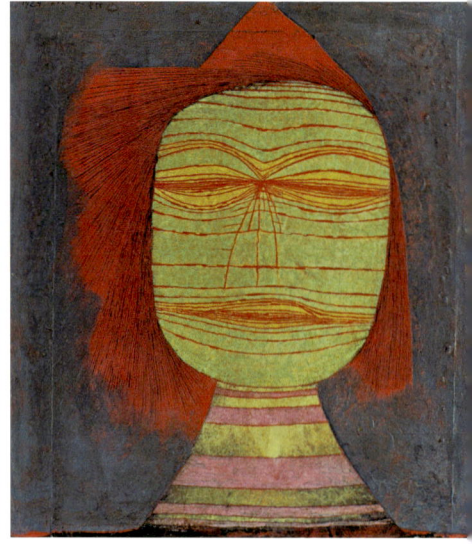

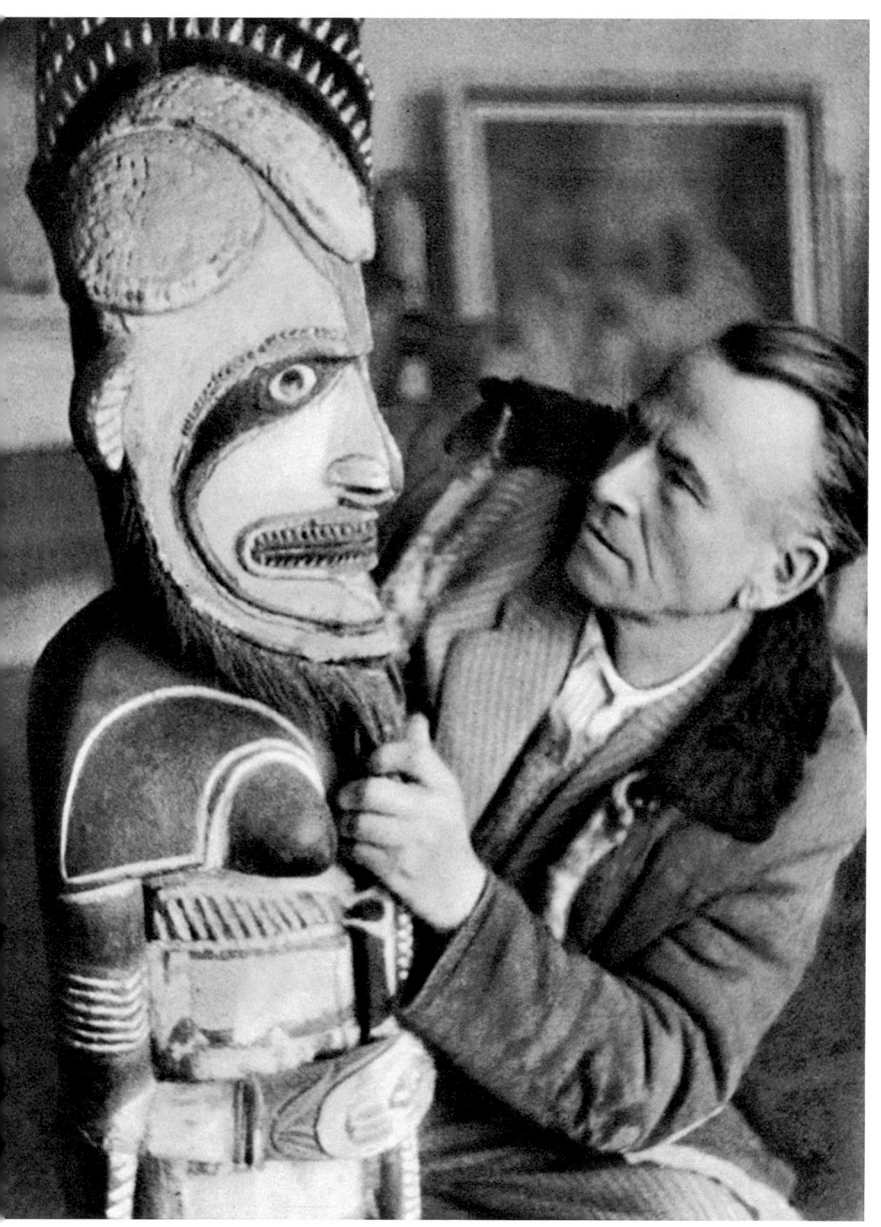

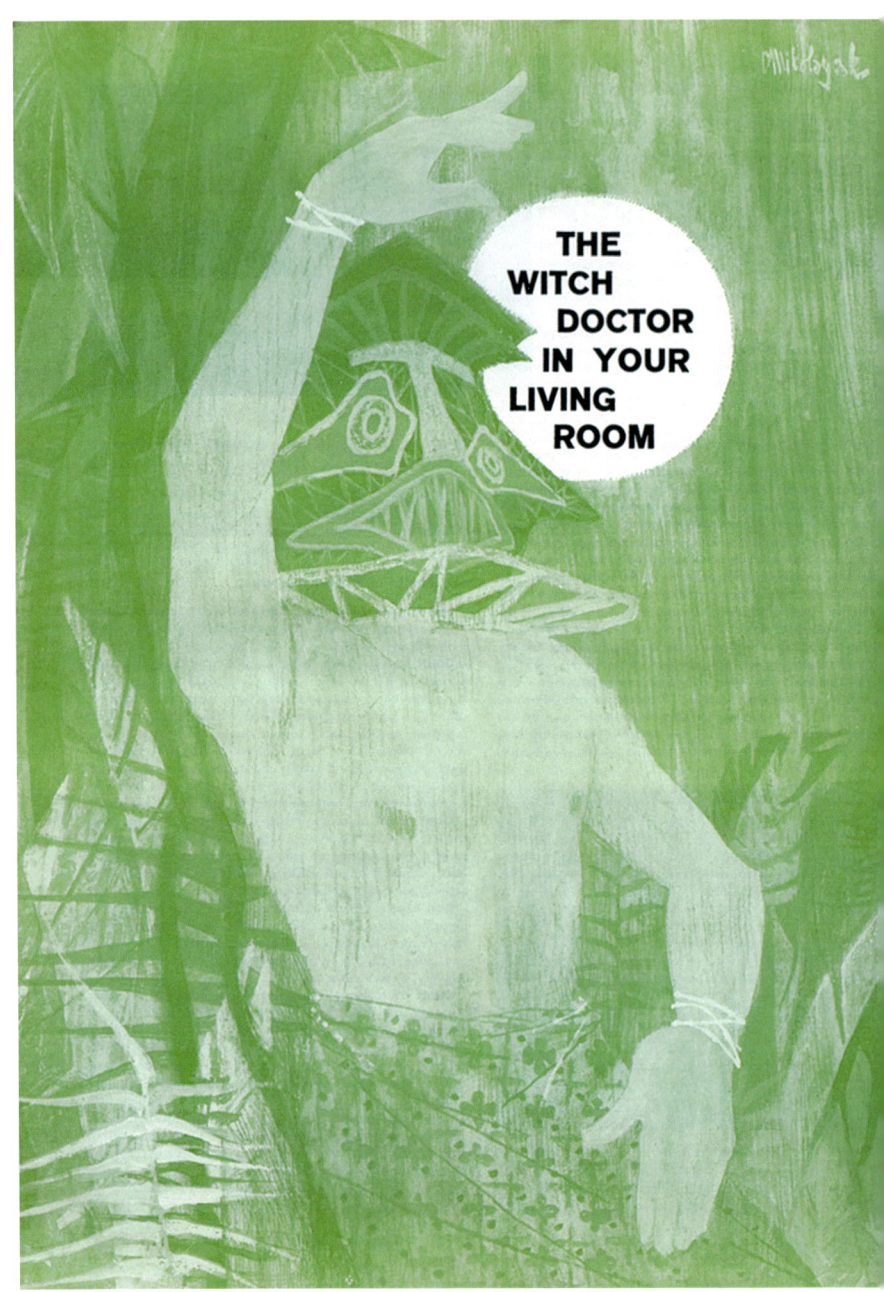

THE
WITCH
DOCTOR
IN YOUR
LIVING
ROOM

they saw in native carvings to their own new art. When the Nazis began to denounce these works as "degenerate," some of their creators accepted art doyenne Peggy Guggenheim's invitation to come to America.

Emigrating from Nazi rule, the European artists brought their sensibilities to the New York art scene. In 1946, The Museum of Modern Art in New York mounted America's first major exhibition focusing on the arts of the South Seas. *Life* magazine published an elaborate article on the show, and its imagery entered pop culture.

Other museums throughout America followed with exhibitions on the "primitive" theme, and tribal art became a status symbol for the cultural elite. Interior decorators used it in conjunction with modern furnishings, and at cocktail parties new acquisitions were favorite conversation pieces. Since Polynesian art was so singular that most of it had already wandered into museums, private collectors turned to Melanesian art.

The quintessential movie to capture this element of the mid-century zeitgeist is the 1958 romantic comedy *Bell, Book and Candle*. Kim Novak stars as the owner of a New York gallery specializing in tribal art who literally bewitches regular guy James Stewart to fall for her. Novak's character is an artsy bohemian type clad in black leotards. Her brother, played by Jack Lemmon, is a bongo-playing beatnik, while Ernie Kovacs portrays the doubtful urban witchcraft researcher.

In the early 1900s, the modern avant-garde had discovered original tribal-art pieces as a revelation that helped them to deconstruct figurative art. By mid-century their cubist, abstract stylings had become the accepted art of the times and they were used in contemporary graphic design. Young artists

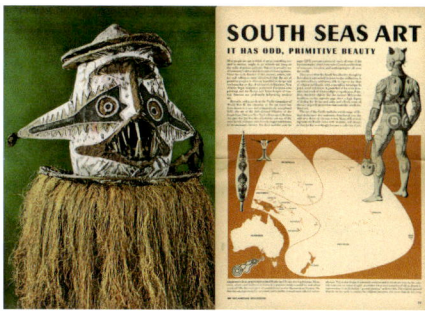

OPPOSITE: *Hi-Fi Stereo* magazine illustration for the first article on exotica music, 1960 *(Dean Curtis Collection)*

ABOVE: *Life* article on the "Arts of the South Seas" exhibition, 1946

BELOW: *South Pacific* record cover with art clipped from the article about the exhibition, 1950s

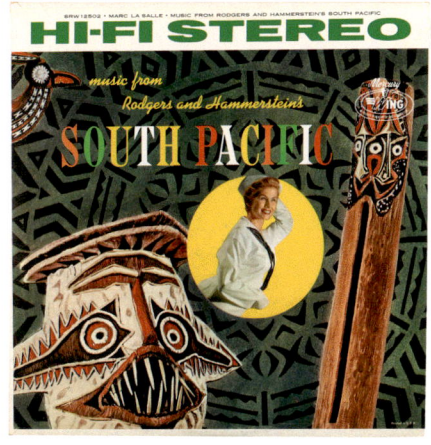

now applied this aesthetic to their modern renderings of Oceanic art. The evolution of modern primitivism had come full circle.

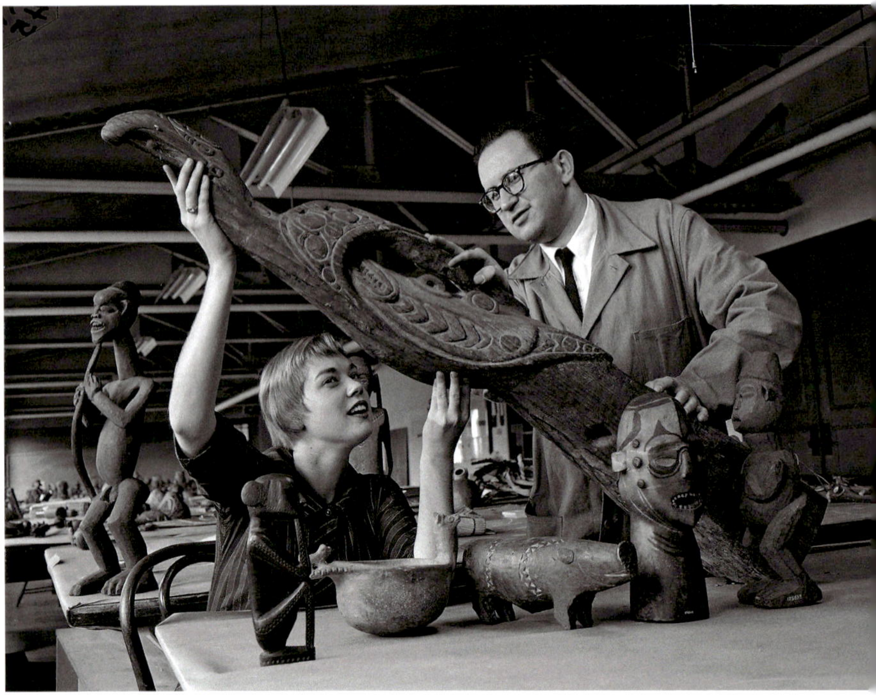

The stylistic elements of mid-century-modern Tiki art were composed of a good dose of this modernist verve, sometimes veering toward naïve brutalism, sometimes using cartoony influences. The best examples of the style all share a creative ingenuity and whimsy unique to the time and place in which they were fashioned.

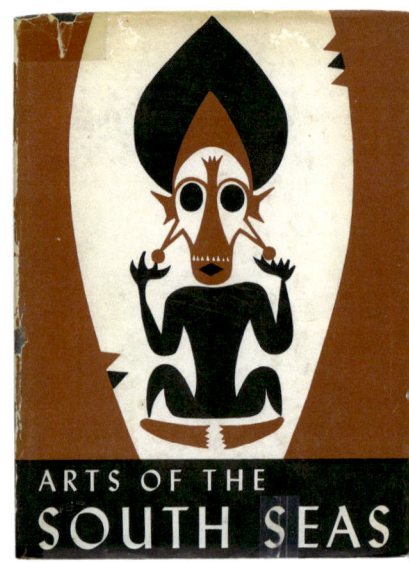

ARTS OF THE
SOUTH SEAS

OPPOSITE ABOVE: 1958 exhibition
"What Is Primitive Art?," Chicago
Natural History Museum

OPPOSITE BELOW: The catalog for
the Museum of Modern Art show

RIGHT: Society ladies ogling
Oceanic art

BELOW: Modern living room
with tribal-art accents

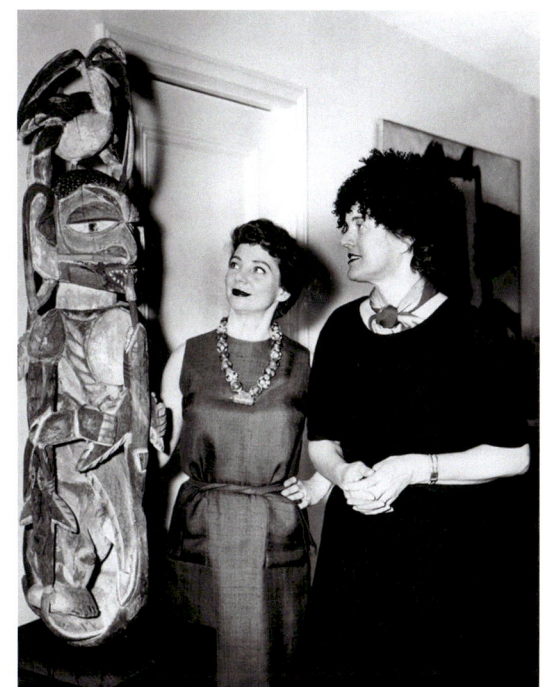

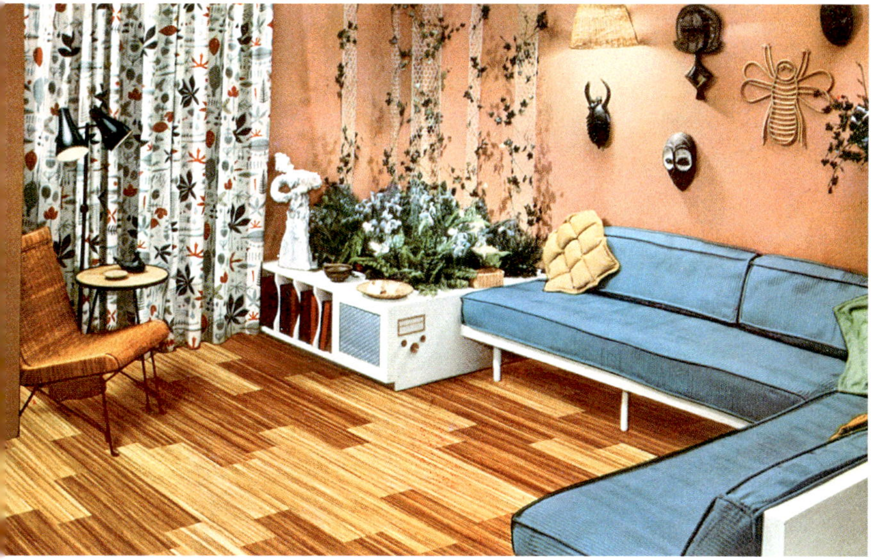

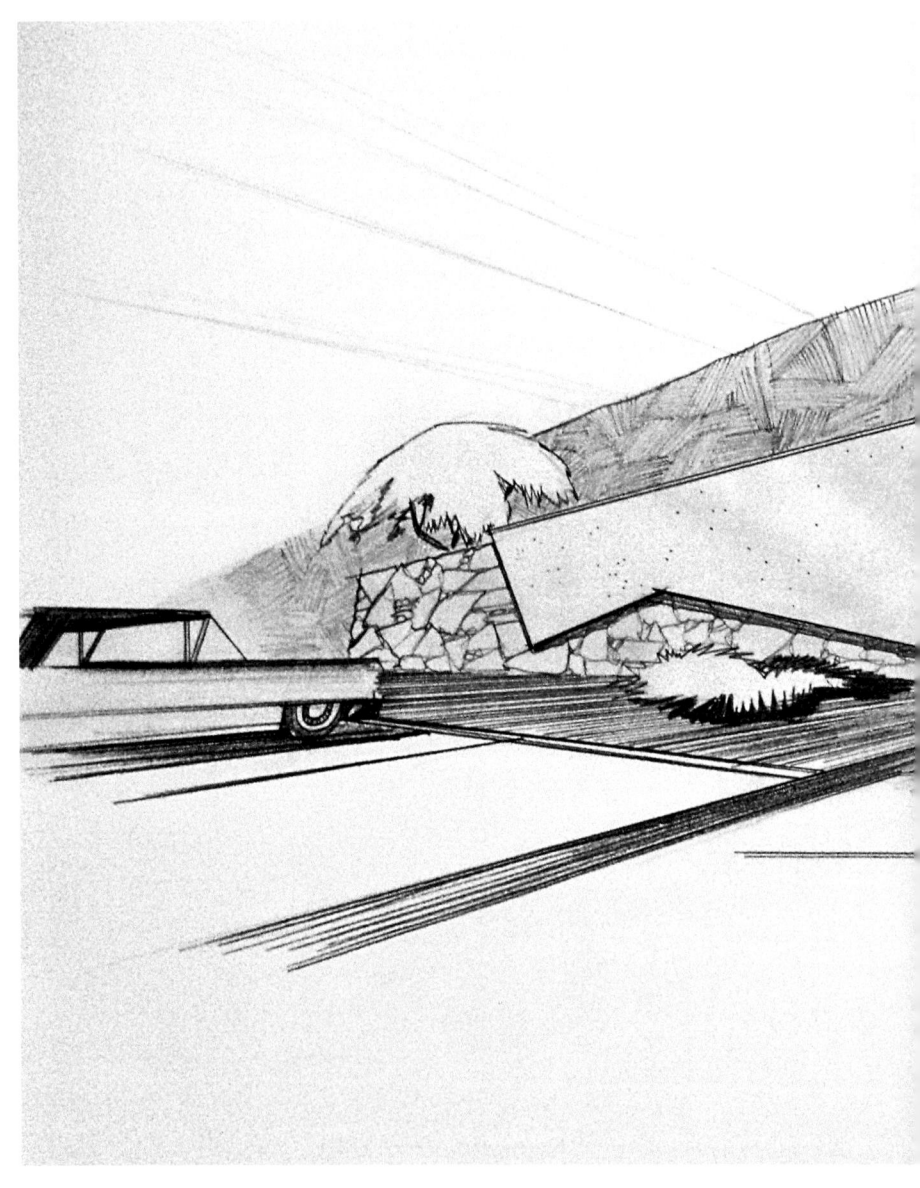

Architectural rendering for a
Palm Springs apartment by
Hugh Kaptur, 1960

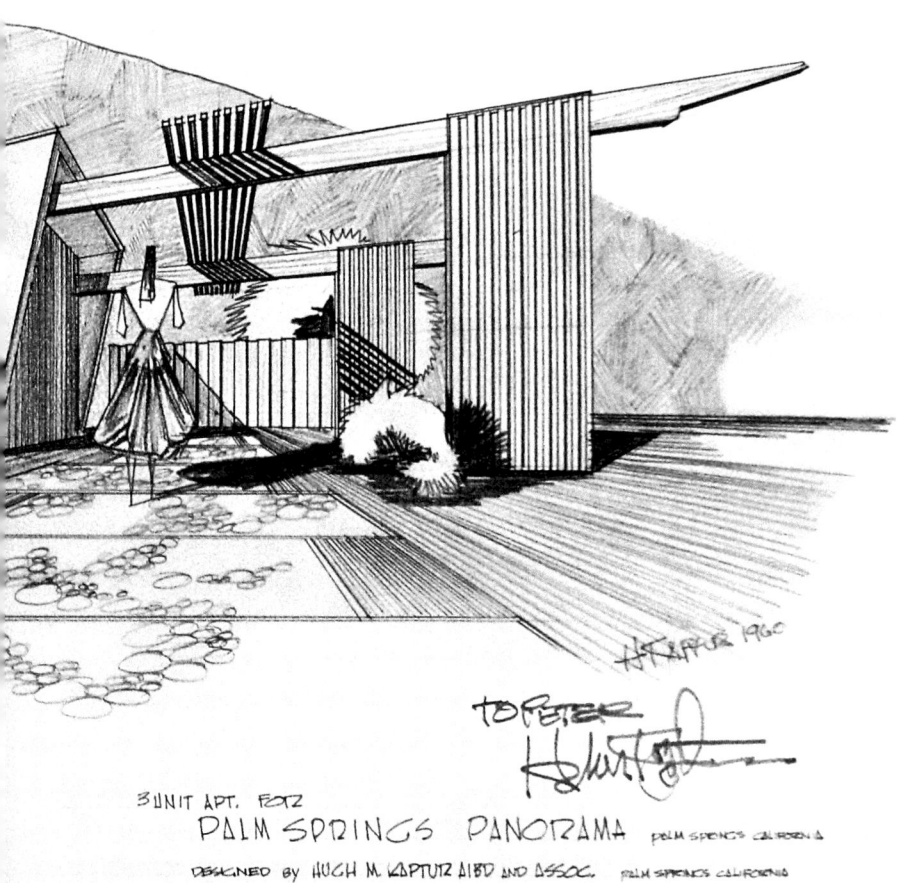

HKAPPUR 1960

TO PETER

3 UNIT APT. FOR

PALM SPRINGS PANORAMA PALM SPRINGS CALIFORNIA

DESIGNED BY HUGH M. KAPTUR AIBD AND ASSOC. PALM SPRINGS CALIFORNIA

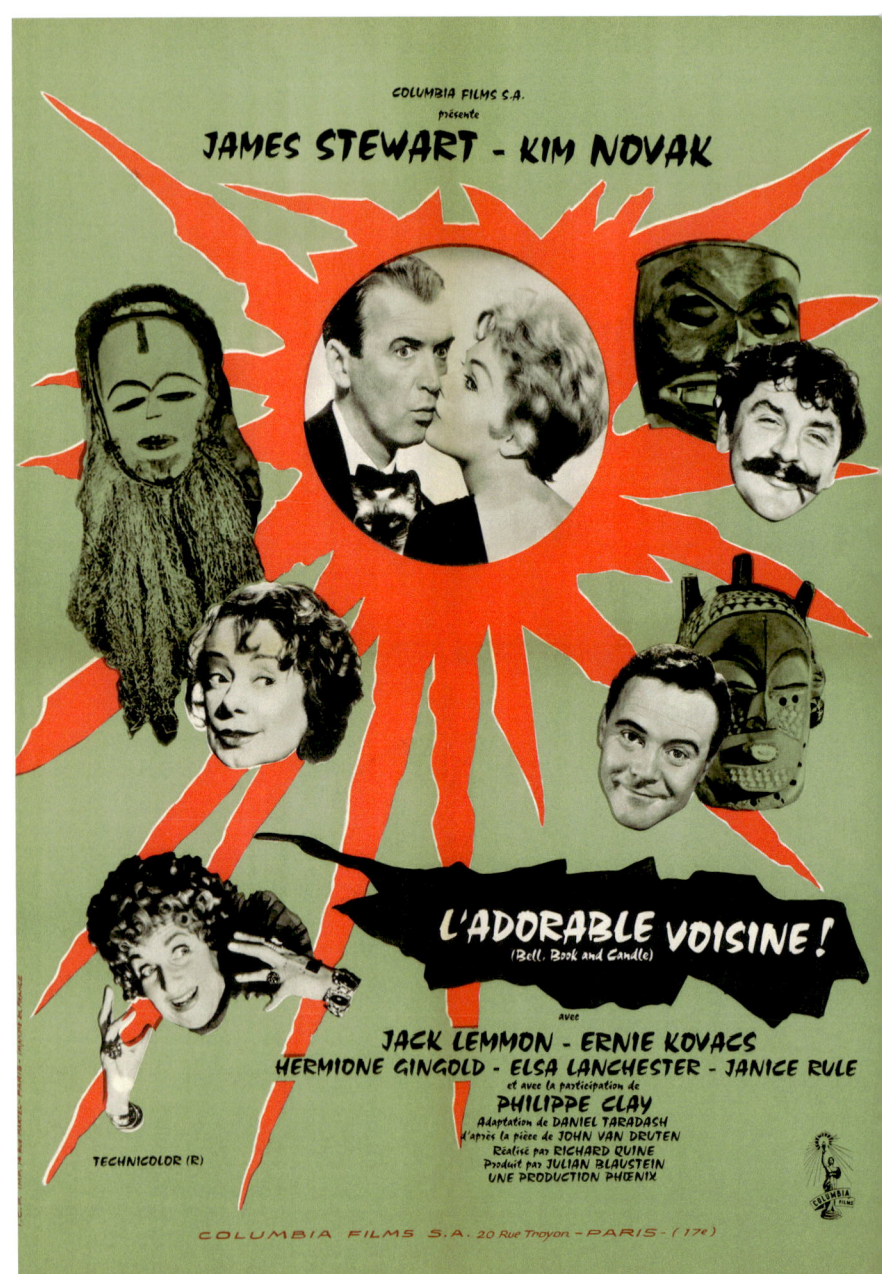

DURCH DEN BEITRITT HAWAIIS ZU DEN
Vereinigten Staaten wurde das Faible der
Amerikaner für Polynesien sozial und öko-
nomisch auf ein neues Level gehoben. Was
aber führte dazu, dass Tiki dem Hula-Girl
Mitte der 1950er-Jahre die Zügel aus der
Hand nahm? Ein Faktor war, dass sich der
amerikanische Geschmack langsam für die
sogenannte Primitive Kunst öffnete. Der
Mittelstand entdeckte, dass sich indigene
Skulpturen gut mit moderner Wohnungs-
einrichtung kombinieren ließen.

Diese Entwicklung wurde Anfang des
20. Jahrhunderts durch die modernen europäischen Künstler initiiert. Pablo Picasso
und seine Zeitgenossen in Paris ließen
sich von afrikanischen und ozeanischen
Stammesskulpturen inspirieren. Für sie

waren sie ein Beweis, dass es in der Kunst
mehr gab als den Naturalismus und die
realistische Porträtmalerei. Der Anführer
der Surrealisten, André Breton, schrieb ein
Gedicht namens „Tiki". Künstlergruppen
wie die „Brücke" in Berlin proklamierten
ihr Recht und ihre Pflicht, die subjektiven
und spirituellen Formen der Stammeskunst
in ihre eigenen Werke fließen zu lassen. Als
die Nazis begannen, diese Werke als entar-
tet zu denunzieren, nahmen manche ihrer
Schöpfer die Einladung der Kunstmäzenin
Peggy Guggenheim an und immigrierten
in die USA.

Den Nazis entflohen, bereicherten die
europäischen Künstler die New Yorker
Kunstszene. 1946 stellte das Museum of
Modern Art in New York Amerikas erste

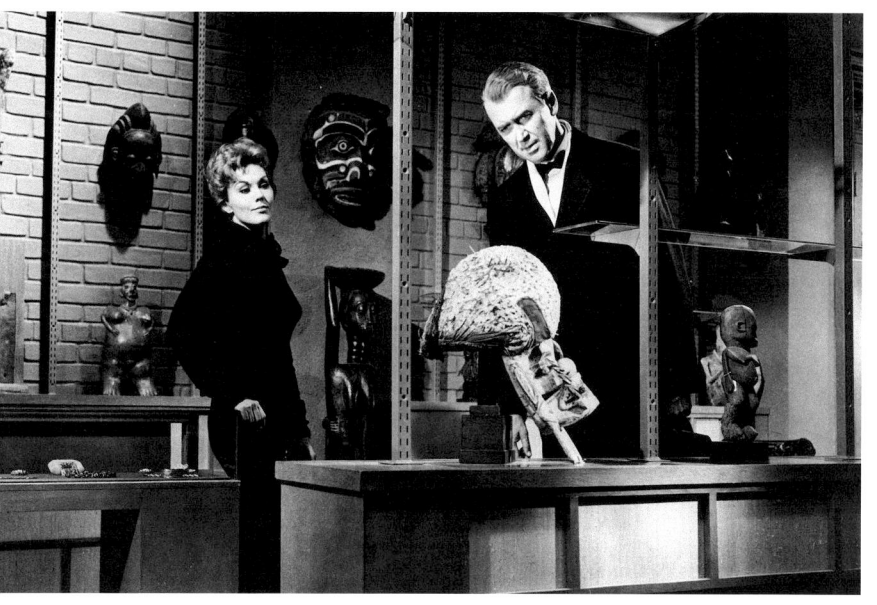

OPPOSITE: French poster for *Bell,
Book and Candle*, 1958

ABOVE: James Stewart inspects
an Oceanic mask

Großausstellung über die Künste der Südsee zusammen. Das Magazin *Life* veröffentlichte einen ausführlichen Artikel über die Ausstellung, deren Bildsprache fortan in die Popkultur einging.

Andere Museen in Amerika schlossen sich mit Ausstellungen zur Primitiven Kunst an. Stammeskunst wurde zum Statussymbol der Bildungselite. Innenarchitekten kombinierten sie mit modernen Möbeln und auf Cocktailpartys waren die entsprechenden neuen Errungenschaften das beliebteste Gesprächsthema. Da die polynesische Kunst so einzigartig war, dass sich das meiste davon bereits in Museen befand, wandten sich Privatsammler der melanesischen Kunst zu.

Der Film, der diese Facette des Mittfünfziger-Zeitgeists am besten festhält, ist die Liebeskomödie *Meine Braut ist übersinnlich* von 1958. Kim Novak spielt die Besitzerin einer New Yorker Galerie, die auf Stammeskunst spezialisiert ist. Durch Zauberei sorgt sie dafür, dass sich Shepard Henderson (James Stewart) – ein ganz normaler Kerl – in sie verliebt. Novaks Figur ist eine künstlerische, unkonventionelle Frau in schwarzen Gymnastikanzügen. Ihr Bruder, gespielt von Jack Lemmon, ist ein bongotrommelnder Beatnik, während Ernie Kovacs den dubiosen Hexenforscher gibt.

Im frühen 20. Jahrhundert hatte die moderne Avantgarde die urtypische Stammeskunst als Offenbarung für sich entdeckt; mit ihrer Hilfe ließ sich die figurative Kunst auseinandernehmen. Bis Mitte des Jahrhunderts war diese kubistische, abstrakte Gestaltungsweise die akzeptierte Kunstform ihrer Zeit geworden und fand sich im zeitgenössischen Grafikdesign wieder. Junge Künstler wandten den Look auf ihre modernen Interpretationen ozeanischer Kunst an. Die Entwicklung des modernen Primitivismus war wieder am Anfang angekommen.

Die stilistischen Elemente des Midcentury-modern-Tiki kombinierten modernistischen Elan mit naivem Brutalismus oder karikaturartigen Einflüssen. Die besten Beispiele für diesen Stil bestechen durch ihre kreative Raffinesse und Schrulligkeit, die für die damalige Zeit einzigartig waren.

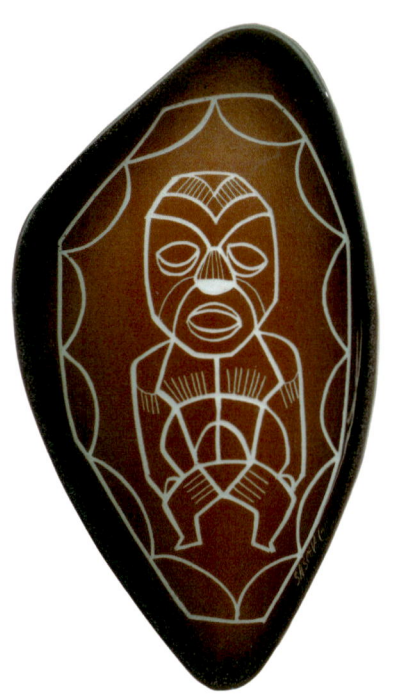

RIGHT: Ashtray design by Sascha Brastoff

OPPOSITE: Menu cover for Aloha Jhoe's restaurant, Palm Springs
(Frank Brajevic Collection)

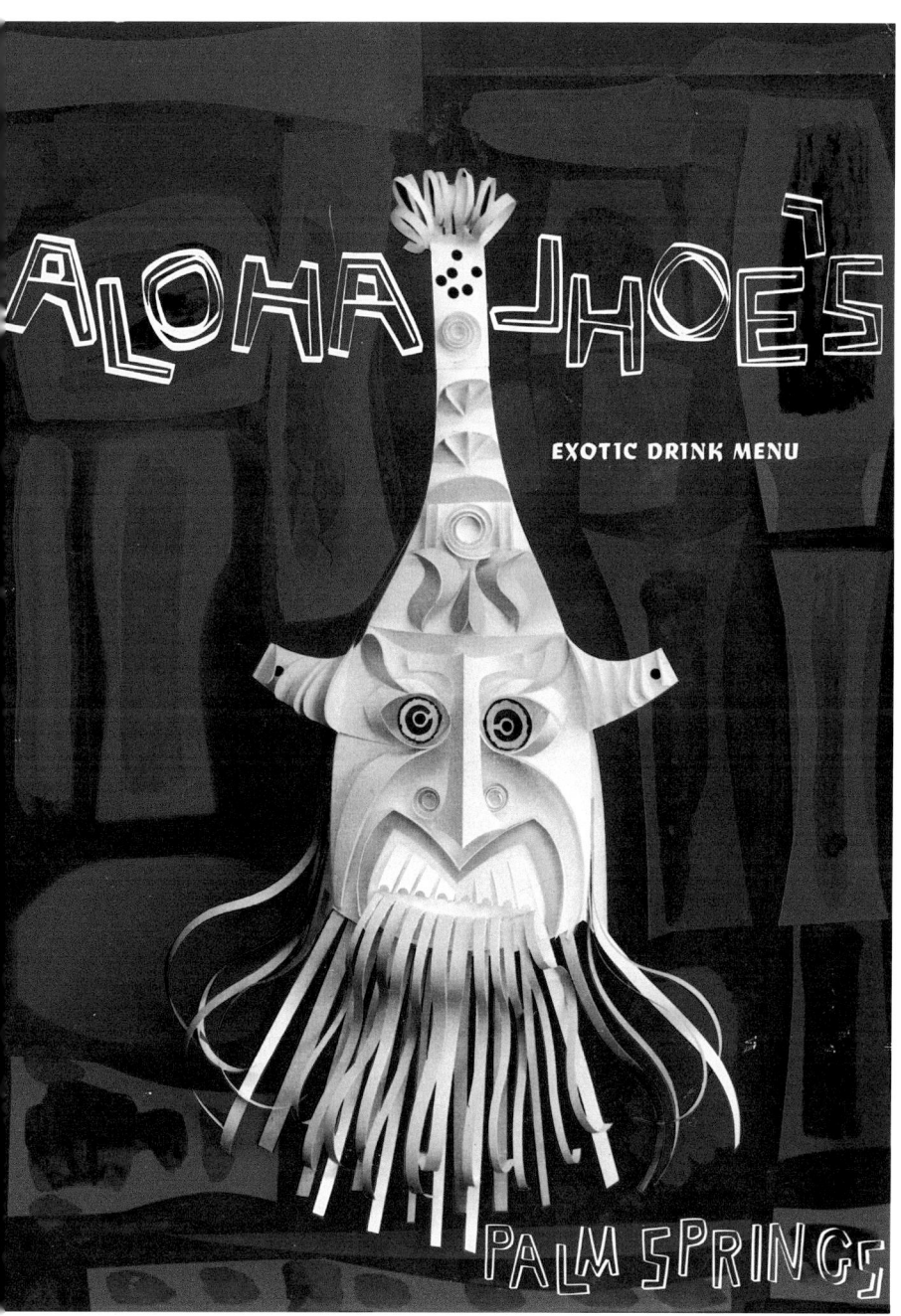

SI L'ÉLAN SOCIAL ET ÉCONOMIQUE

impulsé par l'accession d'Hawaii au rang d'État américain fait encore croître l'amour du pays pour la Polynésie, comment expliquer que le tiki ait supplanté la vahiné sur le trône de l'icône suprême à partir du milieu des années 1950 ? Une des raisons de cette prise de pouvoir est le fait que les Américains ont appris à aimer ce qu'on appelle « l'art primitif ». La classe moyenne découvre que la sculpture « indigène » complète à merveille un intérieur moderne.

Cette évolution du goût occidental puise ses racines au tout début du XXᵉ siècle, avec la première génération d'artistes modernes en Europe. Pablo Picasso et ses contemporains parisiens s'inspirent alors de la sculpture tribale africaine et océanienne, qu'ils considèrent comme la preuve que l'expression artistique ne peut se cantonner au naturalisme et aux portraits d'après nature. Le chef de file des surréalistes, André Breton, écrit un poème intitulé « Tiki ». Les

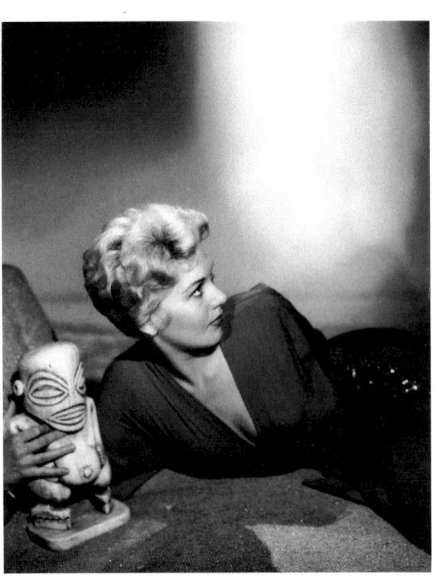

collectifs d'artistes comme le berlinois Die Brücke proclament leur droit et leur devoir d'appliquer à leur art propre et nouveau les formes subjectives et spirituelles qu'ils admirent dans l'art « primitif ». Quand les nazis ont commencé à qualifier ces œuvres de « dégénérées », certains de ces artistes acceptent l'invitation de la mécène Peggy Guggenheim et gagnent l'Amérique.

Fuyant le régime nazi, les artistes européens apportent leur sensibilité à la scène créative new-yorkaise. En 1946, le musée d'Art moderne de New York monte la première exposition majeure du pays dédiée aux arts des mers du Sud. Le magazine *Life* publie un article fouillé sur l'exposition, et cette iconographie entre dans la culture pop.

D'autres musées américains proposent dans la foulée des expositions d'art primitif et tribal, que l'élite culturelle se doit d'apprécier. Les décorateurs d'intérieur l'utilisent en contrepoint à un mobilier moderne, et les dernières acquisitions des ménages font partie des sujets de conversation les plus fréquents au cours de « cocktail parties ». Les rares pièces d'art polynésien ayant déjà été acquises par les musées, les collectionneurs privés se tournent vers l'art mélanésien.

Le film qui incarne la quintessence de cette tendance phare du milieu de siècle est la comédie romantique *L'Adorable Voisine* (1958). Kim Novak y incarne une propriétaire de galerie spécialisée en art tribal qui ensorcelle littéralement un gars lambda, campé par James Stewart. Le personnage de Novak est une femme libre, artiste et

LEFT: Kim Novak as a modern witch

OPPOSITE: Primitive lava stone head

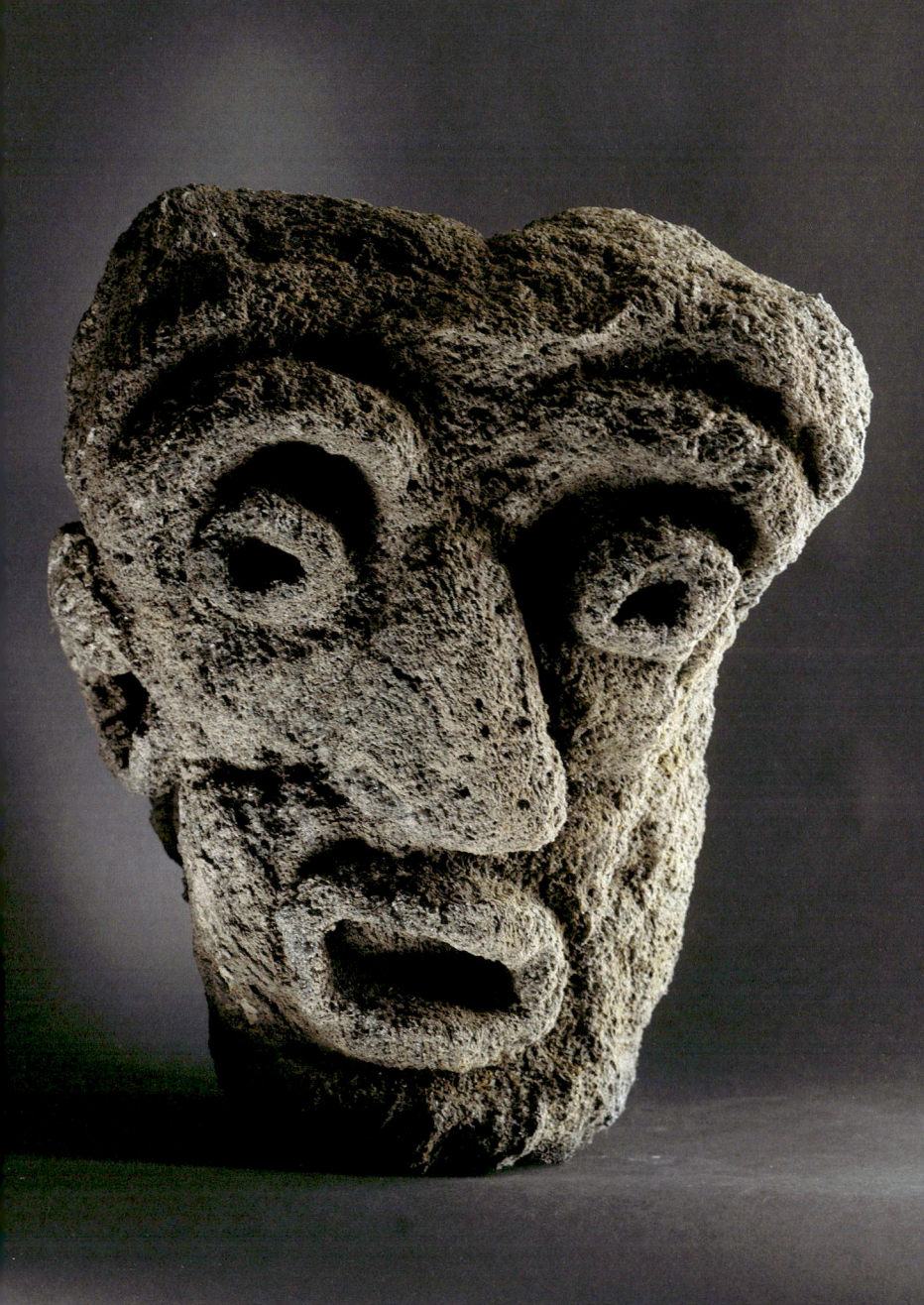

bohème, qui moule son corps dans des bodies noirs. Son frère, joué par Jack Lemmon, est un beatnik joueur de bongo, et Ernie Kovacs complète la bande dans le rôle d'un douteux chercheur en sorcellerie.

Au tournant du XXᵉ siècle, l'avant-garde moderne européenne avait découvert l'art tribal ; certaines pièces avaient été pour eux une révélation, qui leur avait permis de déconstruire l'art figuratif. Cinquante ans plus tard, le cubisme et l'abstrait sont des formes et des styles digérés, que s'approprie le graphisme contemporain. Les jeunes artistes appliquent dès lors cette esthétique métissée à leurs propres interprétations modernes de l'art océanien. L'évolution du primitivisme moderne a parfait son cycle.

Les composants stylistiques de l'art tiki moderne du milieu de siècle étaient en grande partie le fruit de cette verve moderniste, parfois proche d'un brutalisme naïf, parfois pétri d'influences cartoonesques. Les meilleurs exemples de ce style ont en partage une ingénuité et une fantaisie qui sont propres à cette époque et à ces lieux où ils ont été créés.

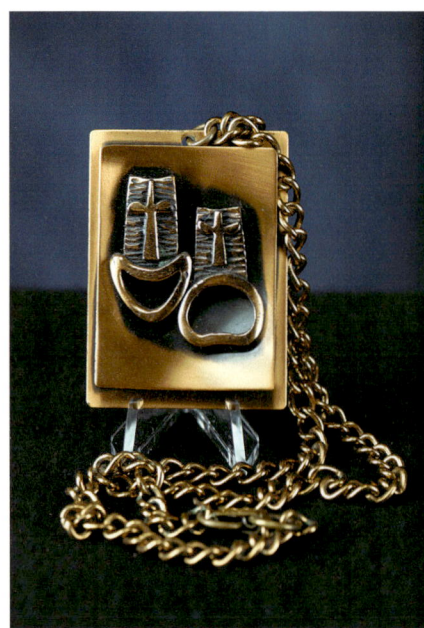

ABOVE: Menu cover for Aku-Aku restaurant, Toledo, Ohio (*Martijn Veltman Collection*)

RIGHT: Modern comedy and tragedy pendant

OPPOSITE: Cartoony salt and pepper shakers

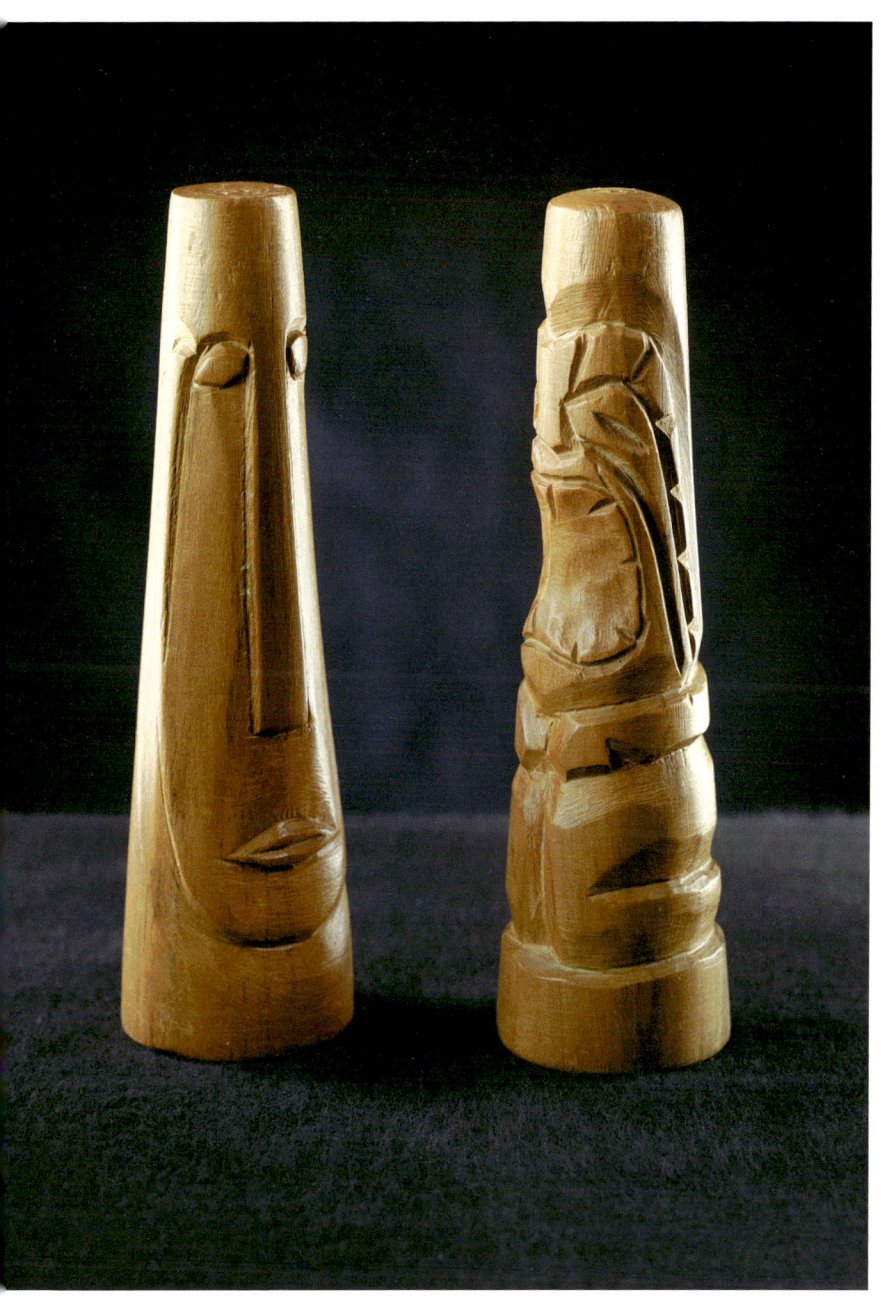

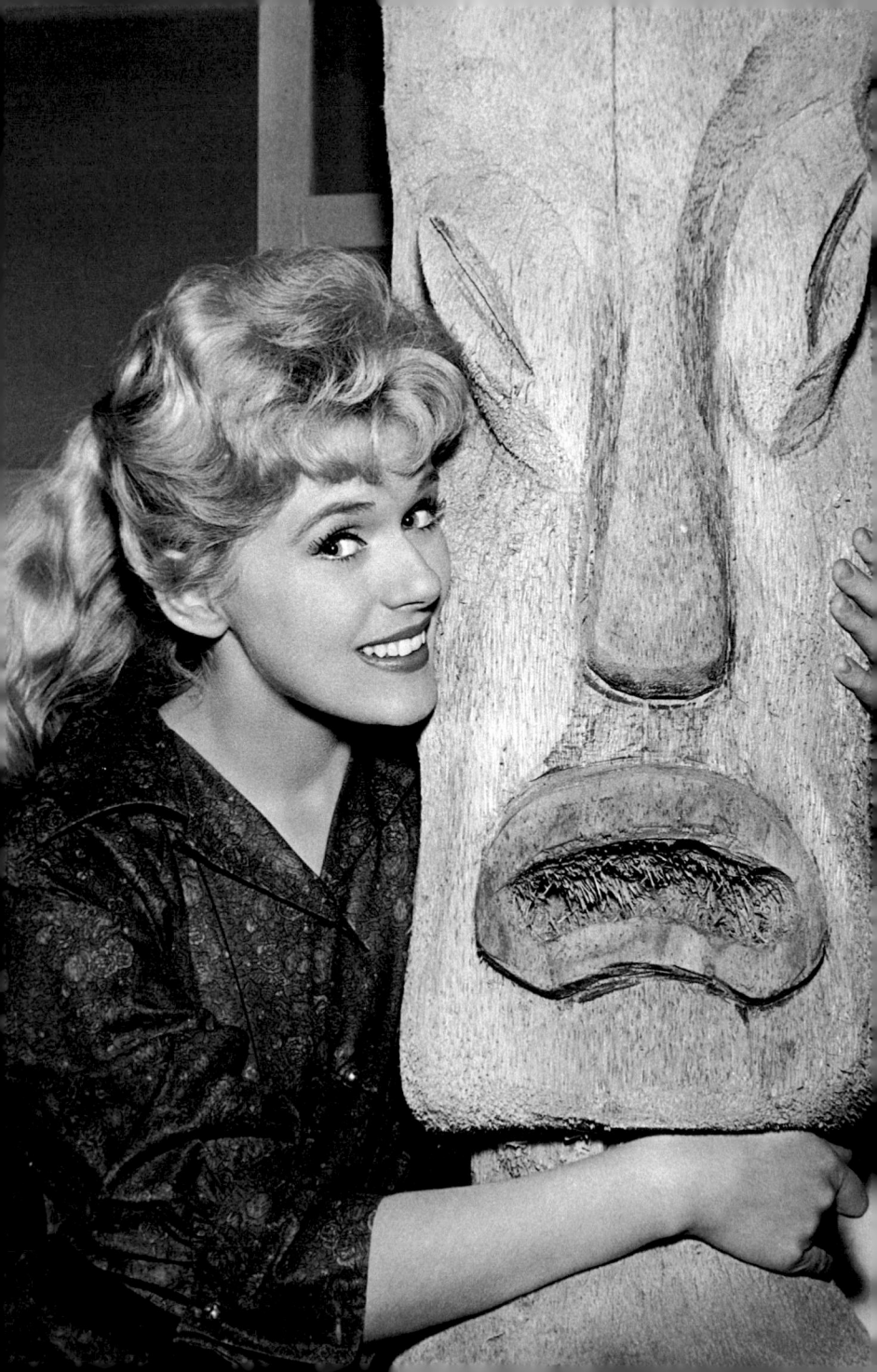

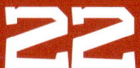

22

TIKI TV

TIKI-TV
LA TÉLÉ TIKI

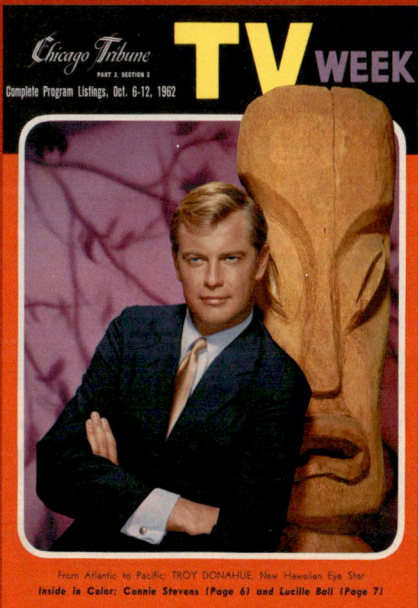

OPPOSITE: "Idol Worship: Connie Stevens learns things about this ancient Hawaiian god on the set of Warner Bros. Hawaiian Eye TV series" (text from 1959 press release)

ABOVE: Teen heartthrob Troy Donahue with the signature Tiki from the *Hawaiian Eye* office *(Kevin Kidney Collection)*

AMERICAN TIKI TRULY CAME INTO ITS
own when its image appeared on the new
mass medium that was supplanting movies
as America's favorite entertainment: television. By the late 1950s, there was a TV in
every American household; and the effect
of the logo Tiki from the *Hawaiian Eye* series
appearing in every living room cannot be
underestimated. TV was the happening
thing in America—Tiki was with it.

Hawaiian Eye was one of the spin-offs
from the successful detective series *77
Sunset Strip*. The "private eyes" of *Hawaiian
Eye* had their office next to Hilton Hawaiian
Village Hotel in Waikiki—actually a set on
the Warner Bros. lot in Burbank, California,
complete with a courtyard swimming pool.
The show ran from 1959 to 1963. Once
every year the cast flew to Hawaii to shoot
exterior location scenes.

The signature Tiki statue stood in the
reception area of the office set and, per
instructions of the producer, had to be
greeted or patted for luck whenever one
passed it. There also was the bamboo-clad
Shell Bar set, where cast member Connie
Stevens (as Cricket) sometimes performed
lounge numbers.

Parallel to *Hawaiian Eye*, another Tiki
TV series premiered in 1959. *Adventures in
Paradise* was developed by novelist James
Michener, and starred Gardner McKay as
a war veteran who plied the South Seas on
his schooner called the *Tiki*. The sailboat
had a figurehead in the shape of a grinning
Tiki, and McKay wore a miniature replica
of it around his neck. *Life* magazine
announced McKay as "the new Apollo for
the ladies," and the series banked on his
being a sex symbol.

Every episode featured a different exotic
beauty in a different port vying for McKay's

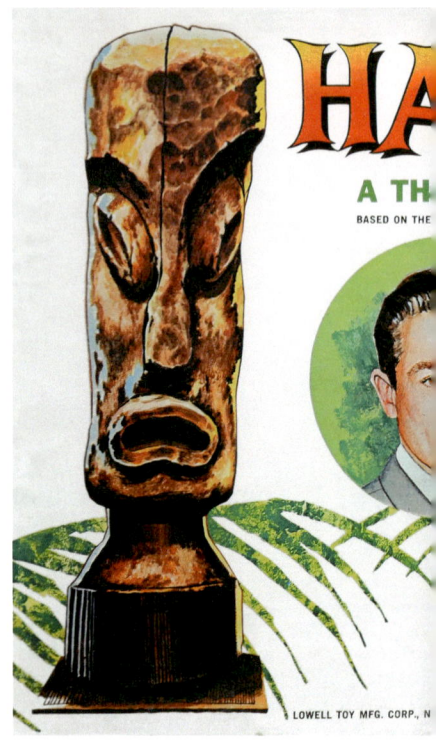

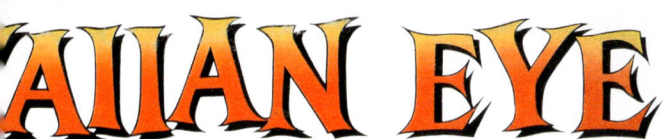

AIIAN EYE

GAME OF INTRIGUE AND SUSPENSE...

**Every Play
a Challenge
of Wits and Skill...**

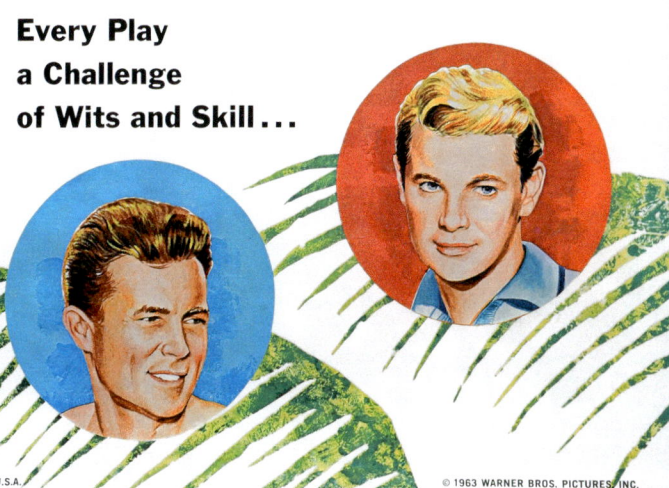

E IN U.S.A.

© 1963 WARNER BROS. PICTURES, INC.

RECOMMENDED
FOR
AGES
10
TO
ADULT

LOWELL
TOY MFG.
CORP.

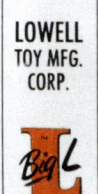

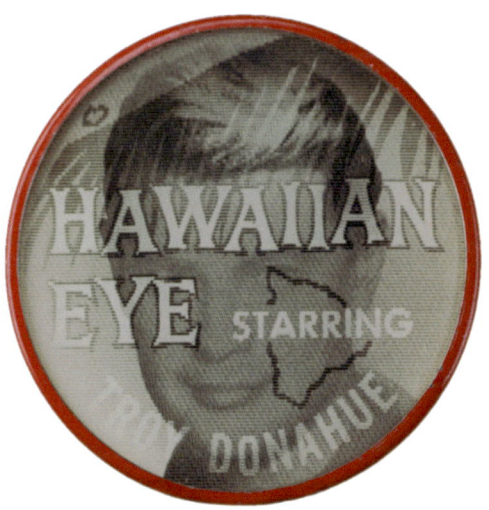

ABOVE: *Hawaiian Eye* board game
(Kevin Kidney Collection)

LEFT: Lenticular button for
Hawaiian Eye fans

WARNER BROS. PICTURES, INC.
BURBANK, CALIFORNIA

INTER-OFFICE COMMUNICATION

To Mr. DIRECTOR

From Mr. STANLEY NISS

Date _____

Subject ALL "HAWAIIAN EYE" PRODUCTIONS

The dressing of the Forecourt, Reception Office, Lanai Office, Shell Bar, Shell Bar Entrance, and Hotel Lobby has been established. There must be no variation from the set dressings established in earlier segments. We have stills available for your guidance.

We must remain consistent in other directions as well. In the daytime, Cricket always wears or carries a hat. She does not use the stroboscope with her camera in the daytime -- she uses an available-light camera. Apply body make-up to Tony Eisley whenever he is seen without a shirt.

A United Airlines poster must be displayed prominently in the window of Cricket's Corner.

We use a receptionist in the Reception Office during the daytime and a uniformed Security Guard the rest of the time.

The position of the cab-stand in relation to the hotel has already been established. Please check stills.

It has also been established that Tom and Tracy salute the tiki whenever they enter the Reception Office.

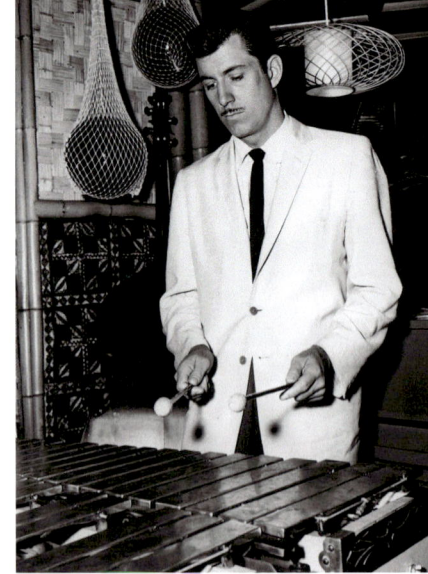

ABOVE: Production memo from producer Stanley Niss mentioning the Tiki *(Kevin Kidney Collection)*

RIGHT: Detective Anthony Eisley tries the vibes at the Shell Bar

OPPOSITE: Title card with logo Tiki

TIKI POP

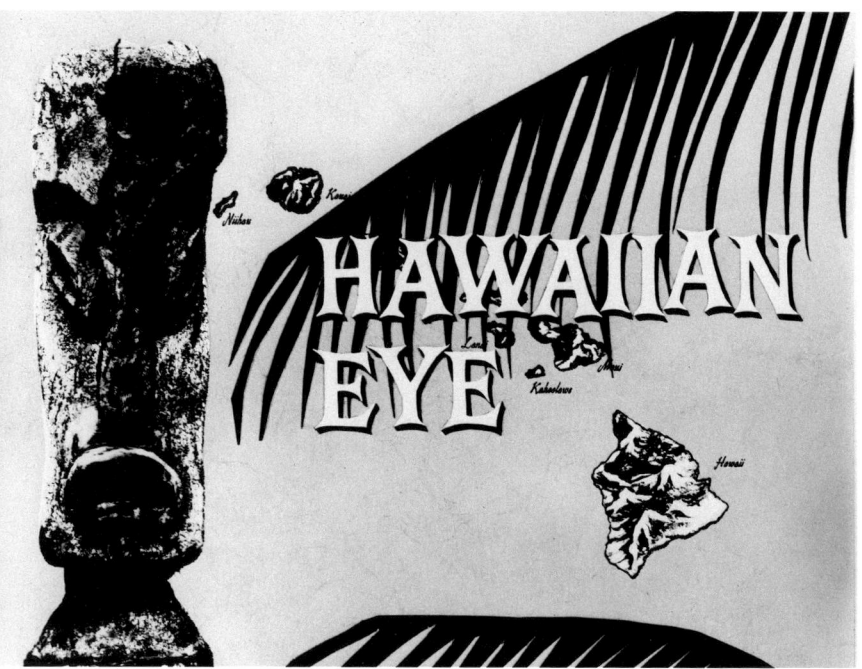

favors. The main location of the Tahitian village where the *Tiki* was anchored was classic Hollywood make-believe: the giant lagoon set on the 20th Century Fox Studios back lot was a water tank in which the ship sat on concrete pillars, the sails merely folded rolls of canvas.

Another South Seas TV series was *Captain David Grief*, based on Jack London's book about the adventures of a South Seas trader. Following in the footsteps of *Hawaiian Eye* was *Follow the Sun*, about two freelance journalists sharing a plush bachelor pad in Honolulu.

The series that best encapsulated the escapist philosophy of Tiki Pop was the short-lived *The Beachcomber*, starring Cameron Mitchell as John Lackland, a dropout from a high-paying executive job in San Francisco. In the trailer for the series, Mitchell addresses the viewer: "Do you ever dream of disappearing from the busy humdrum world, of maybe going to some wonderfully romantic place. . . for the rest of your life?"

The best-remembered, longest-running beachcomber-style TV show was undoubtedly *Gilligan's Island*. From 1964 to 1967, the comical castaways lived the Robinson Crusoe lifestyle, fashioning everything they needed from bamboo and palm fronds. The complete catalog of tropical-island clichés was exploited and parodied, among them the Tiki: in the episode "Waiting for Watubi," the Skipper believes himself cursed after uncovering the carved statue of "Kona."

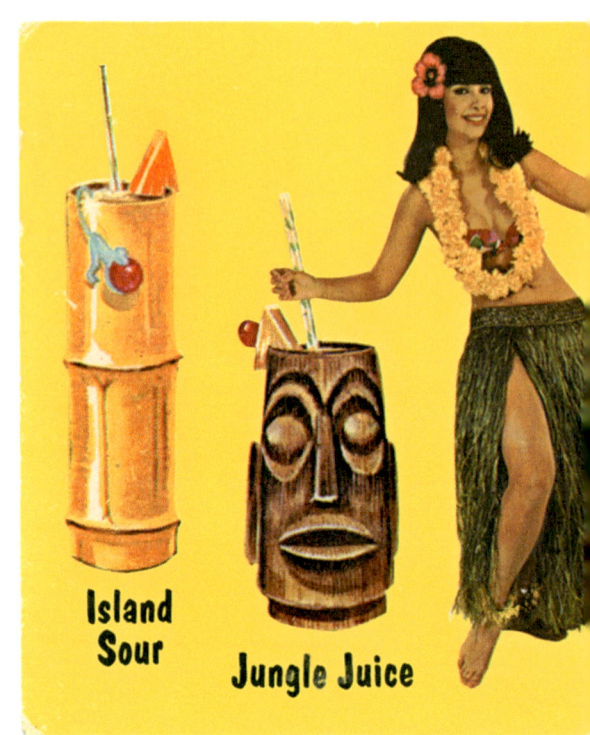

Island Sour

Jungle Juice

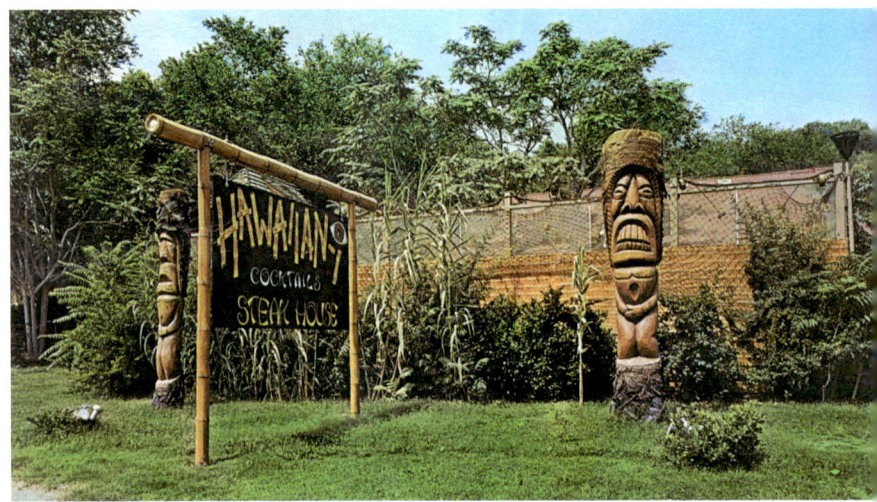

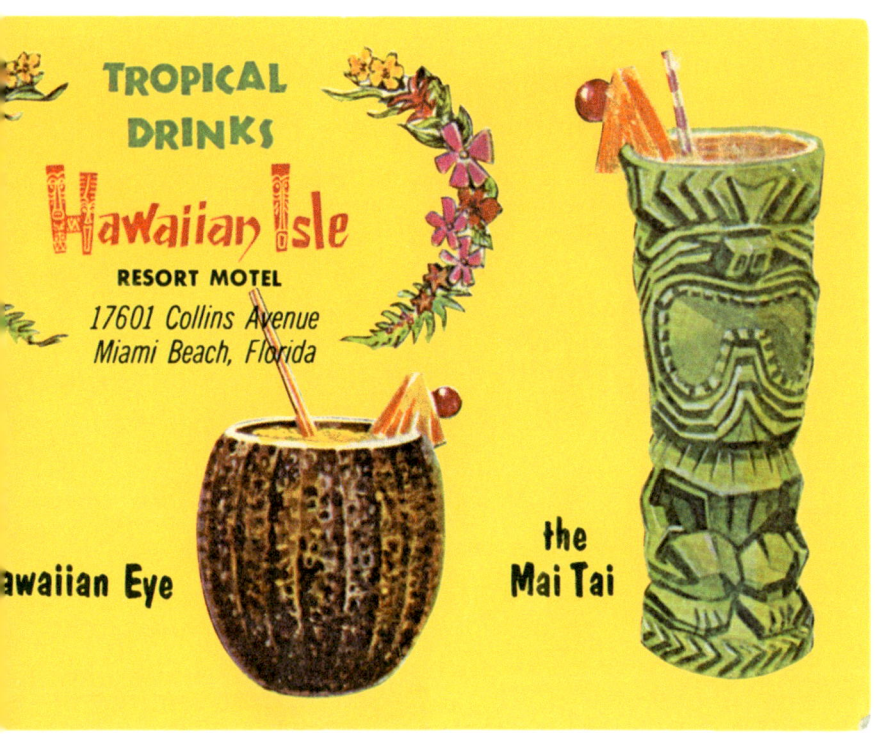

TROPICAL DRINKS

Hawaiian Isle
RESORT MOTEL

17601 Collins Avenue
Miami Beach, Florida

awaiian Eye

the
Mai Tai

DER AMERIKANISCHE TIKI ERREICHTE den Höhepunkt seiner Beliebtheit, als sein Abbild in dem Medium gezeigt wurde, das die Kinos von der Spitze der wichtigsten Unterhaltungsformen verdrängte: dem Fernseher. In den späten 1950er-Jahren hatte jeder amerikanische Haushalt ein TV-Gerät. Der Einfluss des Tiki-Logos der Fernsehserie *Hawaiian Eye,* die in jedem amerikanischen Wohnzimmer lief, darf nicht unterschätzt werden. Das Fernsehen war eine der größten Errungenschaften Amerikas – und Tiki war mit von der Partie.

Hawaiian Eye war ein Ableger der erfolgreichen Krimiserie *77 Sunset Strip.* Die Privatdetektive hatten ihr Büro direkt neben dem Hilton Hawaiian Village Hotel in Waikiki – eigentlich ein Filmset inklusive Pool der Warner Bros. im kalifornischen Burbank. Die Serie lief von 1959 bis 1963. Einmal im Jahr flogen Schauspieler und Crew für Außenaufnahmen nach Hawaii.

Die charakteristische Tiki-Statue stand im Empfangsbereich des Büro-Sets. Der Produzent sah in ihr einen Talisman und verlangte, dass jeder, der sie passierte, sie grüßte oder tätschelte. Es gab auch ein Set der bambusverkleideten Shell Bar, wo Connie Stevens als Sängerin Cricket Blake manchmal auftrat.

Gleichzeitig mit *Hawaiian Eye* startete 1959 eine weitere Tiki-Serie, *Adventures in*

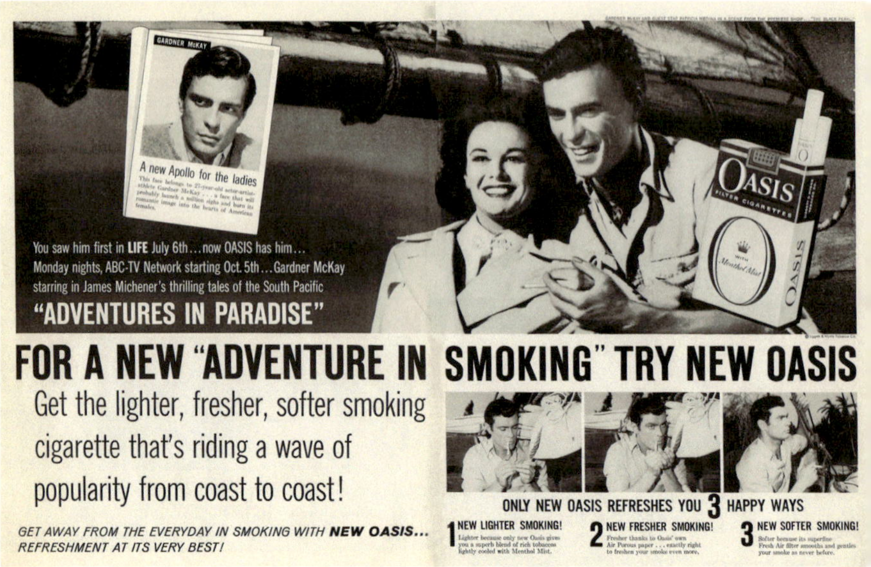

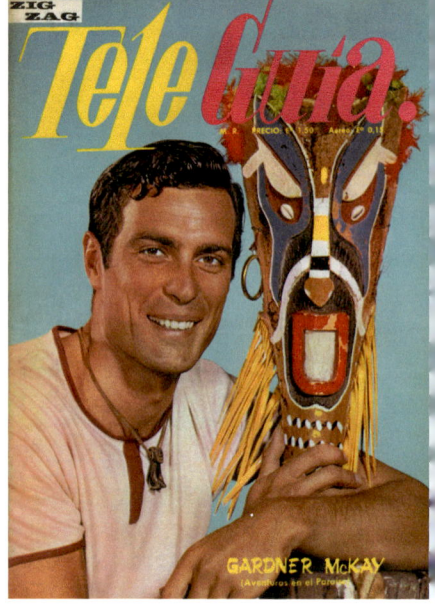
Paradise, die Romanautor James Michener
entwickelt hatte. Gardner McKay spielte
einen Kriegsveteranen, der auf einem Scho-
ner namens *Tiki* durch die Südsee fuhr. Das
Segelboot hatte eine Galionsfigur in Form
eines grinsenden Tiki, die McKay in Miniaturform um den Hals trug. Das Magazin
Life kündigte McKay als „den neuen Apollo
für die Damenwelt" an und die Serie ver-
ließ sich auf dessen Status als Sexsymbol.

In jeder Folge warb eine andere exotische Schönheit in irgendeinem Hafen um
McKays Gunst. Der Hauptschauplatz –
das tahitische Dorf, wo die *Tiki* vor Anker
lag – war ein typischer Hollywood-Schwin-
del. Die Lagune befand sich auf dem
Studiogelände von 20th Century Fox und
war nicht mehr als ein Wasserbecken, in
dem das Schiff auf Betonpfeilern ruhte.
Die Segel waren gefaltete Baumwollstoffe.

OPPOSITE ABOVE: Sponsor cigarette ad quoting the *Life* article

OPPOSITE BELOW: Gardner McKay wearing his Tiki amulet *(Kevin Kidney Collection)*

BELOW: Record cover showing the village set with the good ship *Tiki*

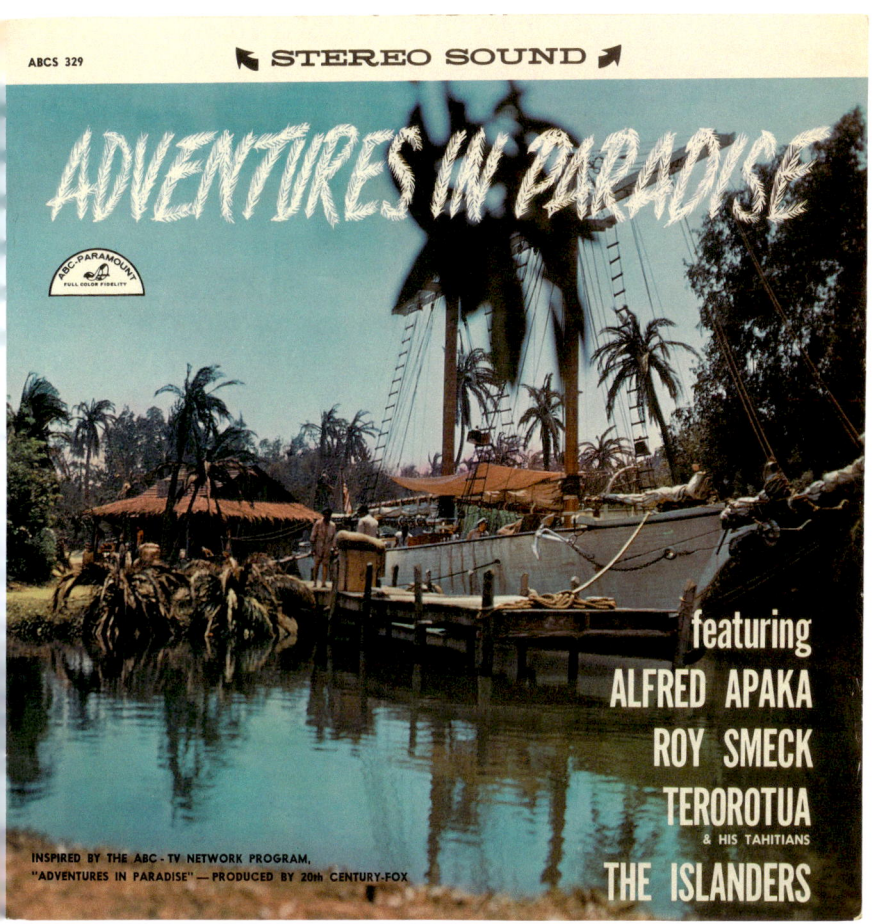

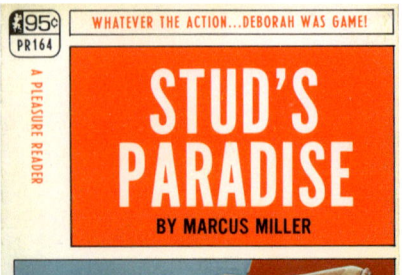

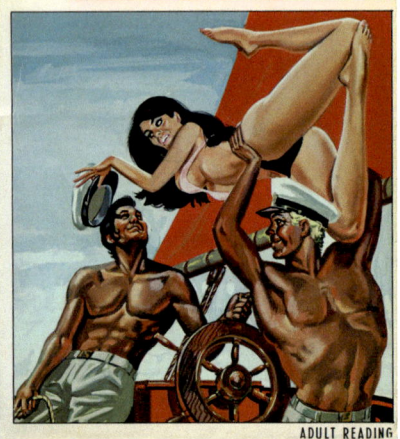

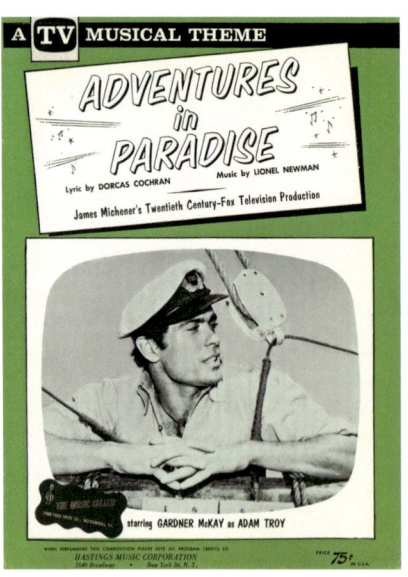

Eine weitere Südsee-Fernsehserie war *Käpt'n Grief an Bord*. Sie basierte auf Jack Londons Buch über die Abenteuer eines Südseehändlers. In den Fußstapfen von *Hawaiian Eye* folgte *Unter heißem Himmel,* eine Serie über zwei freiberufliche Journalisten, die sich eine schicke Junggesellenbude in Honolulu teilten.

Die Produktion, die den eskapistischen Geist des Tiki-Pop am besten einfing, war *The Beachcomber* mit Cameron Mitchell als John Lackland, der seinem gutbezahlten Managerposten in San Francisco den Rücken kehrte. Im Trailer der Serie fragt Mitchell die Zuschauer: „Träumen Sie je davon, dem geschäftigen Treiben dieser Welt zu entfliehen, an einen wundervollen, romantischen Ort zu reisen… vielleicht für den Rest Ihres Lebens?"

Die einprägsamste und langlebigste Beachcomber-Serie war ohne Zweifel *Gilligans Insel*. Von 1964 bis 1967 lebten die ulkigen Schiffbrüchigen den Lifestyle Robinson Crusoes. Alles, was sie brauchten, bauten sie sich aus Bambus und Palmblättern. Hier wurde der vollständige Katalog an Inselklischees ausgeschöpft und parodiert – Tiki inbegriffen. In der Folge „Waiting for Watubi" wähnt sich der Skipper verflucht, nachdem er eine geschnitzte Kona-Statue entdeckt hat.

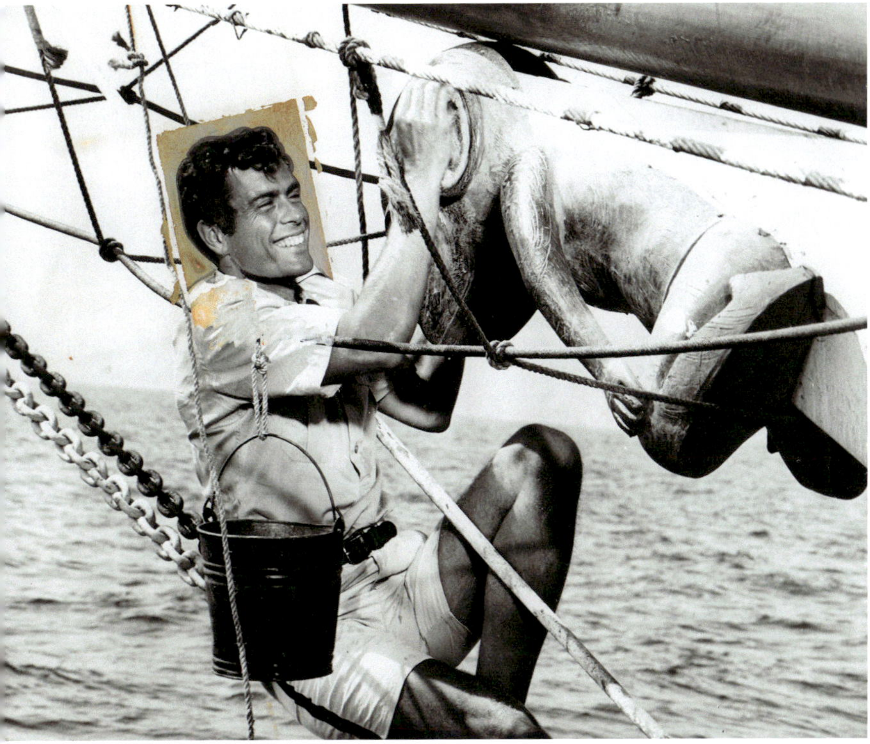

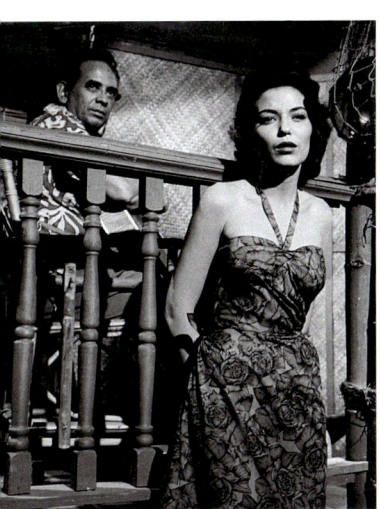

OPPOSITE ABOVE: Exploitation paperback referencing the series

OPPOSITE BELOW: The theme song became a standard covered in countless versions

ABOVE: Gardner McKay polishing his Tiki

LEFT: Actress/singer Linda Lawson appeared in six episodes

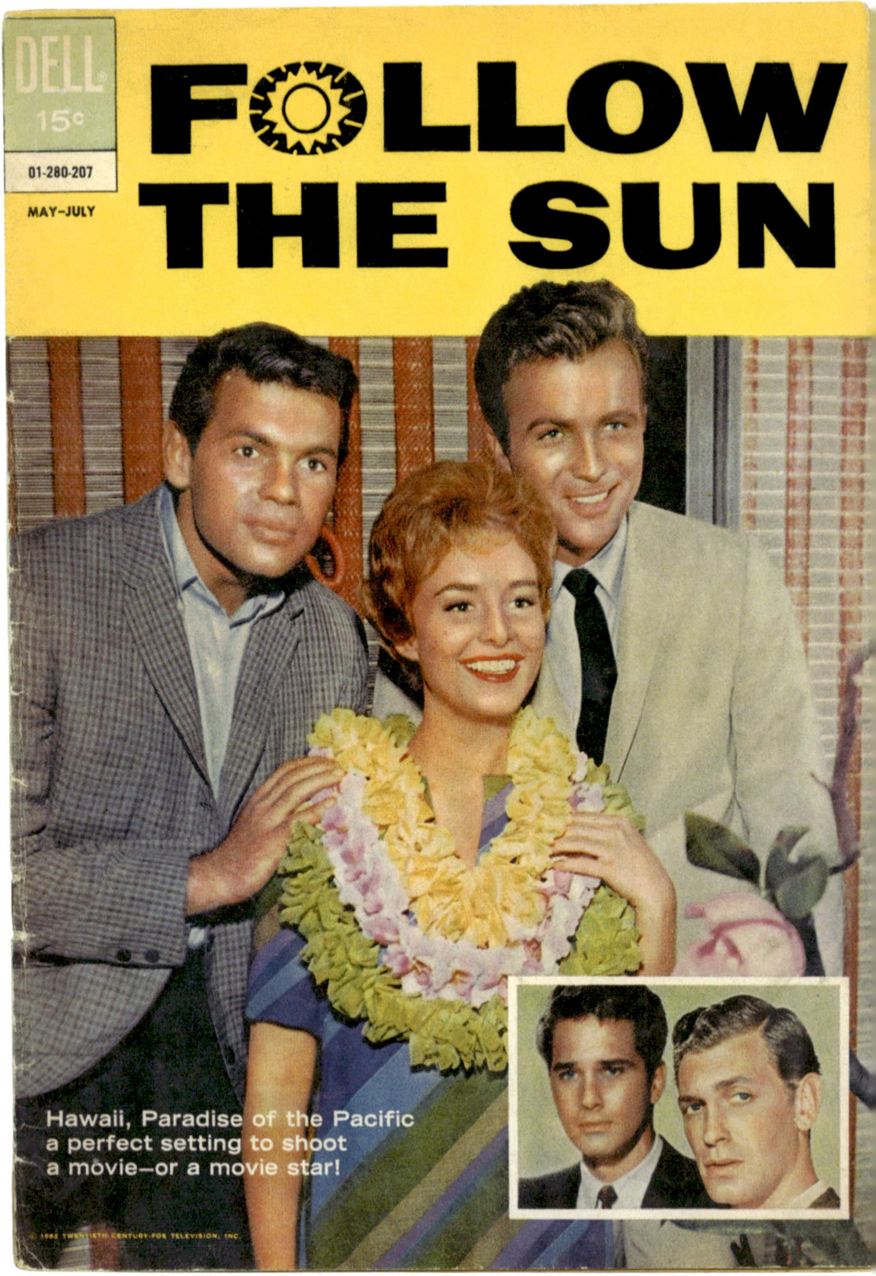

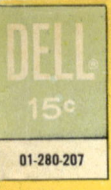

FOLLOW THE SUN

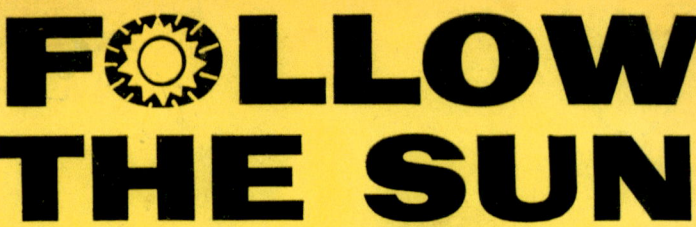

DELL 15¢

01-280-207

MAY–JULY

Hawaii, Paradise of the Pacific
a perfect setting to shoot
a movie—or a movie star!

© 1962 TWENTIETH CENTURY-FOX TELEVISION, INC.

TIKI PO

LE TIKI AMÉRICAIN PREND SON ENVOL

orsque son image apparaît dans le média
le masse qui supplante alors le cinéma au
ang de moyen de divertissement favori
les Américains : la télévision. À la fin des
nnées 1950, chaque ménage possède un
éléviseur, et l'effet produit par le logo tiki
lans le générique de la série *Intrigues à
Hawaï* ne doit pas être sous-estimé. La télévi-
ion est ce qui se fait de mieux à l'époque, et
e tiki *made in America* fait partie du voyage.

Intrigues à Hawaï est l'un des dérivés
le la série policière à succès *77 Sunset Strip*.
Les bureaux des « privés » d'*Intrigues à
Hawaï* sont situés juste à côté du village
hôtelier Hilton Hawaiian de Waikiki – en
éalité un décor appartenant à Warner
Brothers à Burbank, en Californie, équipé
l'une grande piscine. La série est diffusée
le 1959 à 1963. Une fois par an, les acteurs
e rendaient à Hawaii pour tourner d'un
oloc les scènes en extérieur.

Une statue de Tiki reconnaissable entre
mille trône dans le hall d'accueil des bureaux
les « privés », sur instruction des produc-
eurs, qui exigent aussi que tous les membres
le l'équipe le saluent et lui tapotent l'épaule
u passage pour porter chance à la série.
l y a aussi le plateau où a été construit le
Shell Bar bardé de bambou dedans comme
lehors, où l'actrice Connie Stevens (dans le
ôle de Cricket) s'expose parfois dans des
uuméros de music-hall exotique.

Parallèlement à *Intrigues à Hawaï,* une
utre série télévisée débute en 1959 dans
a même veine tiki. *Aventures dans les îles*
st une création du romancier James

Michener, dans laquelle Gardner McKay
joue un vétéran qui a écumé les mers
du Sud à bord de son schooner baptisé
Tiki. Le voilier arbore une figure de proue
en forme de tiki grimaçant, et McKay en
porte une réplique miniature autour du
cou. Le magazine *Life* qualifie McKay de
« nouvel Apollon de ses dames », et la
série repose presque exclusivement sur
ses charmes.

Chaque épisode expose une nouvelle
beauté exotique dans un port différent,
toujours en quête des faveurs de McKay.
Le lieu principal de la série, un village

tahitien où le *Tiki* est amarré, est un grand classique de factice kitch hollywoodien : le lagon géant reconstitué sur un terrain de la 20th Century Fox est en réalité un réservoir dans lequel le bateau est fixé sur des piliers en béton – les voiles sont de simples rouleaux de toile.

Parmi les autres séries situées dans les îles du Pacifique figure *Captain David Grief,* adapté d'un livre de Jack London sur les aventures d'un négociant des mers du Sud. Vient ensuite, sur les traces d'*Intrigues à Hawaï,* la série *Ombres sur le soleil,* sur deux journalistes indépendants qui partagent une garçonnière de luxe à Honolulu.

Les feuilletons qui capturent et traduisent le mieux la philosophie de l'évasion au cœur de la culture pop tiki sont *The Beachcomber,* qui ne resta pas longtemps à l'écran, avec Cameron Mitchell dans le rôle de John Lackland, qui vient de perdre un travail très bien payé à San Francisco. Dans la bande-annonce, Mitchell s'adresse au téléspectateur : « Il ne vous arrive jamais de rêver que vous disparaissez de ce monde trépidant, que vous lâchez votre train-train, peut-être pour vous envoler vers une destination romantique7 et ne jamais en revenir ? »

La série la plus célèbre de cette catégorie et celle qui est restée le plus longtemps sur

WEDNESDAYS 8:00 P.M.
get
away
from
it
all...
with
CAMERON MITCHELL
AS **THE BEACHCOMBER**
WFMY-TV 2

RIGHT: Program-guide ad for *The Beachcomber*

OPPOSITE: Cameron Mitchell as beachcomber John Lackland on the show's set in Florida, 1962

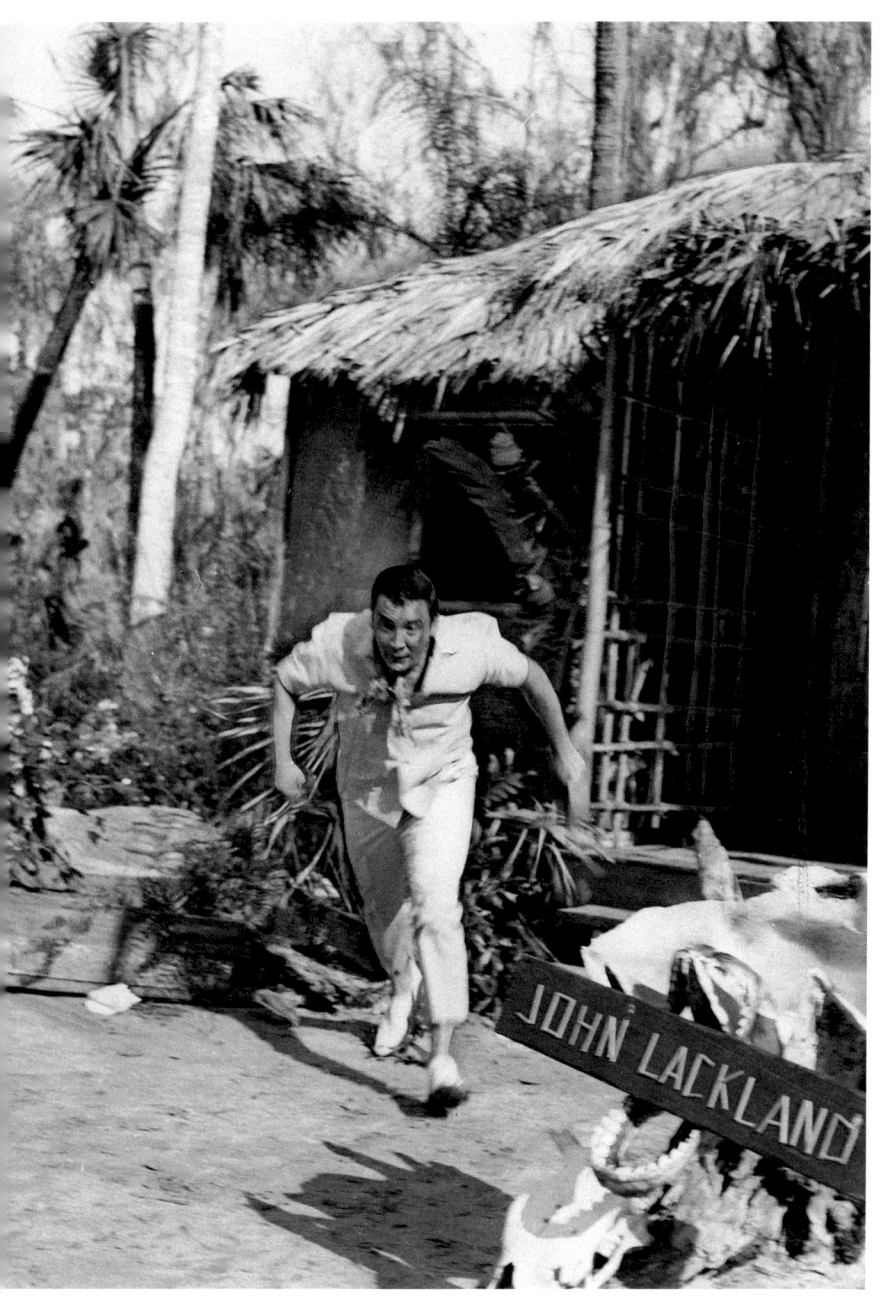

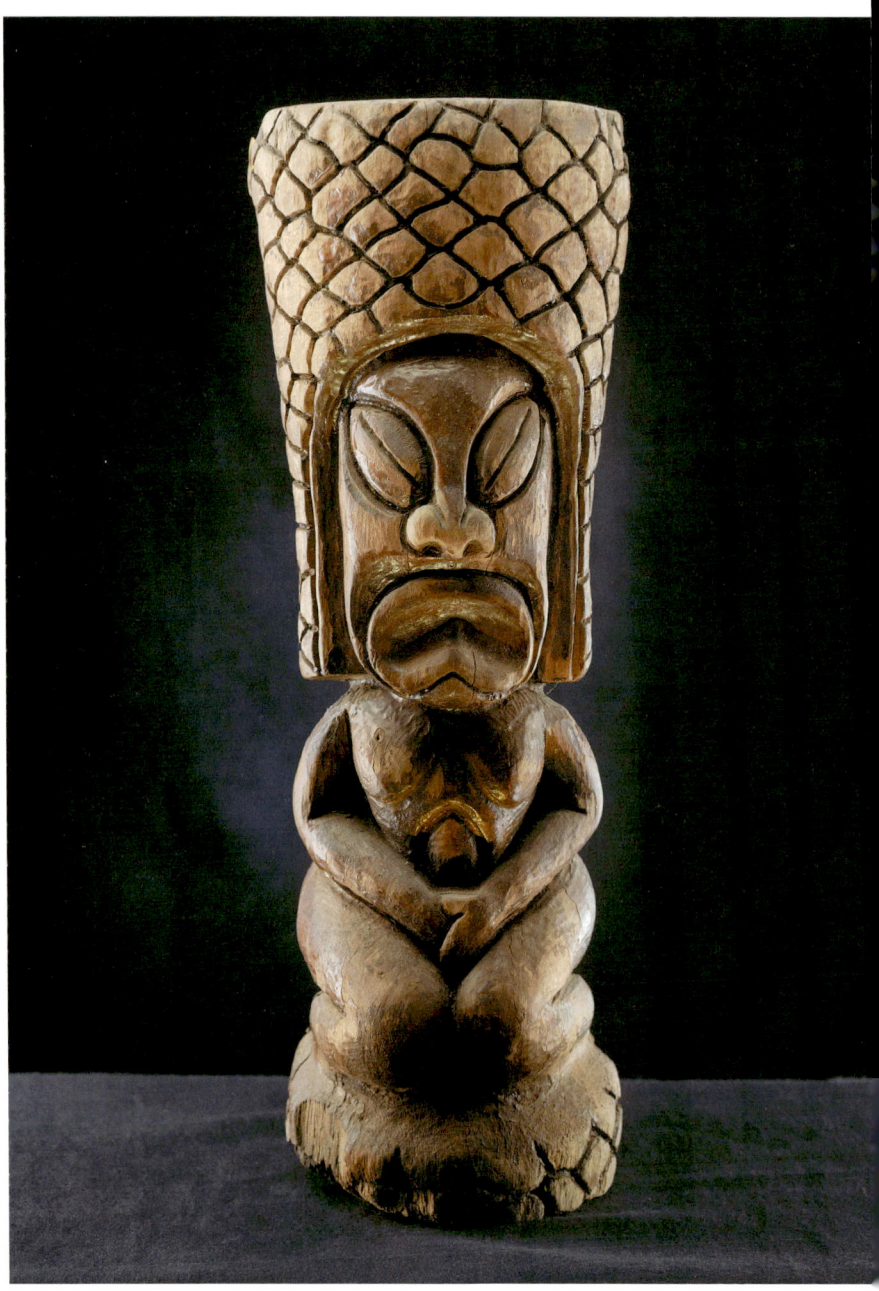

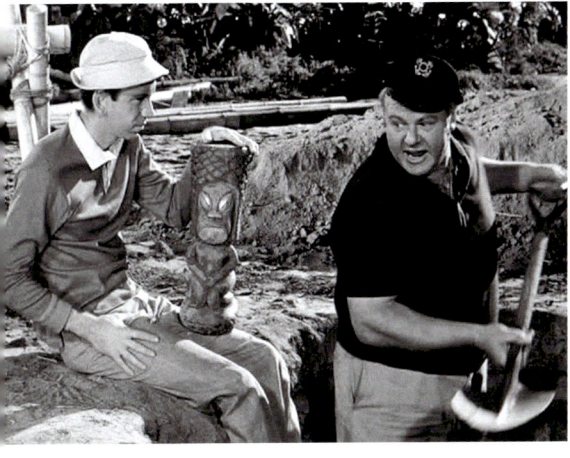

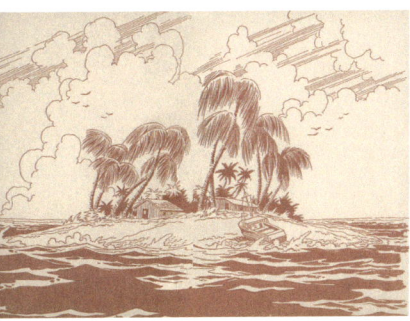

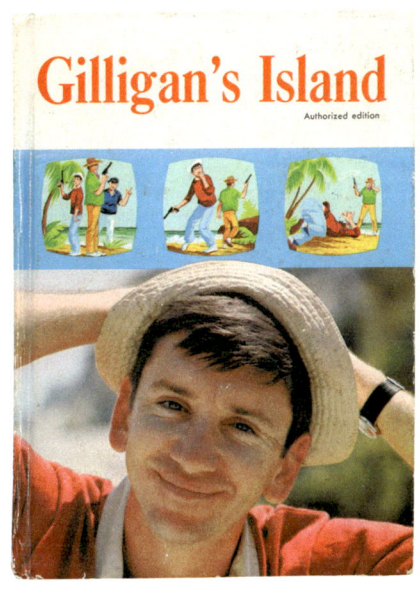

les écrans, est sans aucun doute *L'Île aux*
naufragés. De 1964 à 1967, ces marginaux
omiques vivent comme des Robinson en
abriquant tout ce dont ils ont besoin avec
e bambou et les feuilles de palmier qu'ils
rouvent autour d'eux. La série abuse de
out le catalogue des clichés tropicaux, donc
ussi du tiki, qu'elle exploite et parodie :
lans l'épisode « En attendant Watubi », le
kipper se croit envoûté après avoir déterré
ne statue sculptée de « Kona ».

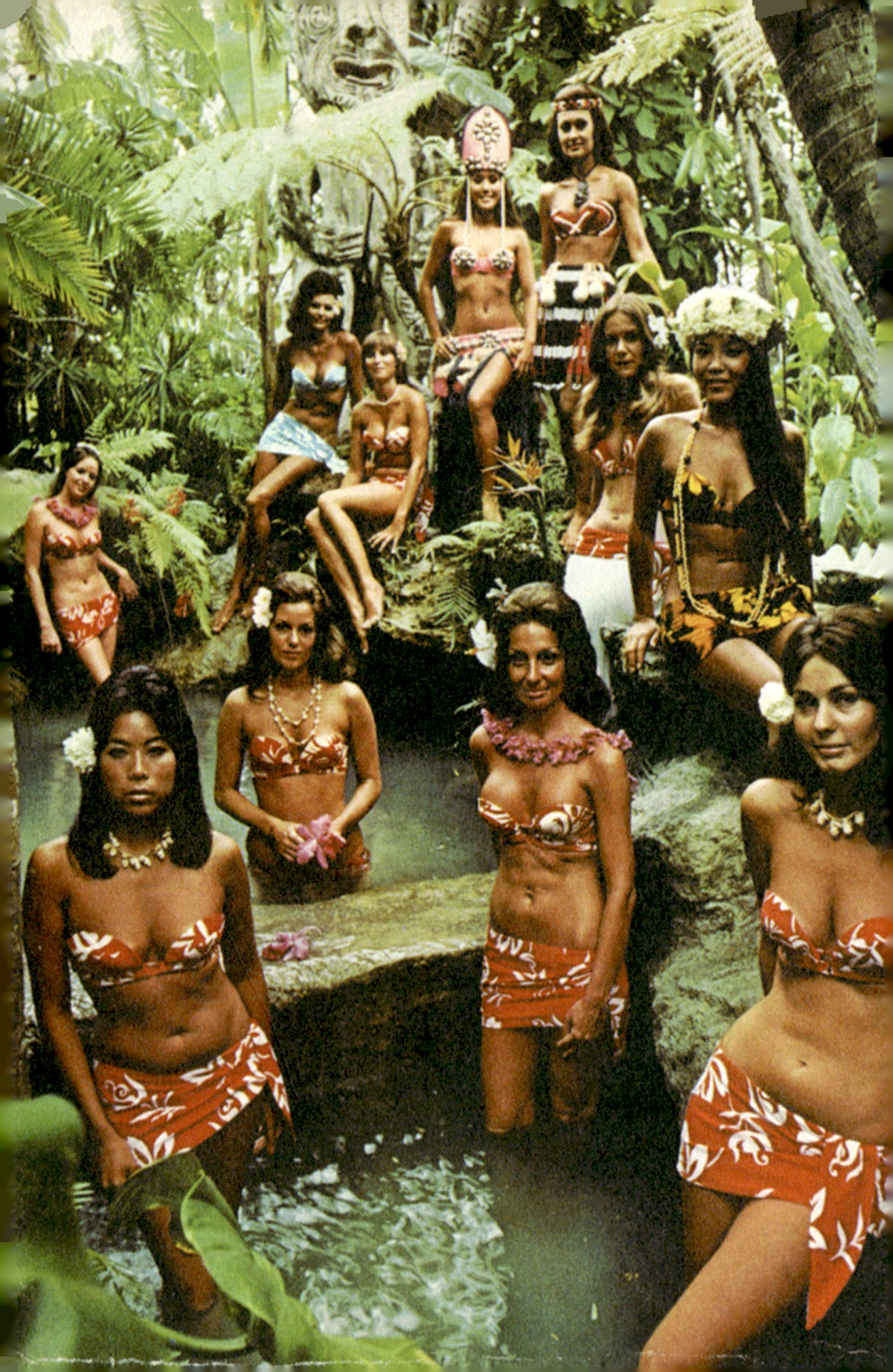

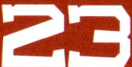

23

GRAND TIKI TEMPLES: THE MAI-KAI

DIE GROSSEN TIKI-TEMPEL – MAI-KAI
GRANDS TEMPLES TIKI – LE MAI-KAI

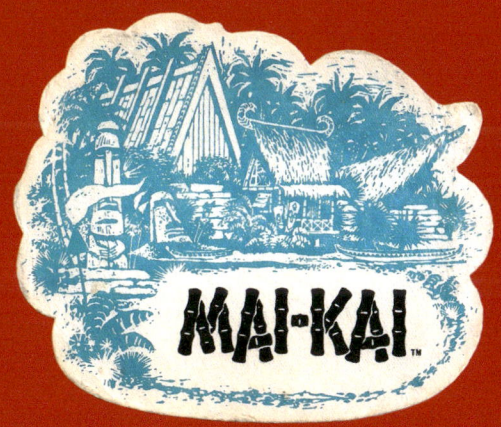

OPPOSITE: The Mai-Kai girls await you on their suburban island
(Tim Glazner Collection)

ABOVE: Drink coaster showing Mai-Kai exterior
(Scott Schell Collection)

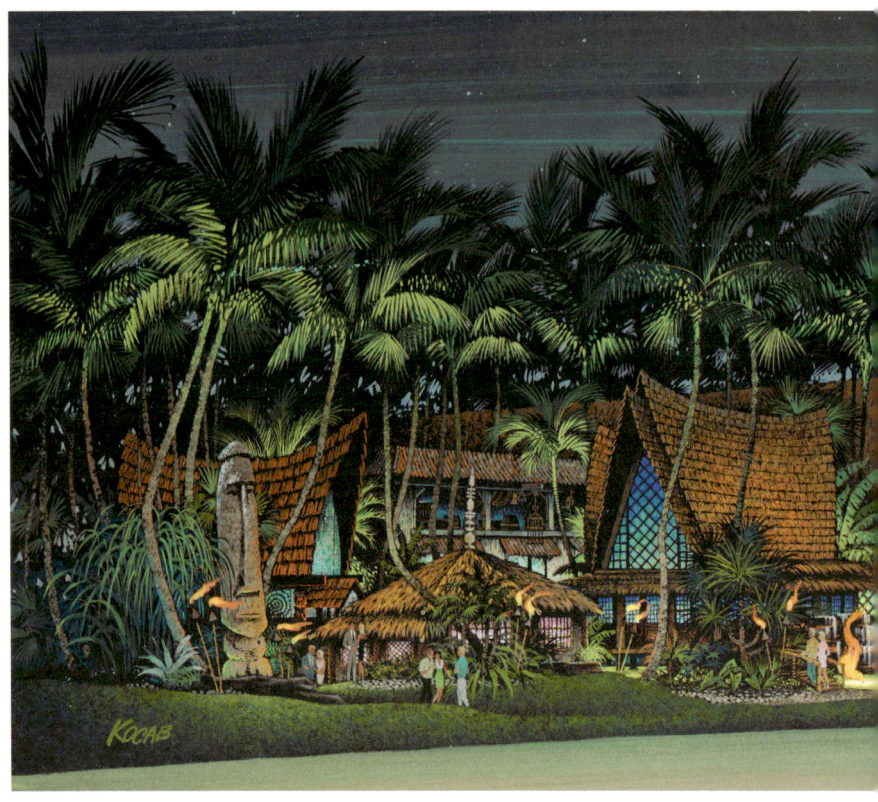

IN THE HISTORY OF TIKI POP THERE
are those places that transcend all of the
other Tiki places, large or small. One of
these is the Mai-Kai in Fort Lauderdale,
Florida, built by brothers Bob and Jack
Thornton in 1956. It is a virtual Taj Mahal
of Tiki and stands today in its original
form—which makes it the last grand Tiki
temple still in existence.

The Thorntons were transplants from
Chicago, where they had been inspired
by the Chicago outpost of Don the Beachcomber. So much so, according to Mai-Kai
researcher Tim "Swanky" Glazner, that
they hired the manager and bar staff away

from Don's to ensure that their new restaurant offered the same quality of service. In
addition, they made one change important
to the birth of Tiki Pop: Don had always
owned a set of mascot Tikis known as the
"Tahitian Cannibal Carvings," but he had
never used them for promotional purposes.
The Thorntons showed themselves as stan-
dard-bearers of the coming Tiki generation
by adopting these figures as the Mai-Kai's
trademark.

While the Mai-Kai's large exterior Tikis
were idols by California carver Barney West,
much of the interior statuary was copied
from the 1956 book *Oceanic Art*. An early

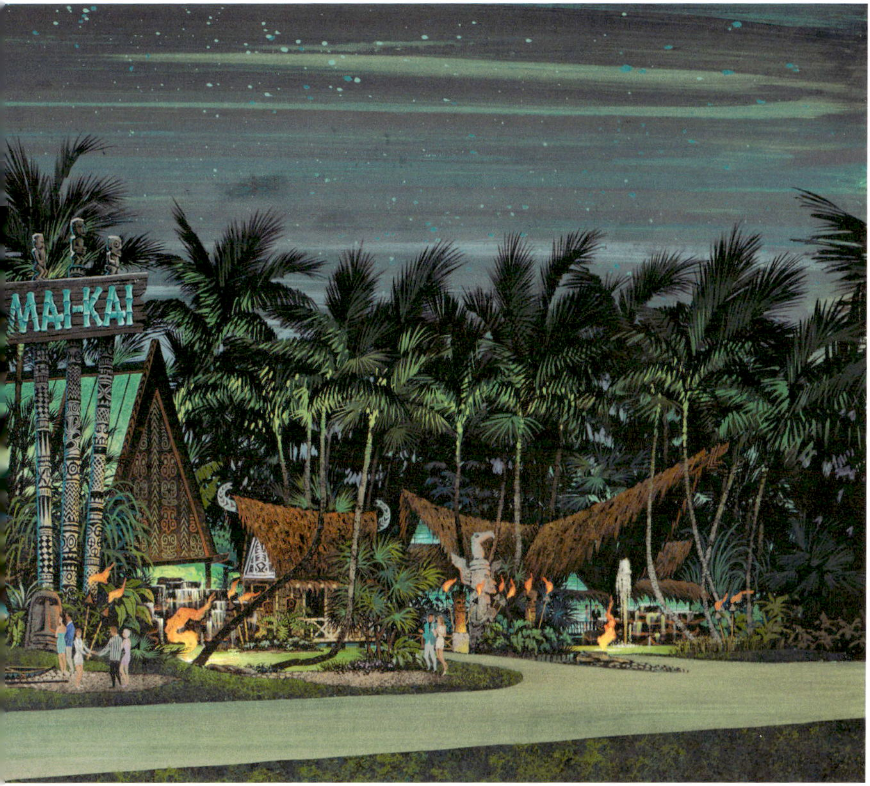

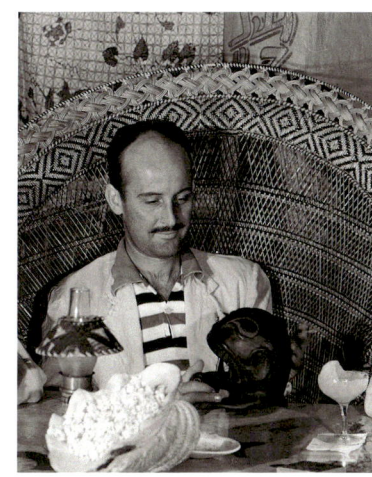

ABOVE: Grand Mai-Kai rendering by
I Kocab *(Mai-Kai Collection)*

GHT: Don the Beachcomber with
ne of his pet Tikis
Vincent Jefferds Collection)

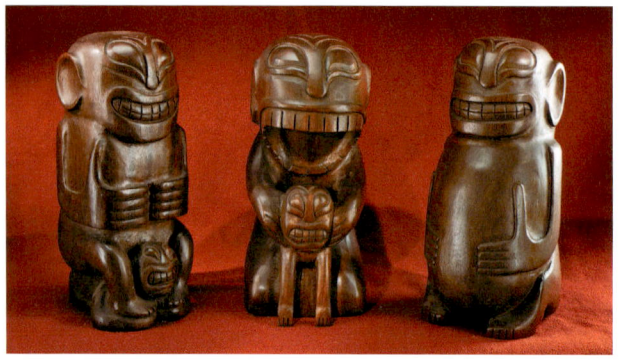

ABOVE: The Tahitian Cannibal Carvings: The Catcher, the Eater, and the Sated (*Kate Simmons Collection*)

BELOW: Grand-opening ad with Cannibal Carving logo Tikis

OPPOSITE: 1958 Mai-Kai ad with logo Tikis (*Tim Glazner Collection*)

REMEMBER!
GRAND OPENING
TOMORROW NIGHT!

MAI-KAI
POLYNESIAN RESTAURANT
3599 North Federal Highway
FORT LAUDERDALE, FLORIDA
For reservations phone **LO**gan **6-1513**

Mai-Kai ad announced: "Our Tiki smiles at you. He smiles because he is a Mai-Kai Tiki. . . he is amidst twenty-odd tons of authentic island décor." Another part of this décor was composed of artifacts from Papua New Guinea, collected by the Thorntons. This led to the Melanesian designs on the Mai-Kai's mugs and menus.

But the Thornton brothers did not forget the hula girl. The female presence was an important factor in the Mai-Kai's appeal. The dancers and waitresses were required to meet certain beauty standards, which were abundantly featured in "Mai-Kai Girl of the Month" calendars and on the cover of the Mai-Kai's *Happy Talk* magazine. The Mai-Kai girls were also sought-after performers at promotional events and parties.

The 1960s were the high times of the swinging bachelor, personified by Hugh Hefner and his Playboy clubs. With its bevy of beauties, the Mai-Kai embodied a Tiki version of the Playboy lifestyle. Projecting the male fantasy of tropical polygamy that was perpetuated in films and magazines, the Mai-Kai was the island every man wanted to be shipwrecked on. Although today's male is more pragmatic, the Mai-Kai is still a place to dream.

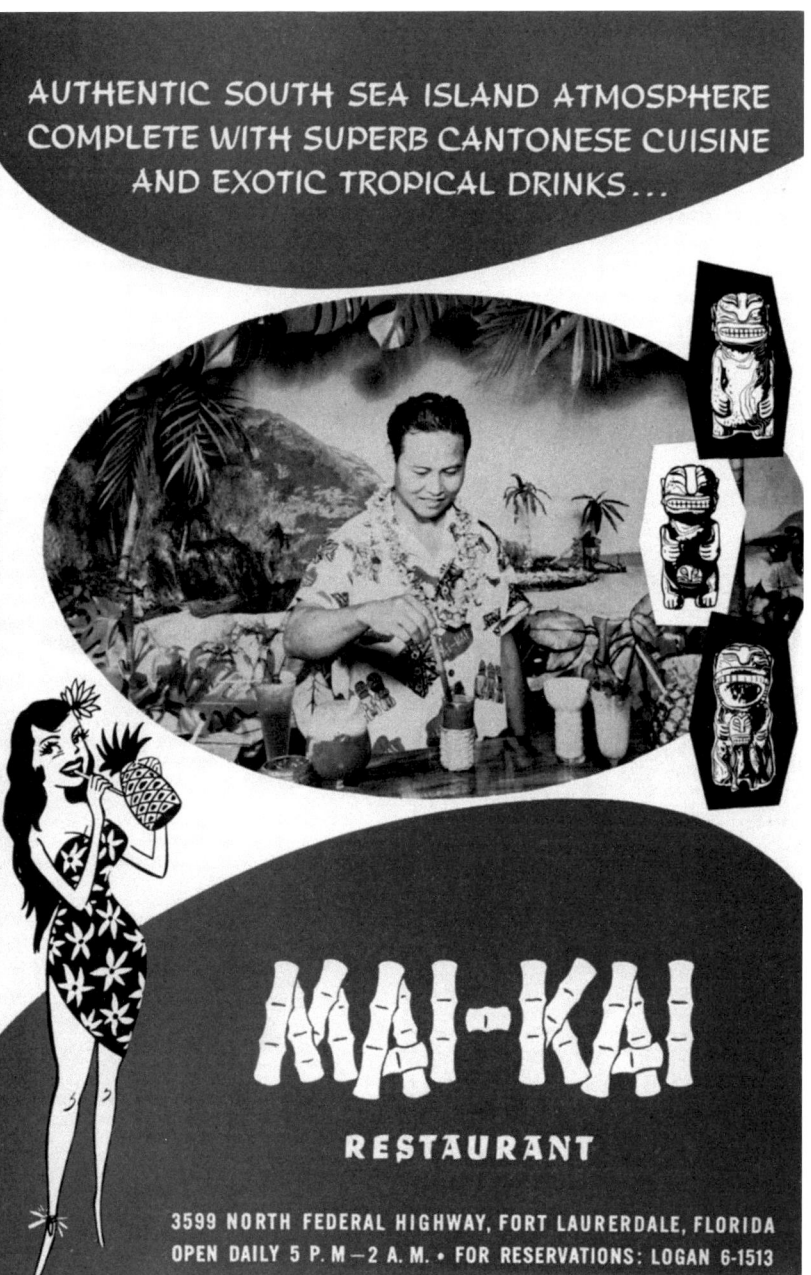

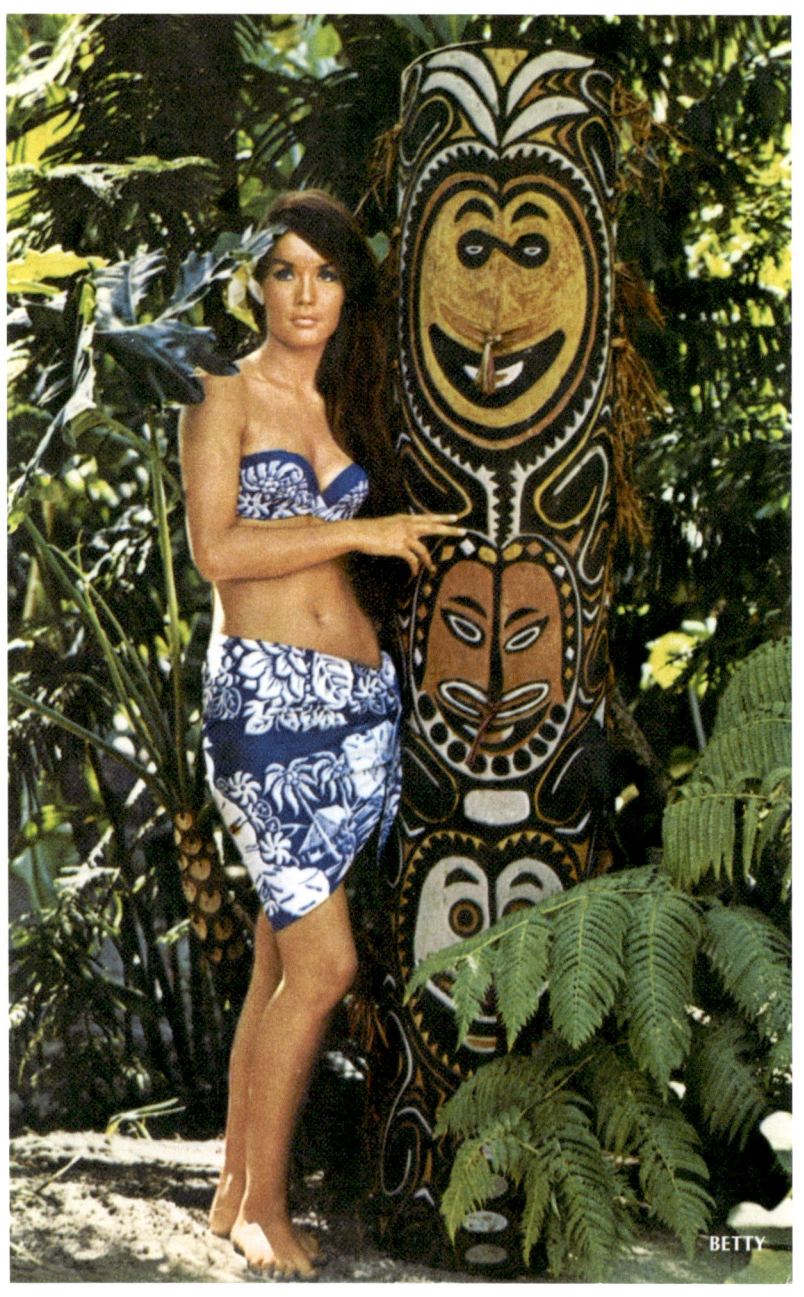

BETTY

TIKI PO

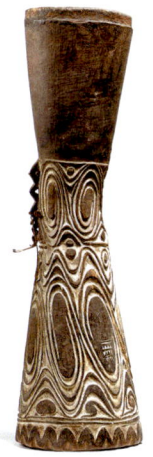

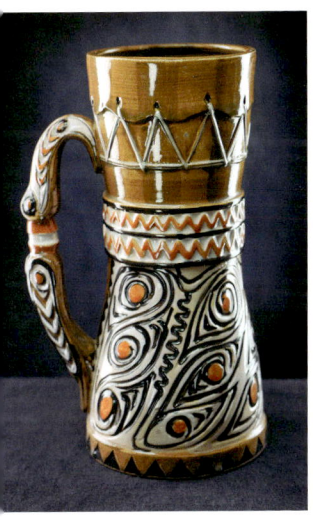

IN DER GESCHICHTE DES TIKI-POP GIBT

es diese Orte, die alle anderen – ob groß oder klein – in den Schatten stellen. Einer davon ist das Mai-Kai in Fort Lauderdale, Florida, das von den Brüdern Bob und Jack Thornton im Jahr 1956 eröffnet wurde. Es ist gewissermaßen das Taj Mahal des Tiki und besteht noch heute in seiner ursprünglichen Form – der letzte große Tiki-Tempel, der bis in die Gegenwart überdauerte.

Die Thorntons stammten aus Illinois und ließen sich von der Filiale von Don the Beachcomber in Chicago inspirieren – und zwar so sehr, dass sie laut Mai-Kai-Forscher Tim „Swanky" Glazner den dortigen Manager und das Barpersonal abwarben, um dieselbe Servicequalität garantieren zu können. Sie führten außerdem eine Änderung ein, die sich als entscheidend für die Blütezeit

OPPOSITE: Betty–exotic temptress in the Mai-Kai gardens, August 1967

ABOVE: Original Papua New Guinea drum (Musée du Quai Branly Collection) and Mai-Kai drum mug (Frank Brajevic Collection)

RIGHT: Appetizer menu cover from the Mai-Kai (Mimi Payne Collection)

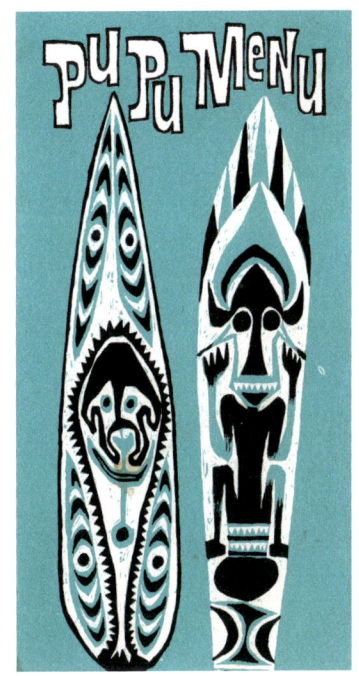

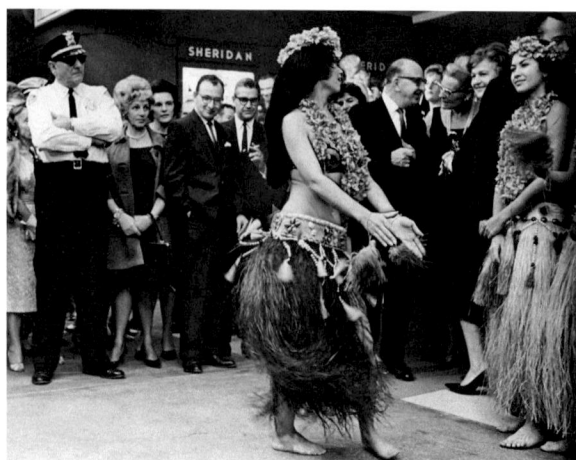

LEFT: The eye-catching Mai-Kai girls swinging their hips at the Miami Beach premiere of *Mutiny on the Bounty*, 1962

OPPOSITE: Seductive Mai-Kai Mystery Girl Linda Spengle holding the Mystery Bowl *(Tim Glazner Collection)*

des Tiki-Pop erwies: Don besaß ein Set aus drei Tiki-Figuren, bekannt als „Tahitian Cannibal Carvings". Für ihn waren sie Talismane und für Werbezwecke hat er sie nie genutzt. Die Thorntons jedoch adoptierten die Figuren als Mai-Kais Markenzeichen und wurden so zu Vorreitern der nachfolgenden Tiki-Generation.

Die großen Tiki-Statuen im Außenbereich des Mai-Kais stammten von dem kalifornischen Bildhauer Barney West. Die meisten Figuren im Innern entstanden nach Abbildungen aus einem Ausstellungskatalog zu ozeanischer Kunst aus dem Jahr 1956. Eine der ersten Mai-Kai-Werbungen verkündete: „Unser Tiki lächelt Sie an. Er lächelt, weil er ein Mai-Kai-Tiki ist… er steht inmitten von mehr als 20 Tonnen authentischem Inseldekor." Zu jenem Dekor gehörten auch Artefakte aus Papua-Neuguinea – Sammlerstücke aus dem persönlichen Besitz der Thorntons. Dementsprechend fügten sich auch die melanesischen Zeichnungen auf den Cocktailbechern und den Speisekarten harmonisch ins Bild.

Auch das Hula-Girl vergaßen die Brüder nicht. Die weibliche Präsenz war ein wichtiger Faktor für die Attraktivität des Mai-Kai. Die Tänzerinnen und Kellnerinnen mussten gewissen Schönheitsstandards gerecht werden und wurden in Mai-Kai-Kalendern und auf den Covern des hauseigenen Magazins *Happy Talk* zur Schau gestellt. Auch für Werbe-Events und Partys waren die Mädchen gefragt.

Die 1960er-Jahre waren die Blütezeit eines Lebensgefühls, das maßgeblich von Hugh Hefner und seinen Playboy-Clubs mitgeprägt wurde. Mit seiner Schar von Schönheiten war das Mai-Kai die Tiki-Version dieses Playboy-Lifestyles. Das Lokal bediente die männliche Fantasie eines polygamen Lebens in den Tropen, die auch in Filmen und Magazinen ihren Niederschlag fand – es wurde so zu einer Insel, auf der jeder Mann gerne stranden wollte. Auch wenn die Männer heutzutage pragmatischer veranlagt sind, ist das Mai-Kai nach wie vor ein Ort zum Träumen.

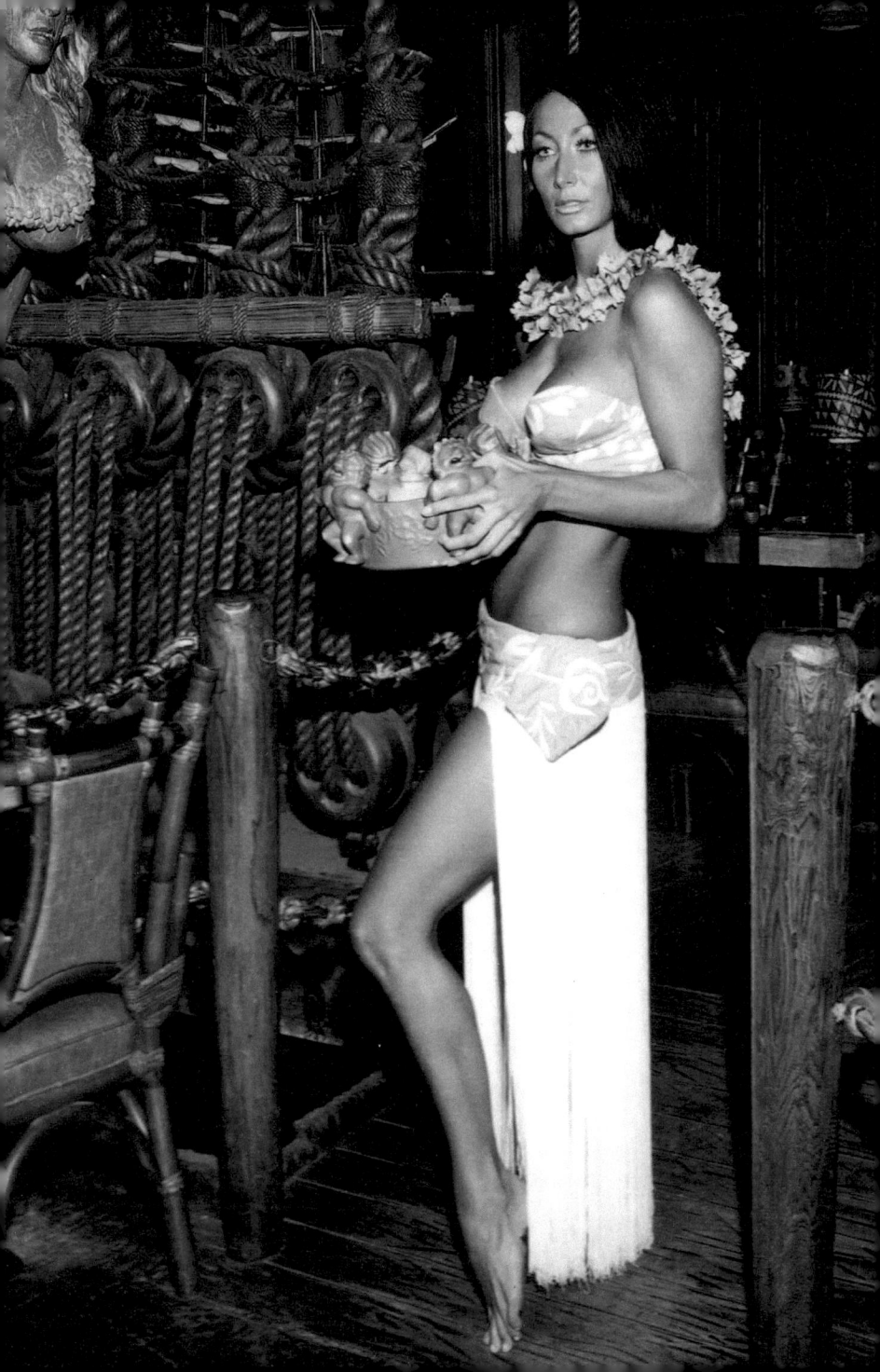

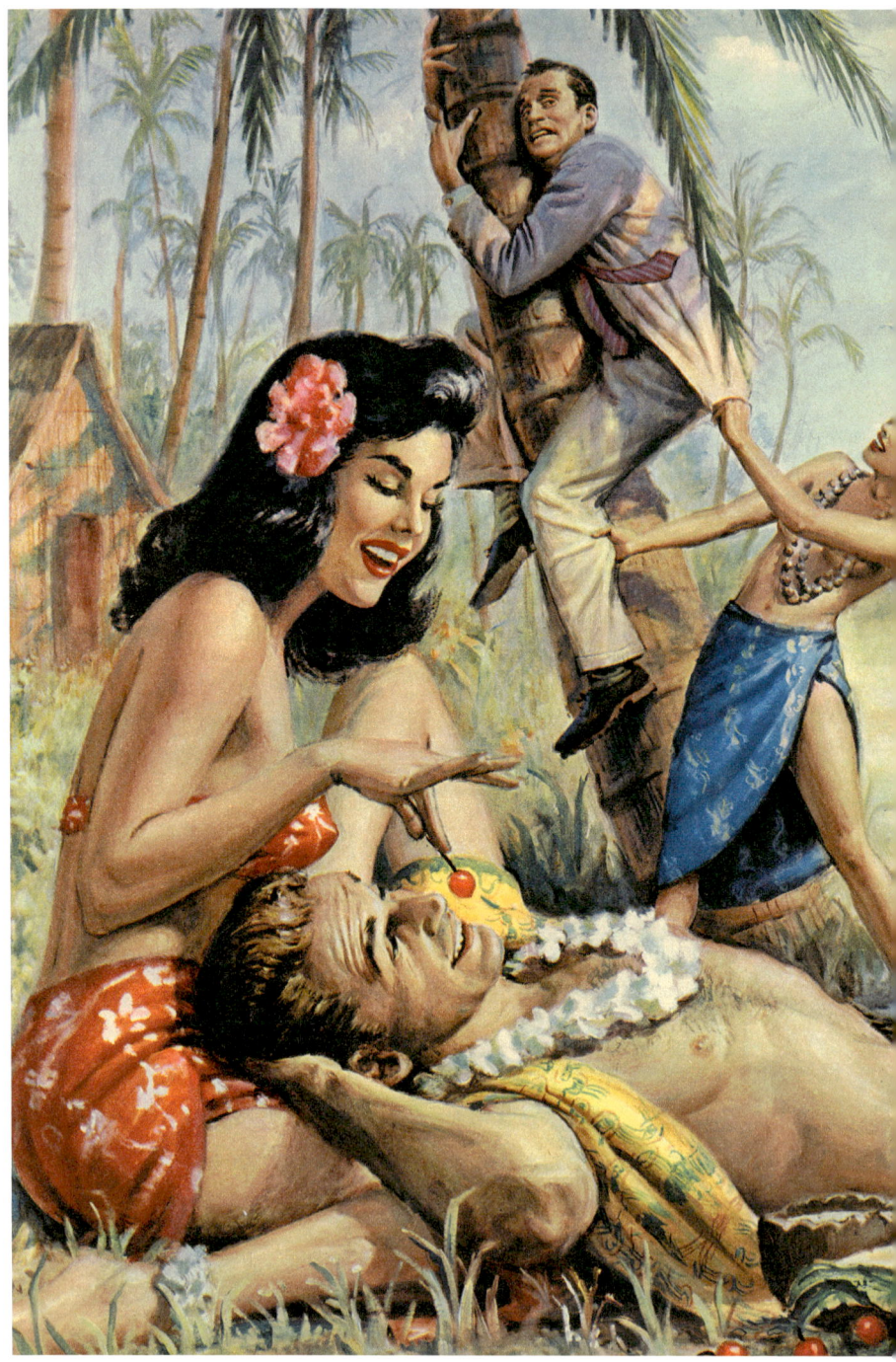

"We were Shipwrecked on an All-Girl Island"

hi . . . Piti . . . Toru . . ."
he cry echoed out through the dark. The fire snapped
ply like a whip. The tom-tom started its slow, insistent
hm as if the sounds the drum made had to travel a
way before they could be heard. The dancers stood
one by one and grouped themselves around the fire.
y started with the *aparima*, which is the "dance of the
ls," the women first letting their long black hair fall

It was a paradise—white sand,
hot sun and lots of *kava* to drink,
while acres of girls ran around
playing a game called "coconut-crazy"

By EVAN TEEL and PRITCHARD RILEY

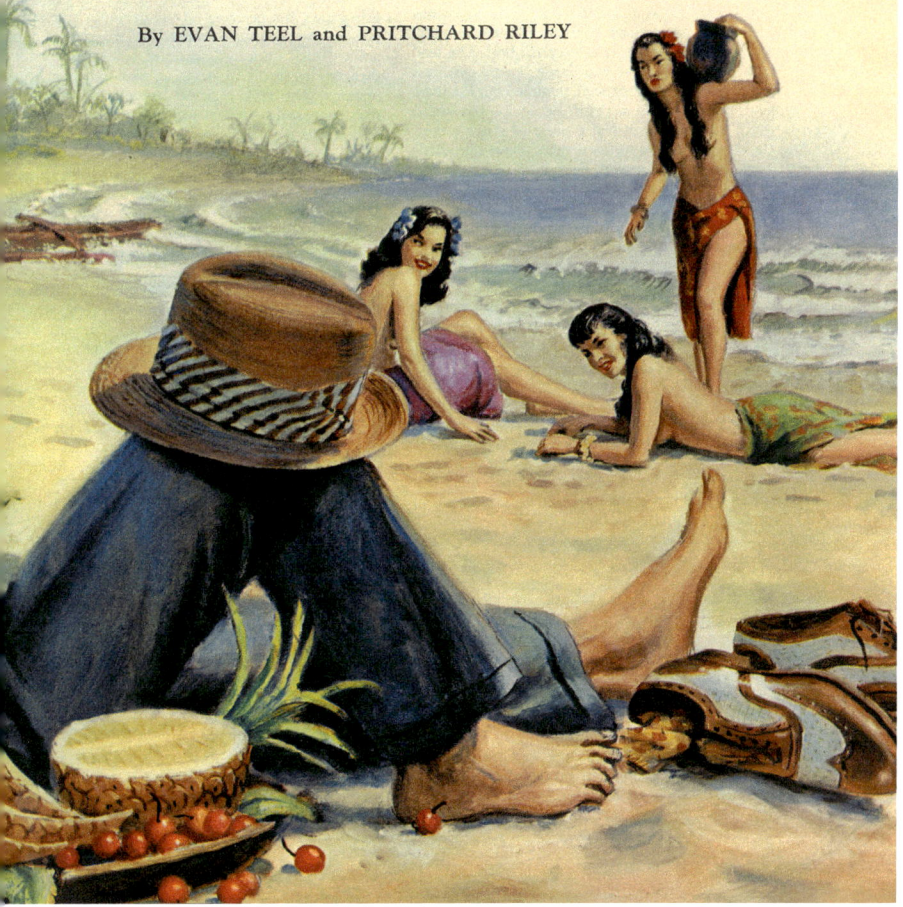

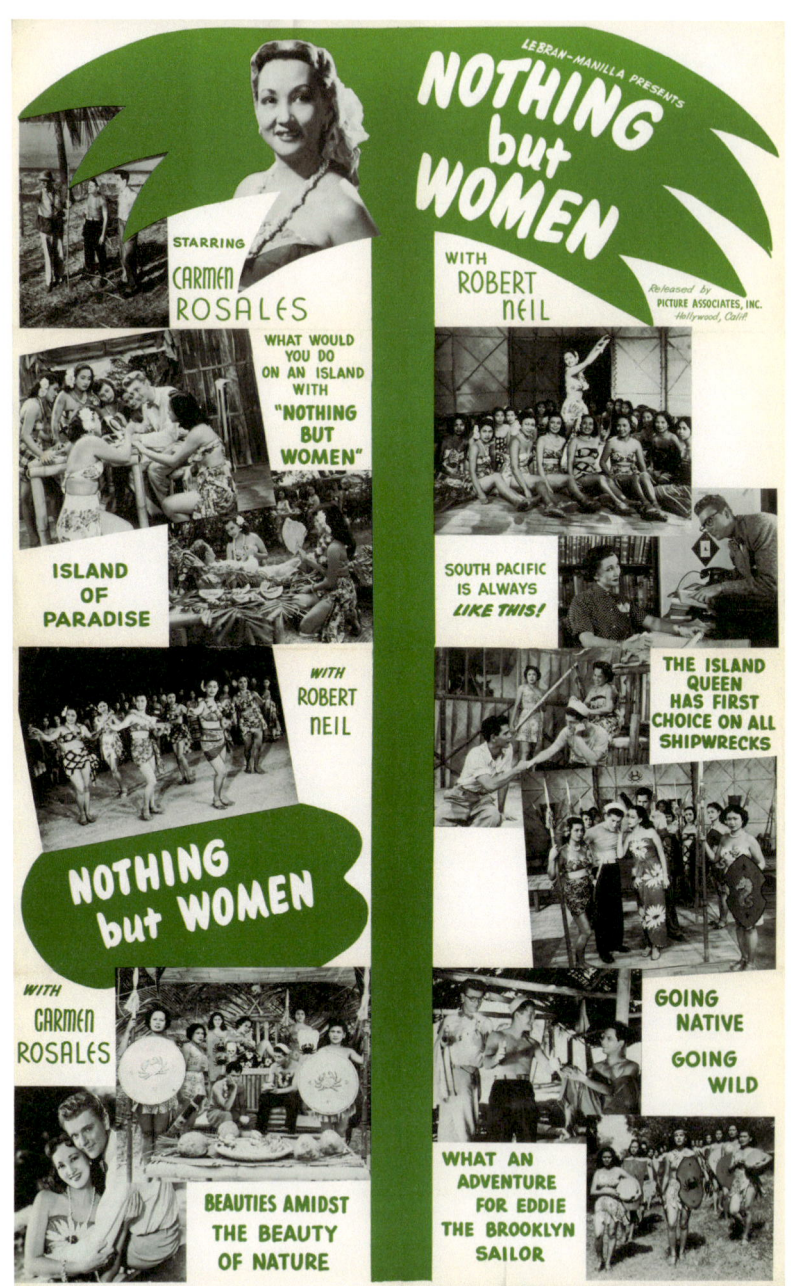

DANS L'HISTOIRE DU TIKI POP, QUELQUES

lieux tiki ont surpassé tous les autres, petits ou grands. Parmi eux, il nous faut citer le Mai-Kai de Fort Lauderdale, en Floride, établi par les frères Bob et Jack Thornton en 1956 : cette sorte de Taj Mahal à la gloire du tiki reste le dernier grand temple, puisqu'il se dresse toujours à son emplacement d'origine.

Les Thornton viennent de Chicago, où ils se sont inspirés de la filiale locale de Don the Beachcomber. À tel point, d'après le spécialiste du Mai-Kai Tim « Swanky » Glazner, qu'ils débauchèrent le gérant et l'équipe du Don's pour s'assurer que leur adresse offrirait la même qualité de service que leur maître. Ils vont toutefois apporter au concept une rupture qui s'avère cruciale dans la naissance du tiki pop. Don avait une collection de mascottes tiki connues sous le nom collégial de « Sculptures tahitiennes cannibales », qu'il s'était toujours gardé d'utiliser à des fins commerciales. Les Thornton, faisant fi des traditions, les choisissent comme emblèmes du Mai-Kai et seront ainsi les chefs de file de la nouvelle génération tiki.

Si les tikis géants plantés à l'extérieur du Mai-Kai sont l'œuvre du sculpteur californien Barney West, la plupart des statues disposées à l'intérieur sont des copies d'œuvres présentées dans l'ouvrage *Oceanic Art* (1956). Une des premières publicités pour le Mai-Kai annonce : « Notre tiki

vous sourit. Il sourit parce qu'il est un tiki du Mai-Kai… Il trône dans quelque vingt tonnes de décor insulaire authentique. » Une autre partie du « décor » est composée d'objets importés de Papouasie-Nouvelle-Guinée par les frères Thornton. Cette combinaison fortuite mène au graphisme mélanésien présent sur les mugs et les menus du Mai-Kai.

Les frères Thornton n'oublient pas non plus la danseuse de hula. Les présences féminines sont un facteur important dans le succès du Mai-Kai. Les danseuses et les serveuses correspondent à certaines exigences de la direction en matière de beauté plastique, et l'une d'elles est honorée chaque mois du titre de « Mai-Kai Girl » et amplement exhibée sur les calendriers et en couverture du magazine *Happy Talk* publiés par l'établissement. Les Mai-Kai girls sont aussi très recherchées pour différents événements promotionnels ou festifs.

Les années 1960 marquent l'heure de gloire du célibataire aux mœurs libres, incarné par Hugh Hefner et ses clubs Playboy. Perpétuellement fréquenté par des beautés dénudées, le Mai-Kai incarnait la version tiki du style de vie Playboy. Projection d'un fantasme très masculin de polygamie tropicale perpétué par le cinéma et la presse magazine, le Mai-Kai est l'île où tout homme rêve de s'échouer. Et si le mâle moderne est plus pragmatique, le Mai-Kai reste l'endroit idéal où rêver.

PAGES 422–423: 1958 men's magazine article telling tall tales

OPPOSITE: An unsung classic of the South Seas B-movie genre

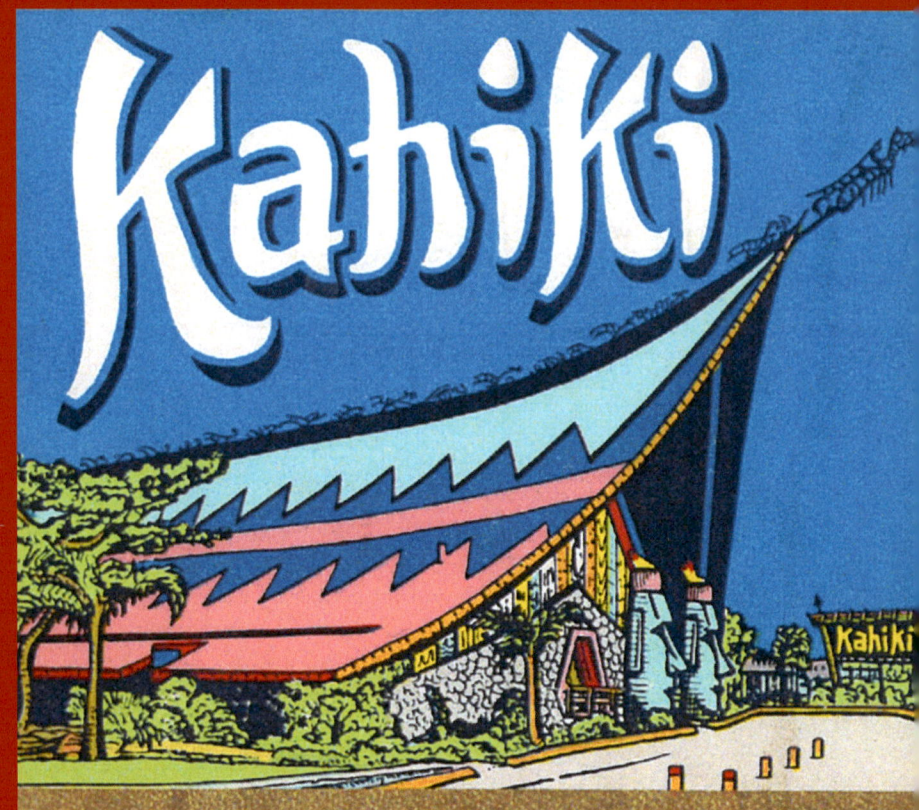

Kahiki

Carta Blanca
RUM
80 PROOF

IMPORTED & BOTTLED BY AUSTIN NICHOLS & CO., INC., NEW YORK, N.
ESPECIALLY FOR

Kahiki

POLYNESIAN SUPPER CLUB, COLUMBUS, OHIO

DISTILLED IN THE VIRGIN ISLAND

24

GRAND TIKI TEMPLES: THE KAHIKI

DIE GROSSEN TIKI-TEMPEL – KAHIKI
GRANDS TEMPLES TIKI – LE KAHIKI

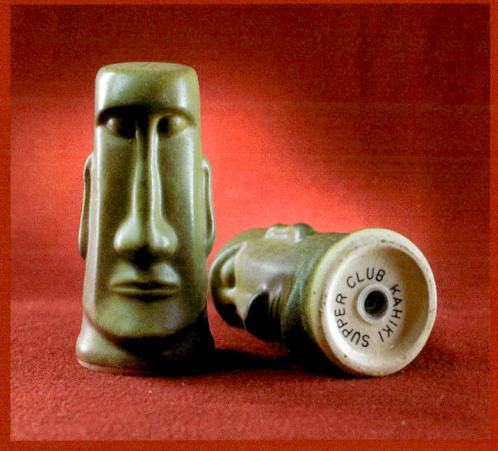

OPPOSITE: Kahiki rum label *(John Holt Collection)*

ABOVE: Moai Salt & Pepper shakers from the Kahiki

THE KAHIKI WAS ANOTHER GREAT
example of independent entrepreneurs
adopting the style features of already established Polynesian-pop havens and then
letting their imaginations create grand new
versions of Polynesia Americana.

Like a spaceship from planet Tiki, the
Kahiki landed in Columbus, Ohio, in 1961.
Its towering scale topped any structure
built in the style before. The promise of
the impressive exterior did not disappoint
when the customer entered: one crossed the
threshold to another place and time.

After passing through the mysterious
Hall of Waterfalls, where the water cast
a milky glow under black lights, one was
greeted by a big Maori head, also a waterfall. On the right was the Beachcomber
Gift Shop. Straight ahead, one would walk
through the Quiet Village, which led down
Kalakaua Street to a two-story-high Moai
fireplace with glowing eyes and a flaming
mouth. The windows on the left side of the
dining room offered views into aquariums,
and on the right, into a rainforest vista.

The Kahiki was a larger-than-life place
that did everything on a big scale—like the
billboard that featured a giant wahine who
gave you the (mechanically) winking eye.
The restaurant had its own rum label and
initially produced its own ceramic ware in
its basement pottery studio.

The logo Tiki of the Kahiki was the
Easter Island head, or Moai. Two concrete
Moai with flaming topknots flanked the

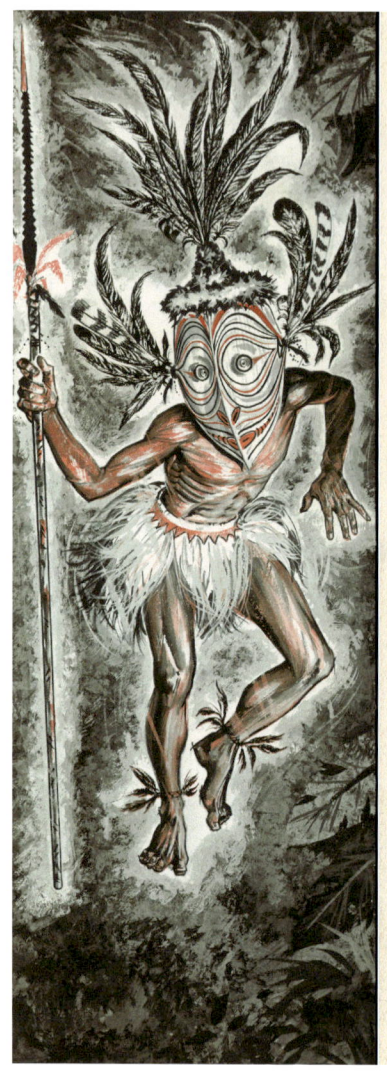

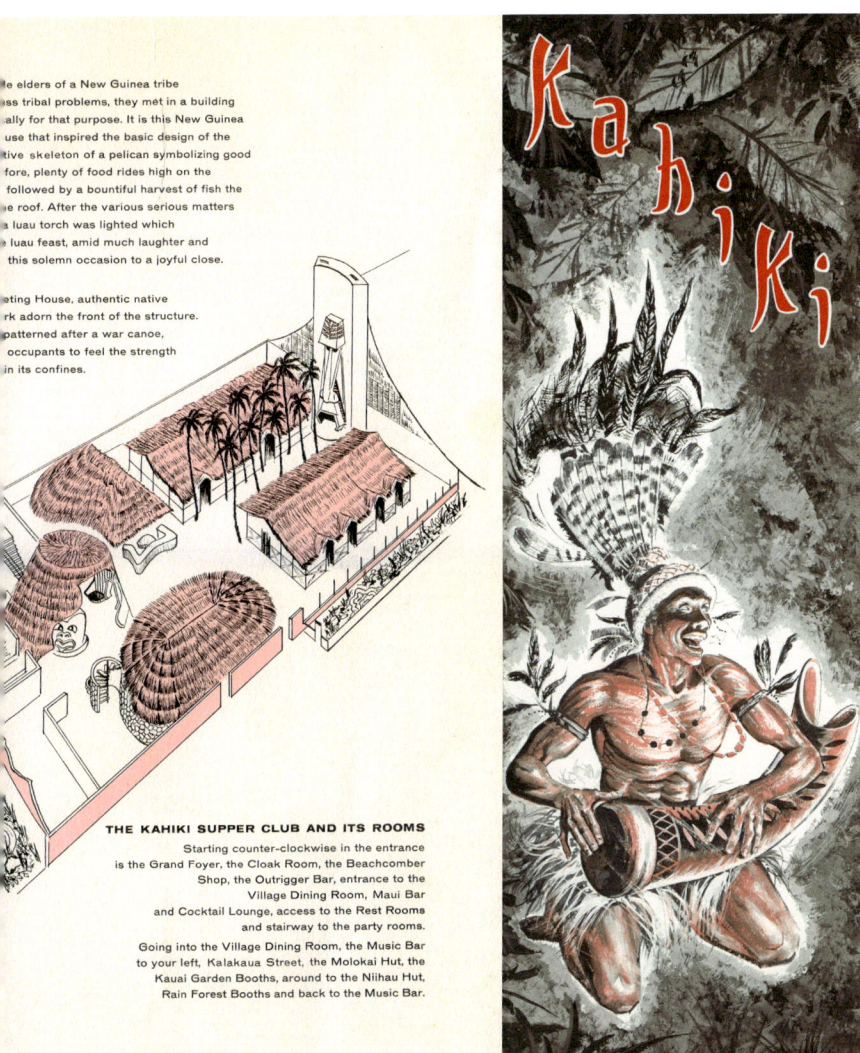

e elders of a New Guinea tribe
ss tribal problems, they met in a building
ally for that purpose. It is this New Guinea
use that inspired the basic design of the
tive skeleton of a pelican symbolizing good
fore, plenty of food rides high on the
followed by a bountiful harvest of fish the
e roof. After the various serious matters
a luau torch was lighted which
luau feast, amid much laughter and
this solemn occasion to a joyful close.

ting House, authentic native
rk adorn the front of the structure.
patterned after a war canoe,
occupants to feel the strength
in its confines.

Kahiki

THE KAHIKI SUPPER CLUB AND ITS ROOMS

Starting counter-clockwise in the entrance
is the Grand Foyer, the Cloak Room, the Beachcomber
Shop, the Outrigger Bar, entrance to the
Village Dining Room, Maui Bar
and Cocktail Lounge, access to the Rest Rooms
and stairway to the party rooms.

Going into the Village Dining Room, the Music Bar
to your left, Kalakaua Street, the Molokai Hut, the
Kauai Garden Booths, around to the Niihau Hut,
Rain Forest Booths and back to the Music Bar.

Kahiki dinner menu, front and back,
with a floor plan of the interior,
describing its various rooms and
architectural features

entrance bridge to the Kahiki, and souvenir Moai statues were sold at the gift shop. While Florida and California Tiki temples benefited from their regions' warm temperatures and abundant tropical flora, the Tiki refuge was also effective in colder climates, heightening the escapist experience by contrast.

Naturally, the Kahiki bar offered a ornucopia of exotic drink presentations. It had adopted the custom of the Mystery Girl from the Mai-Kai, but used Mayan-looking stoneware of its own creation for the Mystery Bowl. The menu espoused the epicurean philosophy of savoring one's Polynesian potion slowly: "Only in that way can one fully sense the world so romantically apart—and yet enable one to practice the art of living à la Polynesienne."

Despite the fact that the Kahiki made it onto the National Register of Historic Places, this great monument to Tiki was torn down in the year 2000 to make room for a Walgreens drugstore—just when American Tiki style was being re-appreciated. Today, only a few cherished artifacts remain.

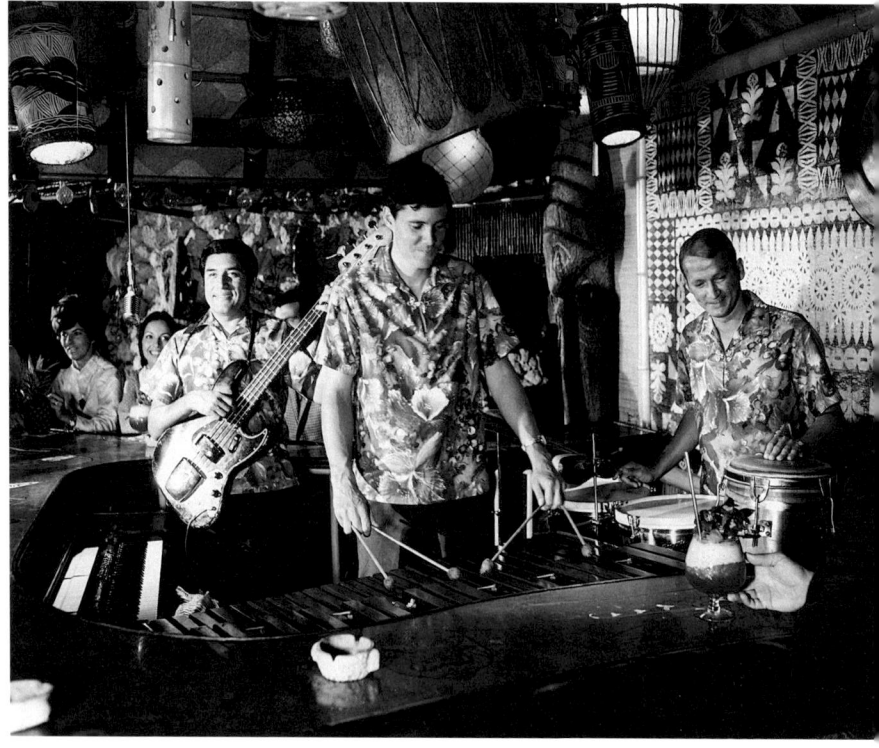

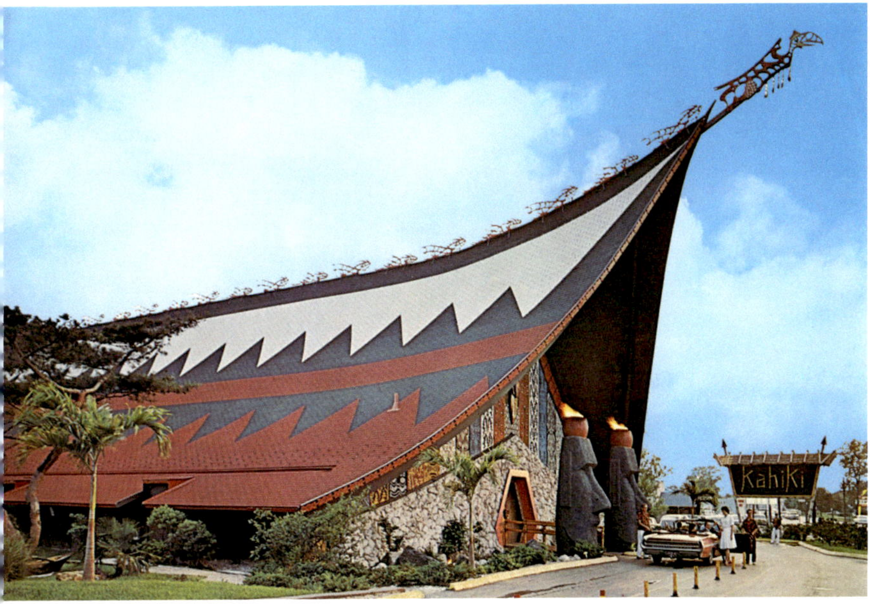

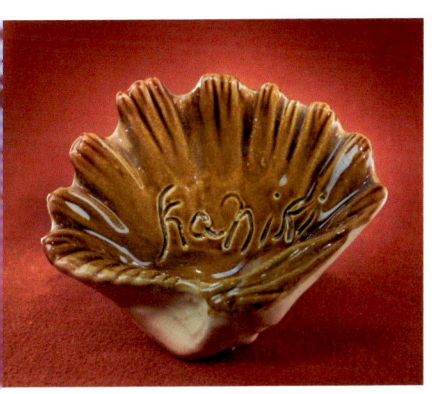

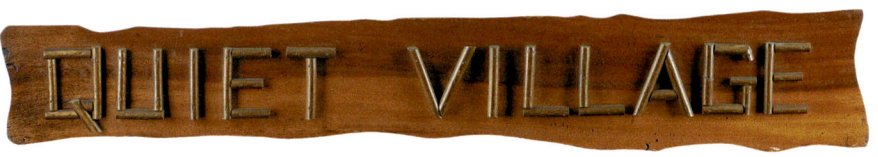

OPPOSITE: The Beachcomber Trio performing at the music bar

ABOVE: The mother ship of Tiki Pop: the Kahiki, Columbus, Ohio, 1961 (*Scott Schell Collection*)

LEFT: Ashtray from the Kahiki

BELOW: Original sign marking the entrance to the Quiet Village (*Kiara Geller Collection*)

EIN WEITERES EXZELLENTES BEISPIEL
dafür, wie Unternehmer den Stil bereits etablierter Oasen des „Polynesian Pop" übernahmen und mit Hilfe ihrer Fantasie daraus eine neue Version des amerikanischen Polynesiens formten, ist das Kahiki.

Wie ein Raumschiff vom Planeten Tiki landete das Kahiki 1961 in Columbus, Ohio. Seine gewaltigen Ausmaße übertrafen alles, was zuvor in diesem Stil gebaut worden war. Die vom äußeren Erscheinungsbild geschürten Erwartungen der Gäste wurden auch im Innern nicht enttäuscht. Sobald man über die Schwelle getreten war, wähnte man sich an einem anderen Ort, in einer anderen Zeit.

Nach dem Durchkreuzen der mystischen Wasserfallhalle, wo die Kaskaden unter Schwarzlicht milchig schimmerten, wurde

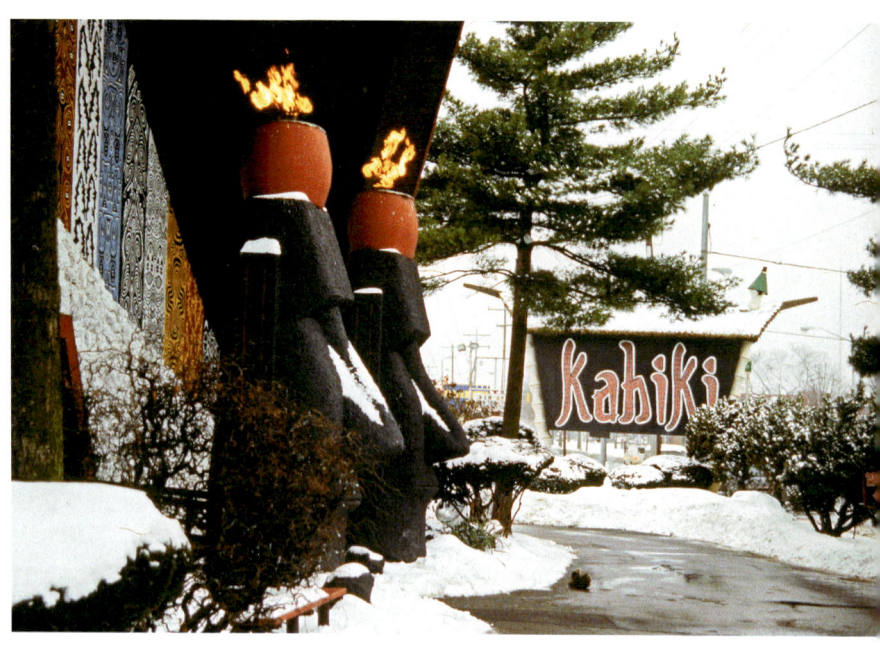

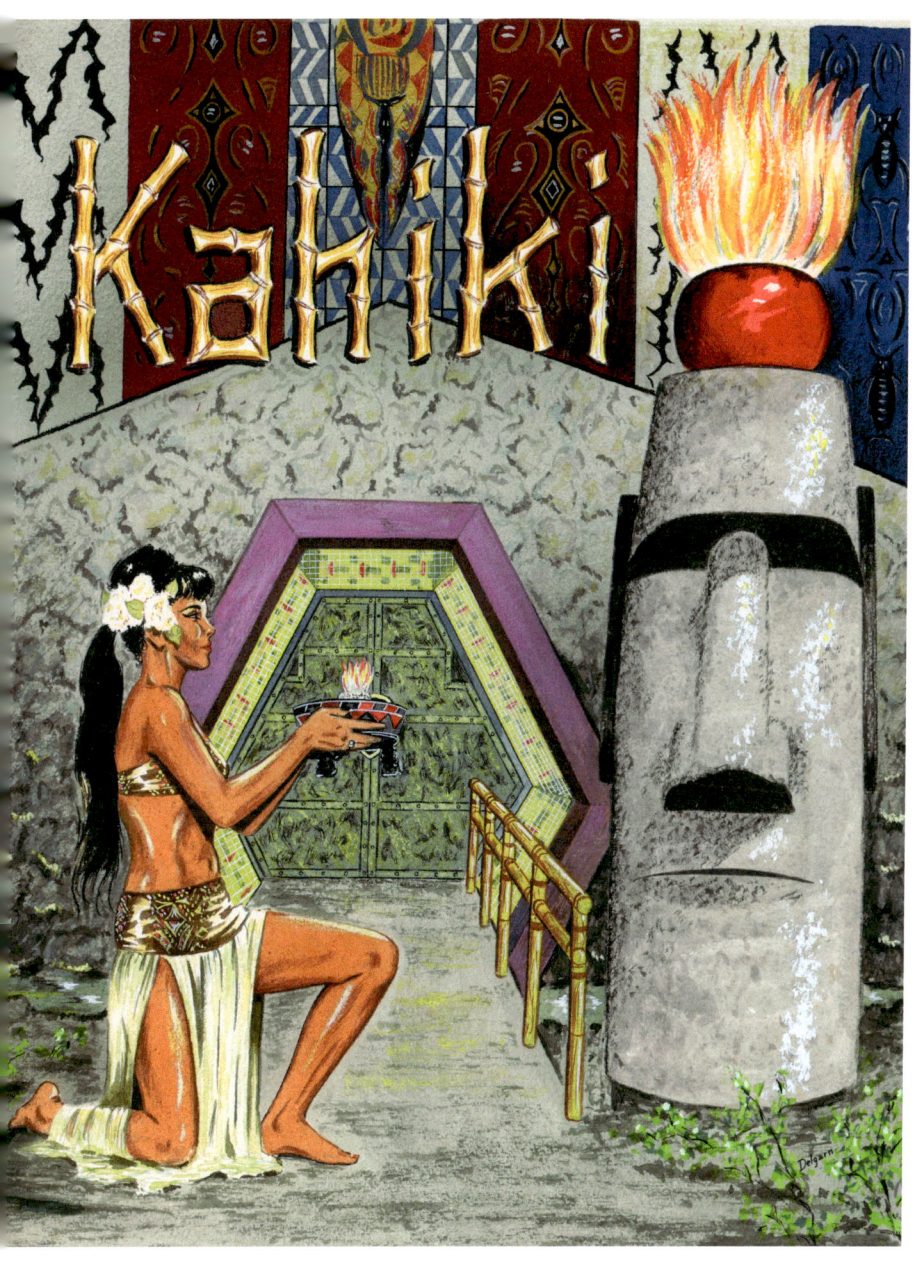

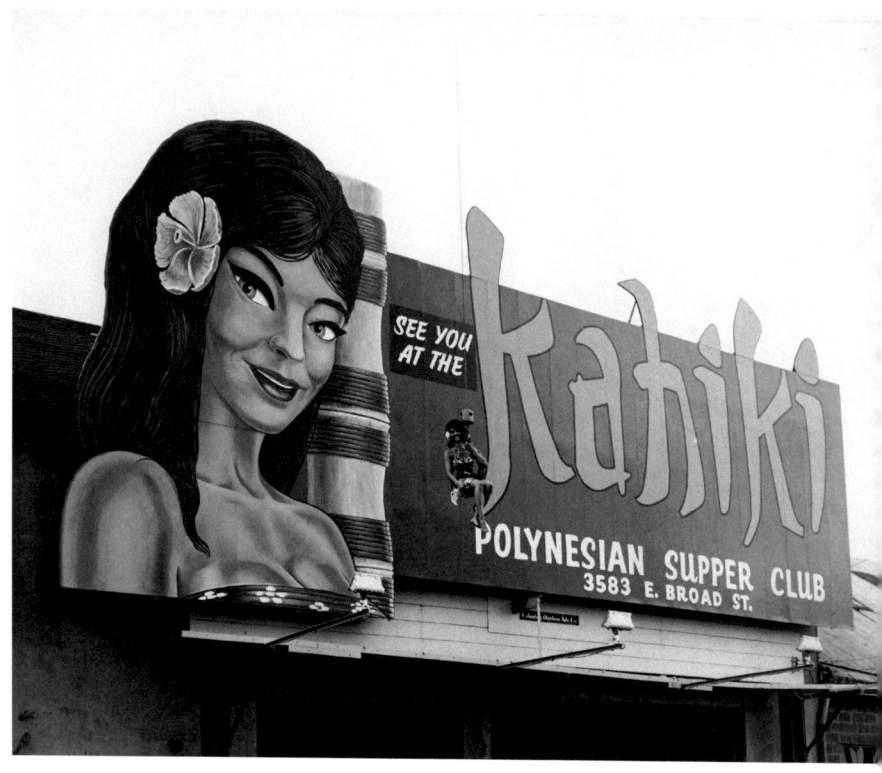

man von einem großen Maorikopf begrüßt, dem ein weiterer Wasserfall entsprang. Auf der rechten Seite befand sich der Beachcomber-Souvenirshop. Geradeaus ging es durch das Quiet Village die Kalakauastraße entlang zu einem zwei Stockwerke hohen Kamin in Form eines Moai, jener berühmten Steinstatuen der Osterinseln, hier allerdings mit glühenden Augen und einem loderndem Feuer in seiner Mundöffnung. Die Fenster auf der linken Seite des Speisesaals blickten in Aquarien, rechts in ein Regenwaldpanorama.

Im Kahiki war alles riesengroß – wie die Werbetafel mit der Wahine, die dem Betrachter (mechanisch) zuzwinkerte. Das

Restaurant schenkte hauseigenen Rum aus und auch die Keramikwaren stammten aus eigener Produktion im Untergeschoss.

Das Logo des Kahiki war ebenfals den Moai nachempfunden, und auch die Brücke am Eingang des Lokals flankierten zwei Moais, auf deren Köpfen ein Feuer loderte. Im Souvenirshop wurden sie in Miniaturform als Andenken verkauft. Obwohl die Tiki-Tempel in Florida und Kalifornien vom warmen Klima und von der tropischen Flora ihrer Standorte profitierten, funktionierte das Konzept auch in kühleren Regionen, wurde doch die Aussteigererfahrung durch die harten Kontraste noch verstärkt.

Selbstverständlich bot die Bar des Kahiki eine Fülle an reich dekorierten exotischen Drinks. Der aus Steingut gefertigte Mystery Bowl etwa erinnerte an Trinkgefäße der Maya. Die Tradition des Mystery Girl, die diesen Cocktail servierte, hatte man vom Mai-Kai übernommen. Die Getränkekarte hielt dazu an, die polynesischen Mixturen langsam zu genießen: „Nur so lässt sich diese ferne romantische Welt wirklich erahnen – und die Kunst des Lebens à la Polynesienne meistern."

Obwohl das Kahiki in das National Register of Historic Places aufgenommen wurde, hat man dieses Monument der Tiki-Kultur im Jahr 2000 abgerissen, um Platz für eine Walgreens-Apotheke zu schaffen – und das, als der Tiki-Stil gerade wieder im Kommen war. Heute sind nur noch einige wenige wertvolle Artefakte übrig.

LEFT: Photo of giant billboard, with suspended Kahiki waitress for scale *(Frank Brajevic Collection)*

BELOW: Happy Kahiki customers enjoying a luau pig (1960s)

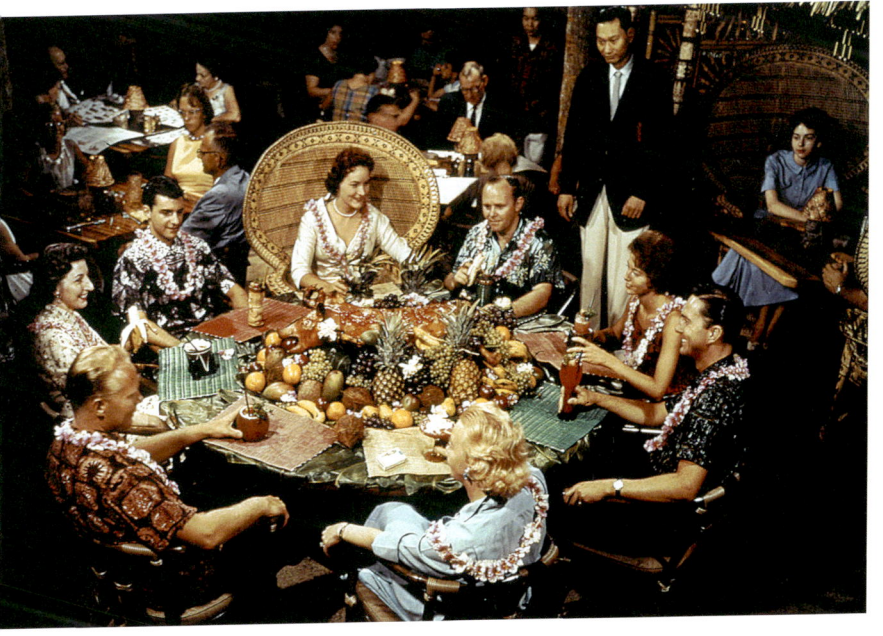

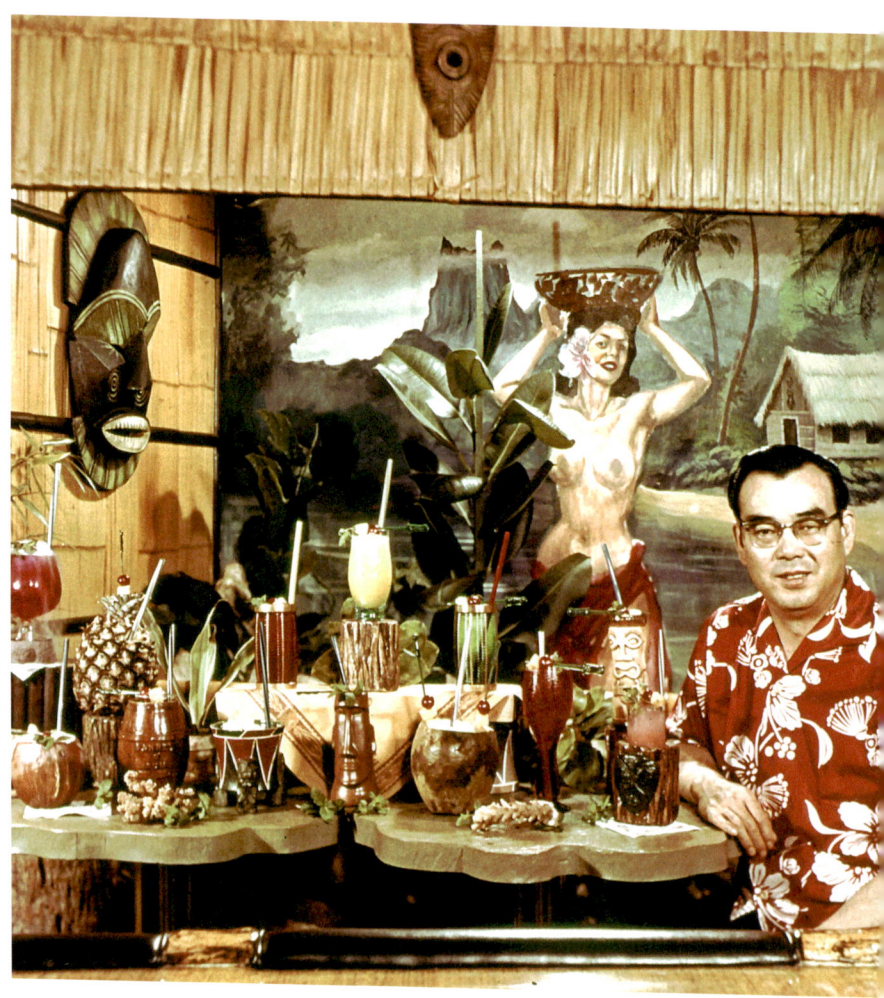

ABOVE: Kahiki bar manager George Ono proudly presenting his creations (*Stephen Sandoval Collection*)

OPPOSITE ABOVE: Idol's cast mug (*Frank Brajevic Collection*)

OPPOSITE BELOW: Rare Kahiki lamp (*Frank Brajevic Collection*)

PARMI LES TEMPLES TIKI, LE KAHIKI EST
né lui aussi de la stratégie d'entrepreneurs
indépendants qui s'approprient les codes
d'un style déjà établi et rendu populaire par
d'autres, tout en apportant les fruits de leur
imagination propre à l'enrichissement de la
culture populaire américano-polynésienne.

Comme un vaisseau spatial venu de
la planète tiki, le Kahiki atterrit à Columbus, dans l'Ohio, en 1961. Ses dimensions
impressionnantes dépassent de loin l'envergure des autres structures du genre. La
promesse faite par l'aspect extérieur était
tenue à l'intérieur : lorsque le client passait
le seuil, il pénètrait dans une autre dimension, un autre lieu, un autre temps.

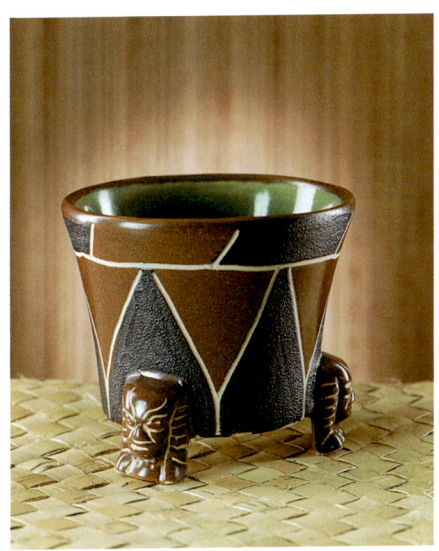

Une fois passé la mystérieuse Salle des
Cascades, où l'eau projette partout une
lueur laiteuse sous la lumière noire, le client
est accueilli par une monumentale tête
maorie, de laquelle s'écoule une source. Sur
sa droite, il découvre la boutique du Beachcomber. En avançant, il traverse le Paisible
Village, dont l'allée centrale, la Kalakaua
Street, mène à un moai haut de deux étages ;
sa bouche énorme abrite une cheminée,
dont les flammes font luire ses yeux vides.
Les baies vitrées ménagées dans les murs
gauches de la salle à manger donnent sur
des aquariums, et celles de droite sur une
reconstitution de forêt tropicale.

Le Kahiki est un lieu qui dépasse l'imagination, où tout est fait à une échelle
immense – jusqu'au panneau monumental
sur lequel une tête de vahiné géante cligne
son œil mécanique. Le restaurant sert son
propre rhum et, au départ, il produit aussi
sa vaisselle dans un atelier de poterie installé dans la cave de l'établissement.

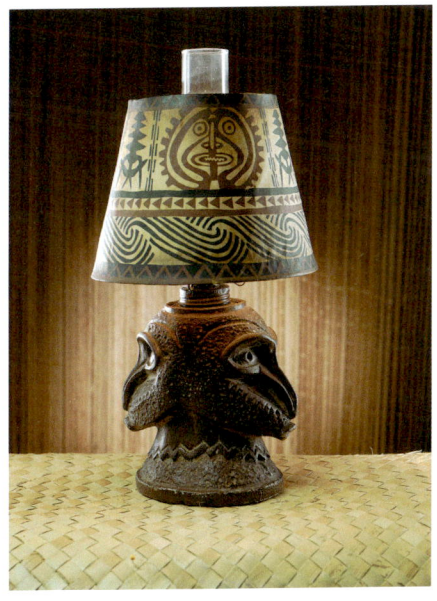

L'emblème tiki du Kahiki est un moai
de l'île de Pâques. Deux moai en béton
coiffés de braseros flanquent l'entrée du

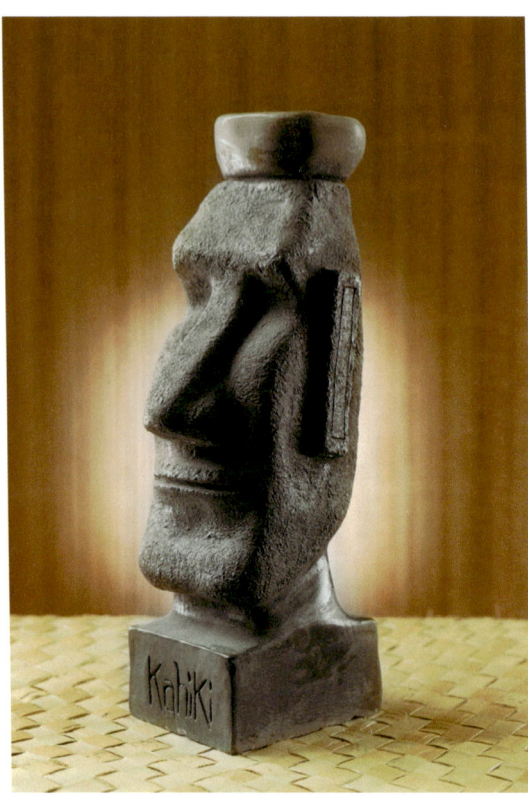

pont qui mène au Kahiki, et la boutique de l'établissement propose des statuettes moai en souvenir. Si en Floride et en Californie les temples du tiki bénéficient de la douceur du climat et de la luxuriante flore locale, l'effet refuge du tiki opérait aussi sous des températures moins clémentes, l'expérience étant même décuplée par le contraste entre extérieur et intérieur.

Le bar du Kahiki propose naturellement pléthore de boissons plus exotiques et spectaculaires les unes que les autres. Il reprend l'idée de la Fille Mystère imaginée par l'équipe du Mai-Kai, mais utilise une pierre creuse façon maya en guise de Bol Mystère. Le menu épouse la philosophie épicurienne d'une dégustation lente : « Le seul moyen de sentir le monde glisser si romantiquement loin de vous, tout en faisant pleinement l'expérience de l'art de vivre à la polynésienne. »

Malgré son classement au registre national des monuments historiques, ce temple majeur du tiki pop a été détruit en 2000 pour laisser la place à un supermarché Walgreens – alors même que le style tiki américain revenait à la mode. Il n'en reste aujourd'hui que quelques objets épars, et très recherchés.

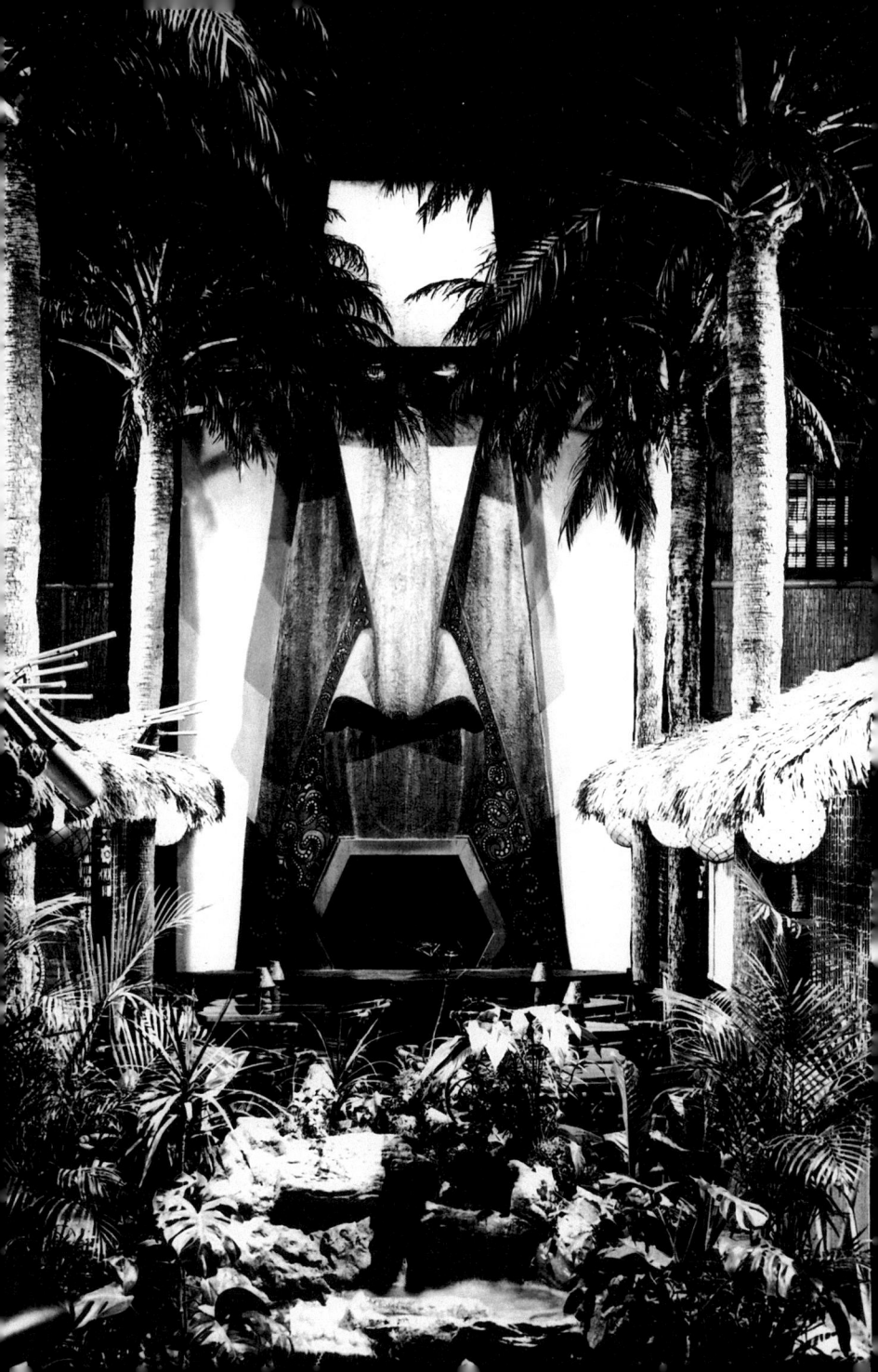

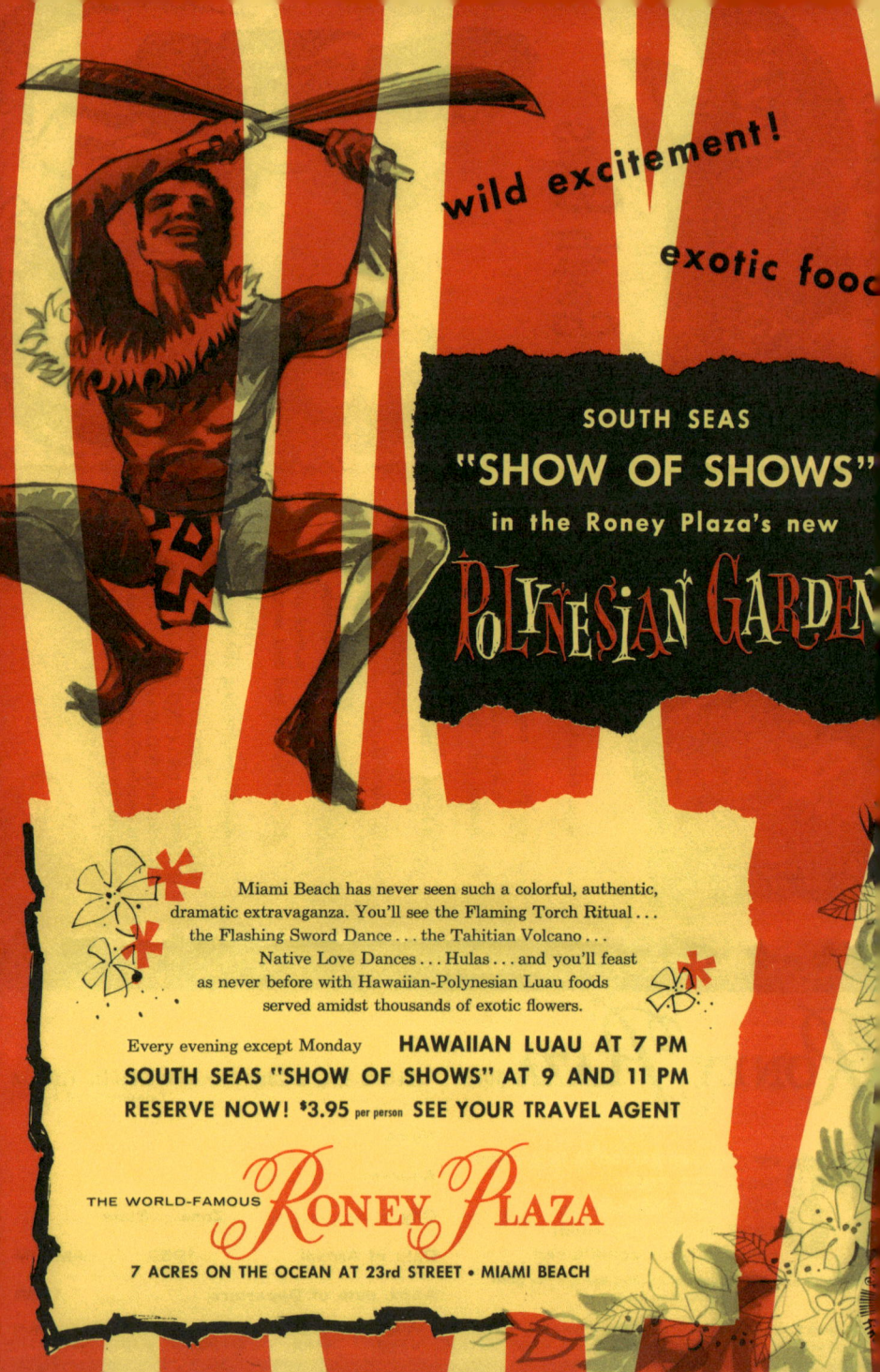

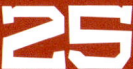

RITUAL AND MAKE-BELIEVE

RITUAL UND SHOW
RITUELS ET FAUX-SEMBLANTS

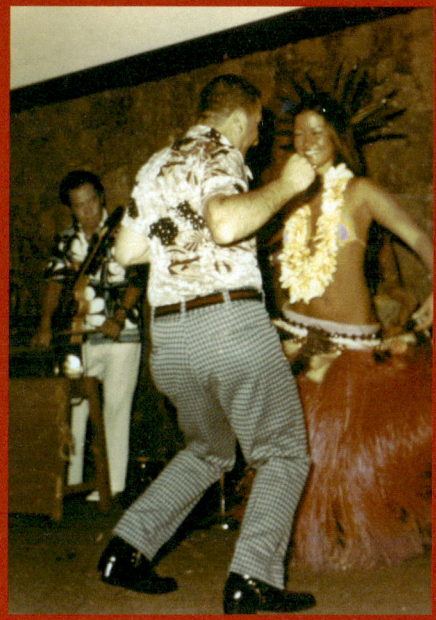

OPPOSITE: "The jet age has brought these wonderful islands only hours away, and the Royal Polynesian Fantasy brings you even closer!"

ABOVE: White men can't dance

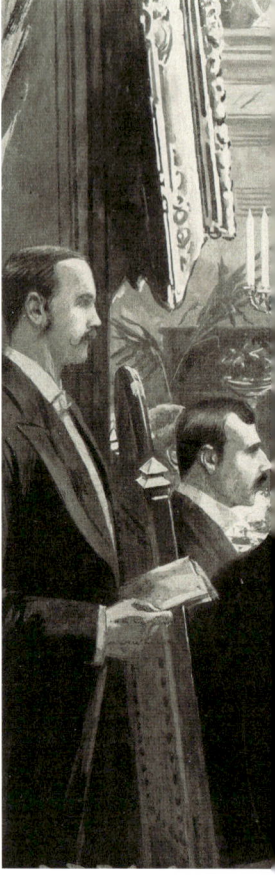

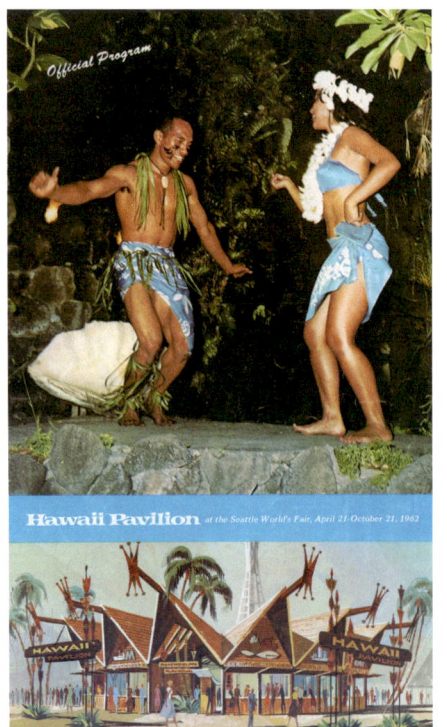

BEGINNING WITH THE FIRST EXPLORERS

who discovered Polynesia, white men were charmed by the rituals and dances that the natives performed for them. This fascination continued into the 20th century, with Polynesian-themed floorshows entertaining urbanites in mainland Tiki resorts. The civilized citizen was captivated by the "exotic other"—and titillated by exposed skin and beautiful bodies.

Polynesian revues usually offered a "United Nations of Polynesia"–style parade

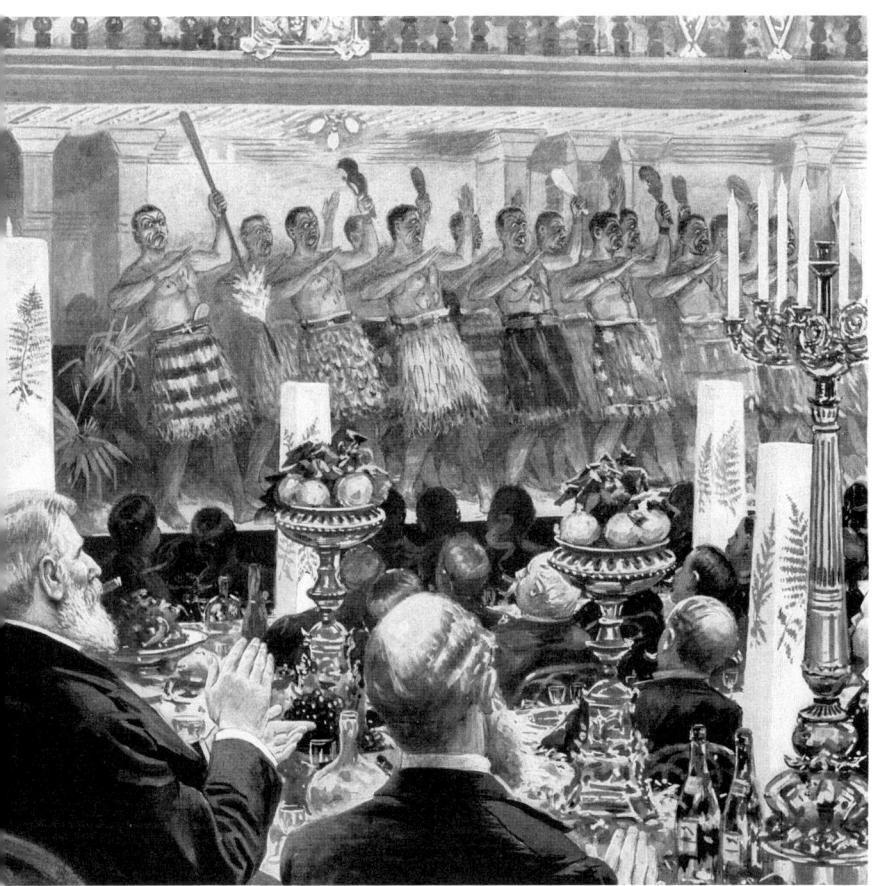

of performances from the various island groups: the Samoan fire dance, the Maori haka, the Hawaiian hula, and the Tahitian drum dance were all standards in most repertoires. Unlike the waitstaff in American Tiki temples, most dance troupes were composed of authentic Pacific Islanders who performed their numbers with an honest and joyful sense of ambassadorship and pride for their culture.

White folks wanted to be in on the fun, too, and dance schools began offering hula

lessons and Maori poi-ball swinging in their curricula. Even the men got to play: since the time of Captain Bligh, it had been a tradition to invite the typically stiff and awkward Western males to swing their hips in a hula dance, which continued to be a source of amusement into the 20th century.

Of course, the ultimate escapist fantasy would be that of *becoming* an islander, of slipping into native skin and merging with the tropical environment. Donning grass skirts was the next best thing, which many

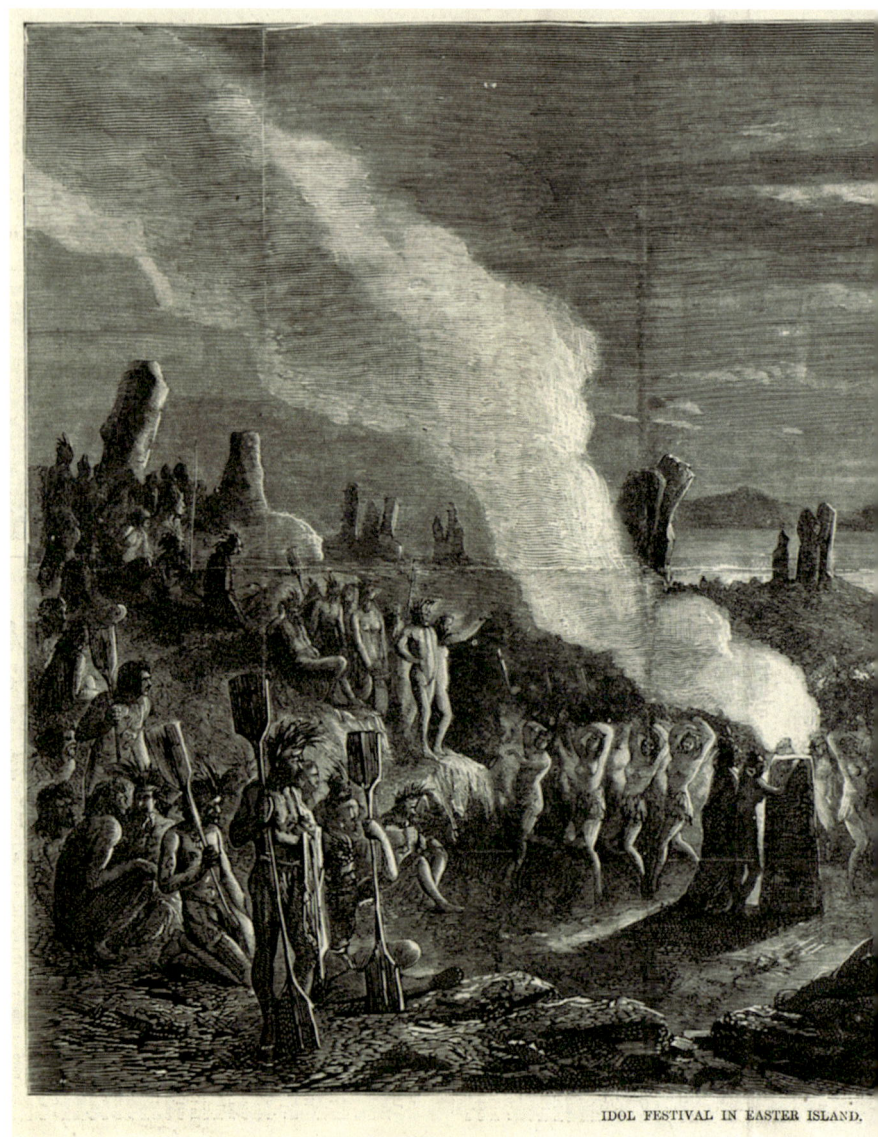

IDOL FESTIVAL IN EASTER ISLAND,

Illustration in *Harper's Weekly,* 1873

TIKI PO

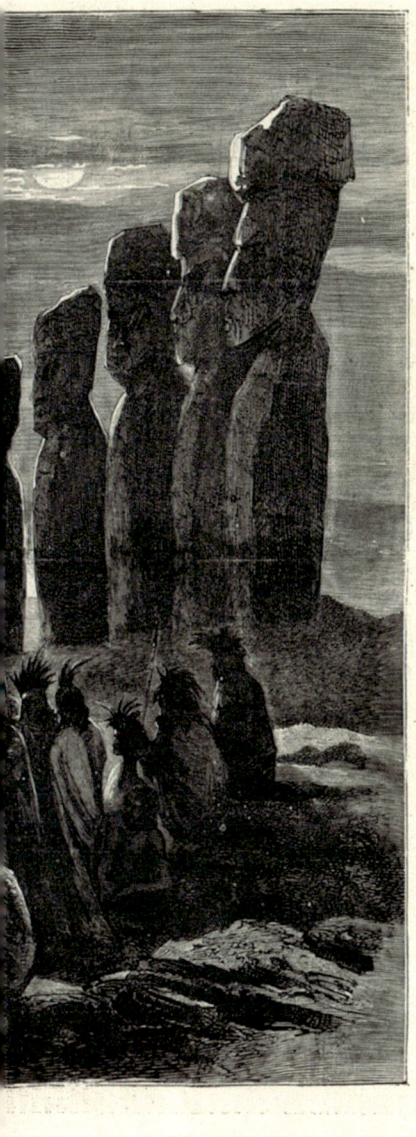

tourists and mainlanders often did. Starting with the Hawaiian-music craze of the 1920s, it continued in the backyard luau phase of the '50s, and culminated with Ava Gardner wearing a grass skirt designed by Christian Dior.

The other fashion device worn in the attempt to "go native" was the Hawaiian shirt. It was the perfect antidote to the constricting suit of the mid-century white-collar worker. Dressed in the wild and colorful patterns of aloha wear, one could become a different person. A Hawaiian outfit meant leisure, it meant fun, it meant partying—it meant being in the "island" frame of mind.

Another classic American attempt to go Polynesian was the reenactment of tribal rituals, like the communal kava-bowl ceremony. Kava was an ancient sedative in Polynesian society, the preparation of which involved mastication by young virgins. Because it was not available in American cocktail culture, a potent rum concoction, the Kava, was used instead. Extra-long straws made parallel consumption possible and fun.

The ultimate example of the ritual-cocktail-bowl concept was without a doubt the Mystery Drink, invented by the Mai-Kai. At the sound of a gong, the Mystery Girl would slowly and seductively approach the customer, then demurely kneel and present the special potion. The routine was such a hit, it was performed on *The Johnny Carson Show* and imitated by several Tiki establishments.

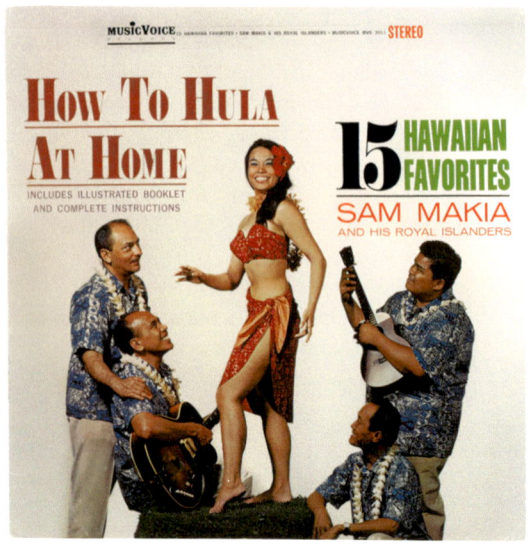

SCHON DIE ERSTEN ENTDECKER

Polynesiens waren von den Ritualen und Tänzen der Einheimischen entzückt. Diese Faszination setzte sich bis ins 20. Jahrhundert fort, wo Städter in Tiki-Resorts des Festlands mit polynesischen Shows unterhalten wurden. Die zivilisierten Bürger waren wie hypnotisiert von dem „exotischen Fremden" – und von der nackten Haut und den schönen Körpern.

Zu den polynesische Revuen gehörten für gewöhnlich Auftritte von Tänzern, die die einzelnen Inselgruppen repräsentierten, eine Show à la „Die Vereinten Nationen Polynesiens". Der samoanische Feuertanz, der maorische Haka, der hawaiische Hula und der tahitische Trommeltanz gehörten zum Standardrepertoire. Anders als die Kellner in den amerikanischen Tiki-Tempeln waren die meisten Tanztruppen mit echten Abkömmlingen der Pazifikinseln besetzt, die ihre Kultur authentisch und voller Freude präsentierten.

Dies weckte bei den Amerikanern den Wunsch, sich an dem Spaß zu beteiligen; Tanzschulen begannen, Hula- und maorische Poi-Tanzkurse anzubieten. Auch die Männer durften mitspielen: Seit den Zeiten von Kapitän Bligh wurden die für gewöhnlich etwas steifen und unbeholfenen Westler dazu eingeladen, beim Hula selbst die Hüften zu schwingen. Dies blieb auch im 20. Jahrhundert eine Quelle der Belustigung.

Natürlich war es die ultimative Aussteigerfantasie, selbst ein Insulaner zu werden, in die Haut eines Einheimischen zu schlüpfen und mit der tropischen Umgebung zu verschmelzen. Das Tragen eines Bastrocks kam dem am nächsten, was Touristen und Besucher entsprechender Veranstaltungen auf dem Festland zur Genüge taten. Dieser Modetrend begann mit der Hawaiimusikwelle der 1920er-Jahre, zog sich durch die Luau-Partys der 1950er und gipfelte schließlich in einem von Christian Dior entworfenen Grasrock, getragen von Ava Gardner.

OPPOSITE AND BELOW: Doing the hula at home

RIGHT: A proud Hawaiian tourist

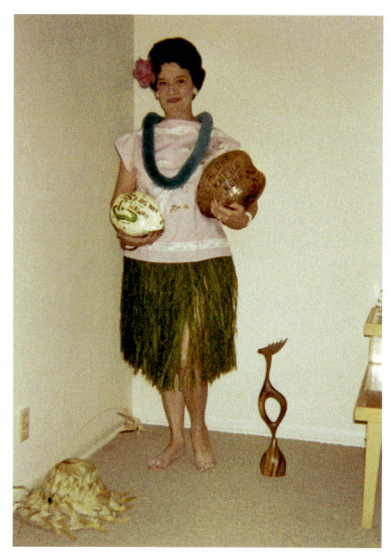

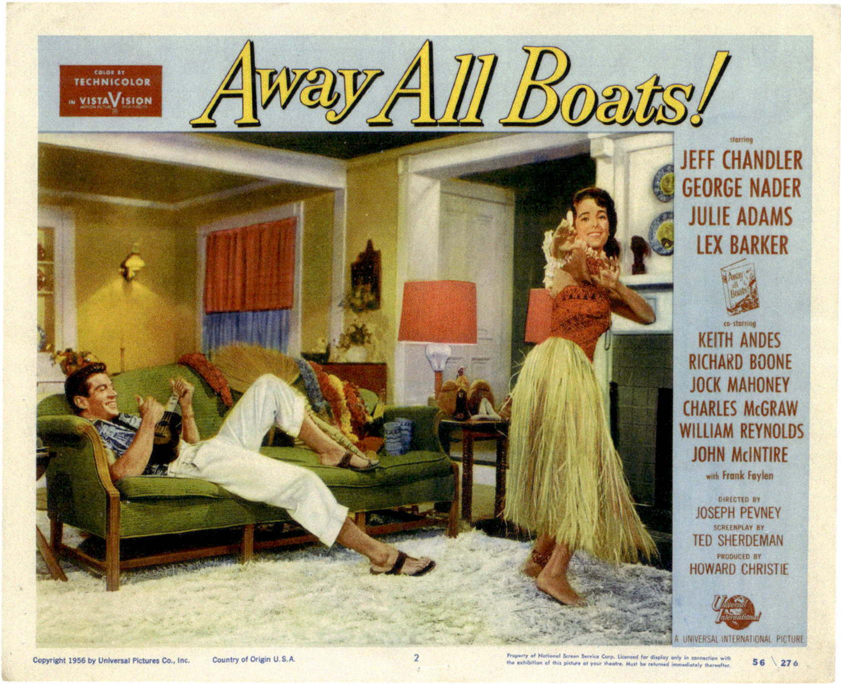

Das zweite Kleidungsstück, mit dem man sich als Insulaner ausgeben konnte, war das Hawaiihemd. In den 1950er-Jahren war es der perfekte Gegensatz zum engen Anzug des typischen Büroangestellten. In wilde und farbenfrohe Muster gekleidet, war man ein ganz anderer Mensch. Ein Hawaiioutfit bedeutete Freizeit, Spaß, Party – es bedeutete, das Lebensgefühl der Polynesier anzunehmen.

Ein weiteres Herantasten an die polynesische Kultur war die Adaption von Stammesritualen wie die der Kava-Zeremonien. Das aus der Kava-Pflanze hergestellte Zeremonialgetränk ist ein Angstlöser und wird in Polynesien unter anderem bei Initiationsritualen genutzt. Da es in den USA für Cocktails nicht zur Verfügung stand, wurde es durch ein starkes Rumgebräu ersetzt. Mittels extralanger Strohhalme konnten mehrere Gäste die Cocktails gleichzeitig genießen.

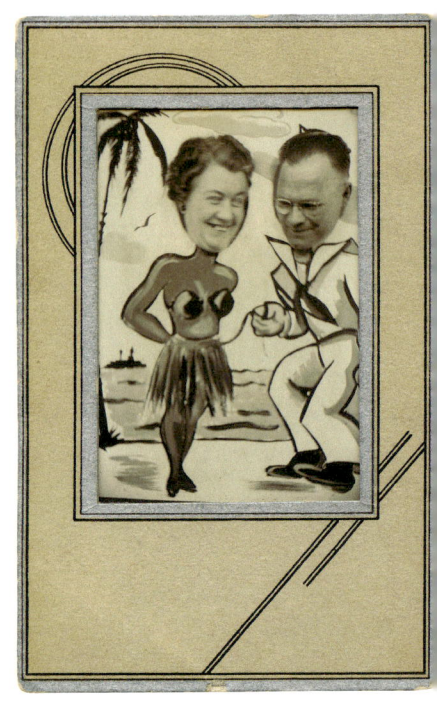

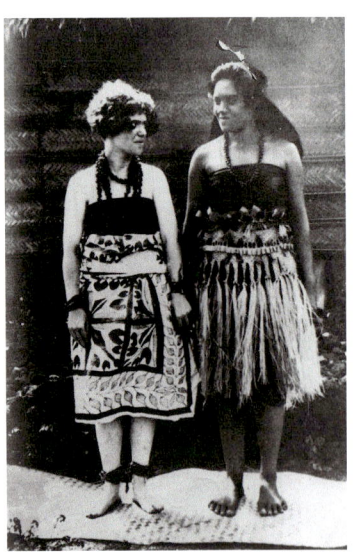

ABOVE: Americans enjoying South Seas role play

LEFT: Anthropologist Margaret Mead in Samoan costume

OPPOSITE: Ava Gardner in Christian Dior threads, on the set of *The Little Hut*, 1957

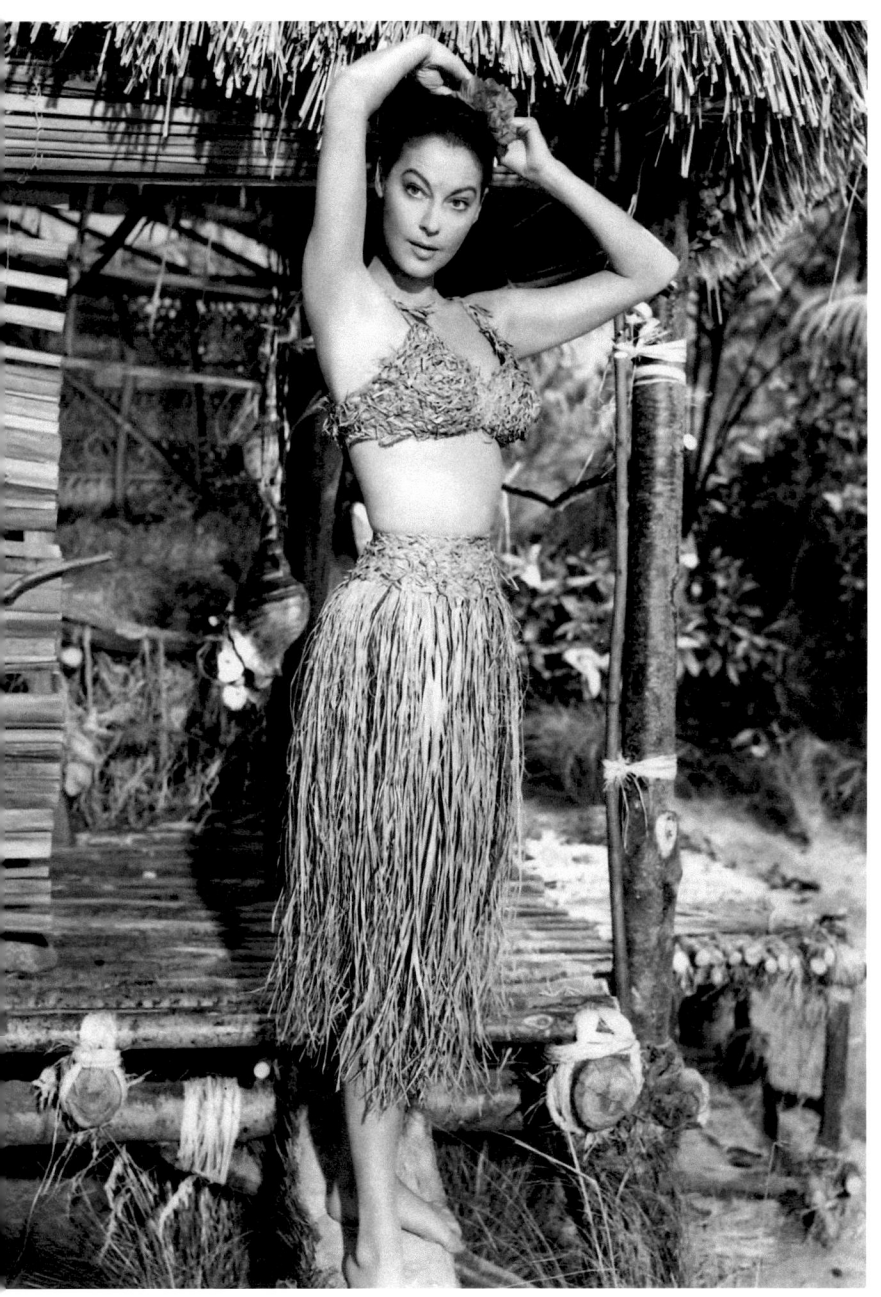

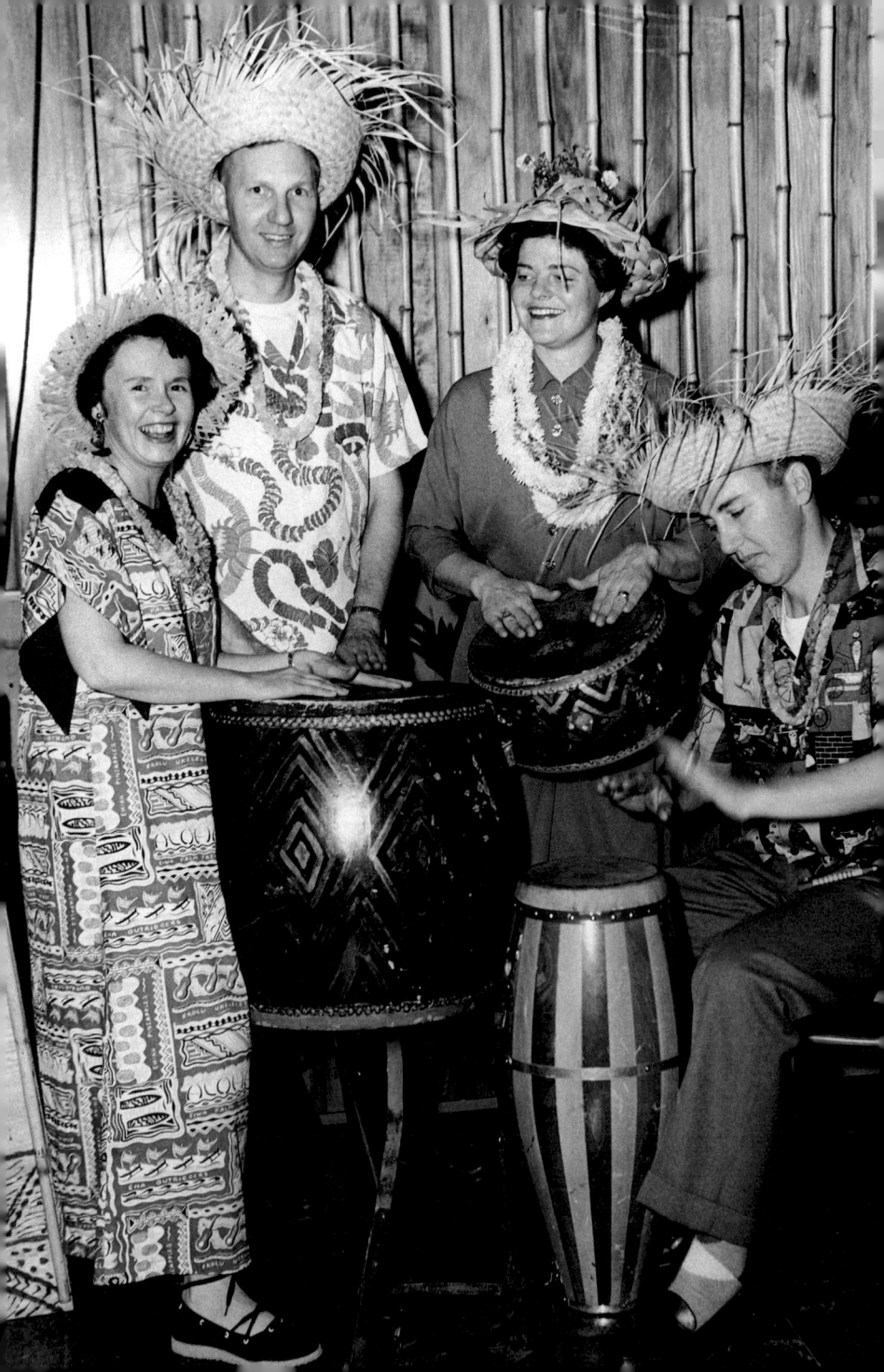

Das beste Beispiel für ein Cocktailritual war zweifelsohne der Mystery Drink, eine Erfindung des Mai-Kai. Nach einem Gongschlag kam das Mystery Girl langsam und verführerisch auf den Gast zu, kniete sich sittsam nieder und präsentierte ihm den besonderen Trank. Das Ritual war ein solcher Erfolg, dass es in der *Johnny Carson Show* vorgeführt und von diversen Tiki-Lokalen übernommen wurde.

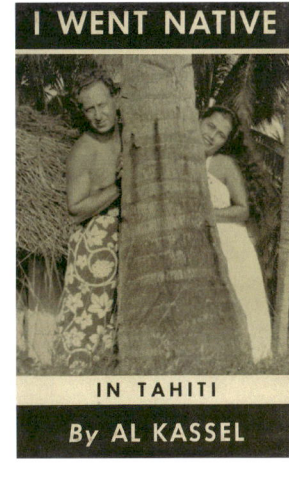

I WENT NATIVE

IN TAHITI

By AL KASSEL

OPPOSITE: American tribal gathering

ABOVE AND BELOW: Ways to go native

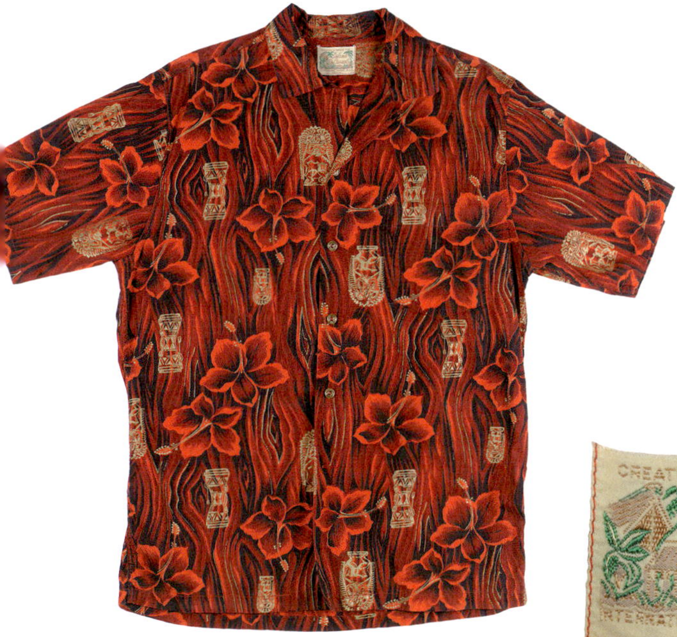

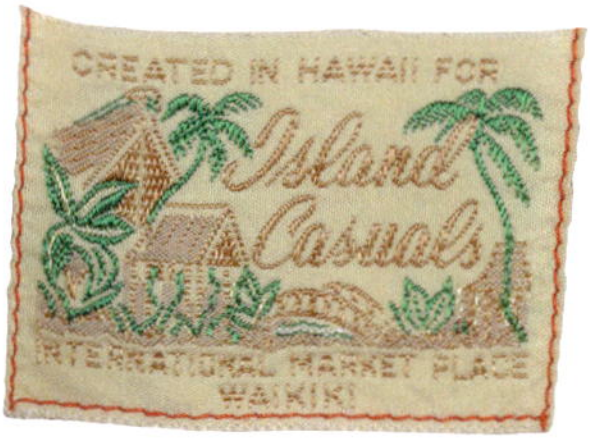

DEPUIS LE JOUR OÙ LES PREMIERS
explorateurs ont foulé le sable polynésien, les hommes blancs ont été charmés par les rites et les danses par lesquels ils y étaient accueillis. Cette fascination s'est perpétuée jusqu'au XXᵉ siècle, en partie grâce aux spectacles proposés par les établissements tiki du continent. Leurs clients urbains, tellement « civilisés », étaient captivés par cet « exotique autre », et bien sûr par la peau et les corps sublimes qui y étaient exhibés.

Les revues polynésiennes proposent en général une parade sur le thème des « Nations unies de Polynésie », où se succèdent des groupes originaires de différentes îles : danse du feu des Samoa, haka maori, hula hawaiien, et danse du tambour tahitienne sont les grands classiques de ce répertoire. Contrairement aux brigades de serveurs des temples tiki américains, la plupart de ces troupes étaient composées d'authentiques insulaires venus du Pacifique,

qui se donnaient en spectacle avec une fierté sincère de représenter leur culture.

Les Blancs veulent participer au spectacle, si bien que les écoles de danse commencent à proposer des cours de hula ou de poi maori, qui consiste à faire danser des balles. Les hommes aussi ont le droit de jouer : depuis l'époque du capitaine Bligh, les mâles occidentaux raides et empotés sont invités à remuer leurs hanches par les vahinés locales, et cette tradition amuse encore les foules au XXᵉ siècle.

Le fantasme d'escapade ultime est bien sûr de *devenir* un îlien, de se glisser dans la peau d'un habitant de ces lieux enchanteurs et ne plus faire qu'un avec son environnement tropical. Enfiler une jupe en raphia peut participer à l'illusion – touristes et continentaux ne s'en privent pas. La tendance née avec l'engouement pour la musique hawaiienne dans les années 1920, qui a perduré dans les années 1950 avec les *luau* d'arrière-cour,

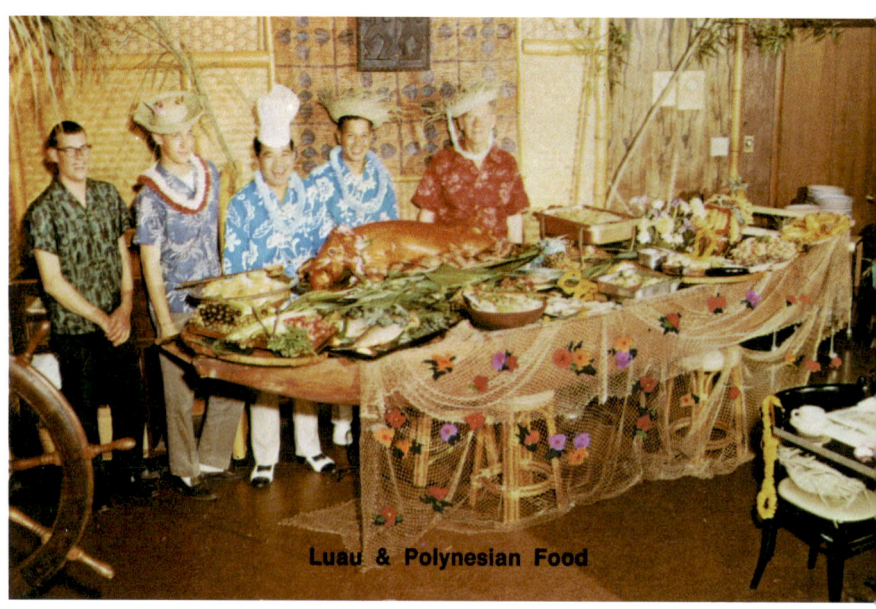

Luau & Polynesian Food

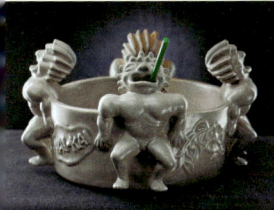

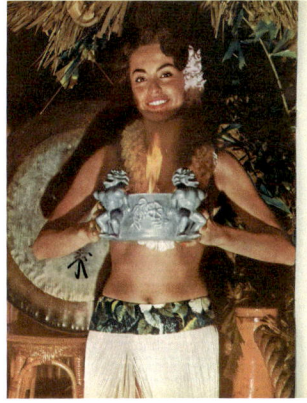

Here's a bit of Polynesian paradise on U.S. Highway 1. Called the *Mystery Bowl*, it's a Mai Kai original—Mai Kai being a million-dollar restaurant in Ft. Lauderdale, Florida—and it's one of forty-eight rum concoctions served in the restaurant's Molokai Bar. But this drink is something special, the only one served by the hula-skirted *Mystery Girl*. This, plus the magic of the Mai Kai chefs, and such atmosphere props as South Pacific Flora, a giant coral-rock waterfall, and machine-driven rain occasionally beating against the windows, often attracts over a thousand Gold Coast guests each night.

mai kai

OPPOSITE: The happy staff at the Zombie Hut, Sacramento, California *(Frank Brajevic Collection)*

ABOVE LEFT: A rare original Mai-Kai Mystery Bowl *(Frank Brajevic Collection)*

ABOVE RIGHT: A Mai-Kai Mystery Girl *(Frank Brajevic Collection)*

BELOW: *Samoan Fire Dance,* rendering by Roger McVicker, 1957

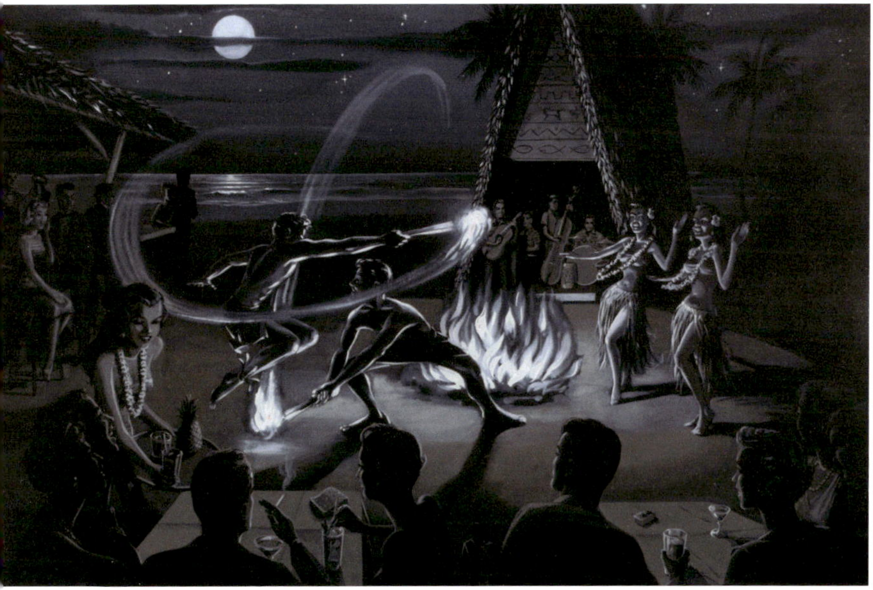

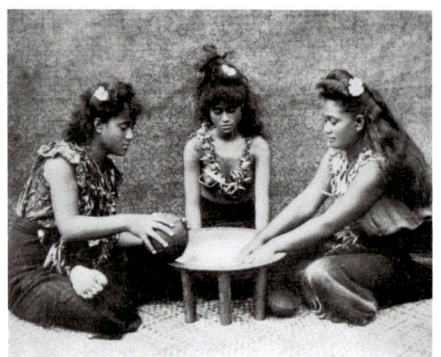

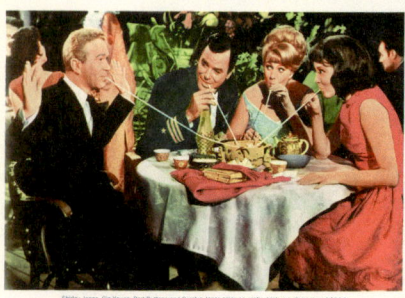

Communal Drinks

SCORPION BOWL **3.85**
(Serves Two or Three Persons)
Originated up the Manoa Valley
in Honolulu. A Rare Punch with
a Touch of Almond and a
Gardenia Float.

SCORPION (for one) . . **1.75**

RUM BARREL **2.50**

LAPU LAPU (Limit Two) **3.00**
(Serves One or Two Persons)
Another One for Those
Who Like to be Alone Together.

RAPA VAHINES **5.50**
(Serves Three or More Persons)
Three's a Crowd, But Not on the Island of Rapa Where
There are Ten Women to One Man. Hence, We Toast
the Vahines on Rapa Island!

SCORPION BOWL

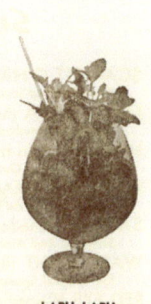

LAPU LAPU

POLYNESIAN KAVA BOWL **3.85**
(Serves Three or Four Persons)
Our Interpretation of the Samoan Welcome
Drink. Served in a Communal Bowl with
Long Straws.

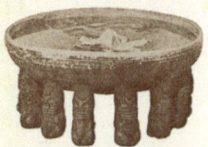

POLYNESIAN KAVA BOWL

TIKI BOWL **2.00**
(Serves One or Two Persons)
A Replica of a Polynesian Ceremonial Bowl is
Employed to Serve You a Tantalizing Light Punch.

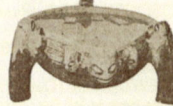

TIKI BOWL

PIJODI BOWL **7.50**
A Drink for the Gods. Only One Bowl is Exclusively Used. Serves Many

ABOVE: Samoan kava preparation
and its American counterpart
(Scott Schell Collection)

LEFT: Cocktail menu offering a
variety of bowl drinks
(Scott Schell Collection)

OPPOSITE: Original kava bowl
from Fiji
(Los Angeles County Museum of Art)

culmine lorsqu'Ava Gardner pose dans une jupe en raphia créée par Christian Dior.

L'autre accessoire de mode supposé « rendre local » est l'inénarrable chemise hawaiienne, parfait antidote à l'étouffant costume-cravate auquel est condamné le col blanc du milieu du siècle. Paré des couleurs chatoyantes et des motifs sauvages typiques du style Aloha, on devient plus facilement quelqu'un d'autre. La tenue hawaiienne est synonyme de détente, de plaisir, de fête, et devient le moyen le plus sûr de se glisser dans l'état d'esprit « des îles ».

Les Américains tentent par ailleurs de devenir aussi polynésiens que possible en se livrant à des rituels tribaux divers, comme la cérémonie collective du kava. Le kava est une plante utilisée de tout temps comme sédatif dans les sociétés polynésiennes, où elle est notamment mâchée par les jeunes vierges. Cette plante étant introuvable en Amérique, elle est remplacée par une décoction très forte à base de rhum, baptisée Kava. Le gros bol était piqué de plusieurs longues pailles afin que les clients puissent boire en même temps, ce qui a multiplié les occasions de rapprochement et d'amusement.

La plus spectaculaire récupération de ce rituel autour d'un bol est l'œuvre du Mai-Kai : le Breuvage Mystère. Lorsqu'un gong retentit, une Fille Mystère s'approche lentement et langoureusement du client, s'agenouille modestement devant lui et lui présente la potion spéciale du soir. Ce numéro remporte un tel succès qu'il est joué jusque sur le plateau du *Johnny Carson Show,* puis imité par plusieurs établissements tiki.

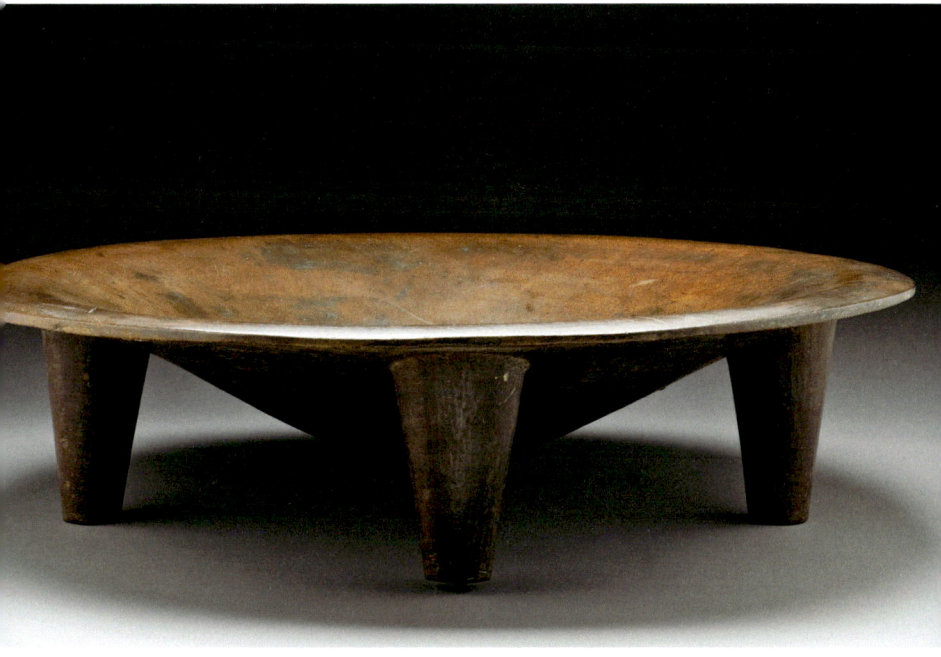

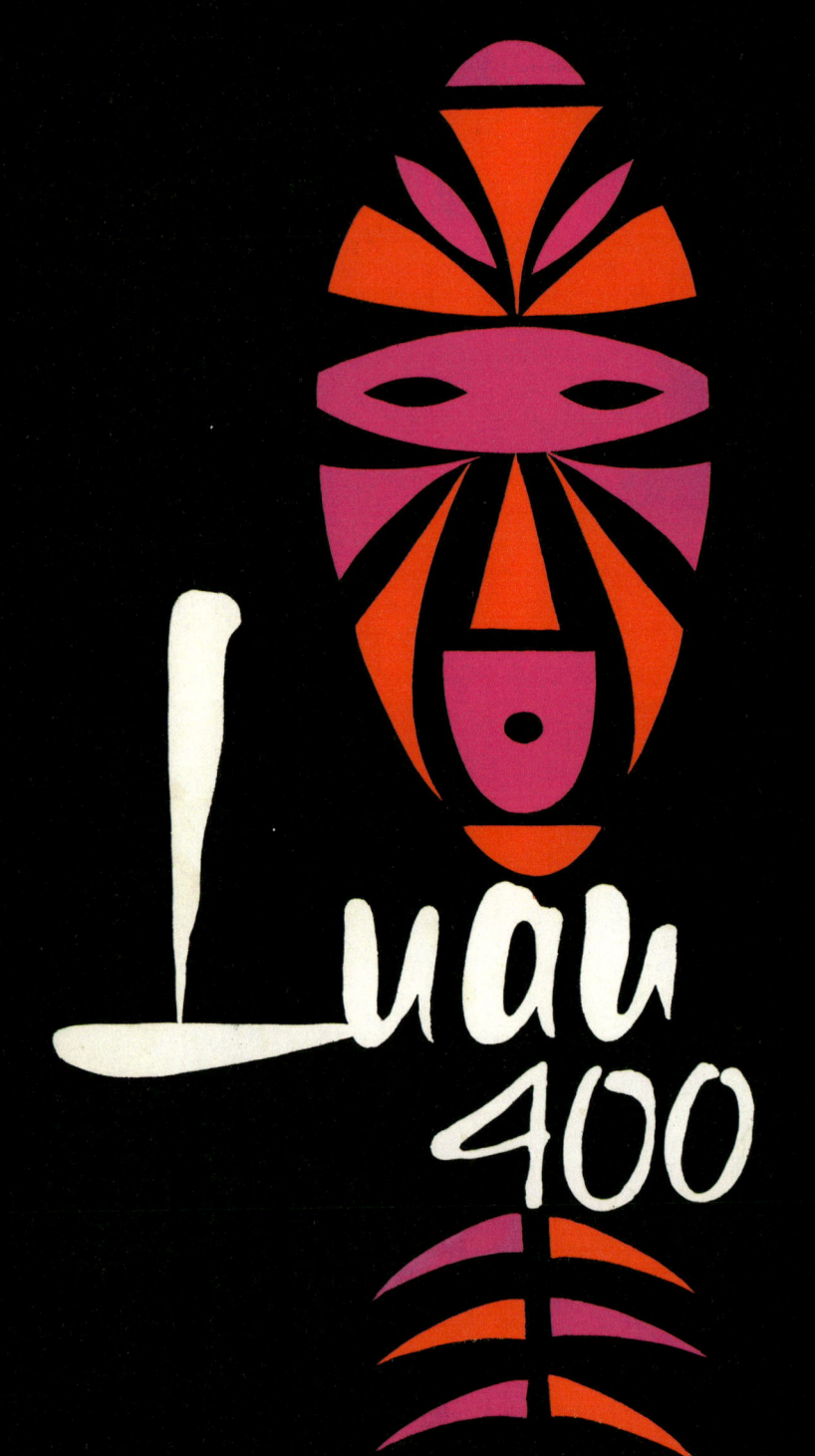

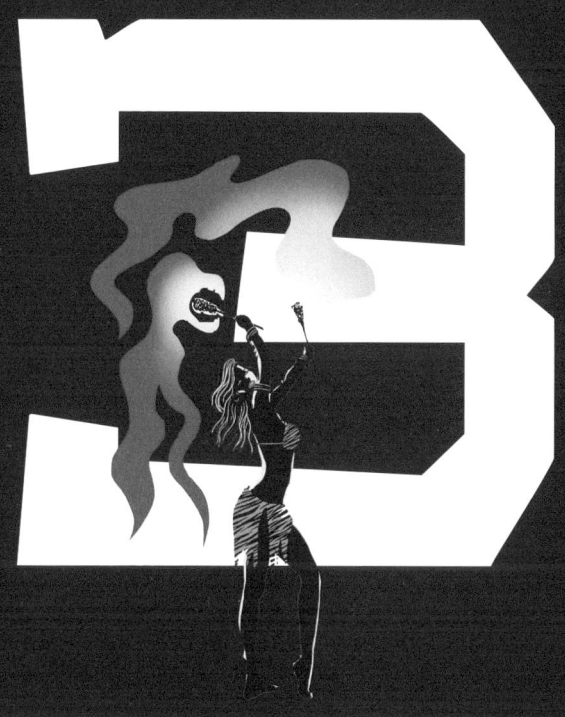

TIKI EXPANSION:
PEAK AND IMPLOSION

TIKIS AUFSTIEG, HÖHEPUNKT UND NIEDERGANG
L'ÉVOLUTION DU TIKI – GRANDEUR ET DÉCADENCE

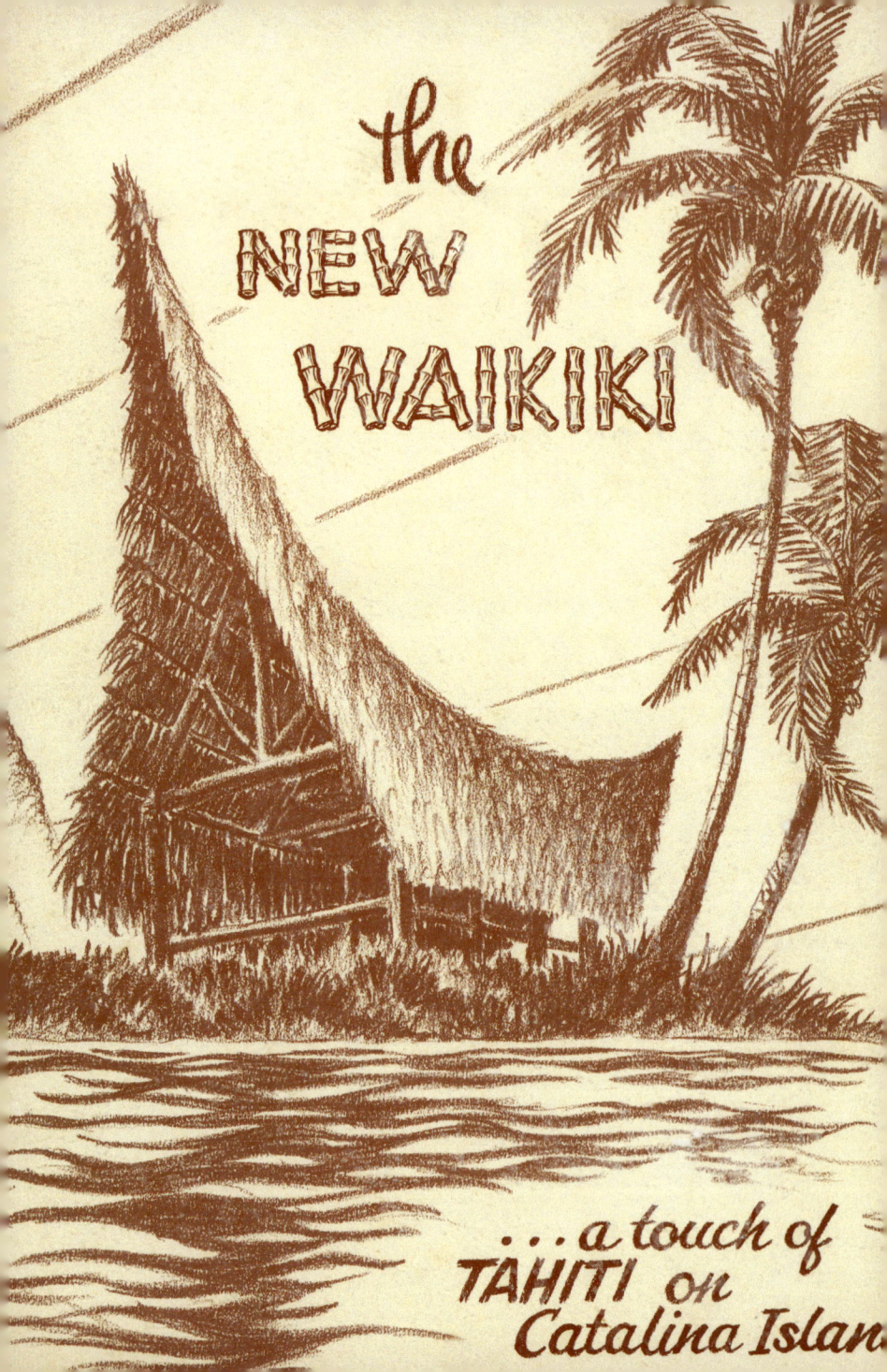

the NEW WAIKIKI

...a touch of **TAHITI** on **Catalina Island**

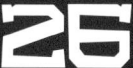

26

TIKI ARCHITECTURE

TIKI-ARCHITEKTUR
L'ARCHITECTURE TIKI

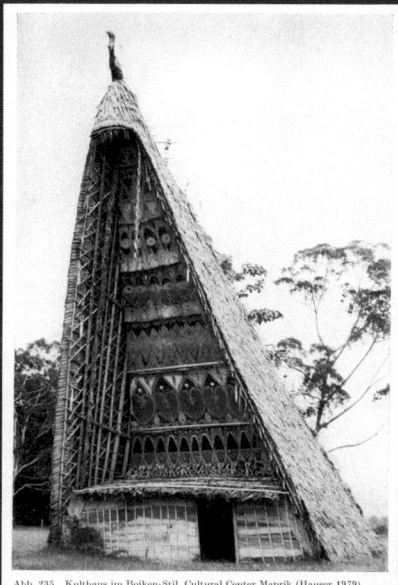

Abb. 235 Kulthaus im Boiken-Stil, Cultural Center Maprik (Hauser 1979).

ALONG WITH THE TIKI FIGURE, ANOTHER significant design feature marked the beginning of Tiki style: A-frame architecture. The peaked roofs of urban bamboo huts began to stretch toward heaven, taking their cues from traditional men's meeting houses from Melanesia.

By timely coincidence, modern architects had chosen the skyward-thrusting "A" shape as the perfect embodiment of the jet-age look, which was making its mark in all design arenas, most notably in the tail-finned cars of the late '50s.

Mid-century architects applied the A-frame to bowling alleys, contemporary churches, and weekend getaways. It seemed only logical, then, to also use this roofline for Polynesian-themed restaurants, motels, and apartment buildings, since the traditional South Seas structures already exhibited similar contours.

The A-frame gables of the original Papua New Guinea tribal huts soared several stories high into the air and featured carved outriggers at their peaks—seamlessly falling in line with the modern look. These meeting houses were complex structures compared to the simple grass huts of other islands, and an inspiration to forward-thinking architects.

The decorations on the men's club-houses of the Palau Islanders were another inspiration to American Tiki-temple architects. These so-called storyboard paintings had

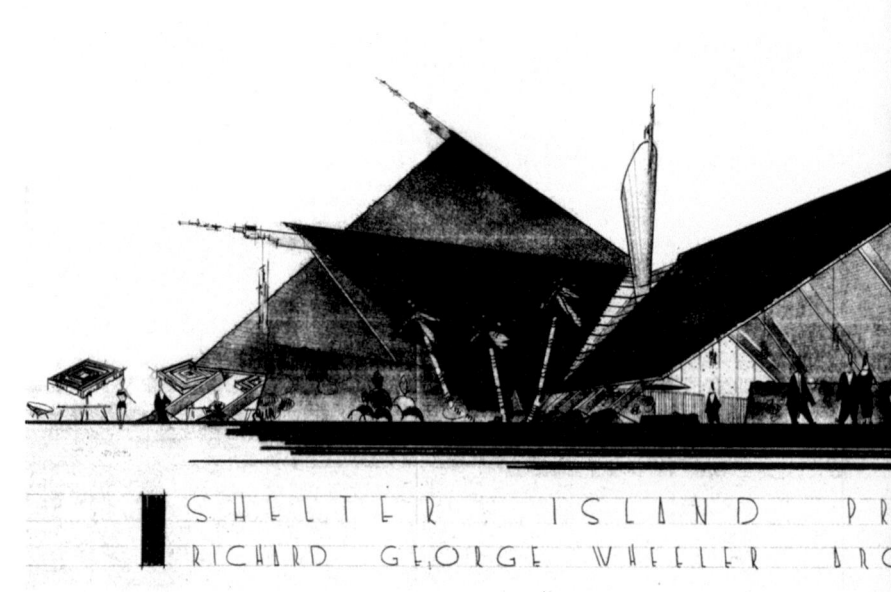

already provided creative inspiration for German Brücke artist Ernst Ludwig Kirchner, and now they were applied to the fasciae of urban A-frame huts. Trader Vic's outposts excelled in the usage of the colorful hieroglyphs, and their designers frequently made up their own stories and characters for them.

The Islander restaurant on La Cienega Boulevard in Los Angeles was one of the classic examples of Tiki Pop architecture: utterly modern with its jutting A-frame shape, its attention-catching entrance featured rickshaw service from the parking lot to the aba-lone-studded ramp that led to a bridge spanning a waterfall-fed moat.

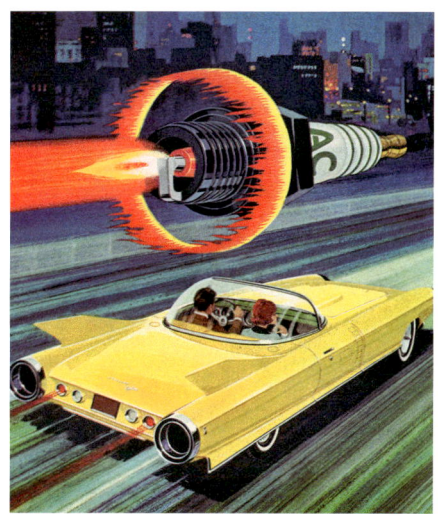

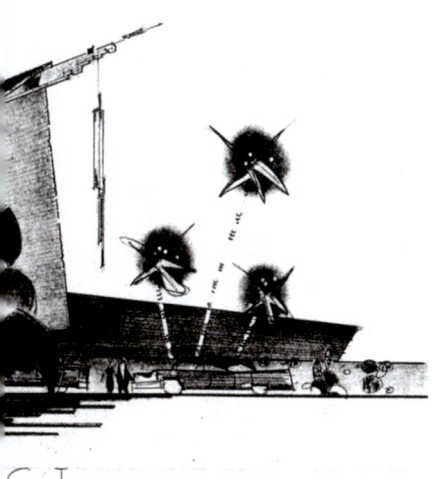

C T

T ₹ A S S O C .

LEFT: A-frame hotel rendering, Shelter Island, San Diego (*Mike Skinner Collection*)

ABOVE: 1959 Cadillac Cyclone

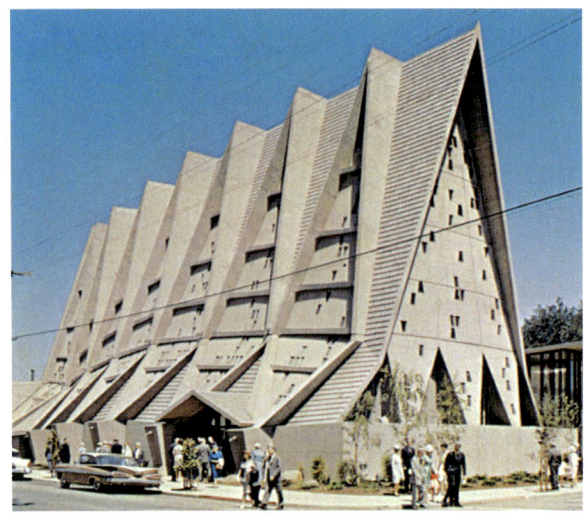

LEFT: Mid-century-modern church, Palo Alto, California, 1964

BELOW LEFT: Sketch for a mountain retreat

BELOW: Rendering of a space-age bowling alley, Arizona

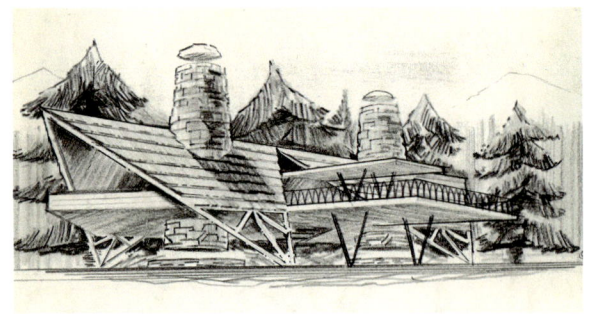

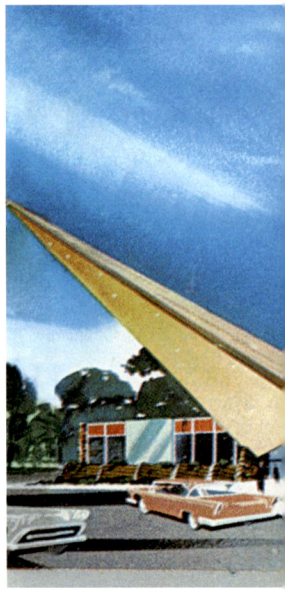

Sometimes multiple interlocking A-frames were used, such as those at the Trade Winds restaurant in Oxnard, California, designed by former 20th Century Fox set designer Fred Moninger.

The elaborate landscaping and use of exotic materials inside and out made such places seem like film sets: artificial waterfalls and streams, flaming torches and volcanoes, lush tropical plantings, and props like boats tied to pier pylons created a suspension of reality. These elements would have made for a quaint and romantic setting as found in the early bamboo bars—if not for the Tiki, who provided a heightened sense of drama to the environs.

Of all the set pieces employed to tell the fable of the Polynesian paradise, the Tiki figure was itself the most striking. Passing under the stern gaze of these idols made one feel like an explorer walking into the Temple of Doom.

The Tiki carvings were used as free-standing décor pieces, or as carved support posts for restaurant roofs. This mirrored their traditional use in the Polynesian Islands as temple statues and house posts that supported the thatched roofs of native architecture. Since many of the American Tiki palaces had interior waterfalls and streams meandering through, Tiki railing posts found ample use, mostly carved in the four-sided Janus style.

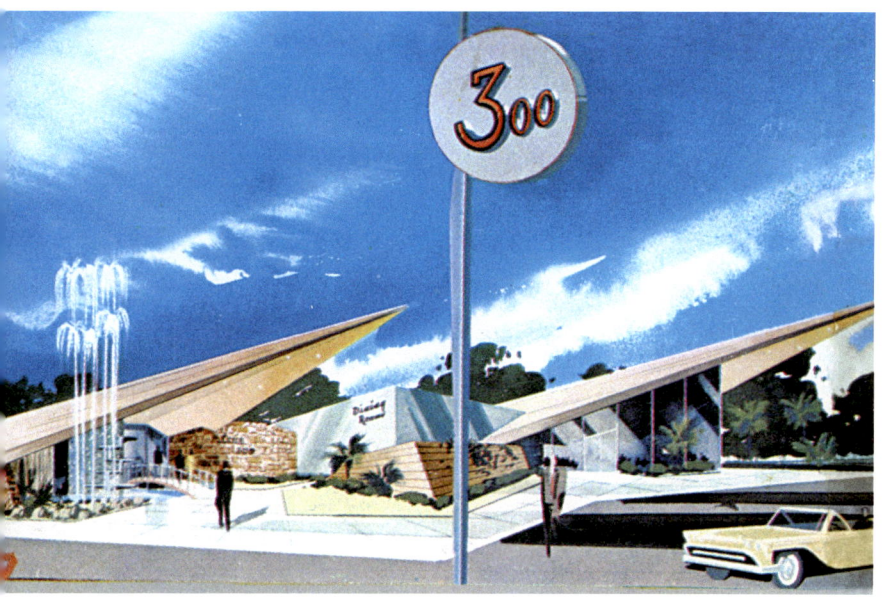

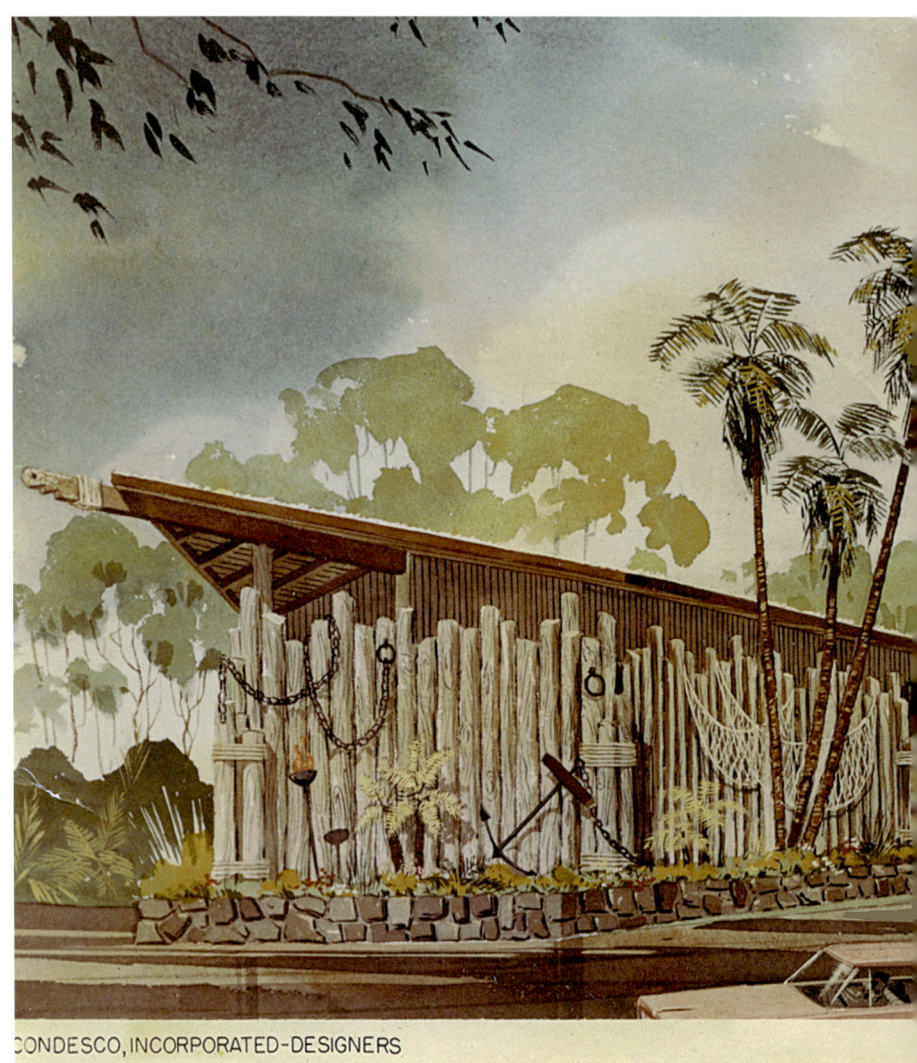

CONDESCO, INCORPORATED-DESIGNERS

Rendering for a Don the Beachcomber
franchise *(Frank Brajevic Collection)*

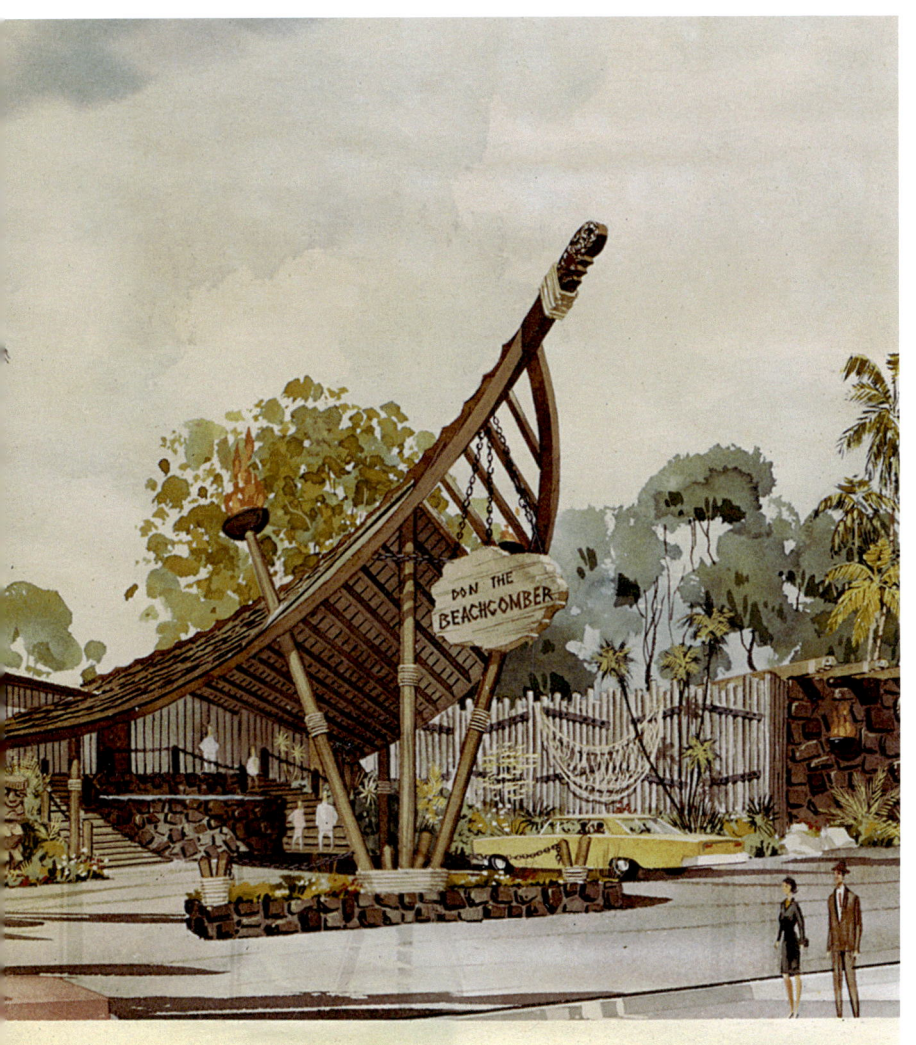

ON THE BEACHCOMBER

CORONA DEL MAR, CALIFORNIA

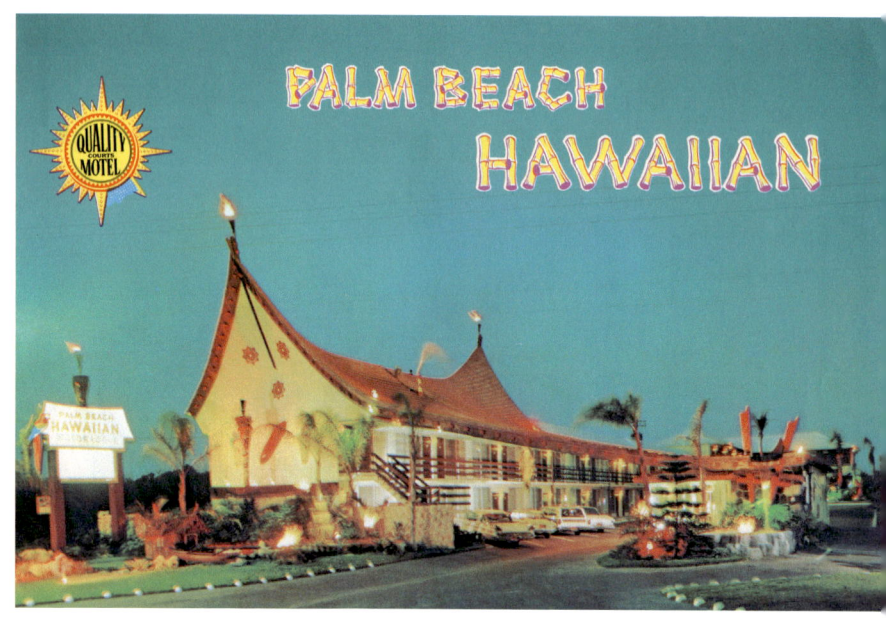

ABOVE: The Palm Beach Hawaiian
Motor Lodge, Florida
(Jackie Zumwaldt Collection)

OPPOSITE ABOVE: Entrance to the
late, great Mauna Loa, Detroit, 1967
(Scott Schell Collection)

OPPOSITE BELOW: Model of a Haus
Tambaran (meeting house), East
Sepik Province, Papua New Guinea
(Musée du Quai Branly Collection)

ZUSAMMEN MIT DER TIKI-FIGUR

markierte noch ein weiteres Gestaltungs-
merkmal die Anfänge des Tiki-Stils: das
Nurdachhaus. Die spitzen Dächer urbaner
Tiki-Tempel streckten sich immer weiter
Richtung Himmel. Ihr Vorbild waren die
traditionellen Männerhäuser Melanesiens.

Es war ein günstiger Zufall, dass sich
zeitgenössische Architekten ebenfalls
für die hoch aufragende A-Form entschie-
den hatten. Sie galt als perfekte Verkör-
perung des Jet-Zeitalters, das sich in allen
Designfeldern bemerkbar machte, insbesondere in den Heckflossen der Autos der
späten 1950er-Jahre.

Architekten verwendeten die A-Form
für Bowlingbahnen, moderne Kirchen und
Wochenendhäuser. Und es schien somit
nur logisch, sie auch für polynesische
Restaurants, Motels und Wohnanlagen
einzusetzen – zumal diese Form in der

ursprünglichen Südseearchitektur bei vielen Gebäuden anzutreffen ist.

Die Nurdachhäuser der Stammeshütten Papua-Neuguineas reichten mehrere Stockwerke hoch in den Himmel und trugen geschnitzte Ausleger an ihrer Spitze, ein Element, das sich problemlos in den modernen Look einfügen ließ. Diese Versammlungsstätten hatten, verglichen mit den einfachen Bambushütten anderer Inseln, komplexe Strukturen und waren eine Inspiration für vorausschauende Architekten.

Die Dekorationen an den Männerhäusern der Palau-Insulaner waren eine weitere Vorlage für die amerikanischen Bauherren der Tiki-Tempel. Die sogenannten Storyboard-Schnitzereien hatten bereits den deutschen Brücke-Künstler Ernst Ludwig Kirchner inspiriert. Nun wurden sie für die Attiken der urbanen Nurdachhäuser verwendet. Trader Vic's Ableger setzten hier farbenfrohe Hieroglyphen brillant in Szene. Ihre Geschichten und Charaktere entstammten oftmals vollständig der Fantasie ihrer Designer.

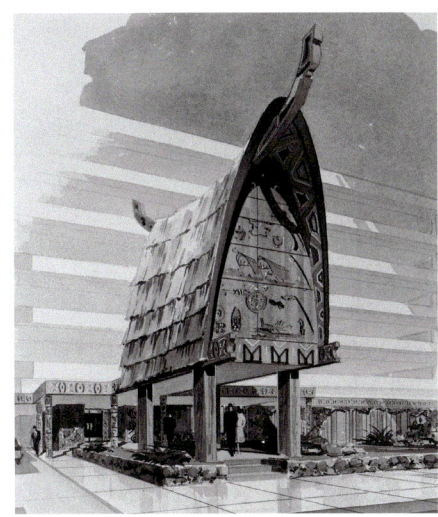

Das Restaurant The Islander am La Cienega Boulevard in Los Angeles war ein typisches Beispiel der Tiki-Pop-Architektur. Am auffällig gestalteten Eingangsbereich mit seiner modernen klaren A-Linie gab es einen Rikscha-Service, der Kunden vom Parkplatz zu einer mit Muscheln verzierten

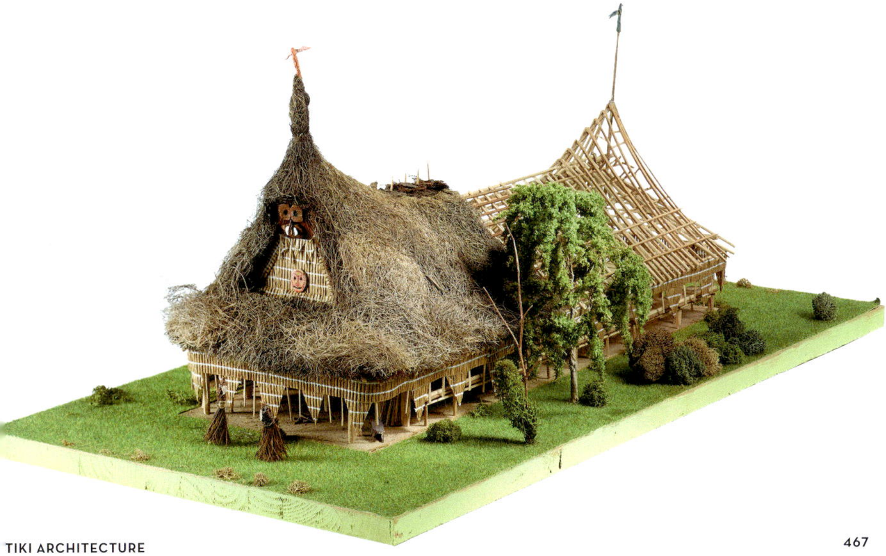

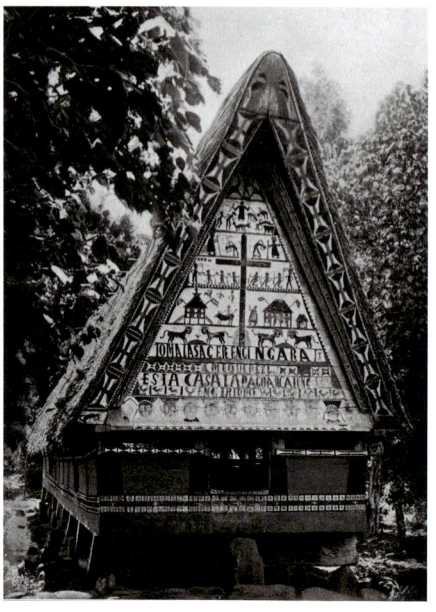

Rampe brachte. Von dort führte eine Brücke über einen Wassergraben, der von einem Wasserfall gespeist wurde.

Manchmal griffen auch mehrere A-Rahmen ineinander. Dies war beim Restaurant Trade Winds im kalifornischen Oxnard der Fall, das vom ehemaligen Bühnenbildner der 20th Century Fox Studios, Fred Moninger, entworfen wurde.

Mit aufwendigen Gartenlandschaften und exotischen Materialien im Innen- und Außenbereich sahen diese Lokale wie Filmkulissen aus. Künstliche Wasserfälle und Bäche, brennende Fackeln und Vulkane, ein üppiger tropischer Pflanzenbewuchs und Requisiten – etwa vertäute Boote – sorgten für die gewünschte Verfremdung der Realität. Die Kulisse hätte so idyllisch und romantisch anmuten können wie die frühen Bambus-Bars – wäre da nicht Tiki gewesen, der dem Ganzen eine dramatische Note verlieh.

Von allen eingesetzten Gestaltungselementen, die die Fabel vom polynesischen Paradies authentisch vermitteln sollten, war die Tiki-Figur das beeindruckendste. Unter ihrem ernsten Blick fühlten sich die Besucher wie Entdecker auf der Schwelle zum Tempel des Todes.

Die Tiki-Schnitzereien wurden als freistehende Skulpturen oder Stützpfeiler für das Restaurantdach eingesetzt. Dies spiegelte ihre traditionelle Verwendung auf den polynesischen Inseln als Tempelstatuen und Stützen für die Strohdächer der Behausungen wieder. Da viele amerikanische Tiki-Paläste Wasserfälle und Bachläufe beherbergten, fanden auch Tiki-Brüstungen reichlich Verwendung. Meist waren diese im vierseitigen Janus-Stil gefertigt.

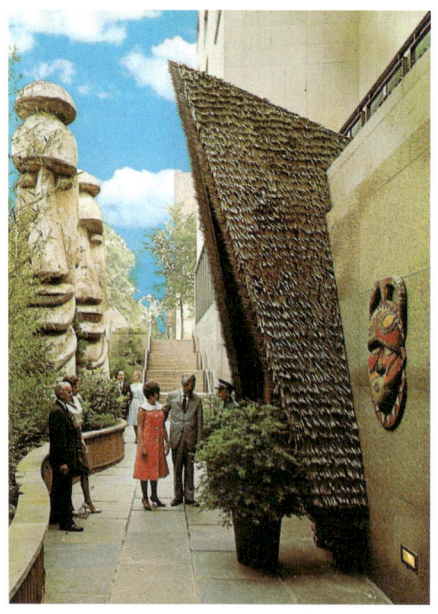

OPPOSITE ABOVE: Authentic men's house of the Palau Islands with storyboard paintings

OPPOSITE BELOW: Side view of A-frame entrance at the Washington, D.C., Trader Vic's

BELOW: Silk scarf depicting Trader Vic's restaurants, many of them A-frames, some with storyboard ornamentation

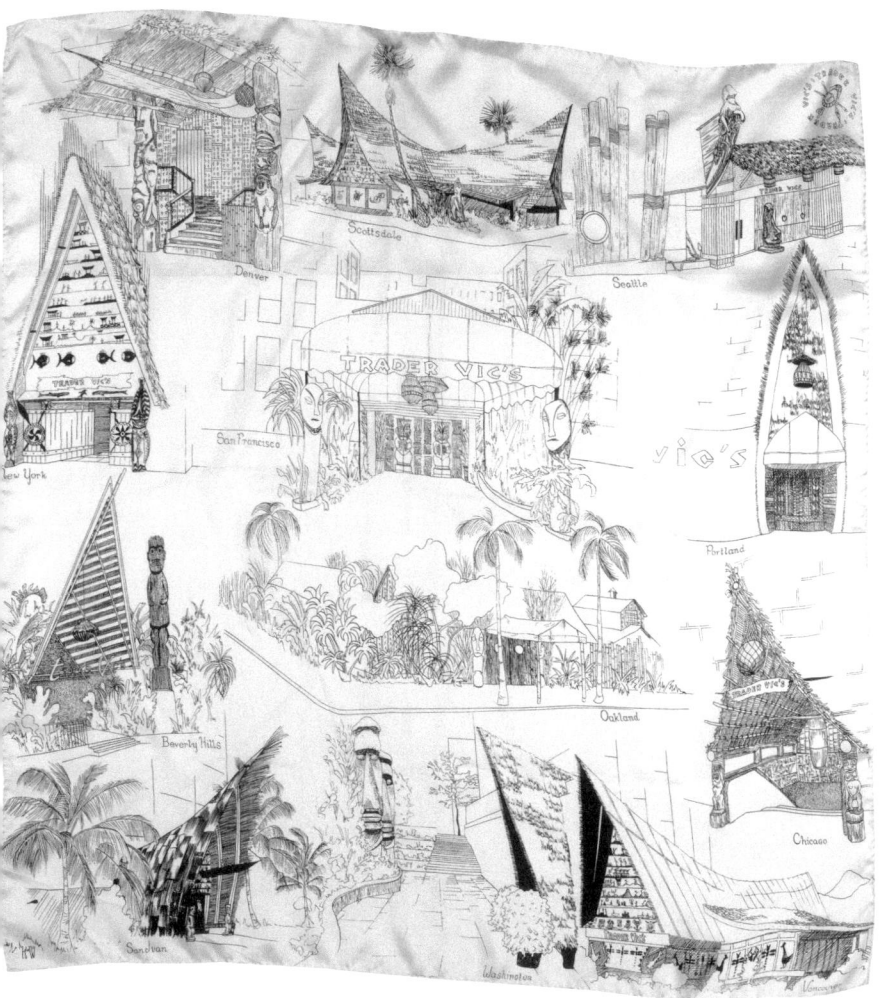

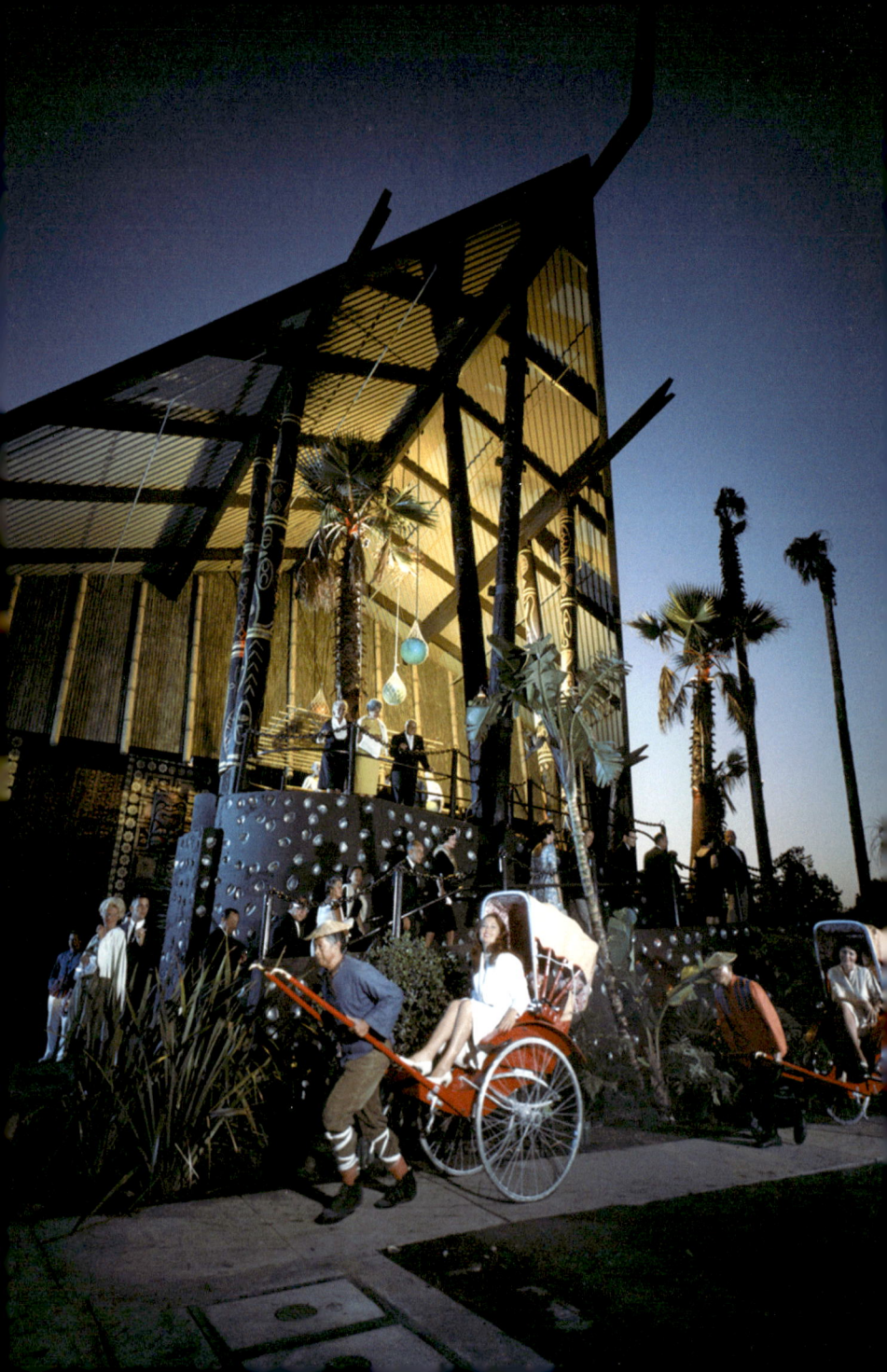

LE TIKI N'EST PAS LA SEULE FIGURE à soutenir l'édifice esthétique tiki. Avec son essor apparaît aussi la charpente en A. Les toits pentus des huttes de bambou urbaines se mettent à pointer de plus en plus haut vers le ciel, s'inspirant ainsi des maisons traditionnelles où se réunissaient les hommes de Mélanésie.

Coïncidence ou air du temps, les architectes modernes jugent aussi que la forme en A est celle qui incarne le plus parfaitement l'ère de l'avion à réaction. Elle imprime d'ailleurs sa marque dans toutes les disciplines du design, et plus particulièrement dans le style des voitures, dotées d'ailerons arrières effilés à la fin des années 1950.

Les architectes du milieu de siècle appliquent la charpente en A aux pistes de bowling, aux églises contemporaines et aux maisons de campagne. Il semble dès lors logique de la retrouver coiffant restaurants, hôtels et résidences de tourisme sur le thème polynésien, puisque les bâtisses du Pacifique possédaient des silhouettes similaires.

Les pignons en A hérités des huttes tribales de Papouasie-Nouvelle-Guinée se dressent à une hauteur de plusieurs étages et présentent des longerons sculptés aux

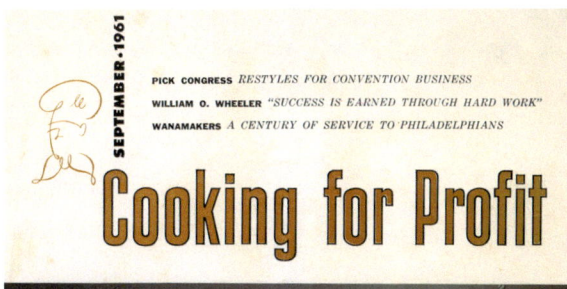

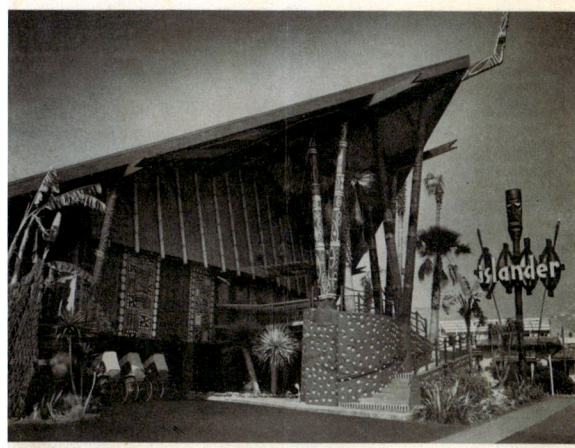

THE EXOTIC ISLANDER, OF LOS ANGELES—A NOVEL VENTURE IN EXQUISITE DINING SERVICE

OPPOSITE: Exotic mode of transportation to an exotic port of call

RIGHT: There was money to be made in Polynesia Americana
(Frank Brajevic Collection)

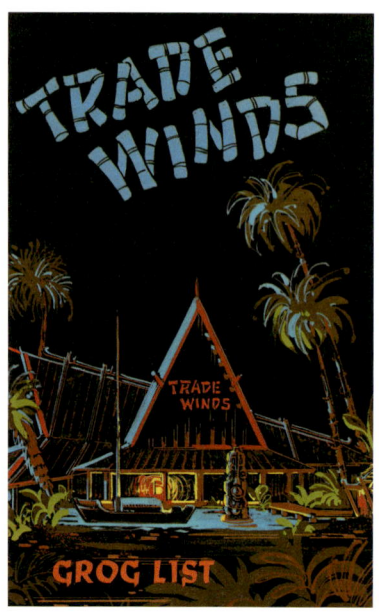

LEFT: Menu cover for Trade Winds restaurant, Oxnard, California *(Frank Brajevic Collection)*

BELOW: Blueprint for Trade Winds restaurant, 1963 *(Ron Ferrell Collection)*

OPPOSITE: Rendering of the Tiki Temple dining hut by Ione Keenan, 1963 *(Tim Keenan Collection)*

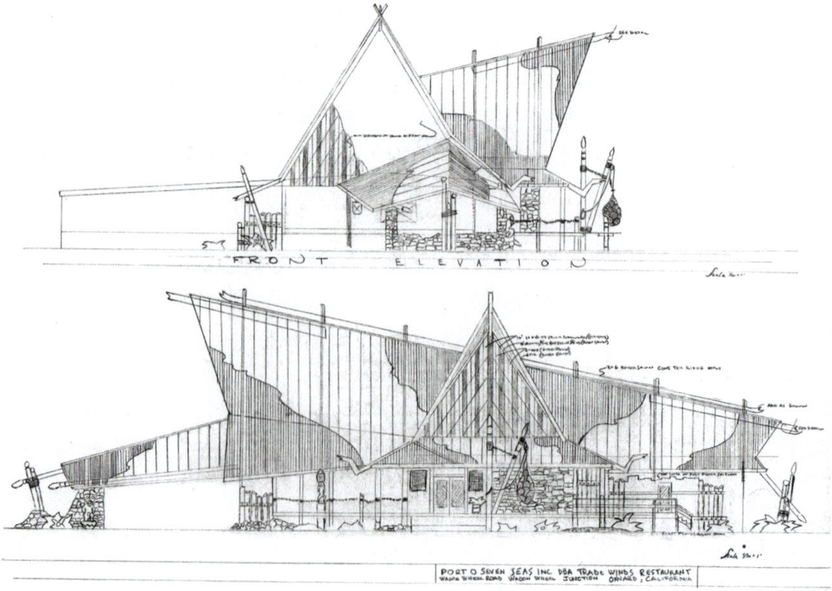

F R O N T   E L E V A T I O N

PORT O SEVEN SEAS INC. DBA TRADE WINDS RESTAURANT
VENTURA HARBOR ROAD WAGON WHEEL JUNCTION OXNARD, CALIFORNIA

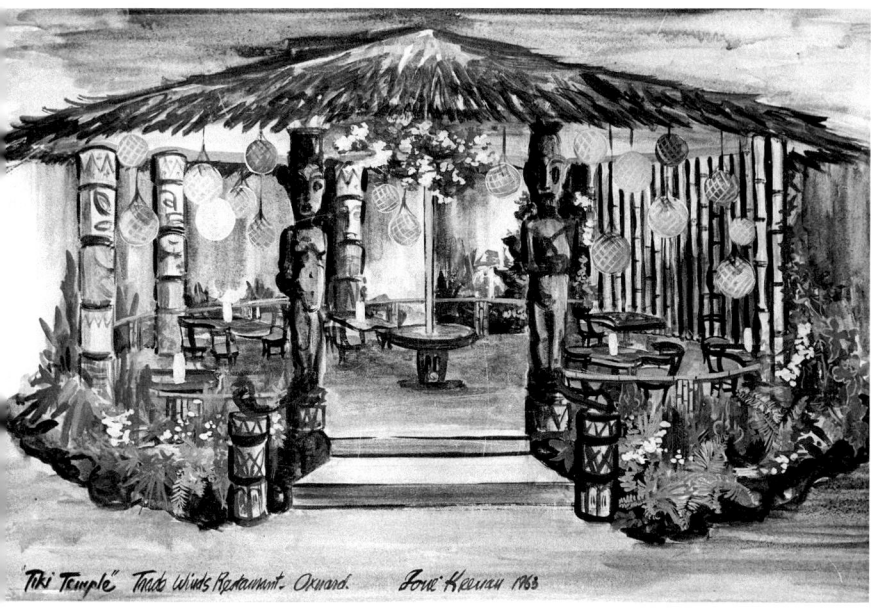

"Tiki Temple" Trade Winds Restaurant Oxnard. Gene Kearney 1963

extrémités, qui s'intègrent parfaitement au paysage urbain moderne. Ces maisons de réunion sont des structures complexes comparées aux paillotes rustiques des autres îles, et inspirent grandement les architectes progressistes de l'époque.

Les architectes des temples tiki américains s'inspirent aussi des décors qui ornent les maisons des hommes de Palau. Ces fresques narratives primitives, qui ont déjà séduit l'artiste allemand du mouvement Die Brücke Ernst Ludwig Kirchner, apparaissent dès lors sur les façades des huttes urbaines en A. Les avant-postes des établissements Trader Vic's maîtrisent le recours à des hiéroglyphes très colorés et les artistes imaginent souvent pour eux des personnages et des intrigues uniques.

Le restaurant Islander de La Cienega Boulevard, à Los Angeles, est un classique de l'architecture tiki pop : brutalement moderne, avec sa typique forme en A et son entrée spectaculaire, où un service de rickshaws conduit les hôtes le long du chemin d'accès planté d'ormeaux, jusqu'à un pont qui enjambe des douves alimentées par une cascade.

Les architectes utilisent parfois des charpentes en A qui s'entrelacent, comme celles du restaurant Trade Winds d'Oxnard, en Californie, conçues par l'ancien décorateur de la 20th Century Fox Fred Moninger.

Les aménagements paysagers sophistiqués et le recours à des matériaux exotiques à l'intérieur comme à l'extérieur ont tout des plateaux de cinéma : cascades et sources artificielles, torches et volcans ardents, plantations tropicales luxuriantes et des accessoires comme une pirogue attachée à un ponton, mettent la réalité en suspens. Ces éléments auraient tout aussi bien trouvé leur place dans le décor plus romantique

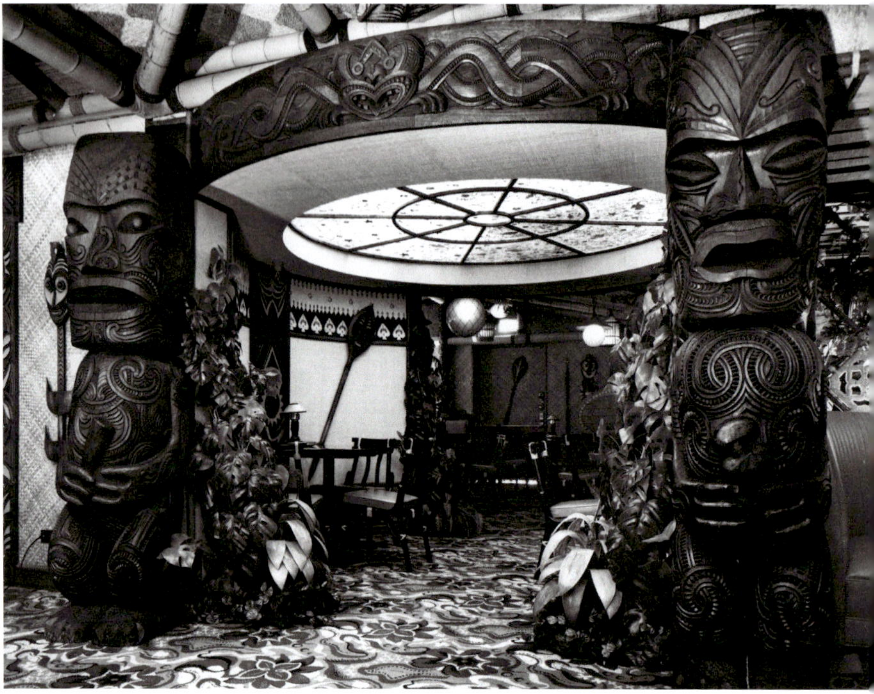

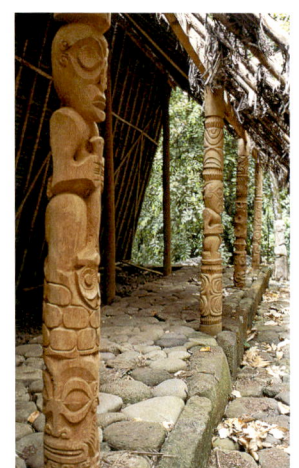

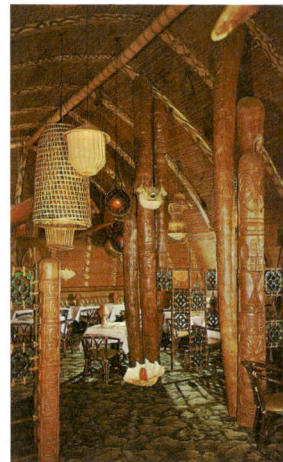

ABOVE: Elaborate entrance to the Kona Kai Restaurant, Philadelphia, Pennsylvania, designed by Armet & Davis, 1961

RIGHT: Original Tiki support posts, Nuku Hiva, Marquesas Islands and Trader Vic's interior, New York

OPPOSITE LEFT: Kona Kai bridge and waterfall *(Kiara Geller Collection)*

OPPOSITE RIGHT: Janus-style Tiki railing post, Kona Kai, Philadelphia *(Jordan Reichek Collection)*

et désuet des premiers bars en bambou – exception faite du tiki, qui apportait à l'ensemble une touche sombre et spectaculaire.

Parmi tous les éléments de décor utilisés pour narrer la fable du paradis polynésien, le tiki est le plus saisissant. Lorsqu'ils passent sous le regard sévère de ces idoles géantes, les clients se sentaient alors comme un explorateur pénétrant dans le Temple maudit.

Les statues tiki sont utilisées comme éléments de décor, ou comme pièces de soutènement de la charpente, reproduisant en cela leur emploi originel dans l'architecture des îles polynésiennes, notamment dans les temples ou les maisons particulières. Nombre de palaces tiki américains étant déjà équipés de cascades intérieures et de cours d'eaux artificiels, ils recourent amplement aux balustrades et aux poteaux tiki, le plus souvent gravés sur quatre côtés, à la Janus.

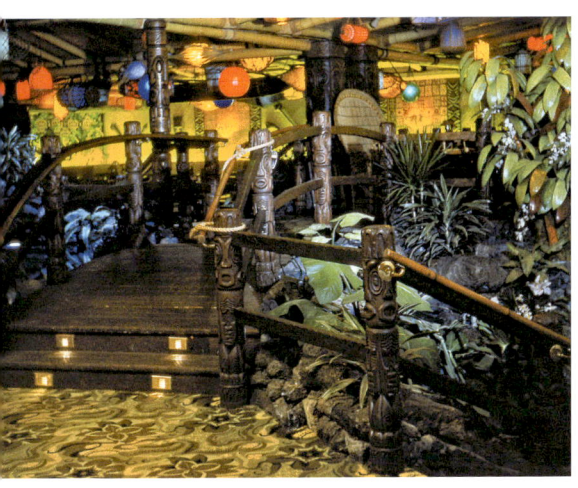

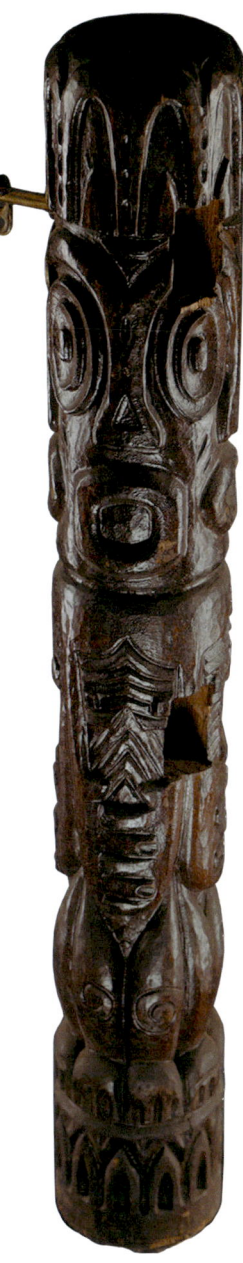

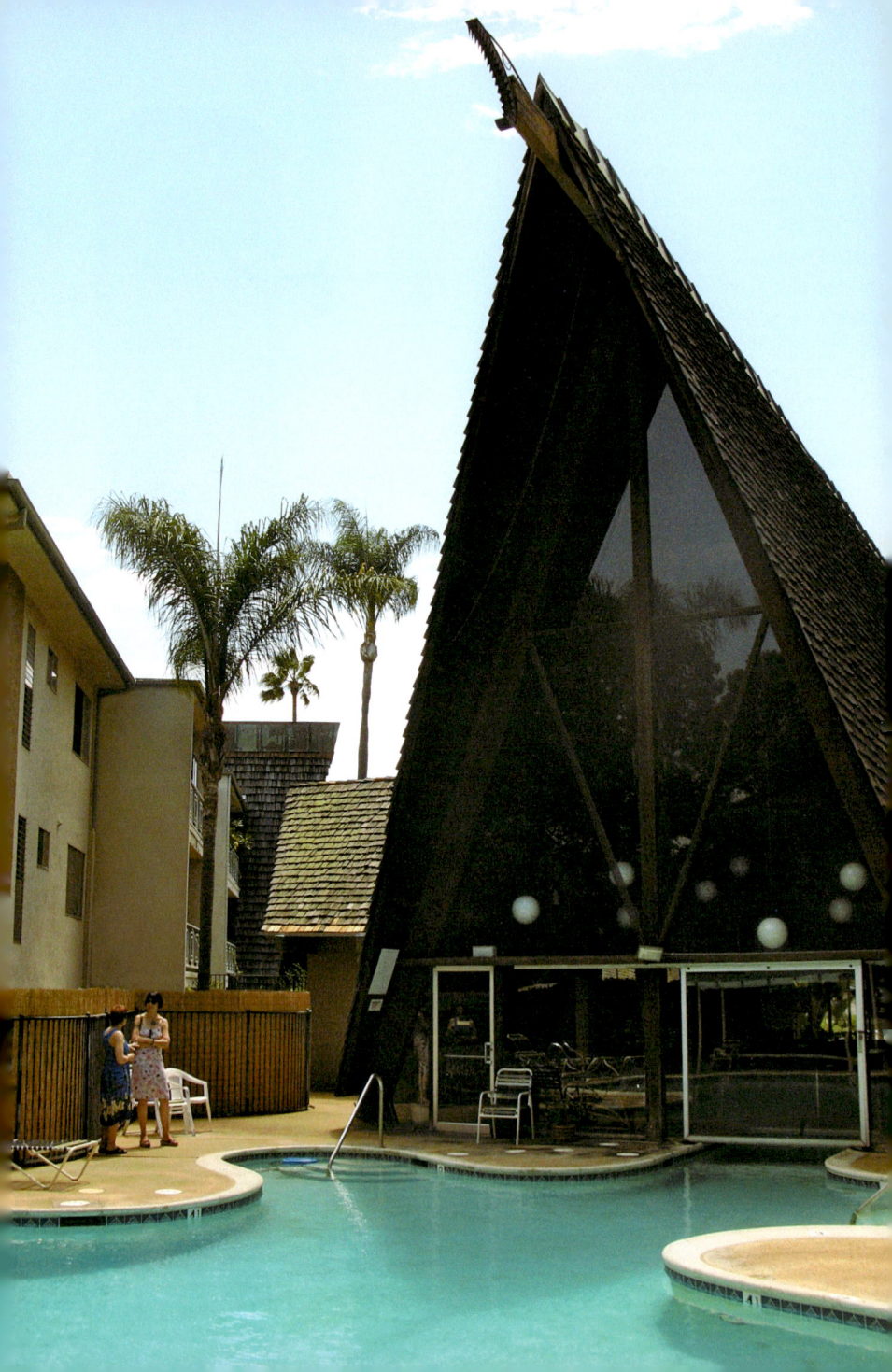

27

TIKI APARTMENTS

TIKI-WOHNUNGEN
LES RÉSIDENCES TIKI

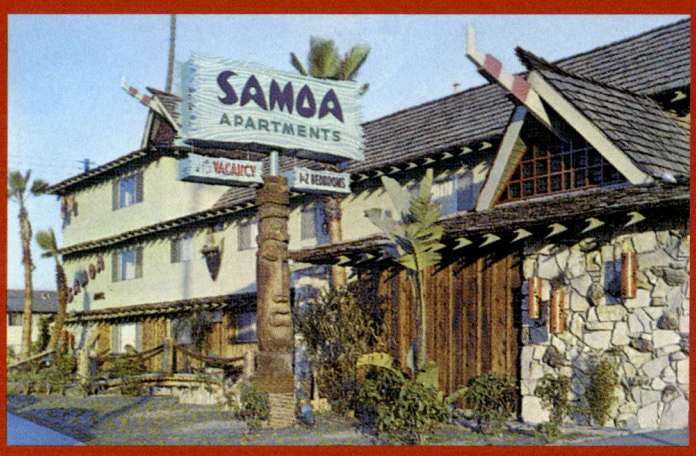

OPPOSITE: Clubhouse for the Halemakai Apartments
(now Point Loma Villas), San Diego

ABOVE: Samoa Apartments, Pico Rivera, California
(Scott Schell Collection)

TIKI POP BECAME A VERITABLE DESIGN
style when it left the realm of restaurant architecture and expanded to other urban sites like apartment buildings, motels, and bowling alleys. All of the concepts used in South Seas supper clubs now appeared in other Polynesian-themed developments: A-frames with outrigger beams on top, landscaping with water features, tropical foliage, flaming gas torches, and especially Tiki carvings as lawn statues and support posts created places for living and leisure the likes of which Americans had never before seen.

Theme apartments were not uncommon in American cities in the 1950s. Building names were considered part of the packaging.

Los Angeles especially had a tradition of applying film-architecture concepts to commercial and residential structures. Buildings could sound and look like English country cottages, Chinese pagodas, or Spanish villas. Your residence could suit your personal taste like your car and clothing.

Much of the style given to a building was just exterior dressing, but nowhere did the theme accouterments become as elaborate as in Polynesian-themed apartment complexes. Their tall A-frame entrances made them visible from far away. Builders topped established ideas when they installed gas torches that shot flames from beneath the surface of streams, or waterfalls flowing from the mouths of wall-mounted Tiki

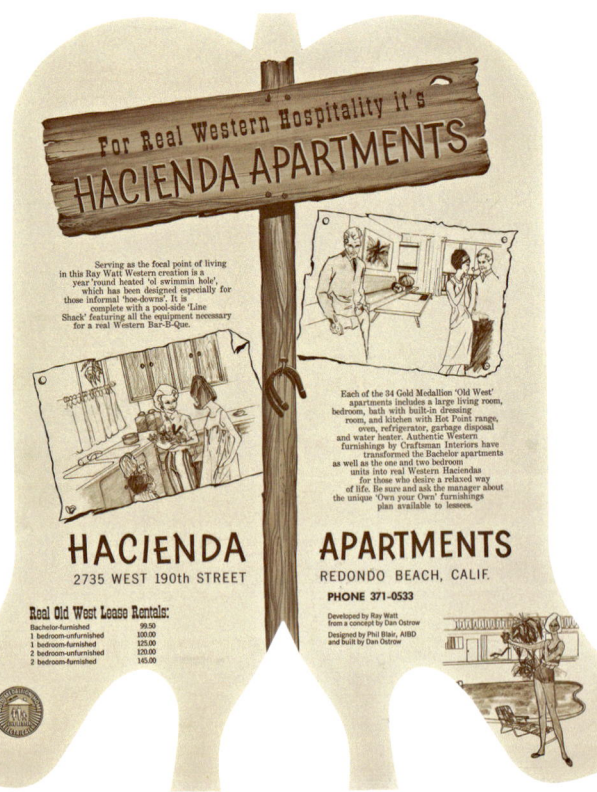

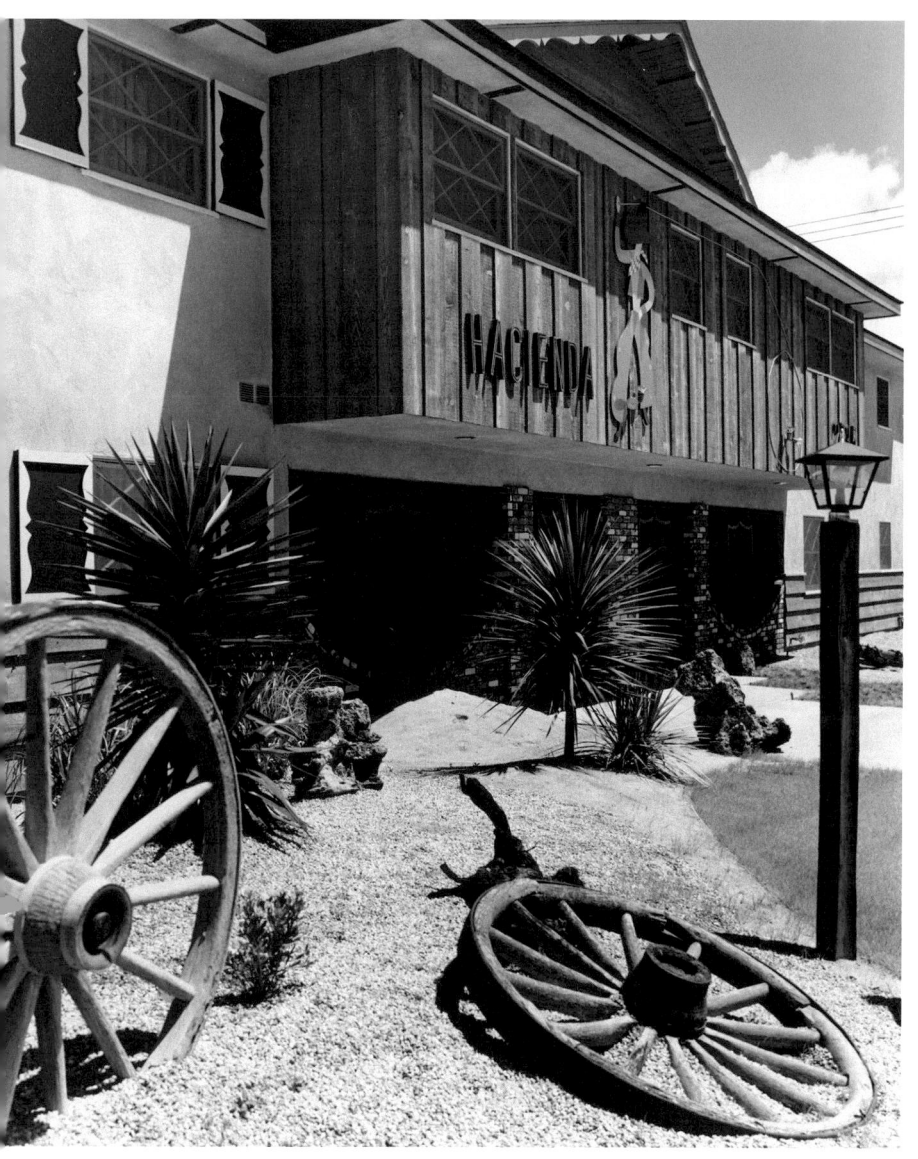

OPPOSITE AND ABOVE: Live like
the hero of a western

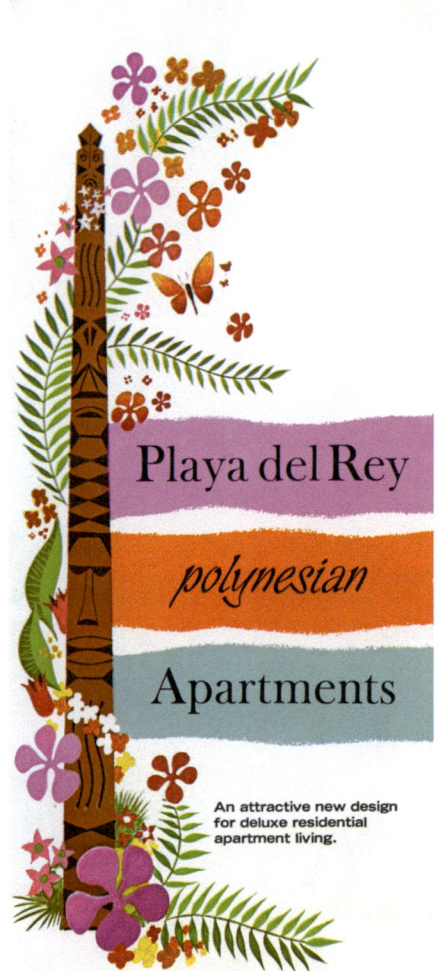

Playa del Rey

polynesian

Apartments

An attractive new design
for deluxe residential
apartment living.

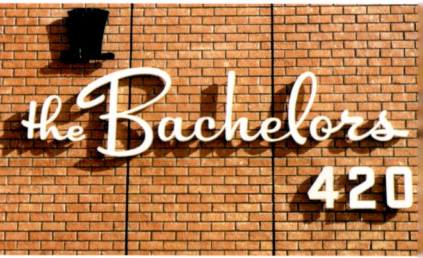

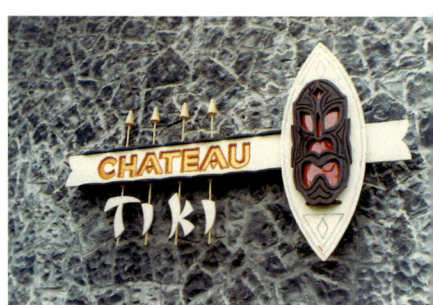

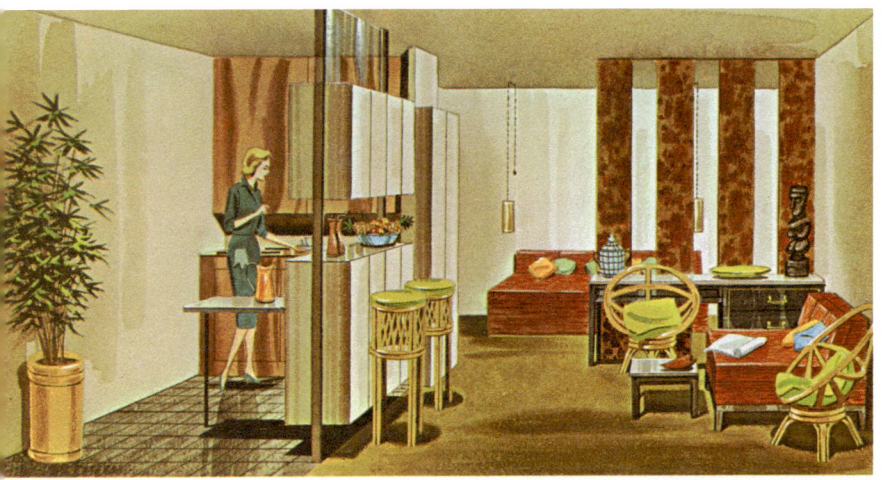

YOU TOO CAN LIVE LIKE A KING IN THIS POLYNESIAN WONDERLAND

masks while their eyes glowed with red light bulbs.

The decorative materials ranged from large bamboo and real *tapa* cloth to anchor chains or thick nautical rope used as railings. Enough lava rock was used as wall covering to downsize a Hawaiian Island.

With its individually carved beams, the Polynesian Village Apartments building in Playa del Rey had more Tikis per square foot than any Polynesian restaurant in the United States. Its brochure enthused: "Polynesian Village is made of carved Tiki gods and concrete block, lush tropical plantings and cascading waterfalls. Flaming lamps silhouette night swimmers. Throw some gardenias in the two pools, get into a muu-muu, serve up the poi, and you've got Diamond Head in Playa del Rey."

Since many Southern California apartment complexes had their own swimming pools, there often was an A-frame pool hut, or rec room, in the courtyard. As described in the advertisement for the Outrigger Apartments: "The shores of the South Pacific have come to Pasadena. Here is Tahitian Island living at a price you can afford. When you walk through the beautifully gabled entrance... past the 10-foot, 4,000-pound giant Tiki god, you will be convinced you are really in the tropics... Overlooking the large pool you will see the original outrigger clad in war paint. The cabana reaches 36 feet into the sky and is in the décor of a true Tahitian Town Meeting Hall..."

Décor was often provided by Oceanic Arts in Whittier, California.

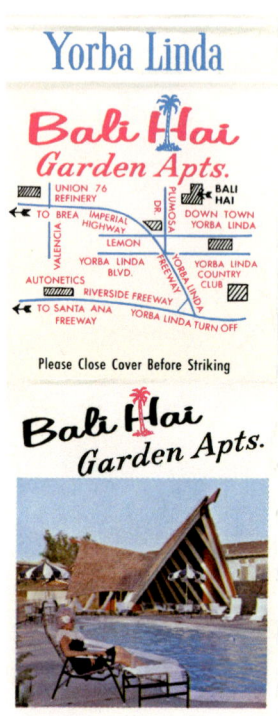

DER TIKI-POP WURDE ZU EINEM ERNST

zu nehmenden Design-Stil, als er von Restaurants auf andere urbane Gebäude wie Wohnkomplexe, Motels und Bowling-bahnen übergriff. Nurdachhäuser mit Auslegerbalken an der Spitze, Gärten mit Wasserspielen und tropischer Bepflanzung, brennende Gasfackeln und insbesondere Tiki-Schnitzereien, die als Statuen im Garten oder Stützpfeiler eingesetzt wurden, ließen Orte zum Wohnen und Wohlfühlen entstehen, wie man sie zuvor noch nicht gesehen hatte.

Themenorientierte Wohnanlagen waren in den amerikanischen Städten der 1950er-Jahre nichts Ungewöhnliches. Besonders in Los Angeles übertrug man gerne Architekturkonzepte aus dem Bereich des Films auf Gewerbe und Wohnkomplexe. Die Gebäude sahen aus wie englische Ferienhäuser, chinesische Pagoden oder spanische Villen. Die eigene Wohnung spiegelte den individuellen Geschmack genauso wider wie der Kleidungsstil oder das Auto.

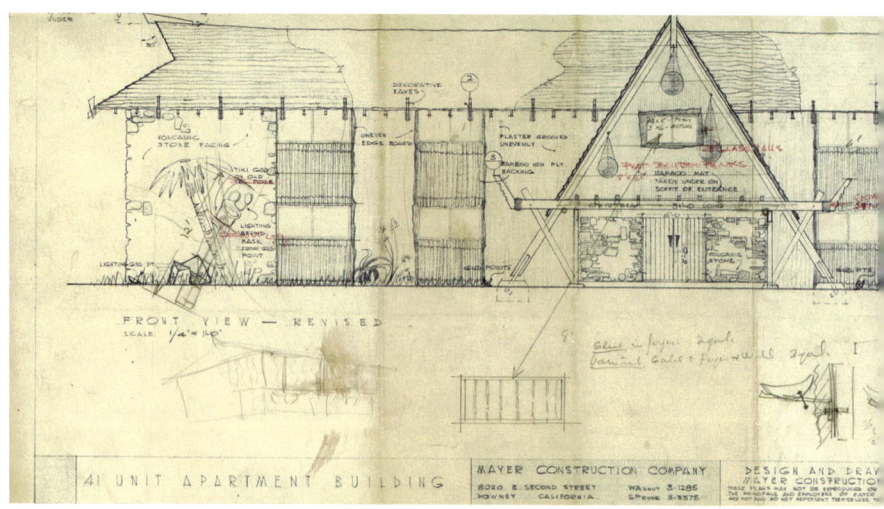

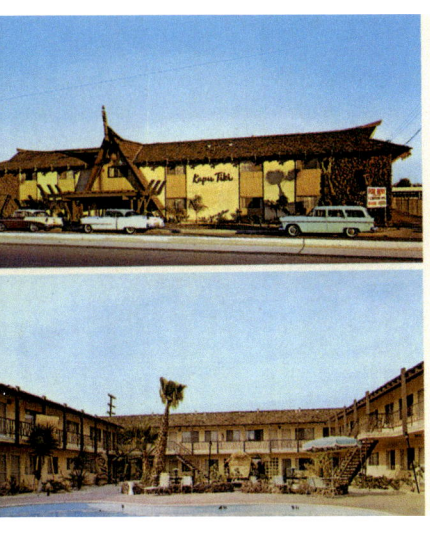

Kapu Tiki Apts.
5400 Rosemead Boulevard
Pico Rivera, California

MODERN - HAWAIIAN

- Fully Draped and Carpeted
- Beautifully Furnished
- Beautiful Tropical Landscaping
- Large Heated Pool
- Walls and Ceilings Insulated and Soundproofed
- Recreation Area has Game Room with Rest Room
- Bar, Sink, Ping-Pong, for Guests and Tenants
- Large Parking Area
- Music (FM) in Patio Area
- Real Tropical Atmosphere

Manager_____ Phone_____
                on premises

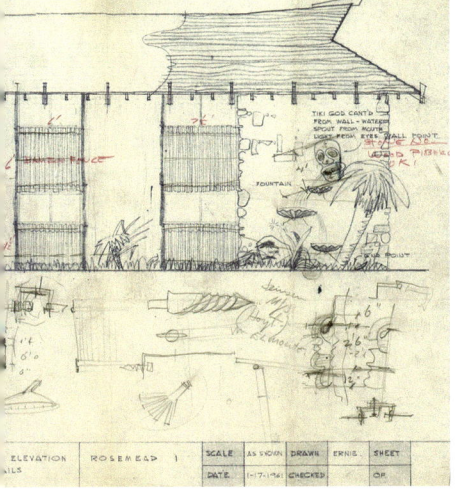

OPPOSITE: Matchbook advertising the Bali Hai Garden Apartments, Yorba Linda, California *(Scott Schell Collection)*

ABOVE: Advertising card for the Kapu Tiki Apartments

LEFT: Blueprint for the Kapu Tiki Apartments *(Oceanic Arts Collection)*

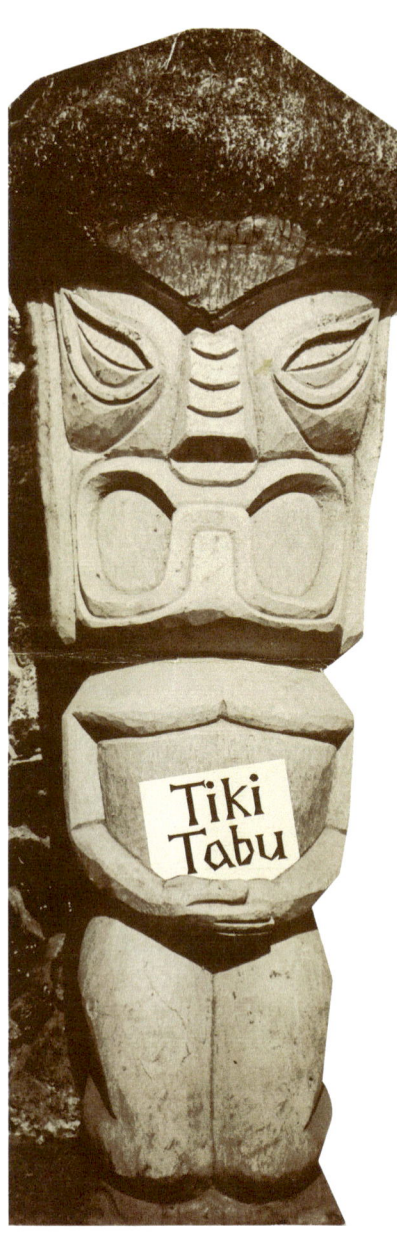

Meist beschränkte sich die spezifische Optik nur auf die Fassade; nirgends jedoch wurden die Themen so extensiv umgesetzt wie bei den Fassaden der polynesischen Wohnanlagen. Mit ihren hohen, A-förmigen Eingängen waren sie schon von Weitem sichtbar. Die Baumeister übertrafen sich selbst, als sie Gasfackeln knapp unter der Wasseroberfläche künstlicher Bäche installierten oder Wasserfälle, die sich aus den Mündern von Tiki-Masken ergossen, deren Augen wie heiße Kohlen glühten.

Die eingesetzten Materialien reichten von großen Bambusstämmen über echten Tapa-Rindenbaststoff bis hin zu Ankerketten und Schiffstauen als Brüstung. Mit der Menge an Lavagestein, das für Wandverkleidungen eingesetzt wurde, hätte man eine kleine hawaiische Insel aufschütten können.

Mit ihren individuell geschnitzten Trägerbalken hatten die Polynesian Village Apartments in Playa del Rey mehr Tikis pro Quadratmeter als jedes polynesische Restaurant in den USA. In einer Werbebroschüre hieß es enthusiastisch: „Das Polyne-sian Village ist aus geschnitzten Tiki-Göt-tern und Betonblöcken gebaut. Es gibt eine üppige tropische Begrünung und Wasserfälle. Des Nachts zeichnen brennende Fackeln den Schattenriss des Schwimmers im Pool. Mit ein paar Gardenien in den beiden Poolanlagen, einem Mu'umu'u [traditionelles hawaiisches Kleid] am Leib und einer Portion Poi holen Sie den Diamond Head nach Playa del Rey."

LEFT: Brochure for the Tiki Tabu Apartments *(Mimi Payne Collection)*

OPPOSITE: The proud owners of the Islander Apartments admire their entrance Tiki, in Torrance, California

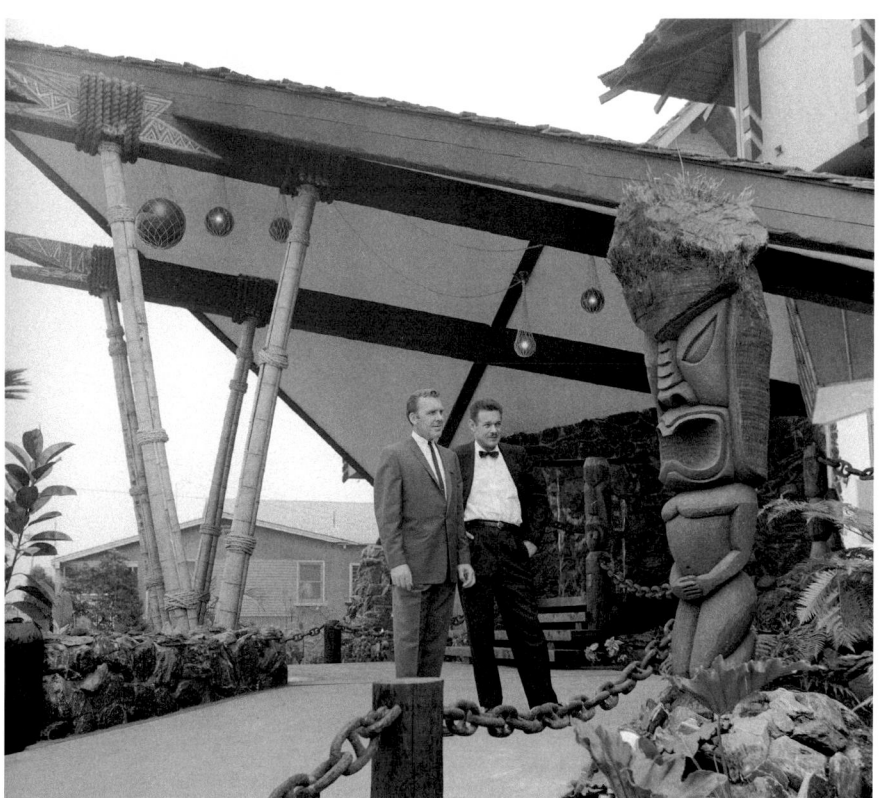

Da viele südkalifornische Wohnkomplexe eigene Poolanlagen hatten, gab es im Garten oft ein Poolhaus oder einen Gemeinschaftsraum in der beliebten A-Form. Eine Anzeige für die Outrigger Apartments beschrieb es wie folgt: „Die Strände des Südpazifiks sind nach Pasadena gekommen. Leben Sie den tahitischen Lifestyle, zu einem Preis, den Sie sich leisten können. Wenn Sie durch den wunderschönen Eingangsbereich treten… vorbei an dem drei Meter hohen und rund zwei Tonnen schweren Tiki-Gott, werden Sie sich in den Tropen wähnen… Die großzügige Poolanlage überblickend, entdecken Sie

ein originalgetreues Auslegerkanu, das in Kriegsfarben bemalt ist. Die Umkleidekabinen ragen 11 Meter in den Himmel und sind einem echten tahitischen Versammlungshaus nachempfunden…"

Die Ausstattung wurde oft von Oceanic Arts in Whittier, Kalifornien, durchgeführt.

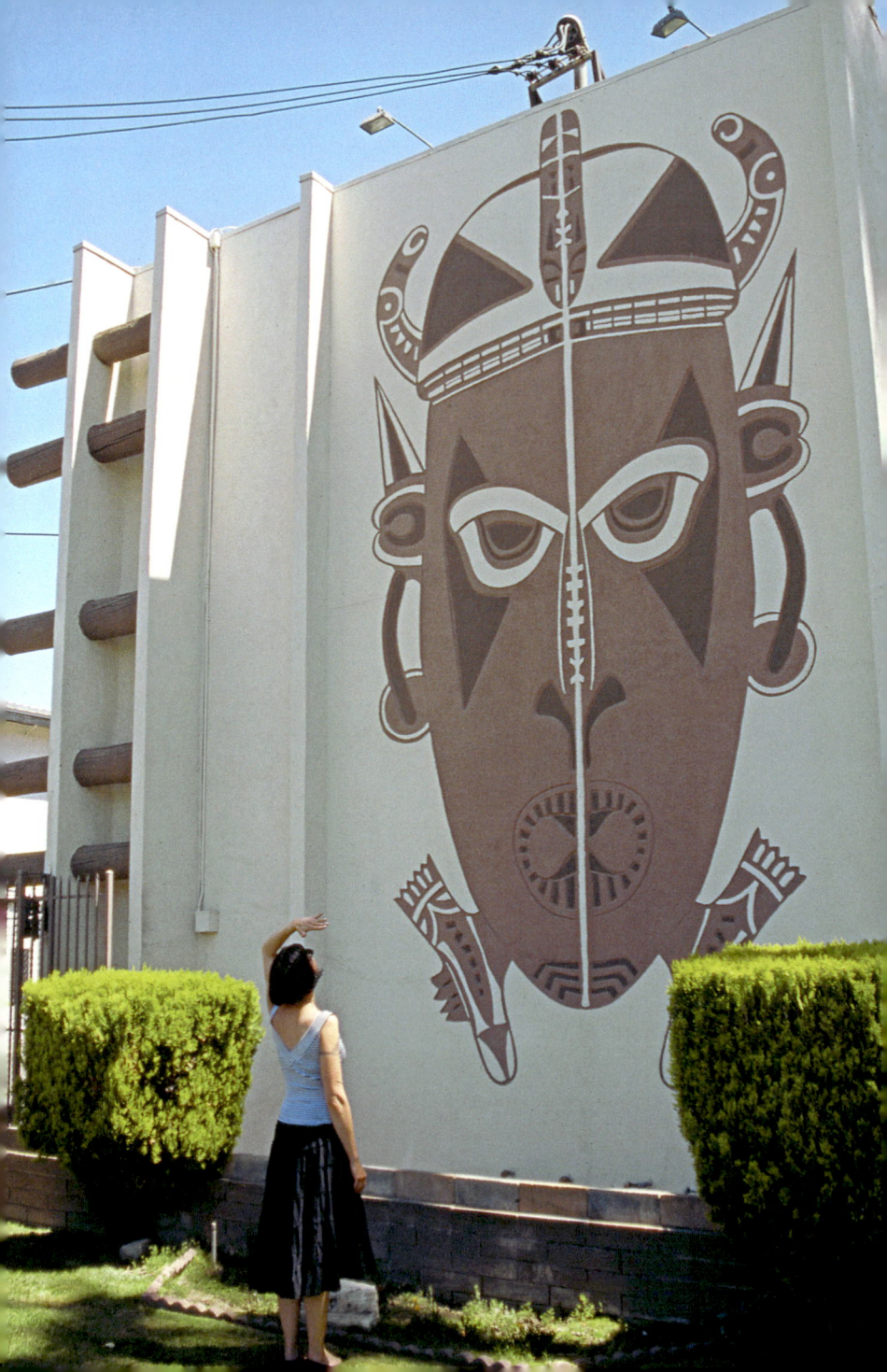

LE TIKI POP DEVIENT UN STYLE À PART

entière lorsqu'il quitte le domaine de la restauration pour s'étendre à d'autres domaines architecturaux comme les immeubles résidentiels, les hôtels… et même les pistes de bowling. Tous les éléments que se sont appropriés les clubs dînatoires polynésiens y passent : charpentes en A avec avant-toits projetés en porte-à-faux, espaces paysagés et pièces d'eau, végétation tropicale, torches à gaz flamboyantes… Quant aux tikis, ils font d'admirables statues de jardin et servent aussi de piliers de soutènement pour former des espaces de vie et de détente jusqu'alors inédits en Amérique.

Ce type d'appartement est presque commun dans les villes américaines des années 1950. Les noms des bâtiments font partie du lot. Los Angeles s'est alors déjà fait une spécialité dans la reprise de concepts architecturaux créés au cinéma pour des constructions commerciales ou résidentielles. Les bâtiments y ont l'aspect et le nom de cottages anglais, de pagodes chinoises ou de villas espagnoles. Il était possible d'assortir sa résidence à ses goûts, comme une voiture ou une veste.

Le style donné à un immeuble tient beaucoup à son aspect extérieur, mais nulle part le thème polynésien n'a été exploité de façon aussi élaborée que dans les immeubles résidentiels. Leurs entrées en A, majestueuses, sont visibles de très loin. Les architectes dépassent les goûts fraîchement établis en plaçant des torches à gaz sous la surface de ruisseaux artificiels ou encore des cascades jaillissant des bouches immenses de masques de tiki accrochés aux murs, dont les yeux irradient une lumière rouge.

Les matériaux décoratifs utilisés vont du bambou et de la toile *tapa* authentique à des chaînes d'ancre et des cordages épais utilisés comme balustres. La pierre de lave tapisse assez de murs pour faire rapetisser une île hawaiienne.

Avec ses poutres sculptées une à une à la main, la résidence Polynesian Village Apartments de Playa del Rey compte plus de tikis au mètre carré que n'importe quel restaurant à thème des États-Unis. Sa brochure doit provoquer l'extase : « Polynesian Village est composé de tikis sculptés dans la masse et de blocs de béton, animé par de majestueuses cascades et de luxuriantes plantations tropicales. La flamme des lampes dessine la silhouette des nageurs

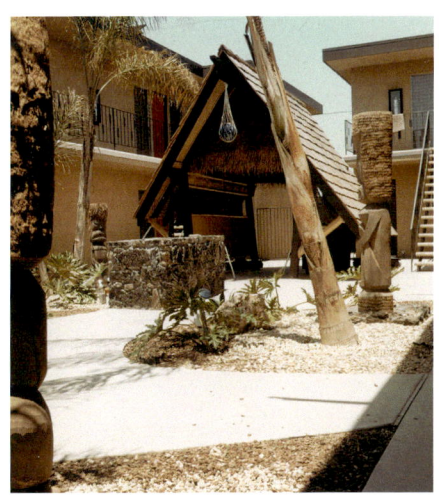

OPPOSITE: 26-foot-tall Tami Mask painting at Polynesia Apartments, Canoga Park, California, built 1961

ABOVE: Rec room at the Tiki Tabu Apartments

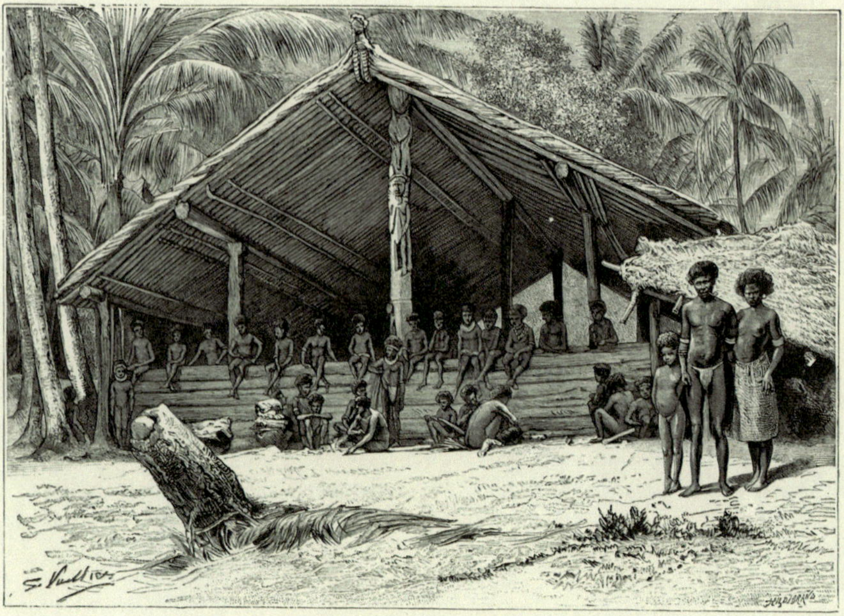

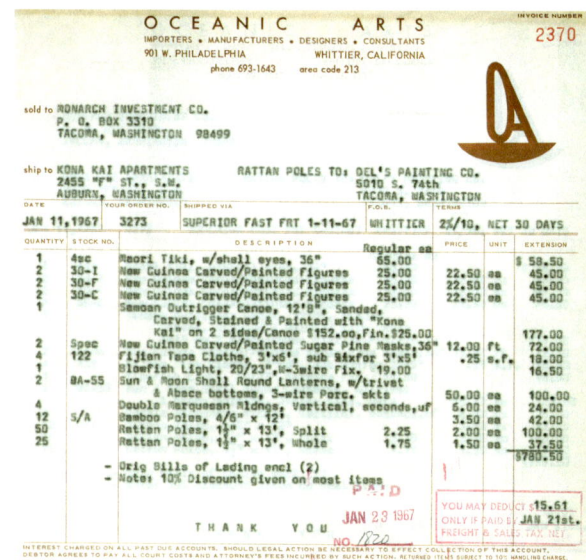

TAMBU AND GROUP OF SANTA-ANA NATIVES, SOLOMON ARCHIPELAGO.

ABOVE: Communal building in the Solomon Islands

RIGHT: Oceanic Arts invoice, providing a classic example of Tiki apartment décor

OPPOSITE LEFT: Rec room at the Kamia Village Apartments, Anaheim, California

OPPOSITE RIGHT: Gas torch from a Tiki apartment building nocturnes. Jetez des gardénias dans les deux bassins, savourez un *muu-muu*, servez-vous du *poi*, et vous voilà à Diamond Head sans quitter Playa del Rey. »

En Californie du Sud, beaucoup de résidences sont dotées d'une piscine privée. On leur adjoint alors souvent des huttes avec une toiture en A ou une salle de jeu côté cour. En témoigne cette description dans une publicité pour la résidence Outrigger : « Les rivages du Pacifique Sud ont été transportés à Pasadena. Ici vous trouverez un mode de vie digne d'une île tahitienne à un prix accessible. Lorsque vous traverserez le hall d'entrée aux majestueux pignons… au pied d'un dieu Tiki géant de deux tonnes et trois mètres de hauteur, vous serez convaincu de fouler le sol des tropiques… Par-delà la vaste piscine, vous découvrirez la pirogue camouflée dans le décor. La cabane s'élève à onze mètres du sol dans un cadre reproduisant une véritable maison à palabres tahitienne… »

La décoration intérieure était souvent fournie par l'agence Oceanic Arts de Whittier, en Californie.

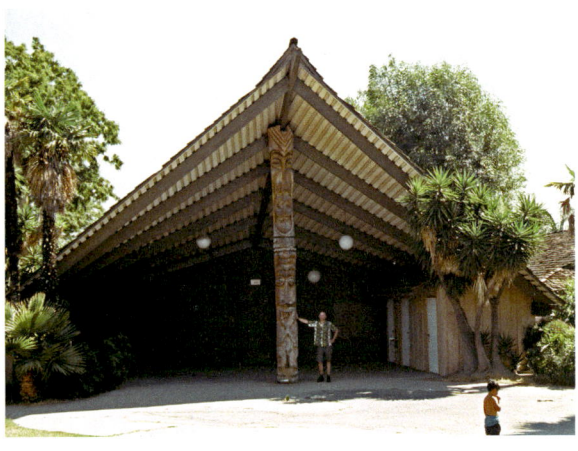

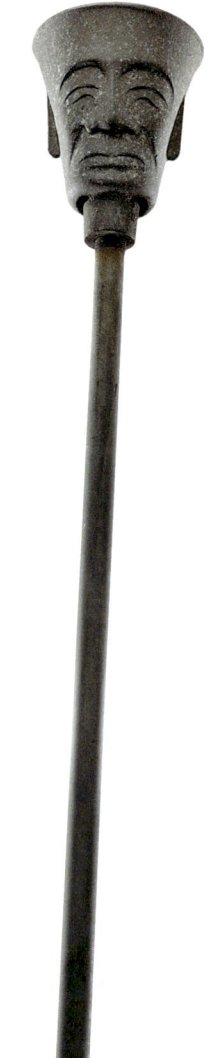

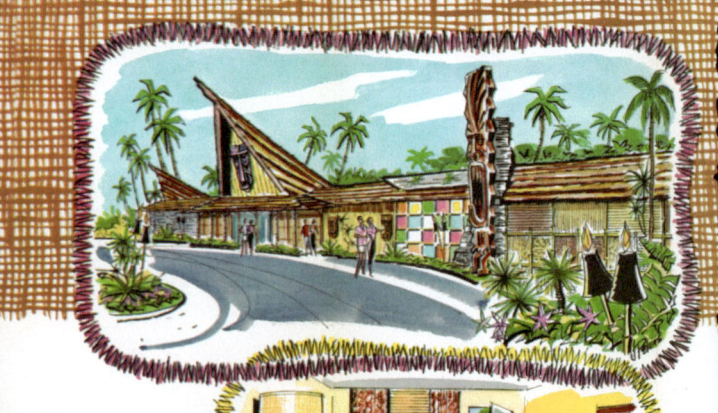

Do you yearn?...

for total, complete escape from the workaday, care-beset world?... where your accommodations offer every feature of comfort and convenience... including individual climate controls, and TV in every room ... where you have your choice of spacious guestroom or modern kitchenette apartment ... where the emphasis is on service, hospitality and cleanliness.

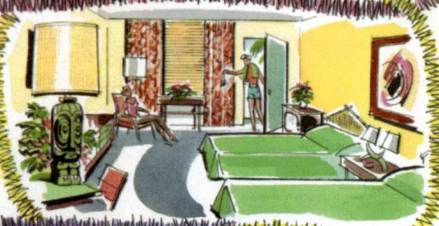

Do you dream?...

of delicious foods served in generous quantities ... in a charming, informal setting, so gaily Hawaiian in mood? Of snacks on the sun-warmed patio or friendly luaus under the stars?

Do you wish?...

for all this? It's yours ... at the HAWAIIAN ISLE. PLUS gay planned social activities (for tots and teeners, too, in their own clubroom, under the keen eye of a special kiddy counselor). PLUS conscientious management, PLUS a sparkling, constant-flow, heated swimming pool, PLUS the delightful Tiki Cocktail Lounge where gaiety is king. PLUS the perfect, near-everything location, just moments from Miami Beach's many sightseeing, entertainment and sports attractions. PLUS — plus — plus — so much more. All vacation-wonderland!

So, stop yearning ... stop dreaming ... stop wishing. Go gaily Hawaiian ... go for the greatest, happiest vacation of your life. Go "Hawaiian Isle". Go soon. Aloha.

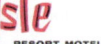

DIRECTLY ON THE OCEAN
17601 COLLINS AVENUE • MIAMI BEACH • FLORIDA
947-0611

Hawaiian Isle
RESORT MOTEL

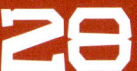

28

TIKI MOTELS

TIKI-MOTELS
LES HÔTELS TIKI

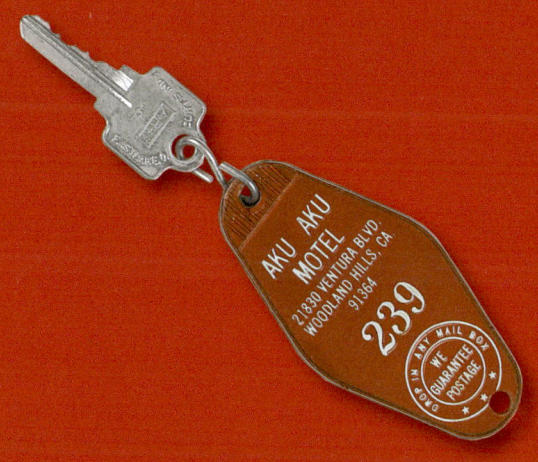

OPPOSITE: Effusive brochure for the Hawaiian Isle Motel, Miami Beach
(Jackie Zumwaldt Collection)

ABOVE: Key to ancient mysteries? *(Ron Ferrell Collection)*

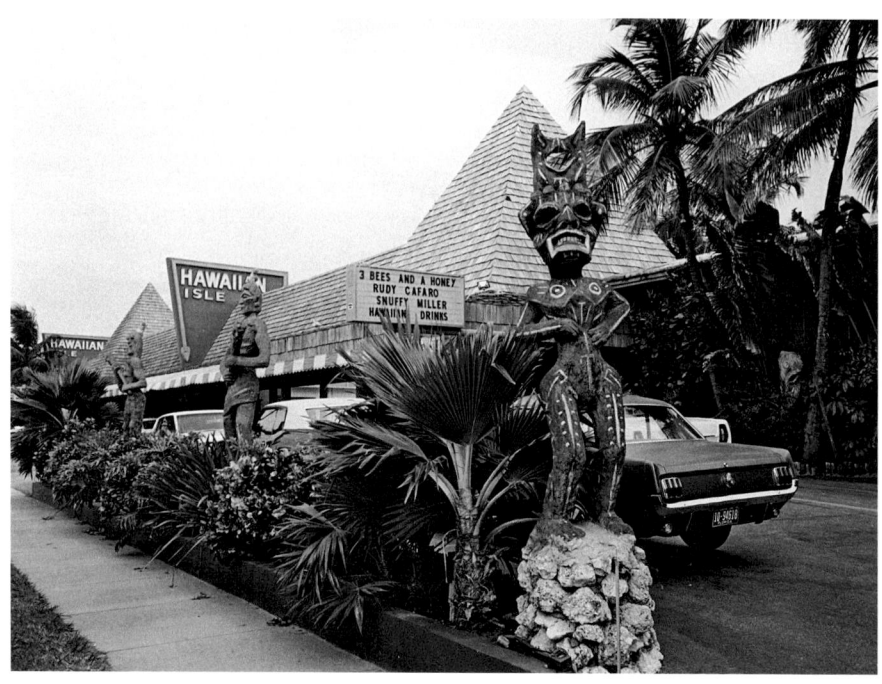

ONE OF THE MORE NOVEL CONCEPTS

that emerged in 20th-century American architecture was the motel. With the proliferation of the automobile and the expansion of the highway system, leisure and commercial road travel had steadily increased, and easy access to roadside resting places became desirable. Road trips were taken by families for fun, and motels mushroomed all over vacation states like Florida and California. At beachfronts in particular, the South Seas Paradise theme was a fitting concept to attract the weary traveler.

But Tiki-themed motels also established themselves in the back country, where they functioned along the same lines as the Tiki eateries in city centers: they were artificial islands that promised rest and recreation, the Polynesian way. More so than even their restaurant counterparts, Tiki motels relied heavily on roadside signage to catch the eye of the passing motorist. Sign-makers constructed giant neon totem poles and blazing gas torches, which functioned as beacons of safe harbor to the tail-finned street boats that sailed down the asphalt roads. The American motel sign became an art form.

In addition to using Tiki masks and torches, sign designers sometimes fashioned shields and spears into a modern-primitive heraldry to signify the Tiki theme. Of course, the exotic architecture itself functioned as a sign, setting these ports-of-call apart from the modern cityscapes they were located in. Additionally, Tiki statuary caught the passing travelers' attention. Some motels used the logo-Tiki concept established by Polynesian restaurants to brand themselves.

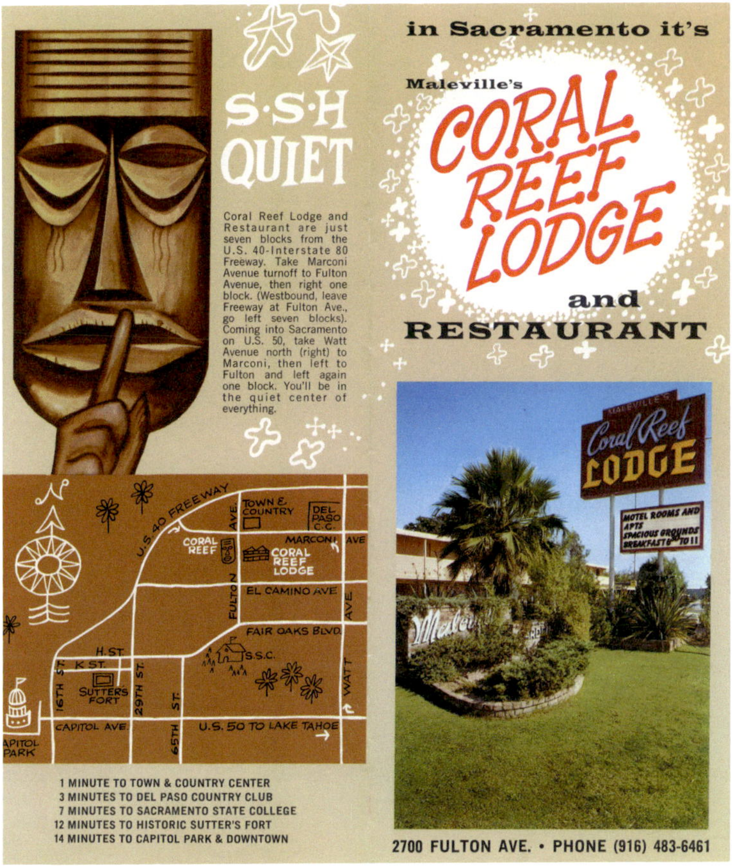

in Sacramento it's
Maleville's
CORAL REEF LODGE
and
RESTAURANT
S·S·H
QUIET
Coral Reef Lodge and Restaurant are just seven blocks from the U.S. 40-Interstate 80 Freeway. Take Marconi Avenue turnoff to Fulton Avenue, then right one block. (Westbound, leave Freeway at Fulton Ave., go left seven blocks). Coming into Sacramento on U.S. 50, take Watt Avenue north (right) to Marconi, then left to Fulton and left again one block. You'll be in the quiet center of everything.
N
U.S. 40 FREEWAY
TOWN & COUNTRY
DEL PASO C.C.
CORAL REEF
MARCONI AVE
CORAL REEF LODGE
FULTON AVE.
EL CAMINO AVE
WATT AVE
FAIR OAKS BLVD.
H. ST.
K ST.
S.S.C.
SUTTERS FORT
16TH ST.
29TH ST.
65TH ST.
CAPITOL AVE
U.S. 50 TO LAKE TAHOE
CAPITOL PARK
1 MINUTE TO TOWN & COUNTRY CENTER
3 MINUTES TO DEL PASO COUNTRY CLUB
7 MINUTES TO SACRAMENTO STATE COLLEGE
12 MINUTES TO HISTORIC SUTTER'S FORT
14 MINUTES TO CAPITOL PARK & DOWNTOWN
MALEVILLE'S
Coral Reef
LODGE
MOTEL ROOMS AND APTS
SPACIOUS GROUNDS
2700 FULTON AVE. • PHONE (916) 483-6461

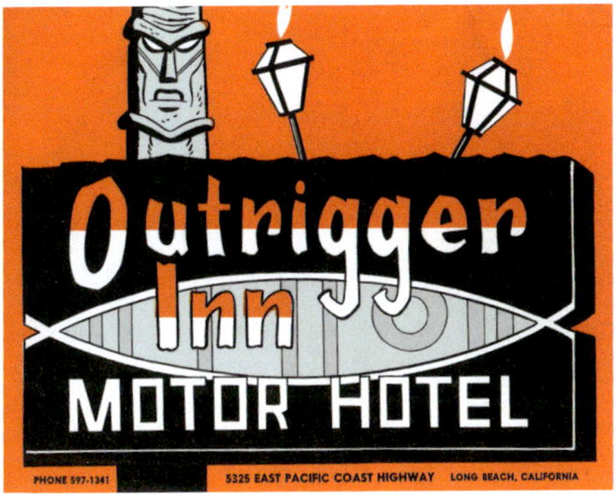

Outrigger
Inn
MOTOR HOTEL
PHONE 597-1341
5325 EAST PACIFIC COAST HIGHWAY
LONG BEACH, CALIFORNIA

OPPOSITE: Strange tribal statues by Lewis VanDercar at the Hawaiian Isle Motel *(Scott Schell Collection)*

ABOVE: Brochure for a Tiki retreat *(Frank Brajevic Collection)*

LEFT: Typical Tiki motel sign, Long Beach, California *(Frank Brajevic Collection)*

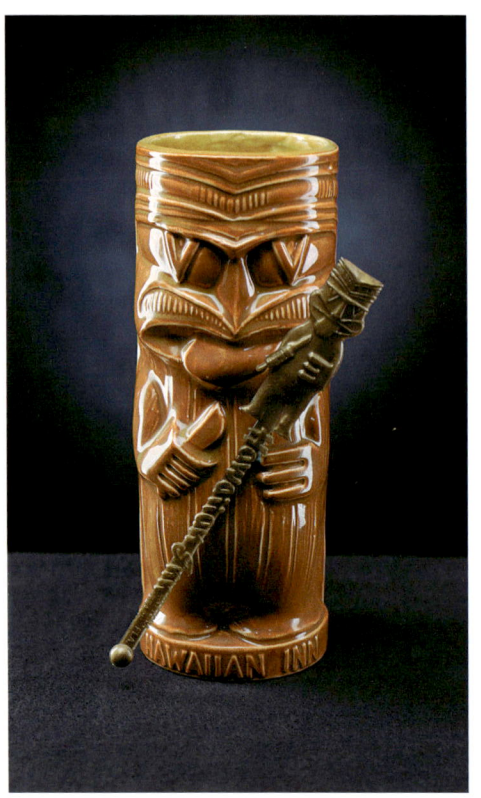

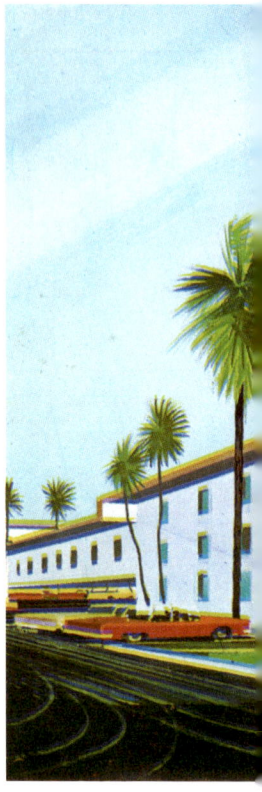

ABOVE: Hawaiian Inn logo Tiki mug and swizzle

RIGHT: Souvenir photo album from the Hawaiian Isle Motel
(Scott Schell Collection)

OPPOSITE: Tiki torch beacon at the Makai Motel, Ormond Beach, Florida
(Scott Schell Collection)

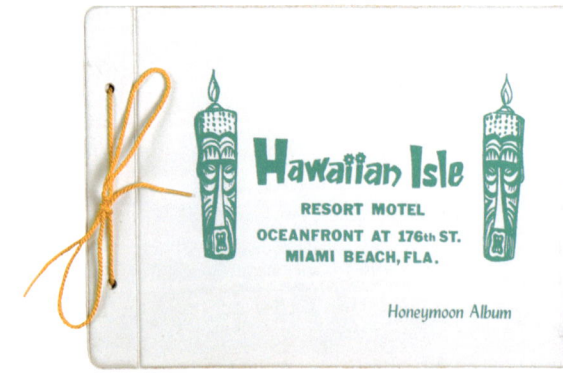

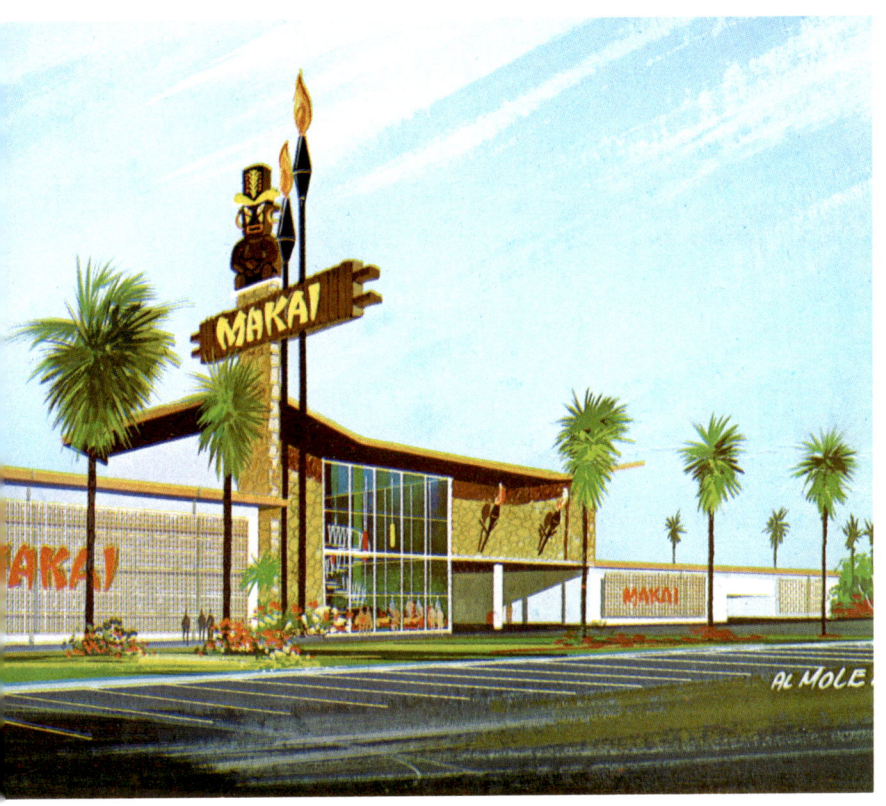

Regional motels employed local artists like Lewis VanDercar and Gerhard Kroll, who exercised their talents with a good dose of artistic license to sculpt their own approximations of primitive Oceanic godheads. The result was that American Tiki art, just like Tiki architecture, spread across America in a diversity of forms and styles, each one unique, making it a pop-art genre of its own.

As larger motel chains started buying out individual mom-and-pop motels, Tiki-themed chain motels sprung up too, like the Tropics motels developed by Ken Kimes. The Rosemead Tropics was located in Los Angeles, and four more Tropics were opened in the desert towns of Indio, Blythe, Modesto, and Palm Springs.

The Modesto and Palm Springs locations still exist, the Palm Springs Tropics being the more elaborate. Past the A-frame entrance, Tikis dotted the pool area; at one time, a bar called the Reef quenched vacationers' thirst. Closed since the 1980s, the bar's Tiki saloon doors have recently been rediscovered.

EINES DER NEUEREN KONZEPTE DER amerikanischen Architektur des 20. Jahrhunderts war das Motel. Mit der Ausbreitung des Automobils und der Erweiterung der Highways war der Reiseverkehr beständig gestiegen, sodass ein einfacher Zugang zu Übernachtungsplätzen entlang der Straßen immer gefragter wurde. Familien fuhren mit dem Auto in den Urlaub und Motels schossen in Ferienstaaten wie Florida und Kalifornien wie Pilze aus dem Boden. Insbesondere entlang der Strände zog das Südseedesign die erschöpften Reisenden an.

Tiki-Motels etablierten sich jedoch auch im Hinterland und nahmen hier dieselbe Funktion ein wie die Tiki-Restaurants in den Städten: Sie bildeten künstliche Inseln für Ruhe und Erholung nach polynesischer Art. Noch mehr als die einschlägigen Speiselokale versuchten Tiki-Motels mit

auffälligen Werbetafeln die Aufmerksamkeit der vorbeifahrenden Autofahrer zu erregen. Hersteller entwarfen riesige mit Neonlicht beleuchtete Totempfähle und lodernde Gasfackeln, die den Straßenschiffen auf dem Asphalt den nahen sicheren Hafen ankündigten. Das amerikanische Motelschild wurde zu einer Kunstform.

Zusätzlich zu Tiki-Masken und Fackeln kreierten die Designer mitunter auch modern-primitive Tiki-Wappen mit Schilden und Speeren. Und natürlich war auch die exotische Architektur selbst, die einen Kontrast zur modernen Stadtlandschaft in ihrer Umgebung bildete, ein Werbemittel. Tiki-Statuen weckten die Neugier der Autofahrer und einige Motels hatten, wie die Restaurants, ein Tiki-Logo als Markenzeichen.

Regionale Motels beauftragten einheimische Künstler wie Lewis VanDercar

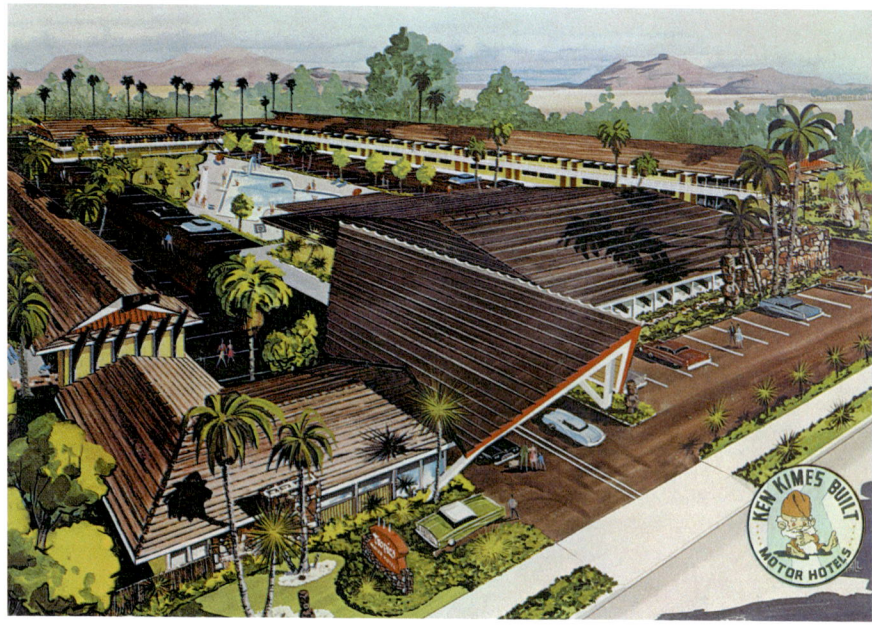

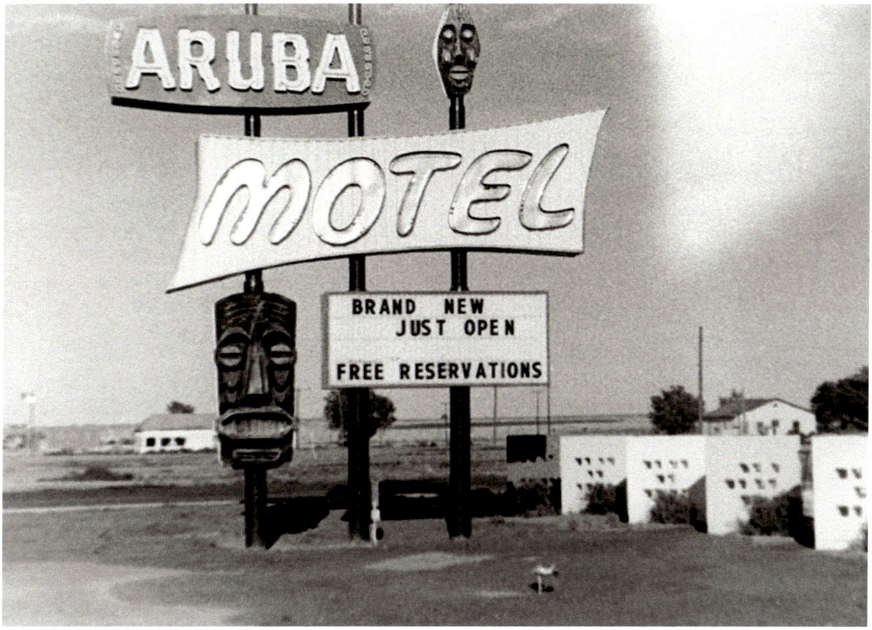

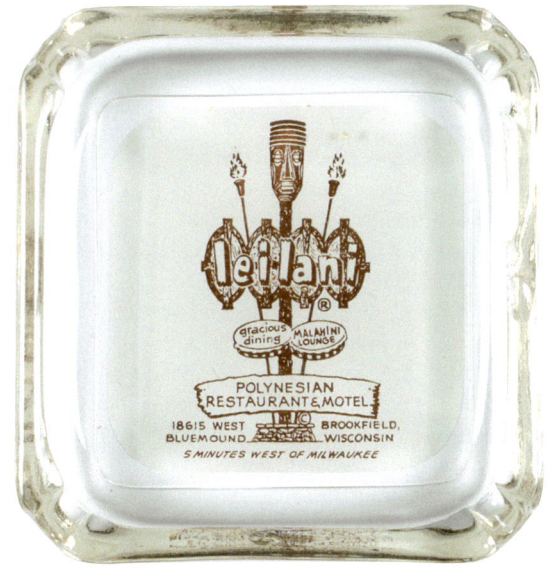

OPPOSITE: Rendering of the Palm Springs Tropics Motel *(Scott Schell Collection)*

ABOVE: Roadside Tiki totems, Tucumcari, New Mexico

RIGHT: Leilani Motel sign on ashtray *(Frank Brajevic Collection)*

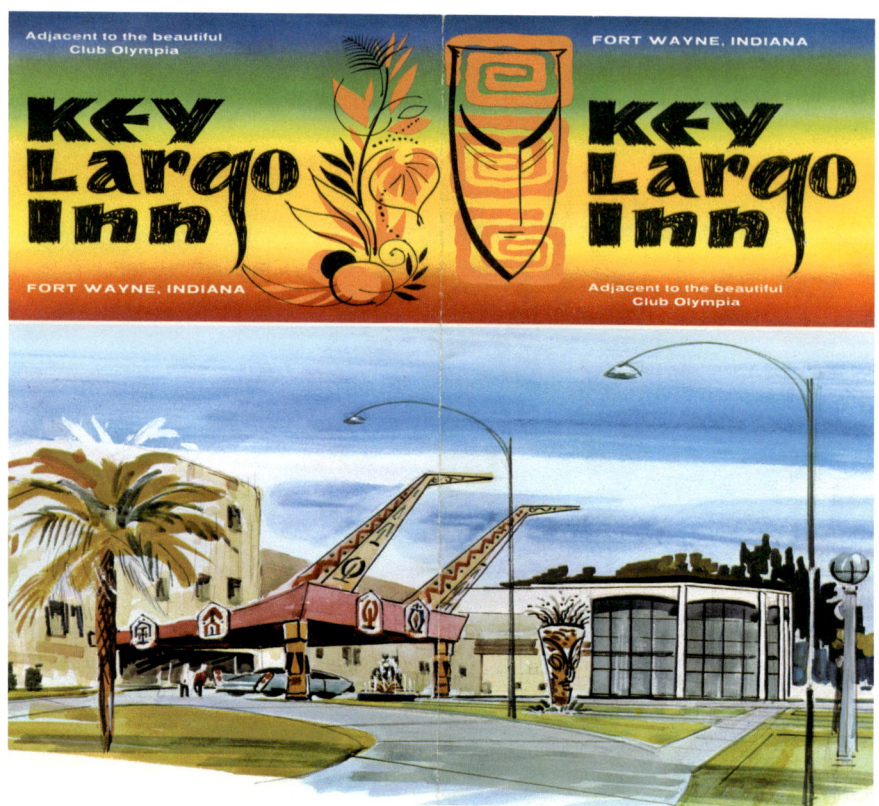

und Gerhard Kroll damit, ihre eigenen Interpretationen der ozeanischen Götterfiguren anzufertigen, wobei der künstlerischer Freiheit kaum Grenzen gesetzt wurden. So verbreitete sich die amerikanische Tiki-Kunst – wie schon die Tiki-Architektur – in vielfältigsten Stilen und Formen über ganz Amerika. In ihrer Einzigartigkeit bildeten die Werke ihr eigenes Pop-Art-Genre.

Als die Motelketten anfingen, kleine Familienbetriebe aufzukaufen, verbreiteten sich auch die Tiki-Motelketten, beispielsweise die Tropics-Motels von Ken Kimes.

Das Rosemead Tropics befand sich in Los Angeles, vier weitere eröffneten in den kalifornischen Wüstenstädten Indio, Blythe, Modesto und Palm Springs.

Die Standorte Modesto und Palm Springs gibt es noch heute, wobei das Palm Springs Tropics das raffiniertere von beiden ist. Hinter dem A-förmigen Eingang waren Tikis links und rechts des Poolbereichs verteilt. Bis in die 1980er-Jahre stillte hier eine Bar namens Reef den Durst der Urlauber. Ihre Tiki-Saloon-Türen wurden vor Kurzem wiederentdeckt.

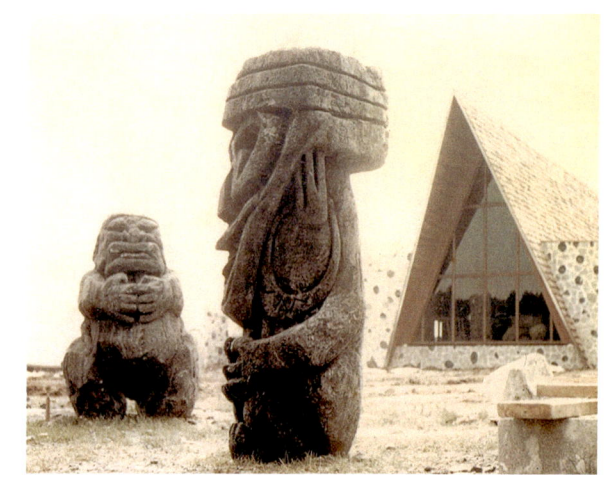

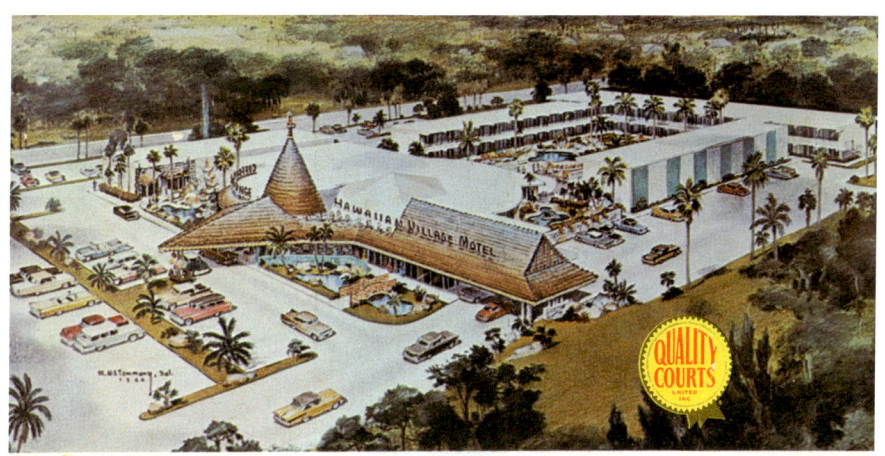

hawaiian village MOTEL AND RESTAURANT

2522 NORTH DALE MABRY • TAMPA, FLORIDA

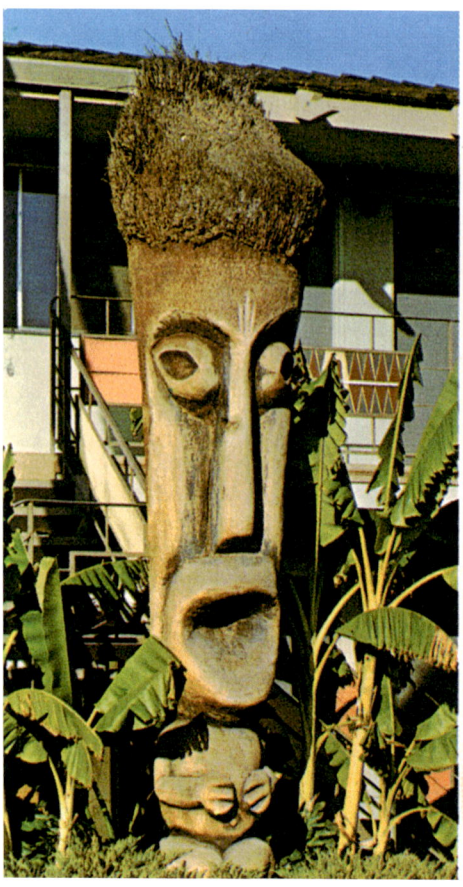

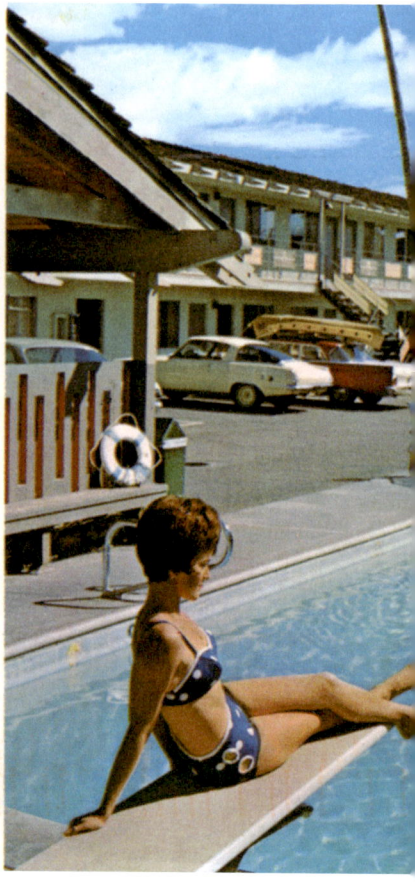

AU XXᵉ SIÈCLE, L'ARCHITECTURE

américaine s'enrichit d'un élément très novateur : le motel. Avec la prolifération automobile et l'expansion du réseau autoroutier, les voyages d'affaires et de plaisir se font de plus en plus en voiture, si bien qu'il devient vite utile de bâtir des établissements hôteliers faciles d'accès depuis les grands axes routiers. Les familles s'adonnent aussi au *road trip*, et bientôt les motels pullulent en Floride et en Californie.

Sur la côte, en particulier, le concept du paradis exotique remporte un succès monstre auprès du voyageur épuisé.

Les motels à thème tiki s'installent aussi dans les terres, où ils jouent sur le même fonds de commerce que les restaurants tiki des centres-villes : ils bâtissent des îlots artificiels promettant détente et divertissement, à la polynésienne. Plus encore que leurs homologues dînatoires, les motels tiki doivent appuyer leur stratégie commerciale

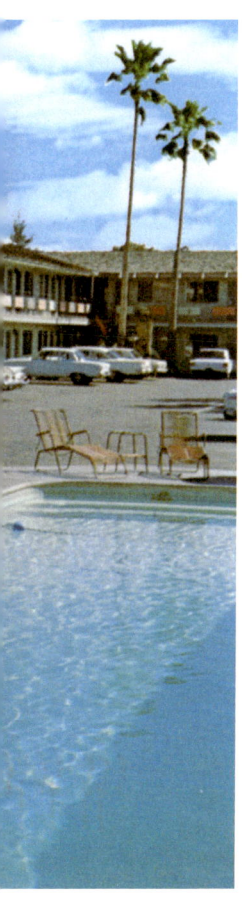

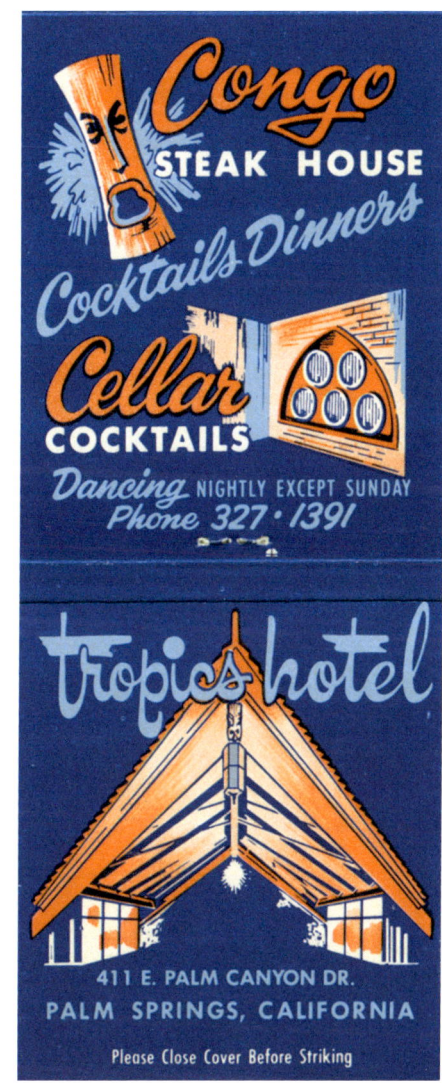

sur une signalétique qui capte le regard… pour attirer l'automobiliste de passage. Les fabricants d'enseignes construisent d'immenses totems bardés de néons et des torches flamboyantes qui apparaissent comme les avant-postes d'une oasis salvatrice aux flottes de vaisseaux flanqués d'ailerons affûtés qui voguent sur l'asphalte des nouvelles routes. L'enseigne de motel américain devient une discipline artistique à part entière.

Outre la réalisation de masques et de torches tiki, les créateurs d'enseignes s'adonnent parfois aussi à la fabrication de boucliers et de lances mêlant formes primitives et modernes qui viennent encore souligner le thème tiki. L'architecture exotique de ces bâtiments, qui les distingue radicalement du paysage environnant, est à elle seule le meilleur des signaux. La statuaire tiki ne

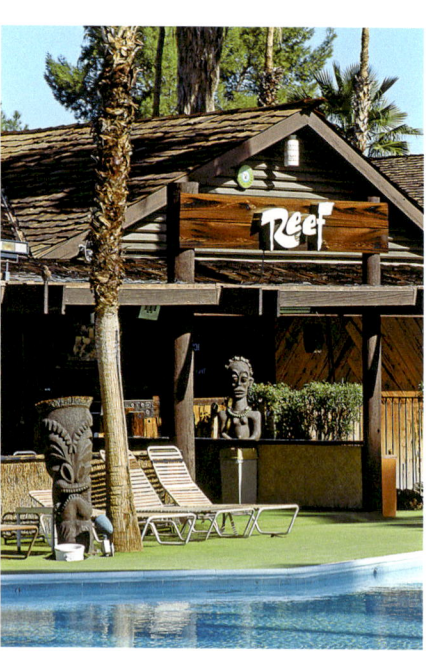

manque bien sûr pas d'attirer aussi l'attention des voyageurs. Certains motels tiki suivent l'exemple éprouvé dans la restauration et se franchisent.

Les motels de province emploient des artistes locaux comme Lewis VanDercar et Gerhard Kroll, qui appliquent une bonne dose de licence artistique à leurs interprétations toutes personnelles des bustes et têtes de divinités océaniennes. La conséquence de cet engouement est que l'art tiki américain s'étend, à la manière de l'architecture tiki, à tout le territoire américain, sous toutes les formes et dans tous les styles, devenant ainsi un genre indépendant du pop art.

À l'heure où les chaînes hôtelières rachètent à tour de bras les motels indépendants à la papa, les chaînes de motels tiki explosent elles aussi, à l'image des motels Tropics de Ken Kimes. Le Rosemead Tropics se trouve à Los Angeles et quatre autres ouvrent dans les villes d'Indio, Blythe, Modesto et Palm Springs, en plein désert.

Les établissements de Modesto et de Palm Springs existent toujours, le Palm Springs Tropics étant le plus sophistiqué. Par-delà la charpente en A de l'entrée, la piscine est parsemée de tikis. Elle fut un temps flanquée d'un bar appelé The Reef, où les vacanciers étanchaient les soifs les plus prosaïques. Fermées depuis les années 1980, les portes affichant un mélange de styles tiki et saloon ont été retrouvées récemment.

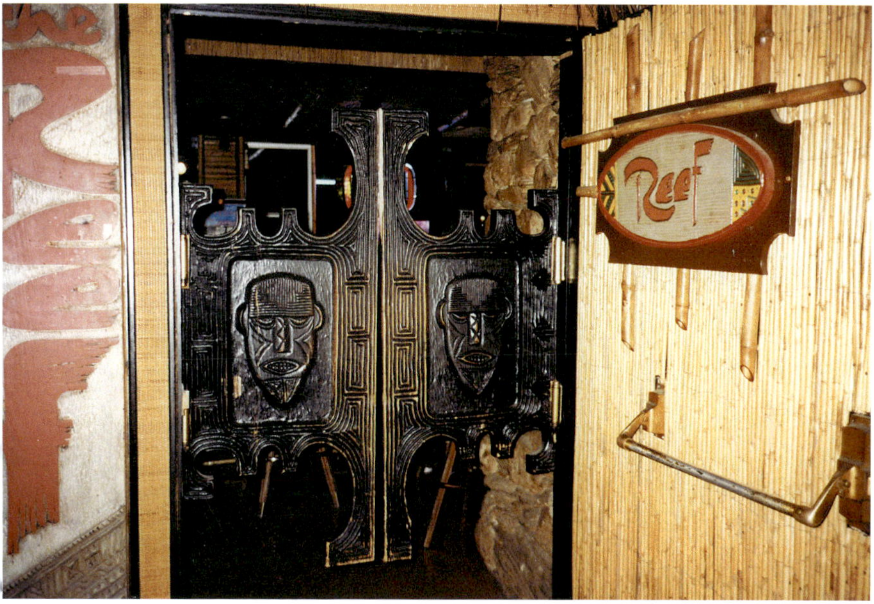

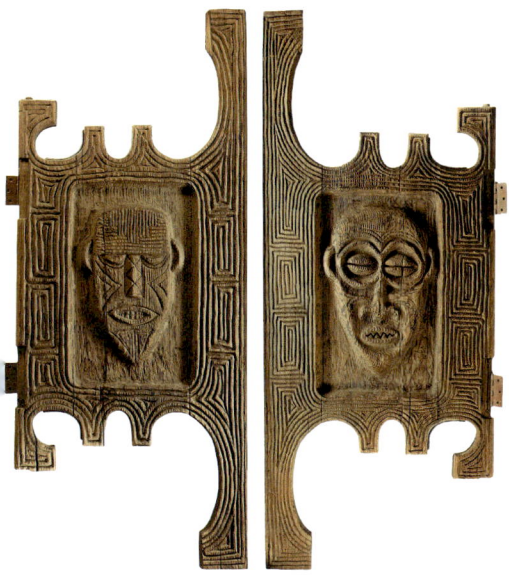

OPPOSITE: Pool entrance to the Reef

ABOVE: The saloon doors *in situ*

LEFT: The Reef's saloon doors by Leroy Schmaltz *(Amy Boylan Collection)*

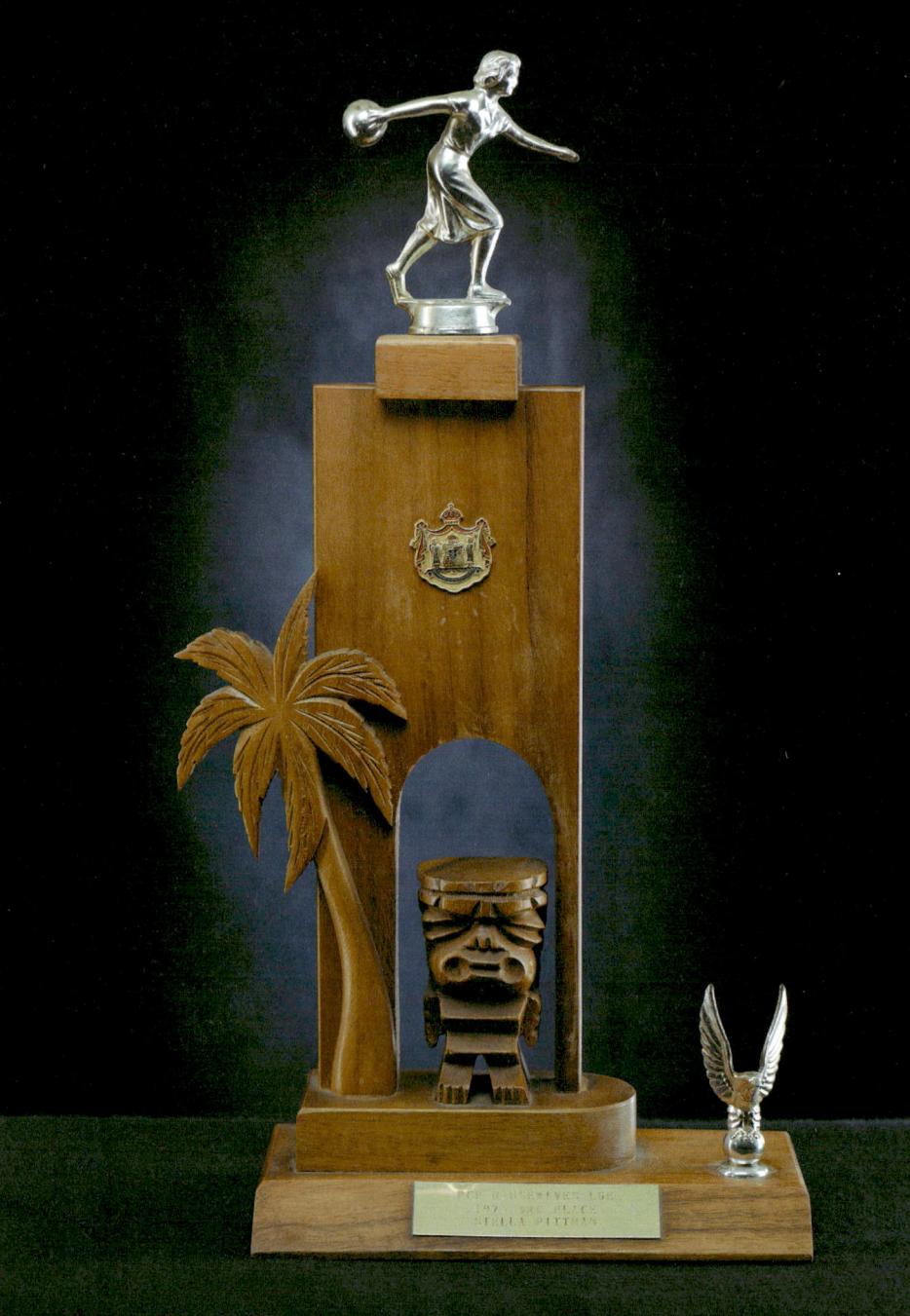

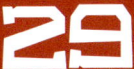

THE TIKI BOWLING ALLEY

DIE TIKI-BOWLINGBAHN
LA PISTE DE BOWLING TIKI

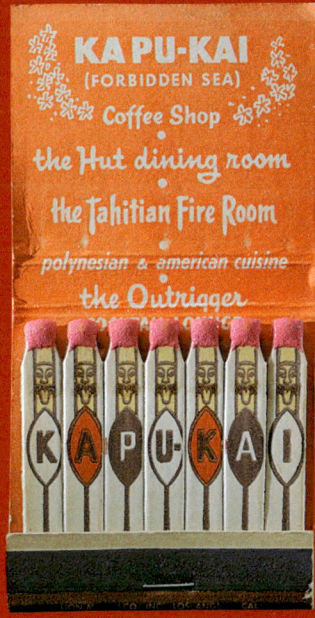

OPPOSITE: Tiki bowling trophy, Hawaii, 1970

ABOVE: Kapu-Kai matchbook *(Oceanic Arts Collection)*

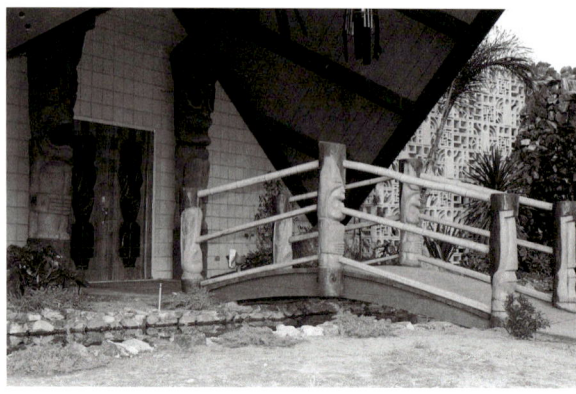

THE ECONOMIC AFFLUENCE THAT

came to the American middle class in the mid-1950s brought on a building boom that expanded the suburbs and created ever-more-fanciful places for leisure and entertainment. The spirit of the California aerospace industry influenced the architecture of coffee shops and bowling alleys, which increasingly looked like space stations. Television was not yet the stay-at-home medium it would become in the '70s, and the Internet didn't exist—people were still going out to have fun. The mid-century bowling alley was a complete entertainment center for the modern family.

The Kapu-Kai in Rancho Cucamonga, California, was one of these Googie-style pleasure domes that not only was a bowling alley, but also offered a coffee shop, a bar, and a restaurant with live entertainment behind its four A-frame gables. Completely furnished in Polynesian style by Oceanic Arts, based in nearby Whittier, with Tikis carved by Milan Guanko, it was a classic Tiki temple to behold. The Tahitian Fire Room served Chicken Kapu-Kai and a cocktail called the Kapu-Kai Cooler in front of

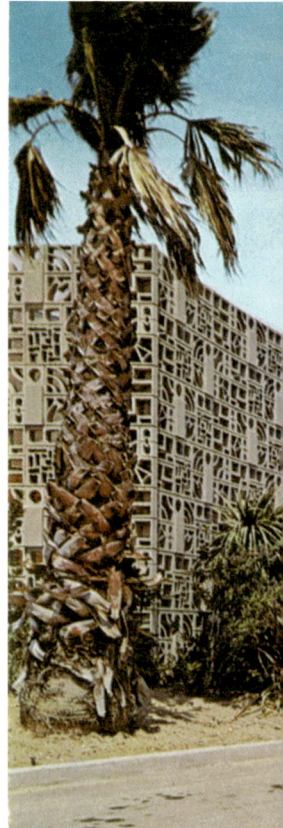

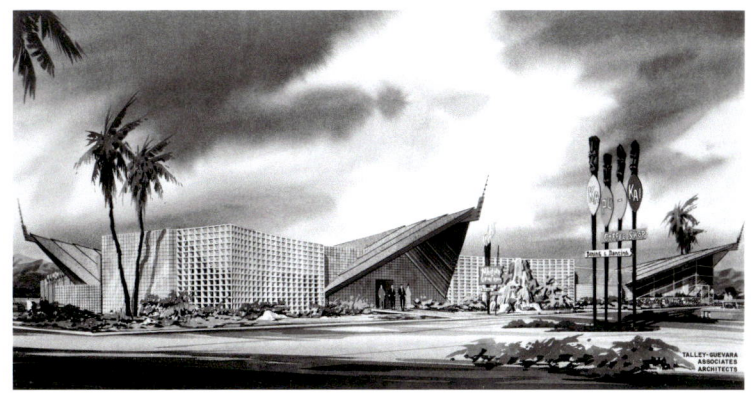

KAPU-KAI

DINING — DANCING — BOWLING
8874 Foothill Blvd., Cucamonga, Calif. — Hwy. 66

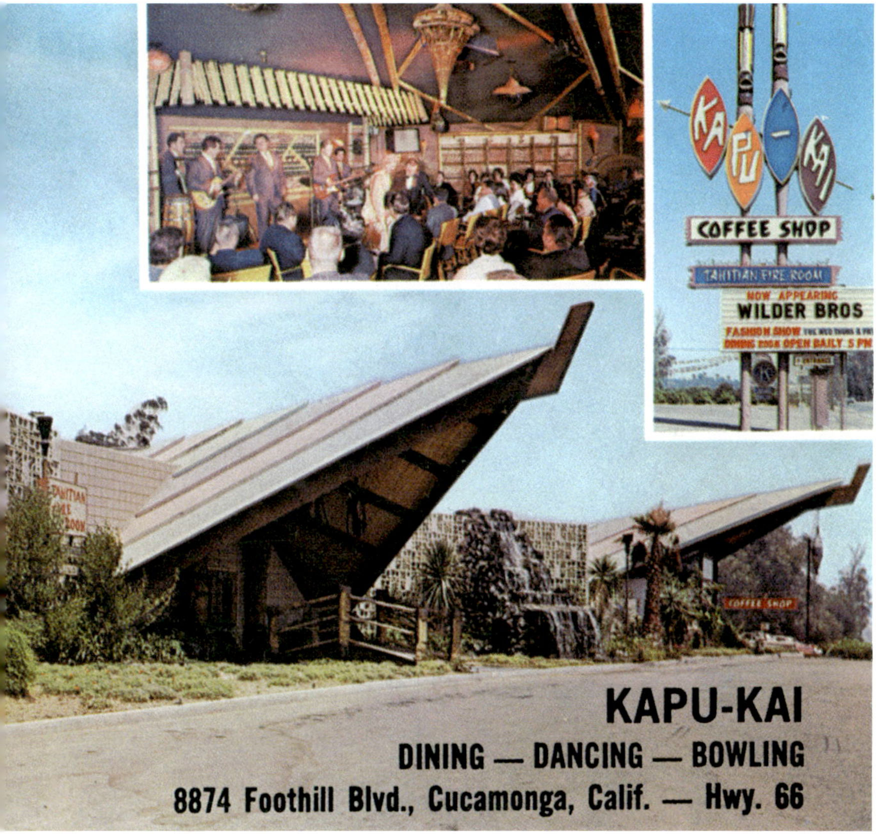

tapa fire murals while bowlers' balls rolled past tall Tiki columns.

At the height of the bowling boom, every fourth American considered himself a bowler. Bowling alleys had become community centers where women could go to the hairdresser while their kids were entertained in child-care rooms and their husbands were having drinks at the cocktail lounge—which was usually themed, from the Egyptian Pyramid Room to the Totem Room or the Kona Cove. The Tiki décor for the Leilani Lanes in Seattle was supplied by William Westenhaver's company, Witco,

which also provided the Tiki trophies for the bowling competitions.

While aloha shirts would not have been out of place in Tiki bowling alleys, the bowling shirt, its more conservative cousin, was the uniform of choice. Like the aloha shirt, it had to have a loose fit, and was not to be tucked in. In the 1950s, company team shirts became popular.

The most striking example of a Tiki bowling-alley interior is not found in one of the impressive A-frame palaces, but in a residential retirement complex called Polynesian Gardens Condominiums in

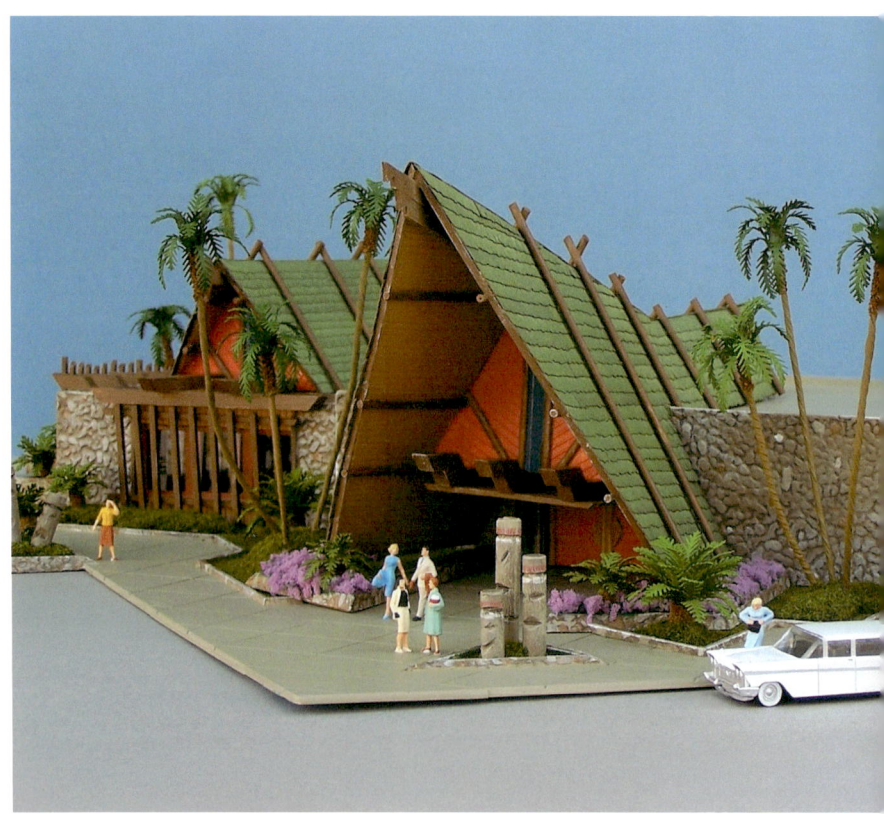

Plantation, Florida, which was endorsed by actress and celebrity Eve Arden.

The four AMF lanes with regulation automatic pinsetters feature scowling Tiki faces whose eyes glow red when a player bowls a strike. While the Polynesian Gardens' pair of logo Tikis leaves much to be desired, the lobby features an amazing mural and a strange copper Tiki fountain.

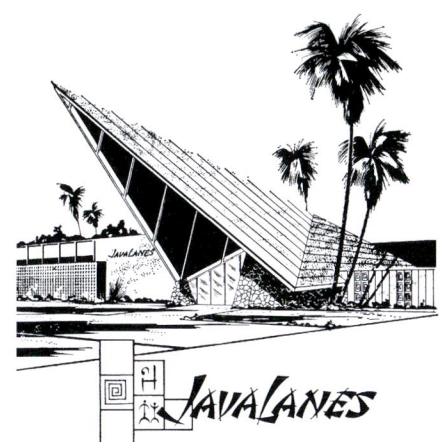

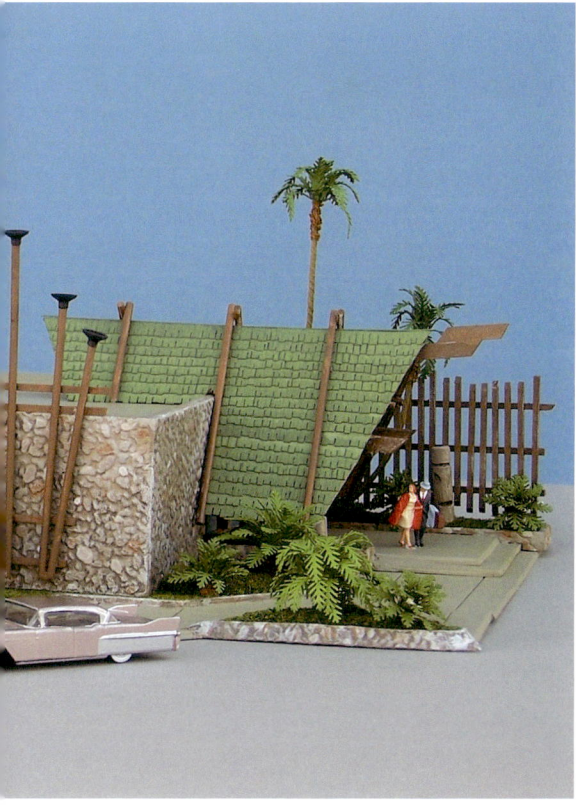

LEFT: Model for a fictitious Tiki bowling alley by Mike Cozart, Los Angeles

ABOVE: Rendering of Java Lanes *(Anders Anderson Collection)*

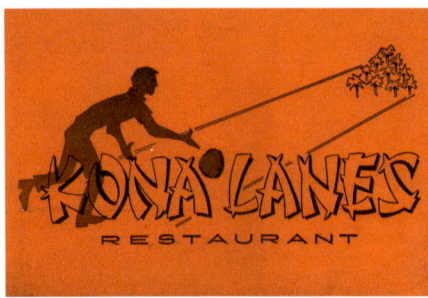

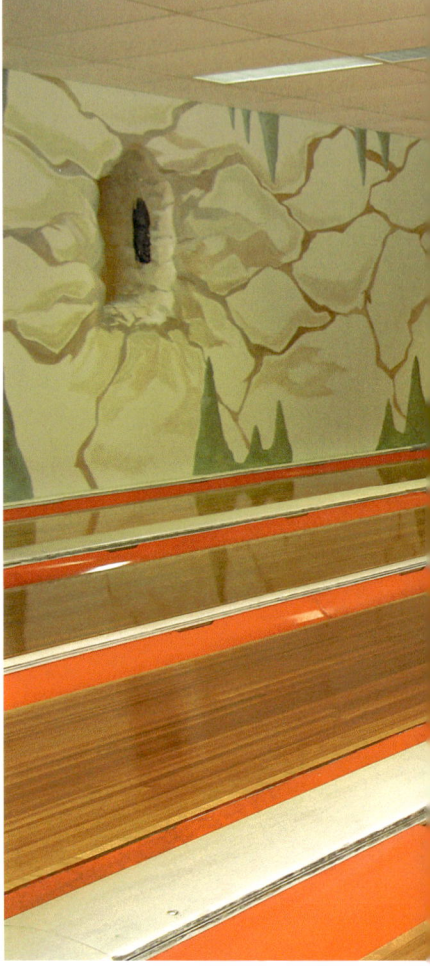

DER WIRTSCHAFTLICHE WOHLSTAND, der die amerikanische Mittelklasse Mitte der 1950er-Jahre erreichte, zog einen Bauboom nach sich. Vorstädte dehnten sich immer weiter aus und mehr und mehr Freizeit- und Unterhaltungseinrichtungen entstanden. Der Geist der kalifornischen Luft- und Raumfahrtindustrie spiegelte sich in der Architektur von Cafés und Bowlingbahnen wider, die zuweilen an Raumstationen erinnerten. Das Fernsehen fesselte die Menschen noch nicht so stark an ihr Zuhause, wie es das in den 1970er-Jahren tun würde, das Internet gab es noch nicht. Die Leute gingen noch vor die Tür, um sich zu amüsieren. Die Bowlingbahnen der 1950er-Jahre waren ein Unterhaltungszentrum für die moderne Familie.

Das Kapu-Kai in Rancho Cucamonga, Kalifornien, war ein Vergnügungstempel im Googie-Design. Hinter seinen vier Giebeln beherbergte es nicht nur eine Bowlingbahn, sondern auch ein Café, eine Bar und ein Restaurant mit Live-Unterhaltungsprogramm. Von Oceanic Arts komplett im polynesischen Stil eingerichtet, war der Bau im nahen Whittier mit den von Milan Guanko geschnitzten Götterfiguren ein Tiki-Tempel wie aus dem Bilderbuch. Der Tahitian Fire Room mit seinen bemalten Tapa-Stoffen servierte Kapu-Kai-Hühnchen und einen Cocktail namens Kapu-Kai Cooler, während die Kugeln der Bowler an Tiki-Säulen vorbeirollten.

Auf dem Höhepunkt des Bowling-Booms zählte jeder vierte Amerikaner den Sport zu seinem Hobby. Bowlingbahnen waren zu Begegnungsstätten geworden, in denen die Frauen zum Friseur gehen konnten, während ihre Sprösslinge im Kinderbetreu-

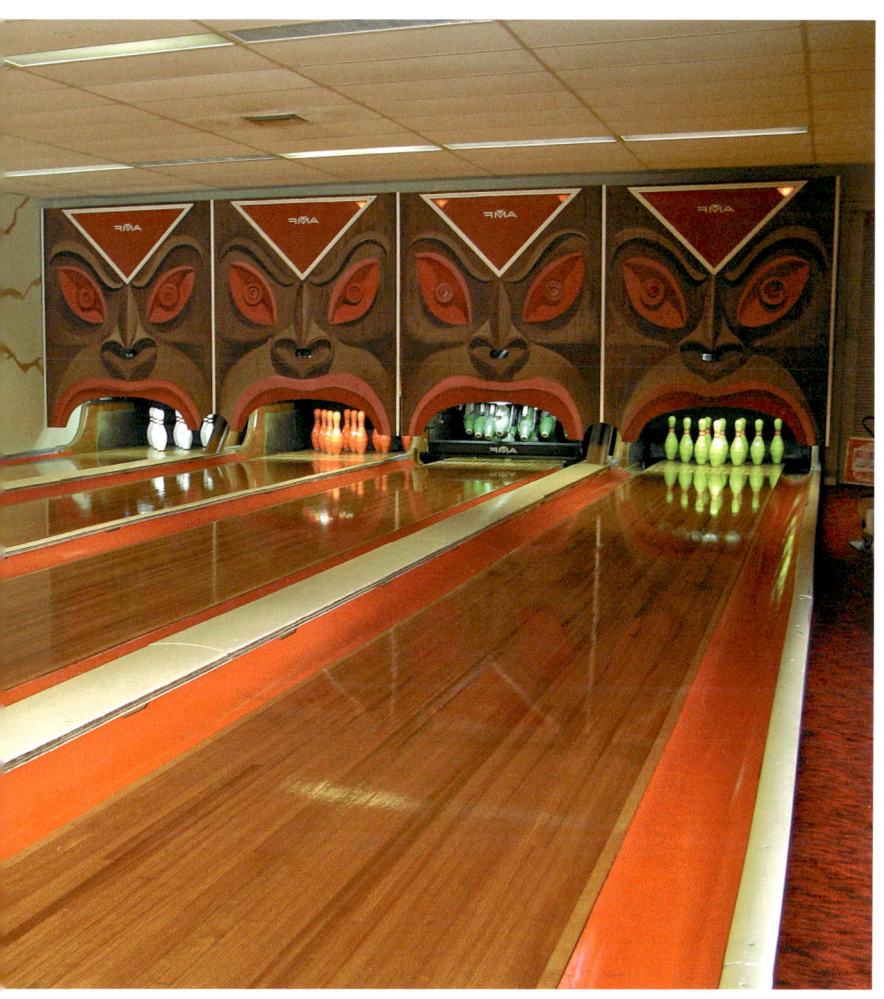

ungsraum spielten und ihre Männer sich
einen Drink in der Cocktaillounge geneh-
migten. Diese war für gewöhnlich thematisch gestaltet, vom Egyptian Pyramid
Room über den Totem Room bis zur Kona
Cove – der Fantasie der Innenarchitekten
waren keine Grenzen gesetzt. Das Tiki-
Dekor der Leilani Lanes in Seattle stammte
von William Westenhavers Firma Witco,

OPPOSITE: Kona Lanes menu cover,
Costa Mesa, California
(Mimi Payne Collection)

ABOVE: Bowling lanes at Polynesian
Gardens, Plantation, Florida
(Christie White Collection)

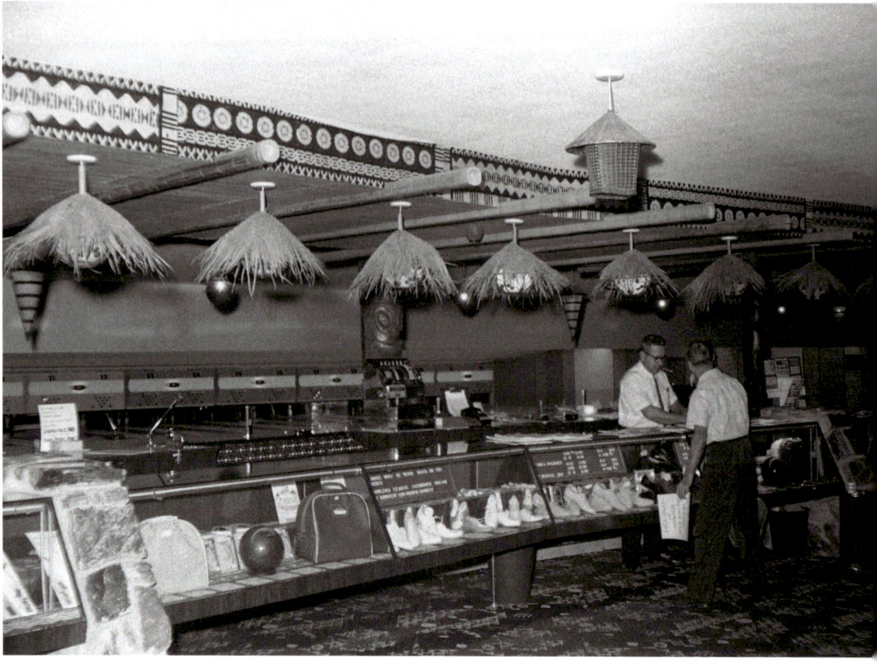

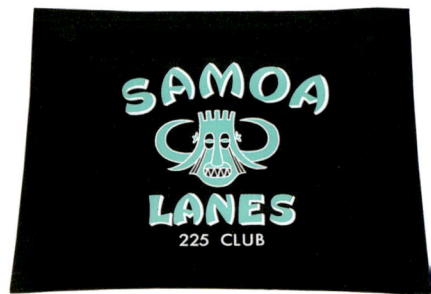

die auch die Tiki-Trophäen für die Bowlingwettbewerbe herstellte.

Auch wenn Hawaiihemden in diesem Umfeld nicht unpassend gewesen wären, trug man doch überwiegend das konservativere Bowlinghemd. Aber wie das Hawaiihemd musste es locker sitzen und durfte nicht in die Hose gesteckt werden. In den 1950er-Jahren kamen auch Teamhemden von Firmen in Mode.

Die bemerkenswerteste Einrichtung unter den Tiki-Bowlingbahnen fand sich nicht in einem der imposanten Nurdachhäuser, sondern in einer Wohnanlage für Senioren namens Polynesian Gardens Condominiums. Sogar die berühmte Schauspielerin Eve Arden sprach sich für dieses Zentrum in Plantation, Florida, aus. Die vier Bahnen mit automatischen

Kegelaufstellern zierten grimmige Tiki-Gesichter, deren Augen bei jedem Strike rot aufglühten. Zwar ließen die zwei Tiki-Köpfe des Logos einiges zu wünschen übrig, doch den Empfangsbereich schmückten ein beeindruckendes Wandgemälde und ein ungewöhnlicher Tiki-Brunnen aus Kupfer.

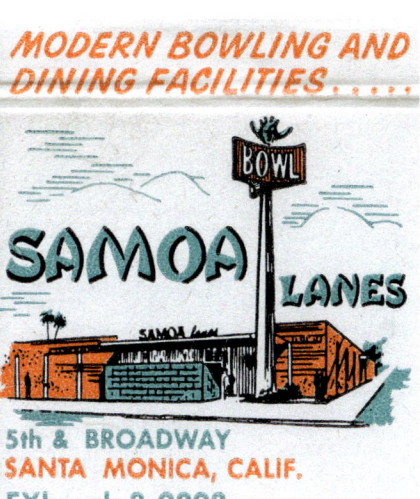

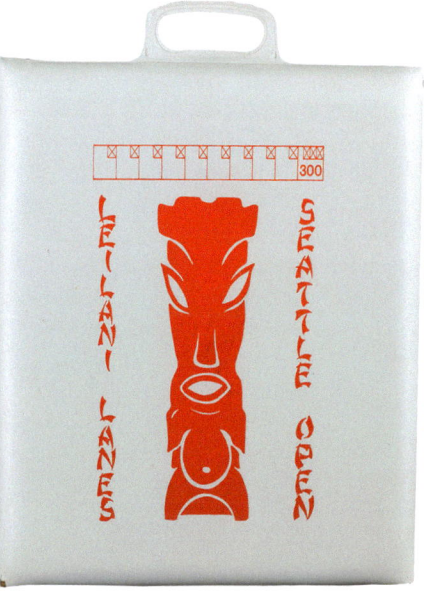

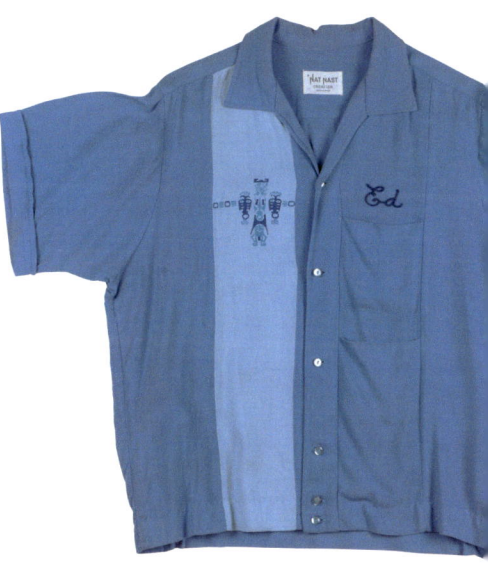

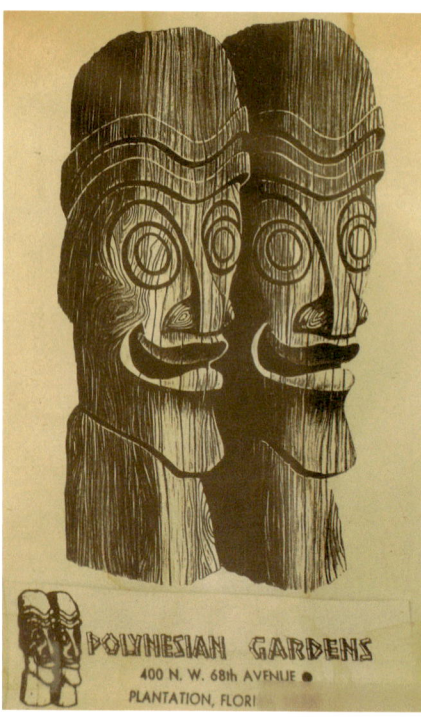

POLYNESIAN GARDENS
400 N. W. 68th AVENUE ●
PLANTATION, FLORI

L'AISANCE ÉCONOMIQUE DONT
bénéficie la classe moyenne américaine
au milieu des années 1950 alimente une
embellie dans la construction immobilière
qui provoque une expansion des villes et de
leurs banlieues, où se multiplient aussi des
espaces spécifiquement dédiés aux loisirs
et à la détente. L'industrie aérospatiale
californienne contribue aussi à l'esprit du
temps et influence l'architecture de certains
commerces, parmi lesquels les salles de
bowling, qui ressemblent de plus en plus à
des vaisseaux spatiaux. La télévision n'est
pas encore le média fétiche d'un nombre
croissant de casaniers, comme ce sera le cas
dans les années 1970 – et l'Internet n'existe
pas – si bien que les gens sortent encore
lorsqu'ils veulent passer un bon moment.

Le bowling devient alors le divertissement
de prédilection des familles.

Le Kapu-Kai de Rancho Cucamonga,
en Californie, est un de ces palais récréatifs,
étendards du Googie. Il abrite non seulement des pistes de bowling, mais aussi
un café, un bar et un restaurant proposant
divers numéros sous sa typique charpente
en A. Entièrement meublé dans le style
polynésien par Oceanic Arts, dont le siège
se trouve à Whittier, non loin, avec des tikis
sculptés par Milan Guanko, c'est un temple
tiki dans toute sa splendeur. Le poulet
Kapu-Kai et un cocktail baptisé le « Kapu-
Kai Cooler » sont servis dans la Salle du
Feu tahitienne, sur fond de tentures en *tapa*,
tandis que les boules des joueurs roulent
entre d'immenses colonnes tiki.

À l'apogée de la passion collective pour
le bowling, un Américain sur quatre dit
pratiquer régulièrement ce sport-divertisse-
ment. Les pistes de bowling sont devenus
de petits centres commerciaux, des lieux de
rencontre où les femmes peuvent aller chez
le coiffeur pendant que de gentils anima-
teurs distraient leurs enfants dans des salles
de jeu et que leurs maris boivent des verres
au bar à cocktail – généralement thématique, de la Pyramide égyptienne à la Salle
des Totems, en passant par l'incontournable
Crique tropicale et autre Kona Cove. La
décoration tiki du Leilani Lanes de Seattle
est réalisée par l'agence de William Westenhaver, Witco, qui fournit aussi les trophées
remis lors des compétitions de bowling.

Les chemises hawaïennes n'auraient pas
déparé sur les pistes de bowlings tiki, mais
la chemise de bowling est aussi une pièce
d'anthologie, bien que plus conservatrice, et
demeure l'uniforme privilégié des passion-
nés. Tout comme la chemise hawaïenne, elle
a une coupe ample pour ne pas entraver

les mouvements, et se porte hors du panta-
lon. Dans les années 1950, les chemises où
figurent un nom d'équipe deviennent elles
aussi très populaires.

L'exemple le plus saisissant de décoration tiki appliquée au bowling ne se trouve
pas dans l'impressionnante enceinte d'un
des palais en A typiques de l'époque, mais
dans une résidence médicalisée de luxe
pour retraités baptisée Polynesian Gardens
Condominiums, à Plantation (Floride), dont

la marraine est l'actrice et célébrité natio-
nale Eve Arden.

Les quatre pistes réglementaires avec
positionneurs de quilles automatiques sont
surmontées de faces de tikis dont les yeux
prennent une lueur rouge quand le joueur
marque un strike. S'il faut avouer que son
logo composé de deux tikis laisse franche-
ment à désirer, le hall d'entrée du Polynesian Gardens abrite une fresque incroyable
et une étrange fontaine en cuivre tiki.

OPPOSITE: Logo Tikis, Polynesian
Gardens, Plantation, Florida

RIGHT: Lobby Mural at
Polynesian Gardens

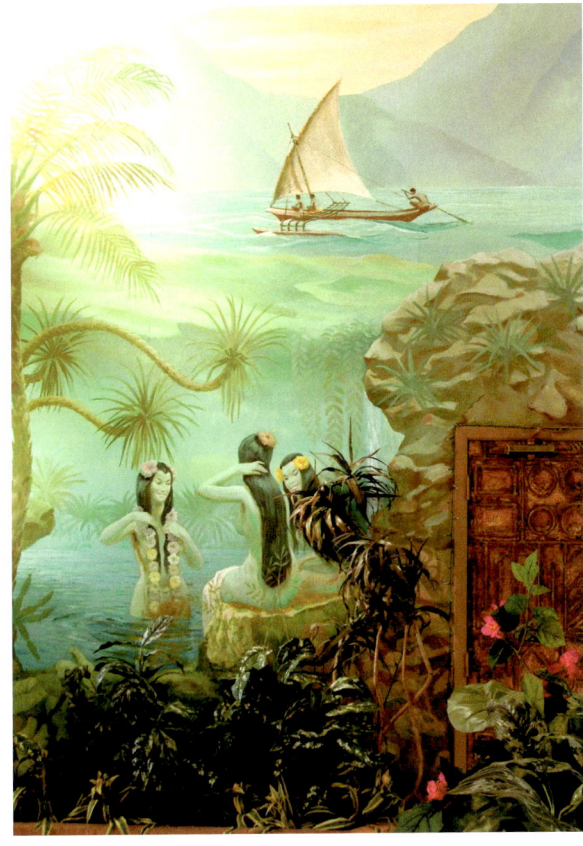

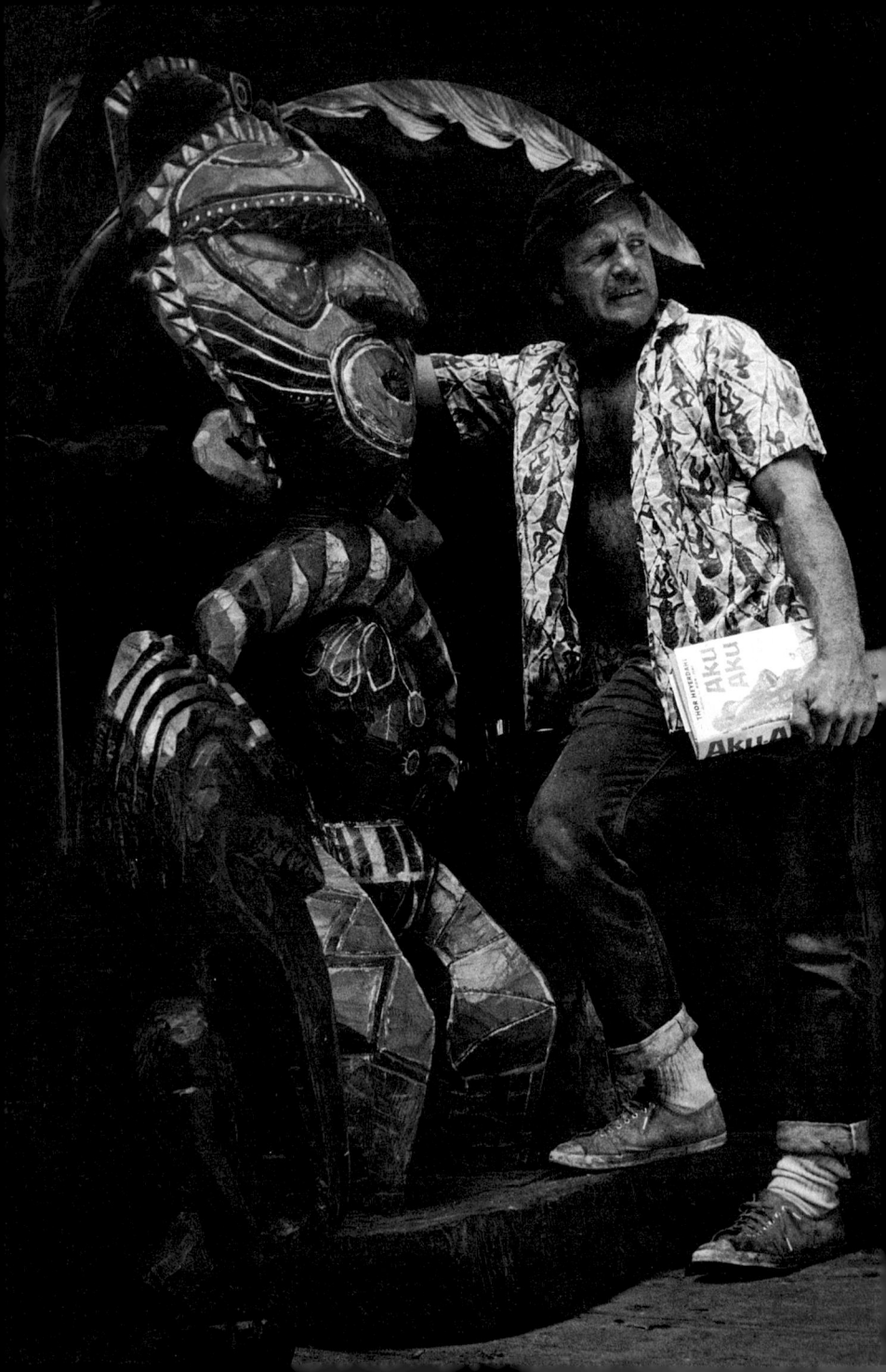

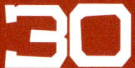

30

ARTISTS
AND CARVERS

KÜNSTLER UND HOLZSCHNITZER
ARTISTES ET SCULPTEURS

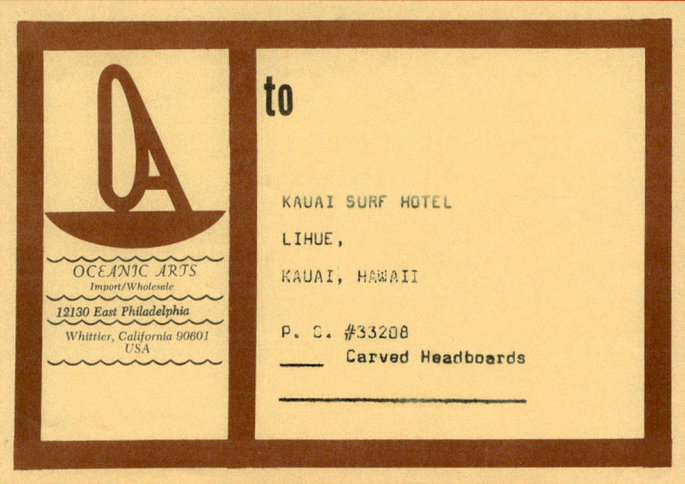

OPPOSITE: Barney West, wearing appropriate attire and clutching apt
literature, strikes a heroic pose with one of his sculptures

ABOVE: Oceanic Arts shipping label

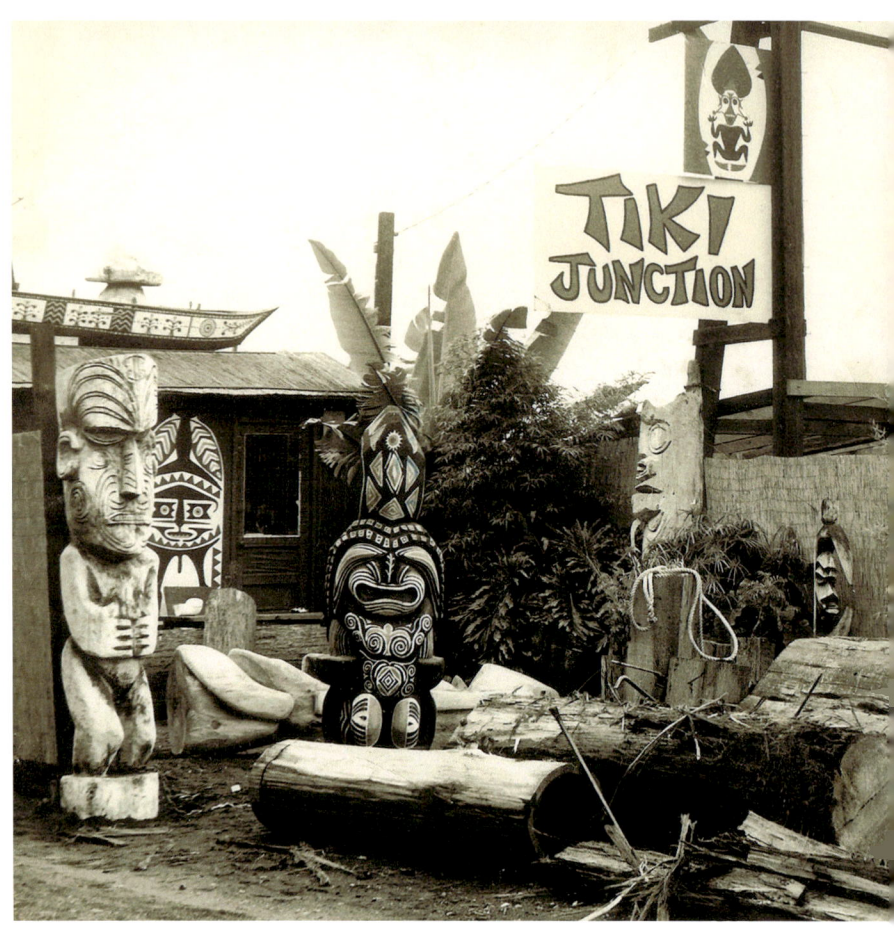

Various Tikis and logs to be carved
at Tiki Junction, Barney West's shop
in Sausalito, California
(both JP Balak Collection)

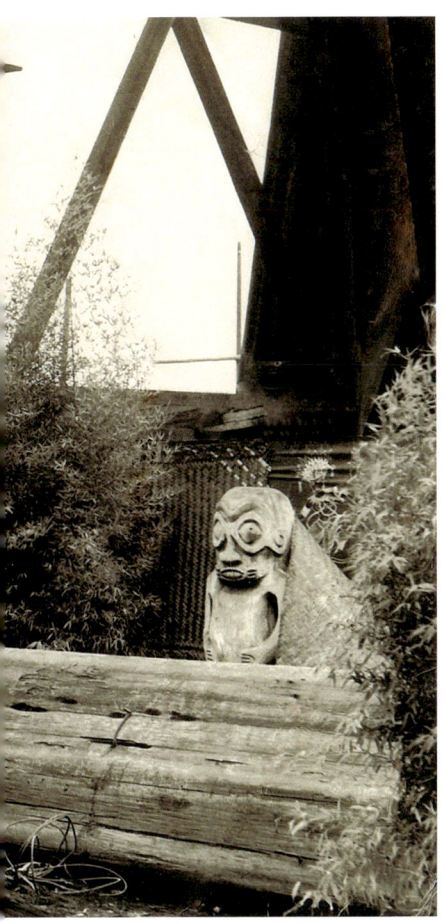

THE COLORFUL PALETTE OF AMERICAN

Tiki Pop was created by a myriad of talented designers, painters, sculptors, and carvers. Only a few can be presented here, representative of the rest.

Barney West was like a character from a South Seas novel: a ruddy old salt who liked his rum. He had served in the merchant marine in the Pacific and opened his Tiki Junction studio in the bohemian harbor town of Sausalito, north of San Francisco. No log was too big for Barney; his giant redwood idols made it all the way to Hawaii, and to the Mai-Kai in Florida. Many of his Tiki carvings were used for Trader Vic's restaurants across the United States. His style was unique and is recognizable to this day.

Founded by Robert van Oosting and Leroy Schmaltz in 1956, Oceanic Arts became the one-stop shop for Tiki décor for restaurants and movie studios during the Polynesian trend. They supplied carvings and materials for virtually all of the great Tiki temples of the day, as well as many apartment buildings along the West Coast and hotels in Tahiti, Hawaii, and Samoa. The business survived the abolition of Tiki Pop, and Leroy still shapes wood into Tikis to this day.

Lewis VanDercar was a sculptor and painter who lived and worked in Miami, Florida, until the mid-1970s. He was a bohemian, a swinger, a prankster, and, later, a warlock. His Polynesian statues were inspired more by fantasy than by Oceanic art and graced several Tiki clubs and motels along the Florida coast. VanDercar's home was festooned with his strange statuary, making it an "outsider art" fixture in Miami. He circulated in Miami Beach's swinging '60s scene of men's magazine characters such as pin-up photographer Bunny Yeager and international playboy Baron Sepy Dobronyi. His Halloween parties were legendary.

After studying at the Pasadena Art Center College of Design, Florian "Gabe" Gabriel applied for a job as the art director for Stephen Crane Associates in 1957. Actor Steve Crane had just taken over the Tropics restaurant in Beverly Hills— renaming it the Luau—and was expanding and Tiki-fying the place. To test Gabe's artistic abilities, Crane sent him to the nearby Trader Vic's and had him sketch a corner of the restaurant. The result was satisfactory, and Gabe began working under head designer George Nakashima. Both were soon tasked with expanding the Luau concept for the Kon-Tiki chain of restaurants that Steve Crane was open- ing for the Sheraton Hotel Corporation. Florian Gabriel's job description was very similar to that of a film-production art director: designing all of the details of the set to support the illusion of another reality. Gabe later conceded that the Tiki had imbued a fresh edge into the old, tired bamboo-hut concept—until it crashed for- ever.After supervising the construction of Kon-Tiki restaurants in Chicago, Portland, Boston, Cleveland, and Dallas, Gabriel and Nakashima went on to help with the expansion of the highly successful Mai-Kai in Fort Lauderdale.Their next job brought them to Detroit to outfit the elaborate Mauna Loa restaurant. A multimillion-dol- lar project, the Mauna Loa opened toward the tail end of the Tiki Pop trend, and did not survive the white flight caused by the Detroit race riots in 1967. The time for the romantic simplification of other societies was coming to an end.

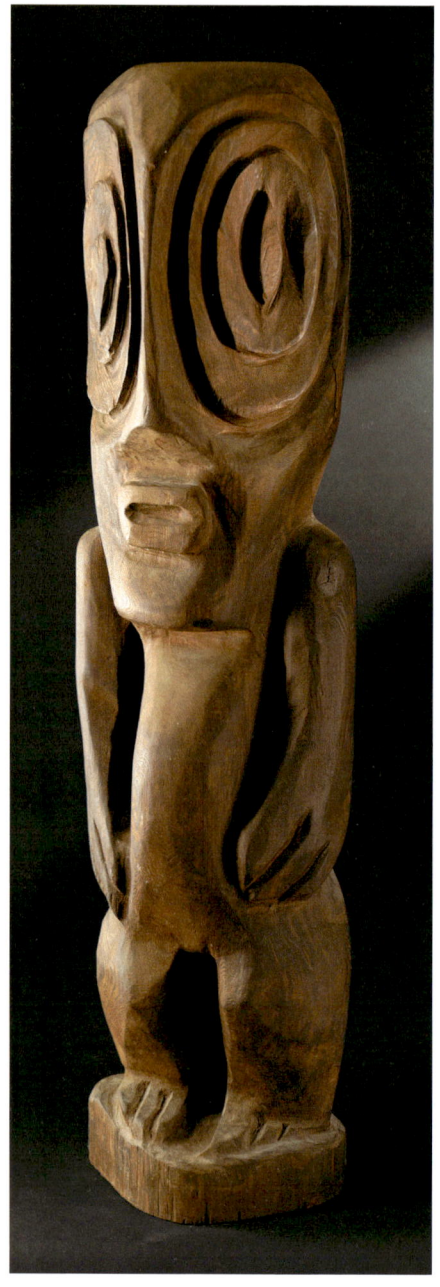

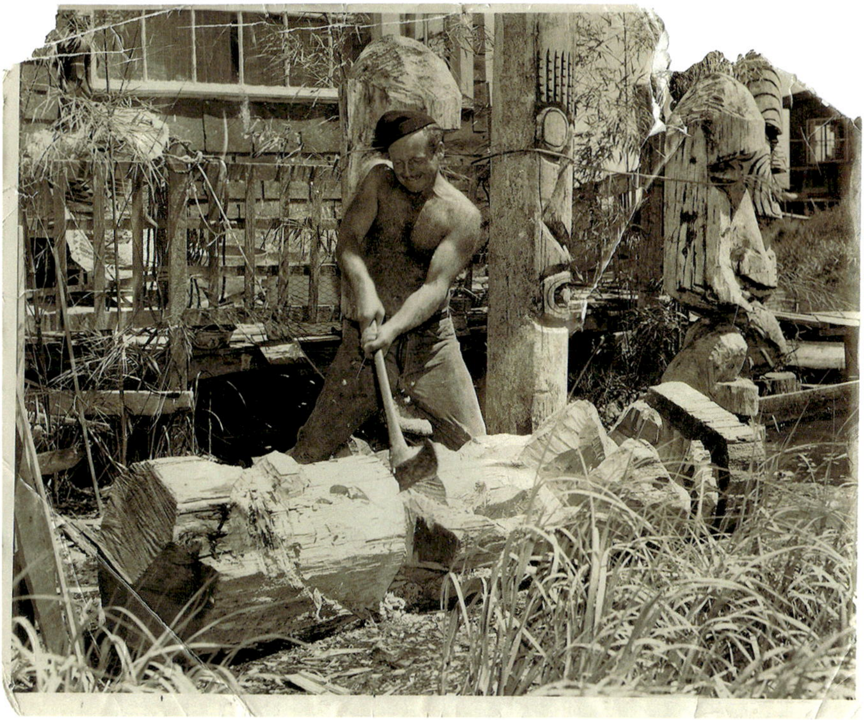

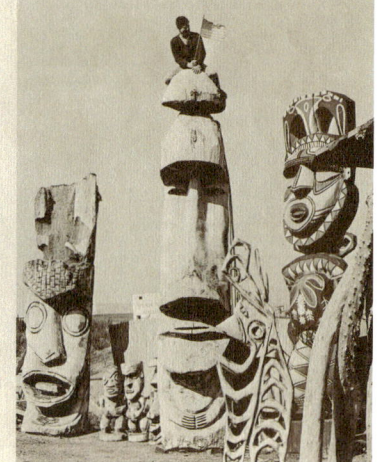

OPPOSITE: A classic Barney West Tiki
(Kiara Geller Collection)

ABOVE: Barney West at work
(JP Balak Collection)

RIGHT: Barney on one of his giants
(O.A. Collection)

In the 1940s, Frank Bowers was a storyboard artist for Warner Bros. Studios in Hollywood, working on films like *A Tree Grows in Brooklyn* and *Edge of Darkness*. He also began painting murals for bars and nightclubs, which were sometimes used for menu covers. While his artworks covered an incredible range of motifs corresponding to the themes of the bars, they had one thing in common: in the classic bar-painting tradition, his females were mostly bare-breasted. This predestined him for Polynesian island scenes, and his work adorned the walls of clubs like the Zamboanga and the Leilani.

Louis Behan was introduced to the Pacific Islands while piloting a B-17 on air force search-and-rescue missions, where he earned silver wings. After he got out of the service, he went to art school and embarked on a career as a commercial artist. Working on mundane jobs such as shower-curtain designs and souvenir art, he never forgot his first love, the South Seas. He chose the traditional Polynesian-pop medium of black velvet to express his fascination with the people and cultures of the Pacific.

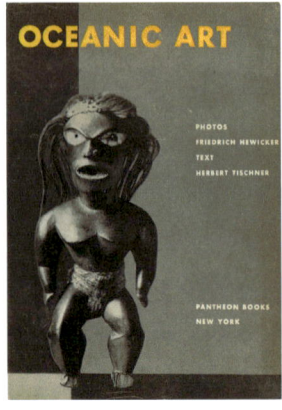

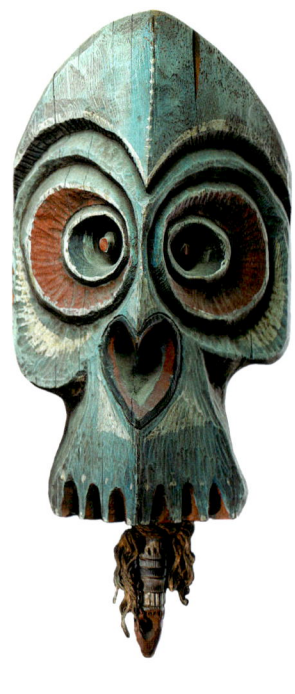

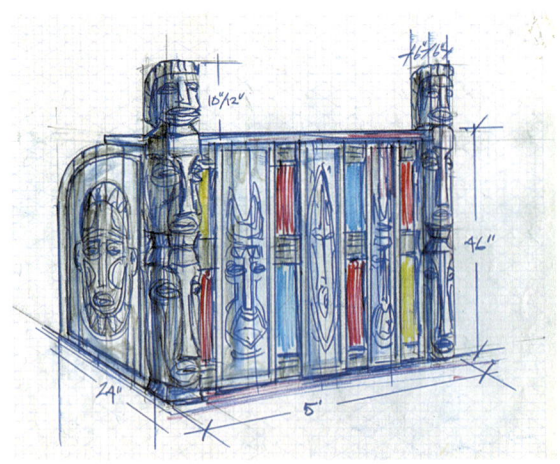

OPPOSITE ABOVE: Reference book for many Tiki carvers

OPPOSITE MIDDLE: Disneyesque skull carved by Leroy Schmaltz

OPPOSITE BELOW: Sketch for a home bar by Leroy Schmaltz

BELOW: 1958 newspaper clipping showing Leroy Schmaltz and Robert van Oosting at work

1958   8813 E. WHITTIER BLVD.   ⁷⁷   7 Cents Per Copy— **16 Pages**

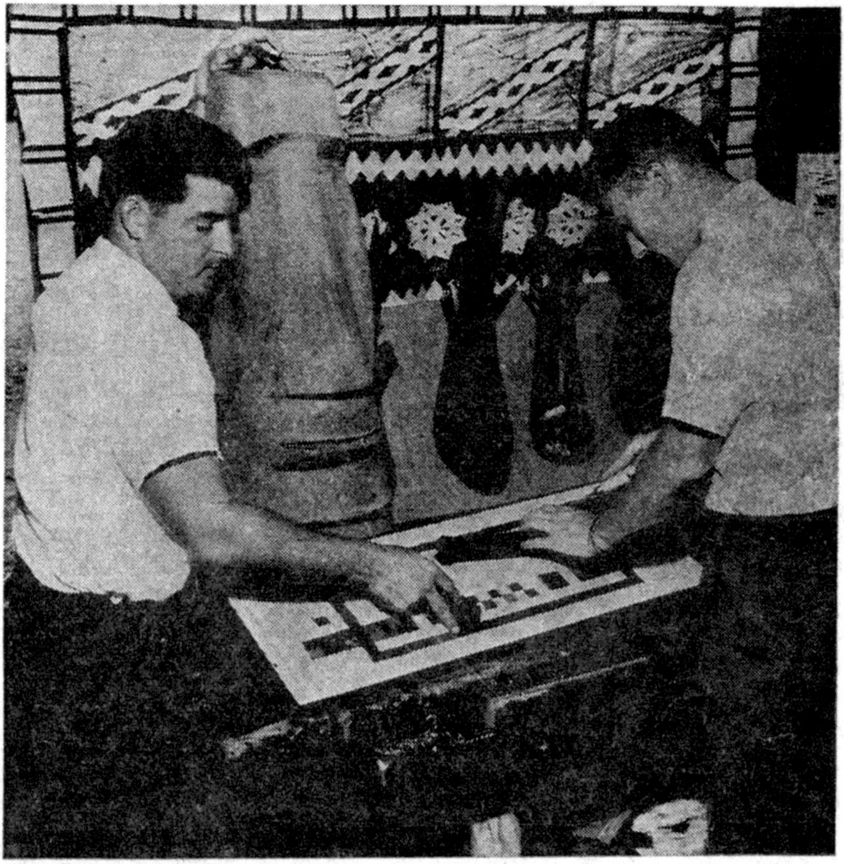

ARTISIANS—Putting the finishing touches on a mosaic table top, Pico Rivera artists Bob Van Oosting and LeRoy Schmaltz pay particular attention to the fine detailing. The young men are turning a fascinating hobby into what promises to be a lucrative business venture. (News Photo).

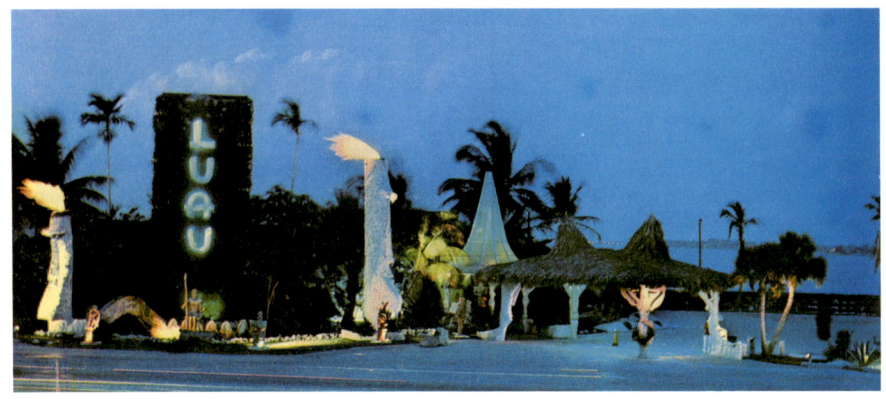

DIE FARBENFROHE PALETTE DES

amerikanischen Tiki-Pop wurde von einer
Vielzahl talentierter Designer, Maler, Bildhauer und Holzschnitzer erschaffen. Im
Rahmen dieses Buches können nur einige
wenige stellvertretend genannt werden.

Barney West erinnerte an eine Figur
aus einem Südseeroman: ein rotgesichtiger
alter Seebär, der seinen Rum liebte. Er hatte
in der Handelsmarine im Pazifik gedient
und eröffnete 1963 sein Atelier namens
Tiki Junction in Sausalito, nördlich von San
Francisco. Kein Holzklotz war Barney zu
groß. Seine riesigen Redwood-Skulpturen
gelangten bis nach Hawaii und ins Mai-Kai
in Florida. Viele seiner Tiki-Schnitzereien
zierten Trader Vic's in den gesamten USA.
Sein Stil war einzigartig und ist noch heute
unverkennbar.

Von Robert van Oosting und Leroy
Schmaltz 1956 gegründet, wurde Oceanic
Arts für Restaurants und Filmstudios zur
Anlaufstelle für Tiki-Dekor. Das Unternehmen belieferte praktisch alle großen
Tiki-Tempel seiner Zeit mit Schnitzereien
und anderem Material. Weiterhin zählten
viele Wohnkomplexe an der Westküste
und Hotels auf Tahiti, Hawaii und den

ABOVE: Impressive array of
VanDercar statuary at Luau
restaurant, Miami Beach

BELOW: VanDercar sculpture of Sea
God for an all-girl-island flick starring
Mai-Kai Mystery Girl Nani Maka

OPPOSITE: Lewis VanDercar at work
in his studio

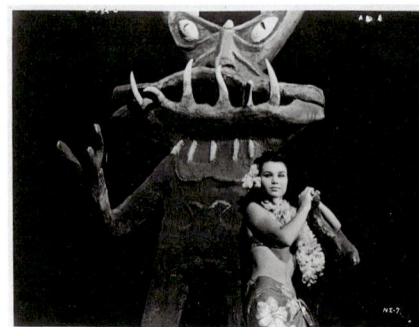

Cinema Syndicate Presents
PAGAN ISLAND
Starring Ed Dew – Nani Maka
Produced & Directed by Barry Mahon

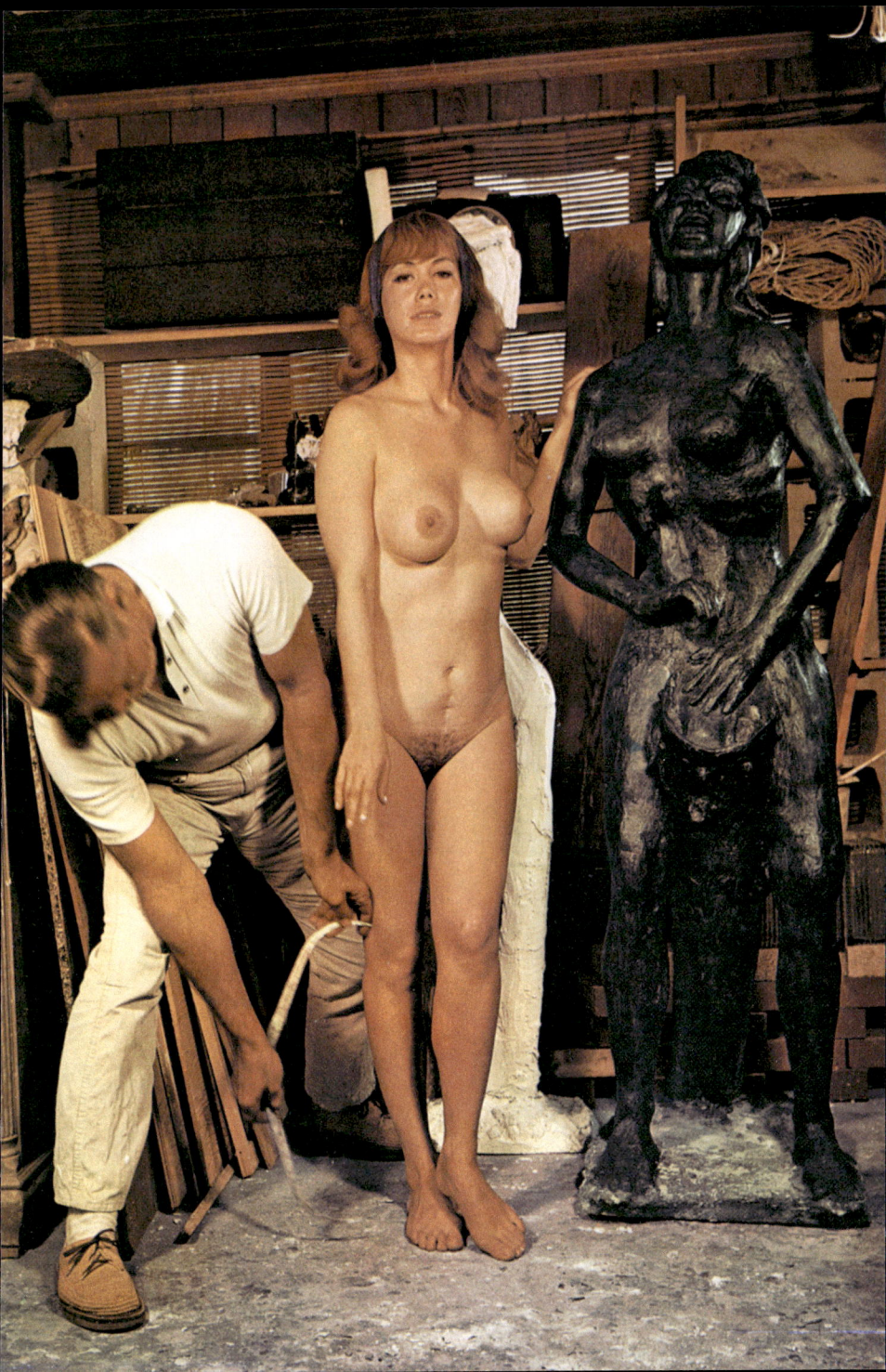

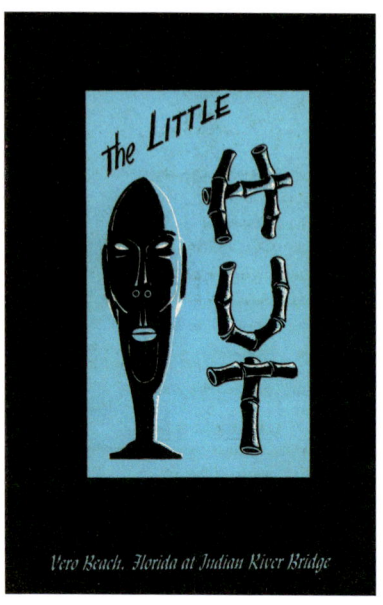

The LITTLE HUT

Vero Beach, Florida at Indian River Bridge

LEFT AND BELOW: Menu and postcard from the Little Hut, Vero Beach, Florida, with alien-style VanDercar Tiki *(Mimi Payne Collection)*

OPPOSITE ABOVE: Lewis VanDercar in front of his Miami home

OPPOSITE BELOW: More primitive art by VanDercar
(Scott Schell Collection)

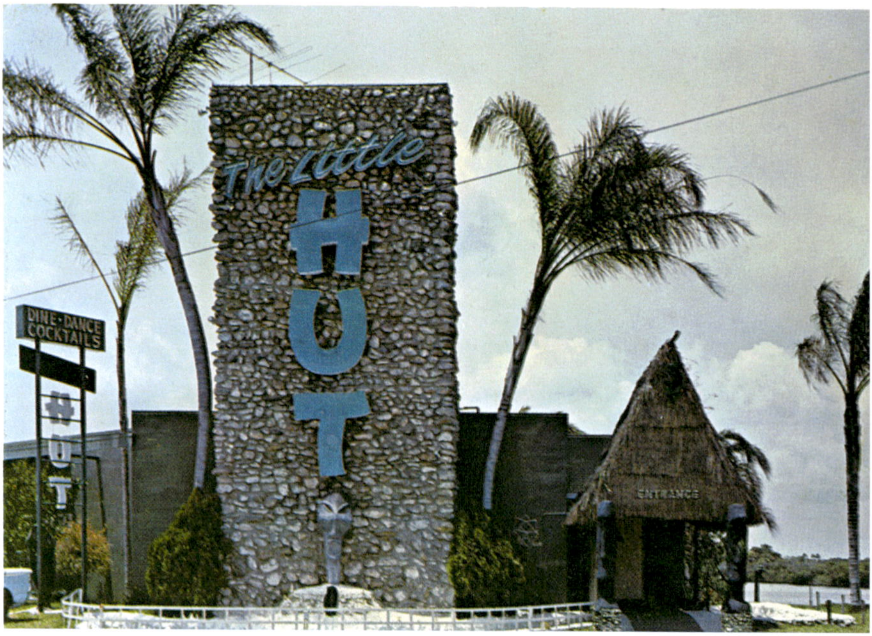

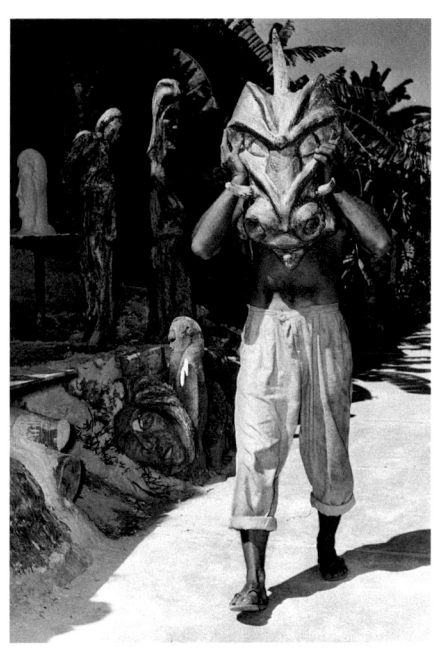

Samoainseln zu den Kunden. Das Geschäft überlebte den Niedergang des Tiki-Pop. Noch heute schnitzt Leroy Tikis aus Holz.

Lewis VanDercar war ein Bildhauer und Maler, der bis Mitte der 1970er-Jahre in Miami, Florida, lebte und arbeitete. Er war Künstler, Swinger und Witzbold – und später auch „Hexenmeister". Seine polynesischen Statuen waren eher von seiner Fantasie als von der ozeanischen Kunst inspiriert und zierten diverse Tiki-Clubs und -Motels entlang der Küste Floridas. Sein Zuhause, angefüllt mit seinen unzähligen außergewöhnlichen Werken, wurde zu einer Institution der Art brut. In der freizügigen 1960er-Jahre-Kunstszene von Miami Beach umgab er sich mit Leuten aus der Welt der Erotikmagazine, etwa der Pin-up-Fotografin Bunny Yeager und dem Playboy und Bonvivant Sepy Dobronyi. Seine Halloweenpartys waren legendär.

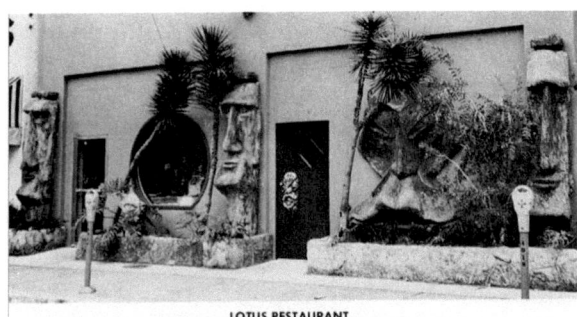

LOTUS RESTAURANT
308 Seabreeze Boulevard, Daytona Beach   32018
Established 17 years in Daytona Beach. Our quality speaks for itself, our guests speak to their friends. Chinese-American cuisine our specialty. 252-9851.

Nach seinem Studium am Pasadena Art Center College of Design bewarb sich Florian „Gabe" Gabriel 1957 als künstlerischer Leiter bei Stephen Crane Associates. Der Schauspieler Stephen Crane hatte gerade das Restaurant Tropics in Beverly Hills übernommen und in The Luau umbenannt; er war im Begriff, das Lokal auszubauen und zu „tikifizieren". Um Gabes künstlerische Fähigkeiten zu testen, schickte er ihn zu Trader Vic's und ließ ihn eine Ecke des Restaurants zeichnen. Das Ergebnis war zufriedenstellend und Gabe begann, unter Chefdesigner George Nakashima zu arbeiten. Schon bald wurden beide damit beauftragt, das Konzept des Luau für die Kon-Tiki-Restaurantkette, die Crane für die Sheraton Hotel Corporation eröffnen sollte, auszubauen. Florian Gabriels Berufsbeschreibung ähnelte der eines Artdirectors beim Film. Er entwarf alle Details des Sets, um die perfekte Illusion einer anderen Welt zu erschaffen.

Später gab Gabe zu, dass die Tikis frischen Wind in das veraltete Bambushütten-Konzept gebracht hatten – bis der Trend in sich zusammenfiel. Nachdem sie den Bau von Kon-Tiki-Restaurants in Chicago, Portland, Boston, Cleveland und Dallas beaufsichtigt hatten, halfen Gabriel und Nakashima beim Ausbau des erfolgreichen Mai-Kais in Fort Lauderdale mit.

Ihr nächster Job brachte sie nach Detroit, wo sie das Restaurant Mauna Loa ausstatteten. Das Lokal war ein mehrere Millionen Dollar teures Projekt, das zum Ende der Tiki-Pop-Ära eröffnet wurde und den Wegzug weißer Einwohner nach den Rassenkrawallen 1967 leider nicht überstand. Die Zeiten romantischer Verklärung fremder Kulturen näherten sich ihrem Ende.

Frank Bowers war in den 1940er-Jahren Storyboard-Zeichner bei Warner Bros. in Hollywood. Er wirkte an Filmen wie *Aufstand in Trollness* (1943) und *Ein Baum wächst in Brooklyn* (1945). Er begann zudem, Wandgemälde für Bars und Nachtclubs zu malen. Seine Werke deckten ein breites Motivspektrum ab, dem jeweiligen thematischen Schwerpunkt der einzelnen Lokale angepasst. Eines aber hatten sie alle gemeinsam: Seine Frauenfiguren waren überwiegend barbusig. Dies prädestinierte ihn für polynesische Inselszenen, die die Wände von Klubs wie dem Zamboanga und dem Leilani schmückten.

Louis Behan lernte die pazifischen Inseln als Pilot eines B-17-Bombers der Air Force kennen. Als Mitglied einer Einheit für die Suche und Rettung in Luft- und Seenotfällen wurde er mit einem silbernen Flugzeugführerabzeichen ausgezeichnet. Nachdem er aus dem Dienst entlassen worden war, ging er auf eine Kunstschule und begann eine Karriere als Gebrauchsgrafiker, als der er so banale Gegenstände wie Duschvorhänge gestaltete. Seine erste große Liebe, die Südsee, vergaß er dabei nie. Um seine Faszination für die Menschen und Kulturen des Pazifik zum Ausdruck zu bringen, wählte er das traditionelle Medium des „Polynesian Pop" – schwarzen Samt.

The original sketch that got Florian Gabriel the job at the Luau

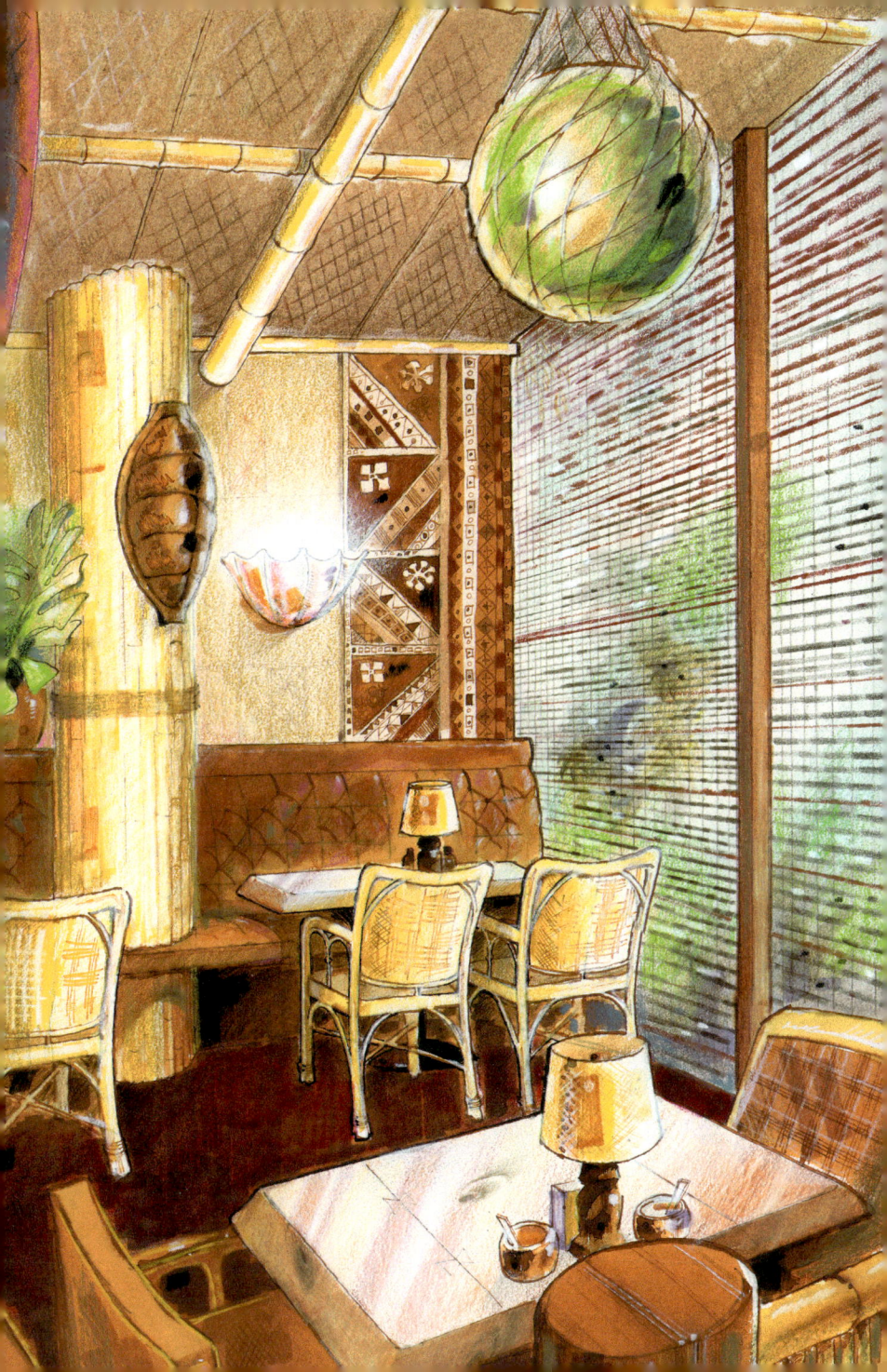

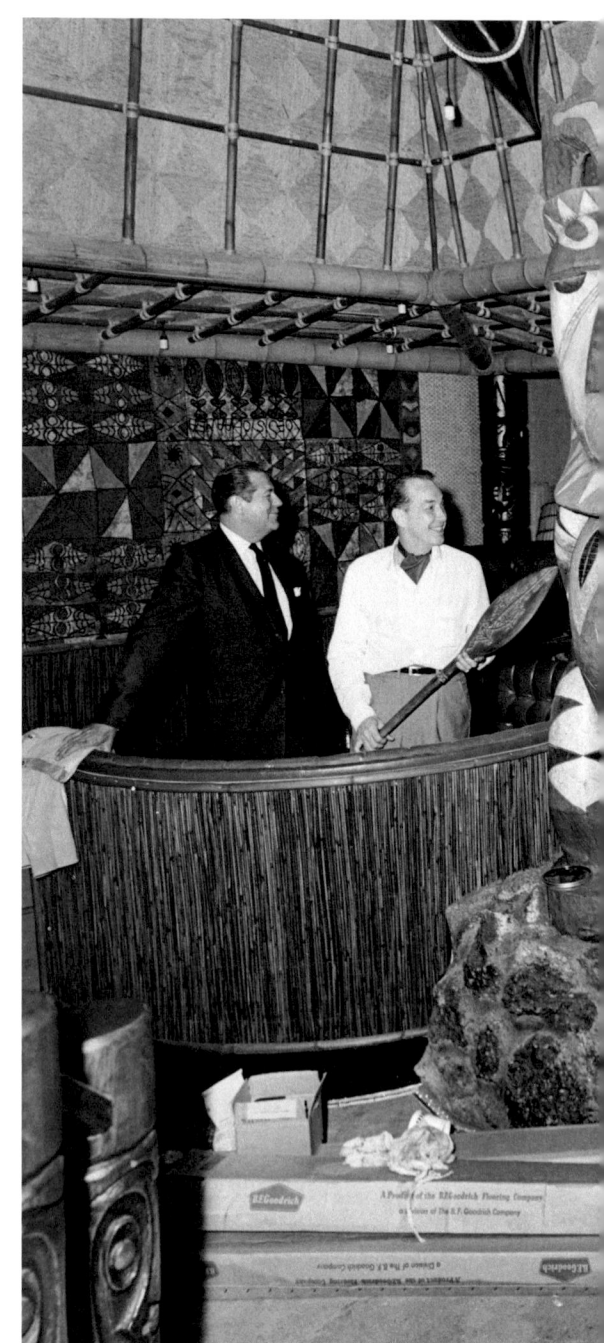

Steve Crane (with spear) inspecting the building of the first Kon-Tiki, Montreal, 1958. Florian Gabriel on the right *(JP Balak Collection)*

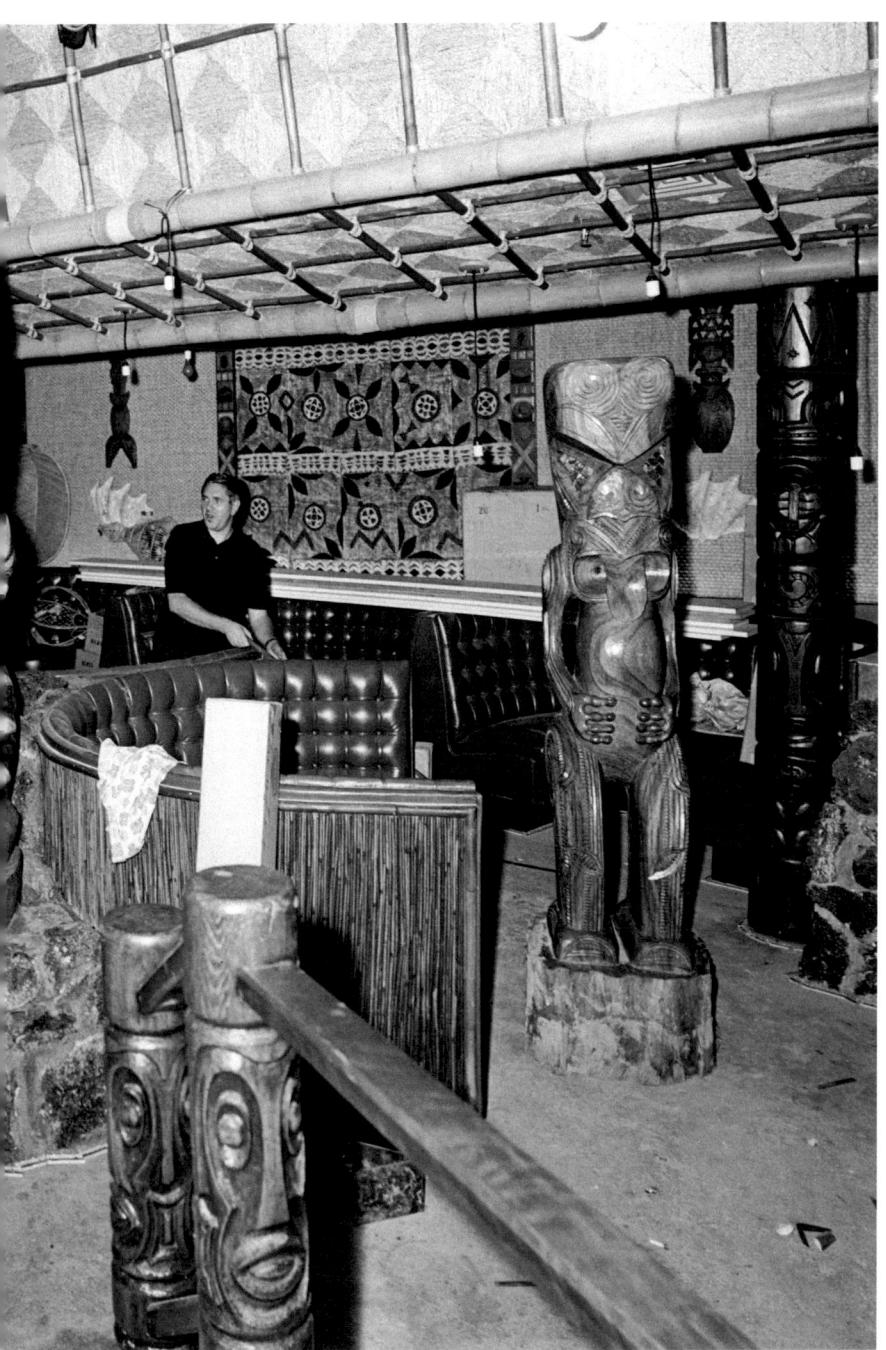

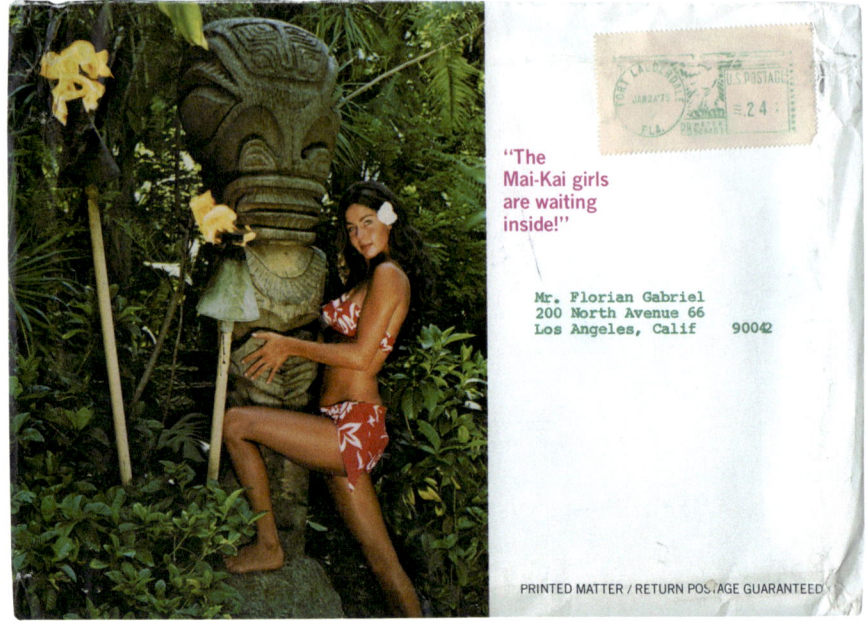

"The
Mai-Kai girls
are waiting
inside!''

Mr. Florian Gabriel
200 North Avenue 66
Los Angeles, Calif   90042

PRINTED MATTER / RETURN POSTAGE GUARANTEED

LA PALETTE BIGARRÉE DU TIKI POP américain fut l'œuvre d'une myriade de designers, de peintres et de sculpteurs talentueux. Il n'est possible ici que d'en présenter quelques-uns, représentatifs de l'ensemble de ces créateurs.

Barney West ressemblait au personnage d'un roman des mers du Sud : un vieux loup de mer buriné très porté sur le rhum. Il avait servi dans la marine marchande, dans le Pacifique, et ouvert son atelier, Tiki Junction, à Sausalito, « ville flottante » et paradis hippie au nord de San Francisco.

Il n'existait pas de bille de bois assez grosse pour résister à Barney. Ses divinités géantes en séquoia ont fait le voyage d'Hawaii et sont allées jusqu'au Mai-Kai en Floride. Nombre de ses sculptures tiki servirent à décorer les restaurants de la chaîne Trader Vic's, aux quatre coins des États-Unis. Son style unique reste reconnaissable entre tous.

Fondée par Robert van Oosting et Leroy Schmaltz en 1956, Oceanic Arts devint, pendant la vague polynésienne, l'adresse par excellence où restaurants et studios de cinéma pouvaient se procurer des éléments de décoration tiki. On y trouvait des sculptures sur bois et des objets qui ornèrent pratiquement tous les grands temples tiki de l'époque, de même que quantité d'immeubles de la côte Ouest et d'hôtels à Tahiti, Hawaii et Samoa. Le commerce a survécu au déclin du tiki pop et aujourd'hui Leroy continue à fabriquer des objets en bois tiki.

Peintre et sculpteur, Lewis VanDercar vécut et travailla à Miami jusqu'au milieu des années 1970. C'était un garçon dans le vent, à la fois hippie, espiègle et même, plus tard, un peu sorcier. Ses statues polynésiennes, émanations de ses fantasmes plus que de l'art océanien orneront plusieurs clubs et motels tiki sur la côte de Floride.

La maison de VanDercar hébergeait un étrange ensemble de statues qui faisait d'elle une installation d'art brut en plein Miami. Il évoluait dans le milieu branché du Miami Beach des sixties, parmi des figures de la presse masculine comme le photographe de charme Bunny Yeager et le baron Sepy Dobronyi, play-boy international. Les fêtes qu'il donnait à l'occasion d'Halloween sont restées légendaires.

En 1957, après ses études au College of Design de Pasadena, Florian « Gabe » Gabriel postula à un poste de directeur artistique au sein de la société Stephen Crane Associates. L'acteur Steve Crane venait juste de reprendre le restaurant Tropics à Beverly Hills. Il l'avait agrandi, « tikifié » et rebaptisé le Luau. Pour tester les compétences artistiques de Gabe, Crane l'envoya au Trader Vic's voisin et

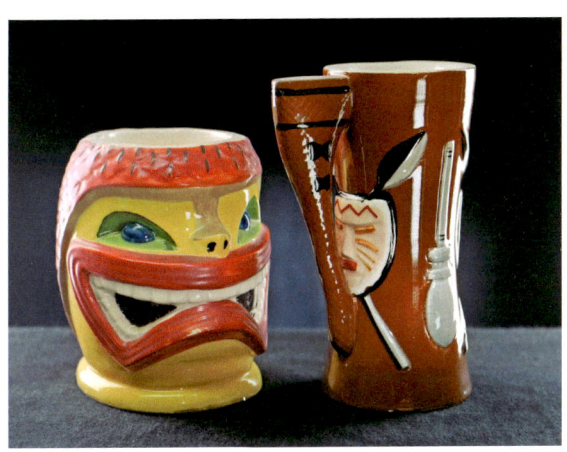

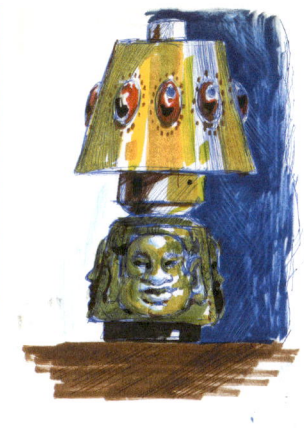

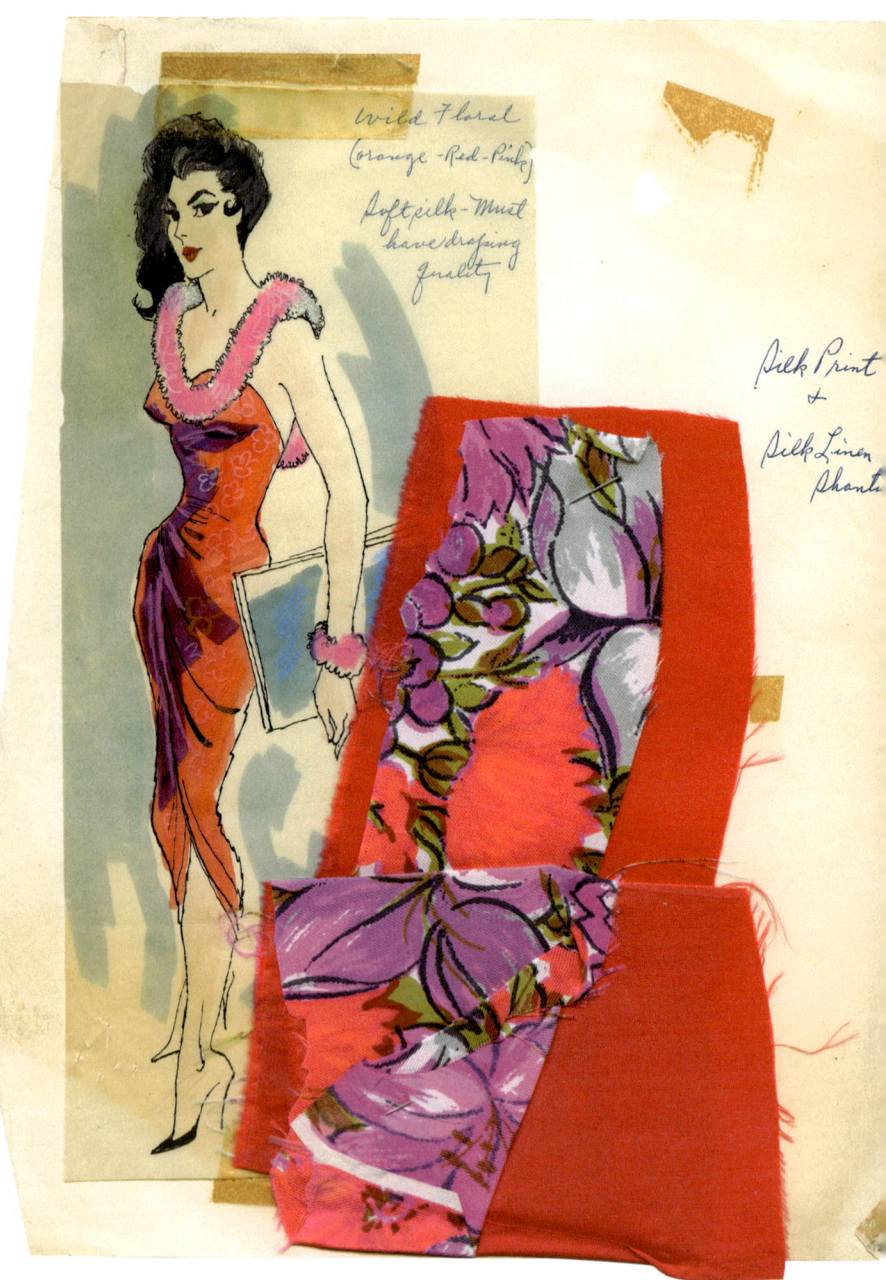

Wild Floral
(orange - Red - Pink)

Soft silk - Must
have draping
quality

Silk Print
&
Silk Linen
Shantu

lui demanda de dessiner un coin du restaurant. Le résultat lui donna satisfaction et Gabe se mit au travail sous la tutelle du designer George Nakashima. Ils s'attelèrent à l'extension du concept du Luau à la chaîne de restaurants Kon-Tiki, que Steve Crane était en train d'ouvrir pour le compte des hôtels Sheraton.

Le profil du poste de Florian Gabriel était très similaire à celui d'un directeur artistique de cinéma : il était chargé de concevoir dans tous ses détails un décor produisant l'illusion d'une autre réalité. Gabe admettra plus tard qu'avant de s'éteindre à tout jamais, le tiki avait fait souffler un vent frais sur le concept vieillot et fatigué de la cabane de bambou.

Après avoir supervisé la construction de restaurants Kon-Tiki à Chicago, Portland, Boston, Cleveland et Dallas, Gabriel et Nakashima participèrent au développement du très prospère Mai-Kai à Fort

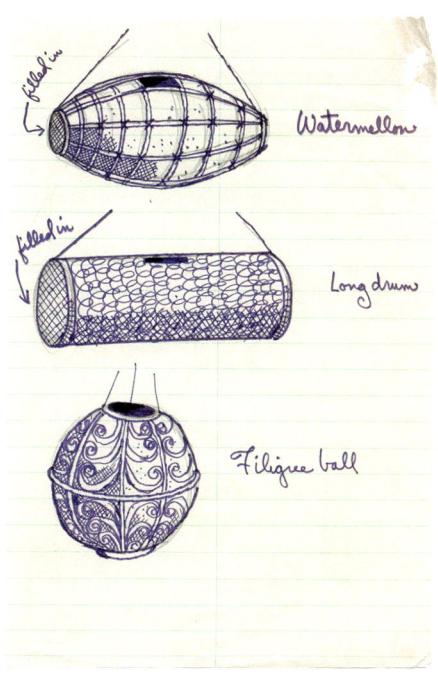

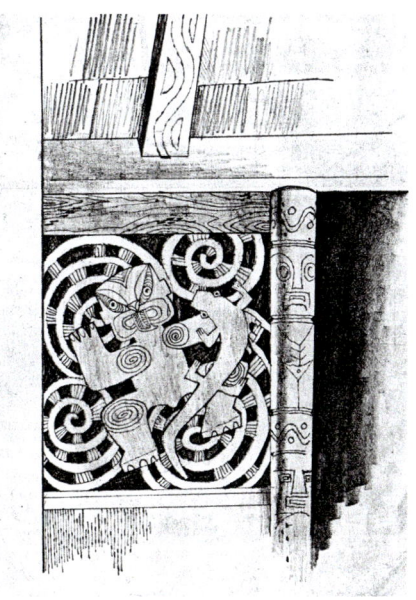

OPPOSITE: Design for a hostess uniform by Florian Gabriel *(JP Balak Collection)*

ABOVE: Design for three exotic beachcomber lamps *(JP Balak Collection)*

LEFT: Sketch for a Maori-style dividing screen

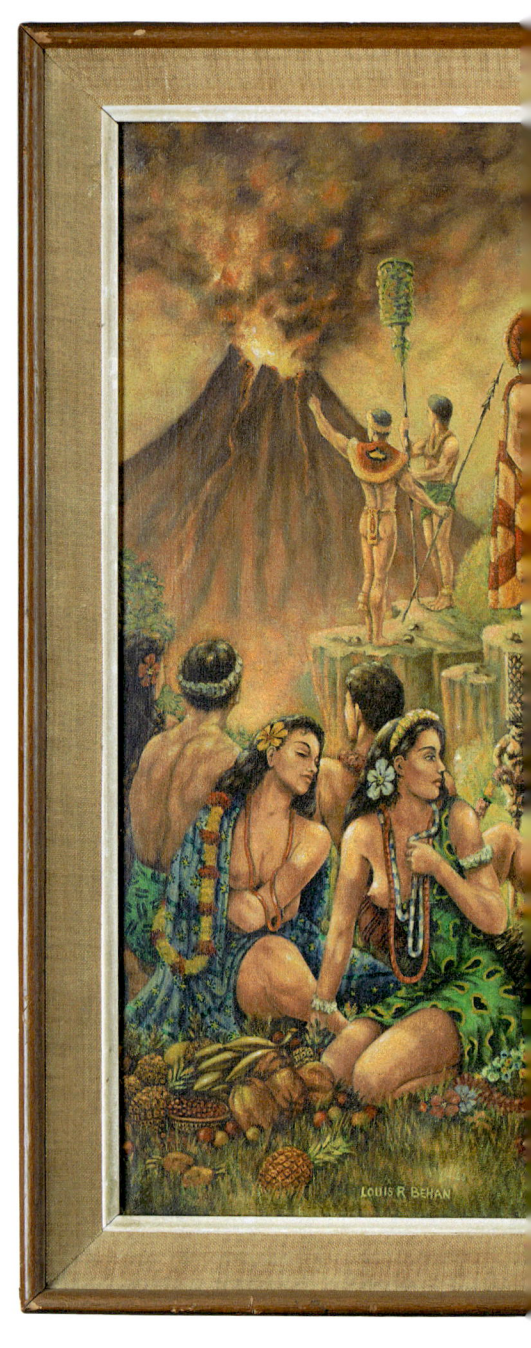

Virgin Sacrifice, early oil painting
by Louis Behan

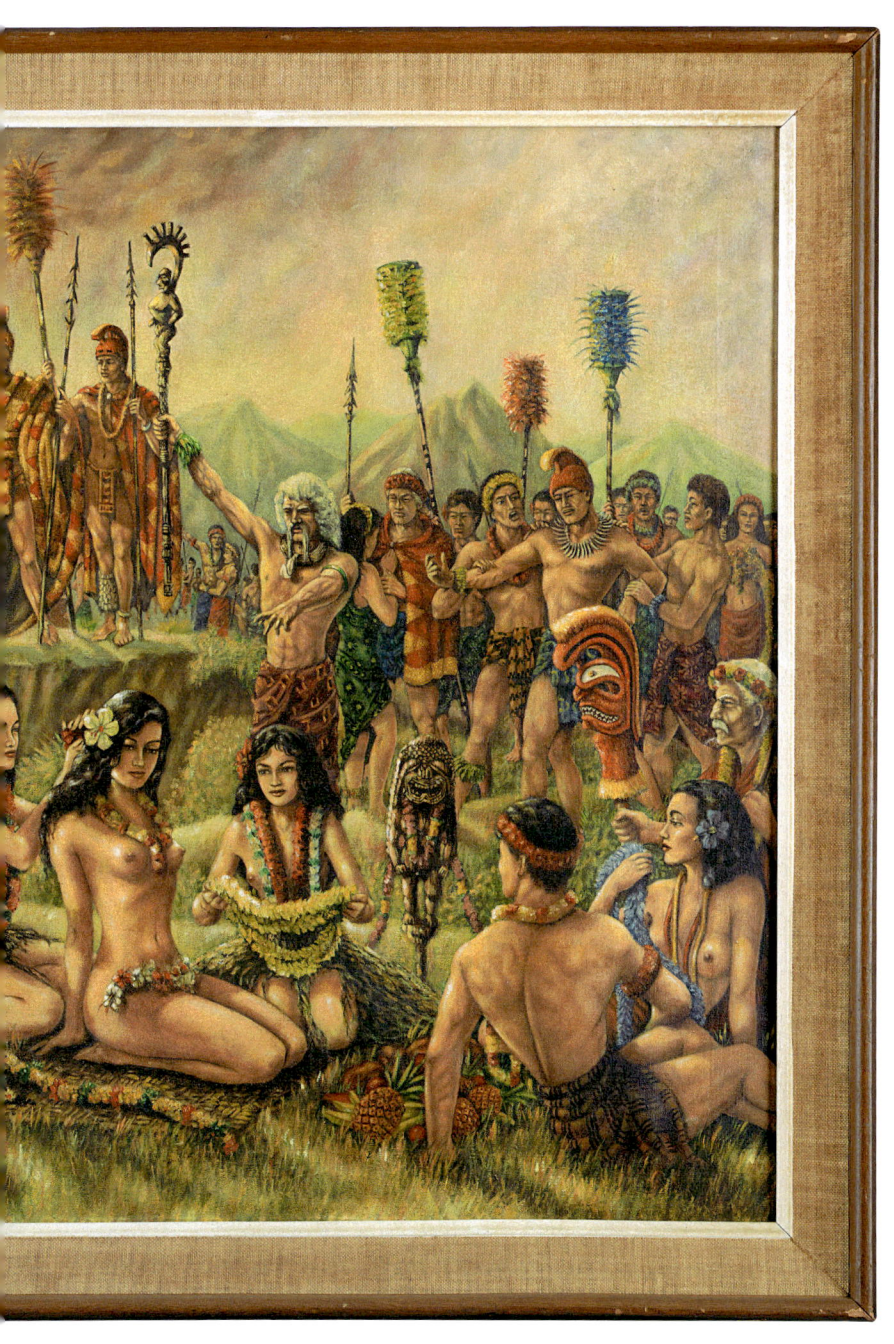

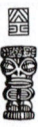

LOU BEHAN

2133 WEST TENTH STREET
BENSONHURST, B'KLYN. N. Y.

DESIGNER ● ILLUSTRATOR
ESPLANADE 2-2139

Dear Sally & Harvey Berger,
                As we did not have much
time for casual talk while you both were
here, I thought I would drop you a
line and give you a slight background
on the painting and myself. I have studied and gathered
research on the peoples of the Pacific for
the past 18 yrs., an interest sparked by a
years military service in the various Islan
groups there. Last year for additional
research I visited the Islands of Tahiti,
Bora Bora, Moorea, Samoa, the Fijis and
Hawaii.   Your Tahitian girl represents
the "HEIVA" dance group from the district
of PAPEETE. This group won the inter-island
annual (1963) contests, for beauty of costume,
dancing, chanting & drumming; winning all
honors and prizes.   They are a large

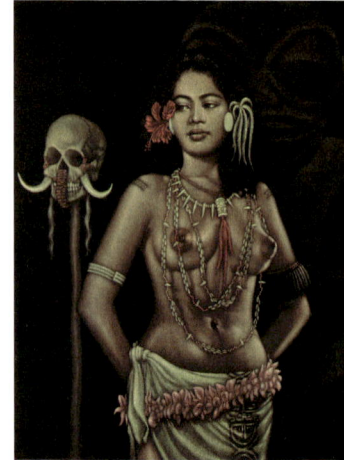

ABOVE AND OPPOSITE: Letter from
the artist to the happy new owners
(opposite) of a Behan black velvet at
the 1962 Seattle World's Fair
(Ron Ferrell Collection)

RIGHT: *NukuHivan Sacrifice* by
Louis Behan

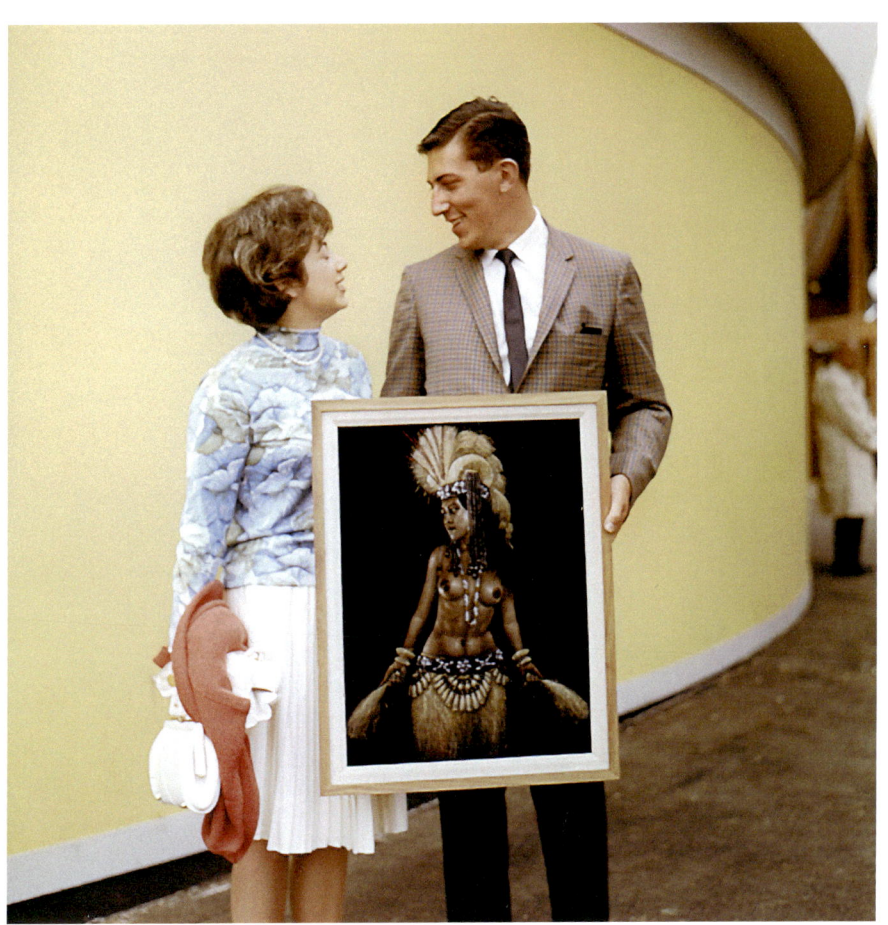

Lauderdale. Leur mission suivante les conduisit à Detroit où ils travaillèrent sur la décoration du très sophistiqué Mauna Loa. Ce restaurant qui avait coûté des millions de dollars ouvrit vers la fin de la vague tiki pop mais ne survécut malheureusement pas au phénomène de « fuite des Blancs » consécutif aux émeutes raciales de Detroit, en 1967. L'imagerie simpliste et romantique des cultures différentes était passée de mode.

Dans les années 1940, à Hollywood, Frank Bowers dessinait des story-boards pour la Warner. Il a ainsi travaillé sur des films comme *Le Lys de Brooklyn* et *L'Ange des ténèbres*. Il commença également à peindre pour des bars et des night-clubs des fresques murales qu'on retrouvait parfois en couverture de leurs menus. Si ses créations couvraient une incroyable variété de motifs correspondant aux thématiques respectives des lieux en question,

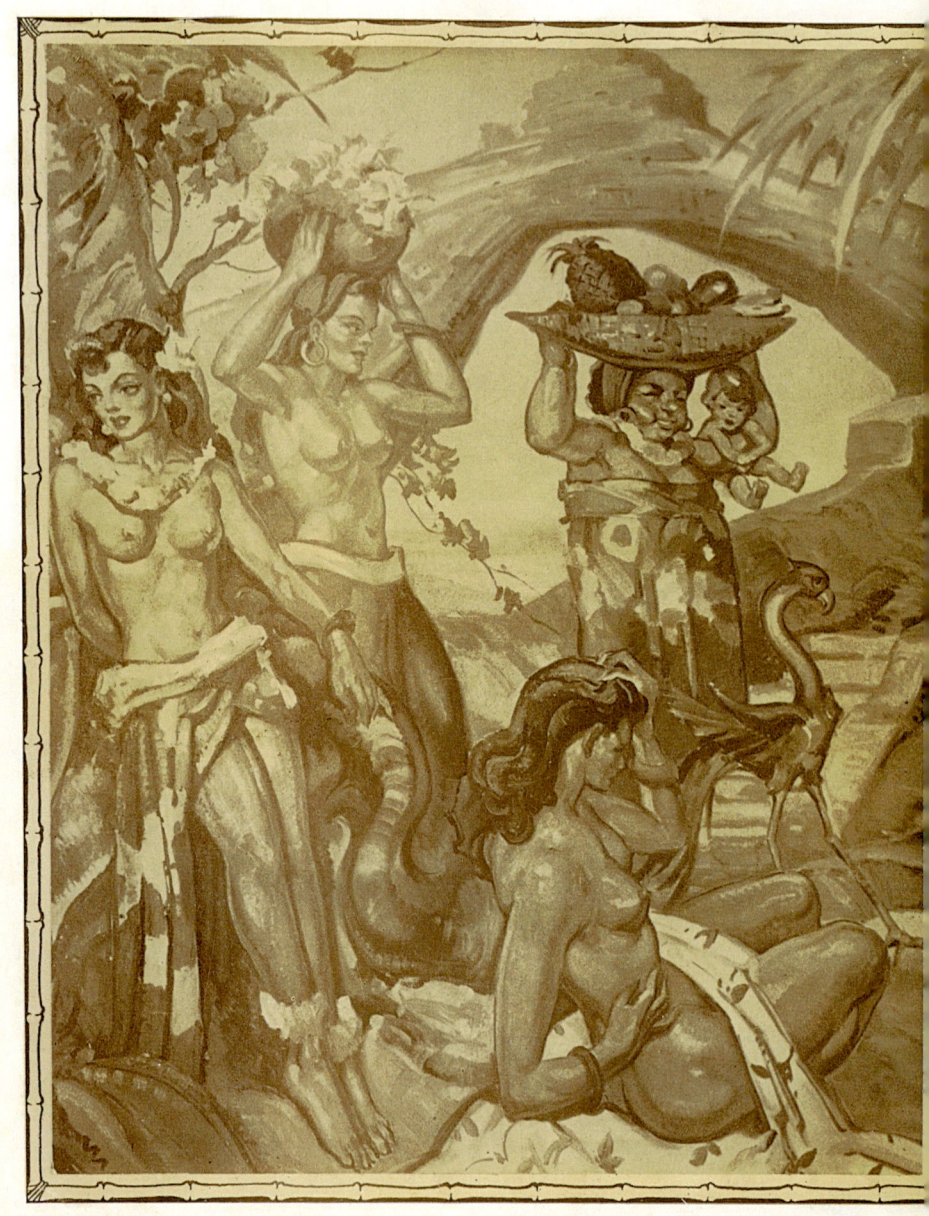

LEILANI

5236 EAST SECOND STREET
BELMONT SHORE • • •
• LONG BEACH, CALIFORNIA •

elles avaient cependant un point commun : fidèles à la tradition classique de la décoration de bar, leurs personnages féminins avaient pour la plupart les seins nus. Voilà qui prédestinait l'auteur à l'imagerie polynésienne : on verra son travail orner les murs de clubs tels que le Zamboanga et le Leilani.

Louis Behan découvrit les îles du Pacique aux commandes d'un bombardier B-17 de l'US Air Force. Ces missions de recherche et de sauvetage lui valurent d'être décoré. Une fois démobilisé, il intégra une école d'art et se lança dans une carrière de designer publicitaire. Tout en travaillant sur des projets ordinaires comme la conception de rideaux de douche ou d'objets-souvenir, il n'oubliait jamais son premier amour, les mers du Sud. Il choisit la matière caractéristique de la pop polynésienne, le velours noir, pour exprimer sa fascination envers les peuples et les cultures du Pacifique.

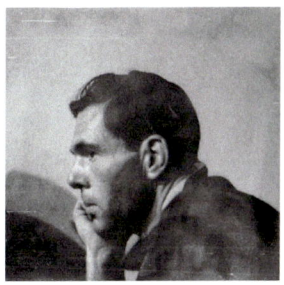

OPPOSITE: Frank Bowers menu cover for the Leilani
(Frank Brajevic Collection)

ABOVE AND BELOW RIGHT: A photo of the artist and instructional booklet by Bowers

BELOW LEFT: Framed fragment of a Bowers mural

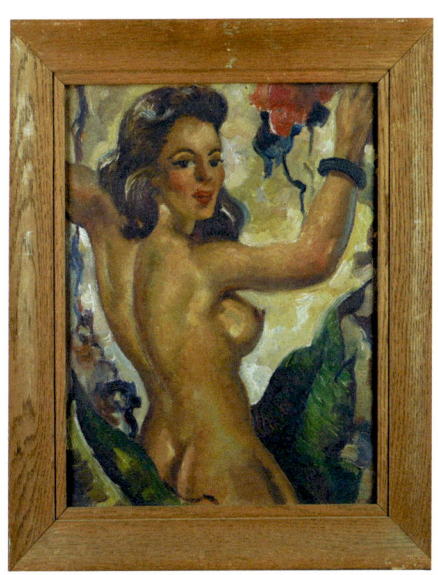

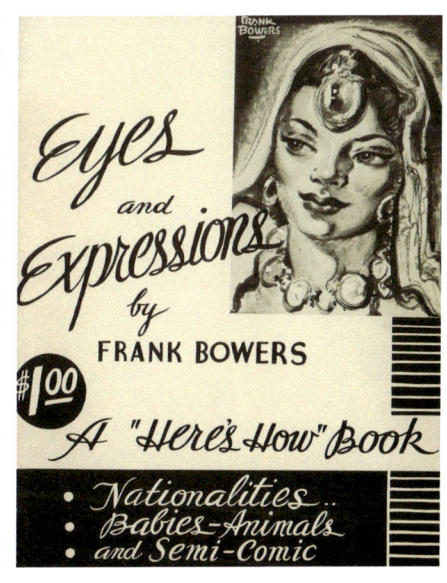

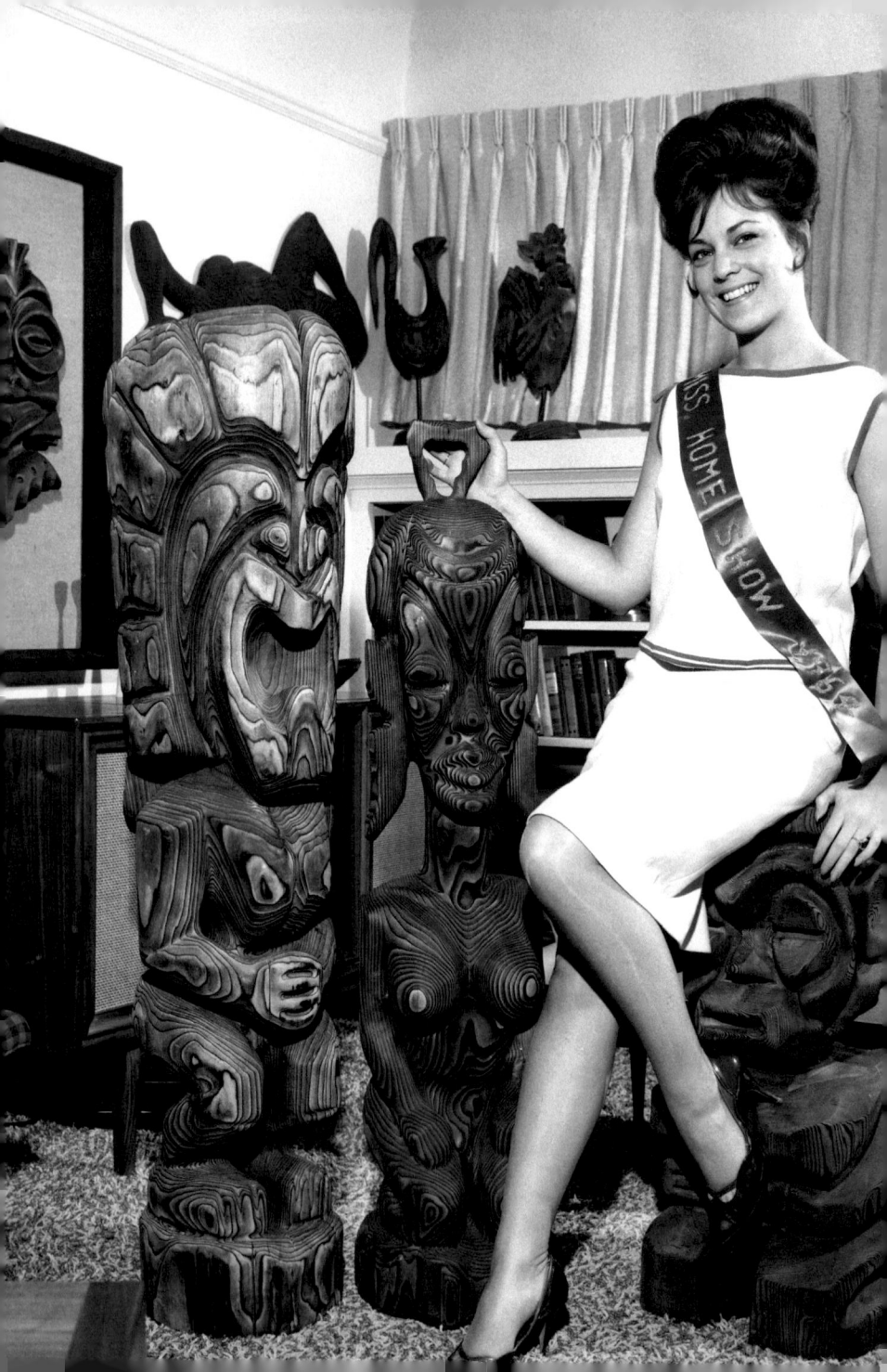

TIKI AT HOME

TIKI IN DEN EIGENEN VIER WÄNDEN
TIKI À LA MAISON

OPPOSITE: Miss Home Show having fun with some modern-primitive house idols, Tacoma Home Show, 1964

ABOVE: Luau party invite (*Frank Brajevic Collection*)

WHILE TIKI POP EXPANDED ACROSS the American cityscape, it also entered the privacy of the suburban family home. Like everything Hawaiian, island-themed parties were the social-event concept of the decade. In supermarkets, tropical-fruit aisles were emptied of pineapples and coconuts as basement party rooms and backyard patios were dressed up with fishnets and leis for the tropical festivities. The final touch to create the right mood for pagan revelry was some form of tribal art, preferably that native idol known as Tiki. The luau feast was transplanted to American backyards from Hawaii, where no visitor would leave the islands without having been at one.

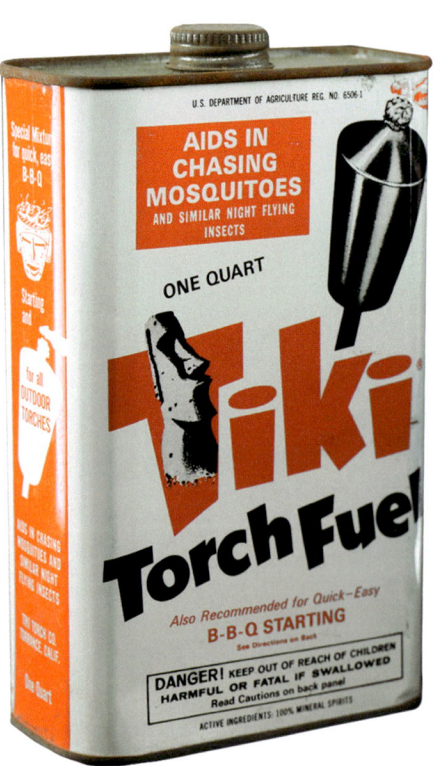

Not every luau had to boast a roasted pig at its center; what mattered was the spirit of casualness: eating with your fingers while sitting on the floor, dressed in colorful aloha wear. This was a marked release from the restraining etiquette of mid-century society. The Tiki torch was an important element in backyard luaus: the open flame gave the proceedings a ritualistic feel. Important, too, was the drinking: whereas a laid-back hostess might simply serve up a big bowl of spiked punch, others prided themselves on their abilities to mix a mean Mai Tai or a sumptuous Lapu Lapu. When you could not pronounce the name of the drink anymore, you knew you had had enough. Intoxicated revelry was part of the spirit of the luau, too.The traditional Hawaiian household was rather simple: most of its utensils were not much more sophisticated than Stone Age tools—the ornately decorated ones were reserved for chiefs and rituals. In the Maori and Marquesan cultures, the Tiki image was used more liberally as ornament.

In the American Tiki Pop household, the use of the Tiki image was fully democratized: from mugs to bowls to spice racks, the housewife could exercise her personal taste and decide where she wanted to "go native" in her kitchenware. Besides the availability of complete Tiki tableware sets, the crafty homemaker could try her hand at do-it-yourself Tiki pottery. Making ceramics was a favorite hobby for American housewives in the 1950s; a home kiln was added to the list of household appliances. An entire industry developed of suppliers of pottery clays and glazes, of which Duncan Ceramics became one of the leading firms, offering a whole range of Tiki molds. Another material that found

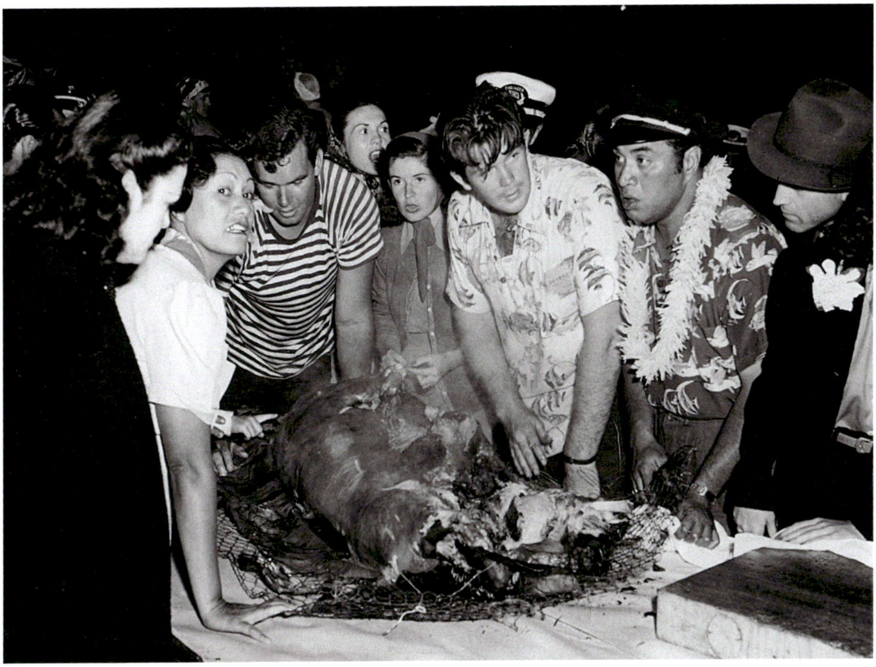

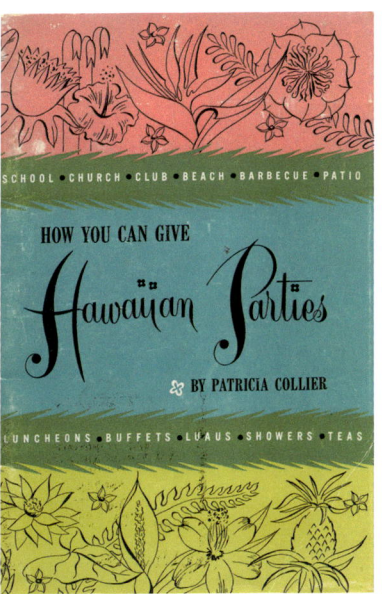

OPPOSITE: Tiki Torch Fuel can

ABOVE: Earliest example of a mainland luau: movie actors and friends having a traditional luau on Santa Catalina Isthmus in 1940

LEFT: Hawaiian-party tips for the housewife

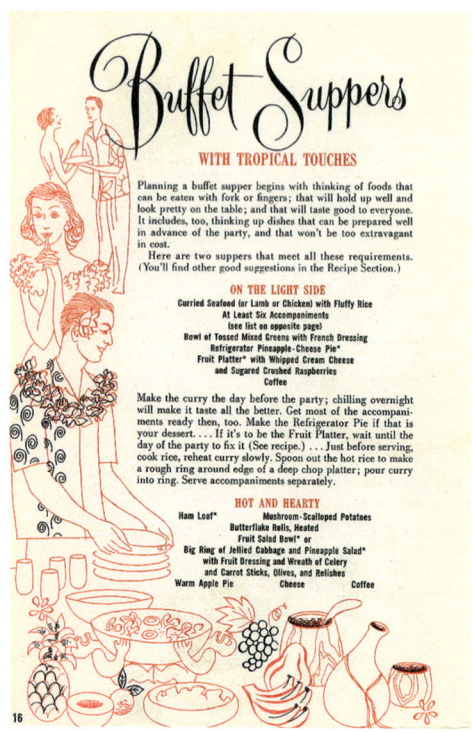

Buffet Suppers

WITH TROPICAL TOUCHES

Planning a buffet supper begins with thinking of foods that can be eaten with fork or fingers; that will hold up well and look pretty on the table; and that will taste good to everyone. It includes, too, thinking up dishes that can be prepared well in advance of the party, and that won't be too extravagant in cost.

Here are two suppers that meet all these requirements. (You'll find other good suggestions in the Recipe Section.)

ON THE LIGHT SIDE

Curried Seafood (or Lamb or Chicken) with Fluffy Rice
At Least Six Accompaniments
(see list on opposite page)
Bowl of Tossed Mixed Greens with French Dressing
Refrigerator Pineapple-Cheese Pie*
Fruit Platter* with Whipped Cream Cheese
and Sugared Crushed Raspberries
Coffee

Make the curry the day before the party; chilling overnight will make it taste all the better. Get most of the accompaniments ready then, too. Make the Refrigerator Pie if that is your dessert. . . . If it's to be the Fruit Platter, wait until the day of the party to fix it (See recipe.) . . . Just before serving, cook rice, reheat curry slowly. Spoon out the hot rice to make a rough ring around edge of a deep chop platter; pour curry into rice ring. Serve accompaniments separately.

HOT AND HEARTY

Ham Loaf*   Mushroom-Scalloped Potatoes
Butterflake Rolls, Heated
Fruit Salad Bowl* or
Big Ring of Jellied Cabbage and Pineapple Salad*
with Fruit Dressing and Wreath of Celery
and Carrot Sticks, Olives, and Relishes
Warm Apple Pie   Cheese   Coffee

16

LEFT: American luau setting and recipes

BELOW: The leisure life with Tiki touches *(Timothy Haack Collection)*

OPPOSITE: Canned-food fun at the luau *(Frank Brajevic Collection)*

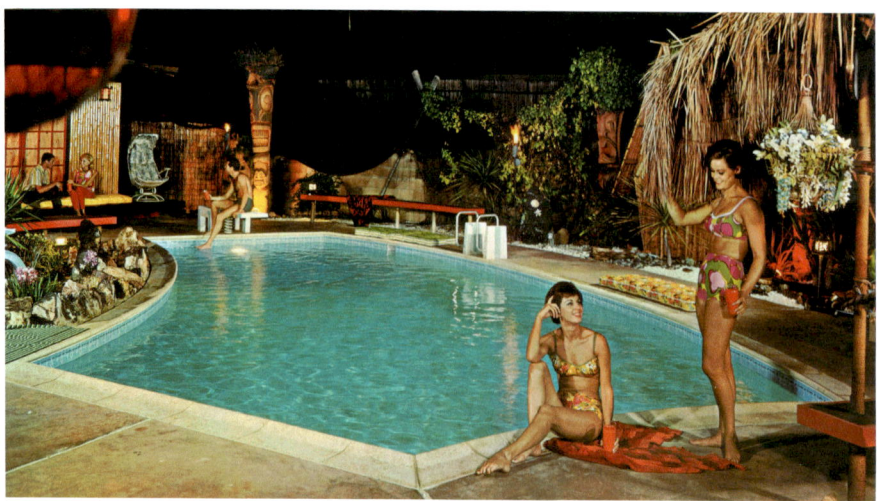

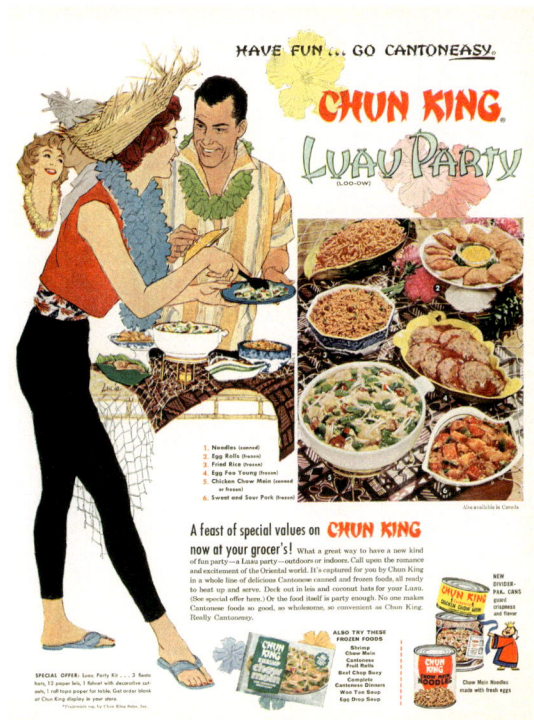

ample use in the Tiki home was monkeypod wood. Fashioned into bowls and dishes perfect for luau snacks, these items were created expressly for the Hawaiian tourist industry.

The Marquesan-style Tiki design that was used for the mugs created by Paul Marshall Products was perhaps the Tiki shape most fashioned into utilitarian objects. It could be found in ceramic as salt and pepper shakers, cigarette lighters, and coffee mugs; and in plastic, in patio string lights, luau torches, more salt and pepper shakers, and condiment squeeze bottles. It also inspired a line of Amway "Tonga" soaps and toiletries. With the growing

affluence and expanding leisure time of the post–World War II generation, the demand for patio furniture increased. Herb Ritts (father of the photographer) successfully introduced rattan furniture to America and made the tropical look fashionable for interior home décor. He opened a chain of Tropic Shops across the United States, and rattan furnishings became the preferred trappings for pre-Tiki rumpus rooms of the early '50s. Everything from home bars to TV cabinets was shaped from the flexible palm wood. It took William Westenhaver's company, Witco, to elevate interior design to the Tiki Pop stage. Expanding its interior décor line annually from the early '60s onwards, Witco's oeuvre soon comprised every aspect of home furnishings. The outrageous use of figural shapes was applied to everything from entire living-room sets to lamps to bedroom ensembles. Witco freely mixed Polynesian and African influences to create functional primitive sculptures in their "Contemporary Idol" line. This shunning of preconceived notions of "good taste" appealed to self-made pop-culture style-makers like Elvis Presley and Hugh Hefner. Presley outfitted his Jungle Room in Graceland with Witco furniture, and Hefner embellished his swimming pool at the Playboy headquarters in Chicago with Witco Tikis and masks. Although Elvis is known for his song "Blue Hawaii," his music cannot be considered Tiki Pop music. This distinction belongs to Martin Denny, who created the genre of exotica music based on the work of composer and musician Les Baxter.

Baxter was an all-around musical talent, working in Hollywood first as a conductor and arranger, then eventually as a film composer. The first movie he scored was the 1953 Tahiti documentary *Tanga Tika*. He continued writing film scores for various adventure movies while recording his own albums, which often resembled soundtracks from exotic ports of call. In 1957, Hawaiian resident Martin Denny recorded the Les Baxter composition "Quiet Village" from Baxter's 1951 album *Ritual of the Savage*. Denny had come up with the concept of using bird sounds as an added effect while performing live in Hawaii and now used it on the recording, which made it a chart-topping success. The hit song was part of Denny's first album, *Exotica*, which contained several tracks that combined jungle sounds with exotic percussion instruments and gave rise to the name of the new genre: exotica music.

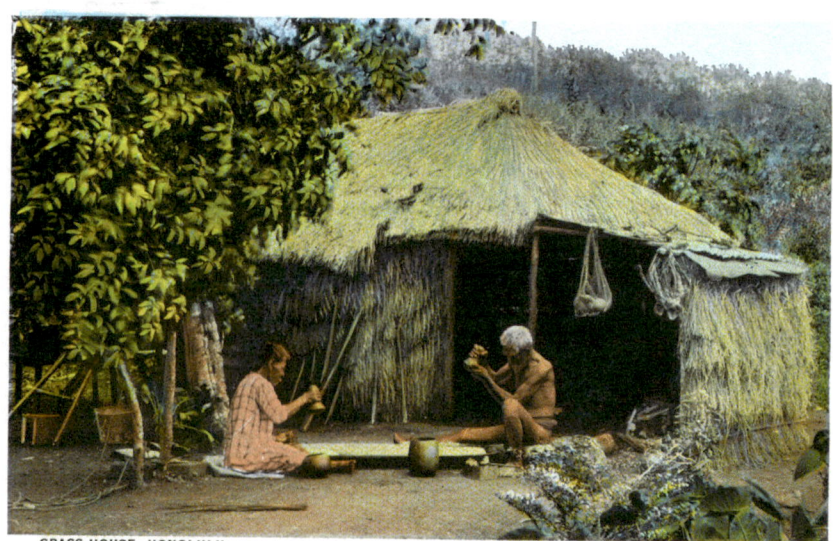

GRASS HOUSE, HONOLULU.

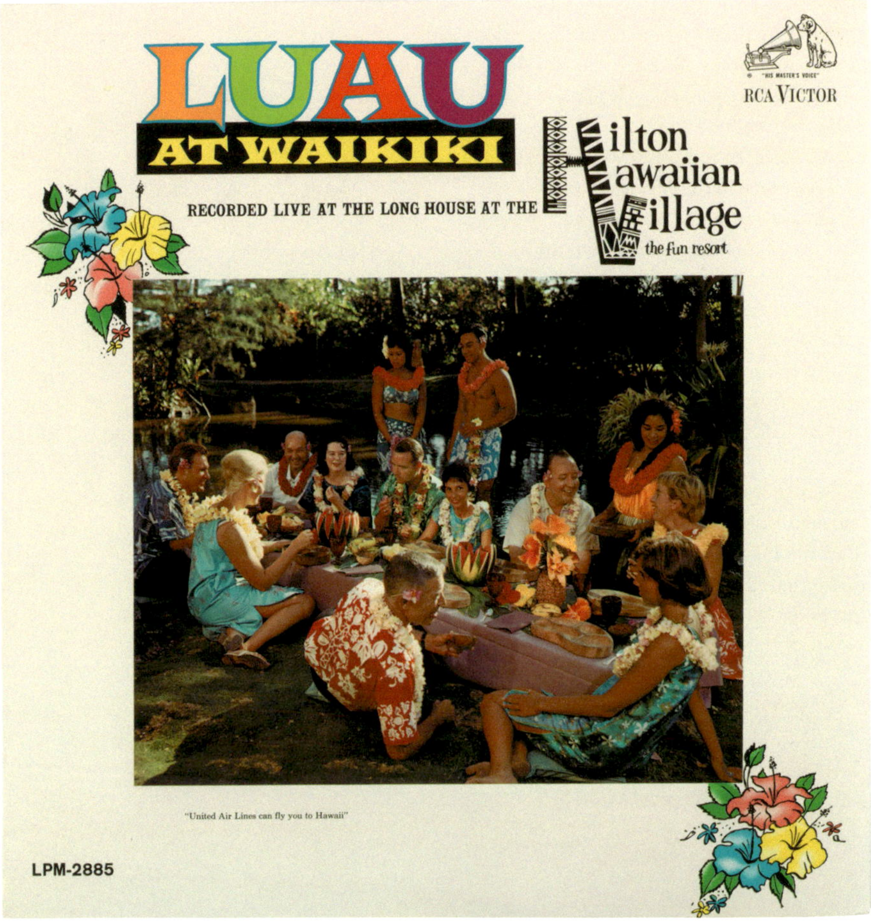

LUAU
AT WAIKIKI

RECORDED LIVE AT THE LONG HOUSE AT THE **Hilton Hawaiian Village** *the fun resort*

RCA VICTOR
"HIS MASTER'S VOICE"

"United Air Lines can fly you to Hawaii"

LPM-2885

OPPOSITE: A Hawaiian family pounding poi

ABOVE: Typical tourist luau in Hawaii

RIGHT: A Tiki spice rack
(Kate Simmons Collection)

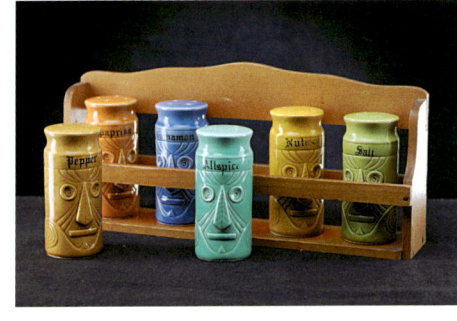

ALS SICH DER TIKI-POP IN DEN

amerikanischen Städten ausbreitete, bahnte
er sich auch seinen Weg in die Familien-
haushalte der Vorstädte. Wie alles Hawaiische feierten Inselthemen für Partys Hoch-
konjunktur. In Supermärkten wurden
alle Vorräte an Ananas und Kokosnüssen
aufgekauft, und zu Hause dekorierte man
die Partyräume und Terrassen mit Fischernetzen und Blumenketten. Den letzten
Schliff verlieh man den heidnischen Lust-
barkeiten mit Elementen vermeintlicher
Stammeskunst, bevorzugt in Form der als
„Tiki" bekannten Götterfigur. Der Besuch
von Luau-Partys war ein Muss für jeden
Hawaii-Urlauber, der solche Feste nun auch
zu Hause feiern wollte. Nicht jede Luau
bedurfte eines Spanferkels – die gelöste
Stimmung war das Wichtigste. Man aß mit
den Fingern, saß auf dem Boden und trug
bunte Aloha-Kleidung, um so ein deutliches

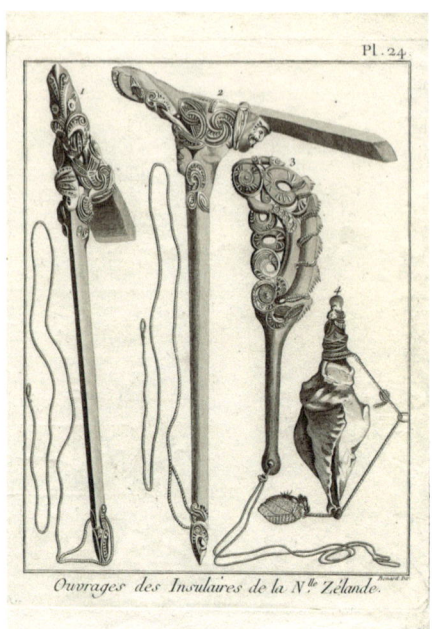

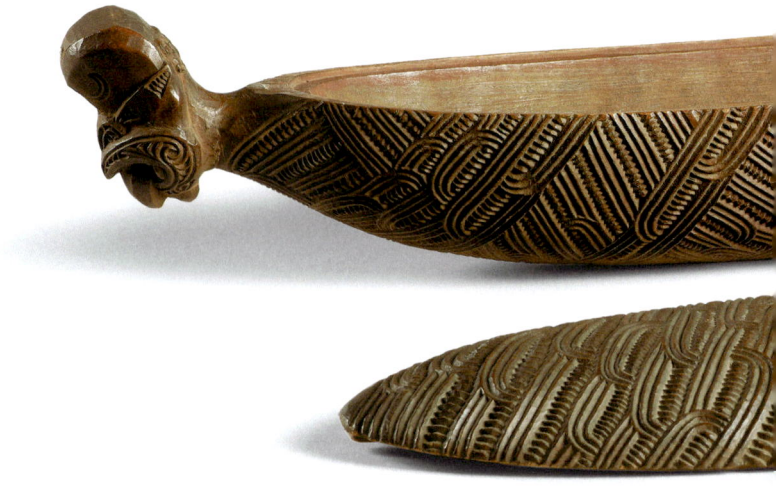

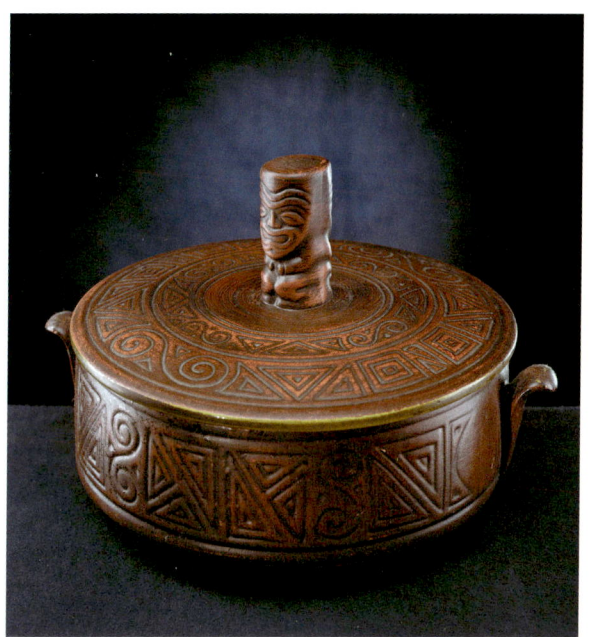

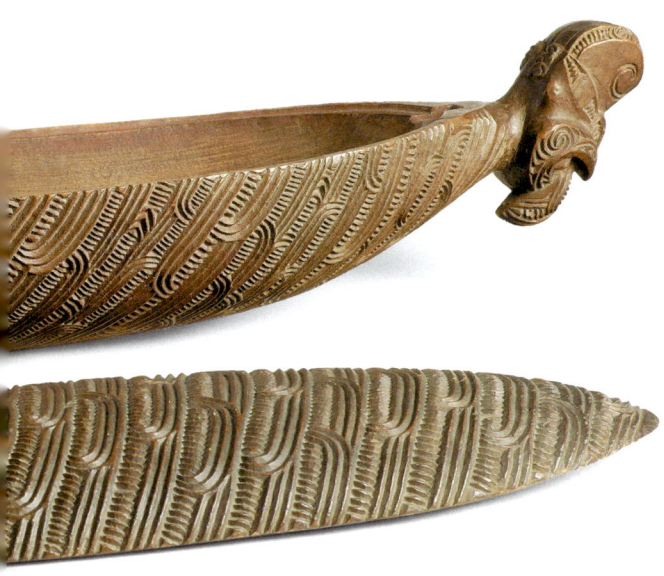

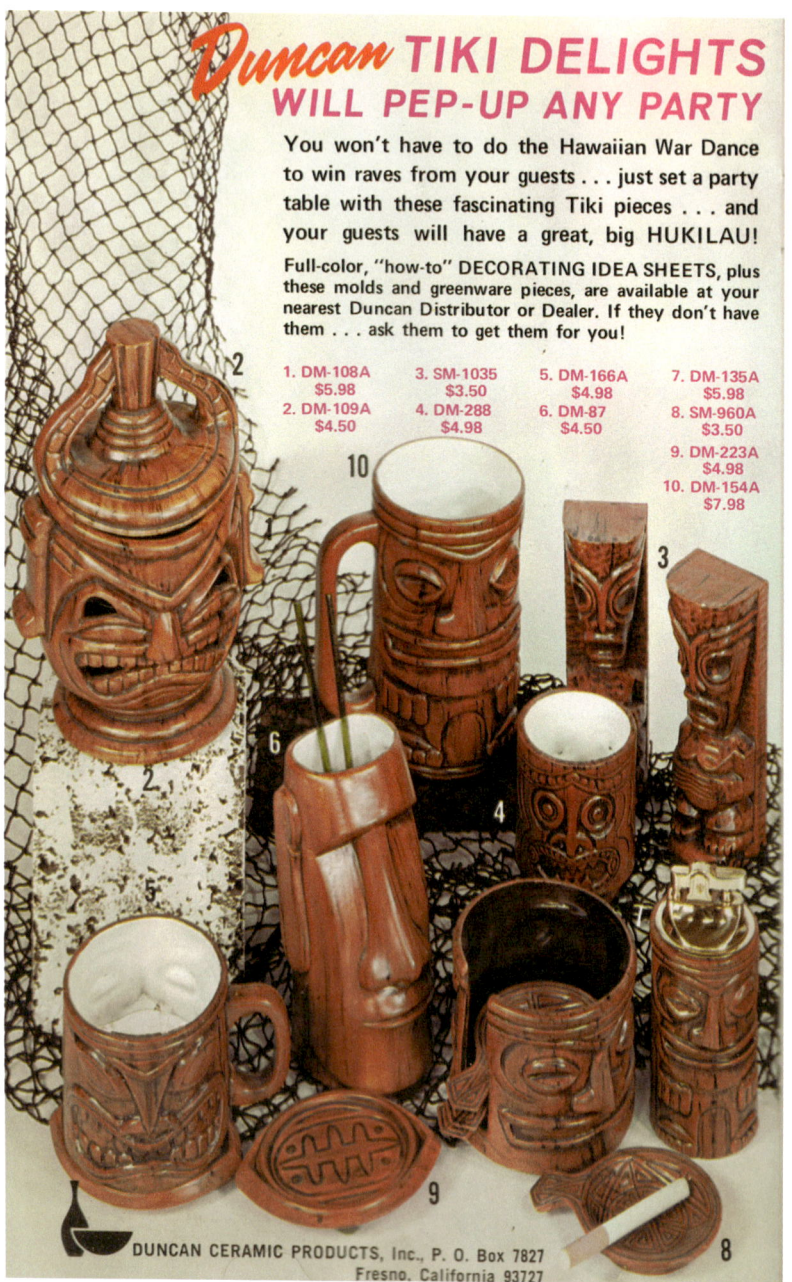

Duncan TIKI DELIGHTS
WILL PEP-UP ANY PARTY

You won't have to do the Hawaiian War Dance to win raves from your guests . . . just set a party table with these fascinating Tiki pieces . . . and your guests will have a great, big HUKILAU!

Full-color, "how-to" DECORATING IDEA SHEETS, plus these molds and greenware pieces, are available at your nearest Duncan Distributor or Dealer. If they don't have them . . . ask them to get them for you!

1. DM-108A $5.98	3. SM-1035 $3.50	5. DM-166A $4.98
2. DM-109A $4.50	4. DM-288 $4.98	6. DM-87 $4.50

7. DM-135A $5.98	
8. SM-960A $3.50	
9. DM-223A $4.98	
10. DM-154A $7.98	

DUNCAN CERAMIC PRODUCTS, Inc., P. O. Box 7827
Fresno. California 93727

Zeichen gegen die einengende Etikette der damaligen Gesellschaft zu setzen, wobei die offene Flamme der Tiki-Fackeln dem Ganzen eine rituelle Atmosphäre verlieh. Eine große Rolle spielten selbstverständlich auch die Getränke. Während sich eine entspannte Gastgeberin vielleicht mit einer großen Schale hochprozentigem Punsch begnügte, brüsteten sich andere mit ihrer Fähigkeit, exzellente „Mai Tais" oder aufwendige „Lapu Lapus" mixen zu können. Wer den Namen seines Drinks nicht mehr aussprechen konnte, wusste, dass er genug hatte. Das Saufgelage gehörte zu einer richtigen Luau dazu.

Während der traditionelle hawaiische Haushalt eher schlicht ausgestattet war und reich verzierte Gegenstände den Häuptlingen bzw. rituellen Zwecken vorbehalten waren, wurde in den Kulturen der Maori und Marquesas Tikis Bildnis freigiebiger eingesetzt – so auch im amerikanischen Tiki-Pop-Haushalt, in dem die Verwendung der Götterfigur vollständig demokratisiert war: von Bechern über Schüsseln bis zu Gewürzregalen – die Hausfrau konnte frei wählen, welchen Teil ihrer Küchenausstattung sie „polynesisch" gestalten wollte. Es gab ganze Geschirrsets mit Tiki-Motiven zu kaufen, zudem konnte man sich auch an Tiki-Keramiken zum Selbermachen versuchen. Töpfern war ein beliebtes Hobby unter den amerikanischen Hausfrauen der 1950er-Jahre und zwischen den üblichen Küchengeräten fanden sich bald auch Brennöfen.

Es entwickelte sich eine ganze Industrie für Töpferton und Glasuren. Die Firma Duncan Ceramics bot eine enorme Vielfalt an Tiki-Formen an und wurde zu einem der Marktführer. Ein weiterer Werkstoff im Tiki-Heim war Regenbaumholz. Schalen und Geschirr wurden explizit für die hawaiische Tourismusindustrie gefertigt und eigneten sich perfekt fürs Servieren von Luau-Snacks.

Der Tiki im Stil der Marquesas-Inseln, den die Firma Paul Marshall Products für ihre Becher verwendete, war die wohl häufigste Variante im Bereich der Gebrauchsgegenstände. Es gab ihn als Salz- und Pfefferstreuer, Feuerzeug und Kaffeebecher, Lichterketten und Luau-Fackeln und sogar als Squeeze-Flasche für Ketchup. Amway produzierte Seifen und andere Hygieneartikel mit Tiki-Motiven. Mit dem wachsenden Wohlstand der Nackriegsgeneration, einhergehend mit der Zunahme von Freizeit, stieg der Bedarf an Terrassenmöbeln. Herb Ritts, der Vater des gleichnamigen Fotografen, brachte erfolgreich Rattanmöbel auf dem amerikanischen Markt und machte den Tropenlook in den eigenen vier Wänden populär. Er war Inhaber der Tropic-Shop-Kette mit Filialen in den gesamten USA und so wurden Rattanmöbel landesweit zur beliebtesten Einrichtung für die Prä-Tiki-Partyräume der frühen 1950er-Jahre. Von Bars bis zu TV-Schränken wurde alles aus dem biegsamen Palmholz gefertigt.

Der Tiki-Pop trat im Bereich der Inneneinrichtung erst mit William Westenhavens Unternehmen Witco in Erscheinung. Von den 1960er-Jahren an baute Westenhaven seine Kollektionen jedes Jahr weiter aus und hatte bald alle erdenklichen Möbelstücke im Sortiment. Die geschnitzten Figuren wurden exzessiv überall eingesetzt – in

The Duncan family of Tiki molds
(Rick Henderson Collection)

Schlafzimmern, für Lampen und in Form ganzer Wohnzimmergarnituren. Für die Skulpturen seiner Linie „Contemporary Idol" vermischte Witco freimütig polynesische und afrikanische Stile. Dieses Abwenden vom vermeintlich „guten Geschmack" sprach Stilikonen wie Elvis Presley und Hugh Hefner an. Presley stattete seinen Jungle Room in Graceland mit Witco-Möbeln aus und Hefner dekorierte seinen Pool im *Playboy*-Haupt-sitz in Chicago mit Witcos Tikis und Masken. Auch wenn Elvis mit „Blue Hawaii", dem Titelstück aus seinem gleichnamigen Film, große internationale Erfolge in den Charts feierte, war er kein

Vertreter der Tiki-Pop-Musik. Dieser Ruf gebührt Martin Denny, dem Urvater der Exotica-Musik, die auf den Werken des Komponisten Les Baxter basiert.

Baxter war ein großes musikalisches Talent. In Hollywood arbeitete er zunächst als Dirigent und Arrangeur und schließlich als Filmkomponist. Sein erster Film war die Tahiti-Dokumentation *Tanga Tika* (1953). Anschließend schrieb er die Musik für diverse Abenteuerfilme und nahm nebenbei eigene Alben auf, die oft an exotische Klänge aus fernen Häfen erinnerten. 1957 nahm Martin Denny, der in Hawaii lebte, Les Baxters Stück „Quiet Village" von

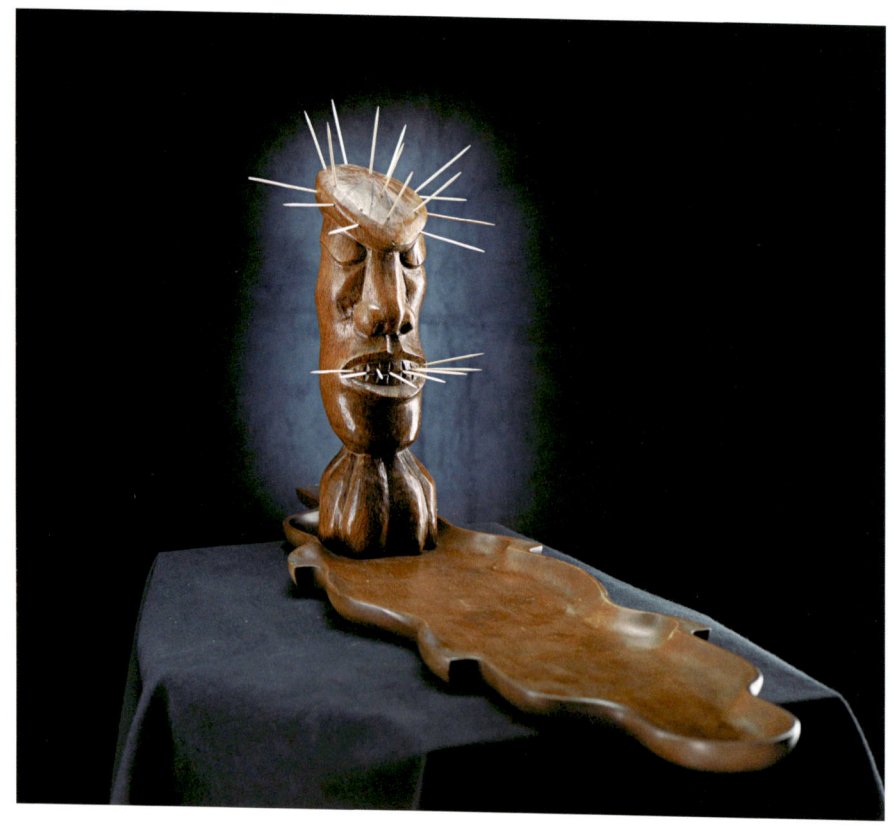

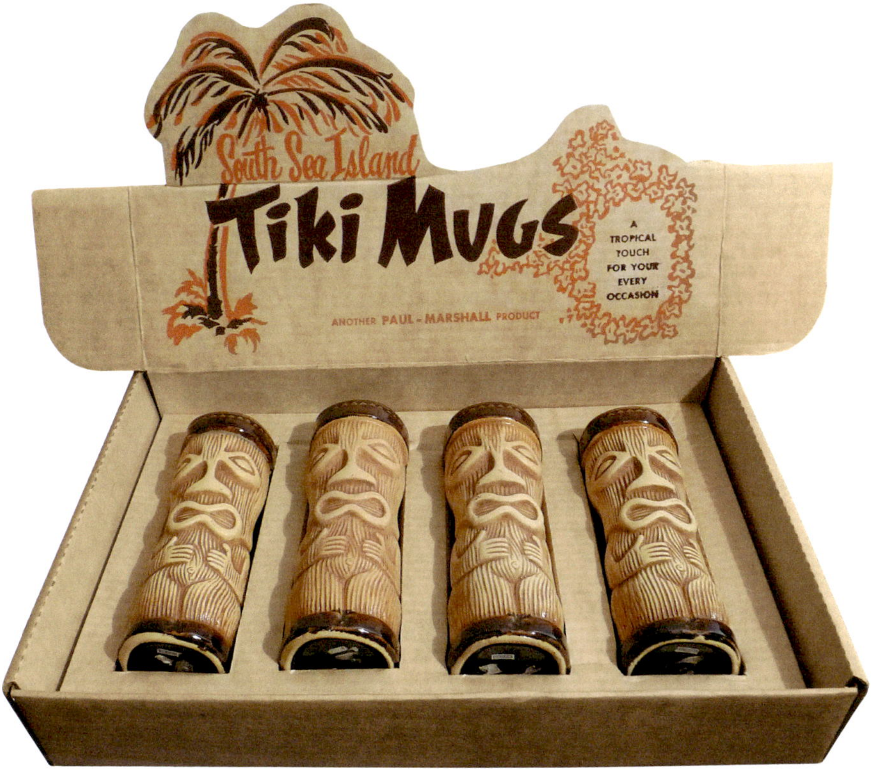

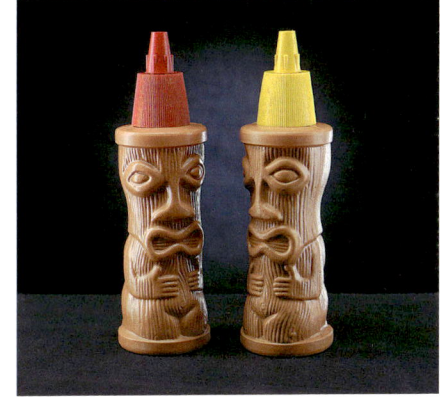

OPPOSITE: Tiki hors d'oeuvres platter made of monkeypod wood

ABOVE: The mother mug of many molds *(Jimmy Virani Collection)*

RIGHT: Some of its children *(Kate Simmons Collection)*

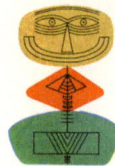

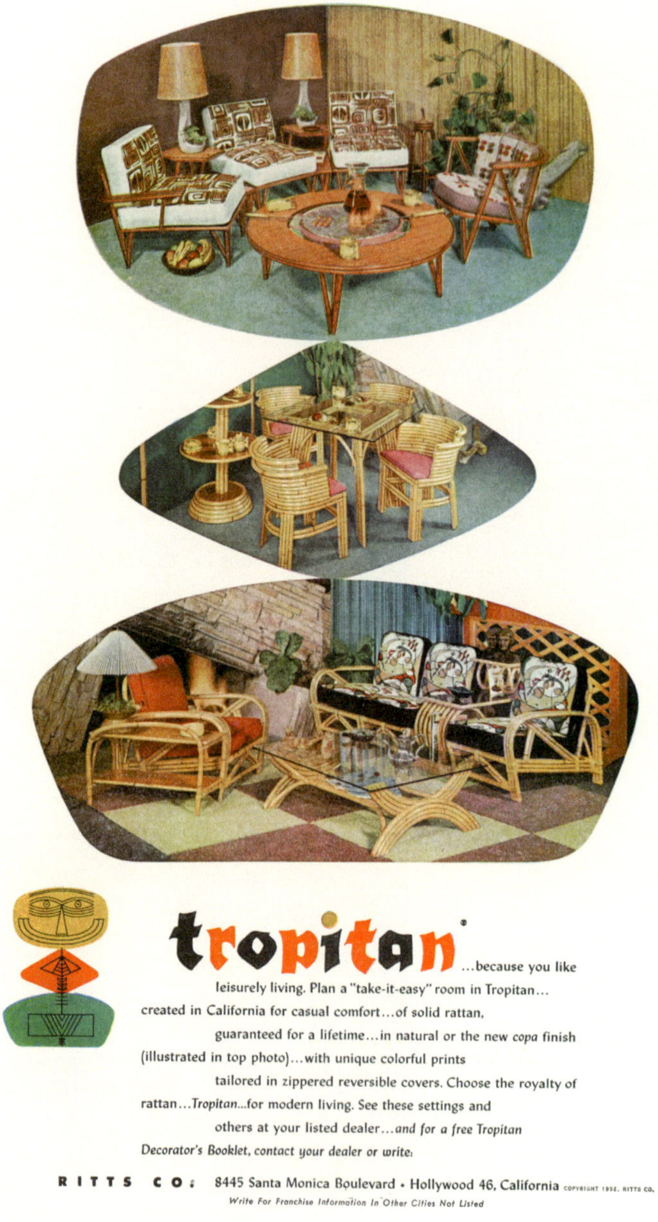

tropitan®

...because you like leisurely living. Plan a "take-it-easy" room in Tropitan... created in California for casual comfort...of solid rattan, guaranteed for a lifetime...in natural or the new *copa* finish (illustrated in top photo)...with unique colorful prints tailored in zippered reversible covers. Choose the royalty of rattan...*Tropitan*...for modern living. See these settings and others at your listed dealer...*and for a free Tropitan Decorator's Booklet, contact your dealer or write:*

RITTS CO. 8445 Santa Monica Boulevard · Hollywood 46, California COPYRIGHT 1953, RITTS CO.
Write For Franchise Information In Other Cities Not Listed

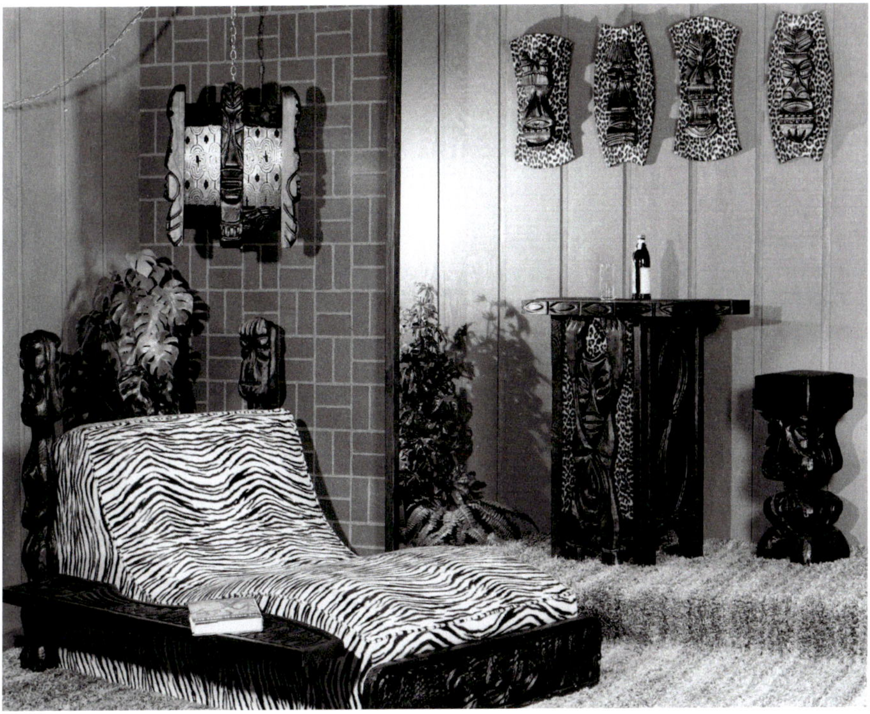

dessen Album *Ritual of the Savage* (1951)
auf. Während einer seiner Live-Auftritte
in Hawaii war Denny die Idee gekommen,
Vogelstimmen in die Stücke einzubauen.
Bei der Aufnahme von „Quiet Village" ließ
er einen seiner Musiker Vogelstimmen imi-
tieren – und die Platte stürmte die Charts.
Der Hit erschien auf Dennys erstem Album
Exotica. In mehreren Liedern hatte er
Dschungelgeräusche mit exotischen Schlag-
instrumenten kombiniert und markierte
so die Geburtsstunde eines neuen Musik-
genres – Exotica.

OPPOSITE: 1952 ad for Herb Ritts
rattan furniture

ABOVE: The baroque Tiki Pop of Witco

BELOW: Matchbook from one of
Ritts's many Tropic Shops

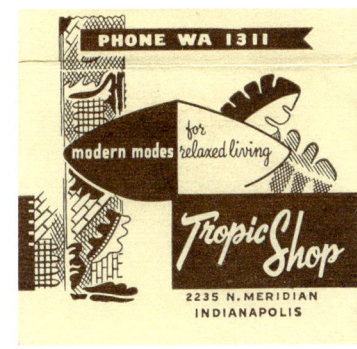

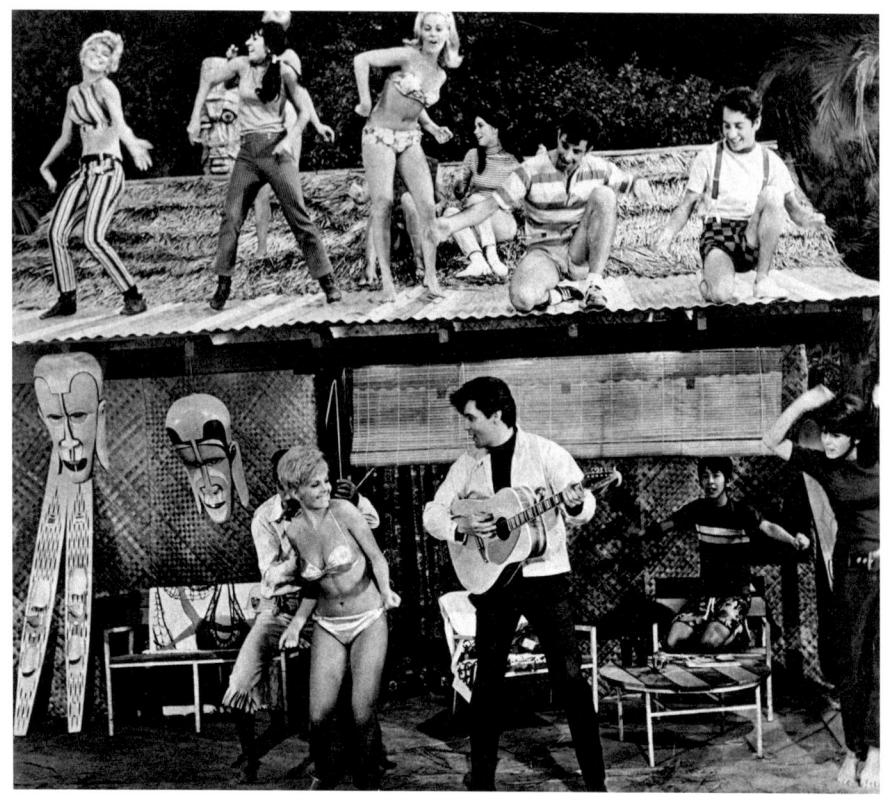

PARALLÈLEMENT À SA DIFFUSION
dans le paysage urbain des États-Unis,
le tiki pop pénétrait les faubourgs et la
vie intime des familles qui les peuplaient.
À l'instar de tout ce qui venait du Pacifique,
les soirées à thème hawaiien constituèrent
le concept festif de la décennie. Dans les
supermarchés, le rayon des fruits tropicaux
était régulièrement vidé de ses ananas et
de ses noix de coco. Dans le même temps,
terrasses et jardinets, à l'arrière des maisons, et les caves aménagées pour les sur-
prises-parties se remplissaient de filets de
pêche et de colliers de fleurs assurant à ces
soirées tropicales leur couleur locale. Pour

renforcer l'atmosphère de rigueur pour
ces agapes païennes, rien ne valait l'art
tribal, et de préférence cette idole indigène
qu'on appelle tiki.

Le banquet *luau*, passage obligé de
tout visiteur des îles, se retrouva trans-
planté d'Hawaii aux jardins américains.
Une fête digne de ce nom pouvait fort bien
se passer d'exhiber le traditionnel cochon
rôti ; l'important, c'était la décontraction du
moment. On mangeait avec les doigts, assis
par terre, en tenue hawaiienne – bariolée.
L'occasion par excellence d'échapper aux
conventions sociales étriquées du milieu
du XXᵉ siècle.

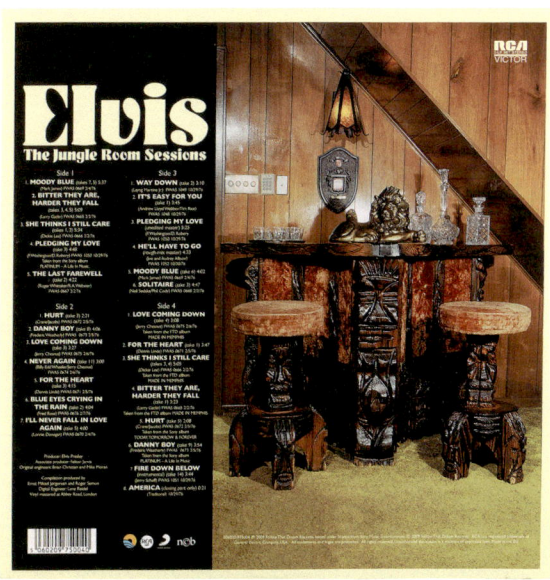

Elvis
The Jungle Room Sessions

Side 1
1. MOODY BLUE
2. BITTER THEY ARE, HARDER THEY FALL
3. SHE THINKS I STILL CARE
4. PLEDGING MY LOVE
5. THE LAST FAREWELL

Side 2
1. HURT
2. DANNY BOY
3. LOVE COMING DOWN
4. NEVER AGAIN
5. FOR THE HEART
6. BLUE EYES CRYING IN THE RAIN
7. I'LL NEVER FALL IN LOVE AGAIN

Side 3
1. WAY DOWN
2. IT'S EASY FOR YOU
3. PLEDGING MY LOVE
4. HE'LL HAVE TO GO
5. MOODY BLUE
6. SOLITAIRE

Side 4
1. LOVE COMING DOWN
2. FOR THE HEART
3. SHE THINKS I STILL CARE
4. BITTER THEY ARE, HARDER THEY FALL
5. HURT
6. DANNY BOY
7. FIRE DOWN BELOW
8. AMERICA

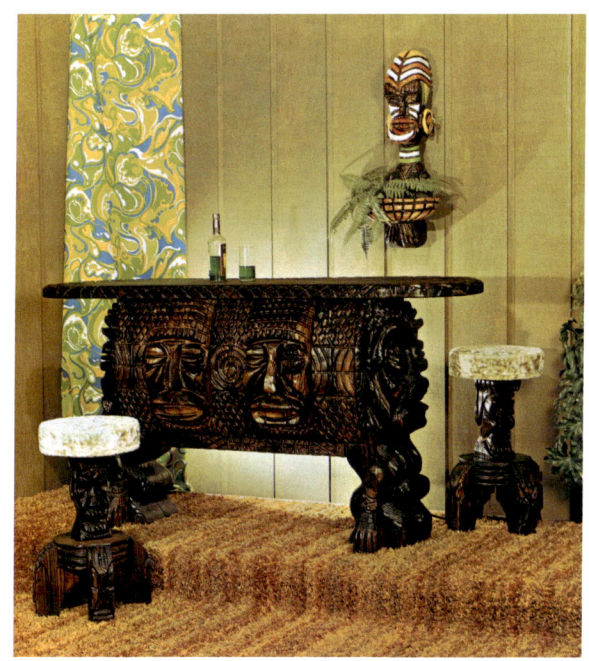

OPPOSITE: Elvis Presley rocks out in front of a Tiki beach shack in *Clambake*, 1967. From 1961 to 1966, Elvis made three films in Hawaii

ABOVE: Witco furniture in Elvis's home. He sometimes used the Jungle Room to record his songs

LEFT: Witco's stunning "Tahiti" bar

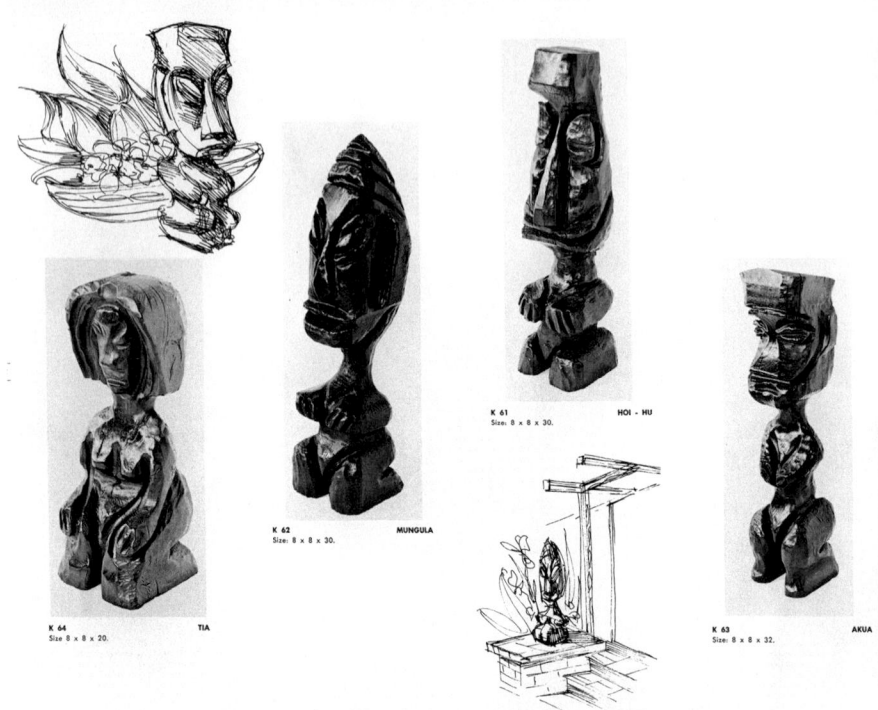

K 64
Size: 8 × 8 × 20.   TIA

K 42
Size: 8 × 8 × 30.   MUNGULA

K 61
Size: 8 × 8 × 30.   HOI - HU

K 63
Size: 8 × 8 × 32.   AKUA

La torche de type tiki était un accessoire important du banquet organisé dans les jardinets : cette flamme libre conférait à l'événement une dimension rituelle. Tout aussi importantes étaient les boissons. Tandis que certaines maîtresses de maison décontractées se contentaient d'offrir à leurs invités une grande bassine de punch alcoolisé, d'autres s'enorgueillissaient de leur expertise dans la préparation d'un super Mai Tai ou autre somptueux Lapu Lapu… Quand vous n'étiez plus capable d'articuler le nom de ce que contenait votre verre, c'est que vous aviez votre compte. Festoyer en état d'ivresse faisait aussi partie de l'esprit du *luau*.

Home idols from the 1964
Witco catalog

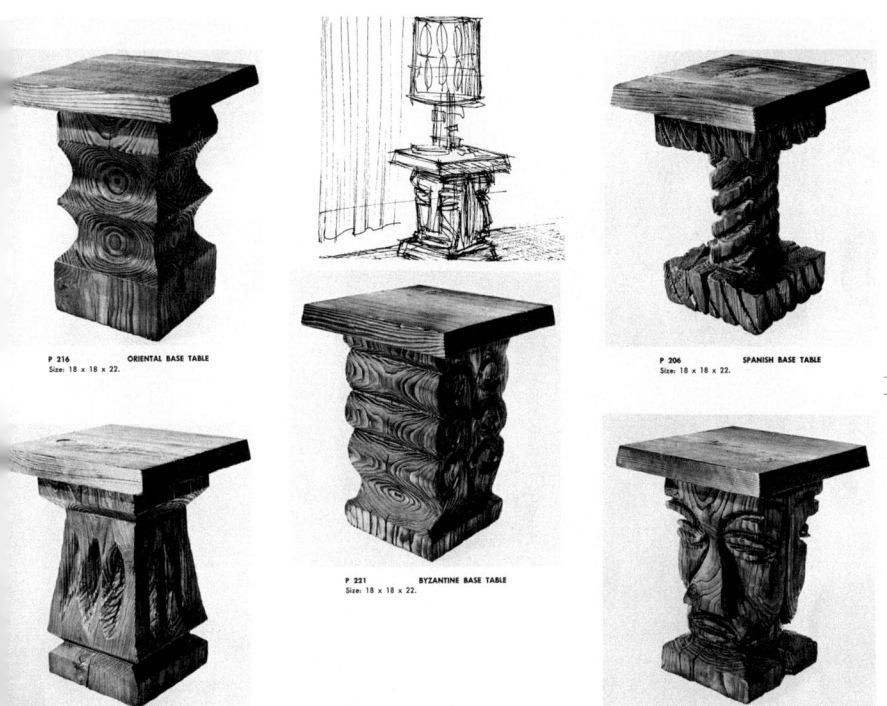

P 216   ORIENTAL BASE TABLE
Size: 18 x 18 x 22.

P 206   SPANISH BASE TABLE
Size: 18 x 18 x 22.

P 221   BYZANTINE BASE TABLE
Size: 18 x 18 x 22.

P 231   EGYPTIAN BASE TABLE
Size: 18 x 18 x 22.

P 201   TIKI BASE TABLE
Size: 18 x 18 x 22.

La maisonnée traditionnelle hawaiienne était plutôt simple. La plupart de ses ustensiles n'étaient guère plus sophistiqués que les outils de l'âge de pierre – les plus ornementés d'entre eux restant réservés aux chefs et aux cérémonies rituelles. Dans les cultures maori et marquisienne, la figure du Tiki était utilisée plus librement, comme élément de décoration.

Les foyers tiki pop américains démocratisèrent complètement l'usage de l'image du tiki. Des mugs aux assiettes en passant par le carrousel à épices, la maîtresse de maison avait tout le loisir de cultiver ses préférences personnelles et de choisir dans sa vaisselle les pièces les mieux adaptées

à une « immersion au cœur de la culture autochtone ».

Outre une vaisselle de table complète aux couleurs tiki, la ménagère habile pouvait s'essayer à la poterie. Dans les années 1950, la fabrication de céramiques était en effet l'un des passe-temps préférés des « housewives » américaines. Un four approprié venait alors s'ajouter à l'équipement de la maison. Pour fournir argiles et émaux, une industrie se développa, emmenée par la firme Duncan Ceramics, qui proposait tout un éventail de moules d'inspiration tiki.

Un autre matériau largement utilisé dans les foyers tiki était le bois d'arbre à pluie, également appelé bois noir d'Haïti. On en

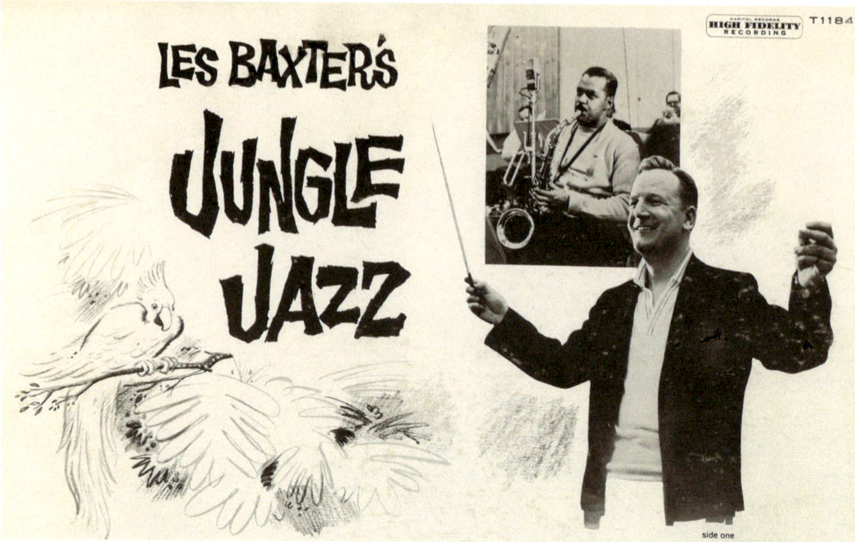

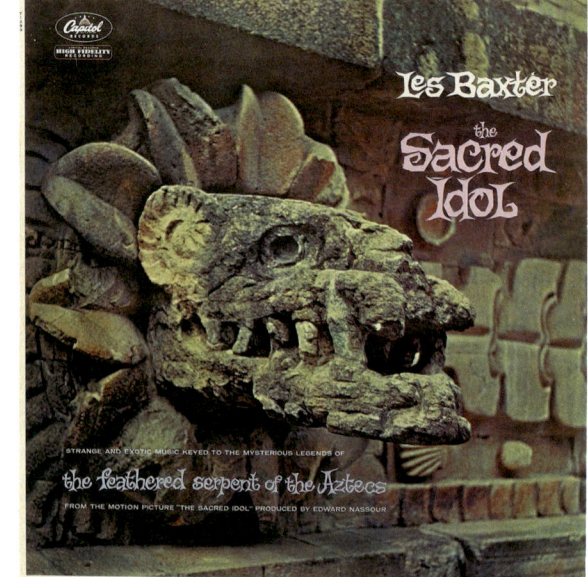

ABOVE: Les Baxter conducting his *Jungle Jazz*

RIGHT AND OPPOSITE: The soundtracks of forgotten civilizations, *Sacred Idol* (1960) and *Barbarian* (1959) faisait des bols et des plats tout indiqués pour accueillir le buffet des *luau*, et créés spécialement à l'intention de l'industrie touristique hawaïenne.

Le design tiki d'inspiration marquisienne utilisé pour les mugs créés par Paul Marshall Products était sans doute la forme tiki la plus répandue dans les objets utilitaires. On s'en servait pour faire des salières ou des poivriers en céramique, des briquets et des tasses à café. En plastique, il inspirait lampes de suspension pour terrasse, torches pour *luau*, ainsi que moult salières et poivriers et autres flacons à condiment. Il insuffla aussi à la marque Amway une ligne de savons et d'articles de toilette appelée « Tonga ».

La génération d'après-guerre consacrant de plus en plus de temps aux loisirs, la demande de mobilier de jardin s'accrut comme jamais. Herb Ritts (le père du photographe) introduisit ainsi avec succès aux États-Unis les meubles en rotin. Il réussit à rendre « tendance » les décorations d'intérieur d'inspiration tropicale. Il lança une chaîne de Tropic Shops à travers le pays, de sorte que l'ameublement en rotin devint le décorum favori des salons prétiki au début des années 1950. Tout, du *home bar* au meuble TV, était fabriqué en bois de palmier. Il reviendra à Witco, l'entreprise de William Westenhaver, d'accompagner le design d'intérieur pendant l'époque du tiki pop.

Enrichissant chaque année sa gamme de décoration intérieure, le catalogue Witco, à partir du début des années 1960, englobe bientôt tous les types possibles d'ameublements. L'usage immodéré de formes figuratives s'applique à tout : salons-séjours complets, lampes, chambres à coucher… Pour sa gamme « Contemporary

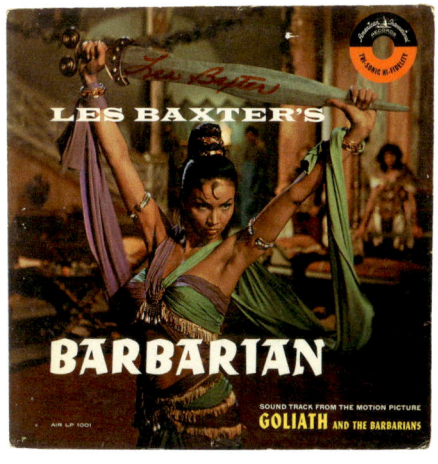

Idol », Witco mélangeait très librement les influences polynésiennes et africaines afin de créer des sculptures primitives fonctionnelles. Ce refus du « bon goût » conventionnel séduisit certains inventeurs de tendances autodidactes déjà consacrés par la culture pop, tels Elvis Presley ou Hugh Hefner. Presley équipa sa Jungle Room, à Graceland, avec du mobilier Witco, quant à Hefner il orna la piscine installée au siège de *Playboy* à Chicago, de tikis et de masques Witco.

Même si sa chanson « Blue Hawaii » a marqué l'époque, on peut difficilement considérer la musique d'Elvis Presley comme de la musique tiki pop. Pas d'ambiguïté, en revanche, dans le cas de Martin Denny, à qui l'on doit la création de ce genre musical exotique basé sur l'œuvre du compositeur Les Baxter.

Baxter était un musicien polyvalent qui travailla à Hollywood, d'abord en tant que chef d'orchestre et arrangeur, puis comme compositeur de musiques de film. Le premier film dont il signa la bande originale

QUIET VILLAGE

By LESLIE BAXTER

ARRANGED BY MARK LAUB FOR HAMMOND ORGAN (ALL MODELS WITH PERCUSSION EFFECT)

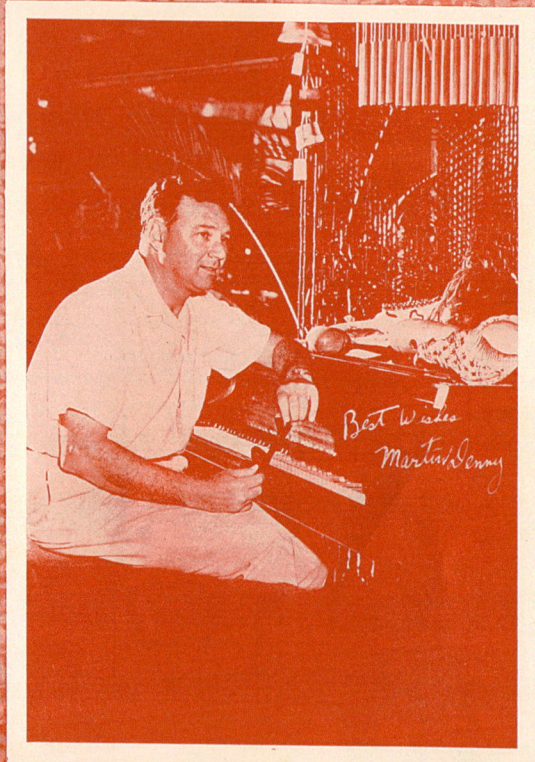

$ 1.25

ATLANTIC MUSIC CORPORATION
and
BAXTER WRIGHT MUSIC CO., INC.
150 West 55th St. • New York 19, N. Y.

fut le documentaire *Tanga Tika* consacré
à Tahiti (1953). Il continuera à écrire des
musiques pour divers films d'aventure
tout en enregistrant ses propres albums,
qui évoquaient souvent l'univers sonore
d'escales lointaines et exotiques.

En 1957, Martin Denny, qui résidait à
Hawaii, enregistra le titre « Quiet Village »,
composé six ans plus tôt par Les Baxter
pour son album *Ritual of the Savage*. Denny
avait eu l'idée d'agrémenter de chants
d'oiseaux ses récitals publics à Hawaii. Il
s'en servit pour le morceau de Baxter qui
grimpa rapidement dans les hit-parades.
Le tube inattendu faisait partie du premier
album de Denny, *Exotica*, lequel contenait plusieurs titres combinant sonorités
« jungle » et percussions exotiques. Ce
disque donna son nom à un nouveau genre
musical, l'exotica.

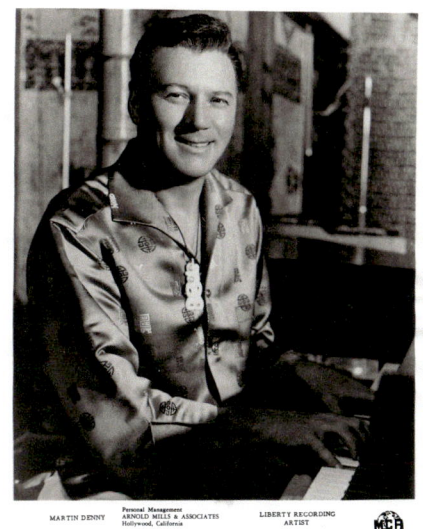

MARTIN DENNY · Personal Management ARNOLD MILLS & ASSOCIATES Hollywood, California · LIBERTY RECORDING ARTIST

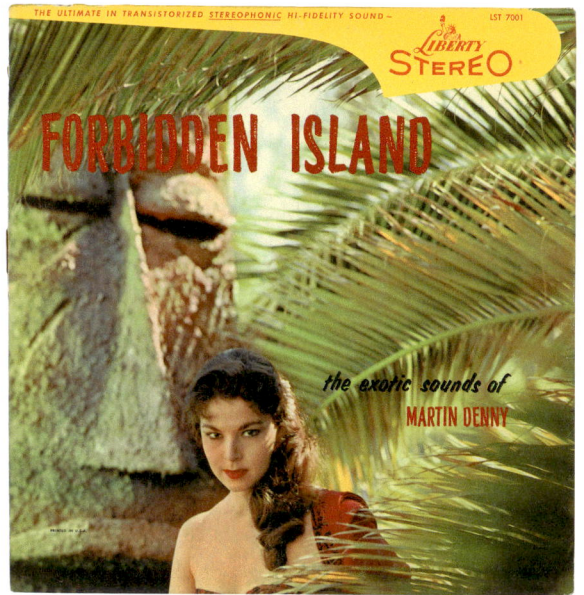

OPPOSITE AND ABOVE: Martin Denny,
the father of exotica music, which
provided the soundscape of the
Tiki lounge

LEFT: The sound of Tiki came in
stereo

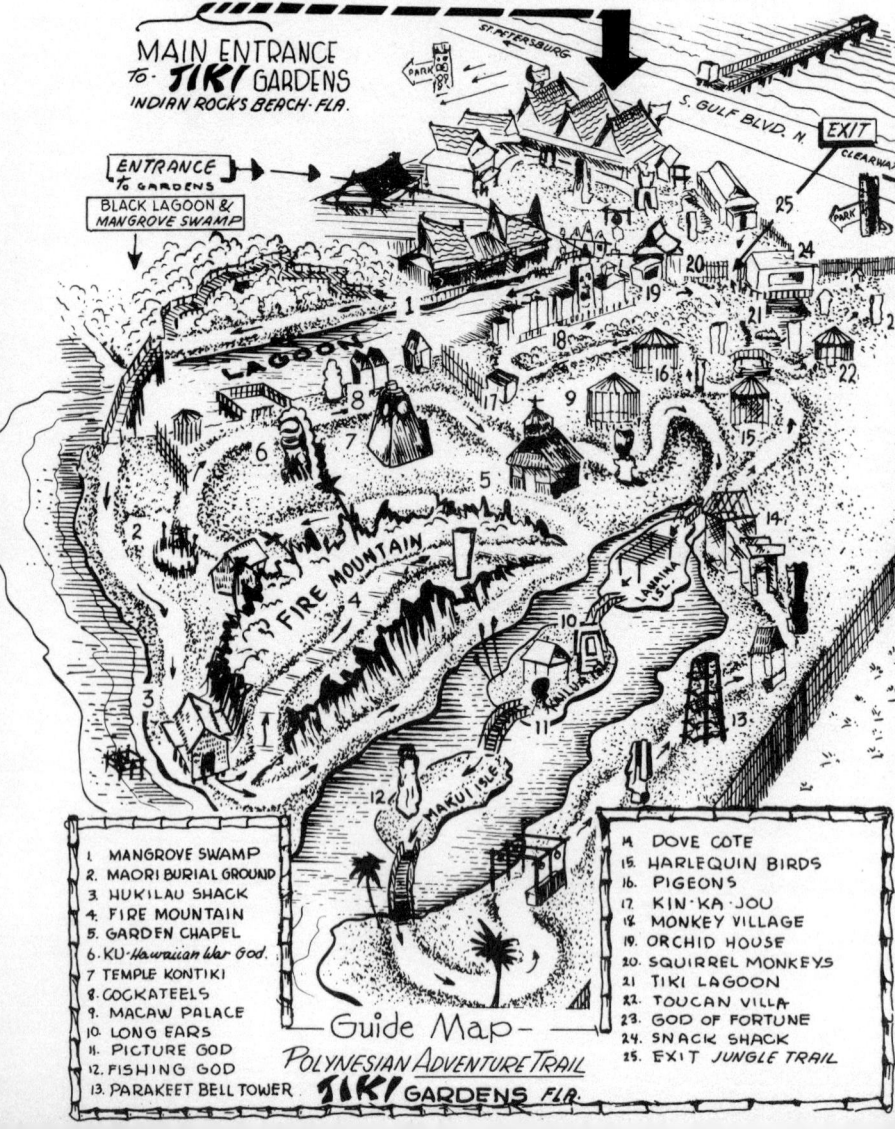

TIKI GARDENS

MAIN ENTRANCE
to · TIKI · GARDENS
INDIAN ROCKS BEACH · FLA.

ENTRANCE
to GARDENS
BLACK LAGOON &
MANGROVE SWAMP

ST. PETERSBURG

PARK

S. GULF BLVD. N.

EXIT
CLEARWATER

PARK

FIRE MOUNTAIN

LAGOON

SABRINA SEA

KAILUA R.

MAKUI ISLE

1. MANGROVE SWAMP
2. MAORI BURIAL GROUND
3. HUKILAU SHACK
4. FIRE MOUNTAIN
5. GARDEN CHAPEL
6. KU·Hawaiian War God.
7. TEMPLE KONTIKI
8. COCKATEELS
9. MACAW PALACE
10. LONG EARS
11. PICTURE GOD
12. FISHING GOD
13. PARAKEET BELL TOWER

14. DOVE COTE
15. HARLEQUIN BIRDS
16. PIGEONS
17. KIN·KA·JOU
18. MONKEY VILLAGE
19. ORCHID HOUSE
20. SQUIRREL MONKEYS
21. TIKI LAGOON
22. TOUCAN VILLA
23. GOD OF FORTUNE
24. SNACK SHACK
25. EXIT JUNGLE TRAIL

— Guide Map —
POLYNESIAN ADVENTURE TRAIL
TIKI GARDENS FLR.

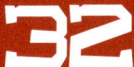

32

TIKI AMUSEMENT PARKS

TIKI-FREIZEITPARKS
LES PARCS DE LOISIRS TIKI

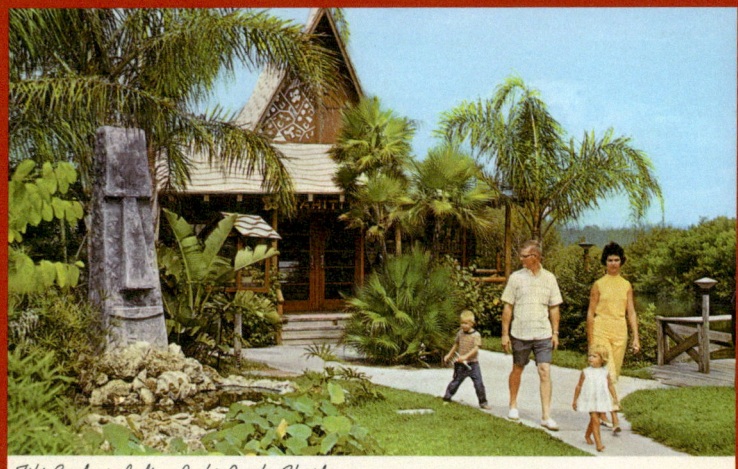

Tiki Gardens, Indian Rocks Beach, Florida

OPPOSITE: Welcome to the Enchanted Isle of the Cement Gods

ABOVE: A god watching his children enjoy Eden
(Scott Schell Collection)

AMERICANS WERE SEEKING THE ALL-
encompassing exotic experience. Since the
artificial landscaping and fabricated sets of
Tiki supper clubs already made them into
little theme parks of their own, it was the
next logical step to create whole amusement
parks revolving around the Tiki concept.
Both enterprises shared the same purpose:
escapism and recreation. The know-how
and materials existed, and what could not
be sourced was handcrafted. In the Tiki
amusement park, the metaphor of the man-
made Garden of Eden was ever more fitting.

In 1964, Frank Byars and his wife, Jo,
followed their passion for Polynesia by
expanding the garden behind their gift
shop, Signal House, in Pinellas County,

Florida, into a Polynesian theme park
named Tiki Gardens. It became one of
the greatest tourist attractions in the area,
drawing over 300,000 visitors annually.

Tiki Gardens offered a "Tropical
Paradise by Day, Polynesian Fantasy by
Night," including a twilight torch-lighting
ceremony accompanied by the blowing
of a conch shell and a Wurlitzer organ.
The exotic jungle sounds were provided
by free-roaming peacocks and the inhabitants of Monkey Village. Several gift shops
promised "A Journey through the Exotic
Marketplaces of the World," and hungry
explorers were fed at Trader Frank's restaurant, a "masterpiece of Polynesian design."
Sadly, Tiki Gardens did not survive Tiki's
demise in the 1980s. It is now a public
beach-access parking lot.

Tiki Gardens's main attraction was
the giant idols, poured out of concrete,
inhabiting this "Enchanting Land of Pagan
Customs." A sign explained that Tiki gods
were descendants of "big-boned white
men" worshipped by the natives of Easter
Island. This pantheon included the God of
Fortune; the Fishing God; Ku the War God;
and even a temple to Kon-Tiki, the Sun God.

While Tiki Gardens was a charming, self-
made pop-art installation, the Enchanted
Tiki Room at Disneyland represents the
high-tech side of the Tiki-attraction genre.
Conceived by the master of the modern
theme park himself, Walt Disney, it featured
early computer-controlled animatronic
Tikis both inside and out. In the courtyard
of the still-operational attraction, an
assembly of gods entertains guests with

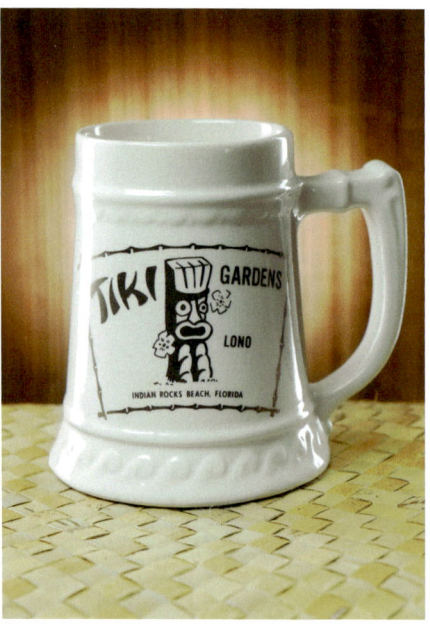

ABOVE: Lono, here on a beer mug, was the logo Tiki of Tiki Gardens

OPPOSITE: Kahona was another oft-used idol created by Tiki Gardens *(Frank Brajevic Collection)*

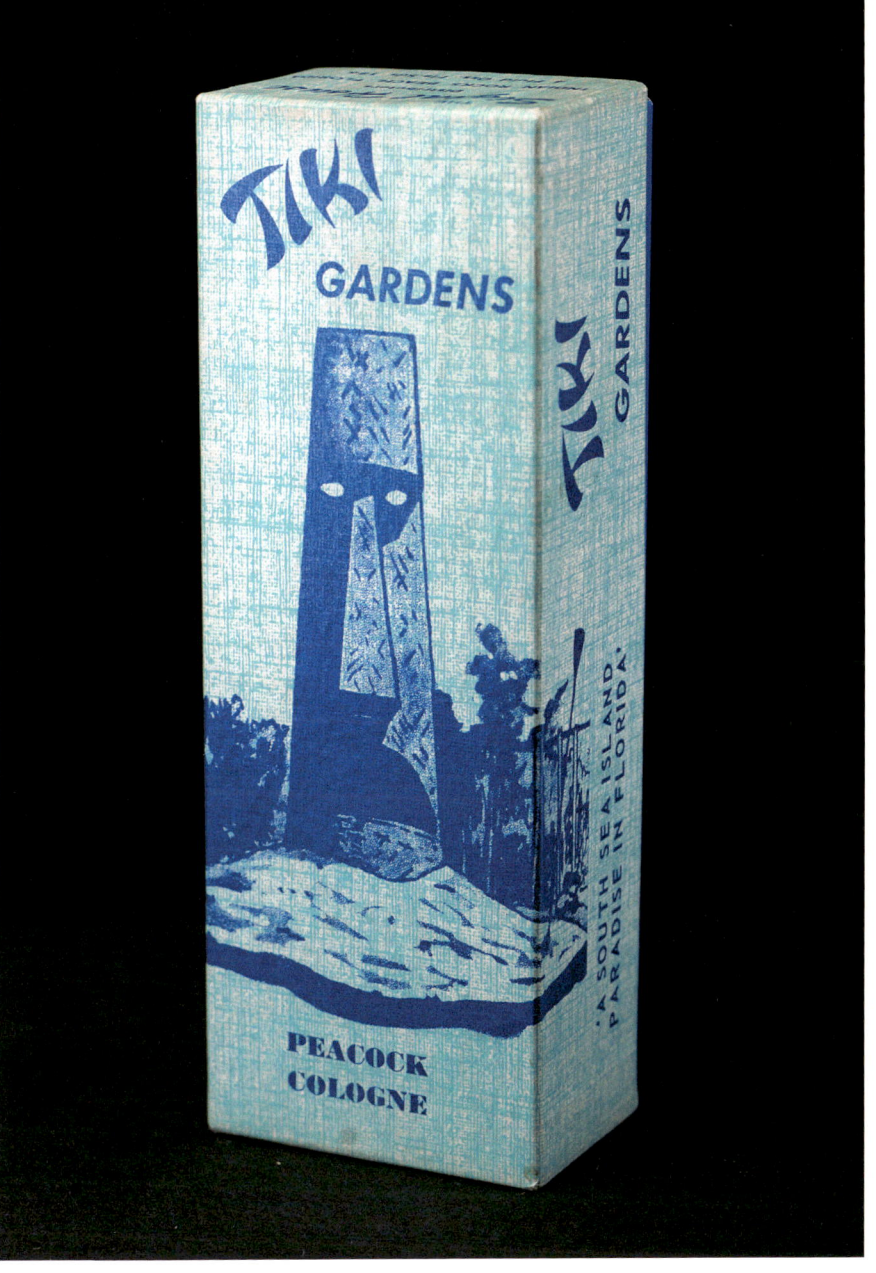

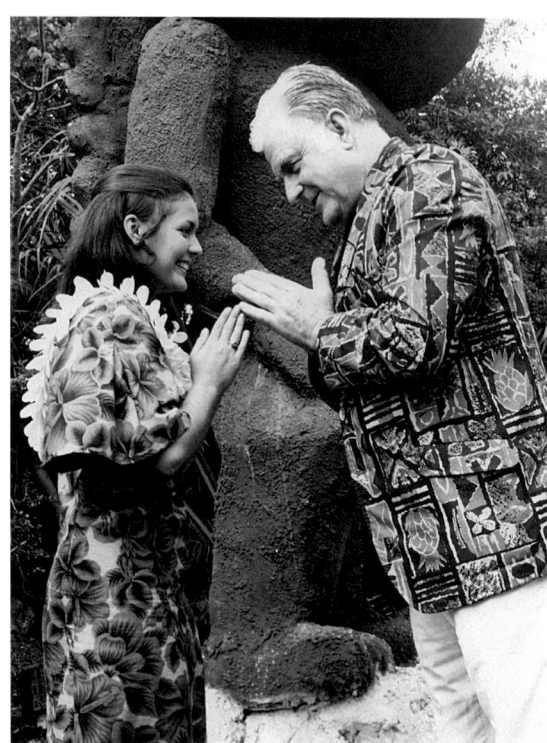

their mythological prowess, and inside, the visitor is dazzled by a symphony of singing tropical flora and fauna, while mechanically moving Tiki gods drum and chant in unison. Walt was a regular at Southern California Polynesian restaurants, and he yearned to give the Polynesian concept the famous Disney touch.

Next to the Tiki Room was the Tahitian Terrace restaurant. It featured a Polynesian floor show in which dancers appeared through an artificial waterfall. Further on, a shop called Tiki's Tropical Traders stood in front of the Jungle Cruise ride, selling Tikis and Tiki pendants by Randotti. Today, only the Enchanted Tiki Room still stands

nearly unaltered, one of Disneyland's oldest classic attractions.

Pacific Ocean Park was an amusement park built in 1958 on the remains of a pleasure pier on the Santa Monica beach. A gigantic volcano arose out of the Pacific, perched atop the water on a platform of stilts. Dubbed Mystery Island, it was reached by a bridge suspended over a waterfall that plummeted into the ocean below. Visitors circled the artificial isle on a banana train steered by a "carefree beachcomber" to see "cannibals, monkeys, and other inhabitants of the South Sea jungles." In a unique public-relations stunt sanctioned by a Samoan chieftain, *South*

Pacific star Mitzi Gaynor officially inducted Mystery Island as part of the Samoan chain. The illusion had been made complete.

Another amusement park, the Tikis, materialized from the vision of Danny Balsz. It began with a chicken ranch on the outskirts of Los Angeles that Balsz converted into luau-style party grounds available for rent during the Polynesian boom. Balsz had a natural talent for landscaping, and he let the plaster and concrete flow into a moonscape of volcanoes and lava tubes that grew into a veritable Planet Tiki. He needed to populate this lava land, and hearing that Tikis brought good fortune, he called the place the Tikis and filled it with pagan statuary from local idol-makers like Oceanic Arts. Hundreds of luau-happy customers were bussed in from nearby aerospace plants and entertained with a Las Vegas-meets-Polynesia extravaganza that climaxed with a virgin being thrown into an 80-foot volcano by a gorilla. Things got too wild, however, and Balsz was evicted. Undaunted, he rebuilt his empire further south. But times had changed, and the Tikis never reopened. By the time urban archaeologists rediscovered it in the early 1990s, it had become a lost civilization.

The fantasy of a self-made Polynesia reached its peak with the creation a South Seas paradise in the middle of the desert. What had worked for Las Vegas would succeed in the arid lands near Newberry Springs, California, insisted Gus Raigosa, a former airplane-factory plumber from Los Angeles. By drilling into the dusty soil, Raigosa's crew could tap aquifers and create private lakes with their own island ecosystems. Of several proposed projects, like Lake Aloha and Lake Tahiti, only one came to fruition.

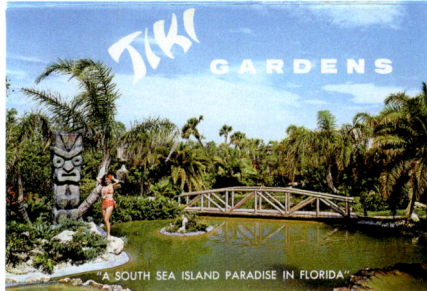

"A SOUTH SEA ISLAND PARADISE IN FLORIDA".

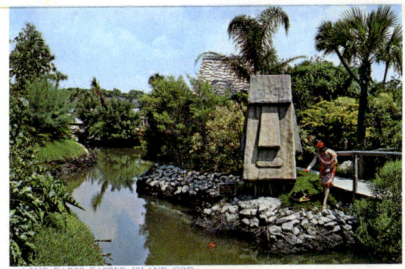

"LONG EARS" EASTER ISLAND GOD

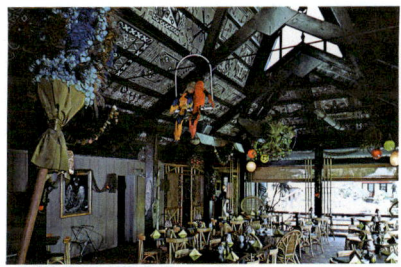

TRADER FRANK'S RESTAURANT

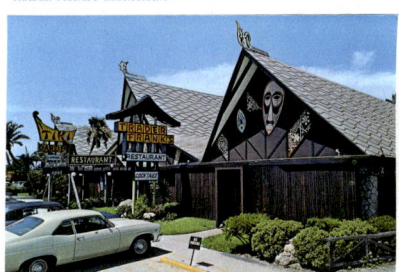

MAIN ENTRANCE

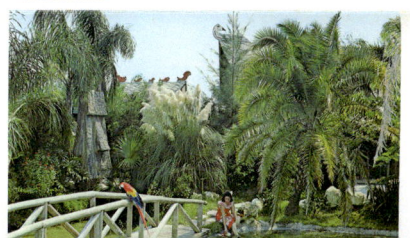

DIE AMERIKANER WAREN AUF DER
Suche nach dem ultimativen exotischen
Erlebnis. Die Tiki-Supper-Clubs glichen
dank ihrer Gartenlandschaften und künstlichen Tropenatmosphäre sowieso schon
kleinen Freizeitparks. Da war es nur logisch,
einen Schritt weiterzugehen und eigen-
ständige Tiki-Erlebnisparks zu eröffnen.
Der Zweck blieb derselbe: Realitätsflucht
und Entspannung. Das Know-How und
die Mate-rialien gab es bereits. Was nicht
beschafft werden konnte, wurde selbst hergestellt. Im Tiki-Vergnügungspark passte
die Metapher vom menschengemachten
Garten Eden besser denn je zuvor.

1964 folgten Frank Byars und seine Frau
Jo ihrer Leidenschaft für Polynesien und
bauten den Garten hinter ihrem Souvenir-
laden Signal House in Pinellas County,

Florida, zu einem polynesischen Freizeitpark namens Tiki Gardens aus. Mit mehr
als 300 000 Besuchern im Jahr wurde er
zu einer der größten Touristenattraktio-
nen der Region.

Das Tiki Gardens bot seinen Gästen ein
„Tropisches Paradies bei Tag" und einen
„Polynesischen Traum bei Nacht". Mit Ein-
setzen der Dämmerung wurden mit großer
zeremonieller Geste die Fackeln entzündet,
begleitet von den Kängen eines Schnecken-
horns und einer Wurlitzer-Orgel. Für exotische Dschungelgeräusche sorgten die frei-
laufenden Pfauen und die Bewohner des
„Monkey Village". Diverse Souvenirläden
versprachen „eine Reise zu den exotischen
Marktplätzen der Welt" und hungrige Entdecker bekamen in Trader Frank's Restaurant „Meisterwerke nach polynesischer Art"

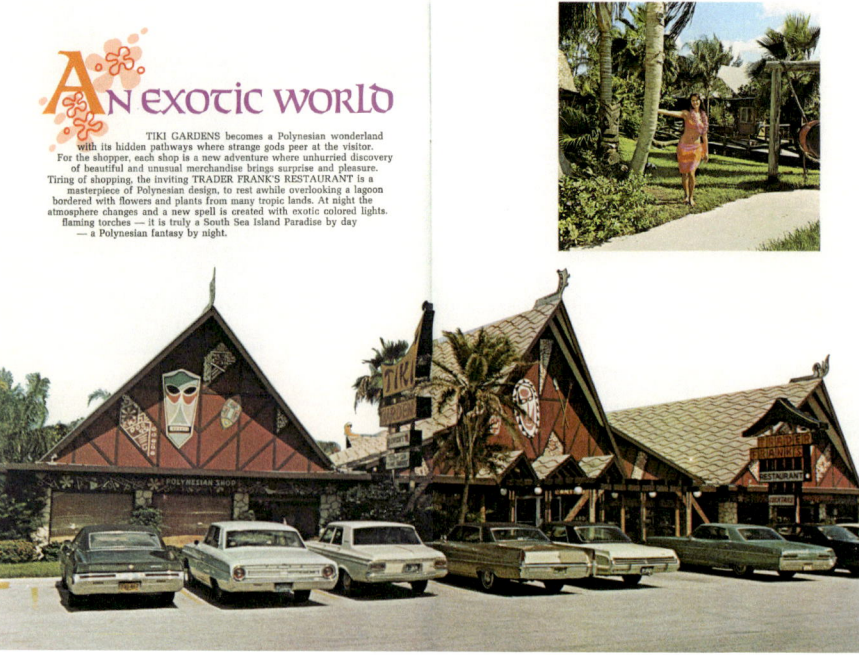

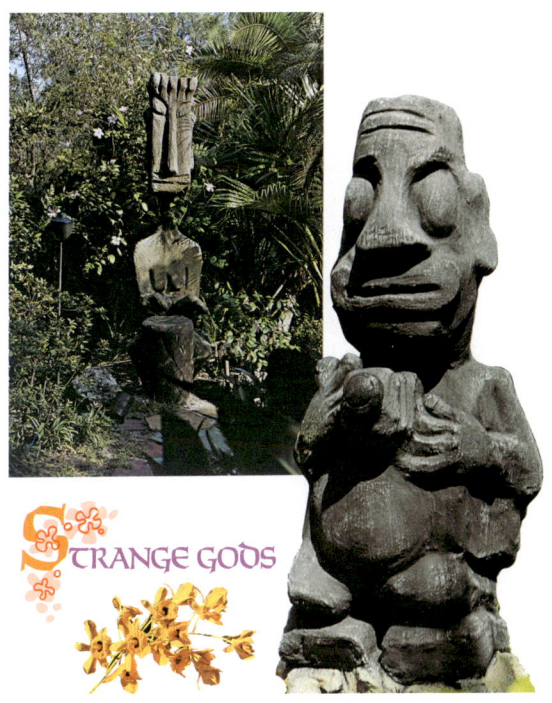

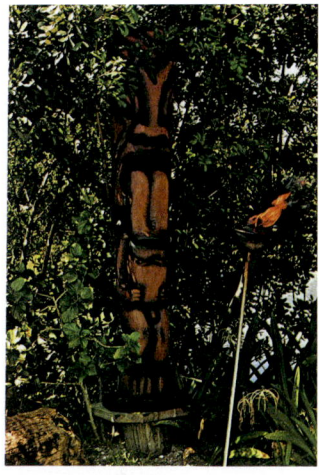

Strange Gods

POLYNESIANS worshipped many gods — Family gods, ammakuas or akuas, gods of nature and of creation. These gods had their public temples or heiau. In Hawaii the main god was KANE, in the other islands, TANE. Other gods were LONO, god of rain and peace, and KU, god of war. Every family had a sacred fishing god. Here in TIKI GARDENS we have tried to give you a bit of Polynesian culture — with our many stone and wooden gods. With the coming of the missionaries, our neighbors of the 50th State of the Union, became Christians, so today all these customs are a thing of the past — only MADAM PELE the fire goddess seems to continue to reign in the islands with her many volcanoes as she also lives atop FIRE MOUNTAIN in TIKI GARDENS.

OPPOSITE: Your one-stop Polynesian shop—actually seven shops offering exotic fashions and gifts

ABOVE: Tiki Pop mythology: the strangest of the strange gods, including Kula the Picture God

RIGHT: The *Tiki*, about to leave the dock for a scenic cruise *(Scott Schell Collection)*

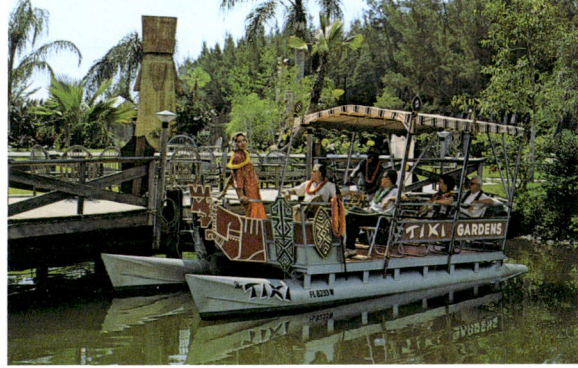

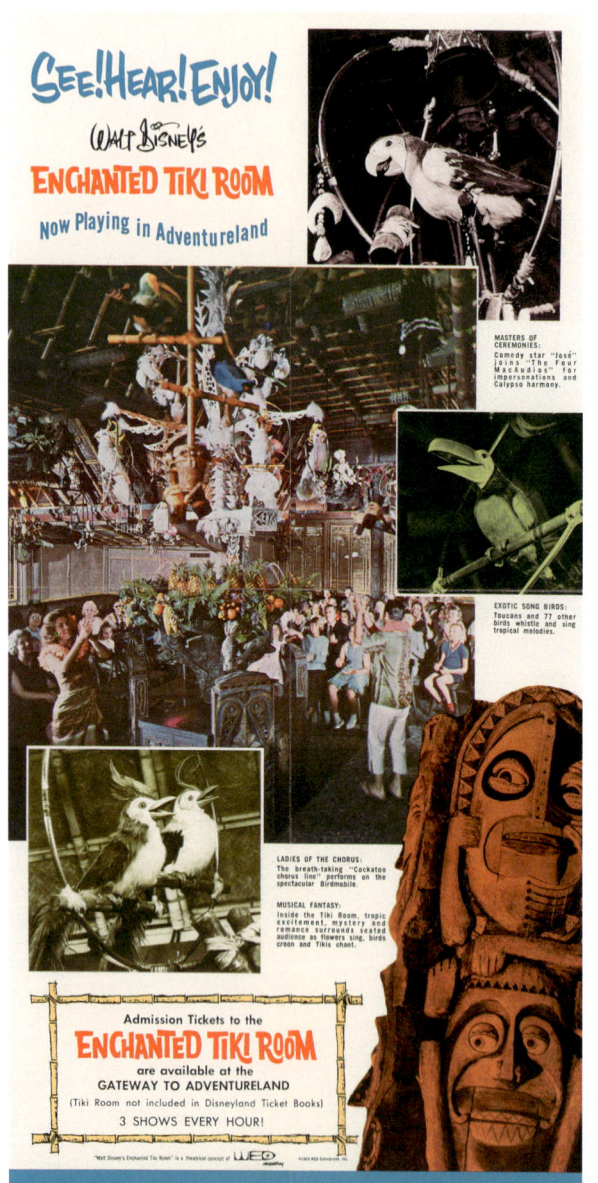

LEFT: Enchanted Tiki Room brochure, 1963 *(Kiara Geller Collection)*

OPPOSITE: The Enchanted Tiki Room entrance at Disneyland

PAGES 576–577: Conceptual rendering for the Tahitian Terrace serviert. Leider überlebte das Tiki Gardens das Abebben der Bewegung in den 1980er-Jahren nicht. Heute ist es ein öffentlicher Parkplatz für Strandbesucher.

Die Hauptattraktion des Tiki Gardens waren die riesigen Götterfiguren aus Beton, die das „bezaubernde Land heidnischer Traditionen" bewohnten. Ein Schild erklärte, dass Tikis die Abkommen „grobknochiger weißer Männer" waren, die von den Einheimischen der Osterinsel verehrt wurden. Zu dem Pantheon gehörten der Gott des Glücks, der Fischergott und der Kriegsgott Ku. Und es gab sogar einen Tempel für Kon-Tiki, den Sonnengott.

Tiki Gardens war eine charmante Pop-Art-Installation der Marke Eigenbau. Ihre High-Tech-Version war der Enchanted Tiki Room in Disneyland. Vom Meister moderner Freizeitparks, Walt Disney, selbst entworfen, gab es dort computergesteuerte Tikis im Innen- und Außenbereich. Die Attraktion existiert in veränderter Form noch heute. Im Hof unterhält eine Gruppe aus Göttern die Gäste mit ihren mystischen Fähigkeiten, im Innern überwältigen eine singende Flora und Fauna und mechanisch trommelnde Tiki-Götter die Besucher. Walt Disney war Stammgast in den polynesischen Restaurants Südkaliforniens und bestrebt, dem Thema seine berühmte Disney-Note zu verleihen.

Neben dem Tiki Room befand sich das Restaurant Tahitian Terrace. Hier gab es eine polynesische Show, bei der die Tänzer durch einen künstlichen Wasserfall auf die

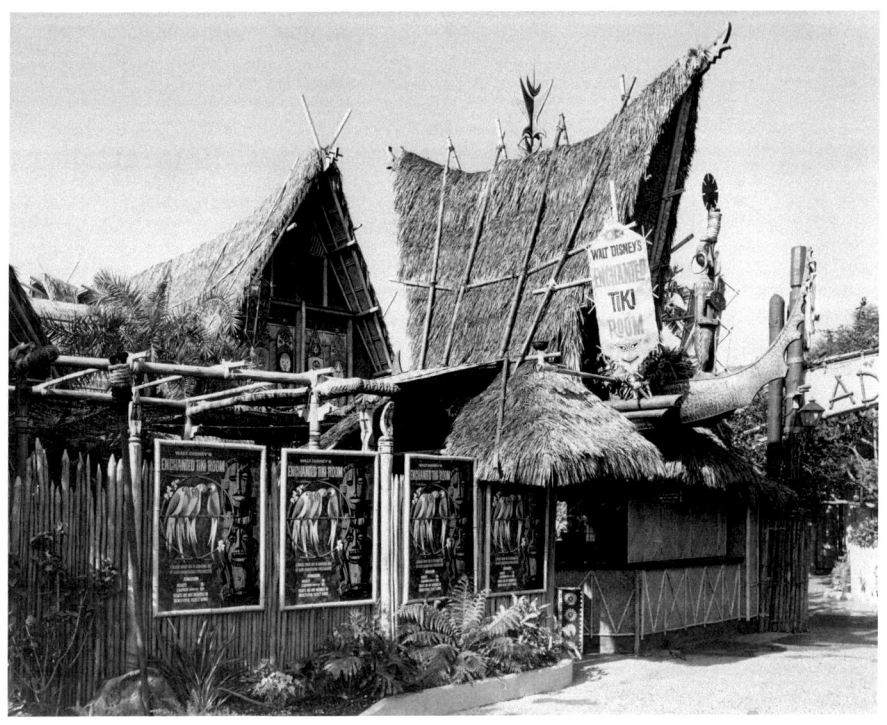

Bühne traten. Ein Stück weiter verkaufte ein Laden namens Tiki's Tropical Traders Tiki-Figuren und -Ketten der Firma Randotti. Direkt dahinter befand sich das Fahrgeschäft Jungle Cruise. Heute gibt es nur noch den Enchanted Tiki Room, eine von Disneylands ältesten Attraktionen.

Der Pacific Ocean Park war ein Erlebnispark, der im Jahr 1958 auf den Überresten eines Vergnügungspiers am Santa Monica Beach errichtet wurde. Hier ragte ein riesiger Vulkan auf einer Stelzenplattform aus dem Pazifik. Die sogenannte Mystery Island erreichten die Besucher über eine Brücke, die über einen Wasserfall führte, der in den Ozean herabdonnerte. In einem „banana train", der von einem „sorglosen Strandbummler" gesteuert wurde, konnten Besucher die künstliche Insel umfahren und dabei „Kannibalen, Affen und andere Bewohner des Südseedschungels beobachten". Mit Einverständnis eines samoanischen Häuptlings erklärte *South Pacific*-Star Mitzi Gaynor in einem einzigartigen PR-Gag Mystery Island offiziell zu einer samoanischen Insel. Die Illusion war perfekt.

Ein weiterer Freizeitpark, The Tikis, ist Danny Balsz' Vorstellungskraft entsprungen. Alles fing mit einer Hühnerfarm in den Außenbezirken von Los Angeles an. Balsz baute sie zu einem thematisch gestalteten Veranstaltungsort um, den Gäste für ihre privaten Luaus mieten konnten. Der Mann hatte ein Talent für Landschaftsgärtnerei. Aus Gips und Beton schuf er Mond- und Vulkanlandschaften mit Lavagrotten – einen veritablen Tiki-Planeten. Sein Lavaland musste belebt werden und da er gehört hatte, dass mit dieser Mode gutes Geld zu verdienen war, nannte er es The Tikis und füllte es mit heidnischen Statuen von amerikanischen Herstellern

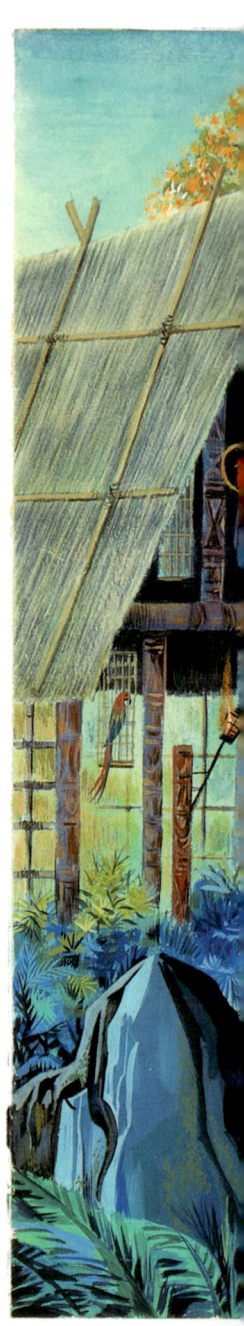

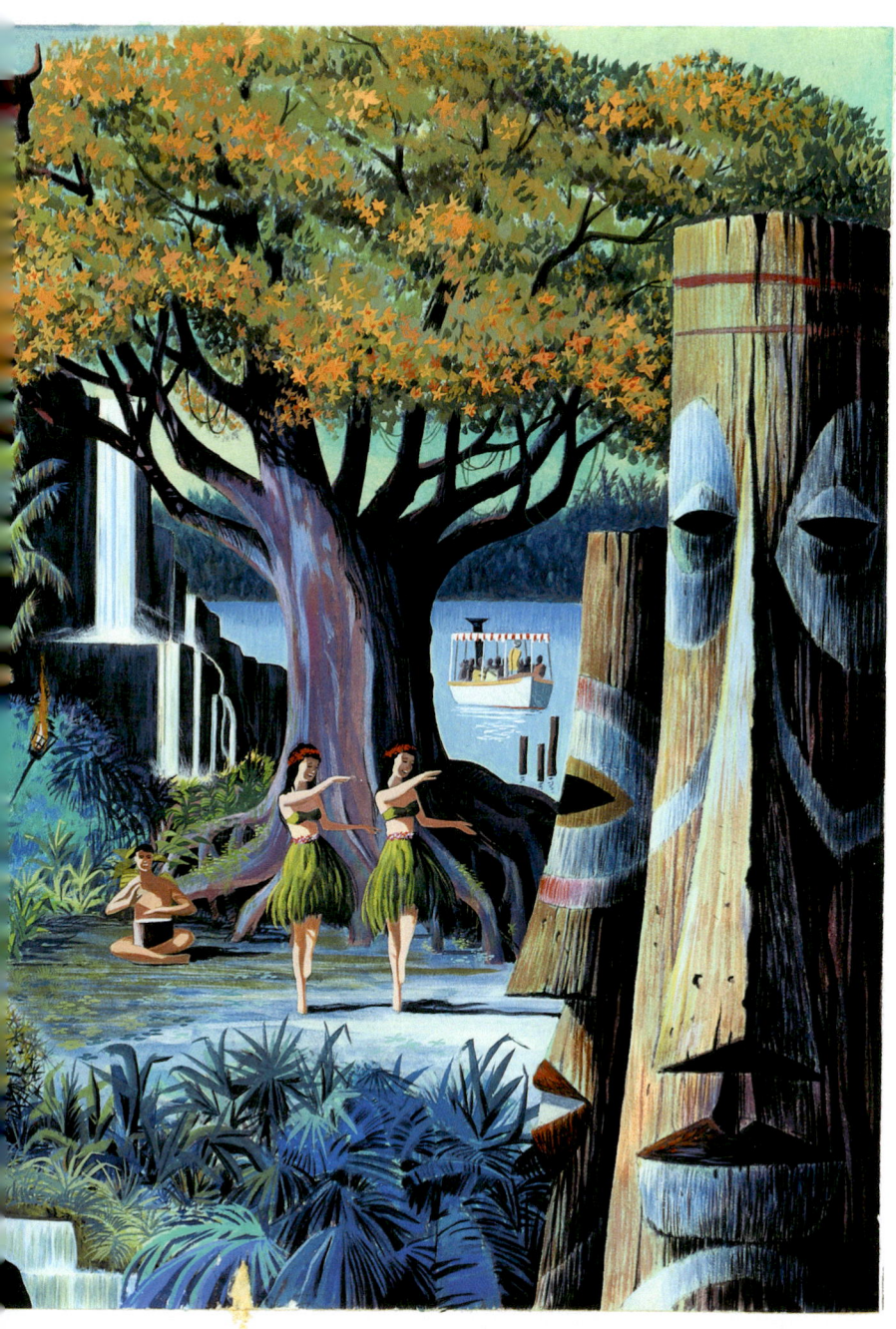

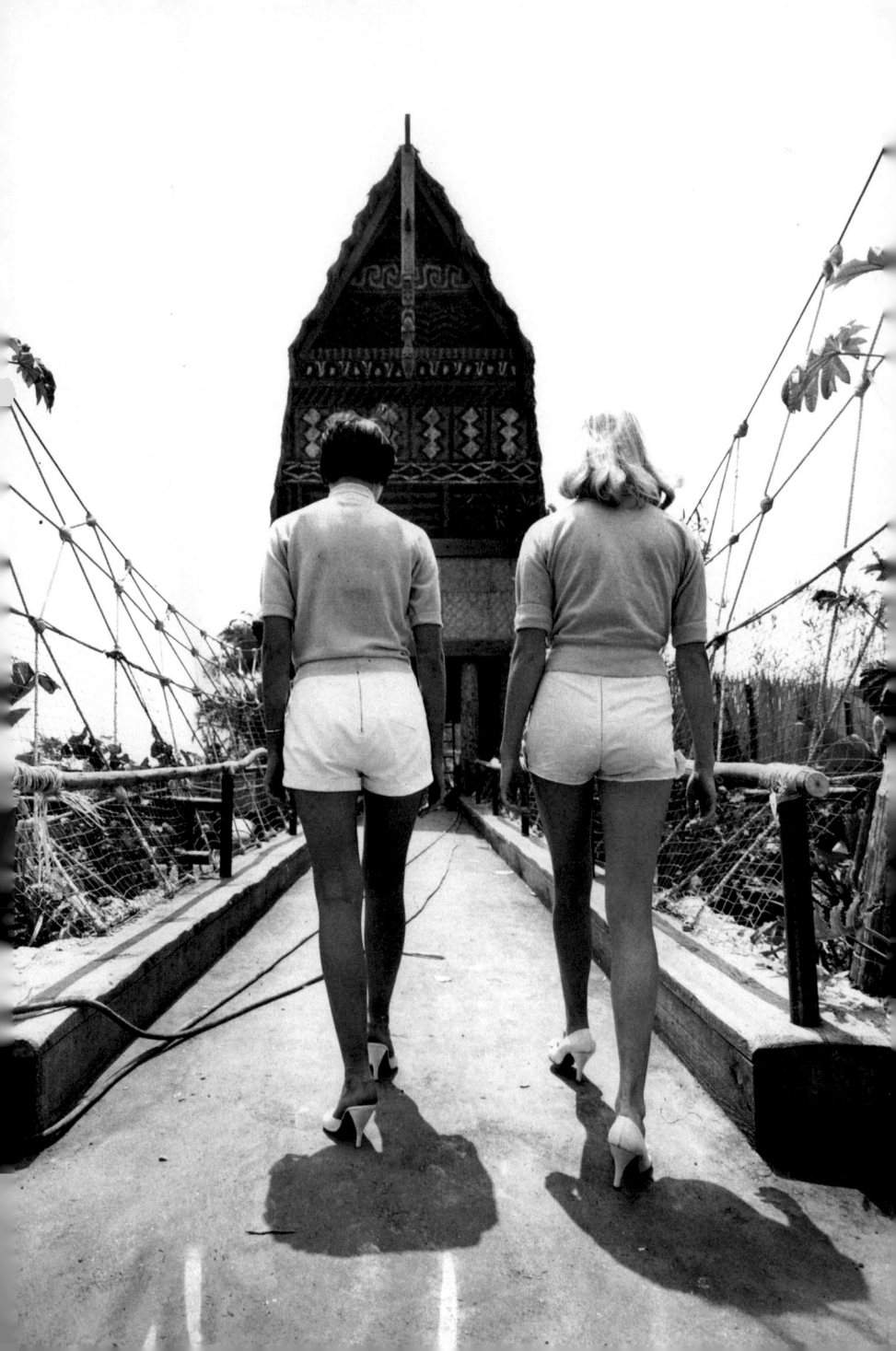

wie Oceanic Arts. Hunderte Luau-freudige Besucher kamen von den nahegelegenen Fabriken der Luft- und Raumfahrtindustrie ins Tikis, um sich von der „Las-Vegas-trifft-Polynesien-Zauberposse" unterhalten zu lassen. Höhepunkt der Show war eine Jungfrau, die von einem Gorilla in einen 24 Meter hohen Vulkan geworfen wurde. Irgendwann trieb es Balsz jedoch zu wild und das Gelände wurde zwangsgeräumt. Unverdrossen baute er sein Reich etwas weiter südlich wieder auf. Aber die Zeiten hatten sich geändert und das Tikis sollte seine Tore nie wieder öffnen. Als es Stadtarchäologen in den frühen 1990er-Jahren entdeckten, waren nur noch Ruinen übrig.

Der Traum eines selbst erschaffenen Polynesiens erreichte seinen Höhepunkt, als mitten in der Wüste ein Südseeparadies entstehen sollte. Was für Las Vegas funktioniert hatte, würde auch in der unfruchtbaren Landschaft nahe Newberry Springs, Kalifornien, Erfolg haben, war sich Gus Raigosa, ehemaliger Installateur in einer Flugzeugfabrik in Los Angeles, sicher. Man müsse nur in den staubigen Boden bohren, um das Grundwasser anzuzapfen. So ließen sich Seen mit einem eigenen Ökosystem kreieren. Von diversen vorgeschlagenen Projekten wie Lake Aloha und Lake Tahiti wurde nur eines umgesetzt.

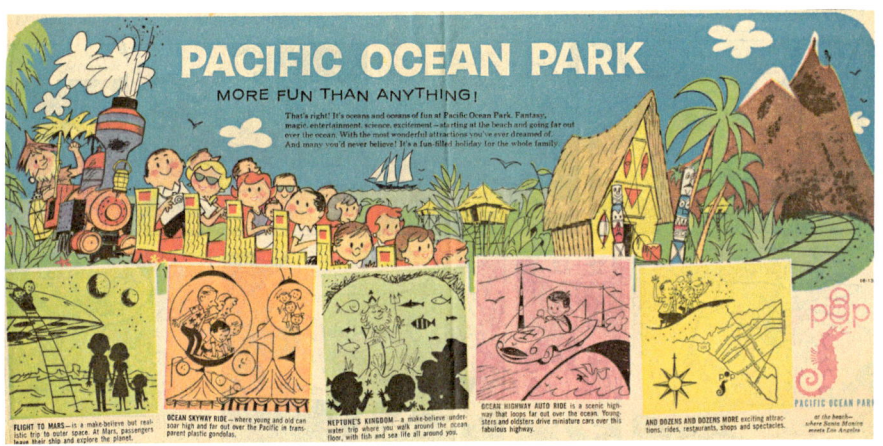

OPPOSITE: Attractive visitors explore the attraction

ABOVE: Newspaper ad for Pacific Ocean Park
(Timothy Haack Collection)

LES AMÉRICAINS CHERCHAIENT
l'expérience exotique intégrale. Dans la
mesure où le décor artificiel et les ambiances montées de toutes pièces des clubs
dînatoires tiki en faisaient déjà de petits
parcs à thème, l'étape suivante, logiquement, devait conduire à créer de vrais parcs
de loisirs basés sur le concept tiki. De fait,
les deux projets partageaient le même objectif : évasion et détente. Le savoir-faire et les
ressources existaient, et ce qui n'était pas
disponible pouvait de toute façon être fabriqué artisanalement. La métaphore du jardin
d'Éden créé par l'homme allait vraiment
comme un gant au parc d'attraction tiki.

En 1964, Frank Byars et sa femme Jo
suivirent leur passion commune pour la
Polynésie en transformant le jardin situé
derrière leur boutique de souvenirs, Signal
House, à Pinellas County en Floride, en
un parc à thème polynésien nommé Tiki

Gardens. Il devint l'une des plus grosses
attractions touristiques de la région, attirant
plus de 300 000 visiteurs chaque année.

Tiki Gardens proposait un « paradis
tropical le jour, une fantasmagorie polynésienne la nuit ». Au programme figurait
une cérémonie d'allumage des feux au clair
de lune, accompagnée du bourdonnement
émis par une conque et d'un piano électrique Wurlitzer. Les ambiances sonores
évoquant la jungle étaient assurées par
des paons en liberté et par les habitants du
Monkey Village (le village des singes). Plusieurs magasins de souvenirs promettaient
« un voyage à travers les marchés exotiques
du monde entier », quant aux explorateurs
affamés, un restaurant Trader Frank les
attendait, « chef-d'œuvre de design polynésien ». Hélas Tiki Gardens ne survécut
pas à la disparition du tiki dans les années
1980. L'endroit abrite désormais un parc de

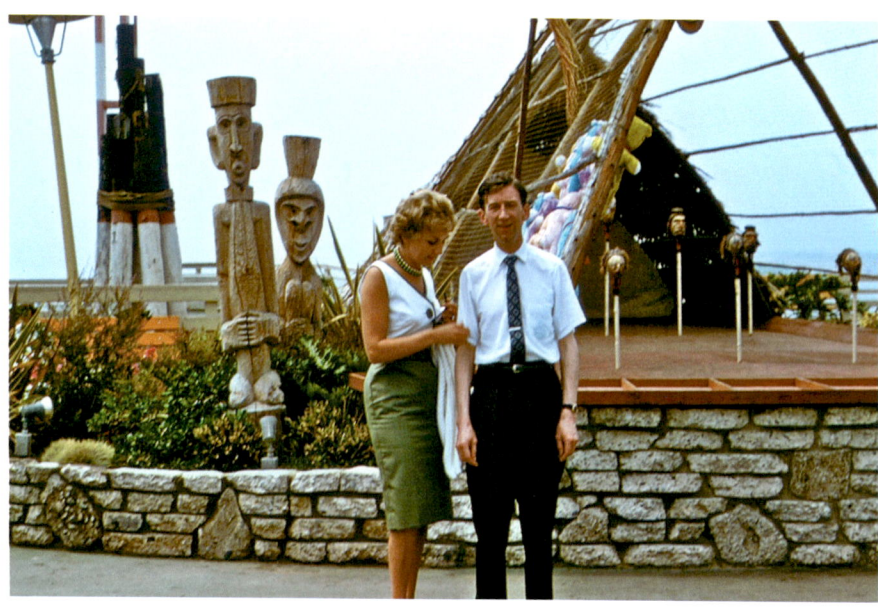

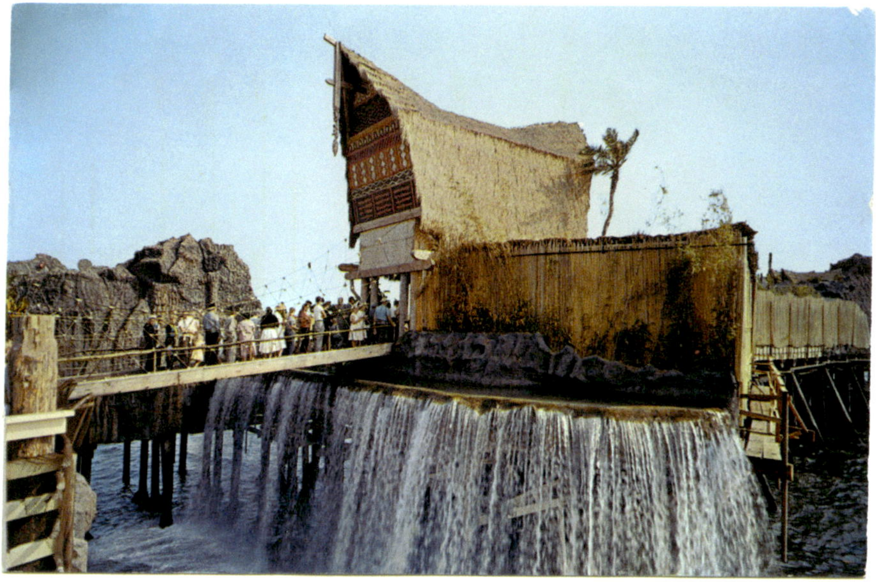

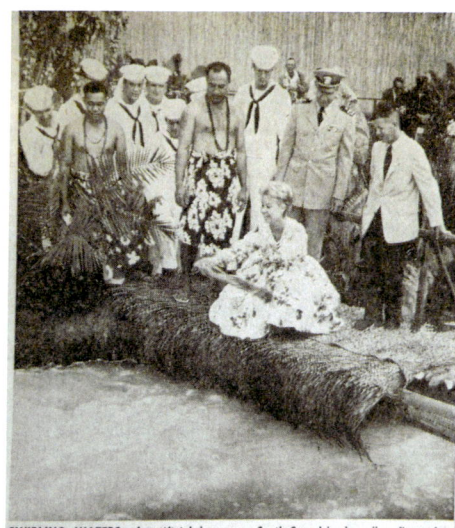

OPPOSITE: Effigies and California natives *(Charles Phoenix Collection)*

ABOVE: An island in the sky *(Scott Schell Collection)*

RIGHT: The fantasy becoming reality *(Chris Merrit Collection)*

SWIRLING WATERS of artificial lagoon on South Seas Island swallow flower leis at dedication featured by Mitzi Gaynor. Others are (from left) Samoans Asovalu Tuiasosopo and Malaetia Tufele, Lt. Cmdr. Oliver E. Emmons, Santa Monica Naval Reservists and James MacLeod, representing British consul. New Zealand shares trusteeship of Samoan group. (Evening Outlook Photos by Norman Wexler.)

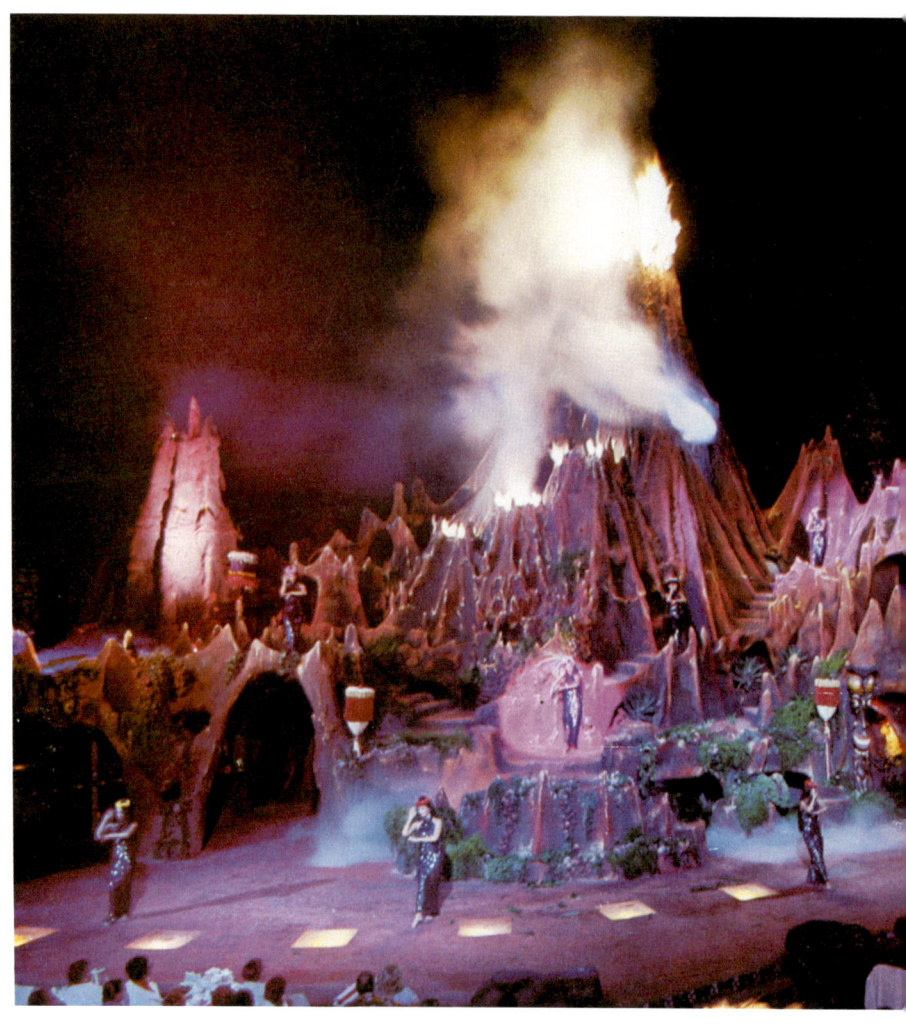

ABOVE: Pele would be proud: the grand Polynesian show in front of the 80-foot volcano at the Tikis (*Scott Schell Collection*)

OPPOSITE: A Polynesian Hollywoodland

stationnement en bord de plage. L'attraction principale de Tiki Gardens, c'était son aréopage d'idoles géantes en béton, résidentes permanentes du « pays enchanté des coutumes païennes ». Un panonceau expliquait que les divinités tiki descendaient des « robustes hommes blancs » vénérés par les populations indigènes de l'île de Pâques.

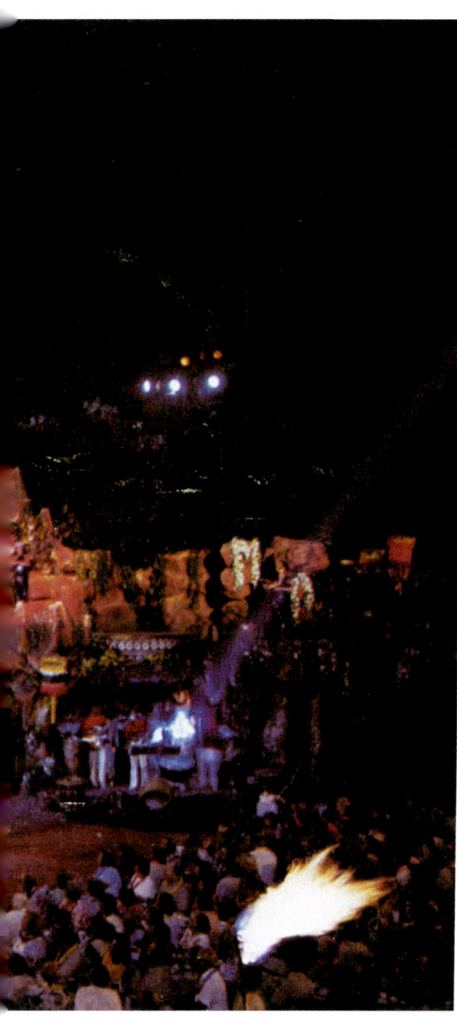

high-tech. Conçue par le roi du parc à thèmes moderne, Walt Disney lui-même, il comprenait les premiers robots tiki téléguidés par ordinateur, aussi bien à l'intérieur qu'à l'extérieur. Côté cour, cette attraction – toujours en activité – abrite une assemblée de divinités chargées de divertir les visiteurs avec leurs prouesses mythologiques. À l'intérieur, ce même visiteur en prend plein les yeux et les oreilles, accueilli par une symphonie végétale et animale, tandis que des dieux tiki tambourinent et chantent à l'unisson. Walt Disney qui était un habitué des restaurants polynésiens de Californie, eut à cœur d'insuffler au concept la fameuse « Disney touch ».

À côté de la Tiki Room se trouvait le restaurant Tahitian Terrace qui proposait un spectacle de cabaret polynésien dans lequel on pouvait admirer les danseurs émergeant de chutes d'eau artificielles. Un peu plus loin, une boutique nommée Tiki's Tropical Traders attendait ses clients devant l'entrée de la Jungle Cruise ; elle proposait

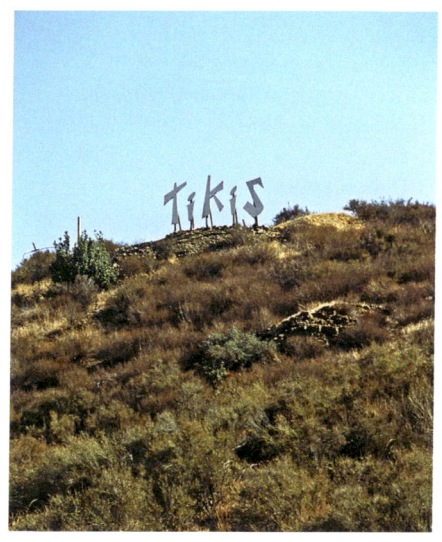

Ce panthéon accueillait notamment le dieu de la Fortune, le dieu de la Pêche, Ku le dieu de la Guerre et même un temple dédié à Kon-Tiki, dieu du Soleil.

Si Tiki Gardens tenait de l'installation pop art « faite maison », la Enchanted Tiki Room de Disneyland, dans le registre du parc de loisirs tiki, en représente la face

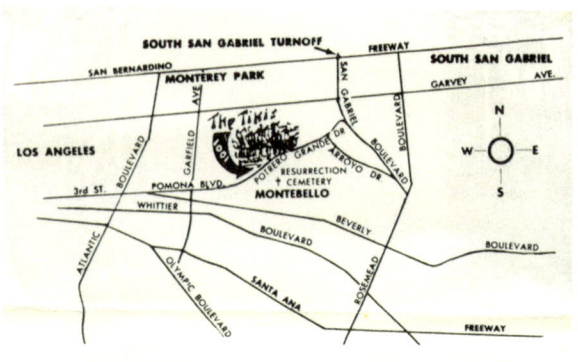

Three Acres of Lush Atmosphere
310 Foot Entrance — 200 Foot Underground Volcanic Cave
Erupting Volcano — Waterfalls — Large Lagoons
Thunder — Rain — Bird Calls — Monkeys Chattering
3 Dance Areas — Many Individual Huts
100 Foot Sunken Snake Bar — Outside Barefoot Bar
Complete Indoor and Outdoor Banquet Facilities
3 Acres of Paved Parking   Holiday Parties
Serving Up to 1500 Persons

The Tikis **1001 N. POTRERO GRANDE DRIVE**
South San Gabriel   **ATlantic 0-1209**

des tikis et des pendentifs tiki fabriqués par Randotti. Aujourd'hui l'Enchanted Tiki Room est la seule attraction à avoir conservé, presque inaltérée, sa forme originelle. C'est l'une des plus anciennes de Disneyland.

Le Pacific Ocean Park a lui été construit en 1958 sur les vestiges d'un parc de loisirs situé sur la plage de Santa Monica. Un volcan gigantesque surgissait du Pacifique, surplombant les eaux grâce à des colonnes immergées. Baptisé Mystery Island, on y accédait par un pont suspendu au-dessus d'une cascade qui se jetait dans l'océan. Les visiteurs faisaient le tour de l'île artificielle à bord d'une banane montée sur rails pilotée par un « beachcomber insouciant » pour admirer « cannibales, singes et autres

habitants des jungles des mers du Sud ». Dans le cadre d'une opération de relations publiques hors du commun entérinée par un chef de clan samoan, Mitzi Gaynor, l'actrice de la comédie musicale *South Pacific*, déclara officiellement Mystery Island partie intégrante de l'archipel des Samoa. L'illusion était complète.

Un autre parc de loisirs, The Tikis, concrétisa le rêve de Danny Balsz. L'aventure démarra par un élevage de volaille des environs de Los Angeles que Balsz transforma en terrain aménagés pour des fêtes *luau*, disponibles à la location pendant la vague polynésienne. Balsz avait un don inné pour l'aménagement paysager. Ainsi le plâtre et le béton donnèrent-ils vie à un panorama lunaire fait de volcans et de tunnels de lave qui finirent par former une véritable planète tiki. Comme il lui fallait faire connaître ce « lavaland », et qu'il avait appris que les tikis portaient bonheur, il appela l'endroit The Tikis et le remplit de statues païennes dues au talent de sculpteurs locaux tel Oceanic Arts. Des centaines de visiteurs avides d'ambiance *luau* étaient amenés en bus depuis les usines aéronautiques voisines et divertis avec une extravagance mariant allègrement Las Vegas et la Polynésie. Le dispositif atteignait son paroxysme lorsqu'un gorille jetait une jeune vierge au fond d'un volcan de 25 mètres. Cependant, après quelques dérapages fâcheux, Balsz dut abandonner la direction du parc. Sans se démonter il alla rebâtir son empire un peu plus au sud, mais les temps avaient changé et The Tikis ne rouvrit

jamais ses portes. Quand les archéologues de l'histoire urbaine le redécouvrirent au début des années 1990, il n'était plus qu'une civilisation perdue.

Le rêve d'une Polynésie fabriquée de toutes pièces connut son apogée quand un paradis des mers du Sud surgit au milieu du désert. Pourquoi ce qui avait marché à Las Vegas ne pourrait-il pas réussir sur les terres arides entourant Newberry Springs, en Californie ? Tel était le pari de Gus Raigosa, un ancien plombier d'une usine aéronautique de Los Angeles. En forant le sol poussiéreux, son équipe prévoyait d'exploiter des nappes d'eau souterraine et de créer des lacs privés dotés de leur propre écosystème insulaire. Parmi les projets alors envisagés, comme le lac Aloha et le lac Tahiti, un seul aboutira.

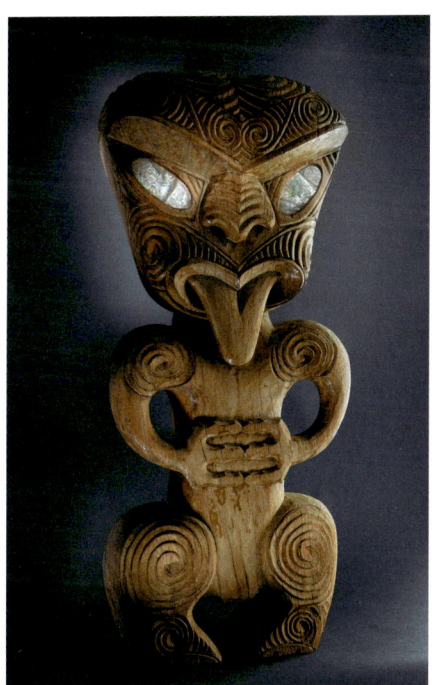

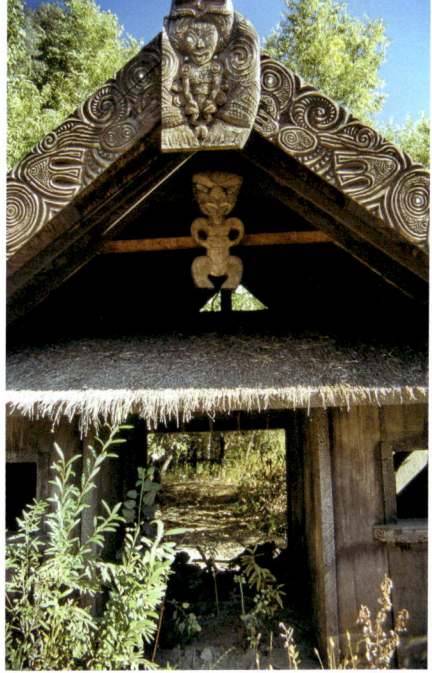

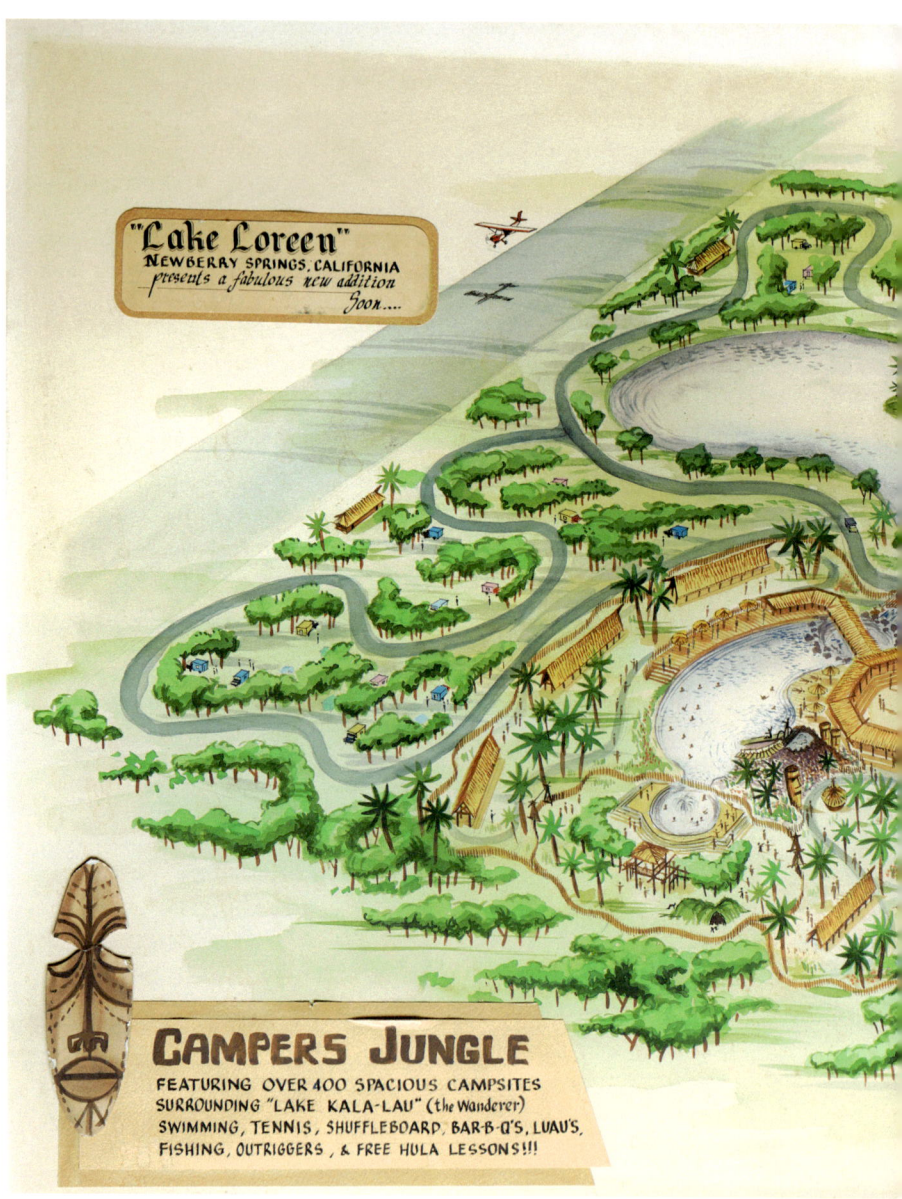

"Lake Loreen"
NEWBERRY SPRINGS, CALIFORNIA
presents a fabulous new addition
Soon....

CAMPERS JUNGLE

FEATURING OVER 400 SPACIOUS CAMPSITES
SURROUNDING "LAKE KALA-LAU" (the Wanderer)
SWIMMING, TENNIS, SHUFFLEBOARD, BAR-B-Q'S, LUAU'S,
FISHING, OUTRIGGERS, & FREE HULA LESSONS!!!

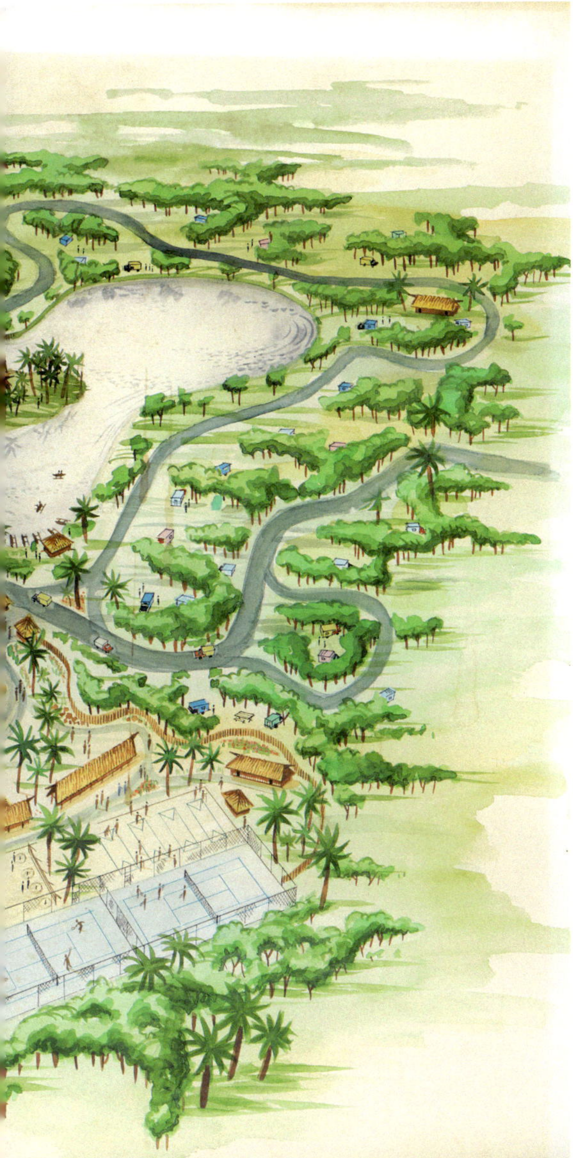

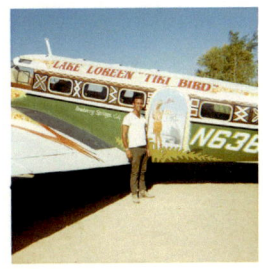

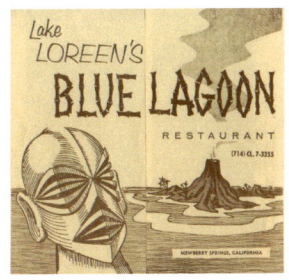

LEFT: After Lake Loreen, other lakeside Polynesias were planned (*Amy Boylan Collection*)

ABOVE: The *Tiki Bird*, your air taxi to a desert isle

BELOW: A Tiki oasis in the California desert (*Oceanic Arts Collection*)

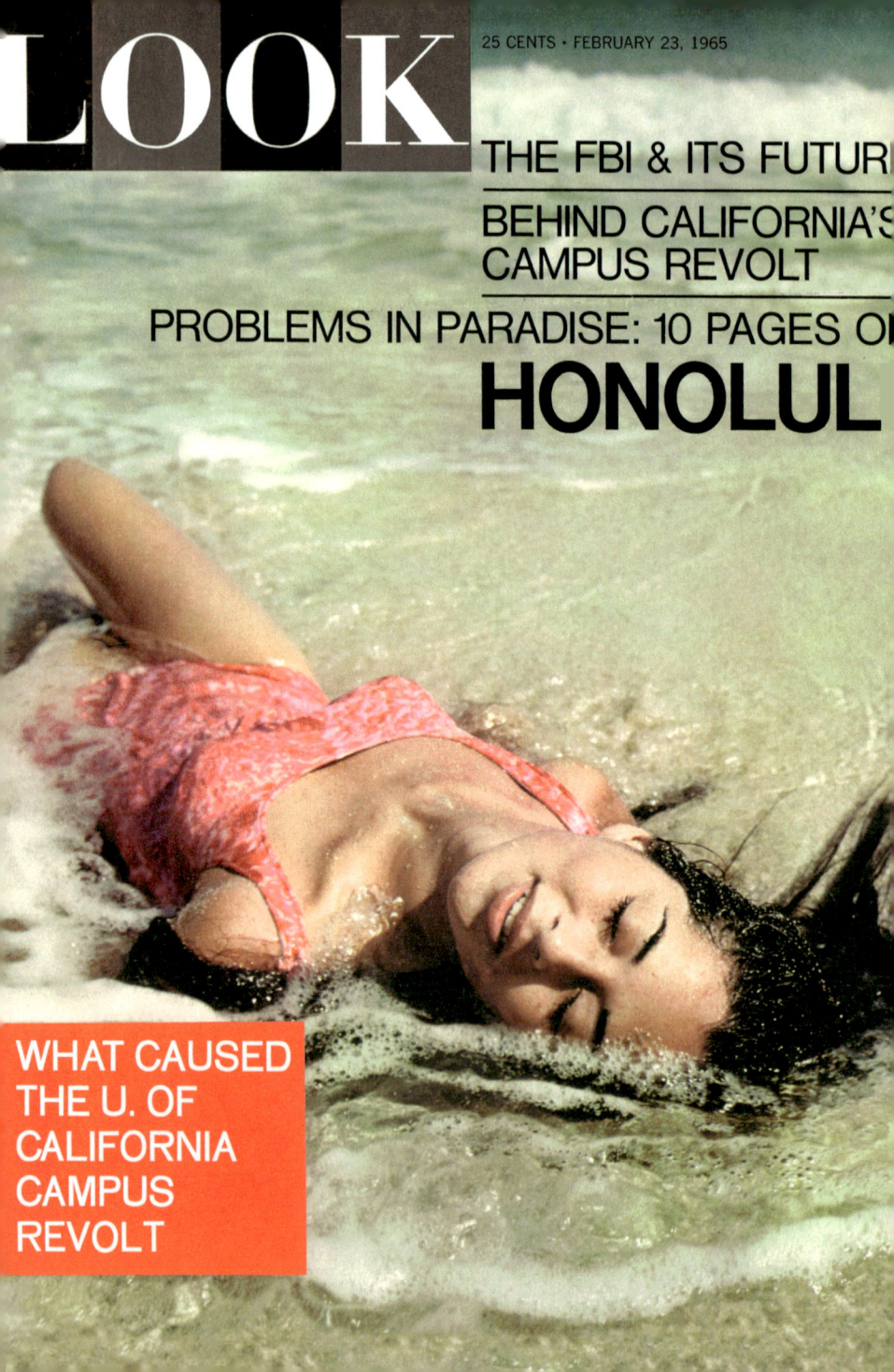

LOOK

25 CENTS · FEBRUARY 23, 1965

THE FBI & ITS FUTUR

BEHIND CALIFORNIA'S CAMPUS REVOLT

PROBLEMS IN PARADISE: 10 PAGES O

HONOLUL

WHAT CAUSED THE U. OF CALIFORNIA CAMPUS REVOLT

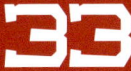

TIKI DEVOLUTION

TIKIS NIEDERGANG
LA DÉCADENCE DE TIKI

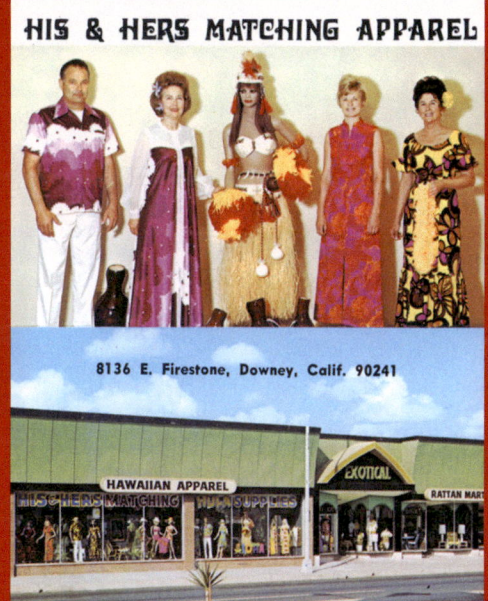

BY THE MID-1960s, AMERICA'S tropical fantasy was fading: Tiki Pop was losing its mass appeal. Postwar baby boomers found their parents' Polynesian posturing somewhat ridiculous, their attitudes toward native cultures patronizing. *Look* magazine sported a Hawaiian cover girl decidedly not dressed in the iconic hula skirt, and its cover lines told of "Problems in Paradise" and California university students revolting. Commercialism had begun to corrupt the very core of the Tiki Pop concept: the fantasy of a paradise in its pristine state, uncontaminated by civilization. Developers, seeing dollars, began destroying exactly what Americans were seeking. Beaches were bulldozed for high-rise resorts; cars raced feet from the sand on multilane highways. Capitalism had found its vacation spot.

Somehow, too, the South Seas fantasy had become its own punch line, a parody of itself to those not engaged in it. While there were still many who frequented Polynesian restaurants and participated in backyard luaus, they were mostly people who were now being labeled as "the establishment": middle-aged, well-off, conservative whites, out of touch with America's changing ideals. These people were "square"—embarrassingly so to their kids.

In 1965, half of the American population was under the age of 25. They benefitted from a better standard of living than their Depression-era parents had, and they were better educated: whereas less than half of all pre-World War II Americans had graduated from high school, by the 1960s, three out of four young people were attending college.

With their financial stability and perceived intellectual superiority, '60s youth formed their own opinions and shunned

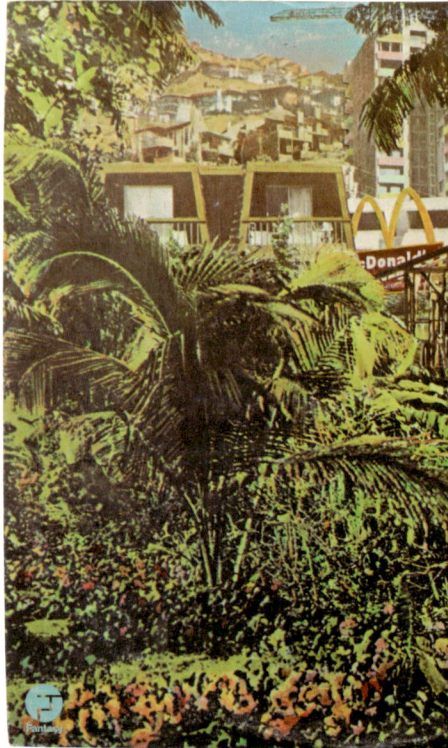

their parents' values and modes of entertainment. The titillation of *Playboy* magazine and depictions of bare-breasted wahines were now considered sexist.

The "future generation" was intent on changing America's values. From a woman's place in the working world to racial equality, beliefs once held sacrosanct by Americans were turned on their heads. The young rebelled against their elders however they could: psychedelic music and long hair aggravated hardworking fathers and worrying mothers. The gap between the beliefs and ideologies of the two generations widened to never-before-seen proportions.

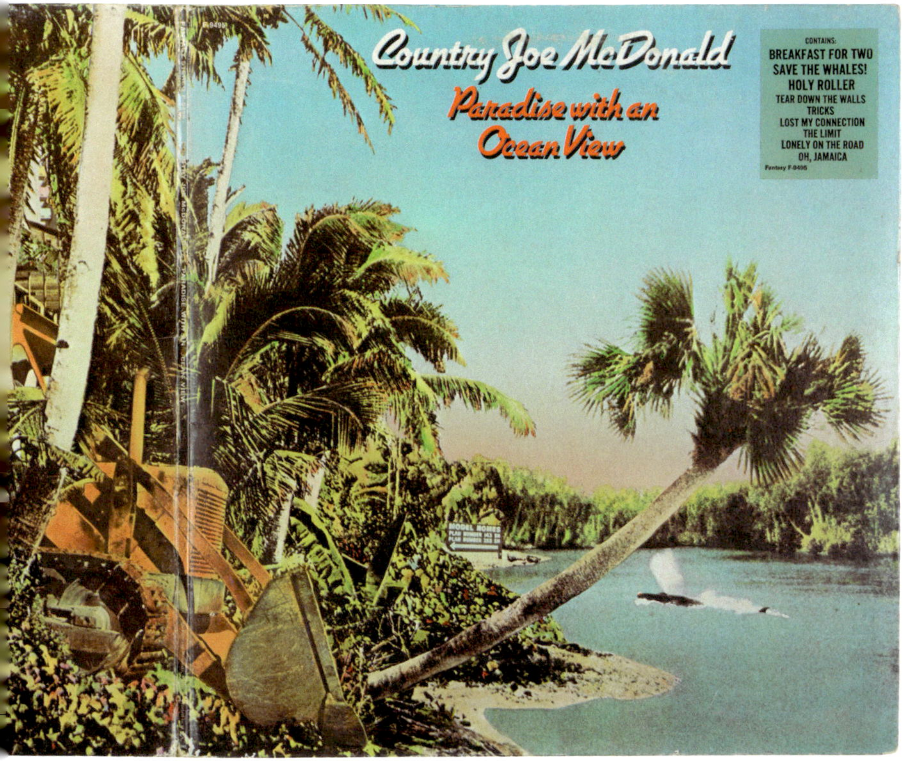

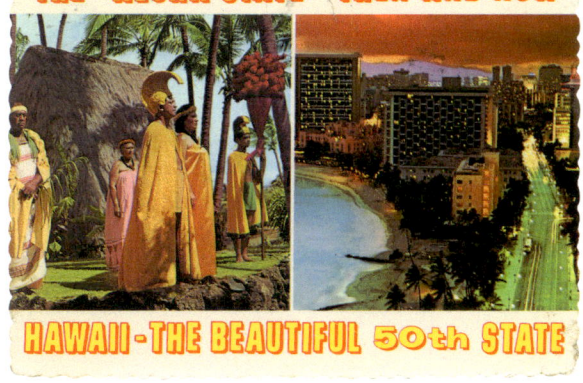

ABOVE: "They paved paradise and put up a parking lot"
—Joni Mitchell, 1970

LEFT: Before and After: paradise lost through its construction

A gallery of Tiki Pop clowns,
as seen by their children:
BELOW: Old fogey!
OPPOSITE ABOVE, LEFT: Nerdsville!
OPPOSITE BELOW: Embarassing!

OPPOSITE ABOVE, RIGHT: Their
children's form of recreation

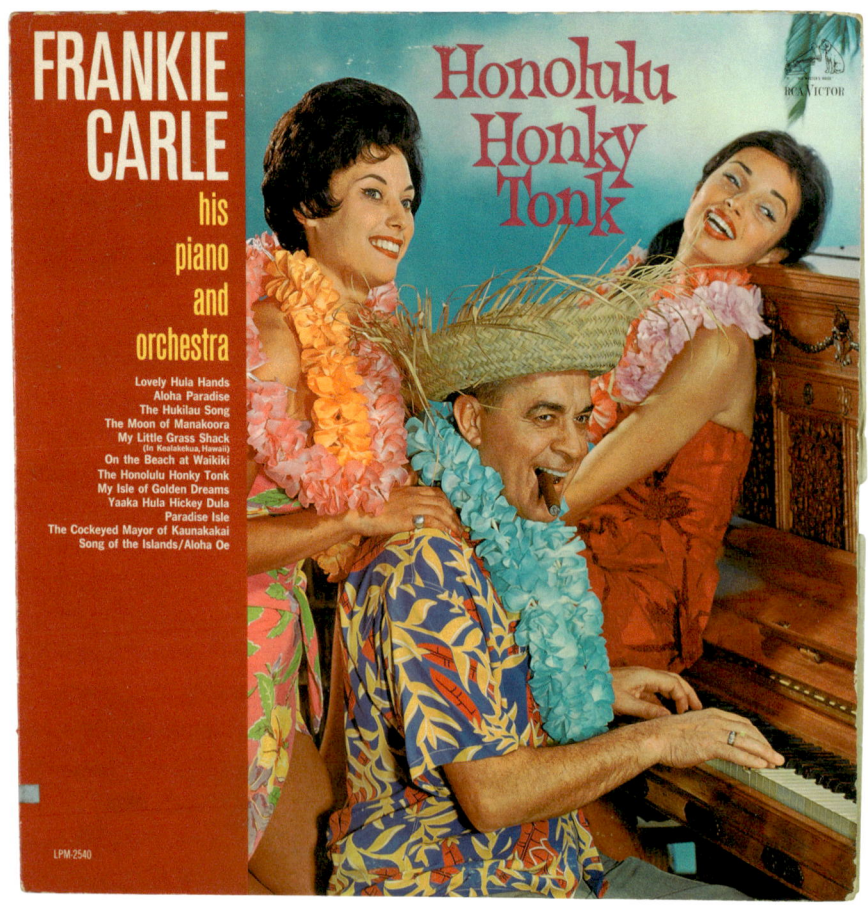

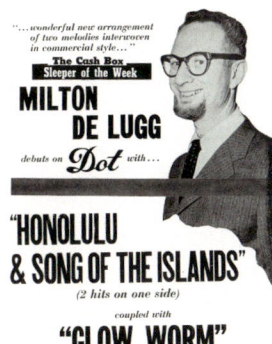

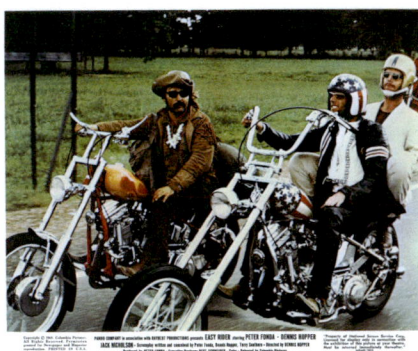

As the Tiki cocktail devolved into artificially flavored, syrupy concoctions, marijuana and LSD became the preferred recreational drugs of the young set. Whereas their parents sought temporary refuge from civilization, '60s youth wanted their psychedelic paradise now. They expanded their consciousnesses with alternative forms of religion and mind-altering drugs; to them, the definition of an earthly Eden was finding a new way of thinking that would lead to a state of peace of love.

With the shocking assassination of President Kennedy in 1963, the American dream began to fracture. The violent underbelly of America emerged, giving way to expressions of anger that World War II vets couldn't have imagined would ever occur on their home front. Homicide rates more than doubled between 1955 and 1970. The growing dissatisfaction affected popular culture. Instead of lighthearted Technicolor musical comedies set in faraway lands, movies began to portray "real life": films full of car chases and shoot-outs revolved around antiheroes whose frustration landed them on the wrong side of the law. Underdogs and misfits became the central characters, trying to find justice in

an America that had traded its humanistic values for the corporate dollar.

The escalation of the Vietnam War (1956–1975) polarized America: whereas the more conservative population supported the fight, most opposed putting the nation's young men in harm's way on faraway shores. The U.S. was not being threatened by foreign oppressors; instead, it was seen

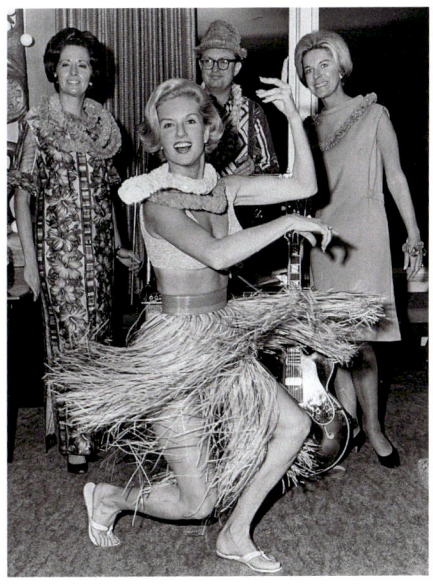

as the aggressor. The My Lai Massacre of 1968 confirmed the worst fears: not all American soldiers were the noble liberators of mankind they had been in World War II. The ghosts of Wounded Knee came haunting.

With the anti–Vietnam War movement, the old guard's politics were called into question. Their children viewed their Machiavellian maneuverings as corrupt and immoral, and they worked hard to expose their leaders' criminal dealings. The new Americans refused to participate in the status quo and everything that had been part of it. Tiki Pop had been the favorite pastime of the establishment and was now deemed outdated and politically incorrect.

American Tiki met the same fate as its Polynesian antecedents. Its idols were abandoned and discarded on the trash heap of passé pop cultures. Almost as fast as Tiki rose to prominence, it was disowned with a sense of embarrassment and denial. By the 1980s, most Tiki temples had been shuttered, and the word *Tiki* faded from the American language.

In America's wholesale rejection of Tiki Pop, works of artistic merit—wood carvings, interiors, signage, and architecture—were destroyed to make way for "better" things, and soon Tiki was completely forgotten. Another generation passed before what little still remained was rediscovered and reappreciated for its creative value.

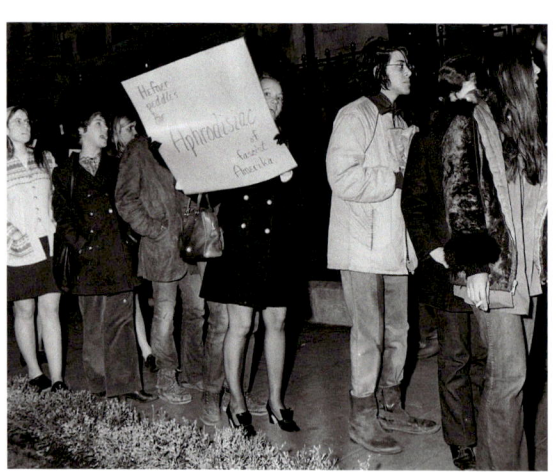 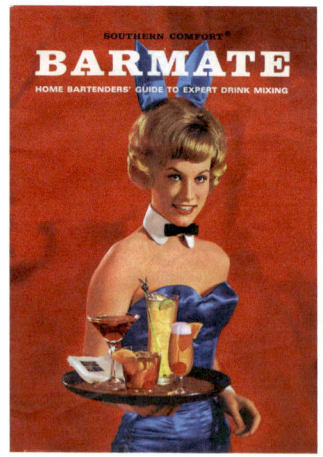

ABOVE LEFT: Once Nazi hunters, now fascists?

ABOVE RIGHT: Not sexy—sexist!

OPPOSITE: Tiki-geezers leering after a nude maiden

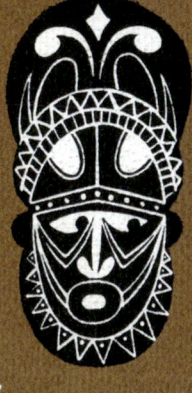

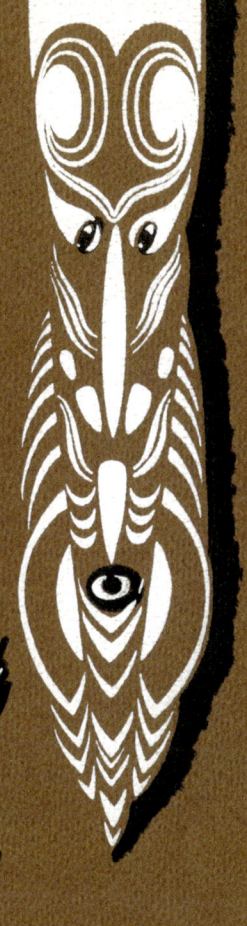

TRADER VIC'S

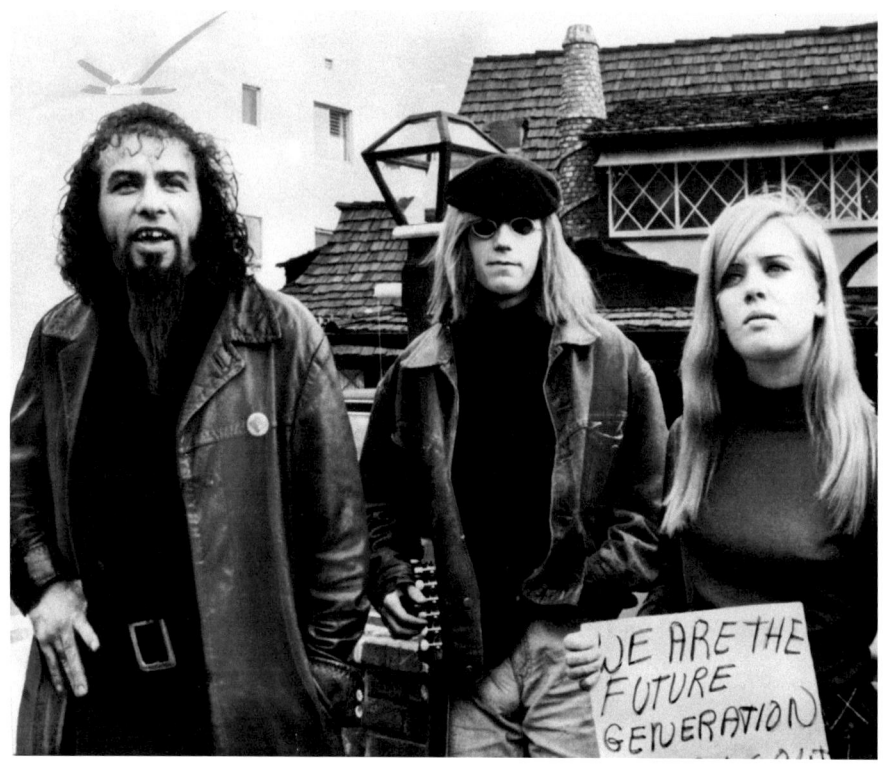

MITTE DER 1960er-JAHRE BEGANN
Amerikas Tropenfantasie zu verblassen:
Der Tiki-Pop verlor seinen Reiz für die
Massen. Die Babyboomer fanden das
polynesische Getue ihrer Eltern lächerlich,
ihre Haltung gegenüber einheimischen
Kulturen herablassend. Das Magazin
Look zeigte ein hawaiisches Mädchen
auf seinem Cover, das bewusst nicht in
einen Hula-Rock gekleidet war. Der Titel
verkündete „Probleme im Paradies" und
berichtete über rebellierende Studenten
an den Universitäten Kaliforniens. Die
Kommerzialisierung hatte begonnen, das
Konzept des Tiki-Pop in seinem Kern zu
zerstören: den Traum von einem Paradies

in seiner reinsten Form, unbeschadet von
der Zivilisation. Bauunternehmer mit
Dollarzeichen in den Augen zerstörten
genau das, wonach die Amerikaner suchten. Strände wurden mit hoch aufragenden
Resorts zugebaut, Autos rasten nur wenige
Meter vom Strand entfernt auf mehrspu-
rigen Highways vorbei. Der Kapitalismus
hatte sein Urlaubsziel gefunden.

Die Südseefantasie war zu ihrer eigenen
Parodie geworden für jene, die nicht an ihr
teilhatten. Es gab immer noch viele Menschen, die in polynesische Restaurants gingen oder Garten-Luaus veranstalteten – nur
wurden diese jetzt dem „Establishment"
zugerechnet: wohlsituierte, konservative

Weiße mittleren Alters, die den Bezug zu den sich verändernden Idealen Amerikas verloren hatten. Es waren „Spießer", die ihren Kindern peinlich waren.

1965 war die Hälfte der Bevölkerung der USA jünger als 25 Jahre. Die jungen Amerikaner genossen nicht nur einem besseren Lebensstandard als ihre Eltern, die während der Weltwirtschaftskrise aufgewachsen waren, sondern auch eine bessere Bildung. Hatte in der Vorkriegsgeneration kaum die Hälfte der Jugendlichen einen Highschool-Abschluss, gingen in den 1960er-Jahren drei von vier aufs College. Ihre finanzielle Sicherheit und ihre gefühlte intellektuelle Überlegenheit waren mitverantwortlich dafür, dass sich die Jugend der 1960er-Jahre von den Werten und Unterhaltungsformen ihrer Eltern abwandte. Der *Playboy* und die Abbildungen barbusiger Wahine galten nun als sexistisch.

Die „Generation der Zukunft" war fest entschlossen, Amerikas Wertvorstellungen zu verändern. Von der Stellung der Frau in der Arbeitswelt bis zu Fragen der Diskriminierung von Afroamerikanern – die Jugend rebellierte auf jede nur erdenkliche Weise gegen die Älteren. Psychedelische Musik und lange Haare verärgerten hart arbeitende Väter und besorgte Mütter. Die Lücke zwischen den Glaubenssätzen und Ideologien beider Generationen wuchs auf nie zuvor gesehene Dimensionen an.

Als der Tiki-Cocktail zu einem künstlich aromatisierten siruppartigen Gebräu verkam, wurden Marihuana und LSD die bevorzugten Drogen der jungen Leute. Während ihre Eltern der Zivilisation nur temporär entfliehen wollten, kämpfte die Jugend der 1960er-Jahre für ein psychedelisches Paradies im Hier und Jetzt. Sie erweiterte ihr Bewusstsein mit alternativen

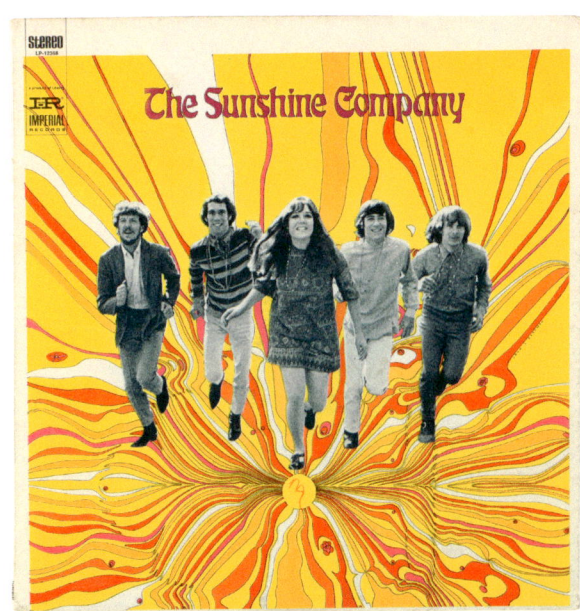

OPPOSITE: We know where it's at!

RIGHT: The new look

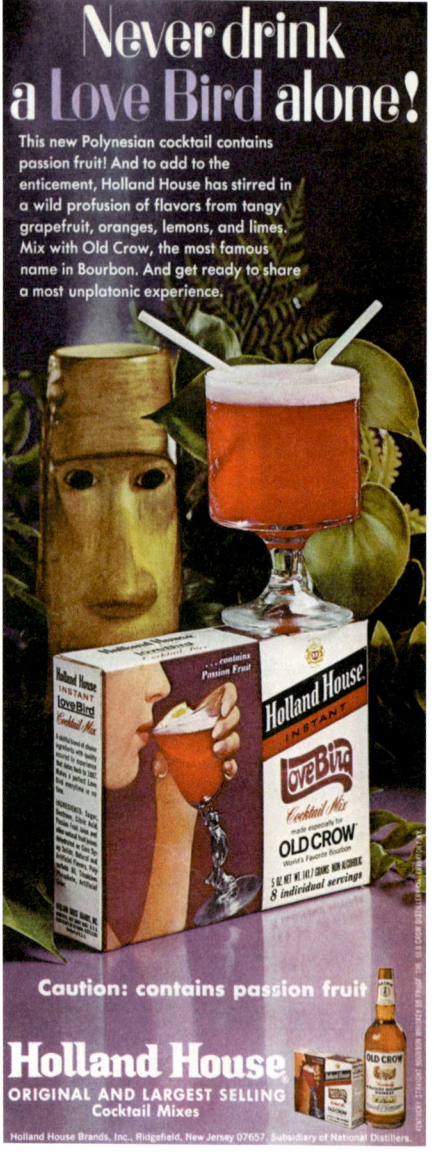

Im abgebildeten Werbebild:

Never drink a Love Bird alone!

This new Polynesian cocktail contains passion fruit! And to add to the enticement, Holland House has stirred in a wild profusion of flavors from tangy grapefruit, oranges, lemons, and limes. Mix with Old Crow, the most famous name in Bourbon. And get ready to share a most unplatonic experience.

...contains Passion Fruit

Holland House
INSTANT
Love Bird
Cocktail Mix
made especially for
OLD CROW
World's Favorite Bourbon
5 OZ NET WT. 141.7 GRAMS NON ALCOHOLIC
8 individual servings

Caution: contains passion fruit

Holland House
ORIGINAL AND LARGEST SELLING
Cocktail Mixes

Holland House Brands, Inc., Ridgefield, New Jersey 07657. Subsidiary of National Distillers.

Religionsformen und bewusstseinsverändernden Drogen. Für sie definierte sich ein irdischer Garten Eden durch neue Denkweisen, die Frieden und Liebe förderten.

Nach der Ermordung von Präsident Kennedy im Jahr 1963 begann der amerikanische Traum zu bröckeln. Die gewalttätige Schattenseite der USA kam zum Vorschein, wie sie sich die Veteranen des Zweiten Weltkriegs nie hatten vorstellen können. Zwischen 1955 und 1970 verdoppelten sich die Mordraten. Die steigende Unzufriedenheit nahm auch Einfluss auf die Popkultur. Statt fröhlichen Musikkomödien, die in fernen Ländern spielten, porträtierten die Filme nun das „wahre Leben". Die Geschichten waren gespickt mit Verfolgungsjagden und Schießereien. Im Zentrum standen oft Antihelden, deren Frust sie auf die falsche Seite des Gesetzes trieb. Underdogs und Außenseiter suchten in einem Amerika nach Gerechtigkeit, das seine humanistischen Werte gegen Geld eingetauscht hatte.

Die Eskalation des Vietnamkriegs (1956–1975) spaltete das Land: Die konservative Bevölkerung unterstützte die Kämpfe, doch die meisten waren dagegen, dass die jungen Männer in der Ferne täglich ihr Leben aufs Spiel setzten. Die USA wurden nicht von fremden Mächten unterdrückt, sie waren die Angreifer. Das Massaker von My Lai 1968 bestätigte die schlimmsten Ängste: Nicht alle US-Soldaten waren die noblen Befreier, die man aus dem Zweiten Weltkrieg kannte. Die Geister von Wounded Knee suchten das Land erneut heim.

Die Anti-Kriegsbewegung sorgte dafür, dass die Politik der alten Garde infrage

An instant Tiki cocktail—how convenient!

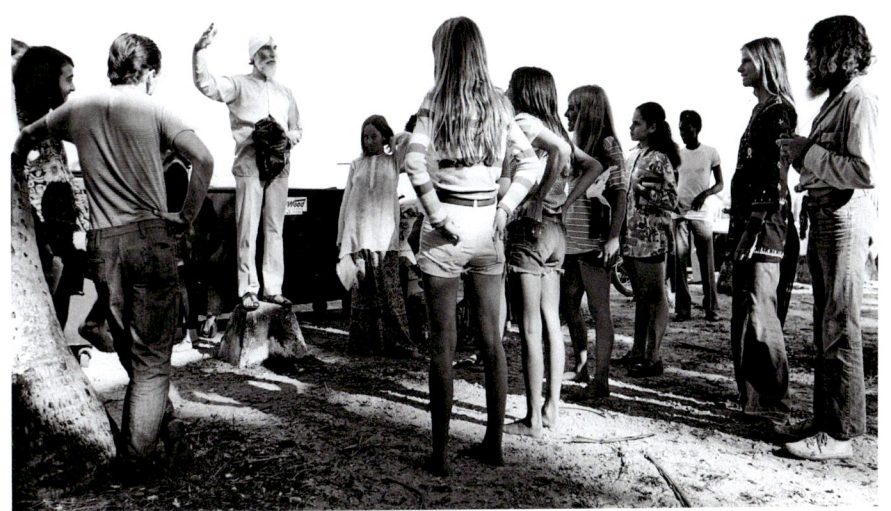

gestellt wurde. Die Jugend empfand deren machiavellistisches Verhalten als korrupt und unmoralisch und arbeitete hart daran, die kriminellen Machenschaften der Landesführer aufzudecken. Der Tiki-Pop hatte zur Freizeitkultur des Establishments gehört und galt somit nun als überholt und politisch inkorrekt.

Den amerikanischen Tiki ereilte dasselbe Schicksal wie seine polynesischen Vorfahren. Von der einstigen Zuneigung zu den Götterfiguren wollte man nichts mehr wissen und sie wurden auf dem Müllberg vergangener Popkulturen entsorgt. Fast so schnell wie Tiki aufgestiegen ist, wurde er mit einem Gefühl von Verlegenheit wieder verstoßen. Bis zu den 1980er-Jahren waren die meisten Tiki-Tempel verlassen und der Name begann

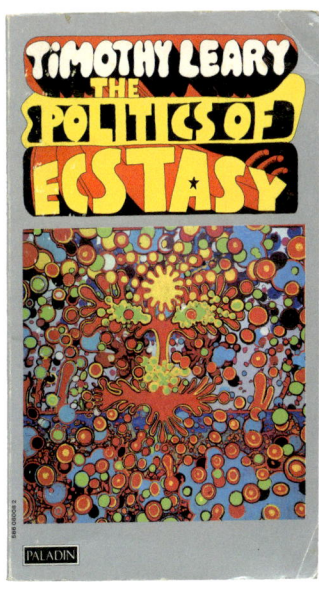

TOP: Yogi Rama prophesizes a new age on Miami Beach, Florida

ABOVE: Wisdom in a pill

aus dem amerikanischen Sprachgebrauch zu verschwinden.

Diese generelle Zurückweisung des Tiki-Pop führte dazu, dass Werke von hohem künstlerischen Wert – Holzschnitzereien, Einrichtungsgegenstände, Schilder und Gebäude – zerstört wurden, um Platz für „Besseres" zu schaffen. Bald war der Tiki in Vergessenheit geraten. Erst eine ganze Generation später wurden die kärglichen Überreste wiederentdeckt und aufgrund ihrer künstlerischen und kulturgeschicht-lichen Bedeutung geschätzt.

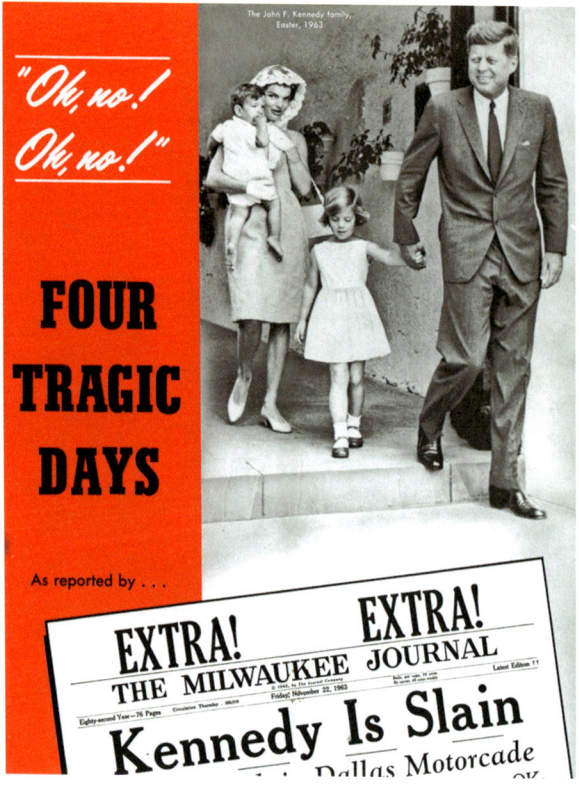

LEFT: America's fall from grace

OPPOSITE ABOVE: Tiki Liquors was now a crime scene *(Scott Schell Collection)*

OPPOSITE BELOW: Car-chase/shoot-out movies became a genre of their own

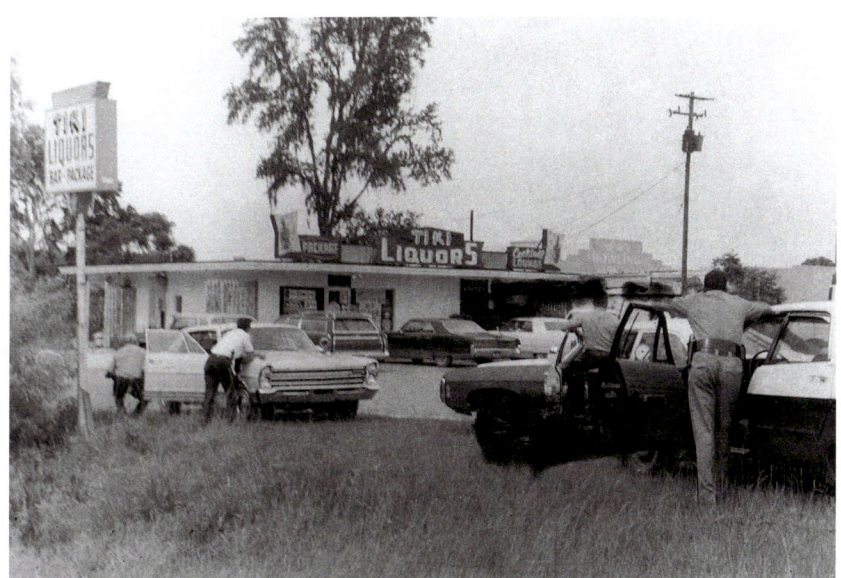

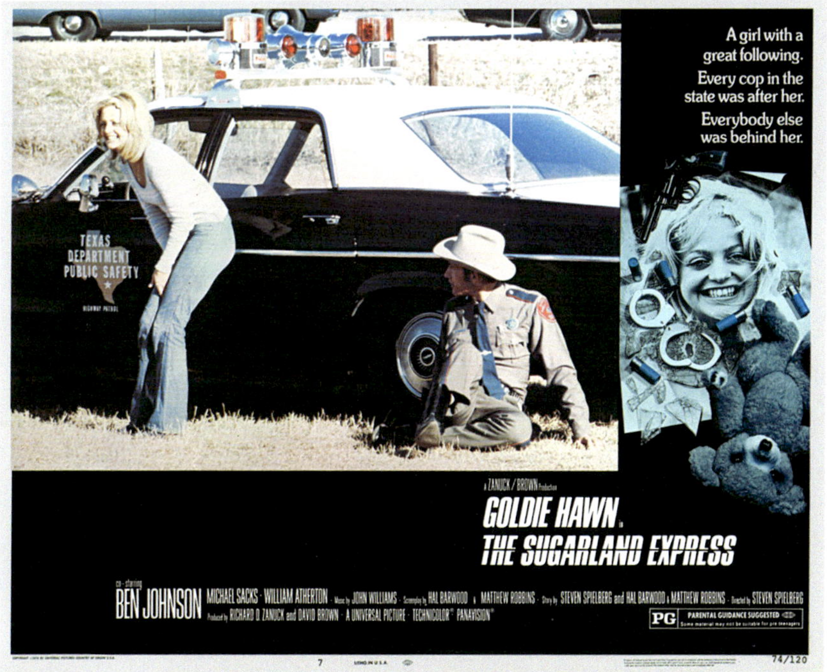

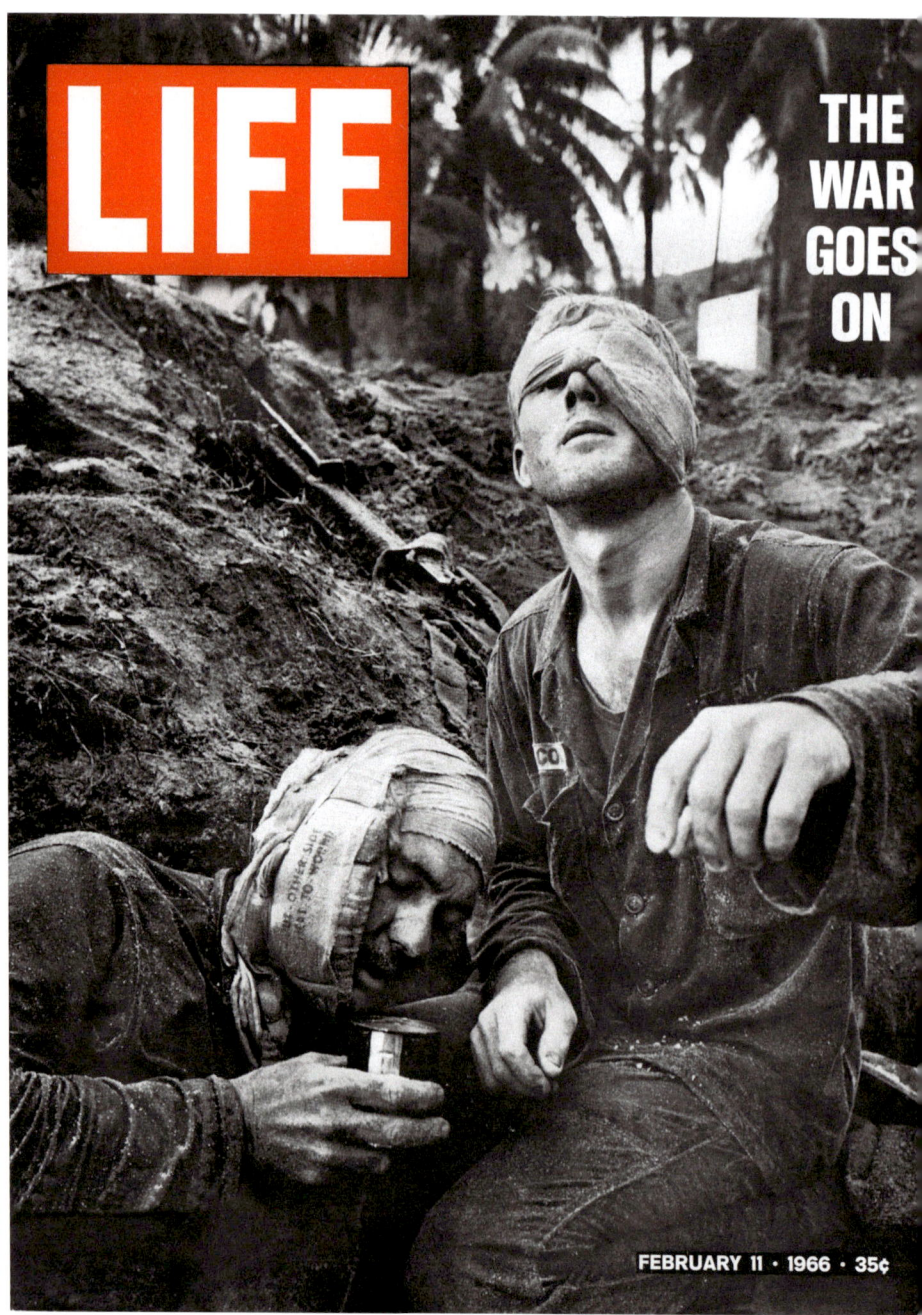

LIFE

THE
WAR
GOES
ON

FEBRUARY 11 · 1966 · 35¢

VERS LE MILIEU DES ANNÉES 1960, l'imaginaire tropical américain était en perte de vitesse : le style tiki pop avait cessé de fasciner le grand public. Les baby-boomers d'après-guerre jugeaient les simagrées polynésiennes de leurs parents un peu ridicules, leurs attitudes envers les cultures autochtones plutôt condescendantes. Le magazine Look arborait en couverture une cover-girl hawaiienne surtout pas vêtue de la jupe hula emblématique, et son titre évoquait des « Problèmes au paradis », faisant allusion aux étudiants californiens alors en pleine révolte.

Le mercantilisme avait commencé à corrompre le cœur même du concept tiki pop : le fantasme d'un paradis demeuré intact, non contaminé par la civilisation. Les promoteurs du divertissement, ayant flairé le bon filon, commencèrent à détruire exactement ce que recherchaient les Américains. Les plages furent passées au bulldozer pour bâtir des stations balnéaires de grande hauteur ; les voitures fonçaient sur des autoroutes à plusieurs voies à quelques mètres seulement du sable chaud. Le capitalisme avait bel et bien jeté son dévolu sur les lieux de vacances.

D'une certaine manière aussi, le fantasme des mers du Sud avait fini, pour ceux que le concept laissaient de glace, par virer au gag, réduit à une simple parodie de lui-même. Si un large public fréquentait encore les restaurants polynésiens ou organisaient des *luau* dans leur jardin, il s'agissait pour la plupart de gens appartenant à l'establishment des Blancs conservateurs, plutôt nantis, d'âge mûr, ayant perdu le contact avec

l'évolution des idéaux de l'Amérique. Ces américains-là étaient « vieux jeu » – au point d'embarrasser leurs enfants.

En 1965, la moitié de la population américaine était âgée de moins de 25 ans. Ces jeunes gens bénéficiaient d'un meilleur niveau de vie que leurs parents nés pendant la Grande Dépression et ils étaient mieux éduqués : alors que moins de la moitié des Américains d'avant la Seconde Guerre mondiale avaient décroché son

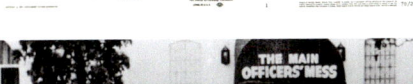

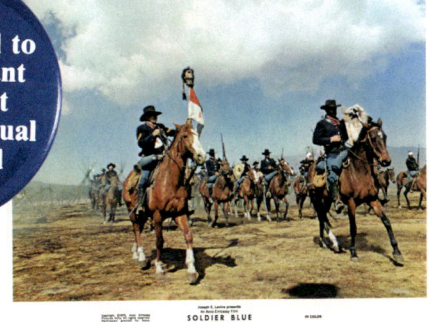

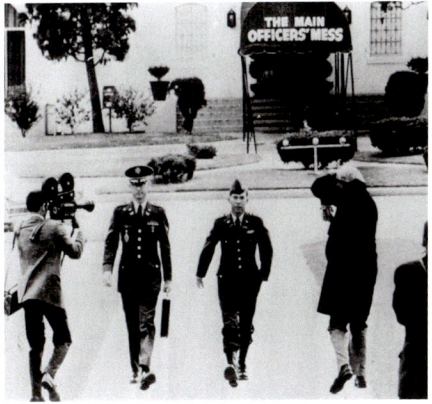

OPPOSITE: How long was this supposed to go on?

ABOVE: The crimes of the forefathers repeated themselves

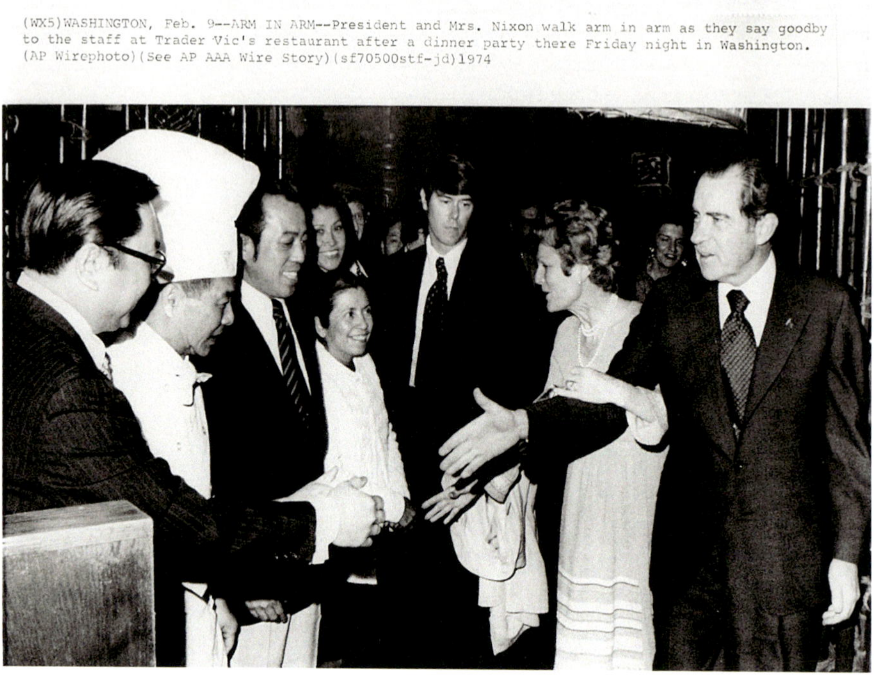

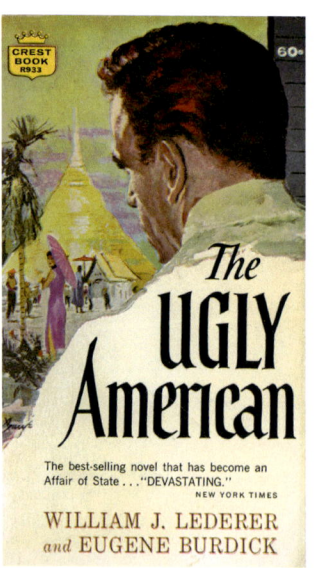

The

UGLY
American

The best-selling novel that has become an Affair of State..."DEVASTATING."

NEW YORK TIMES

WILLIAM J. LEDERER
and EUGENE BURDICK

ABOVE: Richard Nixon at his favorite restaurant, six months before he was forced to resign

LEFT: His image was tainted

OPPOSITE ABOVE: It was time for Tiki to retire *(Timothy Haack Collection)*

OPPOSITE BELOW: American Gothic, Polynesian pop-style

diplôme d'études secondaires, dans les années 1960, trois jeunes gens sur quatre fréquentaient l'université.

Leur stabilité financière et leur supériorité intellectuelle supposée encouragea la jeunesse des sixties à se forger ses propres opinions et à refuser les valeurs et les distractions de leurs parents. L'excitation que pouvaient offrir des magazines comme *Playboy*, ou les représentations de vahinés aux seins nus étaient désormais considérées comme sexistes.

La « génération future » avait la ferme intention de changer les valeurs de l'Amérique. De la place des femmes dans le monde du travail à l'égalité raciale, les opinions jusque-là révérées par les Américains se virent déboulonnées. Les jeunes se révoltaient contre leurs aînés comme ils

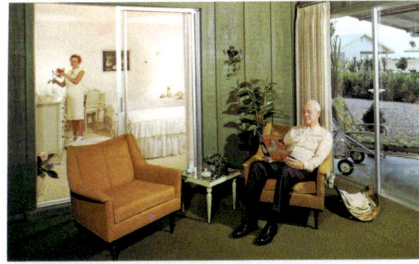

The lanai provides a place for those golden moments of privacy

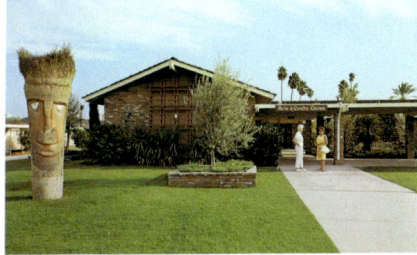

The beautiful Arts and Crafts building is typical of Sun City's facilities

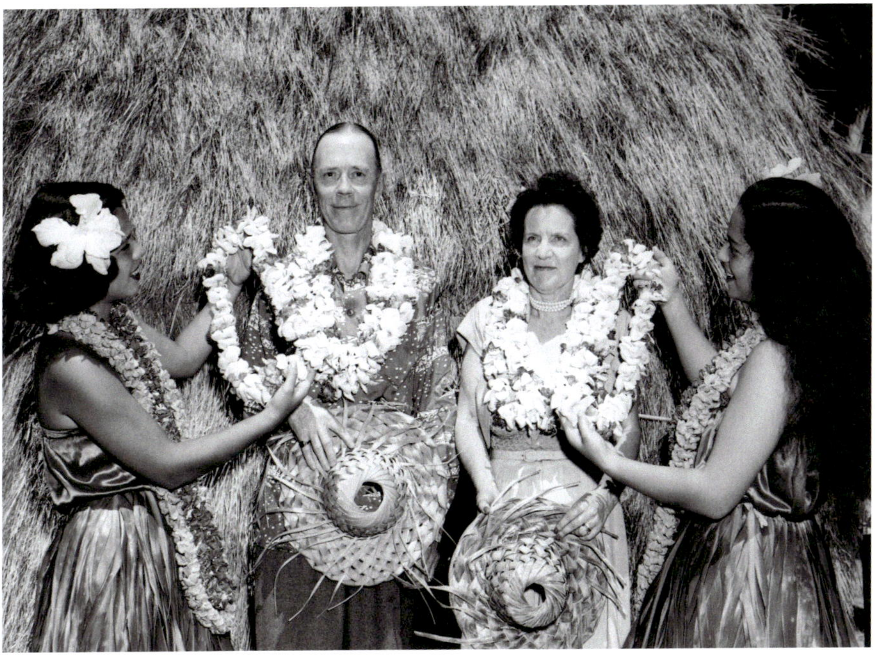

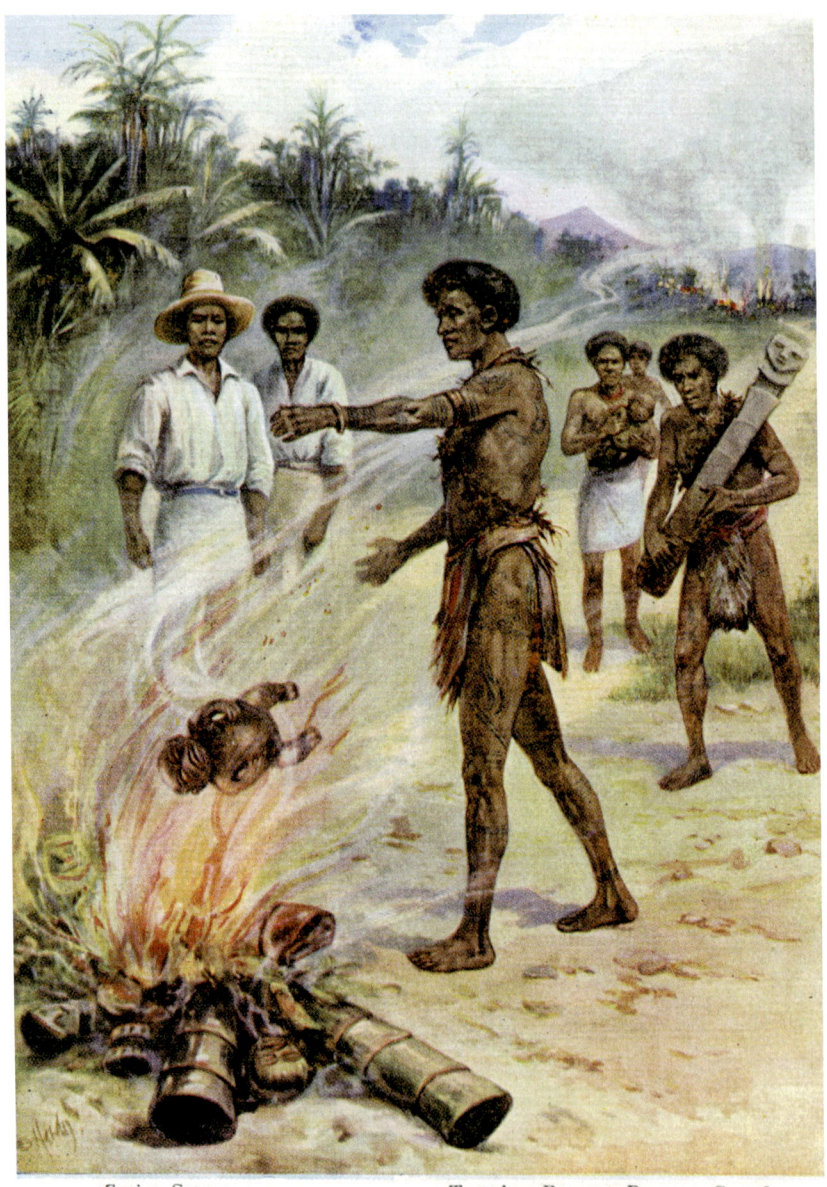

Series Seven.   THE ALL BRITISH PICTURE CO., LTD

The burning of the idols.

le pouvaient : musique psychédélique et cheveux agaçaient les pères qui travaillaient dur, comme les mères inquiètes. Le fossé entre les croyances et les idéologies des deux générations se creusa alors dans des proportions jusque-là inédites.

Tandis que le cocktail tiki tournait à la décoction sirupeuse d'arômes artificiels, la marijuana et le LSD devenaient les drogues récréatives préférées de la jeunesse. Là où leurs parents avaient cherché un refuge temporaire hors de la civilisation, les jeunes des années 1960 voulaient leur paradis psychédélique tout de suite. Ils élargissaient leur champ de conscience en recourant aux religions alternatives ou aux psychotropes ; pour eux, la définition du paradis terrestre consistait à trouver une nouvelle façon de penser qui devait conduire à l'instauration de l'amour et de la paix.

Avec le choc de l'assassinat du président Kennedy en 1963, le rêve américain commença à se lézarder. La violence souterraine de l'Amérique déborda, avec des manifestations de colère que les vétérans de la Seconde Guerre mondiale n'auraient jamais imaginé devoir affronter dans la mère patrie. Le taux d'homicides fera plus que doubler entre 1955 et 1970. Une insatisfaction croissante ronge la culture populaire. Au lieu de comédies musicales légères en technicolor tournées dans des contrées lointaines, les films commencent à représenter la «vraie vie » : bourrés de poursuites en voiture et de fusillades, ils sont interprétés par des antihéros qui accumulent les frustrations et finissent par se révolter contre les lois. Laissés-pour-compte et marginaux sont désormais des figures centrales en quête de justice dans une Amérique qui a troqué ses valeurs humanistes contre une poignée de dollars.

L'escalade de la guerre du Vietnam (1956-1975) coupe l'Amérique en deux : alors que les secteurs les plus conservateurs de la population soutiennent l'option militaire, la plupart des Américains refusent de voir les jeunes hommes de la nation risquer leur vie sur des rivages lointains. Les États-Unis ne sont pas menacés par des agresseurs étrangers ; tout au contraire, ce sont eux qui sont considérés comme les agresseurs. Le massacre de My Lai en 1968 confirme les pires craintes : certains soldats américains sont bien loin des nobles libérateurs de l'humanité qu'ils furent lors de la Seconde Guerre mondiale. Les fantômes de Wounded Knee reviennent hanter la mémoire collective.

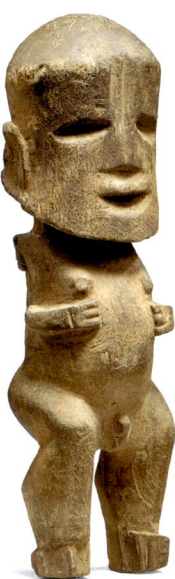

OPPOSITE: Casting out the old gods
(Scott Schell Collection)

ABOVE: A weathered Tahitian deity
(Musée du Quai Branly Collection)

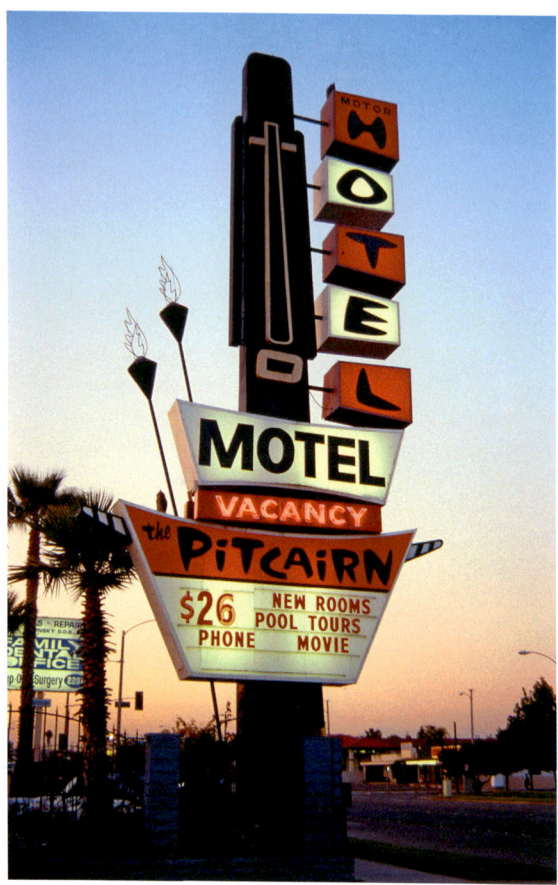

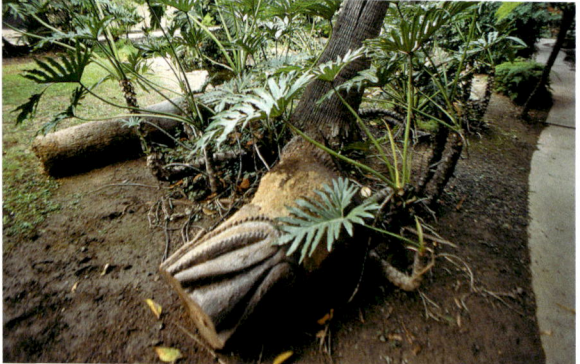

LEFT: Pitcairn Motel sign, Anaheim, California, 1961

BELOW: Tiki chainsaw massacre

OPPOSITE LEFT: Tiki termination: the end of a dream
(Frank Brajevic Collection)

OPPOSITE RIGHT: The Pitcairn sign before its imminent demise in 1998

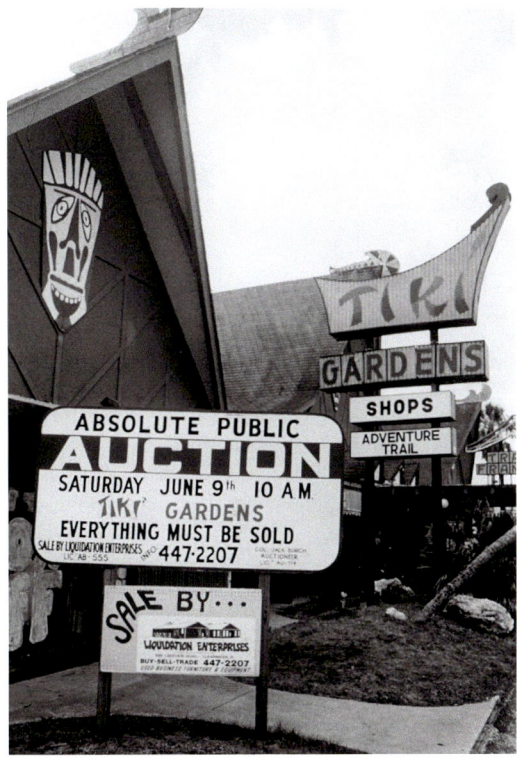

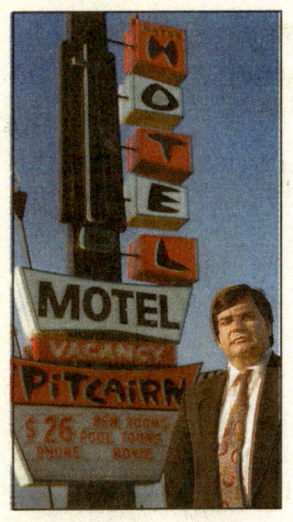

Avec le mouvement anti-guerre du Vietnam, la politique de la vieille garde est remise en question. La jeune génération juge corrompues et immorales ses manœuvres machiavéliques, et elle s'évertue à démasquer les agissements criminels de ses dirigeants. Les nouveaux Américains refusent de participer au *statu quo* et à tout ce qui le constituait. Passe-temps favori de l'establishment, le tiki pop est désormais considéré comme dépassé et politiquement incorrect.

Le tiki américain aura donc connu le même sort que ses prédécesseurs polynésiens. Ses idoles seront abandonnées et jetées sur les tas d'ordures des cultures populaires du passé. Presque aussi vite qu'il a accédé à la notoriété, Tiki sera désavoué dans un mélange d'embarras et de déni. Dans les années 1980, la plupart des temples ferment, et le mot « tiki » disparaît de la langue américaine.

Avec le rejet global du tiki pop par l'Amérique, des œuvres de valeur, sculptures en bois, décors, panneaux de signalisation, et bâtiments divers sont détruits pour faire place à des objets « meilleurs » et Tiki ne tarde pas à sombrer dans un complet oubli. Une autre génération s'écoulera avant que le peu qui avait subsisté soit redécouvert et sa valeur créative réappréciée.

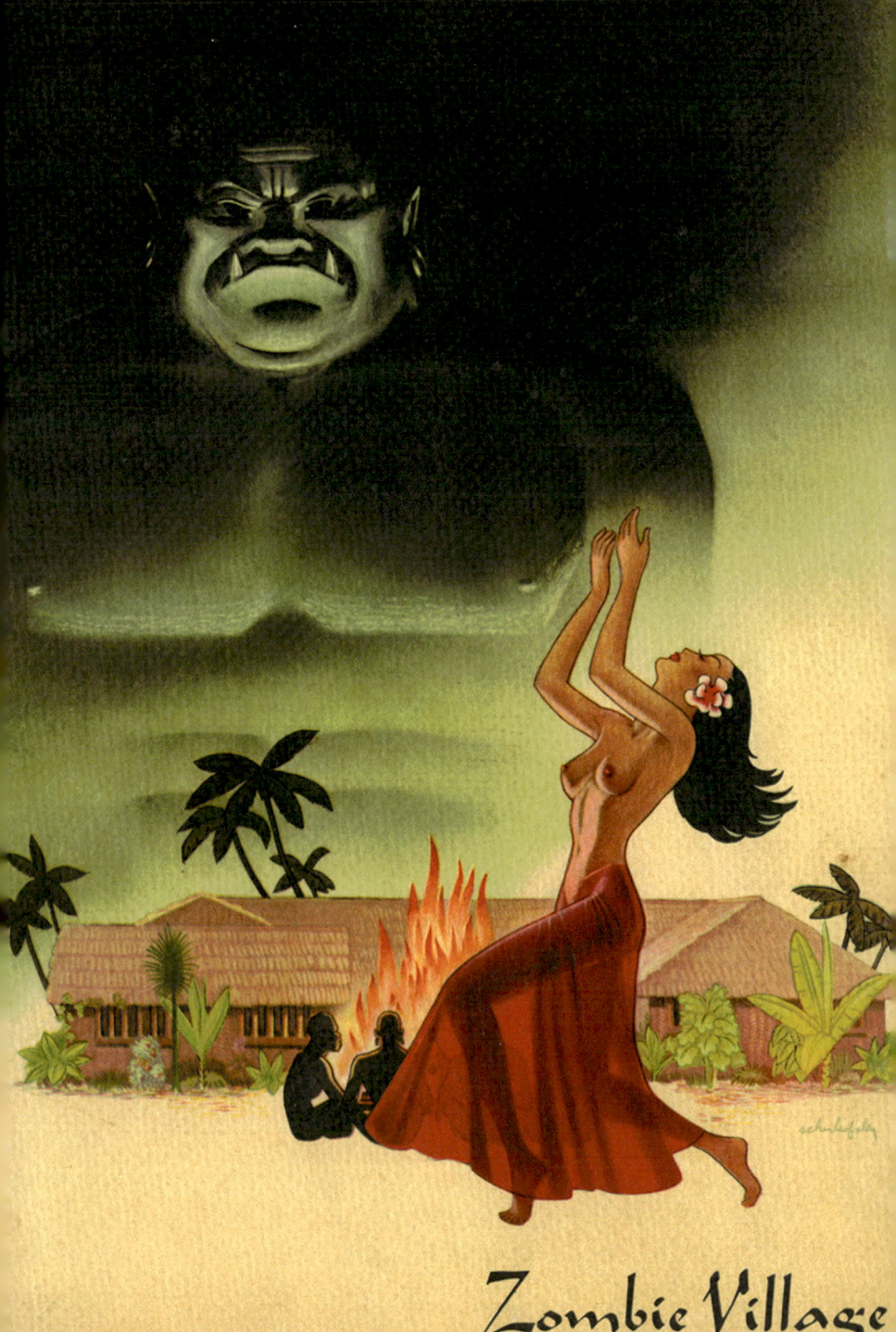

Zombie Village

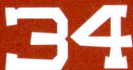

34

THE TIKI REVIVAL

DAS TIKI-REVIVAL
TIKI, LE RETOUR

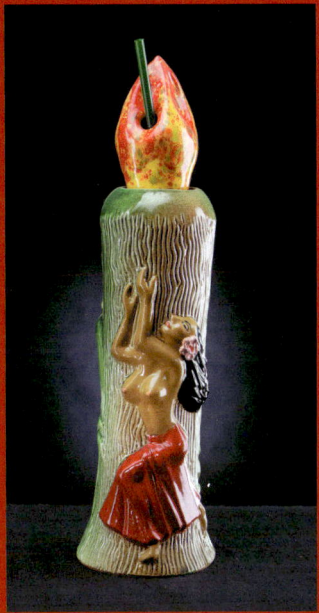

OPPOSITE: Zombie Village menu cover, 1950s
(Frank Brajevic Collection)

ABOVE: Zombie Village mug by Wendy Cevola
(Scott Mabbutt Collection)

BY THE EARLY 1990s, TIKI WAS ALL BUT forgotten. But ex-adherents of punk and new wave music, always fond of the different and obscure, began to appreciate the then-unfashionable lounge and exotica tunes of the cocktail generation. While excavating old LPs from record stacks at secondhand stores, vinyl archaeologists also came across Tiki mugs, and they began to collect them as well. Other remnants, like restaurant matchbooks and menus, also surfaced.

Although these were pre-Internet days, aficionados managed to network, and they met at homes and restaurants to share their finds. In Los Angeles, early enthusiasts included this book's author; the musician, artist, and vintage-store owner Josh Agle—now better known as Shag—whose colorful Tiki- and cocktail-laden paintings are highly collected; and Otto von Stroheim, who in 1995 published the first Tiki-related magazine, *Tiki News*. Now isolated Tiki seekers scattered across America realized that they were not alone.

Also in this mix was Jeff "Beachbum" Berry, who not only collected mugs, but also was unearthing long-lost tropical-drink recipes, which were to inform the "craft cocktail" movement in the ensuing decade. His first book, 1998's *Grog Log*, is now the standard of every Tiki Revival bar.

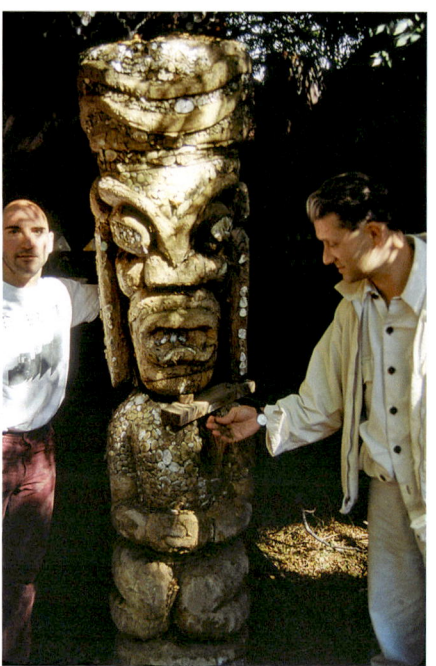

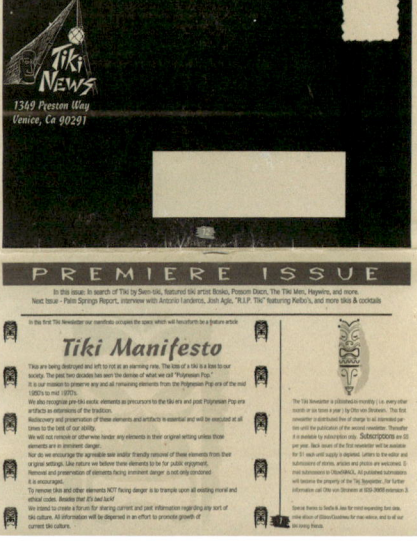

ABOVE RIGHT: Urban archaeologists Otto von Stroheim and Sven Kirsten inspect a find at the Tikis, 1994

RIGHT: First issue of *Tiki News*, 1995

OPPOSITE: Limited-edition barstool, collaboration between Paul Frank and Shag, 2000
(Naomi Alper Collection)

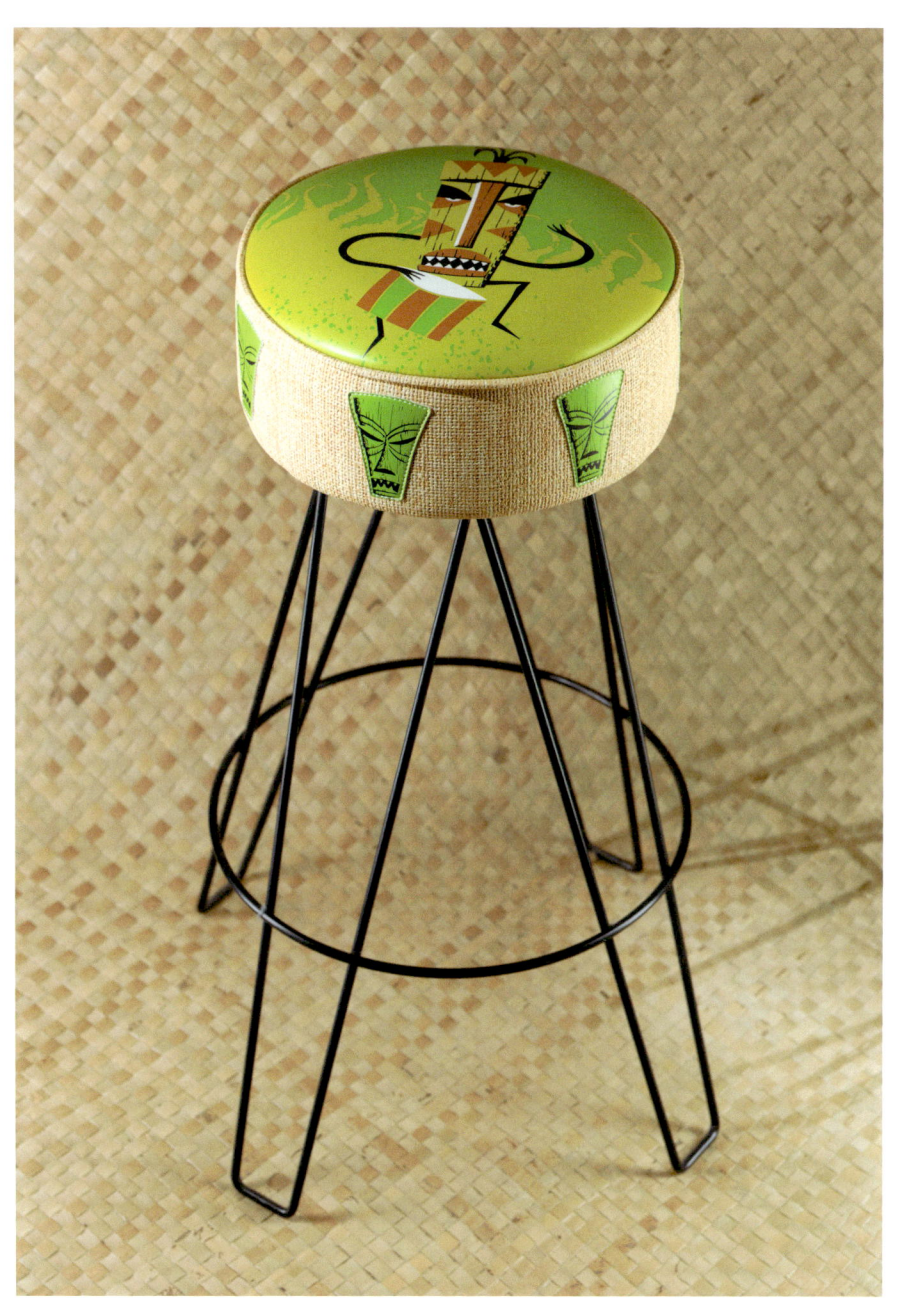

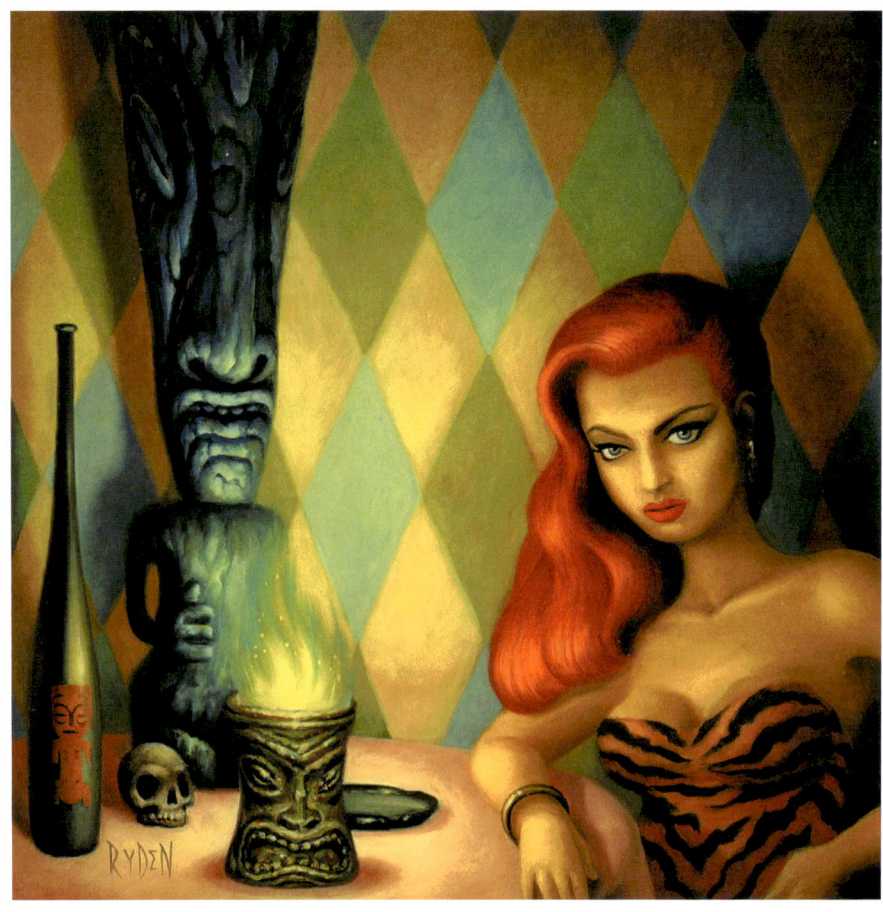

Concurrently, an underground art movement was emerging. This scene, which came to be called Pop Surrealism, was influenced by pop-culture references from the past—Tiki among them. The god of the artists was inspiring a new generation of artists such as Mark Ryden, Bosko, Coop, and Moritz R. (creator of the *Book of Tiki* cover) to incorporate his image in their work. Besides appearing on canvas, the Tiki's likeness resurfaced in a multitude of forms and materials, rivaling the icon's proliferation in its mid-century heyday.

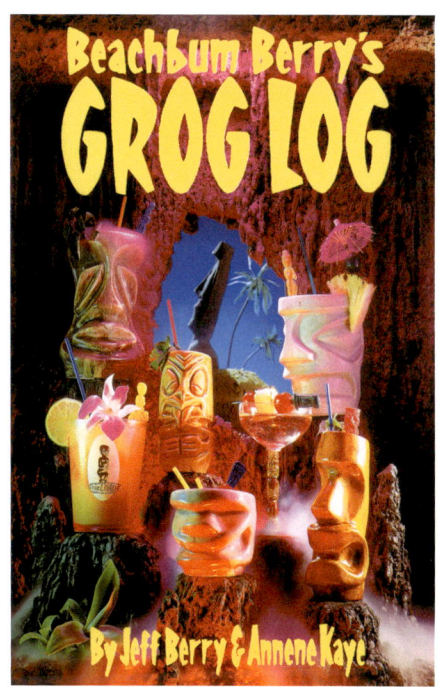

While *Tiki News'* and James Teitelbaum's *Tiki Bar Review Pages* on the then-fledgling Internet broadened the awareness of Tiki, it remained relatively underground. The decisive push for the Tiki Revival came in the year 2000, when urban archaeologist Sven Kirsten compiled 10 years of research into *The Book of Tiki*, defining and naming Tiki as a genre. "Tikiphiles" convened at Tiki festivals: Tiki Oasis in 2001 and the Hukilau in Florida in 2002 were the first of many to follow.

As *TikiCentral.com*, Tiki Farm, and then *Tiki Magazine* emerged and started spreading the Tiki gospel, more and more artisans picked up the chisel and began hacking wooden logs into modern idols. The availability of Tiki books and imagery on the World Wide Web spread the art form to Europe and other countries where there had been no Tiki Pop before. Talented artists from Mexico to Germany, even Japan, heeded the call of Tiki, each culture adding one more layer to the diversity of the art form. From small pendants to giant godheads, the traditional Polynesian deity was reinterpreted as a pop-culture icon, decorating new bars or the homes of Tiki collectors.

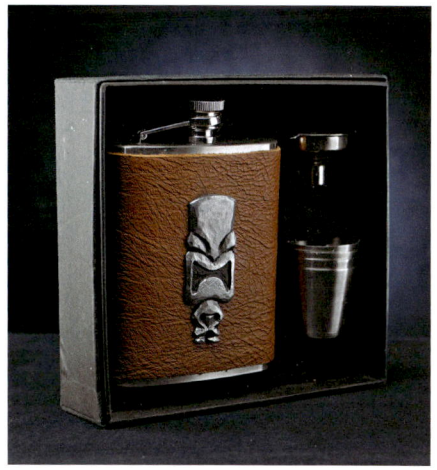

After collecting old Tiki mugs for years during the early '90s, artist Bosko Hrnjak decided it was time to try his luck on sculpting his own. His first generation of mugs ended up gracing the cover of *Grog Log*, and many more followed. Artists like Cass McClure, Danny Gallardo, Crazy Al, and Munktiki were now creating Tiki mugs as art objects, often referencing classics from Tiki's Golden Age. These were collectibles but were also used as containers for the newly appreciated cocktails prepared by hobby mixologists at their home Tiki bars. It wasn't long before Holden Westland's Tiki Farm was producing mugs for new Tiki restaurants and bars.

Tiki-themed group art shows at galleries like La Luz de Jesus, Copro Nason, and M Modern gave new artists a platform to showcase their talent. At its best, 20th- and 21st-century Tiki was and is inspired equally by classic Polynesian art, mid-century American Tiki Pop and modernism, and cartoons. Because the Tiki Revival has not been wholly embraced by the art intelligentsia—much as it was in Tiki Pop's first incarnation—artists are not constrained by the definitions of "good" and "bad" as decreed by the cultural establishment. The results are full of playful irreverence, humor, and new creative concepts untried anywhere else—all in the confines of the Tiki-style language.

In Los Angeles, where many artists are employed by the film and animation industry, their new appreciation of Tiki has translated into their work. Nickelodeon Studios' *SpongeBob SquarePants* has introduced Tiki to a whole new generation. The playful side of Tiki partners well with cartoons and toys.

By looking backwards to its most primal beginnings, creative minds have brought Tiki—both its original sources and its new incarnations—to the forefront of consciousness again. Thanks to the work of countless artists, writers, musicians, and entrepreneurs, our connection to humanity's collective past and our archetypal dreams of paradise have never fully died, even when they were constrained by concrete and stone.

America's Tiki Pop movement, both in the 20th century and today, is simply our culture's way of reminding ourselves of the ancient and sacred roots that connect all of mankind. The colorful pop patina with which Americans painted Tiki, and its places of expression—films, restaurants, bars, and communal gatherings—should not discredit this art form, but be treated as another page in Tiki's creation story.

Long live Tiki, in all its forms!

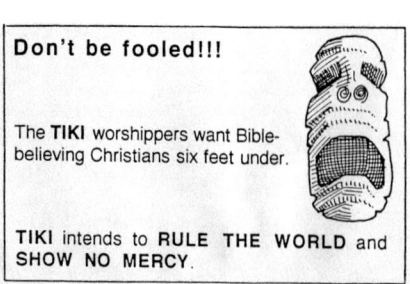

Don't be fooled!!!

The **TIKI** worshippers want Bible-believing Christians six feet under.

TIKI intends to **RULE THE WORLD** and **SHOW NO MERCY**.

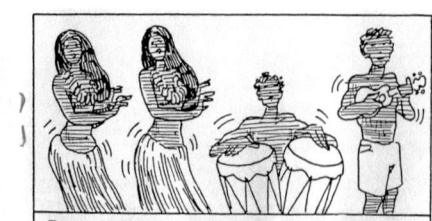

Paganism runs rampant in the ceremonies and practices of this new **TIKI** culture.

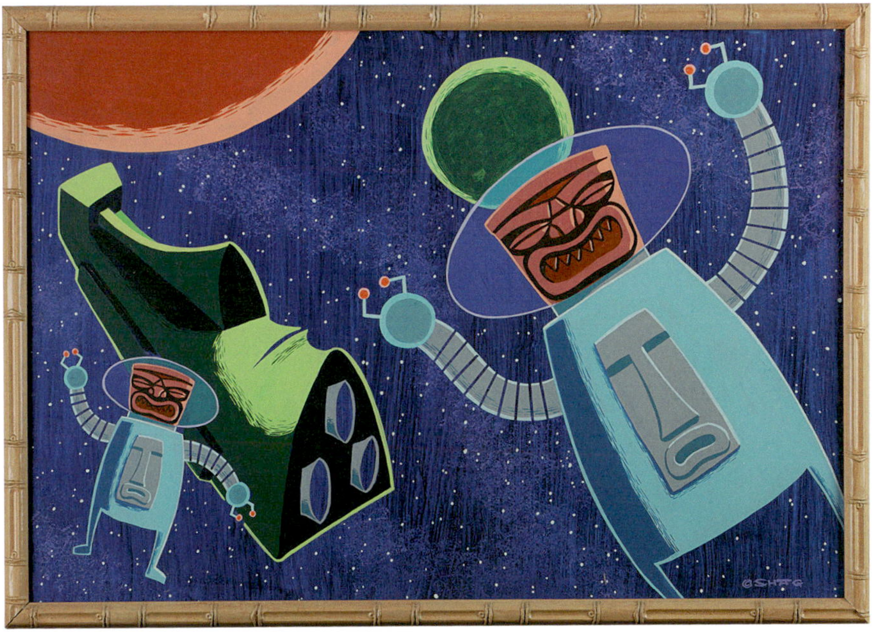

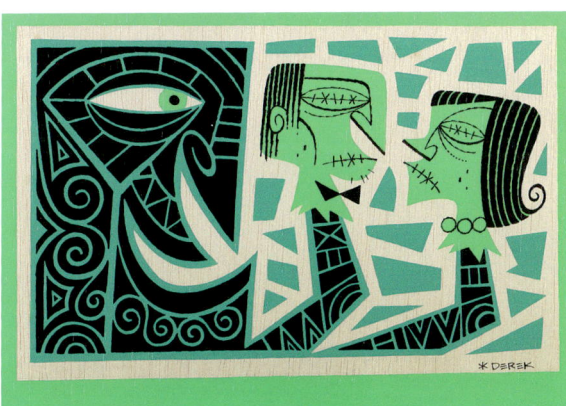

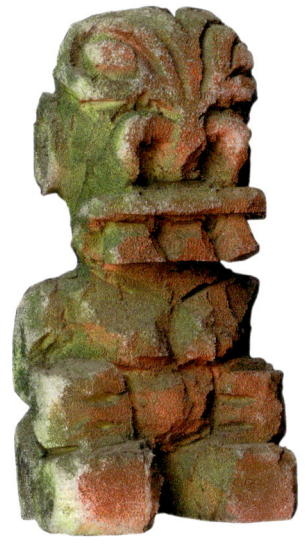

OPPOSITTE: Chick tract parody by unknown artist

TOP: *Interstellar Tiki* by Shag, 1996

ABOVE: *Witchdoctor* by Derek Yaniger

RIGHT: Styrofoam Tiki from Combustible Edison's *Tiki Wonder Hour*, 1991

THE TIKI REVIVAL

ANFANG DER 1990er-JAHRE WAR TIKI
in Vergessenheit geraten. Doch ehemalige
Anhänger der Punk- und New-Wave-
Musik – Anhänger des Anderen, des
Unbekannten – begannen, eine Vorliebe
für die damals unpopulären Lounge- und
Exotica-Klänge der Cocktailgeneration zu
entwickeln. Während sie in Secondhandläden nach alten LPs suchten, stießen diese
Musik-Archäologen auch auf Tiki-Becher,
Tiki-Streichholzbriefchen, -Speisekarten
etc. – Gegenstände, die nach und nach
zu neuen Sammlerobjekten wurden.

Obwohl es das Internet damals noch
nicht gab, gelang es den Liebhabern, sich
zu vernetzen. Sie trafen sich in Wohnungen und Restaurants, um ihre Funde zu
teilen. Zu den frühen Fans in Los Angeles
zählen der Autor dieses Buchs, der Musiker, Künstler und Vintage-Store-Besitzer
Josh Agle – besser bekannt als Shag – dessen farbenfrohe Gemälde von Tikis und

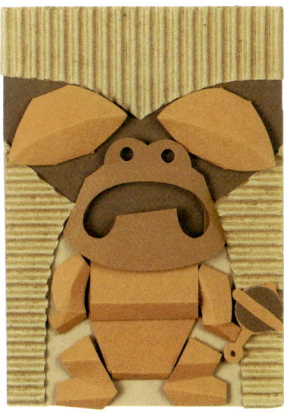

OPPOSITE: The Tiki torch was relit in
the 21st century

ABOVE: Baby-shower invite by Eric
October (*Humu Humu Collection*

BELOW: A gathering of Tiki revivalists,
Arizona, 2010 (*photo by Alfonso Elia*)

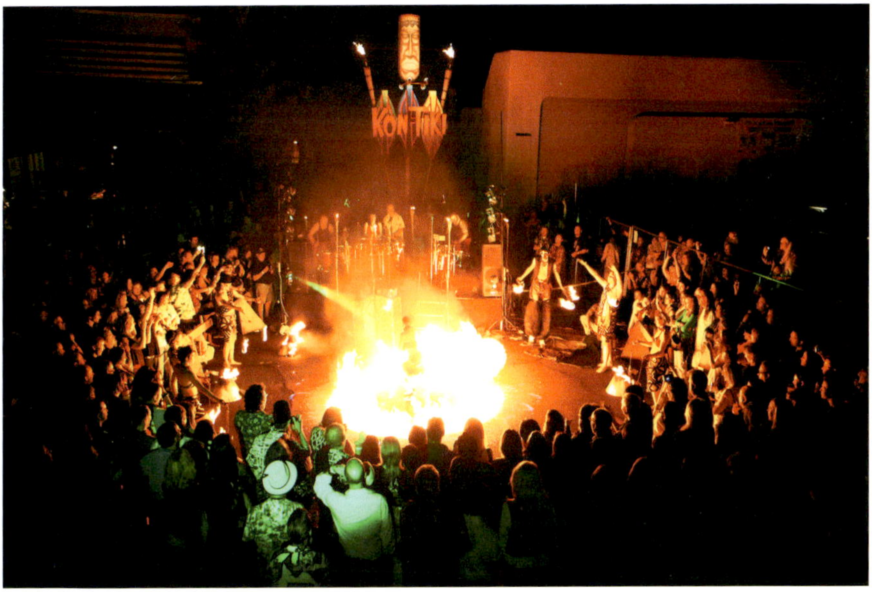

Cocktailpartys heiß begehrt sind, und Otto von Strohheim, der 1995 das erste Tiki-Magazin – *Tiki News* – auf den Markt brachte. Einsame Tiki-Liebhaber in ganz Amerika wussten nun, dass sie mit ihrer Leidenschaft nicht alleine waren.

Mit von der Partie war auch Jeff „Beachbum" Berry, der nicht nur Becher sammelte, sondern auch lang verloren geglaubte Rezepte tropischer Cocktails ausgrub. Diese sollten im folgenden Jahrzehnt die Craft-Cocktail-Bewegung inspirieren. Sein erstes Buch, das *Grog Log* von 1998, ist heute ein Standardwerk in jeder Tiki-Revival-Bar.

Gleichzeitig begann sich eine Untergrundkunstbewegung zu formen. Der sogenannte Pop Surrealism nahm Bezug auf vergangene Popkulturbewegungen – auch auf die des Tiki. Der Gott der Künstler inspirierte eine neue Generation von kreativen Köpfen, sein Abbild in ihre Arbeiten einfließen zu lassen, beispielsweise Mark Ryden, Bosko, Coop und Moritz R. (Gestalter des Covers für *The Book of Tiki*). Tikis Bildnis wurde nicht nur auf der Leinwand, sondern in diversen anderen Formen wiederbelebt, ein Revival, dass sich durchaus mit seiner Ausbreitung

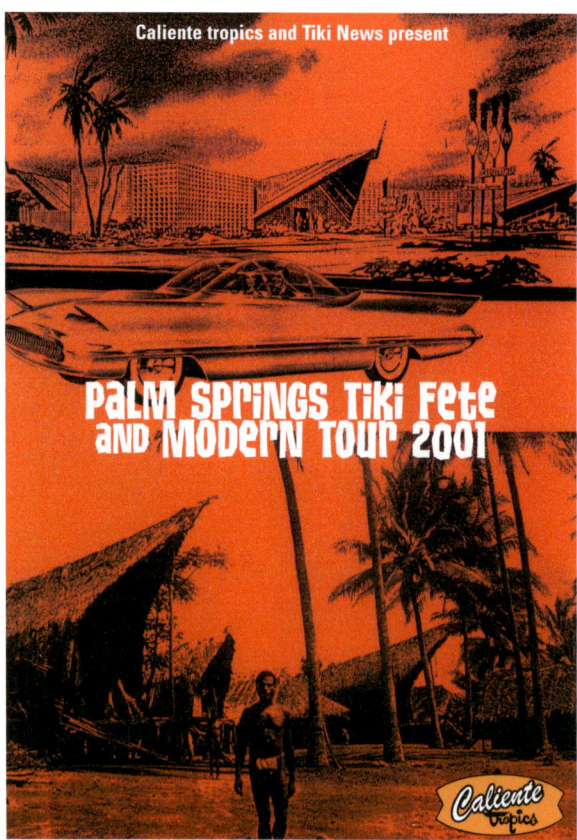

LEFT: The first Tiki Oasis flyer

OPPOSITE: Giant Tiki bar by Notch Gonzalez at Oasis

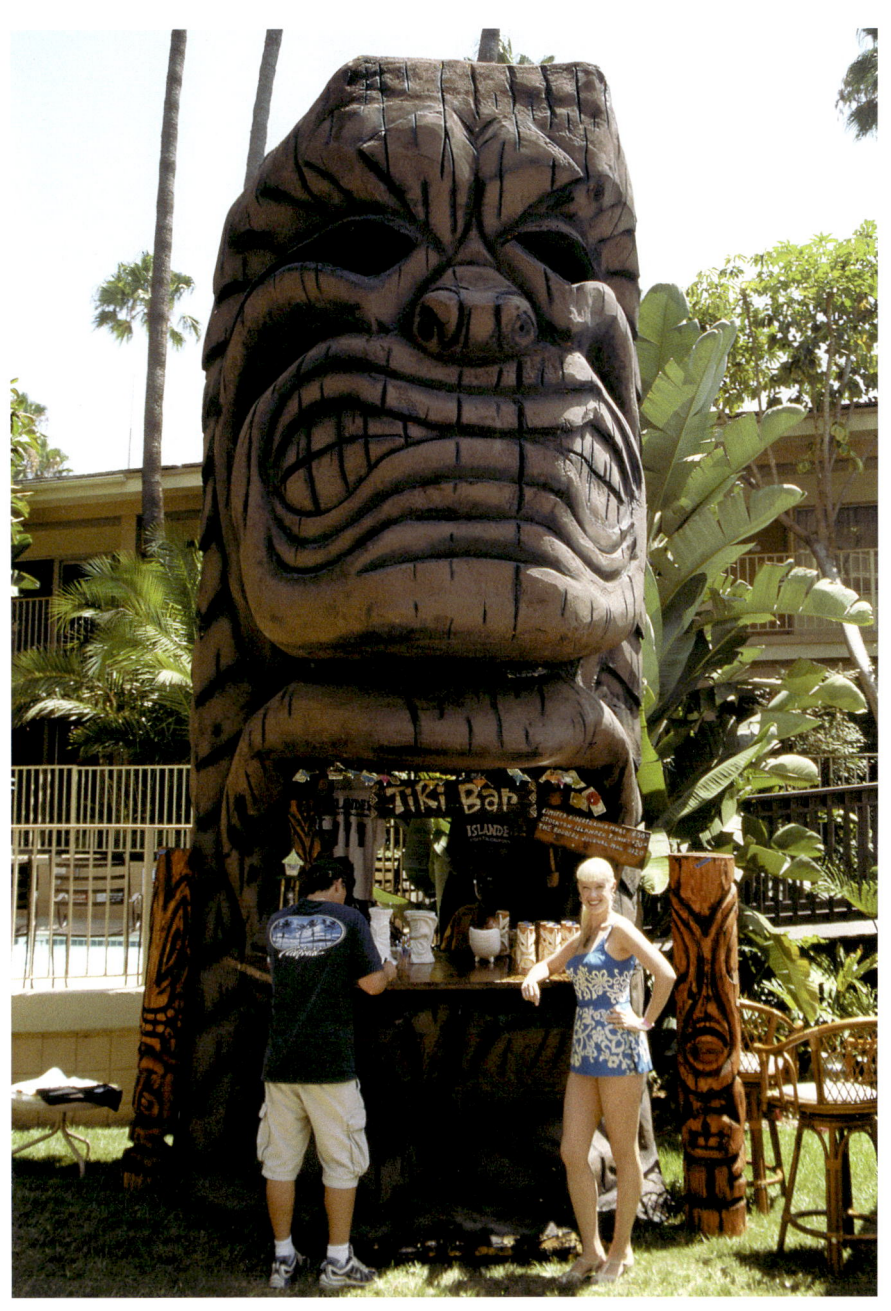

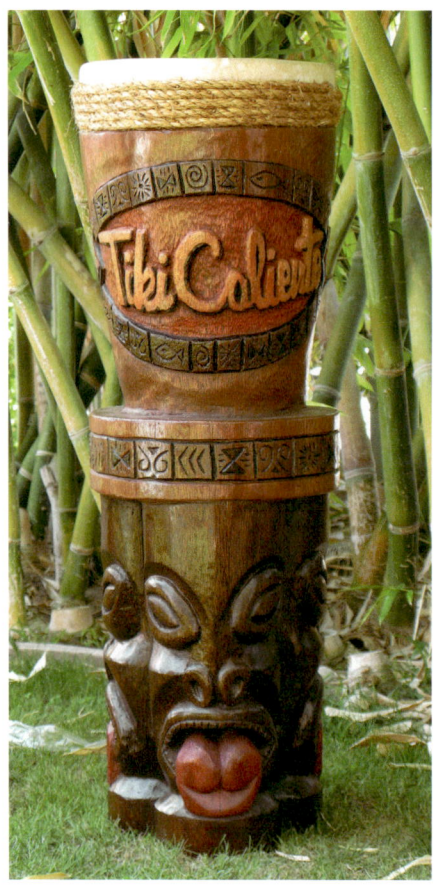

zu seinen Glanzzeiten in den 1950er-Jahren vergleichen lässt.

Obwohl sich Tikis Bekanntheit im aufkommenden Internet durch *Tiki News* und James Teitelbaums *Tiki Bar Review Pages* erhöhte, blieb es eine Untergrundbewegung. Der entscheidende Schub des Tiki-Revivals kam im Jahr 2000, als der Stadtarchäologe Sven Kirsten zehn Jahre Forschung in *The Book of Tiki* festhielt und Tiki als Genre definierte und benannte. „Tikiphile" versammelten sich auf einschlägigen Festivals. Tiki Oasis in 2001 und das Hukilau in Florida 2002 waren die ersten von vielen.

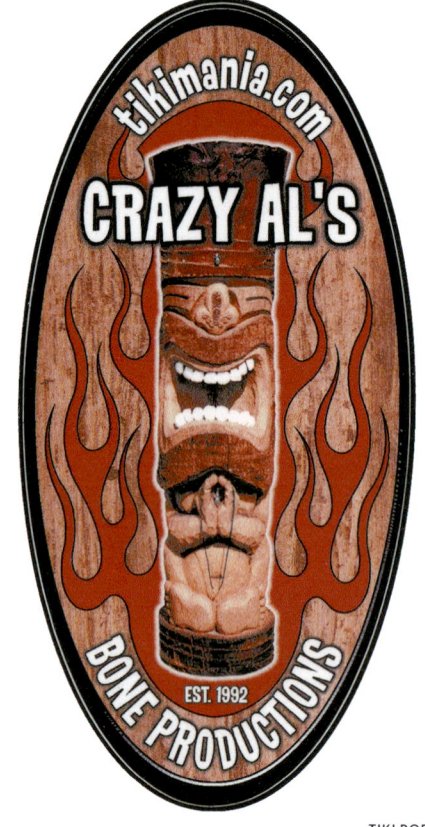

ABOVE: Tiki Caliente festival drum by Buzzy Meeker

RIGHT: Crazy Al Evans sticker

OPPOSITE ABOVE: Carver Kai "Haikai" Sarnes at work

OPPOSITE BELOW: Disneyland Rongo bowl by Jody Daily and Kevin Kidney, 2008

Als *TikiCentral.com*, Tiki Farm und dann *Tiki-Magazine* anfingen, das Tiki-Evangelium zu verbreiten, griffen mehr und mehr Kunsthandwerker zu Hammer und Meißel und begannen, Holzklötze in moderne Götterfiguren zu verwandeln. Die Verfügbarkeit von Tiki-Büchern und -Bildern im Internet machte die Kunstform auch in Europa und anderen Ländern bekannt, die zuvor noch nie etwas davon gehört hatten. Von Mexiko bis Deutschland und sogar in Japan folgten talentierte Künstler Tikis Ruf. Jede Kultur verhalf der Kunstform zu mehr Vielschichtigkeit. Von kleinen Amuletten bis zu riesigen Statuen – der polynesische Gott wurde als Popkultur-Ikone neu interpretiert und dekorierte Bars und die Wohnungen von Sammlern.

Nachdem der Künstler Bosko Hrnjak in den 1990er-Jahren jahrelang Tiki-Becher gesammelt hatte, befand er, es sei an der Zeit, sich an eigenen Entwürfen zu versuchen. Seine erste Generation Becher landete auf dem Cover des *Grog Log*, viele weitere folgten. Nun schufen Künstler wie Cass McClure, Danny Gallardo, Crazy Al und Munktiki Tiki-Becher als Kunstobjekte, die oftmals den Klassikern aus Tikis Glanzzeit ähnelten. Es waren Sammlerstücke, aber auch Trinkgefäße, in denen Hobby-Barkeeper wiederbelebte Cocktails in ihrer Tiki-Hausbar servierten. Es dauerte nicht lange, bis Holden Westlands Firma Tiki Farm Becher für neue Tiki-Restaurants und -Bars produzierte.

Galerien wie La Luz de Jesus, Copro Nason und M Modern veranstalteten Ausstellungen zum Thema und boten jungen Künstlern eine Plattform, auf der sie ihre Werke präsentieren konnten. In seiner besten Form wurde und wird der Tiki des 20. und 21. Jahrhunderts von klassischer,

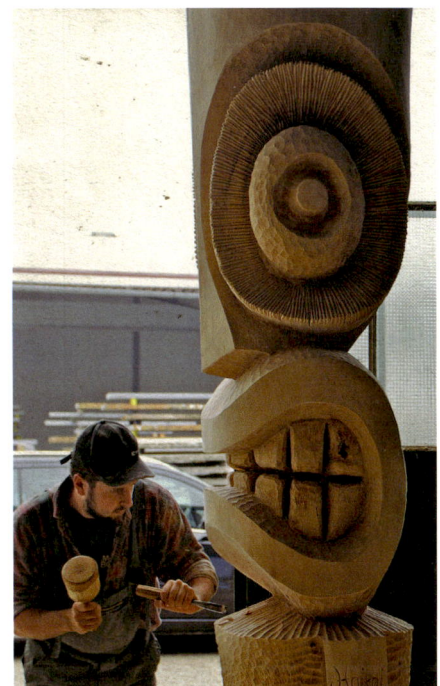

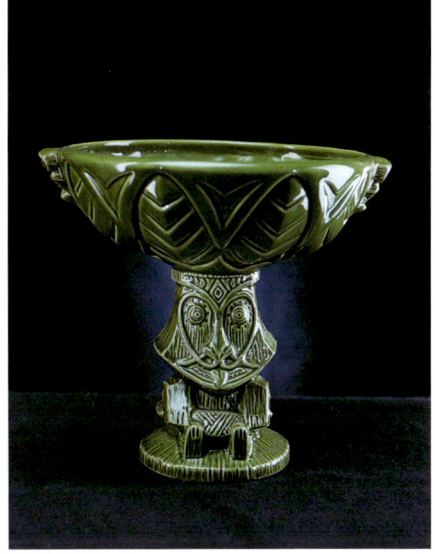

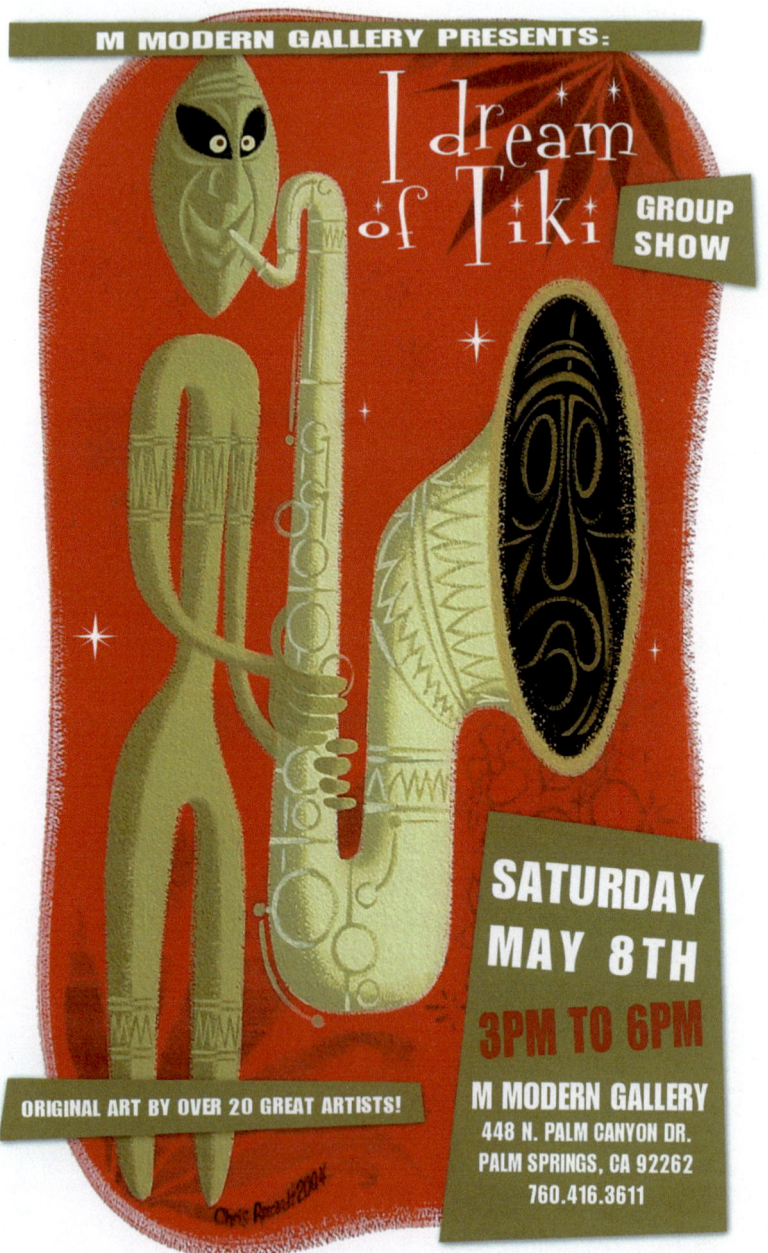

polynesischer Kunst, dem amerikanischen Tiki-Pop der 1950er-Jahre, vom Modernismus und von Karikaturen gleichermaßen inspiriert. Tikis Wiedergeburt wurde – wie bei seinem ersten Aufkommen auch – von der Kunstszene nur teilweise aufgegriffen. Die Künstler sind somit frei von der einschränkenden Unterscheidung des kulturellen Establishments in „gut" oder „schlecht". Das Ergebnis sind Werke von spielerischer Pietätlosigkeit und Humor sowie innovative kreative Konzepte, wie sie anderswo kaum zu finden sind – alles im Rahmen des Tiki-Stils.

Auch in Los Angeles, wo viele Künstler für die Film- und Animationsindustrie tätig sind, fließt deren neu gefundene Wertschätzung für Tiki in ihre Arbeit ein. Die Episode „Thaddäus im Tiki-Land" der Zeichentrickserie *SpongeBob Schwammkopf* stellte Tiki einer ganz neuen Zuschauergeneration vor. Seine verspielte Seite harmoniert gut mit Cartoons und Spielzeug.

Indem sie sich Tikis Ursprüngen zuwandten, haben kreative Köpfe sowohl das Original als auch seine neueren Inkarnationen zurück ins Gedächtnis der Öffentlichkeit gerufen. Dank der Werke zahlreicher Künstler, Autoren, Musiker und Unternehmer ist unsere Verbindung zur gemeinsamen Vergangenheit der Menschen und unseren archetypischen Träumen vom Paradies nie ganz abgebrochen, auch dann nicht, als wir uns zwischen Stein und Beton eingezwängt fühlten.

Amerikas Tiki-Pop-Bewegung – im 20. Jahrhundert wie auch heute – ist ganz einfach ein Medium unserer Kultur, mit dessen Hilfe wir uns an die alten, heiligen Wurzeln erinnern, die alle Menschen miteinander verbinden. Weder die farbenfrohe Pop-Patina, die Tiki von den Amerikanern bekam, noch die Orte, an denen der Tiki-Lifestyle ausgelebt wurde – in Filmen, Restaurants, Bars und auf Partys – sollten diese Kunstform diskreditieren. All ihre Erscheinungsformen stehen vielmehr für eine weitere Seite in Tikis Schöpfungsgeschichte.

Lang lebe Tiki, in all seinen Formen!

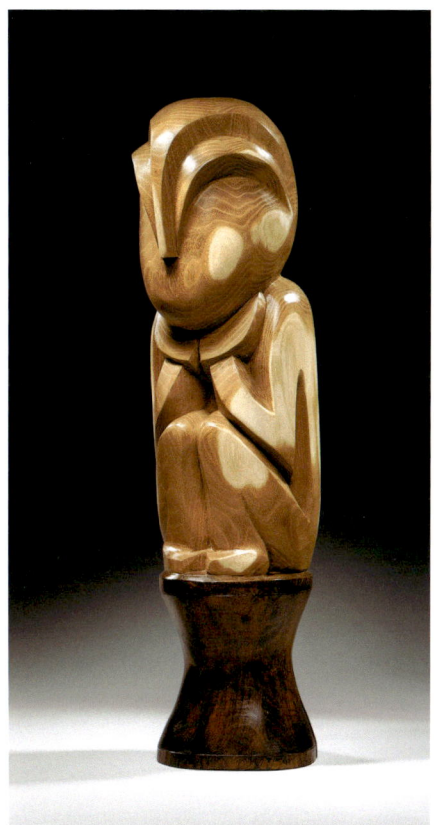

OPPOSITE: Tiki group-show flyer by Chris Reccardi

RIGHT: Pogany Tiki by Jérôme Laojia Hansel, 2009

AU DÉBUT DES ANNÉES 1990, TIKI EST
complètement oublié. Mais les ex-fans
de musique punk et new wave, toujours
friands d'ambiances différentes et sombres,
commencent à apprécier les airs exotica et
lounge alors démodés, la génération cocktail. En exhumant les vieux vinyles dénichés
dans les piles de magasins de disques
d'occasion, ces archéologues retrouvent
aussi des mugs tiki qu'ils se mettent à collectionner. D'autres vestiges, boîtes d'allumettes ou menus de restaurants, refont
alors surface – autant d'indices renvoyant
à une culture oubliée.

Bien qu'il s'agisse encore de la période
pré-Internet, les aficionados réussirent à former un réseau, et à organiser des rencontres
chez eux ou au restaurant pour partager
leurs trouvailles. À Los Angeles, l'auteur de ce
livre a compté parmi les premiers amateurs.
Citons aussi le musicien Josh Agle, artiste et
propriétaire d'un magasin vintage – mieux
connu sous le surnom Shag – dont les
peintures colorées bourrées de tikis et de
cocktails sont très recherchées, ou encore

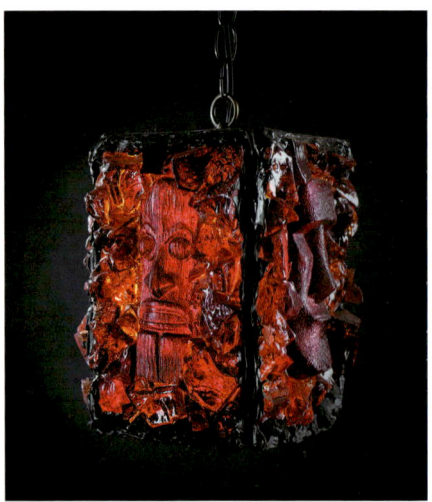

Otto von Stroheim, qui en 1995 a publié le
premier magazine sur le thème du tiki : *Tiki
News*. Les chercheurs d'objets tiki, isolés et
éparpillés aux quatre coins de l'Amérique,
ont alors réalisé qu'ils n'étaient pas seuls.

On trouve aussi dans ce cocktail Jeff
« Beachbum » Berry, qui non seulement
collectionnait des mugs, mais redécouvrait
aussi depuis longtemps des recettes de
boissons tropicales qui devaient initier le
mouvement « craft cocktail » dans la décennie suivante. Son premier ouvrage, *Grog
Log* (1998), a imposé le code de tous les bars
Tiki Revival.

Parallèlement, un mouvement d'art
underground était en train de voir le jour.
Cette mouvance, baptisée par la suite
« surréalisme pop », subit l'influence de
références de la culture populaire passée
– notamment du tiki. Le dieu des artistes
a ainsi conduit une nouvelle génération
d'artistes comme Mark Ryden, Bosko Coop,
et Moritz R. (créateur de la couverture du
Book of Tiki) à intégrer son image dans leur
travail. Outre ses incarnations picturales,
l'image du Tiki a refait surface sous une
multitude de formes et de matériaux, rivali-
sant avec la prolifération de l'icône, à son
apogée au milieu du siècle dernier.

Malgré les efforts des sites *Tiki News* et
Tiki Review Pages de James Teitelbaum, sur
un Internet encore balbutiant, pour élargir
le public du tiki, ce dernier est resté relativement marginal. Le coup de pouce décisif
vers le Tiki Revival s'est produit en 2000,
quand l'archéologue urbain Sven Kirsten a
compilé dix ans de recherche dans *The Book
of Tiki*, définissant et baptisant le genre tiki.
Les « tikiphiles » se retrouveront dès lors
dans les festivals tiki, tels Tiki Oasis (2001)
et Hukilau en Floride (2002), les premiers,
bientôt suivis de nombreux autres.

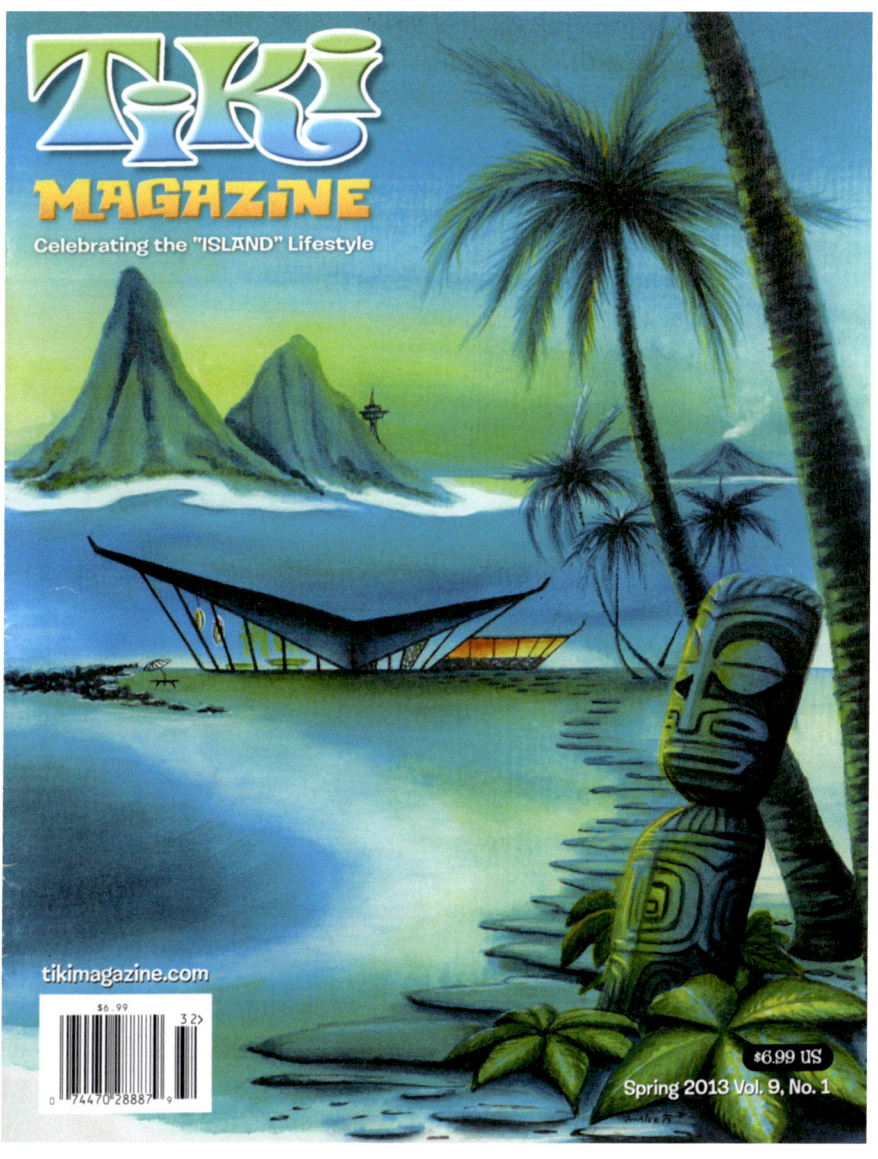

OPPOSITE: Resin lamp by Wendy Cevola and Roger Bodine

ABOVE: *Tiki Magazine* cover by Dawn Frazier, 2013

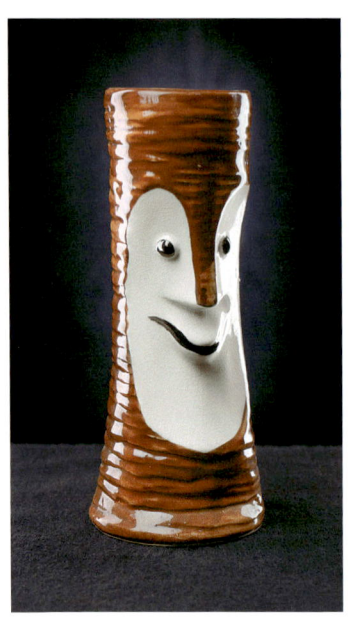

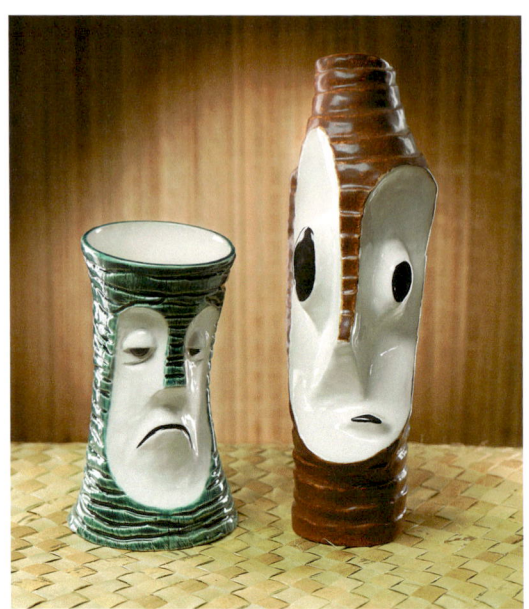

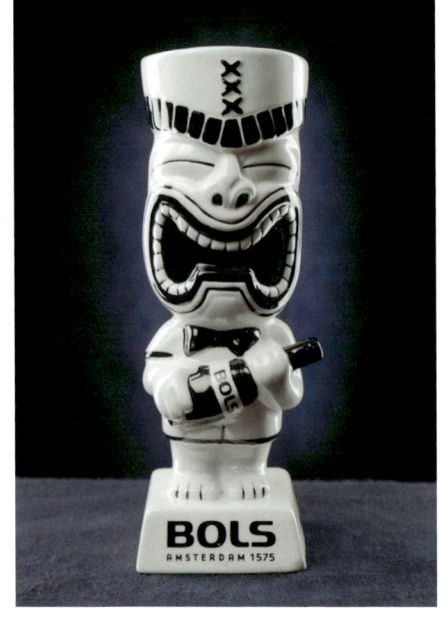

ABOVE LEFT: The original Tiki Bob's mug from the 1950s

ABOVE RIGHT: Blue Bob by Grog and Picasso Bob by Bosko, both made in homage to the original Tiki Bob's mug

RIGHT: Bols Tiki mug by Dirk Rehder

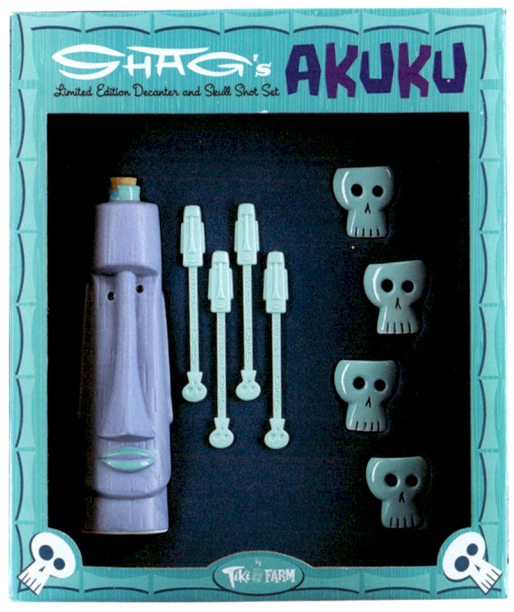

LEFT: Akuku decanter set by Shag, manufactured by Tiki Farm, 2002

BELOW LEFT: Witco God of Fortune mug by Bai

BELOW RIGHT: Mug sculptor Gecko and fan Bullet at Oasis

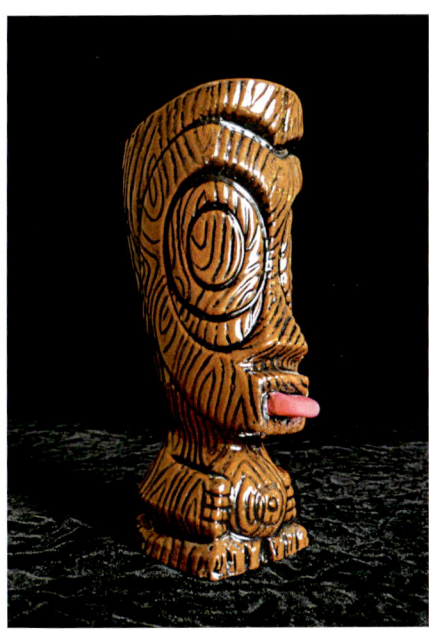

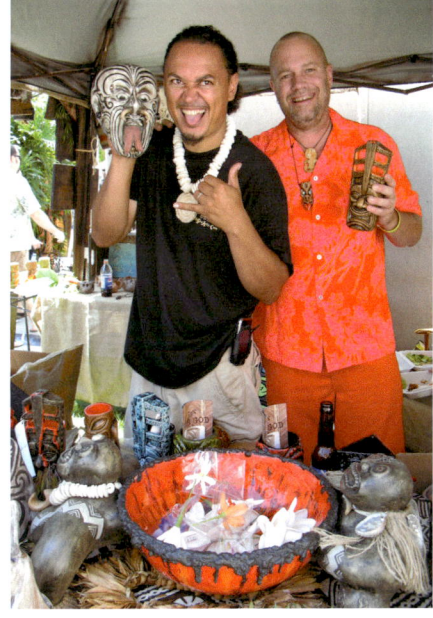

BELOW: Kai Sarnes's New Zealand sketchbook

RIGHT: Mata Hari 45 record cover by Michel Casarramona

OPPOSITE: Found thrift-store painting in original frame, with Tiki added by Moritz R., 1996

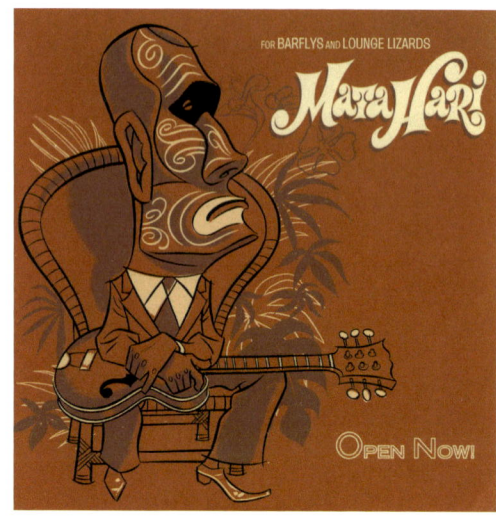

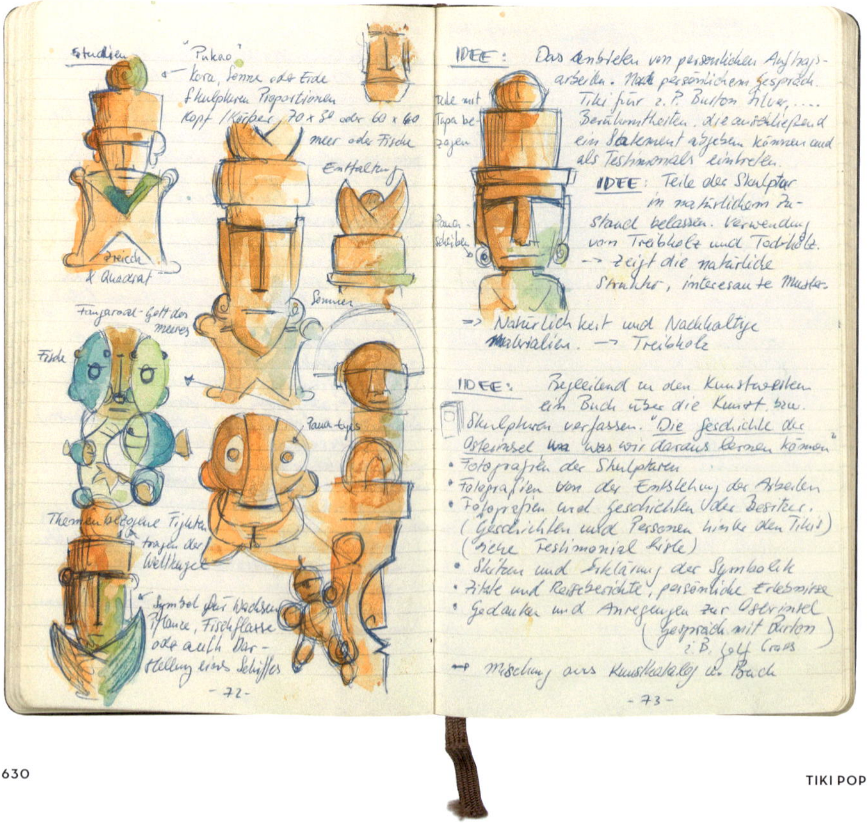

Avec l'apparition de *TikiCentral.com*, Tiki Farm, puis *Tiki Magazine* qui commençaient à répandre l'évangile tiki, un nombre croissant d'artisans ont empoigné le ciseau à bois et se sont mis à transformer des rondins en idoles modernes. La disponibilité des livres et des images tiki sur le World Wide Web a contribué à propager cette forme d'art en Europe et dans d'autres pays qui avaient échappé à la vogue tiki pop. Des artistes talentueux, du Mexique à l'Allemagne, voire au Japon, ont répondu à l'appel de Tiki, chaque culture ajoutant une facette supplémentaire à la diversité de cette forme d'art. Des petits pendentifs aux divinités géantes, la divinité polynésienne traditionnelle fut réinterprétée comme une icône de la culture pop, ornant de nouveaux bars ou les intérieurs de collectionneurs d'objets tiki.

Après avoir collectionné de vieux mugs tiki pendant des années, au début des années 1990, l'artiste Bosko Hrnjak décide qu'il est temps de tenter sa chance en sculptant les siens. Sa première génération de mugs sera célébrée en couverture de *Grog Log*, et beaucoup d'autres suivront. Des artistes comme Cass McClure, Danny Gallardo, Crazy Al, et Munktiki élèvent au rang d'objets d'art les mugs tiki qu'ils créent, se référant souvent aux classiques de l'âge d'or tiki. Ces objets de collection sont également utilisés comme récipients pour les nouveaux cocktails tendance préparés par les barmen amateurs sur leur bar

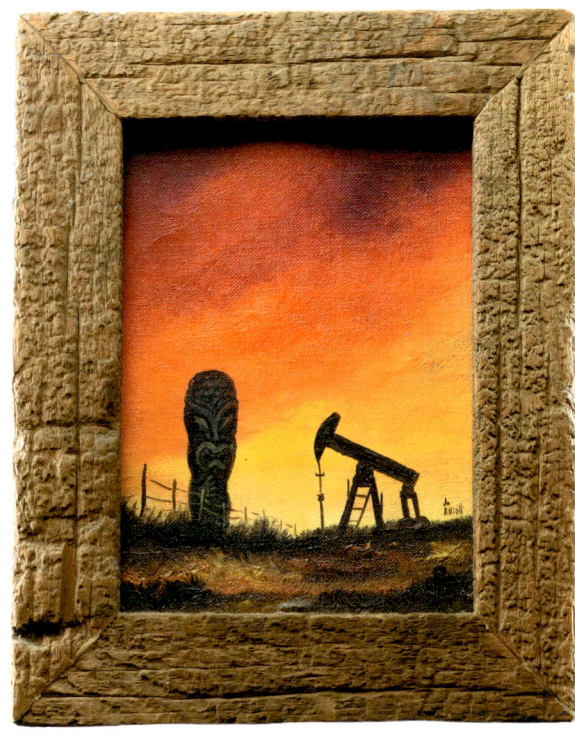

tiki. Peu après, la compagnie Tiki Farm de Holden Westland lancera à son tour sa production de mugs destinée aux nouveaux bars et restaurants tiki.

Les expositions collectives sur le thème tiki, montées dans des galeries comme La Luz de Jesus, Copro Nason, et M modern ont procuré à ces nouveaux artistes une plateforme pour faire connaître leur talent. À son meilleur niveau, le tiki des XXᵉ et XXIᵉ siècles fut et reste inspiré par l'art classique polynésien, le tiki pop américain et le modernisme du milieu du XXᵉ siècle, ainsi que par le dessin animé. Le Tiki Revival n'ayant pas encore été entièrement reconnu par l'intelligentsia artistique – comme c'est déjà le cas autant lors de sa première incarnation – les artistes tiki pop ne sont pas limités par les étiquettes « bon » ou « mauvais » telles qu'édictées par l'establishment culturel. Les résultats sont pleins d'irrévérence ludique, d'humour et de nouveaux concepts créatifs encore inédits ailleurs, le tout dans les limites du lexique stylistique tiki.

À Los Angeles, où de nombreux artistes travaillent pour l'industrie du cinéma et de l'animation, cette réhabilitation du style tiki s'est exprimée dans leur travail. *SpongeBob SquarePants* de Nickelodeon Studios a fait connaître le tiki à une toute nouvelle génération. Le côté ludique des personnages tiki a trouvé un bon moyen d'expression dans les dessins animés et les jouets.

En opérant un retour à ses tout premiers commencements, les esprits créatifs ont su ramener au premier plan les sources originales du tiki comme ses nouvelles incarnations. Grâce au travail de nombreux artistes, écrivains, musiciens et chefs d'entreprise, notre connexion au passé collectif de l'humanité et nos rêves archétypaux de paradis ne sont jamais totalement morts, même s'ils

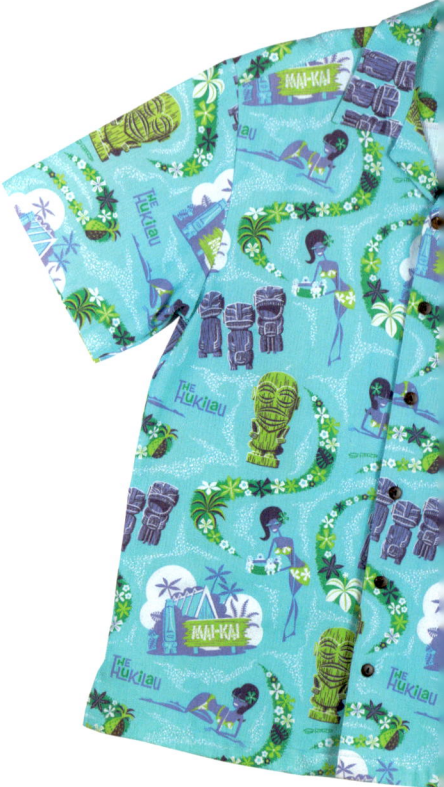

sont enfermés dans le béton et la pierre. Le mouvement américain du tiki pop, aussi bien au XXᵉ siècle qu'aujourd'hui, n'est rien d'autre que la façon dont notre culture se remémore les racines anciennes et sacrées qui relient l'humanité tout entière. La patine pop colorée dont les Américains ont recouvert Tiki et ses lieux d'expression – qu'il s'agisse de films, de restaurants, de bars ou de rassemblements informels, ne devrait pas discréditer cette forme d'art, mais être traitée comme une autre page de l'histoire créative de Tiki. Longue vie à Tiki, sous toutes ses formes !

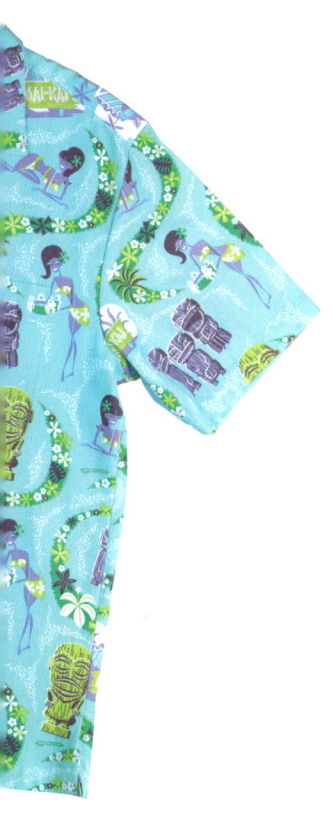

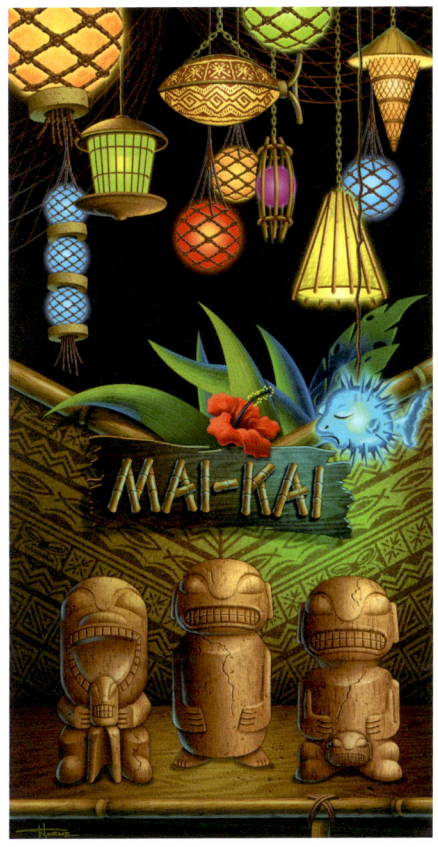

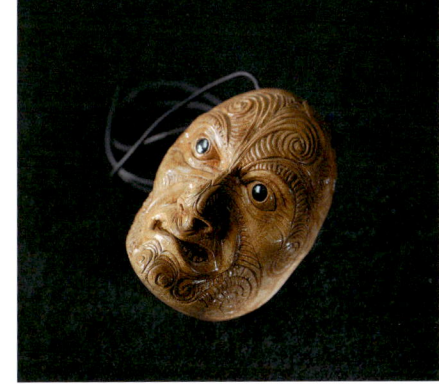

ABOVE LEFT: Hukilau Festival aloha shirt by Shag

ABOVE RIGHT: *Mai-Kai Cannibals* by Doug Horne

RIGHT: Maori mask pendant by Benzart

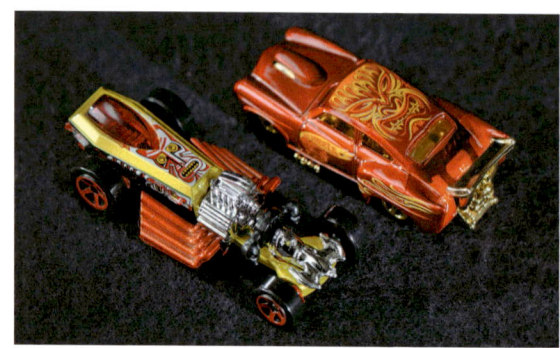

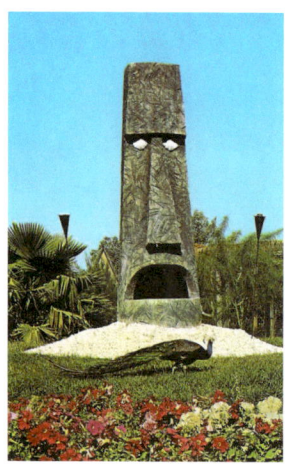

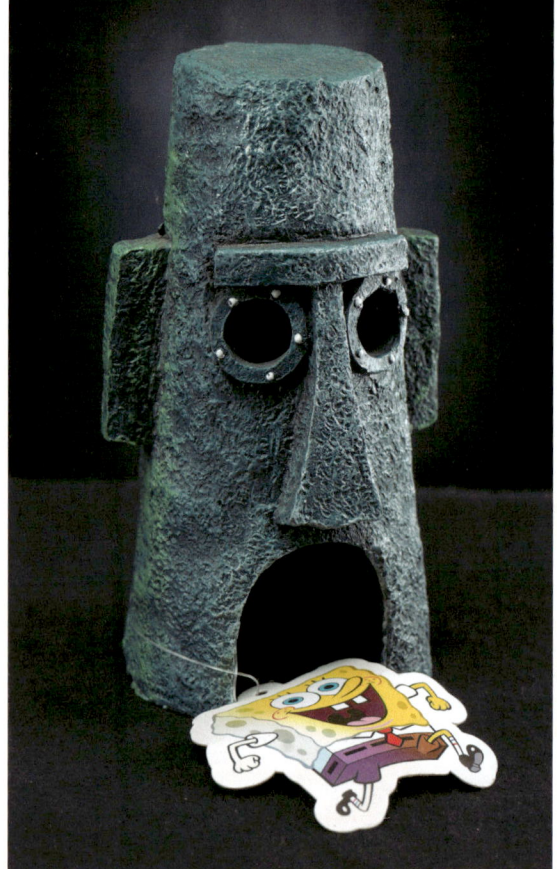

ABOVE: Original Tiki Gardens postcard

ABOVE RIGHT: Tiki Hot Wheels by Mattel *(Amy Boylan Collection)*

RIGHT: Squidward home from *SpongeBob SquarePants*

OPPOSITE: *Song of the Puffer Fish* by Ken Ruzic

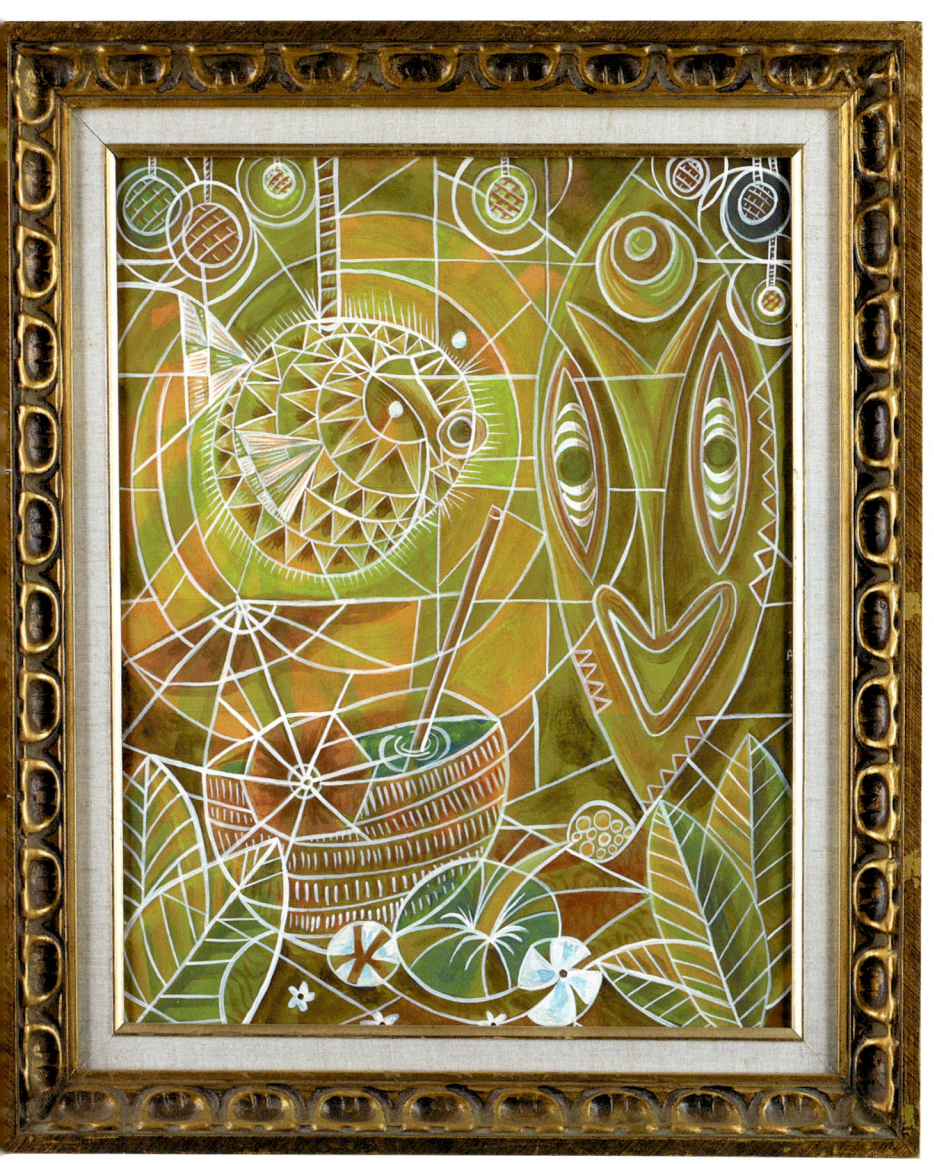

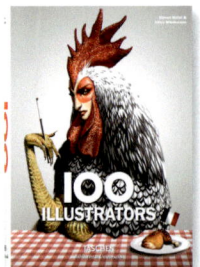

100 Illustrators

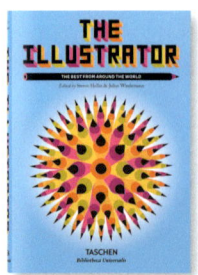

The Illustrator

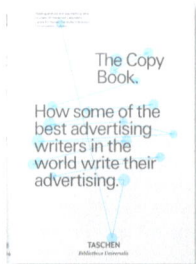

D&AD.
The Copy Book

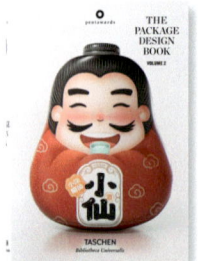

The Package Design
Book. Volume 2

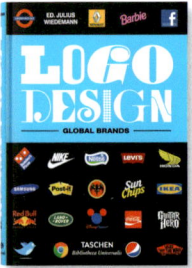

Logo Design.
Global Brands

Bookworm's delight: never bore, always excite!

TASCHEN
Bibliotheca Universalis

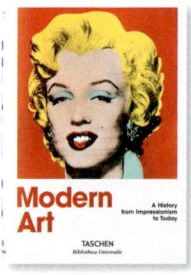

Modern Art

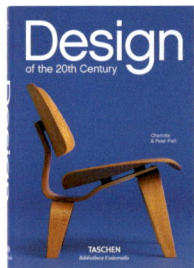

Design of the 20th Century

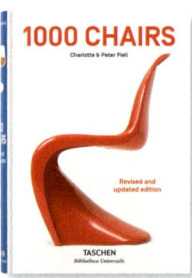

1000 Chairs

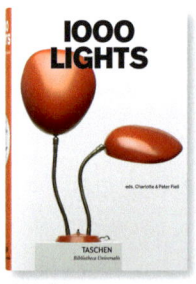

1000 Lights

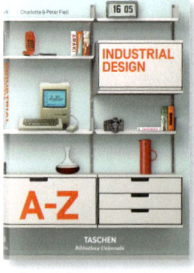

Industrial Design A–Z

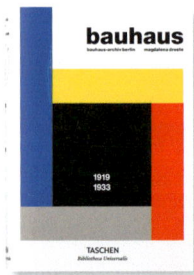

Bauhaus

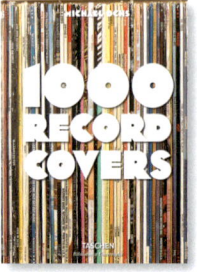

1000 Record Covers

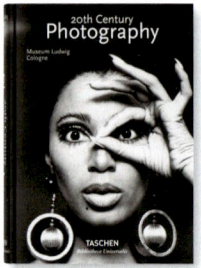

20th Century Photography

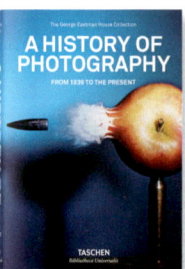

A History of Photography

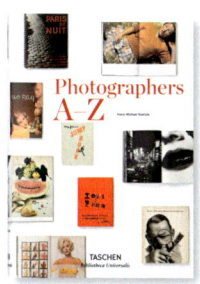

Photographers A–Z

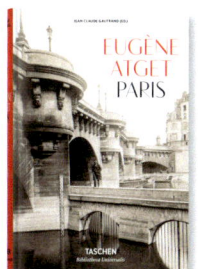

Eugène Atget. Paris

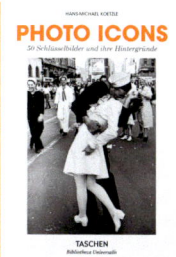

Photo Icons

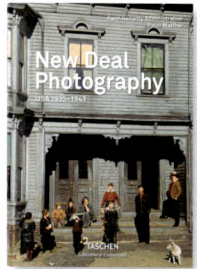

New Deal Photography

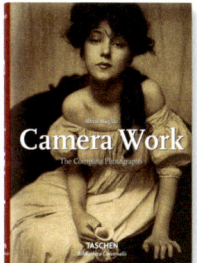

Stieglitz.
Camera Work

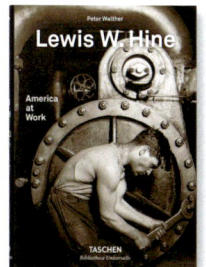

Lewis W. Hine

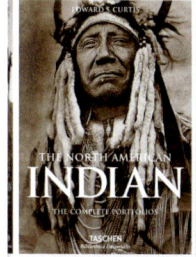

Curtis. The North
American Indian

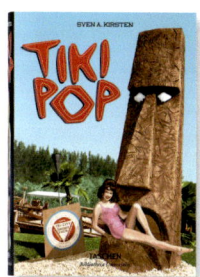

Tiki Pop

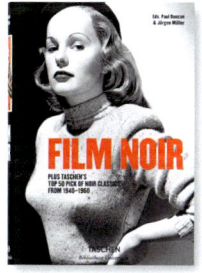

Film Noir

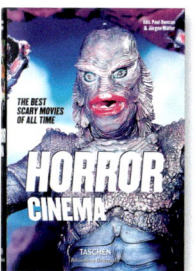

Horror Cinema

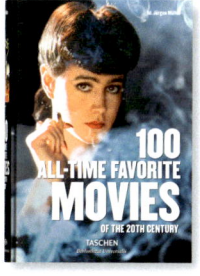

100 All-Time
Favorite Movies

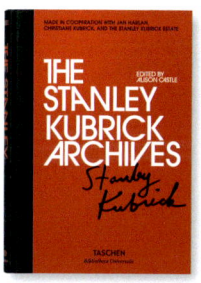

The Stanley Kubrick
Archives

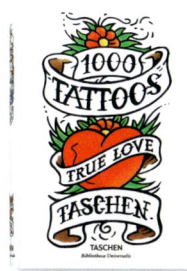

1000 Tattoos

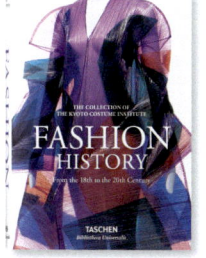

Fashion History

20th Century Fashion

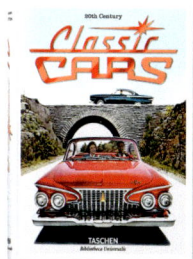

20th Century Classic Cars

YOU CAN FIND TASCHEN STORES IN

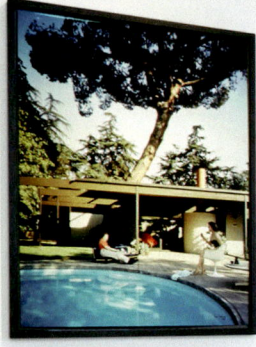
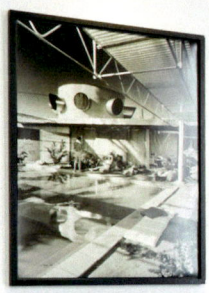
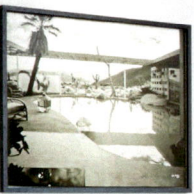

Berlin
Schlüterstr. 39

Beverly Hills
354 N. Beverly Drive

Brussels
Place du Grand Sablon /
Grote Zavel 35

Cologne
Neumarkt 3

Hollywood
Farmers Market,
6333 W. 3rd Street, CT-10

Hong Kong
Shop 01-G02 Tai Kwun,
10 Hollywood Road,
Central

London
12 Duke of York Square

Madrid
Calle del Barquillo, 30

Miami
1117 Lincoln Rd.

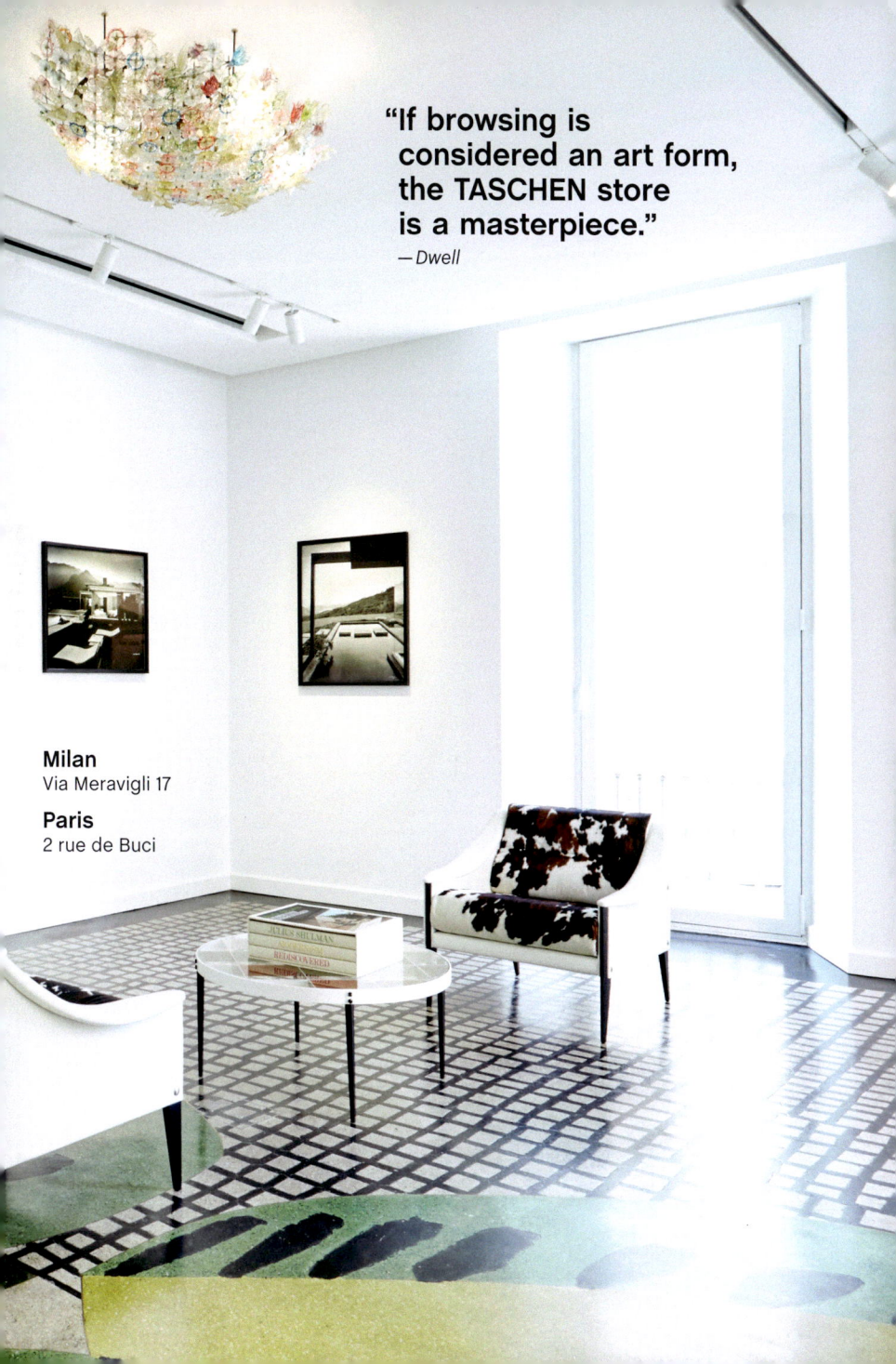

"If browsing is considered an art form, the TASCHEN store is a masterpiece."
—*Dwell*

Milan
Via Meravigli 17

Paris
2 rue de Buci

My sincerest gratitude for making this elaborate project possible goes to Stéphane Martin, director of the Musée du Quai Branly, and to Benedikt Taschen, for putting this culmination of my work in print.

Furthermore, I would not have been able to complete this opus without the support, patience, and hands-on editing and writing of my wife Naomi Alper.

This book and the museum exhibit would not have been possible without these fellow researchers, hunters, and collectors of Tiki's past, who selflessly donated their knowledge and artifacts:

Frank Brajevic, Scott Schell, Kiara Geller, Jon Paul Balak, Mimi Payne, Martijn Veltman, Timothy Haack, Bob van Oosting, Leroy Schmaltz, Ron Ferrell, Amy Boylan, Jackie Zumwaldt, Kevin Kidney, Jody Daily, Geoff Sundstroem, Tim Glazner, Steve Luchsinger, Vincent Jefferds, Rick Hamilton, Eric Stollsteimer, Travis Szekely, Tom Duncan, Duane Orzol, Chris Merritt, Mark Noland, Charles Phoenix, Jeff Berry, Mike Cozart, Jimmy Virani, Cheryl and Chester Crill, Cheeky Tiki, Dug Miller, Pete Moruzzi, Chris Nichols, Ben Dickow, Jochen Hirschfeld, Frieder at Kino Flo, Dean Allen, Mike Skinner, Carl and Caren at the Velveteria, all the Tiki archeologists on Tiki Central, Boris Hamilton, and Kate Simmons.

—Sven Kirsten

The following are credits for copyrighted material; all illustrations not mentioned here are from the collection of the author or have been credited in the captions.

© Fine Arts Museums of San Francisco: 324
© The Huntington Library, photo by Joseph Fadler: 485
© The Huntington Library, photo by Maynard Parker: 120, 171
© Los Angeles County Museum of Art: 130 bottom, 455
© Los Angeles Public Library Photo Collection: 270–271, 578
© 2014 Musée du quai Branly/ Scala, Florence: 252 top
© 2014 Musée du quai Branly, photo Claude Germain/Scala, Florence: 34 top, 35 bottom, 146–147, 419 top, 467 bottom, 607, 625
© 2014 Musée du quai Branly, photo Thierry Ollivier/Michel Urtado/ Scala, Florence: 550–551
© New York Public Library: 168
© RMN-Grand Palais (Musée d'Orsay), Hervé Lewandowski: 63
© Jacob Stelman Collection, The Athenaeum of Philadelphia: 474 top
© Tacoma Library: 542
© Time & Life Pictures/Getty, photo by Ralph Crane: 337, 470
© Bruce Torrence, Hollywood Photograph Collection: 140 bottom

EACH AND EVERY TASCHEN BOOK PLANTS A SEED!
Each year, we offset our annual carbon emissions with carbon credits at the Instituto Terra, a reforestation program in Minas Gerais, Brazil, founded by Lélia and Sebastião Salgado. To find out more about this ecological partnership, please check: www.taschen.com/institutoterra.
Inspiration: unlimited.
Carbon footprint: (almost) zero.

Want to see more? Visit taschen.com to view our current publications, browse our latest magazine, and subscribe to our newsletter.

This book was first published on the occasion of the exhibition "Tiki Pop — America Imagines Its Own Polynesian Paradise," on show at the Musée du Quai Branly from June 24 to September 28, 2014.

© 2025 TASCHEN GmbH
Hohenzollernring 53, D-50672 Köln
www.taschen.com

Printed in Bosnia-Herzegovina
ISBN 978-3-8365-8154-7

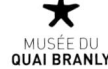

MUSÉE DU
QUAI BRANLY

EDITED AND WRITTEN BY:
Sven A. Kirsten, Los Angeles
ART DIRECTION:
Josh Baker, Los Angeles,
GERMAN TRANSLATION:
Carolin Polter, Berlin
FRENCH TRANSLATION:
Alice Pétillot, Bordeaux;
Daniel Roche, Paris

FRONT COVER:
Tri-City Queen Rita Mathies at Tiki Gardens, 1962
© Photograph by Karl E. Holland, courtesy of the State Archives of Florida, Florida Memory
SPINE:
Zombie Village mug by Wendy Cevola (*Scott Mabbutt Collection*)
BACK COVER:
Mai-Kai Cannibals by Doug Horne

THE AUTHOR:
Sven Kirsten is a cinematographer and urban archaeologist. It was his love for visuals that inspired him to collect and photograph the remnants of the forgotten culture of Polynesian pop in America, leading him to identify the Tiki as its icon. He published his findings in the Book of Tiki in September 2000. Four books later the cult of Tiki has made a spectacular comeback.